CURRENT BIOGRAPHY

CURRENT
BIOGRAPHY

WHO'S NEWS AND WHY
1 9 5 2

EDITED BY

Anna Rothe

Evelyn Lohr

THE H. W. WILSON COMPANY
NEW YORK, N. Y.

THIRTEENTH ANNUAL CUMULATION—1952

PRINTED IN THE UNITED STATES OF AMERICA

Copyright 1953
by
THE H. W. WILSON COMPANY

International Standard Book Number 0-8242-0118-3

Library of Congress Catalog Card No. (40-27432)

Preface

During 1952 CURRENT BIOGRAPHY presented an average of thirty articles monthly. Of the total of 335 biographies published in those eleven current issues and here cumulated in one alphabet, thirty-four biographies were about women and seventy-one were about individuals outside the United States. Following the practice begun in 1946, this Yearbook also contains the usual "bonus" of twenty biographies of authors which were originally printed during the year in the WILSON LIBRARY BULLETIN. These are indicated in the Yearbook's indexes by "WLB."

CURRENT BIOGRAPHY continues to publish superseding articles about people whose biographies first appeared in the 1940 or 1941 Yearbook, the two volumes now out of print. Among the thirty-five biographees in that group are General Fulgencio Batista, Danny Kaye, Marshall Field 3d, Frank Lloyd Wright, Dimitri Mitropoulos, Helen Rogers Reid, and John R. Steelman. These as well as all other biographies published in the course of 1952 were subject to revision to provide for any major changes in an individual's position during the year.

We call the attention of readers to a new cumulated index which was begun in 1951 and which is planned to cover the years 1951-1960. The index for the years 1940-1950, which appears in the 1950 Yearbook, is available separately for fifty cents a copy.

The assembling of material for these biographies entails thoroughgoing research. Files of clippings are drawn upon when a name is selected for inclusion in CURRENT BIOGRAPHY. Indexes to magazine articles and books guide writers to a mass of information which is culled for biographical and background facts. Various "Who's Who's," encyclopedias, and other reference works contribute data. Information is also obtained from government offices and a variety of commercial and educational organizations. Whenever it is possible to get in touch with the subjects of the biographies, they are asked to confirm or correct facts; it should be pointed out, however, that these are not authorized biographies in the usual sense of that word.

Special acknowledgement is due Anna Rothe, whose eight-year editorship of CURRENT BIOGRAPHY ended with the September 1952 issue.

E. L.

Contents

Explanations

Authorities for biographees' full names, with few exceptions, are the bibliographical publications of The Wilson Company. When a biographee prefers a certain name form, that is indicated in the heading of the article. For example, "Steelman, John R(oy)" means that Steelman commonly uses only the initial of his middle name; and when a professional name like "Garland, Judy" appears in the heading, the original name is given in the article itself.

The heading of each article includes the pronunciation of the name if it is unusual, date of birth (if obtainable), and occupation. The article is supplemented by a list of references to sources of information, in two alphabets: (1) newspapers and periodicals, (2) books. Space limitation requires that these bibliographies be confined to sources of strictly biographical nature.

References to newspapers and periodicals are listed in abbreviated form; for example, "Sat Eve Post 217:14-15 S 30 '44 por" means *Saturday Evening Post*, volume 217, pages 14-15, for September 30, 1944, with portrait. (See the section "Periodicals and Newspapers Consulted" for full names of the publications.) The books given as references are limited to those of a biographical nature, including such reference works as *Who's Who in America, Living Musicians,* etc. (See the section "Biographical References Consulted" for complete list.) The reference following each obituary notice is to the New York *Times*; these notices appear for persons whose biographies have been published in CURRENT BIOGRAPHY.

As indicated in the table of contents, this volume contains three name indexes, the purposes of which are self-evident. The 1940-1950 cumulated index is to be found in the 1950 Yearbook and is also available separately at fifty cents a copy.

KEY TO PRONUNCIATION
(Based on Webster's Guide to Pronunciation*)

ā	āle	N	Not pronounced, but indicates the nasal tone of the preceding vowel. as in the French bon (bôN).	û	ûrn; French eu, as in *jeu* (zhû); German ö, oe, as in *schön* (shûn), *Goethe* (gû'tĕ)		
â	câre						
ă	ădd						
ặ	ặccount						
ä	ärm						
á	ásk			ŭ	tŭb		
ȧ	sofȧ			ü	circŭs		
		ō	ōld	ü	Pronounced approximately as ē, with rounded lips: French u, as in *menu* (mē-nü'); German ü, as in *grün*.		
ē	ēve	ô	ôrb				
ĕ	ĕnd	ŏ	ŏdd				
ê	makêr	oi	oil				
		oo	ooze				
g	go	ŏŏ	fŏŏt				
		ou	out				
ī	īce			zh	azure		
ĭ	ĭll	th	then				
		th	thin	′ = main accent			
ᴋ	German ch as in *ich* (īᴋ).			″ = secondary accent			
		ū	cūbe				

(*Exceptions: th in then; main and secondary accents.)

KEY TO ABBREVIATIONS

AAA — Agricultural Adjustment Administration
A.A.A.A. — Amateur Athletic Association of America
A.A.U. — Amateur Athletic Union
ABC — American Broadcasting Company
A.C.L.U. — American Civil Liberties Union
ADA — Americans for Democratic Action
AEC — Atomic Energy Commission
AEF — American Expeditionary Force
AFL — American Federation of Labor
Ag — August
A.L.A. — American Library Association
A.M.A. — American Medical Association
AMG — Allied Military Government
Ap — April
A.P. — Associated Press
ASCAP — American Society of Composers, Authors and Publishers
ASNE — American Society Newspaper Editors
AVC — American Veterans Committee

b. — business address
B.A. — Bachelor of Arts
BBC — British Broadcasting Corporation
B.D. — Bachelor of Divinity
B.L.S. — Bachelor of Library Science
B.S. — Bachelor of Science
CAA — Civil Aeronautics Administration
CAB — Civil Aeronautics Board
C.B. — Companion of the Bath
C.B.E. — Commander of (the Order of) the British Empire
CBS — Columbia Broadcasting System
CCC — Civilian Conservation Corps
C.E. — Civil Engineer
CEA — Council of Economic Advisers
C.E.D. — Committee for Economic Development
CIO — Congress of Industrial Organizations
C.M.G. — Companion of (the Order of) St. Michael and St. George
Com. — Commodore
CWA — Civil Works Administration
CWS — Chemical Warfare Service

D — December
D.A.R. — Daughters of the American Revolution
D.C.L. — Doctor of Civil Law
D.D. — Doctor of Divinity
D.Eng. — Doctor of Engineering
D.F.C. — Distinguished Flying Cross
D.J. — Doctor of Jurisprudence
D.Lit. — Doctor of Literature
D.Mus. — Doctor of Music
DP — Displaced Person
D.Pol.Sc. — Doctor of Political Science
D.Sc. — Doctor of Science
D.S.C. — Distinguished Service Cross
D.S.M. — Distinguished Service Medal
D.S.O. — Distinguished Service Order

ECA — Economic Cooperation Administration
ECOSOC — Economic and Social Council
ERP — European Recovery Program
ESA — Economic Stabilization Administration

F — February
FAO — Food and Agriculture Organization
FBI — Federal Bureau of Investigation
FCA — Farm Credit Administration
FCC — Federal Communications Commission
FEPC — Fair Employment Practice Committee

FERA — Federal Emergency Relief Administration
FHA — Federal Housing Administration
FSA — Federal Security Agency
FTC — Federal Trade Commission
G.B.E. — Knight or Dame Grand Cross Order of the British Empire
G.C.B. — Knight Grand Cross of the Bath
GHQ — General Headquarters
h. — home address
H.M. — His Majesty; Her Majesty
HOLC — Home Owners' Loan Corporation
ICC — Interstate Commerce Commission
I.C.F.T.U. — International Confederation of Free Trade Unions
I.L.A. — International Longshoremen's Association
I.L.G.W.U. — International Ladies' Garment Workers' Union
I.L.O. — International Labor Office
I.L.P. — Independent Labour Party
INS — International News Service
IRO — International Refugee Organization
I.T.U. — International Typographical Union
J — Journal
Ja — January
J.C.B. — Juris Canonici Bachelor
J.D. — Doctor of Jurisprudence
Je — June
j.g. — junior grade
Jl — July
K.B.E. — Knight of (the Order of) the British Empire
K.C. — King's Counsel
K.C.B. — Knight Commander of the Bath
L.H.D. — Doctor of Humanities
Litt.D. — Doctor of Letters
LL.B. — Bachelor of Laws
LL.D. — Doctor of Laws
LL.M. — Master of Laws
M.A. — Master of Arts
M.B.A. — Master of Business Administration
MBS — Mutual Broadcasting System
M.C.E. — Master of Civil Engineering
M.D. — Doctor of Medicine
M.E. — Master of Engineering
MGM — Metro-Goldwyn-Mayer
M.Lit. — Master of Literature
M.P. — Member of Parliament
M.P.P.D.A. — Motion Picture Producers and Distributors of America
Mr — March
MRP — Mouvement Républicain Populaire
MSA — Mutual Security Agency
M.Sc. — Master of Science
Msgr. — Monsignor, Monseigneur
MVA — Missouri Valley Authority
My — May
N — November
NAACP — National Association for the Advancement of Colored People
NAB — National Association of Broadcasters
NAM — National Association of Manufacturers
NATO — North Atlantic Treaty Organization
NBC — National Broadcasting Company
N.E.A. — National Education Association
NLRB — National Labor Relations Board
N.M.U. — National Maritime Union
NRA — National Recovery Administration
NRPB — National Resources Planning Board
NWLB — National War Labor Board
NYA — National Youth Administration

O — October
OCD — Office of Civilian Defense
OEEC — Organization for European Economic Cooperation
OPA — Office of Price Administration
OPM — Office of Production Management
OPRD — Office of Production Research and Development
OSRD — Office of Scientific Research and Development
OWI — Office of War Information
PAC — Political Action Committee
P.C. — Privy Councilor
PCA — Progressive Citizens of America
P.E.N. — Poets, Playwrights, Editors, Essayists and Novelists (International Association)
Ph.B. — Bachelor of Philosophy
Ph.D. — Doctor of Philosophy
por — portrait, -s
PWA — Public Works Administration
Q.C. — Queen's Counsel
R — Review
RAF — Royal Air Force
RCA — Radio Corporation of America
REA — Rural Electrification Administration
RFC — Reconstruction Finance Corporation
RKO — Radio-Keith-Orpheum
ROTC — Reserve Officers' Training Corps
S — September
SEC — Securities and Exchange Commission
s.g. — senior grade
SHAEF — Supreme Headquarters, Allied Expeditionary Force
S.J.D. — Doctor of Juridical Science
SPA — Surplus Property Administration
SSB — Social Security Board
S.T.B. — Bachelor of Sacred Theology
S.T.D. — Doctor of Sacred Theology
S.W.O.C. — Steel Workers' Organizing Committee
T.U.C. — Trades Union Congress
TVA — Tennessee Valley Authority
T.W.U.A. — Textile Workers Union of America
U.A.W.A. — Union Auto Workers of America
UMT — Universal Military Training
U.M.W.A. — United Mine Workers of America
U.N. — United Nations
UNESCO — United Nations Educational, Scientific, and Cultural Organization
UNRRA — United Nations Relief and Rehabilitation Administration
U.P. — United Press
USO — United Service Organizations
U.S.S.R. — Union of Socialist Soviet Republics
U.S.W.A. — United Steel Workers of America
VA — Veterans Administration
V.F.W. — Veterans of Foreign Wars
WAA — War Assets Administration
W.C.T.U. — Woman's Christian Temperance Union
WFA — War Food Administration
W.F.T.U. — World Federation of Trade Unions
WHO — World Health Organization
WLB — War Labor Board
WMC — War Manpower Commission
WPA — Work Projects Administration
WPB — War Production Board

ABDULLAH, MOHAMMAD (äb-dōol'ä)
Dec. 5, 1905- Prime Minister of Jammu and
Kashmir

Address: Srinagar, Kashmir

Through the leadership of Prime Minister
Sheikh Mohammad Abdullah one hundred and
five years of dynastic rule in Jammu and Kashmir was ended in August 1952, with the decision of this state's Constituent Assembly to
abolish the powers and title of the maharaja
and install an elected head of the government.
This move, which Abdullah hailed as a "triumph of the people's struggle against one-man
rule," followed the Assembly's approval of an
agreement that Abdullah had made with the
Indian Government in New Delhi to give Kashmir a near independent status within the Republic of India. Abdullah has headed the Kashmir Government since 1947, when the controversy arose between India and Pakistan as to
which country would control Kashmir. He had
earlier been president of the Moslem Conference
and president of the All-India Peoples Conference.

Mohammad Abdullah (the "sheikh" preceding his name is a courtesy title which originally meant elder or chieftain) was born
December 5, 1905, in the village of Soura—
seven miles from Srinagar, the capital of
Jammu and Kashmir—in the extreme northwest
of what was then the British Indian Empire.
The boy was reared by his elder brothers because his father, a dealer in shawls, had died
shortly before his birth and his mother had
died during his childhood. Abdullah attended
school first in Srinagar and then in Jammu,
whence he proceeded to the University of
Lahore, being graduated from this institution
with distinction.

Meanwhile Abdullah's social consciousness
had been aroused by conditions in his native
mud-hut village. "All around me were the
poor," he told Mary Harrington of the New
York *Post* (February 16, 1948). "I could always compare myself with those people; boys
with whom I had played grew up wearing
rags." An Associated Press correspondent,
Harold K. Milks (Washington *Post*, October
28, 1951), has credited Abdullah's "entry into
the freedom struggle" to "the death—from virtual starvation—of a boyhood friend" when
Abdullah was eighteen years old. While attending Kashmir College, Abdullah in 1927 formed
a Students' Union there. Three years later he
completed what Michael James of the New
York *Times* (February 3, 1952) has called "the
virtually impossible task of working his way"

MOHAMMAD ABDULLAH

through India's Moslem University of Aligarh,
where he received his M.Sc. degree in 1930.

After graduation Sheikh Abdullah went back
to Kashmir to become a science teacher in the
State High School. "When I returned to my
place," he told Mary Harrington, "I collected
a few friends around me, and we began to
press for reforms. We were arrested, and that
led to a large-scale upheaval. The maharaja
was forced to release us." This was in 1931—
the same year that the Moslem Conference was
organized with Abdullah as first president.
According to the New York *Times* (February
3, 1952), the Conference originally was limited
to Moslems and was "little more than an agency
through which skilled young Moslems attempted
to get jobs." While touring the country (in
which the predominantly Moslem population was
ruled by a Hindu maharaja) Sheikh Abdullah
found that not only Moslems but also Hindus
and Sikhs were living in poverty; he has attributed this situation to the fact that there were
"two classes, the exploiters and the exploited"
(New York *Post*).

In 1939 Abdullah persuaded the Moslem Conference to change its name to Kashmir National Conference and at the same time open
its membership to everyone who was "for the
establishment of a democratic form of government." The movement (wrote Michael James)

ABDULLAH, MOHAMMAD—*Continued*

"joined forces with other dissident groups in Kashmir and eventually with Gandhi's powerful forces in India proper," with the consequence that Abdullah "became one of the Gandhi-Nehru group's 'bright young men'" and formed a close association with Jawaharlal Nehru which later became very important. Pressure for reforms by the Conference were steadfastly opposed by the maharaja, and Sheikh Abdullah was sent to jail six times before 1946, when he launched the "Quit Kashmir" movement dedicated to abolishing the prince's feudal rule. For this defiance the Sheikh (widely known as "Sher-I-Kashmir" or "Lion of Kashmir") was again sentenced to jail in August 1946.

The "Lion of Kashmir" had served five months of his seventh sentence when on February 20, 1947, the British Labor Government of Clement Attlee announced its intention to divide its Indian Empire into two dominions—India and Pakistan, the first predominantly Hindu and the second Moslem. On August 15, 1947, both dominions came into being, with the status of Jammu and Kashmir remaining undecided. The Hindu Maharaja of Kashmir, Sir Hari Singh, favored his country's joining India and in this he was supported by Sheikh Abdullah, who had been elected President of the All-India States Peoples Conference while in jail. As explained by Margaret Parton of the New York *Herald Tribune* (December 2, 1948), Abdullah's reason for favoring alliance with India rather than Pakistan was that "India, at least in theory, is a secular state."

Released from prison, Abdullah organized a "peace brigade" to maintain harmony in Jammu-Kashmir. Then, on October 22, 1947, mountain tribesmen from the North, "perhaps at the instigation of Pakistan" (New York *Times*), "came galloping down in the direction of the valley." Two days later the maharaja left Srinagar for the safety of Jammu, where on October 25 he proclaimed the accession of Kashmir to the Dominion of India and asked for Indian troops to stem the invasion. In Srinagar, meanwhile, Mohammad Abdullah became head of the government through a *coup d'état*. He stated at this time (according to a subsequent Kashmir Government release) "that the invasion was meant to compel the people of Kashmir to accede to Pakistan and that every Kashmiri resented this compulsion on his will." He called on the people to "come forward and raise the banner of Hindu-Moslem unity. . . .In Kashmir we want a people's government. We want a government which will give equal rights and equal opportunities to all men, irrespective of caste or creed. The Kashmir Government . . . will be a joint government of the Hindus, the Sikhs and Moslems. That is what I am fighting for."

When in January 1948 the United Nations Security Council began debate on the future of Kashmir, Sheikh Abdullah became a member of the Indian delegation to the U.N. and made his first trip to the United States. In a fifty-minute speech at Lake Success, New York, on February 5 he defended the legality of his government and attacked the move in the

Council to set up a neutral interim government in Kashmir to conduct a plebiscite.

Upon his return to Srinagar in March Abdullah established a semidemocratic government with himself as Prime Minister and a Cabinet of seven (five of whom were Moslems), gaining from the maharaja concessions which stripped that prince of most of his powers. The civil war continued with an invading force from Pakistan pushing back the Indian-Kashmiri troops and occupying most of northern Kashmir. A military stalemate developed which enforced postponement of the plebiscite decided upon by the United Nations in April, and caused damage to agriculture and craft industries alike. Abdullah endeavored to relieve the situation by increasing the rice ration to peasants, declaring a moratorium on debts, canceling the land holdings of feudal chiefs to give the land to the peasants, and encouraging the export of rugs and shawls by setting up a government-sponsored Arts Emporium to get Kashmir goods into India. By the end of 1948 his government was secure in the area he controlled, and order was being maintained. Moslems favoring alliance with Pakistan, however, charged that Abdullah had "instituted a police regime" in Kashmir (New York *Herald Tribune*, December 2, 1948).

On January 1, 1949, under pressure from the United Nations, both India and Pakistan ordered an immediate cease-fire to end their fourteen months of warfare in Kashmir and announced their agreement to a plebiscite to decide which country should control Kashmir. However, it soon became apparent that India would not abide by a vote which might conceivably result in a Pakistan victory. The following June Sheikh Abdullah was appointed to the Indian Constituent Assembly which drafted the present basic law of the Republic of India, and subsequently he was named a member for Kashmir in the Indian Parliament. By December 1949 Abdullah returned to New York to argue before United Nations that "Pakistan has no legal position in Kashmir, because Kashmir has acceded to India" (New York *Times*, December 16, 1949). During 1950 it became increasingly clear that neither India nor Pakistan would abide by a plebiscite decision.

Gradually Abdullah began to move toward establishing Jammu-Kashmir as a more or less autonomous state, which would (as he said) maintain "intimate relations with the Indian Government." When the Kashmir Prime Minister called a Constituent Assembly in Srinagar in November 1951 to "decide the state's future political affiliation," he told delegates: "You are the sovereign authority in this state." Later the same month he announced that Crown Prince Karan Singh (who assumed active reign from his father in 1949) had signed an amendment to the existing constitution by which "all legislative and executive powers formerly vested in the maharaja" were to be "surrendered to the state government and legislature" (New York *Times*, November 22, 1951). Conferences between Abdullah and Prime Minister Nehru of India in New Delhi in July 1952 resulted in an agreement by which Kashmir was to receive special status within the Republic of

India, while retaining its own flag and its own land laws. In most other respects the Indian constitution was to apply to Kashmir; the title and hereditary position of the maharaja were to be abolished and a head of state, acceptable to the Indian government, was to be chosen by the Kashmir legislature. Subsequently, on August 21, the 105-year-old dynastic rule was formally abolished by a majority vote in the Kashmir Constituent Assembly.

Sheikh Mohammad Abdullah and Begum Akbar Jahan were married in 1932; they are the parents of two daughters and three sons, one of whom is named Mustafa Kemal, after the father of modern Turkey. The Prime Minister has told Mary Harrington that his greatest personal regret was that he had "too little time" for his children. "I like best to play with my children. I like to read history and biography, and I find that for me the best time to read is in jail. I have had no time except for those periods behind bars." Abdullah is six feet four inches tall. He wears his country's traditional gray karakul fez, although in other respects he prefers western attire. His religion is the Moslem.

References

N Y Herald Tribune p26 D 2 '48; II p3 D 18 '49 por
N Y Post p33 F 16 '48 pors
N Y Times Mag p10+ F 3 '52 pors
Washington (D.C.) Post p3B O 28 '51 por

India and Pakistan Year Book and Who's Who, 1952
International Who's Who, 1952

ADAMS, SHERMAN Jan. 8, 1899- Governor of New Hampshire
Address: b. State House, Concord, N.H.; h. Lincoln, N.H.

Governor Sherman Adams of New Hampshire, who in July 1952 was named the personal campaign manager of the Republican candidate for the Presidency of the United States, was chosen on November 24 by President-elect Dwight D. Eisenhower to become in January Assistant to the President. New Hampshire's chief executive, now serving a second two-year term in the gubernatorial office in Concord, was one of Eisenhower's earliest political champions and was floor manager of the pro-Eisenhower forces at the Republican National Convention in Chicago. Adams, who was a forester and lumber executive prior to his entering politics, served as speaker of the New Hampshire House of Representatives and as a member of the Seventy-ninth Congress in Washington, before his election as Governor in November 1948. He was re-elected in 1950 for the term ending January 1953.

A native of the small village of East Dover in Windham County, Vermont, Sherman Adams was born to Clyde H. and Winnie Marion (Sherman) Adams on January 8, 1899, and through his father is descended from the Henry Adams who established the famous Quincy, Massachusetts, branch of the family in the early Colonial period. Clyde Adams, the owner of the East Dover grocery store at the time of his son's birth, moved shortly afterward to Providence, Rhode Island, where the boy was reared and graduated from both elementary school and the local Hope High School. He saw World War I service with the United States Marine Corps in 1918 and two years later (1920) received his B.A. degree from Dartmouth College in Hanover, New Hampshire, the State he was subsequently to make his home and to serve in various political capacities. Adams was president of the Outing Club during his senior year at Dartmouth and hiked some 400-odd miles over trails in the White and the Green mountains.

Early attracted to the life of the woods, Sherman Adams began his career in the lumber industry as a clerk and scaler in the logging camp of the Black River Lumber Company in Healdville in southern Vermont, about half way between Bellows Falls and Rutland. In a biographical sketch in the *Journal of Forestry*—a publication to which Adams himself has contributed a number of articles—R. H. Monahan recorded that soon afterward when the camp foreman became ill, young Adams was placed in charge. Appointed treasurer of the Black River concern in 1921, he reduced costs of operation with such dispatch that in 1923 he was transferred to Lincoln, New Hampshire, as woods superintendent of the controlling lumber and pulp enterprise, the Parker-Young Company. He in time rose in the latter to be general manager and was also made a director of the Pemigewasset Railroad operating between Plymouth, New Hampshire, and Lincoln, and of the Pemigewasset National Bank in Plymouth. Adams entered politics in the summer of 1940 when he campaigned, as a Republican, for election to the New Hampshire House of Representatives from Lincoln; victorious in November in what the New York *Herald Tribune* reported was considered "a three-to-one Democratic town," he was made chairman of the House Committee on Labor when the session began in 1941. In this session Adams authored a State law creating forestry advisory boards. Two years later, having been re-elected, he became speaker of the New Hampshire House, the country's largest State legislative assembly, numbering well over four hundred members. He was made chairman of the Republican Committee for Grafton County (in which Plymouth is located) in 1942 and was a delegate to the Republican National Convention of 1944, supporting Governor Thomas E. Dewey of New York for the Presidential nomination.

In November 1944 Sherman Adams was elected to the Seventy-ninth Congress in Washington as representative of the Second New Hampshire District comprising most of the northern and western parts of the State; soon after the Congress convened on January 3, 1945, he was assigned to the House Labor Committee, Flood Control Committee, and Elections No. 2 Committee. In the first session of this Congress he supported a measure for a permanent Committee on Un-American Activities, an

SHERMAN ADAMS

anti-poll tax bill, and antitrust exemption for railroads. Adams' votes in May 1945 for extension of the Reciprocal Trade Agreements Act and in October of the same year for the government reorganization bill reflected his interest in international matters and in efficient administration, and were followed on November 30 by his signing a statement by thirty-one "Young Republicans" headed by Representative Augustus Bennet of New York that they "intend to express their own views on major matters and not allow party leaders to speak for them." Early in the second session of the Seventy-ninth Congress (1946) Representative Adams defied the "Old Guard" leadership of his own party by proposing a more liberal substitute for the Case Strike Control Bill, although he subsequently cast a "yea" vote for enactment of the latter. In May he favored President Truman's Strike Control Bill, but voted in June to override the Presidential veto of the Case measure. The New Hampshire Congressman, who had opposed extension of price controls in June 1945, voted for the assurance of "reasonable profits" under OPA ceilings in April 1946. He also gave his support to the $3.75 billion loan to Great Britain in the following July. Other votes cast by Adams in the second session of the Seventy-ninth Congress were for an extension of the draft to 1947 and against draft exemption for teen-agers.

When Adams during the summer of 1946 sought the Republican nomination for the Governorship of New Hampshire, he lost in the August primary by a very narrow margin to the incumbent Governor, former Mayor Charles H. Dale of Portsmouth, who was seeking a second term, and consequently the following January found himself out of political office. Adams, who had relinquished his executive position with the Parker-Young Company when

he went to Washington, remained a director of the Northeastern Lumber Manufacturers Association. Thus early in 1947 he undertook representation of the American pulpwood industry in New York City and for a period of nearly two years was especially active in promoting good trade relations with Canada. In the summer of 1948 he again sought, this time successfully, the Republican nomination for the Governorship of New Hampshire and won the election over his Democratic opponent in November. He began his first two-year term as Governor in January 1949.

By his policies and actions as the Granite State's chief executive, Sherman Adams "is known as a moderate conservative who believes the government should offer a measure of security to the individual" (*United States News and World Report*) and as the proponent of business-like State administration. Early in his first term in the gubernatorial office in Concord he called upon his Legislature to authorize a State reorganization study along the lines recommended by the Hoover Commission. The outcome was the setting up of the New Hampshire Commission on State Administrative Organization, with State Senator Curtis C. Cummings as chairman and John D. Langmuir as secretary, a body which accomplished its function largely through fifteen citizen "task forces" at a cost of less than $15,000 (Edgar M. Mills in the *Christian Science Monitor*). Governor Adams personally campaigned for adoption of its recommendations, which were passed by the Legislature and have resulted in cutting the State administrative departments from 83 to 43, consolidating accounting, purchasing, public works, conservation, and other functions, among various "streamlining" reforms. The program, which was the first of its kind to become effective in New England, was in operation by the summer of 1950 and is thought to have had much to do with Adams' re-election as Governor for the term expiring in January 1953. He defeated his leading opponent in the September 1950 primary by a vote of 57,499 to 16,943 and his Democratic adversary, State Senator Robert P. Bingham, by a 26,742 majority in November. Shortly after beginning his second term in January 1951 the Governor "brought together . . . a number of top New Hampshire industrialists" to form the New Hampshire Business Development Corporation, the primary objective of which is "to encourage new construction to replace outmoded facilities" and which has $2 million available to qualified individuals who desire to start new enterprises within the State. A State fund of $4 million to "promote, assist, and encourage development and advancement of the business prosperity and economy of the State" had been set up by August 1951.

Nationally New Hampshire's chief executive is best known as one of the earliest proponents of General Dwight D. Eisenhower's becoming Republican candidate for President in 1952. At the forty-third annual Governors' Conference in Gatlinburg, Tennessee, on September 30, 1951, he was one of six Republican Governors to urge the nomination of Eisenhower and predicted that the General's name would be filed

by petition in his State's Presidential preference primary on March 11, 1952, and that Eisenhower would not request its withdrawal. A
notable speech by Adams, nationally broadcast,
to the National Republican Club in New York
City on January 29, 1952, may be considered
the opening gun of an active "Eisenhower for
President" campaign, the New Hampshire Governor stating that Eisenhower "stands the best
chance of election" among available Republicans
and that "on his own merits must be outstand-
ingly the best qualified candidate for President
of the United States." In the New Hampshire
campaign preceding the March preferential
primary, Adams threw the weight of his own
political influence behind Eisenhower, the latter
winning easily over Senator Robert H. Taft,
who stumped the State on his own behalf.
Adams was selected as floor manager of the
"Eisenhower for President" forces at the Republican National Convention in July; and on
the 22nd of the same month, after the General
had been nominated, he was offered and accepted the post of "chief of staff" in the candidate's personal campaign organization. He took
a three-month leave of absence from his gubernatorial duties commencing August 1, and on
August 19 Adams was appointed by Eisenhower to head his own four-man committee to
coordinate activities with the Republican National Committee and was directed to open a
"political end strategy office" in Washington.
"The announcement," commented W. H. Lawrence of the New York *Times*, "means that in
a very real sense Governor Adams will be the
supreme director of the Eisenhower victory
drive, taking orders only from General Eisenhower." A month later, the *United States News
and World Report* observed that the "shrewd,
quiet Yankee businessman" named Adams
"the man you want to see if you want to see
Eisenhower." On November 24, 1952, President-elect Eisenhower announced his decision
to appoint Adams as Assistant to the President
when he takes office in January 1953.

Governor Adams is a trustee of both Dartmouth College and the University of New
Hampshire; he received an honorary M.A. degree from the former and an LL.D. degree
from the latter in 1950 and a C.L.D. degree
from New England College in 1951. His
fraternity is Sigma Alpha Epsilon; Adams'
service organizations are the American Legion
and the Forty-and-Eight. He is a member of
the Ancient and Honorable Artillery Company
and the secretary of the New Hampshire chapter of the Sons of the American Revolution.
The Granite State Governor became a junior
member of the Society of American Foresters
in 1930 and a senior member in 1942; he is a
Mason (Shriner) and an Elk. His church is the
Episcopal. Sherman Adams and Rachel Leona
White were married in July 1923 and are the
parents of three daughters, Marion, Jean, and
Sarah, and one son, Samuel. The blue-eyed,
gray-haired Governor is five feet eight inches
in height and 150 pounds in weight. Golf, fishing, skiing and snowshoeing are his recreations.

References

Journal of Forestry 47:307-8 Ap '49
N Y Herald Tribune II p1 Ag 3 '52 por
U S News 33:20 S 26 '52 por
Biographical Directory of the American
Congress, 1774-1949 (1950)
Congressional Directory (1946)
International World Who's Who, 1948-
49
Who's Who in America, 1952-53
Who's Who in United States Politics
(1950)
World Biography (1948)

ADLER, MORTIMER J(EROME) Dec.
28, 1902- Philosopher; educator; author
Address: b. c/o Institute for Philosophical Research, 2090 Jackson St., San Francisco, Calif.;
h. 3340 Jackson St., San Francisco, Calif.

NOTE: This biography supersedes
the article which appeared in
Current Biography in 1940.

In June 1952 Mortimer J. Adler announced
plans to found an institute for philosophical
research at San Francisco for the analysis of
the basic ideas and issues in the thought of
the Western world. To devote himself to this
new project he resigned from his post as professor of the philosophy of law at the University of Chicago, where he was considered a
stimulating, controversial, and influential figure
for more than two decades. He went to Chicago from Columbia University in 1930 at the
invitation of President Robert M. Hutchins, who
brought him there to be his aid in instituting
a "return to the classics" program of education. With Hutchins he was instrumental in
establishing the Great Books Program and he is
the associate editor of *Great Books of the
Western World* and editor of its two-volume
Syntopicon.

Mortimer Jerome Adler was born in New
York City on December 28, 1902, the son of
Ignatz Adler, a jewelry salesman, and Clarissa
(Manheim) Adler, a former schoolteacher. Although he was a brilliant student at DeWitt
Clinton High School and editor of the paper
there, he did not graduate—"I had a difference
of opinion with the principal as to who was
running the school." He left high school after
two years, then aged fifteen, and became
the secretary of Edward Page Mitchell,
editor of the New York *Sun*. Early an omnivorous reader, at seventeen he was dismayed
to learn that John Stuart Mill, the nineteenth
century English philosopher, had read Plato's
Dialogues at the age of five. Adler, who had
not even seen the *Dialogues*, promptly bought
a copy, read it, and decided to become a
philosopher instead of a journalist. In 1920 he
obtained a scholarship to Columbia, where he
finished the four-year course in three years,
highest in his class and first on the Phi Beta
Kappa list. But he did not receive the baccalaureate degree, said *Time*: one requirement
was to take the test in swimming, which Adler
refused to do. However, after he had been
teaching for five years Columbia awarded him

Halsman

MORTIMER J. ADLER

the Ph.D. degree in psychology in 1928. The title of his thesis was *An Experimental Approach to the Measurement of Music Appreciation*.

It was as an instructor in psychology that Adler began teaching. Following the lead of John Erskine, who exercised one of the strongest influences on his thinking, he conducted a course on great books at Columbia for several years. From 1923 until 1929 he taught psychology there, and during the same period lectured at the College of the City of New York and at the People's Institute, of which he was an assistant director from 1928 to 1930. A comment he wrote on the law of evidence attracted the attention of Robert Maynard Hutchins, then acting dean of the Law School at Yale University, and shortly after Hutchins became president of the University of Chicago in 1929, he invited Adler to join the faculty. But some members of the philosophy department so strongly opposed Adler's ideas on education and philosophy, according to *Time*, that Hutchins had to create a new post for him, and appointed him associate professor of the philosophy of law. Adler held this rank from 1930 until 1942, when he became a full professor. In 1937 he became visiting lecturer at St. John's College at Annapolis, Maryland. There, as at Chicago, a return to the traditional basis of education was established: close study of the classics of the Western world.

It is Adler's opinion that the dominant influence on current American thought and education—that of John Dewey, who taught him philosophy at Columbia—has been a disastrous one. Adler has always been opposed to the pragmatic view that truth is whatever is useful to a given society at a specific stage in its history. On the contrary, he affirms, there are absolute and universal truths and values, and

the failure to recognize their existence results from the application of scientific method in areas where it is not competent. "The fundamental ideals and concepts on which education should be based," he wrote in the *Rotarian*, "are not merely the *mores* and beliefs which happen to be current in twentieth century America. They are universal truths about what constitutes a good education for all men at all times and places just because they are men." Progressive education, he believes, with its emphasis on individual expression and inclinations, is based on false and dangerous principles. The elective system, under which a student is free to choose any course in the curriculum he wishes, encourages aimlessness and superficiality. Genuine freedom, according to Adler, is identical with duty, and can be achieved only through discipline; a genuine liberal education "consists in the moral and intellectual disciplines which liberate men by cultivating their specially rational power to judge freely and to exercise free will."

Adler propounded his views in numerous articles, books, and lectures, which, because of their controversial character, have generally provoked mixed reactions. *Art and Prudence* (1937), one of his early books, not only received the approbation of scholars, but came to wider public notice because of its discussion of motion pictures as both an art and an agency of social education. The book is for the most part, however, a formal, academic analysis of the views of Plato, Aristotle, and St. Thomas Aquinas (of whom Adler is a disciple) on the relation of art to morals. The *Nation* described the book as "scholasticism in full dress." *Commonweal* remarked that Adler "is one of our best American expositors of medieval culture; in this work he turns his vast knowledge in this field to practical account and enriches Thomistic philosophy with a fresh application to a modern art."

Adler's best-known work, *How to Read a Book; the Art of Getting a Liberal Education*, was published in 1940. Written in sixteen days, a chapter a day, in the hope of earning $1,000, the book instead topped the best-seller lists for months and brought its author $30,000. *How to Read a Book* is another projection of Adler's theories on the meaning of a liberal education. It is his belief that a smaller proportion of Americans is literate now, in the real meaning of the term, than in the eighteenth century. Any book worth reading, he maintains in the book's first section, requires "the most intense mental activity" for real understanding and must be read three times—for analysis, for interpretation, and for evaluation. In the second section he sets down rules for reading (as necessary, he says, as for playing tennis or driving a car), such as noting clue words and sentences, pivotal paragraphs, and central ideas. His third section is concerned with the connection between reading and freedom. Albert Guerard wrote of the book in the New York *Times*: "Its excellent sense is plain and unadorned, and the sole recipe it recommends is hard work. That such an austere, conservative manual . . . should prove a favorite with the general public is a high tribute to the seriousness of the American mind." Clifton Fadiman was also favorably impressed. "This is a condensed book," he wrote in the *New Yorker*, "written without literary charm, without trickery. It makes no empty promises. It says flatly that proper reading is serious work, but it shows concretely how that serious work may be accomplished and how much it may yield in the way of instruction and delight." The *Atlantic* was one of the few dissenting voices in the general chorus of praise. "We could think more highly of Mr. Adler's effort, conscientious as we are sure it is, if he had frankly labeled his educational plan as a makeshift, and had given due warning against the danger of putting any extravagant expectations on it."

Adler's next popular book, *How to Think about War and Peace* (1944), also evoked a mixed response. *Library Journal* saluted it as "a necessary guide for intelligent comprehension and criticism of the hundreds of books which have been (and will be) published about peace and postwar planning." The New York *Times* regarded it as "a challenge that anyone who is seriously interested in peace in our time and the years to come must accept. It leads to a brilliant exercise in plain and fancy thinking, during which Mr. Adler lays low one popular illusion after the other by the simple process of requiring precise definitions of all the terms used in the discussion." Malcolm Cowley, however, who reviewed the book for the *New Republic*, found it "an exercise in scholastic logic, presented in the almost geometrical style."

One offshoot of the undergraduate seminar on classics at the University of Chicago was the launching, in 1946, of the Great Books Program, a plan by which hundreds of discussion groups composed of adults from many walks of life were organized in numerous cities. The members of the "classes" prepare for the biweekly, two-hour meetings, which are presided over by two leaders, by reading a certain work. Included on the first list of authors are Greek philosophers, St. Augustine, St. Thomas, Montaigne, Shakespeare, Locke, Rousseau, Adam Smith, and Marx. The movement has been summed up as "free, universal, liberal education of adults."

During the course of a discussion in 1943, Adler and Hutchins conceived the idea of reprinting the great books of the Western world, the selection of which would be based on the courses they had taught at Chicago. An important part of the project was the compiling of an index to, or concordance of, the main ideas in the collection. Adler became the editor in chief of the two-volume guide, entitled *Syntopicon*, ("a synthesis of topics") which *Time* called "the first Baedeker to thirty centuries of Western thought." The complete set of *Great Books of the Western World*, of which Adler is associate editor, comprises 54 volumes containing 443 works by 74 authors from Homer to Freud. The cost of the undertaking (completed in 1952) was sponsored by *Encyclopædia Britannica* and the University of Chicago.

The *Syntopicon* represents to Adler a step on the way to a comprehensive analysis of the basic concepts and issues in Western thinking, a step necessary for the promotion of the advancement of learning. He regards his new project in San Francisco, an institute for philosophical research, as a further step in the same direction. The institute (plans for which were announced in June 1952) will be endowed with grants totaling $655,000 by the Old Dominion Foundation and the Fund for the Advancement of Education. It is expected to have a staff of twenty-five and to produce at least twenty-five books. As the New York *Times* reported, it "will try to find questions worth answering, the possible answers that have been or are being given, and the connections between questions and answers."

The philosopher is also the author of *Dialectic* (1927), *Crime, Law, and Social Science* (with Jerome Michael, 1933), *Diagrammatics* (with Maude Phelps Hutchins, 1935), *Art and Prudence* (1937), *What Man Has Made of Man* (1938), *St. Thomas and the Gentiles* (1938), *Problems for Thomists: The Problems of Species* (1940), and *A Dialectic of Morals* (1941). He has contributed numerous articles to magazines, among them *The Thomist*, *The Saturday Review of Literature*, *Harpers*, *Commonweal*, *Ladies' Home Journal*, and *Social Frontier*. Aside from his activities as philosopher, teacher, writer, and editor, Adler has been an adviser to the Motion Picture Association of America ("Hays office"), lecturer for the United States Air Transport Command, and consultant to the Ford Foundation. He is a member of the American Catholic Philosophical Association, the Mediaeval Academy of America, and the Thomistic Institute.

Adler and Helen Leavenworth Boynton were married May 2, 1927, and have two children, Mark Arthur and Michael Boynton. Tennis is the philosopher's favorite form of outdoor exercise. Of his appearance and tastes *Time* wrote that "his friends have compared him to a better-fed Savonarola. He likes Brooks Brothers suits, good leather, fast cars, fine food . . . but whatever he enjoys, he usually enjoys in a hurry."

References

> Harper 183:377-88 S '41
> N Y World Telegram p20 Mr 21 '40
> Time 59:76+ Mr 17 '52
> Who's Who in America, 1952-53
> Who's Who in American Education, 1947-48
> Who's Who in Chicago and Illinois (1950)

AHLGREN, MILDRED CARLSON *See* Ahlgren, Mrs. O. A.

AHLGREN, MRS. OSCAR A(LEXANDER) Nov. 7, 1902- Women's organization official

Address: b. c/o General Federation of Women's Clubs, 1734 N St., N.W., Washington 6, D.C.; h. 1735 Stanton Ave., Whiting, Ind.

As president of the General Federation of Women's Clubs, Mrs. Oscar A. Ahlgren heads

AHLGREN, MRS. OSCAR A.——*Continued*

the largest international organization of women, composed of about eleven million members living in various parts of the world. Before her election to the presidency on May 16, 1952, in succession to Mrs. Hiram Cole Houghton, she traveled widely in a number of executive capacities for the federation. Mrs. Ahlgren announced that as leader of the G.F.W.C. she intends to engage in a crusade for Americanism by stimulating civic interest and by developing programs of education in democratic ideals.

Born on November 7, 1902, in Chicago, Illinois, Mildred Carlson Ahlgren is the daughter of August John and Hilda Sophia (Peterson) Carlson, both of whom came to the United States from Sweden. (She has a brother, who is now president of the Indiana Manufacturers Association.) Mildred was reared in Indiana Harbor, Indiana, and attended the East Chicago (Indiana) High School, from which she was graduated in 1917. She became a student at the Columbia College of Expression in Chicago and also took courses at the University of Chicago. On June 6, 1923, she was married to Oscar Alexander Ahlgren, who had been her teacher in public speaking seven years earlier at high school. Their daughter Adrienne is now Mrs. Charles Haeuser. Ahlgren, who was speaker of the House of the Indiana legislature at the time of his marriage, later became an attorney in Whiting, Indiana, where they make their home. Since 1935 Mrs. Ahlgren has been a columnist and special correspondent for the Hammond (Indiana) *Times*, contributing society news and feature articles.

Mrs. Ahlgren commenced her work as a clubwoman in 1932 as a member of the Whiting Women's Club. Her first step toward leadership in women's organizations occurred when she offered to serve as that club's delegate to the Lake County Federation meeting, where, to her surprise, she was nominated president. After her election to this office, Mrs. Ahlgren became business manager of the *Indiana Club Woman*. Her position as treasurer of the Indiana State Federation was followed by the post of first vice-president. Then, as president of the Indiana State Federation from 1941 to 1944 she organized civic interest discussions in various Indiana colleges, in cooperation with the Daughters of the American Revolution, the League of Women Voters, the National Federation of Business and Professional Women's Clubs, the American Legion Auxiliary, and the Parent-Teacher Association. The forums were designed to encourage women's participation in politics and candidacy for public office. The *Christian Science Monitor* pointed out that in this period Indiana elected its first woman Senator to the State Legislature and sent seven women to its House of Representatives.

From 1944 to 1947 Mrs. Ahlgren was the recording secretary of the General Federation of Women's Clubs, from 1947 to 1950 its second vice-president, and from 1950 to 1952 its first vice-president. Previously, in 1943-44, she had been dean of directors on the executive committee of the G.F.W.C. Other offices Mrs. Ahlgren had filled were those of member of the resolutions committee and chairman of the

federation's United States saving bonds committee. On May 16, 1952, at the sixty-first annual convention of the General Federation of Women's Clubs, in Minneapolis, Minnesota, she was elected president without opposition, succeeding in this office Mrs. Hiram Cole Houghton of Iowa.

During her years as an officer for the G.F.W.C., Mrs. Ahlgren was also active in many other groups. By appointment of the Governor she was during 1941-43 a member of the Indiana State Planning Commission (the only woman member), and during 1943-46 served as the woman member of the Indiana State Personnel Board, which supervises the State's merit system. Governor Henry F. Schricker commissioned her as a member of the Mid-Century White House Conference on Children and Youth and as a trustee of the Indiana State Employes Retirement Fund from 1949 to 1952. She was chairman of the Women's Division of the Indiana War Finance Committee (1940-46), of the Women's Committee of the Indiana War History Committee (1945-48), and of the National Advisory Committee for Savings Bonds for the United States Treasury (1951). Mrs. Ahlgren has also served on the national sponsoring committee for Allied Youth. In the course of her years as vice-president of the General Federation, she visited women's clubs in most of the States in the Union, Alaska, and seven Latin American countries. In 1950 she took part in a good-will tour of nine European countries, meeting members of American women's clubs who were traveling abroad and contacting organizations affiliated with the General Federation of Women's Clubs.

As head of the G.F.W.C., Mrs. Ahlgren leads about eleven million women members in the United States and forty other countries. She lives in the G.F.W.C.'s headquarters in Washington, D.C., the center of the world organization. Her duties require her membership in more than thirty committees, foundations, and councils, and she frequently is called upon to officiate at public ceremonies. The federation is comprised of eight departments: American home, communications, education, fine arts, international relations, legislation, public affairs (recently changed to Americanism), and welfare. The G.F.W.C. international program advocates mass education on the United Nations and world problems, legislative proposals to strengthen the U.N. and other groups working for world peace, world good will and rehabilitation, and an international scholarship plan.

Mrs. Ahlgren's two primary objectives are the encouraging of women to participate more fully in civic affairs and the awakening of American religious feeling. "I feel we're in a mess today because of a spiritual collapse. We must get back to faith in God," she has stated. "Children must not be allowed to grow up without religious teaching as many of them are doing." She calls for a re-establishment of basic values—"the old virtues of hard work, integrity in the individual and in government." Announcing in Washington on June 5, 1952, that she was starting a "crusade for Americanism," she outlined her program as follows: the stimulation of voting in the November 1952 elections; the education of all people to the advantages of representative government; the development of an awareness of the importance of great Americans; a campaign to make American history a required subject in high schools and colleges; and the encouragement of women's participation in public affairs. In other statements since assuming her new post she has called for more action and fewer resolutions.

The sixty-fifth annual convention, at which Mrs. Ahlgren was elected president, reaffirmed the federation's support of the United Nations and resolved to attempt to develop an appreciation for the U.N. among the American people. The convention also placed itself on record as condemning any blanket order for the censorship of information. Mrs. Ahlgren announced that the federation would cease to support Federal aid to education, explaining, "We believe in States' rights." Another important resolution passed by the federation at the convention was the revoking of its previous ban on the admittance to membership of clubs on the basis of sectarian affiliations. The new president stated that in the following year the federation would again sponsor a contest which would encourage youths to participate in community work, and announced that in the following January and February another group of federation women led by herself, would undertake a tour of the world in order to exchange ideas for solving international conflicts.

Mrs. Ahlgren has also been active in the National Citizens Commission for the Public Schools (advisory board member), the Parent-Teacher Association, the League of Women Voters, the All-American Conference to Combat Communism (advisory board member), Indiana Civic League, Indiana Committee for the George Foster Peabody Radio Awards, the Hoosier Art Patrons' Association (vice-president). She is a member as well of Business and Professional Women's Club, the National Federation of Press Women, National League of American Pen Women, the Indiana Women's Press Club, Alpha Delta Pi, Phi Beta, and Beta Gamma Upsilon; and of the Order of the Eastern Star, the P.E.O. Sisterhood, and the American Legion Auxiliary. Clubs outside Indiana which claim her membership are the San Antonio (Texas) and Chautauqua (New York); she has been given an honorary life membership in the Whiting Women's Club, of which she remains a director. Her country club is Lake Hills, and she attends the Plymouth Congregational Church.

The Ahlgrens, said Dorothea Pattee of the Washington Post, usually give a Christmas party for as many as 800 fellow members in twenty-five clubs. Mrs. Ahlgren speaks Swedish fluently. She has gray eyes and brown hair, is five feet five inches tall, weighs 136 pounds. Since her school days, reported the Indianapolis News, she has liked "art, the theater, good books, white ruffled curtains, and

MRS. OSCAR A. AHLGREN

friends." She has been characterized as having "a great gift for recognizing and calling out the best in others."

References

Christian Sci Mon p3 My 12 '52
Indianapolis (Ind.) News p3 M 1 '52
Time 59:27 My 26 '52
Washington (D.C.) Post p45 Je 8 '52
por
Who's Who in America, 1952-53

ALI, MOHAMMED Oct. 19, 1909- Ambassador from Pakistan to the United States
Address: b. c/o Embassy of Pakistan, 2201 R Street, N.W., Washington, D.C.; h. 2343 S Street, N.W., Washington, D.C.

In January 1952 Mohammed Ali, then serving as Pakistan's High Commissioner in Canada, was named Ambassador to the United States from Pakistan. Ali began his career as a statesman in the early 1930's in the position of vice-chairman (deputy mayor) of the Bogra municipality and of honorary magistrate. Among the posts he has held since then are Finance Minister of Bengal, acting Premier, and member of the Constituent Assembly of Pakistan. The Ambassador has founded a number of schools and colleges in his country and has established charity dispensaries.

Mohammed Ali was born October 19, 1909, in Barisal, East Bengal, Pakistan, one of the seven children (six boys and one girl) of Altaf Ali and Meher Banu Begum. His grandfather was Nawab Bahadur Syed Nawab Ali Chaudhury of Dhanbari, the first Muslim minister in Bengal, to whose career Ali attributes some

MOHAMMED ALI

influence on the choice of his own lifework. In Calcutta, where the boy grew up, he attended two schools, Hastings House in Alipore and Calcutta Madrassah; at the latter school he was chosen secretary of the debating society. After graduating from high school in 1926, he continued his education at Islamia College, where he founded the student union and became its secretary. He also studied at Presidency College of Calcutta University and received the degree of B.A. with distinction in 1930.

Entering public service in 1932, Ali Mohammed became the vice-chairman of the district board (deputy mayor) of the Pakistan municipality of Bogra. A year later he was made deputy chairman of the Padmpara Central Cooperative Bank, in 1933, and a member of the Bengal Wakf Board the following year. He held the chairmanship of the Muslim League of his district from 1937 to 1948. During the early years of his career he also served as an honorary magistrate (justice of the peace). As the chairman of the Bogra district board he directed the non-official local administration from 1938 to 1943 and from 1944 to 1946. In 1938 he also became a member of the Bengal Agricultural Board and the Court of the University of Dacca, and in 1939 he was made a fellow of Calcutta University. Another post held by Ali at this time was the honorary chairmanship (1940-46) of the Central Cooperative Bank at Bogra, which provided credit facilities to rural societies. After a year (1944-45) as the parliamentary secretary to the Premier of East Bengal, he occupied the office of president of the Bogra school board in 1945, having jurisdiction over primary education in the district.

While in the position of Finance Minister of Bengal in 1946-47, Ali also acted as the Premier for short periods. He was elected in 1947 to the Constituent Assembly of Pakistan, of which he remained a member until 1949. The legislator received a diplomatic appointment in 1948 when he was sent to Burma as Pakistan's first Ambassador to that country. The following year he became the Pakistani High Commissioner in Canada and served as such for three years. When Mirza Abol Hassan Ispahani, the Pakistan Ambassador to the United States, was appointed High Commissioner in London, Mohammed Ali (as announced on January 13, 1952) was named to succeed him in the Washington assignment.

Soon after his arrival in Washington, Ali stated in a newspaper interview that he intended to study production methods in the United States in order to introduce them into Pakistan, believing that this was the only way in which his country's standard of living could be raised. On April 21, 1952, the new Ambassador spoke at a luncheon given by the Far East-America Council of Commerce and Industry, Inc., discussing in his address tax concessions which would be made by the Pakistan government to encourage investment and industrial enterprises. He also referred to Pakistan's need for capital goods and industrial services which could be supplied only by the West and expressed his belief that with the continuation of his country's development greater earnings in foreign exchange would become available to purchase such commodities. At a ceremony in April 1952 in which he presented Pakistan's flag to the State University Maritime College, Fort Schuyler, the Bronx, Ali told of his country's plans for rebuilding a merchant fleet (since most of her ships and ports were lost in the partition of India) and for establishing a Merchant Navy Academy at Juldia Point, Chittagong. Speaking at Colgate University's Conference on American Foreign Policy on July 30, 1952, he stated that Pakistan is ready to assume the role of "interpreter of the Middle East to the Western World and of the Western World to the Middle East." He also stated that Western economic aid to the Moslem countries might be received with suspicion because those nations have been "dominated politically and exploited commercially" by other powers.

Boards and committees in Pakistan on which Ali has served are the Board of Industries, the Bengal Board of Film Censors, the Central Parliamentary Board, and the Eastern Bengal Railway Advisory Committee. He has also been a member of the governing bodies of the Indian Football Association and the Bengal Hockey Association. The Pakistani official owns an estate in Bogra, where he was founder and president of a college which offers the baccalaureate degree. He also established several junior and high schools and a number of charity dispensaries. Ali has been awarded the Jubilee Medal, the Coronation Medal, the Medal of Merit, and the Khan Bahadur (lately relinquished). He gave up his title of Nawab in 1946 and, as reported in the Washington *Post*, will soon surrender his properties in Pakistan in accordance with a law (that he helped make) by which lands will be sold at low prices to the government and then parceled out to farmers. "We feel the time has come," the *Post* quoted Ali as saying, "when 'have-nots' should have the benefits of freedom and should not be subjected to that type of bondage where they serve without owning land."

Ali and Hamida Banu were married March 30, 1934; they have two sons, Hammad and Hamde. The Ambassador's political affiliation is the Muslim League. His clubs are the Calcutta Club, the Dacca Club (Pakistan), the Royal Calcutta Turf Club, and the Calcutta South Club. He is an enthusiastic amateur photographer and enjoys shooting, bowling, curling, and golf. Other interests are deep-sea trolling and trout casting. Ali has dark brown eyes and black hair, is five feet eight inches tall, and weighs one hundred and seventy-five pounds.

References

> Washington (D.C.) Post p5C F 29 '52; p75 S 7 '52
> Ansari's Trade Directory of Pakistan, 1951-52
> Indian and Pakistan Yearbook and Who's Who, 1950
> International Who's Who, 1951
> Nalanda Yearbook and Who's Who in India and Pakistan, 1950-51
> Who's Who in India, 1946-47
> Who's Who in the United Nations (1951)
> World Diplomatic Directory (1951)

ALLEN, RAYMOND B(ERNARD) Aug. 7, 1902- United States Government official; university administrator

Address: b. c/o Office of the Chancellor, University of California, Los Angeles 24, Calif.

The appointment in December 1951 of Dr. Raymond B. Allen to occupy the newly created office of chancellor of the University of California at Los Angeles occurred at about the same time that he was assigned to direct the Psychological Strategy Board of the National Research Council. When Allen took office on the PSB in early January 1952, it was expected that he would remain in that position until September, at which time he would assume his duties as university chancellor. His appointment to the PSB, where he is responsible for planning and coordinating American propaganda abroad, is the third of Allen's Government posts. The two earlier ones—both occupied while he was president of the University of Washington—were director of the Defense Department's Office of Medical Services and Chairman of the Salary Stabilization Board. Before his appointment to the University of Washington in 1946, Allen was engaged in medical practice and research and in the administration of medical schools.

The son of Anthony J. and Ellen (Faulkner) Allen, Raymond Bernard Allen was born August 7, 1902, in Cathay, North Dakota. The five boys and one girl of the Allen family are of Scotch, Irish, English, and French descent; their father, a Methodist minister, and mother had gone to North Dakota from their native Kentucky. They later moved to Minneapolis, where Raymond Allen attended East High School until graduation in 1920.

James O. Sneddon

RAYMOND B. ALLEN

His advanced education was acquired at the University of Minnesota, from which he received the B.S. degree in 1924, the M.A. in 1925, and his medical degrees (M.B. and M.D.) in 1928. While studying medicine he held a teaching fellowship in anatomy at the university. Following general medical practice from 1928 to 1930 centering about Minot, North Dakota, and concurrent with an assistant surgeonship at the Northwest Clinic, Allen returned for further study at the university. He studied on a Mayo Foundation fellowship, which he held until 1934, when he was awarded his Ph.D. degree by the Mayo Foundation Division of the university's Graduate Division. His thesis was entitled *Experiments on the Physiology and Causes of Compensatory Renal Hypertrophy* (1935). His interest in science, Allen has said, was stimulated by Professor Richard Scammon, anatomist and biometrician, and his interest in education and administration by Dr. Hugh Cabot, surgeon at the Mayo Clinic.

In 1933 Dr. Allen entered upon his first post as a medical school administrator by becoming associate director of the New York Post-Graduate Medical School and Hospital. The following year he was named, in addition, associate dean in charge of graduate studies of Columbia University's College of Physicians and Surgeons. He left both positions in 1936, the year of his appointment as dean of the College of Medicine of Wayne University. From Wayne, Allen went in 1939 to the University of Illinois, becoming executive dean of the Colleges of Dentistry, Medicine and Pharmacy, all in Chicago; and from 1943 to 1946 he was, besides, dean of the College of Medicine. While an educational official in Chicago, where he remained until 1946, he wrote for a committee of the council of the New York Academy of Medicine a study with the title *Medical Education and the Changing Order* (1946). In

ALLEN, RAYMOND B.—*Continued*

this work, in which he discusses problems of professional preparation, Allen sets forth his medical creed: "Medicine, with its age-old concern for the sick—the poor as well as the rich, the weak as well as the strong—has been an influence for good surpassed only by the moral precepts of religion." Allen is a fellow of the American College of Physicians and a member of the Detroit Academy of Surgery and of the Chicago Institute of Medicine.

The physician moved into the field of general educational administration with his appointment in 1946 as twenty-first president of the University of Washington. During his stay there he saw the establishment of schools of medicine and dentistry and the institution's admission to the Association of American Universities, considered the "blue ribbon" group among university organizations.

While Allen was president at Washington controversy arose over his action following an investigation of subversive persons at the university by a committee of the Washington legislature. Three accused instructors were ordered by him to stand trial before a faculty committee as to their fitness to teach in view of Communist party membership. Allen approved the majority view of the committee that jurisdiction to try was lacking but that in principle dismissal was proper. He defended the dismissal as being in furtherance of free inquiry: "We can have no quarrel with philosophies, economic, political or otherwise, honestly held, which do not require the teacher holding such philosophies be subject to outside dictation. We maintain, however, that an active member of the Communist party, subject to outside dictation, is not a free seeker after truth" (quoted by the New York *Herald Tribune*). Shortly afterward Allen characterized a request of the House Un-American Activities Committee for a list of the texts used by his university as an attempt to investigate a matter outside legislative cognizance, purely for decision by qualified educators.

Problems of administering medical service also occupied Allen at this period. As a member of the Eberstadt Committee of the Commission on Organization of the Executive Branch of the Government (Hoover Commission) he participated in making recommendations for establishing a medical advisory board in the office of the Secretary of Defense. Such a body, the Armed Forces Medical Advisory Committee, was formed in 1948, with Allen a member. Subsequently, June 1949 saw Allen installed as first director of the Office of Medical Services in the Defense Department. This office had the tasks of coordinating and supervising Army, Navy, and Air Force use of medical personnel and facilities. Allen, according to Harold B. Hinton (writing in the New York *Times*), was one of those said to favor the restriction of such medical care to the armed services. After Allen's resignation from this post in October 1949, he supported the action of his successor, Dr. Richard L. Meiling, in reducing the number of military hospitals in the United States.

In July 1951 Allen took leave of absence from the University of Washington to serve as chairman of another newly created Government agency, the Salary Stabilization Board, which was set up under the general supervision of the Office of Price Stabilization to make policy decisions for the already existing Office of Salary Stabilization. Among the policies announced by Allen during his chairmanship was one generally limiting bonuses for salaried persons to the 1950 levels instead of allowing a percentage increase in them as the Wage Stabilization Board had done in relation to wage earners' bonuses. Allen said that his board was considering the situation arising when such salaried personnel as foremen receive less compensation than overtime wages plus regular wages given to the workmen under them. Data was being gathered, he explained, on the customary spread of compensation between·the two types of employees.

Allen returned only briefly to the university after leaving his SSB post in late 1951, for in December the regents of the University of California, on the nomination made by university president Robert Gordon Sproul, elected Allen the chancellor of the Los Angeles campus, largest of the eight comprising the university. Among the reasons given by President Sproul for this selection was that Allen had extensive experience in administering institutions of higher learning, was young enough to devise plans and see them through much of their development, and was firmly opposed to communism. Allen succeeded Dr. Clarence A. Dykstra, who had died in May 1950; Dykstra had held the title of provost, but the university decided that the independence exercised in most matters by the heads of the campuses at Los Angeles and Berkeley justified the use of a title connoting greater authority.

Allen's new educational duties, however, were not to occupy him immediately. Instead, in December 1951, he was appointed to succeed Gordon Gray, the first director of the Psychological Strategy Board. A subsidiary of the National Security Council, it has as its specific function the formulation of policies for conducting American propaganda—open and secret—in the countries behind the Iron Curtain. Allen's role is administrative: he directs the seventy-some employees in making studies and preparing recommendations, while actual policies are decided by the three board members, one each from the State Department, the Defense Department, and the Central Intelligence Agency. Decisions reached are transmitted to the State Department and other branches of the Government for action. As announced on August 14, 1952, Alan G. Kirk, former Ambassador to Moscow, was appointed to succeed Allen as director of the PSB. Allen remained as senior consultant to the board until taking up his duties at U.C.L.A.

Dr. Allen has been active as well in other phases of the educational field. In May 1950 he was elected chairman of the board of trustees of the Educational Testing Service, which was formed in 1948 by consolidating the testing activities of the American Council on Education, the College Entrance Examination Board, and the Graduate Records Examinations of the Carnegie Foundation. At one time he belonged to the committee of ten college presidents established by the American Council of Education to investigate intercollegiate sports. He also served (as of March 1952) on the council's problems and policies committee; is a trustee of the Institute for International Education and of the Carnegie Foundation for the Advancement of Teaching; a member of the board of directors of the American Committee on a United Europe and of the Board of Visitors of the Air University. Allen's academic eminence has been recognized by the award of several honorary degrees: the LL.D. degrees from Tulane University (1946), University of Illinois (1946), Lake Forest College (1946), University of Hawaii (1948), Boston University (1948), Gonzaga University (1949), and University of Southern California (1951). His Greek-letter societies are Phi Beta Kappa, Sigma Xi, Alpha Omega Alpha, Phi Delta Kappa, and Phi Beta Phi; his clubs, the University of New York and the Cosmos of Washington, D.C.

National and local organizations with which Allen is affiliated are Freedoms Foundation (member of the board of directors), Seattle Symphony Orchestra (member of the board of trustees), Pacific Coast Banking School (member of the board of directors), American Cancer Society (member of the board of directors of the Washington division), Washington Tuberculosis Association (honorary vice-president), March of Dimes Campaign (member of the State committee), Associated Boys Club, Inc. (member of the board of advisers), Washington State Heart Association (member of the advisory council), Seattle Community Chest (member of the board of trustees).

Raymond Allen married Dorothy Sheard on August 29, 1931; they had six children, Charles Anthony, Raymond Bernard, William Sheard (deceased), Blanche Elizabeth (deceased), Dorothy, and Barbara Jean. The Los Angeles *Times* described Allen as "a man of decision, a man who gets things done," and to *Time* he is "a big, affable man who has a knack for getting along with almost anyone." His height is five feet, eleven and a half inches, his weight 185 pounds, and he has hazel eyes and brown hair. His church is the Episcopal.

References

Am Med Assn J 140:634 Je 18 '49
American Medical Directory, 1950
Leaders in Education (1948)
Who's Who in America, 1950-51
Who's Who in American Education, 1947-48
Who's Who in the West (1951)

ALLYSON, JUNE Oct. 7, 1923- Motion picture actress

Address: b. c/o Metro-Goldwyn-Mayer Studios, Washington Blvd., Culver City, Calif.; h. Bel-Air, Los Angeles, Calif.

JUNE ALLYSON

Among Metro-Goldwyn-Mayer's most popular young stars is June Allyson, who by 1951 had appeared in over twenty of that studio's motion pictures. She began her career in 1938 as a chorus girl on the Broadway stage and played her first featured role three years later in the musical comedy hit *Best Foot Forward*. Signing a motion picture contract with MGM in 1942, she made her screen debut in the film version of *Best Foot Forward* the following year. The actress scored such a success in her first important film role as the feminine lead in *Two Girls and a Sailor* (1944) that she attained stardom later that year in *Music for Millions*. Since then she has played light comedy, musical, and dramatic roles on the screen.

June Allyson was born Jan Allyson in New York City on October 7, 1923, the only daughter of Arthur and Clare Allyson. Six months later, when her parents were separated, Mrs. Allyson went to work in a card-engraving business and the child lived for a time with her grandmother. She attended public schools in New York and in Pelham in Westchester County. An injury sustained at the age of eight necessitated her wearing a corrective back brace for several years. Once freed from the brace, she took up swimming to strengthen her muscles and eventually won a Greater New York City free-style swimming championship. She also taught herself to dance by watching Fred Astaire-Ginger Rogers motion pictures (she reportedly saw *The Gay Divorcée* eighteen times) and then imitating the dance routines as soon as she got home. While a student at Theodore Roosevelt High School in the Bronx she once announced to her friends that she could dance like Ginger Rogers. When they dared her to try out for a Broadway show, she won a place in the chorus line of *Sing Out the News* in the fall of 1938. "The only honest

ALLYSON, JUNE—*Continued*

way to describe it is to say that they hired me for laughs," she later explained. After two months her mother insisted that she quit the show (her employers did not know she was only fifteen) and return to high school for the senior year. She graduated with a certificate of merit for the highest scholastic average (97.3) in the class of 1939.

In the fall of 1939 Miss Allyson returned to Broadway in the chorus line of *Very Warm for May*, and when that musical comedy closed early the next year, she next danced in *Higher and Higher*. The following season, in October 1940, she was one of the chorus girls in *Panama Hattie* and later understudied Betty Hutton, who played the comedy part of Florrie. Miss Allyson had a chance to show her talents in five performances while Miss Hutton was ill with measles in May 1941. Among those who saw her were George Abbott, the Broadway producer, and Arthur Freed, a producer at Metro-Goldwyn-Mayer. Although the latter suggested a film contract, Miss Allyson felt she was not yet ready for the screen. Later she was given a specialty dance in *Panama Hattie*, but left the show in the summer of 1941 when Abbott offered her a small featured ingénue role (at $125 a week) in his forthcoming production of *Best Foot Forward*. In this musical comedy with a prep school background, she danced, spoke some lines, and had the opportunity to sing three numbers: "Don't Sell the Night Short," "What Do You Think I Am?" and "The Three B's." When *Best Foot Forward* opened to enthusiastic notices in October 1941, Brooks Atkinson of the New York *Times* singled out Miss Allyson among the "notably talented" members of the youthful cast as "a sunny blonde with considerable charm"; and the *Christian Science Monitor* critic called her "pretty and energetic and hearty-voiced."

During the run of *Best Foot Forward* Miss Allyson made several screen tests, which brought offers of contracts from two Hollywood studios. In the summer of 1942, acting as her own agent, she and four other teen-age players from *Best Foot Forward* signed with MGM, which had acquired the film rights to that Broadway show. Arriving on the West Coast in September 1942, she made her motion picture debut in her former stage role as Minerva in the Technicolor picturization of *Best Foot Forward*, starring Lucille Ball. The first day on the set, according to a frequently quoted story, she was told to go home and cure her cold. "But I haven't got a cold," she protested, "I talk like this all the time." Since then the trace of huskiness in her voice has reportedly proved to be an asset, helping to individualize her screen personality. Following the release of *Best Foot Forward* in June 1943, the New York *World-Telegram*'s Alton Cook commented that the actress had "transplanted her jolly spirit from the stage to the screen," *Variety* described her as "both a looker and a good vocalist," and the *Hollywood Reporter* found her "an attractive newcomer." In her next brief screen appearance she sang and danced "Treat 'Em Rough" with Mickey

Rooney in a remake of the Gershwin musical comedy, *Girl Crazy* (1943). After doing a specialty song number in the musical *Thousands Cheer* (1943), she had a small part, singing "I Like to Recognize the Tune" with Vaughn Monroe's band in *Meet the People* (1944), in which the stars were Lucille Ball and Dick Powell.

It was the MGM producer Joe Pasternak who gave Miss Allyson her first important role as the acting-singing-dancing feminine lead in *Two Girls and a Sailor* (1944), opposite Van Johnson. According to *Life*, the "fresh and exuberant" performances of Miss Allyson and Gloria De Haven as a sister-act team proved to be "the most delightful" feature of the picture, which marked "the real beginning of their movie careers." On the strength of her work in this musical, she received star billing and graduated to a dramatic role in another Pasternak production, *Music for Millions* (1944), in which she impersonated a troubled Army wife who played the bass fiddle in José Iturbi's symphony orchestra. To Irene Thirer of the New York *Post*, it seemed that she was "an exceptionally clever actress—probably 1944's most promising." Pasternak then cast the young star in *Her Highness and the Bellboy* (1945), a "fairy tale in modern dress," with Hedy Lamarr and Robert Walker. A *Variety* reviewer thought Miss Allyson came "close to stealing the picture" in the "difficult" role of an invalid. Later in 1945 she was again co-starred with Walker in *The Sailor Takes a Wife*, a domestic farce about a couple of wartime newlyweds. "Miss Allyson holds her own well in the frivolous and sentimental proceedings," was the verdict of the *Christian Science Monitor*'s film critic.

One of Miss Allyson's most popular characterizations was as Kathryn Grayson's demure young sister in *Two Sisters from Boston*, a period musical produced by Pasternak in 1946. "The comedy falls to Miss Allyson," observed Bosley Crowther in the New York *Times*, "and she charmingly demonstrates again that her talent in this department is extensive and captivating." She next appeared briefly in a musical biography of Jerome Kern, *Till the Clouds Roll By* (1946), singing several numbers from that composer's *Leave It to Jane*. Her "sensitive" portrayal of an adolescent with a father fixation in *The Secret Heart* (1946), a psychological drama costarring Claudette Colbert and Walter Pidgeon, was rated the best acting performance of her career up to that time by the *Variety* and *Christian Science Monitor* reviewers. As Van Johnson's childhood sweetheart who later became a Navy nurse in *High Barbaree* (1947), Miss Allyson was "excellent," according to *Time*'s critic, who added that she seemed "incapable" of giving a "superficial performance." The actress was said to welcome her next role in *Good News* (1947), a remake of the Broadway musical about college life in the 1920's, because the story did not require her to cry. "It seems like that's all I've been doing on the screen lately," she told one interviewer. Howard Barnes of the New York *Herald Tribune*

wrote of her work in this picture: "Her singing is pleasant, she dances nicely, and she succeeds in giving a bit of tension to the tatter-
demalion script."

The year 1948 saw Miss Allyson again
teamed with Van Johnson in the comedy *The
Bride Goes Wild*. Playing the part of a prim
New England school teacher, she was "at her
cutest" in the opinion of the New York *Sun*'s
Eileen Creelman, who considered Miss Allyson
"one actress who is not only bearable but
amusing when she's cute." This was followed
by the role of the ill-fated Constance Bonan-
cieux in a lavish, "tongue-in-the-cheek" version of Alexandre Dumas' *The Three Muske-
teers* (1948), with Gene Kelly and Lana
Turner. Subsequently she sang and danced the
"Thou Swell" number in *Words and Music*
(1948), a musical based on the lives of Richard
Rodgers and Lorenz Hart. The next year she
essayed the role of Jo March, previously
brought to the screen by Katherine Hepburn,
in a Technicolor remake of Louisa May Al-
cott's *Little Women*. The critics disagreed
over her interpretation of this character, several of them believing that she had been mis-
cast. Bosley Crowther, however, praised her
portrayal of Monty Stratton's wife in *The
Stratton Story* (1949), which was based on
the life of the noted White Sox pitcher (played
by James Stewart). Writing in the New York
Post, Archer Winsten expressed the opinion
that both stars did some of their best work
in this picture.

Ever since her marriage, on August 19, 1945,
to the screen and radio star, Dick Powell, Miss
Allyson had wished to play opposite her husband in a film. Her ambition was realized in
1950 when they were first costarred in a romantic comedy, *The Reformer and the Redhead*, and then teamed together in *Right Cross*,
a drama about prize fighting. Reviewing the
former picture for the New York *Herald
Tribune*, Otis L. Guernsey, Jr., said: "Miss
Allyson has a hard time bringing her character (a zoo-keeper's daughter) into any sort
of life, and she tries to do it with a super-
abundance of fresh feminine eagerness." In
the latter film Thomas Pryor thought that she
did "nicely" in the "somewhat trying role" of
the manager of a Mexican boxer, played by
Ricardo Montalban. More recently, in 1951,
she was cast opposite Van Johnson for a fourth
time in *Too Young to Kiss*, in which she is
a pianist who pretends to be a thirteen-year-old
prodigy in order to win a concert booking.
Time's verdict was that the role was "the
perfect outlet" for her "little-girlishness."
Toward the end of 1951 Miss Allyson completed *The Girl in White* and was committed
to two other pictures, *A Steak for Connie* and
One for the Road.

The screen star has won a number of popularity polls. In a nation-wide survey conducted
by the Motion Picture Research Bureau in
1946, she was chosen as the "Most Typical
American Girl," and editors of 250 college
papers voted her 1947's "Most Lovable Movie
Actress." Selected as one of the five top
women stars in *Photoplay*'s polls from 1947
through 1950, she was also named second to

Bette Davis as the most popular feminine star
in *Woman's Home Companion*'s 1949 and 1950
polls. According to *Boxoffice* magazine's year-
end survey, she was United States moviegoers'
favorite star in 1950.

The Powells adopted a baby girl, whom
they named Pamela, in 1948, and two years
afterward their son, Richard Keith, was born.
Miss Allyson, who stands five feet one inch
tall and weighs 97 pounds, has blonde hair and
"crinkly" blue eyes. She is said to be modest
about her talents, sensitive, energetic, impulsive.
Her mild interest in sports is confined mostly
to tennis, swimming, and golf. Among her
hobbies are collecting miniature china pigs and
records of classical music, particularly those
by Sibelius, Tchaikovsky, and Beethoven.

References

Am Mag 139:124 F '45 por
Boston Sunday Post (Your Week) p5
    Jl 9 '44
Collier's 114:24 N 11 '44 por
Life 19:87 O 1 '45 por
Look 23:79 Ja 22 '46
N Y Daily Mirror Mag p8 N 10 '46
N Y Post Mag p12 Mr 30 '46; p2 Ja 25
    '47; p12 Je 12 '49; p11 Ap 28 '50
Photoplay 25:57 O '44; 26:30 D '44; 26:
    32 Ja '45
Sat Eve Post 223:34-5 Ja 20 '51
Time 47:94 Mr 11 '46
International Motion Picture Almanac,
    1950-51

ALSOP, JOSEPH W(RIGHT), JR. (ôl'
sŭp) Oct. 11, 1910- Newspaperman; author
Address: 2720 Dumbarton Ave., N.W., Washington 7, D.C.

**ALSOP, STEWART (JOHONNOT OLI-
VER)** May 17, 1914- Newspaperman; author
Address: b. 2720 Dumbarton Ave., N.W.,
Washington 7, D.C.; h. 3139 Dumbarton Ave.,
N.W., Washington 7, D.C.

The brothers Joseph W. Alsop, Jr., and
Stewart Alsop became associated in journalism
in 1946 when they began for the New York
Herald Tribune their syndicated column *Matter of Fact*, interpretative news reports from
Washington and other news centers of the
world. Since that time they have gained the
reputation, according to *Newsweek*, of being
"among the nation's top political commentators,"
and in 1950 and again in 1952 won a citation
from the Overseas Press Club for the "best
interpretation of foreign news." The younger
member of the partnership, Stewart Alsop,
earlier an editor for the Doubleday Doran publishing company in New York, had had no
newspaper experience before joining his brother
in writing the Washington by-lined column.
Joseph Alsop had been for five years a reporter for the New York *Herald Tribune* and
from 1937 to 1940 was co-author with Robert
E. Kintner of a syndicated column entitled
Capitol Parade. With Kintner, he also wrote
two books on Washington political affairs. Both
brothers served in World War II—Joseph in

JOSEPH W. ALSOP, JR.

the Far East, as a member of General Chennault's American Volunteer Force in China and Chief of the Lend-Lease Mission to China, and Stewart in the European theater, as a volunteer in the British Army and later as a parachutist for the Office of Strategic Services. After the war, in collaboration with Thomas Braden, Stewart wrote *Sub Rosa*, an account of the work of the OSS.

Avon, Connecticut, is the birthplace of both Joseph Wright Alsop, Jr., who was born October 11, 1910, and Stewart Johonnot Oliver Alsop, born May 17, 1914. Their father, Joseph Wright Alsop, an insurance executive, has been a member of the upper and lower houses of the Connecticut Legislature, chairman of the State Utilities Commission, and (until 1950) senior member of the board of control of the Connecticut Agricultural Experiment Station. Also prominent in Connecticut public life, their mother, Corinne Douglas (Robinson) Alsop, who is a relative of the late President Franklin D. Roosevelt, was elected to three terms in the State Legislature, took a leading part in Connecticut defense organizations during World War I and II, and has been active in Republican State politics. Joseph and Stewart Alsop have a brother, John deKoven, and a sister, Corinne Roosevelt (Mrs. Percy Chubb).

Joseph Alsop spent his early years on his parents' farm in Avon before being sent to Groton School, Massachusetts. Having completed his preparatory school training, in 1928 he entered Harvard University, where his interests were literature, the arts, and philosophy. When he was graduated from Harvard *magna cum laude* with the B.A. degree in 1932, the young man had no idea of journalism as a career. At the suggestion of his parents, however, that he try newspaper work, with their help he became a beginning reporter for the New York *Herald Tribune*. In this capacity he worked in the city room from 1932 to 1935,

at first (as related by *Newsweek*, March 13, 1950) the subject of some criticism for his erudite manner and his preference for the works of James Joyce and Marcel Proust, but later respected for his concise, comprehensive reporting, notably his coverage of the Hauptmann trial. Sent to Washington, D.C., in 1936 to cover the capital news for the same New York paper, he met Robert E. Kintner, another reporter on the *Herald Tribune* staff. The two young men in 1937 collaborated in writing a nationally syndicated column from Washington called *The Capitol Parade*, which was distributed by the North American Newspaper Alliance to almost 100 newspapers throughout the United States. The column established both men as top-ranking news commentators.

While reporting from Washington in this prewar period, Joseph Alsop became the joint author of three books: the first, *The 168 Days* (1938), was written with Turner Catledge; and two others, *Men Around the President* (1939) and *American White Paper; the Story of American Diplomacy and the Second World War* (1940), in collaboration with Kintner. The first work, a chronological account of the Supreme Court crisis when President Roosevelt disclosed his plan to enlarge the Court, was judged by the *Saturday Review of Literature* an "excellent piece of journalism . . . free from that quality of smart aleckism which has disfigured much Washington correspondence . . . and [carrying] conviction of authenticity on every page." Of Alsop's second book, a widely read study of the inner circle of Roosevelt's advisers, the critic for the *New Republic* wrote: "Alsop and Kintner are doing a remarkable thing. In their newspaper column and in this book, they are writing about Washington as if it were a police precinct. . . .In the present book . . . [they] preserve an admirable impartiality." The New York *Times* commented: "The authors have mastered the difficult job of being fair without being stilted." In the best-seller *American White Paper* they give a sympathetic account of the Administration's foreign policy from the time of the Munich agreement to the outbreak of war in Europe. *Commonweal* judged the work to be "assertively journalistic and written by one of Washington's most facile and able reportorial teams." The *New Yorker* commented: "Enlightening stuff, not official but fairly convincing."

The journalistic partnership of Joseph Alsop and Robert Kintner came to an end in 1940 when Alsop joined the United States Navy as a lieutenant. (Kintner later joined the United States Army and after the war became a radio executive.) Since Alsop had been assigned to what he later called a "do-nothing job" in India, he resigned from the Navy in August 1941 in order to join the staff of General Claire L. Chennault, who was then directing the American Volunteer Group in China. In a letter to the editors of *Time* magazine relating his war services, Alsop wrote, "My service in the A.V.G. under General Chennault was the hardest and the most interesting work I have ever done." In the same letter he related the sequence of events during this period of his life: "In late November 1941, General Chennault sent me to Manila to negotiate with General MacArthur. . . .On my way back to Burma, I was caught in Hong Kong by the outbreak of war. During the fighting there, I placed myself under the command of our military observer. . . .When the surrender came, Colonel Condon instructed me to burn my A.V.G. papers and enter civilian internment with false papers as a newspaper man." Alsop remained a prisoner of the Japanese until June 1942, when he was repatriated and returned to the United States on the *Gripsholm.* As a civilian official in the Lend-Lease Mission to Chunking, Joseph Alsop in December 1942 returned to China, where on the request of Chennault he was commissioned as a Captain in the plans section of the 14th (China) United States Army Air Force. He remained in China until the conclusion of the war, his services being recognized with the award of a Legion of Merit and the Chinese Cloud Banner Medal. By the end of 1945 Alsop was ready to resume his newspaper work, and looking for a collaborator for a new column, he chose his brother Stewart.

After passing his early boyhood on the family farm in Connecticut, Stewart Alsop, like his brother, attended Groton School. From Yale University, where his father had been a student and which Stewart entered in 1932, he received his B.A. degree in 1936. Shortly afterward he began his career as an editor for the publishers, Doubleday Doran and Company of New York City. With the entrance of America into World War II, Stewart Alsop volunteered for service in the United States Army; rejected on medical grounds, he went to England in 1942 and there became a member of the 60th Regiment, Kings Royal Rifle Corps. He was commissioned a second lieutenant the next year and in 1944 was promoted to the rank of captain. Later in that year Alsop was transferred to the United States Army as a parachutist with the Office of Strategic Services. Having completed the Jedburgh training course in the special techniques of that service, shortly after D-Day he parachuted into France in order to join the forces of the Maquis, the French underground resistance army. In 1945 he resigned his commission and returned to the United States. He was awarded the French Croix de Guerre with palm.

Stewart Alsop's firsthand knowledge of the Office of Strategic Services was incorporated into a volume, *Sub Rosa; the O.S.S. and American Espionage,* written in collaboration with Thomas Braden, another parachutist in the OSS, and published in February 1946. Like *Cloak and Dagger; the Secret Story of OSS,* by Corey Ford and Alastair MacBain, which appeared at about the same time, the book described the achievements and failures of the special intelligence office, the Jedburgh training given the international force, and the aid furnished the guerrilla armies in the various theaters of war. Lewis Gannett, reviewing the two volumes for the New York *Herald Tribune,* found the Alsop-Braden work more realistic, giving "an at once terrifying and glowing sense of sweating, frightened men doing a job." Other critics recommended *Sub Rosa* as exciting

STEWART ALSOP

reading, but pointed out its limitations as a history of the OSS.

By the end of 1945 the two brothers had agreed on a collaboration and in the early part of 1946 the jointly by-lined Washington column, syndicated through the offices of the New York *Herald Tribune,* was appearing in an increasing number of newspapers throughout the United States (137 papers carried the column in 1950, *Newsweek* estimated). Gathering their information by telephone, by interviews with informants (upwards of 40 such a week, according to *Time*), and by regular visits to all parts of the globe, the Alsop brothers write three times a week and often on Sundays a two-column, approximately 1,000-word report on special aspects of national or international affairs. Described by *Time* as a "blending of political and economic punditry, forecasts and crusades, e.g. their defense of Dean Acheson and attacks on Louis Johnson while Defense Secretary," the column received the acclaim of other newspapermen when in 1950 and in 1952 Joseph and Stewart Alsop were named award winners by the Overseas Press Club for "best interpretation of foreign news." While many of the journalists' predictions, such as the Communist coup in Czechoslovakia, have become realities, others, such as their prediction that Estes Kefauver would not gain more than one delegate in the 1952 New Hampshire primary, have fallen short of the eventual developments.

Joseph Alsop has described the column as one of information—"halfway between pure opinion and what is essentially gossip." The authors "have no fights on policy," he has explained. "Our arguments are on points of emphasis—and on how far out on a limb we should go." Ever since his first trip to the Orient showed him that some of his ideas had been incorrect, Joseph Alsop resolved never to write about foreign affairs without making regular trips to

**ALSOP, JOSEPH W., JR., and STEW-
ART**—*Continued*
the countries involved. Thus, during a major
portion of the year, one of the brothers is interviewing and reporting from one of the news
centers of the world, while the other handles
events from Washington. They have contributed to the *Saturday Evening Post, Life,* the
New Yorker, and the *Atlantic Monthly.*

The authors of a number of reports on
aspects of Western defense, Joseph and Stewart
Alsop were denounced before the United Nations General Assembly in November 1949 by
Soviet Foreign Minister Andrei I. Vishinsky
because they had advised the creation of new
air bases in northern India, the Middle East,
and North Africa. In May of 1950, when
investigations into charges of Communist infiltration in the State Department were being
conducted by a Senate foreign relations subcommittee, Joseph Alsop wrote a letter to the
chairman, attacking the methods used by the
group, presenting his own knowledge of the
Chinese situation, which was then under scrutiny, and defending the loyalty and integrity of
several individuals in the State Department
accused by Senator McCarthy of Communist
affiliation. At a subsequent Senate Committee
inquiry Alsop appeared to testify about events
in China and to defend Henry A. Wallace and
John Carter Vincent from charges made by
Louis Budenz, former Communist editor.

The Alsop brothers have their office in the
Georgetown home of Joseph, who defied the
Georgian traditions of that residential area of
Washington by designing for himself a modern
house. Joseph Alsop is a member of the Links
Club and the Brook Club of New York, the
Metropolitan Club of Washington, D.C., and
the Porcellian Club of Cambridge. He is five
feet nine inches in height, has blue eyes and
brown hair. Stewart is taller, being six feet in
height, and has brown hair and gray eyes. He
is a member of the River Club of New York
City and the Metropolitan Club of Washington, D.C. He was married in October 1944 to
Patricia Hankey, an English woman whom he
met while a member of the British Army.
They have four children—Joseph Wright, Ian
Alexander, Elizabeth Winthrop, and Stewart
Johonnot Oliver. The journalists are Protestants in their religious affiliation. Contrasting
the two, *Time* noted that Stewart Alsop is
"scholarly, quiet"; his brother, "aggressive,
facile, gregarious."

References

Newsweek 35:55 Mr 13 '50 por
Time 51:49 Je 7 '48; 58:55 Jl 9 '51
Sat Eve Post 220:10 S 6 '47
International World Who's Who (1949)
Who's Who in America, 1952-53

ANDERSON, LEROY June 29, 1908-
Composer; conductor
Address: b. c/o Mills Music, Inc., 1619 Broad-
way, New York 19

Conductor-composer-arranger Leroy Anderson "captured the entire country's fancy" when

his instrumental composition *Blue Tango*
reached the No. 1 position on the *Hit Parade*
with a sale of over one million recordings.
Among his other popular compositions are *The
Syncopated Clock, Sleigh Ride, Promenade,* and
Fiddle-Faddle. Anderson, who began his career
as a teacher of the theory of music at Radcliffe College, has been the director of the
Harvard University Band and guest conductor
of, and arranger for, Arthur Fiedler's Boston
Pops Orchestra.

Leroy Anderson, of Swedish ancestry, was
born to Brewer A. and Anna M. (Johnson)
Anderson on June 29, 1908, in Cambridge,
Massachusetts. He received his first music
lessons from his mother, a church organist,
and later studied the organ with Henry Gideon.
He was taught the bass viol by Gaston Du-
fresne. While in attendance at the Cambridge
High and Latin School in his native city, Anderson wrote the music for the school's graduation class song for three consecutive years.
Upon graduation from secondary school in
1925, he entered Harvard University, where
he took his major in music. He studied theory
under Walter Spalding and Edward Ballantine
and orchestration and composition under Walter Piston and Georges Enesco. He served
as president of the Pierian Sodality of 1808
(Harvard University Orchestra) and conducted the Harvard University Band.

During these days the humor in Anderson's music first became evident. He wrote his
impressions of college activity into his *Harvard
Sketches.* One of these impressions, "Freshman
in Harvard," has been described as a "happy-
go-lucky theme played slightly out of tune" on
the clarinet. Another sketch portrays a college
library scene. When Anderson received his
B.A. degree in 1929, he was graduated *magna
cum laude,* a member of Phi Beta Kappa, and
a recipient of the Borden scholarship. On an
Elkan Naumberg fellowship Anderson continued his studies in music at Harvard University and there took his Master of Arts
degree in 1930.

Anderson began his career as a teacher of
music theory and interpreter of classical music
by accepting a position at Radcliffe College.
He then undertook a four-year (1930-34) study
of Scandinavian languages, working toward a
Ph.D. degree. In 1932 he became the director
of the Harvard University Band, a position he
held for the next three years. It is reported
that the band still uses his arrangements. According to a comment in the Boston *Post,* Anderson's strength lies in his ability to "arrange
for all manner of instrumental combinations up
to and including the symphonic orchestra."
Using his knowledge of the organ, he served
as organist and choir master of the East Congregational Church in Milton, Massachusetts,
from 1929 to 1935.

In 1935 Anderson left his studies to begin
free-lance arranging, composing, and conducting in Boston and New York. On one occasion,
when he was a guest conductor at a "Pops"
Harvard night, his arrangement of Harvard
songs brought him to the attention of Arthur
Fiedler, leader of the Boston Pops Orchestra.

The result was that Anderson was invited to arrange the scores for that orchestra and from time to time he also conducted the orchestra. His arrangements for Fiedler included classical works, ballet, and musical comedy selections. His orchestrations are said to show a "high degree of perceptiveness in the matter of orchestral color and the required skill at balancing and contrasting sonorities; they also exhibit a high abundance of fancy humor" (Warren Storey Smith in the Boston *Post*, May 10, 1952). From his free-lance composing arose *Jazz Pizzicato* (1939) and *Jazz Legato* (1944).

In 1942 Leroy Anderson entered the United States Army for duty in Iceland, where he did translating and liaison work with the Icelandic press and radio. Later he served in Washington, with Military Intelligence. Discharged in February 1946 in the rank of captain, he returned to the Boston Pops. Fiedler now encouraging him to resume writing original music, Anderson next composed *Chicken Reel, The Syncopated Clock*, and *Fiddle-Faddle*. After receiving an enthusiastic welcome from Boston audiences Anderson was approached by the vice-president of Decca Records, Inc., who wanted to issue Anderson compositions first on classical labels and then as "pops" singles. *Pathfinder* reported that Anderson, who doubted that he would "ever make the *Hit Parade* . . . rounded up an orchestra and went to work." One of the first tunes that he recorded was *The Syncopated Clock*, which became widely known through television as the theme song of WCBS-TV's *The Late Show*. Words were subsequently written for the *Clock* as well as for several other of his compositions. For his Decca performances Anderson uses a fifty-piece orchestra. The musician, whose compositions show "ingenuity and charm," employs the same elaborate orchestration in his other original melodies: the waltz measures of *Belle of the Ball*, the "casual" Western swing of *Horse and Buggy*, the "witty" pizzicato of *Plink, Plank, Plunk*; and *Serenata, Ticonderoga, Saraband, Trumpeter's Lullaby, A Christmas Festival, Song of Jupiter, The Penny-Whistle Song, The Phantom Regiment*, and *China Doll*. Commissioned by the Eire Society of Boston, Anderson wrote the *Irish Suite*, which, said Smith, "exhibits a high abundance of fancy humor."

According to Anderson, his ideas are the result of constant search. "Alertness for ideas soon becomes an unconscious habit that is always at work," states Anderson. Often he thinks of a new melody while at work on the score of another. *The Syncopated Clock*, for example, came to him while he was occupied with *Promenade*. His latest hit, *Blue Tango*, was the first purely instrumental number in popular music history to win the No. 1 position on the *Hit Parade*. Over one million records were sold, surprising the experts who believed that it would be a "flop."

Recalled to active duty after the Korean crisis began, Captain Anderson was stationed with the army intelligence branch at Fort Bragg, North Carolina, to serve until August 1952. While in service he made a guest appear-

Marcus Blechman

LEROY ANDERSON

ance on Ed Sullivan's television program, *Toast of the Town*; and a musical program of WQXR (the New York *Times* radio station) was dedicated to him.

Anderson is a member of the American Society of Composers, Authors and Publishers and of the American Federation of Musicians. Married to the former Eleanor Jane Firke since October 31, 1942, he is the father of Jane Margareta, Eric Russell, and Rolf Fredric. The composer is five feet eleven and one half inches tall, weighs 160 pounds, and has gray hair and blue eyes. His hobbies are reading, home carpentry and photography.

References

Boston (Mass.) Post My 19 '52
Newsweek 39:88 My 26 '52
Pathfinder p30 My 7 '52
Who is Who in Music, 1951

ANDREWES, SIR WILLIAM (GERRARD) Nov. 3, 1899- British naval officer
Address: b. Admiralty House, Bermuda, B.W.I.; h. Wharf House, Winchester, England

When the United States Admiral Lynde Dupuy McCormick was named Supreme Allied Commander of the Atlantic in the North Atlantic Treaty Organization on January 30, 1952, British Vice-Admiral Sir William Andrewes was appointed Deputy Supreme Commander. Andrewes, who was awarded the American Silver Star for his leadership of British Commonwealth naval units in the Inchon landings in Korea in July 1950, had been serving immediately before his recent appointment as commander in chief of the British Atlantic-West Indies station, with headquarters at Bermuda.

William Gerrard Andrewes, born in Winchester, Hampshire, England, on November 3,

British Inf. Services

VICE-ADM. SIR WILLIAM ANDREWES

1899, is the son of the Reverend Canon Gerrard Thomas Andrewes and of Helen Louisa (Kirby) Andrewes, the granddaughter of a naval officer. Four generations in the direct Andrewes' line previous to his father had been Church of England clergymen, and William Andrewes' elder brother, now deceased, also took holy orders. (There is one sister, now resident in Canada.)

"I always—to the limit of my memory," Vice-Admiral Andrewes has said, "recall an intention to enter the Royal Navy." Thus, after attending nearby Twyford School, he entered the Royal Naval College at Osborne when he was twelve and a half years old. Two years later, when World War I broke out, he was transferred to the Royal Naval College at Dartmouth. At fifteen the young midshipman was on sea duty, and before the end of the war he had been promoted to sublieutenant in the Grand Fleet. Aboard the battleship *Canada* he participated in the Battle of Jutland; he also saw war duty with the destroyer *Walrus*.

Remaining with the destroyer fleet, Andrewes served through the 1919 Baltic campaign against Bolshevik Russia. In the rank of lieutenant, to which he was advanced in 1920, he was assigned to specialized work in torpedoes and mining in 1921-23; he then was ordered to China as submarine flotilla torpedo officer for two years beginning in 1925. Promoted to lieutenant commander in 1927 he was appointed to the staff of the Royal Navy Torpedo School; and in 1930 he returned to the China station as fleet torpedo officer. In 1934 Andrewes, who two years earlier had been made a commander, attended the Staff College and on graduation was appointed fleet torpedo officer of H.M.S. *Nelson*. He became executive officer of H.M.S. *Rodney* in 1937, attained a captaincy the next year, and in 1939 took the course at the Imperial Defense College. When World War II

broke out, he was in command of H.M.S. *Albatross*, a seaplane carrier.

After a few months on the bridge of the *Albatross* in Atlantic and West African waters, Captain Andrewes was reassigned as chief of staff at the Dover naval base in 1940 and still later in the same year became naval joint planner attached to the War Cabinet. He returned to line duty in 1942 as commander of H.M.S. *Uganda*, a new cruiser, which he commanded first in the Atlantic and afterward through the invasion of Sicily, winning mention in dispatches. As a unit of Mediterranean Task Force "K," the *Uganda* subsequently participated in the invasion of the Italian mainland, and for gallantry in the Salerno landing operations Andrewes was made a Companion of the Distinguished Service Order. The vessel was severely damaged and was taken across the Atlantic by its commander to Charleston, South Carolina, for repair, before completion of which Captain Andrewes was reassigned (1944). His new post was officially described as "chief staff officer for administration and turn-around invasion duties to the commander in chief" at the principal home naval base at Portsmouth, and he participated in the invasion of Normandy. Created Commander of the Order of the British Empire (C.B.E.) at this time, Andrewes flew to Australia following his appointment in December 1944 as chief staff officer to the vice-admiral's administration of the British Pacific Fleet, and was serving as such when hostilities ended in 1945.

Named commander of the fleet carrier H.M.S. *Indomitable* in 1946, Andrewes returned to Portsmouth in the following year as chief of staff to the commander in chief. Still later in 1947 he was assigned as aide-de-camp to King George VI, and in the following year was promoted to rear admiral. For the next two years Admiral Andrewes was the senior naval directing staff officer at the Imperial Defense College; then, in January 1950 he became flag officer commanding the 5th Cruiser Squadron and flag officer, second in command, of the British Far East Station. As commander of British and Allied Naval Forces operating in Korea, Andrewes was honored with a special complimentary signal from United States General MacArthur for the contribution, made by him and his forces, to the success of the Inchon landing of July 1950; and on the following October 1 he was presented with the American Silver Star in recognition of his part in the same achievement. Andrewes was advanced to vice-admiral in His Majesty's Fleet as of December 1, 1950. Two months later (February 2, 1951) he became Sir William Andrewes through promotion to the grade of Knight Commander in the Military Division of the Order of the British Empire (K.B.E.) for "distinguished service in Korea" since the previous July.

On February 19, 1951, Vice-Admiral Sir William Andrewes succeeded United States Rear Admiral Allan E. Smith as commander of United Nations Task Force 95, comprising ships of eight nations engaged as a blockading, escort, and support force off the Korean coast. He remained as such, however, for two months, being reassigned in April 1951 as commander in chief of the Royal Navy's Atlantic-West Indies Station, with headquarters at Bermuda. Andrewes was so serving when on January 30, 1952, Prime Minister Winston Churchill—following conferences with President Truman and in accordance with an understanding entered into by his predecessor, Clement Attlee—agreed "reluctantly and with some reservations" to the appointment of an American naval officer as Supreme Allied Commander of the Atlantic in the North Atlantic Treaty Organization. United States Admiral Lynde Dupuy McCormick was named to the post, with Vice-Admiral Andrewes as Deputy Supreme Commander. Andrewes was later to say that he would "be proud to act as deputy" to Admiral McCormick. The two have since worked on plans for the setting up of the Supreme North Atlantic Ocean Command, early steps toward which were taken in March when both McCormick and Andrewes began a twenty-six day, 24,000-mile air visit to ten NATO capitals. In addition to serving as NATO Deputy Naval Commander, Vice-Admiral Andrewes retains his command of the British Atlantic-West Indies station.

Honors awarded to the Vice-Admiral, besides those already mentioned, have made him Companion of the Order of the Bath, Officer of the American Legion of Merit, and recipient of the Greek Military Cross. He stands five feet eleven and a half inches in height, weighs 178 pounds, and has hazel eyes and graying dark-brown hair. Lady Andrewes is the former Frances Audrey Welchman, also of Winchester; the couple, who married February 26, 1927, are the parents of one son, Gerrard John Michael, a naval lieutenant who has seen action aboard a frigate in the Korean War, and one daughter, Jennifer Mary. The Admiral is a communicant of the Church of England; his club is the United Service in London. In his cadet days at Osborne and Dartmouth, Andrewes played football, hockey, and tennis. "I am a keen gardener and carpenter," he writes of his present-day recreations. "I enjoy walking, fishing, and tennis, though I now play tennis very quietly."

References

Illus Lond 220:225 F 9 '52 por
N Y Herald Tribune p1 Ja 31 '52
N Y Times p1 Ja 31 '52
Who's Who, 1952

ANDREWS, STANLEY Dec. 18, 1895-
United States Government official

Address: b. c/o Technical Cooperation Administration, Department of State, Washington 25, D.C.; h. 3031 S. Columbus, Fairlington, Va.

To succeed the late Dr. Henry Garland Bennett as director of the Point IV Program of technical aid to underdeveloped areas of the world outside the United States, President Truman on April 21, 1952, nominated Stanley Andrews, until recently the head of the Office of Foreign Agricultural Relations of the Department of Agriculture. His precise title in his new post is Administrator of the Technical

STANLEY ANDREWS

Cooperation Administration in the Department of State. Before entering Government service Andrews, a journalist, was editor of the *Arkansas Farmer* and the *American Cotton Grower*.

Stanley Andrews was himself a country boy, having been born and reared in rural Excelsior, near High Point, Missouri. He was born on December 18, 1895, to George R. and Martha Ann (Beard) Andrews. When he was a student at the University of Missouri, the United States entered World War I. Joining the army as a private in 1917, he was sent to France with the American Expeditionary Force, rose to the grade of first sergeant in the 354th Infantry, 89th Division, and was subsequently commissioned a second lieutenant.

After demobilization Andrews returned to the University of Missouri to receive the Bachelor of Journalism degree in 1921. He now began his newspaper career, as editor of the Sedalia (Missouri) *Capital,* which he left in 1922 to work for a short time as a political reporter on the Kansas City *Journal.* His next employment took him in the same year to Arkansas, where he was appointed editor of the El Dorado *News and Times.*

In April 1926, in the fourth of his five years with the El Dorado daily, Stanley Andrews purchased and assumed the editorial direction of the *Arkansas Homestead and Farmer,* a farm and livestock monthly established in 1898 and published at Little Rock. Shortening the name to the *Arkansas Farmer,* he also announced in the periodical's November 1928 issue that his editorial policy would advocate, among other things, equality of tax burden on farm and city property, the supplementing of the State highway system with farm-to-market roads, and cooperative marketing of farm products. He also acquired radio station KARK at Little Rock in 1931 and managed it for three years. Andrews' direct supervision of both the radio station and the *Arkansas Farmer* came to an

ANDREWS, STANLEY—*Continued*

end in 1934 when he moved to New Orleans, Louisiana, to become editor of another agricultural magazine, the *American Cotton Grower*. He remained, however, associated with the Little Rock monthly as executive editor until 1940, and in the view of the present publisher, Thomas J. Anderson, was "one of the most outstanding editors the *Arkansas Farmer* has ever had."

Andrews first entered the service of the Federal government in 1940 when, after six years in charge of the *American Cotton Grower*, he was appointed assistant to the president of the Commodity Credit Corporation. In the year following he became general agent for the Farm Credit Administration at New Orleans and remained as such until June 25, 1943, when, in the World War II emergency, he was commissioned a major in the Army. Dispatched to North Africa, he served there as a planning adviser on food and later was assigned to duty with the American Military Government in Italy. In Western Germany in 1945 Andrews was promoted to lieutenant colonel and named Deputy Chief of the Food, Agriculture and Forestry Group of the Military Government of the United States occupation zone. He was advanced to colonel and became Chief of the group before his return to America in 1946.

For a period Andrews was a special writer on the staff of the Little Rock evening newspaper, the *Arkansas Democrat*. Recalled to Government service in 1947, he was appointed special assistant and consultant on food problems to Secretary of Agriculture Clinton P. Anderson. A year later (1948) he returned to Western Germany to become Chief of the Food, Agriculture and Forestry Division of the American-British Control Group under Lieutenant General Lucius D. Clay. "There," stated the New York *Times*, "he supervised a system of planning production quotas, collections, distribution and rationing of food, and acted as adviser in supervision of the procurement, distribution, and supply of food for the Berlin airlift." For his achievement at this time he was awarded the War Department medal for extraordinary civilian service. Other honors he has received are the Legion of Merit and the Order of the Crown of Italy.

On July 5, 1949, Andrews was named Director of the Office of Foreign Agricultural Relations in the Agriculture Department at Washington. A few months after taking office he represented the United States at the second session of the International Wheat Council in London. In late November 1949 he also represented his country at the fifth annual conference of the United Nations Food and Agriculture Organization and joined with J. Harold Wilson, president of the British Board of Trade, in blocking a move to create a billion-dollar "food bank" to channel food surpluses under U.N. supervision. "We do not believe in accumulation of soft currencies in another international organization," Andrews declared, adding that President Truman's recently launched Point IV Program would "accomplish the same thing more easily."

The President's proposal that the United States "embark on a bold new program for making the benefits of our scientific advances and industrial progress available for the improvement and growth of the underdeveloped areas" of the world was the fourth point in the "program for peace and freedom" recommended by the Chief Executive in his inaugural address on January 20, 1949. It was approved by Congress the following May, and in September an initial appropriation of about $28 millions was voted to implement the plan in its first year. The Technical Cooperation Administration was established within the Department of State, and on December 1, 1950, Dr. Henry G. Bennett, president of Oklahoma Agricultural and Mechanical College and *doyen* of American land-grant college presidents, was sworn in as its head. Under Bennett's direction American technicians were sent to eleven countries in the Near East and South Asia "on a variety of projects, mainly in the fields of agriculture, national resources development, health, and sanitation and education" (stated an official State Department release) in an endeavor to offset the spread of Communist ideology and general unrest in these areas. (It has been reported that in most of those areas 80 per cent of the inhabitants are "chronically" hungry, 70 per cent are ill, and approximately the same percentage are illiterate.)

Bennett's direction of the Technical Cooperation Administration came to an abrupt end on December 22, 1951, when while on a tour of inspection he lost his life in an airplane crash in Iran. One week later Stanley Andrews, who as Director of the Office of Foreign Agricultural Relations had been closely associated with Bennett as an adviser, was granted temporary leave from the Department of Agriculture to become Special Consultant to the Secretary of State to assist in the development and execution of the Point IV Program, and immediately left for Asia to complete Bennett's mission. On April 21, 1952, Andrews was nominated by President Truman as Bennett's successor, relieving Acting Administrator Jonathan B. Bingham. According to Thomas L. Stokes (in the New York *World-Telegram*), about 72 per cent of the Point IV appropriations (for which Congress, it is expected, will approve $200 millions for the fiscal year or 1952-53) will be used for technical "know-how" to increase food production, and more than 15 per cent for health and education.

Commenting editorially on the selection of Andrews for the post, the *Christian Science Monitor* felt that Andrews would inspire confidence in a "continuity of purpose." In 1952, 900 experts were sent where needed, in 1953 there may be 1,500. The paper pointed out that "these men and women . . . must be experts in public relations" as well as in engineering, agronomy, and other specialties; it was therefore important that the policy instituted by Dr. Bennett of drawing heavily on "the experience of the United States farm services" and "the county agent type of expert" should not be interrupted. The Washington *Post* also approved of the nomination of Andrews. "One of his outstanding characteristics" it said, "is his ability to talk to people on their own terms. . . .At the same time he has a reputation for hardheaded management." Andrews took the oath of office in the first week of May 1952.

Stanley Andrews and Florence V. Cox were married June 28, 1924, and have one daughter, Florence Walker, now Mrs. Jack Chestnut. The Point IV administrator is a Mason and a member of Acacia. He belongs to the Christian Church. His clubs are the Round Table in New Orleans and the University in Washington.

References

N Y Herald Tribune p15 Ap 22 '52 por; II p1 Ap 27 '52 por

N Y Times p1 Ap 22 '52 por

International World Who's Who (1949) Who's Who in America, 1952-53

EIKICHI ARAKI

ARAKI, EIKICHI (ä-rä-kē ä-kē-chē) April 1891- Ambassador from Japan to the United States

Address: b. c/o Embassy of Japan, 2514 Massachusetts Ave., N.W., Washington, D.C.

For the first time since Japanese Ambassador Kichisaburo Nomura left the United States in 1941, an envoy from Japan was appointed in May 1952 when Eikichi Araki was named by Premier Yoshida to represent that country in Washington. This appointment also marked the first time that a businessman, instead of a career diplomat, had been chosen to speak for Japan in a major post abroad. As an employee of the Bank of Japan, Araki, who had been partially educated in the United States, served in the New York office of that institution in the 1920's and 1930's before returning to his native country to work in banking there. After a year (in 1944) as an economic adviser in Nanking, China, for the Japanese Government, Araki held the governorship of the Bank of Japan in 1946 before the purge by the Allied Military Government brought about his retirement for five years. At the time of his acceptance of the Ambassadorship, he was chairman of the board of the Tokyo Electric Company. As Ambassador, Araki will be primarily concerned with the strengthening of mutual understanding between his nation and the United States.

The eldest son of Tokutaro Araki, Eikichi Araki was born in April 1891, in the Ishikawa Prefecture of Japan. On receiving his degree in law from the Tokyo Imperial University in 1916, he joined the Bank of Japan as a junior clerk. From 1923 to 1926 he was assigned to the New York office of the bank, during which time he undertook a brief course of study at Princeton University and later at Cornell University. In addition to the regular business of the bank, he was particularly interested in the theory and practice of the Federal Reserve System, which contributed greatly to his subsequent banking career. On his return to Japan, he worked in the Fukushima and Kobe branches and as chief of the bank's examining department. From 1936 to 1938 he was once again assigned to New York, this time as a representative of the Bank of Japan. When he returned home from this assignment, he served for two years as chief of the newly created foreign exchange department and then for an additional two years as chief of the business department. In 1942 he was appointed director.

During World War II Araki held the post of vice-governor of the Bank of Japan, being promoted to full governorship in October 1945. The previous year, 1944, he had been economic adviser to the Japanese Government installed at Nanking, China. Araki functioned as governor of the Bank of Japan for eleven months, before being placed on the purge list of the MacArthur military government in September 1946. Four years later, in October 1950, his name was removed from that list, an act which enabled him to become chairman of the board of the Tokyo Electric Power Company in May 1951.

The peace treaty signed in San Francisco in September 1951 restoring full sovereignty to Japan formally went into effect in April 1952. Early in the following May, Araki was named by Premier Shigeru Yoshida as Ambassador to the United States, the first envoy from Japan to be sent to Washington since the outbreak of World War II, when Kichisaburo Nomura was the Japanese Ambassador. "His appointment was a surprise," commented the New York *Herald Tribune*, because "he has no diplomatic or political background." *Time* reported: "Araki tried to turn down the Washington appointment on the ground that he was not a diplomat, but Premier Yoshida insisted that Araki's financial experience was required in the main business of the Embassy: straightening out Japan's debt to the United States and arranging for loans from the United States Government." Upon accepting the post, Araki

ARAKI, EIKICHI—*Continued*

became the first Japanese businessman to fill such an Ambassadorship, hitherto reserved to career diplomats.

When Japan's new Ambassador arrived in Washington on June 7, 1952, he told newspaper correspondents that there were two outstanding features of Japan's foreign relations: "One is that Japan is firmly encamped in the free democratic world. The other is that Japan is inseparably linked with the United States by the security treaty concluded at the same time as the peace treaty." Two days earlier, in a stopover at San Francisco, the Ambassador had voiced Japan's desire to be admitted to the United Nations. With the new Ambassadors from Brazil and Thailand, Araki presented his credentials to President Truman on June 12, at which time he expressed his feeling of being honored in representing his country to a nation whose "untiring efforts and farsighted leadership" had been instrumental in restoring the independence and sovereignty of Japan.

At the first meeting of the Japan Society to be held in fifteen years, Ambassador Araki in June 1952 stated that never "has there existed such a broad identity of interests" between Japan and the United States as at the present, partly because of the good effect American occupation troops had had in Japan. Speaking of the readiness of the Japanese people to work for the economic reconstruction of their country, Araki said, "They ask for access to the raw materials they need, access to the markets that would let in their goods. . . .They ask for humane and human rights and privileges. Foreign trade and higher industrialization are essential to their well-being." (The Japan Society, founded in 1907 to further Japanese-American relations, is in 1952 under the presidency of John D. Rockefeller 3d.) On August 13, 1952, the Japanese Ambassador signed the articles of agreement by which Japan became a member of the International Bank for Reconstruction and Development and the International Monetary Fund.

By his marriage to Takiko Matsumoto (who is deceased), the Ambassador is the father of four children, three sons and a daughter, Tomiko. She and her twenty-nine-year-old brother, Fumio, accompanied the Ambassador to Washington, where Fumio Araki will serve as an Embassy attaché and as secretary to his father. The Washington *Post* said of the Ambassador, "A studious man, he reads a great deal and has little time for other recreation." For outdoor exercise the Ambassador likes an occasional game of golf and early morning walks.

References

N Y Herald Tribune p6 My 6 '52; II p1 Je 15 '52
N Y Times p4 Je 5 '52; p1+ Je 8 '52
Time 59:26 Je 16 '52
Who's Who in Japan, with Manchukuo and China, 1940-41

ARMSTRONG, GEORGE E(LLIS) Aug. 4, 1900- United States Army officer; surgeon
Address: b. c/o Office of the Surgeon General, United States Army, Washington 25, D.C.; h. 4219 25th St., North Arlington, Va.

Major General George E. Armstrong, who was sworn in as Surgeon General of the United States Army on June 6, 1951, began his army career in 1923 when he enlisted as a private in the National Guard. An army medical officer since 1926, Armstrong has been stationed at posts in Washington, D.C., Georgia, and California, and during World War II served thirty-four months overseas in the China-Burma-India theater. In accordance with the Surgeon General's duty to "provide and conduct programs and direct certain aspects of the medical service to insure the health of the Army," Armstrong has reported progress on a drug for the cure of malaria, a dressing for atomic burns, and new artificial hands for amputees. He also reported that the Korean war death rate among the wounded has been cut to 2½ per cent, half the World War II rate.

George Ellis Armstrong was born in Springville, Indiana, on August 4, 1900, to Frank T. and Jennie G. (Norvell) Armstrong. After his secondary schooling he enrolled at the University of Indiana, where he took premedical courses. Upon receiving the B.A. degree in 1922 he remained at that university for his medical training; the M.D. degree was conferred on him in 1925. While a student, he enlisted in the National Guard of Indiana as a private, from which he rose to the rank of technical sergeant. On June 26, 1925, the young doctor was discharged from the National Guard to accept a commission as first lieutenant in the Army Reserve Corps.

After serving a year's internship (1925-26) at Letterman General Hospital, San Francisco, Armstrong was commissioned first lieutenant in the Regular Army Medical Corps in July 1926. In 1927 he graduated with honors from the Army Medical School, in Washington, D.C., and from the Medical Field Service School, at Carlisle Barracks, Pennsylvania. The following year (1928) he was promoted to captain. From 1931 to 1935 Armstrong was assistant chief surgeon at Walter Reed Hospital, in Washington. The following two years he served on the staff at Fort Benning, Georgia, in the same capacity. When Armstrong began his overseas service in 1937, he had risen to the rank of major. He was sent to Tientsin, China, as assistant surgeon, later assuming the responsibilities of chief surgeon there.

In 1938 Armstrong was transferred to Fort Stotsenburg, in the Philippine Islands, as chief surgeon in the venereal disease ward. Returning to the United States in 1939, he graduated from the advanced course at Pennsylvania's Medical Field Service School in 1940. This was followed in 1941 by another graduate course, at the Command and General Staff School, Fort Leavenworth, Kansas. Armstrong was promoted to the rank of lieutenant colonel (temporary) in February 1942 and two years later began his overseas World War II service as assistant theater surgeon in the China-Burma-India theater. He remained in China until 1946, by which time he was surgeon of that theater and had advanced to a permanent colonelcy (July 1945).

Returning to Washington in July 1946 after thirty-four months of service abroad, Armstrong became Chief of Personnel, Surgeon General's Office. About a year later, in June 1947, he received the appointment of Deputy Surgeon General and in the same month the rank of brigadier general (temporary), a promotion confirmed as permanent in May 1948. He advanced to the rank of major general (temporary) in May 1949 with date of rank from May 1948, and received that permanent rank in June 1951 to date from August 1949.

As Deputy Surgeon General Armstrong in September 1950 represented the army before a House Armed Services Subcommittee inquiring into fees paid for X rays. In defense of the news stories reporting the "large sums received by some private physicians" (New York *Times*, September 8, 1950), Armstrong testified that the alleged "big earnings" reaped from X-raying draftees were the result of the Army's effort to save money. Armstrong reported to the committee that when the Korean war began, only twenty-two of the nation's one hundred eight induction centers were equipped with X-ray facilities.

Major General Armstrong was sworn in as Surgeon General of the Army on June 6, 1951. It is customary for a new Surgeon General to be appointed every four years; thus Armstrong succeeded Major General Raymond W. Bliss, who had taken office in 1947. It is Armstrong's responsibility as Surgeon General to "plan and formulate medical and sanitary policies and procedures; provide and conduct programs and direct certain aspects of the medical service to insure the health of the Army; and provide and service medical material for the army as assigned to the Surgeon General" (*United States Government Organization Manual*). In line with his duty to provide for the health of the army, Armstrong reported in September 1951 on a new drug (primaquine), which may prove to be a fast and permanent cure of malaria. The General stated that the drug should rid Korean war veterans "of the malarial parasites in their bloodstreams without ever knowing they have been victims" (New York *Herald Tribune*, September 9, 1951). At a conference of military surgeons in Chicago in October 1951, Armstrong was one of the three Surgeons Generals who announced a new artificial hand for the servicemen amputees. This device was developed at the army's research laboratory of Walter Reed Hospital, "after many months of hard work" (*Newsweek*). The army has recently released the artificial limb for civilian use.

According to Austin Stevens of the New York *Times*, Armstrong reported in an interview on February 17, 1952, that the army's research program for 1952 will cost $10 millions, a large portion of which is being devoted to "medical aspects of atomic warfare." (Army and civilian agencies have already developed a dressing for atomic burns.) A search for a

U. S. Army

M^J. GEN. GEORGE E. ARMSTRONG

substitute for blood plasma will also receive attention—Armstrong reported that the Korean War is draining the army's supply of blood plasma faster than it is being replaced. He testified that the most outstanding lesson learned by military medicine in Korea is the realization of the "enormous importance of human blood and plasma and the importance of prompt treatment of wounded on the battlefield" (New York *Sunday News*). Lauding the army's program of preventive medicine, Armstrong stated that the army medical service has "relearned the old lesson that it pays to prepare for disease and injury before they strike you down."

At a dinner of the American Pharmaceutical Manufacturers' Association in New York on November 27, 1951, Armstrong reported a drop in the Korean war death rate to 2.5 per cent, or half the World War II rate. He attributed this improvement to five factors: rapid evacuation of wounded by helicopter, more use of whole blood, increased use of mobile surgical teams, better trained doctors, and germ-killing drugs (New York *Herald Tribune*). In March 1952 the General gave out the latest mortality figure: 1.8 deaths for every 100 patients reaching a forward hospital as against 4.5 deaths for every 100 in World War II (New York *Times*).

Armstrong is the recipient of the American Legion of Merit, Army Commendation Ribbon, Army Defense Service Ribbon, Asiatic Pacific Campaign Ribbon with three bronze stars, World Wars I and II Victory Ribbons, Chinese Cloud Banner with Ribbon, and the Chinese Honorary Nobility Ribbon. He is a member of the American College of Surgeons and the American Medical Association. His fraternities are Phi Kappa Psi, Phi Rho Sigma, and Alpha Omega Alpha, and he is a member of the Scabbard and Blade. A Mason, he belongs to the

ARMSTRONG, GEORGE E.—*Continued*

Blue Lodge, Scottish Rite, and Shrine. He is a Protestant. Married to Lillian T. Ott on March 20, 1937, he has one son, George B.

Reference

Who's Who in America, 1951-52

ARNAZ, DESI *See* Ball, L., and Arnaz, D.

ASGEIRSSON, ASGEIR (äs'gärs-sōn äs'-gär) May 13, 1894- President of Iceland

Address: Reykjavik, Iceland

In the first popular election for the presidency of Iceland, which took place on June 29, 1952, Asgeir Asgeirsson became the President of the republic. The newly chosen executive has taken part in his country's public life for many years, having been a member of the Althing (the parliament of Iceland) since 1923, Prime Minister from 1932 to 1934, and a delegate to the United Nations General Assembly in 1947 and 1948. He is a member of the Social Democrat party, which has been described by the *Political Handbook of the World* as advo-

ASGEIR ASGEIRSSON

cating "the ordinary program of moderate socialism." Iceland has acquired new importance in the last few years because of its strategic defense position in the sea and air lanes between the United States and Europe.

Asgeir Asgeirsson was born in Koranesi, Iceland, on May 13, 1894, the son of A. Eythorsson and the former Jensina Bjorg Matthiasdóttir. His father, a merchant for a time, later became an accountant. Asgeirsson received his secondary education in the Reykjavik High School, of which he is a 1912 graduate. Receiving a degree in theology in 1915, in that

year and 1916 he served as secretary to the Bishop of Iceland. He then worked for a year (in 1917-18) as an assistant in the National Bank of Iceland and in 1918 became a teacher at the Teachers' College of Iceland, a post he held until 1926.

Asgeirsson began his service with the government of Iceland in 1923, when he became a member of the Icelandic parliament (Althing). The Althing is the oldest parliamentary institution in the world, having existed almost continually since 930. When a committee was formed in 1926 to arrange the celebration of the one thousandth anniversary of the assembly Asgeirsson was named a member. On July 19, 1926, he was appointed chief of the Government Bureau of Education, serving until 1931, and in another capacity, from 1927 to 1935, was chairman of the Currency Committee of the Althing. The statesman has been a member of the Althing's Foreign Relations Committee from 1928 to 1931 and again since 1938. He was elected as the speaker of the Althing in 1930 for the term of one year.

From 1931 to 1934 Asgeirsson was the Minister of Finance of Iceland, and in 1932 he became the Prime Minister of the country, an office he filled until 1934. He again served for four years as the chief of the Government Bureau of Education, beginning in 1934. In 1938 Asgeirsson then assumed the managing directorship of the Fisheries Bank of Iceland (Utvegsbanki Islands). Because of the island's strategic position in the Western defense line during World War II, British forces landed there in May 1940 and American marines arrived in July 1941 with Iceland's approval. In the following month Asgeirsson went to Washington, D.C., as a member of the delegation that carried on negotiations with the United States on financial, trade, and shipping problems. The Icelandic delegation to the United Nations General Assembly included the statesman in 1947 and 1948. He has been Iceland's representative on the board of directors of the International Monetary Fund since 1947.

The first President of the Icelandic republic (its independence from Denmark was proclaimed in 1944), Svein Björnsson, died in January 1952, thus making a presidential election necessary. Björnsson had been appointed President by the Althing in 1944, and re-elected by acclamation in 1945 and again in 1949 with no candidate opposing him either time. The 1952 election therefore was the first presidential election by popular ballot ever to be held in Iceland. The three candidates for the presidency were Asgeirsson, Bishop Bjarni Jonsson, and Gipsi Sveinsson, former Minister to Oslo. Bishop Jonsson was a nonpolitical candidate supported by the Conservative and the Progressive parties. Sveinsson was backed by the Independents. Asgeirsson, formerly a member of the Progressive party, now belongs to the Social Democrat party, which, however, did not campaign actively for him so as to make clear the nonpolitical character of his candidacy. The election was held June 29, 1952, with Asgeirsson receiving 32,925 votes, Jonsson 31,040, and Sveinsson, 4,255. Commenting on the election the New York *Herald*

Tribune said, "Now that American troops are in Iceland by invitation of the Icelandic government, to aid Iceland's defense under the North Atlantic alliance, it is important and highly encouraging to know that the administration is friendly to the United States and has wide popular support."

In 1918 Denmark (which had held Iceland since 1380) recognized Iceland as an independent state by a treaty between the two countries. The Danish King, however, was still to be recognized as the sovereign of Iceland and was to exercise certain powers for that country, such as the management of foreign affairs. This treaty was subject to revision in 1940; if a new treaty should not be agreed upon in three years from that time the treaty would lapse. As the German occupation prevented the Danish King from exercising his treaty powers the Althing delegated the royal functions to the Cabinet and in 1944 declared the treaty terminated. The question of independence and of a constitution was then put to a popular vote and the formal restoration of the Icelandic republic took place on June 17, 1944.

Dora Thorhallsdóttir, the daughter of Thorhallur Bjarnason, the Bishop of Iceland, is the wife of the new President of Iceland. Asgeirsson has received many decorations for his services, among them the Grand Cross of the Icelandic Order of the Falcon, the Grand Cross of the Orange Nassau Order of the Netherlands, and the Grand Cross of Finland's Order of the White Rose.

References

N Y Herald Tribune II p6 Jl 6 '52
N Y Times p4 Jl 2 '52
World Biography (1948)

AVENOL, JOSEPH (LOUIS ANNE)
June 9, 1879—Sept. 2, 1952 Former secretary general of the League of Nations; began government career in the French Treasury (1905); served as French member of the League financial committee (1920-23); League deputy secretary general (1923-33); headed League during period after Hitler came to power (1933) and Germany withdrew from the organization; resigned from the League (1940) and retired first to France and later to Switzerland. See *Current Biography*, 1940.

Obituary

N Y Times p29 S 3 '52

AYDELOTTE, FRANK (ā'dĕ-lŏt) Oct. 16, 1880- Educator; former college president
Address: b. c/o Institute for Advanced Study, Princeton, N.J.; h. 88 Battle Rd., Princeton, N.J.

NOTE: This biography supersedes the article which appeared in *Current Biography* in 1941.

Former college president and the Director Emeritus of the Institute for Advanced Study,

Dr. Frank Aydelotte is widely known as an educator and administrator. As president (for nineteen years) of Swarthmore College, he developed an Oxford plan for American universities, an outgrowth of his study at Oxford University as a Rhodes scholar and his many years as American Secretary of the Rhodes Trust. Another post he filled, for twenty-five years, was that of chairman of the educational advisory committee of the Guggenheim Foundation.

Frank Aydelotte was born October 16, 1880, in Sullivan, Indiana, the son of William Ephraim and Matilda (Brunger) Aydelotte. His father, the owner of a woolen mill, was descended from a Huguenot who settled in Delaware early in the eighteenth century; his mother was a native of Canada. Brought up in Sullivan, Frank Aydelotte graduated from the local high school in 1896. The future educator then passed his college undergraduate years at Indiana University, where he majored in English, played football, was elected to the Sigma Nu fraternity, and received a Phi Beta Kappa key. Graduating with the B.A. degree in 1900, he began his career that year as an instructor in English at the Southwestern State Normal School of Pennsylvania. A year later he returned to Indiana University as an English instructor, but after twelve months proceeded to Harvard University to work for the M.A. degree. That he received in 1903, whereupon followed years (1903-05) as an instructor at the Boys' High School in Louisville, Kentucky.

Aydelotte resumed his studies in England, entering Oxford University as the successful competitor for one of the two Rhodes scholarships allotted to the State of Indiana. Accepted at Brasenose College, he remained there for the usual three years (although his scholarship was terminated by his marriage in 1907) and took the B.Litt degree in 1908. (The Ph.D. was not conferred at either Oxford or Cambridge until some years later.) His thesis, *Elizabethan Rogues and Vagabonds*, was published in 1913 as the first of a series of "Oxford Historical and Literary Studies," projected by two English scholars. The aim of the study, which (said the *American Oxonian*) is still regarded as unexcelled in its field, was (according to the preface) "to make as complete a picture as possible" of the life of the Elizabethan vagabond "by piecing together historical and literary material."

The Rhodes scholarships, provided under the last will of Cecil John Rhodes, multimillionaire founder of the DeBeers Mining Company in South Africa, former Oxford student and later Premier of Cape Colony, were first awarded in 1904; they were envisaged by their doner as a means of advancing the ultimate federation of all English-speaking peoples. The will provided for three-year scholarships at Oxford for sixty recipients each year from the British Dominions, two from each State of the United States, and (by codicil) fifteen from Germany; aspirants were (and normally still are) required to be unmarried and to be under twenty-five years of age. As Aydelotte

Harris & Ewing

FRANK AYDELOTTE

has written, Rhodes was "emphatic in his desire that his Scholars should not be mere bookworms, but men chosen upon a broad basis of intellectual and personal qualities including, besides scholastic ability and achievement . . . solidity of character, interest in their fellows and instincts for leadership, and proficiency in manly outdoor sports."

When Aydelotte returned to the United States it was as a lifelong exponent of Anglo-American amity and as a firm believer in the Oxonian system, then unknown in American universities. The system is approximately self-education under guidance: attendance at lectures is voluntary, and the student working under the direction of a tutor is required to take only final examinations. Thus, at both Indiana University (where he was an associate professor of English from 1908 to 1915) and at the Massachusetts Institute of Technology (as professor of English from 1915 to 1921) Aydelotte kept in close touch with Oxford and contributed articles on English university life to various periodicals. He became the editor of the *American Oxonian* for four years beginning 1914, and in 1917 published under the title of *The Oxford Stamp* a collection of essays which he describes as "articles from the creed of an American Oxonian." Also during this period appeared his textbook *College English* (1913), and two other books of his editing—*Materials for the Study of English Literature and Composition* (1914) and *English and Engineering* (1917), the latter a collection of essays for use in English classes in engineering schools.

During the first thirteen years of the Rhodes Trust, as many as thirty-six United States scholarships went unfilled for want of candidates, partly because a knowledge of Greek and Latin was required for admission by the English university, and partly because the various State committees selecting the candidates were composed of men who (as Aydelotte has put it) "knew for the most part nothing about the University of Oxford." To correct this situation the trustees approved in 1918 a suggestion that in the future an American Secretary act with the State committees, the latter (with the exception of the chairman) to be composed of former Rhodes scholars. Aydelotte (who in that year gave World War I service as national director of the War Issue Course of the War Department Committee on Education and Special Training) was selected for the post of American Secretary of the Rhodes Trust, a position that he occupied for some thirty-five years before announcing in July 1952 that he planned to retire on January 1, 1953. In the year 1922 the new American Secretary, in collaboration with L. A. Crosby and A. C. Valentine, further acquainted Americans with Oxonian ways through the book *Oxford Today* (of which a revised second edition appeared in 1927). In 1924 he came forward with a plan to correct inequities in competition caused by the method of distributing scholarships on a State basis through the substitution of six districts of eight States each, with appointments available to the United States being evenly divided among these districts. This change was authorized by Britain's Parliament in May 1929. (When, in 1946, scholarship awards were resumed after World War II, Aydelotte was largely responsible for inducing Oxford to relax its restrictions on age and bachelor status in favor of former servicemen.) In 1930 Aydelotte was elected president of the Association of American Rhodes Scholars.

A new phase in Aydelotte's career began in 1921 when he was offered the presidency of Swarthmore College in Pennsylvania, a small but highly regarded Quaker institution founded in 1864. He accepted the post largely because he saw in the attitude of the board of managers and the faculty a "favorable opportunity" to experiment in America with a modification of the Oxford system. The project, which went into effect in 1922, became famous as the "Swarthmore Plan," whereby the more brilliant students were, from the beginning of the junior year, given the opportunity to work for honors. Tutored in small seminars, they were permitted to concentrate on two or three subjects, were relieved (as at Oxford) from compulsory attendance at lectures, and were required to submit only to final examinations, written and oral, conducted by scholars from outside the college. Details of the scope and general impact of the system, which was followed elsewhere, may be found in the chapter Dr. Aydelotte contributed to the book *Five College Plans* (1931); the collaborative account by members of the Swarthmore faculty, *An Adventure in Education* (1941); and Aydelotte's own later and longer work, *Breaking the Academic Lock Step* (1944). During his nineteen years as president of Swarthmore, Aydelotte was the recipient of honorary degrees: the LL.D. from Allegheny College in 1923, the L.H.D. from the University of Pennsylvania in

1924, the D.Litt. from the University of Pittsburgh and Oberlin College in 1925 and 1926, respectively, and LL.D.'s from Yale and Indiana universities in 1928 and 1937, respectively. An honorary fellow of Brasenose College, he received the D.C.L. from Oxford in 1937.

While serving as president of Swarthmore the educator became (in 1922) a trustee of the Carnegie Foundation for the Advancement of Teaching, the chairman (beginning in 1925) of the advisory board of the John Simon Guggenheim Memorial Foundation, a trustee (in 1927) of the World Peace Foundation, and a trustee (in 1930) of the new Institute for Advanced Study endowed in that year at Princeton, New Jersey, by the Newark department store owner Louis Bamberger and his sister, Mrs. Felix Fuld.

The Institute for Advanced Study, which is independent of Princeton University, but which works in close cooperation with the latter, has as its aim to "provide a place where a few highly qualified students" may "engage in productive scholarship." It draws its membership largely from advanced students and college professors on sabbatical who desire the opportunity to pursue their own special researches under the guidance of a small faculty in which Dr. Albert Einstein is probably the most famous luminary. No degrees are conferred. Dr. Abraham Flexner was the first director, and when he resigned in 1939 Dr. Aydelotte was chosen as his successor. For one year Dr. Aydelotte held both this position and the presidency of Swarthmore, but resigned the latter in 1940. Honorary LL.D. degrees were conferred on him at this time by both New York University and Pomona College, while Swarthmore itself gave him an L.H.D. degree. He received honorary LL.D. degrees from the Universities of Iowa and California in 1941 and 1942, respectively.

During World War II Dr. Aydelotte served (beginning 1942) as chairman of the committee of scientific personnel of the Office of Scientific Research and Development. Subsequently (1945-46) he served also on the Anglo-American Committee of Inquiry on Palestine. His book *The American Rhodes Scholarship: A Review of the First Forty Years* (published also in England under the title of *The Vision of Cecil Rhodes*) appeared in 1946. As director of the Institute for Advanced Study, Dr. Aydelotte had reached the normal retirement age a year earlier, but was persuaded to stay on for another two years, or until October 15, 1947, when he was given the title of Director Emeritus and succeeded as director by Dr. J. Robert Oppenheimer. In his farewell address Dr. Aydelotte said that it "was a good satisfaction to know" that he was "leaving with the budget balanced, the faculty considerably enlarged, and the enrollment of students greater than ever before" (New York *Times*). He remains a trustee of the Institute as well as of Swarthmore College and the Carnegie Foundation, but resigned the chairmanship of the Guggenheim advisory board in 1950. Upon his seventieth birthday Dr. Aydelotte was honored in seven essays, tributes by associates and friends, in the January 1951 issue of the *American Oxonian*.

The educational administrator has been active in a number of learned societies. He is a member of the Modern Language Association of America; American Historical Association; American Philosophical Society (twice a member of its council and vice-president in 1941-43); Council on Foreign Relations; American Academy of Political and Social Science; (member of the Phi Beta Kappa senate since 1931 and vice-president during 1946-49); college of electors of the Hall of Fame of New York University; president of the Association of American Colleges (1925); honorary member of the American Association of University Professors.

Mrs. Frank Aydelotte, who died on June 1, 1952, was the former Marie Jeannette Osgood of Boston. They were married on June 22, 1907, in England, and had one son, William Osgood. The blue-eyed educator is five feet nine inches in height and weighs about 170 pounds. A Quaker since 1940, during 1940-47 he was a member of the board of directors of the American Friends Service Committee. In political alignment he is a Democrat. His clubs are the Cosmos in Washington, the Thames in New London, the Century in New York city, the Franklin Inn and University in Philadelphia, the Harvard in Boston and New York, the Nassau in Princeton, and the Athanæum in London Golf remains his favorite outdoor recreation.

References

American Oxonian 38:1-23 Ja '51 por
Friends Intelligencer 97:671-3 Tenth month 19 '40
N Y Times VII p5+ Ja 5 '41 por; p11 D 23 '46 por; p29 O 16 '47 por
Newark (N.J.) Sunday Call p12 Mr 16 '41 por
Newsweek 11:34 Ja 3 '38 por
Science ns 91:566 Je 14 '40
Time 25:47 Je 5 '33; 33:57 Ja 12 '39; 35:42-3 Mr 4 '40 por

Author's & Writer's Who's Who (1948-49)
Banta, R. E., comp. Indiana Authors and Their Books (1949)
Directory of American Scholars (1942)
Leaders in Education (1948)
National Cyclopædia of American Biography, Current vol F, 1939-42
Who Knows—and What (1949)
Who's Who, 1951
Who's Who in America, 1950-51
Who's Who in the East (1951)
World Biography (1948)

BABSON, NAOMI LANE Nov. 30, 1895-
Author

Address: b. Harcourt Brace & Company, Inc., 383 Madison Ave., New York 17; h. Durston Rd., Bozeman, Mont.

Reprinted from the *Wilson Library Bulletin*, October 1952.

The work of Naomi Lane Babson is familiar to many American readers, for her stories and

Schlechten

NAOMI LANE BABSON

articles, and half a dozen novelettes have appeared in magazines reaching millions—*The Saturday Evening Post, Collier's, Ladies' Home Journal, Redbook, Cosmopolitan, McCall's,* and *Good Housekeeping.* Many of the short stories have been widely republished in England, Australia, New Zealand, and the Scandinavian countries. Since 1936, she has also had four novels published. In locale, Miss Babson's fiction is divided between her native America and China, where she spent twelve years, plus a return visit in 1948-49.

Born in Pigeon Cove, near Rockport, Massachusetts, November 30, 1895, in the very house where her father, Frederick Babson, had been born, she and her two sisters and a brother grew up there, and as the Cape Ann scene left indelible early impressions, it still figures large in her writings. Both her father and her mother, Ella (Bailey) Babson, came of old New England stock. As Miss Babson puts it, "My ancestry is straight Yankee, going back in four lines to Colonial New England."

Finishing high school in 1913, she taught several years in country schools in Massachusetts and Connecticut, then attended Radcliffe College, majoring in English. After that came the Chinese interlude. She taught the school for children of the Western staff members of Lingnan University in Canton, China, where her husband-to-be, Paul Alfred Grieder, was professor of English. They were married in 1926, and their two children were born there. The oldest died in 1933 when only three years old. The second, Jerome Bailey Grieder, is in 1952 a student at Brown University.

Although she had sold a group of stories to *Youth's Companion* about 1920, she did not begin serious and sustained writing until after the death of her little son. She had stopped writing when she went to China, being "too busy living." But she thoroughly absorbed the atmosphere, so that even today her Chinese stories have the authority that comes only from long, close association with a people.

She and her family returned to America in 1935, locating in her present home, Bozeman, Montana, where Mr. Grieder teaches at the State College. The four war years were spent in New York; and in 1948 they went back to China, Mr. Grieder as a Fulbright professor. Here they remained "until the Communists came uncomfortably close."

In 1936, her first novel, *The Yankee Bodleys,* was published. It records nearly eighty years in the life of an American family on the Massachusetts coast. This theme of several generations in one family is a favorite of Miss Babson's, three novels being concerned with it. Of this one, Stanley Young, in the New York *Times,* comments: "She does not grapple with burning issues or concern herself with current isms. . . . She simply draws objectively some very knowing portraitures." The novel was awarded the *Prix Fémina Americaine.*

The author's second novel, *All the Tomorrows* (1939), tells a story of transition in China, from 1860 to the present, from the days of the Emperors to the coming of the Communists and the Japanese invasion. Mary Ross, in New York *Herald Tribune Books,* says of it: "Vivid scenes and characters that illumine the news from China . . . more realistically than is comfortable . . . likely to stay in one's remembrance as the story of persons one has known well, rather than of a people half a world away." The *New Yorker* agreed that she knew her China, "but in trying to get everything in, from the old priests in their noisy, crowded temples to the young revolutionaries, she . . . has spread her material a little thin."

Look Down from Heaven (1942) is the story of an American-born daughter of Finnish parents, and her young days in a Massachusetts seaport village from 1905 to 1919. Mary Ross recommended it in *Books* as having "the originality of a quietly told tale which illuminates the persons of the story with sufficient clarity to reveal their uniqueness." In the *Saturday Review* M. T. Bacon wrote: "A moving and charming story. Her prose is delicately punctuated with lyric and poetic passages. She has maintained a remarkable unity . . . through her three main divisions."

In her latest book, *I Am Lidian* (1951), the author tells the story through the lips of the ninety-year-old heroine, from her pampered girlhood in Massachusetts, through hard days crossing the plains in a singing troup with her husband, and finally settling in Montana with her second husband. Evelyn Eaton, in the New York *Times,* approves it thus: "A vivid recreation of pioneer mores, it is also a well-drawn portrait of a pioneer woman in youth and in age—has the timeless quality of all good fiction." It was a 1951 choice of the Book League.

In her home in Montana, looking mountainward in four directions, Naomi Lane Babson is in 1952 at work on a fifth novel. A small woman with a charming smile, brown eyes, and gray hair, she is an Episcopalian and a political independent. Travel, keeping a private journal, and reading the journals of others give her pleasure. Her favorite authors are Shakespeare, then Jane Austen, the Brontës, Dorothy Wordsworth, Dickens, Tolstoy. She lectures at writers' conferences occasionally, such as the Drury College Conference and the Regional Round Up of the Arts, at the University of Montana.

BACKMAN, JULES May 3, 1910- Economist; college professor
Address: b. c/o New York University, School of Commerce, Washington Sq., New York 3; h. 59 Crane Rd., Scarsdale, N.Y.

Economist and educator Jules Backman, who has been a member of the faculty of New York University since 1938, has frequently been a consultant on questions of wages, prices, and economic policy for major industrial and economic research organizations. In early 1952 he was consultant for the steel industry at hearings before the Wage Stabilization Board on the issue of increased wage rates for members of the United Steelworkers Union. Employed in 1935 by the Securities and Exchange Commission and in 1942 by the Office of Price Administration, Backman worked with the several Government bodies concerned with establishing economic controls. He has been active as an author and editor: his writings comprise reports, editorials, and several books; and for ten years he was economic editor for *Trusts and Estates Magazine*. In 1950 Backman was named professor of economics at New York University's School of Commerce, Accounts and Finance.

Jules Backman was born in New York City on May 3, 1910, one of three sons of Nathan and Gertrude (Schall) Backman. He spent his early years in his native city, and attended Franklin K. Lane High School, in Brooklyn. After receiving his high school diploma in 1927, he began to study at New York University, majoring in economics. Though he completed his undergraduate studies in the usual four-year period, all his classes were in the evening hours so that he was able to hold a job during the day.

From 1927 to the beginning of 1930 he worked as a statistician for Newberger, Henderson & Loeb. After taking his Bachelor of Commercial Science degree *cum laude* in 1931, he worked during the year 1932-33 for Sydeman Brothers, stockbrokers. Having become interested in economics and finance as a result of this introduction to Wall Street, Backman continued his studies at New York University, receiving in 1932 the M.A. degree from the School of Education, and in 1933 a degree as Master of Business Administration. His thesis for the latter degree was on foreign exchange. In 1935 he was granted the degree of Doctor of Commercial Science, for which his doctoral thesis was a report on government price fixing. While still a graduate student, Backman served from 1933 to 1935 as vice-president and editor for Economic Statistics, Inc.

JULES BACKMAN

On the completion of his studies Backman accepted an appointment in 1935 with the Securities and Exchange Commission. The next two years he did research in public utilities for Madden and Dorau, economic consultants, and also began an eight-year association with *Trust and Estates Magazine* as its economic editor. In 1938 he returned to his alma mater as instructor in economics in the School of Commerce; in 1944 he was promoted to an assistant professorship, and two years later to an associate professorship. In September 1950 he was named professor, a position he continues to hold in 1952.

Backman, whose career as a consultant had begun in 1935, worked in 1942 with the Office of Price Administration as head economic consultant. The next year he made two special studies for the Brookings Institution, and in 1944 he began an association with the steel industry when he acted as director of special studies and as economic adviser to the Steel Case Research Committee in connection with the steel wage mediations of that year. During the same period he was a technical adviser to the industry members of the President's Cost of Living Committee; another Federal service, in 1945, was as economic adviser to the OPA Retail Reconversion Pricing Committee. From 1947 to 1949 he was a member of the New York Milkshed Price Committee, and since 1946 he has been an economic adviser to the railroads in cases involving both national wage and national rate disputes. In the year 1949 and again in 1950 he headed the economic staff handling the steel producers' position in wage increase hearings and mediations. Other industries whose economics he has studied and whose management position he has represented include cotton textiles, potash, coal, frozen foods, carpets, and the surety groups. He has also acted as consultant to New York

BACKMAN, JULES—*Continued*

City department stores and to the newspaper publishers of the city.

In 1944, when the National War Labor Board was conducting hearings on the steel workers' request for increased wages, Backman, as chief of the economic staff representing the producers, warned against granting the wage request. He contended that such increases would mean a general rise in wages for the entire country, which in turn would mean higher war costs, the creation of strong inflationary trends, and distortions in the national economy. He further claimed that while corporate profits, after taxes, had increased $5 billions during the war, wages and salaries had expanded by more than $50 billions since before the war. In December 1946, when the Nathan Report, issued by the CIO, stated that a 25 per cent increase in wages could be granted by industry without raising prices, he described the report as "statistical trickery replete with figures based upon false premises." According to the New York *Sun* summary of his criticism, Backman declared that "reducing profits by raising wages [would] make price reductions impossible," and that too high profits could be better combatted by price competition than by cost increases. Again, in 1947 he made a study of wage demands (which was financed by the eastern, western, and southeastern railroads and published by the National Industrial Conference Board) in which he described the Heller Budget, prepared by a research staff of the University of California and used by the union as the basis for its requests, as "unrealistically high." To provide the workers with the goods and services included in the budget of the average four-person family, Backman asserted that the national production rate would have to exceed by more than $35 billions the highest rate of consumer goods production ever achieved in the nation's history.

In the disputes, in early 1952, over the workers' demand for a wage increase, Backman represented the steel industry in its case before the Wage Stabilization Board. The economist centered his arguments around the belief that the 1950 wage increases had enabled steel workers to keep step with the rise in the cost of living and that they were thus in a better financial position than the employers, since wages, before taxes, had risen 14 per cent since the outbreak of the Korean conflict, while profits of the industry, after taxes, had dropped about 15 per cent. If the wage demands were met, Backman predicted the conversion of "the inflation lull into an inflation gallop," according to the New York *Times* report of his opinion.

In connection with his consultant assignments as well as with his university teaching, Backman has been the author and coauthor of more than fifty books and pamphlets and of numerous articles for trade and economic journals. These writings began in 1936 with the issuance of *Adventures in Price Fixing*, followed two years later by *Government Price Fixing*. During the years of World War II he wrote several works on prices, wages, and government controls. He also issued studies on price controls and rationing in Great Britain and Canada. His research work with the Brookings Institution, the National Industrial Conference Board, the American Potash Institute, the American Iron and Steel Institute, the Foundation for Economic Education, and the National Retail Dry Goods Association resulted in special reports on the statistics, particular economic problems, and the relations of wages with prices for each of these groups and industries. In addition to these reports, Backman from 1943 to 1948 wrote several editorials weekly for the New York *Times*. Two recent publications are *Multi-Employer Bargaining* (1951) and *War and Defense Economics* (1952), the latter a textbook which he edited and coauthored. He has also been a frequent participant in radio and television forums.

Backman is a member of the American Economic Association, the American Statistical Association, the New York University Men in Finance, and the Trade and Industry Law Institute (vice-president). He belongs to Beta Gamma Sigma and is an honorary member of Phi Lambda Delta, Lambda Gamma Phi, Sigma Eta Phi, and Alpha Phi Sigma. A founder and treasurer of the New York University Graduate School of Business Administration Alumni Association, Backman is also a member of the board of directors of the university's Alumni Federation. For the latter group he served as vice-chairman of the fund drive from 1939 to 1943, receiving the Fund Award for three of the four years of service. In addition, in 1943, he was the recipient of the university's Alumni Medallion Award for "distinguished service to the university."

The economist has gray eyes, brown hair, stands five feet ten inches tall, and weighs 180 pounds. He is a trustee of the Jewish Community Center of White Plains and treasurer of the Jewish Culture Foundation at New York University. Married on October 18, 1935, to Grace Straim, a high school teacher at the time, Backman has two children, Susan Patricia and John Randolph. He lists golf as his favorite sport.

References

Who Knows—and What (1949)
Who's Who in Commerce and Industry (1951)
Who's Who in the East (1951)

BACON, SELDEN D(ASKAM) Sept. 10, 1909- Sociologist; college professor

Address: b. c/o Center of Alcohol Studies, Laboratory of Applied Physiology, Yale University, New Haven, Conn.; h. 10 West Slope Lane, Hamden 14, Conn.

The point of view which holds that alcoholism is primarily an illness has been scientifically developed by the Yale Center of Alcohol Studies, of which Dr. Selden D. Bacon became the director in 1950. Placing prevention "far above" rehabilitation and believing that "education is essential," Bacon has called the work of the Yale Center and Alcoholics Anonymous "humanitarian . . . efficient . . . dramatic." Bacon, a professor of sociology at Yale, previously taught at Pennsylvania State College.

Selden Daskam Bacon was born in Pleasantville, New York, on September 10, 1909, the son of Selden and Josephine Dodge (Daskam) Bacon. Among his forebears, who settled in New England in 1640, were several clergymen, his great-grandfather Leonard W. Bacon having been a Congregational minister who was active in the abolitionist movement. Bacon's mother is the novelist and author of stories for children, and his father was a well-known constitutional lawyer. In the Bacon family there were six children, of whom Selden and his two sisters are the offspring of the elder Bacon's second marriage.

In 1927 Bacon graduated from the Taft School, a preparatory school in Watertown, Connecticut, the headmaster of which, Horace D. Taft, was a major influence in Bacon's choice of a career; another was Albert G. Keller. The youth then entered Yale University, selecting history as his main subject. His Bachelor of Arts diploma is dated 1931. The recipient of a Social Science Research Council field fellowship and a Henry A. Page fellowship, he remained at Yale for graduate study. He was given the Master of Arts degree in government in 1935 and the Ph.D. degree in sociology in 1939. His doctoral dissertation was on the rise and development of American municipal police. During 1935-36 he was resident assistant in charge of surveys in that field in Pennsylvania.

During the years Bacon was an instructor of sociology at Pennsylvania State College (from 1937 to 1939) he served as editor of the Pennsylvania State Chiefs of Police *Bulletin*, and was a member of the State Commission for In-Service Training for Police Departments. Upon obtaining his doctorate, Bacon became an instructor in Yale's Department of Sociology in 1939 and an assistant professor in 1942 (the same year he was named a Fellow of Branford College, Yale); he was promoted to associate professor in 1947 and spent that summer at the University of Utah as a visiting professor. His status at Yale in 1952 is that of full professor.

At Yale Bacon became associated with the Center of Alcohol Studies, which had grown from the experimental program conducted by Dr. Howard W. Haggard and his colleagues in the Yale Laboratory of Applied Physiology in 1930. A pioneer in research on the physiological effects of alcohol, Haggard concluded that "physiology alone could not give . . . an adequate answer" (*Newsweek*, September 10, 1945), a point of view which led to the inclusion of sociologists, psychiatrists, economists, and statisticians in the research group. (The biometrician who joined the researchers, Dr. Elvin M. Jellinek, became the first director of the Center of Alcohol Studies.) In 1939 the enlarged unit of investigators began publishing the *Quarterly Journal of Studies on Alcohol.*

Bacon, who became the director of the Yale center in 1950, is concerned with a number of problems connected with alcoholism. Accord-

Yale Univ. News Bureau (Alburtus)
SELDEN D. BACON

ing to the *Directory of American Scholars*, his studies have included drinking behavior, excessive drinking and the institution of the family, alcohol and complex society, mobilization of community resources, and new legislation for the control of alcoholism.

The Yale program is composed of two major activities: (1) a free clinic for alcoholics, which was both a model for community hospitals and a place of treatment for alcoholics in need of medical and psychiatric aid; and (2) the Summer School of Alcohol Studies (begun in 1943), attended by ministers, educators, physicians, social workers, probation officers, and others vocationally interested in the problems of the alcoholic. In an accelerated curriculum of four weeks, the summer students consider five major aspects of alcoholism: the effect of alcohol on the body; its bearing on personality; its relation to society; agencies and factors controlling alcoholism; and the rehabilitation of inebriates.

One result of the Yale summer sessions was the 1945 publication of *Alcohol, Science and Society*, a collection of twenty-nine lectures and discussions held at the 1944 session. Called by H. M. Parshley in the New York *Herald Tribune Weekly Book Review* (February 3, 1946) "a good example of genuine science and free discussion in a nontechnical manner," the Yale lectures were also judged "a most useful and authoritative body of material, much of which is outstanding in originality and significance," by Niles Carpenter in the *American Sociological Review* (June 1946). "The reading public should be very wide," wrote Haven Emerson in the *American Journal of Public Health* (October 1946), and the psy-

BACON, SELDEN D.—*Continued*

chiatrist J. A. Kindwall found the book "well worth reading, even studying" (*Annals of the American Academy of Political and Social Science*, January 1946).

Two of Bacon's lectures are included in *Alcohol, Science and Society*. One entitled "Alcohol and Complex Society" maintains that while alcohol can "reduce tension, guilt, anxiety, and frustration," it can also "reduce operational efficiency below the minimum necessity for social existence, or even for existence at all." The lecture also pointed out that "the complexity of society increases the needs . . . for sharp discrimination, caution, accurate responses, timing, cooperation, and the acceptance of responsibilities. Alcohol, taken excessively, can deteriorate all of these." In another lecture, "Excessive Drinking and the Family," Bacon asserted that excessive drinking and marital happiness are incompatible, that "both are products of a complex of social and psychological factors."

At a later summer session, in 1948, Bacon stated that while most habit patterns are taught to a child at a very early age in life—as well as the guilt-feelings if he breaks them—"there are no such fixed rules about drinking behavior." As a result, an individual often learns his drinking habits "from persons who are equals or perhaps even his inferiors." For this reason Bacon places emphasis on the educational value of the Yale Center, in that it seeks to prevent alcoholism. "What do young people learn from the message of Alcoholics Anonymous or of the clinic?" he wrote in the *Christian Science Monitor* (June 15, 1949). "They learn about rehabilitation, they learn about the success story . . . they are keenly appreciative. . . .They are not spoken down or ordered around. The ways of their parents or family friends are not cursed or sneered at. And this works. This is prevention."

A service which the Yale Center has helped to inaugurate and expand since 1948 is that of advising industry on alcoholism among employees—on policies of discipline, termination of employment, insurance and pension payments, labor-management relations, and health services. Statistics indicate a billion-dollar yearly loss to industry because of alcoholism, a yearly loss of 24,000,000 man-hours of work, and the cause each year of 1,500 preventable factory accidents.

Bacon, who has served as chairman of the Connecticut Commission on Alcoholism since 1945 and as editor of the *Quarterly Journal of Studies on Alcohol* since 1946, is also the author of two studies in that field: *Sociology and the Problems of Alcohol* (1944) and *Inebriety, Social Integration, and Marriage* (1945). From 1945 to 1950 he was secretary-treasurer of the National Committee for Education on Alcoholism, and has been a member of the board of directors of the Council of Social Agencies since 1947. He is also a member of the Industrial Medical Association, the Connecticut Academy of Arts and Sciences, the Connecticut Conference of Social Work, the Eastern Sociological Society, the American Sociological

Society. His clubs are the Yale, Faculty, and Old Fields Community. He belonged to Pi Gamma Mu (a social science honor society) at Yale. He is an Episcopalian.

By his first marriage—to Cornelia Howard on December 20, 1934—Bacon has a daughter, Anne; by his second marriage—to Margaret Keller (who is an assistant professor of psychology) on May 25, 1948—there are two sons, Michael and Selden D., Jr. The sociologist has gray eyes, brown hair, stands five feet eleven inches in height, and weighs 190 pounds. His chief recreation is reading.

References

Directory of American Scholars (1951)
Who's Who in American Education (1949-50)
Who's Who in the East (1951)

BALL, LUCILLE Aug. 6, 1911- Motion picture actress; television producer

ARNAZ, DESI (är'nĕz dĕ'zĭ) Mar. 2, 1917- Musician; motion picture actor; television producer

Address: c/o CBS-TV, 1313 Vine St., Hollywood, Los Angeles, Calif.

In May 1952, for the first time, the four national television rating services were in agreement as to the country's most popular television program—the Columbia Broadcasting System's *I Love Lucy*. A "warmly human," farcical domestic comedy series, it is produced, owned, and starred in by Lucille Ball, who had appeared in about fifty-five motion pictures, and her husband, Desi Arnaz, hitherto best known as the leader, vocalist, and drummer of a rumba band. Acclaimed for her skill at pantomime and slapstick comedy, Miss Ball "belongs to a rare comic aristocracy: the clown with glamour."

The daughter of Henry D. and Désirée (Hunt) Ball, Lucille Ball was born in Jamestown, New York, on August 6, 1911. Much of the information about her early life is vague and contradictory. Henry Ball, her father, was (according to *Time*) a telephone lineman who died when his daughter was four years old. Lucille began taking music lessons in her fifth year from her mother and later attended the Chautauqua Institute of Music for two seasons. Her ambition, however, was to be an actress. Every spring, she has told, she would run away and walk in the direction of New York City until someone found her and brought her home.

Appearing in a local Masonic revue, Lucille Ball put so much gusto into an apache dance that she dislocated an arm. *Time* quoted her remark about a high school performance of *Charley's Aunt*: "I played the lead, directed it, cast it, sold the tickets, printed the posters, and hauled furniture to the school for scenery and props." At fifteen she left high school to enroll in the John Murray Anderson dramatic school in New York. After her first year in dramatic school, her teacher advised her to choose another occupation. Having tried secretarial work and found it dull, the girl applied for chorus work in musical productions. She was engaged to dance in the third road company of Ziegfeld's *Rio Rita*, but after five weeks of rehearsal she was told, "You're not meant for show business. Go home." This experience occurred again after she was engaged for *Stepping Stones* and two other musicals. Each time she returned for another attempt. Her first permanent job was as a soda fountain clerk in a drugstore on New York's Broadway.

Next Miss Ball earned twenty-five dollars a week modeling dresses in a wholesale showroom and subsequently was employed in fashionable department stores and the Hattie Carnegie salon. As a result of an accident (reported a CBS-TV release) she was disabled for three years. When she was able to work again she entered the more lucrative field of photographic modeling and she used the name Diane Belmont. One year she was the "Chesterfield Girl," with a contract to appear in a series of national advertisements. In 1934 she was selected for the group of "poster girls" which Samuel Goldwyn was engaging for six weeks' work in the chorus of *Roman Scandals*.

The six weeks of work were extended to the six months required to complete the Eddie Cantor comedy. When it was over, Lucille Ball remained in Hollywood, where a succession of small speaking and nonspeaking parts kept her "busy but not prosperous"; one part required her to be the target of squirted seltzer and tossed pies. When Columbia Pictures engaged her for its stock company, Miss Ball telegraphed to her mother, grandfather, and sister to join her in California. The next day Columbia decided to disband its stock company, and when the family arrived, they found her working at Paramount as an extra.

After a part in the musical *Roberta* (with Irene Dunne, Fred Astaire, and Ginger Rogers), Miss Ball received a RKO contract, starting at fifty dollars a week. Since much of her working time was spent as a show girl in musical numbers, between assignments she gained experience in acting in RKO's Little Theater. Her performance in the second lead of *The Girl from Paris* brought her a leading role in a short-lived Broadway musical *Hey Diddle Diddle*. Back in Hollywood, Miss Ball was one of the girls in the Ginger Rogers-Katharine Hepburn *Stage Door*. Erich Pommer hailed her as a "new find" on the basis of her performance as a burlesque queen in *Dance, Girl, Dance*. Then came her largest part, the leading lady of *Too Many Girls*, in which she sang some of the year's most popular songs. The third male lead was played by Desi Arnaz, to whom she was married seven months later, on November 30, 1940.

Desiderio Alberto Arnaz y de Acha, 3d, was born in Santiago, Cuba, on March 2, 1917. He is an only child. His father was mayor of the city, and his mother, Lolita de Acha was known as a beauty. During Desi's childhood the family owned three ranches, a town house, an island in Santiago Bay, a racing stable, and several cars and speedboats. At the time of the Cuban revolution in August 1933, the elder

LUCILLE BALL and DESI ARNAZ

Arnaz, a follower of President Machado, was a member of Congress. When Machado was deposed, the Arnaz property was confiscated and members of Congress imprisoned. Señora Arnaz and her son then left for Miami, Florida, where Desi, who had been attending the Colegio de Dolores in Santiago, entered St. Patrick's High School. He earned money by driving taxis and trucks, as a checker in a railroad yard, and as a store and office clerk.

After six months Arnaz' father rejoined the family in Miami and for a time was in the export-import business. About this time, in 1934, young Arnaz found steady employment as guitarist in a four-piece Cuban band. According to *Time*, the youth was liked for his personality, but, theater owner Carlos Montalban is quoted as saying, "He was always off-beat." Arnaz was playing the guitar and singing with a seven-piece rumba band at the Roney-Plaza Hotel when he came to the attention of "rumba king" Xavier Cugat.

After a year (1936-37) as featured vocalist with Cugat's orchestra, Desi Arnaz organized his own Latin dance band, which made its first appearance at La Conga Café in Miami in 1938, and was soon playing for conga lines in night clubs in other cities. In 1939 Arnaz went on the stage in the part of a Cuban football star, the third lead in George Abbott's hit musical, *Too Many Girls*. When the screen rights were purchased by RKO, the studio brought Desi Arnaz to California to re-create his stage role.

Toward the end of 1940, Lucille Ball arrived in New York, where Arnaz was then appearing on the stage of the Roxy theater and in November they were married in Greenwich, Connecticut. Although they bought a five-acre ranch in the San Fernando Valley and built a home on it, Arnaz was able to spend little time there. His heavy accent limited the roles he could play, so that his motion picture en-

BALL, LUCILLE, and ARNAZ, DESI
—*Continued*

gagements were for occasional specialty musical numbers. Most of the time he was traveling with his band, playing in theaters and night clubs—he and his wife estimate that, in the first eleven years of their marriage, they spent a total of three years together, and spent some $29,000 on telephone calls and telegrams.

While Desi Arnaz was on tour with his rumba band, his wife worked on many B-grade pictures, usually cast as a chorus girl, actress, or other entertainer. Her salary rose to $1,500 a week, but few good parts were assigned to her. She had roles as foils for comedians, among them Jack Oakie, Joe Penner, and the Marx Brothers—the last-named in *Room Service*. Then, according to *Look*, Miss Ball's friend Carole Lombard introduced her to Damon Runyon, who in turn recommended her for the part of Her Highness in his *The Big Street*, which was screened in the summer of 1942. *Life's* comment on Miss Ball's performance was that it was "superb"—"the girl can really act." As an immediate result she was signed to a long-term starring contract with MGM on her birthday in 1942.

Desi Arnaz was to have his first real opportunity at about the same time; there was a brief part as Private Felix Ramirez in the war film *Bataan* (starring Robert Taylor). Arnaz was considered "convincing" in the role, but parts for his type were still lacking. The bandleader reportedly declined a commission in the Cuban Army before he was drafted into the Army of the United States in February 1943. Because of a kneecap broken in basic training, Arnaz was assigned to limited service with the Army Medical Corps, entertaining hospitalized servicemen. He was discharged as a staff sergeant in November 1945, and resumed his life of travel.

Meanwhile Lucille Ball was starred in the title role of the lavish *DuBarry Was a Lady* (MGM), opposite Red Skelton and Gene Kelly. This was followed by two other Technicolor musicals, the gay *Best Foot Forward* (MGM) and *Meet the People* (MGM), roles which required her to wear beautiful clothes, dance a little, make a few "wisecracks," but offered little opportunity to show acting ability. She played a temperamental heiress opposite Victor Mature in *Seven Days Leave*. Among other Ball films were *Without Love, Affairs of Annabell, Valley of the Sun, Love from a Stranger*. What the New York *Sun* reviewer called "her biggest part and her funniest" came in *Easy to Wed* (1946) in which she was co-starred with Van Johnson and Esther Williams. One comment was, "Lucille Ball with her flaming red hair and doll eyes furnishes the comic highlights . . . a superb farceuse . . . as scatterbrained and indignant as a wet hen." Another reviewer wrote, "Keenan Wynn and Lucille Ball . . . make it clear that they are the funniest comic team on the screen just now —and by a wide margin." Another successful farce was *Her Husband's Affairs*, in which she played opposite Franchot Tone. After its completion, Miss Ball went on tour in the starring role of Elmer Rice's play *Dream Girl*,

a part which gave her the opportunity to show her versatility as an actress. She then returned to the screen with RKO's *Interference* (with Victor Mature and Sonny Tufts).

Lured, a 1947 Scotland Yard melodrama, with Boris Karloff and George Sanders, gave Lucille Ball a chance for both comedy and drama. *Variety's* critic said, "Miss Ball registers best in comic bits as a wisecracking show girl and less effectively in the emotionally distraught scenes." She was Bob Hope's leading lady in *Sorrowful Jones* and *Fancy Pants*. Comments were: "Lucille Ball . . . knows her small place and keeps it"; "Lucille Ball . . . handicapped by lack of comic lines, gives what help her pert presence can afford"; "She is a fine foil for the star, building up bits of business to a point where they are comically consequential, even though they have next to nothing to do with the original plot." She was "wasted," said some critics, in *Easy Living* and *Miss Grant Takes Richmond*. The only picture to make use of her talent for "rubber-faced slapstick clowning" was *The Fuller Brush Girl* (1950, with Eddie Albert). While making it, Miss Ball suffered several sprains and emerged with pneumonia.

Besides brief appearances in such pictures as *Father Takes a Wife, Four Jacks and a Jill*, and *The Navy Comes Through*, Arnaz had two commitments in low-budget "B" musicals suited to his talents: Universal's *Cuban Pete* in 1946 (*Variety* said, "Arnaz tries hard, and his songs and music are an aid"); and three years later, Columbia's *Holiday in Havana*. The latter included two songs of Arnaz' composition, the title song and "The Arnaz Jam," both percussive Latin numbers. "Arnaz is boyishly enthusiastic about all this," wrote the New York *Herald Tribune* reviewer. "His performance in front of the band has color and authority. This is not quite enough to redeem a mediocre Cuban-accented show." In the interval Arnaz served as musical director of the Bob Hope radio show in 1946-47, and toured the United States and Canada the rest of the time. A review of his appearance at Ciro's Hollywood in November 1950 (typical of reviews of his performances), described his "pulse-pounding prancings with the conga and bongo drums," and commented, "Maestro's showmanship, tremendously improved over the years, is flashy, and even when he muffs a line, which is often, he holds the ringsiders in his palm." The Arnaz band also made recordings, occasionally with Lucille Ball as guest vocalist.

While Arnaz was on the road, his wife studied languages and literature with a tutor three evenings a week. When the band was playing nearby night clubs Lucille Ball watched the performances. In 1950 the couple decided to form a corporation, Desilu Productions, with the husband as president and the wife as vice-president, to handle their business affairs and to promote joint contracts that would enable them to work together in pictures and on the air. As a first step Miss Ball undertook a radio program, a domestic comedy series called *My Favorite Husband*, and later Arnaz went on a sustaining program. To test their theory that they would be a successful comedy team they went on a nation-wide vaudeville tour, playing six or seven shows a day before enthusiastic audiences. With that encouragement, they left film, radio, and band contracts estimated at half a million dollars a year, to "gamble" on a television show of their own.

Toward the beginning of 1951 Desilu made a sample film of their planned show, and within two days sold the show to the Philip Morris Company for a reported $30,000 a week. The first of the series was filmed four months later, one month after the birth of Lucie Désirée Arnaz in July 1951. The program, called *I Love Lucy*, was written by the trio who had authored Miss Ball's radio program; to photograph it, Desilu had engaged Karl Freund, who had won the Academy Award for *The Good Earth*. The production method is original with Desilu: basically, each show is a three-act play, studied, rehearsed, and performed in sequence before an audience, filmed as it is performed (close-ups are done later), recorded (with audience laughter), edited, scored, and released on television. The entire process takes five weeks. The Arnazes own the films and retain the re-release rights. Hitherto filmed TV programs were of poorer quality than "live" telecasts, presumably because they employed production methods usual in Hollywood but unsuited to the fast pace and smaller budgets of TV. By playing before an audience and shooting in sequence, *I Love Lucy* was considered to gain spontaneity and conviction. An average total of ninety-three actors and technicians was employed for each show, and the production cost was said to be $23,000 to $25,000 a week, leaving an average corporate profit of $5,000 to $7,000 a week during 1951-52.

I Love Lucy was first telecast over the CBS-TV network in October 1951. It achieved such popularity that by February 1952, when Red Skelton received an award from the Academy of Television Arts and Sciences as the best television comedian of the year, he said, "I don't deserve this. It should go to Lucille Ball." Critics agreed in praising Miss Ball's "high-quality slapstick", "ebullient" charm and talent for making outrageous situations believable. "The viewer is somehow persuaded," said *Pathfinder*, "that *any* wife might buy $700 worth of meat for a deep freezer, or glue a beard on her face in a campaign against her husband's mustache." Opinions on Desi Arnaz were: "Refreshingly unpretentious", "a sprightly sense of fun, a young and handsome facade, acting ability . . . and a marvelous parallel aptitude for nonsense that bounces slickly and affectionately alongside his wife's." The plot, which casts Arnaz as Ricky Ricardo, preoccupied leader of an obscure rumba band, employs his musical abilities and gives Lucille Ball (as the harebrained wife) the opportunity to wear a wide variety of costumes and to engage in antics like stealing an elephant, setting fire to her husband's morning newspaper to attract his attention at the breakfast table, and posing as a hill-billy, a circus clown, or Oriental queen. "This is fun, not work," said Miss Ball

of a weekly routine of three six- to ten-hour days of rehearsal and an all-day rehearsal followed by the actual performance.

The success of the Ball-Arnaz production methods led to contracts to produce other shows. During 1952 Desilu Productions did the commercials for the Red Skelton show, six pilot (sample) films for Leo Durocher and Laraine Day, and one for Eve Arden's *Our Miss Brooks*. As a result of the last-named, Desi Arnaz was signed to produce that show for CBS-TV, thus causing an "indefinite" postponement of his and Lucille Ball's summer appearances in New York and Boston. (According to *Variety*, they were to have received $57,000 for two weeks "plus overages on $100,000 weekly" at New York's Roxy theater.) "All my life," Arnaz has said, "I've worried what I'd do when I got too old, too fat, too ugly to be in front of a band. Now I don't worry. We're learning to produce television films."

The comedy situations of *I Love Lucy* are said to be only an exaggeration of the hilarity which characterizes the couple's home. The couple "dabble in farming," like to dance, give frequent parties, collect symphonic and popular records, and fish from their 34-foot cabin cruiser, the *Desilu* (also the name of their ranch and the rumba band). Lucille Ball is "fascinated by Desi's boundless energy"—he rides, swims, repairs the boat, plays tennis, takes pictures of the baby, and cooks elaborate dishes. His red-haired slender wife never diets, but sometimes forgets to eat. She "collects stray dogs and cats," reported *Look*, paints in oils, and has complete beauty-shop equipment which she uses on her mother, mother-in-law, friends, and sometimes on women interviewers. On television Miss Ball's theatrical beauty and chic clothes bring as much fan mail as her comedy, but in private life she wears sweaters and skirts or slacks. In personality she is described as unpretentious and outspoken. While her husband gained much practical business experience in managing his band, Lucille Ball "hasn't seen her pay check in years," and leaves what she calls "the gruesome details" to her business manager. Miss Ball's church is the Presbyterian. Nine years after the couple's marriage, they were remarried by the rites of Arnaz' Roman Catholic faith.

References

Collier's 108:16 Ag 16 '41 por
Life 13:116 O 5 '42 pors; 15:65 Ag 9 '43 pors
Look 16:77 Je 3 '52 pors
N Y Post p5 My 25 '52 por
Newsweek 39:67 F 18 '52 pors
Time 59:62 My 26 '52 pors
TV Guide 5:4+ Je 6 '52 pors
Graham, A. P. Strike up the Band! (1949)
International Motion Picture Almanac 1951-52
Who is Who in Music, 1951
Who's Who in America, 1952-53

BALL, STUART S(COBLE) Sept. 5, 1904-
Business executive
Address: h. 2331 Orrington Ave., Evanston, Ill.

Montgomery Ward and Company, second largest merchandising organization in the United States, received a new president in 1949 when Stuart S. Ball was elected to that office. The executive, a corporation lawyer, had entered that company's employ in 1932 after practicing law for five years. On September 25, 1952, it was announced that Ball had resigned from the presidency of Montgomery Ward.

Wide World Photos·

STUART S. BALL

Stuart Scoble Ball, son of Amos and Jessie Edna (Wildman) Ball, was born in Marshalltown, Iowa, on September 5, 1904. He was educated at East High School in Des Moines, from which he graduated in 1921. After a year at Grinnell College in Iowa, he entered Northwestern University, where he received his B.A. degree in 1924 and was elected to the Order of Coif (the honorary legal society) and to Delta Sigma Rho. Ball remained at Northwestern for postgraduate studies, taking the M.A. and Doctor of Jurisprudence degrees in 1927. In the same year he was admitted to both the Illinois and Iowa bars.

Ball then returned to Des Moines to become a member of the law firm of Parrish, Cohen, Guthrie and Watters. After five years, in 1932 he entered the employ of Montgomery Ward and Company as an assistant secretary. From 1933 to 1949 he held the office of secretary, working most of that time as a legal assistant to Sewell Avery, who in 1937 had become board chairman of the mail-order house. Avery had been invited to take the chief executive post in Montgomery Ward when the company was faced with a heavy deficit. Under his administration, however, the firm began to flourish, wiping out its deficit and expanding

until, by 1939, it was close behind Sears, Roebuck in profits and in volume of business.

The legal assistance on which Avery relied in his disagreements with the United States Government, said *Fortune*, had in large measure been provided by Stuart Ball. The conflicts between Montgomery Ward and the NLRB (and the WLB) meant long and complicated litigation, in which Ball had a major role. He is credited with working out the legal strategy of the company's conflict with Federal agencies which resulted in the Army's seizure of the plant in 1944. This had followed upon Ward's dispute with CIO's United Mail Order, Warehouse and Retail Employees Union, in which the WLB recommended an extension of the contract until a new election could be held. Upon the company's refusal to recognize the WLB directive, a strike was called; when the dispute was referred to President Roosevelt, he ordered the seizure of the plant by troops.

While Avery registered his protest against Federal intervention by refusing to leave the plant Ball and his legal staff prepared for court action. The Government sued to have its seizure of the property declared legal, but the case was dismissed when, after thirteen days, the Army left the plant. Later a Federal District Court held that the seizure was illegal and in violation of the Constitution. This decision, in turn, was reversed by the Circuit Court of Appeals. The plant was returned by the Government before the Supreme Court could act on the case, and the highest court thereupon vacated judgment of the Circuit Court and ordered the case sent back to District Court to be dismissed as moot. In 1946 Ball summarized the outcome: "The situation today is as if no litigation had ever been brought."

The office of president of Montgomery Ward became vacant in 1946 upon the resignation of Clement D. Ryan. At that time Avery admitted to interviewers that he was looking for "an heir" and, *Fortune* reported, "would undoubtedly prefer to tap one of his own men if any could qualify." The qualifications for the job, as Avery listed them, were as follows: "(1) You must have a man who knows the mail order machine; (2) he must have been successful, but ripe for greater successes; (3) he must have borne the brunt of a national responsibility; (4) he must be able to implement Ward's historic economy in terms of quality and good taste." *Fortune* listed five executives from the company who were considered candidates for the post (Ball's name was not among them), and one of the five, Wilbur H. Norton, was elected president in 1946.

In 1948 Avery was faced with a management "revolt" as several directors and other executives had resigned. As told in *Business Week*, under pressure from his board of directors Avery yielded certain of his powers to top executives in the firm. New bylaws were passed to give the president wider powers in merchandising and personnel operations, while Avery retained control over all major financial and expansion policies. Less than a month later. however, these new bylaws were canceled when, according to the New York *Times*, Ball "rendered the legal opinion that the change in bylaws was meaningless because of the vagueness of its language and the fact that it did not change the position of the chairman as the chief executive of the company." President Norton was out of town at this time, and Ball was commissioned to telephone him requesting his resignation.

The office of president remained vacant for eleven months. In April 1949 Ball was elected one of eight new vice-presidents of Montgomery Ward's, and a month later, at a meeting of the company's executive committee, he was elected president. He was (to quote from *Time*) "the only experienced senior officer. . . who had remained true to Avery and . . . had always got along with him." Ball was elected to the board of directors in April 1950.

Montgomery Ward, which had its origin in a mail-order business established in Illinois in 1872, was incorporated in that State in 1919. According to the report covering the year that ended January 31, 1952, it owns 610 retail stores (in every State except Delaware and Massachusetts), 242 mail-order sales units, and three factories, and employs 60,300 persons. More than 130,000 items are advertised in its catalogue. The second largest merchandising organization in the country, its net sales for that year totaled approximately $1.1 billions, its net income $54.34 millions.

President Ball's outlook in questions of management and company policy was generally similar to Avery's. In a speech which he delivered to the National Founders Association meeting in Chicago on November 7, 1946, he expressed his disapproval of intervention by the Federal Government in business, especially in matters of labor disputes. The solution to the labor problem, he said, is "to keep Government out, put management and organized labor as nearly as possible into positions of approximate equality, take from each the power to destroy the other, and rely upon collective bargaining." He also stated his opposition to the closed shop and urged management to seize every possible opportunity for "self-defense" in court. Ball's resignation as president of Montgomery Ward was announced on September 25, 1952.

Ball lives in suburban Evanston, near Chicago. He has been married to the former Marion Wolcott Watrous since September 5, 1930; they have two daughters, Marion Watrous and Eleanor Wolcott, and a son, Stuart Scoble, Jr. The business executive is a member of a number of professional organizations: the Chicago Association of Commerce and Industry (of which he is a director), and the American, Chicago, and Illinois bar associations; his clubs are the Chicago, the Economic, the Legal, the University, the Law, the Commercial, Chicago Literary, Cliff Dwellers, and Glenview. From time to time he has contributed articles to law reviews.

References

N Y Times My 10 '49
Newsweek 33:64-5 My 23 '49
Time 53:86 My 23 '49
Vital Speeches 13:300-8 Mr 1 '47

Who's Who in America, 1952-53
Who's Who in Chicago and Illinois (1950)
Who's Who in Commerce and Industry (1951)

BATISTA (Y ZALDÍVAR) FULGENCIO (bä-tēs'tä ē säl-dē'vär fōōl-hän'syō) Jan. 16, 1901- Provisional President of Cuba
Address: Presidential Palace, Havana, Cuba

NOTE: This biography supersedes the article which appeared in *Current Biography* in 1940.

The "Strong Man of Cuba," General Fulgencio Batista, in his second army coup in nineteen years unseated the President of the island republic on March 10, 1952. His first revolution—"My destiny," he has said, "is to carry out revolutions without bloodshed"—was accomplished in 1933, which marked the beginning of his seven years as the "maker and unmaker" of Presidents. After a four-year term as President himself (1940-44) Batista left Cuba upon the defeat of his candidate for that office. Having returned to Cuba in 1948, he became a presidential candidate in 1950, for which office elections were to be held in June 1952. A few weeks after his coup in March, the United States recognized his government. Batista assumed office as Provisional President of Cuba on April 4, 1952.

Fulgencio Batista y Zaldívar was born in Banes in the Santiago (now Oriente) province of Cuba on January 16, 1901, less than three years after his native land was liberated from Spanish rule and somewhat less than two years before it became an independent republic. He is of mixed racial origin—Spanish, Indian, Negro, and Chinese. His father, Belisario Batista Palerma, was a farm laborer; his mother was the former Carmela Zaldívar Gonzales. Both his parents died before their son had reached his thirteenth year. He now left the Quaker missionary school he had entered at the age of nine and went to work as a tailor's apprentice. A miscellany of jobs—as laborer in the canefields, grocery clerk, bartender, railroad brakeman, and barber—followed before twenty-year-old Batista made his way to Havana and joined the National Army as a recruit in April 1921.

At the end of his two-year enlistment period Batista worked for a few months in a supervisory position on a sugar plantation in his native province. Then he resumed military service as a private and began seven years of study at night. In 1928, having meanwhile graduated from the Escuela Nacional de Periodistas with a command of shorthand and typewriting, he was advanced to sergeant, first class (the highest noncommissioned officer grade in the Cuban Army) and assigned as chief clerk and stenographer at Camp Colombia, near Havana. The dictatorship of General Gerardo Machado Morales was then at its most ruthless, and Sergeant Batista was called upon to record the military trials of a number of Machado's political opponents. "This experi-

United Press Photo.

GEN. FULGENCIO BATISTA

ence," stated the New York *Times*, "inspired
him to join the A.B.C., one of the many groups
plotting President Machado's downfall."

Hatred of the "butcher-dictator," the world
depression, a general strike in Havana, and
direct action by what has ben described as a
"clique of politicians and army chiefs" resulted
on August 12, 1933, in the flight of Machado
from Cuba. The scholarly and elderly Dr.
Manuel de Céspedes was set up as provisional
president. But violent disorders prevailed for
twenty-three days, whereupon, on September 4
Sergeant Batista and other sergeants (linked
with radical university intellectuals) staged a
coup before officers could organize the revolt.
Seizing control of Camp Colombia, Batista
brought about the ousting of Céspedes and the
naming of a new provisional president, Dr.
Ramón Grau San Martín, leader of the young
intellectuals. Batista was promoted to the rank
of colonel and made Chief of Staff of the
Army. Shortly afterward, however, Dr. Grau
announced a prolabor and "Cuba for Cubans"
policy (four-fifths of the country's wealth was
controlled by foreigners) with the consequence
that recognition of his regime was withheld
by Washington. Batista, describing himself as
"an idealist, but a practical one," accordingly
forced out Dr. Grau in January 1934 and after
an interval of two days installed as president
the conservative Colonel Carlos Mendieta,
whom the United States recognized. "The
Army was invoked to break up strikes and unrest," stated the New York *Times* in summarizing the period that ensued. "Stability returned to the sugar industry as the United
States reduced tariffs. The new regime won
a nationalist victory with an agreement abrogat-
ing the Platt amendment that had permitted
United States intervention in Cuba."

From that time on through the next six
years Colonel Batista was known as the

"Strong Man of Cuba" and "the maker and unmaker of presidents." Mendieta, whose presidency ended after two years, was followed by
José Barnet, Mariano Miguel Gómez, and
Federico Laredo Brú, all of whom were dependent on the support of Batista for tenures
of office which varied from a few weeks to
about three years. In the meantime, Batista
increased the size of the army from 8,000 to
20,000 men, restored its morale, and (given
charge of education as well) established about
1,300 new schools, many of which were staffed
by military personnel. In the late 1930's (according to *Time*) Batista (influenced perhaps
by the example of the New Deal) began not
only to speak of "disciplined democracy," but
"started to curry civilian support." He "encouraged opposition, pardoned political prisoners, even legalized the Communist party." In
line with this changed attitude he resigned—
with the rank of major general—from command of the army in February 1940. When
this action led to a revolt in the army and
navy, Batista again placed himself at the head
of the army, suppressed the uprising, and in
June 1940 endorsed the new constitution under
which Cuba is administered today. He called
a general election for the following month
(July), himself ran for the presidency as the
candidate of a Democratic-Socialist coalition,
and was elected by a decisive margin over his
principal opponent, Dr. Grau.

Batista took office as constitutional President
in October 1940, and a little over one year
later, following the Pearl Harbor attack,
brought Cuba into World War II on the side
of the Allies. He "took energetic measures
against Axis sabotage and arrested all aliens
suspected of dealings with the enemy powers"
(*10 Eventful Years*), and gave aid in the antisubmarine campaign. In addition (stated the
New York *Herald Tribune*) he "directed the
men who sold the annual sugar output of more
than 4,000,000 tons to make it available to the
United States for war uses." Meanwhile, at
his inauguration he had declared that the "revolutionary cycle" had closed and that he wished
"to be kind and to be loved" by the people.
The ensuing four years accordingly witnessed
the launching of large-scale public works projects (partly financed by American loans), establishment of rural hospitals, minimum wage
legislation, and increased salaries for people
in private as well as government employ. He
saw to it that the men in the armed services
received higher pay, pensions, better food, and
modern medical care. He "respected the laws
he had set up" (New York *Times*), and in
June 1944, when the time came for the choosing
of a new president, the election was duly held
and proved the "cleanest" in Cuba in thirty
years.

Under the 1940 constitution a Cuban President, elected for a four-year term, may not
seek re-election until after an interval of eight
years. In the 1944 campaign Batista backed
Dr. Carlos Saladrigas as his successor, but
the latter was defeated by former President
Grau. Batista, who handed over the reins of
government to Dr. Grau in October, left Cuba,
made an extensive tour of Central and South

America, and eventually went to live at Daytona Beach, Florida. That he did not regard his career as over was demonstrated by the publication, in Mexico City in 1946, of his book *Sombras de América*, in which he surveyed his life and policies and set forth his views on current and future Latin American problems. Two years later (June 1948) he re-entered the Cuban political scene by supporting Ricardo Nuñez Fortuondo for the presidency against Dr. Carlos Prío Socarrás, the candidate of the outgoing Dr. Grau, and by himself running (as a Liberal) for the post of Senator from Santa Clara province. Prío Socarrás emerged the victor in the presidential race, but Batista won the Senatorial contest. He returned to Cuba in November and began to organize his own party (Unitary Action), which in the biennial elections of 1950 gained five seats in the House of Representatives. In December 1950 Batista announced that he would again be a candidate for the presidency in June 1952, assailing "graft and corruption" in Cuba and declaring that "the people are sick of it and they have shown their desire for a change in many ways."

In the early morning of March 10, 1952, three months before the date set for the presidential election, General Batista accomplished his second military coup. With a group of officers he seized control of the same Camp Colombia which had been the scene of his "sergeants' revolt" of nearly twenty years earlier. After a "77-minute, practically bloodless" revolution (two guards were killed at the Presidential Palace), he was in control of the army, navy, and air force, and by noon he had occupied the Palace, from which President Prío had fled to Mexico. Batista explained that he had been forced to action to save Cuba "from those who have taken the country to the border of chaos," and because of the alleged intention of Prío to establish a dictatorship in April in order to assure the election as president, in June, of Secretary of Agriculture Carlos Hevia.

While it was recognized that the Cuban Government was disorganized and that there was widespread graft as well as gang warfare, editorials in the United States criticized the method used by Batista, whose victory in June was not regarded as assured. The General suspended constitutional guarantees for forty-five days, banned strikes, suspended Congress, and canceled the elections scheduled for June 1, promising that they would be held later. He raised police and army salaries and installed his own officers in both those branches throughout Cuba. His Cabinet, in which he has the titles of Chief of State and Prime Minister, includes nine men who had served under him previously. On March 27, 1952, the United States formally recognized the new Batista Government: it had met with two criteria outlined by Secretary of State Dean Acheson—the Cuban people had "acquiesced" to the change, and the new regime would carry out its international obligations. Batista, who became Provisional President of Cuba on April 4, 1952, is expected to hold that office until a new government is elected in 1953.

Batista has been married twice, first to the former Elisa Pilar Godínez Gómez, by whom he has three children, Marta, Rubén, and Elisa Aleida. The union was dissolved by a Mexican divorce in November 1945, and shortly afterward Batista and Marta Fernandéz Mircada were married. There are two children by that marriage, Carmela and Jorge. A picturesque figure, General Batista has been described as having "a body of steel, a jaw of bronze, his crowning glory a glistening comb of black hair." He combines a sense of the dramatic with a sense of humor, and is a rapid speaker with a flowery vocabulary. While living in Florida, he was up each morning at seven to row on the Halifax River, and he played tennis at the Dayton Beach Country Club. For spectator diversions he likes cockfighting and motion pictures.

References

Collier's 99:12+ Je 19 '37 por
Life 16:30-1 My 8 '44 pors; 32:21+ Mr 24 '52
N Y Herald Tribune p10 Mr 11 '52; II p1 Mr 16 '52 por
N Y Times p13 Mr 11 '52
N Y World-Telegram p7 Mr 13 '52
Newsweek 12:15-16 N 21 '38 por; 17:34 F 17 '41 por; 39:44 Mr 17 '52 por
Read Digest 39:61-5 Ag '41
Sat Eve Post 211:8-9+ My 20 '39 pors
Scholastic 60:26 Mr 15 '52
Time 29:21-3 Ap 26 '37 por; 34:30+ D 4 '39 por; 37:28 F 17 '41; 43:37-8 Je 12 '44 por; 51:44 Ap 12 '48 por; 59:36 Mr 17 '52 por
Batista, F. Sombras de América (1946)
Collier's Encyclopedia (1949)
Columbia Encyclopedia (1950)
Fernsworth, L. A., ed. Dictators and Democrats (1941)
Gunther, J. Inside Latin America (1941)
Strode. H. Pageant of Cuba (1934)
10 Eventful Years (1947)
Thorning, J. F. Builders of the Social Order (1946)
Who's Who in Latin America (1951)
World Biography (1948)

BELKIN, SAMUEL Dec. 12, 1911- University president

Address: b. c/o Yeshiva University, Amsterdam Ave. & 186th St., New York 33; h. 65 E. 96th St., New York 28

Under the administration of Dr. Samuel Belkin, who assumed the presidency in June 1943 of New York's Yeshiva University, this first university in the United States to be established under Jewish auspices has attained extensive physical and academic expansion. Belkin, who came to the United States from Poland in 1929, a year after his ordination as a rabbi, joined the teaching staff of Yeshiva in 1935 and before being elected president served for three years on the institution's sevenman executive board. In the fall of 1951 the university president was granted a partial leave of absence from his executive duties so that

Fabian Bachrach

SAMUEL BELKIN

he could devote most of his time to Yeshiva's State-wide drive to raise $10 million to construct a medical school as part of its $25 million nonsectarian medical center.

Born on December 12, 1911, in Swislicz, Poland, Samuel Belkin is the son of Solomon and Mina (Sattir) Belkin. At the age of eleven, after having received his first instruction from his father, he was sent to Yeshiva school at Solonina. Following later study at the Yeshivoth of Radin and Mir, he was ordained a rabbi in 1928, at the age of seventeen, by Rabbi Simeon Shkop, head of the Rabbinical College of Grodno. The following year Belkin immigrated to the United States, where during the academic year 1929-30 he was occupied as a lecturer in Talmud at the New Haven Rabbinical Seminary in Cleveland. He continued his education at Harvard University (1934) and at Brown University, where he was awarded his Ph.D. degree in 1935. At Brown he also attained election to Phi Beta Kappa society and in the year 1934-35 held an honorary fellowship.

Thus equipped with the Talmudic learning of European rabbinic centers and with the training of American universities, Belkin was appointed in 1935 to the staff of Yeshiva College of Arts and Sciences in New York as instructor in Greek. The next year he assumed the additional duties of instructor in Talmud at Yeshiva's Rabbi Isaac Elchanan Theological Seminary and in 1937 became instructor in Hellinistic literature in the newly organized graduate school now known as the Bernard Revel Graduate School, where he was advanced to a full professor in 1940. While continuing to teach until 1943, Belkin accepted a number of administrative positions, his first being the appointment in 1937 as secretary to the faculty. In 1939 he became a member of Yeshiva's executive committee and in 1940, after the death

of Dr. Bernard Revel, founder of the College of Arts and Sciences (who had been head of the Rabbi Isaac Elchanan Theological Seminary since 1915 and president of the college since 1928), Belkin was named dean of the seminary and a member of the seven-man executive board, which exercised presidential functions pending the selection of a successor to Revel. In June 1943 Belkin, then thirty-two years old, was elected president of the Rabbi Isaac Elchanan Theological Seminary and Yeshiva College. At the ceremonies on May 23, 1944, inaugurating Belkin as the second president in the institution's history, Chief Justice Harlan Fiske Stone referred to the educator as a "distinguished teacher of spiritual values in the modern world."

"Rigorously orthodox Yeshiva" was described by *Newsweek* magazine in 1944 as "the only college in the United States offering a curriculum of liberal arts and sciences under Jewish auspices, and the largest of its kind in the world." With an enrollment of some 2,000 students (in 1951) from the United States and about twenty foreign countries, Yeshiva, which became a university in 1945, comprises eight schools and graduate divisions providing courses leading to fifteen different undergraduate and graduate degrees. These schools are the Rabbi Isaac Elchanan Theological Seminary (founded in 1897), the Talmudical Academy High Schools (which maintain branches in Brooklyn and Far Rockaway on Long Island), the Teachers Institute, Yeshiva College of Arts and Sciences, the Institute of Mathematics, the Bernard Revel Graduate Division, the Harry Fischel School for Higher Jewish Studies (a graduate summer division), and the School of Education and Community Administration. Other facilities offered by the university are a psychological clinic, audio-visual service, a community service bureau, and an educational service bureau. "Yeshiva retains the traditional chanting manner of study developed at the Babylonian academies of Sura and Pumbeditha," reported *Newsweek* (June 23, 1952). "The skull-capped scholars also maintain one of the most grueling academic schedules in the United States."

When the Regents of the University of the State of New York granted Yeshiva the status of "a full-fledged university" on November 16, 1945, President Belkin under the new charter began plans for a $7,500,000 expansion program in adult education, in undergraduate facilities in arts and sciences, and in mathematical studies. Among the projects brought to completion under his administration have been the establishment of the Harry Fischel School (1945) and the School of Education and Community Administration (1948) and the setting up of a graduate department of mathematics as part of the university's Institute of Mathematics (1952). In November 1948 the Society for the Establishment of a Medical School at Yeshiva launched a program for a proposed $25 million non-sectarian medical center. Three years later, in June 1951, Dr. Belkin announced his acceptance of New York City's offer to unite the university's medical schools with the city-sponsored $36 million Bronx Municipal Hospital Center, comprising a 500-bed tuberculosis hospital, a 750-bed general hospital, and an out-patient department. The Yeshiva medical school will appoint the professional staff of the hospital and in practice university professors will be in charge of the hospital program.

"In creating a $61,500,000 hospital-medical center," noted the New York *Times* (June 16, 1951), "the Bronx will have one of the largest and most comprehensive centers of its kind in the city if not the entire country." Dr. Belkin was quoted by the *Times* as saying that a "medical school sponsored by the Jewish community and particularly under the auspices of an established and accredited university such as Yeshiva University will have a salutary effect on many problems which confront, today, Jewish young men who wish to pursue the field of medicine." The four hundred students for whom Yeshiva will provide facilities will be admitted on the basis of merit, without discrimination in race or creed. To raise funds for the construction of a $10 million medical school building expected to be completed in 1953 (other buildings for schools in dentistry and public health will follow), Belkin in November 1951 received a partial leave of absence from his administrative work so that he could direct an eight-month special gifts campaign.

At the graduation exercises in March 1947 at the Rabbi Isaac Elchanan Theological Seminary, Belkin urged the newly ordained rabbis "to continue in Yeshiva's orthodox tradition in order to preserve the Jewish community as a 'separate entity.' In America, he said, each racial group is encouraged to give expression to its own religious and cultural ideas, because this 'plurality of culture is the essence of democracy'" (New York *Herald Tribune*, March 17, 1947). Noting that he disapproved of some of the more modern sects of Judaism, *Time* quoted him as stating, "The world today suffers from a laxity of faith and the great need of this moment is not so much 'the watering down' of particular religious beliefs but rather a greater and firmer conviction of one's own religion."

Belkin's first book, *The Alexandrian Halakah in Apologetic Literature of the First Century C.E.*, was published in 1936. *Philo and the Oral Law; the Philonic Interpretation of Biblical Law in Relation to the Palestinian Halakah*, Belkin's second book, became volume XI of the Harvard Semitic Series, published in 1940. Among the articles he has contributed to the *Journal of Biblical Literature, Jewish Quarterly Review, Pardes, Horeb,* and *Talpioth* are "The Religious Background of Paul," "Dissolution of Vows and Oaths in the Gospel and Contemporary Jewish Literature," and "Alexandrian Source of Contra Opionem." In 1939 he acted as an associate editor of Rabbinics for the *Universal Jewish Encyclopedia* (published in 1940). He is a member of the Society of Biblical Literature and Exegesis Art, the Union of Orthodox Rabbis of the United States and Canada, the Publication Committee of the Jewish Publication Society of America (honorary), the Jewish Academy of Arts and Sciences, the New York Academy of Public Education, the American Academy of Political and Social Science, and is a cochair-

man of the New York State Citizens Committee on Housing.

On November 10, 1935, Samuel Belkin married Selma Ehrlich of Philadelphia, granddaughter of Rabbi B. L. Leventhal, dean of American Rabbinate. The Belkins have a daughter, Linda Rose, and a son, Salo Maurice. The brown-eyed, dark-haired educator became a citizen of the United States in 1941. He received in Philadelphia on May 20, 1951, the award of the Tri-State Region of the Union of Orthodox Jewish Congregations of America.

References

Newsweek 23:68 Jl 3 '44 por; 39:86 Je 23 '52 por
Time 49:75 Mr 31 '47 por

National Cyclopædia of American Biography Current vol G, 1943-46
Universal Jewish Encyclopedia (1940)
Who's Who in America, 1952-53
Who's Who in American Jewry, 1938-39
World Biography (1948)

BELL, MARGARET ELIZABETH Dec. 29, 1898- Author

Address: b. c/o William Morrow & Company, Inc., 425 4th Ave., New York 16; h. Loring, Alaska

Reprinted from the *Wilson Library Bulletin*, June 1952.

Juvenile authors who write about Alaska are rare; those who write of that Arctic outpost with the authority of the native-born are even rarer. Best of that select company surely is Margaret Elizabeth Bell, Alaskan by birth and by inclination, whose junior novels have done so much to make her homeland vivid and real for us all.

Margaret Elizabeth Bell was born in Thorn Bay, Alaska, on December 29, 1898, to Robert Biggar Bell and Florence (Millar) Bell. Both parents were of Scottish stock and had come to Alaska from Canada. They met and married in the Territory, at a Presbyterian Indian mission. Mr. Bell operated a salmon cannery. There were three children. Miss Bell says of her childhood: "Our lives in Alaska were unusual in that we never lived in towns, but in the wild, mountainous coastal country where we learned to know the forest, the wild animals, and the sea. Later my brother, sister, and I were sent to school in the States to be 'civilized.'"

Margaret Bell attended the Annie Wright Seminary at Tacoma, Washington, graduating in 1918. She then spent two years at the University of Washington in Seattle. She lived for some time in Portland, Oregon, and for ten years in San Francisco. During the war, as a Red Cross recreation worker, she returned to the Northwest, spending two years in the military hospitals of British Columbia and Alberta, and one year in the Aleutian Islands.

"People," Miss Bell says, "seemed to like to hear about my early life in Alaska. It seemed natural to write about it." Her first writing venture was a full-length book for older boys,

MARGARET ELIZABETH BELL

based upon the early experiences of her own family. *The Pirates of Icy Strait* was published in 1943. A. M. Jordan wrote in *Horn Book*: "The bleak Alaskan coast is well described and the hazards of the canning industry made real in this absorbing story." Anne Eaton in the New York *Times*: "The tale, though packed with adventure, is never overdrawn. . . . She allows her characters to speak for themselves, and the reader closes the book with a strong feeling that he has made the acquaintance of some very real individuals."

Danger on Old Baldy (1944) was an adventure-mystery story of Alaska and Japanese spies, salmon fisheries, and mountain climbing. Mary Davis said in the *Saturday Review*: "Boys and girls will like it for its plot and action, for the humor and realism of its characters. Mike and Ole and Long Paul fit perfectly into their environment."

Enemies of Icy Strait (1945) impressed Nellie McCalla of *Library Journal* as "Of special interest to boys of junior high school age." Virginia Kirkus: "Competent background, intimate woodland and hunting scenes, but the plot drags at times and the interest is only moderately well sustained."

For the next two books the author left the contemporary Alaskan scene and turned to the pioneer period of her parents' youth. *Watch for a Tall White Sail* (1948) goes back to 1887. Dorothea Dawson in the *Library Journal* called it "an extraordinary story for teenage girls—fine style, fast pace, good character delineation, and the ring of truth." Quall Hawkins in the San Francisco *Chronicle*: "Reality and romance, so blended, make a very satisfactory novel for older girls: one above the milk-and-water trash so often offered them. The love story rings true, and will be cherished by those who appreciate the depth of feeling beneath the prim manner of a day gone by."

This book was followed by a sequel, *The Totem Casts a Shadow* (1949). Louise Bechtel in the New York *Herald Tribune* said, "The book is written with feeling for the strangely beautiful country and with delicate sensitiveness as to the heart of a girl of eighteen." *New Yorker*: "A fine 'novel' for older girls, with a delicately handled love story."

Ride Out the Storm (1951), telling of an Alaskan girl's experience in a California boarding school, was an honor book in the *Herald Tribune's* spring festival. Margaret Walraven in the *Library Journal* said: "Good characterization, family relationships, values. Enriched by the author's ability to describe the beauties of nature without being dull, and with homey, intimate details of life in a girl's school."

Miss Bell, a sturdy, energetic redhead who can turn her hand to anything, lives now at Loring, Alaska, in an old-time cabin overlooking Naha Bay. She saws her own wood for her Franklin stove, and sails her own skiff. Her cabin is well stocked with books: the works of Homer, Carlyle, Swift, Jane Austen, Henry James, George Meredith, Shakespeare, and Blake. Besides reading, she names as her recreations, "Fishing and gathering wild berries to put by for the winter; getting in wood for winter; watching birds and wild animals and natural phenomena for material to use in writing; talking with oldtimers and newcomers."

She is now (in mid-1952) at work on a short biography of Kit Carson and a novel for young people. She makes occasional trips to the States, where she has appeared on several radio programs. But the wild country of her youth will always be home to her. In her own words: "It is a beautiful country, both wild and tender, and one loves it as one loves the errant child who persists in his own way. There is a lesson to learn in this wild nature that is too subtle for words. It has to do with *being* with nature—be with it, but let it alone."

BENDER, GEORGE H(ARRISON) Sept. 29, 1896- United States Representative from Ohio

Address: b. House Office Bldg., Washington 25, D.C.; h. 495 North St., Chagrin Falls, Ohio

Seven times the voters of the State of Ohio have chosen Republican George H. Bender, a Cleveland insurance executive, as their Representative-at-large in Congress. Previously he had been a member of the Ohio General Assembly for ten years, in which he emerged as an opponent of the Anti-Saloon League. Although he has frequently criticized the Truman Administration and is regarded as an isolationist of Taft sympathies, Congressman Bender is often cited for the independence of his opinions, which do not always follow the Republican party line. His most important committee assignment has been to the House Committee on Expenditures in the Executive Departments.

George Harrison Bender is the son of Joseph and Anna (Sir) Bender; his mother was descended from Moravian missionaries who settled on the banks of Ohio's Cuyahoga River at a time when Indians still occupied that region. He was born September 29, 1896, in Cleveland, Ohio, where he was to attend the grade schools and the West Commerce High School. Attracted at that period to debating, public speaking, and newspaper work, the sixteen-year-old student campaigned in his community for Theodore Roosevelt in the Bull Moose campaign of 1912, an activity which enabled him to meet his idol and which stimulated his interest in politics.

For a period, at twenty-one, Bender published his own newspaper, which was devoted to appeals for good government. Following his service in World War I, he returned to Cleveland in 1920 to become advertising manager of the Bailey Company. His next employment, after two years, was as general manager of the Bedell Company. In 1934 he established the G. H. Bender Insurance Company, of which he is still president.

Elected on the Republican ticket to the Ohio General Assembly in 1920—and thus becoming its youngest member—Bender served as a State Senator for five successive terms, until 1930. These ten years were marked by his opposition to the activities of the Anti-Saloon League. "Though an ardent dry himself," Jack H. Pollack wrote of Bender in *This Week*, "the young legislator rebelled against league practices—mainly the indiscriminate raiding of homes by snooping justices of the peace." One of the homes raided was Bender's own, and in the ensuing court battle over this act Bender was awarded $25,000 in damages, Delos W. Lovelace reported in the New York *Sun*. In the legislative sphere, Bender in 1927 was responsible for the defeat of a bill sponsored by the league, receiving the support of a 500,000 majority in this effort, as well as nation-wide interest. While he was a State Senator, Bender also conducted the Ohio campaign for Hiram Johnson, in one of the latter's unsuccessful attempts to secure the Presidency.

Resuming his work as a publisher and editor in 1934, Bender began the publication of the *Ohio Republican* and the *National Republican*. That same year he was made president of the League of Republican Clubs of Cuyahoga County, a post he held for six years. In 1936 he was chosen chairman of the Republican Central Committee, a chairmanship he retains. The Ohio Republican entered the national political scene in November 1938, when he was elected to the Seventy-sixth Congress. He was re-elected to the Seventy-seventh (November 5, 1940), Seventy-eighth (November 3, 1942), Seventy-ninth (November 7, 1944), and Eightieth (November 5, 1946) Congresses. Defeated in his campaign for election to the Eighty-first Congress, Bender was, however, returned as Ohio's Congressman-at-large to the Eighty-second Congress, on November 7, 1950. He was elected to the Eighty-third Congress on November 4, 1952.

During his many years in Congress, Bender's name has been associated with several major issues. Prominent from 1943 to 1947 in efforts to repeal the poll tax, he presented bills to accomplish this purpose, one of which was

Blackstone Studios
GEORGE H. BENDER

passed by a House vote of 290 to 112 on July 22, 1947. Congressman Bender has written several articles on this issue: "The Poll Tax" (*Free World*, May 1944), "Citizens Without Ballots" (*This Week*, October 20, 1946), and "The Poll Tax Disgrace" (*Christian Century*, July 23, 1947).

In August 1947 Bender was named chairman of a Congressional subcommittee assigned to investigate price increases in the Middle West, one of three such committees created for regional studies. Operating as a subsidiary of the Senate-House Joint Committee on the Economic Report, Bender's subcommittee, with a Republican majority, was instrumental in the formation of an anti-inflationary program which was presented to Congress in November 1947. This report, ascribed high prices to the necessity for supporting President Truman's plans for European aid, criticized Administration projects for restoring price controls, and called for the exercise of economy in Government.

Subsequent to this inquiry, Bender held the chairmanship of a subcommittee of the House Committee on Expenditures in the Executive Departments. "Chief purpose of the Bender committee," Pollack wrote, "is to uncover fraud and overpayment in settling war contracts." Using material unearthed by the Government's General Accounting Office, the Bender committee set about its investigation with a declaration of its intention of avoiding the sensationalism that marked other recent Congressional hearings, of protecting witnesses and allowing them to be represented by counsel, and of permitting them to reply to allegedly defamatory charges. This objective brought Representative Bender editorial praise in the columns of *PM* and the *Christian Science Monitor*. The Ohio Representative also announced his intention of recovering as much as possible of the more than $500,000,000 overpaid in war contracts.

BENDER, GEORGE H.—*Continued*

Another Government contract which came to Bender's attention in 1948 was that of the agreement between the Permanente Metals Corporation and the Kaiser-Frazer Corporation under a War Assets Administration agreement. Upon his return to Congress for the Eighty-second's first session, Bender in 1951 again participated in the work of a similar subcommittee, investigating tax concessions given to steel companies operating under the defense production program.

In connection with another investigation before the House, Bender was instrumental in the moves to prolong the life of the Tolan Defense Investigating Committee, originally devoted to the study of migration of defense workers and subsequently to other aspects of the war effort, described by the New York *Post* in 1943 as having made "an outstanding and liberal record." That year, too, he urged an investigation of State Department policies, as well as of statements made by Ambassadors Standley, Hayes, and Murphy, the United States envoys to Russia, Spain, and French North Africa, respectively. Bender in 1945 sponsored the plan to sell directly, through Government retail stores, war surplus goods. In 1947 he was one of the chief opponents of the Greek-Turkish aid bill and charged President Truman with moving from one "international crisis to another in order to establish himself as a leader who should not be abandoned in the midst of a virtual state of war." Toward the end of that year he urged an investigation of security measures and censorship imposed by Government agencies, which he considered "completely unwarranted" and against the national interest. In criticism of the war in Korea, Bender stated in 1951 that the United Nations forces were predominantly American and characterized the United Nations designation as "a shabby and disgraceful farce, designed to deceive the American people."

During his first term in Congress, Representative Bender voted for supplementary defense appropriations, supplementary aid for Great Britain, the repeal of Section 6 of the Neutrality Act, the passage of the Selective Service Act, and for the mobilization of small businesses for the war effort; and against the alteration of the weight of the dollar and the requisitioning of foreign merchant vessels. In the subsequent Congress—the Seventy-eighth—he voted affirmatively on the increase of the national debt, the settlement of war contract claims, appropriations for the National Military Establishment, the extension of lend-lease and mustering-out pay for servicemen. He cast no vote for the simplification of income tax, for example, or the investigation of the Montgomery Ward seizure, or maternity and infant care for servicemen's wives. The Seventy-ninth Congress found him opposed to a permanent Committee on Un-American Activities (1945), the Case strike control bill (1946), the loan to Great Britain (1946), and to a proposal to shelve the atomic energy control bill (1946); and in favor of a second $1,350 millions for

UNRRA (1945) and of the President's strike control bill (1946).

In the following Congress the Ohio Republican supported a proposal to limit the Presidential term to two years (1947), rent control extension bills (1947 and 1948), a measure to recommit the loyalty test bill (1947), subversive activities control bill (1948), the $6 billion foreign aid authorization (1948), and the displaced persons bill (1948). He objected to a measure to restore cuts in reclamation funds (1947), the *Voice of America* bill (1947), and a proposal for a new TVA steam plant (1948). During 1951 he voted for a cut in government's civil payrolls and for a $10 million cut in reclamation funds. While favoring a $350 million cut for economic aid to Europe, he supported a $7½ billion foreign assistance bill.

Besides the special Tolan Committee on Interstate Migration and the House Committee on Expenditures in Executive Departments (on which he still serves in 1952), Bender was a member of the Rivers and Harbors Committee in the Seventy-seventh, Seventy-eighth, and Seventy-ninth Congresses and of the Committee on Public Works in the Eightieth Congress. His speeches, "Should the Voice of America Project Be Established by Congress?" and "A Faith for Fifty-One" have been reprinted in the *Congressional Digest* (February 1948) and *Vital Speeches* (July 1, 1951), respectively. His book, *The Challenge of 1940*, was considered by Delos W. Lovelace of the New York *Sun* "a practically unanswerable summation of Democratic shenanigans." To bring current issues to the attention of the public in a terse form, Bender in 1951 began the practice of inserting short questions (some addressed to Government officials) in the appendix to the *Congressional Record*.

Bender, upon the opening of the Eightieth Congress, distributed new brooms to Republican members of that body. In his office, reported *Newsweek*, are to be seen a number of small statues of elephants. Married to the former Edna Eckhardt, Bender is the father of two daughters, Virginia and Barbara (Mrs. Ernest Stevenson). The Congressman has brown eyes and brown hair, stands five feet eleven inches tall and weighs 185 pounds. He has been described by Jack Pollack as a host who "entertains lavishly." He enjoys flying, practical jokes, and rich desserts, but does not indulge in smoking or drinking. His club is the City Club of Cleveland. A Methodist who is fond of joining in the hymn-singing of his church, Bender has been a Sunday school teacher at the Church of the Savior in Cleveland Heights, where he resides. Once, when an interfaith group visited the Ohio Representative at his office, he knelt and prayed with them.

References

N Y Sun p18 S 18 '45
This Week p5 D 14 '47
Biographical Directory of the American Congress, 1774-1949 (1950)

Congressional Directory (1951)
Who's Who in America, 1950-51
Who's Who in United States Politics
(1950)
World Biography (1948)

BENDETSEN, KARL R(OBIN) Oct. 11,
1907- United States Government official; lawyer

Address: h. 1017 Sherman St., Alameda, Calif.

Former Under Secretary of the Army, Karl
R. Bendetsen, who assumed office on May 7,
1952, and resigned soon afterward in September
1952, had previously held a number of posts in
Washington—in the office of the Judge Advocate General, on the War Department's General Staff, and as a special consultant to the
Secretary of the Army and later Assistant
Secretary of the Army. Before entering active
service in World War II, Bendetsen practiced
law in the State of Washington for six years.
As Assistant Secretary he had supervision
of the over-all programs of management, fiscal
and budget work, and aspects of military procurement. In addition, beginning August 1950,
when the country's railroads were taken over
by the Government to avert a nation-wide
strike, Bendetsen was the nominal director of
all the railroads of the United States.

Karl Robin Bendetsen was born in Aberdeen,
Washington, on October 11, 1907, to Albert
M. and Anna (Benson) Bendetsen. During
his high school years (1921-24) he was a
member of the Washington State Guard. A
student at Stanford University in California,
he received the Bachelor of Arts degree in
1929 and the Bachelor of Laws degree in 1932.
By that time he had entered the Officers Reserve Corps, in which he remained for about
eleven years, until 1940. The young lawyer
was admitted to practice in the courts of California, Oregon, and Washington, and in 1934
he opened his law office in Aberdeen. He continued to practice until 1940, when he was appointed to the office of the Judge Advocate
General for the Army, Washington, D.C., with
the rank of captain. Subsequent promotions
brought him the rank of major in 1941, and
of lieutenant colonel and colonel in 1942.

Soon after joining the War Department office, Bendetsen acted as the Army's representative on the board which drafted and processed
through Congress the Soldier and Sailor Civil
Relief Act of 1940. Another duty of his in 1941
was to serve as special representative of the
Secretary of War to General MacArthur.
That year, too, he drafted the executive order
and operating instructions for the seizure of
the Air Associates Plant in Bendix, New Jersey, for the United States Government.

In 1942 Colonel Bendetsen, appointed to the
Department of War's General Staff, was as-
signed to direct the evacuation of persons of
Japanese origin from the West Coast area.
Bendetsen also established the Prisoner of War
Information Bureau and served as one of four
officers who organized the Provost Marshal
General's office, the Army Military Police

Wide World Photos
KARL R. BENDETSEN

Corps, and the School of Military Government. Another responsibility of his during
World War II was to set up the Alaska
Travel Control program. Toward the end of
the war he was named United States Chief
of civil affairs for Northwest Europe and
later was appointed to the rank of Deputy
Chief of Staff for the United States Communications Zone in Normandy. With the completion of this mission Bendetsen became Chief
Combat Liaison Officer for the European campaign.

In 1946 Bendetsen resumed his law practice
in the State of Washington. After a year as
a management counsel he became director of
several real estate organizations: the Shoreland
Properties, Inc., the Productive Properties,
Ltd., the Indian Beach Yacht Harbor, Ltd.,
and the Saginaw Logging Company. In 1948
he returned to public life, accepting the position
of counsel and special assistant to the Secretary of Defense. In August of the ensuing
year he became a special consultant to the
Secretary of the Army, Gordon Gray. From
this he moved to the rank of Assistant Secretary of the Army, having been nominated to
the position by President Truman on January
24, 1950, and shortly afterward confirmed by
the Senate. Upon taking office on February
2, he entered upon the third highest civilian office in the Department of the Army.
That he had been selected for the second
highest was made known April 23, 1952, when
President Truman nominated him for promotion to Under Secretary.

As one of two assistant secretaries of the
Army, Bendetsen was responsible for the general management of the Department. As stated
in the *United States Government Organization
Manual*, Bendetsen directed and supervised the

BENDETSEN, KARL R.—*Continued*

"performance of comptroller functions . . . the administration of guaranteed loans and related matters in support of procurement activities; and the Management Improvement Program. . . .He [supervised] . . . over-all program management; fiscal and budget management; the provision of reports and statistics within the Department of the Army; matters relating to improvement in organization and management practices; activities of the Army Efficiency Awards Committee; general management aspects of the Panama Canal, the Canal Zone Government, and the Panama Canal Company; and the activities of the Army Policy Council as Executive Secretary."

Soon after entering upon this post Bendetsen issued a plan to increase the number of officers and men in the Organized Reserves who are available for immediate combat duty. In the fall of 1949 he had made a study of reserve affairs in the Army as a member of the Civilian Components Policy Board. The purpose of the Bendetsen plan, which will take five years to carry out, is to bring together the various units of trained and active reserve forces, thus separating them from those in the inactive and honorary reserves. It is hoped that such a program will increase combat readiness of the reservists so that they can be called upon quickly to fill out the Regular Army's divisions. In May of 1950 he answered charges of fraud and lapses of security made against the Army Finance Center at St. Louis. Testifying before the House Armed Services subcommittee investigating alleged improper operations at the center, particularly with respect to overpayments by the Office of Dependency Benefits, Bendetsen stated that their unrecovered overpayments represented only one-fifth of 1 per cent of the total benefit payments made at the St. Louis center. A *New York Herald Tribune* report on the hearings quoted Bendetsen as explaining that the overpayments occurred because "it was virtually impossible to gear notices of separation to the wartime demand of promptly paying the allotments." In February of 1952 Bendetsen and other department officials were present at an unusual display before Congress of the new weapons of war. The objective of the exhibition was to show the unavoidable and high costs of modern warfare.

When the Secretary of the Army was authorized by the President in August 1950 to take control of the nation's railroads, Bendetsen was named to carry out the executive order. The seizure order was issued after seventeen months of unsuccessful negotiations between the four operating railroad unions and management over hours and wage increases and the threat by two of the unions to call a nation-wide strike. Since that time Bendetsen was the nominal head of all the railroads in the United States. Although the day-to-day operations were conducted by regular railroad managers, with assistance from Army personnel, Bendetsen from time to time had to take action in the settlement of problems arising out of the seizure by the Government. In December of 1950,

when an agreement had been reached between the union leaders and the carriers, he announced the intention of the Army to return the railroads to their owners. However, when the agreement was submitted to union members, it was rejected, and subsequent negotiations failed to reach a settlement until May 1952, when the Army formally turned the railroads back to their private owners. Bendetsen, who in May took office as Undersecretary of the Army, resigned that position on September 26, 1952.

Bendetsen is the holder of a number of military awards: the Distinguished Service Medal, the Legion of Merit with two Oak Leaf Clusters, the Croix de Guerre with Palm, membership in the Order of the British Empire, and the rank of officer in the French Legion of Honor. He is a member of the Washington, Oregon, California, San Francisco, and American bar associations. From 1934 to 1940 he was counselor and trustee of the Washington State Taxpayers' Association; he is past vice-chairman of nine San Francisco Bay companies and director of the Alameda Company. He is a director of the American Red Cross and past vice-president of the American Red Cross Mutual Aid. Married on March 10, 1938, to Billie McIntosh, he has a son, Brookes McIntosh. His second wife is the former Maxine Bosworth; their marriage took place in 1948. Bendetsen's fraternity is Theta Delta Chi; his clubs are the Commonwealth, the Washington Athletic, and the University. He professes a Protestant faith.

References

N Y Herald Tribune p21 Ja 25 '50
N Y Times p9 Ja 25 '50
Who's Who in America, 1950-51

BENNETT, HENRY G(ARLAND) Dec. 14, 1886—Dec. 22, 1951 United States Government official; college president; appointed superintendent of schools in Hugo, Oklahoma (1910), president of the Southeastern State Teachers College, Oklahoma (1919), president of Oklahoma Agricultural and Mechanical College (1928); delegate to U.N. Food and Agriculture Organization conference, October 1946; named Administrator of the Technical Cooperation Administration in the Department of State (director of the Point IV Program) in November 1950. See *Current Biography,* 1951.

Obituary

N Y Times p1+ D 24 '51

BENNETT, IVAN L(OVERIDGE) Apr. 18, 1892- Chaplain

Address: b. c/o Office of the Chief of Chaplains, Department of the Army, Washington 25, D.C.

Ivan L. Bennett was made the United States Army Chief of Chaplains, with the rank of major general, on April 29, 1952, succeeding Roy H. Parker, who retired. A minister of the Southern Baptist Church, Bennett has been an

Army chaplain since World War I; during World War II he served in the Pacific area. From 1949 until he assumed his present post, he had been command chaplain of the United States Army's Far East Command, with headquarters in Tokyo.

On April 18, 1892, Ivan Loveridge Bennett was born in Regan, Brunswick County, North Carolina, the son of Henry Iredell and Zillah (Russ) Bennett. His father and grandfather, both deacons for many years in the Baptist Church, were farmers in North Carolina, where Ivan was reared along with two brothers and seven sisters. After graduating from the Winterville (North Carolina) High School in 1912, he entered Wake Forest (North Carolina) College, from which he received his B.A. degree in 1916. As an undergraduate, Bennett participated in religious organization work, in intercollegiate debates, and in intramural tennis and football. In 1927, while on active duty with the Army, he received his LL.B. degree through the LaSalle College extension program.

"My associations with the young men who were being drafted during World War I prompted me to offer my services as a chaplain in 1918," Bennett has said. "Later Dr. John R. Sampey, professor of Hebrew and Old Testament interpretation at Southern Baptist Theological Seminary, Louisville, Kentucky, took an interest in my problem when I was offered a commission in the Regular Army." Bennett was assigned to duty at Fort Belvoir, Virginia, in 1918 and was commissioned in the Chaplain's Corps of the regular Army of the United States in 1920—the same year this Corps was established. Under authorization of the Continental Congress in 1775, chaplains had become associated with the armed forces during the Revolutionary War. As defined in the *Army Almanac* (1950), the duty of a chaplain is "to serve the religious and moral needs of the personnel of the command to which he is assigned." His responsibilities include conducting religious services, counseling, visiting the sick and wounded, and supervising religious education.

Following a brief period with the 2d Field Artillery at Camp Knox, Kentucky, Bennett spent three years (1921-24) attached to the Tank School at Camp Meade, Maryland. His first period of duty in the Pacific area was from 1924 to 1926, with the 31st Infantry stationed at the Sternberg General Hospital in Manila, Philippine Islands. He returned to the United States in March 1926 to spend four years at Fort Brown, Texas, a brief period at Fort Eustis, Virginia, and three years (1930-33) at Fort Monroe, Virginia, before going back to the Philippines in March 1933 for three years' service at Fort William McKinley. In April 1936 he was named post chaplain at Fort Benning, Georgia, where he remained until October 1940, when he was assigned to Fort Meyer, Virginia, serving there for two years, first as post and regimental chaplain to the 3rd Cavalry and then as corps chaplain with the Headquarters 6th Corps.

The World War II years, from 1942 to 1946, saw Bennett stationed in the Pacific area,

U. S. Army

MAJ. GEN. IVAN L. BENNETT

part of that time with troops in Australia. His first postwar assignment (October 1946) was to Fort Monmouth, New Jersey, as post chaplain. From March 1947 to October 1949, in the position of Army chaplain, he was successively attached to the 2d Army Headquarters at Fort George G. Meade, Maryland, the 1st Army Headquarters on Governor's Island, New York, and the 4th Army Headquarters at Fort Sam Houston, Texas. In the fall of 1949 Bennett was made command chaplain of the Far East Command with headquarters in Tokyo, a post he held until March 1952. Shortly after the outbreak of fighting in Korea, he was given in July 1950 added duties as United Nations Chaplain. During the latter year he was appointed a member of the Military Chaplains Association's committee, which presented this organization's 1950 award to General of the Army Douglas MacArthur.

His nomination to the four-year assignment as Chief of Chaplains of the United States Army was announced by President Truman on April 10, 1952, and approved by the Senate on April 29. The Chief Chaplain is the officer who "advises the Secretary of the Army and the Chief of Staff on moral and religious matters and formulates plans for, and supervises, moral training and religious ministration in the Army" (*United States Government Organization Manual*). Bennett's predecessor in this office was Roy H. Parker, also a Southern Baptist Minister, who had held the post from 1949 until his retirement on May 31, 1952. With Bennett's new appointment came an advance in rank from colonel to major general.

During the course of his chaplain's career Bennett compiled *The Hymnal, Army and Navy* and the *Song and Service Book for Ship and Field, Army and Navy*. In an article, "Our Hope For Peace," which he wrote for the *Christian Century* (November 14, 1951), he

BENNETT, IVAN L.—*Continued*

urged the establishment of the Japan International Christian University Foundation, toward which Christian and non-Christian Japanese are now contributing money. "It is not enough," he wrote, "to meet force with force, to burn cities and bomb miserable populations. . . .There is need for positive action to build in Japan the foundations of Christian faith and brotherhood." Speaking in July 1952 at the twenty-first annual convention of the Military Chaplains Association at Fort Slocum, New York, General Bennett defended the principle that military service involves no link between church and state. He was quoted by the New York *Times* (July 24, 1952) as saying: "Religion should never be the echoing voice of government and, thank God, in all my experience the chaplain service is the word of religion speaking to government. . . .Religion should be utilitarian in the sense that it makes for better men"; he added that "the best soldiers are spiritually motivated."

The chaplain has been awarded an honorary Doctor of Divinity degree by Payne Theological Seminary, Zenia, Ohio, (1944), the Distinguished Service Medal (1945), and the Legion of Merit (1946) with Oak Leaf Cluster (1952). Major General Bennett is a member of the Masonic Order, York Rite, and a fellow of the Hymn Society of America. Married on December 26, 1917, to the former Ruby Jenrett, he is the father of three sons, Ivan L., Jr., John C., and Richard T. His height is five feet seven inches and his weight 175 pounds; he describes his eyes as clay-colored and his hair as light brown.

BERRA, LAWRENCE (PETER) May 12, 1925- Baseball player
Address: b. c/o New York Yankees, 745 5th Ave., New York 22; h. Woodcliff Lake, N.J.

Lawrence ("Yogi") Berra, New York Yankees' catcher, was chosen by the Baseball Writers Association to receive the Landis Memorial Award as the most valuable player in the American League during 1951. The selection of Berra, whose first contract with the Yankees was signed in 1942 when he was eighteen years old, was based on the player's "formidable" hitting, his base-running prowess, and his skillful batting teamwork with his pitchers.

Born in St. Louis, Missouri, on May 12, 1925, Lawrence Peter ("Yogi") Berra is the second youngest child in the family of Pietro Berra, a brickyard worker. He was seven years old when, with his parents, his three elder brothers, and his younger sister, he went to live in the so-called "Hill" or Italian district of his native city. There from twenty to twenty-five neighborhood boys—including the four Berras and Joe Garagiola (later catcher with the St. Louis Cardinals)—played such outdoor sports as baseball, softball, roller hockey, soccer, and football, and in due course were organized as a YMCA team known as The Stags. Berra was later to tell Harry Paxton of the *Saturday Evening Post*: "The sport I

liked most was baseball. I wanted to be a ballplayer. My brothers wanted to be ballplayers too. But my pop comes from Italy, and he didn't know anything about this baseball business. The family needed extra money, and he wanted his boys to work at something that would bring in steady wages."

Consequently fourteen-year-old Berra, after completing the eighth grade at the Wade Grammar School, got a job in a coalyard. Later he drove a truck for a soft-drink company, next became a tack-puller in a shoe factory. He continued to play ball in his free time, and in 1941 was invited to join the Stockham Post American Legion junior team, managed by Leo Browne, a former umpire. Jack Maguire, later an outfielder with the New York Giants, was another member of this team. "It was Jack," Berra told Paxton, "who gave me my nickname of Yogi. Some of us went to a movie with a yogi in it, and afterwards Jack began calling me Yogi. It stuck." (Berra, who sometimes signs himself as "Larry," is "Lawdy" to his parents, "Lawrence" to his brothers.)

Berra played left field with the Legion team, but at one time or another in his pre-professional days filled all nine positions on the diamond. In 1942, when with his teammate Garagiola he tried out for the St. Louis Cardinals, he was advised by Leo Browne that he would stand his best chance as a catcher. Garagiola was quickly signed by the Cardinals organization, but General Manager Branch Rickey told Berra there was no future for him in big league baseball. However, through the good offices of Browne, Johnny Schulte, a Yankee coach, offered Berra a minor league contract. "Things weren't so tough at home any more, with the other boys working," Berra was quoted as saying in the *Saturday Evening Post*. "This time my pop said yes."

In his first year (1943) in professional baseball, Berra was assigned to the Norfolk (Virginia) Tars, the Yankee farm in the Piedmont League. His work as a catcher was not faultless—he made sixteen errors—but his feat in driving in twenty-three runs in two days left little doubt as to his promise as a batting star, even though his season's hitting average was .253. After a year at Norfolk he was "moved up" to Kansas City, the Yankee farm in the American Association. He never played for Kansas City, however, but instead joined the Navy for World War II service. As a gunner he saw action for fifteen consecutive days on a rocket boat in the Normandy invasion. When returned from overseas duty, he was assigned to the welfare and recreation section at the Navy's submarine base near New London, Connecticut.

Berra, who played on the New London team, displayed such good stickwork against the New York Giants in an exhibition game that the management of that National League team offered the Yankee organization $50,000 for his contract. The Yankees refused the offer and, after Berra's discharge from the Navy in May 1946, sent him to the Newark (New Jersey) Bears of the International League, then their top-level farm. In his single season

(1946) with Newark he batted .314 and hit fifteen home runs.

One of two International League players to join the Yankees for the final week of the 1946 major league season, Berra made his presence conspicuous by hitting a home run his first time at bat. Retained by the New York Yankees for 1947, Berra made sports headlines for other reasons as well. Short and squat, and with a gait described by Tim Cohane in *Look* as "a sort of swift, purposeful waddle," he was overanxious to make an impressive showing both at and behind the plate. Thus the promise revealed during 1947 in his fifteen two-base hits and eleven home runs was offset by his tendency to hit at bad pitches, which held his batting average down to .280. Although in a game with the St. Louis Browns on June 15, 1947, he tied a catchers' major league record by making an unassisted double play, his throwing was at times so erratic that before the season was over he was shifted to the outfield, where he did not improve. In the World Series of that year between the Yankees and the Brooklyn Dodgers, Berra started again behind the plate; but the National League team stole five bases in the three and one-third games he caught before he was moved back to the outfield and subsequently benched. Later, however, he scored a pinch-hit home run.

The Yankee manager, Bucky Harris, still had confidence in Yogi Berra: he was once reported to have offered to wager that Berra "would someday be one of baseball's best catchers and a .300-plus hitter" (Gordon Manning in *Collier's*). Berra fulfilled the latter prediction in 1948, hitting 14 homers, batting in 98 runs, and striking out 24 times in 125 games, for a season's average of .305. Bucky Harris was succeeded by Casey Stengel, who added to his coaching staff the former Yankee catcher, Bill Dickey. "Bill told me the trouble was that I threw flatfooted," said Berra. "Another thing he told me was to get down on both knees when a pitch went into the dirt." Writer Manning observed further that while the coach taught Berra much, he helped even more by "awakening Yogi's pride." The result was that in 1949 Yogi's fielding average rose to .989, although because of a thumb injury incurred in August his batting dropped to .277. (Berra bats left-handed but throws right-handed.) He fielded 1.000 in the midseason All Star Game and in the 1949 World Series.

In the following year (1950) Yogi Berra had the best all-round season of his career thus far. His batting average went up to .322, seventeen points above his best previous figure, and he hit 28 homers. Afield he led all American League catchers in double plays, was again chosen to play in the All Star game, and, in the World Series with the Philadelphia National League club, hit an important home run. Named by the Baseball Writers' Association of America as catcher on the *Sporting News* ideal team, he placed third in the fall balloting by the same association for the "Most Valuable Player" award. Berra was the highest-paid catcher in the American League in 1951—his salary is said to have been about $30,000—and his manager Casey Stengel rated him the

Wide World Photos
LAWRENCE BERRA

best in either major league. "I don't care who the hitter is," Frank Graham of the New York *Journal-American* has quoted Stengel as saying. "He knows just how he should be pitched to. . . .He knows when they get on the bases too. They try to run on him and he sticks that ball down there and he's got them."

Berra encountered a "slump" in the last two months of the regular 1951 season, and although he hit 27 home runs during the year, his batting average dropped to .294. Because of this, his victory over pitchers Ned Garver and Allie Reynolds in the November voting by the Baseball Writers' Association for the Landis Award as the "Most Valuable Player" in the American League during 1951 surprised some sports authorities. The choice was explained by Joseph M. Sheehan of the New York *Times*: "He was the solid man of the Yankees on a day-to-day basis. . . .To Yogi's astute handling of his pitchers belongs a good share of the credit for the twenty-four shutouts turned in by the Yankee staff. This was the biggest whitewashing job in the American League since the Red Sox accounted for twenty-six shutouts in the 'dead ball' days of 1918." Berra, who is the first catcher since Mickey Cochrane of the Philadelphia Athletics (in 1934) to be voted the American League's most valuable player, was formally presented with the Landis Award at the reopening of the Yankee Stadium in New York City on April 18, 1951.

Mrs. Berra, who was born Carmen Short, taught dancing and worked in an office and an aircraft plant before her marriage, on January 26, 1949; there are two sons in the Berra family, Lawrence and Timothy. Brown-eyed, black-haired Yogi Berra weighs 185 pounds; he has a height of five feet eight inches. "He greets the world with a broad, good-humored face," is one description of him. He likes

BERRA, LAWRENCE—*Continued*
moving pictures, comic books, and mystery
stories. His church is the Catholic.

References

Collier's 124:21+ Ag 13 '49 pors
Life 27:71+ Jl 11 '49 pors
Look 13:65-7 Ag 2 '49 pors
N Y Journal-American p23 Ag 2 '51
N Y Post p53 My 20 '48; p56 S 1 '48;
   p96 Mr 24 '50
N Y Times V p2 Mr 20 '49; p42 N 14
   '51 por
N Y World-Telegram p16 Ag 29 '49
   por; p45 Mr 8 '50
Sat Eve Post 222:32-3+ Ap 29 '50 pors
Baseball Register (1951)
Epstein, B. Yogi Berra, the Muscle
   Man (1951)
Gross, M. Yankee Doodles (1948)
Hopkins, L. Real Book About Baseball
   (1951)
Turkin, H. & Thompson, S. C. Official
   Encyclopedia of Baseball (1951)
Waldman, F. Famous American Ath-
   letes of Today (1951)

BERRA, YOGI *See* Berra, L. P.

**BIRNIE, WILLIAM A(LFRED)
H(ART)** (bûr'nĭ) Aug. 4, 1910- Magazine
publisher; editor

Address: b. c/o Woman's Home Companion,
640 5th Ave., New York 21; h. Greens Farms,
Westport, Conn.

The editor of the *Woman's Home Companion* for nine years, since 1943, William A.
H. Birnie was appointed to the post of publisher of the magazine in August 1952. In 1938

WILLIAM A. H. BIRNIE

he had come to the Crowell-Collier Publishing
Company, which also publishes *Collier's* and
the *American Magazine*, as the associate editor of the *American*, in which many of his
articles appeared. A number of months before
becoming the publisher of the *Companion*
Birnie was named a director of the publishing
company.

William Alfred Hart Birnie was born August 4, 1910, to Walter Birnie, a paper manufacturer, and Loraine Field (Hart) Birnie, in
Springfield, Massachusetts. The family (in
which there is another son, now an engineer)
is of Scotch-English stock. For his secondary
education William Birnie attended the local
Central (now Classical) High School, from
which he received his diploma in 1926. There
he had been the editor and business manager
of the school paper and vice-president of the
senior class.

He next enrolled at Williams College, selecting English as his major. Continuing his
activity in school journalism, he was chosen
senior associate editor of the campus newspaper. He became a member of the Chi Psi
fraternity and of the Gargoyle Society, and he
joined the swimming team. By 1931, the year
he was graduated with the B.A. degree, he
had been the recipient of several essay awards
and had also won a German exchange fellowship which made it possible for him to study
abroad. Thus, during 1931-33 he took courses
in modern history at the universities of Munich
and Bonn.

Birnie's first position upon his return to the
United States in 1933 was as a newspaper reporter on the *Berkshire Evening Eagle* of
Pittsfield, Massachusetts, for the depression-
period salary of fifteen dollars a week. He
secured the position, he once remarked (as told
in the *Westporter-Herald*, Westport, Connecticut), because the father of his college roommate
was the owner of the paper. After about a
year he went to New York City to join the
staff of the *World-Telegram*. There in the
course of four years (1935-38) he was, successively, reporter, rewrite man, and drama
editor.

In the meantime Birnie had been writing articles for magazines. As reported in the *Town-
Crier* (also of Westport), he was encouraged
to continue with feature writing when the
Reader's Digest requested permission to reprint
an article of his. Becoming known in the
magazine field, in 1938 he left newspaper work
to accept the position of associate editor of the
American Magazine, a periodical of the Crowell-Collier Publishing Company. For approximately four years, while on the staff of that
magazine, he was engaged in editorial duties
and in writing numerous articles and some short
stories. Most of them appeared in the *American
Magazine* and a number were reprinted in
Reader's Digest.

In 1942 Birnie was appointed managing editor of the *Woman's Home Companion*, another
of the Crowell-Collier periodicals. His succession to the chief editorship of the *Companion*
came on April 1, 1943; and nine years later,
on August 1, 1952, he became the publisher

of the magazine, to take the place of Edward Anthony (who became the publisher of *Collier's*, likewise a Crowell-Collier property). Some months earlier, in January 1952, Birnie had been elected a director of that publishing company.

The *Woman's Home Companion*, which was given that name in 1897, was established in 1873 as the *Home Companion*. In 1886, as the *Ladies' Home Companion*, it was enlarged, as a monthly, from eight to sixteen pages. For the purpose of aiding women as homemakers, it initiated the first women's service departments. It had become a thirty-two-page magazine with a larger format and was publishing fiction and nonfiction by leading writers by 1897. That year also marked the appearance of advertisements of products which have since become nationally known brands. Around the turn of the century (according to an official statement) the *Woman's Home Companion* was being read in 325,000 homes, a high figure at that time. Its present circulation is over 4,300,000.

When Birnie became editor of the *Companion* in 1943 he introduced innovations to strengthen and modernize all departments to serve the interests of thousands of war brides and the widened horizon of women generally, for whom the crises of war and the looming issues of the postwar period created new problems. To the original concept of service to women as homemakers (in the kitchen, nursery, at the dressing table, and in interior decorating) was added a distinct editorial formula of "servicing women's minds." With woman's interests extending into sociological and political fields, she was concerned with such topics as world affairs, government medicine and health, the school child and the child delinquent, race relations, and interreligious movements. In these she is a positive force. Birnie believes, and therefore reads to be moved to action. The *Companion* maintains an "opinion poll," a monthly survey by means of questionnaires submitted to a panel of two thousand readers. Another phase of the magazine's editorial policy is the distribution of reprints of "service" articles—approximately one and a third million reprints were sent out between July 1946 and December 1951. In discussing fiction, Birnie has said that its appeal to today's woman is more subtle. In a radio program in 1950 he spoke of the end of the old "hearts and flowers" theme and the new treatment in fiction (which also entertains) of problems and situations women experience.

Birnie and the former Jean Whittlesey, who were married on September 22, 1939, have four children: Loraine Jean, Whittlesey B. H., William A. H., Jr., and Christine. In New York City the publisher-editor is a member of the Dutch Treat Club. He is an Episcopalian, and he names his political position as independent. With a height of six feet, he weighs 170 pounds, and the color of his eyes and hair is brown. Music holds first place in his list of interests: his collection of records numbers approximately five thousand, including rare examples and many operatic compositions and lieder. Working about his Connecticut place

and reading also occupy his free hours; and swimming remains his favorite outdoor sport. A daily commuter to New York City, Birnie likes to ride his motor bicycle to the suburban station.

References

> Town Crier (Westport, Conn.) Ja 4 '51
> Westporter-Herald (Westport, Conn.) Ja 29 '52
> Who's Who in America, 1952-53

BJÖRNSSON, SVEINN Feb. 27, 1881 - Jan. 25, 1952 President of Iceland; began law practice in 1907; was elected to the Althing in 1914 and re-elected in 1916; in World War I was sent on diplomatic missions to the United States and Great Britain; Minister to Denmark (1920-41); Regent of Iceland (1941-44); was elected President of Iceland in 1944 by the Althing, and was re-elected in 1945 and 1949. See *Current Biography*, 1944.

Obituary

> N Y Times p13 Ja 26 '52

BLAKE, FRANCIS G(ILMAN) Feb. 22, 1887—Feb. 1, 1952 Physician; educator; joined Yale University faculty in 1921; was Sterling Professor of Medicine (1927-52), dean of the School of Medicine (1940-47); Government adviser on epidemic diseases in World War II; chairman of the commission on medical science of the Research and Development Board, Department of Defense (1948-51); civil director of Army Medical Research (1952). See *Current Biography*, 1943.

Obituary

> N Y Times p13 F 2 '52

BLANK, THEODOR (blänk tā'ō-dōr) Sept. 19, 1905- German Government official

Address: b. Der Bundeskanzler, Bundesrepublik Deutschland, Bonn, Germany; h. Dortmund, Germany

As the principal representative of Chancellor Konrad Adenauer, Theodor Blank participated in the 1951-52 negotiations to determine the nature and extent of the military participation of the Federal Republic of Germany (the Bonn Government) in the European defense plan. A prominent labor leader who has been a Christian Democratic deputy to the Bundestag, the Bonn parliament, Blank has been mentioned by political observers as being in line for the position of West Germany's first postwar Defense Minister when the Western Allies have ratified the pending German peace treaty.

Theodor Blank was born September 19, 1905, in Eliz on the Lahn in the Province of Hesse-Nassau, Germany. After attending the Volksschule (public school) in the Ruhr Valley, Blank was apprenticed at the age of fourteen to a wood-pattern maker; that was his trade for many years. In 1930 he was appointed

Wide World Photos

THEODOR BLANK

secretary of the central association of the Christian Factory and Transport Workers Union, from which post he was dismissed by the Nazis in 1933. Blank then studied at the Essen-Steele Gymnasium (high school), graduating in 1936. During four years of unemployment preceding his military service, Blank attended the University of Münster in Westphalia and the Technische Hochschule (institute of technology) at Hannover, where he studied mathematics, physics, and mechanical engineering.

In the army in World War II Blank served as a first lieutenant in Russia and in the Battle of the Bulge (*Newsweek*). The war over, he resumed his interrupted organizational activities among the workers as secretary and member of the executive board of the Independent Miners Union. Since August 1949 Blank, a member of the Christian Democratic Union party headed by Dr. Konrad Adenauer, has sat in the Bundestag (lower house) of the Parliament of the Federal Republic of Germany as a deputy for the precinct of Borken-Bocholt-Ahaus.

The Federal Republic of Germany (Bundesrepublik Deutschland), with its capital at Bonn and its jurisdiction in an area coinciding with the British, French, and American occupation zones, was authorized by a constitution adopted and approved in May 1949. It began functioning on September 21, 1949, when the Allied High Commission turned over to it the civil administration of that part of the former Reich lying west of the Elbe river. An election held shortly thereafter resulted in a victory for the Christian Democrats over the Socialists led by Kurt Schumacher, and Dr. Adenauer formed a government of which he became Chancellor. Pending the conclusion of a formal peace, however, control of foreign policy and military

security was reserved to the Allied Commission. The matter of maintaining harmonious relations with the Commission on the implementation of security policy, one of prime importance from the beginning, became especially vital as the question of the nature and degree of West German participation in the joint West European defense effort neared the discussion stage. To millions of Germans any prospect of involvement in future fighting was unpopular, and in October 1950, accordingly, Chancellor Adenauer replaced his first security adviser, Lieutenant General Count von Schwerin, with the civilian Theodor Blank. Don Cook of the New York *Herald Tribune* characterized this move as designed "deliberately to de-emphasize the military aspect and status of the job." Blank was given the title of Deputy of the Federal Chancellor for Questions Connected with the Increase of Allied Troops. "His personality was as anonymous as his name," George Boultwood of the Associated Press commented in the Washington *Post*.

The significance of the appointment became apparent two months later (December 1950) when Blank was named by Chancellor Adenauer to head a three-man German team to negotiate with the Western powers on the measure of West German cooperation in the North Atlantic Treaty Organization's defense establishment. His associates were Lieutenant General Adolf Heusinger, former operations chief of the *Wehrmacht*, and Lieutenant General Hans Speidel, formerly Marshal Erwin Rommel's chief of staff. The place of meeting was in the mountain region of Petersberg, near Koenigswinter, where toward the end of January 1951 was evolved the so-called "Petersberg Plan" to provide for the raising of a West German army of twelve divisions (250,000 men), a tactical air force, and small naval units. It would have a national integrity under over-all NATO command. The Petersberg Plan was believed by Germans to have the endorsement of United States Commissioner John J. McCloy, who later came out in favor of an attempt to reconcile this proposal and an alternate plan advanced by the French Premier René Pleven. In July 1951 Blank went to Paris to take over from lower-level delegates the German representation in the revived discussions. On July 24 the European Army Conference issued an interim report recommending that Europe "be defended by a unified continental army plus the British army plus an American army" all under the authority of the NATO supreme commander (New York *Times*).

In the months that followed, Blank and his associates worked in secret on a program for the recruiting and arming of the proposed twelve German divisions, details of which were first disclosed early in January 1952 through a supposedly private talk by Blank to fellow members of the C.D.U. party, but at which several German newspapermen were present. "According to their accounts," wrote New York *Herald Tribune* correspondent Russell Hill, "there is to be an eighteen-month military service period. There will be three Panzer divisions with between 280 and 300 tanks each, three Panzer-grenadier divisions with 150 tanks each and six motorized infantry divisions with 70 tanks apiece. There will be a 75,000 man air force equipped with jet fighters and fighter-bombers. There will be a German defense ministry. Mr. Blank did not say so, but he is apparently in line for the post." On January 19 an official announcement was made through a special broadcast by Blank to the German people. It was then revealed that youths between the ages of 19 and 21 would be conscripted to raise the 300,000 to 400,000 men of the twelve German divisions in a forty-three division European army. Blank made it clear in his broadcast that this army "would be organized on a national basis only to the extent of divisions, the army corps to include a variety of national units" (New York *Times*).

With this radio address Theodor Blank "came into the public eye as the No. 1 salesman for German rearmament" (George Boultwood), subsequently broadcasting to mothers on the need for armed defense. He also addresses young men who will be conscripted. Placing stress on the international character of the rearmament program, Blank has pledged that Prussian-type militarism and rigid caste distinctions will be "rooted out" of the new German divisions—"We want to see a private and a colonel having coffee together." In working out the organizational details of the new German army an important role has been played by Blank's military assistant, Count Johann Adolf von Kielmansegg, and by General Heusinger; the implementation of their work, however, must await formal ratification, by all powers concerned, of both the West German Peace and European Defense Community treaties. Should the latter go into effect by January 1, 1953, Blank estimates it will take until January 1954 to organize twelve divisions, while six additional months would be needed for training.

Blank, who is married and is the father of one boy, has a home in Dortmund. *Newsweek* described the blue-eyed German statesman as short in stature, of stocky build. Don Cook observed that he has "an outspoken way about him."

References

Life 32:104+ Je 9 '52 por
N Y Herald Tribune II p2 Ja 14 '51
    por; II p2 Jl 13 '52 por
Newsweek 37:36-8 F 5 '51 por
Washington (D.C.) Post p2B Jl 6 '52
    por
Wer Ist Wer? (1950)

BLODGETT, KATHARINE BURR Jan. 10, 1898- Research physicist and chemist
Address: b. c/o Research Laboratory, General Electric Company, River Rd., Schenectady, N.Y.; h. 18 N Church St., Schenectady, N.Y.

NOTE: This biography supersedes the article which appeared in *Current Biography* in 1940.

A research scientist in surface chemistry, Katharine Burr Blodgett has received widespread recognition for the practical application of her work on thin films, for the invention of a device for measuring the thickness of films within one micro-inch, and for the development of nonreflecting "invisible" glass. Her lifelong scientific associate, Dr. Irving Langmuir, Nobel Prize winner in chemistry, has described Dr. Blodgett as "a gifted experimenter" with a "rare combination of theoretical and practical ability." She has been associated with the General Electric Laboratories in Schenectady since 1918, except for two years of study under Sir Ernest Rutherford at the Cavendish Laboratories of Cambridge University, where she was the first woman student to receive a Ph.D. degree in physics.

Born in Schenectady, New York, on January 10, 1898, Katharine Burr Blodgett is the daughter of George Bedington and Katharine Buchanan (Burr) Blodgett, who also had an older child, a son. The father, a patent attorney for the General Electric Company, moved from Boston soon after the company became established in Schenectady. Katharine was born a few weeks after her father's death; Mrs. Blodgett later took her son and daughter to New York City, where they lived for three years. Following a sojourn in France, they returned to the United States for a few years, after which the children traveled to Germany. Katharine Blodgett's education was begun at the age of eight, when for one year she attended a public school in Saranac Lake, New York. For the remainder of her elementary and her secondary schooling she was enrolled in a private institution in New York City. Her grades in a competitive examination won her a matriculation scholarship to Bryn Mawr College in Pennsylvania for the year 1913-14. Here the teaching of James Barnes inspired an interest in physics, which became her major study.

Because of her father's work, Katharine Blodgett had a sentimental feeling for Schenectady. Thus, during the Christmas vacation of her senior year the eighteen-year-old college girl visited the General Electric plant in that city. Her guide through the laboratories was Irving Langmuir, who advised her to take further scientific training. Accordingly, after graduation in 1917, she enrolled for postgraduate studies at the University of Chicago. The following year (1918) Miss Blodgett obtained the M.Sc. degree, for which she had submitted a thesis on problems in the chemistry of gas masks.

Despite the prevailing bias against women scientists, in 1918 Miss Blodgett, aided by her scholastic standing, a wartime shortage of personnel, and her father's old friends, became the first woman research scientist in the General Electric laboratories. Working in the borderline area between physics and chemistry, she assisted Dr. Langmuir for the following six years on such studies as the quantitative measurement of flow of electric current under prescribed conditions. During this period she and Langmuir jointly published several research

KATHARINE BURR BLODGETT

papers in technical journals. Langmuir, appreciating her potentialities, advised her to increase her knowledge by studying at Cambridge University. In 1924 she was admitted to the British institution, where she studied under Sir Ernest Rutherford, Nobel Prize-winner, at the Cavendish Laboratories. Two years later she received the first Ph.D. degree in physics ever awarded to a woman by Cambridge.

Then, back in Schenectady, Dr. Blodgett pursued her work with Dr. Langmuir for about five additional years on the improvement of tungsten filaments in electric lamps and on other problems, the two researchers continuing to publish joint papers. In 1933 Langmuir asked her to work on phenomena related to his discovery that oily substances on the surface of water form a single molecular layer. It was in the course of many years of research along these lines that Dr. Blodgett made her main contribution to science—methods of constructing films of infinitesimal thinness.

The invention of the "color gauge," which permits film measurement within one microinch, began with Dr. Blodgett's discovery in December 1933 that monomolecular layers of stearic acid, each about one ten-millionth of an inch in thickness, could be successively deposited on to a plate lowered into the solution. This enabled her to construct films in a series of progressive thicknesses, of which each reflects a characteristic color in white light. Her method of depositing sheets of barium stearate on plates enables a standardized color gauge to be constructed. "Anyone who wishes to measure the thickness of a film which is only a few millionths of an inch thick," she said, "can compare the color of his film with the series of colors in the gauge. The step on the gauge that matches his film in color will give him a measure of its thickness." This device eliminates expensive optical instruments in the measurement of transparent or semitransparent

films by metallurgists, physicists, chemists, and other technicians. Dr. Blodgett also showed interest in the application of this method to the measurement of the thickness of biological tissues.

The General Electric Company announced in December 1938 that Katharine Blodgett had succeeded in developing a nonreflecting "invisible" glass. Ordinary glass is visible because of the light rays which are reflected from its surface, and when a film is placed upon the glass, there is a reflection from the film as well as from the glass. Dr. Blodgett discovered that a coating of forty-four layers of one-molecule-thick transparent liquid soap, of about four-millionths of an inch or one-fourth the average wave length of white light, made sheets of glass invisible. Since the reflection from the soap film neutralizes the reflection from the glass itself, the crests and troughs of the two sets of light waves cancel each other, thereby eliminating reflected light. At the same time, the soap varnish is a good conductor of light, permitting 99 per cent of the light striking it to pass through. The one aspect of Dr. Blodgett's work on nonreflecting glass requiring further research was the development of harder coatings which could not be wiped off. Some of the applications of the invention are seen in automobile windshields, shop windows, showcases, cameras, spectacles, telescopes, picture frames, and submarine periscopes. Within two days after the woman scientist's discovery was made known, two other scientists announced that they had also devised an "invisible" glass by depositing the condensed vapor of metallic fluorides on glass.

One of Dr. Blodgett's assignments in World War II was the problem of ridding airplane wings of ice. She also helped devise a new kind of smoke screen which, according to *Science Illustrated*, saved thousands of lives in the North African, Italian, and later invasions. She did research in 1947 for the Army Signal Corps on the use of thin films for the development of an instrument to measure humidity which could be carried into the upper atmosphere by weather balloons; the available devices did not react with sufficient rapidity during the balloon's fast ascent, nor were they adequately sensitive at high altitudes. Her current work, as reported by *Chemical & Engineering News* on April 9, 1951, involves the construction of a high-resistance electrical material obtained by heating lead glass in hydrogen, a process producing a low-conductivity thin surface film which is stable at high electric potentials. During the course of her years at GE, the woman scientist was instrumental in bringing to Langmuir's staff Vincent J. Schaefer, who invented the technique of producing artificial rain by having airplanes drop dry ice pellets into clouds. Another of her colleagues has been Robert Smith-Johannsen, who worked on coatings to prevent icing on airplane propellers.

Scientific journals have published Dr. Blodgett's papers, which deal with discharges in gases, surface chemistry, and the development of nonreflecting glass. She has received honorary doctorates from Elmira College (1939), Western College (1942), Brown University (1942), and Russell Sage College (1944). The American Association of University Women on March 29, 1945, presented her with the Annual Achievement Award of $2,500 for her research on thin films. In April 1951 she received the Francis P. Garvan Medal, honoring women in chemistry, from the American Chemical Society for her work in surface chemistry. On the occasion of this meeting she addressed the society on the subject "Interference Colors Reflected by Thin Films." Two other honors came to her in 1951. She was the only scientist, reported *Look*, honored by Boston's First Assembly of American Women of Achievement (in May); and in that summer Schenectady celebrated Katharine Blodgett Day. A fellow of the American Physical Society, she is also a member of the Optical Society of America.

In all her career as a research scientist Dr. Blodgett has used a battered old table and scarred wooden stool, with which she refused to part when her laboratory was moved into the new glass and steel building in Schenectady. Active in Schenectady civic affairs, she has served as treasurer of the Travelers Aid Society, is a member of the Zonta Club, and is a past president of a GE employees' club. Her church affiliation is Presbyterian.

Katharine Blodgett lives in a house in downtown Schenectady. Gardening is her favorite vacation recreation, though the *Times* has reported that she "is thrown into a shrieking panic in meeting face to face a common garter snake." Her other hobbies are amateur astronomy and collecting antiques. She is five feet tall and has been described as "a modest, plump, pleasant-faced woman with an uptilted nose and merry eyes."

References

Chem & Eng N 29:1408 Ap 9 '51
Christian Sci Mon O 24 '44 por
Ind Woman 19:29 Ja '40 por p3
Look Ag 28 '51 por
N Y Post Je 4 '41 por
N Y Times S 24 '39; Mr 15 '51 por
Sci Ilus 2:9-11 D '47
Time 33:33 Ja 9 '39 por
American Women, 1939-40
International Who's Who, 1950
Who's Who in America, 1950-51
Yost, E. American Women of Science (1943)

BOATNER, HAYDON L(EMAIRE) Oct. 5, 1900- United States Army officer
Address: b. c/o Department of the Army, The Pentagon, Washington 25, D.C.

Major General Haydon L. Boatner was the fourteenth commandant within sixteen months of the United Nations prisoner-of-war camp on Koje Island off South Korea. Appointed mid-May 1952 to succeed Brigadier General Francis T. Dodd, Boatner was confronted with the task of re-establishing order and reasserting authority. He has among other qualifications a

U. S. Army
MAJ. GEN. HAYDON L. BOATNER

reputation for being a "tough" disciplinarian, a master of the Chinese language, and a trainer and leader of Chinese troops during World War II. On September 1, 1952, Boatner left Korea for the United States to assume his new post as deputy commander of the Fourth Army at Fort Sam Houston, Texas.

Born in New Orleans, Louisiana, on October 5, 1900, Haydon Lemaire Boatner is the third son in a family of four boys and two girls, the children of Judge Mark Mayo Boatner and the former Byrd Elizabeth Bryant. There have been Boatners in the United States Army since the American Revolution, and Judge Boatner himself had expected to become a soldier before he turned to law. It was his hope that his sons would carry on the family tradition of military service, to which end he imbued them with such an interest in military life that three of them became graduates of West Point (John Gardner in the New York *Sunday News*). Haydon graduated from high school in the spring of 1918, some months before the end of World War I.

The seventeen-year-old boy wanted to enlist immediately, but because of his mother's objections waited until October 8, 1918, three days after his eighteenth birthday, to join the United States Marines as a private. When he was mustered out on March 31, 1919, his father and he took steps toward securing for him an appointment to the United States Military Academy. He became a West Point cadet on July 1, 1920, after studying at Tulane University in his native city for one academic year (1919-20).

Having received a B.S. degree as well as his second lieutenant's commission at West Point on June 12, 1924, Haydon Boatner was assigned to the 29th Infantry at Fort Benning, Georgia. In September 1928 he entered the Infantry School at Fort Benning, and after

BOATNER, HAYDON L.—*Continued*

graduation in the following June he was sent to Tientsin, China, to join the 15th Infantry. Boatner was promoted to first lieutenant (permanent) on May 29, 1929, and in September 1930 became a language student at the California College of Chinese Studies at Tientsin, where he received his M.A. degree in Chinese in June 1934. (His principal work in scholarship up to the present time has been a translation and interpretation of the military history of the Manchu conquest of China.) In command of a mounted patrol when the Japanese, having invaded Manchuria in 1931, moved into north China, he led his men into "the thick of the trouble, trying to protect American citizens and American lives," stated John Gardner in the *Sunday News*. He was sent on missions into the interior, to search out the sources of illegal opium and report on the operations of Chinese bandits.

Following completion of his language studies, Boatner was assigned as assistant military attaché at the American Embassy in Peking (Peiping), then the Chinese capital, and placed in charge of translation. Six months later (December 1934) he returned to the United States for duty with the 30th Infantry at San Francisco, California. Advanced to captain (permanent) on August 1, 1935, Boatner was transferred in the following October to Baltimore, Maryland, as aide to the commanding general of the Third Corps Area. In September 1938 he entered the Command and General Staff School at Fort Leavenworth, Kansas, and upon graduation in June 1939 joined the 38th Infantry, with which he served at Fort Sill in Oklahoma and Camp Bullis and Fort Sam Houston in Texas. Promoted to major (temporary) on January 31, 1941, Boatner became in the following May an assistant in the Chinese Unit of the Defense Aid Section of the War Department General Staff. A month later (June 12) Boatner received the permanent rank of major and was serving as such in Washington when the United States entered World War II. He has been credited with organizing the Magruder military mission and the original mission of Lieutenant General Joseph W. Stilwell to China.

On December 24, 1941, about two weeks after Pearl Harbor, Boatner was promoted to lieutenant colonel (temporary) and sent to San Antonio, Texas, as assistant to the plans and training officer of the Third Army. In February 1942 he returned to Asia to become, under General Stilwell, the Chief of Staff of the Chinese Training Project at Ramgarh, India; he was promoted to colonel (temporary) on June 17 and to brigadier general (temporary) on November 1; then, in 1943 he was made Chief of Staff of the Chinese Army in India, stationed at Ramgarh. Meanwhile operating from what has been described as "a fantastic headquarters hidden away in a bamboo forest," he had converted 60,000 "demoralized" Chinese troops into an efficient combat force, and had displayed "aggressiveness, informality, contempt for red tape, and a command of invective" which became legendary throughout the China-Burma-India theater of operations. The quo-

tation is from a dispatch to the New York *Herald Tribune*, which added: "He runs around in shorts, shirt, work cap and boots, with no insignia of rank." This was in November 1943, following an attack by the Boatner-trained Chinese, who drove the Japanese from the upper Hukawng Valley in northern Burma and from the vicinity of the Ledo road. Boatner himself compared this fighting to Indian warfare in early American history.

The final weeks of the war found General Boatner the deputy commander of the Chinese Combat Command and seated with General Hsaio Yu-shu in the August 1945 conference to arrange for the surrender of Japanese troops in China. (During the following month Boatner was insistent that the surrender at Nanking should be "a 100 per cent Chinese show" with the Americans remaining in the background.) Boatner (who has been awarded the Distinguished Service Medal and the Legion of Merit with one Oak Leaf Cluster) was back in the United States in October 1945 and in February 1946 was reassigned to Fort Sam Houston as assistant personnel officer of the Fourth Army, having meanwhile reverted to the peacetime rank of colonel (temporary). He took over as personnel officer of the Fourth Army in May of the same year and was advanced in permanent rank to lieutenant colonel on June 12, 1947, and to colonel on June 10, 1948. In the following August he began the first of three years as professor of military science and tactics at Texas Agricultural and Mechanical College and was also commandant of cadets.

Elevated on July 28, 1951, to brigadier general (temporary) with date of rank from July 16, 1951, Boatner was transferred to the Far East Command in the ensuing month and shortly thereafter became deputy commander of the 2d Infantry Division in Korea. He was serving in the "Heartbreak Ridge" area when on May 14, 1952, he was made commandant of the prisoner-of-war camp on Koje Island. This camp, which confined some 79,000 North Koreans and Chinese in seventeen barbed wire compounds more or less self-administered according to the Geneva Convention, had been the scene of violence and bloodshed among Communist and anti-Communist internees, and had seen thirteen different commandants within sixteen months. The twelfth of these, Brigadier General Francis T. Dodd, going to the gate of Compound 76 on May 7, 1952, to discuss complaints by P.O.W. leaders, was seized, dragged within the compound, and held as a hostage. Brigadier General Charles F. Colson was then sent to Koje as commandant and secured General Dodd's release on May 10. In bargaining with the leaders of the compound, however, Colson signed a letter in which he promised that there would be "no more forcible screening of prisoners" (to determine whether or not they wished to be repatriated) and gave assurance that "in future P.O.W.'s can expect humane treatment." The expressions "no more" and "in future" played into the hands of the Communist negotiators at the stalemated armistice conference at Panmunjom.

The Dodd kidnapping occurred during the final days as United Nations Far Eastern Commander of General Matthew B. Ridgway, who had already been named to succeed General Dwight D. Eisenhower in Europe. His successor, General Mark W. Clark, had the problem of establishing order on Koje and of restoring "if possible . . . some of the Army's lost face in Korea." The quoted words are those of Lindesay Parrott of the New York *Times,* who added that as "an old Far East hand" with a "reputation as a tough disciplinarian," Brigadier Haydon L. Boatner "seemed the man to do it." On the same day (May 14) Boatner's assignment to Koje was announced, General Clark formally repudiated the Colson letter as signed under duress. Boatner at the same time proclaimed that his policy on Koje would be "tough but fair," and when asked about negotiations with prisoners, replied sharply, "Prisoners do not negotiate" (*Time*). He also characterized past disturbances on the island as "symbols of defiance—not mutiny," and was quoted by the Associated Press as saying: "It's just like a child who throws a tantrum at bedtime. You let them get away with it once, they will throw a tantrum every night."

The 187th Airborne Regiment, of three thousand men, went to Koje as re-enforcement, and by May 18 American medium tanks were placed in position with guns pointed at the compounds. On the following day Mac R. Johnson of the New York *Herald Tribune* defined Boatner's "progressive plan" for restoring order as one based (in the General's words) on "no terror, no shooting of prisoners, and no incidents." Boatner, continued this correspondent, "is educating the Communists in their rights and obligations, and if they do not respond to his 'no bloodshed' policy, there is still time to use force." Force was necessary by mid-June when the General had the prisoners removed from the large camp to smaller compounds, with Communist ringleaders segregated. After thirteen months in Korea, Major General Boatner on September 1, 1952, left for the United States to become deputy commander of the Fourth Army at Fort Sam Houston. On the day of his departure he was presented with an Oak Leaf Cluster to the Distinguished Service Medal for his work on Koje Island.

The army officer and Dorothy Gowen were married in China on April 16, 1929; they are the parents of one son, James Gowen, an army lieutenant, and one daughter, Helene Lemaire. The six-foot General has been described by *Newsweek* as talking "out of the corner of his mouth to make up for his appearance as a bespectacled intellectual." A polo player in his early China days, Boatner still likes active sports, particularly tiger hunting. His interest in writing continues—according to his sister, he has for many years been collecting material for a military history of the War of 1812.

References

N Y Herald Tribune p38 N 21 '43; II p1 My 18 '52 por
N Y Sunday News p78-79 Je 1 '52 pors
N Y Times IV p4 My 18 '52

N Y World-Telegram p13 My 17 '52 por
Newsweek 39:36 My 26 '52 por
Time 59:30 My 26 '52
International World Who's Who (1949)
Who's Who in America, 1952-53

BORBERG, WILLIAM Nov. 3, 1885-
Danish representative to the United Nations
Address: b. c/o Danish Delegation to the United Nations, Room 6300 B, Empire State Bldg., New York 1; h. 630 Park Ave., New York 21

Among the delegates to the General Assembly of the United Nations, few have been active in international affairs longer than William Borberg, since 1947 Denmark's permanent representative to the United Nations. Entering the Danish Foreign Office in 1919 as a specialist in trade negotiations, Borberg was later a counselor to his country's London legation. Then for twelve years, beginning in 1928, he was Denmark's permanent delegate to the League of Nations in Geneva, Switzerland. A member of the United Nations Preparatory Commission in London in 1946, he also served as *rapporteur* of the Committee on Procedures and Organization in 1947 and represented Denmark on the Economic and Social Council from 1948 to 1950.

Descended from a family of farmers, manufacturers, clergymen, and teachers, William Borberg was born in Copenhagen, Denmark, on November 3, 1885, one of the six sons of Dr. Niels Christian Borberg, a physician, and Dorothea Caroline Amalie Ernestine (de Hofman-Schmidth) Borberg. (His eldest brother, Dr. Niels Christian Borberg, is an eminent neurologist.) The boy, who became an orphan at the age of eleven (his mother died in 1892 and his father four years later), was reared in Copenhagen, where he was graduated in 1904 from the Metropolitanskolen (Metropolitan High School). Two years later came the publication of his book, *Spiritualistic Phenomena and Danish Science: A Case of Prejudice.* After receiving his M.A. degree in political economy from the University of Copenhagen in 1911, he went abroad to study sociology, social psychology, and political psychology, first at the University of Munich (1911-12) and then at the London School of Economics (1912-13). He spent these years surveying the economic and social conditions of Germany, Great Britain, the United States, Hawaii, Japan, Korea, China, Australia, and New Zealand.

The outbreak of World War I brought the young Danish economist back to his native land, where in 1915 he was appointed secretary of the Merchants' Guild of Copenhagen. The following year he became general manager of the Guild's Office for Foreign Trade, filling this position for the next three years. In 1919 Borberg was chosen secretary to the Committee of Commercial Treaties organized for preparatory work on Denmark's postwar commercial policy and was named a vice-consul on service in the Foreign Office. From 1921 to 1926 he was a member of the Treaties Committee, at the same time filling the position of a section chief in

United Nations

WILLIAM BORBERG

the Foreign Office and attending, in 1922, international conferences in Geneva and The Hague as a member of the Danish delegation. He left the Copenhagen Foreign Office in 1926 for an assignment in London as counselor to the Danish Legation for the next two years.

Named as Denmark's permanent delegate to the League of Nations in 1928, he served as such until 1940, being a member of all the League's general assemblies since 1928 and holding the rank of Envoy Extraordinary and Minister Plenipotentiary since 1934. When Denmark gave notice of its withdrawal from the League in 1940, Borberg returned to the Foreign Office in Copenhagen, where he remained until 1946. That year he represented his country on the U.N. Preparatory Commission in London and became a member of the Danish delegation to both sessions of the first General Assembly, one in London and the other in New York City. Early in 1947, before the second General Assembly convened in New York, Borberg was named permanent representative of Denmark to the United Nations. After serving in that session as *rapporteur* of the Committee on Procedures and Organization, he was named to the Economic and Social Council for a two-year term in 1948 when the U.N. met in Paris. As his country's representative to the United Nations, Borberg has participated in all subsequent sessions of the General Assembly.

Over the years Borberg has continued his early interest in the social sciences, contributing articles to learned journals and addressing scientific organizations. At the 1950 annual meeting of the American Psychiatric Association in Detroit, Michigan, he delivered his paper "On Methods of the Social Sciences in their Approach to International Problems," which was subsequently published in the *American Journal of Psychiatry* (March 1951). In it he said: "It is my conviction that the General Assembly

and other organs of the United Nations, including the Secretariat, have more men and women of the modern outlook than had the League of Nations. . . .The part of the United States in the United Nations has, I believe, been contributive to this."

In another article, "On Active Service for Peace" (*Bulletin of the World Federation for Mental Health*, August 1950), Borberg pointed out that "sociological development, at least twice in our lifetime, has brought to the leadership of 'great powers' men who are mentally unfit to undertake that integration and coordination of 'states' necessary for the avoidance of war under modern conditions of man's development." Quoting from the preamble of the United Nations Educational, Scientific and Cultural Organization, which says that "since wars begin in the minds of men, it is in the minds of men that the defenses of peace must be constructed," Borberg urged that "in every country and in international organizations ways and means should be sought" by social scientists "for getting into contact with the 'policy leaders,' to explain what the social sciences, and particularly the psychological sciences, might do, and to ask that they may be given a chance to study whether they may be of practical service." He reiterated this idea in an address, "Mental Health and International Cooperation," before the United States Committee for the World Federation for Mental Health on June 15, 1952.

Borberg has been honored in his native land by the award of the Silvercross of Dannebrog and by the decoration of Commander, Danish Dannebrog Order. He has also been decorated Knight Commander, Icelandic Falcon; Grand Cross, White Rose Order of Finland; Commander, Orange Nassau Order; Commander, Polonia Restituta (Poland); Knight, North Star Order; Swedish Vasa Order; and Norwegian St. Olaf Order. The Danish diplomat has blue-gray eyes and gray hair and weighs 157 pounds. His hobby is science reading.

References

U N Bul 3 :376 S 16 '47 por
Kraks Blaa Bog (1951)
Who's Who in America, 1952-53
Who's Who in the United Nations (1951)
World Biography (1948)
World Diplomatic Directory (1951)

BOYER, HAROLD RAYMOND Feb. 25, 1899- United States Government official; engineer

Address: h. 17700 E. Jefferson Ave., Grosse Pointe 30, Mich.

In an effort to bring military plane production up to the minimum goal of 5,000 planes a year, the Aircraft Production Board, with Harold Raymond Boyer as chairman, was created in the Defense Production Administration in July 1951. Boyer, on leave as director of production engineering for the General Motors Corporation, was also named deputy director of DPA. The recently appointed aviation executive had previously served in an administrative capacity for the United States Government as chief of the plane manufacturing division of the War Production Board during World War II. Before and after World War II Boyer was for twenty-five years an engineer and executive with various machine and automotive firms. Announcement was made on April 18, 1952, that Boyer would resign at the end of the month as aircraft production expediter in the Defense Production Administration to return to General Motors.

Harold Raymond Boyer was born February 25, 1899, the only child of Frank Custer and Mathilda (Grube) Boyer. In his native city of Springfield, Ohio, the future engineer spent his early life and attended the Springfield High School. In 1916, after graduating from the secondary school, he became a student at Wittenberg College, also in Springfield. There he remained until 1919, when he entered the Massachusetts Institute of Technology, from which in 1922, with a major in the field of engineering administration, he received the B.S. degree. While at the institute he played on the basketball team and became a member of the Delta Kappa Epsilon fraternity. Boyer's first employment was with the Maxwell Motor Company of Detroit, Michigan, where as stockroom attendant in 1922 he began his career in the automobile industry, "shoveling nuts and bolts" (as *Time* described the job).

In 1923-24 Boyer was an engineer in Detroit for the Fisher Body Corporation, manufacturers of parts, particularly bodies, for automobiles. During the next five years he was general works engineer for the Oakland Motor Car Company, in Pontiac, Michigan, and at the end of that time (1929) he became president and general manager of the Allen Corporation, in Detroit. In 1940, when the United States defense program was becoming established, Boyer was chosen chief of the Aircraft Manufacturing Branch of the War Production Board. During the subsequent three years of his Washington service he worked in close association with William S. Knudsen, former president of the General Motors Corporation and director, in the early years of World War II, of the industrial production program. Boyer is credited by *Time* with having "helped push output up to 100,000 planes a year."

Accepting an offer by the General Motors Corporation, Boyer in 1943 returned to private industry and in 1946 he was promoted to the position of director of production engineering for the automobile company. It was while he served in that capacity that his company's production of passenger cars represented 43 per cent of the total of such vehicles produced in the United States and its net income for a year (1949) amounted to $656,526,969.

On leave of absence from his General Motors position, Boyer on July 25, 1951, became chairman of the Aircraft Production Board, newly created within the Defense Production Administration. Director of Defense Mobilization Charles E. Wilson was reported by the New York *Times* to have chosen Boyer because of his familiarity with mass production problems. In his new position, Boyer, whose

HAROLD RAYMOND BOYER

responsibility covers all output of planes, also has the title of deputy director of the DPA. At a news conference held after his swearing-in ceremony, Boyer stated, according to a report in the New York *Times*, that "there is a serious bottleneck in machine tools that must be eliminated if our aircraft production schedules are to be met," and that there was "a serious shortage in aluminum and alloy metal castings required for jet engine production." While agreeing that airplane production for defense purposes was behind schedule, Boyer explained that many planes were 99 per cent completed and needed only "some gadget or other" in order to be put to use. To relieve this situation, he explained, he intended to study the desirability of reactivating the airplane "modification centers" of World War II where innovations and improvements could be added after the planes had been completed at mass production plants.

An analysis (in *Newsweek*, November 19, 1951) of the delay in defense airplane production mentioned criticism leveled against the Defense Production Administration for the bottleneck as well as criticism of the armed services for not assisting sufficiently in obtaining material allocations for their airplane contractors. Boyer's task is to help plane contractors get all allocations from the combined Defense Production Administration-National Production Authority, which is charged with balancing the requests of the armed services against civilian consumption needs. In late October Boyer was successful in getting much-needed aluminum, steel, and copper to a manufacturer of jet engines whose allocations had been miscalculated and then cancelled. Some of the problems to be met by Boyer's new agency were outlined by the chairman in an article for the December issue of *Planes*, the magazine of the Aircraft Industries Association of America. He wrote that defense needs cannot con-

BOYER, HAROLD RAYMOND—*Cont.*

tinue to be subordinated to civilian demands if the ultimate monthly goal of 1,800 to 2,000 planes is to be met. Boyer, who was said to have "brought order out of chaos" in military aircraft production, resigned from the Aircraft Production Board at the end of April 1952 to take up an assignment at General Motors.

Boyer's other financial and industrial affiliations are with the Industrial National Bank, Square D Manufacturing Company, and Gear Grinding Machine Company, all of Detroit; Parker Appliance Company of Cleveland; and Lear, Inc., of Grand Rapids. His clubs are the Detroit, the Detroit Country, Metamora Hunt, Grosse Pointe, Yondotega, and the Economic. He is also a member of the Aero of Michigan and of the Society of Automotive Engineers, and is director of the Detroit Civic Opera and of the Detroit Red Cross. His church is the Presbyterian. On October 6, 1928, he married Frances Alger; their children are Frances (Mrs. Hudson Mead), Mary, Harold, Jr., and Frederick Alger. The DPA official stands six feet two inches tall, weighs 200 pounds, and has black hair and blue eyes. He enjoys hunting and sometimes travels in his own plane on big-game expeditions.

References

    Time 58:77 Ag 6 '51

    Who's Who in Commerce and Industry (1951)

BRANDO, MARLON Apr. 3, 1924- Actor
Address: b. c/o Twentieth Century-Fox Studios, 10201 W. Pico Blvd., Los Angeles, Calif.

One of the most discussed of the younger American stage and screen actors is Marlon Brando, whose career began in 1944 in a supporting Broadway role which shortly led to the part of Marchbanks in Katharine Cornell's production *Candida*. Impressed by his forceful acting in *A Streetcar Named Desire*, Hollywood introduced him to the film public in 1950 as the hero in *The Men*. Subsequently he was screened in the male leads of *A Streetcar Named Desire* and *Viva Zapata!*

Marlon Brando was born in Omaha, Nebraska, on April 3, 1924. His father, Marlon Brando, Sr., whose French forebears spelled the family name Brandeau, is a manufacturer of chemical feed products and insecticides. When the boy was six, his family moved to Evanston, Illinois, and later to Libertyville in the same State. Young Brando, who had been on the track squad, left the Libertyville High School to continue his education at Shattuck Military Academy, in Faribault, Minnesota, from which he withdrew shortly before graduation, in 1943. In later years he took several courses, in art, French, and other subjects at the New School for Social Research in New York.

A short period of work in Libertyville as a tile-fitter for a drainage construction company was ended after a few months when Brando accepted his father's offer to finance his prep-

aration in a professional field. With a family interest in the theater (his mother had been an actress in the Community Playhouse of Omaha and his sister Jocelyn Hammer has appeared in the play *Mister Roberts*), he chose dramatics. The youth first spent the remainder of the summer of 1943 in the New York City home of his sister Frances, an artist, and in the fall entered the Dramatic Workshop of the New School for Social Research. Brando's student performances under the direction of Erwin Piscator, were noticed by George Freedley, drama critic of the New York *Morning Telegraph*, who commented that Brando gave the best performance in the production on May 24, 1944, of Gerhart Hauptmann's *Hannele's Way to Heaven;* in it Brando filled the roles of the schoolteacher and, in the dream sequence, an angel. He also appeared in an adaptation of two of Molière's plays and in Shakespeare's *Twelfth Night*. In the summer of 1944 he played in the stock company of the theater in Sayville, Long Island, also directed by Piscator. Brando's principal teacher during his student days was Stella Adler, exponent of a thorough study of the character to be played. After launching his stage career Brando studied with Elia Kazan, under whose supervision he directed a student performance of Ibsen's *Hedda Gabler*.

The first Broadway part of the young actor was in Kathryn Forbes's highly successful play, *I Remember Mama*, opening October 19, 1944, in which as the fifteen-year-old Nels he drew from the New York critics some brief favorable comment. During 1945 he did not appear on the stage, but returned on February 7, 1946, to fill the role of Sage McRae, a war veteran who kills his faithless wife in Maxwell Anderson's short-lived *Truckline Café*. His portrayal of remorse, which drew critical praise, was seen by Guthrie McClintic, who offered Brando the role of Eugene Marchbanks, the young poet, in Katharine Cornell's revival, opening April 3, 1946, of Bernard Shaw's *Candida*. While Lewis Nichols in the New York *Times* complained that Brando was a "somewhat monotonously intoning poet," *Variety*'s critic saw him as giving "at times . . . a remarkable performance"; and Howard Barnes of the *Herald Tribune* found that he made the final act "exceedingly" satisfying. Other critics, notably *PM*'s Louis Kronenberger, thought Brando's interpretation of the part not "particularly successful."

After *Candida*, Brando took the role of the refugee Jew David in Ben Hecht's *A Flag Is Born*, a story about the newly formed state of Israel, in which the young actor was much interested. Later on in 1946 he acted the male lead opposite Tallulah Bankhead in Jean Cocteau's *The Eagle Has Two Heads*, but left the cast before the play reached New York.

Following a period of about a year spent in study and foreign travel, Brando returned to the stage on December 3, 1947, as Stanley Kowalski in Tennessee Williams' Pulitzer Prize-winning play, *A Streetcar Named Desire*, directed by Elia Kazan. His interpretation of the factory worker whose brutality is decisive in reducing to madness his already de-

graded alcoholic sister-in-law was generally
given very high praise. Howard Barnes called
him "convincing"; William Hawkins of the
World-Telegram thought "his stilted speech
and swift rages were ingeniously spontaneous";
and Kronenberger referred to his "brilliant performance . . . the more astonishing for being
like nothing else he has ever played." In 1948
and following years Brando attended classes at
the Actors Studio, an experimental workshop
in New York with which Robert Lewis, Kazan,
and Cheryl Crawford are associated. One of
the roles played by Brando in the course of
his study at the Actors Studio was that of a
Hapsburg prince in *Reunion in Vienna.*

For *The Men*, his first motion picture, directed by Stanley Kramer and released by
United Artists in mid-1950, Brando played the
part of the paraplegic veteran, who at first re-
pulses all attempts at treatment. To prepare
himself for an authentic portrayal, Brando spent
some weeks observing the regimen of a paraplegic at Birmingham Veterans Hospital in Van
Nuys, California. Bosley Crowther commented
in the New York *Times*: "The illusion is complete. His face, the whole rhythm of his body
and especially the strange timbre of his voice,
often broken and plaintive and boyish, are
articulate in every way." *Time*, praising his
"wholehearted concentration on his craft,"
called his achievement in *The Men* "magnificent."

The actor, who makes a contract for each
of his pictures and has not bound himself to
any one studio, was next engaged in duplicating
his role of Stanley Kowalski for Warner
Brothers' production of *A Streetcar Named
Desire*, costarring Vivien Leigh and again directed by Elia Kazan. While *Variety* noted a
garbled pronunciation, other reviewers were
unstinting in their expression of admiration.
Time attributed the film's "highest voltage" to
Brando, and Otis L. Guernsey, Jr., of the
Herald Tribune wrote, "This performance is
as close to perfect as one could wish." Bosley
Crowther felt a heightened tension when compared with his acting in the stage play.

Intensive study of history and of Mexican
types was part of Brando's preparation for his
next screen role, that of the title role in John
Steinbeck's *Viva Zapata!* the story of Pancho
Villa's principal confederate. This biography
of Mexico's agrarian rebel was filmed in
Mexico and Texas under Kazan's direction and
was released early in 1952 by Twentieth Century-Fox. The critical response to Brando's
acting was on the whole less warm than it
had been. However, Bosley Crowther, while
considering him less adequate than in earlier
roles, discovered "power enough in his portrayal to cause the screen to throb."

Known for the intense and naturalistic style
of his performances, Brando has said that he
follows no particular school of acting. In
the opinion of Robert Lewis, he belongs to the
tradition of dramatic artists whose technique is
so great as to be invisible. John Mason Brown
has commented in the *Saturday Review of
Literature* on the striking variety in Brando's
emotional range and on his skill in quickly

MARLON BRANDO

changing his moods. "Surely his voice and diction in any other actor would count as liabilities," Brown has further observed, "but he converts them into assets. His slurred speech
and frequently thin tones convey his feelings
with overwhelming clarity." For his work in
The Men Brando was paid $40,000, for the mo-
tion picture *Streetcar* $75,000, and for
Viva Zapata! $100,000 (New York *Herald
Tribune*, October 10, 1951). Newspaper reports
early in 1952 were that Paul Graetz, French
film producer, had a one-picture contract with
Brando. In the summer of 1952 it was announced that the young actor had accepted the
role of Mark Antony in MGM's film version of
Julius Caesar.

Brando, who is the subject of numerous
legends, enjoys books on serious subjects, visiting art museums, playing Afro-Cuban drums,
and travel. Writers have commented on his
informality of dress. He has invested some of
his earnings in a cattle-raising enterprise,
Marsdo, Inc., operated by his father. Robust
in build, Brando stands five feet ten inches and
weighs 170 pounds; he has gray eyes and
brown hair.

References

Life 29:49+ Jl 31 '50
N Y Post Mag p19 Ag 13 '50
Photoplay 38:41+ D '50
PM Mag p7-9 My 16 '48
International Motion Picture Almanac,
1951-52

BRANIFF, T(HOMAS) E(LMER) Dec.
6, 1883- Airline executive

Address: b. c/o Braniff International Airways,
Love Field, Dallas, Tex.; h. 5039 Seneca Rd.,
Dallas, Tex.

T. E. Braniff is founder, president, and board
chairman of the only major American airline

T. E. BRANIFF

that still bears its owner's name—Braniff International Airways, which in early August 1952 .merged with Mid-Continent Airlines under the name of Braniff. The executive established his company, which flies routes through the Midwestern United States and into Latin America, after he had built a million-dollar fortune in the insurance business in Oklahoma. Interested in world brotherhood, Braniff also serves as Catholic co-chairman of the National Conference of Christians and Jews.

Braniff's Irish-born forebears settled first in Pennsylvania and later moved to the Kansas prairies. Thomas Elmer Braniff was born in Salina, Kansas, on December 6, 1883, to J. A. and Mary Catherine (Baker) Braniff. The family next lived in Kansas City, Missouri, where young Tom attended public school. When Oklahoma Territory was opened to settlers under the Homestead Act, the Braniffs moved there; and a year later, in 1901, young Braniff, who had remained in Missouri, followed his family to Oklahoma City. There he joined his father in the insurance business, the teen-aged youth driving a buckboard through the Kiowa and Comanche Indian country of Western Oklahoma to sell tornado and fire insurance to new settlers. By 1902 he had opened an insurance office in Oklahoma City, in partnership with Frank Merrill. When Merrill, twenty-two years older than Braniff, retired in 1919, Braniff bought his interest.

The insurance business grew to the point where by 1923 Braniff was erecting one of the city's earliest skyscrapers—the Braniff Building—not then in the heart of the city, but in what has since become its most valuable business district, a growth Braniff foresaw. Braniff "had a fortune" by 1927, reported Time. More recently the 265 agents of the T. E. Braniff Company have been writing, according to

Newsweek (March 5, 1951), more than $1.5 millions in premiums a year.

Braniff entered a new field in 1928 when he helped finance and later took over an airline that flew oilmen the 116 miles between Oklahoma City and Tulsa. At that time the company owned one single-engine five-place Stinson-Detroit plane and employed a staff of three. Braniff expanded his route northward, flying routes between Chicago and Houston. At first he lost money, but a mail contract awarded him in 1934 helped the firm "break even" by 1935. And in 1938, according to Time (April 16, 1945) Braniff Airways earned its first profits, $28,000. The 1944 profits amounted to $773,000.

Meanwhile Braniff was venturing into international transportation. First he formed a Mexican company, Aerovias Braniff, S.A., which would make connections with his American routes. In April 1945 a Douglas DC-3 made its first flight over the new airline, to Mexico City. Three DC-3's, converted from Army transports, were to fly the 569-mile route between Mexico City and Nuevo Laredo on the Rio Grande, a junction point for the American Braniff lines. But competition from Compañia Mexicana de Aviación, an affiliate of Pan American, created some difficulties: among other things, facilities were denied Braniff's planes at Mexican airfields. By 1947 Braniff had been forced out of Mexico, for which, according to the New York Times January 4, 1952, he "has never ceased to blame Pan American."

In 1946 the Civil Aeronautics Board had granted Braniff certificates permitting his line to fly to Rio de Janeiro and Buenos Aires, but Pan American Airways and Panagra (50 per cent of which is owned by Pan American) had refused Braniff joint use of their airport facilities in South American stopping points. Braniff thereupon built his own radio station in Ecuador, reportedly at a cost of $100,000, to provide radio beams for his planes, and set about inaugurating plane service to Lima, Peru. In May 1948, when service was about to begin, the Peruvian Government acting, it was thought, to protect Peruvian International Airways, suspended the license it had granted to Braniff. Later, pressure from the United States Government, said Aviation Week, led to Peru's honoring the agreement, and in June Braniff began regular flights to Lima by way of Havana.

With Buenos Aires still his goal, Braniff equipped a stopover station at La Paz, Bolivia, and in Rio de Janeiro arranged with the Scandinavian Airlines System to share its facilities. By 1950 his planes were making the 2,500-mile flight from Lima to Rio de Janeiro "across the heart of South America," in what was described by the New York Times as "a heretofore unheard-of hop that is one of the longest regularly scheduled flights in the world." Braniff next routed planes from Lima to Buenos Aires by way of La Paz and Asuncion, "thus opening Paraguay to four-motor travel for the first time," the Times writer pointed out. In May 1950, when the first Braniff DC-6 landed at Buenos Aires after an express flight from Houston with stops at Panama City and Lima, *Newsweek* called it "a victory over climatic conditions, hostile foreign governments, and competing Pan American Airways." Braniff's fleet of 33 planes was now flying routes totaling 10,583 miles, from Chicago to leading South American cities. To stimulate trade with Latin America, the airline company set up the Braniff Business Bureau, and advertised lower fares to attract more tourists.

The magazine *Aviation Week* reported in April 1948 that for 1947, although Braniff airlines had carried more passengers, mail, and cargo than in any other year, its records showed a loss of $1,148,761. Braniff had reduced its personnel from a peak of 2,530 in 1946 to 2,030, and appealed for an increase in payment for mail. Retroactive mail pay adjustments were granted in September 1948 by the Civil Aeronautics Board, which commended the Braniff and Delta airlines for having the lowest unit operating costs among the companies carrying mail. Braniff airlines' profits for 1948 (as noted in *Aviation Week*) were $191,634, and the following year, with operating revenues at a record high ($18,438,000) the domestic lines made a profit of $446,000, more than enough to cover the $224,000 loss incurred by the international routes.

In 1951 Braniff International Airways was flying a total of 11,161 route miles. Of its personnel of 2,712 persons, over 1,600 were employed at 50-acre Love Field in Dallas. The company could point to a safety record of one billion eight hundred million passenger miles flown in safety. (The National Safety Council presented its 1946 plaque to Braniff for the best safety record in the industry.) In January 1952 a plan for merging Braniff International Airways and Mid-Continent Airlines was approved by the directors of the two companies, subject to the approval of stockholders and the CAB. The new company, formed in August 1952 under the name Braniff, is the sixth largest American airline. Braniff International Airways had served 31 cities in nine States and nine Latin American countries, and Mid-Continent 35 cities in twelve States.

Braniff's other business interests are directorships of the Republic National Bank, Dallas, and of the Kansas City Fire and Marine Insurance Company; he is president of the T. E. Braniff Company and of the Braniff Investment Company, and board chairman of the Prudential Fire Insurance Company of Oklahoma. He is a member of the United States council of the International Chamber of Commerce, chairman of the transportation and commerce committee of the United States Inter-American Council on Commerce and Production, trustee of the United States Inter-American Council, member of the united business committee of the National Association of Manufacturers, director of the Air Transport Association of America and of the National Safety Council.

Of his civic, educational, and philanthropic activities, the airline executive is perhaps best known for his work with the National Conference of Christians and Jews, which elected him national Catholic cochairman in April 1946. (Serving with him as cochairmen in 1952 are Benson Ford, Protestant, and Roger Straus, Jewish.) In 1947 Braniff was one of a small group associated with Charles Evans Hughes in the founding of a World Council of Christians and Jews, devoted to promoting religious tolerance, and during 1950 he was in Europe setting up the World Brotherhood Organization. The National Conference of Christians and Jews sponsors the National Brotherhood Week (of which Braniff was the Texas chairman), promotes religious tolerance, working with community and church organizations and in industry, and maintains a news service. Braniff is also chairman of the board of directors of the Texas division of the American Cancer Society, a director of the Dallas Community Chest, chairman of the University of Notre Dame Foundation, and a member of the advisory council of that university's College of Commerce, a trustee of Oklahoma City University, a member of the advisory committee of the Dallas Pilot Institute for the Deaf, a trustee of the Institute of International Education, and a member of the advisory council of the Institute of Fiscal and Politcal Education. He is, as well a director of the Dallas Grand Opera Association and a member of the Dallas branch of the English Speaking Union of the United States. He is active in the Boy Scouts. In 1944 Braniff and his wife established the Braniff Foundation, the purpose of which is to support religious, educational, and scientific projects.

The highest honor bestowed by the Pope on a layman came to Braniff in 1944 when he was named Knight Commander of the Order of St. Gregory; he is also a Knight of the Order of the Holy Sepulchre. His clubs in Dallas are the Critic, Brook Hollow Country, Rotary, Downtown, and Notre Dame; in Washington he belongs to the Burning Tree Club; in Kansas City, to the Serra Club and the River Club; in Oklahoma City to the Lotus Club; at the University of Texas, to the Newman Club. He is also on the roster of the Conquistadores del Cielo, an aviation fraternity.

Mrs. Braniff, the former Bess Thurman, daughter of a Missouri judge, was married to Braniff on October 26, 1912. Their two children, Thurman and Jeanne, are deceased. Described as pink-cheeked and affable (the press often speaks of him as Tom Braniff), the airlines head is said to find time to know his employees, and to dress as Santa Claus every Christmas for their children. He plays a leisurely game of golf and likes to take hunting trips.

References

N Y Times Ja 4 '52 p46; D 21 '51, p18
Newsweek 35:67 Je 5 '50; 37:71 Mr 5 '51
Time 45:77+ Ap 16 '45; 55:93+ My 22 '50
Who's Who in America, 1950-51
World Biography (1948)

BRANSOME, EDWIN D(AGOBERT)
(brăn'sŭm dă'gō-bērt) June 18, 1893- Business executive
Address: b. c/o Mack Trucks, Inc., 350 5th Ave., New York 1; h. Rumson, N.J.

Since 1949 the president and chairman of the board of directors of Mack Trucks, Inc., the oldest truck manufacturer in the United States, has been Edwin D. Bransome. Bransome, who has gained a reputation for putting corporations "back on their feet," was president, from 1935 to 1949, of the Vanadium Corporation of America. His earlier connections in the industrial world had been with a welding and metals company and with General Motors. In 1934 he was the deputy administrator of the rubber industry code of the National Recovery Administration and in 1940 he served on the labor divi-

EDWIN D. BRANSOME

sion of the National Defense Commission.

Edwin Dagobert Bransome was born in Philadelphia, Pennsylvania, on June 18, 1893, the son of Dagobert Emile and Marie (Dowd) Bransome. From 1906 to 1908 he was a student at Rockhill Academy, at Ellicott City, Maryland. On completion of his studies at that preparatory school, he enrolled at Ursinus College, at Collegeville, Pennsylvania, from which he was graduated in 1912. Immediately after his college training he became partner in the firm of Reid Waples Company, Philadelphia, a contracting firm which, according to Bransome, took on "any job that came along." One of the jobs was to repair the bulkheads of the Deleware River between tides. In 1917, having for some years been interested in flying, Bransome decided to enlist in the United States Navy as an aviation cadet for World War I duty. Later he was promoted to the rank of lieutenant and air pilot. After two years of military service he accepted a position with the General Motors Company, in New York City.

Beginning as a trainee in the export division of General Motors, Bransome soon became operating manager of the division. He was with GM until 1921, the year he became vice-president and general manager of Wilson Welder & Metals Company, Inc. At that time electric welding was a new industry, in the development of which Bransome is regarded as a pioneer. Nine years later, in 1930, he joined the executive staff of the Air Reduction Company, Inc., as coordinator of business relations. Here he remained for five years. Then, in 1935 he was appointed president of Vanadium Corporation of America, a mining concern which was going through a difficult financial period when Bransome joined it. Within a year, said *Time*, it earned profits of $152,000, its first in six years. He reorganized the mining operations of the company, which was to supply some of the uranium ore for the first atom bomb experiments. By 1944 profits reached $459,000. In 1949 Bransome, who had been on the board of directors of Mack Trucks, Inc., was appointed president and chairman of the board of directors of the truck-making corporation, at a salary of $100,000 a year.

The concern which Bransome heads was founded by three Mack brothers, machinist-blacksmiths and wagonmakers, who in 1900 produced the first gasoline-driven bus in the United States. (It was made for Isaac Harris, who operated it as a sight-seeing bus in Brooklyn's Prospect Park.) The company expanded, producing busses, trucks, and in 1910, the first motor-propelled hook-and-ladder fire department unit in the United States. In time the corporation became the leading heavy truck producing organization in the country, with sales in 1947, a peak year, reaching a total of $124 millions and profits a total of more than $8 millions. The company's products, each carrying the bulldog trademark, became the basis for the common expression, "built like a Mack truck." In the period immediately before Bransome became president, however, the corporation's sales and earnings were well below the average, with a deficit of $3.9 millions.

It became President Bransome's task to correct the situation. He reorganized the executive branch of the company, cut production costs by reducing the number of models manufactured and the number of parts, improved the advertising and public relations program, brought coordination between the sales and production divisions; to cut production costs he enlarged Mack's engine plant in Plainfield, New Jersey, to which he moved its transmission and gear production from a nearby town. By July of 1950 he was able to report to the stockholders a net gain of $64,402 for January-July as compared to a net deficit of $1,653,294 for the first six months of the previous year. By the end of 1950 sales had increased 50 per cent and net income for the year had climbed to $1.3 millions. *Time* magazine, reporting on the improved position of the company and on the executive ability of its president, wrote that Bransome's own formula for success was: "First find out what's wrong, then correct it." Giving credit to his five "top" men, he added:

"We're not supermen doing a superman's job, you know. We just apply common sense."

The industrialist has twice been appointed to posts in the United States Government. In 1934 he served in the National Recovery Administration, heading the rubber industry code. Later commenting on the assignments, he said: "I didn't know one thing about rubber and told NRA that, but they said: 'Then you're just the man we want.'" In 1940, before the War Labor Board was established, Bransome was asked to serve as a member of the National Defense Commission, and to be responsible for assisting industry settle labor disputes that threatened to slow production of defense materials. According to a report of his activities in *United States News,* he earned the respect of both labor and management. In the spring of 1941 Bransome accepted an appointment as chairman of the group of industrial consultants for the Office of Production Management, available for assistance in the adjustment of labor disputes in defense plants.

Since becoming head of Mack Trucks, Inc., Bransome has addressed groups on the relation of the trucking industry to the defense needs of the country. At the twenty-second annual Boston Conference on Distribution, held in October 1950, he maintained that truckers pay more taxes than do railroads while they also are a vital means of transportation. Believing that all types of transportation are needed, he recommended a "live and let live" policy. On March 20, 1951, at a luncheon given in his honor by the transportation section of the New York Board of Trade, he again asked the railroads to cooperate in a program to meet the national emergency by fair competition, instead of issuing "unwarranted and distorted" attacks on the highway users. He spoke in favor of a. increased road-building program, as well as for uniform State laws for trucks.

The business executive has the reputation for being "rough and ready" and "hardfisted." On February 10, 1932, he married Margaretta Homans O'Sullivan; they have three children— Joseph DeWitt, Margaretta Homans, and Edwin Dagobert. His clubs are the Leash, Cloud, Racquet and Tennis, Links of New York, and the Rumson Country in New Jersey.

References

Time 57:93 F 19 '51
U S News 9:36 D 13 '40
Who's Who in America, 1950-51
Who's Who in Commerce and Industry (1951)
Who's Who in the East (1951)
World Biography (1948)

BRAUN, WERNHER VON *See* Von Braun, W.

BRICKELL, (HENRY) HERSCHEL
Sept. 13, 1889—May 29, 1952 Editor and writer; former United States Government official; worked on newspapers in the South and in New York as reporter, editor, copyreader, book columnist (1911-28); editor of Henry Holt and Company, New York (1928-33); cultural relations officer at the United States Embassy in Colombia (1941-44); held other posts in cultural affairs in the Department of State (1944-47); editor of the *O. Henry Memorial Prize Short Stories* since 1940; wrote reviews and literary articles for magazines and newspapers. See *Current Biography,* 1945.

Obituary

N Y Times p10 My 30 '52

BRIND, SIR (ERIC JAMES) PATRICK
(brĭnd) May 12, 1892- British Naval officer
Address: b. c/o Headquarters of Commander in Chief, Allied Forces, Northern Europe, Oslo, Norway.

Named by General Dwight D. Eisenhower in March 1951 as the North Atlantic Treaty Organization's Commander in Chief in Northern Europe as well as Commander of Naval Forces in Northern Europe, British Admiral Sir Patrick Brind during September 1952 directed "Exercise Mainbrace"—a twelve-day, ten-nation land, sea, and air maneuver which tested the defenses of Scandinavia. Prior to his NATO command, he had spent World War II years fighting the German submarine campaign, which was launched from the same ports he is now charged with defending. Brind was one of the British Admiralty's chief naval planners for the Normandy invasion in 1944; six years later he commanded Britain's Far Eastern Fleet in operations at the beginning of the Korean War.

Eric James Patrick Brind is from a family of Army men: the late General Sir James Brind was his grandfather; his father was an officer of the famous Connaught Rangers; and General Sir John Edward Spencer Brind of the Royal Artillery is his eldest brother. Born May 12, 1892, Eric James Patrick Brind, the third son of Colonel E. A. Brind, was brought up at the family home in the ancient English county town of Dorchester. The boy entered the Royal Naval College at Osborne, Isle of Wight, in 1905, about three months before his thirteenth birthday, and two years later proceeded to the Royal Naval College at Dartmouth, Devonshire, for the second half of his officer's training, being "passed out" as midshipman in 1909. Brind served on the gunboat *Excellent* at the beginning of World War I (1914-15) and in 1916 was transferred to H.M.S. *Malaya,* fighting aboard this ship as a lieutenant in the two-day battle of Jutland in May 1916.

Shortly before the fighting ended in 1918, Lieutenant Brind was assigned to the monitor H.M.S. *Moore.* In 1919 he specialized in gunnery on H.M.S. *Excellent,* where he served on several occasions, at one time as senior instructor and at another as second-in-command, being promoted with each transfer until he attained the rank of captain in 1933. His first command was H.M.S. *Orion;* his second was the cruiser *Birmingham,* which was operating from the China Station when World War II began. Brind's "most famous exploit" oc-

British Inf. Services

ADM. SIR PATRICK BRIND

curred in 1939 when he took the *Birmingham* "into the Japanese naval base at Tsingtao and calmly rescued the British merchant ship that had been detained." He did this in the face of a threat "to blow [the] ship and the merchantman out of the water" (John Allan May, *Christian Science Monitor*, March 21, 1951).

For six months during 1940 Captain Brind commanded H.M.S. *Excellent*; then in December 1940 he was appointed chief of staff to the Commander in Chief, Home Fleet, with the rank of commodore, first class. Under Admiral Sir John Tovey he participated, aboard H.M.S. *King George V*, in the sinking of the German battleship *Bismarck* on May 27, 1941, and in the following October was made a Commander of the Order of the British Empire "for distinguished services in the masterly and determined action" which brought about the destruction of the Nazi raider. On February 5, 1942, after having taken part in the first convoy operations to Russia over the northern route, Commodore Brind was promoted to rear-admiral and in May was assigned to the Admiralty in London as an Assistant Chief of Naval Staff. Here he remained for two and a half years, helping to plan naval operations ranging from small raids to large-scale cooperative actions involving the Navy and the invasion forces in North Africa, Italy, and Normandy.

In July 1944 Rear-Admiral Brind was made a Companion of the Order of the Bath "for distinguished services in the planning and execution of the successful allied landings in Normandy." Assigned at the end of 1944 to his first seagoing command since reaching flag rank, Brind joined the newly formed Pacific Fleet as rear-admiral commanding the 4th Cruiser Squadron and participated in the bombardment of Truk and other Japanese strongholds. He was present in Tokyo Bay in Sep-

tember 1945 when Japan surrendered, and the next month he was promoted to vice-admiral. In January 1946 he was recalled from the Pacific for special duty with the Admiralty in London and was so engaged when that summer he was created a Knight Commander of the Bath for his services in the Pacific. (Previously he had been referred to in naval dispatches and releases as Eric J. P. Brind, but after receiving the accolade of knighthood he preferred to be called Sir Patrick Brind.) From October 1946 to the end of 1948 Sir Patrick was on shore duty as president of the Royal Naval College in Greenwich, near London, where this "expert on naval history" (British Central Information Office release) spent much of his spare time browsing in the museum.

With the rank of full admiral, Brind in January 1949 returned to the Orient as Commander in Chief of the British Far East Station and as such "was associated with the dramatic escape in 1949 of the battered British frigate *Amethyst*, which Chinese Communists had attacked and held as hostage in the Yangtse River" (J. A. May in the *Christian Science Monitor*). When the Korean War began in June 1950 Admiral Brind's fleet of twenty-two ships, including the aircraft carrier *Triumph* and three cruisers, was on a summer cruise in Japanese waters. The Admiral dispatched ten warships to convoy United States troops to Korea and to cover their first landings, while directing another part of the fleet to assist in land resistance to Communist-backed bandits in Malaya.

Recalled to England in February 1951, Admiral Brind, who a month earlier had been elevated to Knight Grand Cross Order of the British Empire, relinquished his Far East command to Admiral Sir Guy Russell. On March 20, 1951, Brind was named by General Dwight D. Eisenhower, then Supreme Commander, Allied Powers in Europe, to be the North Atlantic Treaty Organization's Commander in Chief, Northern Europe, and Commander of Naval Forces, Northern Europe. In this double capacity Brind "is to act as General Eisenhower's chief representative in that area, in an over-all military sense, and will also be in command of Allied naval forces in the area" (*Christian Science Monitor*, March 21, 1951). Hanson W. Baldwin of the New York *Times* pointed out that the water around Norway and part of the North Sea assigned to British Admiral Brind were specifically excluded from the NATO Atlantic command then assigned to United States Admiral William M. Fechteler.

Brind set up headquarters in Volksenkollen, near Oslo, and in September 1952 supervised and conducted the twelve-day NATO naval maneuvers known as "Exercise Mainbrace." Characterized by Hanson W. Baldwin as "the biggest Allied naval exercise in modern history," and designed to test the defense strategy for Scandinavia, this operation covered 500,000 square miles of water and engaged more than 180 warships, 1,000 aircraft, and 80,000 men of ten nations. Action of "orange" and "blue" attacking and defense forces was based on a supposed pincers movement on Scandinavia launched from the east southward across the northern frontier of Norway and up from occupied Germany into southern Denmark. After the Mainbrace exercise, Brind stated in a press conference: "First that the Atlantic alliance European and Atlantic commands should conduct another exercise like Mainbrace to provide additional training and iron out the 'wrinkles' revealed by the operations of the last two weeks; second, that the exercise showed great progress in the development of an international military team" (in the words of the New York *Times*, September 27, 1952).

Admiral Sir Patrick Brind holds the American Legion of Merit among his decorations. His club is the United Service in London. By his first wife, the former Eileen Margaret Apperly, whom he married in 1918, he is the father of one daughter, Patricia Helen, who was married to Captain John Hanson in 1944. His first wife died in 1940 and on January 22, 1948, the admiral married Edith Gordon Blagrove, widow of Rear-Admiral Blagrove. Admiral Brind, stated a British Central Information Office release, "has great personal charm and is known throughout the Royal Navy for his kindliness and humor and for the keen interest he takes in the welfare of those who serve under him." The British admiral, as described by Hanson W. Baldwin, "has white hair, a patina of laughter wrinkles around his eyes, and bushy tufted eyebrows." He stands six feet four inches tall and has a "husky" build.

References

Christian Sci Mon p4 Mr 21 '51

Debrett's Peerage, Baronetage, Knightage and Companionage (1952)
International Who's Who, 1952
Kelly's Handbook to the Titled, Landed, and Official Classes, 1952
Who's Who, 1952

BRITTON, EDGAR C(LAY) Oct. 25, 1891- Chemist

Address: b. c/o Dow Chemical Company, Midland, Mich.; h. 2306 Eastman Rd.; Midland, Mich.

For the year 1952 the president of the American Chemical Society is Edgar C. Britton, director of organic research at the Dow Chemical Company and holder of more than 260 patents for synthetic organic chemicals. Associated with the chemical corporation since 1920, Britton has directed the research which developed new insecticides, weed killers, and pharmaceuticals. The chemist began his career as a teaching assistant at the University of Michigan in 1914, where he later became an instructor and for one year was the acting head of the Chemistry Department.

Edgar Clay Britton was born in Rockville, Indiana, on October 25, 1891, the son of Joseph Albert and Bertha Elizabeth (Hirshbrunner) Britton. His father had practiced law in Kansas before moving to Indiana; in Rockville he became a builder of covered wooden bridges. Edgar Britton, who attended the local schools and sold newspapers in his spare time, helped

EDGAR C. BRITTON

on the building of six of the twenty bridges constructed by the elder Britton. Money earned in this work as well as from waiting on table, clerking in a men's clothing store, and teaching in the Indiana grade school system, paid for the youth's college education. This was begun in 1911 at Wabash College (in Crawfordsville, Indiana), which he entered with the intention of studying to become a lawyer. However, according to an account in *Chemical and Engineering News*, on the train taking him to his first year at Wabash Britton met an upperclassman who suggested that he talk over his future courses with Professor Garner, then head of Wabash's Chemistry Department. A brief conversation with the chemistry professor resulted in Britton's choosing chemistry as his major.

Britton remained at Wabash for three years, studying chiefly under Professor Garner, who, according to Britton, "was the type of man—well, you either got interested in chemistry or you got out of the course." For the last year of undergraduate study, Britton attended the University of Michigan, which awarded him his B.A. degree in 1915. During the next three years, as a graduate chemistry student he was employed as a teaching assistant at Michigan. His advanced work in organic chemistry was carried out under the direction of William J. Hale, and on its completion in 1918 he received the Ph.D. degree. For two years, from 1918 to 1920, the chemist was an instructor at the University of Michigan and for one year served as acting head of the Chemistry Department. At the end of that time, Hale, who had become director of organic research for the Dow Chemical Company (in Midland, Michigan) asked his former student to become his assistant. After twelve years as a research chemist for the organization, Britton in 1932 was appointed to the position which he continues to hold in 1952, that of director of the organic

BRITTON, EDGAR C.—*Continued*

research laboratory. He is also vice-chairman of Dow's executive research committee, as well as a director and the secretary of the board of the Dow Corning Corporation, a subsidiary of the Dow Chemical Company.

When Britton joined the chemical company its research facilities were limited to a small, one-room laboratory, and its personnel consisted of Hale and Britton. In 1952 Dow's organic chemical research is carried on by approximately fifty chemists in a modern three-story building. According to *Chemical and Engineering News*, Britton's research interests have ranged widely—"all the way from the photochlorination of cyclohexane to the synthesis of complex amino acids." He has worked on the phenols, amines, and halogen compounds; the acetic acids, insecticides, fungicides, pharmaceuticals, veterinary medicines, essential amino acids, detergents, and plastics and plasticizers. During the more than three decades that Britton has been associated with Dow his research has produced many new synthetic organic chemicals; more than 260 patents for these chemicals have been issued in his name. In addition, his work has resulted in the development of new catalysts, to speed up the conversion of oil refinery by-products into synthetic rubber. He has also improved methods for producing carbolic acid and acetic acid. Britton's articles and reports of findings have appeared in various scientific journals, and he is the coauthor of several articles on the phenol process in chlorobenzol Freidel-Craft reaction, on phenols in industry, and on the synthesis of methionine.

The organization to which Britton is attached is one of the larger chemical companies in the United States, principally producing industrial, pharmaceutical, and agricultural chemicals, and plastics and magnesium. Though its main plants are located at Midland, other plants of the parent company and the plants of its four wholly owned subsidiaries (engaged in the production of natural gas, magnesium, styron, and other chemical products, as well as in the treatment of oil and gas wells) are located elsewhere in the United States and in Canada.

For many years a member of the American Chemical Society, Britton in 1933 was chairman of the Midland Section of the scientific organization and from 1933 to 1951 was one of the councilors. His other activity in the society has consisted of serving as acting chairman of the division of organic chemistry in 1935, as head of the committee on the revision of the constitution and by-laws in 1947, and as member of the committee on hazardous chemicals and explosives. In 1949 he was elected a director at large of the society; the next year he was chosen president-elect; and in December of 1951 the membership of 67,000 elected him president for 1952, to succeed Professor N. Howell Furman. The American Chemical Society, founded in 1876, is the largest scientific association in the world. Its publications, *Chemical Abstracts, Chemical and Engineering News,* and *Industrial and Engineering Chemis-*

try, are among the most widely circulated journals in science and applied science.

Britton, who was an appointee to the United States National Defense Research Committee, maintains memberships in a number of professional societies: the American Association for the Advancement of Science, the American Institute of Chemists, the Society of Chemical Industry, and the Chemical Society of London. His fraternities are Alpha Chi Sigma, Pi Lambda Upsilon, and Sigma Xi; other of his associations are the Chemists' Club of New York, the Torch, Kiwanis Club, the Odd Fellows, and the Midland Country Club. He is a Republican and a Methodist. Britton's marriage to Grace Van Huss, which took place on June 29, 1916, terminated in divorce in 1937. The couple had three children, Harold E., Joseph H., and Leunis G. On December 25, 1937, he married Mildred A. Proud, from which union there are two children, Linda Ann and Daniel E.

Britton is known among his associates as a "working" chemist—he may be found during the day in any one of his nine laboratories at the Dow plant, carrying out the details of experiments himself. "No chemist," he says, "knows what he should about a reaction he has obtained until he has accounted for every chemical put into it." Research chemists under him find they have considerable freedom in their work and in their choice of projects. "If a boy has an idea," *Chemical and Engineering News* reported Britton as commenting, "we tell him to go ahead. After all, I never say 'no' to anybody." With fishing, hunting, gardening, golf, and "the whole outdoors" as his hobbies, Britton spends his free time at a cabin fifty miles north of Midland.

References

Chem & Eng N 25:3058 O 20 '47; 27: 3108 O 24 '49; 30:80 Ja 7 '52
Oil Paint & Drug Rep 158:7 D 18 '50
American Men of Science (1949)
Who's Who in America, 1950-51
World Biography (1948)

BRO, MARGUERITTE HARMON Aug. 5, 1894- Author

Address: b. c/o Doubleday & Company, Inc., Garden City, N.Y.; h. Cable, Wis.

Reprinted from the *Wilson Library Bulletin,* Sept. 1952.

When a high school principal asked the then eleven-year-old daughter of Margueritte Harmon Bro what her mother did in her spare time, the youngster replied, "I don't know. She never had any."

This succinct statement is supported by the list of Mrs. Bro's published works, and the truth becomes more apparent when the usual biographical data of birth, school, marriage, and subsequent career are listed.

Margueritte Harmon Bro was born a Midwesterner and a P.K. (preacher's kid), in David City, Nebraska, August 5, 1894, to the former Alice Gadd and Andrew Davison Harmon, who was pastor of the First Christian Church there. Then he was called to a parish in Minnesota, and young Margueritte began her education in St. Paul. High school was interrupted by another transfer of the father to northern Wisconsin, where Margueritte was able to finish those important years at Ashland Academy. Her college work with a B.A. degree and a philosophy major was completed at Cotner College in Lincoln, Nebraska, in 1917. This was followed by graduate study at Butler University in Indianapolis, Indiana, and the University of Chicago.

In May 1918, Margueritte Harmon was married to Albin Carl Bro, whom she had met at Ashland Academy in Wisconsin, and the following year they went to China, where Mr. Bro was in educational work.

Three of their four children were born in China, a bit spectacularly. Harmon Hartzell arrived in Nanking on Christmas Eve, and when the caroling students sang "Hark the Herald Angels" for him, the young mother said she felt "the messiahship in all new babies." Kenneth appeared in Tsingtao in a new house by the sea, where the doctor had to climb a ladder because the stairs were not yet in. Alice, young number three, was born in Kuling in the mountains, during a typhoon. Andrew is the only one of the boys who can qualify for the American presidency. He was born in Chicago.

It was during the China years that Mrs. Bro began to write, though one suspects writing was latent in her blood. She had been a contest winner with a first story when in the seventh grade. The prize was a copy of *Helen's Babies*, which was a precious property up to the time it was stolen by bandits in China.

Her versatile activities in the preparatory years, as teacher, pastor's assistant, editor for *Harper's*, book reviewing, some ghost writing, additional graduate study at the University of Nanking, all helped to lay the foundation for the variety in her published books. *Let's Talk About You* (1945) is a book for teen-age girls, dealing with their problems in the social structure. In reviewing it for the Chicago *Sun Book Week*, Phyllis Whitney said, "Here, if ever, is a handbook of good sense for girls from twelve to eighteen."

More than We Are (1948), a book on prayer, had an even wider audience. Virginia Kirkus called it "among the best of the recent devotional books, both as to content and style." Also, the *Christian Century* said, "Its excellence lies partly in its simplicity and directness . . . that its language is completely understandable."

Mrs. Bro's first book-length story, *Sarah*, a junior novel, was published in 1949. It was listed in the *Library Journal* with this comment, "Reality which goes below the surface and a noble character who is convincing make this a fine book for older teen-age girls and young adults." Mary Gould Davis wrote in the *Saturday Review*, "A thoughtful book in which a philosophy of life is analyzed by interesting, convincing people."

MARGUERITTE HARMON BRO

Sarah is the story of a girl's unfolding, from her eleventh year, when her doctor father died, through her development as a concert pianist. The scene is New England.

From Vermont Mrs. Bro turned to China for her next book, *Su-Mei's Golden Year* (1950). It is the story of a young Chinese girl and of the clash between ancient Chinese superstitions and modern farming methods. Of it the New York *Herald Tribune* said, "A rich variety of people and of ideas, as well as good story quality, make this a rewarding book for any reader of ten or older."

Mrs. Bro now lives in Indonesia, where her husband is cultural officer in the United States Information Service. Bali will provide the background for the next book, the story of a little girl who wants to be a *legong* dancer. This is an ancient, precise, difficult dance performed by girls between the ages of nine and fourteen, after rigorous training. It will be an authentic book, for Mrs. Bro has traveled extensively, witnessing actual ceremonies and gathering material to make the story real. Following the publication of the Bali story, there are plans under way for an adult book on marriage problems, and a teen-age book on comparative religions.

Between China and exciting escapes from mobs and bandits—one of them a sort of marathon to reach the last boat down the Yangt-ze for many months—and present life in Bali, there was a period of service in Korea, and a longer one when Dr. Bro was president of Shimer College in Illinois; and always the writing, a steady flow of magazine articles and reviews.

Mrs. Bro is a poised five feet five, with graying hair now and eyes that remain gray or green according to mood, with a fine sense of humor—she can laugh at herself and is her own severest critic. She likes to swim and walk, and reading is a must.

BROPHY, THOMAS D'ARCY Oct. 18, 1893- Advertising executive; patriotic organization official
Address: b. c/o Kenyon & Eckhardt, Inc., 247 Park Ave., New York 17; c/o American Heritage Foundation, 25 W. 45th St., New York 36; h. 45 Brewster Rd., Scarsdale, N. Y.

For more than thirty years Thomas D'Arcy Brophy, chairman of the advertising agency Kenyon and Eckhardt, Inc., has been engaged in various phases of advertising, and for more than twenty of those years he has been associated with the firm he now heads. He joined the organization in 1931, after ten years in

Jean Raeburn

THOMAS D'ARCY BROPHY

sales and promotion, was elected president in 1937, and became chairman in 1949. Active in a number of civic and patriotic organizations, he has been president of the American Heritage Foundation since its establishment in 1947.

Thomas D'Arcy Brophy was born October 18, 1893, in Butte, Montana, to Patrick Jerome and Margaret (D'Arcy) Brophy. His father, born in Ireland, was a merchant who became Fuel Administrator for Montana during World War I. Young Brophy received the B.A. degree in 1912 from Gonzaga College in Spokane, Washington, and four years later the B.S. degree from the Massachusetts Institute of Technology. During World War I he rose from second lieutenant to major, serving successively as instructor at the Artillery School at Fort Monroe, Virginia, and as Assistant to the Chief of Artillery in Washington, D.C.

Following a brief association, during 1919-20, with the South Atlantic Maritime Corporation of New York, where he was assistant to the president, Brophy joined the Anaconda Copper Mining Company in 1921 to establish a department of sales research and promotion.

He remained with the company until 1929, heading that department and serving in the same capacity for the American Brass Company and affiliated companies. During the same period he also became vice-president and director and a member of the executive committee of the Copper and Brass Research Association. His next post, which he occupied from 1929 until 1931, was as vice-president and chairman of the sales committee of Revere Copper and Brass, Inc.

Joining Kenyon and Eckhardt, Inc., the advertising firm, as vice-president in 1931, Brophy was elected president on December 9, 1937, succeeding Henry Eckhardt. A year later, on December 19, 1938, the company opened a Canadian office in Montreal, and since 1949 Brophy has been chairman of both branches of the firm. During 1942 and 1943, and again from 1943 to 1945, he was vice-president and director of the American Association of Advertising Agencies; in April 1947 he was elected vice-chairman of the association's board of directors and a year later, on April 8, 1948, its chairman. Addressing a convention of the Advertising Federation of America in June of that year, Brophy asserted, as reported in the New York *Sun*: "Advertising has the public's eye and ear through all the hours of the day, and people are forming many of their strongest opinions about free competitive business from what the advertising industry is saying. . . .As a consequence, advertising men must ask themselves when looking at an advertisement not only 'will it sell?' but also 'does it serve?' " On April 9, 1949, at a meeting of the American Association of Advertising Agencies, he again urged the advertising profession to gain and hold public confidence, and to observe the truth strictly in its relations with both clients and the general public.

During World War II Brophy placed his services as an advertising executive at the disposal of the USO, acting as director and chairman of its committee on public information (1941-47). He described the campaign he directed in behalf of the USO in these words: "Known and proven techniques of advertising were employed, and it is believed that, for the first time, advertising methods which have been so successful in selling the mass production products of American industries, have been applied in full to a patriotic effort." From 1943 to 1945 he was also a director and member of the executive committee of the National War Fund.

A more recent affiliation of Brophy's is with the American Heritage Foundation, a nonpartisan group brought into existence in February 1947 "to awaken pride in our past, a wider recognition of our obligation to maintain our free institutions, and a more extensive participation by citizens in the processes of democracy." As president of the foundation since 1947, he headed the campaign to publicize the Freedom Train, which carried to many cities in the country some 150 basic, original documents of American history. On September 25, 1947, at the ceremonies attending the departure of the Freedom Train from New York City, the American Legion presented its Americanism medal to Brophy. A year later, when the train paid a return visit to New York in December 1948, he was awarded a good citizenship medal by the Sons of the American Revolution for his "skillful organization" and "tactful direction" in making the train a symbol of rededication to the ideals of America's past.

When the American Heritage Foundation announced plans in June 1951 for a national Year of Rededication to the principles of the Declaration of Independence, Brophy pointed out, "Only by active personal participation in the affairs of our country, locally and nationally, can we safeguard our freedom." On April 2, 1952, the foundation announced a campaign, to be conducted in association with the Advertising Council, of which Brophy has been a director since 1941, to bring 80,000,000 citizens to the polls in 1952, a figure 30,000,000 higher than the number of voters in the 1948 Presidential election. Brophy proposed on April 29, 1952, that a committee of citizens be formed to plan for the celebration in 1953 of the three hundredth anniversary of the incorporation of New York City as New Amsterdam.

Brophy was a trustee of the Village of Scarsdale, New York, during 1936-38; he is also a director of the National Outdoor Advertising Bureau, a member of the committee on public interest of the Community Service Society, chairman of the public information committee of the United Negro College Fund, director of American Youth Hostels, vice-president and chairman of the committee on education of the Greater New York Civic Center Association, alumni member of the corporation of the Massachusetts Institute of Technology, member of the executive committee and chairman of the visiting committee of the Department of Business and Engineering Administration of the same institution. He is an honorary commander of the Order of the British Empire. In addition to the awards cited, he received the Civic Service Award of the National Conference of Christians and Jews in 1950 and the Distinguished Service Medal of the School of Journalism of Syracuse University in 1951. Brophy is a member of Chi Phi fraternity, the University Club of New York, Scarsdale Golf Club, Shenerock Shore Club, and Fox Meadow Tennis Club. The advertising executive married Jessie Milligan on October 9, 1923. Their son, Thomas D'Arcy, Jr., died in the Philippine Sea area in World War II. Their daughters are named Cynthia Ann (Mrs. John L. Cleveland, Jr.), and Joan Sheila.

References

Business Executives of America (1950)
Who's Who in America, 1952-53
Who's Who in Commerce and Industry (1951)

BURDELL, EDWIN S(HARP) (bûr-děl')
Feb. 2, 1898- College president; sociologist
Address: b. c/o The Cooper Union for the Advancement of Science and Art, Cooper Sq., New York 3; h. 32 Washington Sq., New York 11

Dr. Edwin S. Burdell, who was installed in November 1938 as the sixth director of the Cooper Union for the Advancement of Science and Art, New York City, is known as an exponent of the educational philosophy of scientific humanism. He is also an authority in the

Fabian Bachrach
EDWIN S. BURDELL

fields of urban sociology, town and city planning, European theories of adult education, housing conditions and projects, and problems of youth and unemployment. For four years (1934-38) a professor of sociology at the Massachusetts Institute of Technology, he was also, for the last of those four years, the institute's Dean of Humanities. Dr. Burdell's official title was changed from director to president of Cooper Union in the summer of 1951.

Youngest of the three sons of William Frederick and Jennie Nottingham (Kelsey) Burdell, Edwin Sharp Burdell was born February 2, 1898, in Columbus, Ohio. His father, who died in 1945, was president (later chairman) of the board of the local Huntington National Bank; he was (in the words of Karl T. Compton, former president of the Massachusetts Institute of Technology) "all his life a leader in the work for good citizenship," and to his example may be ascribed in large measure his third son's subsequent interest in sociology. The boy's early ambition, however, was to become an engineer; and after attending the Columbus public schools (until 1911), the Asheville School in North Carolina (1911-15), and the Chauncey Hall School in Boston, Massachusetts (1915-16), he entered the Massachusetts Insti-

BURDELL, EDWIN S.—*Continued*

tute of Technology. Burdell's engineering studies were interrupted (1918-19) by service as a second lieutenant of infantry in World War I, in the course of which (again quoting Dr. Compton) he "received experience in executive procedures in the army." For this and other reasons he decided, after demobilization and one additional year as a student of engineering administration at M.I.T., to change his objective. After studying at the Harvard Graduate School of Business Administration (1920-21) and teaching for a time in 1922 at M.I.T., he joined his father's banking enterprise, and in the next three years acquired a grasp of finance. Already interested in civic improvement, he began in 1923 nine years of service as vice-chairman of the Columbus Board of Zoning Adjustment, while in the following year he began a three years' visit of observation and study in Europe, Mexico, and Central America. Burdell was the first American to be graduated from the French National Scout Leaders' training school at Château Cappy.

In 1928 Burdell entered Ohio State University for postgraduate study, took his M.A. degree in the following year, and was appointed to an instructorship in urban sociology and social research. He became a member of the Ohio State Commission on State Unemployment Insurance in 1932, served also as director of the Ohio State University School for the Unemployed, and in 1933 was named director of the Ohio Emergency Schools Administration. Burdell also contributed articles on social service problems and training (for example, his "Apprenticeship for Board Members" and "What's the Matter with Volunteers?" to *Survey* for December 15, 1930, and April 15, 1932, respectively) to various periodicals before completing his doctoral dissertation entitled *A Method of Investigating the Administration of the Zoning Ordinance in Columbus, 1923-31.* He received his doctorate in sociology from Ohio State University in 1934. (Ten years later (1944) he was elected to Phi Beta Kappa, Epsilon Chapter, "in recognition of his high attainments in liberal scholarship.")

Largely on the strength of his record in what Compton has characterized as "organizing a remarkable system of education at all levels" among the Ohio Unemployed, Burdell was invited in 1934 to return to M.I.T. as an associate professor of sociology. In 1935 he added to his duties those of director of the M.I.T. Summer School, and in the ensuing year also assumed the chairmanship of the institute's museum committee. A paper he published in *School and Society* for November 12, 1936, on "Scientific Humanism" (a term which he later defined as meaning "a marriage of science and the accumulated culture of the past") led in 1937 to his appointment as Dean of Humanities at M.I.T. with the rank of full professor and with the departments of English, history, modern languages, economics, and social science under his supervision. While a professor at M.I.T. Burdell served also (1935-38) as a member of the Massachusetts State Board of Prison Industries, and for two-year periods as

a consultant of the Massachusetts Planning Board (zoning administration), the Cambridge Board of Family Welfare Service, and the Boston Housing Association. Since 1946 he has been a member of the visiting committee in the departments of English and history at M.I.T.

The Cooper Union for the Advancement of Science and Art, in the directorship of which Dr. Burdell was installed November 3, 1938, was established by Peter Cooper in 1859 with the purpose (among others) of offering young men and women free college-level education. The main building occupies an "island" plot at the north end of the Bowery in New York City, and its "great hall" (at present used for the well-known Cooper Union Forums) is celebrated as the scene (in 1860) of one of Abraham Lincoln's most important speeches. The bachelor's degree is granted by the School of Engineering in chemical, civil, electrical, and mechanical engineering, while the School of Art "trains talented young people in the fine or graphic arts or in architecture." In the words of a Union brochure, "potential talent" is the "primary requirement for admission . . . without regard to race, creed, color, or place of residence in the U.S.A." Applicants for the Union's day and evening courses are selected through competitive examinations, and standards have been and remain exceptionally high. Graduates in the school's earlier days included such famous men as Michael Pupin, Justice Felix Frankfurter, and the sculptor Augustus Saint-Gaudens; but later (according to an article by Roger Burlingame in the *American Mercury*) there was a lapse from "its early tradition of vitality."

When the electrical engineer Gano Dunn became president of the board in 1935 he was (said Burlingame) "disturbed by what he saw, which seemed to him a departure from Peter Cooper's declaration of 1859: 'The great object I desire to accomplish . . . is to open the volume of nature by the light of truth.' ". To improve a curriculum which provided "little inspiration to leadership, no understanding of history, philosophy, literature, economics or government," Dunn turned to Edwin Burdell.

"As an undergraduate . . . twenty years ago," stated Dr. Burdell in his installation address as director of Cooper Union on November 3, 1938, "I saw the intellectual narrowness of the man who 'does things,' who regards music, languages, literature and especially the social sciences with indifference." He then outlined a policy of "scientific humanism," inaugurating six required courses in civilization.

In his thirteen years as head of Cooper Union, Dr. Burdell has maintained numerous sociological, educational, and professional affiliations. Chairman of the Community Service Society's Committee on Housing since 1938 and a trustee of the society since 1942, he is also a member of the board of the Citizens Housing Council. Burdell was a member of the commission of the Society for the Promotion of Engineering Education which wrote *Aims and Scope of Engineering Education* (1940), and of another commission which was responsible for *Engineering Education After the War* (1944); he is the author of the chapter

"Architects and Sociologists in a Post-War World" in Paul Zucker's symposium *New Architecture and City Planning*. For many years, too, Dr. Burdell has been an authority on adult education in Denmark, and in 1946 was awarded the King Christian X Medal of Liberation for his interpretation of Danish education and culture to America. In 1949 the educator was appointed by the president of the American Institute of Architects (of which he became an honorary member in 1951) to the chairmanship of a national commission to survey architectural education and registration. He is a cofounder of United Medical Service, a nonprofit medical and surgical indemnity plan operated in conjunction with Associated Hospital Services.

In the summer of 1951 the Cooper Union constitution was amended to change Burdell's official title from director to president, and that of Gano Dunn to chairman of the board. Burdell's annual report for the same year was largely devoted to a forecast of the probably adverse impact of universal military training on American colleges and students. He said further: "Quite independent of wars and their consequences, I am convinced that the traditional four years of high school and college can be regrouped to advantage. To begin with, I would consider combining junior high school and the first two years of senior high school into one four-year experience, which for want of a better term I would call 'middle school.' I would follow that by a two-year terminal junior college course, at the end of which I would award associate in arts or science degrees to young men and women at the ages of eighteen or nineteen."

Burdell is a fellow of the American Academy of Arts and Sciences, and a member of the Newcomen Society, the American Society for Engineering Education, the Architectural League, the American Sociological Society, the Municipal Art Society (member of the board since 1946), the American Institute of Planners, and board of visitors to Letchworth Village. He belongs to the Sigma Chi fraternity, the Sons of the Revolution, the Pilgrim Society; and to the Century, Technology, and Church clubs in New York City. An Episcopalian, he is a vestryman of Grace Church, New York, and a member of the Episcopal Diocesan Committee on College Work. Mrs. Burdell is the former Emma Metthea Mathiasen; married on April 2, 1917, they are the parents of Mrs. Karla Kelsey Fender and Mary Metthea Burdell. The Cooper Union president is above medium height and gray-haired. His hobbies are gardening and cats.

References

Am Mercury 70:231-8 F '50
N Y Times p21 F 21 '38 por
Newsweek 12:34-5 N 14 '38 por
Sch & Soc 48:605-19 N 12 '38
Time 32:36 N 14 '38 por
America's Young Men, 1938-39
Directory of American Scholars (1942)
International World Who's Who (1949)
Leaders in Education (1948)
Who's Who in America, 1950-51
Who's Who in American Education, 1947-48
Who's Who in Government, 1932-33
Who's Who in New York, 1947
Who's Who in the East (1951)
World Biography (1948)

BURDICK, USHER L(LOYD) Feb. 21, 1879- United States Representative from North Dakota

Address: b. House Office Bldg., Washington 25, D.C.; c/o Burdick & Burdick, Williston, N.D.; h. Williston, N.D.

One of the elder members of the House of Representatives in point of age, though not of party seniority, is Congressman Usher L. Burdick of North Dakota, an Independent Republican supported by the Nonpartisan League. A lawyer, rancher, and writer on Western history, Burdick is also a past Lieutenant Governor of his State. First elected to Congress in 1934, he retained his seat until 1944, when he ran for the Senate and was defeated. He was re-elected to the Eighty-first Congress in November 1948, to the Eighty-second in 1950, and to the Eighty-third in 1952.

Youngest of the children of Ozias Warren and Lucy (Farnum) Burdick, Usher Lloyd Burdick was born February 21, 1879, on a farm near Owatonna, Minnesota. His father, a native of Vermont, was a descendant of the Robert Burdick who came to the American colonies from England in 1634; his mother, born in New York State, was of Norman ancestry. The couple had settled in Minnesota's Steele County shortly after the end of the Civil War, through which Ozias Burdick had fought in the Union Army. After discouraging efforts at farming, the elder Burdick decided to move farther westward, to homestead in the Dakota Territory. Usher Burdick was three years old at that time. At Graham's Island the future Congressman attended a district school established in 1885, learned to shoot and to lasso, and acquired from the Indians his knowledge of the Sioux tongue. (Details of his boyhood years may be found in Burdick's "Recollections and Reminiscences of Graham's Island," which ran in three issues of *North Dakota History* in 1949.) He was ten years old when North Dakota was admitted to the Union as the thirty-ninth State, and seventeen when he entered the North Dakota State Teachers College at Mayville, where he majored in history and from which he received his teacher's certificate in 1900. (He was later to receive the B.A. degree in education.)

Burdick was appointed deputy superintendent of Benson County schools, but a year later his marriage to Emma (Rassmussen) Robertson (on September 5, 1901) and a local political feud caused him to change his objectives and seek to fit himself for the practice of law. He enrolled at the University of Minnesota, where his 220 pounds and record of running a hundred yards in 10.5 seconds put him on the football team—he played right end on the Minnesota teams of 1903 and 1904, which won the "Big Ten" championship. To meet expenses for him-

Vincent A. Finnigan

USHER L. BURDICK

self and his wife, who also entered the university, he taught in a business college. Burdick acquired his LL.B. degree from Minnesota in 1904; he also holds a Ph.B. degree.

Admitted to the North Dakota bar in 1904, Burdick began practicing at Munich, where he also became credit manager for the First National Bank. Three years later (1907) he was elected to the State legislature as a progressive-minded Republican (his chief influences, he says, have been Washington, Jefferson, Lincoln, and "Teddy" Roosevelt); and after re-election in 1909 he became its speaker, the youngest in the United States. In 1910 Burdick moved to Williston, the administrative seat of Williams County, his present place of legal residence. He was elected Lieutenant Governor in 1911. As judge of the State Senate he presided over the only impeachment trial ever held in North Dakota and, on completion of this executive term at Bismarck, held the office of States Attorney for Williams County (1913-14). Subsequently, he served as a special prosecutor (1915-20). It was during this latter period that he made his only try, as a Progressive Republican, for the governorship. Arthur Townley's Nonpartisan League had gained power in 1917, and Burdick, who was sympathetic with its aims, withdrew his own candidacy after two weeks of campaigning.

From 1920 to 1929 he was engaged in law practice, livestock breeding, and farming, and to some extent also in writing. In 1929 he published *The Last Battle of the Sioux Nation* (the Custer battle), the first of importance among the twenty-two pamphlets or books on Western history or Americana that bear his name. Among his subsequent longer works in this field were to be *The Life of George Sperry Loftus* (1939), *Tales from Buffalo Land*; *the Story of Fort Buford* (1940), *The Last Days of Sitting Bull* (1941). Burdick has brought

to light rare short items of Lincolniana, and in 1944 published in a limited edition his own *History of the Farmers Political Action in North Dakota.*

Named Assistant District Attorney in 1929, Burdick served as such until March 1932, when he announced his candidacy for the Republican nomination for one of North Dakota's two Representatives at large in Congress. His experience as a Federal prosecutor of "dry law" cases having convinced him that the Prohibition amendment had been a mistake, he advocated repeal, at the same time supporting Franklin D. Roosevelt over Herbert Hoover for President. Burdick was defeated in 1932, but tried again two years later and was elected, with Nonpartisan League support, to the Seventy-fourth Congress, which convened in January 1935. On the Indian Affairs, Pensions, and Territories committees, the North Dakotan cut across party lines by casting his first important vote in favor of the Democratic Administration's work relief bill, though he later opposed both Social Security and the Eccles banking bill. In the summer of 1936 he gave another indication of unorthodoxy by supporting the candidacy for President of his fellow Representative at large from North Dakota, William Lemke, and managing the campaign of the latter's short-lived Union party. In consequence, when he himself took his seat in the next (Seventy-fifth) Congress, he lost his seniority rights by order of the Republican high command.

In the Seventy-fifth Congress (1937-38) Burdick voted in favor of the Roosevelt Supreme Court retirement bill, against investigation of sit-down strikes, and for the Wagner housing bill; and during the Seventy-sixth (1939-40) he opposed a majority of his party in voicing approval of the nomination of Frank Murphy as Attorney General and declaring in debate that while "monumental mistakes" had been made by the New Deal, "it must be admitted by all that the President has been actuated by the highest motives." Also, during this Congress he introduced for the first time his bill to restrain "any Congressman, Cabinet member, Federal judge, or appointive executive officer from making public addresses for pay, on penalty of forfeiture of his office." The bill was brought up again by Burdick in 1941, but was buried in a subcommittee.

In the matter of foreign and military policy, Usher Burdick, like most of the other legislators from the prairie States, was an isolationist until Pearl Harbor. As early as March 1937 he was voting for embargo on the peacetime exporting of munitions. He opposed naval expansion in 1939, conscription in 1940, and lend lease in 1941. He stated his general position at a Washington Peace Rally in June 1940, when he asserted that "this nation is in no position to tell others what to do or to assist them in their wars when we are unable to stop their wars." After Pearl Harbor he "openly and publicly recanted" (New York *Post*), declaring that "when the country is engaged in war" he is "for this country, right or wrong." Subsequently, Burdick further declared that he favored "straight-out participation in some international organization" to prevent another world conflict. Thus he voted for the Fulbright resolution in 1943 and in March 1944, while serving his tenth consecutive year in the House, was chosen by the Nonpartisan League (and Senator William Langer) to fight the renomination of isolationist Senator Gerald P. Nye as Republican candidate for the Senate. Burdick, who made Nye's isolationism his chief issue, lost to Nye on that issue in the June primaries. His Senate candidacy also cost him his seat in the House, since he could not in the circumstances seek re-election as Representative at large.

The North Dakotan returned to his ranch at Williston and his law practice (as senior partner of the firm of Burdick & Burdick) at Williston and Fargo. Offering himself again for Republican nomination as Representative at large in the State primaries of 1948, he defeated (with Nonpartisan League support) the incumbent Representative Charles S. Robertson (who had the backing of the party "regulars") and went on in November to victory over his Democratic opponent by approximately a 2-to-1 vote. When he returned to Washington for the opening of the Eighty-first Congress, he was assigned to the Post Office and Civil Service Committee. On domestic issues in the first session (1949) he cast votes in favor of rent control extension (March) and long-range public housing (June); and against repeal of Federal taxes on oleomargarine (April). Of the Truman foreign policy he was skeptical: while he supported extension of the Trade Agreements Act (February), he voted against continuation of the Marshall Plan (April) and in favor of cutting European arms aid by 50 per cent (August). Regarding assistance to the economy of Great Britain he asserted, "It is absolutely asinine for us to go any further with loans to England. She will never repay a cent of it because she cannot."

Shortly before the Eighty-first Congress reconvened for its 1950 session, Burdick announced that he intended to "ask the House to set up a special investigating committee to find out whether payroll padding is a widely prevalent Congressional practice" (New York World-Telegram). In his own experience, he declared, he had "found members of Congress honest generally," but recent convictions of two Representatives for venality had, he believed, caused "many folks back home to think we're all a bunch of crooks" and he thought "the facts should be brought out." He introduced a resolution to this effect in January 1950, but the resolution was tabled in May by the Rules Committee.

Re-elected to Congress in November 1950, Burdick renewed the attack by introducing in the Eighty-second Congress in January 1951 a bill to require members to publish their payrolls and swear that they were not taking salary "kickbacks." Another anticorruption measure launched by Burdick (September 1951) would make it illegal to require fees for employment on any Government-financed project. The North Dakotan's voting record in 1951 included votes in favor of universal

military training (April) and the tidelands oil bill (July), and he occasioned some surprise by supporting the Truman Administration's plea to include cattle price rollbacks in the price-control policy, even though this would mean a personal financial loss to himself (Time). In August he favored a $350 millions cut in economic aid to Europe, and in December he assailed the clause in the proposed United Nations Covenant on Human Rights reading: "Freedom to manifest one's religious belief shall be subject only to such limitations as are pursuant to law and are reasonable and necessary." This he regarded as sounding "like the language of a dictator," in comparison with the guarantee contained in the United States Bill of rights. In the June 1952 North Dakota primary Burdick won renomination for Congress and was re-elected the following November.

The two sons and the daughter born to Usher and Emma Burdick hold law degrees: Quentin Northrop and Eugene Allan are their father's partners at Fargo and Williston, respectively, while Eileen Rosemary practices law in Ohio. Described by Drew Pearson as "a big, shaggy bear of a man," the septuagenarian Representative from North Dakota has a height of six feet two inches and weighs about 270 pounds. His eyes are brown, his hair is gray. He is, said Time, "a great success with small groups of farmers when he rips off his coat and speaks in unvarnished and untechnical language." A Thirty-second Degree Mason, an Elk, a Moose, a Knight of Pythias, and a Son of the American Revolution, the Congressman is also a member of the Phi Delta Phi fraternity and of the "M" Club of Minnesota. He names football as his hobby.

References

North Dakota History 16:5-29 Ja '49; 16:101-130 Ap '49; 16:165-191 Jl '49
PM p4 Ap 3 '44 por
Time 43:20 Je 19 '44 por; 58:7-8 Jl 23 '51 por
Washington (D.C.) Post p9B Ja 28 '50
Biographical Directory of the American Congress, 1774-1949 (1950)
Congressional Directory (1951)
Who's Who in America, 1950-51
Who's Who in United States Politics (1950)

BUSHNELL, ASA S(MITH) Feb. 2, 1900-
Organization official
Address: b. c/o Eastern College Athletic Conference, Biltmore Hotel, New York 17; h. 71 Palmer Sq., Princeton, N.J.

The commissioner of the Eastern College Athletic Conference, which started in 1938 as the Central Office for Eastern Collegiate Athletics, is Asa S. Bushnell, former graduate manager of athletics at Princeton University. In his present post Bushnell has major credit for formulating the revised college football code nationally adopted in 1945, and for authorship in 1951 of a seven-point program for the safeguarding of strict standards for amateurs

Orren Jack Turner

ASA S. BUSHNELL

in campus athletics. Bushnell is also the Secretary of the United States Olympic Committee.

Asa Smith Bushnell, a descendant of the Francis Bushnell who left England for the Connecticut colony in the middle of the seventeenth century, is a grandson and namesake of the Asa Smith Bushnell who settled in Springfield, Ohio, in 1851, became the president of a mower and reaper manufacturing concern, and from 1895 to 1899 served as the fortieth Governor of the Buckeye State. He is himself a native of Springfield, having been born there to John Ludlow and Jessie Manton (Harwood) Bushnell on February 2, 1900; his father was president of the First National Bank. The boy was prepared for Princeton University at the Hill School at Pottstown, Pennsylvania. Graduated in 1917, he spent a period as an apprentice seaman in the United States Naval Reserve during World War I in 1918. When he took his B.S. degree at Princeton in 1921 he was a member of the senior council and secretary of his class. He was not, however, prominent in athletics. "Although as a boy I played the usual outdoor games," he tells, "I was never good at any of them, even at 'prep' school."

Following his graduation from Princeton, Bushnell studied for several months at the Columbia University Law School and in 1922 entered the employ, as a teller, of the Morris Plan Bank in his native Springfield. In 1924, the year he was made a director of the bank, he also was appointed office manager and treasurer of the Direct Products Company and became associated with a printing establishment called the Lagonda Publishing Company. "I was not altogether happy in the kind of work I was doing," Bushnell related in an interview. "Like most college men I guess I had a hankering to get back to the campus." Accordingly, when the editorship of the *Princeton University Alumni Weekly* was offered to him in 1925, he

accepted and moved to the New Jersey town, where he has since made his home.

Bushnell's active connection with college sports began in 1927, the second of his five years as editor of the *Alumni Weekly*, when he was named graduate manager of the Princeton University Athletic Association, a position which he occupied until the end of 1937. In this course of this ten-year period he founded (in 1932) the *Princeton Athletic News* (which he edited for the next five years) and originated (in 1934) the Princeton Invitation Track Meet, which he directed until 1939. Bushnell also became a member of the American Olympic Association (serving as assistant treasurer in 1936-37), the U.S.A. Sports Federation (beginning eight years of service on the executive committee in 1937), and various other university and amateur sports bodies.

The Central Office for Eastern Collegiate Athletics (which later became the Eastern College Athletic Conference) was created on January 1, 1938, as an "experimental federation" of eleven intercollegiate leagues and associations in seven branches of sport. Its purpose, as quoted (in part) from the preamble of its constitution, is "to promote the establishment, maintenance, and implementation of the highest standards of integrity, honesty, and efficiency in the administration, policies, and scope of amateur athletic activities in member colleges, and to enact rules . . . designed to achieve those purposes." Among the original member organizations were the Intercollegiate Association of Amateur Athletes of America, the Eastern Intercollegiate Baseball and Basketball Leagues, and the Eastern Intercollegiate Football Association. He left the Princeton post to become executive director of the new body, with offices in New York City.

During the following year the Eastern Intercollegiate Tennis Association and the Collegiate Basketball Officials Bureau became connected with the Central Office, while the football group took an important step in a decision "not to employ in collegiate games men who are also officiating in the professional leagues." Early in 1941 the Intercollegiate Rowing Association joined the federation, with the result that the Bushnell office was assigned chief responsibility for staging the annual Poughkeepsie regatta. In August of that year Bushnell was named by Nelson A. Rockefeller as sports director in the Office of the Co-ordinator of Inter-American Affairs. He also served as acting director of athletics at Princeton for two years beginning 1942 and was a member of the National Committee on Physical Fitness in 1943. During 1944 Bushnell was made assistant to the director of schools and training in the Office of Strategic Services and a special consultant to the athletics director of the Army's Special Services Division.

In the summer of 1944, largely at the instance of Coach Lou Little of Columbia University, the question was raised in the rules committee of the National Collegiate Athletic Association as to whether certain "radical alterations" should be made in the collegiate football code. The proposal was voted down by 9 to 1 on the ground that such changes were undesirable while a world war still continued. Bushnell, the minority of one, then "took his case for rules reform to the newspapers" (said Chairman William Bingham of the rules committee) and for this "mutiny" was dropped from the committee. The Eastern Intercollegiate Football Association (in which Bushnell held the executive post of commissioner) then drafted its own changes, the most important of which legalized passing from anywhere below the line of scrimmage, allowed the defensive team to run with a fumble, and authorized use of a one-inch tee at the kickoff. This revised gridiron code was used in Eastern Intercollegiate games in the following fall with such success that in the spring of 1945 the N.A.A.A. adopted all the Bushnell changes except the one relating to running on a fumble.

This endorsement of Bushnell's ideas further augmented the prestige of the Central Office for Intercollegiate Athletics. At the beginning of 1946 the name was changed to Eastern College Athletic Conference, with Bushnell receiving the title of commissioner; and on November 1, 1947, a new constitution was adopted which (in the words of the organization's handbook) "transformed" the E.C.A.C. "into an organization of colleges with the unit of membership the college itself." (The original member bodies became "affiliated leagues or associations.") Fifty-three colleges and universities in eleven Atlantic States and the District of Columbia were voted charter memberships; though one of these later resigned, twenty-four more were added by December 1948. The number increased by ten in 1949 and five in 1950, making the 1952 E.C.A.C. membership (of ninety-one private, State, and municipal colleges) the largest in the country.

Bushnell returned to the executive committee of the N.A.A.A. in 1947, was elected president of the National Association of Collegiate Commissioners in the same year, and in May 1948 was made secretary of the National Football Shrine and Hall of Fame, to be located at Rutgers University in New Jersey. As secretary-general of the executive committee of the United States Olympic Committee since 1945, Bushnell became the editor of the committee's official report on the 1948 games at St. Moritz and London, a volume praised by Red Smith of the New York *Herald Tribune* as "a handsome job . . . rich in detail." Early in 1950 Bushnell became the center of a controversy in consequence of action taken on the apparent "dead heat" finish of Don Gehrmann and Fred Wilt in the "Wanamaker Mile" event in the Millrose Athletic Association track meet on January 28 of that year. The judges were divided on the outcome, and Bushnell (as chief judge) resolved the deadlock by declaring Gehrmann the winner. Wilt protested to the Metropolitan Amateur Athletic Union Registration Committee, which awarded the decision to Wilt in February. Ten months later (December 9) the board of governors of the N.A.A.A. reversed this action, upholding Bushnell's right to vote (which had been questioned), and pronounced Gehrmann the victor.

On December 5, 1951, Commissioner Bushnell outlined a new seven-point E.C.A.C. plan to combat professionalism, subsidies, and academic deficiency in intercollegiate athletics. This program stipulated that there should be "no lowering of standards for students who are also athletes," made mandatory "loss of athletic eligibility by students not making normal progress towards an academic degree," reserved loans and grants-in-aid to "those students who actually need them," and stated that there must be "no recruiting by coaches, no proselyting or subsidizing, no try-outs or all-expenses-paid campus visits, no lavish entertainment, no extravagant promises by alumni." The principles of the Bushnell code were adopted on December 14, and the constitution and rules of eligibility were accordingly amended. Further amendments to the rules—to govern the appearance of college basketball players in all-star games and to allow students who had played hockey in foreign countries to represent their colleges in interscholastic competition— were adopted by the E.C.A.C. at a special meeting on May 29, 1952.

Bushnell contributed the sections on amateur football to the Britannica and Collier's encyclopedias. In Princeton, from which he commutes daily to his office in New York, his club is the University Cottage and his church is the Episcopal. Mrs. Bushnell is the former Thelma Lucille Clark; married February 11, 1924, they have one son, Asa Smith, and one daughter, Barbara Clark (now Mrs. John C. Leonard). The commissioner, who is above medium height, has slightly graying light-brown hair and gray eyes; he has been described as mild-mannered. None of his diversions is athletic.

References

N Y Journal-American p26L F 10 '52
   por
N Y Times V p14 Ag 31 '41
Who's Who in America, 1952-53

BYROADE, HENRY A(LFRED) (bī′rōd)
July 24, 1913- United States Government official; engineer
Address: b. c/o Department of State, Washington 25, D.C.; h. 4410 20th St., North Arlington, Va.; Woodburn, Ind.

Henry A. Byroade was named Assistant Secretary of State for Near Eastern, South Asian, and African Affairs in November 1951. An army man whose specialty is engineering, Byroade in World War II initiated and supervised air supply and base construction in Assam and China. In 1946, at the age of thirty-two, he was advanced to the temporary rank of brigadier general. Later he was right-hand man to General George C. Marshall in the latter's mission to reconcile Nationalist and Communist factions in China; and still later (1949) was "loaned" by the Army to become first acting deputy director and subsequently director of the State Department's Bureau of German Affairs. Byroade took the oath of office as Assistant Secretary of State for Near Eastern Affairs on April 14, 1952.

(Continued next page)

HENRY A. BYROADE

A native of Indiana, Henry Alfred Byroade was born July 24, 1913, in Maumee Township, Allen County, and was brought up on the farm of his parents, Ernest C. and Carrie Byroade. He acquired his elementary and secondary education in local public schools. Receiving an appointment to the United States Military Academy as of July 1, 1933, he was a member of the academy's basketball and football teams until a broken leg and ankle halted his athletic activities. He ranked in the upper fourth of his class when graduated on June 12, 1937, with the B.S. degree. Commissioned a second lieutenant in the Corps of Engineers, he served two years (1937-39) with the 3d Engineers Regiment in Hawaii and then returned to the continental United States to begin a postgraduate course in engineering at Cornell University. After his advancement to first lieutenant in June 1940, Byroade was assigned in August to the 21st Engineers Regiment at Langley Field, Virginia. This experimental Aviation Engineers unit, the first of its kind, brought the young officer promotion to captaincy (temporary) on September 9. Byroade received his M.Sc. in engineering from Cornell in 1941.

Following the attack on Pearl Harbor and the entrance of the United States into World War II, Byroade was placed in command of a battalion of Aviation Engineers dispatched to the Army Air Base at Mitchel Field, Long Island, New York, to construct installations. In March 1942 he was appointed engineer for the "Haynes Mission" to the Far East, and one month later, having been transferred to the Services of Supply, China-Burma-India Theater, assumed command of Advance Section No. 2 in Assam, India. In the words of a State Department biographical release, Assam was "to become the take-off point for plane flights pouring supplies into China over the famed 'Hump' route, jumping over the long,

tortuous and hazardous Burma road"; and Byroade (who was advanced to the rank of major, temporary) "had to supervise the flow of supplies by railway and barge from Calcutta to the Assam area as well as by air over the 'hump'." For his "resourcefulness, outstanding efficiency, energy and devotion to duty" in this assignment he received the Legion of Merit decoration to which two Oak Leaf clusters were subsequently added.

Promoted to lieutenant-colonel (temporary) in January 1943, Byroade was placed in the following August in command of Advance Section No. 4, supporting the forward echelon of the 14th Air Force in Eastern China. Four months afterward (December) he was assigned to initiate and supervise the construction (by some 500,000 native workers) of forty-three bases to accommodate the forthcoming B-29 heavy bombers, a "task compared in engineering difficulty to building the pyramids in Egypt" (New York Herald Tribune). In February 1944 Byroade was transferred back from Services of Supply to the Army Air Forces, and thereafter served as engineer both of the 14th Air Force and the China Air Service Command, with responsibility for all Air Force construction in China. This assignment brought him promotion to full colonel (temporary) in April 1944, and the award of the Air Medal, with a citation stressing his more than 300 flight hours in search of air base sites "over territory where enemy fire was probable and expected and where landings were necessarily made on difficult terrain."

In September 1944 Colonel Byroade was transferred to the Pentagon in Washington, D.C., to serve as deputy chief and later acting chief of the Asiatic Theater Section of the Operations Division in the office of Army Chief of Staff General George C. Marshall, and was so engaged when World War II came to an end. When, in mid-December of 1945, the officer (who had meanwhile retired from active duty) was sent by President Truman to China as special ambassador to mediate between the Kuomintang Government of Generalissimo Chiang Kai-shek and the Chinese Communists, Colonel Byroade was assigned as military attaché and functioned as Marshall's chief of staff. On January 17, 1946, Byroade, then thirty-two, was promoted to brigadier general (temporary), the youngest ground officer at that time, and one of the youngest ever to hold that rank. While Chiang Kai-shek agreed to include Communists in his Cabinet, dissent developed in the Kuomintang, and the civil war broke out anew. Early in May, Byroade personally concluded with Nationalist and Communist generals a cease-fire covering the Central China area, and later in the same month was sent to Peiping as director of operations, executive, and commanding general of a Headquarters Group formed to activate a truce in Manchuria; he was pursuing this objective when he was stricken with typhoid fever and virus pneumonia and was forced to return home. On September 25, just before embarking, he was decorated by General Marshall with the Distinguished Service Medal, the accompanying citation mentioning the "exceptional diplomacy, tact, and sound judgment that enabled him to hold the confidence of strongly opposed parties." Byroade also wears the Special Breast Order of the Yun Hun (3d and 4th Class) of Nationalist China.

After a short convalescence in the United States, Byroade was assigned to attend the Armed Forces Staff College at Norfolk, Virginia. In November 1947 he went to Europe as an adviser to General Marshall (who had become Secretary of State) at a four-power Foreign Ministers' conference which attempted to reach an agreement with the Soviet Union on unification of Germany; and through 1948 he served as chief of the Army's International Affairs Group, an advisory body. (On July 1, 1948, peacetime tables of organization having become again effective, Byroade reverted to the ranks of permanent lieutenant colonel and temporary full colonel.) Byroade was a strong advocate of early replacement of United States military government by civilian administration in Germany, and at the time of the Berlin blockade and airlift became known in Army circles as the "Berlin expert."

When the State Department established the Bureau of German Affairs (first called "Office of German and Austrian Affairs") in March 1949, Dean Acheson, successor to General Marshall as Secretary of State, requested the Army to assign Byroade thereto as acting deputy director. He was so named on a "loan" basis (retaining Army rank and status, and drawing Army pay instead of a State Department salary), and on the following October 7 was advanced to director, in succession to Robert Murphy, who had been named Ambassador to Belgium. As such he attained a State Department rank equivalent to Assistant Secretary. The Bureau (states the *United States Government Organization Manual*) "executes responsibility for the general conduct of United States affairs in Germany by applying overall . . . policies" and "provides policy guidance for the United States High Commissioner in Germany." Byroade, who has been quoted as viewing the Bureau as "primarily . . . a source of supply and support" for the High Commissioner, has further defined American objectives as "to combat Soviet designs" and "to get a Germany . . . that will live and cooperate in peace, as an equal member of the family of nations" (State Department release). The author, in July 1950, of a paper outlining a formula for a European army, he urged in a speech at Frankfort on the February 15 following that German strength be added "as quickly as possible" to the North Atlantic Treaty Organization's military effort; and at the same time expressed the opinion that West German assumption of defense "responsibilities and obligations" should be "accompanied by a significant change in political relationships" between the occupying powers and the German Federal Republic (New York *Times*). This change was expected to take the form of a "contractual agreement," on which Byroade had already been working for a considerable time.

The naming of Byroade in November 1951 to the post of Assistant Secretary of State in charge of Near Eastern, South Asian, and African Affairs came about as the result of changes in the course of which Assistant Secretary of State George C. McGhee, previously in charge of those areas, was named United States Ambassador to Turkey. "The shift of Mr. Byroade from German-Austrian affairs to what is perhaps the most politically sensitive area in the world," the New York *Times* commented, "is a sign that the United States government is now eager to put a fresh mind to work on Middle East policies. The continuing hostility between the Arab states and Israel, the explosive Anglo-Iranian and Anglo-Egyptian disputes—at a time when the Western world is hurrying to set up a Middle East defense pact—has focused attention on the region to a greater extent than ever before." Byroade assumed his new duties as Assistant Secretary of State for Near Eastern Affairs on April 14, 1952.

Byroade is of medium height (five feet eleven inches), dark-haired, and youthful in appearance. At conference tables he is said to be insistent on the free airing of divergent ideas. "He is," an associate has commented, "interested in achieving a coordination of views, rather than in imposing a single viewpoint." Mrs. Byroade, born Mary K. Richard, is, like her husband, a "Hoosier," and was a graduate nurse at the time of her marriage on June 12, 1937. The Byroades have three sons, Gene Richard, Alan Marshall, and John Douglas. For recreation Byroade likes to work with his hands—he recently rebuilt a 38-foot boat on a Potomac tributary.

References

Life 30:74 Ja 1 '51 por
N Y Herald Tribune p24 Ja 23 '46
N Y Times p9 N 29 '51 por
N Y World-Telegram p15 D 1 '51 por
U S News 28:32-3 My 5 '50
Official Army Register (1951)
Who's Who in America, 1950-51

CALDERONE, FRANK A(NTHONY)
(käl'dẽr-ōn) Mar. 10, 1901- United Nations official; physician

Address: b. c/o United Nations, New York 17; h. 245 Kings Point Rd., Great Neck, N.Y.

Dr. Frank A. Calderone is medical director of the Health Service of the United Nations Secretariat. An authority on preventive medicine and on public health, he served as first deputy health commissioner in New York City's Department of Health from 1943 to 1946. In the latter year he was appointed director of the headquarters office of the Interim Commission of the World Health Organization (WHO). Calderone assisted in the organization of services and staff in the creation of WHO as a permanent agency of the U.N. in 1948, and at that time became chief technical liaison officer and director of its New York office. During 1950 he was executive director of the New York City Cancer Committee and

FRANK A. CALDERONE

early the next year was named to his present U.N. post.

A native of New York City, Frank Anthony Calderone was born in the Lower East Side of Manhattan on March 10, 1901. He is one of the three children of Salvatore and Rosaria (Spoleti) Calderone. His father, who had come to the United States from Sicily in 1895, engaged in newspaper work for several years and later built a chain of vaudeville and motion picture theaters in Nassau County, Long Island. Young Calderone attended local public schools, in 1916 graduating from Stuyvesant High School. Following premedical studies at Columbia University he entered the Medical School of New York University, which granted him an M.D. degree in 1924. Aside from his medical profession, for some years after his father's death he served as chairman of the board of directors of the Calderone Corporation from 1930 to 1946, managing the family investments and real estate holdings. From 1931 to 1936 he was on the staff of the New York University Medical School as an instructor in pharmacology and did research in pharmacology and anesthesia. Upon receiving his Master of Public Health degree from the School of Public Health at Johns Hopkins University in 1937, he was promoted to assistant professor of preventive medicine at the New York University Medical School, teaching public health subjects, with special emphasis on statistical analysis of populations and on administrative methods in public health. He remained at that institution until 1940.

During 1937 and 1938 Calderone was associated with the New York State Department of Health as an epidemiologist-in-training. On February 1 of the latter year he joined the New York City Department of Health as a district health officer. In this capacity he was instrumental in the promotion of the Lower East Side Health and Teaching Center, which opened in 1939. Later he and his associates established the Mothers' Health Organization of the Lower East Side with the aim of bettering community health through an understanding of nutritional problems—this group attracted national attention for its work in community organization. Calderone was named acting secretary of the New York City Department of Health on May 18, 1942, and two months later received the permanent appointment. After serving for eight months in this post, on February 15, 1943, he was named first deputy commissioner of health by Dr. Ernest L. Stebbins, the commissioner. During the absence overseas of Stebbins in 1945, Calderone served as acting commissioner. He resigned from the Department of Health on January 23, 1946.

Between 1946 and 1948 Dr. Calderone served as director of the headquarters office, in New York City, of the Interim Commission of the World Health Organization (WHO) of the United Nations. The International Health Conference, which met for the first time in New York City during the summer of 1946, drafted the constitution for WHO, a document stating that "the health of all peoples is fundamental to the attainment of peace and security and is dependent upon the fullest cooperation of individuals and states." Until the constitution had been officially ratified by the governments of at least twenty-six of the U.N. member nations, WHO functioned through an Interim Commission composed of representatives from eighteen nations. The Interim Commission planned for the establishment of a permanent organization and assumed numerous technical functions and duties formerly performed by the League of Nations Health Organization and the Office International d'Hygiene Publique. It took action on the world's most pressing health problems, coordinated and improved existing epidemiological reporting services, assumed administration of work in biological standardization, set up expert committees in medical and allied health fields, and carried forward the UNRRA program of technical aid to the health administrations in fourteen countries.

One of the contributions of WHO's Interim Commission to the advancement of international health and collaboration among nations was its assistance in fighting the cholera epidemic in Egypt in the fall of 1947. During this outbreak, the headquarters office of the commission, under Calderone's direction working in cooperation with the various governments of the world, procured and shipped by air to the striken area more than five million cubic centimeters of anticholera vaccine—enough to inoculate over three million persons. To this action was credited in large measure the rapid control of the epidemic. The disease was confined to Egypt and brought under control within two months. According to Dr. Calderone, this was the first time in medical history that an epidemic which spread at the rate of more than a thousand new cases a day had been checked in so short a time.

By April 1948 the twenty-sixth U.N. member had ratified WHO's constitution, and the

Interim Commission called the first World Health Assembly, which met in Geneva, Switzerland, two months later to organize WHO on a permanent basis and shape its policies. Calderone attended this assembly as assistant secretary in charge of the headquarters and regionalization, legal, and administration and finance committees. The headquarters and regionalization committee recommended that Geneva be selected as the permanent site of WHO and that regional offices be set up in five major geographical areas—Eastern Mediterranean, Western Pacific, Southeast Asia, Africa and Europe, and the Americas. The legal committee gave its approval to regulations concerning the methods of procedure to be used by the various member countries in the compilation of data on diseases and causes of death. It was agreed that WHO would concentrate its activities in 1949 on six major health problems: malaria, tuberculosis, venereal disease, the promotion of maternal and child health, improved environmental hygiene, and nutrition. On September 1, 1948, WHO began official operation as a permanent specialized agency of the U.N. with a membership of fifty-eight countries. Calderone then became chief technical liaison officer and director of WHO's New York liaison office and later served as one of WHO's representatives in sessions of the U.N. General Assembly, Economic and Social Council, and Trusteeship Council.

On December 21, 1949, Dr. Calderone announced his resignation to accept appointment as executive director of the New York City's Cancer Committee. (He continued, however, to act as consultant and adviser to WHO and as consultant to the U.N. Health Service.) Dr. Brock Chisholm, director-general of WHO, stated that he had accepted the resignation "with greatest reluctance," writing to Calderone: "You have given great service in establishing the permanent organization as a sound administrative structure. You have been largely responsible for building up the relationships with the U.N. and many of the specialized agencies, and in negotiating agreements with these bodies, and your services in arranging for WHO headquarters in Geneva and assisting in the arranging of financing the organization have been invaluable."

Dr. Calderone assumed his new duties as executive director of the New York City Cancer Committee at the beginning of 1950. During the year he filled the post he helped reorganize that group. A local branch of the American Cancer Society, the committee serves the more than three million people living in the boroughs of Manhattan and the Bronx, where its research, service, and educational activities are conducted in cooperation with medical and public health authorities and community organizations. During April-May 1950 the committee conducted its annual fund-raising drive to finance the continuation of this program. A total of $1,204,917 was collected in contributions from the two boroughs in 1950.

It was announced on January 10, 1951, that the physician had been appointed medical director of the Health Service of the U.N. Secretariat, upon which office he entered at the beginning of February. The health Service is a diagnostic and referral service in the field of preventive medicine; it does not provide medical care and treatment other than first-aid treatment in emergencies. It has a fully equipped dispensary on the fifth floor of the Secretariat Building at U.N. headquarters in New York. By means of periodic examinations of staff members, consultations by staff members, the record of illnesses suffered by the staff and the examination of staff members going to and returning from missions, the Health Service learns the status of health of the 3,600 Secretariat staff members from the U.N.'s sixty member countries. Its other functions include inoculations; health counseling and environmental hygiene; reviewing and advising on applications for sick leave; medical group insurance and service-linked disability compensation; and establishing and advising on medical standards for appointment and for the Joint Staff Pension Fund.

Articles and papers by Dr. Calderone have appeared in the *Journal of Laboratory and Clinical Medicine, Journal of Pharmacology and Experimental Therapeutics, American Journal of Hygiene, Medical Care, Industrial Medicine, British Medical Journal, American Journal of Nursing, Journal of Educational Sociology, Food, Drug and Cosmetic Law Quarterly,* and the *Physicians Forum Bulletin.* During World War II he acted as a consultant to the United States War Department; he received a citation for meritorious service. A fellow of the American Public Health Association, he served as chairman of its war health information commission in 1943. Other organizations in which he holds membership are the American Medical Association, New York County Medical Society, Society of Medical Jurisprudence, Harvey Society, and Alpha Omega Alpha. His first marriage (in 1929), to Mrs. Lola P. Calderone, was dissolved in 1941. On November 26, 1941, he married Mary Steichen, a physician active in public health; they have two daughters, Francesca and Maria. The "mild-mannered" U.N. medical director, who stands five feet nine inches tall and weighs 145 pounds, has gray hair and hazel eyes. His favorite recreation is sailing.

References

N Y Sunday News II p6 Ap 6 '52 por
N Y Times p36 Je 28 '42; p22 F 16 '43; p13 D 22 '49 por
U N Bul 8:113 Ja 15 '50 por
Who's Who in the United Nations (1951)

CALKINS, ROBERT D(E BLOIS) Jan. 19, 1903- Economist
Address: b. c/o Brookings Institution, 722 Jackson Pl., N.W., Washington 6, D.C.; h. 5415 Connecticut Ave., Washington 15, D.C.

Robert D. Calkins is the president of the Brookings Institution in Washington, D.C.,

CALKINS, ROBERT D.—*Continued*

which was organized in 1928 as a non-profit corporation to promote research and training in economics and government. A graduate in economics from the College of William and Mary and Stanford University, Calkins served as dean of the College of Commerce at the University of California from 1937 to 1941 and as dean of the School of Business at Columbia University from 1941 to 1946. The following year he became vice-president and director of the General Education Board and he remained in this position until July 1952, when he took office as head of the Brookings Institution.

Born in Lebanon, Connecticut, on January 19, 1903, Robert De Blois Calkins, Jr., is the son of Robert D. and Ethel Mae (Chambers) Calkins. His ancestors had settled in Connecticut and Massachusetts in 1640 and in Nova Scotia in 1760. Robert spent his boyhood in Florida and his youth in Virginia, where he graduated from the Williamsburg High School in 1921. As an undergraduate at the College of William and Mary majoring in business and economics, he reportedly had no time for athletics, since he had to work his way through school as a telephone operator and drug store soda jerker. Receiving his B.S. degree in 1925, he began his career that same year as a research assistant with the Food Research Institute of Stanford University and later (1925-27; 1930-32) was a junior research associate at the institute. At Stanford he also served as a university fellow (1928-29) and as a teaching assistant and instructor (1929-30). That institution awarded him the M.A. degree in 1929 and the Ph.D. degree in economics four years later. The subject of his dissertation was *Price Leadership Among Major Wheat Futures Markets*. Appointed lecturer in economics at the University of California in 1932, Calkins was made an assistant professor of economics the next year, promoted to associate professor in 1936, and then attained the rank of full professor in 1940. Meanwhile, he held the positions of chairman of the economics department at the University of California from 1935 to 1940 and of dean of its College of Commerce from 1937 to 1941.

Calkins was chosen to succeed Dr. Rosewell C. McCrea as professor of business economics and dean of the School of Business at Columbia University on April 7, 1941 (he assumed the duties of this post the following September). At the time of his appointment it was reported that he planned to expand the school's curriculum to include studies in the economics of enterprise, organization, and administration and in regional business development, fields in which he had specialized at California. "We don't want merely to train managers of business; we are going to train business statesmen," he told a *Columbia Alumni News* interviewer shortly after he assumed direction of the school, which then had some 330 students enrolled. A year later he said that schools of business should train men and women to operate the economic system in which government would play "an increasingly important role as director and co-

ordinator." In November 1943 he revealed that the School of Business had formulated a postwar program to permit returning servicemen to resume their studies under a special curriculum featuring revised admission requirements for veterans and refresher and reorientation courses.

In an article titled "A Challenge to Business Education" (*Harvard Business Review*, Winter 1945), Calkins stated: "Schools of business have a broader educational function than they have recognized. They must, in effect, become schools of business and economic affairs dedicated to the education of men, not for business alone, but to direct and operate the wide variety of economic institutions of modern society. By enlarging the concept of their educational objectives and by developing appropriate instruction, they may attain maturity as professional schools and materially improve the preparation of students for the tasks of later life. There has never been a time when this step was needed more urgently than now, as preparations are made for the great influx of students after the war."

Appointed vice-president and director of the General Education Board in New York City on December 8, 1946, to succeed Jackson Davis, Calkins took up his work with the board at the beginning of the next year and served as the associate director until April of 1947 when Davis died. The General Education Board was established in 1902 by John D. Rockefeller, Sr., to promote education in the United States "without distinction of race, sex, or creed," and by 1952 it had appropriated over $300 millions for that purpose. Originally, the board's activities were national in scope, but since 1940 it has been devoting its attention primarily to higher education in the South. The four "strategic points of attack" have been: (1) the development of stronger graduate programs in a few promising educational centers; (2) the improvement of undergraduate instruction in a few key Negro colleges; (3) the acceleration of educational improvements in the four low-income States; and (4) the advanced training of graduates and younger staff members of Southern institutions. In his 1950 annual report, Calkins stated that barring a world war the South should be able to raise the quality of its educational services "very substantially" in the "foreseeable future." The report of the following year read, in part: "In a nation that demands ever greater and greater educational qualifications, the South can overtake the national procession only by developing its intellectual resources as rapidly as possible; and this requires a speeding up of its educational advance. The great need is for more, and the greater need is for better, education at all levels."

The election of Calkins to succeed Dr. Harold G. Moulton as president of the Brookings Institution in Washington, D.C., was announced on September 19, 1951. The Brookings Institution is a privately endowed, non-profit corporation organized for scientific and educational purposes and devoted to the public interest. Its objects, as stated in the charter, are "to promote, carry on, conduct, and foster scientific research, education, training, and publication in the broad fields of economics, government administration, and the political and social sciences generally . . . without regard to and independently of the special interests of any group in the body politic, whether political, social, or economic." The origin of the institution dates back to 1916 when a group of educational and business leaders decided to establish in the nation's capital the Institute for Government Research to study with scientific objectivity the expanding structure of government and to promote efficiency and economy in public administration. Largely through the initiative of Robert S. Brookings, a St. Louis businessman, the institute was able to continue its activities after World War I. In 1922 Brookings persuaded the Carnegie Corporation to finance a second unit, the Institute of Economics, for the purpose of "ascertaining the facts about current economic problems and interpreting these facts for the people of the United States." Two years later he launched a third unit, the Brookings Graduate School of Economics and Government, to provide for advanced students a research training program leading to the Ph.D. degree. These three organizations were merged to form the Brookings Institution in 1928. By 1951 the institution had published its studies in 175 books and 62 pamphlets.

As president of the institution Calkins, who assumed office on July 1, 1952, the date of Dr. Moulton's retirement, is responsible "for formulating and coordinating general policies, for recommending projects for investigation, for selecting the scientific staff, and for administering the financial and business affairs of the Brookings Institution." *Business Week* (November 3, 1951) reported that Calkins was glad to be returning to his first love, economic research, and that he hoped actually to do some himself, not merely organize it and raise money for it. What Calkins calls "intermediate" research will receive heavy emphasis at Brookings, *Business Week* predicted. "He doesn't want to get too involved in immediate research of the day nor exclusively in long-run 'fundamental' research. 'What are the prospects,' he asks, 'for economic stability three to five years ahead?' "

An arbitrator of labor disputes from 1935 to 1946, Calkins was also vice-chairman of the San Francisco Regional Labor Board in 1934 and its public representative the following year. He served as a mediator on the War Labor Board (1942-45) and was a member of the Railway Labor Panel (1943-45). From 1933 to 1935 he was a temporary representative on the staff of the National Recovery Administration and of the Agricultural Adjustment Administration. He has also been a consultant to the Bureau of Reclamation of the Department of the Interior (1939-40); the National Resources Planning Board (1940-42); the Office of Price Administration (1942); and the War Department (1942). From 1942 to 1948 he held membership on the research advisory board of the Committee of Economic Development. He was a Class C director of the Federal Reserve Bank of New York from 1943 to 1949.

Leet Brothers

ROBERT D. CALKINS

The head of the Brookings Institution is a coauthor of *An Economic and Industrial Survey of the San Francisco Bay Area* (1941, with Walter E. Hoadley, Jr.) and has contributed a number of articles to various periodicals. Since 1930 he has been a member of the American Economic Association, and he also holds membership in the Royal Economic Association. He has served as vice-president (1933-34) of the San Francisco chapter of the American Statistical Association and as vice-president (1938) and president (1941) of the Pacific Coast Economic Association. From 1939 to 1941 he was chairman of the Pacific Coast regional committee of the Social Research Council. A member of the American Council of the Institute of Pacific Relations (1937-40), he was chairman of its executive committee from 1943 to 1945. In 1942 the College of William and Mary awarded him an honorary LL.D. degree. His Greek letter societies are Phi Beta Kappa and Sigma Alpha Epsilon, and he belongs to the Century Club. On September 11, 1929, he married Mary Gertrude Gilmer, of Seattle; they have two children—Elizabeth Dixon and Robert Gilmer. The economist, who has been described as "tall, vigorous, with an easy smile," has brown hair, stands five feet eleven inches and weighs 200 pounds.

References

Bsns W p112-17 N 3 '51 por
Columbia Alumni News S '41 por
Fortune 44:122 N '51 por
N Y Times p16 S 19 '51 por
Directory of American Economic Association (1948)
Directory of American Scholars (1951)
Leaders in Education (1948)
Who's Who in America, 1952-53

(Continued next page)

CALKINS, ROBERT D.—*Continued*

Who's Who in American Education (1951-52)
Who's Who in Commerce and Industry (1951)
Who's Who in the East (1951)
World Biography (1948)

CAPPER, ARTHUR July 14, 1865—Dec. 19, 1951 United States Senator from Kansas; publisher; worked as typesetter, reporter, and city editor on Topeka *Daily Capital* (1884-1892); became publisher of *Capper's Weekly, Kansas Farmer,* and other farm journals; elected Governor of Kansas in 1914 and re-elected in 1916; elected to the Senate in 1918 and re-elected for five successive terms; noted as an isolationist and leader of the farm bloc; retired in January 1949. See *Current Biography*, 1946.

Obituary

N Y Times p31 D 20 '51

CARLSON, WILLIAM S(AMUEL) Nov. 18, 1905- University president
Address: b. c/o State University of New York, State Capitol, Albany 1, N.Y.; h. 40 Marion Ave., Albany, N.Y.

Dr. William S. Carlson took office as president of the State University of New York on April 1, 1952, succeeding Dr. Alvin C. Eurich.

WILLIAM S. CARLSON

Carlson, whose teaching career began in Michigan and Minnesota schools, had been dean of the University of Minnesota and president of the University of Delaware and of the University of Vermont before coming to the chief administrative post of the State University of

New York. A geologist, he is considered an authority on the Arctic, to which he had led several expeditions.

On November 18, 1905, William Samuel Carlson was born in Ironwood, Michigan, to Samuel Carlson (a mine operator) and Mary (Lamsted) Carlson. He attended the town high school, where he played on its football team. Before graduating with the Bachelor of Arts degree in geology from the University of Michigan in 1930, Carlson had acquired field and professional experience in his specialty. In 1927 he was an assistant in geology at the University of Michigan, during 1928-29 a field leader in the University of Michigan Greenland Expedition, and during 1929-30 again an assistant in geology at the University of Michigan. For a period in 1928 he held the position of special observer for the United States Weather Bureau.

On completing his undergraduate studies, Carlson became the leader of Michigan's fourth expedition to Greenland (1930-31), which was undertaken to chart an air route to Europe. During 1931-32 he studied at the University of Copenhagen, Denmark, as a fellow of the American-Scandinavian Foundation. Taking the Master of Science degree in 1932 at the University of Michigan, Carlson remained there for a year as an instructor in geology. His next appointments in the State took him to the Ironwood High School as teacher (1933-34), to the Wakefield High School as principal (1934-36), and to the East Lansing High School as principal (1936-37). Sometime in 1935 he studied at Columbia University. One year after his 1937 appointment as an assistant professor at the University of Minnesota, Carlson was awarded the degree of Doctor of Philosophy by Michigan, writing as his dissertation the *Report of the Fourth University of Michigan Greenland Expedition.*

On the basis of data gathered during a year in southern Greenland and a winter near the most northerly settlement (primarily to study air currents), Carlson wrote *Greenland Lies North* (1940). Of it *Christian Century* said: "Mr. Carlson gives an informative and interesting account of the country and climate, the ways of the Eskimos, the Danish administration, and practically everything else that one would care to know in view of the growing importance of Greenland." In his review in the New York *Herald Tribune Books* H. M. Shaw attributed to Carlson's account "a deeper value than of a mere travel-and-adventure book." While two critics felt that the book moved slowly, the New York *Times* reviewer found its style had an "easy spontaneity," and the *Scientific Book Club Review* praised Carlson's "interesting, often humorous" manner of writing.

Meanwhile, at the University of Minnesota Carlson was promoted to associate professor in 1939 and appointed director of admissions and records in 1941. During World War II, from 1942 to 1945 he was on leave of absence while serving with the United States Air Force, first as a major, later as a colonel: he was assistant chief of the Special Projects Branch, Plans Division, Army Air Force Headquarters

(1942-43); executive officer, Western Hemisphere Branch, Plans Division (1943-44); and director of Arctic, Desert, and Tropic Branch, AAF Tactical Center (1944-45). Carlson was awarded the Asiatic-Pacific Theatre Campaign, the American Theatre, and the European-African-Middle East medals, and the Legion of Merit. He has served as a member of the board of visitors of the Air University and since 1945 has retained the rank of colonel in the Organized Reserve Corps.

Returning to academic life, Carlson was appointed dean of the University of Minnesota in 1946. In July of the same year he entered upon a four-year tenure as president of the University of Delaware. There he awarded the university's first Ph.D. degree, admitted its first Negro student, and set up a new department of biological sciences, a speech clinic, and a psychological services center for war veterans.

The December 31, 1949, issue of *Collier's* (the day before the various annual "Bowl" football games were played in the United States) carried Carlson's article which criticized the annual football "classics" as well as the general overemphasis on collegiate sports. "Our universities should exist for the books in the library and all that goes with their accumulated wisdom," he wrote. "Intercollegiate athletics are one of the activities that a university can offer; they should not be the crux of the educational program." He stated that the University of Delaware had adopted the policy of "refusing to participate in post-season games," which he called the "most commercialized angle of a commercialized business" and a "carnival of prostituted education."

Having accepted the presidency of the University of Vermont in November 1949, Carlson was installed July 1950. There his position on athletics challenged by an alumnus, the new president reiterated his views in a letter which was released to the press. Mentioning that Vermont is in the upper tenth among universities whose graduates are in *Who's Who in America*, he wrote further: "This is, it seems to me, the kind of record that every alumnus should look on with pride. Would you have us divert our meager resources to a big-time football team, and ignore . . . high educational standards? . . . I don't mean that we are opposed to a sound athletic program. . . . We do insist, however, that whatever success we have . . . be achieved honorably and by the maintenance of educational standards at a high level."

An article of Carlson's in the January 1952 *American Scholar*, entitled "The Roughest Profession: The College Presidency," attracted attention in the educational world. Condemning the selection of nonacademic men or political figures, rather than scholars, for the presidencies of colleges and universities, he also criticized the educators for failing to qualify. "When confronted with the opportunity to seize the presidencies themselves," Carlson wrote, "our scholars too often display ineptitude which throws the burden on their boards of trustees to go out and find someone, even though off the campus, who seems to know

what the score is." The colleges are also blamed for seeking a "name" instead of a man with such qualities as courage ("the habit of taking responsibility"), integrity, tact, patience, physical endurance, intellectual flexibility, a sense of humor, a platform presence, an ability to say "no" pleasantly, and "a score of other attributes."

Carlson remained at the University of Vermont nearly two years. In January 1952 it was announced that the trustees of the State University of New York had selected him as its president, which office he assumed April 1, 1952. The State University of New York, which is not actually a university in the usual sense, is an educational system comprising twenty-two schools and colleges and eleven two-year technical institutes with a total enrollment of 33,000 full-time and 14,000 part-time students. At the time of the appointment, Dr. Oliver C. Carmichael, chairman of the university's board of trustees, announced that the choice of Carlson climaxed a six-month search for a "worthy successor" to Dr. Alvin C. Eurich, who had resigned to accept the vice-presidency of the Ford Fund for the Advancement of Education. Carlson (whose salary is $19,000) heads a faculty of 3,000 and manages a $33-million budget. He was called "admirably equipped" for his task by the New York *Times* (January 5, 1952); and the judgment expressed in an editorial in the New York *Herald Tribune* was: "Dr. Carlson seems to be a foresighted administrator as well as a first-class educator. He is just the man, fresh and vigorous, that our new university needs." On assuming his new duties Carlson said that he would devote himself to "building further on the sound foundation of the university system that has already been laid."

From time to time the educator speaks on problems related to his field. In the high tuitions that prevail in colleges in the United States he sees a possibility of Federal aid to students; in that connection he cited particularly the expensive preparation for the medical profession. In an effort to ease the shortage of teachers, Carlson and several other college presidents are members of a committee pledged to support teacher-training courses for graduates of liberal arts colleges.

Among other writings of the educator are articles for periodicals; and two books: *Report of the Northern Division of the Fourth University of Michigan Greenland Expedition* (1941); a *Student Teacher's Handbook* (1940), with C. W. Boardman. He edited a *Manual for the Supervising Teacher* (1940). His honorary degrees are the Doctor of Letters from the universities of Delaware and Michigan and from Middlebury and Dickinson colleges. Carlson was a member of the 1941 Minnesota Governor's Advisory Committee on Education. He belongs to the American Association for the Advancement of Science, the Minnesota Academy of Science, the National Education Association, the Society for the Advancement of Education, the American Swedish Historical Museum, and the American Legion. During 1937-41 he was the secretary of the Minnesota Association of Secondary School

CARLSON, WILLIAM S.—*Continued*

Principals. His fraternities are Sigma Xi, Sigma Gamma Epsilon, and Phi Delta Kappa; his clubs are the Explorers (New York) and "M" (University of Michigan).

In May 1952 it was announced that a fifteen-room house had been purchased in Albany as a home for President Carlson. In approving the purchase by the university the trustees said that the house would not only provide a residence for Carlson but also serve as a meeting place for the officers of the State university's member institutions. Occupancy is planned for August 1, 1952. The educator and the former Mary Jane Rowe, who were married December 17, 1932, have a daughter, Kristin Rowe. *Time* has described him as a "genial six-footer."

References

Collier's 124:13 D 31 '49 por
N Y Herald Tribune p3 N 23 '49 por; p1 Jan 5 '52 por; p6 Jan 6 '52
N Y Times p7 Nov 3 '49 por; p1 Jan 5 '52 por
Time 59:67 Jan 14 '52 por
American Men of Science (1950)
Leaders in Education (1948)
Who's Who in America, 1952-53
Who's Who in American Education, 1947-48
Who's Who in the East (1951)

CARR, WILLIAM G(EORGE) June 1, 1901- Educator

Address: b. c/o National Education Association, 1201 16th St., N.W., Washington 6, D.C.; h. 3600 Connecticut Ave., N.W., Washington 8, D.C.

On January 26, 1952, the National Education Association announced that William G. Carr would succeed Willard E. Givens on August 1, 1952, as executive secretary of the teaching profession's organization, a position described by A. C. Flora, chairman of the NEA board of trustees, as "one of the most influential educational posts in the world." Carr, who has been active in UNESCO and other groups concerned with international education, began his association with the NEA in 1929 and became associate secretary in 1940. He is the author of books, pamphlets, and magazine articles on educational subjects, particularly in the fields of international relations, school finance, and school administration.

William George Carr was born June 1, 1901, in Northampton, England, the son of Alfred S. and Alice (Bailey) Carr. In 1915 the family went to the United States to make its home in California. Young Carr attended the University of California from 1920 to 1923; he then became a student at Stanford University, from which he received his B.A. degree in 1924. After his graduation he taught for a year at Roosevelt Junior High School in Glendale, California. Taking postgraduate studies at Stanford, he was given his M.A. degree in 1926. At the end of a year (1926-27) as a professor of education at Pacific University in Forest Grove, Oregon, he returned to Stanford

as a Cubberley Fellow to take his Ph.D. degree in 1929. The educator in 1928 had been for a year the director of research for the California Teachers Association.

In 1929 Carr began his association with the National Education Association in the position of assistant director of research, a post he filled until 1931. Simultaneously he began to serve as visiting professor or lecturer in summer sessions of universities, at Stanford for three summers, at Michigan for six, at California for two, at Pennsylvania and Oregon for one each. The educator became the director of research of the NEA in 1931; in that year he also served on the board of consultants of the National Survey of School Finances, and in 1933 he was a member of the National Conference on Financing Education.

Carr has been the secretary of the Educational Policies Commission of the NEA and the American Association of School Administrators since 1936. At the Sixth International Documentation Conference held in Oxford, England, in 1938 the educator was a member of the United States delegation. He became the associate secretary of the NEA in 1940 and held this position until 1952. At the White House Conference on Children held in 1941 he was among those on the organization committee. In his speech before the convention of the American Association of School Administrators, in San Francisco in 1942, Carr voiced an internationalist stand. He urged American high schools to teach "as vigorously as possible" that the United States "is now and forever bound up in the affairs of the world; that it is foolish for it ever again to retreat to the position of isolation." He advocated including in the school curriculum a study of the Atlantic Charter, the Four Freedoms, and similar documents, and an emphasis on the interdependence of all nations, particularly those of the Western Hemisphere. In 1942 he also served as a member of the United States delegation to the Eighth Pan-American Child Congress, which was held in Washington, D.C.

As secretary of the Educational Policies Commission, which functioned in 1943 as a commission on postwar education, Carr announced that the ideas of the American commission and those of its British counterpart agreed on most of the leading policy questions. Both groups recommended that a permanent international organization for education be incorporated into a future world government and that the United Nations deal with the educational reconstruction in the Axis-occupied countries. When the International Education Assembly met in New York in 1945, it selected Carr, chairman of the assembly, to represent it at the United Nations Conference on International Organization at San Francisco, at which was adopted a resolution urging the establishment of an international office of education. Carr also acted as consultant to the United States delegation at the San Francisco conference, where he worked for the setting up of the United Nations Educational, Scientific, and Cultural Organization (UNESCO). In 1945 he also was chosen as the deputy secretary of the Conference on Educational and

Cultural Organization which met in London. The following year he became a member of the United States National Commission on UNESCO (he served on this commission until 1950) and was the UNESCO month lecturer at the Sorbonne.

Carr, who has been the general secretary of the World Organization of the Teaching Profession since its founding in 1946, was also adviser to the United States delegation to the Second General Conference of UNESCO held in Mexico City in 1947. At the 1947 convention of the Association of School Administrators he again discussed the importance of education in international relationships, stressing the necessity of obtaining through education the proper attitude toward other countries.

In a report on a two-year study of education for international understanding given before the 1948 convention of the NEA, Carr emphasized the need for a realistic approach. Too much of such education has been "either sentimental or pacifist," Carr said, and it does not recognize, as it should, "the legitimate role of a national power as a means of achieving international order." The educator took part in the international educational conference in London in 1948, one at Berne the following year, and one at Ottawa in 1950. "Universal education is important as a barrier to communism," Carr stated at the conference of the World Organization of the Teaching Profession in Ottawa in 1950. In August 1952, at the international meeting of teachers of the free world in Copenhagen (which Carr attended), a new organization was formed, the World Confederation of the Teaching Profession (WCOTP).

Carr was appointed on January 26, 1952, by the board of trustees of the National Education Association to the office of executive secretary for a four-year term. He succeeded Willard E. Givens upon the latter's retirement on August 1, 1952. The educational body, originally known as the National Teachers Association, was founded in Philadelphia in 1857 and now has 875,000 direct or affiliated members. Its purpose is "to elevate the character and advance the interests of the profession of teaching and to promote the cause of popular education in the United States."

On a Columbia Broadcasting System program, "How Can We Keep Teachers in Our Schools?" Carr in 1946 discussed the reason for the shortage of teachers. Stating that less than one college student in ten is enrolled in a teachers college, the NEA secretary put the blame for the teaching shortage on "editorial writers who imply that all teachers are willy-brained, absent-minded incompetents; cartoonists who invariably portray teachers as ugly gargoyles; school board members who require women teachers who marry to resign as though they had committed a mortal sin; legislators who are quite willing to leave the tenure and professional reputation of good teachers to chance; and snobbish parents who treat their children's teacher more like a servant than like a trusted colleague."

Chase News Photo.

WILLIAM G. CARR

Carr has written a number of books and pamphlets dealing with international education, among them: *Education for World Citizenship* (1928), *Educational Leadership in this Emergency* (1942, a discussion of ways to teach internationalism); *Only by Understanding, Education and International Organization* (1945, a comparison of educational systems and an educational program to further understanding between nations); and *One World in the Making; the United Nations* (1946, an explanation of the United Nations Charter). His writings on school administration include *County Unit of School Administration* (1931), *The Lesson Assignment* (with John Waage, 1931), and *School Finance* (1933). The educator has also written *Purposes of Education in American Democracy* (1938), *Learning the Ways of Democracy* (with others, 1940), and *Education and the People's Peace* (1943). He is the author of *John Swett, the Biography of an Educational Pioneer* (1933) and the editor of *Frontiers in International Education* (1944). As an editor, he serves on the editorial board of *The Education Digest* and is an associate editor of *The School Executive*. The titles of some of the many magazine articles Carr has written are "Recipe for a Warlike Nation" (*School and Society*, December 28, 1935), "Efficiency through Democratic Administration" (*National Education Association Journal*, March 1942), "You Can Change Human Nature" (*Parents' Magazine*, November 1948), "How Good Are Your Schools?" (*Ladies' Home Journal*, April 1948), and "Five Years of UNESCO" (*National Education Association Journal*, October 1950).

Carr serves on the board of trustees of the Institute of International Education. He holds a life membership in the American Educational Research Association of the NEA; honorary memberships in the Philip-

CARR, WILLIAM G.—*Continued*

pine Public School Teachers Association and the Malta Union of Teachers. He is a member of Sigma Pi and Phi Delta Kappa; in Washington he belongs to the Cosmos Club. He and Elizabeth Vaughan were married August 20, 1924, and have one son, Wilfred James.

References

Nat Ed Assn J 41:67 F '52
Leaders in Education (1948)
Presidents and Professors in American Colleges and Universities 1935-36 por
Who's Who in America, 1952-53
Who's Who in American Education, 1951-52
World Biography (1948)

CASHMAN, ROBERT Jan. 12, 1886- Congregational Church official; seminary executive

Address: b. c/o Chicago Theological Seminary, 5757 University Ave., Chicago 37, Ill.; h. 1360 E. 58th St., Chicago 37, Ill.

In June 1952, at its eleventh biennial meeting, the General Council of the Congregational Christian Churches of America elected Robert Cashman to its top-ranking post as National Moderator. An authority on church financing

ROBERT CASHMAN

and administration, Cashman has been associated with the Chicago Theological Seminary for nearly thirty years, as business manager and assistant treasurer from 1923 to 1951 and since then as vice-president in charge of finance and development. Before that he had handled organizational and financial matters for the World's Sunday School Association and for the International Sunday School Association (1908-20).

Robert Cashman was born in Sioux Falls, South Dakota, on January 12, 1886, to Leonard W. and Nettie Ione (Brown) Cashman. Pioneers in South Dakota, his mother and his father (a carpenter and builder) reared five sons and one daughter. While attending Sioux Falls elementary and high schools, Robert became interested in music and played the violin in the school orchestra.

In 1903, at the age of seventeen, the young man secured a job as a clerk in a grocery business, which he left two years later to accept a clerk's position in a life insurance firm. He stayed there until 1908 when he moved to Chicago to enter the employ of the International Sunday School Association, in which he later directed affairs of national and international scope. After joining the staff of the World's Sunday School Association in 1911, Cashman traveled extensively in North America and Europe in the promotion and administration of the World's Sunday School Convention in Switzerland in 1913. The following year (1914) he was named business manager of the International Sunday School Association, a post he held until becoming in 1920 Chicago manager for the University Society of New York (publisher of children's books) with the responsibility of training salesmen. Cashman left this position in 1923 upon his appointment as business manager and assistant treasurer of the Chicago Theological Seminary. In these various capacities he also had duties in teaching, writing, lecturing and counseling. In 1951 he was promoted to his present post as the seminary's vice-president in charge of finance and development.

Cashman was elected on June 18, 1952, to a two-year term as Moderator of the General Council of the Congregational Christian Churches of America, the highest office in the Congregational denomination, and as such he is the titular head of more than 6,000 churches with a total membership of 1,250,000. In accordance with church custom that a layman alternate with a minister as moderator, Cashman succeeded the Reverend Dr. Vere V. Loper of Berkeley, California. The Congregational Christian Churches are the result of the merger in 1931 of two denominations, the Congregational Church and the Christian Church. (The Congregational Church, the second oldest Protestant religious body in the United States, dates back to early seventeenth century settlers in Massachusetts. With a similar emphasis on the autonomy of the local congregation, the Christian Church was organized at the time of the eighteenth century Wesleyan and revival movements.)

In the words of Frederick L. Fagley, secretary emeritus of the General Council of Congregational Christian Churches, "The denomination maintains a democratic structure. The local churches elect delegates, first to the Association, which includes the churches of the county (in New England) or restricted territory, second to the State Conference, and third to the General (National) Council. . . .The General Council meets biennially and is made up of delegates elected by local units which number at least 1,000 members, and also of delegates elected by the State conferences." The Congregational churches support three major missionary agencies—the Board of Home Missions, the Council for Social Action, and the American Board of Commissioners for Foreign Missions.

In 1949 a majority of the General Council had voted to merge with the Evangelical and Reformed Church (which has a membership of about 800,000), but Cadman Memorial Church of Brooklyn objected to the proposed union and took the problem to court, arguing, as *Time* (June 30, 1952) reported, "that individual congregations could not be forced to abide by a general church decision." On January 26, 1950, New York State Supreme Court Justice Meier Steinbrink stated in a declaratory judgment that he was going to decide in favor of Cadman Memorial. Consequently, during the meeting of the General Council at which Cashman was elected in June 1952, delegates voted "to continue to look forward" to a merger but agreed to take no positive steps until the merger argument had been settled in the courts.

An expert in the field of church financing, Cashman is the author of two books on the subject. In a review of his first book, *The Business Administration of a Church* (1937), *Christian Century* magazine noted: "Mr. Cashman is a layman with many years of business experience. He writes only on those phases of church organization and administration which his experience qualifies him to discuss, leaving to preachers to write of the many problems of worship, education and committee administration which demand their energy." Also commenting on the book in *Christian Century*, W. H. Leach observed: "Some will criticize it as reaching conclusions too quickly and laying down rules with too flexible precision. Others will appreciate the brisk, to-the-point chapters, which assume that the minister is not versed in business terminology and executive procedure. This assumption is probably correct and the approach of the volume will be welcomed by the many ministers who will buy and read it." C. T. Holman in *Journal of Religion* said of the book: "No better author could have been chosen to write this book . . . Robert Cashman is a very able executive who has also the gift of clear and precise speech. The order and thoroughness of the book reflect the orderliness and competency of the author's mind."

Cashman's second book, *Finances of a Church* (1949), was also reviewed in *Christian Century*: "Here [Cashman] considers all phases of church finance—budgets, campaigns, accounting, risks and losses, debts, pensions, endowments, and the functions of trustees, women's organizations and other groups in relation to a church's solvency and property." In evaluating the book the magazine stated: "Those who have this volume and Cashman's earlier one . . . will have a pretty complete library on this aspect of the church." Cashman has written a number of articles for *Church Management* and other church periodicals.

Dr. Cashman has said that he was influenced in the choice of his lifework by three men— Marian Lawrance of the International Sunday School Association, and Dr. Ozora S. Davis and Clarence S. Funk of the Chicago Theological Seminary. "These were great men with whom I worked closely, and from whom I learned much," he has remarked, "but fundamentally I believe that my life has been guided by 'a higher power.'" Cashman was awarded an honorary LL.D. degree by Bradley University in 1950. He is a past president of the Chicago Congregational Club (1930) and a member of the Union League Club of Chicago and of the Quadrangle Club. The seminary executive married Virginia Morris Linn on October 10, 1912; he married his present wife, the former Zelma Chappell, on September 1, 1935. He is the father of four children—Robert Linn, Anne Frances (Mrs. Robert Van Valkenburgh), Chappell F., and Marjoree (Mrs. George F. Rung, Jr.). Cashman stands five feet seven inches tall, weighs 160 pounds, and has blue-gray eyes and brown hair. He is a Republican and a Congregational member of Chicago's Bryn Mawr Community Church.

References

N Y Times p30 Je 19 '52

Who's Who in Chicago and Illinois (1936)

CASSADY, JOHN H(OWARD) Apr. 3, 1896- United States naval officer

Address: b. c/o Department of the Navy, The Pentagon, Washington 25, D.C.; h. 227 N. Main St., Spencer, Ind.

As commander of the United States Sixth Fleet, Vice-Admiral John H. Cassady directs the naval unit operating in the Mediterranean in conjunction with the fleets of several European countries in preparation for the defense of the southern flank of the North Atlantic Treaty Organization's SHAPE command in the event of war. Cassady, whose service began in World War I and whose first assignment in naval aviation was made in 1928, became one of the Navy's leading experts on carrier warfare in World War II. Before assuming his present duties on May 27, 1952, in succession to Vice-Admiral Matthias B. Gardner, he had held, since January 1950, the post of Deputy Chief of Naval Operations for Air.

John Howard Cassady was born on April 3, 1896, in Spencer, Indiana, the son of William Franklin Cassady and Samantha (Haxton) Cassady. He attended Spencer High School and the Army and Navy Preparatory School at Annapolis, Maryland, before his appointment to the United States Naval Academy in 1915. While a midshipman, he played baseball and basketball. His Annapolis training accelerated because of the World War I emergency, he was graduated and was commissioned ensign in June 1918 with the class of 1919.

A period of two months aboard the battleship U.S.S. *Virginia* preceded his joining the U.S.S. *Cassin* in August 1918 for duty with the destroyer forces based at Queenstown, Ireland. From December 1918 to March 1920 he served on the cruiser U.S.S. *Olympia*, flagship, Com-

VICE-ADM. JOHN H. CASSADY

mander, U.S. Naval Forces, Eastern Mediterranean. He was promoted to the rank of lieutenant (j.g.) on July 1, 1920. Returning to the United States, he was assigned successively to the destroyers *Wilkes*, *Dixie*, and *Truxton* until June 1922. From that date until February 1924, he saw duty on the U.S.S. *McCormick*, flagship, Destroyer Detachment, Naval Forces, Europe, becoming in the latter part of that period the executive officer of the *McCormick*.

On assignment to the Office of Naval Communications, Cassady was stationed in Washington until February 1925, when he reported for duty as "district communication superintendent with additional duty as radio material officer of the San Juan Communication District, San Juan, Puerto Rico" (in the words of the biography supplied by the Navy Department). From September 1926 he served in the mine-layer U.S.S. *Aroostook* until being sent in March 1928 to the Naval Air Station at Pensacola, Florida, for flight training. Since his designation on December 22, 1928, as naval aviator he has served uninterruptedly in naval aviation. In December 1928 he joined Scouting Squadron 2, based on the U.S.S. *Saratoga*, with which squadron he remained until May 1930. Following three years at the Naval Air Station in Pensacola, Cassady reported in October 1933 for duty on the aircraft carrier U.S.S. *Ranger,* where he served from her commissioning in June 1934 until June 1935. The next year he commanded Scouting Squadron 4, based on the U.S.S. *Langley*, another aircraft carrier. After a year at the Naval Air Station in Norfolk, Virginia, he filled the position of Assistant Naval Attaché and Assistant Naval Attaché for Air at the American Embassy in Rome from August 1937 to May 1939.

Back again in the United States, he was assigned duty in connection with the fitting out of the aircraft carrier U.S.S. *Wasp* as air officer from her commissioning on April 25, 1940, until April 1941. His next appointment was as operating officer on the staff of the Commander of Aircraft of the Atlantic Fleet. From May 1942 to March 1943 he was Chief of Staff and Aide to the Chief of Air Operational Training at the Naval Air Station in Jacksonville, Florida. He then directed the aviation training division of the Bureau of Aeronautics in Washington until August 1943, at the same time representing the Navy on the Joint Committee of Air Training in North America.

On August 22, 1943, Captain Cassady assumed command of the U.S.S. *Saratoga*, which under his direction participated in two raids on Rabaul, an important enemy naval base, forcing the Japanese fleet to withdraw to Truk, 900 miles to the north. The *Saratoga* then moved north to take part in the capture of the Gilbert Islands, in the occupation of Eniwetok Atoll, and in raids on Sabang on April 19, 1944, and on Soerabaja on May 17, 1944. Cassady was awarded the Legion of Merit for "exceptionally meritorious conduct" (read the citation) "in the performance of outstanding services to the Government of the United States as Commanding Officer of the U.S.S. *Saratoga* during action against enemy Japanese forces in the Buka-Bonis Area, Bougainville, British Solomon Islands, on November 1-2 and against Rabaul, New Britain, on November 5 and 11, 1943." He was also awarded a Gold Star with Combat Distinguishing Device for his part in the raids on Sabang and Soerabaja.

When he returned to the United States, Cassady was named Director of the Aviation Planning Division of the Office of the Chief of Naval Operations on July 24, 1944; he was nominated Rear Admiral on September 20 and on October 5 of that year was designated Assistant Deputy Chief of Naval Operations for Air. For outstanding performance in both capacities, he was again awarded a Gold Star. From October 1945 until January 1946 he served as Commander of Carrier Division 4 of the Atlantic Fleet, and on January 7, 1946, he was transferred to the command of Carrier Division 1. In March 1946 he headed the Navy's "Operation Frostbite," a three-week expedition designed to test the effectiveness of the 45,000-ton carried *Midway* (described in the *Herald Tribune* as "beyond question the most powerful fighting machine in existence") under sub-Arctic conditions. The operation, Cassady told newspaper correspondents, proved "that it is possible to wage carrier warfare effectively in sub-Arctic regions" and that "it is far easier to wage war from a carrier deck in cold regions than from an air base on land."

Commanding Carrier Division 1, Cassady participated in Eighth Fleet maneuvers in the Western Atlantic and Caribbean areas from April 19 to May 27, 1946, the Navy's first large-scale postwar training operation, and in August and September he took part in maneuvers in the Mediterranean. On April 23, 1948, following service as Commander of Fleet Air at Quonset, Rhode Island, he was transferred to Washington as Assistant Chief of

Naval Operations for Air. A year later, on May 23, 1949, he was appointed to what the New York *Times* called "one of the most responsible posts in naval aviation" as Commander of Fleet Air in Jacksonville, Florida. He returned to Washington in January 1950 as Deputy Chief of Naval Operations for Air and was promoted to Vice-Admiral upon assuming his new duties.

Testifying before a closed session of a House Appropriations subcommittee in February 1950, Cassady stressed the importance of antisubmarine warfare and the Navy's need for modernized planes to accomplish its task. In May 1951 he informed the same body that the Navy was executing a "vigorous" program of modernizing its aircraft, but warned that "we are not ahead of the enemy in all phases of technical aviation development." Writing in the magazine *Flying* in November 1951, he stated: "The Navy believes that its aviation program was shown to be fundamentally sound when operations in Korea put it to the test. . . .The plane types were more than adequate; the training and doctrine effective in the support of United Nations Forces; and the ability to work with other Services and with allies gratifying in the extreme." In an interview in *United States News and World Report* he disclosed in January 1952 that the Navy had 10,000 planes and 18,700 fliers and that in the eighteen months since the outbreak of the Korean war, Navy planes had dropped "more than three fourths the tonnage of the total bombs dropped by the Navy and Marine Corps in the Pacific during all of World War II." The Navy had two jets in Korea, he stated, the Grumman Panther and the McDonnell Banshee, which "have over twice the range and twice the endurance of the MIG-15."

To a closed session of the Senate Preparedness Committee he revealed in April 1952 that the Navy had developed attack aircraft and long-range fighters capable of delivering "the small atomic bombs," and that it also had carrier planes able to deliver "the big bombs." In Congressional testimony he disclosed also that to provide defense against modern-type underwater craft, an array of new weapons had been devised, including an antisubmarine airplane, an antisub helicopter, an antisub blimp, a magnetic locating device, and homing torpedoes designed "to seek out the enemy craft, being drawn to it by a sonar device that is attracted by the submarine's underwater noise" (New York *Times*, May 29, 1952).

Cassady assumed command on May 27, 1952, of the United States Sixth Fleet, "a rotating fleet" of warships variously estimated as between forty and seventy in number. In this assignment he succeeds Vice-Admiral Matthias B. Gardner in directing the training and preparation of the American fleet in the Mediterranean, cooperating with naval units of Great Britain, France, Italy, Greece, and Turkey to take part in the North Atlantic Treaty Organization's defense of southern Europe in the event of a major war. On an official visit to Yugoslavia in September 1952, Vice-Admiral Cassady spoke of the strategic importance of the Adriatic Sea and "praised Yugoslav efforts to build a de-

fensive power capable of 'tying up large forces of any potential enemy'" (*Christian Science Monitor*, September 13, 1952).

Besides the decorations mentioned, Cassady is the recipient of the Victory Medal, Destroyer Clasp (U.S.S. *Cassin*), and is authorized to wear the American Defense Service Medal, Fleet Clasp, the American Campaign Medal, the Asiatic-Pacific Campaign Medal, and the World War II Victory Medal. Great Britain has awarded him the degree of Honorary Commander of the Military Division of the Most Excellent Order of the British Empire, and Greece has conferred on him the Order of the Phoenix. The naval officer and his wife, the former Miss Sallie Dold, who were married on February 3, 1925, are the parents of two sons—John Howard, Jr., and William Francis. *Time* magazine has described Cassady as "reedy" and "rugged."

References

N Y Times p21 S 21 '44
Who's Who in America, 1952-53

CHAPMAN, ALBERT K(INKADE) May 31, 1890- Business executive
Address: b. c/o Eastman Kodak Company, 343 State St., Rochester 4, N.Y.; h. 810 Allen's Creek Rd., Rochester 18, N.Y.

The president of the Eastman Kodak Company, the world's largest manufacturer of photographic equipment, is Albert K. Chapman, who on May 20, 1952, succeeded Thomas J. Hargrave, now chairman of the board. The new president has been associated with the Eastman organization since 1919 and in that time has held the offices of production manager, vice-president, general manager, and director.

Albert Kinkade Chapman was born May 31, 1890, in Marysville, Ohio, one of the three sons of Charles S. and Anna T. (Kinkade) Chapman. In 1912 Chapman received his bachelor of arts degree from Ohio State University, where he was a member of Sigma Xi and was elected to Phi Beta Kappa. After taking his M.A. degree a year later from the same institution, he attended Princeton University on a fellowship for three years and was granted the degree of Ph.D. in 1916. The subjects of his theses were "Spectra of Compounds" and "Corbino Effects in Metals and Alloys." Next he spent a year (1916-17) at Clark University in research work on physiological optics.

In 1917 Chapman entered the United States Army with the rank of first lieutenant in the Science and Research Division of the Signal Corps. Transferred to the United States Air Corps, he held the rank of lieutenant and later of captain. At the end of a year of service in Washington, D.C., he was stationed in 1918 at Kodak Park in Rochester, New York, where for a year he took charge of the development work on the aerial camera and film, filters, paper, and chemicals for the Science and Research Division of Army Ordnance. He returned to civilian life in 1919, and from

Eastman Kodak Co.
ALBERT K. CHAPMAN

1924 to 1927 held the rank of major in the Ordnance Reserve

Having become interested in the Eastman Kodak Company while he was stationed at Kodak Park, Chapman in February 1919 joined the organization as head of the development department, which he helped establish. After three years, in January 1922 he was named assistant to the vice-president in charge of manufacturing. He became the production manager of the company in January 1930, an office which he held until 1941. In 1930 he was also made a director of the Eastman Gelatine Corporation, of Peabody, Massachusetts, the first of several executive positions he was to fill with Eastman subsidiaries. He was elected in April 1931 a director of the Canadian Kodak Company, Ltd., and was also a director of the Tennessee Eastman Corporation at Kingsport, Tennessee, from May 1934 to December 29, 1950, when the organization became the Tennessee Eastman Company. From February 1936 to December 1943 he filled the vice-presidency of the Eastman Gelatine Corporation, to which he was again named on September 18, 1944.

While holding the title of assistant vice-president of the Eastman Kodak Company, which he was given on May 13, 1936, Chapman served as director of Distillation Products, Inc., Rochester, from August 1, 1938, until August 24, 1948. He was made vice-president and assistant general manager of the parent company in May 1941, and two years later, in November 1943, he became general manager and a director of the company. He has been vice-president of the subsidiary Canadian Kodak Company, Ltd., since 1944. At the annual meeting of the board of directors of the Eastman Kodak Company on May 20, 1952, he was elected president of the company, when Thomas

J. Hargrave, the former president, became chairman of the board.

What was to become the Eastman Kodak Company began in 1880 as a small factory owned by George Eastman, a young Rochester bank clerk, who produced "dry" photographic plates according to a method which he had worked out. In 1888 Eastman developed the Kodak box camera combining the roll film principle and the plate camera, and in 1891 daylight loading was marketed. The company, which changed its name to Eastman Kodak Company in 1892, has continued its pioneering in the photographic field. The founding of the Kodak Research Laboratories in 1912 has produced improvements and new developments in photography and allied sciences. During World War I Kodak introduced the first aerial camera using film instead of plates. The Cine Kodak, the first amateur motion picture camera, was produced in 1923, and Kodacolor, a film permitting amateurs to take motion pictures in color, was developed in 1928. An improved film, Kodachrome, was introduced in 1935 and was adapted for taking still pictures in color. One of its subsidiaries, the Tennessee Eastman Corporation, which was organized to provide certain raw materials for the parent company, has since manufactured many plastic products generally. The Eastman company in May 1952 announced the termination of fair-trade contracts with retailers. This decision, made known shortly after Chapman became president of the company, was reached, according to an Eastman official, because some Kodak dealers were consistently undercutting others who had signed the contracts and because Kodak has long felt that the contracts were unenforceable.

Chapman is a member of the American Optical Society and the Photographic Society of America. He has served as a director of the Rochester Institute of Technology since 1930 and secretary since 1944. From 1940 to 1943 he acted as a director of the American Standards Association. He is a member of the board of trustees and an executive committee member of George Eastman House, Inc., a museum set up in the former home of George Eastman, which contains exhibits tracing the development of photography from its earliest days. He is a director of the Lincoln Rochester Trust Company and A. M. Tenney Associates, Inc. Chapman serves as both trustee and director for the Rochester Chamber of Commerce; he is a director of the Rochester Chapter of the American Red Cross and a member of the Corporation of the Rochester Community Chest. He belongs to the Army Ordnance Association and the National Rifle Association, the Princeton Alumni Association of Rochester, and the YMCA. Other societies of which he is a member are the Newcomen Society, the Royal Society of the Arts, and the Masons. Among his clubs he numbers the University Club of Rochester, the Genesee Valley Club, and the Country Club of Rochester. He is a Republican and a Presbyterian.

On August 14, 1916, Chapman married Ercil Howard; they have two children, Ercil H. (Mrs. George Haywood Hawks, Jr.) and Elizabeth (Mrs. Hiram G. Hanson). Hunting and golf are the sports Chapman enjoys; and his garden and farm are other interests. He collects antiques, prints, oil paintings, and Oriental rugs.

References

Business Executives of America (1950)
Who's Who in America, 1952-53
Who's Who in Commerce and Industry (1951)
Who's Who in New York, 1952

CHARLES-ROUX, FRANÇOIS (-JULES) (shàrl"rōō' frän"swä' zhül) Nov. 19, 1879- Canal company official

Address: b. c/o Compagnie Universelle du Canal Maritime de Suez, 1 rue d'Astorg, Paris 8, France; h. 7 bis rue des Saints-Pères, Paris 6, France

Rising tension between Great Britain and Egypt over the Suez Canal and the Sudan has brought world attention to the international company that owns that waterway in Egypt. Its president François Charles-Roux, has had a long career as a diplomat, serving in French embassies in St. Petersburg, Constantinople, London, and Prague, and during 1932-40 as French Ambassador to the Vatican. A member of the Institut de France, Charles-Roux is also an historian whose works deal with problems of Egypt and the Suez Canal. He accepted the position of director of the Compagnie Universelle du Canal Maritime de Suez in 1944, and in 1948 became president of its board of directors.

François-Jules Charles-Roux was born November 19, 1879, in Marseilles, France, the son of Jules and Claire (Canaple) Charles-Roux. His father, a shipowner and former deputy of Marseilles, served for a time as vice-president of the Compagnie Universelle du Canal Maritime de Suez. François-Jules spent his childhood in Marseilles. He studied for a degree in law and in literature at the University of Paris, and also received a diploma for advanced studies in history and geography. He then attended the Ecole des Sciences Politiques, obtaining his diploma in 1902, the year he entered the diplomatic service.

After working for a short time in Paris, Charles-Roux was assigned on June 2, 1902, to the French Embassy in St. Petersburg. On February 1, 1905, he was transferred to Constantinople, where he became secretary, third class, on January 11, 1906; in 1907 he was assigned to Cairo, where he became secretary, second class, on March 27, 1911. He was made a member of the embassy staff in London on January 27, 1912. When World War I broke out, he joined the army and was sent to Seddul-Bahr; there his record won him the Medal of the Dardanelles and the Croix de Guerre. On February 4, 1916, he was assigned to the French Embassy in Rome, becoming its first secretary on September 29, 1917, and Embassy counselor on January 8, 1921.

The diplomat became inspector of embassies and consulates on November 21, 1924, and minister plenipotentiary, second class, on April 5,

Harcourt, Paris
FRANCOIS CHARLES-ROUX

1925. He was appointed a delegate to the International Conference on the Danube on August 1, 1925. Two months later he was made a member of the jury of admissions to the diplomatic services. After his Danubian assignment ended in 1926, in 1927 Charles-Roux became envoy extraordinary and minister plenipotentiary to Czechoslovakia; he was promoted to minister plenipotentiary, first class, on December 26, 1931. His appointment as Ambassador to the Vatican on May 6, 1932, kept him there until July 8, 1940. It was during those years that he gained a reputation as an orator, an "adroit and discreet diplomat," and an official capable of realistic cooperation. In his next post he was named secretary-general of the Ministry of Foreign Affairs in Paris. He was placed on inactive status on October 27, 1940. At the trial of Marshal Pétain in 1945 he gave evidence.

Throughout his diplomatic career, Charles-Roux has made studies of historical and contemporary affairs, contributing articles to the *Revue des Deux-Mondes, Revue Historique, Revue Politique et Parlementaire,* etc. He is the author of a number of books, most of them dealing with Egypt and the Suez Canal: *Les origines de l'expédition d'Egypte* (1910); *Alexandre II, Gortchakoff et Napoléon III* (1911); *L'Angleterre, l'isthme de Suez et l'Egypte au XVIIᵉ siècle* and *Le projet de conquête d'Egypte sous de règne de Louis XVI* (1922); *L'Angleterre et l'expédition française d'Egypte,* two volumes (1925); *Trois ambassades françaises à la veille de la guerre* (1928); *Les échelles de Syrie et de Palestine au XVIIIᵉ siècle* (1928); *France et Afrique du Nord avant 1830* (1932); *Bonaparte, gouverneur d'Egypte* (1936); *France et Chrétiens d'Orient* (1936); *Histoire de la Nation Egyptienne* (1937); *Huit ans au Vatican* (1947); *Cinq mois tragiques aux Affaires Etrangères* (1949);

CHARLES-ROUX, FRANCOIS—*Cont.*

La paix des Empires Centraux; *Thiers et Méhémet Ali* (1951). The author was made a member of the Academy of Moral and Political Science of l'Institut de France on December 8, 1934. In 1944 he was elected vice-president and in 1945 president of the academy. Many of his works have been given honorary awards by the institute.

On December 21, 1944, Charles-Roux became a director of the Compagnie Universelle du Canal Maritime de Suez, which owns the 100-mile waterway connecting Port Said on the Mediterranean with Port Taufiq, near Suez, on the Red Sea. Though Great Britain owns 44 per cent of the company's stock, a majority of the stockholders have always been French, and a Frenchman has always been president of its board of directors. Charles-Roux became president on April 6, 1948. In 1951 he headed a board comprised of sixteen Frenchmen, ten Britons, four Egyptians, one Dutchman, and one American. Since World War II, nearly 70 per cent of the canal traffic has been British or American. Revenue in 1949 came to $80,000,000, leaving a profit of $28,000,000. The company completed a $14,000,000 improvement program in November 1951, providing a new by-pass, called the Farouk Canal, which eliminated a bottleneck for passing convoys.

Founded in 1856 by engineer Ferdinand de Lesseps to raise funds for building the Suez Canal (at a cost of nearly $74,000,000), the company holds a 99-year concession dating from November 17, 1869, when the canal was opened. At the expiration of the concession in 1968, ownership will revert to the Egyptian Government. However, the question of immediate nationalization of the canal has often been an issue. On March 7, 1949, the company signed an agreement providing for greater participation by Egypt in management and profits, making the government a "privileged partner" in the company. Since 1882 the canal has been guarded by British troops, and since 1888 it has been operated under a convention making it an international waterway, open to ships of all nations in war and peace. However, since 1949 Egypt has been denying passage through the canal to ships of all nationalities bound for Israel, most of them tankers carrying oil to Haifa. A United States-British-French resolution demanding that Egypt cease her restrictions was passed by the United Nations Security Council in September 1951, which Egypt has not observed.

In October 1951 Premier Mustafa Nahas Pasha asked his parliament to abrogate Egypt's 1936 treaty with Great Britain, force British troops out of the canal zone and take over full control of the Anglo-Egyptian Sudan. Calling this action "illegal," the British sent additional troops to canal bases. According to the British view, expressed by Robert Fedden in the New York *Times* (March 11, 1951), abandoning the canal would be "suicidal," for in the event of war it would leave exposed the strategically important Middle East with its oil resources. When labor trouble and incidents costing the lives of several British soldiers and Egyptians

occurred at canal bases during October-November 1951, the question of company intervention was raised. The New York *Times* quoted a Suez Canal company official as saying that under international regulations the company could not interfere, for its sole function was to provide for the safe passage of ships through the canal. It was expected, said the New York *Herald Tribune* on November 26, 1951, that the company would "come under fire during forthcoming debates in the Egyptian Parliament."

François Charles-Roux is a Grand Officer of the French Legion of Honor, a member of the Institut d'Egypte and administrator of the Land Bank of Egypt. He is a member of the Catholic Church and president of Catholic Aid in France. He and his wife, the former Sabine Gounelle, have a son, Jean, and two daughters, Cyprienne (Princesse del Drago) and Edmonde. Of medium build, Charles-Roux is five feet five inches tall; he has brown eyes. A tennis enthusiast, he is honorary president of the International Tennis Club (French section), and an honorary member of the English section of the club.

References

Annuaire Diplomatique et Consulaire (1939)
Dictionnaire Biographique Français Contemporain (1950)
International Who's Who, 1951
Who's Who, 1951
Who's Who in Egypt and the Middle East, 1949

CHASE, WILLIAM C(URTIS) Mar. 9, 1895- United States Army officer

Address: b. c/o Military Assistance Advisory Group of Formosa, APO 63, c/o Postmaster, San Francisco, Calif.

An officer of the United States Army Cavalry for more than thirty-five years, Major General William C. Chase has headed the American Military Assistance Advisory Group in Formosa since its inception in the spring of 1951. The mission's purpose is to help train Chiang Kai-shek's Nationalist forces on the island to resist possible Communist assault. Before assuming his present command, General Chase served with the Third Army from 1949 until 1951, first as chief of staff and then as deputy commander. During World War II he became known for three "firsts"—he commanded the landing troops that seized the first foothold on the Japanese Admiralty Islands; the 1st Cavalry Division under his command was the first to re-enter Manila in February 1945 and the first to enter Tokyo the following September.

William Curtis Chase was born in Providence, Rhode Island, on March 9, 1895, to Ward Beecher and Dora Evelyn (Curtis) Chase. While serving in the field artillery of the Rhode Island National Guard from 1913 to 1916, he attended Brown University in Providence, receiving his B.A. degree there in 1916. In November of that year he was commissioned a second lieutenant of Cavalry in the Regular

Army and was then promoted to first lieutenant. After attending the Army General Service School in Fort Leavenworth, Kansas, he was assigned in April 1917 to the 3d Cavalry in Fort Sam Houston, Texas, and three months later was transferred to the 6th Cavalry in Marfa, Texas. He then took courses at the Machine Gun School and the Infantry School of Arms in Fort Sill, Oklahoma, from October 1917 to February 1918, when he rejoined the 6th Cavalry. The following month he was transferred to the 11th Machine Gun Battalion in Camp Green, North Carolina, and in May 1918 he sailed with that unit to France, where he participated in the World War I offensives of Aisne-Marne, St. Mihiel, and Meuse-Argonne.

Upon his return to the United States, Chase was assigned to the 16th Cavalry, being stationed in Texas at Camp Mercedes and at Fort Sam Houston. He was promoted to the permanent rank of captain on September 2, 1919. After four years (1921-25) as Assistant Professor of Military Science and Tactics at Michigan Agricultural College, Chase enrolled in the Cavalry School at Fort Riley, Kansas, from which he was graduated in June 1926. Three months later he entered the Infantry School at Fort Benning, Georgia, where he completed the Advanced Course in May 1927, subsequently accepting assignment with the 14th Cavalry at Fort Sheridan, Illinois. In July 1929 Chase, whose promotion to the permanent rank of major had become effective on December 29, 1928, was made plans and training officer of the 14th Cavalry; he then attended the Command and General Staff School in Fort Leavenworth, graduating in June 1931.

From 1931 until 1934 Chase was stationed in the Philippine Islands, first as post plans and training officer at Fort Stotsenburg and later as post intelligence officer, as chemical warfare officer, and as commander of the 2d Squadron, 26th Cavalry. Following his graduation from the Army War College, which he attended from August 1934 to June 1935, he filled for the next three years the assignment of instructor in tactics at the Cavalry School at Fort Riley, Kansas. Chase was promoted to the permanent rank of lieutenant colonel on October 1, 1938. That year a new teaching post took him to the Command and General Staff School, Fort Leavenworth, Kansas, where he remained until his return in November 1940 to Fort Sam Houston, Texas, as assistant chief of staff for intelligence of the Eighth Army Corps. After commanding the 113th Cavalry from February 1942 to February 1943, he assumed command of the 1st Cavalry Brigade, which the following June was sent from Fort Bliss, Texas, to the southwest Pacific.

On February 29, 1944, Chase led dismounted units of the 1st Cavalry Division, including the famous Custer's 7th Regiment, in the landing on Los Negros Island in the Admiralty-Islands group and directed the capture there of Momote airfield. The New York newspaper PM (March 1, 1944) predicted that this invasion would "bring about the collapse of the entire Japanese defense system in the southwest and south Pacific." Chase took the brigade into

U. S. Army

MAJ. GEN. WILLIAM C. CHASE

Leyte on D-Day and later into Luzon; then in February 1945 the 1st Cavalry Division under Chase became the first to re-enter Manila. "At dusk on the evening of February 3," as recounted by Newsweek (February 12, 1945), "after a dash of 100 miles in 66 hours, a flying column of tanks and motorized infantry of the 1st Cavalry Division led by Brig. Gen. William C. Chase broke into Manila from the east. Storming through barricades against intense sniper fire, the Americans rushed first to Santo Tomás concentration camp, where about 3,700 emaciated civilians were interned. . . . Next, the 1st Cavalry seized Malacanan Palace, the residence of the Philippine Presidents." In May of that year Chase was awarded the Distinguished Service Cross by General Douglas MacArthur for "extraordinary heroism" in this action.

As commander of the 38th Infantry Division, Chase in February 1945 led the assault on Mariveles harbor on the southern tip of the Bataan Peninsula—an action regarded by George E. Jones of the New York Times as being of considerable importance in gaining control of Manila Bay. The next month Chase supervised the combined airborne and amphibious operation against Caballo Island, off Corregidor, and in April he participated in the demolition of Fort Drum, an immovable "concrete battleship" at the entrance to Manila Bay. After six weeks of intense fighting, he directed on May 28 the seizure of the Wawa Dam on the Marikina River, thereby assuring Manila and its environs of an adequate water supply and helping to solve sanitary problems facing the High Command in establishing Manila as the chief base for operations against the enemy.

Chase's desire "to be the first general into Tokyo," just as he had been the first into Manila (New York Times, August 19, 1945), was realized on September 8 when he led the 1st Cavalry Division, having become its com-

CHASE, WILLIAM C.—*Continued*
mander in July 1945, into the Japanese capital.
In the rank of major general, to which he was
advanced in January 1948, Chase remained in
command of the 1st Cavalry in Tokyo until
February 1949. During World War II (wrote
Peter Edson in the New York *World-Telegram*,
April 30, 1951) "General Chase was a GI's
general and ate out of the mess lines, wherever
he was, in preference to private dining rooms.
He gained considerable fame by the signs he
had put up as a morale booster for his troops,
reading: 'Welcome to Tokyo—Courtesy 1st
Cavalry.'"

Following his return to the United States in
1949, General Chase was assigned to the Third
Army at Fort McPherson, Georgia, where two
months later he was made chief of staff. In
December 1950 he was named deputy commander of the Third Army with headquarters
in Atlanta, Georgia. Concurrently with the Defense Department's announcement in April 1952
of the formation of a Military Assistance Advisory Group to aid Chiang Kai-shek's Nationalist forces in Formosa under the Mutual
Defense Assistance Program came news of the
appointment of Chase as head of the mission.
The object of the group, as reported by the
New York *Times* (April 21, 1951), was to
study "the needs of the Chinese Nationalist
troops and recommend to officials here [in
Washington] what types of arms, weapons,
communications, aircraft and other 'hard' items
are most needed. The group will also take
charge of the training of the Nationalists in the
use of the American-made equipment." Shortly
after his arrival in Formosa in May, Chase explained at a press conference that he was not
there to lead an invasion, that his group was
formed under the same law "as are twenty to
thirty of these advisory groups operating
throughout the world" (New York *Times*,
May 2, 1951), and that all such bodies were
guided by directives issued by representatives of
the State and the Defense Departments and of
the Economic Cooperation Administration. The
next month he expressed satisfaction with the
general progress being made by his group in
integrating its program "with all phases of
Nationalist China's armed forces without touching the Chinese organization or administration"
(New York *Times*, June 25, 1951).

In a report from Formosa by Henry R.
Lieberman, Chase was said to have objections
to both the "organization of the Chinese services of supply and the political commissar system established in the armed forces under the
direction of General Chiang Ching-kuo, the
Moscow-educated elder son of Generalissimo
Chiang Kai-shek" (New York *Times*, November 11, 1951). Lieberman added that Chase was
also handicapped by equipment delivery delays
which had been caused by priority demands
from Korea, Europe, and Indo-China. New
York *World-Telegram* correspondent Jim G. Lucas stated the following month that Chase had
managed to accomplish "a great deal," including the improvement of the average Chinese
soldier's diet, the procurement of new uniforms
and shoes, the establishment of a revised training program, and, by virtue of his tactfulness,

the creation of goodwill between the Nationalists and the American advisory mission. In a
New Year's statement delivered on December
31, Chase described the United States and Nationalist China as "equal partners in the fight
against the evil of communism" (New York
Herald Tribune, December 31, 1951) and mentioned the possibility that Chiang Kai-shek's
troops might be used in places other than
Formosa. On May 1, 1952, the first anniversary
of his arrival in Formosa, Chase said that
the combat efficiency, morale, and physical condition of the Nationalist Army had improved
considerably during the last year.

In addition to the Distinguished Service
Cross, the cavalry officer has been awarded
the Distinguished Service Medal, the Legion of
Merit, the Bronze Star Medal with two Oak
Leaf Clusters, the Army Commendation Ribbon,
and the Purple Heart. In 1946 he received an
honorary LL.D. from Brown University. He
is a member of Phi Beta Kappa and Delta
Kappa Epsilon. His club is the Army and
Navy Country Club, Washington, D.C. On
September 4, 1922, he married Dorothea Marie
Wetherbee.

References

N Y World-Telegram p18 Ap 30 '51
N Y Herald Tribune II p1 Jl 1 '51
Who's Who in America, 1952-53

CHELF, FRANK L(ESLIE) Sept. 22,
1907- United States Representative from
Kentucky
Address: b. House Office Bldg., Washington 25,
D.C.; h. 216 E. Main St., Lebanon, Ky.

Frank L. Chelf, Democratic Representative
from the Fourth District of Kentucky, was
first elected to the United States Congress in
1945, and as of 1952 has been continually re-
elected to the national legislature. Since
March 1945 he has been a member of the House
Judiciary Committee, and on February 5, 1952,
he was appointed chairman of a Judiciary subcommittee to investigate corruption in the
United States Department of Justice. After
initial difficulties, the subcommittee secured Presidential agreement to its getting
data from Governmental departments and agencies. Chelf was one of the leading Congressional supporters of the displaced persons program in 1947. Prior to becoming a Representative he served for three consecutive terms as
attorney of Marion County, Kentucky.

Frank Leslie Chelf, the son of Judge Weed
S. Chelf and Hallie (Wrather) Chelf, was
born on a farm near Elizabethtown, Kentucky,
on September 22, 1907. Both his grandfather
and father were lawyers. (He had two sisters and five brothers; one of the latter is
now deceased.) At the age of five, upon the
death of his father and mother, Frank was
placed in the Masonic Widows and Orphans
Home of Kentucky. A public school pupil,
he was graduated in 1926 from Elizabethtown
High School, where he was a member of the
debating society and participated in football
and other sports. Chelf was a student also at

Wide World Photos

FRANK L. CHELF

St. Mary's College and Centre College, both in Kentucky, and in 1931 he received the LL.B. degree from the law school of Cumberland University, in Lebanon, Tennessee.

After being admitted to the Kentucky bar in 1931, Chelf practiced law in Lebanon. From 1934 to 1944 he was County Attorney of Marion County, serving as prosecutor for three consecutive terms. He received national attention in 1941 in the trial of a murderer. By locating the gun, despite the killer's efforts to confuse the police by "planting" a spurious weapon, Chelf was able to discover and successfully to prosecute the criminal.

During World War II Chelf served as an officer in the Army Air Force. Taking a leave from his position as County Attorney in 1942, he volunteered in the United States Army and was commissioned as a first lieutenant in the Air Corps, in which post he saw active duty. He also served as chief code designator for the Intelligence Division of the Air Transport Command, as executive officer of the Plans and Liaison Division, and as assistant chief of Air Staff Training. By August 10, 1944, when he was discharged because of a physical disability, he had attained the rank of major.

Chelf became active in national politics early in his career, serving in 1936 as a delegate to the Democratic National Convention at Philadelphia. Shortly after leaving the Air Corps, he was elected to the United States House of Representatives, beginning his legislative duties on January 3, 1945, in the Seventy-ninth Congress. The Fourth Kentucky District, which Chelf represents, comprises nineteen counties. The lawyer was subsequently re-elected to the Eightieth, Eighty-first, and Eighty-second Congresses. His main committee assignment has

been the House of Representatives Judiciary Committee, to which he was appointed in March 1945.

On the opening day of the Seventy-ninth Congress (1945), Chelf cast his first legislative vote—against Democratic Representative Rankin's proposal to elevate the Un-American Activities Committee to the rank of a standing committee in the House. He supported the Government reorganization bill and the antitrust exemptions for railroads. In May the Kentuckian voted for a constitutional amendment requiring only a majority of the full membership of each house of Congress for approval of treaties, and in June he supported the anti-poll tax bill. Regarded by Truman as of "the first order of importance" for the success of his administration, the Hull reciprocal trade program was extended to 1948, with the aid of Representative Chelf's "Yea" in May. Chelf also voted in December for the second appropriation, of $1.35 billions, to the United Nations Relief and Rehabilitation Administration. In the second session (1946) he expressed himself in favor of the loan of $3.75 billions to enable Great Britain to re-establish its foreign trade (July). Also, in 1946 he favored the extension of the draft to 1947 and opposed exemption of teen-aged youths; he supported the President's strike-control bill.

Representative Chelf voted in February 1947 against establishing a two-term limit for the Presidency in the first session of the Eightieth Congress and supported in the same month the banning of portal-to-portal pay suits. He voted (May) in favor of the Greek-Turkish aid bill. In the summer of 1947, as a member of a House Immigration subcommittee, Chelf together with Jacob K. Javits and James G. Fulton visited more than 200 DP camps in Germany and Austria, interviewing about 2,000 displaced persons. At the opening meeting of the subcommittee in June, the newspaper *PM* had commented, Chelf seemed to be the only "receptive" person on the subcommittee. Back from the tour of the refugee camps, Chelf, the leading Congressional supporter of the DP program, said that if the United Nations worked out allocations rapidly enough he would favor a special session of Congress to pass a new immigration bill to admit the United States quota.

In the second session of the Eightieth Congress (1948), Chelf expressed himself in favor of a bill extending $6 billions aid to members of the European Recovery Program (March), concerning which the President had stated, "This measure is America's answer to the challenge facing the free world today." The Representative from Kentucky voted for action to control subversive activities (May), and he supported the admission of 200,000 displaced persons into the United States (June). During this session Chelf introduced a bill, approved unanimously by the House Judiciary Committee, authorizing the Attorney General to award medals to American servicemen for unusual bravery and achievement.

Representative Chelf voted to extend rent controls (March) in the first session of the

CHELF, FRANK L.—*Continued*

Eighty-first Congress (1949) and cast his ballot against the repeal of the Federal oleomargarine taxes (April). He affirmed extension of the Marshall Plan (April), and opposed a 50 per cent reduction in military aid to Europe (August). In December of 1949 he introduced legislation to make sex crimes a Federal offense, with a ten-year minimum penalty and with required psychiatric treatment; the purpose of this law, he stated, would be not only to penalize, but to prevent the repetition of such crimes. In the second session of this Congress (1950) Chelf voted against a voluntary fair employment practice bill (February) and in favor of a measure to abolish the electoral college (July). He supported economic aid for Korea and Formosa in February, as well as a $2.7 billions extension of the ECA in March. Another measure he favored was the extension of the rent control act, and he voted against overriding the veto of the Communist control bill.

Shortly after the beginning of the Eighty-second Congress (1951), Chelf introduced a bill which would raise the House membership from 435 to 450, thereby taking account of population shifts reported by the previous census. It was during this same year that the Kentucky Democrat declared that Czechoslovakia had resorted to "barefaced lies" in imprisoning William N. Oatis, Associated Press correspondent, in Prague, and said to the new Czechoslovakian Ambassador, "You are about as welcome in this country as a swarm of red ants at a family picnic gathering." In the first session of this Congress Chelf voted to restore to the House Rules Committee the power to withhold legislation from floor action (January). In July he opposed authorizing the President to build and operate defense plants and voted against an amendment to the Defense Production Act permitting packers a "reasonable margin of profit" on each type of meat which was processed. Chelf opposed a bill giving coastal States title to submerged oil fields in adjacent specified waters (July). A foreign aid bill granting about $7.5 billions in aid met his approval (August).

On February 5, 1952, Chelf was appointed chairman of a seven-man Judiciary Subcommittee investigating corruption in the Department of Justice, and shortly afterward Harold E. Stassen demanded that this group consider reports that Attorney General J. Howard McGrath had become a millionaire while holding public office. Appearing before the subcommittee in March, McGrath saw no necessity for probing the Justice Department; but Representative Chelf insisted that, had such a probe been made in the past, the irregularities of Theron Lamar Caudle, Assistant Attorney General (dismissed the prior November by Truman), would have been revealed. When the subcommittee wished to see tax returns of McGrath and nineteen other high officials in the Justice Department, the Attorney General refused to comply, and the President instructed all Government Departments not to furnish certain data to the Congressional investigators.

McGrath resigned at the President's request. On April 12 Truman requested all executive departments and agencies to cooperate to the fullest extent with the subcommittee. Chelf declared himself to be "very much pleased." The Representative was elected to the Eighty-third Congress on November 4, 1952.

Chelf is a member of the Kentucky Bar Association, the County Attorneys Association of Kentucky, the national and Kentucky peace officers associations, the International Aviation Association, the American Legion, and the Veterans of Foreign Wars. His fraternity is Phi Delta Theta. He was chairman of the Sixth Bar District of Kentucky during 1940-41. Other memberships of his are in the Masons (Knights Templar, Order of the Eastern Star) and the Kiwanis Club.

Frank L. Chelf married Louise Rash on June 12, 1935; their three children are named Carolyn Jane, Angela Bonnie, and Frank L., Jr. The Representative is a Presbyterian. He has blue eyes and brown hair, is five feet nine inches tall, and weighs 140 pounds. His favorite sports are boxing and football, and his hobby is amateur photography. Shortly before adjournment in 1948, he participated in a singing act on the floor of the House of Representatives, playing the harmonica.

References

> Biographical Directory of the American Congress, 1774-1949 (1950)
> Congressional Directory (1951)
> Who's Who in America, 1952-53
> Who's Who in United States Politics (1950)

CHERWELL, FREDERICK ALEXANDER LINDEMANN, 1ST BARON (chär'-wĕl) 1886- British Cabinet member; university professor

Address: b. & h. Christ Church, Oxford, England; 11 Downing St., London, S.W. 1, England

A friend and counselor of Winston Churchill since the 1920's, Frederick Alexander Lindemann, 1st Baron Cherwell, has as his main tasks in the Conservative Government the supervision of Britain's atomic energy program and the direction of the statistical branch of the Prime Minister's office. He has accompanied Churchill on the latter's travels, being prominent among the negotiators who went with the Prime Minister to the United States for conferences in January 1952. Cherwell's official title is Paymaster-General, a Cabinet office he was given in October 1951 when the Conservatives returned to power and which he had held during several of the World War II years. A scientist, he has been professor of experimental philosophy at the University of Oxford since 1919.

Frederick Alexander Lindemann, who was born in 1886, is of Alsatian extraction, one of the four sons of Adolphus Frederick Lindemann, a wealthy businessman and scientist (who had settled at Sidmouth, Devonshire, England), and of an American mother, the former Olga Noble Davidson. His education was unconventional. Instead of going to Eton or Winchester, and then to Oxford or Cambridge (as did most sons of wealth), he was sent to a private school, Blairlodge. This was followed by schooling in Darmstadt, Germany, and later by studies in astrophysics and the quantum theory under Professor Nernst at the University of Berlin, which awarded him his Ph.D. degree. He took further studies in Paris.

Lindemann was employed from the early days of World War I as research scientist at the headquarters of the Royal Flying Corps (as it then was named) at Farnborough, Hampshire. "It was there," noted H. R. Trevor-Roper in the New York *Times*, "that he achieved one of his most dramatic exploits." "At one time," stated the London *Observer*, "there were serious losses of planes and pilots from the apparently incurable disease known as 'tail spin.'" Lindemann, said Trevor-Roper, produced a solution on paper and submitted it. Then, impatient of delay, he set about proving it himself. After training as a pilot for three weeks, he took his plane up to a high altitude, put it into a tail spin, and, at the risk of his life, showed that his theory had been correct.

Lindemann's position as director of the Aeronautical Research Laboratory through the war at Farnborough brought him into contact with men prominent in public life, among them two statesmen, Lord Birkenhead and Winston Churchill. In 1919, without either an Oxford or a Cambridge degree, he was appointed professor of experimental philosophy at Oxford. He was also made a fellow of Wadham College that year and two years later of Christ Church, at which college he has since spent his academic life. It was there that he earned the sobriquet of "The Prof," although, remarked the *Observer* writer, "he was in every way remote from the conventional image of a professor . . . neither amiable nor absent-minded nor other-worldly."

Lindemann's chief work in his first years at Oxford was to initiate research (at the Clarendon Laboratory) on very low temperatures. In university life he became a person of mark— unorthodox, mysterious, and influential. He himself was rich and moved about to lectures or on country house visits in a limousine, always wearing a derby hat in which (according to Trevor-Roper) he even made a parachute jump at the Moscow Air Exhibition. In a decade when young Oxford liked to be "pink" in politics he was "blatantly" conservative. As time went on he became more closely associated with Winston Churchill as political supporter and intimate friend. In the years immediately preceding World War II, when the official Conservatives hoped that Hitler might be stalled off by appeasement, he supported Churchill and Eden in their denunciation of the dictator's aggression.

In 1937 Lindemann came actively into the political scene as a by-election candidate for one of the University of Oxford Parliamentary seats, opposing two fellow dons. He

British Inf. Services

LORD CHERWELL

came out a "bad third" in the voting, but on July 4, 1941, about two years after the outbreak of the war, he was raised to the peerage, choosing for his title Cherwell, Oxford's little river. As a member of the House of Lords, he frequently gave advice to Prime Minister Churchill (he was Churchill's personal assistant, says *Who's Who*), particularly on matters wherein his skillful interpretation of statistics could be applied. He supplied data on which the high strategy of Britain was founded, said Trevor-Roper: "He became the sole channel for all scientific inventions submitted to the Government, and was charged with the duty of drawing attention to vital shortages wherever they might occur." In December 1942 he had been appointed to the Churchill Cabinet as Paymaster-General, the paying agent for Government departments other than the revenue department. Since that office entails few duties, Cherwell was available for such advisory tasks the Prime Minister might assign to him. On January 13, 1943, Lord Cherwell was made a Privy Counselor.

After Churchill's fall from power in 1945 Cherwell remained his close friend and constant adviser, and a pillar of the Conservative cause in the House of Lords and in public controversy. In April 1947 he initiated a discussion in the *Times* by denying the Socialist Government's contention that the British people, as a whole, were better fed than ever before, using "compelling" statistics to argue his case. In regard to the atomic energy program, one of his chief concerns, Cherwell in July 1951 argued in the House of Lords that the program should be removed from civil service control and put under "a free organization which could move fast and tighten up security arrangements" (New York *Herald Tribune*). In September and October of that year he toured centers of

CHERWELL, FREDERICK ALEXANDER LINDEMANN, 1ST BARON—*Cont.*
scientific research in both the United States and Canada.

When the Conservatives displaced Labor as the governing party in October 1951, Cherwell again became a member of the Cabinet as Paymaster-General, who may undertake such duties as the Prime Minister directs. For Cherwell those duties chiefly comprise statistical interpretation and the supervision of developments in atomic energy. He refuses to accept any salary. A prominent member of the group of negotiators brought over to Washington in January 1952 by Churchill, Lord Cherwell is generally credited with being the prime mover, on the British side, in producing the agreement whereby the United States will furnish steel to Britain in return for tin and rubber. As reported later, at the Washington meeting there also were conversations about the pooling of British and American atomic secrets.

Lord Cherwell's London address is a specially provided apartment at 11 Downing Street, next door to the famous official residence of the Prime Minister, No. 10. "The illusion of mystery" about Cherwell dissolves, wrote Trevor-Roper, when one meets him: "He turns out to be a sociable, convivial figure, a witty (if sometimes acid) conversationalist." He is tall, massive, and clean-shaven; a bachelor, a teetotaler, a nonsmoker, and a vegetarian. The *Observer*'s pen portrait gives him a "sad but insensitive face" with "indrawn eyes." His published works include *The Physical Significance of the Quantum Theory* and papers on physical, chemical, and astrophysical subjects in the *Proceedings of the Royal Society*, the *Philosophical Magazine*, and other journals; he is a fellow of the Royal Society. His recreations are lawn tennis and golf; his club is the Athenæum.

References

N Y Times Mag p11 Ja 6 '52
U S News 32:42+ F 29 '52

Burke's Peerage (1949)
Kelly's Handbook to the Titled, Landed, and Official Classes, 1949
Who's Who, 1951

CHEVRIER, LIONEL (shĕv″ryā′) Apr. 2, 1903- Canadian Cabinet Minister

Address: b. c/o Department of Transport, Hunter Bldg., Ottawa, Ontario, Canada; h. 5 Linden Terrace, Ottawa, Ontario, Canada; Cornwall, Ontario, Canada

Plans for the development of the St. Lawrence waterway project began to take definite shape early in 1952 with the formation of the St. Lawrence Seaway Authority of Canada. The spearhead in this enterprise is Lionel Chevrier, Canadian Minister of Transport since 1944, who introduced legislation in the Canadian Parliament to establish the seaway agency. Chevrier, who was first elected to the House of Commons in 1935, has served on several Parliamentary committees and has represented the Dominion at international conferences. By profession a lawyer, he was appointed King's Counsel in 1938.

Lionel Chevrier was born April 2, 1903, to French-Canadian parents in Cornwall, Ontario (a town with relatively few inhabitants of French descent), of which his father, Joseph Elphège Chevrier, was elected Mayor for a number of years, holding that office during World War I. Mrs. Chevrier, reported Corolyn Cox in the Canadian periodical *Saturday Night*, was born Malvina de Repentigny, a member of the family of St. Anne de Bellevue celebrated in the Canadian romance *The Golden Dog*. During the years that he attended the local elementary school in Cornwall, Lionel Chevrier frequently accompanied his father on trips to the United States. After graduating from the Cornwall Collegiate Institute in 1917, the youth entered the University of Ottawa, from which he received the B.A. degree in 1924 and the Ph.B degree. At the university he won medals in chemistry and debating, and captained the football and hockey teams. With his law degree from Osgoode Hall in Toronto (received in 1927), Chevrier was admitted to the bar of Ontario in 1928. For a year and a half he practiced with a law firm before returning to Cornwall in 1928 to form the general law partnership of Chevrier and Latchford, now known as Chevrier, Latchford and Fitzpatrick. Chevrier was named a King's Counsel in 1938.

It was in 1935 that Chevrier was first elected to the Canadian House of Commons as representative of the constituency of Stormont, Ontario, which re-elected him in 1940, 1945, and 1949. A member of the Liberal party, Chevrier in 1940 was named deputy chief Government whip. In World War II he became chairman of the Special Parliamentary Subcommittee on War Expenditures in 1942 and was named Parliamentary assistant to C. D. Howe, the Minister of Munitions and Supply, in 1943. Nominated to the Privy Council April 18, 1945, Chevrier was at that time also appointed Minister of Transport, a portfolio which was again assigned to him November 15, 1948, in the Cabinet of Louis St. Laurent. The Department that Chevrier heads was organized in 1936 to bring under one authority the supervision of harbors, canals, railways, marine and shipping, civil aviation, radio, and meteorology (*Canada Year Book*, 1950). Since June 8, 1948, the Minister of Transport has also been responsible for the operation of telegraph and telephone services, which had formerly been a function of the Department of Public Works.

As Minister of Transport, Chevrier has been prominent in pressing for a joint Canadian-American St. Lawrence waterway and power project, particularly the St. Lawrence Seaway. At a February 1951 meeting of the Montreal Board of Trade and Chamber of Commerce, Chevrier stressed the necessity for the project: "From the point of view of national defense, I believe that the immediate development of the St. Lawrence deep waterway is of the greatest importance. Without construction of the seaway, the large deposits of high-grade iron ore in

Labrador cannot move economically and expeditiously to the Great Lakes steel centers. . . .You would find within the Montreal area 6,000,000 horsepower of electrical energy. . . . When this power is fully developed I would venture the opinion that this will be one of the richest areas on the North American continent."

In the expectation that the United States Congress would not immediately approve the joint project, Canada prepared to undertake the venture alone, with the result that in late 1951 Chevrier presented a plan for a St. Lawrence Seaway Authority to the Canadian Parliament. When this was passed in January 1952, the way was open for Canada to provide funds for the construction, which might be begun in 1953. Under the Authority's legislative powers, it could borrow up to $300 millions (Chevrier estimates that the seaway will cost Canada $250 millions). To circumvent Congressional disapproval, President Truman in April 1952 agreed with Canadian Foreign Minister Lester B. Pearson to submit plans for the two-nation hydroelectric project to the International Joint Commission; American participation would be secured, possibly, by the New York State Power Authority under licensing by the Federal Power Commission. This agreement left Canada free to undertake the river-deepening project alone, thus making it necessary for United States deep-draught ships in the future to pay toll to Canada for use of the waterway. Robert Mc-Keown, Canadian Parliamentary correspondent, itemized the pros and cons of the question in a May 20, 1952, article for *Look*, pointing out that Canada's vastly increased postwar industry requires improved water freightways and intensified power facilities. On the other hand, as opponents of the project argue, the waterway would be frozen five months yearly; it would be vulnerable to enemy attack; and it would draw traffic from other transportation facilities, one of the reasons it is opposed by railroad companies, coal operators and unions, and Great Lakes vessel owners, chiefly in the United States.

In the Canadian Parliament Chevrier has been a member of the Sessional Committee on Railways and Shipping since 1945. In international affairs he represented his country at the Empire Parliamentary Association meeting held in Washington, D.C. (1943); the United Nations Monetary and Financial Conference held at Bretton Woods, New Hampshire; and the third United Nations General Assembly meeting in Paris, where in 1948 he headed the Canadian delegation. Present at the first meeting of the Interim Assembly of the Provisional International Civil Aviation Organization convened at Montreal in May 1946, the Transport Minister also served as head of the Canadian delegation to the 1949 conference on civil aviation in London between Canada and the United Kingdom, and in New York between Canada and the United States.

From 1928 to 1934 Chevrier was secretary to the Board of Trade in Cornwall, and in 1932 a member of the Centennial Committee of his native town. There he also belongs to the Cornwall Club and the Cornwall Golf and Country Club; in Ottawa his Club is the

LIONEL CHEVRIER

Rideau. The Stormont, Dundas, and Glengarry Highlanders in 1949 made Chevrier an honorary colonel of that regiment. Another honorary post he holds is that of the presidency of the Alumni Association of the University of Ottawa, which institution awarded him an honorary LL.D. degree in 1946. His fraternity is Phi Delta Phi, the legal society. He and the former Lucienne Brûlé, who were married October 22, 1932, have six children, Lucie, Robert, Jean, Bernard, Adèle, and Marie. Roman Catholic, he is a Knight of Columbus. Because of Chevrier's equal fluency in French and English, Corolyn Cox has observed, he is well qualified to interpret the points of view of the two great sections of Canadian citizens.

References

Sat Night 58:2 Jl 10 '43
International Who's Who, 1951
Les Biographies Françaises d'Amérique, 1950
Who's Who in America, 1952-53
Who's Who in Canada, 1949-50
Who's Who in the United Nations, 1951
World Biography (1948)

CHRISTENBERRY, ROBERT K(EA-TON) Jan. 27, 1899- Boxing commissioner; hotel executive

Address: b. c/o New York State Athletic Commission, 80 Centre St., New York 13; c/o Hotel Astor, Times Sq., New York 18; h. Shawnee-on-Delaware, Pa.

The chairmanship of the New York State Athletic Commission is filled by Robert K. Christenberry, who was appointed to the post by Governor Thomas E. Dewey in September 1951. Because of the large number of boxing and wrestling matches held in that State, the

ROBERT K. CHRISTENBERRY

rulings of the commission are regarded as particularly important. Christenberry's career has almost exclusively been in the hotel field—he is general manager and president of Hotel Astor, to which he came in 1935.

Robert Keaton Christenberry, the son of William C. and Rebecca A. (Keaton) Christenberry, is a native of Huntington, in western Tennessee; the date of his birth is January 27, 1899. For his secondary education he attended high school in nearby Milan. At the age of sixteen Christenberry enlisted in the Marine Corps; and in 1917, when the United States entered World War I, he was sent to France with the 5th Regiment. The young marine, who was enthusiastic about boxing, was in the middleweight class. In 1918, however, a grenade he was holding exploded prematurely, resulting in the loss of his right hand. Released from service he was sent to Vladivostok, Russia, as United States vice-consul. At Santo Domingo (now Ciudad Trujillo) in the Dominican Republic, to which he was transferred in the following year (1919), he remained until resigning from the consular service in late 1921 to fulfill an early ambition to become a newspaperman.

Upon joining the staff of the Washington (D.C.) *Herald*, Christenberry was assigned to the general news and sports desks. It was as a sportswriter that he had "his first view of a boxing contest, a battle in which the late Pancho Villa, world flyweight champion in 1922, was a participant" (James P. Dawson in the New York *Times*). Christenberry also took courses at George Washington University during his three years with the *Herald*. Then, attracted by the land boom in Florida in 1925, he went to Jacksonville, where he continued newspaper work on the staff of the *Times-Union*.

Christenberry's initiation into hotel operation came in 1926, through his appointment as chief deputy hotel commissioner for the State of Florida. This position he held until 1929, when he was engaged as public relations and promotion manager by the Hotel Winton (now the Carter) in Cleveland, Ohio. Two years later he moved to Michigan, as director of sales and business promotion for the Book-Cadillac of Detroit, and the year 1932 found him as manager of the Jefferson at Peoria, Illinois. In 1934 he moved to Pittsburgh, Pennsylvania, where he was the general manager of the Roosevelt Hotel until November 1935, when he was called to New York to fill the position of vice-president and general manager of the Hotel Astor under a three-year contract. The contract was renewed in 1938 and again in 1941. Christenberry was elected to the presidency of the Astor in mid-June 1944; he is also the treasurer and a director of the hotel corporation.

The 1,000-room Hotel Astor, located on the west side of Broadway in the heart of the Times Square theatrical district, was considered New York's most palatial hotel when it opened in 1904. By the time Christenberry assumed the position of manager, Madison and Park Avenues had become the city's more fashionable hotel thoroughfares. He met the challenge by changing the hotel "from the red-velvet place it had been into a not-too-flashy modern," noted Alice Davidson in a New York *Post* article. Other writers have mentioned as contributory to the hotel's present prestige Christenberry's promotion of it as convention and banqueting headquarters and his cultivation of a distinguished theatrical residential clientele. He has also been president, since 1941, of the Broadway Association, a merchants' organization formed thirty years earlier "to work for the improvement of the thoroughfare." In 1942 he became chairman of an American Hotel Association "temperance committee" formed to "combat future moves by dry forces for the return of prohibition" (New York *Times*). To Alice Davidson a year later he explained: "Now, some people say that if you are chairman of a temperance committee . . . you must have the same goal as the W.C.T.U., but this is not correct. I do believe in temperance in its true meaning—in liquor, food, dress, play, work. But everybody knows the evils of trying to put a tight lid on drinking."

In the years of World War II Christenberry was the Times Square zone's first air-raid warden, and by the middle of 1943 he had worked on two USO campaigns and American Red Cross and Greater New York Fund drives. In addition to fulfilling his managerial duties at the Astor, he held directorships in the affiliated Ritz-Carlton Hotel, the West Side Association of Commerce, and the 42nd Street Merchants' and Property Owners' Association. In December 1943 the Astor manager was appointed consultant to the OPA restaurant branch, and in 1945, at the request of General Dwight D. Eisenhower, he accompanied General Mark Clark through France, Holland, Belgium, Germany, and Austria on a War Department mission to set up recreational facilities for American troops in liberated or occupied areas. Also, in 1945 (July) the hotel executive was elected president of a veterans' political committee formed for "protection of the basic American form of government against the inroads of any subversive or power-hungry group or elements," and in the following year was a member of the national executive committee of American Action, Inc., announced as "dedicated to a practical doorbell-ringing campaign against Communist-line candidates" (New York *Times*). Christenberry, a Republican, was a participant in the 1950 movement to draft Thomas E. Dewey for a third term as Governor of New York. In addition to the affiliations already mentioned he is currently a director of the Colonial and Central Real Estate Associations, the Columbia Baking Corporation, and the New York City Hotel Association; a member of the New York Convention and Visitors Bureau, of the national council of the Boy Scouts of America, and of the New York City Advisory Committee on Civil Defense.

The New York State Athletic Commission "issues licenses for, and has the sole direction, management and control of, all professional boxing, sparring and wrestling exhibitions in the State" (*New York Legislative Manual*). It is headed by a commission of three members appointed by the Governor with the consent of the State Senate. The commissioners' terms of three years each are "staggered" so that one appointment expires every year; the chairman receives a salary of $9,378 per annum.

In the summer of 1951 Lieutenant Colonel Edward P. F. Eagan, who had been chairman for about six years, resigned from the commission; on September 25 of that year Governor Dewey announced the appointment of Robert Christenberry to Eagan's vacated post. This announcement was accompanied by a statement of five objectives which the Governor wished to see attained in order to improve boxing conditions. "Fullest reliance," Dewey instructed, "must be placed on the Medical Advisory Board as it will be reconstituted and other scientific agencies whose research is available to the commission in order to reduce to a minimum the hazards of the sport." It was further stipulated that "every avenue must be kept open so that free competition exists in every licensed club" and that "all the business of professional boxing must be conducted in the open."

Governor Dewey's choice caused some comment among managers, promoters, and sportswriters, because Bob Christenberry's spectator interest in sports had been largely confined to watching wrestling contests on television. "This we imagine is just as well," a New York *Herald Tribune* editorial observed. "The best approach to boxing at the present moment is from the outside." The new chairman told the press when questioned as to his plans: "I'll do the best I can. I don't know the problems involved. For me to go off the deep end would be the height of stupidity, and I hope the Governor didn't appoint a stupid man." Christenberry's first important decision—a decision described as "stern"—was made on October 6 when he applied the highest legal penalty by revoking the boxing license of Sandy Saddler and suspending Willie Pep for "violating every rule in the book" in a featherweight championship match ten days previously. About a month afterward Christenberry issued instructions to all licensed clubs in the State to install safety pads perfected by the Cornell Aeronautical Laboratory at the instance of his predecessor, and in December launched an investigation of the International Boxing Club's exclusive contracts for bouts at Madison Square Garden, the Polo Grounds, and the Yankee Stadium in New York City. In January 1952 he ordered the world's heavyweight champion, "Jersey Joe" Walcott, to sign within fifteen days a contract to defend his title, and in the same month upheld the referee Ruby Goldstein in halting an uneven but "lackadaisical" bout between Livio Minelli and Johnny Saxton.

Christenberry, whose appointment as chairman of the Athletic Commission was formally confirmed by the New York State Senate on January 28, spends part of his time at his Astor Hotel office and part at the boxing commissions' office. He says that he attends at least four fights in the course of a week and about two out-of-State fights each month on the television. "Like the hotel business," he said in the interview for the *New Yorker*, "it's a twenty-four-hour-a-day job. . . .You're on call all the time."

Robert Christenberry and Edna Joan Le Roy were married August 14, 1929, and have one son, Robert Keaton, Jr., and one daughter, Sally Joan. The family resides at Shawnee-on-Delaware, Pennsylvania, where Christenberry, when he can take time away from New York, may find recreation at the local country club. Despite the loss of one hand, he reportedly plays an excellent game of golf. Other clubs to which he belongs are the New York Exchange (of which he is a charter member and past president), the New York Athletic, and the Circus Saints and Sinners. He is a Mason (Shriner), an Elk, an American Legionnaire, and a member of the Veterans of Foreign Wars. Christenberry, who is a Protestant, formed the habit of regularly reading the Bible while he was a reporter on the Washington *Herald*. He still speaks with a Tennessee accent, and has been described in the *New Yorker* as a "lively, talkative, robust individual who seems to live, work-wise and socially, with much gusto." He is tall and has graying hair and a small gray mustache.

References

Cue 20:10-12+ Je 16 '51 por
N Y Herald Tribune p1 S 26 '51; II p1 S 30 '51 por
N Y Post p33 Jl 13 '43 pors
N Y Times p42 S 26 '51 por
New Yorker 25:17-18 Ja 5 '52
Sat Eve Post 224:29+ F 16 '52

Business Executives of America (1950)
International World Who's Who, 1948-49
Who's Who in Commerce and Industry (1951)

CHUBB, L(EWIS) WARRINGTON Oct. 22, 1882—Apr. 2, 1952 Research engineer; director emeritus of the Westinghouse Research Laboratories; joined Westinghouse Electric and Manufacturing Company in 1905 as engineering apprentice; manager of radio engineering department (1920-30); helped establish radio station KDKA in Pittsburgh; director of Westinghouse Research Laboratories (1930-48); in World War II worked on method of producing fissionable material; was awarded the John Fritz medal for 1947; holder of some 150 patents. See *Current Biography*, 1947.

Obituary

N Y Times p35 Ap 3 '52

CLARK, JOHN Sept. 10, 1888- Labor union official

Address: c/o International Union of Mine, Mill and Smelter Workers, Tabor Bldg., Denver 2, Colo.; h. 3403 S. Lincoln, Englewood, Colo.

The International Union of Mine, Mill and Smelter Workers is headed by John Clark, who in 1951 was elected to his third two-year term as president. Now an independent union, it was expelled from the Congress of Industrial Organizations (CIO) in 1950 for alleged Leftist sympathies. At the time of the 1951 strike in the nonferrous industries, which affected production of metals vital to the defense program, President Truman sought an injunction in order to effect a settlement, in which the union and several major copper producing companies were involved. Clark, an American citizen of British birth, has been a copper miner and an official of copper-mining unions for a number of years. During World War II he served on three Federal boards.

JOHN CLARK

The son of Francis and Elizabeth (Lee) Clark, John Clark was born September 10, 1888, in England, where he spent his childhood and early youth. Subsequently, in his late teens he immigrated to the United States, of which he became a citizen in 1936. Working as a miner in the copper mines of America's West, Clark at the age of twenty became interested in trade unions, "influenced," he has said, "by working conditions and wages in the nonferrous metals industry—which were bad."

In 1908 Clark joined the Western Federation of Miners, which had been founded in 1893; by 1905 it was the one well-organized group which, with other dissatisfied AFL unions and independent unions, founded the Industrial Workers of the World (I.W.W.). A number of years later he was elected secretary of Local No. 16 of the International Union of Mine, Mill and Smelter Workers at the Great Falls (Montana) branch of the Anaconda Smelting and Refining Company. Clark held this office from June 1, 1936, until 1946, when he was chosen by the executive board of the international union to fill the office of vice-president. A year later, in 1947, Clark also became secretary-treasurer of the organization.

During the national defense effort of World War II and the attendant need for certain critical metals, the membership of the I.M.M.S.W. had risen to about 100,000, reported *Fortune*. This enrollment had diminished considerably by 1947, because forty-nine locals and about 30,000 members had withdrawn from it. Further decreases brought the membership down to 44,000 in February 1950, when the union was expelled from the Congress of Industrial Organizations for alleged pro-Communist domination. Clark denied the charges and condemned the action as antilabor. Later, votes taken in a number of mines and plants brought more than 12,000 new members into the union. Clark, elected president of the independent union in 1947, was re-elected to that post for two additional terms, in 1949 and 1951. One reason for his being chosen as president, reported *Fortune*, is that he is a known non-Communist, while the two previous presidents had been considered "Stalinists."

In August 1951 the I.M.M.S.W. called a nation-wide strike affecting operations at the four chief copper and nonferrous metal producers, Kennecott, Anaconda, Phelps-Dodge, and American Smelting and Refining, and at a number of smaller producers, after contract negotiations directed by the Federal Mediation and Conciliation Service had failed. Besides the 60,000 members of the I.M.M.S.W., 40,000 more workers were involved, since members of sympathetic AFL unions also walked out. Proposals for wage increases and pension contributions made by Federal Mediator Cyrus L. Ching had been acceptable to the union, but not to the operators. This impasse led President Truman to refer the matter to the attention of the Wage Stabilization Board, whose chairman, George Taylor, immediately invited the disputants to a Washington conference. In accepting, Clark declared, "We want to cooperate in any way consistent with the interests of our membership and the general welfare," and added that a return to work depended upon industry's acceptance of the mediation proposal. Appealing for either seizure or an injunction, Clark voiced the union's objections to collective bargaining under the Wage Stabilization Board. "Our sworn enemies," said Clark, "are part of it"—considered a reference to CIO members of the board. Because of the strike, the WSB declared itself ineligible to act after a preliminary hearing, thus delivering the dispute again to the President, who then named a three-man fact-finding board to undertake further investigations.

On August 30, 1951, acceptance by the Kennecott Copper Corporation of a package increase of 22 cents an hour led Clark and other of the union's officials to predict that this agreement would set an industry-wide pattern. When Phelps-Dodge, Anaconda, and American Smelting and Refining refused to follow Kennecott, President Truman invoked the terms of the Taft-Hartley Act and directed the United States Attorney General to obtain a temporary injunction against the union and thirty-one mining concerns, ordering operations to resume. In a statement to the press, Clark said: "This is the first time such an injunction has been thrown against workers who many days ago accepted the proposal of the Government. . . . It is [the] companies that have arrogantly and stubbornly refused the Government's proposal, not us. . . .The Truman Administration is determined to keep wages of metal workers down while profits of the metal corporations rise to new fantastic heights." The objections of the other major companies, said *Business Week*, were based on the hourly wage increase (which would exceed WSB ceilings) and a contract renegotiation clause in the Kennecott agreement. Adopting a resolution to accept a 19½-cent hourly package increase as basis for closing negotiations, the I.M.M.S.W. by early October 1951 had reached settlements with the chief copper mining operators: 20½ cents with Phelps-Dodge and American Zinc; 21 cents with United States Metal Company; and 16½ cents with American Smelting and Refining.

At the September 1951 convention of the United Electrical, Radio and Machine Workers of America, at which Clark was invited to speak, he disclosed a tentative plan for the uniting of the eleven unions, ousted from the CIO for alleged Leftist policies, with John L. Lewis' United Mine Workers. Representatives of eight of these unions, including Clark, met the following month in New York for discussions concerning "a national campaign to break the wage freeze."

During World War II John Clark served on the Selective Service Board of Cascade County, Montana; the tripartite panel of the War Labor Board; and the War Manpower Commission. His fraternal organizations are the Eagles' Lodge and the Knights of Pythias. In his political alignment Clark is a Democrat, in his church membership, an Episcopalian. Clark and his wife, Malvina, live in Englewood, a suburb of Denver. Prior to their marriage, on July 13, 1914, Mrs. Clark was a nurse. With a height of six feet seven inches he weighs 184

pounds; he has gray eyes and medium-brown hair. He names fishing as his favorite pastime.

Reference

Fortune 44:59 O '51

CLARK, JOSEPH S(ILL), JR. Oct. 21, 1901- Mayor of Philadelphia
Address: b. City Hall, Philadelphia 7, Pa; h. 440 Rex Ave., Chestnut Hill, Philadelphia 18, Pa.

When Joseph S. Clark, Jr., a Philadelphia attorney was elected Mayor of that city on November 6, 1951, he broke a sixty-seven-year-old tradition—he is the first Democrat since 1884 to fill the top elective post of the nation's third largest city. Clark, who took office on January 7, 1952, had previously served as Pennsylvania's Deputy Attorney General in 1934-35, as an Army Air Force colonel during the World War II years, and as City Controller of Philadelphia for two years prior to his election as Mayor.

Joseph Sill Clark, Jr., was born in Philadelphia, Pennsylvania, on October 21, 1901, the son of Joseph Sill Clark (a lawyer and, more than half a century ago, a national tennis champion) and Kate Richardson (Avery) Clark. He grew up in Chestnut Hill, a residential section of Philadelphia. For his college preparatory study young Clark attended Middlesex School in Massachusetts, where he played on the school's baseball and football teams, and graduated in 1919 as the class valedictorian. As an undergraduate at Harvard College from 1919 to 1923, Clark specialized in history, government, and economics, winning the John Harvard scholarship for high academic distinction and two other prizes. In sports he became a member of the baseball and track teams. A Phi Beta Kappa student, he graduated *magna cum laude* with the B.S. degree in 1923. Three years later, in 1926, Clark took his LL.B. degree at the University of Pennsylvania Law School, where he was an editor of the *Law Review*. In December of that year he was admitted to the bar of Pennsylvania; whereupon he established a general law practice in Philadelphia as an associate of Clark, Clark, McCarthy and Wagner, which he left in 1934 to join the firm of Dechert, Bok, Smith and Clark.

Breaking with the Republican tradition of his family, Clark left that party in 1928 to support Alfred E. Smith for the Presidency against Herbert Hoover. His reason, he said, was: "You can't get anything done in the Republican party" (New York *Herald Tribune*, November 7, 1951). Described by a friend in Philadelphia as "a rebel by nature," Clark developed his political philosophy in sympathy with what he has called the "Right-wing New Deal." He first sought public office in 1934, when he ran unsuccessfully as a Democratic candidate for the City Council. As Deputy Attorney General of Pennsylvania during 1934-35, he was engaged in trial work in connection with the closing of banks.

(Continued next page)

JOSEPH S. CLARK, JR.

At the age of thirty-nine Clark entered the Army Air Force as a captain. "A friend of mine called me from Washington and said war was surely coming," Clark is quoted as saying in a *Collier's* article (November 3, 1951). "He was an accurate prognosticator, and I got in before Pearl Harbor." His military service, which began in August 1941 and continued through World War II to September 1945, comprised the following assignments: Captain in the Officers' Reserve Corps Headquarters, Army Air Force, Washington, D.C. (doing organizational and administrative work on the staff); Director, Organizational Planning Headquarters, AAF; Deputy Chief of Staff with General George E. Stratemeyer in the Eastern Air Command (integrated with the Royal Air Force), the India-Burma-China theater; Executive Officer and for a brief time Acting Chief of Staff with General Stratemeyer's staff. Altogether Clark spent twenty-three months in that theater of operations. He reached the rank of colonel on October 15, 1943, and was awarded the Bronze Star, the Legion of Merit, the Military Order of the British Empire, and Honorary Wings of the Chinese Air Force. Upon his return to the United States after the war, Clark was called to Mitchel Field, Long Island, by General Stratemeyer to assist in reviewing the staff organization of the Continental Defense Command, of which Stratemeyer was then Commanding General.

In 1947 Clark resumed his political activity in a reform movement, as campaign manager for a fellow Democrat, Richardson Dilworth, who entered the electoral contest for the mayoralty of Philadelphia; as chairman of the citizens' committee for Truman and Barkley in 1948; and as chairman of the Philadelphia

chapter of the Americans for Democratic Action in 1948-49. In the municipal elections of 1949 Clark was a candidate for the office of City Controller, and Dilworth ran for the office of County Treasurer. Despite a Republican enrollment of 700,000 to the Democrats' 300,000 in Philadelphia, Clark and Dilworth were elected by margins of more than 100,000 votes. Speaking of his achievements in "reform and efficiency," Clark stated (as told by John Denson in *Collier's*) that he found the City Controller's office, with a staff of 92 employees, was giving poor service. "I cut this to 67, and I'm convinced we're giving real service to the taxpayers. I've been able to conduct complete and frequent audits—and that's my job." Among civic organizations in which Clark was active were the Pennsylvania Merit League; the Public Charities Association of Pennsylvania; the Bureau of Municipal Research; Philadelphia's Committee of Seventy, which conducted a drive for civic decency; and the Citizen's Council on City Planning.

For the 1951 elections Democrats Clark and Dilworth joined forces again, Clark as the nominee for Mayor and Dilworth as the nominee for District Attorney. With a broom as their symbol, they pledged themselves to sweep corruption out of Philadelphia's City Hall. "I've always had a desire to see if we couldn't fix this town up—which it certainly needs," Clark declared in campaign speeches. Clark rejected national political issues as not pertinent to the Philadelphia contest, concentrating on local issues of machine politics and corrupt municipal practices. He criticized the Republican city government of the previous four years, pointing to such scandals as the embezzlement of $208,000 in amusement taxes, imprisonment of the fire marshal and two aids, falsification of records by the director of supplies and purchases, corruption in the water bureau, several suicides, embezzlement of court funds, and indictment of building, sewer, and plumbing inspectors for extortion.

With the support of most of the labor unions, labor's League for Political Education, Americans for Democratic Action, various independent citizens' groups formed especially to work for him, and of the Philadelphia *Inquirer* (a politically independent newspaper), Clark defeated his Republican opponent, the Reverend Daniel A. Poling (the Baptist clergyman and editor, who was also pledged to wipe out corruption) by a vote of 442,133 to 319,923. (Clark's running mate, Dilworth, won the election as District Attorney by a vote of 438,009 to 318,361 for his Republican rival, Michael A. Foley.) The final tally showed that the Democrats were victors by the largest majority recorded in an off-year local election since 1935. Hailing the Democratic victory as one for "all decent people in Philadelphia," Clark said that his party was "proud to be chosen as the instrument which will bring decent government to the city." The new Mayor was inaugurated on January 7, 1952.

The city government that Clark heads was "streamlined" in April 1951 by the adoption of a new city charter, which also extended civil service. The Philadelphia city and county governments were merged, all county offices becoming city offices. The new charter also increased the Mayor's administrative, investigative, and legislative powers. Clark has under him a managing director, a director of finance, and a city representative; he appoints all subordinates, but the city solicitor must be confirmed by the Council. Another provision of the new charter was the increase of the Mayor's annual salary from $19,800 to $25,000.

In April 1952 the Mayor launched a television series, *Tell It To the Mayor*, on which he and other Philadelphia officials answer questions concerning his administration. *Variety* described it as "an entertaining and visually satisfying offshoot" of his newly established Bureau of Information and Complaints. Taking a different stand from that of other leading Democrats in the State, in May 1952 Clark and Dilworth announced that they would support the Presidential candidacy of Senator Estes Kefauver.

The blue-eyed, black-haired Mayor of Philadelphia is five feet nine inches tall and weighs 145 pounds. On April 6, 1935, he married Noel Hall; they have a son (Joseph S., 3d) and a daughter (Noel Clairborne). Clark, who received an honorary LL.D. degree from Temple University in 1952, is a member of the Philadelphia, Pennsylvania, and American bar associations, the Juristic Society, Sharswood Law Club, Junior Legal Club; Americans for Democratic Action; American Legion and Veterans of Foreign Wars; and the Harvard Club in Philadelphia and New York, the Racquet Club, the Philadelphia Club, Sunnybrook Gold Club, and the Philadelphia Cricket Club. His church affiliation is Unitarian. He lists tennis, horseback riding, and chess as his favorite recreations.

References

Christian Sci Mon p11 N 7 '51
Collier's 128:38+ N 3 '51 por
N Y Herald Tribune II p3 O 21 '51; p1 N 7 '51 por
N Y Times p19 N 7 '51; p23 N 8 '51
Who's Who in United States Politics (1950)

CLARK, ROBERT L(INCOLN) June 12, 1903- United States Government official

Address: b. Executive Office Bldg., Washington 25, D.C.; h. 5528 Bradley Blvd., Chevy Chase 15, Md.

When three offices of the National Security Resources Board were combined in 1950 to form the Office of Human Resources, Robert L. Clark was named director of this office, whose function it is to plan for providing the necessary skilled manpower in the event of full mobilization and to devise facilities for carrying out a manpower control program. This office is also responsible for mobilization planning in regard to housing and health. The year before he accepted his present post, Clark had held the position of director of the Manpower Office of the NSRB, which had similar though narrower areas of responsibility. He entered government service in 1934 as the as-

ROBERT L. CLARK

sistant supervisor of the cost of living survey for the New Hampshire Department of Labor.

Robert Lincoln Clark was born June 12, 1903, in North Stratford, New Hampshire, the only son of a Baptist clergyman, John Lew Clark, and his schoolteacher wife, Lena Sophia (Frederiksen) Clark, who reared Robert and their three daughters in New England. Clark's paternal ancestors had come to America from England in 1630 and had settled for a time in Massachusetts, moving to New Hampshire a few years later: John Clark, a major in the Revolutionary War, helped to establish the settlement of Clarktown, which is now a part of Barnstead, New Hampshire; Lewis Whitehouse Clark, Robert Clark's grandfather, was the attorney general of the State of New Hampshire and the chief justice of the New Hampshire Supreme Court. His maternal grandfather, a cabinetmaker, emigrated from Denmark as a young man.

Young Clark was graduated in 1924 from the Phillips Exeter Academy in Exeter, New Hampshire, where he had been the president of the debating society and the editor-in-chief of the yearbook. He then majored in political science at Dartmouth College, Hanover, New Hampshire, but had to discontinue his studies in 1929 to work as an advertising and printing salesman at the Free Press Printing Company, Burlington, Vermont, in order to earn money to complete his education. In college he had been a member of Kappa Kappa Kappa and had worked as a photostat operator in the school library. For three summers Clark, who had had previous experience as a camp counselor and swimming instructor, was director of Camp Camelot, Dover, New Jersey, a fresh air camp operated by the New York City East Side Settlement.

Upon graduating with his B.A. degree from Dartmouth in 1932, Clark became the assistant

CLARK, ROBERT L.—*Continued*

to the Director of Admissions of Phillips Exeter Academy, a position which he left in 1934 to begin his government career as the assistant supervisor of the cost of living survey for the New Hampshire Department of Labor in Concord. After five years (1935-40) as the senior interviewer and manager of the New Hampshire State Employment Service, Clark went to Washington, D.C., where for the next two years he served as assistant to the chief of the Field Management Division of the Social Security Board. Promoted in 1943 to chief of the Employment Service Division of the War Manpower Commission (which was responsible for programing wartime operations of the United States Employment Service), Clark directed the importation of workers from Mexico, Canada, Puerto Rico, and Central America, supervised WMC offices in other countries, and negotiated agreements with foreign governments. During his year in this office Clark was a member of a four-man commission, two from the United States and two from Mexico (one of whom was Padilla Nervo, later president of the United Nations General Assembly), which met to settle a dispute between the two governments regarding utilization of Mexican workers on United States railroads. When the negotiations were concluded, the commissioners agreed to continue the importation of Mexican workers.

From 1944 to 1949 as Principal Budget Examiner for the United States Bureau of the Budget in Washington, Clark was responsible for all manpower and educational agencies of the government and for reviewing their policies, operation, and financial budgets. While in this post he became adviser to the United States delegation to the Thirtieth Session of the International Labor Conference, which was held in 1947 in Geneva, Switzerland. Clark in 1949 was named director of the National Security Resources Board's Manpower Office, a body concerned with planning for sufficient skilled manpower, should full mobilization become necessary, and responsible for developing a manpower control program and for setting up an administrative structure to carry it out. In 1950 union leaders, objecting to Clark's lack of labor background, asked W. Stuart Symington, chairman of the NSRB, to appoint a labor man as the NSRB's vice-chairman, over Clark. Instead, Symington agreed to name a union man to head a separate labor affairs section in the NSRB.

When the NSRB was reorganized in 1950 and three offices—the Manpower, the Health Resources, and the Housing and Community Facilities—were combined to form the Office of Human Resources, Clark was named to head this new office, whose functions are similar to those of the Manpower Office but include also the mobilization aspects of housing and the supervision of medical and other health personnel and facilities, including hospitals. In an address on August 22, 1951, before the In-

stitute of Manpower Utilization and Government Personnel at Stanford University in California, Clark discussed the mobilization of manpower for national security. He stated that the United States must develop military strength sufficient to prevent armed aggression from other powers and must, among other things, create better relationships with peoples who might unite with America in a quest for mutual security. "Manpower is not to be dealt with like other resources," he said. "It is the activating force for all national effort. The unique character and role of manpower, therefore, requires above all else deep understanding, leadership, and wise guidance both for its effective development and for its use."

In another speech, at the opening session April 17, 1952, of the seventh annual National Conference on Higher Education in Chicago, Clark pointed out: "Our nation is short of men today, and women too. There simply are not enough people to do everything that we need to do to defend ourselves, to help our allies, to produce material goods necessary for our national defense, and to maintain a civilian economy that will enable us to push ahead into an even happier, more virile, more enlightened civilization in the future." The only way to combat the greater numbers of the potential enemy, Clark said, would be to use our technological superiority and to do this we would need men trained in specialized skills. He maintained, however, that the number of men receiving advanced degrees in the physical sciences would decrease in the next few years; as for the social sciences, Clark said that there was a shortage of personnel who knew foreign lands, their languages, customs, and psychology—knowledge indispensable for arbitrating with unfriendly powers and for cooperating with friendly states. Toward this end, he continued, "The National Security Resources Board and the Office of Defense Mobilization in collaboration with other Federal Government agencies as well as representatives of business, industry, and the academic world are making a concerted attack on the problem of equipping the United States with persons who are adequately prepared to represent their country abroad either as public servants or as private citizens."

Clark and Pauline Keysar (a former teacher) were married July 5, 1935, and have three children: Carol Ann, Peter Lincoln, and Christopher John. The government official is a member of the International Association of Public Employment Offices and the Society of Public Administration. He belongs to the Kenwood Country Club. He is a Democrat and his church affiliation is Congregational. With a height of five feet seven inches, he weighs 180 pounds and has brown hair and brown eyes. Fishing and travel are his hobbies; he also enjoys reading, particularly biography and history.

Reference

Who's Who in America, 1952-53

CLIFT, DAVID H(ORACE) June 16, 1907-
Librarian; library association official

Address: b. c/o American Library Association,
50 E. Huron St., Chicago 11, Ill.; h. 3054
Hartzel St., Evanston, Ill.

David H. Clift, the executive secretary of
the American Library Association, was installed
in July 1951 as successor to John Mackenzie
Cory and entered upon his new duties two
months later. A graduate of the University of
Kentucky and of the Columbia University
School of Library Service, Clift subsequently
served as a reference assistant in the New
York Public Library, as assistant to the director of libraries at Columbia University, and
as associate librarian of Yale University. During World War II he was assigned to the Office of Strategic Services, and in 1946 he spent
six months in Germany as a member of a
Library of Congress mission seeking books for
American research libraries.

Born in Mason County, Kentucky, on June
16, 1907, David Horace Clift is the son of
Charles Lawson and Mary Ethel (Tomlin)
Clift, whose family consists of three sons (one
of whom, Glenn, is also a librarian) and three
daughters. A Clift forebear settled in Marsh-
field, Massachusetts, about 1650, and a branch
of the family later migrated to North Carolina, Virginia, and Kentucky. Charles Clift
(who wanted his son David to be a lawyer)
was a tobacco farmer until the mid-1920's,
when he was elected Circuit Clerk of Mason
County, an office he still holds, while tobacco
growing remains a side line. Young Clift attended Washington (Kentucky) High School—
his extracurricular activities, he says, were those
of a farmer's boy. He was graduated in 1924.
As an undergraduate at the University of Kentucky, where he majored in economics, he
earned money by working as a waiter in a
small restaurant, as a drugstore soda-jerker,
and as a newspaper deliverer. With the title
of "scribe" he was active in the local chapter
of the Order of DeMolay, and became a member
of that order's Legion of Honor. In 1930 he
was granted his B.S. degree in commerce by
the university, where he had been elected to
Delta Sigma Pi, the honorary commerce fraternity.

Although Clift had originally intended to
become a certified public accountant, his interest
in library work had developed while he was a
student assistant in the University of Kentucky
Library (1927-30) and a desk assistant at the
Lexington Public Library in the summer of
1930. Important factors in his decision to enter
the library field were the sense and understanding of the profession and the encouragement
he gained from his superiors at those libraries
—"I have always been fortunate in my bosses,"
Clift has said. In the fall of 1930 he enrolled
in the School of Library Service at Columbia
University; while studying there he worked
as an assistant in the school's library. After
obtaining his B.S. degree in library science
from Columbia in 1931, he was a reference
assistant at the information desk of the New
York Public Library for six years. He returned to Columbia in 1937 as administrative

Koehne

DAVID H. CLIFT

assistant to Dr. Charles Clarence Williamson,
who at that time was director of the university's
libraries.

For World War II duty Clift entered the
United States Army as a private in 1942, to
serve briefly in the Medical Department. Then,
transferred to the Office of Strategic Services
in Washington, D.C., he was first made chief
of the publication section, next chief of the
analysis and abstract section, and finally rose
to the post of deputy chief of the OSS's Interdepartmental Committee for the Acquisition of
Foreign Publications. Upon his discharge from
the Army with the rank of first lieutenant in
November 1945, he received the Commendation
Ribbon.

Shortly thereafter Clift became a member,
and later acting chief, of the Library of Congress Mission to Germany. A cooperative acquisition project managed by about fifteen members, it undertook the acquisition, for American
research libraries, of copies of publications
which had appeared in former enemy countries
during the war years. In the course of his tour,
which included Austria and Switzerland as well
as Germany, Clift entered the Russian-occupied
zone of Germany to spend six days in Leipzig
in March 1946. In that city, once the book
publishing center of Germany, he got in touch
with publishers and book agents, many of
whom, he found, had set aside books throughout the war for American libraries. The mission was engaged not only in a search for
books, state documents, sheet music, phonograph records, radio broadcast transcripts, and
other materials for American collections, but
also in the study of the possibility of establishing normal intellectual intercourse between libraries in the two countries.

Returning to the United States early in July
1946, Clift assumed his duties as associate li-

CLIFT, DAVID H.—*Continued*

brarian of Yale University, a post to which he had been appointed in 1945, while he was still with the OSS. James T. Babb, librarian at Yale has summed up (in *College and Research Libraries*) Clift's chief task during five years at that university as "drafting and putting into operation a classification and pay plan for librarians . . . activity in school and departmental library matters . . . efficient and diplomatic dealing with scholars . . . and . . . constant work for the welfare and proper recognition of the librarians at Yale." (The operation of Yale's classification and salary plan, which was adopted in July 1947, has been described by Ralph R. Shaw in the *Library Journal*, June 1, 1949.) Clift's contribution to the life at Yale was recognized by his being named an associate fellow of Trumbull College, one of the university's ten residential colleges.

From 1947 to 1951 Clift was a member of the American Library Association's board on personnel administration, and he served as the board's chairman for 1950-51. In January of the latter year John Mackenzie Cory, who had served as A.L.A.'s executive secretary since September 1948, submitted his resignation. In May the association's executive board met to select a successor, and on June 2, 1951, it was announced that Clift had been unanimously chosen as the association's new executive secretary. He was formally installed at the final general session of the A.L.A.'s seventy-fifth anniversary conference, in Chicago, on July 13, 1951, and took over his new duties at the beginning of September, after relinquishing his position at Yale. In her welcome to the new executive secretary, Mrs. Loleta D. Fyan, president of A.L.A., wrote: "Emerging from a difficult period of financial retrenchment and reorganization, so ably handled by Mr. Cory, we are confident that, with Mr. Clift's guidance, the association will move ahead to further structural improvements and a vigorous and expanded program of activities."

The A.L.A. executive secretary is in charge of the association's headquarters in Chicago and its personnel, carries out the activities provided for in the budget, and performs such other duties as may be assigned to his office. He serves as an officer, without the right to vote, of both the A.L.A. council—the legislative body which meets twice a year—and of the executive board, which administers the affairs of the association between these meetings. He is required to submit a monthly report to the board.

David Clift has been a consultant on library matters to the United States Department of State and a member of the technical advisory committee for regional libraries of the Connecticut State Department of Education. He has been secretary (1947-49), first vice-president (1949-50), and president (1950-51) of the Connecticut Library Association, and at various times a member of its legislative committee, nominations and elections committee, and committee on the certification of public libraries.

During his period of activity with the Connecticut association he promoted studies for the improvement of public and rural library service in the State, which resulted in the presentation of bills to the legislature in 1951 for the establishment of a regional library program. He was treasurer (1949-50) of the Connecticut Valley chapter of the Special Libraries Association, and he has also been active as program chairman (1950-51) of the Friends of the Hamden (Connecticut) Library.

A member of the program committee for the midwinter meeting of the Association of College and Reference Libraries in 1950, since 1947 Clift has also been secretary and a member-at-large of the microcard committee. He assisted in the surveys made of the University of Minnesota Library (1949, with Keyes D. Metcalf) and of the West Haven (Connecticut) Public Library. In the summer of 1949 he taught at New Haven State Teachers College. He has contributed reviews to the *Library Journal* and the *Library Quarterly*, and his *Memo to Members* appears regularly in the *ALA Bulletin*. Other associations in which he holds memberships are the American Association of School Administrators, the Society for the Advancement of Education, the Kentucky Library Association, the New York Library Club (president, 1941-42), the Illinois Library Association, and the Chicago Library Club. He is an honorary member of the Connecticut Library Association (president, 1950-51). In New York City he belongs to the Yale Club and The Leos—the latter (named for the lions on the Fifth Avenue steps of the Public Library) is a small social club formed by men who are or were members of that library's staff.

Mrs. Clift, who was Eleanore Flynn before her marriage on November 4, 1933, is also a graduate of the Columbia University School of Library Service. (When she left the Brooklyn Public Library in 1943, she had the title of head librarian in the Central Childrens Room; and she has from time to time since then held various library posts.) The library association official, who stands five feet six inches tall and weighs 135 pounds, has light-brown hair and hazel eyes. His political party is the Democratic, his church the Presbyterian. He finds recreation in bowling, picnicking, and taking snapshots; and when he gets home to Kentucky he plays pool with his father, "winning occasionally."

References

A.L.A. Bul 45:249 Jl-Ag '51 por
Col & Research Lib 12:205 Ap '51; 12:
   375 O '51 por
Library J 76:982 Je 15 '51
New Haven (Conn.) Register Jl 21 '46;
   Mag p2 Ag 14 '46 pors
Wis Lib Bul 47:139 Je '51
Yale Univ Lib Gaz 20:36 O '45
Who's Who in America, 1952-53
Who's Who in Library Service (1943)
Who's Who in New England (1949)

COCKE, C(HARLES) FRANCIS June 10, 1886- Bankers organization president; lawyer

Address: b. c/o American Bankers Association, 12 E. 36th St., New York 16; c/o First National Exchange Bank, Roanoke, Va.; h. 28 Cardinal Road, Clermont Heights, Roanoke, Va.

The president, for the 1951-52 term, of the American Bankers Association is C. Francis Cocke, formerly vice-president of the seventy-seven-year-old organization and president since 1938 of the First National Exchange Bank of Roanoke, Virginia. Succeeding James E. Shelton of Los Angeles, Cocke, who had been active in committee work for the organization since 1941, was elected to office at the annual convention of the A.B.A., on October 3, 1951, in Chicago. The banking executive had practiced law for some thirty-five years in Virginia, where he is also director of a number of business firms.

Charles Francis Cocke was born in Roanoke, Virginia, on June 10, 1886, one of four children of Lucian Howard and Lelia Maria (Smith) Cocke. His father, a prominent lawyer and banker in the Virginia city, served as general attorney for the Norfolk and Western Railroad, as vice-president of the National Exchange Bank, as city solicitor, and from 1882 to 1884 as Mayor of the city. Charles Cocke attended the University of Virginia and received his B.A. degree in 1908. This was followed by two years at the university's Law School. Admitted to the Virginia bar in 1910, he began his law practice in Roanoke, in which he was engaged for more than thirty-five years, except for a period during World War I (1917-19) when he served as a second lieutenant in the Air Service Aeronautics. In January 1947 he retired (as senior member) from Cocke, Hazelgrove & Shackelford, a firm specializing in financial law.

Cocke, whose law firm had been closely associated with the First National Exchange Bank of Roanoke, in 1927 was elected vice-president and director of the bank, and in 1938 he became president, a position he continues to hold in 1952. One of the four major banking firms in Roanoke (a city with a population of 91,000), the First National Exchange Bank has total resources, according to the Rand McNally *Bankers Directory* (1951), of more than $72,000,000 with total deposits amounting to over $67,000,000.

Cocke's first executive position with the American Bankers Association began in 1941 when he was chosen a member of the committee on Federal legislation, on which he served until 1950, the last four years as chairman. From 1946 to 1950 he was also chairman of its Federal legislative council; in 1949 he was elected to the executive council; and the next year, at the association's Diamond Anniversary Convention in New York City, he was chosen vice-president, a selection which customarily carries with it the presidency for the following year. Thus, on October 3, 1951, at the seventy-seventh annual convention held

J. Etheridge Ward

C. FRANCIS COCKE

in Chicago, Cocke was elected president, succeeding James E. Shelton. Representing approximately 15,480 of the more than 16,350 banks in the United States, the American Bankers Association also represents banks in Canada and Mexico. The aims of the association are, in the words of the *Encyclopedia of Banking and Finance,* "to promote the general welfare and usefulness of bank and financial institutions; secure uniformity of action; obtain the practical benefits of personal acquaintance and discussion of subjects important to banking and commerce, especially proper consideration of financial and commercial usages, customs and laws affecting the banking interests of the entire country; and to provide for protection against crime." To achieve these purposes, some thirty departments have been established to handle such specialized programs as employee training, taxation, public relations, real estate mortgages, insurance, etc., and an extensive financial library has been set up in the New York offices. Affiliated with the national group are the various State banking organizations, such as the Virginia Bankers Association, of which Cocke was president during the 1948-49 term.

Shortly after becoming president of the American Bankers Association Cocke spoke before a meeting of the Mid-Continent Trust Conference of the national group, discussing the capacity of the United States to produce the goods demanded by the military and foreign aid programs. He emphasized the need of minimizing as far as possible nondefense spending as an anti-inflation measure, as well as the necessity for arousing "a feeling of individual responsibility" among the members of the community toward Federal expenditures. At a later conference the bank executive urged noninterference by the government in the private credit system of the country, asserting (accord-

COCKE, C. FRANCIS—*Continued*

ing to a report of his speech in the December 4, 1951, issue of the New York *Herald Tribune*) that the private banks of America "can be counted on for appropriate action for the best interests of our economy." In response to a statistical study being conducted by the Federal Reserve System concerning the excess profits tax applied to earnings of banks, Cocke in a letter to members requested their cooperation in the study, stressing the possible advantages to banks that might result in terms of future legislation and in new conditions for strengthening bank capital.

Cocke is associated as director with the Peoples Federal Savings and Loan Association, the Lawyers Title Insurance Corporation, and the Virginia Iron, Coal and Coke Company. From 1943 to 1948 he was vice-chairman of the Virginia War Finance Committee. He is a member of the Virginia State Library Board, president of the board of trustees of Hollins (Virginia) College, and a trustee of the Roanoke Hospital. He holds membership in the Virginia State and the American bar associations, and in the American Legion, of which he was chosen a deputy commander in 1919. His fraternal organizations are Sigma Chi and Phi Delta Phi; his clubs, the Commonwealth of Richmond, the Shenandoah, the Roanoke Country, and the Rotary of Roanoke (president). Cocke married Frances Tilghman Mingea on October 1, 1914, and is the father of a daughter, Lelia Smith. An Episcopalian, he serves as chancellor of that church's diocese of Southwestern Virginia. Politically he is a Democrat.

> *References*
>
> Bsns W p148 O 13 '51 por
> Who's Who in America, 1950-51
> Who's Who in Commerce and Industry (1951)
> Who's Who in the South and Southwest (1950)

COMPTON, WILSON (MARTINDALE)
Oct. 15, 1890- United States Government official; former college president

Address: b. c/o International Information Administration, Department of State, Washington 25, D.C.

Wilson Compton was selected by President Truman and the United States Department of State to head the new International Information Administration, established in January 1952. For six years previously he had been the president of Washington State College, and prior to that for twenty-six years the secretary and general manager of the National Lumber Manufacturers Association. Primarily an expert in forestry and the development of wood products, Dr. Compton represented the lumber interests in the days of the National Recovery Administration. In 1949 he was an alternate United States delegate to the General Assembly of the United Nations. In his new post Compton has charge of the *Voice of America*

broadcasts and other informational propaganda functions of the State Department.

The domestic circle into which Wilson Martindale Compton was born on October 15, 1890, has been called the "first family" of American education. His father, the Reverend Elias Compton, a Presbyterian minister, was for about forty years a professor of philosophy and for twenty-two years the dean at the College of Wooster in Ohio; Wilson's mother, Otelia Catherine (Augspurger) Compton, was the recipient in 1932 of an honorary LL.D. from Western College at Oxford, Ohio, for "outstanding achievement as a wife and mother," and was named "American Mother of the Year" for 1939. The eldest of their three sons, Karl Compton, became president of the Massachusetts Institute of Technology; the youngest, Arthur Compton, now chancellor of Washington University at St. Louis, was a cowinner of the 1927 Nobel Prize in physics, in recognition of his discovery of the "Compton phenomenon"; their sister, Mary Elesa, is the wife of C. H. Rice, once head of a Christian college in Pakistan. All four Compton children were born in Wooster, Ohio, and all were trained (in the words of their mother) "on the Bible and common sense." Each of the three boys (who are said collectively to hold more honorary degrees than any other American family) helped to pay his own way through the College of Wooster, where they were prominent in athletics and were graduated with Phi Beta Kappa keys.

Wilson, the second son, took his Ph.B. degree at Wooster in 1911, remained to acquire an M.A. degree in 1912, then proceeded on a history, politics, and economics fellowship to Princeton University, where he received the Ph.D. degree in 1915. Attracted to forestry ever since a childhood vacation in the woods of northern Michigan, Wilson Compton chose the lumber business for his doctoral thesis, the full title of which is *The Organization of the Lumber Industry, with Special Reference to the Influences Determining the Prices of Lumber in the United States* (1916).

Young Dr. Compton had been an assistant professor in economics and political science at Dartmouth College for about a year when his doctoral thesis aroused governmental interest. Accordingly, in the fall of 1916 he left Dartmouth to go to Washington, D.C., as an economist with the Federal Trade Commission. He received a law degree (LL.B.) at the Hamilton College of Law in Chicago in 1917, and in World War I year of 1918 served as assistant chief dispatcher for the United States Emergency Fleet Corporation.

Late in 1918 Compton left his Federal office to begin twenty-six years of service as secretary and general manager of the National Lumber Manufacturers Association, with headquarters in the nation's capital. This organization, established in 1902, had declined somewhat in effectiveness when Compton joined it. In 1919 he called together the first American Lumber Congress, which adopted a program for revision lumber grading methods. Compton served as economic adviser to a special

United States Senate committee of reconstruction and production in 1921. A contributor to periodicals in the lumber field, he is the author of a monograph, *Legal Aspects of Trade Associations*, which appeared in 1930. In that year he became a member of the advisory committee of the United States Timber Conservation Board. He was appointed chairman of its survey committee in 1931, the year in which the National Lumber Manufacturers Association was commended by Secretary of Commerce Robert P. Lamont for "sane and constructive leadership of an enlightened character and ever-widening scope in a difficult field." In 1932 Compton helped to found and became vice-president and manager of American Forest Products Industries, Inc., an affiliated enterprise.

When the National Recovery Administration was established in 1933, Wilson Compton was appointed special policy adviser representing the lumbermen. As such he helped in that and the following year to draft the code for the lumber industry, and was made chief of the Trade Associations Division of NRA "to utilize his exceptional talents as an organizer" (William E. Berchtold in the *New Outlook*). He added a professorship in economics at George Washington University to his other activities in Washington in 1934. (In the year following he was the recipient of an honorary LL.D. degree from the College of Wooster, with his mother placing the hood denoting the doctorate on him.) Compton also helped, during the 1930's, to initiate the Federal Forest Conservation Conferences, the problems and aims of which he described in the address *Forest Conservation: a Task in Engineering*, published in 1939; while in 1940 he became cofounder of what a biographical sketch in the New York *World-Telegram* summed up as "the system of American Free Farms which gradually is converting forest industries into self-perpetuating permanent operation." Filling several wartime posts, Dr. Compton was appointed chief consultant on lumber and timber products with the Office of Production Management in 1941, a member of the advisory board on materials and equipment for the Quartermaster General of the Army in 1942, and consultant to the research committee of the Office of Scientific Research and Development in 1943.

In November 1944, the announcement was made from Washington State College at Pullman, Washington, that Dr. Wilson Compton had accepted the presidency of that institution. "Forestry engineering is Dr. Compton's specialty, and a program of the study of wood utilization which he is expected to promote ties in exactly with the regional need," explained a *Christian Science Monitor* dispatch, which added that he was also expected to place "greater emphasis . . . on the liberal arts" in a curriculum hitherto largely confined to agricultural, domestic, and mechanical sciences. During the six years, following his assumption of presidential duties at the beginning of 1945, he founded (1947) the first national industry-owned wood research and testing laboratories, increased the college registration from 1,500 to 6,000, and raised funds for the erection of a

Hutchison

WILSON COMPTON

new Institute of Technology, a new library, and the doubling of dormitory facilities. He served, in 1946, on the United States Education Mission to Japan, and in 1949 as an alternate representative to the United Nations General Assembly where, as a member of the Economic and Financial Committee, he interpreted the Point Four Program and American plans to extend foreign trade, and in countering criticism from the Soviet bloc.

At Washington State College, though, he found himself increasingly at odds with the board of regents over faculty rating and student counseling services which he introduced, and also over the disposition of funds (*Life*). On April 27, 1951, accordingly, the statement was made that he had submitted his resignation as president and had asked to be relieved of his duties not later than January 1, 1952.

On September 17, 1951, the announcement was made by the State Department that the university administrator had been appointed staff director of an Advisory Committee on Information with authority to correlate the work of six subsidiary committees in the "Campaign of Truth" which President Truman had directed the State Department to develop. This was preliminary to the action of the Department in completely reorganizing its foreign information and education staff so as to meet Congressional demands that its overseas propaganda and good will media (including the *Voice of America* broadcasts and the Division of Overseas Information Centers) be put under a new office.

Thus, on January 18, 1952, an International Information Administration was established, with Dr. Compton as its head; he has "full authority over the operation of the Government's radio, press, publication and exchange of persons programs abroad" (New York *Times*), and reports directly to Secretary of State Dean

COMPTON, WILSON—*Continued*

Acheson. (Compton is "advised" on "informational and psychological strategy" by the Assistant Secretary of State for Public Affairs, Howland H. Sargeant.) Accepting the position, Dr. Compton announced that, in line with the President's views, he intended to make the *Voice of America* an information service rather than a propaganda-spreading medium: "I think we'll stick mostly to facts," he declared. "Of course, we'll put our best foot forward, but . . . we can't say black is white." He also laid stress on exchange of students and leaders, and asserted that the problem confronting him was "essentially" managerial. "We need more people," he was quoted in the New York *Post* as explaining. "In our new budget we recommend 3,000 new positions, 90 per cent of them overseas. Our budget request is up from 87 million to 133 million." A highlight of the first months of his tenure of office was the launching (March 4, 1952) of the coastguard vessel *Courier*, which will be used as a "roving broadcasting station" to penetrate the Iron Curtain.

Dr. Wilson Compton has been described by William V. Shannon of the New York *Post* as "a sturdily built, broad-shouldered man of medium height" who "makes a striking appearance with a crest of white hair, deep-set blue eyes, and a bronzed complexion." His "chief hobby and relaxation" is the large farm in Virginia where he lives with Mrs. Compton, who was Helen M. Harrington before their marriage on December 29, 1916. Their four children, who now have homes of their own, are Wilson Martindale, Jr., Catherine Ross, Ross Harrington, and Helen Case. Wilson Compton is a Republican in his political views; an active Presbyterian layman, he is a former vice-president of the Washington (D.C.) Federation of Churches. His fraternities, in addition to Phi Beta Kappa, are the Alpha Tau Omega and the Sigma Delta Chi; his clubs are the Cosmos and the Congressional Country (Washington). Dr. Compton is a fellow of the Royal Economics Society of England as well as a member of numerous United States organizations, such as the American Educational Association, the American Bar Association, the American Forestry Association (vice-president in 1946), the Academy of Political Science, and the American Academy of Arts and Sciences.

References

Christian Sci Mon p4 N 13 '41
Life 30:49-50+ Je 11 '51 pors; 31:5 Jl 2 '51
N Y Post Mag p2 F 10 '52 pors
N Y Times IX p2 N 15 '31; p16 Je 18 '35; p2 Ja 19 '52
N Y World-Telegram p13 Ja 26 '52 por
New Outlook 163:45 Mr '34
Pub W 161:919 F 16 '52
Time 45:74+ F 12 '45 por
Bolton, S. K. & Sanderson, E. W. Famous Men of Science (1946)
Directory of American Scholars (1951)
Leaders in Education (1948)
National Cyclopædia of American Biography, Current vol G, 1943-46
Who Knows—and What (1949)
Who's Who in America, 1950-51
Who's Who in Law, 1937
Who's Who in the West (1951)
World Biography (1948)

COOK, DONALD C(LARENCE) Apr. 14, 1909- United States Government official; lawyer

Address: b. c/o Securities and Exchange Commission, 425 2d St., N.W., Washington 25, D.C.; h. 3055 N. Ohio St., Arlington, Va.

The Chairman of the United States Securities and Exchange Commission is Donald C. Cook, who was appointed by President Truman to that post in February of 1952. Cook had served on the quasi-judicial financial agency as one of its five commissioners since October 1949. Earlier, from 1935 to 1945, in the SEC he had been a financial examiner, then a utilities analyst, and finally an assistant director of one of the SEC divisions, where he gained the reputation for being "one of the ablest staff members of the agency." A lawyer as well as business administrator by training, Cook has been employed in the United States Department of Justice, has been a partner in a Washington law firm, and in 1943 began a two-year assignment as special counsel to the United States House of Representatives Committee on Naval Affairs. In 1950 he was appointed chief counsel for the preparedness subcommittee of the Senate Armed Services Committee, a post he resigned in March 1952.

Donald Clarence Cook was born in Escanaba, Michigan, on April 14, 1909, the son of N. Nelson Cook, Jr., and the former Edith Bryant. His father, who was of German descent, and his mother, who was of English ancestry, had two other children, a son and a daughter. Donald Cook spent his early years in the Michigan city, attending the local high school and earning his first money as a newsboy. After graduating from the secondary school in 1926, he spent another year at study there. For his college education he enrolled at the University of Michigan. Here he was able to pay for part of his expenses by working in the school library. Additional extracurricular activities were his service as publication manager of the *Gargoyle* and other publication projects of the student body.

After being granted the degree of Bachelor of Arts in 1932, Cook remained at the university for postgraduate courses, which brought him the degree of Master of Business Administration in 1935. That year he moved to Washington, D.C., to accept a position as financial examiner in the registration division of the Securities and Exchange Commission. He continued his studies by taking law courses at night at George Washington University. In 1937 he was promoted to the rank of utilities analyst in the Public Utilities Division of the SEC.

Having completed his professional training at George Washington University, Cook in 1939 received the Doctor of Jurisprudence degree and in 1940 the degree of Master of Laws. At that time he was admitted to practice before all the courts of Michigan, the Court of Appeals of the District of Columbia, and the United States Supreme Court. He also was certified as a public accountant in the State of Maryland. After five years in the Public Utilities Division of SEC, Cook in 1943 was named assistant director of that division. That was his title until 1945, when he became executive assistant to the United States Attorney General. While still with the SEC he had been special counsel for two years to the Committee on Naval Affairs of the United States House of Representatives. A year later, in 1946, he became director of the Office of Alien Property in the United States Department of Justice. In this latter position his responsibilities involved the control of foreign-owned property, administered in accordance with the Trading with the Enemy Act, and the preparation of legal opinions involving alien property and foreign funds. Cook left Federal service in 1947 to enter private law practice as a partner in the firm of Cook and Berger. On October 27, 1949, he was appointed one of the five commissioners of the SEC. In July of 1950 he was chosen vice-chairman, and in February of 1952 President Truman named him to the post of Chairman.

The agency which Cook heads was created by Congress in 1934 to administer laws designed to "protect the interests of the public and investors against malpractices in the securities financial markets." According to the *United States Government Manual*, these laws provide "for public disclosure of pertinent facts concerning new security offerings to the public and securities listed on exchanges; regulation of trading in securities on exchanges, and in over-the-counter markets; . . . enforcement of sanctions against companies and persons guilty of security frauds; . . . integration and simplification of holding company systems of electric and gas utilities; . . . improved protective provisions in mortgage indentures under which debt securities are sold to the public; . . . supervision of the activities of investment companies engaged in the purchase and sale of securities and elimination of abuses in the conduct of their businesses; regulation of the activities of investment advisers; . . . and advisory services to courts in reorganization proceedings for bankrupt corporations." The five members of the Commission (only three of whom may belong to the same political party) are appointed by the President for a five-year term; the vice-chairman is elected from among the commissioners, and the President designates the chairman. There are three main operating divisions: corporation finance, public utilities, and trading and exchanges, with regional offices in ten key cities of the country. During the fiscal year ending June 30, 1951, almost $6.5 billions' worth of securities were registered with the Commission, and 922 broker-dealer inspections were completed.

On the occasion of his 1952 appointment, Cook told the *Time* writer that when he first joined the SEC he "wanted some day to be a

Fabian Bachrach

DONALD C. COOK

commissioner and if the fates were kind . . . Chairman." With his ambition fulfilled, he said that his goal would be to "get up some of the old fizz and vinegar that SEC had in the '30's." One of his first acts as Chairman was to propose new and increased fees to be paid by the concerns which the Commission regulates. These increased fees will double the revenue previously collected by the Commission, but approximately $3.5 millions will still come from Congressional appropriations to cover the costs of operating the agency.

Another plan of the SEC Chairman is to ask Congress for the right to compel companies to file "understandable" statements when they register new securities to be offered to the public. Admitting that other chairmen had had a similar goal, Cook also promised a "concerted drive" to end proceedings on those public utility holding companies still failing to meet the requirements that they be well integrated and simple in corporate structure. He also declared his intention of placing the agency "beyond suspicion" by inaugurating strict rules to prevent any former employee from appearing before the SEC in connection with any case on which he had worked while on the staff of SEC.

From 1950 until March 1952 Cook held the post of chief counsel for the preparedness Subcommittee of the Senate Armed Services Committee: he compiled its special reports on military spending, tin, and other aspects of the defense program. He is also a partner in the Cook-Halquist Properties, and president and director of Mitchell Gardens, Inc., of Arlington, Virginia; he was formerly associated with the Housing Corporation of America. In the course of his studies and work he has contributed articles to the University of Michigan's *Business Review*, the *Investment Dealers' Digest*, and the law reviews of George

COOK, DONALD C.—*Continued*

Washington University and the University of Chicago. He is a member of the Michigan and American bar associations, the American Accounting Association, and the American Institute of Accountants. His clubs are the National Press Club and the Quadrangle, and his fraternity is Theta Xi; his political party is the Democratic, his church the Episcopal.

On December 4, 1943, Cook married Winnifred V. Carlsen, an employee of the SEC. Cook has a height of five feet eight inches, a weight of 170 pounds. The brown-haired, blue-eyed official has been described as "tough-talking, fast-moving." His hobbies are horseback riding, gardening, photography, and carpentering.

References

    Bsns W p27 Ja 19 '52
    Newsweek 38:21 D 3 '51
    Time 59:89 Mr 10 '52
    Who's Who in Commerce and Industry
    (1951)
    Who's Who in the South and Southwest
    (1950)

COOKE, (ALFRED) ALISTAIR Nov. 20, 1908- Journalist

Address: b. c/o British Broadcasting Company, 630 5th Ave., New York 20; c/o Manchester Guardian, 53 E. 51st St., New York 22; h. 1150 5th Ave., New York 28

The journalist Alistair Cooke, who is British by birth and upbringing but a citizen of the United States, is considered one of the most successful promoters of good will and understanding between the two countries. Three years after joining the British Broadcasting Company's staff in 1934, Cooke went to the United States as the BBC's commentator on

ALISTAIR COOKE

American affairs. There he has also represented the London *Times* and is now the chief American correspondent of the *Manchester Guardian*. His Britain-beamed radio program, *Letter From America*, was begun in 1946; and a collection of the "letters" was published in 1952 in the United States under the title of *One Man's America*. He is also known as the author of *A Generation on Trial*, a study of the Alger Hiss trial.

Alfred Alistair Cooke was born in Manchester, England, on November 20, 1908, the son of a Wesleyan preacher, Samuel Cooke, and the former Mary Elizabeth Byrne. Brought up in his native Lancashire, he was in his final year at Blackpool Grammar School in the same county when he passed the "Little Go," the entrance examination for Cambridge University, and was accepted as a scholar, or candidate for an honors degree, at Jesus College. The youth, who looked forward to becoming an actor, helped in 1928 to found the Cambridge University Mummers, a dramatic society. In 1929 he passed the first part of the English tripos examination and a year later, the second half.

After being awarded his B.A. degree in 1930, Cooke remained at Cambridge for an additional year (during which he became editor of the students' literary journal *The Granta*) to receive the Diploma in Education in the summer of 1931. His article on the Cambridge Festival Theatre was the first (in November 1931) of a number of contributions to *Theatre Arts Monthly*, the American periodical. In the following year he visited the United States on the first of two successive one-year Commonwealth Fund fellowships in dramatic research, which took him to Yale University in 1932-33 and to Harvard in 1933-34.

It was during those sojourns, said *Look*, that Cooke "fell in love with America." Three years were to pass, however, before he became a permanent resident of the United States. On termination of his second fellowship he returned to England, where he joined the British Broadcasting Company staff as cinema critic, a post he retained until 1937. The first book which bears his name on the title page is the anthology of British and American film criticism, *Garbo and the Night Watchmen* (1937); this he edited. In 1936 Cooke became the London correspondent of the National Broadcasting Company; he covered the abdication of King Edward VIII (and later also the Munich Conference) for the American network. His broadcast account on August 4, 1937, of the Wimbledon tennis match between Donald Budge and Baron von Cramm received much attention: *Vital Speeches*, which referred to Cooke as "the most brilliant of the new generation of radio commentators," printed the text of his tribute to the sportsmanship of Budge under the caption "Oh, Baby! A Study in Good Ambassadorship." It also appeared in John Gehlmann's anthology of essays, *Challenge of Ideas*, published in 1950.

Cooke's success on the NBC Blue Network in explaining to Americans the British reactions to events brought him permanently to the

United States to interpret Americans to Britons. Early in 1938 he began his present work as commentator on American affairs for the British Broadcasting Company. For two years beginning with 1938 Cooke served, too, as special correspondent of the *Times* of London, and he also began to contribute occasional articles to such publications as the American *New Republic* and the English *Fortnightly Review* and *Spectator*. His continued interest in the art of motion pictures was reflected both in his piece on Charlie Chaplin in the *Atlantic Monthly* for August 1939 and in his second book, *Douglas Fairbanks: The Making of a Screen Character*, a critical biography published by the Museum of Modern Art in 1940.

Cooke became a United States citizen in 1941 and in the same year began a two-year connection with the British Labor newspaper the *Daily Herald* as American feature writer. The following year, as roving correspondent for the London *Times*, he made a 20,000-mile, six-month automobile trip to every part of the United States to observe "what the war has done to community life, to the American highway, everything from orchids to peanuts . . . from the turpentine industry to the effects of rationing." In 1944 Cooke was instrumental in setting up the BBC's *Transatlantic Quiz* program, a sort of international *Information Please*.

In the spring of 1945 the journalist became connected for the first time with the *Manchester Guardian*, the old, internationally known Liberal daily paper published in his native city: its editor, A. P. Wadsworth, commissioned him to report on the United Nations organizational conference at San Francisco. Continuing to cover U.N. affairs for the *Guardian* until 1948, he became the paper's chief American correspondent. He covered both the perjury trials (1949-50) of Alger Hiss, filing 2,000 words a day. Later he told Harvey Breit of the New York *Times* that he looked upon the Hiss case as "the biggest trial in American history," and that he had considered it as the theme for a tragic novel before he finally wrote it up as a nonfictional study of "the trials of a man who was judged in one decade for what he was said to have done in another."

That phrase is quoted from the opening sentence of the book, which was published in late 1950 under the title *A Generation on Trial: U.S.A. v. Alger Hiss*. The volume was hailed by R. H. Rovere in the *New Yorker* as "one of the most vivid and literate descriptions of an American political event that have ever been written," and by *Time* as "a model of balance and lucidity." Sidney Hook, reviewing it for the New York *Times*, also thought it a "dramatic and absorbing book." *A Generation on Trial* pronounces no judgments on the justice of the outcome of the Hiss case; and Cooke, who has stated that his purpose was to "place the reader on the jury," told Harvey Breit that he was glad that he himself did not have to decide upon the innocence or guilt of the defendant.

During the spring of 1947 the British Broadcasting Company proposed that Cooke begin a new series of peacetime broadcasts (fifteen minutes every Friday evening). Thus was launched the weekly *Letter From America*, which in 1951 (stated *Look*) reached one British listener in every nine and was already "the longest series in BBC history." *Letter From America*, differing from the conventional newscast, has as its purpose to acquaint Britons with American folkways, ideals, tastes, habits and customs; and it has fulfilled its function with such success that one American diplomat was led to refer to Cooke as "our ambassador without portfolio to Great Britain." "It's something America doesn't have, and perhaps ought to have—the radio essay," Cooke told Breit in 1950. "People in America, when listening to the radio, like to lean forward; people in Britain like to lean back. That's the difference." For his broadcasts from America Cooke was given a Peabody Award, radio's highest prize, in May 1952.

In the course of nearly six years Cooke has traveled thousands of miles in search of material and has broadcast between two and three hundred "letters" on such varied topics as a typical Fourth of July celebration, the personality of Margaret Truman, the reconstruction of Williamsburg, the street noises of New York, the Southerners' admiration for Robert E. Lee, New England foliage in autumn, table manners, Joe Louis, baseball, and American slang. About thirty of these radio "essays" were published in London in 1951 under the title *Letters From America* and in New York as *One Man's America* in April 1952. "After reading them," commented Lewis Gannett in his daily book column in the New York *Herald Tribune*, "I should guess that they were worth more to the cause of Anglo-American understanding than . . . most of the work of the embassies." Writing in the Sunday book section of the same paper, Gerald W. Johnson said that the collection "has all the lucidity and analytical skill that characterized *A Generation on Trial*," and remarked that "any intelligent American will congratulate himself that we have an interpreter at once so genial and so well informed." The historian Henry Steele Commager called *One Man's America* "all in all a very entertaining book and a shrewd one" in his New York *Times* review. "There is only one reservation," he added. "This offering is too fragmentary by far."

Alistair Cooke has been married twice, first to Ruth Emerson on August 24, 1934. He has one son by this union. On April 30, 1946, he married Jane (White) Hawkes, widow of Major A. Whitfield Hawkes; they are the parents of one daughter. (Mrs. Cooke has two children by her previous marriage.) "Mr. Cooke may appear English—he is tall, slim, nattily dressed, and all in all has a kind of King George look—but he hardly ever sounds it," Harvey Breit has observed, while *Time* has described Cooke as "lanky, hardworking, cogent, farsighted." He belongs to the National Press Club in Washington; his recreations are photography, chess, music, motion pictures, beachcombing, and the American West.

(Continued next page)

COOKE, ALISTAIR—*Continued*

References

Look 15 :18 S 11 '51 por
N Y Herald Tribune VII p3 O 1 '50
por; IX p14 O 28 '51 por
N Y Times Mag p27 O 8 '50 por
Time 57 :71-2 Mr 19 '51 por

Who's Who, 1951
World Biography (1948)

COOPER, JOSEPH D(AVID) May 25,
1917- United States Government official
Address: b. c/o Salary Stabilization Board,
Washington 25, D.C.; h. 8601 Leonard Dr.,
Silver Spring, Md.

In May 1951 Joseph D. Cooper was named
Executive Director of the Salary Stabilization
Board, which was created by Economic Stabi-
lizer Eric Johnston to regulate salary increases

JOSEPH D. COOPER

of executives and nonunion white-collar workers who are not under the jurisdiction of the
Wage Stabilization Board. Since becoming a
government employee in 1934 as a messenger
at the Federal Trade Commission, Cooper has
been advanced to increasingly responsible positions in connection with personnel management
and administrative procedures. Before being
named executive director of the Salary Stabilization Board, he was an examiner of organization and methods for the State Department.

Joseph David Cooper, born May 25,
1917, in Boston, Massachusetts, spent his early
childhood in New York City. There his father,
Samuel Cooper, a cabinetmaker, and his mother,
Hinde (Bryner) Cooper, reared a family of
four, a son and three daughters. The future
government administrator attended Boys' High
School in Brooklyn, where before his gradua-

tion in 1934 he was active in the science and
mathematics clubs. At the suggestion of one
of his sisters he had taken a Federal Civil
Service examination for the position of messenger and in the year of his graduation he
received the appointment with the Federal
Trade Commission. The next year he became
messenger and clerk in the Department of
Agriculture, where he began to interest himself in the extracurricular activities of the employees of that Department and thus became
acquainted with personnel problems. This interest led in 1939 to an assignment as a training assistant in the personnel office which he
held until 1942.

Meanwhile Cooper began to study political
science at nearby George Washington University. In 1942, at the suggestion of one of his
supervisors and stimulated by a growing interest in the field of administration, he decided
to complete his undergraduate work and in 1944
he received the B.A. degree. He then attended
the American University for graduate studies
leading to his M.A. degree (1947) in public
administration and his Ph.D. (1951) in the
same subject. Cooper's thesis, *Decision-Making
and the Action Process in the Department of
State*, grew out of the work in which he was
then engaged for the government. At American
University, Cooper has stated, he was much
influenced in the development of his thinking
by Dr. Catheryn Seckler-Hudson, chairman of
the department of political science and public
administration.

In the course of time Cooper's appointments
in the government had become more closely
associated with administrative procedures and
techniques. In 1942 he joined the staff of the
Office for Emergency Management to work in
personnel techniques and in 1944 took an assignment in the War Shipping Administration
and the United States Maritime Commission as
a manpower utilization officer. After a year
(1945) as procedures analyst in the Office of
Price Administration, he moved to the United
Nations Relief and Rehabilitation Administration, to become chief procedure analyst. While
with UNRRA he also was an instructor during
the 1945-46 school year at George Washington
University. In 1947 he received an appointment as management analyst with the United
States Department of State. This was followed
the next year by promotion to the status of
organization and methods examiner, and in January 1950 to a post of higher rank on the
management staff of the department.

Cooper's next Federal appointment came in
May 1951 when Eric Johnston, Economic
Stabilization Administrator at that time, created the Salary Stabilization Board and named
Cooper its Executive Director to administer
the rulings of the three-member board (of
which Justin Miller is chairman). While pay
increases for most employees are under the
jurisdiction of the Wage Stabilization Board,
Cooper's agency will rule on salary increases
for all executives and all administrative and
professional workers not covered by the regulations of the Wage and Hour Law and not
included within union bargaining contracts.

Rulings by the board, the purpose of which is to prevent pay inflation, have permitted salary increases, bonuses, stock options, promotions, and merit and length of service raises comparable to those granted by the Wage Stabilization Board. Approximately 5,000,000 employees are affected by the board's rulings which enable employers to re-establish and maintain historical or customary relationship and differentials between their salaried employees and the workers such employees supervise. (Rulings as to raises were discussed in two issues of *United States News & World Report,* June 29, 1951, and November 30, 1951.)

In permitting bonus and profit-sharing payments to executive officers and salaried employees, the board limits the amount to the 1950 total or to one-third of the total of such payments made during any three years of the 1946-1950 period. (Cooper prepared a detailed explanation of the board's bonus regulations for *United States News & World Report,* December 14, 1951.) Overtime pay for foremen and supervisory workers has also been permitted, and in November 1951 the Salary Stabilization Board ruled that companies do not need its approval to give employees options to buy company stock provided the option price is at least 95 per cent of the market price. Although the board has a staff of field inspectors to check compliance with its regulations, it has been established as a policy, at the suggestion of Cooper, that the salary restrictions be "self-enforcing," with employers being given considerable leeway in applying the board's decisions.

The executive director of the SSB is a member of the American Society for Public Administration and has served as consultant on employee relations to the Federal Personnel Council, an interdepartmental committee for promoting the development of personnel policies and practices. Cooper, who enjoys writing, has prepared articles on personnel management. He married on February 11, 1942, and he and his wife, Mrs. Ruth Z. Cooper, a former government employee, have a daughter and a son (Lenore and Byron). Cooper has blue-gray eyes, black hair, stands five feet ten and a half inches tall, and weighs 185 pounds. He likes to "putter" about the basement of his house. He has said (in 1952) that, as yet, he is not sure what his lifework will be—"I suppose this is because I have become something of a generalist as a result of my insatiable curiosity."

Reference

Biographic Register of the Department of State, 1951

COPPERS, GEORGE H(ENRY) Nov. 29, 1902- Business executive

Address: b. c/o National Biscuit Company, 449 W. 14th St., New York 14; h. 370 Lydecker St., Englewood, N.J.

George H. Coppers, president and director of the National Biscuit Company, is the head of the world's largest baking company. This

Fabian Bachrach

GEORGE H. COPPERS

concern, which distributes its products under the trademark "Nabisco," has been, since it was founded in 1898, the leader of the American cookie and cracker industry. Coppers, a lawyer and an accountant, joined the National Biscuit Company in 1920 as an office boy; he became the president of the corporation in September 1945. After entering that office he initiated a large-scale expansion and modernization program ultimately to cost $120,000,000. Holding directorships in four other corporations, he also fills executive posts in a number of organizations associated with the baking industry.

The son of George Henry and Letitia (McGrath) Coppers, George Henry Coppers was born in New York City on November 29, 1902. He attended the New York City public schools and was graduated from high school in 1920, at which time he began his career with the National Biscuit Company as an office boy in the company's general office. While working at Nabisco, Coppers attended the Pace Institute of Accountancy and Business Administration, from which he graduated in 1925, after three years of studying at night. By this time he had become a member of Nabisco's legal department. Coppers then enrolled at the law school of Fordham University, attending evening classes for four years, and in June 1929 was graduated *cum laude* with the LL.B. degree. He was admitted to the bar in January 1930.

Coppers, who was promoted to a clerkship in the accounting department shortly after taking his first position with Nabisco, remained in that position until 1923, when he was transferred to the legal department to assist in tax problems. Appointed to the post of assistant secretary of the company on October 1, 1930, he continued with legal work and the supervision of tax questions. By 1937 his title was

COPPERS, GEORGE H.—*Continued*

assistant general counsel and in July 1938 he was raised to the post of general counsel, in which office his successful handling of a tax refund problem arising out of the Agricultural Adjustment Act brought him favorable attention from Roy Tomlinson, then president of the company. When Tomlinson, who had previously occupied the position of general counsel, became chairman of the board in 1945, he recommended Coppers as the next head of the National Biscuit Company. Coppers entered upon that office in September 1945.

The new president of Nabisco inherited large but somewhat outdated manufacturing facilities. During his first three years in office Coppers spent $11 millions on an improvement and expansion program, and by January 1, 1951, had disbursed $60 millions for this purpose. Most of these funds were allocated to equipment for making biscuits and crackers, such as Premium Saltines, Ritz, and Vanilla Wafers, which, according to *Newsweek*, comprise about three quarters of the company's total sales. In 1951 Nabisco spent about $6.5 millions for construction and $8.5 millions for new machinery and other facilities. The Portland (Oregon) bakery, which was officially opened in January 1951, cost $10 millions and is the largest in the West. Equipped with six band ovens, this plant is capable of producing annually fifty-five million pounds of cookies, crackers, and ice cream cones.

The National Biscuit Company expansion program for 1952 included the allocation of approximately $5 millions for construction and about $10 millions for machinery and equipment. In accordance with Coppers' business philosophy, "You have to spend money to make money," Nabisco plans to continue to reinvest a large part of its earnings in its expansion and modernization program, which by 1956 will have cost $120 millions. As of 1950, Nabisco owned twenty-two bakeries in the United States and Canada; with the consummation of its building plans, the number of plants will be reduced to fifteen units, of which the total capacity will be one-fifth larger than that which previously existed. Of the total national production in that industry, National Biscuit's sales amount to one half.

Coppers, whose salary was reported by *Fortune* to be $90,000 a year in 1948, introduced improved methods to Nabisco's production and packaging. In his first three years as president he expended nearly $180,000 for the employment of management consultants. The modernization program is expected to reduce labor expenses by the installation of band ovens, three-hundred-foot units which operate automatically, thereby eliminating hand operations in baking processes. By 1955 Nabisco plans to do about 95 per cent of its baking in band ovens. Bulk loading methods have also been introduced in order to reduce costs; new ways of packaging biscuits and crackers automatically are being studied; and research has continually been in progress to develop packages which preserve the freshness of the bakery products. The company predicted in 1950 that its new facilities would reduce labor costs by 3 per cent.

With the introduction of these new methods, the task of management will become even more vital to smooth and effective functioning. Coppers wrote in an article for *Advanced Management*: "The development of technological improvements in baking and packaging our products will require an even closer degree of coordination between sales planning, production scheduling, and supply procurement, in all of which the tool of budgeting can provide a more effective means for management to control production costs, quality of product and quantity of inventory." A major portion of the production and distribution which Coppers coordinates is concerned with the biscuit division, which makes such products as Uneeda Biscuits, Social Tea Biscuits, Nabisco sandwich wafers, Fig Newtons, Lorna Doones, Oreo Creme Sandwich, Premium Saltine Crackers, and Ritz Crackers. Among the many other items which the company manufactures are bread and cake, packaged cereal such as Shredded Wheat and Wheatsworth, and pretzels, potato chips, ice cream cones.

The president of the National Biscuit Company, which employs some 30,000 workers, emphasizes the importance of organizational plans that establish the duties and authority of the employees. He is concerned, too, with the necessity of establishing good communications between management and workers, so as "to foster a sense of belonging and a desire to cooperate on the part of the employee." Without satisfactory human relations within a company, he has stated, no organizational and control techniques will bring about the success of an enterprise.

Since Coppers was appointed president of Nabisco, sales of the company have increased, according to *Standard & Poor's*. The volume of $204,995,178 in 1945 rose to $296,408,934 in 1950, and profits moved upward from $10,-534,453 to $21,110,431 for the same respective years. The company announced a rise of 11 per cent in sales during 1951, but rising operating costs reduced the net profit to $16,202,212. Coppers stated that not before August 1951, when the company was allowed to increase its prices, was it possible to recover part of the higher costs.

George H. Coppers is a director of the Citizens National Bank & Trust Co., Englewood, New Jersey; National Biscuit Company; Commerce & Industry Association of New York; Trade and Industry Law Institute, Inc., New York; and the Home Life Insurance Company. He is a director and vice-president of the Biscuit and Cracker Manufacturers Association of America, a governor of the American Bakers Association, and is a director and second vice-president of the Grocery Manufacturers of America. Other offices held by Coppers are vice-president of the New York chapter of the Quartermaster Association, trustee of the Nutrition Foundation and of the Citizens Budget Commission, and chairman of the executive committee of the Chamber of Commerce of the State of New York.

A member of the Association of the Bar of the City of New York and the New York State Bar Association, Coppers also belongs to the New York County Lawyers Association. His clubs are the Bakers Club of Chicago and New York, the Economic Club of New York, the Englewood Club (of which he is a governor), the Englewood Field Club, the Knickerbocker County Club in Tenafly (New Jersey), and The Links in New York City. He is a Mason, a Republican, and a Protestant Episcopalian. Coppers married Eleanor Sherwin on August 10, 1929. His hobbies are golf, bowling, and skeet shooting.

References

Bsns W p19 Ap 30 '49 por
Fortune 37:86-91+ Je '48 por
Business Executives of America (1950)
Who's Who in America, 1950-51
Who's Who in Commerce and Industry (1951)

CORDON, GUY Apr. 24, 1890- United States Senator from Oregon
Address: b. Senate Office Bldg., Washington 25, D.C.; h. Roseburg, Ore.; 2480 16th St., N.W., Washington, D.C.

The senior United States Senator from Oregon, Republican Guy Cordon, first entered Congress in March 1944 to fill the interim vacancy created by the death of Senator Charles L. McNary. In the following November election he succeeded in being returned for the remaining four years of that term, and in 1948 was re-elected to a term which will end in January 1955. Before his entrance into the Senate, Cordon spent some time in Washington as an adviser to the Oregon Congressional delegation on matters concerning public lands, and as Senator he is a member of the Senate Committee on Interior and Insular Affairs.

Guy Cordon was born in Cuero, Texas, on April 24, 1890, to Jacob and Caroline (Terry) Cordon. In his early childhood the family moved to Roseburg, Oregon, where he was educated in the public elementary and secondary schools. After leaving high school the youth began to study law by himself. In 1920 he passed the State bar examination.

Most of Cordon's career has been spent in, or in close association with, public office. He first served as deputy assessor of Douglas County, Oregon, from 1906 to 1916 and then as county assessor from 1917 to 1920, except during 1918, when he was in the United States Army as a private in the Field Artillery. In 1923, three years after his admission to the bar, the young lawyer was elected District Attorney of Douglas County, an office he held until 1935. Cordon then returned to his law practice in Roseburg, at times going to Washington, D.C., as attorney for the Interstate Association of Public Land Councils, an organization of eleven Western States, and for the Association of Oregon Counties. During the period, beginning in 1926, in which he worked with the Oregon legislators in Con-

Moss Photo.

GUY CORDON

gress as an adviser on public lands, the future Senator helped draw up public land measures which were introduced in the Senate by his predecessor, Senator McNary. As a tax expert, Cordon also advised Governor Earl Snell of Oregon on revenue measures.

Governor Snell's interim appointment of Cordon to the Senate on March 4, 1944, came as something of a surprise since it had been believed that Snell would resign his office to become a Senator himself. Cordon, who at first declared himself undecided about remaining in the Senate beyond the interim service, entered the Republican primary election in May and, winning the nomination, was elected in November to serve out the remainder of Senator McNary's term. In the same election Oregon's other Senator, Rufus Holman, was replaced by Wayne Morse; thus Cordon became senior Senator by virtue of his ten months in the Seventy-eighth Congress. He was subsequently re-elected in November 1948 to his present term, which will end in January 1955.

During the second session of the Seventy-eighth Congress (1944) Cordon was a member of the Senate Committee on Commerce, Indian Affairs, Irrigation and Reclamation, Library, and Post Offices and Post Roads. He retained membership on the Library and Irrigation and Reclamation committees in the Seventy-ninth Congress (1945-46); and in that and the three following Congresses (1945-52) he was a member of the Appropriations Committee and the Committee on Public Lands and Surveys, which became the Committee on Interior and Insular Affairs after the Congressional Reorganization in 1947. In the Seventy-ninth Congress, the Oregon Senator also served on a Special Senate Committee on the Conservation of Wild Life Resources, and from 1946 through 1950 he was a member of the Repub-

CORDON, GUY—*Continued*

lican Policy Committee headed by Robert A. Taft.

During the two years of the Republican-controlled Eightieth Congress (1947-48) Cordon conducted several field investigations for the Senate. As chairman of the Senate Subcommittee on Territories and Insular Affairs he was sent to Hawaii in January 1948 as a committee of one to investigate the qualifications of the territory for statehood. He "returned with one of the most factual, down-to-earth reports ever to come out of the island, strongly recommending Hawaiian admission to the Union" (Josephine Ripley in the *Christian Science Monitor*, May 5, 1948). "Hawaii," said Cordon, "is able and ready to accept the social, political and economic responsibilities of State government as well as the advantages." The Senator offered evidence to refute the charges of statehood opponents that there was a widespread infiltration of Communist influence in Hawaii. The racial harmony he found in the Islands also pleased Cordon, who in May 1950 expressed the fear that a distrust of non-Caucasian races was at the base of much of the opposition to Hawaiian statehood. He headed the fight for statehood legislation in the Committee on Interior and Insular Affairs, but the bill was blocked in committee. Later statehood bills were also shelved in the Eighty-first (1949-50) and Eighty-second (1951-52) Congresses. Cordon made a second trip to the Pacific in November 1948, this time as chairman of a twelve-man committee to investigate the American administration under United Nations Trusteeship of islands formerly under Japanese mandate.

In April 1947 Cordon headed a committee consisting of himself, Joseph C. O'Mahoney, and Henry C. Dworshak in an investigation of a mine explosion in Centralia, Illinois, which killed 111 miners on March 25, 1947. Cordon's report to the Senate on June 5 stated that "almost everyone concerned was guilty of negligence to one degree or another—management, the miners, the mine workers' union, State bureau and Federal bureau."

The Oregon Senator has usually taken his stand in foreign policy with the Senate group headed by Taft and the late Kenneth S. Wherry. He supported the Bretton Woods Agreement and the United Nations Charter (July 1945), the Greek-Turkish Aid Bill (April 1947), Senate ratification of the Italian Peace Treaty (June 1947), the European Recovery Program (March 1948), and the Vandenburgh Foreign Policy Resolution (June 1948). He voted against cutting economic aid to Europe (May 1947, March and April 1948) and against a $500 millions cut but in favor of a $250 millions cut (August 1951). Measures Cordon opposed were the North Atlantic Security Pact (July 1949), the Foreign Military Aid Bill (August 1949), sending troops to Europe without Congressional approval, and an appropriation of $45 millions for the President's Point Four Program (May 1950). His only recorded vote in favor of extension of the Trade Agreement Act came in June 1948,

when limitations were placed on the President's authority to lower tariffs.

Cordon has placed himself on the side of economy in Federal spending with his support of two proposals to cut all Federal appropriations by 5 to 10 per cent (August and September 1949), of a 10 per cent cut in nondefense spending (August 1950), of a 25 per cent cut in the Government's publicity payrolls, and of a shorter annual leave for Government employees (1951). Income tax reduction also received his support in 1947 and 1948, but on August 28, 1951, he voted for a $5.5 billions tax increase. On the two emergency strike control bills presented in Congress in May 1946, Cordon voted for the Case bill and against the President's emergency strike control bill. In May 1947 he favored the Taft-Hartley Labor-Management Relations Act, although he voted against amendments to curb industry-wide bargaining and to outlaw union as well as closed shops; and he supported the 1949 coalition revision of the act. In the attempt to impose cloture on the antipoll tax filibuster of May 1944 and the FEPC filibusters of February 1946 and July 1950, Cordon voted "Yea"; he opposed Vice-President Barkley's ruling in March 1949 that cloture could be applied at any stage in the consideration of a measure, a ruling which would have made it possible to limit debate on a motion to take up a measure as well as on the measure itself. The Senator favored the exemption of servicemen in the armed forces from poll taxes (1948) and voted against the elimination of segregation among draftees (1950).

On economic controls Cordon voted, in June 1944, for a bill to end subsidies a year later; in June 1946, for price-fixing formulas which would have set ceilings for both manufacturers and distributors based on 1941 prices plus the average industry-wide increase in unit price; in July 1946, for the OPA revival bill; in August 1950, to tie wage controls to price controls; and in June 1951, for a ban on price rollbacks and on livestock slaughter quotas. He opposed price control extension in June 1945; meat, poultry, and egg ceilings in July 1946; and lower farm price supports and an increase in borrowing power for the Commodity Credit Corporation in June 1950. In June 1947 the Senator favored an eight-month rather than a twelve-month extension of rent control, and in June 1950 he voted against rent control altogether. He supported proposals for rent increases in May 1947 and in June 1951 and local option rent control in March 1949. He voted against the long-range housing bill presented in the Eightieth and Eighty-first Congresses, and in June 1951 he opposed the limitation of public housing to five thousand units. On the Federal Aid to Education Bill, Cordon voted "Yea" in April 1948, after opposing a ban on aid to church schools, and "Nay" in May 1949. He also opposed a rise in the old age tax base and Federal aid to the needy disabled in June 1950 and favored opening State relief rolls to inspection in July 1951.

Cordon cast his vote against two of President Truman's controversial appointments, that of Henry Wallace as Secretary of Commerce in March 1945 and that of David Lilienthal as Chairman of the Atomic Energy Commission in April 1947. He voted in July 1950 to permit the appointment of General George Marshall as Secretary of Defense by exempting the General from a provision forbidding the appointment of any man who had served as a commissioned officer in the Armed Forces within ten years. Of the three Constitutional amendments which have come before the Senate during his two terms in office, Cordon supported the Equal Rights Amendment in July 1946 and the two-term limit for Presidents in March 1947, and opposed the Lodge-Gossett Amendment which would have split Presidential electoral votes in each State among the candidates on the basis of their popular vote. In June 1947 he voted in favor of the bill which changed the Presidential succession, in the event of the death of both President and Vice-President, from the Secretary of State to the Speaker of the House of Representatives.

The Senator and his wife, the former Ana Lucille Allen, whom he married on September 30, 1914, have two children living, a son, Allen, and a daughter, Margaret Anne (Mrs. P. A. Laurance) ; a second daughter, Mrs. Carolyn Crouch, is deceased. Cordon is a director of the Umpqua Savings and Loan Association of Roseburg. He has been active in the American Legion and in the Oregon District Attorneys' Association, and is a former Oregon State Commander of the first-named and a past president of the latter.

References

> Biographical Directory of the American Congress, 1774-1949 (1950)
> Congressional Directory (1951)
> Who's Who in America, 1950-51
> Who's Who in the West (1951)
> Who's Who in United States Politics (1950)
> World Biography (1948)

CORNELL, KATHARINE Feb. 16, 1898-
Actress-manager
Address: b. c/o Katharine Cornell Productions, Inc., 1270 6th Ave., New York 20; h. Sneeden's Landing, Palisades, N.Y.

> NOTE: This biography supersedes the article which appeared in *Current Biography* in 1941.

Katharine Cornell, who appeared in her first starring role in 1925, in *The Green Hat*, and has managed her own productions since the first presentation of *The Barretts of Wimpole Street*, in 1931, has also been acclaimed for her performances in *Candida*, *Romeo and Juliet*, *No Time for Comedy*, and *The Doctor's Dilemma*, among other roles. The 1951 opening of *The Constant Wife* marked the thirtieth year since her debut on Broadway and the twenty-fifth year she has been directed by her producer husband, Guthrie McClintic.

The only child of Dr. Peter Cortelyou Cornell and Alice Gardner (Plimpton) Cornell,

Katharine Cornell was born February 16, 1898, in Berlin, Germany, where her father was taking a postgraduate course in surgery. Three months later the family returned to the United States to settle in Buffalo, New York. There, she tells, her father (who was an excellent amateur actor, as was his father also) later left the medical profession and became the manager of a theater. Another influence in Katharine Cornell's early life was her aunt, Miss Lydia Cornell, who had an unusual dramatic talent. As a student at Oaksmere School, a finishing school in Mamaroneck, New York, the young girl wrote allegorical plays, designed the sets, and directed and appeared in them. Excelling in athletics, she was a runner-up for the Buffalo championship in tennis as well as the city's amateur swimming champion.

When Edward Goodman, of the Washington Square Players, went to Oaksmere in 1916 to help coach a play Miss Cornell had written, he suggested that she try out for the Players. This she did, but because of nervousness she read poorly. Subsequently, after Florence Enright had given her some coaching Miss Cornell was offered a part when one of the company did not appear at a rehearsal. Then followed a two-year period of bit roles with the Washington Square Players, during which time she earned a total of $40 from 1916 to 1918. However, since Miss Cornell had an inheritance from her mother, she was able to continue her apprenticeship with the Players. Her first part with that group was in *Bushido*, in which she spoke four words: "My son, my son."

Not long afterward Katharine Cornell joined a touring stock company owned by Jessie Bonstelle, who was a friend of the Cornell family. During the summer of 1919 Miss Cornell played secondary roles in Bonstelle stock productions in Buffalo and Detroit. Later that year, at the age of twenty-one, the young actress received her first critical recognition as Jo in Miss Bonstelle's London production of *Little Women*. Returning to the United States in 1920, she played leading parts in summer stock with the same company in Detroit. In 1921 she made her first Broadway appearance, in *Nice People*. That year, too, on September 8, she was married to the director Guthrie McClintic, who had once scribbled on his program about her acting: "Interesting—monotonous—watch."

Because of the press notices on her performance in London, Miss Cornell was offered the feminine lead in the 1921 production of Clemence Dane's *A Bill of Divorcement*, in which she had her first "personal triumph." A comment, in *Theatre Magazine*, read: "Katharine Cornell is wholly delightful as the cheeky, young flapper." After two seasons in that play, Miss Cornell was assigned the lead in Clemence Dane's *Will Shakespeare* (1923), as the Dark Lady of the Sonnets, and for the first time she played a scene as Juliet. Two other productions in which Miss Cornell appeared in 1923 were Pinero's *The Enchanted Cottage* and Sidney Howard's adaptation of *Casanova*. In *The Way Things Happen* (1924) she made her first appearance in a Guthrie McClintic production, and later that year acted in *The Outsider*

KATHARINE CORNELL

(by Dorothy Brandon) and in *Tiger Cats* (by Karen Bramson).

The title role in *Candida* (1924) was Miss Cornell's first of a number of portrayals of Bernard Shaw heroines. The reaction of the critics was summed up by one: "The tenderness, the poetry, the supreme womanliness of Katharine Cornell's impersonation of the title part puts this actress a notch ahead of anything she has yet attempted. It is an impersonation touched by the wand of genius." (A museum in Buffalo, the city in which she had grown up, commissioned Eugene Speicher—also from that city—to paint a full-length oil portrait of her, posed in the red gown that had been designed for her role in *Candida*. The portrait was presented by her to New York's Museum of Modern Art in 1939.) Three other times, in 1936, 1942, and 1946, she was to return to Broadway in revivals of *Candida*, a performance that evoked a letter from Bernard Shaw: "I don't think I was ever so astonished by a picture as I was by your photograph. Your success as Candida, and something blonde and expansive about your name, had created an ideal suburban British Candida in my imagination. Fancy my feelings on seeing in the photograph a gorgeous dark lady from the cradle of the human race—wherever that was—Ceylon, Sumatra, Hilo, or the southernmost corner of the Garden of Eden!"

Michael Arlen's *The Green Hat*, in which Miss Cornell played the lead during 1926-27, brought her stardom in the traditional theatrical sense, for her name went up in lights on the marquee. The New York *Herald Tribune* critic wrote that she played the part "with such enchantment that the audience . . . was . . . spellbound." The production of this play marked another milestone in her career: it was directed by her husband, who has since been the director of all of Miss Cornell's plays. The three dramas which followed were Somerset Maugham's *The Letter* (1927), an adaptation of Edith Wharton's *The Age of Innocence* (1928), and *Dishonored Lady* (1930), her last appearance under a management other than her own, in this case Gilbert Miller's.

Miss Cornell's sensational success as Elizabeth Barrett, the poet, in Rudolf Besier's *The Barretts of Wimpole Street* in 1931 marked the beginning of her career as actress-manager. Brooks Atkinson, the New York *Times* drama critic, said of her work: "Miss Cornell might be showier, but she could hardly be more discriminating, true, and exacting. *The Barretts of Wimpole Street* is a triumph for her and the splendid company with which she has surrounded herself. Everything about the performance is genuine." Brian Aherne played opposite her as Robert Browning for the New York run of 370 performances; and together they were to re-create their roles in revivals on Broadway, on tours, and before Armed Forces audiences in Europe in 1945, until more than a thousand performances had been given. (A later recognition came in the form of an invitation to the actress and actor to attend the dedication of the Browning collection at Baylor University in 1951.)

After *The Barretts*, Miss Cornell played the title role in Thornton Wilder's *Lucrece* (1932), again with Brian Aherne as the male lead. In *Alien Corn* (1933), written for Miss Cornell by Sidney Howard, the "vitality" and "restrained intensity" of her acting won much critical praise. She "has superbly mounted the play with distinction that is nothing short of remarkable" was *Billboard*'s observation on the production. The next year, 1934, in *Romeo and Juliet*, her first Shakespearean role, she was described by the New York *Times* critic as playing "with an all-consuming fervor." James Mason Brown wrote in the New York *Evening Post*, "She has given *Romeo and Juliet* one of the most beautiful, most spirited, and best-acted Shakespearean productions of our time." *Flowers of the Forest* (1935) was followed by Shaw's *Saint Joan* in 1936, about which John Anderson commented, "It is Shaw's greatest play, and Miss Cornell is superb."

Her next production, Maxwell Anderson's *The Wingless Victory*, was alternated with a second revival of her role in *Candida*. After a sabbatical year (1937-38)—a world tour planned for the season had to be abandoned—Miss Cornell appeared in *Herod and Marianne,* the Hebbel classic. This was followed by *No Time for Comedy* (1939), her first light touch, which remained in New York a year and which she took on a coast-to-coast tour, traveling 15,240 miles and playing in fifty-six cities in twenty-nine States and Canada. Miss Cornell feels strongly about the necessity of taking only first-rate companies on the road. "If the road is to continue to recover, we must give it the best we can offer," she declared. "Everybody says the movies killed the road, but that isn't the whole truth. The theater itself helped to kill it by sending out inferior attractions. . . . We can only win them back to the theater by giving them their money's worth."

When the actress applied for the right to produce Shaw's *The Doctor's Dilemma*, the dramatist cabled from England, "Yes, dear Katharine, yes." Opening as a revival of that drama in 1941, Miss Cornell's production had the longest run ever enjoyed by the Shaw comedy. She also appeared in Chekhov's *The Three Sisters* in the 1942-43 season, bringing together a cast which included Judith Anderson, Ruth Gordon, Edmund Gwenn, and Alexander Knox. "As usual with Miss Cornell the manager," Lewis Nichols wrote in the New York *Times*, "she has stinted on nothing, and her cast comes from the top drawer of what would be any other manager's remote dream." Its run of 230 performances was a record for any Chekhov play in English.

"The greatest experience, the most rewarding, I ever had," Miss Cornell has said, was the 143-performance tour of *The Barretts of Wimpole Street* in 1945 for American soldiers in Italy, France, and Holland. Back on Broadway in 1946, she produced an adaptation of *Antigone* which drew some critical disagreement, but a revival of *Candida* (with Marlon Brando) later that year was applauded. After welcoming her 1947-48 *Antony and Cleopatra*, which had the longest run on record for that play, for its "beauty, power, and grandeur," the critics showed mixed reactions toward *That Lady* in 1949. (During 1948-49 she had had another sabbatical year.) On December 8, 1951, Miss Cornell revived Somerset Maugham's 1927 play, *The Constant Wife*, in which she was praised for her "grand manner and great warmth." This comedy, in which the actress-manager appears with Brian Aherne and Grace George, was described by *Variety* in January 1952, on the basis of its first four weeks' run, as one of the biggest commercial successes of Miss Cornell's career.

Miss Cornell has rarely ventured into fields other than the theater. In 1939 her autobiographical *I Wanted to be An Actress* was published, in which she gave encouragement to young people with dramatic talent. Of Miss Cornell herself, as revealed in the book, one critic said: "It is not a glamorous person who emerges but someone who in some indefinable manner is essentially native to the soil of America." In November 1940 Miss Cornell made a radio appearance in which she did three scenes from *The Barretts of Wimpole Street* for a Red Cross benefit. She admitted to nervousness and has declined subsequent offers to act before a microphone. In 1943 she played in her first Hollywood motion picture, the all-star *Stage Door Canteen*, in which she did a scene from *Romeo and Juliet*.

Miss Cornell has received the Chancellor's Medal at the University of Buffalo in 1935, the New York Drama League Award in 1935 for her performance as Juliet, the Gold Medal of the National Achievement Award for 1936, and the Jane Addams Medal Award at Rockford (Illinois) College in 1950. She has also been the recipient of honorary doctor's degrees from the University of Wisconsin (Litt.D., 1936), Elmira College (Litt.D., 1937), Cornell University (Litt.D., 1937), Smith College (L.H.D., 1937), Hobart College (Litt.D.,

1938), University of Pennsylvania (Litt.D., 1938), and Doctor of Fine Arts from Clark University (1941), Ithaca College (1947), and Princeton University (1948). Another recognition (in 1946) was the art citation by the National Conference of Christians and Jews.

For thirty-one years the McClintics lived in a Beekman Place house in New York. In 1952 they joined the ranks of commuters by moving to Palisades, into a home which McClintic decorated. Miss Cornell, who is five feet six inches tall and weighs 130 pounds, has brown eyes and brown hair. Her clubs are the Colony and Cosmopolitan, and she names her chief interests as golf, weaving, and dogs.

References

Cue 10:15 Mr 8 '41
Life 10:83 My 5 '41 por
Look 16:92 F 12 '52
Mademoiselle 11:123 My '40 por
N Y Times Mag p14+ F 25 '45
New Yorker 6:23-5 F '31
Newsweek 31:82-3 Ja 19 '48
PM p44 Mr 9 '41
Sat R Lit 32:132 Ag 6 '49
Theatre Arts 21:36-51 Ja '37; 29:67 F '45 por; 32:41 Ag '48
Bower, W. New Directions (1937)
Cornell, K. I Wanted to be An Actress (1939)
Who's Who in America, 1950-51
Who's Who in the Theatre (1947)
World Biography (1948)

CORTINES, ADOLFO RUIZ *See* Ruiz Cortines, A.

COWDEN, HOWARD A(USTIN) May 18, 1893- Cooperative organization executive

Address: b. c/o Consumers Cooperative Association, 318 E. 10th St., Kansas City, Mo.; h. R.F.D. 4, Kansas City, Mo.

A pioneer of the farm cooperative movement in Missouri, Howard A. Cowden is the founder, general manager, and president of the Consumers Cooperative Association, which started in Kansas City in 1929 as a small oil purchasing and distributing medium. Under his guidance the C.C.A. reached in its twenty-third year a membership of 450,000 families, to which in 1950-51 it distributed $75 millions' worth of home and farm supplies. He is also prominent as secretary-treasurer of the International Petroleum Cooperative Association, chartered in 1946, and is a leading advocate of the creation of an international oil authority.

Born near Bolivar, Polk County, Missouri, on May 18, 1893, Howard Austin Cowden is the seventh of the nine children (one daughter and eight sons) of John Porter and Margaret (Burns) Cowden. His forebears were Scotch-Irish farmers; the 500-acre Ozark Mountains farm at Pleasant Hope on which he was reared was a government land grant to his pioneering grandfather. His father, described by Howard Cowden as "a very intelligent man, a hard

Farnan Foto

HOWARD A. COWDEN

worker, a man who built the first silo in the community," was regarded as one of the area's more progressive-minded agriculturalists and livestock breeders, and was a lecturer for the Grange and an adherent of the Populist movement. "From him," the son has said, "I gained the philosophy of cooperation." The family farm, however, was "not too fertile," and the Cowdens were hard put to meet mortgage payments, largely because of the inequities of a marketing system which forced farmers to sell their produce and livestock to wholesalers and packers at buyers' prices. "Well I can remember," Howard Cowden has recorded, "how we used to ship our livestock to Kansas City after growing the steers for two years and feeding them all winter in the cold and slush the corn we ourselves had grown. When they were shipped to the Kansas City market, my father would come back and say to the boys: 'Well, the market was off 75 cents or $1.00 per hundred, and the packer buyers didn't come into the alleys until about noon.' They were actually carrying on a sit-down strike against the sellers of cattle."

At Pleasant Hope High School young Cowden was a member of the debating team and also an all-around athlete, winning the hundred-yard dash and the high jump at a Polk County track meet and playing basketball and baseball. The Polk County folk nicknamed him "Shell" after Shell Cunningham, a local boy who had gone on to big-league baseball, and for a while Howard Cowden thought of becoming a professional player. He was graduated from the Pleasant Hope High School in 1911.

Encouraged by his father, Howard Cowden entered a corn-raising contest sponsored by the St. Louis and San Francisco Railroad, the prize for which was a four-month "short course" at the University of Missouri's College of Agriculture. Cowden won the prize

and on completion of the course became a teacher, first at one of the Polk County elementary schools in 1914, and a year later at the Pleasant Hope High School, where two of his pupils won prizes in a State pig-feeding contest conducted by the *Missouri Farmer*, published by William Hirth. "In that pre-World War I period," stated Richard Fowler, in an article on Cowden in the Kansas City *Star*, "Hirth was promoting the idea of school house farm clubs for adults that would one day develop into the Missouri Farmers Association." Cowden organized a number of such clubs before enrolling for a general college course at the Springfield Normal School (now the Southwest Missouri Teachers College), where during his first year he supported himself by many odd jobs and also played basketball. This was during World War I; and he spent part of his second year in the Student Army Training Corps, but was released in November 1918.

Returning to Polk County, Cowden was aware that the same marketing conditions which had resulted in his father losing his farm through mortgage foreclosure also applied to other farm produce, including eggs. "The price of eggs," he recalls, "always went down when the hens were laying plentifully, because all other farmers' eggs were going to market then and the buyer took advantage of the farmers." On February 10, 1919, accordingly, Cowden called a meeting of the local farm clubs and proposed the organization of the Polk County Farmers Association and of a farmers' exchange to ship eggs to Kansas City, where prices were higher than in the local market. The suggestion was adopted and Cowden was made manager of the Farm Club Exchange which opened at Bolivar on March 19 and eventually grew into the Producers Produce Company of Springfield, now one of the largest egg and poultry concerns in the country. The exchange was the first to be set up under the auspices of the Missouri Farmers Association, launched by William Hirth in the preceding year. Cowden became secretary of the M.F.A. at Columbia, Missouri, on August 1, 1920, and in the next eight years (stated a release) "helped organize hundreds of local co-ops and many terminal marketing and purchasing co-ops." He resigned to organize the Consumers Cooperative Association in 1929, and has been president and general manager of the C.C.A. and its subsidiaries ever since.

Cowden started the Consumers Cooperative Association in a small Kansas City office with one stenographer and $3,000. "In the beginning," Richard Fowler wrote, "he bought oil that was distributed under the association's label to a few small farmer co-ops. When he ran into complaints on the quality of the oil he won the agreement of his directors to make their own in a little shell of a building behind a two-car garage in North Kansas City." Another article (in *Time*) stated that "by the end of the year he had 22 member co-ops and had sold $310,000 worth of oil products." Throughout the countryside he organized oil co-ops in which shares were sold to the farmers at $10 apiece, until by 1934 the association was in a position to buy the Pennsylvania Petroleum Company's plant at a "depression" price of $57,000. In the same year the C.C.A. began exporting lubricating oil to European cooperatives; this took Cowden on his first trip across the Atlantic, and in the spring of 1935 he attended the International Cooperative Alliance's Congress at London as the first United States representative. Two years later (1937) at the I.C.A.'s next congress, in Paris, he proposed that a world oil cooperative be formed "to take the profit out of one of the most troublesome cooperatives in international trade." Unsettled conditions, however, postponed further action in this regard until after World War II.

In order to insure a source of oil supply, Cowden raised $350,000 from $10 shares sold to C.C.A. members and built an association refinery at Phillipsburg in northwestern Kansas. When the supply of crude oil was shut off a month after the opening of the refinery in 1939, more money was raised from the members for the purchase of oil wells and pipelines (*Time*). Drilling for oil at Phillipsburg met with success in the winter of 1940-41, and within two years the refinery had paid for its cost. In the interim, a second refinery, erected at Scottsbluff, Nebraska, was opened early in December 1941. During World War II Cowden served on the Petroleum Industry War Council, the National Petroleum Council and various price and oil-marketing committees.

At the first postwar session of the International Cooperative Alliance at London in September 1945, Cowden resubmitted the idea of an international petroleum cooperative and proposed the creation of an international allocation authority to resolve conflicting American, British, and Dutch rivalries for the oil of the Middle East. Within another twelve months Cowden had assurances of support in fifteen nations, and at Zurich, Switzerland, on October 1, 1946, the delegates to the next I.C.A. congress agreed that the International Cooperative Petroleum Association should be chartered. Today the I.C.P.A., with headquarters at New York, has a membership of twenty-one large regional cooperatives in thirteen countries and does a multimillion-dollar business.

As its secretary-treasurer, Cowden was responsible for the drafting of a plan to create an international authority to administer Middle-East oilfields "with the consent of the states involved," which was on the agenda of the United Nations Economic and Social Council, 1947. Four years later (1951) Cowden came forward with a "middle way" to settle the Anglo-Iranian oil dispute. "In July," he stated in his latest annual report to the C.C.A., "I proposed to President Truman that Iran's nationalization of oil be recognized and that a world oil co-op, financed by loans from the World Bank, be organized to produce, refine, ship, market, and distribute Iranian oil." Subsequently the plan was said to have aroused the "serious interest" of Iranian Premier Mohammed Mossadegh (Richard Fowler in the Kansas City *Star*).

The annual report above quoted covered the fiscal year 1950-51 and was presented to 2,854 delegates assembled in the Kansas City Municipal Auditorium in December 1951 to mark the Consumers Cooperative Association's twenty-third year of existence. In 1950-51 Cowden revealed, "C.C.A. distributed $75 million worth of home and farm supplies to 450,000 families." It had become (stated *Time*) "the largest cooperative of its kind" in the United States, with assets of $52,200,000. The owner of about 1,000 producing wells and more than 900 miles of pipelines, it also sold (in addition to oil) food, agricultural supplies, machinery, home appliances, automotive supplies, and building materials. In October 1951 it announced expansion in the fertilizer field through undertaking the erection of a $16,000,000 nitrogen plant at Lawrence, Kansas. The C.C.A., which publishes the twice-monthly periodical *Cooperative Consumer* (circulation 322,500), gives news and market reports over five Midwestern radio stations, and sponsors investment services and recreational camps for its members, has as its most important subsidiary the Cooperative Refining Association. Cowden is the president of the latter unit. He is also a board member (and former president) of the National Cooperative Refining Association, vice-president of the Cooperative League of the U.S.A., and a member of the executive councils of both the International Cooperative Alliance and the International Trading Agency at London. When awarded an honorary LL.D. by St. Francis Xavier University at Antigonish, Nova Scotia, on May 24, 1950, he was cited as "the number one cooperative businessman of America."

Howard Cowden has been married twice, first to Thelma Lundy on November 1, 1917. She became the mother of two sons, Keith L. and John Henry. The present Mrs. Howard Cowden, a secretary before her marriage on April 23, 1932, is the former Edna May Reno. Cowden has blue eyes and graying brown hair; he stands six feet and one inch tall and weighs 210 pounds. He is a Presbyterian and a Mason. Organizations to which he belongs include the Chamber of Commerce of Kansas City, the Oil Men's Club, and the Missouri Farm Bureau. He is also chairman of the Clay County (Missouri) Planning Commission and a member of the Citizens' Planning Council of Kansas City. At his home, "Cowdena," a farm near Kansas City, the C.C.A. president makes a hobby of raising purebred Hereford cattle. He takes a keen spectator interest in baseball.

References

Kansas City (Mo.) Star p40+ Ja 27 '52 por

Time 58:89 D 10 '51 por

Business Executives of America (1950)
Who's Who in America, 1950-51
Who's Who in the Midwest (1949)

COWLES, FLEUR (FENTON) (kōlz)
Jan. 20, 1910- Magazine editor
Address: c/o Cowles Magazines, Inc., 488 Madison Ave., New York 22

Associate editor of *Look* and *Quick* magazines and editor of *Flair* from January 1950

Michael Vaccaro

FLEUR COWLES

until the discontinuance of that magazine a year later, Fleur Cowles is also author of *Bloody Precedent* (1952), a comparative study of two Argentine dictatorships. Mrs. Cowles, who was active in the field of advertising before entering publishing, is the wife of Gardner Cowles, president of Cowles Magazines, Inc., publishers of *Look* and *Quick*. She gave voluntary wartime service in Washington during World War II, was appointed special consultant to the Famine Emergency Committee by President Truman in 1946, and in November 1950 was named consultant to the Chief of Staff, Headquarters United States Air Force.

Fleur Fenton Cowles was born January 20, 1910, in Montclair, New Jersey, where her father, Matthew Fenton, was a businessman-manufacturer. Her mother's maiden name was Eleanor Pearl. At the age of eleven Fleur Cowles began to record her impression of the things about her. "I was terribly self-conscious about what I wrote," she says, "and would hide my work under the mattress. But the main thing is that I wrote every day." Reared in New Jersey (and Boston) she was graduated in 1926 from the Montclair High School, and she continued her education at the School of Fine and Applied Arts in New York. (Her sister is Mildred Fenton, president of her own radio productions company.)

While studying at the latter institution, Fleur Fenton began six years of "spasmodic" work in advertising by responding to a department store advertisement for an experienced copywriter. Obtaining the positon (in the advertising department of Gimbel Brothers) she asked and received a weekly salary of $100. Later she was promoted to the rank of assistant advertising manager. "A natural huckster," Mort Weisinger wrote of her in the 1950 *Writer's Year Book.* Adept at devising slogans and sales

promotion ideas, she left Gimbels to open her own advertising agency in Boston.

This enterprise, of which she is said to have made "a reasonable success," was followed by two years (1931-32) during which she wrote a by-lined daily column for the first page of the second section of the New York *World-Telegram.* The *Writer's Year Book,* in speaking of her *World-Telegram* column, refers to Miss Fenton as "a sort of female Lucius Beebe" who "gave dull fashion news sparkle."

Miss Fenton returned to the field of advertising, and by 1936, according to *Time* (June 7, 1948), "had an agency of her own" and "was making $20,000 a year." By the time she was twenty-seven she and her first husband, advertising executive Atherton Pettingell, owned the Dorland International Pettingell and Fenton Advertising Agency, of which she was executive vice-president. (The Pettingells were divorced in the mid-1940's.)

During World War II Miss Fenton gave voluntary speech-writing and campaign service to Government war agencies, serving in 1944 as a dollar-a-year executive. At the end of the war she sold her interest in the Dorland International agency, stated an official biography, went to Europe, and was the first American woman civilian to enter several liberated countries. She returned home early in 1946 to become special consultant to the Famine Emergency Committee by Presidential appointment. In November 1950 she was named consultant to the Chief of Staff, Headquarters United States Air Force.

Miss Fenton was married on December 27, 1946, to Gardner Cowles, president of Cowles Magazines, Inc. (publishers of *Look, Quick,* and the now discontinued *Flair*), president of the Des Moines *Register* and the Des Moines *Tribune,* president of the Cowles Broadcasting Company (which operates four radio stations), and chairman of the board of the Minneapolis *Star* and *Tribune* Company. Mrs. Cowles' association with *Look* had begun earlier in the year, when she created the women's department in the magazine, introducing sections on food, fashion, and family problems, and also representing the woman's point of view on the executive editorial board. She is the only woman on the board of directors of Cowles Magazines, Inc. According to a statement of publisher Gardner Cowles, this editing of the magazine with "the whole family . . . in mind" is responsible for the fact that *Look*'s advertising lineage and circulation (now placed at 3,200,000) doubled in two years. Mrs. Cowles became associate editor of *Look* in 1947.

Mrs. Cowles' encouragement of the idea is said to have been partially responsible for the capsule-sized (four by six inches) weekly pictorial, *Quick,* a "newsstand best-seller" four months after it was launched in July 1949; it reached a circulation of about 850,000 in fifteen months. Mrs. Cowles is associate editor of the magazine. To it her departments contribute the women's interests sections, covering home life, food, fashion, art, and a special feature entitled "For Women Only."

In February 1947 Mrs. Cowles first discussed with her huband her idea for *Flair*—a monthly "class" magazine designed to utilize new advances in the graphic arts. It would combine, said Mrs. Cowles, "for the first time under one set of covers the best in the arts, literature, fashion, humor, decoration, travel and entertainment." The result of several years of planning and experimentation, the magazine, with Mrs. Cowles as its editor, appeared in January 1950 and was financed by what she described as "a very generous three-year budget." It incorporated a variety of paper stocks and printing processes, included pages differing in size and texture, featured a double cover, embossed and with a die-cut on the outside revealing a portion of the inner cover, and employed a new method of binding which eliminated stapling and permitted pages to lie flat. After a total of thirteen monthly issues (January 1950-January 1951), *Flair* discontinued publication in December 1950. Publisher Cowles gave as his reason for this action the expense of paper and difficulty in obtaining it— and an increase in production costs. The name *Flair* appears on the masthead of *Look* as being incorporated in that magazine. In an interview given to Harvey Breit for the New York *Times Book Review* in February 1952, Mrs. Cowles revealed that she planned to revive *Flair* as an annual publication; the book, a hard-bound volume to sell for $10, was at that time on the press.

In her book *Bloody Precedent* (1952) Fleur Cowles compared the Perón rule in Argentina with that of a nineteenth century dictator, Juan Rosas. The half of the book dealing with the Peróns, whom Mrs. Cowles met during her visit to Argentina in 1950, contains what V. L. Warren in the New York *Times* called "perhaps the most perceptive and accurate picture of Evita [Señora Perón] published to date." Other reviewers, while admitting the readability of the book, commented on an uneven quality in regard to organization and preciseness of expression.

Mrs. Cowles was decorated by the French Government in 1951, as a Chevalier of the Legion of Honor; she is the recipient of the 1950 Nieman-Marcus Award for service to fashion, is a member of the Women's National Press Club and of Theta Sigma Phi. For one year chairman of the women's division of the Urban League, she is also chairman of the Reconstructive Plastic Surgery Unit of the New York University-Bellevue Rehabilitation Center, and a member of the board of the Society of the Rehabilitation of the Facially Disfigured. A former licensed aviatrix, she has given up flying and now names painting as her hobby. She recently won a silver medal for her water-color painting entered in the Art News Annual Competition. She is a Republican in politics and a Methodist in her religious affiliation. Weighing 110 pounds, she is five feet five inches in height, has ash-blonde hair and hazel eyes. Mrs. Cowles has been described as "sensitive, alert, candid," and as giving the impression of "a person of forthright purpose and determination." She wears large, black-rimmed glasses, likes softly tailored clothes, and is said always to wear a rose and a large, one-inch square uncut emerald ring.

References

> Ed & Pub 83:41 Oct 7 '50
> Magazine Industry Winter '50
> N Y Post Mag p3 Jl 26 '47
> Newsweek 34:59 S 12 '49
> Time 51:48 Je 7 '48
> Who's Who in the East (1951)
> Writer's Year Book, 1950

COWLES, MRS. GARDNER *See* Cowles, F. F.

CRIPPS, SIR (RICHARD) STAFFORD Apr. 24, 1889—Apr. 21, 1952 Former British Cabinet Minister; became a Labor member of Parliament in 1931; Ambassador to Russia (1940-42); Lord Privy Seal and Leader of the House of Commons (1942); Minister of Aircraft Production (1942-45); President of the Board of Trade (1945); Minister for Economic Affairs (1947); Chancellor of the Exchequer (1947-50). See *Current Biography*, 1948.

Obituary

> N Y Times p1+ Ap 22 '52

CROFT, ARTHUR C(LARENCE) May 26, 1890- Arbitration organization official; publisher

Address: b. c/o American Arbitration Association, 9 Rockefeller Plaza, New York 20; c/o National Foremen's Institute, 100 Garfield Ave., New London, Conn.; h. 2 Beekman Pl., New York 22; 14930 Corona del Mar, Pacific Palisades, Calif.

Arthur C. Croft, who has headed the National Foremen's Institute, Inc., of New London, Connecticut, since 1937, has twice (in 1950 and 1952) been elected president of the American Arbitration Association, an organization engaged in furthering voluntary arbitration. The National Foremen's Institute is concerned, among other things, with the training of foremen in their relations with labor and employers and issues a number of publications in that field.

Arthur Clarence Croft was born in Cleveland, Ohio, on May 26, 1890, the son of John Henry and Lucetta (Shirk) Croft. He received his education in the public schools of Cleveland and began his career by becoming a foreman in a metal working shop in the same city. In 1911, however, at the age of twenty-one, Croft moved to Chicago to work on the magazine *Factory*, thereby entering the publishing field. From 1912 until 1928 he was associated with the A. W. Shaw Company, Inc., of Chicago, filling the position of circulation manager. Going East in 1928, he took a post with the McGraw-Hill Publishing Company in New York, where he helped establish

ARTHUR C. CROFT

Business Week magazine and later became its director of circulation.

Croft, who remained with McGraw-Hill through 1936, accepted in 1937 the presidency of, and a directorship on, the National Foremen's Institute, Inc., in New London, Connecticut, a position he continues to hold. The National Foremen's Institute is an organization devoted to the training of foremen to handle workers properly, and to the educating of employers in their relationship with foremen. The institution concentrates heavily on training in scientific methods in solving employee grievances with the aim of creating harmonious relations between labor and management and thus making for maximum production, an aim which is also furthered by the publication of *The Foreman's Letter* and other literature associated with business, labor relations, and supervisory training. Since Croft became head of the institute, its volume of business as of 1950 had increased fifteenfold, according to the New York *World-Telegram*, which quoted Croft as saying, "Employers now pay us $2,000,000 a year to carry on our work." Croft is also president of the International Foremen's Institute, Inc., of Montreal.

On November 14, 1950, Croft accepted another administrative position, this time in succession to Spruille Braden as president of the American Arbitration Association, a nonpartisan and nonprofit-making organization established in 1926 for the purpose of advancing the knowledge and use of voluntary arbitration in many kinds of disputes. These range from minor everyday difficulties, such as the spoiling of a dress by a cleaner, to controversies such as those arising from automobile accidents to major differences between labor and management in large industrial firms. Cases which involve crimes, domestic relations, minors, and boundary disputes lie outside the

province of the association. With its headquarters in New York City, the association has regional offices throughout the United States and arbitrators in twenty-two countries of the Western Hemisphere and in an increasing number of countries in Europe, Asia, and Africa.

The American Arbitration Association maintains a national and an international panel of arbitrators chosen from professions and trades covering nearly every occupational group. When a dispute is referred to the association, a list of qualified arbitrators in the region is sent to the disputing parties. From this list the arbitrator preferred by both sides is selected. A hearing follows, and the arbitrator's verdict is accepted as binding, thus saving the time and costs of the usual court proceedings. From time to time the association expresses its views on pertinent issues: in its journal, *Arbitration News*, in April 1952 it maintained that the Wage Stabilization Board's handling of the steel dispute showed that the "neutral" members, in seeking support from either side, lost their impartiality. It recommended that each WSB panel include three public members and one each from labor and industry, thus insuring a public majority. (The Washington *Post* thought this proposal the most constructive one offered.)

Upon election to the presidency of the association in November of 1950, Croft announced that the organization was gearing its operations so that "arbitration proceedings can be started within twenty-four hours after disputants have agreed to submit their controversy." A few days later he expressed his aim of promoting the use of arbitration in aiding the national defense effort, the association having urged upon W. Stuart Symington, chairman of the National Security Resources Board, the establishment of arbitration machinery in every community with a defense plant, and the inclusion of arbitration clauses in contracts.

Second on Croft's list of objectives, also announced in November 1950, was the expansion of a network of tribunals to help settle foreign trade disputes out of court. For the attainment of this end, Croft planned an extensive tour of the United States, Canadian, and Latin American cities and a comparable tour of Europe to urge the greater use of arbitration clauses in contracts between businessmen. In June 1951 he flew to Portugal to present an award to the International Chamber of Commerce (convening in Lisbon) for its role in promoting the out-of-court settlement of commercial disputes between American and foreign businessmen. At the same time he brought to the attention of the eight hundred businessmen attending the meeting his plans for further expanding the existing facilities for arbitrating international disputes. At the annual meeting of the association's board of directors in February 1952 (at which he was re-elected president), he was able to announce that the group's greatest advance in 1951 was in the foreign trade field, the use of arbitration in this area being 86 per cent higher than it had been in 1950.

In New London, Connecticut, Croft has also been active as a director of the Greater New London Chamber of Commerce and as president of the Housing Foundation, Inc. In the latter capacity he addressed a letter to the editor of the New York *Times* (March 3, 1947) recommending a substantial reduction in building costs as a possible remedy for the housing shortage. Since April 6, 1948, he has been a director of the Western Foundry Company in Chicago. A contributor to the *Arbitration Journal* and other publications in the field of labor-management and industrial relations, Croft is also publisher of the *Employee Relations Bulletin, Educator's Washington Dispatch, Executive's Labor Letter, Foreman's Letter,* and *Teacher's Letter.*

Arthur C. Croft and Christine (Marquis) Croft, who were married September 9, 1920, have one son, Noyes Marquis. Politically, the arbitration specialist is a Republican; he is a member of the Church of Christ, Scientist. He has brown eyes and gray hair, is five feet ten inches tall, and weighs 215 pounds.

References

N Y World-Telegram p40 N 15 '50
Who's Who in America, 1952-53
Who's Who in Commerce and Industry (1948)

CUSHING, RICHARD J(AMES), ARCHBISHOP Aug. 24, 1895- Roman Catholic prelate

Address: b. Lake St., Brighton, Mass.; h. 2101 Commonwealth Ave., Boston, Mass.

The Most Reverend Richard J. Cushing, the Roman Catholic Archbishop of Boston, Massachusetts, administers the second largest archdiocese, in population, in the United States. He was consecrated in November 1944, some months after the death of William Cardinal O'Connell. Ordained as a priest in 1921, Father Cushing served as pastor of several churches in the Boston area before his assignment within a year to the Boston branch of the Society for the Propagation of the Faith, of which he became director in 1929, when he was named Monsignor. His fund-raising activities for the society, for which he became widely recognized as an eloquent speaker, were to continue until 1939. That year marked his elevation in the hierarchy to Auxiliary Bishop.

Richard James Cushing was the third of five children (two sons and three daughters) born to Patrick and Mary (Dahill) Cushing. His birthplace is South Boston, Massachusetts, his birth date August 24, 1895. Patrick Cushing, a blacksmith who repaired wheels at the Boston Elevated Street Railway carbarns, had come from County Cork; Mary Dahill, who also was Irish-born, had emigrated from County Waterford. For his elementary education Richard Cushing went to the Oliver Hazard Perry Public Grammar School in South Boston; as a schoolboy he earned some money in his free time by carrying water to railway construction gangs. He then enrolled at Boston College High School, the Catholic institution

Wide World Photos

ARCHBISHOP RICHARD J. CUSHING

from which he received his diploma in 1915. There, said Joseph F. Dineen in an article for *Collier's,* the athletic youth had been a good infielder and batter and might have become a baseball player had not debating and public speaking interested him more.

By the time young Cushing was a student at Boston College he had decided to enter the priesthood. Accordingly, after two years at college, he began his training for the religious office at St. John's Seminary in Brighton. His oratorical gifts and powers of persuasion early revealed themselves when, in his first year, he surpassed all previous records in collecting funds among the students for the Society for the Propagation of the Faith. On May 26, 1921, he was ordained by William Cardinal O'Connell in Boston's Holy Cross Cathedral, and celebrated his first Mass at St. Eulalia's Church, the church of his old neighborhood. During the subsequent six months he served as curate at St. Patrick's Church in Roxbury (for two months) and at St. Benedict's Church in Somerville (for four months).

The young priest's next assignment was to St. Mary's Church in Lynn, to assist its pastor, who was director of the Boston office of the Society for the Propagation of the Faith. From that time (1922) dated Father Cushing's seventeen years in the service of the society, the purpose of which is "to solicit prayers and alms for the support of missions in every part of the world" (*National Catholic Almanac*). At the end of seven years he succeeded Monsignor McGlinchey as the director of the society, the office he was to fill for about a decade. For his success as an administrator and fund raiser whose organizing techniques and platform and pulpit manner brought "unprecedented" results, he became known as "The Bishop of the Missions."

(Continued next page)

CUSHING, RICHARD J., ARCHBISHOP
—Continued

With his elevation to domestic prelate on April 1, 1939, Father Cushing received the title of Monsignor. And a few months later, on June 29, he was consecrated Auxiliary Bishop of Boston and Titular Bishop of Mela by Cardinal O'Connell, whose assistant in the archdiocesan administration he now became in succession to Bishop Francis Spellman, who was named Archbishop of New York. At the same time, Father Cushing began serving as pastor of the Sacred Heart Church in Newton Center.

Upon the death of Cardinal O'Connell on April 22, 1944, Bishop Cushing acted as administrator *ad interim* of the archdiocese for about five months. On September 28 Pope Pius XII announced the elevation of the Boston ecclesiastic to Archbishop. When he was consecrated on November 8, he became, at forty-nine, the youngest man to reach that rank in the Catholic hierarchy in the world, and the third native-born son of Irish immigrants to hold that office in the Boston Metropolitan See, which is the second largest diocese, in population, in the country—its more than 1,300,000 Catholics represent 74 per cent of the population. The archdiocese comprises 23 cities and 124 towns and maintains 169 parochial schools, 71 high schools, and 25 private schools, with an inclusive enrollment of 117,000. The church also maintains general and special hospitals, homes for convalescents, and refuges for the needy (17 in all), and guidance centers and educational clinics for children. In process of being built are 6 new hospitals, 6 colleges and high schools, a seminary, and a number of chapels. Also under the Archbishop's jurisdiction are nearly 3,000 priests and members of various religious orders. The communicants themselves have formed clubs, societies, sodalities, fraternities, and guilds. (The statistics are from *Collier's*.)

Archbishop Cushing, who has been called "the most pervasive social force" in Boston, addresses many gatherings of Catholics and nonreligious groups, making known Catholic opinion on doctrinal and other matters. He was called upon to silence the Reverend Leonard Feeney, the Jesuit priest who declared there was no salvation outside the Catholic faith. Calling for aid to Archbishop Stepinac of Yugoslavia, the Boston churchman criticized the United States for giving aid to Marshal Tito's country while withholding it from Spain. He supports the right of parents to choose the schools their children should attend, pressing for a greater integration of religion and education and denouncing the ban on religious teaching in the public schools. In socialized medicine and in Federal legislation for increased activity in child welfare he sees steps toward totalitarianism. He has criticized the Taft-Hartley Act, asked for labor-capital amity, and urged labor to oust Communists and "fellow travelers" from unions. He has stated his opposition to the military draft as a road to war and has urged Catholic youth to interest themselves more in the peace movement. Speaking in behalf of fund drives conducted by non-Catholics, he has aided campaigns for better educational opportunities for Negroes and for the United Jewish Appeal, on several occasions contributing large sums himself. He has urged that war-maimed veterans be given employment and that displaced persons be absorbed into the life of communities. Indecency in entertainment and the misuse of intoxicants have received his censure.

Except for a brief visit to Bermuda, Archbishop Cushing had not traveled outside the United States until 1948. That year he led a pilgrimage of five hundred Catholics to Rome to receive an audience with Pope Pius XII, to visit shrines there and in France, and to present a petition for the canonization of Pope Pius X. In 1949 he led a similar number of Catholics to Ireland, and the next year he shared another pilgrimage to Rome. On a journey to Europe in 1951 he visited Spain, where he talked with Generalissimo Franco.

A number of the Archbishop's sermons and addresses have been reprinted in *Vital Speeches* and several are included in collections, among them *Best Sermons*, edited by G. P. Butler; *The Challenge of Ideas*, edited by J. Gehlmann. His articles on moral, social, and ecclesiastic questions have appeared in the *Pilot*, the weekly publication of the Boston archdiocese, or as separate publications of the Society for the Propagation of the Faith. For his civic, relief, and youth work he is the recipient of many awards. Among those bestowed on him in recent years are the Knight of the Grand Cross and Prior of the Eastern Lieutenancy of the Order of the Knights of the Holy Sepulchre (1946); the Human Rights Award of the Committee of Catholics for Human Rights for his service in furthering those rights and interracial unity (1947); Officer of the French Legion of Honor (1948); the award of the Silver Buffalo from the Boy Scouts for "distinguished service to boyhood" (1949); the gold medal of the American Irish Historical Society "in recognition of his services to the Republic" (1951).

Nearly all articles on the Catholic prelate mention his stature: he is six feet tall and has the carriage of "a well-trained athlete." Joseph Dineen wrote of him in *Collier's*, "Lest lines queue up to kiss his episcopal ring, he departs from ceremonies quickly, hands clasped over his head, a symbolic personal handshake in farewell. If an elderly man or woman tries to bend a knee to kiss the ring, he is quick to put his hands under their elbows to prevent it and raises the ring to make it unnecessary." He has a reputation for quick-wittedness, and his laugh is described as hearty. In his forthrightness, said an associate, he is "utterly unsubtle."

References

Boston (Mass.) Sunday Advertiser O 1 '44
Boston (Mass.) Sunday Post Je 18 '39
Collier's 128:24 N 10 '51
American Catholic Who's Who, 1952-53
Who's Who in America, 1952-53
World Biography (1948)

DANIEL, ROBERT PRENTISS Nov. 2, 1902- College president

Address: b. c/o Virginia State College, Petersburg, Va.

In February 1950 Dr. Robert Prentiss Daniel became president of Virginia State College, where his father had served as secretary for twenty-eight years. Before his appointment as fifth president of the Virginia institution, the Negro educator had taught at Wayland Academy in Richmond, Virginia, where he began his educational career as an instructor of mathematics, and at Virginia Union University, also in Richmond, where he became a professor in 1928. From 1936 to 1950 Daniel held the position of president at Shaw University in Raleigh, North Carolina.

Robert Prentiss Daniel, who was born in Ettrick, Virginia, on November 2, 1902, is one of the six surviving children of Charles James and Carrie Tabitha (Green) Daniel. The Daniels' four sons and one of their daughters are Doctors of Philosophy and the other daughter is a Master of Arts; all of them except a son (who is an investment counselor) are active in the field of education. Having been brought up on a college campus as they were, Robert Daniel remarks, they were "exposed to the many cultural advantages of a college community." The elder Daniel was trained as a shoemaker by his father; in addition to working on his father's rented land by day and making shoes by night Charles Daniel managed to carry out a program of self-education which permitted him to enter Richmond Institute in 1871. In 1882 he went to Danville, Virginia, as teacher-principal and remained there until 1888, when he accepted the position of secretary of the Virginia Normal and Collegiate Institute at Petersburg, Virginia (later Virginia State College), which he held until his death in 1916.

After graduation in 1920 from Wayland Academy of Virginia Union University in Richmond, Robert Daniel entered Union University itself, where he took a major in education. During his college years he was secretary and president of the Gamma chapter of Alpha Phi Alpha fraternity, a member of the college debating team as a senior, and class valedictorian when he graduated in 1924 with the degree of Bachelor of Arts. Concurrently with his entrance into the teaching profession upon his graduation from college, Daniel took postgraduate studies at Columbia University, receiving the M.A. degree in education in 1928 and the Ph.D. degree in educational psychology in 1932. During five summers between 1940 and 1945 he devoted himself to a study of Biblical literature at Union Theological Seminary in New York City. The educator's dissertation for his doctorate was *A Psychological Study of Delinquent and Non-Delinquent Negro Boys*.

During the academic year 1924-25 Daniel taught mathematics at Wayland Academy, and in 1925, a year after his graduation from college, he returned to Virginia Union University as an instructor of mathematics and education. He remained there until 1936, becoming an as-

ROBERT PRENTISS DANIEL

sistant professor of education in 1926 and a full professor at the age of twenty-six in 1928. He also served as director of the Division of Education, Psychology, and Philosophy and of the Extension Division from 1928 to 1936. In this latter capacity he was instrumental in the establishment of the Norfolk Division of Virginia Union University, which later became a branch of the administrator's present school, Virginia State College. He spent the summers of 1935 and 1936 as a visiting professor of education at Hampton Institute.

In 1936 Dr. Daniel left Virginia to become president of Shaw University in Raleigh, North Carolina, where his thirteen years in that office prompted laudatory newspaper editorials when his election to the presidency of Virginia State College was announced on December 15, 1949. The Raleigh *News and Observer*'s comment was: "He had settled the question of whether it is wise for Negro institutions in the South to have Negro presidents. That question was a disputed one at Shaw not many years ago. During his thirteen years at the institution Dr. Daniel has settled the question to the satisfaction of all members of both races who are familiar with his work." "It is not often," said the Durham *Carolina Times*, "that . . . any . . . Southern State . . . has within its borders a Negro college president who is uncompromising in his stand on the problems of his race. Dr. Daniel afforded . . . that kind of leadership and was dynamic and wise enough in so doing to protect the interest of the school he headed." Daniel accepted the presidency of Virginia State College on February 1, 1950, and was inaugurated at the Negro institution on October 14 of the same year.

Established by the Virginia General Assembly in 1882, Virginia State College has been a land-grant institution since 1920 and has at present a physical plant of more than forty

DANIEL, ROBERT PRENTISS—*Cont.*

buildings on the 202-acre campus on the Appomattox River and a 425-acre experimental farm, a faculty of more than 250, and a student body of about 5,000. Educational facilities consist of divisions of agriculture, arts and sciences, education, home economics, mechanic arts, and graduate studies; a Reserve Officers' Training Corps established in July 1947; an extension department, providing night school and correspondence courses; and a junior college division at Norfolk, Virginia. The coeducational college awards four degrees: Bachelor of Arts, Bachelor of Science, Master of Arts, and Master of Science.

Among Daniel's writings are articles entitled "Negro-White Differences in Non-Intellectual Traits and in Special Abilities", "One Consideration of Redirection of Emphasis of the Negro College", "Impact of War upon the Church-Related College and University," all of which appeared in the *Journal of Negro Education*; "Basic Considerations for Valid Interpretations of Experimental Studies Pertaining to Racial Differences," in the *Journal of Educational Psychology*; and an article written in collaboration with his brother Walter Green Daniel "The Curriculum of the Negro College," in the *Journal of Educational Sociology.* He also contributed articles to *College and University Business*, the *Virginia Teachers Bulletin*, and the *North Carolina Teachers Record.* The educator received the Certificate for Distinguished Service in Education from the National Urban League in 1948 and the Leadership in Education Certificate from the Eastern Regional Conference of the Alpha Phi Alpha fraternity in 1950. Morris Brown College of Atlanta, Georgia, and Virginia Union University both bestowed the degree of Doctor of Laws upon him in 1949.

Daniel, who was given the Silver Beaver Award of the Boy Scouts of America in 1942, has been active in the Boy Scout movement since 1928, serving on the advisory board of the Colored Scouts, Richmond Area Council of the Boy Scouts of America from 1928 to 1936; as chairman of the district committee of the Occoneechee Council in Raleigh from 1936 to 1939 and as chairman of the area divisional committee from 1939 to 1948; as a member of the committee on interracial activities of the National Council of Boy Scouts of America since 1939 and of the committee on relationships since 1945; and as a member of the executive board of the Robert E. Lee Virginia Council since 1951. He also belongs to the American Psychological Association, the National Education Association, the Virginia Society for Research (president in 1930-31), the National Association for the Advancement of Colored People, the American Teachers Association, the National Association for the Study of Negro Life and History, the American Association of School Administrators, Sigma Phi Pi Boule, Alpha Phi Alpha Fraternity (national budget director from 1935 to 1949), the Virginia State Teachers Association (educational research secretary from 1926 to 1934 and president from 1934 to 1936), the Masons (he is a Shriner and a Thirty-second Degree Mason), and the Frontiers of America.

Among Dr. Daniel's other professional activities has been his service as president of the North Carolina Negro College Conference in 1938-39, of the Association of Colleges and Secondary Schools for Negroes in 1947, and of the Association of Northern Baptist Educational Institutions in 1948-49. His civic interests have included the Virginia Interracial Commission from 1928 to 1936, the Richmond Community Center from 1932 to 1936, the North Carolina Interracial Commission from 1936 to 1950, the Raleigh Community Chest from 1938 to 1944, the Wake County Defense Council and the North Carolina Council of National Defense from 1941 to 1945, the United War Fund of North Carolina from 1942 to 1944, the International Development Advisory Board of the United States Department of State since 1950, and the Petersburg Community Chest since 1951. As a representative of the King's Mountain Area National Student YMCA, Daniel has traveled in England, Scotland, France, Germany, Italy, Switzerland, Holland, and Czechoslovakia.

The educator's wife, the former Blanche Ardelle Taylor, whom he married on September 11, 1929, is also a graduate of Virginia Union University and holds the M.A. degree in psychology and religious education from Columbia University and Union Theological Seminary. From the time of her marriage until her husband became president of Shaw University in 1936, she was the registrar of Virginia Union University. Daniel has been active in Baptist affairs since 1922, when he helped establish the Baptist Young People's Union Council of Richmond, an organization for which he served as corresponding secretary until 1927. In 1940 he became an ordained minister. In politics his affiliation is Democratic. He is five feet six inches tall and weighs 168 pounds. Baseball, football, and bridge are his favorite pastimes.

References

N Y Times p60 O 15 '50

Leaders in Education (1948)
Who's Who in America, 1950-51
Who's Who in Colored America, 1950

DAVIDSON, JO Mar. 30, 1883—Jan. 2, 1952 American sculptor; began work in sculpture in early 1900's; lived most of the time in France and traveled extensively to find suitable subjects; called himself a "plastic historian"; famous for portrait busts of Woodrow Wilson, Anatole France, and John D. Rockefeller, and statues of Walt Whitman and Will Rogers, among other works. See *Current Biography*, 1945.

Obituary

N Y Times p1 Ja 3 '52

DAVIDSON, WILLIAM L(EE) July 14, 1915- United States Government official; physicist

Address: b. c/o Atomic Energy Commission, 19th St. & Constitution Ave., N.W., Washington 25, D.C.

William L. Davidson, the first director of the newly created Office of Industrial Development of the United States Atomic Energy Commission, has described his task as "enlarging industry's participation in the atomic energy field." A specialist in nuclear physics and technology, Davidson was additionally equipped for his new post by a background in industrial research—as director of physical research for the B. F. Goodrich Company he had been concerned wth problems in the physics of rubber. One purpose of Davidson's office (which was set up in May 1952) is to disseminate to industry AEC technical data of importance in industrial research and development.

Born in Jonesville, Virginia, on July 14, 1915, William Lee Davidson was named for his father, an attorney; his mother, a teacher in the public schools before her marriage, was the former Zelma Albert. The three Davidson children, William and his twin sisters, were reared in Virginia, the boy being graduated in 1931 from Jonesville High School. After school hours he had played baseball and football, but in addition, from the time he was ten, he has recalled, he had "curiosity about things scientific . . . spending much time building crystal radio sets, model airplanes, and the like."

At the College of William and Mary, at Williamsburg, Virginia, the young man majored in physics. When he was graduated in 1936 with the B.S. degree he had been elected to Phi Beta Kappa, national scholastic honor society; Phi Kappa Phi, another scholastic honor society; Sigma Pi Sigma, for outstanding physics students; and Sigma Phi Epsilon, a social fraternity. Davidson went on to Yale University for graduate studies and there worked under Professor Ernest Pollard, who interested him in nuclear physics. By 1940, four years later, he had earned the Ph.D. degree in physics; his thesis subject was *Energy Levels in Nuclei of Medium Atomic Weight*.

Davidson's work with Professor Pollard at Yale's Sloane Physics Laboratory during those years was described in nine articles in the *Physical Review*, some prepared by himself, some in collaboration with colleagues. Davidson was studying the protons resulting from the bombardment of various elements by deuterons. He was one of the group working with Pollard at Yale who constructed in 1940 a cyclotron of moderate size at low cost, which was expected to be adequate for certain types of nuclear research. Davidson and Pollard have stated that work with that cyclotron "concerned itself mainly with the investigation of energy levels in nuclei through a study of the energies of the particles emitted in transmutation reactions." The first experiment, the bombardment of boron by deuterons, was reported in the *Physical Review* by Pollard, Davidson, and H. L. Schultz in April 1940; this article was

WILLIAM L. DAVIDSON

followed by one on the bombardment of carbon and aluminum.

On completing his requirements for the doctorate at Yale, Davidson took a position as research physicist with the B. F. Goodrich Company in Akron, Ohio. He was also at work with Professor Pollard on the book *Applied Nuclear Physics* (1942). Published during the early days of World War II, it was one of the few books of that period to include an account of nuclear fission. A reviewer pointed out that the study was significant for "signaling the development of nuclear physics from a pure science to an applied science." A technical treatment of "artificial radioactivity and transmutation," it was expected by the authors to be of service to chemists, biologists, physicians, and engineers who were using the product of nuclear physics in their own fields.

In a second edition of *Applied Nuclear Physics* (1951) nine years later, the authors recalled how, in 1942 "as the pages came from the presses," other physicists were "giving muscle and sinew to applied nuclear physics" with the research leading to the atom bomb and the "birth of the atomic age," thus making obsolescent the Pollard and Davidson text. The 1951 edition brought the "picture of nuclear science and technology up to date," with additional material on pile theory and nuclear chain reactions, but omitting discussion of atomic weapons. That omission was due to security regulations and to the authors' belief that "in the final analysis it is the constructive, good and useful side of this double-edged sword which will prevail." Reviewers for the technical journals found the revised book "still one of the most readable and useful texts" on the subject.

The physicist spent 1946-47 as a trainee in neutron diffraction and nuclear technology at the Oak Ridge National Laboratory (he attended the first class in reactor technology

DAVIDSON, WILLIAM L.—*Continued*

there). With the exception of that year, Davidson remained with Goodrich as a research physicist from 1940 to 1948, when he became head of the Goodrich physics laboratory, with the title of director of physical research. While his chief concern was defense projects in the physics of rubber, he also worked on X-ray diffraction and radio tracer research, and on self-sealing fuel tanks for war use (he was one of three authors of an article on this subject). Some fifteen papers resulted from these studies, most of them in the *Physical Review* and the *Journal of Polymer Science*.

Davidson had the opportunity to pursue his interest in the peacetime applications of atomic research when in May 1952 he was chosen by the Atomic Energy Commission to head the newly established Office of Industrial Development. To industry the new office would make available technical atomic information of importance in the fields of chemistry, metallurgy, specialized equipment, and power generation. And according to M. W. Boyer, AEC general manager, it would also "foster wider industrial participation in the commission's program and the development, as may be possible, of a more normal competitive approach to the problems and potentials of the atomic energy business." Several industrial and power firms, it was reported, were already studying the possibility of generating atomic power for industrial purposes.

Davidson's published writings comprise the text coauthored with Pollard, twenty-five technical and scientific articles he prepared or collaborated on, and the chapter "X-Ray Diffraction Methods As Applied to Powders and Metals," in the book *Physical Methods In Chemical Analysis* (1951) edited by Walter G. Berl. For *Popular Science* of December 1945 Davidson wrote the article "We Can Harness the Atom," a discussion of the problems to be solved before atomic power could be put to industrial use; he cited experts as estimating that engines to harness atomic power could be developed within ten years. The physicist's affiliations include the Chemical Society, the Physical Society, and the X-Ray and Electron Diffraction Society. *American Men of Science* lists his fields as nuclear physics, radiation chemistry, x-ray diffraction, electron diffraction, bullet-sealing fuel cells, and energy levels in nuclei of medium atomic weight.

The physicist received the Distinguished Service Award for 1949 from both the Akron Junior Chamber of Commerce and the Ohio State Junior Chamber of Commerce. He married Miriam Alloway, then a schoolteacher, on December 20, 1941. His political party is the Republican, and his church is the Methodist. With a height of six feet he weighs 190 pounds; the color of his hair is black, of his eyes, gray.

References

N Y Herald Tribune p28 My 2 '52 por
N Y Times p10 My 2 '52
N Y World-Telegram p29 My 1 '52
American Men of Science (1949)

DAWSON, JOHN A(LBERT) Sept. 3, 1904- Baptist convention president; investment banker

Address: b. c/o John A. Dawson & Company, 1 N. LaSalle St., Chicago 2, Ill.; h. 920 Greenwood Ave., Wilmette, Ill.

At the 1952 annual meeting of the American Baptist Convention (formerly the Northern Baptist Convention) John A. Dawson, a Chicago investment broker, was elected president of the organization. Active for many years in Baptist affairs, he served two terms, from 1950 to 1952, as president of the Chicago Baptist Association. As a member of the North Shore Baptist Church of Chicago he has participated in many of the church activities, serving as Sunday school teacher, superintendent of the high school department, and scoutmaster and troop committee chairman for the church Boy Scouts troop.

One of the three sons of John Henry and Ida Louise (Hellman) Dawson, John Albert Dawson was born in Chicago, Illinois, on September 3, 1904. Both the Dawson and Hellman families were long-time Chicago residents: one of his grandfathers was a member of the Chicago Board of Trade in the 1860's and the other was an early Chicago meat packer. The boy grew up in Chicago and attended local public schools until 1918, at which time he interrupted his education to begin work as an office boy for a law firm. In 1925 having decided to go to college, he attended Northwestern University at Evanston, Illinois, until 1927; his major was liberal arts. He was elected to Purple Key, an honorary society, was a member of Phi Kappa Sigma, and represented the university at Big Ten and Amateur Athletic Union wrestling meets. The wrestling champion of Northwestern in the lightweight field, he earned the fourth position in the National Collegiate Championship.

In 1927 Dawson entered the employ of the Old Dearborn State Bank of Chicago as a bond salesman, the occupation he followed for four years. Becoming an investment broker in 1931, he has operated his own business under the name of John A. Dawson & Company since that time. During World War II he worked in the finance department of the Army Air Force.

Dawson has been an active member of the North Shore Baptist Church of Chicago for many years. For seventeen years he was a member of the board of deacons, and he has been a Sunday school teacher, superintendent of the high school department, and, for ten years, general superintendent. The Baptist layman is a past president of the Chicago Baptist Sunday School Union. Also a member, for more than thirty years, of the Boy Scouts troop connected with the church, he was an Eagle Scout himself and subsequently became a scoutmaster and a troop committee chairman.

Dawson has held several offices in the American Baptist Convention. (The term "convention" refers not to a meeting but to a group of Baptist churches which have come together in an organization. He was a member of the commission on review of this body, and until 1952 he served on the finance committee. For seven years he acted as vice-president of the National Council of American Baptist Men, and he was a member of the board of directors of the American Baptist Assembly at Green Lake, Wisconsin. The committee of fifteen, which raised the funds for the purchase of the American Baptist Assembly grounds at Green Lake, was headed by Dawson. On the local level, from 1950 to 1952 he served as the president of the Chicago Baptist Association.

In May 1952 the American Baptist Convention, which held its forty-fourth annual meeting in Chicago, elected Dawson president to succeed the Reverend Dr. Kenneth S. Latourette. The Chicago sessions were regarded as unique in the history of Protestantism in that they were held concurrently with those of another sect, the Disciples of Christ, with which for many years the American Baptists have been considering unification.

The convention reiterated its objection to "any kind of formal diplomatic relations on the part of our Government with the Vatican." The American Baptists, the Northern organization, then followed the lead of Dr. J. D. Grey, president of the Southern Baptist Convention, who warned political candidates that the Baptists could not support them unless they opposed missions to the Vatican.

Prior to 1845 the Southern and Northern Baptists constituted one convention, but in that year the first-named withdrew from the group to found the Southern Baptist Convention. The Northern Baptist Convention held its first meeting in Washington, D.C. in 1907; at the midcentury meeting the name was changed to the American Baptist Convention. For forty years four missionary societies, the publishing society, and others had carried the name "American Baptist" in their titles. When the name was changed it was stated: "We hold the name in trust for all Christians of like faith and mind who desire to bear witness to the historic framework of cooperative Protestantism." The convention abolished previous territorial limitation which had restricted its activities to certain areas.

The American Baptists are less strict in the matter of church autonomy than are the Southern Baptists. Although the representatives at the meetings are still called "messengers" because theoretically their only function is to carry back to the member churches inspiration and information gained at the sessions, the American Baptist churches may delegate individuals to decide matters for all by majority vote. The greatest difference between the Southern Baptists and the American Convention, stated *Christian Century,* lies in their respective attitudes toward ecumenical Christianity. The Southern sect terms the cooperative church alliances "totalitarian," while the American Baptists work with the National Council of the Churches of Christ and the

JOHN A. DAWSON

World Council of Churches. The American Baptists condemn so-called "innocent" forms of gambling such as bingo and are strongly opposed to universal military training in peacetime, having supported world conferences on disarmament. The convention favors fair employment laws in both State and Federal governments. More than 1,600,000 Baptists are now members of the American Baptist Convention.

Dawson serves on the board of directors of the Baptist Home and Hospital at Maywood, Illinois, and is also on the board of trustees of Shurtleff College at Alton, Illinois. He is a member of the Chicago Crime Commission, a life member of the Art Institute of Chicago, and is a past president of the Illinois Society Sons of the American Revolution. He is also a member of the board of governors of the Society of Mayflower Descendants in the State of Illinois. He belongs to the "N" Men's Club of Northwestern University and gives his political affiliation as "nominally Republican."

Dawson and his wife, the former Annie Joe Howel, were married on March 24, 1934, and are the parents of three children: Ann Catherine, Mary Pratt, and John Howel. The Baptist president is five feet six and one quarter inches tall, weighs 156 pounds, has blue eyes, and describes his hair as "very little and blond." He enjoys golf, swimming, and watching football games. When he owned the yacht *Vandal* for ten years he won several racing trophies.

References

Who's Who in Chicago and Illinois (1950)
Who's Who in the Midwest (1952)

DEANE, MARTHA *See* Young, M.

DEJONG, MEINDERT (dĕ-yŏng' mĭn' dêrt) Mar. 4, 1906- Author
Address: b. c/o Harper & Brothers, 49 E. 33d St., New York 16; h. 321 Plymouth Ave., N.E., Grand Rapids, Mich.

Reprinted from the *Wilson Library Bulletin,* Feb. 1952.

One reason why Meindert DeJong's stories for children are fresh and unusual is that his own childhood was far from ordinary. His birth in Wierum, Friesland, in the Netherlands, March 4, 1906, was accompanied by a seaquake which broke the dike and inundated the village. But the villagers plugged the gap with sandbags; the waters soon subsided, and though women and children were being evacuated, Meindert and his mother, Jantje (whose maiden name was also DeJong, though no relation to her husband's family) were left in peace.

MEINDERT DEJONG

During the boy's first year in school, the teacher went mad, but he was so beloved by the local fishing folk that they refused to let the authorities take him to an asylum. Wierum, a village of 1,000, was in a state of siege for three months before 300 mounted police quelled the riot after several pitched battles with swords, scythes, pitch-forks, and knives. "For three months," says Mr. DeJong, "I lived in our attic, because nightly the stones flew through our windows downstairs and landed in our closet beds." The episode of Crazy Alice in *The Tower by the Sea* (1950) was perhaps suggested by this experience.

The DeJongs were originally Du Jon, a noble French family whose members fled to Friesland during the Huguenot persecutions. At eight the boy came with his parents to Grand Rapids, Michigan, and, he says, "There has been no excitement since." Because of language difficulties, his father, Remmeren DeJong, who had been an architect and builder in

Friesland, became a mason contractor, as did two of his sons. The third, Meindert's elder by only a year, is David Cornel DeJong, the well-known writer who has described their first grim years in Grand Rapids in his autobiography, *With a Dutch Accent* (1944). Meindert's first experience in writing came at Christian High School, where he graduated in 1924, when he cribbed an article on "How to Construct a Box-Kite" from a book in the library. This was so highly praised by his teacher that he began to write his own material. At Calvin College (B.A. 1928) he and brother David cornered the literary market in *The Young Calvinist,* a youth magazine started by the Christian Reformed group. The young Calvinists were paid $5 apiece for stories.

Meindert DeJong graduated into a depression and went to work on the farm his father had bought when his business failed. Writing in the evenings after a sixteen-hour workday, DeJong turned out short stories. The little magazines of the time snapped them up but invariably folded immediately after—even *Hound and Horn,* which was on the point of paying him $60, his first real money. The aspiring author went to peddling eggs, some of them at the public library.

The librarians in the children's room listened to his tales of a pet goose and a duck, and insisted that he write out the story. The result, *The Big Goose and the Little White Duck* (1938), was immediately accepted. Successive titles were *Dirk's Dog, Bello* (1939); what he calls "its unworthy sequel," *Bells of the Harbor* (1941); *Wheels Over the Bridge* (1941), a farm story; and *Little Stray Dog* (1943), which May Lamberton Becker called "a good dog story for any one up to ten," although a *Library Journal* reviewer found it too full of unpleasant adults. Edward Shenton drew the pictures for this one. Jessie Robinson illustrated *The Cat That Walked a Week* (1943), which again ran afoul of the *Library Journal,* but was liked by Mrs. Becker and by Ellen Buell of the New York *Times.* Of *Billy and the Unhappy Bull* (1946) Alice M. Jordan wrote in *Horn Book* that "there is excitement and humor and a truthful picture of family life." She also approved of *Bible Days,* illustrated by Kreigh Collins, which tells how the people of Palestine lived and worked in the days of Jesus.

During World War II DeJong was an historian with the 14th Air Force, probably the only enlisted man so engaged. Though he never rose higher than sergeant, he had to instruct officers in the art of writing history. The children's book he managed to write, "The House of Sixty Fathers," was suppressed by military censors, though it will be published this year (1952). *Good Luck Duck* (1950) was a selection of the Junior Literary Guild; Virginia Kirkus said, "The prose is rhythmic and sparkling, and the dramatic presentation of the story is lively and fun." The *New Yorker* took note of *The Tower by the Sea* (1950), finding it a sort of parable told in a "simple, silken way." *Smoke Above the Lane* (1951), a selection of the Catholic Children's Book Club, was called by Louise Bechtel in the New York *Herald Tribune Book Review* a simple story told with a deep feeling and emotional expression unusual in children's books.

Taking Sinclair Lewis's advice to young authors literally, DeJong became a bricklayer while establishing himself as a writer, finding that "when I held any kind of cerebral job, my writing went dead." He has also been a sexton, gravedigger, and janitor. Mrs. DeJong's name (they were married July 6, 1933) is Hattie. Blue-eyed and blond, standing five feet seven inches, and weighing 155 pounds, DeJong likes gardening, fishing, and Siamese cats. Mexico City and Cape Town, South Africa, are his favorite towns, and his favorite writer is David Cornel DeJong.

DELANY, WALTER S(TANLEY)   Jan. 21, 1891- United States Naval officer
Address: b. 90 Church St., New York 7; h. Quarters A, New York Naval Shipyards, Brooklyn 1, N.Y.

Vice-Admiral Walter S. DeLany took command on July 1, 1952, of the Eastern Sea Frontier, of the Atlantic Reserve Fleet, and of the Western Atlantic subarea of the North Atlantic Treaty Organization naval forces. These combined duties make DeLany responsible for the defense of the Atlantic and Gulf coasts, for supervision of ships in "moth balls" in the area, for control of the naval industrial establishments in forty States east of the Rocky Mountains, and for protection of Allied shipping in the Western Atlantic, under the terms of NATO. Prior to his present appointment, DeLany had served since 1948 as Commandant of the Third Naval District, with headquarters in New York City. During World War II he participated in the Guadalcanal campaign, subsequently going to Washington, D.C., as assistant chief of staff to the Commander in Chief of the United States Fleet (1943-46). From 1946 to 1948 he was in command of all battleships and cruisers in the Pacific Fleet.

Walter Stanley DeLany was born in Reading, Pennsylvania, on January 21, 1891, the son of Irvin F. and Mary E. (Dunkle) DeLany. He spent his early years in his native city, attending Reading High School, where basketball was his main extracurricular interest. After graduating in 1908 he received an appointment to the United States Naval Academy in Annapolis, Maryland, becoming active here as a cheer leader and as a member of the basketball and the lacrosse teams, before receiving his B.S. degree and his ensign's commission in the United States Navy in June 1912. The young officer was assigned for the next three years to service on the U.S.S. *Minnesota,* acting as an aide on the staff of the regimental commander during the occupation of Vera Cruz, Mexico, until he was transferred in 1915 to the U.S.S. *Montana* for torpedo instruction. Having been promoted to the rank of lieutenant (j.g.), DeLany in November 1915 was sent to the Fore River Shipbuilding Company, Quincy, Massachusetts, for duty in fitting out the U.S.S. *Nevada,* on which he was sta-

U. S. Navy

VICE-ADM. WALTER S. DELANY

tioned from her commissioning in March 1916 until May 1917, when he was transferred to the destroyer *Wilkes,* based at Queenstown, Ireland, during World War I.

Back in the United States in August 1918, DeLany assisted in the fitting out of the destroyer *Craven,* two months later becoming her executive officer and serving as such until June 1919. For a brief period thereafter he was in command of the U.S.S. *Paulding,* with the rank of lieutenant. During the next two years (1919-21) DeLany filled the assignment of recruiting officer at the naval station in Albany, New York, and from this position he moved to that of navigator and first lieutenant on the newly commissioned transport, the *Argonne.* In June 1923 he was transferred to duty as executive officer of the destroyer *Lamson,* with the rank of lieutenant commander. After spending the first nine months of 1924 as squadron gunner officer of Destroyer Squadron 9, Scouting Fleet, DeLany in October began a two-and-one-half-year tour of duty in the Training Division of the United States Navy Bureau of Navigation. In 1927 he went back to sea for three years as first lieutenant aboard the U.S.S. *Oklahoma,* returning in 1930 to the Navy Department in Washington, D.C., where for the following three years he worked first in the Office of the Chief of Naval Operations, next in the Bureau of Navigation, and then in the Ships' Movements Division of the Office of the Chief of Naval Operations. Resuming sea duty in 1933, DeLany became navigator aboard the U.S.S. *New York,* a post he held for two years. Then in 1935—twenty-three years after his graduation—DeLany returned to the United States Naval Academy in Annapolis to serve for three years in its executive department.

As commander of Destroyer Division Number 7, attached to the Battle Force of the flag-

DELANY, WALTER S.—*Continued*

ship U.S.S. *Mugford*, DeLany returned to sea in 1938. Less than a year later, in May 1939, he was transferred to duty as chief of staff and aide to the commander of the flagship, U.S.S. *Honolulu*. He left this post in 1941 to become assistant chief of staff and operations officer for the Commander in Chief of the Pacific Fleet, remaining here through the first months of World War II and receiving in 1942 the Legion of Merit award for "contributing materially to the prosecution of the war against Japan." On June 24, 1942, with the newly granted rank of rear-admiral, DeLany assumed command of the cruiser *New Orleans*, then operating in the Pacific, and subsequently participated in the Guadalcanal Campaign. Relieved of this command on November 12, 1942, DeLany returned to Washington, D.C., to take over his new assignments on the staff of the Commander in Chief of the United States Fleet, first as assistant chief of staff for operations and then as assistant chief of staff for readiness. His services in this latter capacity were recognized by his being presented the Gold Star (to be added to his Legion of Merit Award) for "broad vision, unusual initiative, sound judgment, superior professional knowledge, and high executive ability" that "directed the improvement and development of means, methods and practices which kept the United States Fleet in a continually higher state of readiness."

After the reorganization of the various branches of the Armed Forces, the naval officer in October 1945 continued his previous duties as officer in charge of the operational readiness section in the Office of the Chief of Naval Operations. For a short time early in 1946 DeLany headed the Training Policy Board and then became commander of all Pacific Fleet battleships and cruisers, with the U.S.S. *St. Paul* as flagship. Two years later, on July 1, 1948, he was named Commandant of the Third Naval District, comprising the States of Connecticut, New York, and the northern part of New Jersey, with headquarters in New York City. As head of all naval activities within this district, DeLany supervised the operations of the Brooklyn Navy Yard, gun factories, torpedo stations, powder factories, medical centers, hospitals, radio stations, and research laboratories. It was during this command that DeLany and two of his aides received a Distinguished Service Citation, from the Council of American Master Mariners, stating that these officers had administered the merchant marine-Naval Reserve program "in an exceptionally efficient, effective and highly meritorious manner."

At the end of four years in this command, DeLany on July 1, 1952, assumed the rank of vice-admiral in command of approximately 800,000 men in the Eastern Sea Frontier, in the Atlantic Reserve Fleet, and in the Western Atlantic subarea of the North Atlantic Treaty Organization naval forces, succeeding Admiral Oscar C. Badger, who had reached the mandatory retirement age. In his present post, Ad-

miral DeLany is responsible for the defense of the Atlantic and Gulf coasts and for control of the naval industrial operations in forty States east of the Rocky Mountains. The Atlantic Reserve Fleet, which he commands, consists of ships in "moth balls" that can be quickly readied for active service. In his NATO command, DeLany's superior officer is Supreme Allied Commander of the Atlantic, Admiral Lynde D. McCormick, of the United States Navy, head of NATO's West Atlantic area, which is divided into two subareas—the Canadian and the United States. DeLany is in command of the latter and as such is responsible for protecting Allied shipping there. Shortly before assuming his new command, DeLany warned in a National Hospital Day speech that the United States would have to face the "catastrophe of World War III and the catastrophe of defeat" if the nation did not gear its forces to match "communistic hardness and durability" (New York *Times*, May 12, 1952).

The Commander of the Eastern Sea Frontier has gray hair and brown eyes, weighs 163 pounds, and is five feet eight and one-half inches tall. His church is the Episcopal. He married Lou May Sharman on October 2, 1915, and they have two children—Katherine (the wife of Captain Emerson S. Fawkes, of the United States Navy), and Lieutenant Walter Stanley, Jr., a 1945 graduate of Annapolis. In addition to the Legion of Merit with Gold Star, DeLany has received the Mexican Service Medal, the Victory Medal Destroyer Clasp (for service aboard the U.S.S. *Wilkes*), the American Defense Service Medal, the Asiatic-Pacific Campaign Medal, the American Campaign Medal, and the World War II Victory Medal. In 1951 he was awarded an honorary Doctor of Laws degree by Wagner College, Staten Island, New York. DeLany is a member of the Army and Navy Club, the Jonathon Club of Los Angeles, the Pacific Coast Club of Long Beach, California, the Hugenot Society of Philadelphia, and the Sons of the American Revolution.

References

N Y Herald Tribune p6 Jl 1 '52
N Y Times p6 My 8 '52
Who's Who in America, 1952-53

DE SICA, VITTORIO (dā sē′kä vē-tô′ryō) July 7, 1901- Motion picture actor, director, and producer

Address: b. c/o Joseph Burstyn, Inc., 113 W. 42d St., New York 18

One of Italy's top-ranking motion picture directors, Vittorio De Sica is the producer and director of the international award-winning films *Shoe Shine*, *The Bicycle Thief*, and *Miracle in Milan*. His fourth postwar picture, *Umberto D*, which was shown at the Cannes Film Festival in 1952, was at midyear not yet released for general exhibition. De Sica began his career as a "matinee idol" and singer on the Italian stage, became one of his country's most popular motion picture actors, and has continued his acting career simultaneously with his work as a director. He recently appeared in *Tomorrow is Too Late* and the unreleased *Good Morning, Elephant*. In 1952 he made an agreement to direct a film in the United States.

Vittorio De Sica was born on July 7, 1901, in Sora, in the Italian province of Ciociaria, the third of the four children of Umberto and Teresa (Manfredi) De Sica. His father, a native of Naples, was an employee of the Bank of Italy. The family moved to Florence shortly after Vittorio's birth and when he was eleven settled in Rome, where the father became engaged in the insurance business. De Sica recalls having been a shy, timid youth and remembers his boyhood as melancholy. After he achieved a "ragioniere" diploma (an academic award higher than a Bachelor of Arts degree), he enrolled for a course at the Advanced Institute of Commerce, but was unable to continue his studies because of the family's financial difficulties. In 1923, with a compulsory term of military duty behind him, De Sica considered a commercial career in banking or a government position.

A chance meeting with a friend, who had entered the acting company of Tatiana Pavlova suggested a dramatic career to the young man, and with his father's enthusiastic support he applied for and obtained a place in the same company, with which he remained for a year (1923-24). During the next few years he appeared in leading roles on the legitimate stage in drama, musical comedy, and vaudeville. He "preferred character parts to the juvenile parts usually handed him," noted Robert F. Hawkins of the New York *Times*, and in his vaudeville appearances established a reputation as a singer of popular Neapolitan ballads.

De Sica's career in motion pictures began in 1931, when his friend Mario Camerini, a director, cast him in the principal role in *Gli Uomini che Mascatzoni* (a picture considered by some critics as "the basis of the renaissance" of the Italian film). This established him as a popular motion picture actor. Camerini is said to have been responsible for "typing" De Sica as a romantic young dreamer, a role in which he was accepted as the modest ideal of the average Italian. For nine years, in similar parts, he remained one of the leading stars of the Italian screen. In the fall and winter of 1939-40 three comedies starring De Sica were exhibited in the United States—*Il Signor Max, Le Sorprese di un Matrimonio,* and *Napoli d'altri Tempi*. A review in the New York *Times* of May 17, 1940, said of another film: "Vittorio De Sica, one of Italy's better actors, never did a better job than he does in *La Due Madri*. [He] is practically perfect." The reviewer found the picture "disfigured" only by the injection of fascist propaganda. Other films in which the Italian actor had a part are listed in *Chi è?* (1948).

In collaboration with Peppino Amato, a technical expert, De Sica undertook his first directorial work in the production of a light comedy, "Twenty-Four Red Roses" (title trans-

VITTORIO DE SICA

lated), in which he also played the leading role. This picture having proved a commercial success, De Sica continued to direct other popular films, including *Magdalena Zero in Condotta, Teresa Venerdi,* and *Un Garibaldino Al Convento*. The first motion picture in which he attempted a more serious approach was also the first occasion on which he worked with the writer Cesare Zavattini. This was *I Bambini ci Guardano,* adapted from the novel *Prico* by C. G. Viola and released in New York in April 1947 under the title *The Little Martyr*. During World War II De Sica was relieved of having to make a picture in Prague under the sponsorship of Goebbels by an invitation to direct a film for the Catholic Film Center. This was *La Porta Del Cielo,* filmed largely within St. Paul's Basilica.

Since the war De Sica has followed a dual career in acting and producing. As an actor he has appeared more recently in the older character parts he prefers to romantic leading roles. He has said that by acting he was able to support his family, since the pictures he has directed in the last ten years have brought him little commercial success in his own country. He was seen in the United States in a number of pictures released there in 1950. In *Escape Into Dreams,* as the leading figure in one of four episodes on the musings of Italian prisoners of war in a California prison camp, he was described by Alton Cook (New York *World-Telegram*) as "an actor of vigor and charm." *My Widow and I,* a "feckless farce" in the opinion of Howard Barnes (New York *Herald Tribune*), presented De Sica in the role of a corpse restored to life. His portrayal in *Heart and Soul* of the schoolteacher Maestro Perfoni, a role made difficult by sentiment,

DE SICA, VITTORIO—Continued

was praised as "a masterpiece" by Joe Pihodna (New York *Herald Tribune*). Again as a schoolteacher, Professor Lani, he appeared in 1952 in *Tomorrow Is Too Late* (which he is said to have had some share in directing), a story based on the need for sex education among adolescents. The *Saturday Review* critic noted, "As he has proved so many times before, De Sica has a special touch with children." Winner of a number of major prizes in Europe, *Tomorrow Is Too Late* is also the first Italian-language motion picture to run successfully in commercial theaters in the United States. De Sica recently completed an acting part in *Good Morning, Elephant*, not yet released.

As a director De Sica, who has refused in the past few years to compromise his artistic values, has worked against financial odds to produce motion pictures dealing with the subjects which interested him—childhood, poverty, "man's indifference to the needs of other men." He has defined the central message of his best-known films as a "simple Christian sense of solidarity which I believe should be felt by all of us, regardless of the political beliefs we may profess." The first fruit of what De Sica has called his "neo-realistic" approach to motion pictures was *Sciuscia*, released in the United States as *Shoe Shine* (1949), a film based on the director's year-long observation of the boy scavengers of Rome trying to live in the wake of war; it was translated into the "melancholy poetry" of the screen script by Zavattini. The resulting picture, unpopular in an Italy eager for American comedies, was received in the United States and in other countries with appreciation, winning among other prizes the New York Film Critics Award. The New York *Herald Tribune* called it "a brilliant and engrossing screen tragedy," and other reviewers characterized it as "a living experience in truth, human understanding, and tragic beauty" and "a brilliantly executed social document."

In spite of the success abroad of *Shoe Shine*, De Sica found it difficult to raise money for his second serious production, *The Bicycle Thief*, which required three years to make. Written for the screen by Zavattini from 'a novel by Luigi Bartolini, the story "is as simple as the needs and the anguishes of the hungry." While being shown in the United States to nearly universal critical praise, the picture was picketed in New York by the Knights of Columbus because it "glorified a thief," and was refused the seal of approval of the Motion Picture Association of America on the ground that two scenes violated the association's production code. Of this "strong and anguished drama about the ordeal of impoverished life in postwar Italy," film critic Alton Cook wrote: "Unquestionably this is a masterpiece of movie making. There is only the question of whether some slight compromise with its grimness might have been dramatically more sound. But if you are a stout soul equal to this harrowing experience, here is a genuinely great picture." It was voted the best foreign film of 1949 by the New York critics, named the best picture of 1949 by the committee on exceptional films of the National Board of Review of Motion Pictures and by the British Film Academy, awarded the 1949 Grand Prix at the International Film Festival in Belgium, a special award at the festival in Locarno, Switzerland, and given the Seven Silver Ribbons, top Italian film award. De Sica received a Hollywood "Oscar" of the Academy of Motion Picture Arts and Sciences as the director of the best foreign film of 1949.

De Sica's third major production was *Miracle in Milan* (released in the United States in December 1951), a fantasy with passages of irony and social satire adapted for the screen by Zavattini from his own novel *Toto Il Buono*. American critical reaction was expressed by Bosley Crowther (New York *Times*), who called the picture "a little beyond superior but a good bit shy of superb"; it was widely compared with early pictures of Chaplin and René Clair. This production, like its predecessor, was awarded first honors by the Cannes Film Festival, the New York film critics, and the International Film Critics. The fourth De Sica-Zavattini collaboration, *Umberto D*, shown at the Cannes Film Festival in April 1952, was given this comment by Robert F. Hawkins in *Films In Review*: "De Sica's style, colder and more bitter than in previous films, is here at its most refined in the depiction of the solitude of a man and his dog." In his postwar films a primary characteristic of De Sica's work has been his utilization of material close to real life for his stories, of actual places rather than studio sets for his backgrounds, and of nonprofessionals for his actors. He has said of the new Italian school of motion picture making that "production costs and lack of money have been a determining factor in making us take actual life as our subject matter, so that reality is transferred to the plane of poetry" (New York *Herald Tribune*).

In March 1952 the Italian director visited the United States at the invitation of Howard Hughes and the RKO studio. When the contemplated contract with that studio did not materialize, De Sica, who made a cross-continental tour to familiarize himself with the country and to select a locale for a picture, concluded an agreement with the Charles K. Feldman Group Productions. The picture now projected, which will use some ideas from *Miracle in the Rain* by Ben Hecht, will be filmed in Chicago.

On his arrival in the United States, De Sica was described as being about six feet tall, with "high color, pepper-and-salt wavy hair, and a flashing smile." Interviewers noted his "exuberant vitality" and his "combination of strong personality and keen insight." He is married and has a daughter. The actor-director plays the piano, is an amateur composer, and collects contemporary Italian paintings. He has said that he is not concerned with many of the ambitions and problems of the film industry. "When I have something to say I enjoy working in pictures to say it," he told Otis L. Guernsey, Jr., of the New York *Herald Tribune*, "but when it is finished I like to go away for a while. I make films, but I am not a man of the cinema."

References

Cue 21:14 Ap 12 '52
N Y Post Mr 21 '52
N Y Herald Tribune IV p1 Mr 23 '52
N Y Sunday News II p8 Ap 27 '52
N Y Times II p5 Ja 1 '50
New Yorker 28:29 Ap 5 '52
Chi è? (1948)

DEWEY, JOHN Oct. 20, 1859—June 1, 1952 Philosopher, educator, writer; adherent of pragmatism and leading exponent of progressive education; taught philosophy at the University of Michigan, University of Minnesota, and University of Chicago; director of the School of Education, University of Chicago (1902-04); professor of philosophy, Columbia University (1904-30); subsequently emeritus professor; author of *Psychology* (1886), *School and Society* (1899), *Democracy and Education* (1916), *Art as Experience* (1934), and many other books. See *Current Biography*, 1944.

Obituary

N Y Times p1+ Je 2 '52

Homer Page

RENÉ D'HARNONCOURT

D'HARNONCOURT, RENÉ (dȧr-nôn″-kōōr′ rē-nā′) May 17, 1901- Art museum director

Address: b. c/o Museum of Modern Art, 11 W. 53d St., New York 19; h. 333 Central Park West, New York 25

René d'Harnoncourt is the director of the Museum of Modern Art, in New York City, an institution that contains what is considered the most comprehensive collection of twentieth century art in the world. D'Harnoncourt, who is a native of Austria, lived in Mexico from 1925 to 1933. the year he went to the United States. In 1937 he was appointed general manager of the Indian Arts and Crafts Board of the Department of the Interior, and he has served as chairman of the board since 1944. He joined the staff of the Museum of Modern Art in that year as director of its department of manual industries and as vice-president in charge of foreign activities; became chairman of its coordination committee and director of curatorial departments in 1947; and was elected director two years later. An authority on the art of the American Indian and Mexican arts and crafts, he is also considered an outstanding expert on museum installation techniques.

Born in Vienna, Austria, on May 17, 1901, Count René d'Harnoncourt is the son of Hubert and Julie (Mittrowsky) d'Harnoncourt. He comes from a titled family of French origin. After his elementary and secondary schooling in Graz, he studied chemistry and philosophy at the State University there from 1918 to 1921. In his teens he had become interested in art and collected paintings and engravings, but when the family's financial condition greatly deteriorated during and after World War I he decided to take up chemical engineering as a career. He entered the Technische Hochschule

in Vienna in 1922 and wrote the first half of his thesis on "The Creosote Contents of Certain Soft Coals of Southern Yugoslavia." However, two years later he was forced to leave that institution without obtaining his degree, because the part of his great-grandfather's estate from which he derived his income had been expropriated by Czechoslovakia following the dissolution of the Austro-Hungarian Empire.

D'Harnoncourt went to Mexico in 1925 only to find no opportunity for an Austrian chemist in that country. For a time he supported himself by drawing posters, making hand-painted postcards of bull fights for tourists, touching up advertising photographs for a newspaper, and by decorating shop windows for department stores and pharmacies. Then an Austrian antique collector in Mexico City, who had known d'Harnoncourt as an amateur in art in Vienna, commissioned him to sell the collection. In the process d'Harnoncourt met other collectors in Mexico, mostly Americans, who began to commission him to buy for them. Becoming an associate in a Mexico City antique firm in 1927, he built up a department of primitive and contemporary Mexican folk art—pottery, lacquer, and weaving. Two years later he was asked by the Mexican Ministry of Education to make a collection of folk art for the government and to lecture on it as a faculty member of the Seminar for Cultural Relations. During his stay in Mexico he also executed a decorative mural in the Cuernavaca home of Dwight Morrow, who was then American Ambassador to Mexico.

At the suggestion of Ambassador Morrow, d'Harnoncourt was chosen to prepare an exhibition of Mexican fine and applied arts that was to be brought to the United States under the auspices of the Carnegie Foundation and

D'HARNONCOURT, RENÉ—*Continued*

the American Federation of Arts. For this project he made numerous trips into remote parts of Mexico to secure examples of the most primitive art. The exhibition, which included over 1,200 specimens of native workmanship from the time of the Conquest to the present (many of them classified for the first time), opened at New York's Metropolitan Museum of Art in October 1930. As curator of the exhibition, d'Harnoncourt for the next two years toured the United States while the collection circulated among museums in fourteen American cities. In May 1932 a one-man show of his drawings was held at the Weyhe Gallery in New York. According to Edward Alden Jewell (*Times*), d'Harnoncourt was "as romantic and versatile an artists as you will encounter anywhere today." The following year he returned to Austria to obtain a visa and re-entered the United States as an immigrant. (He became a naturalized American citizen six years later.) During 1933-34 d'Harnoncourt was a director of a radio program, *Art in America*, sponsored by the American Federation of Arts. From 1934 to 1937 he served as an instructor in art history at Sarah Lawrence College in suburban Bronxville and in 1936 he lectured at the New School for Social Research in the metropolis.

D'Harnoncourt was made assistant to the general manager of the newly created Indian Arts and Crafts Board of the United States Department of the Interior in 1936, and the following year he was promoted to general manager. "I worked mostly in the field, in the Dakotas and elsewhere," he told a *New Yorker* interviewer. "Our object was to help North American Indians obtain some economic independence through their native crafts." Since one of the functions of the board was to create a new appreciation for the work of Indian artists, d'Harnoncourt supervised a comprehensive exhibit of past and present Indian art and life in the United States and Alaska which was shown at the Golden Gate International Exposition in San Francisco in 1939. Two years later d'Harnoncourt, representing the Indian Arts and Crafts Board and in collaboration with Frederic H. Douglas, curator of Indian art of the Denver Art Museum, directed an exhibition for the Museum of Modern Art which traced the development of North American Indian arts from their earliest beginnings to their contemporary phases. Two years in preparation, "Indian Arts of the United States" contained more than 1,000 items and was reportedly the most ambitious show in the museum's history up to that time. Critics described it as the largest exhibition of American Indian art ever attempted and praised the "superb taste and showmanship" of d'Harnoncourt's installation of the displays.

In January 1944 the Museum of Modern Art announced the establishment of a department of manual industries, with d'Harnoncourt as its director. The function of this department was to study the potential contribution of manual industry to the modern world and to assist in its development. At the same time he

was made vice-president in charge of the museum's foreign activities, with responsibility for conducting relations with cultural organizations in the other American republics. Three years later he became chairman of the museum's co-ordination committee and director of its curatorial departments. (He still holds both of these positions in 1952.) Among the major exhibitions he directed for the museum were "Arts of the South Seas" (1946), "Timeless Aspects of Modern Art" (1948), and "Modern Art in Your Life" (1949), and (in collaboration with members of the museum's staff) exhibitions of sculpture by Henry Moore (1946), Gabo and Pevsner (1948), and Nadelman (1948). On October 18, 1949, he was elected director of the museum, which had been governed by the coordination committee since its founding director, Alfred H. Barr, Jr., resigned that post in 1943 to become director of the museum collections.

Founded in 1929 under the sponsorship of a group of prominent private collectors, the Museum of Modern Art was established with the intention of developing public appreciation for, and encouraging the study of, "the visual arts of our time." The museum has since come to embrace, in addition to painting and sculpture, architecture, industrial and commercial design, motion pictures, photography, and prints and drawings. By the summer of 1952 it had held some 500 exhibitions in New York and published more than 175 books, while its circulating exhibitions had brought modern art before people in hundreds of localities in the United States and Canada and abroad. The museum has the largest library on modern art in the world, and its Film Library, which has acquired some 13,000,000 feet of film, comprises a collection of motion picture films marking stages in the development of the cinema. The museum's permanent collection includes works by the most important contemporary masters and younger experimental artists of Europe and America, and illustrates much of the history of art in the twentieth century. Enriched soon after its foundation by the Bliss bequest of French paintings, the permanent collection has since been constantly augmented by other gifts and particularly by the purchase funds provided by Mrs. John D. Rockefeller, Jr., and Mrs. Simon Guggenheim. The museum, which had a membership of some 15,000 in 1952, has been visited by approximately 7,200,000 persons in the twenty-three years of its existence.

Since d'Harnoncourt became its director, the Museum of Modern Art has continued to present a number of important exhibitions, including retrospective shows of the work of Charles Demuth, Franklin Watkins, Edward Munch, Chaim Soutine, and James Ensor; the record-breaking Matisse survey; such group shows as "Abstract Painting and Sculpture in America" and "Fifteen Americans"; selections from private collections; and the annual "Good Design" exhibits. In September 1951 a $450,000 annex, known as the Grace Rainey Rogers Memorial, was opened adjoining the main museum building. This new annex houses the Young People's Gallery and the studios and workshops of the People's Art Center, which offers about 75 classes for children, young people, and adult laymen. During 1952 a new sculpture court was built in the garden behind the museum, adjacent to the annex and the building (to be completed in 1953) for the Whitney Museum of American Art. The two museums have formed a program for coordinated action in the future.

From 1941 to 1943 d'Harnoncourt was acting director of the Arts Section of the Office of the Coordinator of Inter-American Affairs, in which position he helped organize exchange exhibitions throughout South America. He also served as a member of the Advisory Committee on Art of the Department of State. During the summer of 1946, as senior counselor of visual art of the United Nations Educational, Scientific, and Cultural Organization (UNESCO), he went to London on leave of absence from the museum to develop the program in all forms of the visual arts and museum activities for the Preparatory Commission of UNESCO. Later he became a member of the program committee of the United States National Commission for UNESCO.

The museum director is the author of *Hole in the Wall* (1941), which A. C. Moore (*Saturday Review*) called "a milestone among children's books." Of *Mexicana* (1931), d'Harnoncourt's "picture book for grownups," a *Nation* critic said: "No collection of either the literature or the art of Mexico is complete or even adequate without these eloquent depictions." He also illustrated two children's books by Elizabeth Reeve Morrow: *Painted Pig* (1930) and *Beast, Bird, and Fish* (1933). In addition, he prepared the catalogue, *Mexican Arts*, for the 1930 exhibit, and together with F. H. Douglas wrote *Indian Art in the United States* (1941), which a *Magazine of Art* reviewer described as "the most complete work on the art of the United States Indian ever published." Since 1944 d'Harnoncourt has been chairman of the Indian Arts and Crafts Board, and he is also a member of the board of directors of the National Indian Association and the American Federation of Arts. His club is the Century Association. On May 29, 1933, he married Sarah Carr, who at that time was editor of a fashion trade paper in Chicago. They have a daughter, Anne Julie. A large man, the museum director stands six feet six inches tall and weighs 210 pounds.

References

Art Digest 24:5 N 15 '49
Art N 45:53 Ag '46
N Y Times p30 O 19 '49
New Yorker 25:27-8 D 3 '49
Directory of American Scholars (1952)
Who's Who in America, 1952-53
Who's Who in the East (1951)
World Biography (1948)

DICKSON, MARGUERITE (STOCK-MAN) Nov. 14, 1873- Author

Address: b. c/o Thomas Nelson & Sons, 385 Madison Ave., New York 17

Reprinted from the *Wilson Library Bulletin,* May 1952.

When she was twenty-six, Marguerite Dickson had her first book published, *From the Old World to the New,* which initiated an ultimately highly successful series of American histories used in schools for thirty-five years. She was a bride of a year and a teacher in her native New England at the time. She had complained to a fellow teacher about the textbooks, and her friend retorted, "If you want a better book, write it yourself." So she did.

When Marguerite Dickson was seventy-two, her first junior novel was published, *Bramble Bush* (1945). The Philadelphia *Inquirer* commented: "An exceptionally worth-while juvenile," although *The Booklist* remarked, "Improbable . . . but . . . written with good insight into teen-age problems." This keen insight was back of five other popular junior novels. Mrs. Dickson had never written a line of fiction until she was seventy.

Mrs. Dickson was born Marguerite Stockman in Portland, Maine, November 14, 1873, of colonial American ancestry on both sides. Her father was a physician and, while she was still a baby, the family moved to Cape Ann in Massachusetts, later to Springfield. At fourteen she went to Brooklyn, New York, to live with cousins. After graduation there, she taught in the Brooklyn public schools until she married George Dickson in 1900 and went back to New England.

Mrs. Dickson's husband, who was also a teacher, died when their three children were quite young, so presently she resumed her teaching. While her son and two daughters were still in college, she became director of the Character Education Department of the Women's Municipal League in Boston. Here she remained for ten years. In 1934, her elder daughter opened a dance studio in Cambridge, and until 1946 Mrs. Dickson served as its secretary and registrar.

Her second novel, *Lightning Strikes Twice* (1947), the story of a girl who wants to be a dancer, grew out of her contacts with young people studying ballet. The New York *Times* conceded it was "intelligently written," while the *Library Journal* called it "an inspiration to any girl." The response from readers inspired *Roof over Our Heads* (1948) and *Turn in the Road* (1949). Both are set in the little Maine village where Mrs. Dickson lives every year from May through October. The first is a semi-mystery which *The American Girl* called "dramatic and satisfying." The *Times* commented on its "quality of courage." The second book is about the struggle of a girl from a good family which has suffered severe poverty to better herself and become a librarian. "A plausible and excellent story," was the verdict of the *Horn Book,* while the Chicago *Tribune* applauded thus: "A fine story of youth at its best, ambitious, clear-sighted and forthright."

Stairway to the Sky (1950) is a thoroughly realistic story of a girl who works in a bookshop and wants to write, but has many setbacks before she succeeds in making a start. "Girls who want to write," the *Times* said, "should put this book high on their reading lists . . .

Wilkinson

MARGUERITE DICKSON

warm as well as plausible." The New York *Herald Tribune* called it "surefire with teen-agers."

Five of Mrs. Dickson's books have appeared as serials, and all but one, *Stairway to the Sky,* the most mature title, were selections of the Junior Literary Guild. Her new book (April 1952), *Only Child,* is the story of a girl who is an only child, although not a spoiled one, and of her adjustment to a new and difficult situation.

It was the quality of courage noted about *Roof Over Our Heads* that saw Mrs. Dickson through some trying periods: one, when she was thrown from a wagon and broke so many bones that she spent the entire summer in bed and all that autumn learning to walk again. The second was when an automobile skidded and rolled over, pinning her under it. That time she was in bed twelve weeks and spent a year and a half recovering.

No hint of these experiences is in the trim little figure, just under five feet. Her life is an active one. She appears frequently on radio and television programs, and each Monday night through the winter months she presides over a writing group which meets in her Cambridge, Massachusetts, home. In 1934 she and a number of women who had been studying creative writing decided to work together and have met informally since then under Mrs. Dickson's guidance. Twenty-seven books have come out of this group, which includes Anne Molloy, Sally Barrett, Helene Conway, and the late Amy Wentworth Stone.

Mrs. Dickson's favorite color is red, and a hat in some shade of wine or cranberry is usually perched jauntily on her lovely white hair. She is a great favorite with young

people, and has an ear for present-day teen-talk far better than many writers half her age. One of her hobbies is gardening, which she indulges extensively each summer in her home on the rocky coast of Maine. In 1952 she celebrated her fortieth consecutive year there. When not writing, she works to her heart's content in her beautiful garden beside a white birch grove overlooking the blue waters of the bay, where fog rolls in from the ocean like silver clouds.

DISNEY, WALT Dec. 5, 1901- Motion picture producer
Address: b. c/o Walt Disney Productions, 2400 W. Alameda Ave., Burbank, Calif.

> NOTE: This biography supersedes the article which appeared in *Current Biography* in 1940.

Since launching his *Mickey Mouse* series in 1928, Walt Disney has won international popularity for his animated cartoons and has been responsible for technical advances in sound, color, and photography of cartoon production. With *Snow White and the Seven Dwarfs,* in 1937, the first feature-length cartoon work ever filmed, he scored one of the cinematic successes of the century; and in 1940 with *Fantasia* he introduced visual interpretation of orchestral music. Among other feature-length cartoons, notable for the whimsical quality of Disney's depiction of animals and flowers, are *Bambi* (1942), *The Adventures of Mr. Ichabod and Mr. Toad* (1949), and *Alice in Wonderland* (1951). In *Treasure Island* and *Robin Hood* he used "live" characters, and in the "True-Life Adventures" (*Seal Island, Beaver Valley,* and *Nature's Half Acre* were the first three) he depicted wildlife in widely acclaimed documentary films.

Walt Disney, the youngest of the five children of Elias and Flora (Call) Disney, was born December 5, 1901, in Chicago, Illinois. Walter Elias were his given names. His father, a Canadian of Irish ancestry, was a building contractor at the time; but soon after his youngest child's birth he turned for a while to farming, and with his wife, his four sons and his daughter, moved to a farm near Marceline, Missouri. There Walt Disney acquired his love for animals and made his first drawings. In Marceline, likewise, he began his schooling, which was to continue from 1910 to 1917 at the Benton School, in Kansas City, Missouri, to which the Disney family moved when Walt was a little over eight years old. At the latter time, also, the boy began delivering newspapers before and after school hours. Within another year or so he made what may be regarded as his start as a commercial artist by doing a weekly sketch for a local barber, who gave him in exchange the choice of twenty-five cents or a free haircut. Subsequently, in the summer of 1917, Disney worked as a magazine and candy vendor aboard a Kansas City-Chicago train before continuing his secondary education at the McKinley High School, in Chicago. Here he took a course in photography and also studied in the evenings at the Chicago Academy of Fine Arts. Disney did not graduate from high school; in 1918 he enlisted for World War I service as a Red Cross ambulance driver.

After the war Disney returned to Kansas City and obtained a job as a commercial artist with the Gray Advertising Company. He also studied briefly at a local art school. In 1920 he was hired as an apprentice cartoonist by the Kansas City *Film Advertising*, with which periodical he remained for two years; and during this period he also did some special work making cartoon slides for a film concern. His interest in filmed cartoons thus aroused, he began experimenting in a studio he had made for himself above his father's garage, and in due course turned out a reel of humorous Kansas City incidents which he called *Laugh-O-Grams* for showing in local theaters. Convinced that his future lay in Hollywood, Disney in 1923 left Kansas City for California with a capital of $40 and the first sketches for an experimental film, *Alice in Cartoonland*, which was to combine a living girl with animated cartoon figures.

Disney formed a partnership with his brother Roy, who was already working in the film capital. With their combined savings of $290, and $500 borrowed from a Disney uncle, the two converted a small garage into a studio and during the next three years produced a series of *Alice* comedies. In 1926 Walt Disney contracted with Universal to direct the *Oswald the Rabbit* cartoons and did so for the next two years, until the film concern and the artist disagreed over plans for expansion and Disney relinquished his interest in the Oswald character.

According to one account of the origin of Disney's best-known creation, it was on a train trip between New York and Los Angeles that the artist conceived the idea of Mickey Mouse, remembering a mouse that used to appear on his drawing board when he was in Kansas City. A rough first scenario was completed before the train reached California, and the Disney brothers immediately set to work. Their first two *Mickey* cartoons were scrapped as not up to standard, but the third, *Steamboat Willie*, the first to make use of sound effects, was an instant hit when first shown in October 1928. Mickey, the central figure in over one hundred cartoon "shorts" distributed during the ensuing ten years, enjoyed an international popularity along with such "supporting" characters as Minnie Mouse, Pluto, and Donald Duck, the last-named being subsequently given a series of his own. Mickey, who was known abroad under such names as Michael Maus (Germany), Miki Kuchi (Japan), and Miguel Ratonocito (Spain and Latin America), brought Disney foreign decorations, including that of the French Legion of Honor in 1935 for "creating a new art form in which good will is spread throughout the world."

Shortly after the *Mickey Mouse* pictures first appeared Walt Disney began work on his "Silly Symphony" cartoon series. The first of these, *Skeleton Dance*, was released in July 1929. *Flowers and Trees* (1932) used the Technicolor process for the first time in the

WALT DISNEY

animated cartoon field. *Three Little Pigs* (which popularized the song "Who's Afraid of the Big Bad Wolf?") appeared in 1933, by which time the Disney enterprise was employing over one hundred persons in much enlarged quarters. (By 1940 the personnel numbered seven hundred.) During 1934 work was begun on *Snow White and the Seven Dwarfs* (the first feature-length animated cartoon ever undertaken), which involved an outlay of $1,600,000 and took three years to complete. Among the factors in the extraordinary success of this picture, which was released in December 1937, were its lively songs and the Disneyesque individualization of the dwarfs Grumpy, Dopey, and the rest. *Snow White* grossed $8,000,000 within a short time after its release and held a record as the film industry's greatest money-maker until *Gone With the Wind* appeared about four years later.

Snow White is said to have been the last of his productions to which Walt Disney contributed any of his own work as an artist. While all Disney films since 1928 have reflected distinctively the Walt Disney style and imagination, actual draftsmanship has been done by other artists, working under his direct supervision. His title is chairman of the board and executive of Walt Disney Productions, Ltd.; his brother Roy, as president, handles the finances. While a new fifty-one-acre plant at Burbank was under construction, *Ferdinand the Bull* was completed, its release in 1939 being followed in February 1940 by the first showings of *Pinocchio*, Disney's feature-length cartoon of the Italian children's classic by Collodi. The next November *Fantasia* was released. It was a highly novel film on the development of which Disney and the conductor Leopold Stokowski had worked together in combining classical musical compositions with pictorial conceptions and commentary by Deems Taylor, critic and composer. To

DISNEY, WALT—*Continued*

Bosley Crowther of the New York *Times* the result was "simply terrific, as terrific as anything that had ever happened on the screen," while Howard Barnes of the *Herald Tribune* called the film "brave and beautiful." But the music critics of the same two papers, Olin Downes and Virgil Thomson, were not enthusiastic.

Fantasia was followed on the Disney schedule by *The Reluctant Dragon* and *Dumbo* (both in 1941) and *Bambi* (1942). *Bambi* had at least one new and typically Disneyesque character (Flower, the skunk) worked into Felix Salten's story of a deer, with the fanciful animals against a realistic background. The experiment may be considered as pointing ahead to Disney's success, nearly a decade later, with documentary nature films photographed in color.

Bambi was the last production on Disney's planned program until after World War II: following the Japanese attack on Pearl Harbor, his studios were taken over by the United States Government for quartering of troops and storage of supplies. When film production was resumed there, a somewhat reduced staff of artists was engaged principally in the designing of training, indoctrination, and propaganda films for the armed services and various government departments. Most of these were classified as "restricted," but *Victory Through Air Power*, illustrating the theories of Major Alexander de Seversky, was shown to the general public in 1943. *Saludos Amigos* (1942) and *The Three Caballeros* (1945) were produced to further the "Good Neighbor" policy of the United States toward the Latin American countries.

Disney's first postwar feature-length entertainment was *Make Mine Music* (1946), a cartoon "variety show," which made use of the *Fantasia* manner in Serge Prokofieff's *Peter and the Wolf*. The producer then returned to the depicting of children's classics with *Song of the South* (1947), introducing the Uncle Remus animals, and *The Adventures of Mr. Ichabod and Mr. Toad* (1949), in which Washington Irving's *Legend of Sleepy Hollow* and Kenneth Grahame's *Wind in the Willows* were loosely linked. Other feature-length films produced during these years were *Fun and Fancy Free* (1947), *Melody Time* (1948), and *So Dear to My Heart* (1949). *Cinderella* came to the screen in February 1950, and in the following August *Treasure Island* (filmed in England and the West Indies) was released. The latter was a Technicolor film of Stevenson's pirate story with a "live" cast. *Robin Hood* (1952), Disney's second live-action production, employed an all-British cast and was shot in England. *Variety* praised the actors and called the film a "superb piece of color entertainment. . . .Camera work, settings and decor match the high technical standards of the production."

With *Seal Island* (1948) photographed in the Aleutians, Disney launched a documentary series called "True-Life Adventures," in which wildlife is "starred." *Beaver Valley*, the second of this type of nature film, was voted the best documentary of 1951 by the British Film Academy. The winner of a top prize at the Venice Film Festival in 1951, *Nature's Half Acre*, Disney's third production in that category, was judged "fascinating" by *Variety*. "The tremendous public reaction" to these half-hour subjects, said Thomas M. Pryor in the New York *Times*, "was more than even Mr. Disney expected." In successive years all three of these pictures were awarded Academy "Oscars."

On the afternoon of Christmas Day of 1950 Disney brought his favorite cartoon characters to television for the first time, and with such success that the show was repeated in 1951. In March 1951 the announcement was made that a new series of *Mickey Mouse* cartoons would be put into production. "We never really dropped Mickey, we just drifted away from him," said Disney, who himself supplies the voice for Mickey. *Alice in Wonderland* was released in mid-1951, the day after a European *Alice* had its première. The Disney version evoked varied reactions, depending to some extent on the viewer's receptiveness to a modern-style Alice and Disneyesque Wonderland characters in place of the old conception of Sir John Tenniel. Forthcoming productions on the Disney schedule include Barrie's *Peter Pan*, Jules Verne's *Twenty Thousand Leagues Under the Sea*, Charles Major's *When Knighthood Was in Flower*, and new "True-Life" titles.

The figures and names of Mickey Mouse, Pinocchio, Donald Duck, and other Disney characters have been used by American manufacturers in a wide variety of licensed products—wearing apparel, children's toys, and household goods. Walt Disney's company has produced a number of "Mickey Mouse" and "Silly Symphony" books, *A Sketch Book of Snow White and the Seven Dwarfs* (1938), and syndicated newspaper comic strips. Among other recognitions given Disney by the Academy of Motion Picture Arts and Sciences was a special award in 1932 for the creation of the Mickey Mouse character; for the *Three Little Pigs* he received an Academy certificate in 1933 and for *Snow White and the Seven Dwarfs* a special Academy award in 1938. *Fantasia* brought him a plaque of the Dowling Foundation of Plymouth (Michigan), a scroll of the New York Critics, and a medal of the New York School of Music. Disney is an honorary member of the Art Worker's Guild of London and was the recipient in 1938 of honorary degrees from the University of Southern California (M.Sc.), Yale (M.A.) and Harvard (M.A.). Some 120 awards and honors have been bestowed upon Disney by American and foreign organizations; among these are gold medals from *Parents' Magazine, Look, Cine Revue,* and other publications, and prizes at international film festivals. In early 1952 he was made an officer in the French Academy.

Walt Disney's wife is the former Lillian Marie Bounds of Lewiston, Idaho, and was one of the first two office employees in the Disney brothers' oldest studio. Married on July 13, 1925, they have two daughters, Diane Marie and Sharon Mae. Disney's latest hobby is a model railroad; one eighth of standard gauge, it is capable of carrying passengers. The producer is also an enthusiastic polo player. Disney is described in *Fortune* as "a slender man, just about six feet tall, with black hair, a small mustache and quick bright eyes." He is a Mason and a member of the Order De Molay.

References

Atlan 166:689-701 D '40
Bet Hom & Gard 18:13-15+ Ja '40 pors
Christian Sci Mon p3 Mr 8 '40 por
Fortune 26:90-5+ Ag '42
Ladies Home J 58:20+ Mr '41 pors
Look 15:122 Mr 13 '51 por; 115:15-17+;
    S 25 '51 pors
New Yorker 7:23-7 D 19 '31
Newsweek 35:84+ F 13 '50
Read Digest 41:85-8 O '42
Time 30:19-21 D 27 '37 por; 36:52-5
    N 18 '40; 39:58+ Je 8 '42
Charlot, J. Art from the Mayans to
    Disney (1939)
Cooper, A. C. & Palmer, C. A. Twenty
    Modern Americans (1942)
Feild, R. D. The Art of Walt Disney
    (1942)
Fisher, D. C. American Portraits (1946)
International Motion Picture Almanac,
    1950-51
Logie, I. R. ed. Careers in the Making
    (1942)
Moore, J. A. Famous Leaders of In-
    dustry (1945)
National Cyclopædia of American Biog-
    raphy, Current vol E, 1937-38
Who's Who (1951)
Who's Who in America, 1950-51
Who's Who in the West (1951)
World Biography (1948)

DIX, DOROTHY Nov. 18, 1870—Dec. 16, 1951 Newspaperwoman; reporter and columnist for the New Orleans *Picayune* (1896-1901); began her widely read advice-to-the-lovelorn column, "Dorothy Dix Talks," in 1896; joined staff of the New York *Journal* as special writer, often covering murder cases (1901); joined Wheeler Syndicate staff (1917), Ledger Syndicate staff (1923), Bell Syndicate staff (1933); author of *How to Win and Hold a Husband* (1939), among other books. See *Current Biography*, 1940.

Obituary

N Y Times p31 D 17 '51

DOAN, LELAND I(RA) Nov. 4, 1894-
President of the Dow Chemical Company
Address: b. c/o Dow Chemical Co., Midland, Mich.; h. 1018 W. Main St., Midland, Mich.

To Leland I. Doan, president of the Dow Chemical Company, has been attributed a large part of the development that has made Dow's expansion the greatest in relation to its size of the six major chemical companies in the United States. For a twenty-year period prior to being elected to the presidency in April 1949, Doan, who had joined the Dow Chemical Company in 1917, directed the company's sales activities.

Leland Ira Doan was born in North Bend, Nebraska, on November 4, 1894, the son of Ira Doan, a physician, and Hester (Spencer) Doan. At the University of Michigan, which he entered in 1913, he specialized in chemical engineering until 1916. For a year after leaving college he was in the employ of the Michigan Bell Telephone Company, until late in 1917 he accepted a position as research assistant for the Dow Chemical Company in Midland, Michigan. When he joined the company's industrial sales division in 1918, Doan found sales functions concentrated in the hands of a few people at Midland. In order to expand these activities he established a number of branch offices with a corps of salesmen each specializing in the sale of some specific class of chemical products. As one method of promoting sales, he catalogued information about prospective customers down to their hobbies.

His reputation as an organizer established, Doan became assistant sales manager in 1922, general sales manager in 1929, and director of sales in 1945, watching company sales expand as he discovered markets for such new products as magnesium, plastics, and pharmaceuticals. Meanwhile his standing in the company also advanced: in 1935 he was made a member of Dow's board of directors, in 1938 vice-president, and in 1941 secretary. When Dr. Willard Henry Dow, then company president, was killed in a plane crash on March 31, 1949, Doan was within five days appointed his successor by the unanimous vote of Dow's board of directors.

The company whose presidency Doan assumed in April 1949 had been founded more than half a century before by Herbert Dow for the purpose of separating and marketing the components of extensive native brine deposits in Midland, Michigan. "Beginning with an original process for the electrolytic production of bromine, activities were steadily expanded to include the production of other brine components, coal tar derivatives, solvents, and synthetic, organic chemicals" (*Barron's*, March 6, 1950). When the founder's son, Willard Dow, became president in 1930, he expanded the business to Freeport, Texas, for magnesium from sea water, to the West Coast for a broader chlorine base, and to other areas to produce the bulk of styrene needed for wartime synthetic rubber. The Dow Chemical Company had been the first in the world to extract magnesium from sea water and the first to make commercial the production of styrene. Besides owning a number of plants in the United States, Dow is joint owner of two subsidiaries—the Ethyl-Dow Chemical Company (owned with Ethyl Corporation), which extracts bromine from sea water to produce ethylene dibromide used in making ethyl gasoline, and the Dow Corning Corporation (owned with Corning Glass Works), which makes silicone plastics at Midland. Of Dow's more than six hundred products, 60 per cent are industrial chemicals,

LELAND I. DOAN

with plastics, agricultural chemicals, pharmaceuticals, and magnesium metal also of considerable importance (*Fortune*, March 1950). Dow's research of recent years has included work on processes for producing acetylene from natural gas and work with the Detroit Edison Company on a program for producing atomic power.

When Doan succeeded to the presidency of the company in 1949, it had for a decade been exhibiting the most rapid expansion of any major chemical company in the country (*Barron's*, April 28, 1952). This growth necessitated changes in administration so that of the positions of president, chairman, and general manager, filled simultaneously by Willard Dow, Doan held only the presidency, Earl W. Bennett being appointed chairman and Mark E. Putnam, general manager. To stem a temporary sales decline in early 1949, Doan delegated authority to his department heads and began building a larger sales force trained to become market and production analysts who could help Dow's industrial customers plan their sales. Announcing a $25-million program for expansion and replacement of plant, Doan at the same time directed his energies toward plastics, with the result that mid-year plastic sales increased about 30 per cent above those of the previous year to take up the slack in other products.

Among other developments in the company since Doan became president were the construction of an ammonia plant at Freeport and the expansion of the Freeport-Velasco plant; the purchase of a steel casting plant in Madison, Illinois, to be converted to the rolling of magnesium sheets; and the construction of a plant for the production of plastics near New London, Connecticut. On August 22, 1951, at a meeting of nearly one thousand of the company's stockholders Doan made known plans for new plant facilities to cost approximately $100 millions a year for the next several years. One of Dow's products in increased civilian demand was magnesium, the growth in the commercial uses of which had been pointed out by Doan at a meeting of the New York State Chamber of Commerce in April 1951 as indicative of the fact that the magnesium industry "doesn't need war to remain strong and healthy, or to make progress." In order to increase its export sales from 5 per cent to 10 per cent of its total volume of business, the Dow company formed two new exporting companies (announced in January 1952), the Dow Chemical Inter-American, Ltd., for exports in the Western Hemisphere, and the Dow Chemical International, Ltd., for exports to other countries. Dow's sales for the fiscal year ending May 31, 1952 (as reported by the New York *Herald Tribune*), were $407,158,799, compared with about $340,000,000 for the preceding year.

On the issue of taxation, Doan, speaking before the Providence Analysts Society meeting in Providence, Rhode Island, on December 12, 1951, expressed the opinion that "American business should practice rigid economy" before demanding equal economy on the part of government. In April 1952 he observed at a meeting of the Boston Chamber of Commerce that if heavy taxes destroy incentive and capital, "we will have neither the means nor the desire to continue the creative research which has pointed the way for our national growth and prosperity."

In subsidiary and related organizations of the Dow Chemical Company Doan is secretary and director of the Dow Chemical of Canada, Ltd., vice-president and director of Dowell, Inc., treasurer of the Dow Magnesium Corporation, director of the United States Alkali Export Association, director of the Saran Yarns Company at Odenton, Maryland, director of the Midland Ammonia Company, and director of the Manufacturing Chemists Association. His clubs are the Detroit Athletic, the Canadian (New York), the Chemist's, and the Newcomen Society; he is a member of Sigma Chi and is a Shriner in the Masons.

Leland I. Doan has been married since April 7, 1917, to Ruth Alden (Dow) Doan, sister of the former company president, Willard Dow. He is the father of three children, Leland Alden, Dorothy Margaret (Mrs. Parker Frisselle), and Herbert Dow Doan. Doan's church is the Presbyterian. A Republican, he was elected a regent of the University of Michigan on that party's ticket in April 1951. In 1951 he was also made head of a fund-raising drive to enlarge the community hospital at Midland. Doan owns a summer home on Crystal Lake in the heart of Michigan's cherry-growing country. The Dow executive, called Lee by his friends, is tall and affable, with a ready laugh.

References

Bsns W p26 Ap 16 '49 por
N Y Herald Tribune p23 My 14 '51
Time 60:72-3 Ag 4 '52 por
Business Executives of America (1950)
Chemical Who's Who, 1951
Who's Who in America, 1952-53
Who's Who in Commerce and Industry (1951)

DONNELLY, WALTER J(OSEPH) Jan. 9, 1896- Diplomat

Address: b. c/o Department of State, Washington 25, D.C.

To succeed John J. McCloy as United States High Commissioner for Germany, President Truman on July 18, 1952, nominated Walter J. Donnelly, then United States Ambassador to Austria and High Commissioner for that country. Donnelly, whose resignation from the top position in his country's mission in Germany was announced in December 1952, was in the foreign service since 1929. His first post was as commercial attaché of the American Legation at Bogotá, Colombia. Advanced in 1947, after duty in Brazil, Panama, and Peru, to the rank of Ambassador to Costa Rica, he later became Ambassador to Venezuela. Prior to his first diplomatic assignment he had been for four years a United States trade commissioner in Canada.

Walter Joseph Donnelly was born in New Haven, Connecticut, on January 9, 1896. One of the ten children of Henry Joseph Donnelly, a policeman, and Elizabeth Anne (Kivian) Donnelly, he worked while he was a high school student. For about two years before his country's entrance into World War I he was a reporter on New Haven newspapers. Following his military duty (1917-18) as a second lieutenant in the army he was a scholarship student at the Georgetown University School of Foreign Service in the District of Columbia for two years (1919-21), after which he obtained another scholarship which in 1921 enabled him to attend the nearby George Washington University and to study Latin American history at the University of Caracas in Venezuela. While he was a student at Georgetown, Donnelly paid some of his expenses by working for the Federal Bureau of Investigation, and following his return from Venezuela he was for one year a special agent of the Department of Justice.

Another six or seven years were to pass before Donnelly received a State Department classification. On leaving the Justice Department at the end of 1922 he joined the Bureau of Foreign and Domestic Commerce, a Department of Commerce division first set up ten years earlier to offer businessmen "personal and published aids in the fields of international and domestic commerce and industry" (*United States Government Organization Manual*). Assigned in 1923 to the Boston office as a commercial agent, Donnelly became Assistant Trade Commissioner at Ottawa, Canada, in the year following, and in 1927 was appointed American Trade Commissioner at Montreal. (He is the coauthor, with Charles R. Gruny, of *Trading Under the Laws of Canada*, a Department of Commerce Trade Promotion publication issued in 1928.)

Donnelly's first State Department post (as a Foreign Service Officer, Class 4) came to him in 1929 when he was assigned as commercial attaché to the Legation at Bogotá, Colombia, where Jefferson Caffery, regarded

Wide World Photos

WALTER J. DONNELLY

as one of his country's "model" diplomats, was United States Minister. "Caffery was famous in State Department circles for picking and hanging onto able subordinates," Benjamin Muse has observed in the Washington *Post*. "Caffery held onto 'Don' altogether for sixteen years. . . .It set a kind of record in the Foreign Service for continuous service under one diplomatic chief." There was one interruption—in 1933—when Caffery was appointed Assistant Secretary of State and Donnelly returned to the Commerce Department in Washington; later, when in December 1934 Caffery was named United States Ambassador to Cuba he took Donnelly along as commercial attaché. Donnelly likewise became commercial attaché of the United States Embassy at Rio de Janeiro in 1937, when Caffery began his eight years as Ambassador to Brazil. Five years later (November 1942) the attaché was raised to the rank of embassy counselor for economic affairs. As such he had an important part in coordinating the industrial and agricultural effort of Brazil and the United States in World War II.

When Adolf A. Berle, Jr., relieved Jefferson Caffery as Ambassador to Brazil, Donnelly moved in January 1945 to the United States Embassy at Panama as counselor. Later in 1945 he was assigned in the same capacity to the embassy at Lima, Peru, to serve there until the end of March 1947, when he succeeded Hallett Johnson as United States Ambassador to Costa Rica. He held this, his first, ambassadorial post for the next six months, but during a part of this time was "detached" to assist the United States delegation to the Rio de Janeiro Conference, which produced the Pan-American mutual defense treaty. James E. Warner of the New York *Herald Tribune* has described him as "one of the American diplomats instrumental in helping to draft some

DONNELLY, WALTER J.—*Continued*

of its most important provisions," and as "the delegation's 'trouble-shooter.'" In September 1947 Donnelly was named by President Truman to be United States Ambassador to Venezuela; he presented his credentials in December and (in the words of a statement by President Truman) "served brilliantly" for the better part of the next three years. Donnelly was a member of the United States Delegation to the 1948 Pan American Conference at Bogotá, Colombia, and in Venezuela took an interest in a big highway construction project.

On August 24, 1950, President Truman named Walter J. Donnelly to be Envoy Extraordinary and Minister Plenipotentiary of the United States to Austria and concurrently United States High Commissioner for Austria. The appointment having received Senate confirmation, Donnelly assumed his dual post at Vienna on October 25, and on arrival told newsmen that his appointment signified "a new phase in Austrian-American relationships, in which full emphasis will be placed on normal civilian contacts between our Governments." Replying to a query whether Marshall Plan operations would be continued in Austria as an independent mission, he said that a recently issued Executive Order had stated that the United States High Commissioner should be the "supreme authority." He asserted this authority by making major changes in the Economic Cooperation (Marshall Plan) Administration mission in the following January. In general he showed "in Vienna, where the complications of four-power occupation militate against smooth efficiency of a recognized sovereign government, statesmanlike qualities on major issues" (Seymour Freidin in the New York *Post*). Elevated, by mutual agreement of the two countries, to the rank of Ambassador to Austria in November 1951, Donnelly was a participant (with George Abbott, chargé d'affaires at Budapest) in negotiating the ransom in the following month of four United States airmen forced down in Hungary by Soviet fighter aircraft.

One of Donnelly's later important acts as High Commissioner for Austria was to secure from Chancellor Leopold Figl and Vice-Chancellor Adolf Schaerf a promise that their regime would carry out wide economic reforms and investigate alleged misuse of Marshall Plan funds. In return, a grant of $11 millions of suspended ECA aid was promised to Austria. This was on June 3, 1952, and on the following day, while Donnelly was en route by air to Washington for consultation, his plane was "buzzed" by two Soviet MIG-15 jet fighters. (The Russian Deputy High Commissioner at Vienna replied to American protests by asserting that "the incident could have occurred only because the Soviet Air Force did not know the time when the Ambassador's plane would fly over the Soviet occupation zone.")

By this time Donnelly was already being mentioned as the probable successor, as United States High Commissioner for Germany, to John J. McCloy, who was resigning to return to private law practice; and on July 18, 1952, he was so nominated by President Truman. Commenting on the "complex of issues" to confront the new High Commissioner, Drew Middleton of the New York *Times* wrote a week later: "Mr. Donnelly will face circumstances different from those Mr. McCloy dealt with. The German Government, with the ratification this autumn of the Bonn peace contract with the Western Allies and the European Defense Community Treaty, will assume the role of a powerful equal in the affairs of Europe." Stating that "whatever Mr. Donnelly does will have to be extremely circumspect," Middleton said further that "during that period of somewhat exaggerated nationalism that can be expected to follow ratification of the treaty system and the abolition of the Occupation Statute, the United States will not be served by too heavy an insistence on the adoption of United States views on reunification or other issues. . . . The foreign power that enjoys the greatest influence in the Germany of the next few years will be the one that is most discreet in winning that influence." *Time* also expressed the belief that "Donnelly will need all his tact and firmness to cope with the Germans as they shed the fetters of occupation," at the same time pointing out that "his good manners and good sense and his forceful handling of Communist intrigues in Vienna have prompted the State Department to label Donnelly 'just about the best foreign service officer in the business.'" On December 5, 1952, it was announced that President Truman had officially accepted Donnelly's resignation, effective on December 31, as High Commissioner for Germany.

Shortly before the diplomat left Vienna, Seymour Freidin wrote, "Donnelly also possesses the rather lugubrious distinction of being among the least wealthy of our Ambassadors." Mrs. Donnelly, a Colombian by birth, is the former María Helena Samper de Herrera; they were married January 28, 1936, and of their four children, one is a son named George James. Donnelly, who is described as "handsome, dynamic" and "fluent and intelligent," is a Roman Catholic. A sandlot baseball player in his youth, he remains a "diamond fan"; he helped, while Ambassador at Caracas, to make the game popular in Venezuela. He is a member of several golf clubs.

References

N Y Herald Tribune II p23 D 30 '51 por; p1 Jl 19 '52 por
N Y Post Mag p7 F 24 '52
Time 58:18 D 31 '51 por; 60:20-1 Jl 28 '52 por
U S Dept of State Bul 23:398 S 4 '50
Washington (D.C.) Post p3B O 15 '50 por
American Catholic Who's Who, 1952-53
American Men in Government (1949)
Who's Who in America, 1952-53
World Biography (1948)
World Diplomatic Directory (1951)

DOUGLAS, KIRK Dec. 9, 1916- Actor
Address: b. c/o Paramount Pictures, Inc., 1501
Broadway, New York 18; Hollywood, Calif.

With his portrayal in 1949 of a ruthless
prize fighter in the motion picture *Champion*,
Kirk Douglas, who had previously appeared in
about thirteen stage plays and films, achieved
immediate stardom and in the opinion of some
critics attained the rank of one of Hollywood's
best actors. His subsequent roles in *Young
Man With a Horn*, *Ace in the Hole*, and *Detective Story*, the latter a highly acclaimed
1951 Paramount production, secured his reputation as a convincing dramatic artist.

The only son among the seven children of
Russian immigrant parents, Kirk Douglas was
born Issur Danielovitch on December 9, 1916,
in Amsterdam, New York. While attending
high school in his native city, he worked in a
number of jobs, principally in Amsterdam's
carpet factories, to supplement the family income. An impressionable experience for the
student, who was then acting in school plays,
was his attendance with other members of his
English class at an Albany performance of
Katharine Cornell's *The Barretts of Wimpole
Street*. For a year after graduating from high
school, Issur Danielovitch, who had changed
his name to Isadore Demsky, held a position
as clerk in an Amsterdam department store in
order to earn money for college tuition. At
St. Lawrence University, in Canton, New York,
which he entered in 1935, he continued his interest in acting, becoming president of the
Mummers, the college dramatic group. He was
also chosen vice-president of the German club,
president of the Middle Atlantic Region of
the National Student Federation, and president
of St. Lawrence's student body. A star wrest-
ler on the campus, he won the Intercollegiate
Wrestling Championship and also entered
wrestling matches in carnivals to meet some
of his expenses.

In 1939, with his B.A. degree from St. Lawrence, Kirk Douglas enrolled at the American
Academy of Dramatic Arts in New York City,
where he studied for the next two years. His
vacations reserved for acting in summer theaters at Speculator, New York, and Nuangola,
Pennsylvania, he worked during the rest of the
year first as a dramatics coach at the Greenwich House Settlement and later as a waiter
at a Schrafft restaurant until, in 1941, he made
his debut on Broadway in a minor role as a
singing Western Union messenger in Grace
George's *Spring Again*. His next role, that
of an off-stage echo in Katharine Cornell's
Three Sisters, was followed by a juvenile part
in *Kiss and Tell*, for which he was also assistant stage manager. Gladwin Hill's article
on Douglas in *Collier's* for July 21, 1951, related that the young actor then left Broadway
to enlist in the Navy, was sent to the mid-
shipmen's school at Notre Dame University,
and later was assigned as communications officer on Antisubmarine Unit 1139. Following
action in the Pacific during World War II, he
spent five months recovering from internal injuries at a San Diego (California) hospital.

KIRK DOUGLAS

Upon his discharge from the Navy in 1944,
Douglas returned to New York to appear in
the stage play *Trio*, on radio serial programs,
and later, in January 1945, in the romantic
comedy, *Alice in Arms*, in which he was described as "tolerably good as the Oregon sergeant." Of his next performance, in the *Wind
Is Ninety*, which opened on Broadway in June
1945, Howard Barnes of the New York *Herald
Tribune*, wrote, "Though he plays the impossible role of the Unknown Soldier, he plays it
with a jaunty grace that endows it with dignity
and feeling." After the run of this drama,
Douglas was signed by Hollywood producer
Hal Wallis, to whom he had been recommended
by Lauren Bacall, a former fellow dramatic
student, for a part in the motion picture *The
Strange Loves of Martha Ivers*, starring Barbara Stanwyck. "Kirk Douglas," commented
William Hawkins of the New York *World-
Telegram*, "in his first picture, gives the weak-
ling Walter a convincingly sustained color."
Following a Broadway appearance in the short-
lived Spewack play *Woman Bites Dog* in the
summer of 1946, he was given nonstarring roles
in six motion pictures: *Out of the Past* (1947)
for RKO Radio Pictures as a smiling mobster;
Paramount's *I Walk Alone* (1947) as the sly
Noll Turner in another Hal Wallis production;
Mourning Becomes Electra (1947), an RKO
film starring Rosalind Russell; *The Walls of
Jericho* (1948) as the unsuspecting husband of
Linda Darnell's Algeria for Twentieth Cen-
tury-Fox; *My Dear Secretary* (1949), a United
Artists release; and Twentieth Century-Fox's
A Letter to Three Wives (1949), in which he
played a likeable professor of English.

From these relatively obscure roles Kirk
Douglas was projected to stardom as the pugilist Midge Kelly in the *Champion* (1949), based
on Ring Lardner's short story and produced
on a low budget by Screen Plays, Inc., for a
United Artists release. In his portrayal of an

DOUGLAS, KIRK—*Continued*

ambitious and unscrupulous prize fighter, Douglas won wide critical praise for his "solid and credible" acting and in the opinion of Alton Cook of the New York *World-Telegram* proved himself one of Hollywood's "most accomplished actors, full of the charm of a leading man, a charm that can become an obvious veneer when he chooses, with a few slight gestures, to hint at the depths of a seething deviltry that lies just beneath." This production, which brought Douglas a nomination as the year's best actor by the Academy of Motion Picture Arts and Sciences, led to a lucrative seven-year contract with Warner Brothers for one film a year and the right to make outside engagements. To help publicize the film, he visited New York in the spring of 1949 for a number of radio and television appearances. For his performance in the *Champion* he was presented in February 1950 with an Award of Achievement by his fellow graduates of St. Lawrence University.

Douglas' first motion picture for Warner Brothers was *Young Man With a Horn*, filmed in 1949, the story of a jazz trumpet player. "Acting with communicable intensity," observed a New York *Times* critic, "Mr. Douglas makes a pathetic and interesting person out of the sensitive genius with consuming love for his trumpet." In *The Glass Menagerie*, another Warner Brothers production, starring Gertrude Lawrence and Jane Wyman, he was seen in the role of the Gentleman Caller. He next appeared in Warner Brothers' *Along the Great Divide* (1951) as a grim-faced marshal who enforces the letter of the law without concern for justice. "Just fair entertainment," was *Variety*'s judgment of the film itself.

For Paramount Pictures Douglas starred in Billy Wilder's production of *Ace in the Hole* (1951), giving, in the opinion of Bosley Crowther of the New York *Times*, a "superb" performance as a corrupt and cynical journalist. In Paramount's release of Sidney Kingley's melodrama, *Detective Story*, one of the most highly praised films of 1951, he played the role of the New York detective, James McLeod, who is destroyed through his inability to feel compassion toward wrongdoers. The *New Yorker* found Douglas "never before so convincing"; critics in general applauded his "forceful" and "intense" acting. Warner Brothers' *The Big Trees*, another 1951 motion picture starring Douglas, has been described as a "cliché-ridden" melodrama of lumbering in northern California, in which a grasping villain, played by Douglas, is reformed through his love of a member of a religious sect. *The Big Sky*, also filmed in 1951, presented him in a second outdoor-man role, that of a hard-fighting buckskin hero. Douglas, whose income is estimated at $300,000 a year, in 1951 obtained release from his contract with Warner Brothers: "I bought my contract out because I like to stay free," Erskine Johnson of the New York *World-Telegram* quoted him as saying. "I've never been happy tied to a contract." He plans soon to produce Ben Hecht's

melodrama, *The Shadow*, through his own unit, Byrna Productions.

An actor noted for the "solid" and realistic quality of his performances, Douglas prepares carefully for his roles. In order to look like a professional prize fighter in the *Champion*, the star, who had done no boxing before, trained for a number of months with Mushy Callahan, a retired fighter. For *Young Man With a Horn* he learned to handle the trumpet like a musician by taking lessons for three months from Harry James, who played the trumpet for the picture's sound track. Before the filming of *Ace in the Hole* he familiarized himself with newspaper surroundings by working as a reporter on the Los Angeles *Herald-Express*. In preparation for *Detective Story*, after studying police station routine in New York City, he acted for a week, in January 1951, in the stage version of the play at the Sombrero Playhouse in Phoenix, Arizona. While successful in a variety of roles, Douglas has become best known for his portrayal of a type of screen villain described by Gladwin Hill as "the neurotic heavy, the man with a baneful obsession—essentially weak or unsavory, but with such understandable motivation as to evoke a degree of sympathy." Douglas is said to be constantly in search of stories for filming which emphasize character interpretation and presentation.

Kirk Douglas and Diana Dill, whom the actor had met at the American Academy of Dramatic Arts, were married in 1943 and were divorced in 1951. They have two children, Michael and Joel. Of muscular build, Douglas stands six feet tall and weighs 175 pounds; his hair is light-brown and his eyes are green. Tennis and swimming keep him in trim.

References

Collier's 128:20 Jl 21 '51
Movie Time 1:19 Ja '52
N Y Post p13 My 22 '49
N Y Sun p19 Ja 27 '48
N Y Sunday News p7 O 24 '48

DOWLING, ROBERT W(HITTLE) Sept. 9, 1895- Business executive; organization official

Address: b. c/o City Investing Company, 25 Broad St., New York 4; h. 990 5th Ave., New York 21

Robert W. Dowling, president of the City Investing Company of New York since 1943 and a leader in that city's real estate field, has been associated with such apartment-structure developments as Parkchester, Stuyvesant Town, and Peter Cooper Village in the metropolis. Other of his interests are the City Playhouse Company, which operates several Manhattan theaters; the American National Theatre and Academy, of which he is chairman of the board; and the National Urban League, the country's oldest interracial service agency, of which he was elected president in 1952. Dowling also has a place in the annals of athletics, having been in 1915 the first swimmer to encircle Manhattan Island, a distance of thirty-five miles.

Born in New York City on September 9, 1895, Robert Whittle Dowling is the elder of the two sons of Robert Emmet Dowling (a builder and real estate man who founded the City Investing Company) and the former Minetta Linck. His childhood winters were spent in Manhattan and his summers at Spring Lake, New Jersey—he was taught to swim there by his father. Bob Dowling was enrolled at the age of seven at the Cutler Day School, New York City, where during the next eleven years he "applied himself feverishly to all sports" but was "never good at books" (*Architectural Forum*). When graduated at the age of eighteen he continued to attend the private school for an additional year, receiving special coaching preparatory to taking the College Entrance Board examinations. He also captained the hockey team.

At the same time he started part-time work with the real estate firm of Nassoit and Lanning, gaining practical experience in apartment house management. He also continued under his father the three years of aquatic training which culminated in his famous 35-mile swim around Manhattan Island on September 6, 1915. He was the first to accomplish this feat, which took thirteen hours, during the last four of which the elder Dowling swam beside his son. In the following year (1916) he was proclaimed American National Long Distance Swimming Champion.

When the United States entered World War I in 1917, Dowling enlisted in the Army. First assigned to the Columbia University Unit of the Balloon Training Corps, he was subsequently detached for special service with the Navy, for which he "made special diving studies, and suggested a plan for swimming into enemy harbors and planting bombs, an idea. . . put into effect by the Italian Navy a quarter of a century later" (New York *Herald Tribune*).

Almost twenty-four years old when demobilized in 1919, he gave up all further thought of college and, preferring not to lean on his father in building a career, took a job with the George A. Fuller Company. In this competing firm of contractors he was subsequently made manager of New York City's oldest skyscraper, the Flatiron Building. Later he joined the firm of Starrett Brothers and Ekin, Inc., which erected the Empire State Building; became a vice-president of the Starrett Corporation (1934); and was a member of the board of design for Parkchester, the Starrett-built modern housing development in the Bronx. Dowling also became connected with the United States Realty and Improvement Company and the New York Dock Company (of which he remains a board member) and in August 1942 was elected a director of the Home Title Guaranty Company. He became chairman of the realty committee of the Industrial Savings Bank in the January following.

Less than a month after the death of the senior Robert Dowling on March 16, 1943, his elder son was elected president of the City In-

ROBERT W. DOWLING

vesting Company. (He is also president and a director of the subsidiary R.E. Dowling Realty Corporation and of the Wall and Hanover Street Realty Company—he had been a director of the former since 1920 and vice-president since 1936.) About a month later Dowling was elected to the board of the City Bank Farmers Trust Company, then in the following February was made a director of R.H. Macy & Company, Inc., the department store enterprise; he also became a director of radio station WOR, then owned by a Macy affiliate.

Success of the Parkchester development, which he helped to design, had meanwhile convinced Dowling of the future of this type of residential development—groups of well-spaced, tall, elevator-equipped buildings in pleasant, landscaped grounds. He became housing and planning consultant for similar projects, Stuyvesant Town, Clinton Hill, Peter Cooper Village, and Fordham Hill, all within New York City limits. His enthusiasm for tall residential buildings, suitably isolated to give light and air, was expressed in a series of speeches, notably to the Mortgage Bankers Association of America in April 1944 and to the Real Estate Board of New York in January 1946. Dowling was elected president of the New York Citizens Budget Committee in November 1947 and chairman of the Manhattan Advisory Planning Board in January 1948. He is a director of the Regional Plan Association, the Commerce and Industry Association of New York, Inc., the Equitable Office Building Corporation, the Hilton Hotels Corporation, the Hotel Waldorf-Astoria, and the Fellows Medical Company, and a trustee of the Emigrant Industrial Savings Bank.

As head of City Investing Company, Dowling acquired a large piece of property on Broadway between 45th Street and 46th Street, on which he intended to replace the existing

DOWLING, ROBERT W.—*Continued*

theaters with a center including two theaters, a restaurant, and an office building. When it became necessary to postpone work on this project, Dowling found himself faced with the operation of a chain of theaters for an indefinite period. City Playhouses, Inc., was accordingly formed with Louis Lotito, a former theater treasurer, as president, and has since operated a number of theaters (at which "hit" plays have been presented) as well as several motion picture houses. For the uniform decoration scheme of silver-gray, the refurnishing of formerly "dismal" dressing rooms, and other improvements, Dowling himself was responsible, and for this became in March 1948 the recipient of the American Theatre Wing's Antoinette Perry Award for operating "progressive theaters." For a while also (stated Wambly Bald in the New York *Post*) he helped to finance the *Theatre Arts* magazine.

In November 1950 Dowling accepted the chairmanship of a fund-raising committee for the American National Theater and Academy and the following year, on October 22, 1951, was elected chairman of the board of ANTA. This organization, chartered by Congress in 1935, resulted from a Senate bill permitting the establishment of a nation-wide, tax-free institution which, as provided in the preamble, would be "a people's project organized and conducted in their interests, free from commercialism, but with the firm intent of being as far as possible self-supporting." Not Federally supported, ANTA largely depends upon voluntary contributions for its funds. It established the Experimental Theater in New York, assisted in forming the Dallas Theater '47 in Texas, sponsored, among other groups, two regional repertory companies and a touring company of the Virginia State Theater (the Barter Theater), and planned a Post-Graduate Theater Academy. Among its services ANTA circulates new plays to regional theaters and seeks for them directors, actors, and technicians. Recent ANTA projects include the production of five plays during the 1951-52 season (one being the notably successful *Mrs. McThing*, by Mary Coyle Chase) and the continuation and extension of a national information service conducted by George Freedly, head of the New York Public Library Theater Collection and secretary of ANTA, for the benefit of country-wide community theater movements.

For many years Dowling has been interested in the work of the National Urban League, an organization founded in 1910 for the chief purpose of "achieving equal economic opportunity for Negroes in all fields of endeavor," and now the country's oldest interracial service agency with sixty affiliates in thirty States. Lester B. Granger is executive director of the league, on behalf of which Dowling undertook the national chairmanship of the fund-raising campaign of 1948. He was elected sixth president of the league on May 15, 1952, succeeding Lloyd K. Garrison. Dowling is also active in the National Conference of Christians and Jews and is a director of the Boy Scouts of America.

Dowling has been honored by the Glass Institute with a medal for inventing an all-glass door. His clubs are the Knickerbocker, Racquet and Tennis, Luncheon, and New York Athletic; his political party is the Democratic. He is a trustee of St. John's Guild.

He has been married twice, first to Ethel Robertson in June 1920. This union ended in divorce in 1931, and on January 5, 1934, Mrs. Alice Bevier Hall became Mrs. Dowling; their daughter is named Ruth Alice. The blue-eyed executive, who stands six feet one inch tall, keeps trim by daily exercise and is still a strong swimmer. His favorite reading is Irish poetry.

References

Arch Forum 84:96-9 Ja '46 por
N Y Herald Tribune p23 Je 28 '50 por; p24 Mr 2 '51 por
N Y Post p23 My 3 '48 por
N Y Times II p3 Mr 11 '51
New Yorker 22:16 Jl 13 '46

Business Executives of America (1950)
Poor's Register of Directors and Executives (1952)
Who's Who in America, 1952-53

DOWNS, ROBERT B(INGHAM) May 25, 1903- Librarian; library association official

Address: b. c/o University of Illinois Library, Urbana, Ill.; h. 708 W. Pennsylvania Ave., Urbana, Ill.

NOTE: This biography supersedes the article which appeared in *Current Biography* in 1941.

As first vice-president and president-elect of the American Library Association during 1951-52, Robert B. Downs will automatically assume the presidency of the association for the 1952-53 term at the close of its seventy-sixth annual conference in New York City in July 1952. A member of the A.L.A. since 1929, he has served on its council and has been chairman of a number of its committees and boards. In the course of his career in librarianship Downs has headed the Colby College Library (1929-31), the University of North Carolina Library (1932-38), and the libraries of New York University (1938-43). Since 1943 he has been director of the library and library school, as well as professor of library science, at the University of Illinois.

Born in Lenoir, North Carolina, on May 25, 1903, Robert Bingham Downs is one of the eight children of John McLeod and Clara Catherine (Hartley) Downs. His forebears, of Scotch-Irish and English descent, have lived in North Carolina for many generations. His father was at various times a farmer, school-teacher, postmaster, country storekeeper, and a member of the State Legislature. After his graduation from the Trinity (North Carolina) High School in 1922, young Downs entered the University of North Carolina to specialize in history. There his sports were basketball and tennis. During his youth, Downs has told, he worked on the farm and as a steamfitter's assistant, telephone repairman, ranch hand, and fire ranger.

As a student assistant in the university library for four years he had his first practice in his chosen field. He has stated that his early use of school and public libraries interested him in books and libraries, while in his decision to make librarianship a career he was particularly influenced by Louis Round Wilson, who from 1901 to 1932 was the university's librarian. Receiving his B.A. degree from North Carolina in 1926, Downs continued his studies at the Columbia University School of Library Service, which granted him a B.S. degree in library science in 1927, and an M.Sc. degree two years later. His master's thesis was "A Study of the Reserve Book Problem in College Libraries." In the meantime he worked as a student assistant in the Columbia University Library (1926-27) and as a reference assistant in the New York Public Library (1927-29).

In 1929 Downs was appointed librarian and assistant professor of bibliography at Colby College, in Waterville, Maine. He remained there until 1931, when the University of North Carolina called him back to serve as assistant librarian and associate professor of library science. After Dr. Wilson, the university librarian, was appointed director of the University of Chicago Graduate Library School in 1932, Downs became acting librarian at North Carolina, and a year later librarian of the university and professor of library science. Under his direction strong collections in such fields as Negro history and State documents were built up; passage of a law requiring deposit of twenty-five copies of all State documents in the university library was obtained; and a system of extensive duplicate exchange was developed. He was also concerned with library service to undergraduate students, and the present general college library was created while he was university librarian. Along with his administrative work, he conducted courses in reference, bibliography, and the history of books and libraries in the School of Library Science, and he was chairman of the administrative board of the library and library school for several years. He participated in preparing and implementing a program of cooperation between the University of North Carolina and Duke University in collecting research materials and in instituting other phases of library service. He served as chairman of the committee on intellectual cooperation, which was composed of faculty representatives of these two neighboring universities.

It was announced on March 16, 1938, that Downs had been appointed to succeed Paul North Rice as director of the libraries at New York University. This post had been created three years earlier to integrate the university's library system, which consisted of seven separate libraries so located in the city as to serve the several centers at which the university maintained courses. During Downs's incumbency the machinery for centralized purchasing and cataloging was perfected and the plan expanded so as to increase the efficiency and economy of library operation. Closely related to this cen-

ROBERT B. DOWNS

tralized routine was the maintenance of a union catalogue at the administrative center of the university, covering all library holdings not under the jurisdiction of the Washington Square Library. In the winter of 1942-43 a physical reorganization of stacks, reading rooms, and service desks was effected at the Washington Square Library; throughout this operation, which involved about 100,000 volumes, all books were made available to students and faculty members.

On September 1, 1943, Downs became director of the University of Illinois Library and Library School and a professor of library science there, succeeding Carl M. White. Founded at the Armour Institute of Technology in Chicago in September 1893, the school was moved in 1897 to the University of Illinois in Urbana. Under the guidance of Downs a new curriculum was instituted at the library school in September 1948, offering a full program of undergraduate and graduate courses to students preparing for professional librarianship in all types of libraries. The program emphasized the library as a teaching instrument; the opportunity for graduate study at the doctoral level; research projects employing the Urbana Free Library as a laboratory for the study of professional problems; an extensive publications program; special attention to the provision of financial assistance to students interested in preparing for public library work; and plans to develop the area of work in preparation for public librarianship. The University of Illinois Library has more than 2,400,000 volumes in the main and departmental libraries on the Urbana-Champaign campus, 95,000 volumes on the campus of the Chicago professional colleges, and 60,000 volumes in the undergraduate division in Chicago. With Downs's assistance, a reorganization of the library's staff took place in 1944. As a result, the professional staff of librarians,

DOWNS, ROBERT B.—*Continued*
who had formerly been classified in the university civil service, were given full recognition as an integral part of the academic group.

Since he first joined the American Library Association in 1929, Downs has served as a council member (1940-45); chairman of the subcommittee for the South of the association's committee on resources of American libraries (1934-36); chairman of the board on resources of American libraries (1939-42, 1945-50); a member of the advisory board for the study of special projects; and after 1950 as chairman of the advisory committee on the Japan Library School. During 1940-41 he was chairman of the joint committee on library research facilities for national defense, which had been created by the Library of Congress, the library division of the United States Office of Education, the Special Libraries Association, and the A.L.A. to prepare a guide to the holdings of American libraries on subjects of urgent importance to national defense. He has also been chairman of the joint committee of the Association of Research Libraries and the A.L.A. for the development of the national Union Catalog in the Library of Congress, and from 1946 to 1948 chairman of a joint committee on cooperative acquisition of wartime publications. Elected first vice-president (president-elect) of the A.L.A. for 1951-52, he was installed at the association's seventy-fifth anniversary conference in Chicago on July 13, 1951. He will automatically assume the presidency of the A.L.A. for the 1952-53 term, succeeding Mrs. Loleta D. Fyan, at the close of the annual conference to be held in New York City from June 29 to July 5, 1952.

As special consultant to the Civil Information and Education Section of the General Headquarters of the Supreme Commander for the Allied Powers in Tokyo, Downs visited Japan in the summer of 1948 to assist in the organization of the newly founded National Diet Library. He returned to that country two years later to survey possibilities of establishing the Japan Library School, financed by the Department of the Army and administered and supervised by the A.L.A. In 1949 he served as visiting chief of the Union Catalog Division and consultant in bibliography to the Library of Congress. He has also been a member of the State Department's Committee on Books Abroad, and of the library advisory board of Air University at Maxwell Air Force Base in Alabama. The third president of the Association of College and Reference Libraries (1940-41), he has since 1948 been director of its university libraries section and a member of the editorial staff of that association's publication, *College and Research Libraries.* He was chairman of the college and university section of the New York Library Association (1939-40), and after 1946 has been chairman of the certification board of the Illinois Library Association. Other organizations in which Downs holds membership are the Bibliographical Society of America and Phi Kappa Phi.

A contributor of more than sixty articles (as of 1952) to library and educational periodicals, Downs is best known for his works surveying the resources of libraries for study and research. Most of these surveys were compiled and published under the auspices of the A.L.A. After collaborating with Louis R. Wilson on *Special Collections for the Study of History and Literature in the Southeast* (1934), he edited *Resources of Southern Libraries* (1938), which one critic described as "the first comprehensive survey of the materials for research to be found in any region of the United States." This was followed by *Guide for the Description and Evaluation of Research Materials* (1939) and *Library Specialization* (1941), both of which he edited for the A.L.A. Also sponsored by the association was *Union Catalogs in the United States*, which he edited in 1942; the reviewer for the *Library Association Record* called this study "undoubtedly the most comprehensive work on union catalogues yet produced, or likely to be produced for some time." That same year appeared *Resources of New York City Libraries*; of it observed Wayne Shirley in the *Papers of the Bibliographical Society of America*: "Scholars are much endebted to Mr. Downs for this careful and comprehensive work." In 1951 Downs published *American Library Resources*, which, in the opinion of a *Library Journal* reviewer, "provided the scholarly world with an invaluable practical bibliography of published accounts of the resources of American libraries." Downs has assisted in surveys of the library building situation at Louisiana State University, and of opportunities for library cooperation in the Richmond, Virginia, area (both in 1947), and of the libraries of Cornell University (1948). He is the author of the pamphlets *The Story of Books* (1935) and *American Humorous Folklore* (1950) and, in collaboration with his wife, of *American Humor* (1938).

An honorary Litt. D. degree was bestowed upon the library association official by Colby College in 1944 and an honorary LL.D. degree by the University of North Carolina in 1949. During the academic year 1942-43 he taught as an associate at the Columbia University School of Library Service. In Urbana he belongs to the Rotary and Country clubs. On August 17, 1929, he married Elizabeth Crooks, who had graduated from the Columbia Library School in 1927. They have two daughters, Clara Breckenridge and Mary Roberta. The librarian, who stands six feet two inches tall and weighs 195 pounds, has hazel eyes and auburn hair. His political party is the Democratic. He collects examples of American folklore and humor, enjoys travel and symphonic music, plays golf.

References

    A.L.A. Bul 45:251 Jl-Ag '51 por
    Col and Research Lib 4:312-14 S '43 por
    Ill Lib 25:333 O '43 por
    Library J 68:678 S 1 '43 por
    Library Q 10:264 Ap '40
    Library Service N 7:25 Ap '38
    Sci Mo 62:111 Je '46 por

Directory of American Scholars (1945)
Leaders in Education (1948)
Who's Who in America, 1952-53
Who's Who in Library Service (1943)
Who's Who in the Midwest (1952)
World Biography (1948)

DRAPER, WILLIAM H(ENRY), JR.

Aug. 10, 1894- United States Government official; investment banker

Address: b. United States Special Representative in Europe, 2 Rue St. Florentin, Paris, France; c/o Dillon, Read & Company, 48 Wall St., New York 5

William H. Draper, Jr., the new American Special Representative in Europe, was appointed to that ambassadorial post under the Mutual Security Act in January 1952. Except for eighteen months, since 1940 he served as a member of the War Department General Staff, as a regimental commander in the Pacific, Military Government Economic Adviser in Germany, Under Secretary of the Army, trustee of the Long Island Rail Road, and chairman of the Long Island Transit Authority. Apart from his public life Draper is an investment banker. Ambassador Draper assumed additional duties in Europe in April 1952 when he was named United States Permanent Representative to the North Atlantic Treaty Organization Council.

William Henry Draper, Jr., was born in New York City on August 10, 1894, the son of a dentist, William Henry Draper, and the former Mary Emma Carey. Following his graduation from Yonkers High School, he enrolled at New York University, from which he received the degree of Bachelor of Arts, with a major in economics, in 1916. The next year he earned his master's degree at the same institution. At college Draper was active in sports and in literary and dramatic groups. He was commissioned a second lieutenant in the infantry in May 1917 and served during World War I for a year and a half in New York State, first as an instructor in the officers' training camps at Plattsburg and later as a group commander at Camp Upton. By the time he was demobilized in December 1918, he had risen to the rank of major. (Draper remained a reserve officer, as chief of staff of the 77th Division, Organized Reserve Corps, from 1936 to 1940.)

After his discharge from the army Draper in 1919 entered the banking business in the bookkeeping department of the National City Bank of New York City, to remain there for several years. His next position, from 1923 to 1927, was with the Bankers' Trust Company as assistant treasurer. Since 1927 he has been associated with the investment banking firm of Dillon, Read & Company, becoming treasurer first and, in 1937, vice-president.

Nineteen months before the United States entered World War II Draper was recalled for service, to the War Department General Staff with the rank of colonel. He was assigned in 1940 to the President's Advisory Committee on Selective Service; and in the Office of the Chief of the Morale Branch he

Wide World Photos
WILLIAM H. DRAPER, JR.

headed the Welfare and Recreation Division and later, in 1941, became assistant chief of the Morale Branch. After the Japanese attack on Pearl Harbor, Draper, who was then sent for training to the Infantry School at Fort Benning, Georgia, commanded the 136th Infantry Regiment of the 33d Infantry Division. In July 1943 he accompanied the regiment to Hawaii; about nine months later (March 1944) he was recalled to Washington to take charge of terminating and settling war contracts.

With the end of hostilities in Europe, in May 1945 Draper (a brigadier general since January) was sent to Germany as head of the Economics Division of the United States Group Council (later the American Military Government). In that capacity he was charged with the supervision of German industry and agriculture, covering decartelization, trade and commerce, price control, reparations, and the restitution of assets removed from invaded countries by the German armies. He was also the American member of the Four-Power Economics Directorate in Germany.

Among the problems which faced Draper was the revitalization of German economic life and the liquidation of its war potential. Under the Potsdam Agreement, such industries as munitions, aircraft, and shipbuilding were forbidden in the conquered country, where the Four-Power Allied Control Council later banned the manufacture of a number of other products, among them synthetic gasoline, rubber, primary aluminum and magnesium, heavy farm tractors, and heavy machine tools. Draper believed German economy could not be restored on the basis of agriculture and light industry alone—that under strict Allied supervision the Germans might be permitted to manufacture items not in the "non-belligerent" classification, such as steel, precision instruments, and optical

DRAPER, WILLIAM H., JR.—*Continued*

goods, without the danger of rejuvenating the German war machine. The eventual renewal of a controlled heavy industry, particularly the increasing quota of steel production, was often referred to as the "Draper Plan."

Draper was also concerned with the continuing economic partition of Germany. In an American Military Government pamphlet published in December 1946, the General said, "Without free trade with other parts of Germany, and without a common export program, the United States zone cannot pay its own way." Accordingly he asked that the section of the Potsdam Agreement which called for the treatment of occupied Germany as an economic whole be put into effect or that the entire agreement be revised.

In March 1947 Draper was named Economic Adviser to General Lucius D. Clay and promoted to the rank of major general. At the meeting of the Council of Foreign Ministers in Moscow that same month, he served as Military Government adviser to Secretary of State George C. Marshall. The British-American Conference on Ruhr Coal Production, held in Washington, D.C., in August 1947, was Draper's last duty as a Military Government official. On August 29 he was appointed Under Secretary of War, becoming Under Secretary of the Army the following month, when the War and Navy Departments were unified under Secretary of Defense James Forrestal.

In his new post Draper was concerned with occupation policies in Japan as well as in Germany. Shortly after his appointment he flew to Japan to acquaint himself with the situation there, and in March 1948 he headed an economic mission of American Government officials and industrialists to the Far East. In Japan, as in Germany, American policy had gradually changed from an emphasis on breaking up war industry and monopolies to an attempt to rebuild the country toward self-sufficiency. The Far Eastern Command's economic policies, however, were still guided by the directive which called for a complete removal of monopolies and a purge of other Japanese business. After his return from his visit to Japan, *Newsweek* reported that Draper had expressed the fear that this policy could only end in making Japan permanently dependent on the United States. The directive was later withdrawn. He also favored rebuilding the Japanese merchant marine, 80 per cent of which had been destroyed during the war, and suggested a more lenient reparations policy. In February 1949 Draper resigned his post to return to his banking interests.

In January 1950, six months after he had resumed his vice-presidency in Dillon, Read & Company, Draper made his third trip to Japan to study business conditions and the prospects for American investments. "The time is approaching," he said in an address before the Foreign Policy Association after his return, "to recognize formally that we are at peace with Japan and to turn more and more responsibility over to her government."

Draper obtained a leave of absence from Dillon and Read again, in December 1950, to assume the trusteeship of the bankrupt Long Island Rail Road. Following a Thanksgiving Eve wreck in which seventy-eight persons were killed, the road's two trustees resigned, and Draper's appointment came in response to a demand for a single trustee. (Shortly after his appointment, the financier moved from Scarsdale, New York, to his present home on Long Island in order to become a commuter on the railroad.) On June 30, 1951, he was named chairman of the Long Island Transit Authority by Governor Thomas E. Dewey of New York, and four months later he resigned as trustee of the railroad to avoid any conflict between the two positions. In commenting on his resignation, the New York *Times* noted that he had "restored a considerable measure of public confidence in the Long Island. The road is safer; its financial base, in some respects at least, is sounder." Draper's initial efforts were directed toward trying to reorganize the road as a private enterprise, but in December 1951 he recommended public ownership and private operation as the only workable solution.

President Truman named Draper as Special Representative in Europe on January 14, 1952, to coordinate all American military, political, and economic policies there. In this assignment, according to *Time*, he has the duties and responsibilities both of the top United States civilian official in the North Atlantic Treaty Organization and of the administrator in Europe of the Mutual Security Agency. While Draper will not make American policy in Europe, his recommendations are expected to help shape over-all European defense policies.

Draper has been awarded the Legion of Merit by both the Army and the Navy, the Selective Service Medal, the Distinguished Service Medal, and the Order of Orange and Nassau by the Netherlands. He also holds honorary doctorates of law from New York University, Duke University, and the University of Louisville. A member of the American Legion, Draper was commander of the Westchester County Post in 1933-34. During the 1950 fund drives of the American Red Cross, he served as chairman for the Bronx and Queens.

By his first marriage, to Katharine Louise Baum, on September 7, 1918, Draper has three children: Mrs. Phillips Hawkins, Katharine Louise Draper, and Lieutenant William H. Draper 3d, who in 1952 is serving with the Ninth Army Corps in Korea. Seven years after the death of his first wife, Draper on March 12, 1949, married Eunice Barzynski, the daughter of a retired West Point General and a former WAC captain. Draper is described by Sidney Fields in the New York *Mirror* as "tall, black-browed . . . with a smile that is honestly engaging." He is a Republican and a Presbyterian, and a member of the Bond, Recess, and Downtown Athletic clubs in New York City, the Army and Navy Club in Washington, and the Pacific-Union Club in San Francisco. An amateur magician since his college days, Draper is also a member of the American Society of Amateur Magicians.

References

N Y Herald Tribune p1 Ja 15 '52 por;
    II p1 Ja 20 '52 por
N Y Mirror p33 F 3 '52 por
N Y News p36 D 17 '50 por
N Y Times p1 Ja 15 '52 por
Time 59:4 Ja 28 '52 por
Who's Who in America, 1950-51
Who's Who in Commerce and Industry
    (1951)
Who's Who in the East (1951)

DUBOS, RENÉ J(ULES) (dü-bôs' rẽ-nā' zhül) Feb. 20, 1901- Bacteriologist

Address: b. c/o Rockefeller Institute for Medical Research, 66th St. & York Ave., New York 21; h. Old Albany Post Road, Garrison, N.Y.

René J. Dubos, a specialist in microbiology and experimental medicine and a member of the Rockefeller Institute for Medical Research, is internationally known for his discovery of tyrothricin, a powerful drug extracted from soil microbes which is effective in the destruction of certain types of pneumococci, and for his discovery of a new technique for the cultivation of the tuberculosis bacillus. A pioneer in the development of antibiotic drugs, Dubos also contributed to the development of penicillin and the discovery of streptomycin.

René Jules Dubos was born on February 20, 1901, the son of Georges Alexandre and Adeline Madeleine (de Bloedt) Dubos. A native of Saint Brice, Seine et Oise, France, he lived in France until his twenty-first year. His high school education was acquired in Paris at the College Chaptal, from which he was graduated in 1919. Later in the same year he entered the Institut National Agronomique, Paris, where he specialized in science and in 1921 was granted his B.S. degree. In 1922 he went to Italy to take the position of assistant editor on the staff at the International Institute of Agriculture in Rome.

Leaving Rome in 1924, Dubos came to the United States to attend Rutgers University in New Jersey. While employed as an instructor in bacteriology and research assistant in soil microbiology at the New Jersey Experimental Station of Rutgers University, he studied for the Ph.D. degree, which he received in 1927. At Rutgers he took care of the children of college professors for extra money and has since styled himself "the original baby-sitter." Upon completion of his university work, Dubos became associated with the Department of Pathology and Bacteriology of the Rockefeller Institute for Medical Research in New York City, where he held the successive positions of fellow (1927-28), assistant (1928-30), associate (1930-38), and associate member (1938-41). He has been a member since 1941, except for two years' absence (1942-44) during which he held the positions of George Fabyan Professor of Comparative Pathology and Professor of Tropical Medicine at the Harvard Medical School. As a specialist in microbiology at the Rockefeller Institute, he made a report on August 30, 1938, to the Society of American Bacteriologists meeting in San Francisco on his progress in developing a type of antipneumonia vaccine from a relatively harmless variety of the pneumonia microbe which produced immunity in rabbits against the deadly variety.

The following year came the discovery that was to win him renown. In July of 1939 he reported in the *Proceedings of the Society for Experimental Biology and Medicine* the extraction of a substance from soil bacteria which destroys all streptococci of the gram-positive family (so named because of its ability to retain a type of methylene blue-staining dye developed by Christian Gram). On September 8, 1939, he delivered an oral account of the same discovery before the closing sessions of the third International Congress for Microbiology meeting at the Waldorf-Astoria hotel in New York. For his work in unearthing the new agent he was designated in the following year by the American College of Physicians as the 1940 recipient of its John Phillips Memorial Award, "North America's highest award in internal medicine." The award was announced on March 28 and the medal presented at the annual convocation of the college on April 3, 1940.

Dubos was led to his discovery of the new drug, subsequently named tyrothricin, by experimenting along lines that had been known but little investigated since Louis Pasteur in 1877 had reported that certain soil-dwelling bacteria could destroy the anthrax germ and suggested that such knowledge might be applied to the treatment of human beings. The observation that the soil destroys the germs that destroy men, infected corpses being free of disease within a short while after burial, influenced Dubos to experiment with a small amount of earth taken from the yard of the Rockefeller Institute. Having filled three tumblers with soil and watered them daily with cultures of pneumonia bacteria, streptococci, and staphylococci, he found that after many months a pinch of soil from the tumblers dropped into a test tube containing milky cultures of pneumococci rapidly destroyed the bacteria, leaving the tube clear. Microbes in the soil had been devouring the germs harmful to man and in the process had produced tyrothricin.

Further investigation revealed that tyrothricin was composed of two chemicals, as Dubos reported on March 21, 1940, in the sixth Harvey lecture delivered before the Harvey Society and the New York Academy of Medicine. One of these chemicals, tyrocidin, proved to be of little effect in germ destruction, but gramacidin was found to be deadly to five kinds of pneumococci, as well as to streptococcus, the diphtheria bacillus, staphylococcus, and possibly the tuberculosis bacillus. Experimentation on animals, however, brought disappointment, for the chemical was found to be also destructive of red blood corpuscles and therefore unfit for internal use. Nevertheless its use on non-bleeding external infections is promising, since it has proved effective in the treatment of ulcers, carbuncles, and boils. It has also been helpful when used to treat empyema (an infection of the chest cavity), certain bladder infections, sinusitis, mastoids, actinomycosis (a frequently

Maria Martel

RENÉ J. DUBOS

fatal infection of the jaw), and osteomyellitis (inflammation of the spongy material inside the jawbone). The dairy industry, too, has found the new drug beneficial in treating streptococcus mastitis, an inflammation of the udder of cattle that affects the quality and quantity of milk production.

It was on this new principle in chemotherapy (the treatment of diseases by directly destroying their bacteria) established by Dubos that important advances in penicillin and the discovery of streptomycin were to be made. In 1940, following the precedent set by Dubos the year before, Dr. Martin H. Dawson first proved that the drug penicillin was nontoxic and then undertook a series of experiments to determine the extent of its curative powers. Five years later Dr. Selman A. Waksman, director of Rutgers University Institute of Microbiology, working along lines established by his former pupil Dubos, extracted the drug streptomycin from microbes in the soil. Shortly after the development of tyrothricin Dubos turned his attention to tuberculosis research. In June of 1946 he reported the discovery of a new method of cultivating tuberculosis bacilli to a joint convention of the National Tuberculosis Association, the American Trudeau Society, and the National Conference of Tuberculosis Secretaries then meeting in Buffalo, New York. The same discovery he subsequently described to the Society of American Bacteriologists meeting in Philadelphia on May 14, 1947, and to the International Congress for Experimental Cytology in Stockholm, July 11, 1947. For this work he received the Trudeau Medal of the National Tuberculosis Association on May 16, 1951, at the association's forty-seventh annual meeting in Cincinnati, Ohio. The medal,

established in 1926, has been awarded annually ever since for "the most meritorious contributions on the cause, prevention, or treatment of tuberculosis."

What Dubos had discovered was a technique whereby tuberculosis bacilli could be grown in quantities and with a rapidity hitherto impossible to achieve. Through the introduction into the culture medium of a detergent, "Tween 80," used by the Atlas Powder Company in the manufacture of cosmetics, he was able to penetrate the water-resistant fatty outer layer of the bacilli, thereby promoting their growth. Serum albumin was further added to the medium to remove growth-inhibiting substances produced by the bacilli themselves. Dubos' achievement thus made possible closer observation of tuberculosis bacilli which led to the discovery that there are two distinct types involved differing in their cell structure, one of which is virulent and the other nonvirulent. The ability to study the differences between the two types in order to determine the factor or factors producing virulence is a necessary step in the search for agents to counteract the disease. Under the auspices of the Sigma Xi Research Society, Dubos in April 1948 gave a series of lectures on tuberculosis at twelve colleges in the United States. Special studies made by the bacteriologist, aside from those mentioned, have concerned cellulose decomposition by aerobic bacteria; use of specific bacterial enzymes in biochemistry; antibacterial agents of biological origin; and bacillary dysentery.

Dubos, who in 1946 was editor of the *Journal of Experimental Medicine,* has written technical articles for such periodicals as *Science,* the *National Academy of Sciences of the United States of America Proceedings,* and the *American Philosophical Society Proceedings.* He has also contributed chapters to the volumes *New Worlds in Medicine* (1946), *Medicine in the Postwar World* (1948), and *Science in Progress* (1949). He is also the author of four books, *The Bacterial Cell in its Relation to Problems of Virulence, Immunity, and Chemotherapy* (1945), *Bacterial and Mycotic Infections of Man* (1948), *Louis Pasteur, Free Lance of Science* (1950), and *The White Plague—Tuberculosis, Man and Society* (to be published). Early in April 1952 Dubos was consulted by the New York *Times* on the authenticity of photographs published in the Peiping *People's Daily* of March 15, 1952, in support of the Chinese Communists' accusations that the United States was using germ warfare in Korea. After examining the photographs of what were supposedly meningitis and gangrene germs, Dubos concluded they were fakes, photographs of entirely harmless bacteria, or meaningless blotches.

In recognition of his scientific achievement Dubos has received honorary Sc.D. degrees from Rochester University (1941), Harvard University (1942), Rutgers University (1949), and the University of Paris (1950); and the M.D. from the University of Liege in Belgium (1947). Aside from awards previously mentioned he was the recipient of the Mead Johnson Award (American Academy of Pediatrics) in 1940, the Lasker Award in Public Health

(American Public Health Association) in 1948, and the American Pharmaceutical Award in 1952.

René J. Dubos is a member of the National Academy of Sciences, and since 1951 has been president of the Harvey Society of New York and president-elect of the Society of American Bacteriologists. He was chosen a trustee of Science Service, an institution for the popularization of science, on May 16, 1949, and in August 1951, a trustee of the foundation endowed by Selman A. Waksman to encourage the study of microbiology throughout the world. A naturalized citizen since 1938, he aided the American war effort as a civilian in the Office of Scientific Research and Development. In March 1934 Dubos was married to Marie Louise Bonnet, who died in 1942. Since October 16, 1946, he has been married to Letha Jean Porter, a former bacteriological laboratory technician.

References

American Men of Science (1949)
Who's Who in America, 1952-53

BERNARD C. DUFFY

DUFFY, BERNARD C(ORNELIUS) Jan. 21, 1902- Advertising executive
Address: b. c/o Batten, Barton, Durstine & Osborn, Inc., 383 Madison Ave., New York 17; h. Park Dr. N., Rye, New York

For more than three decades Bernard C. ("Ben") Duffy, president since 1946 of Batten, Barton, Durstine & Osborn, Inc., has worked in advertising, successively as office boy, space buyer, media director, manager, and chief executive. Specializing in media and thus, by the end of 1951, responsible for expending the more than $100 millions clients paid for advertising in that year, he has contributed substantially to the growth of his agency, which in 1950 became the second largest advertising agency in the United States. Ben Duffy is the author of a standard work on advertising media and markets and is a director of the Audit Bureau of Circulations, as well as chairman of the media relations committee of the American Association of Advertising Agencies.

Born in New York City on January 21, 1902, to Irish immigrants from Ulster, Bernard Cornelius Duffy is the son of Bernard and Margaret (Connelly) Duffy. (He is generally known as Ben Duffy—he signs his baptismal names when formal usage so requires.) The Duffy family lived in what was called "Hell's Kitchen," on the city's West Side, where he attended Catholic parochial schools. Before completing his secondary education he left Regis High School in order to work as a messenger for the Arbuckle Coffee Company. Even as an adolescent he became interested in the field of advertising and greatly admired Bruce Barton, a prominent pioneer in the industry. His younger brother, John, had a job as office boy with the advertising agency of Barton, Durstine & Osborn. In response to an inquiry from John's supervisor as to whether there were any other employable boys in the Duffy family, Bernard presented himself and was given a similar job.

When he joined the agency Duffy thought of becoming a commercial artist, but gradually his interests centered on the media aspects of advertising. For his first three years he was successively office boy, shipping clerk, and checker. He spent his spare time learning as much as he could about the business until in 1920 he was promoted to the media department as a space buyer. (The media department selects the publications in which advertisements are placed.) Five years later he was chosen to head the department and in 1928, when the agency merged with the George Batten Company, Duffy continued to direct it. As the number of the agency's accounts increased, Duffy's responsibilities enlarged. In 1935 he became vice-president in charge of media, marketing, and merchandising. In 1938 he became a director of the organization, in 1943 executive vice-president in charge of six Eastern offices and two years later general manager of all operations. The advertising man was named president of Batten, Barton, Durstine & Osborn, Inc., in February 1946.

As chief executive for the second largest advertising agency in the United States (the J. Walter Thompson agency with total billings of $121 millions is rated as the first), Duffy heads an organization that originated in 1891 with the founding of the George Batten Company. In 1919 Barton, Durstine & Osborn was formed, and in 1928 the present organization was incorporated as the result of the merger of the two firms. Known for a number of years as primarily an institutional agency, B.B.D.O., as it is most commonly called, in 1939 instituted a number of organizational changes. As a result, the amount of its advertising billings for the following year increased 16 per cent, and in the course of the decade 1941-51 new advertising accounts brought the

DUFFY, BERNARD C.—*Continued*
gross billings for 1951 to more than $100
millions, of which the usual 15 per cent commission represented the agency's revenue.

In its eleven offices, located in major cities
of the United States and staffed by more than
1,150 employees, B.B.D.O. handles advertising
for some 130 clients—producers and distributors of such diverse commodities and services
as automobiles, safety razors, men's clothing,
blankets, clocks, cigarettes, cranberries, binocu-
lars, and steamship transportation. Its radio
department is twenty-three years old, and the
money its clients spend for television shows is
thought to be the greatest handled by any
agency. According to a detailed report in *Advertising Age* for June 19, 1950, the agency's
"spectacular rise" is the result of high employee loyalty and morale (it has a stock-
purchase plan for employees), efficient organization, thorough training of account executives,
research in media, marketing, and merchandising, and pioneer work in copy testing.

While frequently working as part of a group
to secure clients for B.B.D.O., Duffy is personally responsible for acquiring a number of
outstanding accounts. One involved the annual
expenditure by General Motors of $800,000 for
three years for copy in small-town newspapers;
another was a major campaign by the Crowell-
Collier Publishing Company during the early
years of the depression; and a third, in 1948,
resulted in the acquisition of the $12 millions
account of the American Tobacco Company for
advertising Lucky Strike cigarettes. This last-
named transaction was closed by Duffy after a
one-and-a-half-hour conference with the president of the company at which Duffy presented
a complete factual report on the client's product
and the agency's facilities and proposed programs. Heavy emphasis on all aspects of a
client's business and a scientific understanding
of media are characteristics of Duffy's executive policy. According to *Time* magazine, he
expects the members of his staff to know all
pertinent information on a client's business and
has himself been called a "storehouse of facts."

This same interest in facts showed itself in
1933 when, with H. W. H. Powel, Duffy compiled headlines in American newspapers appearing from February 14 to May 23, 1933, and
had them published in a book entitled *The
World's Greatest 99 Days*. The *Review of
Reviews* found that this "judicious clipping of
the nation's press results in a lively record of
events . . . starting with the Michigan bank
holiday . . . and ending on a happier note three
months later." The year 1939 saw the publication of his second book, *Advertising Media and
Markets*, a volume that was issued in a revised
and expanded form in 1951 under the title
*Profitable Advertising in Today's Media and
Markets*. An account of each step involved in
the selection and most effective use of the
various media, Duffy's book is used in over
twenty-five colleges and universities as a text
for courses in advertising. *Advertising Agency*
wrote of the 1951 edition: "Since its original
publication . . . no other book in this general
field has appeared to challenge its top position";
the *Journal of Marketing* described it as a

"straightforward and unbiased presentation";
and *Western Advertising* felt there was "a
finality and rightness in each stage of the exposition." In a lengthy article for *Business
Week* (June 11, 1949) on the use of television
for advertisers, Duffy discussed costs, coverage, competition, and potentialities of the new
medium.

Duffy is a member of the board of directors
of the Audit Bureau of Circulations, chairman
of the advisory committee on advertising of
the Proprietary Association of America, direc-
tor-at-large of the American Association of
Advertising Agencies, and has served as chairman of the board of governors of the Cooperative Analysis of Broadcasting. A Catholic, he is vice-chairman of the advertising committee of the Cardinal's Committee of the
Laity (for Catholic charities); a member of
the advisory council for the College of Commerce of the University of Notre Dame and
chairman of the Greater New York Chapter of
the president's committee of that institution;
and he belongs to the Friendly Sons of St.
Patrick and is a Knight of Malta. Another
membership of his is in the George Burton
Hotchkiss Chapter of Alpha Delta Sigma. In
his political allegiance he is a Republican. His
clubs are the Westchester Country, the Manhattan, and the New York Athletic.

The "lean, dapper" advertising executive has
the reputation for being "plain-talking, unassuming" and gregarious. With his wife, the
former Marion Edna Brutton, whom he married on April 26, 1930, and their two children,
David Edward and Miriam Margaret, Duffy
lives in a home on the Westchester Country
Club grounds. He is a bridge player and golfer.

References

Adv Agency 44:70 S '51
N Y Herald Tribune p23 Mr 7 '50
N Y Times II p12 F 17 '52
Time 55:81 Mr 6 '50 por

Business Executives of America (1950)
Who's Who in America, 1952-53
Who's Who in Commerce and Industry
    (1951)
Who's Who in New York, 1947
World Biography (1948)

DUGGAR, BENJAMIN MINGE (dŭg'ẽr)
Sept. 1, 1872- Plant physiologist; educator
Address: b. c/o Lederle Laboratories, American
Cyanamid Company, Pearl River, N.Y.; h.
198 Braunsdorf Rd., Pearl River, N.Y.

Upon retiring in 1943 from more than forty
years of college teaching, Benjamin Minge
Duggar accepted an appointment as a research
consultant with the Lederle Laboratories, where
within two years he succeeded in isolating an
organism from which aureomycin, a new "wonder drug," was soon obtained. Before this
major discovery, the scientist had been best
known for his experimental work which resulted in introducing scientific methods in the
United States mushroom-growing industry.

Born in Gallion, Alabama, on September 1,
1872, Benjamin Minge Duggar was one of six

children of Dr. Reuben Henry and Margaret Louisa (Minge) Duggar. Rearing his family in a small village where the chief occupation was farming, Dr. Duggar, a physician, became interested in agriculture and adopted the hobby of experimenting with the grafting and crossing of various plants. Benjamin Duggar's interest in horticulture was stimulated by a friend of his father, Charles Mohr, a druggist in nearby Mobile, who frequently stayed at the Duggar home so that he could search the surrounding countryside for new crude drugs and flora for his business. The boy accompanied the druggist on these field trips and became increasingly fascinated by plant life.

Having completed primary schooling, young Duggar prepared for college under private tutors and beginning in 1887 attended the University of Alabama for one and a half years, until enrolling at Mississippi Agricultural and Mechanical College (now Mississippi State College). "In those days," Duggar has said, "you were supposed to do agricultural work at an agricultural college. This included looking after crops." Duggar was assigned to the State Agricultural Experiment Station connected with the college, where he cared for grass plots containing plant seeds from all over the world and thus had an opportunity to study various plants' reaction to foreign soil and the native soil's reaction to them. After receiving his B.S. degree with highest honors from Mississippi Agricultural and Mechanical College in 1891, Duggar continued his college work at Alabama Polytechnic Institute, where his older brother, J. F. Duggar, was later to be professor of agriculture. While a graduate student, Duggar was also assistant in mycology and plant pathology at the institute, from which he obtained his M.Sc. degree in 1892. The following year on a scholarship he entered Harvard University, where he took his B.A. degree in 1894 and his M.A. degree in 1895, working simultaneously as an assistant instructor in botany at Harvard and at Radcliffe College. In 1897 he became a botany instructor at Cornell University, at the same time undertaking advanced studies in crop diseases and receiving his Ph.D. degree in cytology in 1898. For the year 1899-1900 he studied physiology in Europe with Professor Pfeffer at Leipzig and Professor Klebs at Halle. He went abroad again in 1905-1906 to study at the Botanical Institute of the University of Munich, the University of Bonn, and the University of Montpelier, from which he was sent with a botanical expedition to Algeria.

Duggar began his professional work as an agriculturist during 1892-93 as assistant director of the Uniontown Agricultural Experiment Station (plant sciences) in Alabama. During 1895-96 he was assistant botanist at the Illinois State Laboratory of Natural History, where he studied the control of insects by means of fungus diseases. While studying for his doctorate at Cornell University Duggar was concurrently assistant cryptogamic botanist at the university's Agricultural Experiment Station, specializing in the study of diseases of vegetables and fruits. Upon returning from Europe in 1900, he was made assistant profes-

Wide World Photos
BENJAMIN MINGE DUGGAR

sor of plant physiology at Cornell University, leaving here the next year to become plant physiologist at the Bureau of Plant Industry, United States Department of Agriculture. In this capacity, he took charge of the study of cotton diseases throughout the South and Southwest and went to Europe to study methods of mushroom culture. His study marked the beginning of experimental work which ultimately resulted in the introduction of pure-culture methods, and of scientific methods in general, in the United States mushroom-growing industry.

In 1902 Duggar accepted an appointment as professor of botany and head of that department at the University of Missouri, where he stayed until 1907 when he returned to Cornell University as professor of plant physiology at the College of Agriculture. In 1912 he left Cornell to go to Washington University, St. Louis, as research professor of plant physiology, working concurrently as a physiologist at the Missouri Botanical Garden, and from 1917 to 1919 as a professor of biological chemistry in the medical school of the university. At the beginning of World War I, when it was suspected that some deaths had resulted from eating deteriorated potatoes because of their high solanine (toxic alkaloid) content, Duggar and his graduate student assistant examined the solanine content of potato breeding stocks in the United States and other countries, so that breeders could be warned when deterioration was discovered. As a result, such deterioration is now controlled. Duggar also studied virus diseases of tobacco at a time when (as he has said) "not much was known about viruses." This early work with viruses helped him in his later successful search for an agent to destroy them. When Duggar left Washington University in 1927, he went to the University of Wisconsin in the dual post of professor of

DUGGAR, BENJAMIN MINGE—*Cont.*

plant physiology and economic botany in the College of Letters and Science and of professor of plant pathology in the College of Agriculture. Here he combined research with teaching until he retired from academic life in June 1943.

Soon after his retirement, Duggar was invited by Dr. Yellapragada Subba Row, director of the Lederle Laboratories (a division of the American Cyanamid Company) to become a consultant in mycrological research and production and to do independent research with this company. At first Duggar was reluctant to accept, but his mind was changed (as reported by the Washington *Post*, September 14, 1952) when he read in a scholarly journal that "Dr. Duggar will probably be remembered for his noteworthy inquiry into the physiology of mushrooms." He considered this an insignificant achievement to go on record as his life's work. In September 1945, about a year after he began work at the Lederle Laboratories, he succeeded in isolating and testing the first strain of a new species, later named *streptomyces aureofaciens*, the organism from which aureomycin was shortly afterward obtained.

After being tested in the laboratory for two years, aureomycin was purified in 1947 and that same year was first used on human patients at New York City's Harlem Hospital, where Dr. Louis T. Wright found it effective against a venereal disease called lymphogranuloma. By June 1948, although clinical experiments were still in the early stages, the drug was being produced at the rate of "a pound a day" in the Lederle Laboratories (*Newsweek*, August 30, 1948). Aureomycin was first offered to physicians generally on December 1, 1948—three years after Duggar had discovered its source among the actinomycetes fungi, which had previously been treated by other researchers "with static contempt" (*New York Times*, July 25, 1948).

Besides proving beneficial when used in the treatment of lymphogranuloma venereum, aureomycin was found to be effective against other virus-like diseases and rickettsial diseases including Q-fever, Rocky Mountain spotted fever, rickettsial pox, parrot fever, and typhus fever. In February 1949 a research group, headed by Dr. Harry F. Dowling of George Washington University, reported that "aureomycin was better than any other antibiotic for treating undulant fever (brucellosis), and that it produced good results against streptococcic and staphylococcic infections, scarlet fever, and . . . [virus] pneumonia" (*Time*, March 14, 1949). By March 1949 "aureomycin had taken its place as a standard medicine" (*Time*) and during this same month Lederle doctors reported that the drug had been used successfully to treat whooping cough and rabbit fever (tularemia). While aureomycin (named for its golden yellow color) was being hailed as a new "wonder drug," the British medical journal *Lancet* reported that it had "the widest range of activity of any known antibacterial substance."

Its outstanding quality was the power to reduce high fever quickly. Duggar has stated that the drug is "helpful in preventing secondary infections resulting from weakness of the eyes, throat, or other parts of the body" and that surgeons use it after operations in wounds, often in preference to penicillin because it had a wider effect. "Aureomycin will prove useful to farmers and poultry raisers," Duggar has pointed out, "because it will improve growth in young pigs, chickens, turkeys, calves, and lambs. These animals will mature earlier and at less cost to the farmer." The scientist said that experiments are being conducted now to study the effect of the drug on children who are not showing normal growth.

Having discovered a drug useful in the treatment of diseases caused by what Duggar refers to as some of the "large viruses," he is now looking for one that will inhibit the "small viruses" that produce such illnesses as poliomyelitis, rabies, mumps, smallpox, measles, sleeping sickness, and certain kinds of encephalitis, as well as foot and mouth disease common in cattle. In his research, he and his staff have examined soil samples from the forty-eight States and from Europe, Asia, Africa, South America, and Australia, but Duggar has maintained that "the surface has only been scratched in the search" for miracle drugs (Washington *Post*, February 25, 1951).

In addition to numerous papers on fungi, fungous diseases of plants, physiology of the fungi, physiology of green plants, biological effects of radiation, and photosynthesis, Duggar has written the following books: *Fungous Diseases of Plants* (1909); *Plant Physiology* (1911); *Mushroom Growing* (1915), and *A Textbook of General Botany* (in collaboration with Gilbert M. Smith and others, 1943). He has edited *Proceedings of the International Congress of Plant Sciences* (two volumes, 1929); *The Biological Effects of Radiation* (two volumes, 1936, now being revised); physiology section of *Botanical Abstracts* (1917-1926), and the section on plant physiology in *Biological Abstracts* (1926-33).

Duggar is a trustee of the International Basic Economy Corporation Research Institute, an organization financed by the Rockefeller Foundation and operated to improve the self-sufficiency of Brazil and Venezuela by education in modern methods of agriculture. He is also a trustee emeritus of the Marine Biological Laboratory, Woods Hole Oceanographic Institution, a fellow of the American Association for the Advancement of Science, and the chairman of the division of mycology, New York Academy of Sciences. In 1944 he was awarded an honorary LL.D. degree by the University of Missouri; in 1951 the Medal of Honor of Public Education by Venezuela. The latter year he was elected president of the Society of Industrial Microbiology and in 1952 an honorary fellow by the United States Chapter of the International College of Surgeons. Appointed speaker at the International Congress of Arts and Sciences, section on plant physiology, in St. Louis in 1904, he was also chairman of the organizing committee and general secretary of this organization's meeting in Ithaca, New York, in 1926. During 1925-26 he served as chairman of the division of biology and agriculture of the National Research Council and during 1935-40 as chairman of its committee on the effects of radiation on organisms.

Organizations of which Duggar is an honorary member are the Societa Italiana di Ematologia and of the Societé Botanique de France; he is a corresponding member of La Societa Lancisiana. He also holds membership in Phi Beta Kappa, Sigma Xi, Phi Sigma, the American Philosophical Society, the American Society of Plant Physiology (president 1946-47), the American Chemical Society, the American Phytopathological Society, the American Public Health Association, the Botanical Society of America (president 1912-14; 1923), the National Academy of Sciences, the Philadelphia Academy of Science, the Society of American Naturalists, and the Torrey Botanical Club.

On October 16, 1901, Duggar married Marie L. Robertson, who died in 1922. His children by this marriage are Marie Louise, Benjamin Minge, Anna St. Julian Guerard, George Struan-Robertson, and Emily Westwood. He married Elsie Rist, of St. Louis, on June 6, 1927; they have a daughter, Gene Lorraine. The scientist has a height of five feet five inches and weighs 122 pounds. His hobbies are photography, golf, bowling, and fishing. Duggar is a Democrat and an Episcopalian. "Human relations," he has said, "one's everyday relations, are the most important thing in life."

References

Parade S 14 '52
Time 53:98 Mr 14 '49
American Men of Science (1949)
Who's Who in America, 1952-53

DUNCAN, SIR ANDREW RAE 1884— Mar. 30, 1952 Industrialist; former British Cabinet member; chairman of the Central Electricity Board (1927-35); chairman of the Iron and Steel Federation (1935-40 and from 1945); was elected to Parliament in 1940 and reelected in 1945; President of the Board of Trade (1940-41); Minister of Supply (1940-41 and 1942-45). See *Current Biography*, 1941.

Obituary

N Y Times p19 Mr 31 '52

ECCLES, DAVID (MCADAM) Sept. 18, 1904- British Government member

Address: b. c/o Ministry of Works, Lambeth Bridge House, Albert Embankment, London, S.E.1, England; h. 6 Barton St., Westminster, London, S.W.1, England; "Dean Farm," Chute, near Andover, Hampshire, England

Among the younger, more progressive members of the Conservative party of Britain, David Eccles became Minister of Works in the Government of Prime Minister Winston Churchill in November 1951. Eccles, who has represented Chippenham in Parliament since 1943, attracted national attention through his campaign speeches for the October 1951 election in which he restated the policies of the Conservative party. Prior to his election to

British Inf. Services

DAVID ECCLES

Parliament he was a businessman, an economic adviser to the government, and during World War II a program planner at the Ministry of Production.

David McAdam Eccles was born to William McAdam and Coralie (Anstie) Eccles on September 18, 1904. His great-great-grandfather was John Loudon McAdam, inventor of the macadamized road. David's grandfather and other relatives were doctors, and his father was a surgeon in London's most aristocratic medical street (Harley Street), where the boy was brought up. He went to Winchester College from 1918 to 1923 and then (as is most usual for Wykehamists, as Winchester boys are known) to New College, Oxford, from which he was graduated with the B.A. degree in 1926.

"While still at Oxford he showed talent for making money from his artistic tastes," according to Peter Gladwin, in the Sydney *Daily Telegraph*. "He specialized in buying and selling first editions, and made a nice profit on buying up a number of copies of a limited edition of Lawrence of Arabia's *Seven Pillars of Wisdom*." Eccles went straight from college into the City of London (the commercial center of Greater London) and, says Gladwin, "was quoted as a classic example of a man who entered the City without money or influence and achieved wealth before he was forty." He began as a clerk in the Central Mining and Investment Corporation in 1926 and by 1939 at thirty-five had advanced to the position of a manager of this £4,000,000 investment house. Then he became a chairman of the Anglo-Spanish Construction Company, which owned a railroad in northern Spain. After the war began, in September 1939 he joined the Ministry of Economic Warfare, and later in World War II, from 1939 to 1942, he held the post of economic adviser to His

ECCLES, DAVID—*Continued*

Majesty's Ambassadors in Madrid and Lisbon. Then he went into the Ministry of Production (in 1942-43) as assistant director-general, program and planning.

On August 26, 1943, Eccles began his political career by being elected to Parliament (at a by-election) as Conservative Member for Chippenham, an agricultural-industrial constituency in Wiltshire, winning by 195 votes over an Independent Liberal opponent. He held his seat in the defeat of the Conservatives in 1945, and in the general election of February 1950 was returned with 17,845 votes against a Labor candidate with 13,748 and a Liberal with 8,661.

Eccles, who was heard fairly frequently in debate, has usually specialized in the economic questions which his training has best fitted him to discuss. He is vice-chairman of the Conservative finance committee and was one of R. A. Butler's helpers in working out his party's industrial charter (1947). This charter (stated *Time,*) "opposed Socialist nationalization in principle, but was cagily diffident when it came down to cases." "Some controls," said Eccles, will have to be continued until abundance overtakes scarcity." A pamphlet of his own, following the publication of the charter, caused the *Financial Times* to remark, "Eccles outdoes the Socialists in his worship of planning. He uses the sort of language you'd expect from Bevan or Mikardo" (both Leftists of the Labor party). Eccles favored the loan from the United States and has supported the Council of Europe and the Schuman Plan, but in August 1950, with Harold Macmillan, he put forward an alternative scheme for the management of the first named, according to the New York *Times,* "limiting the supranational authority by placing it under a committee of Ministers within the European council."

On August 4, 1951, at Sturminster, Dorsetshire, David Eccles addressed a rally of Young Conservatives in a speech later reprinted as a pamphlet, *The New Conservatism.* This speech, which crystallized much that progressive British Conservatives have been thinking for years, made Eccles one of the most talked-about figures in British politics. One main point was that the Conservative party could not, and should not, be identified with the rich, but with "the active producers of wealth. The skilled workers with hand or brain. Those who manage or dream they will one day manage a factory, a shop or a farm." The other chief point was that British policy should be directed toward "expanding the national income and taking care to live within it." The speech went on to attack the dividend freeze and the wage freeze as assaults on the standards of life; to advocate "more and fair competition"; to attack the allegedly inflationary policy of Chancellor Hugh Gaitskell; to advocate a policy of expansion. The weekly *Observer's* comment was: "The electorate has to be convinced that if a Conservative Government is returned, it is the progressive outlook of the younger Tories like Eccles and not that of the still influential party die-hards that would prevail."

Eccles followed up his August speech with a feature article, "A Policy of Expansion," in *The Times* of September 20, 1951. Here, as he put it, he gave "the bare bones" of a policy which called for the elimination of waste and inflation and the expansion of production. Among his proposals were a reorganization of the Treasury to improve control of expenditure, reduction in the budget by a 6 per cent cut in government spending, dismantling of exchange controls, maintenance of a national minimum in taxation and social policy, abolition of restrictive practices both of employers and employees, denationalization where possible and decentralization, and guarantee of agricultural prices to encourage farming. Late in October Eccles again attracted national attention by another important campaign speech in which he described the Conservatives as the "creators of wealth" and the "champions of 'The Arriving.'"

Victorious over his Labor opponent, Denger Evans, a Welshman, Eccles was returned to Parliament in the election of October 25, 1951. Soon after, on November 1, he was appointed Minister of Works in Prime Minister Winston Churchill's Government, a post which gives him the rank and salary of a Cabinet officer, but not membership in the Cabinet. As Minister of Works, Eccles is responsible for government construction work and public buildings and for the promotion of "the efficiency of the country's building, civil engineering, and building materials industries (including scientific research and advisory services in this field) and the control of civil building (licensing)" (*Whitaker's Almanac*). One of his more difficult immediate tasks, as the *Manchester Guardian* pointed out, is to provide materials for the 300,000 houses projected by Harold Macmillan, the new Minister of Housing and Local Government. *Newsweek* called Eccles' assignment "an administrative job probably intended to test the internal fortitude of this brilliant leader of the new Tories."

As a scion of medical stock, Eccles, so it happened, chose his wife from a medical family, in 1928 marrying Sybil, daughter of Lord Dawson of Penn, who was physician to King George V. They have two sons and a daughter —John, Simon, and Polly. In the Manchester *Daily Dispatch* Kenneth Pearson noted that Eccles "presents a picture of well-dressed benevolence. His manner is restrained, his features are Hollywood's idea of a successful businessman. He speaks of his convictions with evident sincerity and a singular lack of oratorical passion." The statesman's major private interests are the collection of early English water colors and of books on exploration and travel. At Andover he owns a farm of 300 acres. His London clubs are Brooks's and Burlington Fine Arts.

References

Daily Telegraph (Sydney) S 17 '51 por
Daily Dispatch (Manchester) O 4 '51 por
Newsweek 38:34 O 22 '51 por
Kelly's Handbook to the Titled, Landed, and Official Classes, 1949
Who's Who, 1951

ECKSTINE, BILLY July 8, 1914- (ĕk'stĭn)
Singer

Address: b. c/o The William Morris Agency,
Inc., 1270 6th Ave., New York 20; h. Encino,
Calif.

In his first appearance at the Paramount
theater in New York City in 1950, Billy Eckstine broke the attendance record there for
popular singers which had been held for six
years by Frank Sinatra. After fifteen years
as a singer in night clubs and as a vocalist
with the band of Earl Hines and with his own
musicians, Eckstine had begun to win wide
popularity in 1948. The Negro singer has made
two nation-wide tours with the George Shearing Quintet and is under contract to Metro-
Goldwyn-Mayer to make recordings and motion pictures.

William Clarence Eckstine, the youngest of
the three children of William and Charlotte
Eckstine, was born July 8, 1914, in Pittsburgh, Pennsylvania. Neither of his sisters
was musical. In the *Negro Digest* he recalls,
however, that his father, a chauffeur, bought
a piano for the family when he thought he
saw a talent for music in one of the girls.
When he was eleven years old young Eckstine
sang at a church bazaar, but at that age his
chief interest was football. He attended Armstrong High School in Washington, D.C., St.
Paul Normal and Industrial School in Lawrenceville, Virginia (majoring in physical education), and for one year Howard University
in Washington.

In 1933 Eckstine won the first prize, a week
with the theater band as a singer at ten dollars,
at an amateur show given by the Howard
Theater in Washington. From this beginning
he went on to night clubs in that city and in
Pittsburgh. He was next engaged as the leader
and featured vocalist of a small dance band.
The band dissolved when Earl Hines hired
two of the performers for his own orchestra,
and Eckstine returned to the night clubs. He
had been singing at the De Lisa Club in Chicago two years when Hines, who had earlier
overlooked the young singer, heard him in
1939 and asked him to sing with his band.
Eckstine remained with Hines for four years,
during which time he learned to play the
trumpet.

Leaving the Hines band in 1943, Eckstine
worked as a soloist in New York night clubs
(among them Club Zanzibar) until the 20 per
cent cabaret tax discouraged many club owners
from offering entertainment. He then decided
to form his own band, and by June 1944 he had
arranged for a tour of the South with a group
which included Charlie Parker, Dizzie Gillespie, one of the first exponents of "bop," and
Sarah Vaughan as vocalist. Despite unfavorable wartime conditions (musicians' salaries
were high and travel was difficult), the band
started off well financially, grossing $100,000
in its first ten weeks. Eckstine first played the
trumpet with the orchestra, later took up the
valve trombone because, he remarked, Gillespie
was so expert with the trumpet that no competition was possible. Early in 1946 the singer was
offered a contract by MGM to appear with

BILLY ECKSTINE

Lena Horne in the motion picture *Till the
Clouds Roll By*, but as the band was not included in the offer he refused.

Although the orchestra disbanded in 1946,
by that time Eckstine had gained recognition,
and MGM signed him for a ten-year contract
to make recordings. Unlike many singers, Eckstine did not achieve sudden popularity with
one disc, but gradually built up a following;
MGM sold three million of his records in 1949
and listed him as its leading popular singer
in 1950. At the Oasis Club in Los Angeles in
April 1950 he attracted a record-breaking attendance of 4,587 paid admissions, and his
appearance at the Paramount in New York
City surpassed Frank Sinatra's six-year attendance record.

In the fall of 1950 Eckstine and the George
Shearing Quintet made a cross-country tour,
ending with two concerts in November at Carnegie Hall in New York City. "The time when
jazz in Carnegie Hall was stop-press news is
past," wrote the New York *Times* critic, "but
it is noteworthy when a single attraction fills
the place twice in one day. Billy Eckstine, the
popular singer, and the George Shearing Quintet did it yesterday afternoon and again at night,
when seats were sold on the stage." The entire
tour grossed $262,000, reported *Variety*.

After the Shearing tour Eckstine made a
number of appearances at smart supper clubs,
including the Venetian Room of the Fairmont
Hotel in San Francisco, the Mocambo in Los
Angeles, and the Copacabana in New York
(in the last-named in June 1952 he was to top
Johnnie Ray's record). In March 1951 he returned to the stage of the Paramount, and he
and George Shearing repeated their success of
the previous year with a tour that fall of the
United States and Canada.

Eckstine and Count Basie filled thirty-five
concert and ballroom engagemets on a Southern

ECKSTINE, BILLY—*Continued*

route in the spring of 1952. The Negro singer found the attitude of Southerners on the racial question different from that which he had encountered on his tour in 1945: "It's not the old South any more," he said. On his first tour his audiences were almost entirely Negro, and race prejudice was evident. In 1952 more than half the listeners were white, and, while most of the audiences were segregated, in New Orleans, Miami, and Columbia, there was no separation. *Variety* stated that Eckstine plans about forty Southern commitments in 1953, to include some of the smaller cities and to make such a tour annually.

In 1950 Eckstine signed a contract with MGM to sing in the motion picture *Skirts Ahoy* (1952) starring Esther Williams, in which he was billed as himself in a guest appearance. On television the singer has appeared on *Toast of the Town* with Ed Sullivan as master of ceremonies.

As to his future career, Eckstine, who has a great admiration for Ezio Pinza, says, "In about five years I plan to retire and study voice" (New York *Sunday News*, March 25, 1951). At that time the singer, who has not yet had vocal training, would like to spend three years studying classical music and then make a name for himself on the concert stage. In line with this ambition he has begun to include in his repertoire such semiclassical numbers as "Laugh Clown Laugh."

Serious critical appraisal had indicated that the baritone may have a better chance of achieving success in concert work than would most singers of popular songs. Commenting on his performance at Carnegie Hall on November 11, 1950, the New York *Herald Tribune* said, "Mr. Eckstine begins with considerably more voice than the average crooner, and therefore he is not driven to the usual faking procedures popularized by others. He sings, for the most part, on pitch, cleanly, clearly and with the standard breast-beating and catch-in-the-voice technique that seem the stock-in-trade of novelty crooners. But there is real vocal color to his work, and it is a color which he varies according to the expressive dictates of the song." Several critics have said that he has the most perfect vibrato of any male popular singer, an opinion that earned him the nickname of "The Vibrato"—he is, however, most widely known as "Mr. B." Some critics have said that this vibrato has no place in jazz: Eckstine himself remarked that he did not know he had such a thing until he was told.

Eckstine's records include "I Stay in the Mood for You" and "I'll Wait and Pray" for Deluxe; "In the Still of the Night" for National; and "Fools Rush In", "You Go to My Head", "Caravan," and "Everything I Have is Yours" for MGM. In addition he is heard on discs in trombone solos, "Mr. B's Blues" for MGM and "She's Got the Blues for Sale" and "Cool Breeze" for National. He has also composed songs: "Jelly Jelly", "Stormy Monday Blues," and "That's the Way I Feel."

In 1949 and again in 1950 *Metronome* named Eckstine "Top Male Vocalist," and *Down Beat*'s poll voted him the most popular singer for the same years. He won the *Billboard* 1951 College Poll and in that year was also named "King" of the Sophomore Prom at Columbia University for the third consecutive year. *Our World* reported that there are eighty thousand Eckstine fan clubs in the United States, Canada, and England.

Eckstine and his wife June, an ex-singer, were married in 1942. The singer is nearly six feet tall and weighs about 170 pounds. His wardrobe, said *Our World*, includes forty-five suits, forty pairs of dress shoes, and two dozen pairs of golf shoes; he is said to have popularized "slim-jim" ties and roll-collar shirts. Hunting and swimming are two diversions, but golf is his principal recreation. He has a nine-hole putting range at his home in Encino, California, and takes his own golf professional with him on tours; his 1951 average for eighteen holes was seventy-five.

References

Life 28:101 Ap 24 '50 pors
Negro Digest 9:22 N '50
Newsweek 33:78 My 16 '49
Our World 6:28 Jl '51 pors
PM Mag p2 Ja 19 '47
Time 53:42 Je 20 '49

Who Is Who in Music, 1951
Who's Who in Colored America, 1950

EMERY, ANNE (ELEANOR MCGUIGAN) (măk-wĭg'ĭn) Sept. 7, 1907- Author

Address: b. c/o Westminster Press, Witherspoon Bldg., Philadelphia, Pa.; h. 2307 Park Pl., Evanston, Ill.

Reprinted from the *Wilson Library Bulletin*, Dec. 1952.

Anne Emery is a housewife, ex-schoolteacher, and mother of five who began her writing career twelve years ago, when she started work on short stories for the "slick" magazines, intending, "when established," to write for children. She recalls, however, that it was not long before she discovered a distaste for "the type of slick romance I was struggling unsuccessfully with, wondered what I was waiting for," and turned directly to material for a younger audience. Today, with seven published and three forthcoming novels to her credit, she is popular as the creator of teen-age fiction and has been recognized for what a Chicago *Tribune* reviewer called the "intelligent and understanding fashion" in which she presents young people's problems.

The eldest of five children, Anne Eleanor McGuigan is the daughter of an Irish-born doctor, Hugh A. McGuigan, and a young English teacher, the former Mabel Leininger, whose plans for teaching were interrupted by her marriage. She was born on September 7, 1907, in Fargo, North Dakota.

Anne McGuigan was a year old when her parents took her with them to Heidelberg, Germany, where her father studied for a year on a medical fellowship. During the rest of her first nine years, the family lived in Chicago, later moving to Evanston, Illinois, where she received her education from the fifth grade through Evanston Township High School and Northwestern University. The intervening years she recalls as characterized by "perfectly normal family life and satisfactory social experiences. I took music lessons, was a Girl Scout, went to the Episcopal Church." At Northwestern, where she received the B.A. degree in English in 1928, she was a member of Chi Omega sorority.

In the years since her graduation, she has undertaken what she now calls "desultory" study in American history at the University of Chicago and in French at the University of Grenoble—the latter during a year's travel in Europe after her graduation from college. On her return to Evanston she taught the seventh and eighth grades of the Haven Intermediate School for four years, prior to her marriage, on May 1, 1931, to John Douglas Emery, a dealer in investment securities. In 1934 she resumed teaching at Evanston's Orrington School, where for six years she taught the fourth and fifth grades.

A teaching assignment at the Haven School to work in the library with Mildred Batchelder of the American Library Association aroused Mrs. Emery's lasting interest in children's books. She began writing in 1940, after her retirement from teaching. Her earliest publication was in the church magazine, where she began "at the ground level of 500 word stories for 'tiny tots,' then nine-to-ten-year-old material, then teen-age stories, which I found to be what I really liked best."

After her six-part serial, "The Feathered Serpent," had been purchased by the Westminster Press for its weekly teen-age magazine, Mrs. Emery decided to turn to books and began with a historical adventure story for boys, *Bright Horizons* (1947). It was preceded in publication by the later written *Tradition* (1946), the story of two Japanese-American high schoolers' struggle to win acceptance, which E. L. Buell in the New York *Times* described as "a thoughtful story, very much needed now." Mrs. Emery's next book, *Mountain Laurel* (1948)—which grew out of her own trips through the Great Smoky Mountains—described life in the remote sections of Tennessee as the background of a story for older girls. It was praised by Jane Cobb in the *Atlantic Monthly* as "a charming bit of Americana, and entirely accurate."

The next book, *Senior Year* (1949—like *Mountain Laurel*, it was a Junior Literary Guild selection), marked the beginning of Mrs. Emery's popular books about high schoolers Sally and Jean Burnaby, their family, friends, and beaux. Reviewers have consistently found in the series sound values, entertaining stories, and a skillful, realistic treatment of such serious teen-age problems as sorority life, "going steady," and the pro's and con's of early marriage. *Senior Year*, which was said to reveal "American family life at its best," was followed by *Going Steady* (1950) and *Sorority Girl* (1952).

Among her works-in-progress is a new sequel to the Burnaby family books. Another new

ANNE EMERY

book, *Scarlet Royal*, a Junior Literary Guild selection, was published in October 1952, and a story of a youth hostel called *Vagabond Summer* is scheduled for publication in spring 1953.

Brown-haired, blue-eyed, and petite (she is five feet two inches tall and weighs 118 pounds) Mrs. Emery spends her mornings taking care of her house in Evanston; does her writing in the afternoons, when her five children—Mary, Kate, Joan, Robert, and Martha—are in school or napping.

Mrs. Emery's organizational memberships include the Children's Reading Round Table in Chicago, Midland Authors, and the Authors' League of America. She is an Episcopalian and a Republican, and a member of Evanston civic organizations and the Parent-Teacher Association. Her recreations, in addition to travel, include gardening, furniture refinishing, and reading (Jane Austen, Dorothy Sayers, and Maureen Daly's *Seventeenth Summer* are her favorite reading).

ENTERS, ANGNA (ăng'nä) Apr. 28, 1907-
Dancer; painter; author
Address: b. c/o W. Colston Leigh, Inc., 521 5th Ave., New York 17; h. 113 W. 57th St., New York 19; P. O. Box 848, Beverly Hills, Calif.

NOTE: This biography supersedes the article which appeared in *Current Biography* in 1940.

During her career Angna Enters has touched at some point several of the creative arts. A painter before she made her debut on the stage as a dancer and mime (or dance-mime, a term which she originated) in 1924, she returned to painting with her first exhibition in New York in the fall of 1933. In 1937 she published the

Wide World Photos

ANGNA ENTERS

first of her three books; and she composes much of the music which accompanies her stage performances, designs her costumes, does her own choreography, and plays the piano, guitar, or other musical instruments whenever one of her "Compositions in Dance Form" requires it. Miss Enters has toured the United States, Canada, Hawaii, Cuba, and Europe to present some 150 of her compositions.

Angna Enters was born on April 28, 1907, in New York City, daughter of Edward and Henreitte (Gasseur-Styleau) Enters. Both of her parents had come from Europe, Edward Enters from Austria and Mrs. Enters from France, which Angna visited frequently in her early childhood until the family moved to Milwaukee, Wisconsin, in late 1914. The child attended school only intermittently, receiving most of her education privately both in the United States and in Europe. Her first, and almost her only, formal training in dance was with a ballet master in Milwaukee who, regarding dancing as a social grace, did not encourage professional aspirations in his pupils.

In the fall of 1922 Miss Enters returned to New York City alone to enroll as a student in the Art Students' League, where she studied under John Sloan at night while doing lettering in an advertising agency during the day. At the same time that she continued to think of herself as an embryo painter, her increasing concern with the representation of movement led to an interest in pantomime, which she conceived as painting with the body in movement. Shortly after Thanksgiving in 1922 she received an introduction to Michio Itow, the Japanese dancer, who taught her his system of ten basic gestures.

It was Itow who first suggested that his young pupil become a dancer, a possibility she immediately rejected because she was coming to believe that she could not express her own

ideas within the framework of someone else's system. Eventually she did agree, "for financial reasons," to appear as his partner in a series of recitals in the fall of 1923. That winter in a Broadway revue which Itow organized, she created her first "Composition in Dance Form," *Ecclésiastique*, an evocation in pantomime of the spirit of a Gothic Virgin carved in stone. This number, now entitled *Moyen Age*, is still retained in Miss Enters' repertoire. When the production closed a month after its opening, the young dancer took the part of a Japanese girl in the road company of *The Lady Christalinda*, which starred Fay Bainter.

In the spring of 1924 Miss Enters prepared to give a show of her own at the Greenwich Village Theatre. With no manager and limited funds, she did almost everything herself, ripping up much of her personal wardrobe to make costumes and designing and distributing her own handbills and window cards. The first presentation, on March 2, of what later became known as the Theatre of Angna Enters was followed by others in the next two years and by a growing interest on the part of the public and critics alike. Miss Enters dates the debut of her one-woman theater from her October 17, 1926, appearance at the Little Theatre in New York City—it was the first performance without assisting artists. On December 11, 1926, Stark Young wrote in the *New Republic*: "She remains one of the most individual talents in our theater . . . free of influences foreign to her nature"; he found her numbers "always witty, and sometimes . . . beautiful, profoundly inventive, and never to be forgotten."

In the early days of Miss Enters' career critics were often puzzled by the form of expression which the dancer had chosen. Louis Untermeyer in an article in the *Nation* (December 5, 1928) called her "a dancer who does not dance; an actress who does not speak; a dramatist who makes the audience supply the drama." Of her essential qualities he wrote: "From the complexity of effects, wit emerges first, extraordinarily subtle, almost febrile. . . . But wit alone would make her work dry and overcerebral. Humor saves Angna Enters from a tendency to intellectualize. . . .But . . . the two qualities which distinguish Angna Enters are curiously combined: the macabre. . . .Here is an evocation of all that is masked, twisted, paradoxical, perverse. . . .And then, amazingly, when we have concluded there is no warmth in the woman, she breaks down the last reserve with tenderness." A comment by Louis Kalonyme appeared in *Arts and Decoration* (May 1925): "Any of her dances could, I believe, be squeezed between the trained seal and a 'blues' artiste and 'go over big.'" This pleased Miss Enters because she believed that the clowns and comedians, the dancers and the singers of the popular theater were no less artists than the "serious" performers.

At the beginning of 1927 Miss Enters had managerial assistance for the first time when James Pond presented her in three performances at the Selwyn Theatre in New York City during January and February and also obtained a few touring engagements for her. In England she made her debut at London's St. Martin's Theatre in 1928 and she returned to that city for eight seasons including two-week appearances in May 1950 and October-November 1951 under the sponsorship of the Arts Council of Great Britain. She returned to England in 1952 for a week of performances at the Cambridge University Arts Theatre, beginning on April 28.

Of her latest appearance in London, W. A. Darlington wrote in the London *Daily Telegraph* (October 23, 1951): "It was most rewarding . . . to encounter once again, after many years, the acrid flavor of Angna Enters' personality. . . .In some of her impersonations there is an originality of conception which of itself compels interest—for example, that Spanish boy cardinal of the sixteenth century whose thoughts beneath his reverent pose, are far from holy. But to my mind Miss Enters' most striking talent is her power of making the most trivial and ordinary events and characters significant." In 1929 she went to France to present her compositions at the Salle Gaveau in Paris. After this debut she was invited to make four appearances at the Théâtre des Champs Elysées, where she was accompanied for the first time by an orchestra, the Paris Symphony.

The recipient of a Guggenheim Fellowship Award in 1934 and again in 1935, Miss Enters turned to antiquarian study in Greece and Egypt. From her stay in the first-named country she developed a program of Greek mime, *Pagan Greece*, which she presented on January 25 and 27, 1943, at the Metropolitan Museum of Art, the first theatrical performance ever sponsored by that museum. In this mime she presents "the figure of a hypothetical archaic Greek dance mime entertainer enacting a sequence of various sacred fables." Among the compositions developed from her study of Egyptian art and lore is *Isis-Mary*, in which she expresses the evolution of the ancient Egyptian deity into the Coptic Christian Mary.

From her first European appearances in 1928 until 1938 Miss Enters spent half of each year in Europe. During five summers in Spain, from 1931 to 1936, she composed a series of Spanish mimes including *Auto da Fe, Pavanna*, and *Grand Inquisitor*, which dealt with oppression in Spain under the Inquisition. From her experience of the Spanish Civil War in the summer of 1936 came *Flesh-Possessed "Saint"* —*Red Malaga, 1936*, a satire on Fascist-supporting Spanish monks, and *Spain Says "Salud,"* a depiction of the increasing emancipation of Spanish women under the Republic. In radio appearances and magazine articles she also pleaded the cause of Republican Spain. "Hitherto my activities centered in theater and graphic arts," she said in an article in the September 1936 *New Theater*, "and I sought to communicate my sentiments in those forms—but this 'misunderstanding' [of the Civil War] is so remote from truth that verbal testimony in press and radio became obligatory."

Miss Enters' tours have taken her also to every State in the United States, and to Canada, Hawaii, and Cuba, with the more than 150 compositions which now comprise her "theater." Representative among these are *Dilly Dally* and *Oh the Pain of It—Delsarte Up Until Tonight*, satires, respectively, on surrealist painting and the muscular school of modern interpretive dancing; *The Promenade*, depicting a young French girl waiting for a rendezvous in a street cafe; *Vienna Provincial—1910*, in which a young girl comes home from her prayers, goes to a party, and comes home again with the memory of a waltz lingering in her ears; and *Dance of Death*, which is accompanied only by the rustling of her taffeta skirt. On January 9, 1940, the mime appeared before the President of the United States in an invitational performance at the White House. As a representative of the American National Theater and Academy she was the only American solo performer at the Berlin (Germany) International Arts Festival, sponsored by the United States State Department in September 1951.

The artist's first exhibition of paintings came about as a result of some costume sketches she made while crossing the Atlantic from Europe. A friend traveling with her insisted that she exhibit them; this Miss Enters did, at the Newhouse Galleries, Inc., in New York City on March 4, 1933. Since that time Miss Enters' paintings (which include portraits of herself in costume, a number of Greek and Middle Eastern studies, a series of "personal reminiscences," and a group of paintings inspired by Proust) have been given seventeen exhibitions at the same galleries and "one-man" shows at more than 100 galleries. Among these are the Metropolitan Museum of Art, the Minneapolis Art Institute, the Detroit Art Institute, the San Francisco Museum of Art, the Renaissance Society of the University of Chicago, the Eaton Art Gallery in Toronto, Canada, and the Warren Galleries in London, England. Her paintings are in the permanent collections of the Metropolitan Museum of Art, the Honolulu Museum of Art, and a number of private collections. "Taken either as independent creations or as spadework for her miming," *Time* said on January 3, 1938, "her new paintings and drawings . . . were fresh, economical, expert." In the Hollywood *Citizen-News* on April 20, 1946, Herman Reuter described her painting as "positive, direct. It fairly crackles with electric currents. It is as inevitable and right as it is humanly possible to make a creative work."

Miss Enters' first published book was *First Person Plural* (1937), an exposition of her particular art form and an expression of the ideas aroused in her by her experiences in Spain in 1936. Lloyd Morris, writing in the New York *Herald Tribune* (December 19, 1937) called the book "a story of exceptional interest to everyone concerned with the role of the arts in contemporary American life." *Love Possessed Juana*, a play written in the summer of 1935 about the sixteenth century queen of Spain, was published in 1939 with costume and stage designs by the author. Miss Enters also composed an overture for this play, which she would like some day to develop into an opera. The play was given its initial production by

ENTERS, ANGNA—*Continued*

the Houston (Texas) Little Theatre on October 15, 1946, as was her second play, *The Unknown Lover*, a contemporary comedy-drama, on October 14, 1947. Of her latest book, an autobiographical work entitled *Silly Girl* which appeared in the spring of 1944, Joseph Henry Jackson said in the San Francisco *Chronicle*, "She has succeeded in writing a frank, earnest, open and honest book. . . .This is the story of the making of an artist, and therefore a kind of key to the artist's mind and heart. . . . Angna Enters has done something a long way out of the ordinary." She is at present (in 1952) under contract to her publishers for her first novel. She has also written for magazines: "Mime in Pulpit," *Magazine of Art* (April 1943); "A Mild Jeremiad," *National Theatre Conference Bulletin* (October 1944).

Mama's Angel, an original story by Miss Enters, was purchased by Metro-Goldwyn-Mayer and adapted in 1944 for the motion picture *Lost Angel*, starring Margaret O'Brien. *Silly Girl* and two other original stories, *Tenth Avenue Angel* and *You Belong to Me*, have also been purchased by the MGM studio, to which she has been under contract as a writer and actress since 1945. In August 1951 she created a *commedia dell' arte* sequence for the motion picture *Scaramouche* (1952), an adaptation of the Rafael Sabatini novel.

Since 1938 Miss Enters has spent her summers in Southern California working at the motion picture studio, at her own writing and painting, and developing new compositions for the tours which begin in the fall. Gardening in her Santa Monica home and playing the Spanish guitar are two of her diversions. The artist, who is five feet five inches tall and weighs 118 pounds, has dark eyes set in a pale face and long dark hair. She dresses almost invariably in black because, she says, she can then keep her eye fresh for the colors she needs for her stage costumes.

References

Am Mag 113:74 F '32
Collier's 99:34+ Ap 24 '37 por
Ind Woman 24:352-4 D '45 pors
Mag Art 36:144-7 Ap '43 por
N Y Sun p8 Ja 19 '40 por
Sat R Lit. 17:18 D 18 '37
Twice a Year p187 Fall-Winter '39 Spring-Summer '40
American Women, 1939-40
Dancers' Almanac and Who's Who, 1940
Enters, A. First Person Plural (1937); Silly Girl (1944)
Rosenfeld, P. By Way of Art (1928)
Untermeyer, L. From Another World (1939)
Webster's Biographical Dictionary (1948)
Who's Who, 1950
Who's Who in America, 1952-53
Who's Who in American Art, 1940-47
Who's Who in Dancing, 1932
Who's Who in the East (1951)
Wier, A. E. Thesaurus of the Arts (1943)
World Biography (1948)

ERKIN, FERIDUN C(EMAL) (är-kĭn fär-i-dōōn jâ-mäl) June 3, 1899- Turkish Ambassador to the United States

Address: Embassy of the Turkish Republic, 1606 23d St., N.W., Washington, D.C.; Ministry of Foreign Affairs, Ankara, Turkey

During 1951 Feridun C. Erkin, Ambassador of the Republic of Turkey to the United States, was a key figure in the negotiations that brought his country into the North Atlantic Treaty Organization. Erkin was assigned to the Turkish Embassy in Washington in August 1948, before which he had been Ambassador to Italy. An earlier series of embassy and consulate posts, beginning in 1928, in 1945 was followed by his appointment to Turkey's Foreign Ministry as Secretary General, or the equivalent of Assistant Secretary of State.

Born in Istanbul (then Constantinople), the capital of the Ottoman Empire, on June 3, 1899, Feridun Cemal Erkin is the eldest of the three sons of Mehmet Cemal Erkin and the former Nesibe Tektas. One of his brothers is now a businessman; the other, one of Turkey's leading composers and orchestra conductors, is a professor at the Ankara State Conservatory. "My ancestors were farmers in the Black Sea region," Feridun Erkin has written, "but both my father and my maternal grandfather were government officials. The most prominent Turkish statesmen used to pay frequent visits to my grandfather, who was a very widely respected person. The talks which my grandfather held with these distinguished personalities, among them Ambassadors, left a fascinating impression on my young mind although the subjects were entirely out of my comprehension. . . .I was four years old when one day I innocently asked my grandfather, 'How did these people become great men and Ambassadors?' My grandfather's reply was, 'By studying in school and by hard work in their profession.' My answer was categorical. 'I want to be an ambassador, and I will start school right away.'" His education was directed to that end, and when, after brief military service in World War I, he was graduated from the Galata Saray College at Istanbul in July 1920, he proceeded to the University of Paris. He was a student in the Faculty of Law when, in 1923, Turkey became a republic with Kemal Atatürk as President, and the program of modernization associated with Kemal's name was initiated.

After receiving his law degree at Paris in June 1925, Erkin served until the end of 1927 as secretary to a commission for the resettlement of Greek and Turkish nationals. After a brief period at Prague, he took up his first regular diplomatic appointment, as first secretary at the Turkish Embassy in London, in January 1928. In December 1929 he was recalled to the new Turkish capital of Ankara to become chief of a section of the Ministry of Foreign Affairs. Erkin was promoted to the post of counselor of legations in the Foreign Ministry in February 1932, and as such became during the following year the adviser to a Turkish delegation in Paris, which arranged for the final liquidation of the international obligations of the former Ottoman Empire. In this capacity he helped to complete a work with which his father had been associated as an official of the European Debt Commission. Another assignment in 1932 was as counselor of the Turkish delegation to the Disarmament Conference at Geneva. After going to Berlin as Counselor of the Embassy in January 1934, he later served also as chargé d'affaires in the German capital. In June 1935 he was sent to Beirut, Lebanon, as Consul General.

Erkin returned to the Ministry of Foreign Affairs at Ankara in October 1937 to become Director General of the Economic and Commercial Department. From June 1938 to July 1939 he was Consul General at Berlin, after which he returned to Ankara to begin three years as Director General of the Foreign Ministry's Political Department. One of his duties in 1940 took him to the meeting of the council of the Balkan Entente, at Belgrade. July 1942 saw his advancement to First Deputy Secretary General with the rank of Minister Plenipotentiary (second class); and July 1944 his promotion to Minister Plenipotentiary (first class). Early in 1945 Erkin headed a diplomatic mission to Damascus, Syria, and in the summer of that year he went to San Francisco as Turkish delegate to the United Nations Conference on International Organization.

Promoted with the rank of Ambassador to the post of Secretary General of the Ministry of Foreign Affairs—the equivalent of the Under Secretary of State—in October 1945, the Turkish diplomat became chairman of his country's delegation at the last meeting of the General Assembly of the League of Nations (1946) at Geneva, of which he was vice-president. The London *Sunday Times* has referred to Erkin as "the directing brain of the Turkish foreign policy" in the period 1945-47; while (in a speech introducing Erkin to a New York gathering in 1951) former United States Ambassador Edwin Wilson was to "bear personal witness to the fact that he acquitted himself splendidly" as Secretary General when, the Soviet Government, having ended its nonaggression pact with Turkey, "was . . . demanding cession of the Turkish Eastern Provinces and bases" in the region of the Bosporus and Dardanelles.

In June 1947 Erkin was named Ambassador to Italy, and a year afterward (June 1948) was transferred to Washington, presenting his credentials in August. The New York *Times*, noting that Erkin was "considered one of the main figures of Turkish diplomacy," viewed the transfer as "part of the reorganization . . . being undertaken" by Foreign Minister Necmeddin Sadak with the object of strengthening Turkish relations with both the United States and the United Nations.

On April 27, 1950, as relations with the U.S.S.R. reached new points of strain, Erkin officially announced that "Turkish rejection of Russian proposals for joint control of the Dardanelles was final and conclusive." His subsequent conferences with Secretary of State Dean Acheson prepared the ground for the North Atlantic Treaty Organization's invita-

Luxardo, Rome

FERIDUN C. ERKIN

tion to Turkey (issued on September 19, 1950) to become a consultant to the NATO on problems of defense pertaining to the Mediterranean area (New York *Times*). A month later Erkin signed on behalf of his government the guarantee for a $9,000,000 World Bank loan to Turkey; and on January 23, 1951, by authority of Ankara, he proposed "to the United States that a direct security arrangement between the two countries be arranged by the adherence of the United States to the British-French-Turkish alliance of 1939" (New York *Times*). That treaty, the newspaper noted, obligated Britain and France to "lend all aid and assistance" in the event of Turkish involvement "in hostilities with a European power in consequence of aggression" and includes reciprocal pledges by Turkey.

Subsequently, at the 1951 conference at Ottawa, the decision was taken, on the initiative of the United States, to admit Turkey to the North Atlantic Treaty Organization. Also in 1951, Erkin attended the Japanese Peace Treaty Conference at San Francisco as chief Turkish delegate. Early in November 1951 the Soviet Government sent a note to Ankara warning Turkey against joining the Atlantic Pact. In a speech before the Academy of Political Science in New York during the week following, Ambassador Erkin made no direct reference to that communication, stating, rather, that "Turkey still cherishes the hope that our powerful neighbor will return to a more peaceful conception of international relations." His speech before the National Foreign Trade Council in New York in October was the subject of an editorial in the Washington *Post*, which quoted him: "Turkey [which has renounced any territorial ambitions] has no

ERKIN, FERIDUN C.—*Continued*

other ambition than to work in peace and security, raise the standard of life of her people, and remain a faithful member of the international community."

In the year of his appointment to Washington (1948) Erkin was elected to the International Diplomatic Academy in Geneva, and in 1949 he was decorated with the Grand Cross of the Greek Order of the Phoenix; another decoration he wears is the Lebanese Order of Cedar, awarded in 1946. Ambassador Erkin was active in founding the American-Turkish Society, whereof he was elected an honorary president in the summer of 1949 and later in the year was able to announce his government's decision "in principle to support the initiative of creating a Center of Turkish Studies at Columbia University."

Ambassador Erkin, who is five feet nine inches in height and 178 pounds in weight, has brown eyes and chestnut hair. In a Washington *Post* article, Lee Grove wrote of him as "outwardly grave" but with a "ready, unassuming, natural friendliness. . . .He smokes very little, and finds no time to play the violin, which he studied for about twenty years, nor for tennis." His taste for good music is shared by Madame Mukaddes F. Erkin, who is a pianist and possesses a lyric soprano voice. Another relaxation of the envoy's is the reading of historical works and memoirs.

References

> Washington (D.C.) Post p2 Ag 21 '48
>   por; p3S Ja 22 '50 por
> International Who's Who, 1951
> Who's Who in America, 1950-51
> World Biography (1948)
> World Diplomatic Directory (1951)

ERSKINE, SIR GEORGE (WATKIN EBEN JAMES) Aug. 23, 1899- British army officer

Address: b. c/o Lloyds Bank, Ltd., London, S.W. 1, England; h. "Cheriton House," South Cheriton, Templecombe, Somerset, England

Lieutenant General George Erskine, former commander of the British ground forces in Egypt, took up his new post at the end of April 1952 as the commander in chief of the ground forces of the Eastern Command. Decorated in 1942 with the Distinguished Service Order following the World War II battle of El Alamein, Erskine led Britain's 7th Armored Division through the latter part of the North African campaign and the Italian and Normandy invasions, headed a SHAEF mission to Belgium in 1944, and served as deputy commander in the British occupation zone of Germany two years later.

George Watkin Eben James Erskine, the fifth and youngest child of Major General George Elphinstone Erskine, is the only offspring of the latter's second wife, Eva Constance Sarah (Edwards) Erskine, daughter of a canon of the Church of England. The boy's father, who was on the retired list at the time

of his youngest son's birth on August 23, 1899, had taken part in the suppression of the Sepoy Mutiny in 1857-58; his father, too, was an officer.

The tradition of military service for the Empire was thus strong in the family, and George Erskine went to the Royal Military College at Sandhurst after attending Charterhouse School, Godalming (Surrey). He entered Sandhurst during World War I and received his commission as a second lieutenant in the King's Royal Rifle Corps in April 1918, in time for active duty on the front in France. In the twenty years between the two world wars, Erskine was engaged in regimental and staff service successively in England, India, and Burma. He was promoted to captain in 1928, brevet major in 1936, and major and brevet lieutenant colonel in 1938.

Following his country's declaration of war on the Axis powers in September 1939, Lieutenant Colonel Erskine was assigned to the staff of the First London Division of the Territorial Army (home militia); and in the following year he rejoined the King's Royal Rifle Corps as commanding officer of the 2d Battalion. Breveted a brigadier in December 1940, he led the 69th Infantry Brigade in the Middle East in 1941 and was appointed Chief of Staff of the 13th Corps in the Western desert in 1942. Late in October of that year, announcement was made from Middle East headquarters at Cairo, Egypt, that Brigadier Erskine had been awarded the Distinguished Service Order "on the field" for valor in the Battle of El Alamein. "He was largely responsible for the complete success of this battle," read the citation in part. "He took decisions and issued orders affecting the vital course of operations . . . was a tower of strength throughout the battle, and remained quite unmoved during frequent shelling and Stuka attacks." Almost immediately afterward (November) he was made Chief of Staff of the 8th Army and fulfilled the duties of that post until the following January. The same year (1943) he was advanced to major general and placed in command of the 7th Armored Division, which he led through the remainder of the North African campaign, in Italy at Salerno, and in the Normandy invasion. Erskine was made a Companion of the Bath (C.B.) in 1943.

In September 1944 Erskine was named by the Allied Supreme Commander, General Dwight D. Eisenhower, to head the SHAEF mission in Belgium. "The original scheme," David Anderson of the New York *Times* reported, "called for the administration of Belgium by SHAEF and a Belgian military mission while fighting was going on in the country, SHAEF sliding into the background later in favor of the Belgian government." However, shortage of food and civilian goods, class antagonisms and political rivalries, and other factors, had made the just liberated country ripe for trouble. This was precipitated early in November, when the Conservative Premier Hubert Pierlot announced a policy of disbanding former resistance groups and inclusion in the revived regular Belgian army. Three Left-wing ministers resigned in protest from the Pierlot coalition Cabinet on November 16 and antigovernment demonstrations followed. Pierlot's insistence that all resistance members surrender their arms within three days was backed by General Erskine, who issued a statement reading, in part: "Allied forces will assist the Government with the view of insuring respect for law and maintenance of order because both are essential for the conduct of military operations." He conferred with the resigned Ministers, and on November 18 the Allied Supreme Command was able to announce receipt of a pledge that all weapons would be surrendered. In an article in the London *News-Chronicle* the Resistance Front leader, Fernand Démany, later praised Erskine's "perfect diplomacy," but there was nevertheless some criticism in both Britain and the United States of SHAEF's stand.

In October 1945, after the termination of the SHAEF mission, Major General Erskine was placed in charge of the 43d (Wessex) Infantry Division, a duty retained only until January 1946, when he was sent to Berlin as Chief of Staff of the British Control Commission and deputy military governor of the British occupation zone in Germany. From November 1946, by which time he had been given the rank of lieutenant general, to April 1948 he was General Officer Commanding, British Land Forces, Hong Kong; and from April 1948 to the end of that year the Director General of the Territorial Army of Cadets, with headquarters at the War Office in London. Erskine's appointment, effective January 1, 1949, as General Officer Commanding British Troops, Egypt and Mediterranean Command, was announced November 7, 1948. On May 31, 1950, Erskine received the honor of knighthood, being invested by King George VI with the insignia of a Knight Commander of the Order of the British Empire (K.B.E.).

Sir George was a focal figure of international attention following the announcement by Premier Mustafa Nahas Pasha of Egypt, in the first week of October 1951, of his government's intention to abrogate the Anglo-Egyptian Treaty of Alliance of August 26, 1936. Under this pact Great Britain had reaffirmed her recognition (first given in 1922) of her former protectorate as a sovereign, independent state. Egypt granted to Britain, as an ally, the right to use Alexandria and Port Said as naval bases, to send troops into Egypt in case of war, and to maintain for the next twenty years a force of 10,000 men and 400 aircraft at the Suez Canal for the defense of that waterway. Britain withdrew her troops from Cairo in July 1946.

On October 8, 1951, in an attempt to meet Egypt's nationalist desires, Britain, the United States, France, and Turkey offered to join with Egypt in establishing a Middle East Defense Council which would administer the Suez area, a plan rejected by Egypt. Sanguinary clashes between Egyptians and the British troops followed; and on October 16 the Foreign Office at London announced that the canal

British Inf. Services

LT. GEN. SIR GEORGE ERSKINE

zone garrison would be reinforced. "We are not going to be turned out, forced out or knocked out," General Erskine told his men, and two days later issued an order barring Egyptian troops from the canal zone, except for the purpose of through passage. Reinforcements raised the British garrison total to 40,000 by the end of October. Civil disturbance continued, and while clashes between the Egyptian and British military did not occur, there were warnings by Egypt that she might meet "force with force" if the British proceeded with the building of a 500-yard military road that necessitated the demolition of dwellings. General Erskine had refused to postpone the road construction and an Egyptian offer of police to keep order during the work. With the killing of several British soldiers, he declared the town of Ismailia out of bounds. In mid-December he urged the Egyptians to cease encouraging guerrilla "terrorists" and advocated a cooling-off period as a first step toward an Anglo-Egyptian reconciliation. In late April 1952 Erskine entered upon his new assignment as commander in chief of the ground forces of the Eastern Command, with headquarters in London.

General Erskine has been decorated with the United States Legion of Merit, Grand Cross of the Order of Leopold II, and the Médaille Militaire of Belgium, and is a Commander of the Ordre du Chêne of Luxembourg. Lady Erskine is the former Ruby de la Rue, eldest daughter of Sir Evelyn and Lady de la Rue. The Erskines who were married in 1929, have two sons and a daughter, the latter a godchild of Prince Charles of Belgium, the former Regent. Sir George is a member of the Naval and Military Club.

(Continued next page)

ERSKINE, SIR GEORGE—*Continued*

References

International Who's Who, 1951
Kelly's Handbook to the Titled, Landed,
    and Official Classes, 1949
Who's Who, 1951
Who's Who in Egypt and the Middle
    East (1949)

FAURE, EDGAR (fôr ĕd"gàr') Aug. 18,
1908- Former Premier of France
Address: h. 15 Ave. d'Orsay, Paris 7; Port-
Lesney, Jura, France

In January 1952, Vincent Auriol, President
of France, requested Edgar Faure, of the
Radical-Socialist party and deputy to the National Assembly, to form a Cabinet replacing
the newly fallen one of René Pleven. Faure,

French Embassy Inf. Div.
EDGAR FAURE

belonging to what, despite its name, is a moderate, center party, succeeded in obtaining the
support of all the centrist groups, including the
Socialists, but not of the Communists and
Gaullists. The new Premier, who won the Assembly's approval on January 18 (as did his
Cabinet on January 22) by a heavy vote, had
held a number of Ministry posts in Governments formed after the liberation under Henri
Queuille, Georges Bidault, and René Pleven—
those, successively, of Secretary of State for
Finance, Minister of the Budget, and Minister
of Justice. A lawyer by profession, he was
France's assistant delegate to the International
Military Tribunal in Nuremberg and, before
that, director of legislative services to De
Gaulle's French Committee of National Liberation. On February 29, 1952, Premier Faure
resigned when his forty-day-old Government

failed to win a vote of confidence in the National Assembly.

Edgar Faure was born August 18, 1908, in
Béziers, one of the principal cities of the Department of Hérault, which lies on the Mediterranean. He was graduated from the School
of Oriental Languages in Paris and from the
Faculty of Law, receiving a doctorate from the
latter. Entering the practice of law as an
avocat or barrister, Faure became a lawyer
associated with the Paris Court of Appeal.
France-Amérique has said that he was one of
the youngest doctors of laws and one of
the most brilliant legal men of his time.
During the World War II years, reported the
New York *Herald Tribune*, he made a "distinguished record" in the French underground's
opposition to the Nazis. During 1943 and 1944
he directed the legislative department of the
French Committee of National Liberation,
headed by General de Gaulle in North Africa.

The French Provisional Government, under
de Gaulle, in December 1945 appointed Edgar
Faure assistant delegate to Champetier de
Ribes, the French jurist participating in the
prosecution by the International Military Tribunal of World War II criminals at Nuremberg. The following year, on November 10,
1946, Faure was elected a deputy to the National Assembly on the Radical-Socialist ballot, from the Department of the Jura (where
he has a country home). In the Assembly he
was chosen vice-president of the parliamentary
commission of inquiry into events in France
between 1933 and 1945, and also served as vice-
president of the federalist group in the parliament. Another parliamentary post he held
was that of secretary to the finance committee.

Faure was brought into the Cabinet of
Premier Henri Queuille as Secretary of State
for Finance on February 13, 1949. Speaking
at Meaux on the thirty-fifth commemoration
of the Battle of the Marne that September,
Faure said of France's economic condition:
"We can say today that very great progress
has been made. Financial health is not in de-
flation, not any more in inflation but in stability, and what has been accomplished has not
been accomplished by a party but by all of
France." He pointed out that a general index
figure of 130 had been reached, close to
France's all-time high production figure of
1927. Faure also promised the presentation
of a complete budget to the Assembly, for the
first time since the liberation of France—budgetary measures since then had been voted
through on a temporary basis, because of the
press of other necessary measures before the
parliament.

When the first Queuille Cabinet fell and was
replaced by that headed by Georges Bidault
on October 28, 1949, Faure retained the post of
Secretary of State for Finance until the Bidault Cabinet resigned on June 24, 1950. In
the succeeding Ministry of René Pleven, accepted by a vote of 335 to 226 on July 12 because of its commitment to raise labor's wages,
Faure was given the portfolio of Minister of
the Budget (the same which he had held in the
two-day cabinet—July 2 to July 4—of

Queuille). Visiting New York briefly in August, Faure told a New York *Herald Tribune* interviewer that the French budget had practically achieved a balance, with the help of counterpart funds supplied by Marshall Plan aid, which covered 10 per cent of the expenses. He also expressed interest in French exports to the United States and in adjustment of the high prices prevailing for them in the latter country. When Queuille returned to the Premiership on March 10, 1951, he kept Faure as Minister of the Budget. Controversy over the question of aid to Catholic schools led to the fall of that Cabinet in August, at which time Pleven succeeded in forming a liberal, central, and moderately rightist coalition (without either Gaullists or Communists) which was accepted by a vote of 390 to 222 on August 11. In this fifteenth Government since the liberation, Faure became Minister of Justice, holding that portfolio until the collapse of the six-month-old Pleven Ministry on January 8, 1952. It fell, said the New York *Times*, because the Socialists refused to support it on domestic policies.

The Pleven Ministry's failure to win a vote of confidence made it necessary for President Auriol to seek a new Premier. Faure was the sixth member of the Assembly requested to form a Cabinet in a political situation made complicated by the Socialists' insistence on a sliding scale as a basis for minimum wages, and by the right and center parties' demand for re-formation of the Government-owned railroads and of the social security system. The selection of the former Minister of the Budget was considered encouraging, reported the New York *Times*, because of his "particular competence on the problems that were the direct cause of the Pleven Cabinet's fall." After a week's discussion with the various parties, Faure offered a compromise on the wage scale and the substitution of a specific bill on the railways and the social security questions, instead of the executive decree plan suggested by the previous Premier. The full name of Faure's party is Radical and Radical Socialist party. When it was organized near the end of the nineteenth century, it had some Leftist tendencies, but since it often was the party of the Government, it had leaned toward compromise. Today it is roughly classified as a moderate, center party, with its chief support coming from the urban middle class, the rural population, and small businessmen. While it is still opposed to clerical influence in public affairs, it tends toward conservatism in economic issues.

On January 17, 1952, Faure (reportedly the youngest Premier France has had since 1875) appeared before the Assembly to make what the New York *Times* called "the appeal of a technician for a spirit of compromise and discipline." Following a period of questions directed at him, on January 18 he received the unusually heavy supporting vote of 401 to 101. "He won the vote," reported Lansing Warren of the *Times*, "by the exceptional brilliance of his performance in facing the volley of questions of seasoned political veterans from all sides and by the dazzling effect of the sallies he made extempore." This gained the hitherto uncertain support of the Socialists; the Communists opposed him and the Gaullists abstained. Besides statements on foreign policy (he supported the previous Cabinet's stand on continued war in Indo-China and rearmament, as well as against reviving a German national army), Faure made an appeal to maintain the workers' standard of living, for "the enemies of freedom win points only because there are countries in the world where poverty and misery are so great that freedom does not count." Except for two members, the Cabinet he proposed to the Assembly on January 20 was of the same composition as Pleven's pro-Western coalition, with Robert Schuman remaining as Foreign Minister and Georges Bidault as Defense Minister. Faure, himself, took the portfolio of Minister of Finance in place of René Mayer. Faure's Cabinet received a 396-to-220 vote of approval in the Assembly on January 22, four days after he had been invested as Premier. This approval also endorsed his conciliatory but firm policy toward Tunisia, where disorders had broken out: "France would proceed as in the past to foster Tunisian independence, to be introduced by stages" (New York *Times*). Faure resigned as Premier on February 29, 1952, after the National Assembly rejected his Government's proposal for a 15 per cent tax increase to meet additional expenses for the defense program.

Under the pseudonym of Edgar Sanday, Faure is known as a writer of detective stories. In Paris he has an apartment one block from the Left Bank of the Seine. There he lives with Madame Faure (whose maiden name was Meyer) and their two daughters, Sylvie and Agnès. Faure, reported the *Christian Science Monitor* correspondent, "is known as something of a wit, with an immense capacity for absorbing new facts and figures . . . and a brilliant forensic talent."

References

N Y Herald Tribune p21 Ag 28 '50
Newsweek 39:32 Ja 28 '52
International Who's Who, 1951
Dictionnaire Biographique Français Contemporains (1950)

FAUST, CLARENCE H(ENRY) (foust)
Mar. 11, 1901- Educator
Address: b. c/o Fund for the Advancement of Education, 914 E. Green St., Pasadena 1, Calif.

To be president of the Fund for the Advancement of Education, an independent agency established by the Ford Foundation, the trustees of the parent body elected Dr. Clarence H. Faust on April 4, 1951. Since 1947 he had been the director of libraries and dean of humanities and sciences at Stanford University. Prior to those appointments Dr. Faust, who began his career as a minister of the Evangelical Church, was for seventeen years a member of the English Department of the University of Chicago and was the principal author of a new

CLARENCE H. FAUST

college program introduced there in 1942. In the field of scholarship, Faust is best known as an authority on Jonathan Edwards and Ralph Waldo Emerson. The fund which he now administers made disbursements of upwards of $4,000,000 in 1951, mainly in the form of fellowships for young instructors, and in aid to certain colleges and universities.

Clarence Henry Faust is a native of Defiance, Iowa; born to Henry John and Wilhelmina (Mueller) Faust on March 11, 1901, he was brought up in the Hawkeye State. He was a student at Drake University in Des Moines for one year (1918-19) before enrolling at North Central College, Naperville, Illinois. The college, only a short distance from Chicago, is affiliated with the Evangelical Theological Seminary, also at Naperville. There the young Iowan became a divinity student after receiving his B.A. degree from the college in 1923. Awarded his B.D. degree in 1924 and ordained in the ministry of the Evangelical Church, he was a pastor for four years (1924-28) before acquiring his M.A. degree from the University of Chicago in 1929. As a graduate student at Chicago he made the career and beliefs of the eighteenth century theologian Jonathan Edwards his special field; and it was in the following year, while Faust was holding an instructorship in English at the University of Arkansas, that the newly launched review *American Literature* included in its January 1930 number the first of his published writings, "Jonathan Edwards as a Scientist."

In the fall of 1930, Faust returned to the University of Chicago as an English instructor and candidate for the Ph.D. degree, which he received in 1935. With Thomas H. Johnson, head of the English Department at Hackley School, Tarrytown, New York, he collaborated on the book *Jonathan Edwards: Representative Selections, With Introduction, Bibliography and Notes*, published early in 1935. Later in the

same year he was advanced to an assistant professorship and appointed dean of the University of Chicago's Division of Humanities. Meanwhile he had begun to extend his systematic study of the "history of ideas" into the nineteenth century; the first result of this was the paper "Background of the Unitarian Opposition to Transcendentalism," published in the February 1938 number of *Modern Philology*. Advanced to associate professor in 1939, Faust was on leave of absence from Chicago in 1940-41, having received a Sterling Fellowship at Yale University for that period. He became a member of the editorial board of the *New England Quarterly* in 1940 and continued as such until 1943.

Resuming at Chicago in the summer of 1941, Faust was advanced to a full professorship and made dean of the College. In the latter capacity he was largely responsible for the preparation of the new program of undergraduate education which was announced in January of 1942, and which (in Dean Faust's phrasing) "created a furore in academic circles." As Faust has put it in a report published in the *Educational Review* for April 1945, "the decision in 1942 was to make the College a four-year unit devoted to an integrated program of liberal education, beginning with the junior year of high school, and to award the bachelor's degree for the completion of the requirements of the college." In other words, the B.A. degree could be obtained at what would ordinarily have been the end of the sophomore year at college; and while Faust has stressed that the program was designed for permanence, its adoption was hastened by the entrance of the United States into World War II, since it meant that in many instances students would be able to attain their college degrees before becoming liable for induction into the armed services.

The new four-year course opened in the autumn of 1942 with 200 students largely drawn from the Chicago University High School; but by the end of 1944 the enrollment had risen to 1,887, with students from other parts of the country. Faust administered the new program until the autumn of 1946, meanwhile also pursuing his scholarly work in the nineteenth century field. He collaborated with a fellow faculty member Walter Blair on the article entitled "Emerson's Literary Method," which appeared in *Modern Philology* for November 1944; and "From Edwards to Emerson" was the topic of the series of Clover Lectures he delivered at Brown University in 1945. His paper entitled "Emerson's Literary Theory and Practice" was published in *Modern Philology* in 1946.

A new phase in Faust's career began in October 1946, when he was appointed dean of the University of Chicago's Graduate Library School in succession to Ralph A. Beals, who resigned to become director of the New York Public Library. Slightly less than twelve months later, Faust ended his seventeen years with the University of Chicago to assume (in September 1947) the duties of director of libraries at Stanford University. In April 1948 he became dean of the Faculty of Humanities and Sciences; then, in January 1949 (following the departure of Dr. Alvin C. Eurich to become head of the State University of New York) he was named acting president of Stanford pending the arrival in the following April of the recently appointed president, Dr. Wallace Sterling. Faust, who is a contributor to the symposium *General Education in Transition; A Look Ahead* (1951), continued as dean of the Humanities and Sciences at Stanford until his election, on April 4, 1951, as president of the Fund for the Advancement of Education established by the Ford Foundation.

The Ford Foundation was organized as a corporation in Michigan in 1936 by the late Edsel B. Ford, with a charter defining its purpose as "to receive and administer funds for scientific, educational and charitable purposes." Joseph M. McDaniel, Jr., now assistant director of the foundation, was to point out in an address at Detroit in October 1951, "Both he and his father, Henry Ford, bequeathed important parts of their estates to the foundation," but pending the settlement of these estates, the total grants and disbursements were limited to around $40,000,000. In the autumn of 1948, however, a study committee was appointed to work out a program for future activity; and by 1950, when this committee rendered its report, the estates had been settled and the foundation was in command of resources of nearly $500,000,000 providing income sufficient for annual grants and disbursements of about $25,000,000. The report, which was adopted by the trustees in September, recommended five "areas for action," the fourth of which was "to support activities to strengthen, expand and improve educational facilities and methods to enable individuals more fully to realize their intellectual, civic and spiritual responsibilities" as well as "to promote greater equality of educational opportunity" and "to conserve and increase knowledge and enrich our culture."

It was to expedite a part of this aim that, following the assumption by Paul G. Hoffman of the presidency of the Ford Foundation on January 1, 1951, the Fund for the Advancement of Education was set up (in April) as a separate, nonprofit corporation with its own board of directors headed by Frank W. Abrams of the Standard Oil Company of New Jersey. The purpose of the fund, which received an initial appropriation of $7,154,000, is "to improve education in grade and high schools, colleges and universities," and to this end grants totaling $4,204,530 were made before the end of 1951. "Most of this" (Joseph McDaniel has stated) "has gone to two programs: grants to colleges and universities which permit students under 16½ to enter college without finishing high school, $1,904,400; and fellowships for college teachers, $2,280,000." In announcing the fellowship program on April 26, 1951, Faust explained that it had two major objectives. "First," he stated, "it is aimed at making constructive use of the present national emergency period by enabling a large number of younger teachers to increase their skill in undergraduate instruction. Second, it is intended

to assist colleges to keep a substantial number of promising young teachers who might otherwise be lost to the academic field because of the potential curtailment of college operations due to national mobilization." About 253 instructors received fellowships for the academic year 1951-52 and 250 similar fellowships are planned for 1952-53. The fund's headquarters are at Pasadena, California; and there is also a New York office under the direction of Dr. Eurich, who resigned from the State University in May 1951 to take over operations of the fund in the East.

Clarence Faust and Gladys Lang were married in June 1924, and are the parents of three sons, William Langdon, Dale Henry, and Franklin Paul.

References

Col & Res Lib 8:78 Ja '47 por
Lib J 71:1528 N 1 '46 por

Directory of American Scholars (1942)
International Who's Who (1951)
Leaders in Education (1948)
Who's Who in America, 1950-51
World Biography (1948)

FEINSINGER, NATHAN P(AUL) (fĭn'-sĭng-ẽr) Sept. 20, 1902- Former United States Government official; educator

Address: b. c/o University of Wisconsin, Madison, Wis.; h. Old Middleton Rd., Route 2, Madison, Wis.

Professor of law at the University of Wisconsin, author of books on labor laws, and, beginning on August 30, 1951, chairman of the Wage Stabilization Board in Washington, D.C., Nathan P. Feinsinger has been active in the settling of labor disputes since the late 1930's. He has served successively as a member of the Wisconsin Labor Relations Board, the National War Labor Relations Board, the President's steel and meat fact-finding boards, and as a special representative of the Secretary of Labor in various disputes. In early 1952, as chairman of the Wage Stabilization Board, he figured prominently in negotiations with labor and management in an unsuccessful effort to avert a nation-wide steel strike. The board which Feinsinger headed was disbanded in July 1952 and was replaced by a new WSB under the chairmanship of Archibald Cox.

Nathan Paul Feinsinger was born in Brooklyn, New York, on September 20, 1902, the son of Israel Bernard and Rebecca (Neighstock) Feinsinger. Going to the Middle West for his undergraduate education, he attended the University of Michigan, where he was a member of the varsity track team for three years. His scholastic record won him election to Phi Beta Kappa. After receiving his B.A. degree in June 1926, he entered the university's Law School, where two years later (1928) he was awarded the Doctor of Jurisprudence degree.

Upon completion of his studies at Michigan, Feinsinger returned to New York to engage in postgraduate sociolegal research at Columbia Law School for the academic year 1928-29.

(Continued next page)

NATHAN P. FEINSINGER

In 1929 he was also admitted to the New York bar, but later in that year was back in the Middle West, having accepted an assistant professorship in law at the University of Wisconsin. In the successive ranks of assistant, associate, and full professor Feinsinger has been with the University of Wisconsin ever since, being granted leaves of absence for Government work. Two professorial engagements, for which he also obtained leaves, were as visiting professor of law at the University of Chicago in 1934 and at the University of Michigan in 1936. He had been admitted to the Wisconsin bar in 1931, and in 1937 was chosen special assistant to the attorney general and general counsel of the Wisconsin Labor Relations Board, a post which he held through 1939. In connection with his work for this board, he collaborated with W. G. Rice in a study entitled the *Wisconsin Labor Relations Act,* published in 1937.

Feinsinger began his work for the Federal Government in 1942, upon becoming associate general counsel to the National War Labor Relations Board in Washington, D.C. In this capacity he was active in negotiations of the United Mine Workers strike of 1943, the War Labor Board's fact-finding panel having appointed him on May 6 to represent the United Mine Workers as "stand-in" for John L. Lewis, president of the union, who had refused to appear at meetings of the panel or to negotiate with the War Labor Board.

In 1944, now a representative of the public on the War Labor Board, Feinsinger was again instrumental in settling a labor dispute. This time the nation's whole communications system was endangered by the growing telephone operators' strike, and the army was about to take control. The New York *Sun* said that as he was leaving his office to keep a social engagement for Thanksgiving afternoon, Feinsinger was told that the union leaders were coming.

He sat down again, conferred with the leaders, and within six minutes secured their agreement to a plan to end the strike.

The mediator remained with the War Labor Board through 1945, holding the successive titles of associate general counsel, director of national disputes, alternate public member, and public member. Then, on New Year's Day of 1946 President Truman appointed him to the three-man fact-finding board to investigate and make recommendations concerning the wage dispute between United States Steel and the United Steel Workers (CIO), the union which had scheduled a strike for January 14. Although the strike, the largest and most costly in United States history according to *Time,* was not averted, the fact-finding board of which Feinsinger was chairman was instrumental in bringing about its termination the following month.

In April 1946 Feinsinger acted as chairman and a Government member of the International Labor Office conference held in Cleveland, Ohio, for the purpose of considering methods of improving working, living, and social standards in the iron and steel industry throughout the world. In July he was in San Francisco investigating the West Coast maritime dispute between the Waterfront Employers' Association and the International Longshoremen's and Warehousemen's Union (CIO). The dispute, which had resulted in a strike, was terminated in mid-November partly through the efforts of Federal Mediator Feinsinger, who was special representative of Secretary of Labor, Lewis B. Schwellenbach. Meanwhile, in September Feinsinger had headed the three-man board that prepared and submitted a report to Schwellenbach advocating the use of the fact-finding system as the best current procedure in preventing labor strife.

Again as Schwellenbach's special representative, Feinsinger on November 5, 1946, temporarily interrupted his work on the maritime dispute to make the first of a series of trips to Hawaii, in this case to look into the sugar workers' strike. The sugar strike was scarcely set led, late in December of 1946, before a maritime strike seemed likely to tie up all Hawaiian ports. Feinsinger, acting as Federal labor conciliator, was able to bring about a settlement of the dispute on January 3, 1947, before an actual outbreak of the strike. In July of the same year a strike in the pineapple industry did take place in Hawaii but was terminated within five days, an agreement having been reached on the basis of recommendations made by Feinsinger.

Meanwhile, in June of 1947 Feinsinger returned briefly to San Francisco, where he had been successful in bringing about an interim agreement between West Coast ship operators and the marine cooks and radio operators unions. This dispute, termed a "lockout" by the unions and a "strike" by the employers, had tied up some twenty ships on the West Coast. Then, shortly after his latest return from Hawaii in July, Feinsinger, as chairman, attended the opening meeting of the Pacific Coast Longshore Safety Commission in San

Francisco, the commission having been agreed to the preceeding year in the contract settling the West Coast maritime strike.

Acting in his former capacity of chairman of a fact-finding board appointed by President Truman, Feinsinger went to Washington, D.C., in April 1948 to aid in the settlement of a strike between the United Packinghouse Workers of America (CIO), and major meat packers. In a report that the President described as "objective and clarifying," the board supported the packers' offer of a nine-cent hourly wage increase. But the union considered the proposed increase insufficient, and the strike, which had begun on March 16, remained unsettled until late September of 1948.

Feinsinger delivered a speech in February 1949 to the Senate Labor Committee concerning the deficiencies, from the standpoint of labor, of the 1947 Taft-Hartley Act. On May 3, 1951, President Truman appointed him a public member of the newly reconstituted Wage Stabilization Board. Soon afterward he became vice-chairman of the board, and on August 30, 1951, was appointed chairman to replace George W. Taylor, who had resigned on August 29.

As chairman of the WSB, Feinsinger was faced with the fundamental question of the amount wages could be raised to meet the higher cost of living without increasing the threat of national inflation. To meet this problem a program for wage increases based proportionately on productivity increases was outlined, and on January 27, 1952, in a progress report on the first full year of wage stabilization, Feinsinger announced success in holding wage increases down below the rate of a comparable "prestabilization" period. He also stated in January 1952 that the board would soon grant exemption from wage controls to small employers, probably those with four workers or less, and in February 1952 the question of pensions was handled when the board exempted employee pension plans from wage ceilings.

The Board's principal problems arose in the direct handling of labor disputes. In order to avert strikes that might affect national defense, the Government has been referring critical disputes to the WSB since September 8, 1951, when the President put into effect his executive order which gave the Board fact-finding jurisdiction over such disputes—the occasion was the Utah copper shutdown. Since then the Board has handled disputes in the Douglas Aircraft Company at Long Beach, California, the Wright Aeronautical Corporation at Woodridge, New Jersey, both in October 1951, and in the Wichita (Kansas) plant of the Boeing Airplane Company in December 1951.

A more serious problem confronted Chairman Feinsinger in late 1951, when in November Philip Murray, president of the CIO, announced that the United Steel Workers of America would not submit to wage controls while prices remained "free of any effective check." A strike was scheduled for New Year's Eve, but about four days earlier at Truman's request the union agreed to continue work while the WSB considered the workers' demands for a substantial wage increase as well as a union shop agreement. The ensuing controversy hinged primarily on the question of whether the WSB recommendation of a wage increase agreeable to the union could be granted without a rise in steel prices of sufficient magnitude to threaten the national effort to stabilize the economy. When the WSB recommendation for a wage increase (an action which led to the resignation of Defense Mobilizer Charles E. Wilson) was rejected by the major steel companies, Feinsinger met separately with management and union representatives and on April 6, 1952, arranged a resumption of meetings between the two groups. The WSB Chairman was without authority to discuss prices, but in regard to other matters, as Feinsinger was quoted in the press as saying, he was empowered to do anything he considered necessary or desirable to help settle the dispute. The threatened strike was averted by Government seizure of most of the nation's steel plants on April 9, 1952. (In an interview with Feinsinger the *United States News & World Report* devoted eight pages in the April 18 issue to the topic "What Brought Steel Seizure.") Another important controversy referred to the Federal Board in the spring of 1952 was a wage dispute in the oil industry between 75 major oil companies and 200,000 workers. On July 29, 1952, the WSB headed by Feinsinger disbanded, and a new board, with Archibald Cox as chairman, started functioning the next day.

Nathan Paul Feinsinger is the editor of the fourth edition of A. A. Stearns's *Law of Suretyship* (1934); is author of *Cases and Other Materials on Partnership* (1939), *Cases and Materials on Labor Law* (1940), *Collective Bargaining in the Trucking Industry* (1949), and is coauthor with E. E. Witte of the article "Labor, Legislation, and the Role of Government," published in the *Monthly Labor Review* for July 1950. He holds membership in Kappa Nu fraternity, the Order of the Coif, and the Druids. He has been married to Bettie (Whitney) Feinsinger since January 15, 1940, and is the father of three children, Greg, Ellen, and Peter. A devotee of sports, he enjoys tennis, skiing, skating, and squash, although a near-fatal automobile accident in the winter of 1950 has curtailed some of these activities.

References

  N Y Herald Tribune II p1 Mr 23 '52
  N Y Sun p30 Ag 9 '44

  Who's Who in America, 1950-51
  Who's Who in American Jewry, 1938-39
  Who's Who in Law, 1937
  Who's Who in the Midwest (1949)
  World Biography (1948)

FELLOWS, HAROLD E(VERETT) Mar. 22, 1899- Trade association executive
Address: b. c/o National Association of Radio and Television Broadcasters, 1771 N St., Washington 6, D.C.; h. 423 Puritan Rd., Swampscott, Mass.

The president of the National Association of Radio and Television Broadcasters—the association described in the *Britannica Book of the Year* as "the industry's major trade organization"—is Harold E. Fellows, who had been for seventeen years the general manager of Station WEEI in Boston and for the last seven of those the manager of the New England operations of the Columbia Broadcasting System. Successor to Judge Justin Miller, now chairman of the board, he assumed the presidency of the NARTB on June 4, 1951.

HAROLD E. FELLOWS

Harold Everett Fellows, a native of New England's lower Merrimac valley, is the son of Roscoe Conklin and Grace Adelaide (Hilliard) Fellows. He was born March 22, 1899, in Amesbury, Massachusetts, and passed much of his childhood on a farm at Newton, New Hampshire, just across the State line; then, at the age of twelve he moved with his parents to the nearby shoe-manufacturing city of Haverhill, Massachusetts, where he received his secondary education. At intervals during the four years at the Haverhill High School he worked as a shoe salesman, and by the time of his graduation in 1916 (the year he was president of his class) had decided to follow a business career. Attending New York University where he majored in business administration and advertising, he also worked as a district sales manager for the New York *Herald Tribune*. Later he took courses at Burdett College, a business school in Boston. In the Marine Corps for World War I serv-

ice, he was undergoing specialized training at Harvard College when the armistice was signed. Demobilized, he returned to Haverhill in 1919 to remain eight years as a junior executive with a wholesale provision and cold storage firm.

It was during this period that the sequence of events began which carried Fellows first into vaudeville, then into advertising, and finally into the radio field. "As a paying avocation," stated a biographical sketch supplied by his office, "he sang with a trio. The discovery one night that people enjoy hearing him talk launched him on a career of after-dinner speaking." (It is said that during one five-month period he delivered about 155 postprandial talks.) Attracted to show business, Fellows developed his talent as entertainer in a season of one-night vaudeville stands, and, after leaving the Haverhill provision house in 1927, was for a time in charge of advertising and direct mail with a theatrical costume and scenery firm. "His initial experience in broadcasting," according to the biographical release, "occurred in 1928 when he went on the air . . . in behalf of a paint sponsor. The format of his one-man show included a little singing and a lot of talking, adding up to a lot of sales appeal."

The station was WEEI in Boston, and the young performer soon found himself employed by the Harry M. Frost Advertising Agency as the first radio director in that city. Later in 1928 he established his own agency. In 1930 he became general manager of the Greenleaf Advertising Agency, and two years later (1932) he was appointed assistant manager and commercial manager of WEEI. There he was credited with having doubled the station's billings in his first year as commercial manager. When, in 1936, the station (which was owned by the Boston Edison Company) was leased to the Columbia Broadcasting System, Fellows was promoted to general manager. "Under his direction WEEI has won many industry awards for excellence in promotion, selling, programming, civic leadership and education," reported the magazine *Sales Management*; while *Printers' Ink* characterized his station management and program production as "models of the industry." In 1944 Fellow was made manager of operations of the Columbia Broadcasting System in New England, which he held concurrently with his WEEI position, but from which he resigned when he became the president of the National Association of Radio and Television Broadcasters.

The radio station executive early became a member of the National Association of Broadcasters, the organization established by radio station operators in 1922 "to foster and promote the development of the art of radio broadcasting, and to encourage practices which will be in the best interests of the public and the radio industry." The organization—which is now named the National Association of Radio and Television Broadcasters—has since its inception opposed extension of governmental curbs and of the powers of the Federal Communications Commission and proposals in the Federal Congress and elsewhere to set up boards of review for radio through legislative action. The threat of official censorship seemed particularly serious in 1947, the year in which Fellows was elected to the board of directors of the association. During the same year, when Justin Miller (who had been installed as fifteenth president of the association in 1945) established a special standards of practice committee to draw up a code of self-regulation for the industry, Fellows was named to this body as well as to the finance and public relations committees. The code, which imposes limits on the length of commercial announcements while establishing specific taboos on profanity, attacks on religion, sympathetic treatment of crime and the like, was completed early in 1948. It was adopted by the association in May of that year, to become effective at the beginning of July.

On April 3, 1951, announcement was made from headquarters at Washington, D.C., that Harold E. Fellows had been chosen the sixteenth president of the National Association of Radio and Television Broadcasters in succession to Justin Miller, who was slated to become chairman of the board. The salary, *Variety* reported, is believed to start at $35,000 with annual increases for five years. Commenting on Fellows' appointment, *Printers' Ink* (April 27) remarked that "leading the NARTB is no sinecure" and that the new president would "need all his charm and all his ability to keep broadcasting's competitive segments—AM, FM, and TV—from fighting among themselves so much that they forget that they should be commonly aligned against other media."

President Fellows, who was inducted into office on June 4, 1951, made it clear (in an article he wrote for *Variety* some six weeks later) that he fully comprehended the perils of lethargy; the industry, he pointed out, had permitted itself and its medium "to coast along without acquiring anywhere near the status in the minds of everyone . . . it truly deserves." Thus, at a district meeting in Roanoke, Virginia, at the end of August he mentioned, among improved services to be undertaken by the association, a group insurance plan and the compilation of a "running record of radio's service to mankind." This presumably would come within the sphere of the association's broadcasting advertising bureau, which had been established in 1949. The association has also expressed the belief that "the larger percentage" of its member stations will assist the Ford Foundation in a special study, announced June 11, to determine how commercial television can contribute to "a better level of educational, informative, and more culturally mature programming."

A bill sponsored in Congress by Senator William Benton of Connecticut for the creation of a National Citizens' Advisory Board to examine the program content of radio and television shows and recommend corrective legislation, spurred a committee of the association to complete, after twelve months of deliberation, a code of practices for television. This set of rules, which in the main repeats the provisions of the radio code with additional regulations regarding modesty in dress, was endorsed by some eighty members of the association at a meeting in Chicago on October 18. The latest available figures in 1952 shows that NARTB has a total membership of 1,464. When Columbia Broadcasting System became a member in late 1951 (after withdrawing in May 1950), the return of the network was considered "a feather in the cap" of Fellows.

In the course of his years as a radio executive in Boston, Fellows was active in so many State, city, professional, welfare, and educational organizations that he was known as "Mr. Massachusetts." He has served as president of the Advertising and Radio Executives Clubs of Boston and of the Boston Better Business Bureau; as vice-president and convention committee chairman of the Boston Chamber of Commerce; as a member of the executive committee of Greater Boston Development Committee; as chairman of the Massachusetts State Broadcasters Committee; on the executive committee of the National Conference of Christians and Jews; on the advisory board of Simmons College and the board of visitors of Boston University's School of Public Relations and Communications; on the New England Committee of the National Planning Association; on the board of trustees of the Arthritic Foundation; and on the advertising committee of the United States Chamber of Commerce. His clubs are the Advertising in Boston, the Beach at Swampscott (Massachusetts), and the Tedesco Country, at Marblehead. A member of the Theta Chi social fraternity since his college days, he was also made an honorary member of the Alpha Delta Sigma advertising fraternity on November 18, 1947. He is a Republican and a Congregationalist.

Harold E. Fellows and Janet S. Edgerly were married June 10, 1919, and have two daughters, Barbara Louise (Mrs. Arthur S. Spangler) and Jeanne Edgerly (Mrs. Keith C. Steele), and six grandchildren. The association executive is five feet ten inches in height, weighs 178 pounds, and has hazel eyes and brown hair. He enjoys game fishing in Maine and in the Wisconsin lake country; at his Swampscott home his hobby is gardening.

References

Printers' Ink 238:74 Ap 27 '51 por
Sales Management 66:40 My 1 '51 por
Variety Radio Directory, 1940-41
Who's Who in New England (1949)

FIELD, MARSHALL, 3d Sept. 28, 1893-
Publisher

Address: b. 250 Park Ave., New York 17; c/o Field Enterprises, Inc., 211 W. Wacker Dr., Chicago 6, Ill.; h. Lloyd Harbor, Huntington, N.Y.

NOTE: This biography supersedes the article which appeared in *Current Biography* in 1941.

Marshall Field 3d, the grandson of the founder of the Marshall Field department store in Chicago, is a publisher, radio station owner, and a former investment banker.

(Continued next page)

Halsman

MARSHALL FIELD 3D

In 1939 he began to concern himself with social problems—his interests have ranged from child welfare to the subsidizing of the now defunct liberal newspaper *PM*. In 1952 Field makes most of his philanthropic grants through the Field Foundation, Inc., of which he is president. As president of Field Enterprises, Inc., he directs his publishing and radio properties: the *Sun-Times*, a Chicago newspaper, *Parade* magazine, the *World Book Encyclopedia*, *Childcraft*, five radio stations, and holdings in two book-publishing houses.

The Field forebears were among America's early settlers: in 1630 Zechariah Field left England for America, going first to Connecticut and later settling in Massachusetts. In 1856 there arrived in Chicago, then a young boom town, Marshall Field, the Field descendant who was to amass, through the Chicago department store that bears his name, and banking, real estate, and railroad interests, one of the world's largest personal fortunes. His grandson and heir, Marshall Field 3d, was born September 28, 1893, in Chicago, one of the four children of Marshall Field 2d and Albertine (Huck) Field, the daughter of a Chicago brewer of German descent. (Of the other children, the daughter now lives in Scotland, one son died in infancy, and another in 1917.) Young Field's father died in a shooting accident when the boy was twelve; his grandfather, who lived to the age of seventy-one, died a few months later, in 1906. Shortly thereafter Mrs. Field took her three children to England, where young Marshall attended Eton (graduating in 1911) and then studied history and economics at Trinity College, Cambridge. At the age of twenty-one he returned to the United States to take over a trusteeship of the Field Estate.

Ten days after the United States entered World War I Field enlisted as a private in the 1st Illinois Cavalry, which shortly thereafter became the 122d Field Artillery. He trained at Camp Logan, Texas, and in March 1918 was sent overseas, there to participate in the St. Mihiel and Meuse-Argonne operations and to be decorated for bravery under fire. He held the rank of captain when he was discharged in January 1919.

In civilian life, he became associate director of a Chicago bureau that found employment for ex-servicemen and helped organize community centers for young people. For about a year (1920-21) he was a bond salesman with Lee, Higginson & Company, a brokerage house, before becoming a partner in the investment banking firm, Marshall Field, Glore, Ward & Company, later changed to Field, Glore & Company. As one of its four trustees he was meanwhile helping in the management of the Field Estate, which owns downtown buildings and other property in Chicago as well as stocks and bonds in a number of enterprises. Best known of these is Marshall Field & Company, the Chicago department store which is celebrating its hundredth year in 1952 and of which Field is a stockholder and a director; he owns less than 10 per cent of its common stock and takes little part in its direction, states John Tebbel in his book *The Marshall Fields*.

Field and his family—he had married Evelyn Marshall in 1915—in 1921 moved East, where he built a Long Island country estate, "Caumsett." Its 65-room house and 1,750 acres was run by a staff of eighty-five servants and other employees. There Field maintained stables and a herd of prize cattle, raised prize flowers, flew a private plane, hunted, fished, played polo, tennis, and other sports; he was at the same time managing his investment firm, and serving as director of about twelve corporations. When his first marriage was terminated by divorce in 1930, Field married Audrey James Coats (on a honeymoon trip to Africa, the pair shot a lion, almost lost their lives in a plane crash in the Sudan). Following his second divorce, in 1934, he turned to psychoanalysis to help him account for his growing dissatisfaction with the pattern of his life. The result was that he retired from the banking business and sought to employ a deepening interest in sociological questions.

Early in his philanthropic career Field became interested in child welfare, setting up a New York committee which contributed funds to ten child welfare societies. In addition, problems arising in interracial and intercultural relations continued to be his major concerns after the formation of the Field Foundation, Inc., in October 1940. Field himself has given the reasons for establishing the foundation: "For one thing, I found that a busy schedule of civic and business responsibilities did not allow time to exercise thought and discrimination in deciding upon the merits of the hundreds of appeals for donations addressed to me personally. Moreover, I am opposed to giving of money on a paternalistic or emotional basis. Such gifts, made impulsively and without appropriate study, are frequently resented by the recipients and in any event are extremely unlikely to achieve constructive results." With assets of $11,000,000 the foundation limits itself to making grants for "charitable, scientific, and educational work," does not seek to influence legislation nor engage in propaganda.

One year after the outbreak of World War II, Field became president of the United States Committee for the Care of European Children. When British authorities decided to suspend the child removal program in October 1940 because of the danger of submarine attack, the committee turned its attention to the care of children already in the United States. Marshall Field himself brought five British children into his home, worked in several war relief agencies, and later headed an organization for dispensing hospitality to servicemen on leave in New York City. In 1943 he turned over his estate to the OWI Overseas Branch for use as a school to train combat propaganda teams.

Field was also interested in the furtherance of liberal ideas. Though he had in 1932 contributed to Hoover's campaign fund, by 1934, as he phrased it, "I got rather disgusted with the Republican party and I got interested in Roosevelt and what he was trying to do." His opportunity came in 1940 when he met Ralph Ingersoll, who was seeking funds to establish a liberal crusading newspaper in New York, without accepting advertisements. At first only one of eighteen stockholders in the new paper, which appeared as *PM* in June 1940, when the paper faced a financial crisis (having expended $1,500,000) Field formed a new corporation (in October 1940) by paying the stockholders $300,000 and a 15 per cent interest in the new company in return for the assets of the old.

Probably the only publisher in the country ever to subsidize a newspaper over which he exercised no editorial control, Field was eventually to invest $5,000,000 in *PM*. When the newspaper announced in November 1946 that it would begin to accept advertising, Field wrote that he saw more danger to *PM*'s independence in the fact that one man supported it "than could possibly arise from accepting support from the advertisers of the community. . . .*PM*'s existence cannot permanently depend on whether one man happens to wish to continue to support it." The prolabor, pro-New Deal policy of *PM*, though not determined by Field, had his respect—"I am convinced that [the paper] is paying dividends to me and to all other Americans who care about the promise of American life and the early traditions of freedom in American newspapers." But *PM* was not to survive: in June 1948, it ceased publication, after descending from a peak circulation of 164,686 in 1946 to 140,834.

Meanwhile, Field decided to launch a full-size morning paper of liberal and interventionist policy (but not experimental in format as was *PM*) to compete with the isolationist Chicago *Tribune*. His Chicago *Daily Sun* began publication December 4, 1941. As a member of the paper's editorial board Field set about learning to be a newspaper executive, regularly participating in editorial conferences, occasionally writing an editorial. He determined that, unlike *PM*, the *Sun* should eventually pay for itself. When the *Sun*'s application for Associated Press membership was refused in April 1942, Field filed a complaint with the Attorney General of the United States, charging a violation of antitrust laws. The result of Government action against the A.P. was a Supreme Court decision requiring the A.P. to change its by-laws regulating membership. In November 1945 the *Sun* was admitted to A.P. membership.

The *Sun* was still losing money when in September 1947 Field bought out the stockholders (at a cost of $5,339,000) of the Chicago *Daily Times*, an afternoon tabloid, largely because the *Sun* needed a newspaper plant (it was being printed at high cost in space rented from the afternoon Chicago *Daily News*). Merging the two papers in 1948, Field brought out the *Sun-Times* as an all-day paper. In 1950, nine years after founding the *Sun*, Field withdrew as president, to be succeeded by his son, Marshall Field, Jr., who had been working as assistant to the publisher and who now became editor and publisher. The 1951 Ayer's *Directory of Newspapers and Periodicals* gave the *Sun-Times* weekday circulation as 614,687, its Sunday circulation as 655,155.

Publishing and communications interested Field increasingly. In 1944, attracted by a display of twenty-five cent Pocket Books in Grand Central Station, he wished to buy the firm. On learning that officials of the publishing house of Simon & Schuster owned 49 per cent of the Pocket Books organization, Field negotiated to purchase interests in both book companies, saying afterwards, "I am happy to associate myself in this way with a group of publishers who have pioneered in democratizing the creation and distribution of books in America." In the same year he also organized Field Enterprises, Inc., which in 1952 publishes the Chicago *Sun-Times*, the *World Book Encyclopedia* (which Field bought from the Quarrie Corporation) and *Childcraft*, a set of books for parents. Other interests are Simon & Schuster, Inc.; Pocket Books, Inc.; Parade Publications, Inc. (which publishes the 32-page weekly newspaper supplement *Parade*, founded in 1941); radio stations, WJJD and WFMF-FM (Chicago); Functional Music, Inc. Field's "Project X," which was to be a mass-circulation liberal magazine, was finally abandoned in the planning stage, partly because of high postwar costs. He is, as well, a director of the Continental Illinois National Bank and Trust Company of Chicago. Two of his radio stations, KOIN (Portland, Oregon) and KJR (Seattle, Washington), were sold in July 1952.

Institutions that have been supported by Field also include the Chicago Natural History Museum, which his grandfather founded in 1893 and to which Field himself has given several millions of dollars; its exhibits are valued at $50 millions. It was called the Field Museum of Natural History until 1943, when Field requested that the name be changed to the present one. Another interest of his was the New York Philharmonic-Symphony Society, which he helped subsidize during the depression. He is active in other civic organizations as a director of Hull House, the

FIELD, MARSHALL, 3d—*Continued*

Illinois Children's Home and Aid Society, Provident Hospital, the Public Administration Clearing House, the University of Chicago, and Roosevelt College(all in Chicago) ; and in the East, the New School for Social Research, Sarah Lawrence College, the Metropolitan Museum of Art, and the National Health and Welfare Retirement Association; he is a trustee of the New York Zoological Society, and a governor of the Menninger Foundation. In May 1951 he was elected president of the Child Welfare League of America. Honorary degrees he has received are: Doctor of Humane Letters, from McMurray College, Illinois (1944) and Northwestern University (1948) ; Doctor of Laws, from Grinnell College (1946) and from New York School for Social Research (1948).

On his fiftieth birthday (in 1943) Field came into full control of his grandfather's fortune, which had come to him in a number of transfers: the first five had brought him $93,000,000, the last was estimated to be worth between $70,000,000 and $75,000,000. The same day he bought $10,000,000's worth of war bonds, one of the largest individual purchases ever made. In his book *Freedom Is More Than a Word*, published in 1943, Field attempted to define his understanding of his position as a man of wealth in American society: "I have sought to function," he wrote," as a participating member of a democratic society, with my unusual opportunities to serve because of my financial resources, and not as a man of large property interests actuated by attitudes of self-protection. . . .What private property any of us enjoys represents the acquiescence of society in our private control of it . . and, like every privilege, it carries with it certain obligations."

Field is married to the former Mrs. Ruth (Pruyn) Phipps, who has two sons, Robert and Harry Phipps, by her first marriage. Married in 1936, the Fields have two daughters, Phyllis and Fiona. Field's children by his first wife are Marshall Fied, Jr., Mrs. Barbara (Field) Boggs, and Mrs. Bettine (Field) Goodall. The philanthropist is described as "sturdily handsome" (his heights is five feet nine inches, his weight 170 pounds), with gray hair and brown eyes. He subscribes to a Protestant faith. A member of fourteen clubs in New York, Chicago, and Washington, he lists his recreations as riding, shooting, golf, and tennis. One biographer has noted his slight English accent, quick sense of humor, and "genuine, dignified friendliness."

References

Coronet 25 :99-107 F '49
Cue 10 :34 O 4 '41 por
Life 15 :102-6+ O 18 '43 pors
New Yorker 19 :20-1 N 13 '43
Sat Eve Post 214 :14-15+ D 6 '41
Time 38 :60+ D 1 '41; 40 :51 Ag 10 '42; 42 :44+ S 27 '43; 45 :73 Ap 16 '45
Andrews, W. Battle For Chicago (1946)
Field, M. Freedom is More Than a Word (1945)

International Who's Who, 1951
National Cyclopædia of American Biography Current vol G, 1943-46
Tebbel, J. The Marshall Fields (1947)
Who's Who in America, 1950-51
World Biography (1948)
World Book Encyclopedia (1951)

FIGUEROA, ANA (fē″gā-rō′ä ä′nä) June 19, 1907- United Nations representative from Chile

Address: c/o Chile Delegation to the United Nations, 405 E. 42d St., New York 18; 1533 Agustinas St., Santiago, Chile

Señora Ana Figueroa of Chile, the first woman to be elected to the chairmanship of a major committee of a United Nations General Assembly and the first of her sex to be named an alternate delegate to the Security Council, entered upon these posts in November 1951 and January 1952, respectively, at the U.N.'s Sixth General Assembly in Paris. An educator, she has been general supervisor of the secondary schools of Chile, where she is also prominent in the advancement of women's rights. In November 1952 Señora Figueroa resigned her position as a representative from Chile to the U.N.

The daughter of Miguel Figueroa Rebolledo and Ana Gajardo Infante, Ana Figueroa was born in Santiago de Chile on June 19, 1907. She wished to become a doctor of medicine, but because women were barred from that profession she decided upon teaching as her lifework. For her preparation she enrolled at the University of Chile, from which she graduated in 1928. In the course of her teaching career she attended Teachers College of Columbia University for studies in the philosophy of education, as well as Colorado State College.

Choosing secondary education as her professional specialty, Ana Figueroa became a teacher of English and philosophy in various Chilean high schools. In 1938 she attained her first supervisory post in secondary schools when she was named principal of the Liceo San Felipe, and in the next year she assumed the same position at the Liceo de Temuco. With her promotion in 1946 to be general inspector of secondary education, she entered an office nation-wide in scope.

Besides her academic and administrative work in high school, Señora Figueroa taught psychology at the school for social workers at the University of Chile and wrote a text on sex education in 1934. For a time she observed educational methods in the United States, giving in an article ("On Misunderstanding Good Neighbors") in *School and Society* (August 2, 1947) her criticism of the teaching of Spanish (as if it were a dead language) and of misinforming students about Latin American civilization. Professional organizations to which the educator belongs are the National Society of Teachers, the Syndicate of Chilean Teachers, and the Chilean Federation of Women Instructors.

An advocate of the same opportunities and legal rights for women as men have, Señora

Figueroa administered the Chilean Women's Bureau for a period. The experience gained there is reflected in her article "Fair Deal for the Chilena," which appeared in the issue (May 1950) of the *United Nations World* devoted to Chile. In the field of women's interests she has been in addition a member of the board of the YWCA, president of the Federation of Women's Organizations in Chile, and her country's delegate to the Inter-American Commission of Women (at its sixth assembly in 1949 she was able to report that "the Chilean woman elects and can be elected.")

Señora Figueroa's official association with the United Nations began with her appointment in 1948 as a delegate plenipotentiary to the third regular session of the General Assembly. In a discussion of the international transmission of news (as reported in the *United Nations Bulletin*, June 1, 1949) she gave it as her opinion that "the world lacks sufficient information and that it is threatened by a conspiracy of silence"; in the correction of that condition Chile would "cooperate in the common effort of nations to open the way for democratic realization of fundamental freedoms." In February of 1950 she was appointed alternate permanent Chilean representative to the U.N., with the rank of Envoy Extraordinary and Minister Plenipotentiary. Elected to the Assembly's Trusteeship (Fourth) Committee later in that year, Señora Figueroa (in October) maintained that many who attacked the countries responsible for administering trust territories were themselves chargeable with "neocolonialism"; she praised Great Britain for its policy of gradually introducing self-government among African peoples under British rule. For trust territories she urged (in December) that educational programs be determined by clearly defined social goals and that political progress parallel social and educational advances.

When the United Nations opened its Sixth General Assembly in Paris in November 1951, Ana Figueroa was elected the chairman of the Social, Humanitarian and Cultural (Third) Committee. This sixty-nation committee deals with problems of human rights, refugees, and migration, and seeks to have international treaties made to cover the U.N. Declaration of Human Rights. The first woman to be chosen to head a General Assembly committee, she acknowledges her election as a sign of the U.N.'s pledge to end discrimination against women, but decries the emphasis being placed on the "feminine angle"; she feels it is natural for a woman to be given a high post and that she should not be accorded special privileges. Another responsibility was given to the Chilean representative on January 22, 1952, when her country named her an alternate delegate to the Security Council, where no woman had served before. When General Carlos Ibáñez became the new President of Chile in November 1952, Señora Figueroa, in accordance with Chilean custom, submitted to him her resignation as a representative to the U.N.

Aside from the professional societies to which she belongs, Señora Figueroa is vice-president

United Nations

ANA FIGUEROA

of the Association of Non-Governmental Organizations for the United Nations, is a member of the Athenaeum of Temuco and the Periodical Society of the South, and an honorary member of the Inter-American Cultural Society. She has a son, who is named Arturo. Politically, she is aligned with the Radical party, reported the New York *Times*. Descriptions of the Chilean lady frequently mention her personal attractiveness and modish clothes.

References

N Y Times p4 N 17 '51 por
Time 58:47 N 26 '51 por
U N Bul 11:407 N 15 '51 por
Who's Who in Latin America Pt IV (1947)
Who's Who in the United Nations (1951)

FINKELSTEIN, LOUIS, RABBI (fĭng'-kĕl-stĭn) June 14, 1895- Seminary chancellor

Addres: b. c/o Jewish Theological Seminary of America, 3080 Broadway, New York 27; h. 612 W. 112th St., New York 25

> NOTE: This biography supersedes the article which appeared in *Current Biography* in 1940.

Head of the Jewish Theological Seminary of America since 1940 and its principal professor of theology since 1931, Dr. Louis Finkelstein has long been recognized as one of the foremost of American Jewish scholars, as educator, author, editor, and leader in interfaith and other conferences. He is one of the founders as well as the director of the Institute for Religious and Social Studies and the regularly re-elected president of the annual

Conway Studios

RABBI LOUIS FINKELSTEIN

Conference on Science, Philosophy and Religion in their Relation to the Democratic Way of Life, which first met in 1940. The fourth president of the Jewish Theological Seminary, he was given the new titles of chancellor and president of the faculties in October 1951.

Born to Rabbi Simon J. Finkelstein and the former Hannah Brager in Cincinnati, Ohio, on June 14, 1895, Louis Finkelstein was seven years old when his father, a native of Lithuania, was called to Brooklyn, New York, by the Congregation Oheb Sholom. Rabbi Finkelstein, who was of the Orthodox tenet, started his son early on the path of sacred scholarship. The boy proved an apt and pious pupil: it has been told (in an article in *Time*) that during his youth in the Brownsville area of Brooklyn he would often leave home as early as 5:30 in the morning to study at the synagogue before regular school hours. He was able to finish high school in three years, after which he entered the College of the City of New York, where he became president of the student Zionist organization and also was unusually well liked by his Protestant and Catholic classmates. He took his B.A. degree at C.C.N.Y. in 1915 and his Ph.D. degree at Columbia University three years later in 1918. His doctoral thesis, a new edition of the *Commentary on Isaiah* by the medieval scholar David Kimchi, was published in 1926. The student was awarded a Phi Beta Kappa key.

Dr. Finkelstein prepared for ordination as a rabbi at the institution of which he is now the chancellor, the Jewish Theological Seminary of America, in New York. It had been established in 1886 "for the perpetuation of the tenets of the Jewish religion, the cultivation of Hebrew literature, the pursuit of Biblical and archeological research, the advancement of Jewish scholarship . . . and the training of Jewish rabbis and teachers." Ordained in 1919,

Finkelstein was called by the Congregation Kehillath Israel, in New York; he was to remain there until 1931. (He was awarded Hattarat Horash, the highest form of rabbinical ordination, in 1923). Meanwhile, he had attracted the special interest of the seminary's second president, Dr. Solomon Schechter, and in 1920, the year following his ordination, Dr. Finkelstein was appointed to the faculty as instructor in the Talmud. In 1921 he won the Abraham Berliner award for research in Jewish history with an essay on an assigned subject. This essay was subsequently revised and expanded as the rabbi's first published book, *Jewish Self-Government in the Middle Ages* (1924).

For the six years beginning 1924 Dr. Finkelstein was the Solomon Schechter lecturer in theology at the seminary, as well as an officiating rabbi. He continued his historical research, in 1929 writing for the *Harvard Theological Review* a monograph entitled "The Pharisees; Their Origin and Philosophy." At that time he was in the midst of a two-year term (1928-30) as president of the Rabbinical Assembly of America. In 1930 Dr. Finkelstein was advanced by the seminary's third president, Dr. Cyrus Adler, to an associate professorship in theology, and in the following year, 1931, he left his congregation to assume the Solomon Schechter professorship of theology in the seminary's Rabbinical School, a position which he still retains. He served on the Hillel Foundation Commission for two years beginning 1932, the year he also began the first of seven years on the executive committee of the United Synagogue of America. In 1934 he was appointed assistant to President Adler at the seminary.

In 1935 Dr. Finkelstein was temporarily diverted from his research work on the Pharisees, for in that year Professor A. D. Nock of Harvard informed him that he would be willing to devote a full number of the *Harvard Theological Review* to a biographical monograph on Akiba, the Hebrew sage, who was martyred by the Romans in 132 A.D. Finkelstein immediately put aside other work to concentrate on the suggested monograph. It soon became clear to him, however, that the subject was too large for compression into the pages of a periodical, and accordingly, when *Akiba, Scholar, Saint and Martyr* was published in 1936, it was the form of a book which consolidated Dr. Finkelstein's reputation as a scholar and established him as a writer of distinction. "The volume will take a deserved place with the classics of Jewish literature," said Dr. Abram Sachar in the New York *Herald Tribune*; while Philip Slomovitz, writing for the *Christian Century*, called it "a great book and a great study." During 1937 Finkelstein was a guest lecturer at Johns Hopkins University, and in the same year was appointed provost at his seminary. His two-volume work *The Pharisees; the Sociological Background of their Faith* was published in 1938. Dr. Sachar, again reviewing for the *Herald Tribune*, found that the work proved its thesis that the Pharisees were "the leaders in the movement for economic democracy," and declared that it "should be in every Jewish and Christian home." Dr. Henry Sloane Coffin, writing in the New York *Times*, thought that social forces were "unduly stressed." Also, in 1938, Dr. Finkelstein began another phase of his work, in interfaith understanding by helping to found, and later by becoming the director of, the seminary Institute of Interdenominational Studies (now the Institute for Religious and Social Studies) established "to enable ministers of all faiths to study under the guidance of eminent theologians of the various denominations." He lectured at Oberlin College in 1939 and in the ensuing year was the Carew lecturer of the Hartford Theological Seminary Foundation. By this time he had become the editor in Rabbinics for the *Universal Jewish Encyclopedia* and had contributed many papers to English-, French-, and German-language journals.

The year 1940 was in many respects most important in Dr. Finkelstein's career, for, following the death of Dr. Cyrus Adler in April, he became the fourth president of the Jewish Theological Seminary. He also succeeded Dr. Adler as President Roosevelt's Judaist adviser on steps toward world peace and was the recipient of the 1940 Townsend Harris medal; September of that year saw the first meeting of the Conference on Science, Philosophy and Religion in their Relation to the Democratic Way of Life (proposed by Finkelstein and nine other leaders in those fields), held at the seminary. The results of these convocations have been published in annual symposia, in most years coedited by Finkelstein. His own credo has ben set forth in *Beliefs and Practices of Judaism*, the collections *Faith for Today*, and *Religions of Democracy*, all of which appeared in 1941.

In 1943-44 Dr. Finkelstein gave the Ingersoll lecture on the immortality of man (Harvard University) and in February of the latter year he was awarded an honorary Doctor of Sacred Theology degree by Columbia University "in recognition of the growing spirit of cooperation among religious faiths." (He has also been honored by Boston University with a D.Lit. degree). The Jewish scholar was one of the bicentennial's lecturers at Princeton University in 1946 and edited the collection *American Spiritual Autobiographies*, published in 1948. Addressing the golden jubilee meeting of the Rabbinical Assembly of America in June 1950, Dr. Finkelstein said: "If we can surmount division among ourselves, we may become the instruments to draw together men of all faiths and philosophies for . . . an enduring peace." At another such assembly (in February 1952) he urged a moral and spiritual revolution as the solution of the problems of corruption in government, juvenile delinquency, and other breakdowns in standards of conduct.

In 1950 appeared the 1,400-page *The Jews; Their History, Culture, and Religion*, on which thirty-four scholars, Jewish and Gentile, had worked under Finkelstein's editorship for six years and which was largely financed by the Nehemiah Gitelson Fund. "The special value of this compilation lies in the fact that it furnishes documentary proof that American unity is possible despite the diverse racial, religious and national origins of the American population," wrote W. W. Brickman in *School and Society*. The final chapter, entitled "The Jewish religion: Its Beliefs and Practices," is the work of the editor in chief.

Designation of Dr. Finkelstein in October 1951 as chancellor and president of the faculties of the Jewish Theological Seminary of America, superseding his title of president, was part of a reorganization plan (said *Time*) to "give him more time for scholarship and writing." (Presidential duties have been taken over by a three-man team of two vice-chancellors and the seminary provost.) The seminary, which is located on upper Broadway, near Columbia University, now has about 1,000 students enrolled in its four-year course. Organizations other than those already mentioned with which Dr. Finkelstein is currently affiliated are the American Academy of Jewish Research (fellow and member of the executive committee), American Friends of the Hebrew University (director), Jewish Teachers College Fund (trustee), the American Oriental Society (member), and the New York University Institute of Postwar Reconstruction (board of consultants).

Tall, lean, bearded Dr. Finkelstein and Carmel Bentwich of New York City were married March 5, 1922. They have three children, Hadassah Nita, Ezra Michael, and Faith.

References

Time 58:52-9 O 15 '51 por

Fisher, D. F. American Portraits (1946)
Leaders in Education (1948)
Religious Leaders of America, 1941-42
Who's Who in America, 1950-51
Who's Who in American Jewry, 1938-39
Who's Who in New York, 1947
Who's Who in Philosophy (1942)
Who's Who in the East (1951)
World Biography (1948)

FORBES, JOHN J. (V.) Nov. 21, 1885-
United States Government official
Address: b. c/o Bureau of Mines, New Department of Interior Bldg., Washington 25, D.C.; h. 4822 Chevy Chase Dr., Chevy Chase, Md.

When President Truman appointed John J. Forbes the Director of the Bureau of Mines in November 1951, a White House announcement called the new head "one of the world's foremost mine safety experts and an outstanding career employee in Government Civil Service." Forbes's career in the Bureau of Mines started in 1915 as a probational "first-aid" miner at Pittsburgh, after which he rose to become a supervising engineer in 1927, chief mine inspector at Pittsburgh in 1941, and chief of the Health and Safety Division in 1948. Forbes is well known for his opinion that Federal inspectors should have the power

JOHN J. FORBES

to close mines that do not meet minimum safety standards.

John J. V. Forbes, born November 21, 1885, is one of the twelve children—six boys and six girls—born to John Patrick and Bridget (Buggy) Forbes, both of Irish ancestry. The elder Forbes had worked as a miner, and had later become a sheriff and a tax collector. Young Forbes attended public schools in his birthplace, Shamokin, Pennsylvania, graduating in 1903 from high school.

Born and bred in the heart of Pennsylvania's hard-coal fields, Forbes worked in the mines as a youth to earn funds for his education. At the age of ten he was a breaker-boy, whose duties it is to sort out the slate from the coal. Becoming a mine laborer in 1900, Forbes had advanced to mine "surveying" by 1903. He now enrolled for two years at the State Normal School at Kutztown. A certified teacher, from 1905 to 1907 he taught in the Shamokin public schools. Later resuming his studies, he received the B.S. degree in mining engineering from Pennsylvania State College in 1911. This was followed by employment in several Pennsylvania and Ohio mines.

It was as a probational "first-aid" miner that Forbes started his career with the United States Bureau of Mines in 1915, at the age of thirty. Two years later he was appointed a foreman miner, and in 1919 began service as an assistant mining engineer. For a fifteen-year period, from 1925 to 1940, Forbes served as the Bureau's principal mining engineer, in charge of the Safety Division. After a year as first chief of coal mine inspection, he spent the World War II years, from 1942 to 1945, as chief of the mineral production security division. When Forbes was promoted in 1945 to assistant chief of the Bureau, in charge of health and safety, his appointment was called "another morale booster" for civil servants.

Forbes, who was known by 1951 as "a foremost mine safety expert in Government service," became Director of the Bureau of Mines in November of that year. From the United Mine Workers headquarters came the opinion that it was "an excellent choice." Thomas Kennedy, vice-president of the union, endorsed the appointment more fully: "We have all known Mr. Forbes over the years. . . .He knows the industry, there's no question about that. He's very good and very fair. He knows all the answers. He's been very fair in all his dealings with us and with the industry." Michael J. Kosik, secretary of the Anthracite Conciliation Board and former union president of district in the Scranton-Wilkes-Barre district, commented: "Mr. Forbes is well known to operators and union officers and the rank and file of the anthracite region and is well thought of by people on both sides of the coal industry."

In addition to being charged with the responsibilities of conserving mineral resources and partially regulating the conduct of mine operations, the Bureau of Mines has as one of its major functions the promotion of safety and health in the mineral industries. From 1941 to 1952, for example, the Bureau conducted some 37,000 safety surveys of coal mines, in an attempt to help reduce the number of deaths and injuries resulting from mine accidents and to increase the efficiency of coal production. Representatives of the Bureau investigate the causes of mine disasters and seek ways to prevent them, chiefly by training mine workers and officials in safety methods, accident prevention, and mine rescue and recovery work. The Bureau also assembles statistical data on the number and causes of mine mishaps. Other related activities include tests of flammability and explosive characteristics of metal powders and industrial dusts of mineral origin, and advising on the use of electrical equipment and respiratory devices in mines.

The Bureau of Mines, though active in accident prevention, is without statutory authority to force mine owners to comply with a Federal inspector's recommendations. Of 8,000 safety inspections made in 1950, when Forbes was still in charge of that division of the Bureau, major hazards were discovered in 41 per cent of the mines investigated. The Bureau wrote warning letters to the companies whose mines had major hazards, but only 9 per cent of the letters were answered. Forbes stated at that time that the ratio of replies "is not as bad as it sounds," for larger mines tend to be more safety-conscious and some of the smaller mines might have taken safety action without informing the Bureau. Occasionally, however, Forbes has had to appeal to State Governors for special action where extreme hazards were ignored. The United Mine Workers is empowered by contract to take its members out of a mine which the Federal inspectors have called unsafe, but the union officials would prefer a Federal closure order, rather than take action themselves.

In 1952 President Truman asked Congress to pass a mine safety bill "with teeth in it." Secretary of the Interior Oscar Chapman told a Senate subcommittee on January 24, 1952, that if the Federal government had had authority to enforce safety regulations, it could have prevented the disaster which cost more than one hundred lives at West Frankfort, Illinois, the previous December. (Forbes told the same committee that thirty-one violations had been found at the West Frankfort mine during a July 1950 inspection.) These statements were submitted to the subcommittee studying a bill offered by Senator Neely which would permit a Federal inspector to withdraw all mine employees from a pit deemed unsafe, until the conditions had been corrected. Secretary Chapman favored going still further, by charging violators of Federal safety rules with misdemeanor of felony penalties.

Forbes, who married Irene L. Mudd on March 26, 1917, has two children, Marisse Lee West and John W. The gray-eyed, brown-haired official is five feet nine inches tall and weighs 190 pounds. His faith is the Catholic. The following are the organization memberships and offices he has held: assistant secretary of the Mine Inspectors' Institute of America; program chairman of the coal mining section of the National Safety Council; past president of the Coal Mining Institute of America and the National Mine Rescue Association. Among the other groups to which he belongs are the Mine Rescue Veterans of the Pittsburgh District, Pittsburgh Coal Mining Institute, West Virginia Coal Mining Institute, Monongahela Valley Mining Institute, and Washington Safety Society. Forbes has also written articles on mine safety for technical journals.

References

Bsns W p42 N 24 '51
N Y Times p55 N 11 '51
Who's Who in Commerce and Industry (1951)

FORD, BENSON July 20, 1919- Automobile manufacturer

Address: b. c/o Lincoln-Mercury Division, Ford Motor Company, 6200 W. Warren Ave., Detroit 32, Mich.; h. 100 Kenwood Rd., Grosse Pointe Farms 30, Mich.

Benson Ford, a grandson of Henry Ford, is a vice-president of the Ford Motor Company and the director of its Lincoln-Mercury Division. He received those titles in January 1948, at the age of twenty-eight. Except for a period of service in the armed forces during World War II, he has been associated with the family's industrial empire since 1940. Also active in civic and other affairs, in 1951 Benson Ford was elected Protestant national co-chairman of the National Conference of Christians and Jews.

The second son of Edsel Bryan and Eleanor (Clay) Ford, Benson Ford was born July 20, 1919, in Detroit, Michigan. (His elder brother is Henry Ford 2d, his younger brother is named William, and his sister, Josephine, is now Mrs. Walter Buhl Ford.) Benson was a student at Detroit University School during

BENSON FORD

the years 1927-35 and at Hotchkiss School (in Connecticut) during 1935-38. Following this he studied at Princeton University from 1938 to 1940, when he left to begin working full time at the Ford Motor Company after having spent some summer vacations as a "grease monkey" in the dynamometer division of the River Rouge plant. His first postcollege job was in the experimental garage at the Ford Engineering Laboratories in Dearborn. There (at the suggestion of his father, president of the company from 1918 until he died in 1943) young Ford learned the fundamentals of automobile engine construction through building up and dismantling test motors. With his elder brother (said a release from the Lincoln-Mercury news bureau) he built one of the first experimental jeeps Ford manufactured for the government; during World War II the company turned out 277,896 of these jeeps. During 1940-41 Benson Ford held the position of assistant purchasing agent for the Ford Motor Company, and in 1941-42 was assistant superintendent in its supercharge division. His membership on the company's board of directors dates from April 28, 1941.

Enlisting as a private in the United States Army on October 1, 1942, Ford was assigned to Fort Custer, Michigan, and shortly thereafter to Selfridge Field Air Base, near Detroit, where he remained until January 1943. Until December of that year (in the course of which, in June, he was commissioned a second lieutenant) he was stationed at an induction center in Detroit. In December he was transferred to the 4th Air Force Headquarters in San Francisco, to be aide-de-camp to Brigadier General Samuel M. Connell. His promotion to first lieutenant came in June 1944, and in October he was ordered to the Newfoundland Base Command of the United States Air Corps, where he spent thirteen months. In

FORD, BENSON—_Continued_

January of 1945 he received the bars of a captain.

Upon his separation from the armed forces on February 19, 1946, Ford rejoined the motor company, first going to the Lincoln-Mercury Division, then to the planning division of the Ford Motor Company. In September 1947 he rejoined the Lincoln-Mercury Division on a permanent basis. On January 30, 1948, when he was elected a vice-president of the company, he was chosen director of the Lincoln-Mercury Division, of which he was named general manager on October 18, 1948. He has been a member of the company's administration committee since April 1, 1946, and of its executive committee since July 15, 1949; and he serves on the board of directors of Ford subsidiaries: Ford Motor Experts, Inc., Ford Hydro-Electric Company, Ford International, Inc., Fordson Coal Company, Hamilton & Rossville Hydraulic Company, Seaboard Properties.

Upon the death of Henry Ford in 1947, Benson's elder brother, Henry Ford 2d, president since 1946, made a number of changes in the organization of the Ford Motor Company. Among them was the setting up of the Lincoln-Mercury Division, which had been expanding under a $35,000,000 postwar program, as a nearly autonomous unit, separate from the parent organization except for matters of policy and financial control. In announcing his brother's election to the chief executive post of the Lincoln-Mercury Division on Janury 30, 1948, Henry Ford 2d stated: "The appointment comes when the division is on the threshold of its greatest expansion program which will further establish it as a separate entity. . . .We intend to go after the business in the medium- and high-priced fields, more aggressively. To do this our line of cars is being expanded and completely redesigned." The Lincoln-Mercury Division, one of eleven divisions of the Ford Motor Company, has assembly plants at Detroit, Metuchen (New Jersey), Los Angeles, and St. Louis. Under the direction of Benson Ford, whose chief concerns have been to build up dealer organization, formulate policy, and develop employee good will, the division has expanded. In 1948 production stood at between 600 and 700 cars daily, sold through only 800 dealers. The number of dealers had risen to 1,623 in 1950 and the production rate to 1,579 cars a day. Improved workmanship and styling, Benson Ford has said, explain the increased demand.

At the opening of Lincoln-Mercury's Metuchen plant in June 1948, Benson Ford spoke of the need for a scientific study of labor-management problems to obtain lasting industrial peace. Referring to such evidence of misunderstandings as absenteeism, slow-downs, and strikes, he remarked that "they are no less costly to unions and to individual workers than they are to management. Like wars they are a form of human conflict in which nobody really wins." As a means of improving management planning, Benson Ford holds closed conferences with foremen and supervisors and has given them greater responsibility in the assembly plant. Regarding future production, the automobile executive has said that the primary need is to find a basic metal for cars which would be stronger, lighter, and cheaper to produce than steel.

Under the terms of Henry Ford's will, the controlling share of the voting stock of the Ford Motor Company is in the hands of his four grandchildren. No longer, however, a one-man or family-dominated firm (according to *Pathfinder*, November 1, 1950), the company is now managed by the same type of staff-and-line organization which exists at General Motors or General Electric. Another business connection of Benson Ford is with the Manufacturers National Bank of Detroit, as director.

The automobile manufacturer, who is a member of the Protestant Episcopal Church and has been cited for his work in the cause of racial and religious tolerance, was elected in June 1951 the Protestant national cochairman of the National Conference of Christians and Jews, to serve with Thomas E. Braniff, Catholic representative, and Roger W. Strauss, Jewish representative. The National Conference of Christians and Jews, founded in 1928, carries on a program against bigotry and prejudice in which all religious groups can work together for democratic goals. Through schools, colleges, churches, synagogues, community organizations, business and industrial clinics, as well as through all media of communication, an international educational service is conducted by a corps of technicians and a trained personnel. The council has set up a World Brotherhood organization with headquarters in Paris and other cities, has cooperated with the United Nations on matters of human rights and genocide, and has worked with the Military Governments to promote democracy in Germany and Japan. Benson Ford has also served on the governing body of a number of other organizations: the Detroit Torch Fund, the YMCA, Boy Scouts, and the International Regatta Association. He is a member and trustee of the Ford Foundation, president of the board of trustees of the Henry Ford Hospital and the Henry Ford School of Nursing and Hygiene, trustee of the Henry Ford Trade School, vice-president and trustee of the Edsel B. Ford Institute for Medical Research, president and director of Fordson Estates, Inc., and director of the Wayside Inn. He also holds the presidency of the Edison Institute at Greenfield Village, Michigan.

Clubs to which Benson Ford belongs are the Detroit Country, Grosse Pointe, Economic, University, Cap and Gown, Society of Automotive Engineers, and Automobile Old Timers, Inc. His political preference is Republican. On July 9, 1941, he married Edith McNaughton of Grosse Pointe, daughter of Lynn McNaughton, an executive for the Cadillac Motor Company. The couple, who had known each other since childhood, have a son, Benson, Jr., and a daughter, Lynn McNaughton. Benson Ford has been described by *Pathfinder* as easy-going with a "rather diffident smile and an easy, unassertive way of putting over his ideas." The energetic, stocky, blue-eyed executive names automobiles, photography, and golf as his hobbies.

References

Pathfinder 57:35+ Ja 11 '50; 57:40+ N 1 '50 por
Time 51:84 F 9 '48
Business Executives of America (1950)
Who's Who in America, 1950-51
Who's Who in the Midwest (1949)

FORSYTH, W(ILLIAM) D(OUGLASS)

Jan. 5, 1909- United Nations representative

Address: b. c/o Australian Mission to the United Nations, 350 5th Ave., New York 1; c/o Department of External Affairs, Canberra, Australia

Photo News, Wellington

W. D. FORSYTH

The permanent representative of the Commonwealth of Australia in the United Nations is W. D. Forsyth, appointed in September 1951 with the rank of Minister. Immediately before that appointment he had served for nearly three years as Secretary-General of the South Pacific Commission, a six-power advisory body formed to improve conditions in the South Seas. Still earlier, as an official of the Australian Department of External Affairs, he had represented his country at numerous conferences, in the United Nations General Assembly, and as counselor to the Embassy at Washington. Forsyth is the author of two books, *Governor Arthur's Convict System* (1935) and *The Myth of Open Spaces* (1942), the latter a study of mass population movements.

Of Scottish ancestry on his father's side—his great-grandfather left Scotland for Australia in the 1850's—and English on his mother's, William Douglass Forsyth was born to James Douglass and Martha Alice (Lamborne) Forsyth in Casterton, Victoria, Australia; his birth date is January 5, 1909. (Christopher Russell Forsyth, of the Malayan Civil Service, is his brother; of his three sisters, one is deceased.) A graduate of the Ballarat High School, young Forsyth entered the University of Melbourne in 1927, majored in history and political science, and took his B.A. degree with honors in 1931 and his M.A. degree in 1932.

Beginning his career as a teacher of history, Forsyth was urged by Professor Ernest Scott to make a special study of the attempt made by Governor Sir George Arthur in Tasmania between 1824 and 1836 to reconcile a colonization movement with what had originally been a penal settlement. First results of the research were submitted as a postgraduate thesis to the Imperial Studies Committee of the Royal Empire Society. Grants by the committee and the University of Melbourne then made it possible for Forsyth to complete the book, which was published in London in March 1935, under the title of *Governor Arthur's Convict System: Van Dieman's Land, 1924-36; a Study in Colonization.*

The naming of Forsyth as the recipient of the Harbison-Higginbotham scholarship at the University of Melbourne in the same year enabled the young man to make progress in his study of population and migration trends. He had been keenly interested in that subject ever since the world depression of the early 1930's brought demands that Australia relax her curbs on immigration. A Rockefeller fellowship in social sciences took the Australian to Balliol College, Oxford, in 1936-37. At intervals during his residence there he conferred with authorities on, and students of, demography in London, Northern Ireland, Ireland, and at the International Studies Conference in Paris and at the International Labor Organization in Geneva. After spending 1938 in Melbourne on a research fellowship in 1938, he returned to Balliol in 1939 on another Rockefeller grant, took his B.Litt. degree at Oxford in the same year, and also traveled to Paris, Berlin, and Vienna to examine the new problem of refugee migration.

Forsyth completed, in 1939, the first draft of his book on mass movements of peoples, but the outbreak of World War II made publication at that time seem ill-advised. In 1942, however, when postwar population problems were being anticipated, the book, *The Myth of the Open Spaces: Australian, British and World Trends of Population and Migration*, was published in Melbourne and London. The author's thesis, stated the *Manchester Guardian*, "is, broadly, that there is no longer a sound basis for mass emigration from thickly populated lands to the 'open spaces.'" As Forsyth reiterated in an article, "Stability in the Pacific: Australia's Position" (*Pacific Affairs*, March 1943), "Australia ought not to be called upon to throw open the door of mass migration. . . .The real solution to problems of population is the same as that of the general economic

FORSYTH, W. D.—*Continued*

problem: reduction of trade barriers and stimulation of productivity." Reviewing *The Myth of the Open Spaces* for Columbia University's *Political Science Quarterly*, Henry Pratt Fairchild wrote: "In spite of certain flaws," the book was "a valuable addition to the available material on population and migration." In England the reviewer for the London *Times* called it "a well-written book, lucid in argument, packed with statistics"; and the *Manchester Guardian* was also laudatory.

In the meantime, Forsyth served during 1940-41 as research secretary of the Australian Institute of International Affairs, editor of the *Australasiatic Bulletin*, and had become a member of the staff of the Commonwealth's Department of Information. Then, as Research Officer of the Australian Department of External Affairs at the Federal capital, Canberra, from 1942 to 1946 Forsyth participated in the Australian-New Zealand Conference of 1944 and in 1945 went to San Francisco, California, as an adviser to the Australian delegation to the conference at which the United Nations was charted. In 1946 Forsyth was advanced to First Secretary of the Department of External Affairs and head of the Pacific Division; he attended the United Nations General Assembly in the same year and represented Australia on the Far Eastern Commission. A year later (1947) he received his first appointment to Washington, as counselor at the Australian Embassy. Forsyth was again delegated to the U.N. General Assembly in 1947 and 1948, and represented Australia on the Trusteeship Council. At a Geneva meeting of a special committee on nonself-governing territories (September 1948) Forsyth charged the Soviet Union with attempting "to undermine the confidence of the colonial peoples in the metropolitan governments and to inspire subversive movements."

Australia (which has been administering New Guinea and Nauru for the United Nations) and New Zealand (trustee for Western Samoa) called a six-power South Seas Conference at Canberra on January 28, 1947. The other participants, with colonies or possessions in that area, were the Netherlands (Dutch New Guinea and neighboring islands), France (New Caledonia and other islands), the United Kingdom (Fiji, Gilbert and Ellice Islands) and the United States (American Samoa and other islands). Agreement was reached to establish the South Pacific Commission as an advisory intergovernmental body concerned with economic and social advancement of the peoples of the South Pacific territories, and an interim organization began to function shortly thereafter. The Commission, which became officially effective on July 29, 1948, consists of two members from each participating power, meets twice annually, and has headquarters at Noumea in New Caledonia.

With the appointment in November 1948 of Forsyth as Secretary General of the South Pacific Commission, the Australian soon put forward plans for the first triennial South Pacific Conference, which met at Nasinu (Suva, Fiji), from April 25 to May 5, 1950,

under chairmanship of Governor Sir Brian Freeston of Fiji. Designed as a native forum, it assembled twenty-nine delegates from various parts of Polynesia, Micronesia, and Melanesia, who were thus able for the first time to discuss common problems and to learn the complete scope of the constructive work of the Commission, whose auxiliary Research Council "advises on needed investigations and carries out approved studies." An account of the achievements of the Commission in the three years of Forsyth's Secretary-Generalship may be found in an article by Peter Kihss in the New York *Herald Tribune* for November 7, 1951. It has reported progress in fighting malnutrition in New Guinea and Melanesia, such diseases as infantile paralysis and elephantiasis in other areas, and illiteracy in Melanesia, and has instituted community development projects in Fiji, New Hebrides, and elsewhere.

On September 3, 1951, the appointment of Forsyth as Australia's permanent representative to the United Nations was announced. (In his post as head of the South Pacific Commission he was succeeded by Sir Brian Freeston.) In the rank of Minister, he attended the U.N. General Assembly meetings at Paris in the autumn of 1951, in the course of which he endorsed Western proposals for a tripartite disarmament conference. Speaking at that time (November 23), he expressed the hope that Andrei Vishinsky, the Soviet Foreign Minister, would reconsider Russia's position on that issue; Forsyth said further that Australia approved "the formulation of basic principles as contained in the Western disarmament proposal, leaving the detailed work to be done by the proposed disarmament commission" (New York *Times*).

Forsyth, who is five feet five inches in height and weighs about 135 pounds, has brown hair and hazel eyes. He and Thelma Joyce Sherry were married in 1935, and have one son, Julian Douglass, and two daughters, Katherine and Valerie.

References

　Author's and Writer's Who's Who
　　(1948-49)
　Who's Who in Australia, 1950

FOWLER, HENRY H(AMILL) Sept. 5, 1908- United States Government official

Address: b. c/o Office of Defense Mobilization, Washington 25, D.C.; h. 509 Queen St., Alexandria, Va.

In September 1952, while holding the positions of head of the Defense Production Administration and chief of the National Production Authority, Henry H. Fowler was named Director of Defense Mobilization. In World War II Fowler had been concerned with defense production in the War Production Board, the Office of Production Mobilization, and the United States Mission on Economic Affairs in London. After serving with the Foreign Economic Administration in 1945, he returned to the private practice of law in Washington.

Born in Roanoke, Virginia, September 5, 1908, Henry Hamill Fowler is the son of Mack Johnson and Bertha (Browning) Fowler. Following his graduation from Roanoke College with the Bachelor of Arts degree in 1929, Fowler entered the School of Law at Yale University, where he received his Bachelor of Laws degree in 1932 and his Doctor of Juristic Science degree in 1933. During 1930-32 he was editor of the *Yale Law Journal*. Admitted to the bar of the State of Virginia in 1933, Fowler was employed from 1934 to 1938 as counsel to the Tennessee Valley Authority, of which he became assistant general counsel in 1939.

It was in 1939, too, that Fowler was named a special assistant to the United States Attorney General, to serve as chief counsel to a subcommittee of the Senate Committee on Education and Labor, a post which he filled until 1940. For part of the ensuing year he was special counsel to the Federal Power Commission, before becoming assistant general counsel of the Office of Production Management, with which he spent the remainder of the year. From 1942 to 1944 he was again an assistant general counsel, this time with the War Production Board. Subsequently, after taking an assignment as economic adviser to the United States Mission on Economic Affairs in London for part of 1944, Fowler became special assistant to the Administrator of the Foreign Economic Administration, for which he gathered data on the war potential of Germany, data he presented in October of the following year. He resumed the private practice of law in 1946 as senior partner of the Washington firm of Fowler, Leva, Hawes and Symington.

In September 1951 Fowler rejoined the Government in the capacity of deputy administrator of the National Production Authority, under Manly Fleischmann, who had also been on the War Production Board during World War II. As the operating arm of the Defense Production Administration, which is charged with the planning and programing of the distribution of scarce materials for defense and essential civilian needs, the NPA undertakes execution and implementation of DPA programs. Early in January 1952 Fowler stated before a Washington meeting of the Automobile Passenger Car Manufacturers Industry Advisory Committee that supplies to the industry had been maintained in preference to those for other consumer durable goods industries because of the automobile's vital position in production and labor. On January 8 he was sworn in as Administrator of the NPA, since Fleischmann wished to devote himself entirely to the DPA, of which he was also the head.

In the four months that he headed the NPA, Fowler was principally concerned with supplies, labor, and allocation of scarce metals. As an aid to the more than 3,000 small businesses affected by material shortages, the Administrator in January 1952 announced a program of price differentials in the procurement by the Government of supplies as a means of maintaining production at the smaller plants.

Wide World Photos

HENRY H. FOWLER

A further aid to business, he pointed out the following month, would be the maintenance of civilian goods production on levels established for the second quarter of the business year, without curtailment of metal allocations. In regard to labor, Fowler and other defense mobilization chiefs met with labor union representatives in January to formulate a program for employment, which would involve, the NPA head reported, clinics in fourteen cities to plan for the placement of defense contracts with small concerns and the consideration of employment in allocating materials in the future. With regard to scarce metals and other supplies, Fowler found it necessary in January to tell a group of New York builders that the steel shortage would prevent full allocation of construction materials beyond half-way fulfilment of requirements until defense needs had been met. The following month Fowler amplified this statement by revealing that enough steel would be allotted for certain nonindustrial projects and that foreign steel would be made available "on an individual case basis," provided that copper and aluminum (also in short supply) would not be needed too. Some 645 such applications were approved at the end of February.

About the same time, the NPA reduced copper and aluminum allotments to civilian manufacturers to 30 per cent of pre-Korean War levels, a move balanced afterward by the removal of all controls on stainless chrome steel and of most controls on civilian allotments of lead. To speed the flow of standard components for military and machine tool products, Fowler and Fleischmann on March 31 announced the establishment of a B-5 symbol for priority orders to component manufacturers

FOWLER, HENRY H.—*Continued*

for immediate fabrication to the exclusion of all other orders. By eliminating the special directive system hitherto in use, Fowler said, the new system "represents a solution to a problem never adequately solved during World War II—that of assuring a flow of 'B' products for military production." When, early in April, he found that the nation was "over the hump" of scarce materials, despite the necessity to "prepare . . . for an indefinite period of partial mobilization," he was able to order the relaxing of controls on copper construction materials and on most rubber consumption. Because of the steel strike beginning in the early summer of 1952, Fowler was requested by Secretary of Commerce Sawyer to reimpose recently relaxed steel restrictions for all except defense needs.

With the resignation of Fleischmann, effective May 31, 1952, Fowler was named by President Truman as Defense Production Administrator, the appointment taking effect June 1, 1952; he was sworn in on June 3. As had Fleischmann for a period, Fowler held simultaneously the offices of DPA and NPA head. "In appointing Henry Fowler," said a New York *Times* editorial, "President Truman had picked a successor who has worked closely with the same range of problems the last half year, thus helping to assure continuity and smoothness of both policy and operations."

In May, before his appointment, Fowler had been chairman of a top-level interagency committee on defense production policy, reporting to John R. Steelman, acting Director of Defense Mobilization. Shortly after taking up his DPA responsibilities, Fowler appeared before the House Banking Committee to urge against the adoption of an amendment to the Defense Production Act which would lift controls on imports when domestic production reaches a certain level. On another occasion, later in June, he stated that the United States is capable of achieving far greater industrial preparedness for defense than it now has, without affecting civilian economy and that defense production should be made a permanent part of the national economy. Following the end of the steel strike in July 1952, Fowler outlined the plans formed by the DPA to deal with what the Administrator called "a shortage worse than has been faced since the defense program began."

When Fowler was appointed Director of Defense Mobilization by President Truman on September 5, 1952, he agreed to fill this top mobilization assignment until the end of December 1952. He retained his post as administrator of DPA, but resigned as head of NPA.

Henry H. Fowler is a member of the Metropolitan Club in Washington. His religious affiliation is Episcopal. Married October 19, 1938, to Trudye Pamela Hathcote, he has two daughters, Mary Anne and Susan Maria, and a son, Henry Hamill, Jr.

References

N Y Herald Tribune p15 My 8 '52
Who's Who in America, 1952-53

GALLUP, GEORGE (HORACE) (găl'ŭp)
Nov. 18, 1901- Public opinion statistician
Address: b. c/o American Institute of Public Opinion, 110 E. 42d St., New York 17; c/o American Institute of Opinion, Princeton, N.J.; h. The Great Rd., Princeton, N.J.

> NOTE: This biography supersedes the article which appeared in *Current Biography* in 1940.

Noted as a pioneer in the field of public opinion surveys, George Gallup is the founder and director of the American Institute of Public Opinion, which conducts national polls on questions of political and social interest. During the nine years (1923-32) that Gallup taught journalism he carried on surveys, primarily in the field of newspaper readership, which led to the conception of the Gallup polls. At the time that he established the American Institute of Public Opinion, in 1935, he was associated with the Young and Rubicam advertising agency, of which he was later for ten years a vice-president. Gallup is the author of articles and books on the subject of surveys and polls.

Born in Jefferson, Iowa, on November 18, 1901, George Horace Gallup, the son of George Henry and Nettie (Davenport) Gallup. His father, a speculator in farm and ranch lands, was an advocate of "dry farming" and a logician. When young Gallup was in his second year at the State University of Iowa the family suffered financial reverses; thereafter, he supported himself throughout his college years by means of scholarships and by operating a towel concession in the locker room of the school's swimming pool. As editor of the college newspaper, the *Daily Iowan*, in his junior year, he built the campus journal into one which served the otherwise newspaperless college town and was supported by advertisements of community merchants.

Following his graduation with the B.A. degree in 1923, Gallup remained at the university as an instructor in journalism, concurrently carrying on studies which earned him an M.A. degree in psychology in 1925 and a Ph.D. degree in journalism in 1928. His doctoral thesis, *A New Technique for Objective Methods for Measuring Reader Interest in Newspapers*, contained the idea which later developed into the Gallup polls. At the end of two years (1929-31) at Drake University as head of the department of journalism, he accepted a professorship in journalism and advertising at Northwestern University, which he held for one year. (He was later visiting professor at the Pulitzer School of Journalism at Columbia University during the years 1935-37.) Meanwhile, the theories of reader-interest evaluation which Gallup had devised were being tested in surveys he conducted for several newspapers, including the Des Moines *Register & Tribune*, the Cleveland *Plain Dealer*, and the St. Louis *Post-Dispatch*. Two eventual results of his investigations, as reported by the *National Cyclopædia of American Biography*, were the use of comics for advertising and the publication of *Look* magazine by the Des Moines Register and Tribune Company.

When he accepted a position with Young and Rubicam, an advertising agency in New York City, as director of research in 1932, Gallup began an association with that agency which was to last until 1947. For Young and Rubicam, of which he was made vice-president in 1937, Gallup worked out methods of measuring the public's reaction to the firm's products. By applying the survey principle, he compiled statistics on radio program audience reaction, the readers' interest in printed advertising campaigns, and the consumer appeal of products. The Gallup polls had meanwhile been inaugurated in 1935, with the founding by Gallup of the American Institute of Public Opinion (with offices now in Princeton, New Jersey, and New York City), which is responsible for originating questions, gathering answers and organizing the results. In 1952 the affiliated Publisher's Syndicate distributes the results to over 200 subscribing newspapers. Audience Research Institute, Inc., is an associated organization, founded by Gallup in 1939, primarily to evaluate the public reaction to motion picture titles, casts, and stories. Besides the regular polls, of which there are four a week, the A.I.P.O. from time to time undertakes specialized surveys on subjects such as reader preferences for the selections of the Book-of-the-Month Club, the pulling power of titles for Bantam Books, and the popularity of radio stars. Affiliates of the A.I.P.O. conduct Gallup polls in eleven foreign countries. In 1948 *Time* estimated the annual operating budget of the enterprises at about $750,000 yearly.

The stated purpose of the American Institute of Public Opinion is "impartially to measure and report public opinion on political and social issues of the day without regard to the rightness or wisdom of the views expressed" (*National Cyclopædia of American Biography*). Behind Gallup's claim that his polls are a true representation of the opinions of the whole nation is a theory based on a study of "probable error due to size of sample" made by Professor Theodore Brown of Harvard. As explained by the *New Yorker* (March 2, 1940), Gallup has illustrated the theory by saying that if random samples of 2,500 beans were taken from a barrel containing black and white beans, in only three out of 1,000 samples would the proportion of black to white beans vary from the proportion in the barrel itself. For good measure, he bases his polls on 3,000 samples. The questioning for the polls is carried on by about 1,200 part-time interviewers who are instructed to ask the opinion (usually a "yes," a "no," or a "no opinion" answer is sought) of a number of people chosen from given categories (such as age, sex, income, political allegiance, and locality) in proportions calculated with "near-mathematical exactitude" to form a cross-section of the population of the country. A survey is usually completed in two weeks, but can be made in two days. An innovation in poll-taking is what the institute calls the "quintamensional plan of question design" for complex issues, by which a series of preliminary questions are asked the person polled in

GEORGE GALLUP

order to establish his competency to form an opinion on the issue.

While forecasting the outcome of presidential elections is not the primary service of the Gallup surveys, it is their most spectacular function as far as the public is concerned. The first major success of the A.I.P.O. was in the election of 1936, in which the *Literary Digest* straw vote, previously fairly accurate, erroneously predicted the election of Alfred Landon. The Gallup poll correctly indicated that Franklin D. Roosevelt would be elected, although it underestimated his popular vote by about 7 per cent. In the 1948 presidential election by overestimating the vote for Thomas Dewey by 4.1 per cent and by underestimating that for Harry S. Truman by 5.3 per cent Gallup forecast election of Dewey. This error has been charged by Gallup to ending the poll too far in advance of election day and to disregarding the votes of those who were undecided when questioned. "We are continually experimenting and continually learning," he was quoted by the New York *Times* (February 27, 1949) as saying. "The nation may look to substantial improvement in one of the most useful instruments of democracy ever devised." In the 1952 elections the institute sought to reduce its percentage of error by polling the public on three bases: candidate preference, party preference, and self-interest. The "undecided" voters were also polled on how they voted in 1948 and on economic status, religion, and education for indications as to how they would make their choice. The Gallup poll, like the other major pre-election polls, calculated that Dwight D. Eisenhower had an "edge" over Adlai E. Stevenson in popularity, but underestimated the national Republican vote.

Among criticisms leveled against public opinion polls has been the charge that a poll indicating the probability of the election of a candidate creates a "bandwagon" situation

GALLUP, GEORGE—*Continued*

which influences the result of the election. Another objection to the polls comes from people who believe that in a representative democracy decisions should be based on the judgment of the elected representative rather than on the expression of public opinion. Gallup's answer to the first charge is to demonstrate that in fact this situation never has resulted from an election poll. To the second criticism he has replied that "to the extent that a political leader does take public opinion into account in making his decisions, he should have an accurate and objective measure of that opinion" (New York *Times,* February 27, 1949). On the positive side he has cited the role of the polls as a check on pressure groups and lobbys, and their function in uncovering subjects on which the American public is ignorant. Among opinions which Gallup has publicly expressed are: that the United States should create a $5 billion world relations department to defend democratic ideals and win "converts to our way of thinking" (in a speech to the National Conference on Government in November 1950); that the press of this country is doing "a pretty poor job" in keeping the public "abreast of the times" (in an article in *Time* magazine in November 1951); and that the American people are "intellectually immature," as illustrated by the fact that "fewer people read books in the United States than in any other major democracy" (in a talk before the Washington *Post* Book and Author Luncheon in October 1952).

Gallup is the author of many articles and several books, beginning with *The Business Department of School Publications,* published in 1927. Other titles are *The Place of Public Opinion Polls in a Democracy* (a paper prepared for a meeting of the American Political Science Association in December 1939), *Public Opinion in a Democracy* (1939), *A Guide to Public Opinion Polls* (1944, 1948), and the *Gallup Poll Almanacs* for 1946, 1948, and 1952, printed by the institute. With Saul Forbes Rae, Gallup wrote *The Pulse of Democracy* (1940), described as "an *ad interim* report on the public opinion poll as an instrument for improving self-government." In it the authors deal with the history of straw votes, methods of polling, and evaluations of the surveys as "a useful democratic method." Reviewers called the book "an important document which should be read with profit by politicians, editors and the common man" (New York *Herald Tribune*), "a contribution to sound political thinking" (New York *Times*), and "vastly stimulating and significant reading" (*Newsweek*).

The recipient of honorary Doctor of Laws degrees from Northwestern University, Drake University, and Boston University, Gallup also has honorary doctorates from Tufts College and from Colgate University. Syracuse University conferred on him an award for distinguished achievement, and in 1951 the University of Missouri presented him with the Missouri Honor Award. He founded Quill and Scroll, an international honorary society for high school journalists. He was president of the Market Research Council in 1934 and 1935 and has been vice-president of the National Municipal League since 1942 and treasurer of the Cooperative Analysis of Broadcasting since 1934. Other memberships are in the American Association of Advertising Agencies, the American Marketing Society, the American Political Science Association, Sigma Alpha Epsilon fraternity, Sigma Delta Chi (professional fraternity of journalists), and Sigma Xi (honorary scientific society). He is an associate member of the American Psychological Association, the Council on Foreign Relations, and the National Press Club of Washington, D.C. He founded the British Institute of Public Opinion in 1936.

The pollster has been described as a friendly man with a "comfortable" personality. Genealogical research is among his hobbies; two of his recreations are horseback riding and reading historical novels. He is an Episcopalian. Politically he votes as an independent. On December 27, 1925, Gallup married Ophelia Smith Miller, daughter of a newspaper publisher of Washington, Iowa. Their three children are Alec Miller, George Horace, Jr., and Julia. The family lives in an Early American house on a farm near Princeton.

References

Bsns W p6 Je 19 '48
Forum 103:92-5 F '40
New Yorker 16:20 Mr 2 '40
Scholastic 53:22 N 3 '48
Time 51:21-3 My 3 '48

National Cyclopædia of American Biography Current vol G, 1943-46
Who's Who in America, 1952-53

GARDNER, MATTHIAS B(ENNETT) (mă-thī′ăs) Nov. 28, 1897- United States Naval officer

Address: b. c/o Department of the Navy, The Pentagon, Washington 25, D.C.; h. Coronado, Calif.

The protection of the southern flank of the North Atlantic Treaty Organization command in June 1951 became the primary duty of the United States Sixth Fleet, operating in the Mediterranean in conjunction with British, French, and Italian naval forces. Commanding the Sixth Fleet from March 19, 1951, to May 28, 1952, was Vice-Admiral Matthias B. Gardner, who on the latter date became Deputy Chief of Naval Operations for Air, Washington, D.C. Gardner, whose service extends back to World War I, had become one of the Navy's outstanding directors of aircraft carrier operations in World War II. Following the latter duty Vice-Admiral Gardner served as Chief of the Navy's Strategic Plans Division, commander of Naval Air Bases in Hawaii, and commander of the Second (Atlantic) Fleet.

Matthias Bennett Gardner, who was born November 28, 1897, in Washington, D.C., is the eldest of the three children (two sons and a daughter) of Frank Duane Gardner, a soil expert, and Ellen (Crum) Gardner. The future naval officer was reared in the city of his birth, in Puerto Rico, and in Pennsylvania. For part of his secondary schooling he attended the Tennessee Military Institute during 1913-14. Then he was enrolled for an academic year at Pennsylvania State College (where his father had become professor of agronomy and director of the experimental station) before receiving an appointment to the United States Naval Academy in 1915. There young Gardner boxed and rowed and was on the staff of the *Lucky Bag* and *Log*.

Annapolis training was cut to three years by the World War I emergency: with other 1919 classmen he received his B.S. degree and his ensign's commission in June 1918. There followed brief duty aboard the battleship U.S.S. *North Carolina* before he was ordered to Destroyer Force, based at Brest, France, where he was assigned to the U.S.S. *Drayton*, on convoy duty. From April 1919 to November 1920 Gardner was attached to the newly commissioned destroyer *Biddle*, which, after operating as one of the guard ships for the transatlantic flight of Navy-Curtiss seaplanes, was stationed in Turkish waters. He next reported as engineer officer to the U.S.S. *McFarland*, on duty in the Near East.

Gardner returned to the United States in January 1922 to take flight training at the Naval Air Station at Pensacola, Florida, and to be designated naval aviator on June 9, 1922. Assigned one month later to an observation squadron attached to the U.S.S. *Aroostook* of the Atlantic Fleet, he was with that unit until July 1924. Two years as a flight instructor at Pensacola followed before Gardner was transferred to Kelly Field, Texas, for six months at the Advanced Air Corps Flying School. Having completed the course there in March 1927, Gardner was a member of a fighting squadron (attached first to the aircraft tender *Wright* and afterward to the carrier *Lexington*) until July 1929, when he began another two-year tour of shore duty as Operations Officer at the Naval Air Station at Anacostia, D.C. Here, with the assistance of Captain (then Lieutenant) Aaron P. Storrs and Captain (then Lieutenant) Frederick M. Trapnell, he carried out inverted flight tests considered of much value in determining the necessary load factors for fighter type planes. "Leading his two associates," stated a Navy biographical release, "he developed a series of formation maneuvers which were regarded as the most excellent 'back' flying ever exhibited in this country up to that time."

Four of the six years following Gardner's detachment from Anacostia in July 1931 were spent in the U.S.S. *Saratoga*: he was both executive officer and commander of a fighting squadron which operated therefrom and a staff aircraft gunnery and tactical officer, before reassignment for duty in Pensacola for the period 1934-36. Returning to the *Saratoga* as assistant air officer and carrier representative, Gardner was transferred to the U.S.S. *Ranger* as navigator in June 1937 and to the Navy Department at Washington twelve months later to begin a two-year assignment as officer in charge of the Aviation Section, Ships' Movement Divi-

U. S. Navy

VICE-ADM. MATTHIAS B. GARDNER

sion Office of the Chief of Naval Operations. He returned to the U.S.S. *Wright* in 1940 as executive officer.

In May 1941 Gardner joined the staff of the Commander of Aircraft, Scouting Force, as Chief of Staff and Aide and was thus engaged when the United States entered World War II. Transferred in the same capacity to the South Pacific Command in May 1942, he was during the ensuing six months "largely responsible for . . . the effective cooperation between those air units of the United States, Australia, and New Zealand forces assigned to duty on the island bases." (The quoted words are from the citation accompanying the awarding of the Distinguished Service Medal to Gardner for this achievement.)

Returned to the United States in December to become aviation officer of the plans division at United States Fleet Headquarters, Gardner was advanced in rank to Rear Admiral as of July 19, 1943, and in November was placed in command of the U.S.S. *Enterprise*, flagship of Carrier Division Eleven. Under the Rear Admiral's command the *Enterprise* participated in the invasions of the Gilbert and Marshall Islands, the first and second raids on Truk, the assault and capture of Hollandia and Saipan, and the first Battle of the Philippine Sea. Awarded the Legion of Merit with Combat Distinguishing Device "V" for his "exceptionally meritorious conduct" in these operations, Gardner became Commander of Carrier Division Eleven in July 1944 and of Carrier Division Seven in the following December. In March 1945, when the fleet flagship was put out of action by enemy attack, he "skillfully interposed" his fast carrier task group "between the damaged flagship and the enemy coast" and "maintained vigorous offensive operations against formidable Japanese defenses," thereby

GARDNER, MATTHIAS B.—*Continued*
winning the Bronze Star Medal with Combat
"V" (from the Navy Department's biography).

His own flagship having been seriously damaged in this action, Rear Admiral Gardner was returned to the United States, where, for five months beginning May 16, 1945, he served as Assistant Chief of Staff for Plans for the Commander in Chief, United States Fleet. Gardner was one of the Joint Staff Planners at the Conference of the United Nations Military Staffs at Potsdam, Germany, this service bringing him a Gold Star in lieu of a second Legion of Merit. For ten months beginning October 10, 1945, he was Chief of the Strategic Plans Division in the Office of the Chief of Naval Operations, after which he was for two years in command of Naval Bases at Pearl Harbor, Hawaii. Gardner returned to Washington in August 1948 as Assistant Chief of Naval Operations and two years afterward (August 1950) he was named to relieve Admiral Robert B. Carney as Commander of the United States Second Fleet, operating in the Atlantic. Confirmed by the Senate on September 7, 1950, in the accompanying rank of Vice-Admiral, Gardner assumed his new duties at Norfolk, Virginia, three weeks later. On March 19, 1951, he was transferred to command of the Sixth Fleet, operating in the Mediterranean, in succession to Vice-Admiral John J. Ballentine, who became Commander of the Atlantic Fleet Air Force.

Vice-Admiral Gardner's appointment to operational command of the Sixth Fleet coincided approximately with the transfer thereto of reinforcements which made it the largest battle assemblage ever maintained by the United States in the Mediterranean during a time of peace. It also preceded the announcement on June 5, 1951, that President Truman had "specifically ordered" the Sixth Fleet "to support . . . the southern flank" of General Dwight D. Eisenhower's North Atlantic Treaty Organization SHAPE command. The fleet at the time numbered about seventy vessels, including the aircraft carriers *Franklin D. Roosevelt, Coral Sea,* and *Saipan,* and the heavy cruisers *Newport News* and *Salem.* However, its composition was not to be static. "It's a rotating fleet," said the New York *Post* in the following December. "Except for Admiral Gardner's staff of about 160 officers and men, the fleet gets a new complement of men (and ships) every six months. In this way the Navy is building up a huge reserve of trained men familiar with the Mediterranean area and with the procedures developed in combined exercises with our European allies."

Gardner, who is described in the same article as "an instinctive diplomat" who "knows that the fleet's peacetime mission is also to make and keep friends" as well as to deter Russian moves, took his flagship, the cruiser *Des Moines,* northward into the Adriatic to Fiume in December 1951, flew to Belgrade for conferences with Marshal Tito of Yugoslavia, and in January 1952 paid a good-will visit to Spanish ports with some thirty warships. In February and March the Sixth Fleet participated in nine days

and eight nights of maneuvers ("Exercise Grand Slam"), which, in the words of Arnaldo Cortesi of the New York *Times,* "kept more than 200 United States, British, French, and Italian warships and hundreds of aircraft engaged in a realistic simulated war." The Vice-Admiral, who as early as the end of 1951 had asserted that his Sixth Fleet was "battle-ready," estimated that it would reach peak efficiency early in the summer of 1952. On May 28, 1952, Vice-Admiral John H. Cassady succeeded Gardner as commander of the Sixth Fleet, while Gardner took over Cassady's former post as Deputy Chief of Naval Operations for Air in Washington, D.C.

Aside from the decorations already mentioned, Gardner is the recipient of the Navy Unit Commendation Ribbon, World War I Victory Medal, Destroyer Clasp; American Defense Service Medal, Fleet Clasp; the Asiatic-Pacific Campaign Medal; the World War II Victory Medal; and the Philippine Liberation Ribbon. The naval officer and Mrs. Helen (Shippey) Grant, who were married July 22, 1929, have two sons, Bennett and Joel. Their home is in Coronado, California. In Washington the Vice-Admiral is a member of the Chevy Chase Club.

Reference

Who's Who in America, 1952-53

GARFIELD, JOHN Mar. 4, 1913—May 21, 1952 Actor; associated at the beginning of his career with Civic Repertory group and Group Theater Acting Company in New York; appeared in the stage plays *Having Wonderful Time, Golden Boy, Heavenly Express, Skipper Next to God,* among others; made screen debut in 1938 in *Four Daughters;* starred in *Humoresque, Body and Soul, The Postman Always Rings Twice,* among other motion pictures. See *Current Biography,* 1948.

Obituary

N Y Times p21 My 22 '52

GARLAND, JUDY June 10, 1922- Actress
Address: b. c/o Warner Brothers Studios, Burbank, Calif.; c/o Vern J. Alves, 224 N. Canon Dr., Beverly Hills, Calif.

NOTE: This biography supersedes the article which appeared in *Current Biography* in 1941.

Beginning as a juvenile performer in 1935, Judy Garland in the following fifteen years while under contract to Metro-Goldwyn-Mayer appeared in some thirty-five motion pictures, among them, *The Wizard of Oz, Meet Me in St. Louis,* and *Easter Parade.* On a vacation from acting for the screen, she appeared as a singing and dancing star in 1951-52 at the Palace Theatre in New York, where she set the long-term record for vaudeville in the United States with an engagement of nineteen weeks and 184 performances. Miss Garland has been heard on radio programs and has made recordings for Decca, Metro-Goldwyn-Mayer, and RCA Victor.

Born Frances Gumm in Grand Rapids, Minnesota, on June 10, 1922, Judy Garland is the youngest of three daughters of Frank Avent and Ethel Marian (Milne) Gumm. Both parents were vaudeville players, billing themselves as *Jack and Virginia Lee*. Shortly before Frances was born, her father, a Southerner, became the owner and manager of New Grand Theater in Grand Rapids. Here, the story is told, at the age of thirty months Frances appeared on the stage singing "Jingle Bells" for a Christmas program and responded so favorably to the footlights that she had to be forcibly removed by her father after repeating her song seven times. In 1927, when Frances was five (and her sisters Virginia and Mary Jane seven and twelve, respectively), the family moved to Los Angeles, seeking a climate where Frances would suffer less from her hay fever allergy. Costumed and trained by Mrs. Gumm, who accompanied them at the piano, the three girls formed a singing and dancing trio. For their first public performance, given at the Biltmore Hotel in Los Angeles, they reportedly received $1.50.

After completing elementary school in Los Angeles, Frances studied from 1929 to 1931 at Lawler's Professional School. When her father's health began to fail, the child singing and dancing trio became the principal support of the Gumm family. With their mother, Frances and her sisters toured the principal cities of the United States, appearing in an act in which Frances was billed as "the little girl with the great big voice" (*Hollywood Tintype*, November 21, 1942). At the Oriental Theatre in Chicago, upon the suggestion of George Jessel, Frances changed her name to Judy Garland, and the sister trio was called *The Three Garlands*. *Variety*'s review of the sisters' performance stated that "the youngest, Judy, handles ballads like a veteran and gets every note and word over with a personality that hits audiences. Her sisters merely form a background."

At the close of a series of appearances in Detroit, Indianapolis, and Kansas City, the Garland sisters and their mother returned to Los Angeles in 1934 to get bookings near Mr. Gumm, who was still ill (he died of meningitis the following year). The next summer they accepted an engagement at Lake Tahoe, where Judy's voice was described as "poignant and unforgettable" (*Photoplay*, September 1940). Shortly after singing her favorite song "Dinah" for an agent from Metro-Goldwyn-Mayer Studios, she received a seven-year contract, the only contract, it is said, ever given on the MGM lot with neither screen nor sound tests. When the contract was signed in 1935 (A. E. Hotchner in *Reader's Digest* stated), Judy "couldn't read music, had never had a dancing or singing lesson, but she was bright and inventive and powered with a fantastic drive. . . .She could read pages of dialogue just once, then go through a scene flawlessly." At the beginning of her motion picture career the young actress attended Bancroft Junior High School in Los Angeles (1936-37).

For her first film, a two-reel short called *Every Sunday Afternoon* (1935), with Deanna Durbin, Judy Garland was loaned by MGM to Universal Twentieth-Century Fox Studios. Upon seeing herself on the screen in *Pigskin Parade* (1936), she exclaimed: "I was frightening—a fat little frightening pig with pigtails" (*Hollywood Life Stories*, 1952). MGM put her on a reducing diet with a gymnasium regime and eliminated her natural chubbiness. After an appearance on the Chase and Sanborn radio show in 1936, she gave her first personal stage performance at Loew's State Theatre in New York at the age of fourteen, alternately making her audience laugh and cry and delighting them with her singing. *Variety*'s Hobe Morrison said· "The girl has both the personality and the skill to develop into box office in any line of show business."

Following a role in the film *Thoroughbreds Don't Cry* (1937) Judy Garland became a juvenile singing star in the motion picture *Broadway Melody* (1938), in which she sang "Dear Mr. Gable," a song written for her by Roger Edens. In the opinion of the New York *Post* critic (October 7, 1951), *Broadway Melody* "established Judy as a film personality." She also was seen in 1938 in the films *Everybody Sings, Love Finds Andy Hardy, Listen Darling*, and *The Wizard of Oz*. As Dorothy in *The Wizard of Oz*, in which she sang "Over the Rainbow," she was considered to have given the best juvenile performance of the year and was promoted out of juvenile roles by MGM.

From 1938 to 1940 Judy Garland attended University High School in Los Angeles; she then (1941) entered the school at MGM, taking the subjects she liked, including English literature and music appreciation. When *For Me and My Gal* (1941), in which she played opposite Gene Kelly in her first adult role, was shown at the Astor Theatre, New York, in 1942, Howard Barnes of the New York *Herald Tribune* commented, "Miss Garland is someone to reckon with. Of all the youngsters who have graduated into mature roles in recent years, she has the surest command of her form of make-believe. . . .She turns in a warm, persuasive, and moving portrayal." In 1941 she also had a prominent role in *Life Begins for Andy Hardy*. She returned temporarily to a juvenile role as the leading young lady in *Babes on Broadway*, playing opposite Mickey Rooney, a partner she said she enjoyed because each knew exactly what the other was going to do. On January 26, 1941, Judy Garland appeared on the *Silver Theatre* program of Columbia Broadcasting System in *Love's New Sweet Song*, for which she wrote the original script. The following year, in December 1942, she starred on radio with Walter Pidgeon and Adolphe Menjou in the CBS *Lux Radio Theatre*, presenting an adaptation from the motion picture *A Star Is Born*. While working during this time in radio and pictures, she made recordings for Decca Records.

Singing "Joint is Jumpin' Down at Carnegie Hall," Judy Garland appeared in the all-star film musical of army camp life, called *As Thousands Cheer* (1943), which during its

JUDY GARLAND

première at the Astor in New York added
$534,000 to the third War Loan Drive. In the
motion picture *Presenting Lily Mars*, released
in New York the same year, the actress portrayed a stage-struck girl in a screen adaptation of the Booth Tarkington novel. The film
critic of the New York *Times* on April 30,
1943, described her as having "a perky friendliness that is completely disarming." Her role
in *Girl Crazy* (1943), with Mickey Rooney, a
screen version of the George Gershwin musical
comedy, gave her the opportunity to sing such
songs as "I've Got Rhythm", "Embraceable
You", "They're Writing Songs of Love," and
"Could You Use Me?" Eileen Creelman of the
New York *Sun* thought that "the music and
Miss Garland's performance [were] far above
standard."

Meet Me in St. Louis, Judy Garland's 1944
screen success, a comedy with music and a
period piece based on Sally Benson's sketches
of St. Louis in 1904, provided her with a role
that has been mentioned as her favorite. "Miss
Garland is full of gay exuberance as the second
sister," wrote Bosley Crowther (New York
Times), "and sings with a rich voice that
grows riper and more expressive in each new
film." In 1945 she played her first straight
dramatic role in a screen version of Paul and
Pauline Gallico's *The Clock*, giving a sympathetic presentation of a young girl involved in
a forty-eight hour romance and "showing her
gradual transition from casualness to deep-
feeling" (*Christian Science Monitor*). In *The
Harvey Girls* (1946) she sang "The Atchison,
Topeka and the Santa Fe," adding color to
the story of Fred Harvey's restaurant chain
along the Santa Fe railroad. Her sketch "The
Interview" in *Ziegfeld Follies of 1946*, which
satirized a glamorous motion picture star, led
Bosley Crowther to comment: "Miss Garland
gives promise of a talent approaching that of

Beatrice Lillie or Gertrude Lawrence." She
danced and sang to Cole Porter's music with
Gene Kelly in the screen Technicolor version
of S. N. Behrman's comedy, *The Pirate*, which
Archer Winsten of the New York *Post* called
"the musical of the year." Both Miss Garland
and her partner dropped the tap dancing that
had been their specialty separately or together
in other films and adopted a gymnastic form of
dancing. Dancing with Fred Astaire in 1948,
she was seen on the screen in Irving Berlin's
musical *Easter Parade*, regarded as "altogether her best film performance" by Howard
Barnes.

While making the film *Annie Get Your Gun*,
Miss Garland, who since May 1949 had been
having difficulty in keeping her motion picture
production schedules, was replaced by MGM in
the picture by Betty Hutton, after a million
dollars worth of film had been shot. At the
end of a long vacation during which she tried
to recover her health, the star returned to
MGM to play opposite Gene Kelly in *Summer
Stock*. The studio was said to have promised
her a year's rest as a reward, but within a few
weeks she was recalled to replace June Allyson
opposite Fred Astaire in the motion picture
Royal Wedding. Failing to report for work in
June 1950, she was suspended by MGM and
later released from her $5,000-a-week contract,
which normally would have expired in January
1952.

In New York, where she established a temporary residence, Miss Garland said in October
1950 that she would return to the stage or
screen only on an individual assignment basis.
After a five months' rest, she accepted an engagement for a four-week personal appearance
at the Palladium in London, beginning April 9,
1951, with a salary of $20,000 a week. In a
program, made up of songs from her motion
pictures, her triumph "exceeded expectations"
(*Variety*); a United Press report stated that
a packed house of more than two thousand
stood and roared a three-minute welcome. She
repeated her program in Scotland, where some
critics acclaimed her as the best United States
performer since Danny Kaye, and made further
personal appearances in Dublin and Monte
Carlo. On October 16, 1951, Judy Garland
headed an all-star variety show, playing to a
reserved-seat audience, at the Palace Theatre
in New York, and bringing back the "two-
a-day" vaudeville act. Her nineteen-week run,
grossing nearly $750,000, broke the United
States vaudeville box office record of such stars
as Kate Smith, Eddie Cantor, George Jessel,
and Burns and Allen. Her popularity resulted
in the revival at nearby Loew's State Theatre
of two of her films—*Meet Me in St. Louis* and
Babes in Arms—and a five-year contract with
RCA Victor Records. In January 1952 she
was the initial guest on Columbia Broadcasting
System's capsule interview series presented by
Radie Harris, the columnist.

Judy Garland returned to California in April
1952 to open the Civic Light Opera season at
the Philharmonic Auditorium in Los Angeles
with her Palace vaudeville show. The Associated Press reported that scalpers sold tickets

for $100 a pair, and, during Miss Garland's first week's engagement, a near capacity house grossed over $50,000. She repeated her performance in San Francisco in another four-week run. Following a two-year absence from Hollywood, Judy Garland agreed in September 1952 to star in Warner Brothers Pictures Technicolor film *A Star Is Born,* scheduled to go before the cameras in the spring of 1953.

For her performance in *The Wizard of Oz* Judy Garland was given a special award in 1939 by the Academy of Motion Picture Arts and Sciences. In the Motion-Picture-Herald Fame Poll in 1940, 1941, and 1945, she was voted one of the ten best money-making stars. On November 27, 1951, Judy was honored by the American Guild of Variety Artists, American Federation of Labor, for bringing back the "two-a-day" in vaudeville and giving work to many unemployed in the theater. Harold Clurman has said of her, "Judy Garland has the power that rises from the desire and the ability to give. . . . She brings her excitement right on the stage with her. All she has to do is appear before us and sing" (*New Republic,* November 26, 1951). Part of her appealing quality is in "the wistful eyes and waif-like sadness that match the emotions she pours into her songs" (*Life,* October 29, 1951).

On July 28, 1941, Judy Garland was married to David Rose, a music arranger and composer of "Holiday for Strings." The next year they were divorced, and on June 15, 1945, the actress became the wife of Vincente Minnelli, a stage designer and a motion picture director, who directed her films *Meet Me in St. Louis, The Clock,* and *Ziegfeld Follies of 1946.* They have one child, Liza. About a year after her divorce from Minnelli, Judy Garland on June 11, 1952, married Sid Luft, a film producer. She also has a daughter by this marriage. The star stands five feet three inches tall, weighs about 115 pounds, and has dark brown eyes and red hair. Her favorite color is green; two of her recreations are tennis and swimming.

References

Am W p7 D 30 '51
Newsweek 35:14 Jl 3 '50
Hollywood Life Stories 1:81-4 '52 pors
N Y Post p15 S 12 '41
Photoplay 54:33-4+ S '40; 18:114 Mr '41 por
Read Digest 61:72-6 Ag '52
International Motion Picture Almanac, 1951-52
Winchester's Screen Encyclopedia (1948)
Who's Who in America, 1952-53
World Biography (1948)

GARROWAY, DAVE July 13, 1913- Television and radio personality

Address: b. c/o National Broadcasting Company, 40 W. 49th St., New York 20; h. 710 Park Ave., New York 21

The National Broadcasting Company's early morning, Monday-through-Friday television program *Today,* inaugurated in January 1952, is presided over by Dave Garroway, who is also the star of the Monday-through-Friday radio program *Dial Dave Garroway.* Advertised as "a twenty-first century television news program fifty years ahead of its time," *Today* is considered to have the highest potential for revenue of any program on television. Garroway began his radio career as a $16-a-week page boy at the NBC studios in New York. In the course of eight years he rose from special feature announcer to disc jockey to master of ceremonies of a variety show; he spent three of these years in the Navy in World War II. One of the first television shows originating in Chicago (in 1949) was *Garroway at Large,* a variety show commended for the ingenious use of camera techniques, for inventiveness, and for Garroway's casual, intimate style of delivery.

David Cunningham Garroway, Jr., an only child, was born July 13, 1913, in Schenectady, New York. The senior Garroway, whose wife was the former Bertha Tanner, was of Scottish descent. His work as a General Electric mechanical engineer made it necessary for the family to move frequently. In 1927 the Garroways settled in St. Louis, Missouri. There the son attended University High School; at that time interested in astronomy, the student made several telescopes. After his high school graduation in 1931, he entered Washington University in the same city, majored in English, and received his B.A. degree in 1935.

The following year Garroway worked for three months as a salesman of piston rings before entering upon a short period of study at the Harvard business school. His next project, which he undertook with a friend, was the publication of a list of 800 frequently mispronounced words under the title *You Don't Say! . . . Or Do You?* He was in New York City selling the pamphlet when, in 1938, he was hired as a page at the National Broadcasting Company's studios at a salary of $16 a week. Garroway advanced to guide and then to guide trainer, while at the same time he studied at the company's school for announcers. In the first audition that he received at this school Garroway was rated twenty-third in a class of twenty-four students.

Having completed the course, Garroway went first to radio station KDKA in Pittsburgh, Pennsylvania, as a special events announcer and later, in September 1940, to station WMAQ in Chicago. Garroway's World War II service was in the Navy, which he entered in 1942 with the rating of ensign. He saw sea duty on a mine sweeper and taught in a yeoman's school for radio technicians in Hawaii, achieving the rank of Navy lieutenant (s.g.). At the end of his term of service in 1945 he returned to Chicago to resume his position as a staff announcer at station WMAQ. In January 1946 he began broadcasting his first disc-jockey show, the *11:60 Club,* a midnight program on which he played only the "pure jazz" records he liked and commented on any subject which interested him, in the casual manner which has come to be identified with him.

(Continued next page)

NBC-TV

DAVE GARROWAY

The early Garroway style had two character-istics. One of these was what *Variety* (October 8, 1947) called his "ability to create a cozy 'you-and-me' atmosphere." The other was his use of what John Crosby (New York *Herald Tribune*) termed "distracted prose." He often employed such words as "lissome", "gruesome," "gauzy", "incandescent" with "no great interest in their connotations," and addressed his listeners by such epithets as "old delicate", "my so unfrowzy" or "old tiger eyes." *Variety's* critic felt that Garroway sometimes spoiled his effects "by using two or three adjectives where none would be best." However, his knowledge of jazz, his wide range of interests, and his relaxed, intimate style of delivery increased his popularity to the point where in the fall of 1947 he was conducting, besides the *11:60 Club*, an afternoon daily disc-jockey session and a Sunday night variety show.

An NBC television variety show, originating in Chicago as *Garroway at Large*, which was launched in April 1949, was given three months later a featured Sunday night position. The program, seen in the East and Midwest, consisted of singers, an orchestra, an occasional guest comedian (Henry Morgan and Fred Allen were among those appearing), and of Garroway's "distinctive humor." Innovations were the mobile and creative use of the studio cameras, the use of primarily visual jokes, and the banning of studio audiences. The program was praised for being "pure television," rather than relying on stage, motion picture, or radio technique: Walter Winchell called it "the first show with a professional flavor. Big time all the way." Together with *Stud's Place* and *Kukla, Fran and Ollie*, the Garroway show was cited by several writers as an outstanding example of the "Chicago school" of television, in which imagination and ingenuity offset the lack of high budgets and expensive talent character-istic of programs originating in Hollywood or New York.

On television Garroway retained the "low-pressure" quality of his radio personality. The *Christian Science Monitor's* television columnist said of him: "He is a stylist; his style is calculated unpretentiousness. He cultivates ease of manner, simplicity of address, restraint, understatement, diffidence, almost shyness." Asked in an interview whether he tried to be funny on television, Garroway replied, "I merely try to act natural, so far as the medium will permit. . . .Of course, that a person acts naturally may. in itself seem to be funny."

In November 1949 Garroway signed a five-year contract with National Broadcasting Company which, according to *Variety*, put him in the "top-star bracket" financially. *Garroway at Large*, which began as a sustaining feature, was first sponsored by Congoleum-Nairn, Inc., in February 1950. Dropped by this firm in September 1951, the program was taken on an option by the Armour & Company, which reversed its decision to sponsor the show when the network time available for the program was considered inadequate. The subsequent dropping of the program by the network was called "grounds for genuine misgiving" by Jack Gould (TV and radio critic for the New York *Times*), who said that in technical production the show was "head and shoulders over any other program on the air."

Early in 1952 the National Broadcasting Company initiated an "unprecedented" advertising campaign to publicize its forthcoming two-hour Monday-to-Friday program, *Today*. It was announced that through the television studio, called "the nerve center of the planet," by "all means of communication yet invented," the morning audience would be "in touch with the world." Garroway, chosen for master of ceremonies, or "communicator," of the show, has been quoted as saying, "I came looking for this job. . . .They weren't looking for a lean-against-the-ladder, go-to-sleep-standing-up guy like me. They wanted a guy with dynamics, as they say around here."

Using the large RCA Exhibition Hall in New York as a studio (which is visible from the street), *Today* was first broadcast in January 14, 1952. It employs the transoceanic telephone, telephoto, a TV "walkie-talkie," teletype, tape recorders, records, film, and various electronic devices to present a program of news, weather reports, drama and book reviews, interviews, music, and entertainment features. Garroway broadcasts an additional hour for the Middle West: his first hour is heard only in the Eastern time zone, the second in the Eastern and Central zones, and the last only in the Central zone. With its staff of 75 persons, the show is estimated to cost about $60,000 a week. *Variety* has reported that the potential revenue from the program is $14,560,000 a year. Comments by television columnists on the first presentation were generally not favorable. Some called it "pointless" and "pretentious . . . ostentatious"; the opinion of the New York *Times* reviewer was that it is "the slave rather than the master of its own inventiveness and ingenuity." Seven weeks later, however, *Variety* reported that the program had "shaken down to its essentials. . . .Dave Garroway and his relaxed pace are an obvious asset. . . .*Today* utilized him for only a slice of those capabilities which were wholly reflected in his late and lamented *Garroway at Large*." Since 1949 Garroway has been the star of the NBC fifteen-minute morning Monday-through-Friday radio program *Dial Dave Garroway* (formerly called *Reserved for Garroway*), which *Variety* described as "a pleasant potpourri of song and comedy."

Garroway was given the 1949 gold medal award of the Poor Richard Club of Philadelphia, an advertising association. On the Honor Roll compiled in January 1950 by Jack Gould, of the New York *Times*, Garroway was named as the outstanding "New Male Personality." Another award bestowed on him was the one for the "Most Original in TV" of *Look* Magazine Television Awards in January 1951. His salary has been reported as potentially $300,000 a year for a fully sponsored *Today*.

A man of diversified interests, Garroway has been called by *Time* "an amateur mechanic, gem cutter, tile-setter, photographer, bird fancier, cabinetmaker, and bibliophile." He usually owns four or five foreign sports cars, which he likes to outfit with his own upholstery. His chief recreation is golf—at fifteen he won two round matches in the United States Amateur Golf tournament and later several city championships. On February 15, 1940, he married Adele Dwyer; they have a daughter named Paris and are now divorced. The television star is six feet two inches tall and weighs about 200 pounds. His hair and eyes are brown, he wears large horn-rimmed glasses, and his characteristic dress is tweeds and a bow tie.

References

Collier's p33 Mr 17 '51
N Y Journal-American p10 Ja 17 '51

GARROWAY, DAVID CUNNINGHAM
See Garroway, Dave

GEHRMANN, DON(ALD ARTHUR)
Nov. 16, 1927- Runner
Address: h. Wauwatosa, Wis.

Among the American athletes competing in the 1952 Olympics at Helsinki was Don Gehrmann, outstanding runner with the 800-meter team. Holder of a number of United States and world records (both on cinder and on board), Gehrmann distinguished himself originally as a miler, known for sprint finishes, before becoming equally prominent in races of shorter distance—1,500 and 800 yards.

Donald Arthur Gehrmann was born in Milwaukee, Wisconsin, on November 16, 1927, the son of a machinist of German descent. At Pulaski High School in Milwaukee, recounted Bill Fay in *Collier's*, the youth began to shape into a "record-breaking miler," training for track meets by chasing rabbits in nearby

woods. "I like to run in the country," explained the miler, "It's great for conditioning, even in winter." After entering the University of Wisconsin, from which he was to receive the B.S. degree, Gehrmann in 1946 continued running for the college team, with the result that he became National Collegiate Athletic Association 1,500-meter champion. In 1948 he was placed on the United States Olympic running team and came through in eighth place in the 1,500-meter event. In 1949 he competed in the January Wanamaker Mile, run at New York's Madison Square Garden under the auspices of the Millrose Athletic Association. Gehrmann, victor over nearest contender Willy Slykhuis of Holland, clocked 4:09.5, for a record to that point in his running career and for the fifth fastest mile recorded in that event. Gehrmann's time was somewhat slower—4:15.2—in the February 1949 Michigan State Relays, his college coach stated, because he was used to running on hard clay tracks indoors, and the dirt track had slowed his pace. At the fortieth annual Drake Relays held in Des Moines, Iowa, at the end of April, Gehrmann distinguished himself by sprint finishes in the sprint medley relay and in the distance medley, but was unable to come to the forefront in the one-mile relay.

Emerging as the "nation's premier miler of 1949," Gehrmann went into the 1950 season by winning the Junior Board of Trade Mile in the mid-January Washington (D.C.) *Evening Star* Games. At the end of that month he competed for the first time against Fred Wilt in the eight-furlong, banked track Wanamaker Mile, again run in New York's Madison Square Garden. Both runners appeared to reach the tape simultaneously, so that the judges were forced into disagreement: in a subsequently disputed decision they awarded the first place Rodman Wanamaker cup to Gehrmann, clocked (as was his opponent) at 4:09.3. In March the Metropolitan Athletic Association Union board of managers upheld a reversal of the decision declared by the metropolitan registration committee, which had named Wilt the winner, so that it was not until a balloting taken by the annual convention of the National Athletic Association Union of its membership in December 1950 declared Gehrmann the victor by a 304-to-108 vote.

Gehrmann set a dirt track record of 4:12.7 in the early February 1950 Michigan State Relays, prior to his return meeting with Wilt at the fourteenth annual Chicago *Daily News* Relays in March. There Gehrmann developed an eight-yard lead over Wilt in the Bankers Mile, "came up on his toes like a sprinter in the backstretch about a hundred yards from home," and won, with 4:09.5 on the clock. Competing again in the Drake Relays at Des Moines the following month, Gehrmann, with the University of Wisconsin team, met defeat by the Ohio State relayers. He and his Wisconsin teammates took the mile relay in a May event at Wisconsin's Stadium, losing in other events. Gehrmann individually, however, set a 4:11.8 new record in the mile and clocked a winning 1:53.2 in the half mile. In the fiftieth

DON GEHRMANN

annual Big Ten outdoor track and field meet held in Evanston, Illinois, at the end of May, Gehrmann took an "unprecedented fourth straight mile crown," the first half-mile title he had yet acquired on an outdoor track, and acted as anchor man for the Wisconsin team in its winning mile relay. In his last competition as a member of the Wisconsin team, just prior to his graduation in June 1950, Gehrmann set a 1:50.7 record for the half mile at the Pacific Coast-Big Ten interconference meeting. "It was the fastest half mile run anywhere this year," said the New York *Times,* "and broke the meet and stadium records." At the University of Wisconsin he was also selected as the outstanding miler for the past fifty years in the Big Ten conference. For a time after his graduation Gehrmann worked as an insurance salesman, a job he subsequently gave up: "I didn't like it. I want to work with youngsters." At the end of the year, in a long-distance telephone conversation with Lou Miller of the New York *World-Telegram,* he reported in 1950: "I'm working as assistant public relations director for the Wisconsin American Automobile Association. I'm practicing track six days a week, running after work from 4 to 6 on the University of Wisconsin track."

Opening the 1951 season in January at the fourth annual Washington *Star* Games, Gehrmann won the mile event on a casein-coated track at the National Guard Armory. In this "whale of a race," he beat nearest contender Ingvar Bengtsson of Sweden by 4:16.6 for the eight laps: "It was close, very close, but there is no doubt that he had won." His first 1951 meeting with Wilt was that same month, in a meet sponsored by the Philadelphia *Inquirer*: for a thirty-fourth consecutive victory, the Milwaukee runner chalked up 4:12.4 on the clock for the *Inquirer* Mile, for a seven-yard

margin over Wilt. He was the winner again in their next contest, the mile run in the silver jubilee games of the Massachusetts Knights of Columbus—Gehrmann's thirty-fifth in a row (and fourth over Wilt). "The ease with which the slender Wisconsin graduate won left all observers convinced that he will extend his string of successes indefinitely," observed Joseph M. Sheehan of the New York *Times.* For the third time, Gehrmann late in January placed first in a field of four contestants in the Wanamaker Mile, with a 4:07.5, "which left little doubt that he belongs among the very best." His showing in the victorious mile run at the Boston Athletic Association games in February was 4:07.9, two tenths of a second better than the previous record established by Gil Dodds. "Racing five rivals and the clock," Gehrmann continued his winning streak in the New York Athletic Club's eighty-third anniversary games, to cover the Baxter Mile in 4:08.2, just short of the record. Another disputed mile, run by Gehrmann and Wilt to a simultaneous finish in the Intercollegiate A.A.A.A. meet late in February 1951, was awarded to Gehrmann by a 3-to-1 decision of the judges. In a subsequent contest, Gehrmann went down before Wilt in the Columbian Mile of the thirty-second annual Knights of Columbus games (sports observers felt that Wilt's fellow N.Y.A.C. contestant, Stewart Ray, contributed to his success). With his three-year streak of thirty-nine victories broken, Gehrmann came in second to Lenny Truex for the mile event of the Cleveland (Ohio) Knights of Columbus track meet in March, but redeemed his first place later that month by securing his fourth consecutive Bankers Mile Victory, in the fifteenth annual Chicago *Daily News* relays. Despite a heavy cold he was able to clock at 4:09.1. Sprinting into victory again on March 31 ten yards ahead of Wilt, Gehrmann set a 4:09.1 record for the invitation mile race of the Niagara district A.A.U. meet. The Glenn Cunningham Mile, a feature of the Kansas Relays at Lawrence in April, found Gehrmann in second place. He fell to third in the Penn relays later in the season when, said Lou Miller, "he was as badly out of shape as a model-T flivver."

Of Gehrmann's 4:14 victory in the mile race at the Washington (D.C.) fifth *Evening Star* games in January 1952, Sheehan of the *Times* wrote: "Laying off the pace until the last circuit of the eight-lap flat track, the wiry Badger alumnus cut loose in the final backstretch to snap the tape six yards" ahead of the closest follower. The Wisconsin runner made the "blazing twelve-lap time of 4:10.2" in winning the Philadelphia *Inquirer* Mile for the second consecutive year over Wilt, thus beating by one second the record set by Wilt two years previously. Twenty-four hours later Gehrmann "kicked home a yard ahead" of Wilt and the three other contestants to take the Boston Knights of Columbus Games mile event in 4.09.3. Wilt shortly afterward questioned Gehrmann's style of retaining his strength for a sprint finish, without giving his best speed throughout a race. To this

Gehrmann replied, "I believe the crowd enjoys seeing a sprint finish" and further explained that this style had grown out of the necessity for running in two or three races at each meet during his high school and college days. A one-foot lead over Wilt again brought Gehrmann a triumph in the Wanamaker Mile on January 26, although his time—4:11.2—was the slowest he had yet made in his four tries at that event. After winning the mile run in the Milwaukee *Journal* games (4:08.4) and the Hunter mile in the Boston A.A. games (4:08.9), Gehrman in early February lost the Baxter Mile in the New York Athletic Club meet to Wilt, in a race so close that the judges were obliged to base their decision on a photograph before awarding the 4:10.4 victory to Wilt.

Changing from the mile to the 1,000-yard contest, Gehrmann in mid-February 1952 won his first National A.A.U. senior championship by setting a world indoor record of 2:08.2, in what Jesse Abramson of the New York *Herald Tribune* called "the race of his life." A number of sports commentators expressed awe at the record and spoke of Gehrmann as a potential four-minute mile man. An unexpected upset in a subsequent 880-yard race found Gehrmann behind Reggie Pearman in the Intercollegiate A.A.A.A. special, a defeat repeated by Roscoe Lrowne in the early March New York Knights of Columbus games 880 feature. There, too, Gehrmann, competing in the mile event as well, was defeated by Wilt. With the opening of the Olympic fund campaign in March, Gehrman made an eleven-lap track record of 1:51 in the 800-yard competition at the Olympic Carnival in Madison Square Garden. As the most distinguished performer in 1952 indoor track events, Gehrmann in April received the annual merit award of the New York Track Writers Association. Competing in England Gehrmann was outrun on May 31 in the 1,500-meter international invitation race in London, but returned to top form to win the 1,000-yard feature in 2:11, bettering the British record by one second, and also the 440-yard event in 0:49.2. Exhausted by the time he came home to compete in the Olympic qualifying 1,500-yard and 800-meter tryouts in California, Gehrmann was forced to drop out midway in the former, and made only sixth (and last qualifying) place in the latter. The close programing of the two events brought criticism of the Olympic officials by the sports reviewers, who felt that Gehrmann would have made a better showing in properly distanced events.

Don Gehrmann is in 1952 employed as public relations representative for the Joseph Schlitz Brewing Company. On July 15, 1950, he married his high school sweetheart, Dolores; their sons are Donald, Jr., and Tim Alan. Gehrmann is a member of the Martin Luther Lutheran Church. Customarily referred to as "slight," he is five feet nine inches in height, weighs 131 pounds, according to Bill Fay of *Collier's*. The dark-haired runner wears his spectacles on the track.

References

Collier's 123:64 My 28 '49
Sport 13:42 Ag '52

GEORGE VI, KING OF GREAT BRITAIN Dec. 14, 1895—Feb. 6, 1952 Second son of George V; attended naval training schools at Osborne and Dartmouth; served in Navy and Air Service during World War I; created Duke of York (1920); succeeded to the throne on December 11, 1936, upon the abdication of Edward VIII; was crowned king on May 12, 1937; chief event of his reign, World War II (1939-45). See *Current Biography*, 1942.

Obituary

N Y Times p10 F 7 '52

GIANNINI, L(AWRENCE) M(ARIO) Nov. 25, 1894—Aug. 19, 1952 Banker; president of Bank of America National Trust and Savings Association since 1936; helped his father, Amadeo Peter Giannini build up "the world's largest bank"; filled various positions in the elder Giannini's bank since he entered it as a clearing clerk (1918); member of President Truman's Committee for Financing Foreign Trade (since 1946) and of the Committee on International Economic Policy (since 1947); president and a director of Bank of America-New York (International) since 1949. See *Current Biography*, 1950.

Obituary

N Y Times p19 Ag 21 '52

GILMER, ELIZABETH MERIWETHER *See* Dix, D.

GOEDHART, G(ERRIT) J(AN) VAN HEUVEN *See* Heuven Goedhart, G. J. van

GOLDSTINE, HERMAN H(EINE) Sept. 13, 1913- Mathematician
Address: b. c/o Institute for Advanced Study, Princeton, N.J.; h. Cold Soil Road, R.D. 2, Princeton, N.J.

Electronic computer expert Herman H. Goldstine has been since 1946 a member of the Institute for Advanced Study in Princeton, New Jersey, and assistant director of the institute's electronic computer project. The mathematician, who had previously taught at the University of Chicago and the University of Michigan, served as a ballistics officer during World War II and afterward became a consultant for ordinance research at Aberdeen and Los Alamos. As an observer for the United States at the United Nations Educational, Scientific and Cultural Organization meetings in Paris in 1951, he took part in formulating plans for the establishment of an International Computation Center.

Born in Chicago on September 13, 1913, Herman Heine Goldstine was the only child of

GOLDSTINE, HERMAN H.—*Continued*
Isaac Oscar Goldstine, a lawyer, and Bessie
(Lipsey) Goldstine. When he had completed
his secondary school education at Chicago's
Nicholas Senn High School in 1929, he matriculated at the University of Chicago, where
mathematics was his major subject. Remaining
at the University of Chicago for graduate
courses after he had received his B.S. degree
in 1933, Goldstine took his M.Sc. degree in
1934 and his Ph.D. degree in mathematics in
1936, submitting for the latter a dissertation entitled *Conditions for a Minimum of a Functional*. At the university he had gained election to Phi Beta Kappa, national scholastic
honorary society, and to Sigma Xi, national
scientific honorary society, in 1933 and 1934
respectively.

For three years (1936-39) after finishing his
postgraduate studies Goldstine was employed as
instructor and research assistant at the University of Chicago. He then accepted an appointment as instructor at the University of
Michigan, where he was soon advanced to
assistant professor. At both universities he
taught mathematics to undergraduate and graduate students. Following the outbreak of World
War II Goldstine in 1942 left teaching to become a ballistics officer in the Ordnance Department of the United States Army. In recognition of his services during the years 1942
to 1946, in the course of which he attained the
rank of major, he was awarded the American
Service Medal, the World War II Victory
Medal, the Meritorious Service Unit Plaque,
and the Army Commendation Medal.

In 1946 Goldstine was appointed a permanent
member of the Institute for Advanced Study in
New Jersey and assistant project director of
the institute's electronic computer project. Conceived by Dr. Abraham Flexner, who foresaw
a haven "where scholars and scientists may regard the world and its phenomena as their laboratory," the institute was made possible by an
initial gift of $5 million by Louis Bamberger
and his sister, Mrs. Felix Fuld. It was inaugurated in 1931 on the campus of Princeton
University, moving in 1939 to quarters of its
own at nearby Olden Farm. "Here, under one
roof," wrote Gertrude Samuels in the New
York *Times* (November 19, 1950), "is one of
the most dramatic assemblages of intellectual
power to be found anywhere in the world
today."

Aside from his administrative duties, Goldstine's function as assistant director of the
institute's electronic computer project is, in his
words, "to conduct mathematical investigations
into the numerical methods needed to operate
high-speed, automatic computing devices; with
particular reference to developing methods for
handling the partial differential and integral
equations of mathematical physics on electronic
computing machines." The giant calculator
which has been built at the institute ("a ceil-
ing-high structure of wires and electronic
tubes"), designed by John von Neumann, was
first shown to the public in June 1952. A revolutionary method of weather forecasting, in
which the "mechanical brain" performs high-

speed calculations based on the numerous (there
may be as many as fifty) variables governing
the weather pattern, is now being developed.
In June 1952 the New York *Times* reported
the beginning of a project based on using the
computer for "a series of calculations designed
to throw light on the impact of the nation's
defense program on the economy." Other projected uses for the machine are determining
strategy in games, calculating information for
use in ballistics, and the solution of specific
problems in engineering.

In December 1951 the United Nations Educational, Scientific and Cultural Organization
announced a program, costing $100,000 a year,
to establish an International Computation Center, which would employ for international service "some of man's electronic calculating
brains." Goldstine, who in that year was present
at the UNESCO meeting in Paris as an observer for the United States and who contributed to working out plans for the computation
center, said that "the core of the center is expected to be an electronic machine which might
do 1,000 to 2,000 multiplications," compared
with about 300 a second by the machine at the
Aberdeen Proving Grounds in Maryland (New
York *Herald Tribune*, December 13, 1951).
While the United States has shown interest in
other nations' joining this cooperative undertaking (Goldstine has stated) and while some
American commercial firms have expressed will-
ingness to help, it is not likely that the Government itself will take part.

Goldstine has written a number of papers on
subjects in his special fields of abstract spaces,
calculus of variations, and numerical analysis.
Among the studies that he contributed to the
Bulletin of the American Mathematical Society
are "A Multiplier Rule in Abstract Spaces"
(1938), "Minimum Problems in the Functional
Calculus" (1940), and "The Modular Space
Determined by a Positive Function" (1942,
with R. W. Barnard). For the *Duke Mathematical Journal* he wrote "The Minima of
Functionals with Associated Side Conditions"
(1937), "Weakly Complete Banach Spaces"
(1938), and "The Calculus of Variations in
Abstract Spaces" (1942). In 1946 he collaborated with his wife on a paper titled "The
Electronic Numerical Integrator and Computer." With J. von Neumann and Burks he
wrote "Preliminary Discussion of the Logical
Design of an Electronic Computing Instrument"
in 1946, and in several succeeding published
studies Goldstine and von Neumann analyzed
the problems, theoretical and practical, involved
in the building and use of the electronic computing machine.

Dr. Goldstine has been a consultant for the
Ballistics Research Laboratories at the Aberdeen Proving Ground since 1947 and for the
Los Alamos Scientific Laboratory and the
Ordnance Research No. I at the University of
Chicago since 1948. He was appointed chairman of a subpanel on the computing devices
joint research and development board of the
National Military Establishment in 1948. He
holds membership in the American Mathematical Society, the Mathematical Association

of America, and the Institute of Mathematical Statistics, and is a member of subcommittee A-I on computing centers of the latter organization. The scientist has brown eyes and brown hair, is five feet nine inches tall, and weighs 130 pounds. In 1941 he married Adele Katz, also a mathematician.

References
    American Men of Science (1949)
    Who Knows—And What (1949)

GORE, ALBERT (ARNOLD) Dec. 26, 1907- United States Representative from Tennessee; Senator-elect from Tennessee
Address: b. c/o House Office Bldg., Washington 25, D.C.; h. Arlington Village, Arlington, Va.; Carthage, Tenn.

Democratic Representative from Tennessee's Fourth District Albert Gore was elected Senator from his State in November 1952, after fourteen years in the House of Representatives. For the first four years of his tenure he served on the House Banking and Currency Committee and since 1943 he has been a member of the Appropriations Committee. On most foreign policy issues during his thirteen years in Washington, Congressman Gore has supported the Administration, while his record on domestic matters has not been so regularly consistent. In 1949 he led a House coalition group which defeated the Brannan farm program. Before becoming a legislator, Gore taught school, practiced law, and held the post of Tennessee Commissioner of Labor.

Albert Arnold Gore was born on a farm near Granville, Tennessee, on December 26, 1907, the son of Allen and Margie (Denny) Gore. After attending a one-room country grade school, he graduated from the high school in nearby Gordonsville. He then went on to teach in the rural schools of Overton County, and from 1926 to 1930 in the schools of Smith County. In 1932 he received his B.S. degree from the Middle Tennessee State Teachers College, in Murfreesboro, and was elected superintendent of education for Smith County, a position he retained until 1936. During three years of this period he drove fifty-two miles from Carthage, the county seat, to attend classes three nights a week at the Nashville YMCA night law school, which granted him an LL.B. degree in 1936. That same year he was admitted to the Tennessee bar and began practice in Carthage.

It was the example of Cordell Hull, Carthage's leading citizen, who served as United States Representative from the Fourth Tennessee District for twenty-two years and in 1931 was elected Senator, that made Gore decide to enter politics and become a Congressman. Immediately after the Democratic National Convention of 1932, which nominated Franklin D. Roosevelt for President, Gore entered the campaign and organized Young Democratic clubs on a State-wide basis. He proved so successful as an orator that in 1934 he was made chairman of the speakers' bureau of the State Democratic organization. Following

Chase Statler

ALBERT GORE

the 1936 elections, he was appointed State Commissioner of Labor, and reportedly set up "a model unemployment-compensation plan." Two years later he resigned from that post and announced that he would run for Congress. To help finance his campaign, he mortgaged his only possession, a small hill farm at Carthage. Accompanied by a hillbilly band, the candidate frequently spoke ten or fifteen times a day in towns and villages. A picture of Hull, by that time Secretary of State, appeared on Gore's campaign literature. "He is my ideal in public life," Gore said in his platform. "I will seek the advice and guidance of Judge Hull." Defeating five other candidates for the Democratic nomination, he was elected as Representative from the Fourth District (covering twelve counties with a 1940 population of 206,116) on November 8, 1938, and has been re-elected biennially since that time.

Shortly after taking his seat in the Seventy-sixth Congress on January 3, 1939, Gore was assigned to the House Banking and Currency Committee, on which he served until the end of 1942. "I decided when I hit I would hit hard," the Tennessee Congressman has been quoted as saying: he waited seven months before making his maiden speech on August 3 during a House debate over the Administration's bill expanding the borrowing power of the United States Housing Authority by an additional $800,000,000, to be amortized in sixty years. When the Democrats refused to allot him time to speak against the measure, he appealed to the Republican leadership, and was given the final speech for the opposition, in which he charged that the bill was "in no sense self-liquidating," and would ultimately cost the Government $2,700,000,000. The New York *Times* reported that his address "stopped the show," and was accorded "an ovation of proportions such as are usually reserved for elder

GORE, ALBERT—*Continued*

statesmen." His speech was credited with having changed a number of votes to the opposition. The bill was defeated that same day.

The young Tennessee Representative attracted nation-wide attention during the first session of the Seventy-seventh Congress (1941) by introducing an anti-inflation bill embodying the ideas of Bernard M. Baruch on economic stabilization. As a substitute for what Gore called the "Administration's weak-kneed piecemeal" price-control legislation, his measure provided for a mandatory over-all ceiling on the nation's entire price structure, including wages, commodity prices, rents, services, corporation profits, and farm products at parity. Twice rejected by the Banking Committee, Gore's bill was defeated on the House floor on November 26 by a teller vote of 218 to 63, with party lines obliterated. In May of the second session (1942), he sponsored another bill to freeze wages at the then current levels, impose ceilings on farm prices at parity (instead of the existing 110 per cent of parity), and require compulsory savings by all persons with incomes in excess of $1,500 after tax deductions. Although this measure was equally unsuccessful, an over-all ceiling on prices was ordered that year. Earlier that session Gore had assailed what he termed the "scandalous" compensations and bonuses paid to executives of corporations with defense contracts. Assigned to the House Appropriations Committee in the first session of the Seventy-eighth Congress (1943), he led the fight against rescinding President Roosevelt's salary limitation order.

On December 29, 1943, after waiving his Congressional draft immunity and requesting a leave of absence, Gore was the first Congressman to be inducted into the Army as a private. The following month, however, President Roosevelt issued an order that members of Congress could not retain their seats while serving in the armed forces. At the President's request, Gore shifted to the Enlisted Reserve and resumed his seat in the legislature. He remained in Congress until December 4, 1944, when he resigned to enter active duty as a private. Ordered to Europe as a replacement, he was given a special War Department assignment; three months later it was disclosed that he had been learning at firsthand how the Allied Military Government operated in occupied Germany. During his tour of service, he worked as a prosecutor in a military government court, and also was attached to a spearhead detachment of military government personnel which accompanied regimental teams into the front lines. He returned to the Seventy-ninth Congress in the spring of 1945.

During the second session of that Congress (1946), Gore served as a member of the Select Committee to Investigate Acts of Executive Agencies Which Succeed Their Authority. In February he became head of a group of young House Democrats formed to answer "Republican campaign propaganda" and to instill "aggressiveness into the Democratic party's progressiveness." A year later, under the Republican-controlled Eightieth Congress (1947-

48), the Democratic leadership in the House assigned six of its youngest debaters, including Gore, as a "watchdog team" to "spotlight mistakes of the opposition." The Tennessee Representative led the attack on the GOP fiscal program and assailed Republican claims of economies. As Democratic scorekeeper of Republican savings, he declared in June 1947 that the GOP had cut only $1,800,000,000 from the President's budget estimate, a sum he described as "pitifully short" of the Republican promise to reduce Federal expenditures by $6,000,000,000. In both sessions of this Congress, which he called "the most expensive peacetime Congress in history," he offered amendments to restore funds to various appropriations, but they were rejected by the Republican majority.

In July 1949, during the first session of the Eighty-first Congress (when he was a member of the House Democratic Campaign Committee), Gore led a Democratic revolt in the House against the Administration-sponsored Pace bill, which provided for a "trial run" of the Brannan farm plan. This bill gave Secretary of Agriculture Charles F. Brannan authority to select three commodities, for a two-year test of his proposed production-payment program. Instead of the Government supporting the market by loans and purchases, the measure allowed prices on the "trial run" crops to seek their natural levels and made up the difference between that and parity by direct payments to farmers. Declaring that "we cannot afford to run the risk with the farmer's welfare . . . by taking this leap in the dark and throwing overboard a program that has been built out of sixteen years of experience and farmer cooperation," Gore called the Brannan plan "dangerous"; he said that it had been tried in Germany and Great Britain with results proving that "subsidy on one commodity leads to subsidies on other commodities." He introduced a substitute measure to continue the then existing rigid agricultural price-support system (at the wartime rate of 90 per cent of parity) for another year. On July 21, the Pace bill was defeated by a coalition of Southern Democrats and Republicans in a teller vote of 222 to 152, while the Gore substitute was adopted by a roll-call vote of 239 to 170.

As a member of the "atomic energy" subcommittee of the Appropriations Committee, Gore has recently been closely identified with the Atomic Energy Commission's program, for which he has recommended and supported large appropriations. In April 1951 he made the headlines with his suggestion to President Truman that the United States forces "dehumanize" a belt across the entire peninsula of Korea by radiological contamination, in order to halt further Korean fighting. After witnessing the atomic bomb test at the Nevada proving grounds on October 30, Gore reported that the accuracy with which the bomb was delivered had convinced him that "it might be used in Korea if the cease-fire negotiations break down."

Congressman Gore's voting record on foreign issues during his seven terms in the national legislature thus far shows him in general agreement with the policies of the Roosevelt and

Truman Administrations. He voted against the arms embargo amendment to the Neutrality Act in 1939, and two years later approved of the lend-lease bill and the repeal of the ban on arming merchant ships and on the entrance of American vessels into combat zones and ports of belligerents. His votes were recorded in support of the Fulbright Resolution (1943), authorization of UNRRA (1944), ratification of the Bretton Woods agreement (1945), the British loan (1946), and Greek-Turkish aid (1947). Although he declared himself against the displaced persons bill (1948), he cast his vote in favor of $6,000,000,000 Europe-China foreign assistance (1948), Marshall Plan extension (1949), and in 1950, of both the Korea-Formosa economic aid measure and the $2,700,000,000 ECA extension bill. The year 1951 found him paired against reducing European economic aid by $350,000,000. He is on the record as endorsing the extension of reciprocal trade agreements in 1940, 1943, 1945, and 1949. In his voting on measures involving the armed services, he called "Yea" on conscription (1940), an increase of base pay for servicemen (1942), the Administration's soldier vote bill (1944), draft extension (1946) the Selective Service bill (1948), shelving the veterans' pensions measure (1949) and the combined draft and universal military training bill (1951); while the authorization of the WAAC (1942) and draft exemption for fathers and teen-age youths (1946) drew his "Nay."

On questions of domestic policy, during the Seventy-sixth Congress (1939-40), Gore gave his support to farm parity payments, additional funds for work relief, the Hatch Act, an investigation of the Labor Relations Board, and drastic amendments to the Wagner Labor Act. In the course of the next Congress (1941-42), he rejected cuts in WPA appropriations, the continuance of the CCC, and inclusion of farm labor costs in the parity formula. In the Seventy-eighth Congress (1943-44) he was recorded in favor of the Smith-Connally antistrike bill, the Hobbs antiracketeering bill, extension of the Dies Committee investigation, and revival of the Federal crop insurance program; against cutting OPA appropriations and the Ruml plan. During the following Congress (1945-46), he endorsed both the Case and the President's strike control bills and price control extension. Gore's record in the Eightieth Congress (1947-48) showed him casting affirmative votes for the Mundt-Nixon anti-Communist bill, restoring cuts in farm funds, and the Taft-Hartley labor bill; and negative votes for a two-term limit for the Presidency and for permitting voluntary 15 per cent rent increases.

The succeeding Congress (1949-50) found the Representative favoring the minimum wage amendment to the Fair Labor Standards Act, the Administration's long-range housing bill, rent control extension, and the Communist-control bill; and opposing the FEPC measure, loans for housing cooperatives, and the establishment of a health, education, and security department. In the first session of the Eighty-second Congress (1951), he was against the tidelands oil bill and for the second conference report on a $5,700,000,000 tax increase. Gore voted to sustain Presidential vetos of the anti-subsidy bills (1943, 1944), the tax bill (1944), and the Republican-sponsored income tax reduction bills (1947, 1948); while he favored overriding the Chief Executive's veto of the Smith-Connally, Case, and Taft-Hartley bills. Anti-poll tax measures in 1942, 1945, 1947, and 1949 received his approval. Having defeated Senator Kenneth D. McKellar in the Tennessee nominating primary on August 7, 1952, Gore was elected Senator from his State the following November.

On April 27, 1937, Gore married Pauline La Fon, also of Tennessee, who was at that time a member of the State bar, having worked her way through Vanderbilt University Law School. They have two children, Nancy La Fon and Albert. The Representative has been described as "well-built," with "somewhat heavy features," brown eyes, and dark-brown curly hair. He is part owner of a feed mill in Carthage; a member of the Tennessee Education Association; and belongs to the Missionary Baptist Church. An expert hillbilly fiddler, he is frequently called upon to play at gala occasions in Washington or at the closing sessions of the House.

References

Collier's 109-23 My 30 '42 por
N Y Post Mag p12 Je 13 '42 por
N Y Sun p25 O 31 '41; p20 Ja 7 '44;
   p26 My 24 '46
Biographical Directory of the American
   Congress, 1774-1949 (1950)
Congressional Directory (1951)
Who's Who in America, 1950-51
World Biography (1948)

GORRIE, JACK (OSBORNE) Mar. 21, 1911- United States Government official

Address: b. c/o National Security Resources Board, Executive Office Bldg., 17th St. & Pennsylvania Ave., N.W., Washington 25, D.C.; h. 3175 21st St., North Arlington, Va.

Jack Gorrie, whose appointment as Chairman of the National Security Resources Board was confirmed by the United States Senate on January 29, 1952, first came to the board in 1949. His public career had begun as assistant secretary to United States Congressman from Washington, Democrat Mon C. Wallgren, which was followed by eight years in the Internal Revenue Bureau's Everett, Seattle, and Tacoma offices (1937-44) and four years (1945-48) as assistant to Wallgren, who had become Governor. After graduation from high school, Gorrie was a newspaper reporter for about six years.

Born in Olympia, Washington, on March 21, 1911, Jack Osborne Gorrie (of Scotch, Irish, and English extraction) is the son of Frank Hogarth and Edith Lillian (Goddard) Gorrie, who had another son and a daughter. Frank Gorrie was a painting contractor. At the age of fourteen, by which time the family had

Harris & Ewing

JACK GORRIE

moved to Seattle, Jack Gorrie decided that he wanted to be a newspaperman. That year, when he was in the eighth grade, he got his first job with the Associated Press (where his brother was employed) in Seattle, starting as office boy on the night shift. He went to work after school each day until his graduation from the Queen Anne High School in 1929. (Some years later he studied accounting and taxes through correspondence courses.) While with the Associated Press he learned to punch tele-printer tape and eventually was allowed to write some news stories.

Looking toward a position as editor with the A.P., Gorrie set about acquiring the necessary three years' experience on a daily newspaper. He secured a place in May 1930 as a reporter for the Everett (Washington) *News*, a morning paper. In a working day that started at 11:15 A.M. and lasted until 2:15 the following morning, Gorrie covered a variety of beats, (police, city hall, courthouse, waterfront, and Federal Government offices) and writing sports columns and editorials. In addition, he served as Everett correspondent for the Seattle *Times*, the Seattle *Post-Intelligencer*, and the Associated Press.

It was while covering city, county, and State affairs that Gorrie, who is a Democrat, developed an interest in government, which led eventually to a career in public life. After six months as assistant secretary to United States Congressman Mon C. Wallgren (July-December 1936) Gorrie was appointed field deputy collector in the Seattle office of the Collector of Internal Revenue. Within four months, in April 1937, he was promoted to the rank of deputy collector, in charge of the field division in the Everett office, to supervise collection of all internal revenue taxes in four counties. Among those duties were service of warrant for distraint, filing of liens, service of

levies, assistance to taxpayers in preparation of income tax returns.

Another promotion, in April 1942, made Gorrie the assistant chief of the miscellaneous tax division in Tacoma, directing the staff of 320 supervisory and clerical personnel. From January 1943 to January 1945 he was chief office deputy in Tacoma, in charge of the Washington and Alaska districts. He planned, organized, and directed the operation of all offices, and assumed the duties of his superiors in their absences.

In January 1945 Wallgren, the newly elected Governor of Washington, asked Gorrie to accompany him to Olympia with the title of Assistant to the Governor. In that capacity he was the Governor's "right-hand man" and executive officer, supervising the work of six thousand employees in twenty-two departments, boards, and commissions under the jurisdiction of the Governor. He advised in the selection of top personnel, consulted with directors and board members, made policy decisions, approved quarterly department budgets, served as secretary of the Administrative Board, over which he presided in the absence of the Governor. Other duties included the writing of messages to the State legislature and public appearances in behalf of the Governor, whom he also represented in dealings with the Attorney General and other officials, and the quarterly meetings of the Pacific Coast Board of Inter-Governmental Relations and semiannual conferences of eleven Western Governors; he also attended the national conferences of Governors.

Gorrie's career in the Federal administration began on February 7, 1949, when he joined the staff of the National Security Resources Board. On May 18, 1949, he became executive assistant to the Acting Chairman, John R. Steelman, and served later in the same capacity under the Chairman W. Stuart Symington. He directed the Board's staff, presided at meetings, and represented the chairman in dealings with other Government agencies, the Congress, and the public. For his achievements, Gorrie was officially classified by the National Security Resources Board Chairman as "outstanding," and approved by the Efficiency Awards Committee on May 31, 1951. When Symington became Chairman of the Reconstruction Finance Corporation, on May 5, 1951, Gorrie was designated Acting Chairman of the Board by President Truman. On October 29 of that year he received a recess appointment as Chairman, and on January 29, 1952, the appointment was confirmed by the Senate. "One of the best things about Mr. Gorrie," said a Washington *Post* editorial in October 1951, "is that he understands his mission . . . to do the quiet job of long-term planning that is essential to complement the more immediate work of Defense Mobilizer Wilson. . . . President Truman has used good judgment in giving formal recognition to Mr. Gorrie for the job he already is doing."

The National Security Resources Board was established by the National Security Act of 1947, with the major function of advising the President on industrial and civilian mobilization policies. The Board recommends long-range means for establishing adequate reserves of strategic and critical materials and for the conservation of those materials. One phase of Gorrie's work is the program for the relocation of industries essential to national security. He explained the underlying need for some dispersal of heavy industry by pointing out that the enemy "would fear most the industrial capacity and might that carried the Allied nations to victory in two world wars." Speaking on the possibility of an atomic attack, he emphasized the need for dispersal of industries: "We are determined that an attack should not be a paralyzing blow, or a mortal blow, to our nation." He pointed out, however, that the program was not intended to move established industries, but only to encourage dispersal of new construction to the periphery of built-up areas. Such a program, if skillfully developed, could prove a lasting economic benefit to the nation, both in war and peace, if the new areas continued to develop and expand.

In offering local governments technical assistance and in preparing reports for the President, Gorrie and his staff make extensive use of facilities and resources of other Federal departments and agencies, as well as consulting organizations outside the government. "By this method," Gorrie explained, "we avoid duplication of work and gain the advantage of extensive knowledge and technical skills."

Gorrie, who married Lou Myrtle Dunn on January 1, 1930, has two sons: Jack Osborne, who enlisted in the United States Air Force in 1951, and Gerald Weseley. During the World War II years Mrs. Gorrie was an administrative storekeeper and supply clerk for the Navy. Gorrie is a member of the Elks, Eagles, Knights of Pythias, and Washington State Press Club. He was christened in the Episcopal Church. With a height of five feet ten and a half inches, he weighs 180 pounds; the color of his hair and eyes is brown. He lists playing golf and watching baseball as two of his diversions.

References

Longview (Wash.) Daily News O 8 '51
Washington (D.C.) Post p2 O 4 '51

GOULD, RONALD Oct. 9, 1904- Educator; organization official

Address: b. c/o National Union of Teachers, Hamilton House, Mabledon Place, London, W.C. 1, England; h. 21 Lakenheath, Southgate, N. 14, England

The World Confederation of Organizations of the Teaching Profession, which came into existence at the sixth delegate assembly of the World Organization of the Teaching Profession in Copenhagen on August 1, 1952, elected as its first president Ronald Gould, the secretary general of the National Union of Teachers of England and Wales. Representing some 3,000,000 teachers in the West, the newly formed confederation resulted from a merger of three teaching associations: the World Organization of the Teaching Profession, the

International Federation of Teachers' Associations, and the International Federation of Secondary Teachers' Associations. Gould, who began his career in education as the assistant master of the Radstock Council Boys School and later became headmaster of Welton County Boys' School, has held advisory posts in the British Government and in various teachers' organizations. The educator has also taken part in international education groups such as the Conference of the United Nations Educational, Scientific and Cultural Organization, the United Kingdom Commission for UNESCO, and the International Federation of Teachers' Associations.

Ronald Gould was born in Midsomer Norton, Somerset, England, on October 9, 1904, one of three children (two sons and one daughter) of Frederick and Emma Gould. Ronald's father was a Trade Union leader and twice a member of Parliament for the Frome Division. After his graduation in 1922 from Shepton Mallet Grammar School, which he had entered in 1916, Gould attended Westminster College for training in teaching. There he pursued his interest in football and cricket, as he had done in secondary school, and became a member of the debating society and the Student Christian Movement.

Upon leaving college in 1924, Gould became an assistant master at Radstock Council Boys' School, a post which he held until 1939. Simultaneously for part of this time (1925-29) he filled the position of assistant master of the Radstock Evening Institute. The educator, who had joined the National Union of Teachers in 1924, was three years later made a committee member of the Radstock Association of the National Union of Teachers. Elected unopposed in 1929 to the local government for Midsomer Norton Urban District Council, he became in 1930 the chairman of its rating committee and the following year the chairman of its finance committee.

Beginning in 1931 Gould, who in that year acted as a delegate to the Conference of the National Union of Teachers, served as a representative in Somerset County Teacher's Association. In local government he was the vice-chairman of Norton Radstock Urban District Council from 1933 to 1936, being named its chairman in the latter year (he was then reputed to be the youngest chairman of a local authority in England). Also in 1933 he assumed the governorship of Norton Radstock County Secondary Grammar School. Upon being chosen president of the Radstock Association of the National Union of Teachers in 1935, he also became press secretary of the organization, a post which he held for eight years; he was later its secretary (1940) and its treasurer (1940-41). Succeeding on his first attempt, he was elected in 1936 to the executive of the National Union of Teachers. In 1939, when he was elected "at the top of the poll" to Norton Radstock Urban District Council, Gould began his ten-year term as its chairman and his three-year period as acting Head Master of Radstock Council Mixed School. During the years of World War II he was also selected as the Liaison Officer for Evacuation

RONALD GOULD

and the chairman of the Food Control Committee, the War Emergency Committee, the Civil Defense Committee for Norton Radstock, the Red Cross Fund, the War Allotments Committee, and the Invasion Committee.

When Gould ran for vice-president of the National Union of Teachers in 1941, he achieved immediate election, although, according to *The Schoolmaster*, a candidate must usually make the attempt three times before being successful. Appointed by Ernest Bevin and Hugh Dalton, the educator became a member in 1941 of the Forster Committee to report on conditions of entry into coal mining, and about that time he was chosen a member of the District Advisory Committee of the Ministry of Labor. The year 1941 also marks the beginning of his five-year term as headmaster of Welton County Boys' School, Bath.

At its annual conference in London in 1943, the National Union of Teachers elected Gould as its president for a one-year term. In his presidential address he demanded equality of educational opportunity regardless of the pupil's parents' means or social position or the area in which the school was located. In 1944 he assumed the chairmanship of the International Relations Committee of the National Union of Teachers. With fellow members of the executive, Gould in 1945 founded the Southwestern Federation of County and County Borough Associations of the National Union of Teachers, of which he served as president the next year. Chosen concurrently a member of the Central Advisory Council for England of the Ministry of Education in 1944, the educator became the only member of the council from the Southwest and the only one appointed from a public elementary school. The function of the council was to advise the Minister of Education on educational theory and practice.

Succeeding Sir Frederick Mander, Gould became the general secretary of the National Union of Teachers in July 1946. He was chosen an alternate delegate for the British Government in that year to the first conference of the United Nations Educational, Scientific and Cultural Organization, which was held in Paris. In Mexico City the next year he was the only teacher representative from England with full alternate delegate status at the second UNESCO conference, and in 1948 he attended the third conference of the international association in Beirut in the same capacity. As a representative of the National Union of Teachers, Gould has been a member of the National Foundation for Educational Research, the Council for Education in World Citizenship, the National Council of Social Service, and the council and executive of the Save the Children Fund.

On August 1, 1952, in Copenhagen, Denmark, the World Organization of the Teaching Profession united with two other groups, the International Federation of Teachers' Associations and the International Federation of Secondary Teachers' Associations. In this new organization, the World Confederation of Organizations of the Teaching Profession, now for the first time both elementary and secondary school teachers from all over the world are included in one international group. It was felt that in thus combining the two, the gulf which lies between them in some European countries might be narrowed. Gould who was a member of the executive of the International Federation of Teachers' Associations and of the World Organization of the Teaching Profession, was chosen the first president of the confederation, comprising some 3,000,000 members, by the assembly in Copenhagen.

Among Gould's posts in the national government have been memberships in the Advisory Committee for Education in the Colonies, the Recruitment and Training of Teachers Committee, and the Education Advisory Committee for the Royal Air Force. He represented Somerset on the Lower Paid Areas Association Council and is the secretary and leader of the Teacher's Panel of the Burnham (Main) Committee which is concerned with the question of salaries in private and secondary schools. The official is a member of the executive of the National Foundation for Educational Research in England and Wales, Consultative Committee on Educational Relationships with Germany, and the School Broadcasting Council for the United Kingdom. He is a governor of the Imperial Institute, South Kensington, and a trustee of the Royal Society of Teachers. International organizations in which Gould maintains membership are the International Cooperating Body for Education of UNESCO and the United Kingdom Committee for UNESCO.

"A powerful platform speaker and . . . a skilled debater," as *The Schoolmaster* has described him, Gould has done much public speaking before local and county associations, women's institutes, and discussion groups. He has lectured at the Cooperative Union Summer School and was said to be well known in Somerset, Wilshire, and Bristol as a Brotherhood speaker (he was president-elect of the Bristol and District Brotherhood Federation). Also experienced in expressing his ideas in writing, he managed and edited the *Dawn* (a local political paper), has been London correspondent to the *Scottish Education Journal* since 1941, and has contributed articles to the *Sunday Dispatch, The Schoolmaster*, local papers, gardening journals, and union magazines. His article "Closed Shop and the Teachers" was published in the United States in the *Phi Delta Kappan* in September 1951, and the National Union of Teachers published a pamphlet by him entitled *Challenge of a Changing World*. Gould holds an honorary M.A. degree from Bristol University, conferred in 1943.

Gould and Nellie Denning Fish were married December 26, 1928, and are the parents of two children, Terence and Derek. An enthusiastic amateur horticulturist, the educator is also interested in English literature. He has blue eyes and brown hair, is five feet ten inches tall and weighs 210 pounds. *The Schoolmaster* has commented on his forthright manner combined with "a wealth of humor and a gift of wit."

References

The Schoolmaster p59 Jl 18 '46 por
Who's Who, 1952

GOW, JAMES (ELLIS) Aug. 23, 1907—
Feb. 11, 1952 Scenarist; playwright; on the staff of the New York *World* as assistant in the drama department (1928-31) and film critic (1931); collaborated on scenario of *One Night of Love* (1934), *Paramount on Parade* (1941), *The Man on the Ledge* (1949), and others; with Arnaud d'Usseau wrote stage plays *Tomorrow the World* (1943), *Deep Are the Roots* (1947), and *Legend of Sarah* (1950). See *Current Biography*, 1944.

Obituary

N Y Times p27 F 12 '52

GRAHAM, ELINOR (MISH) Sept. 9,
1906- Author

Address: b. c/o The Macmillan Company, 60 5th Ave., New York 11; h. Flying Point Rd., Freeport, Me.

Reprinted from the *Wilson
Library Bulletin,* Jan. 1952.

The antecedents and personal experiences of Elinor Graham, author of *My Window Looks Down East* (1951), have been radically different from her present environment at Flying Point Road, Freeport, Maine, and undoubtedly have contributed greatly to some of the unique observations expressed in her three published books.

She was born in Hagerstown, Maryland, September 9, 1906. Her father, Frank Winder Mish, was a descendant of Pennsylvania Dutch farmers, and a graduate of Franklin and Marshall College. He attended Heidelberg and Madrid universities and the Sorbonne and, after graduating from Columbia Law School, practiced law in Hagerstown. The inheritance of several farms induced him to renounce the legal profession in order to give his entire attention to farm management. Mrs. Graham's mother, Eleanor Elizabeth (Dubbs) Mish, was the daughter of a professor of history at Franklin and Marshall College. Mrs. Graham's maternal grandfather, great-grandfather and great-great-grandfather, all of Pennsylvania Dutch extraction, were ministers of the Reformed Church. There is also some Scotch, English and Welsh blood in her background, Mrs. Graham says. Elinor Godfrey, the ancestress for whom she was named, had nursed a young Indian chief back to life when he had been shot inadvertently by early settlers. (The Indians camped around the stockade all winter while he recuperated.)

After graduating in 1922 from Washington County High School in Hagerstown, the then Elinor Mish went to the American Academy of Dramatic Arts, from which she graduated in 1924. She joined the Theatre Guild, where she understudied and played in the Sunday night performances of plays that were being considered by the Guild. In 1925-26 she was a walk-on in *They Knew What They Wanted,* Sidney Howard's Pulitzer Prize play. The following year she played Ethel in another Pulitzer Prize play, George Kelly's *Craig's Wife.*

When she left the professional stage she acted in plays at Bowdoin College in Brunswick, Maine, and several years ago acted professionally again in a stock company playing in Bar Harbor, Maine. She has lectured to women's clubs, has worked as a fund raiser for hospitals, and is a well-known collector of antique buttons.

Elinor Graham's first published book, *Our Way Down East* (1943), is a collection of memories of experiences about the making of a home in a new community and the impressions the Grahams got of the natives. There are some well-chosen descriptions of the natives' own impressions of the strangers which add piquancy to the tale. Marguerite Lyon, reviewing the book in Chicago *Sun Book Week,* said, "What appears at first glance to be the world's most scatterbrained story of life on a Maine salt-water farm, turns out to be darned good reading. When you get used to Elinor Graham's way of hopping off the main track and going down all the little byways and side roads of a well-stocked memory, you say, 'Why look! This book's swell!'" In the New York *Times* Winifred Halsted commented, "How to have the farm without the furrows— either in the brow or in the ground—is described by Elinor Graham in a dangerously attractive fashion that will probably set off a whole new batch of deluded city slickers into reaching for the nearest mortgage. . . ."

In 1946, *Maine Charm String* was published —another series of sketches describing Mrs. Graham's button-collecting hobby and the Maine people with whom she came in contact during her avid search for buttons. Jane Voiles in the San Francisco *Chronicle* said, "The social and moral effects of button collecting have many implications, you'll discover.

(Continued next page)

ELINOR GRAHAM

But aside from the buttons there are other interests. Mrs. Graham writes about country living in Maine somewhat in the vein that Zephine Humphreys used to write about country living in Vermont. You get the meaning of country hospitality which extends far beyond threshold, and board to the spirit." L. D. Rich in the *Saturday Review of Literature* added, "The author retains the sense of humor that made her first book so delightful. She can still make fun of herself in a manner that tickles the ribs of the reader."

Most reviewers saw in *My Window Looks Down East* a deeper comprehension of the tragedy of life as well as of its warmth and humor. The book is dotted with candid comments about the neighbors, about her small family and herself, and the pictures portrayed lightly are nevertheless not those to which summer visitors in Maine are accustomed. The Maine coast, specifically Flying Point in Casco Bay, seems to have touched Mrs. Graham's viewpoint as well as her heartstrings. Her many readers will await with interest her first novel, on which she is now working, in 1952.

Among her true loves are her house at Flying Point and her garden. Button collecting is no longer of prime importance to her. Favorite authors and books depend upon the interest of the period, although one gathers from her books that she is an avid reader. She has blue eyes and brown hair, is five feet five inches tall and weighs 140 pounds.

Mrs. Graham and the writer David Livingston Graham are divorced. They had been married October 21, 1933. Their daughter, Florence Beale Graham (called Lani) is one of the more interesting people in *My Window Looks Down East*.

GRAHAM, EVARTS A(MBROSE) (ĕv'-ärts) Mar. 19, 1883- Surgeon
Address: b. c/o Barnes Hospital, 600 S. Kingshighway, St. Louis 10, Mo.; h. Box 485 Old Jamestown Rd., Florissant, Mo.

Prominent American surgeon of international reputation, Dr. Evarts A. Graham is credited with having performed the first successful operation in removing an entire lung in the treatment of cancer. For his pioneer work in lung surgery, which he performed in 1933, he has received a number of honors, among them the Annual Award of the American Cancer Society in October 1951. Dr. Graham, who is emeritus professor of surgery at Washington University School of Medicine and surgeon in chief at Barnes Hospital, St. Louis, has developed cholecystography (the X-ray examination of the gallbladder) and has contributed to knowledge about liver infections, lung suppurations, mechanics of the thorax, and effects of anesthetics on the body.

Evarts Ambrose Graham was born in Chicago, Illinois, on March 19, 1883, one of two sons of Dr. David Wilson Graham and Ida Anspach (Barned) Graham. In the choice of his profession he was influenced by the career of his father, who was professor of surgery at Rush Medical College, Chicago, and a member of the staff of Presbyterian Hospital from 1883 until his death in 1925. For ten years his mother served as president of the women's board of the Presbyterian Hospital. "As long as I can remember," Evarts Graham has said, "I wanted to be a surgeon." Upon completion of his high school education at public schools and at Lewis Institute, Chicago, in 1900, he entered Princeton University for a premedical course. At Princeton, from which he was graduated in 1904 with the B.A. degree, he was active on the board of the *Daily Princetonian* and of the *Nassau Literary Magazine*. Returning to Chicago for his professional training, he took his M.D. degree at Rush Medical College in 1907 and the following year interned at the Presbyterian Hospital. After additional study in surgery as a fellow in pathology at Rush Medical College in 1908-09, he studied chemistry for two years at the University of Chicago. He held the positions of assistant in surgery at Rush Medical College from 1910 to 1914 and member of the staff of Otho S.A. Sprague Memorial Institute for Clinical Research, Chicago, from 1911 to 1914.

A major in the medical corps of the United States Army, Graham served first during 1918 with the School of Neurological Surgery, Chicago, and then with the Empyema Commission at Camp Lee, Virginia, later doing special laboratory research on empyema in Baltimore. (Some years afterward, in March 1948, he wrote for the *North Carolina Medical Journal* an article entitled "Chapters in the History of Thoracic Surgery; Work of the Empyema Commission in World War I." He also wrote the section "Treatment of Acute Empyema" for *Medical and Surgical History of the World War*, published by the Surgeon General's Office in 1924.) From September 1918 to May 1919 he was commanding officer of Evacuation Hospital No. 34 in France.

After the war and his discharge from the Army in 1919 he went to St. Louis to become professor of surgery at the Washington University School of Medicine and surgeon in chief of Barnes Hospital and St. Louis Children's Hospital; in 1952 he retains his association with these institutions with the title emeritus professor. Apart from his practice in St. Louis, he was sent in 1922 by the Rockefeller Foundation to Great Britain to investigate teaching of surgery in British medical schools, and held the posts of temporary surgeon in chief at the Peter Bent Brigham Hospital, Boston, in 1925, and of temporary professor of surgery at St. Bartholomew's Hospital, London in 1939.

It was in April 1933 in St. Louis that Dr. Graham performed the operation which made him famous, for the first time successfully removing one whole lung in the treatment of cancer; his patient was a forty-eight-year-old man. Having made a diagnosis of a malignant tumor, Dr. Graham prepared to remove a lobe of the left lung, but early in the surgery he discovered that both lobes were affected and that cure depended upon the removal of the whole lung. Dr. Graham had previously performed an operation similar to this on animals, but removal of an entire lung of a human being in one stage was until then unknown in medical history. In lung surgery before 1933, Graham has pointed out, there were two instances of removal of a lung for reasons other than cancer, when surgery was performed in two stages. Dr. Graham has explained that because of advances in surgical technique, removal of the lung, which has become standard procedure in treatment of lung cancer, is now possible without removing a rib. "In suitable cases, where the cancer is not too far advanced," he has stated, "the operation can be done with a mortality of only 10 per cent" (New York *Times*, September 30, 1951).

In other phases of medical advancement the St. Louis surgeon, according to *Time* (July 10, 1950) has also pioneered: in aiding diagnoses of gall-bladder diseases by developing a method of making the gall bladder visible on X-ray plates and in his early surgery on the heart valve and the pancreas. With E. L. Wynder, Graham in 1949 undertook the first extensive survey of its kind in examining several hundred patients to investigate a possible connection between smoking and lung cancer.

As a member of a commission appointed by the Secretary of War in 1942, Graham was called upon to take part in a study of the medical department of the United States Army. After World War II, from 1947 to 1950 he served as honorary consultant to the medical department of the Navy. On the National Research Council he filled the posts of member of the medical fellowship board (1925-39), chairman of the committee on surgery (1940-46), member of the committee on growth of the division of medical science (1951, with a

EVARTS A. GRAHAM

tenure of five years). In other positions of national scope, Graham held the chairmanship of the American Board of Surgery (1937-41), membership in the National Board of Medical Examiners (1924-33), and membership in the commission on hospital care of the American Hospital Association to make a two-year study of the nation's hospital resources and needs (1944 and 1945). In 1952 he became a member of the President's Commission on the Health Needs of the Nation.

Early publications of Dr. Graham are *Empyema Thoracis* (1925) and *Diseases of the Gall Bladder and Bile Ducts* (1928). Editor since 1925 of the *Yearbook of Surgery* and since 1931 of the *Journal of Thoracic Surgery*, Graham was also coeditor of *Annals of Surgery* (1934-46) and *Archives of Surgery* (1920-46). Among the more recent of numerous papers which he prepared for medical journals are: "Modern Successful Treatment of Bronchiogenic Carcinoma," *Surgical Clinic of North America*, October 1944; "Medical Education; War Casualty," *Washington University Alumni Quarterly*, July 1945; and "Symposium on Significant Developments in the Field of Chest Diseases; Chest Tumors," *Journal of Missouri Medical Association*, December 1946. For *Postgraduate Medicine* he has written "Surgical Diseases of Lungs," (October 1949), "Changing Concepts in Surgery" (February 1950), and "Diagnosis and Treatment of Pulmonary Suppuration" (March 1950). Between 1924 and 1951 Graham delivered lectures under seventeen special lectureships in the United States, Australia, and England. His Lister lecture, entitled "Some Aspects of Bronchiogenic Carcinoma," was published in the *Annals of the Royal College of Surgeons* (England), November 1947.

(Continued next page)

GRAHAM, EVARTS A.—*Continued*

Dr. Graham has been a fellow of the American Medical Association (chairman of the surgical section, 1925); a member of the American Surgical Association (president, 1937), American College of Surgeons (president, 1940-41, and chairman of the board of regents, 1951), American Association for Thoracic Surgery (president, 1928), Society of Clinical Surgery, American Philosophical Society (1941), National Academy of Sciences (1941), Southern Surgical Association (honorary member, 1949), St. Louis Medical Society (honor member, 1949), and Interstate Postgraduate Medical Association of North America (president, 1948-49). He has also been named honorary member of medical societies in England, Ireland, Scotland, Belgium, France, Greece, Argentina, and Mexico. In 1943 he was made an honorary fellow of the Royal College of Surgeons of England and in 1951 an honorary fellow of the Royal Society of Medicine in England. His fraternity is Nu Sigma Nu, and his honorary societies are Alpha Omega Alpha and Sigma Xi.

For his contributions in the field of lung surgery Dr. Graham received the Annual Award of the American Cancer Society in October 1951. Among earlier awards conferred upon him are the Gold Medal of the Radiological Society of North America (1925), Leonard Research Prize of the American Roentgen Ray Society (1925), John Scott Medal of the City of Philadelphia (1937), Lister Medal (for 1942 awarded by the Royal College of Surgeons of England in 1947), Charles Mickle Fellowship of the University of Toronto (1943), College Award of the American College of Chest Physicians (1949), Mississippi Valley Medical Society-Honor Award (1949), as well as the Roswell Park Medal of the Surgical Society of Buffalo (1949), the Distinguished Service Medal of the American Medical Association (1950), and the Bigelow Medal of the Boston Surgical Society (1951). He holds honorary degrees of LL.D. from Central College (1926) and Glasgow University (1951); D.Sc. from Cincinnati (1927), Princeton (1929), Western Reserve (1931), University of Pennsylvania (1940), University of Chicago (1941), and McGill University (1944); and M.Sc. from Yale (1928).

Dr. Graham's wife, Helen Tredway Graham, whom he married on January 29, 1916, had been trained as a chemist and pharmacologist. They have two sons, David Tredway and Evarts A., Jr. The gray-haired, gray-eyed surgeon stands six feet tall and weighs 175 pounds. His recreation is gardening.

References

J Am Med Assn 143:901 Jl 8 '50
Times 56:34 Jl 10 '50
American Medical Directory (1950)
American Men of Science (1949)
Directory of Medical Specialists (1949)
International Who's Who, 1951
Who's Who in America, 1950-51
World Biography (1948)

GRANIK, (S.) THEODORE 1906- Radio and television director-moderator; lawyer

Address: b. 1627 K St., N.W., Washington, D.C.; h. 4000 Cathedral Ave., Washington, D.C.

When Theodore Granik's *American Forum of the Air* in April 1952 began its twenty-fifth year of broadcasting, President Truman sent a letter to Granik as director and moderator of the program, congratulating him for "outstanding service" in bringing the "facts about important public issues to the public." The oldest show of its kind on the air, the forum was first conducted over a radio network by Granik in 1928; since 1949 it has also been televised (NBC-TV). In 1951 Granik originated the television program *Youth Wants to Know*, which is also concerned with questions of national importance. A lawyer by profession, Granik has served as a district attorney of New York and as an adviser to several government agencies, among them, the United States Housing Authority, the National Selective Service Administration, and the War Production Board.

S. Theodore Granik was born in Brooklyn, New York, in 1906, the son of Charles Granik, a dry-goods store owner, and Minnie Granik. The boy attended public elementary schools and Commercial High School in New York City, entering the College of the City of New York in 1925. That same year he went to work as a secretary to Lee Adam Gimbel, vice-president of Gimbel's department store, which had set up its own small radio station, WGBS. "Soon spending more of his time at the studio than at his secretarial duties," Granik wrote scripts, reported prize fights, and, when a performer failed to appear on schedule, filled in the time with Bible readings (Ben Gross in *Collier's*, April 1, 1950).

Meanwhile Granik, deciding to study law, enrolled for evening courses at St. John's University Law School in Brooklyn. Here he conceived an idea for a weekly radio discussion on legal topics and invited members of the St. John's faculty to participate. The program, *Law for the Layman*, with Granik as moderator, was so successful that when WGBS was sold in 1928 Granik received an offer for his show from station WOR. On the larger network the discussions on law continued until the young moderator persuaded the station directors to allow a nonrehearsed, no-script debate on a highly controversial subject—a practice almost unknown at that time. The subject was prohibition and the speakers were Congressman Emmanuel Celler of New York and Mrs. Ella Boole, then president of the Women's Christian Temperance Union. In this "ad lib" program, the debate became heated, with Mrs. Boole charging that some Washington officials had "subterranean passages between their offices and nearby speakeasies." Promptly her charges, and the program on which she had made them, received nationwide publicity, with the result that WOR approved Granik's idea of launching radio forum discussions in which both sides of an issue could be presented and debated.

While engaged in this new venture, Granik studied at St. John's University Law School for his LL.B. degree, awarded in 1929. The following year he was admitted to the New York Bar, where he found his legal practice successful enough to permit his continuing with the forum, for which WOR paid him only the program expenses and no salary. In 1933 he began a four-year period as assistant district attorney of New York under William C. Dodge, resigning from that post in 1937 to become special counsel to the Federal Housing Authority. Here he remained until 1941 when he was appointed civilian adviser to Brigadier General Lewis B. Hershey, director of the National Selective Service Administration. In 1942 he was named special adviser on public relations to Donald Nelson, chairman of the War Production Board. Granik has also served as counsel to the Senate Select Committee on Small Business and as counsel for the American Business Congress, at the same time conducting his private law practice in both New York and Washington.

When Granik in 1937 became associated with the Housing Authority in Washington, D.C., he moved his broadcast from New York to the nation's capital. At first Congressmen were reluctant to appear on the forum, but later, when they heard of the large mail responses received by their colleagues who had appeared, many became willing participants. It was at this time that the forum began to attract national attention. Gross has estimated that more than 90 per cent of the membership of Congress has at one time or another appeared on the forum, so that it is now known on Capitol Hill as "the unofficial Congress of the United States." Harry S. Truman was a forum guest while he was a United States Senator, Franklin D. Roosevelt when he was Governor of New York. Granik has listed among his "best debaters" Norman Thomas, Senators Robert A. Taft and Owen Brewster, former Senator Claude Pepper, Secretary of Agriculture Charles F. Brannan, former Secretary of State James F. Byrnes, and the late Fiorello La Guardia. The forum has achieved semiofficial status in that it is the only radio program which is reprinted word for word each week in the *Congressional Record,* and discussions begun on the program have been continued later on the floor of Congress. The *American Forum of the Air* has received the George Foster Peabody Award, regarded as the Pulitzer Prize of radio.

Among the topics discussed on the American Forum during its twenty-four years of program life have been various New Deal measures like the AAA and NRA, the League of Nations, isolationism versus internationalism, lend-lease, fascism, communism, civil liberties, government controls, labor unions, foreign relations, and universal military training. Granik, as reported by *Time* (March 24, 1941), places only one restriction on his program—he refuses to allow Communists to debate. Generally Granik searches for discussion topics which are, in his words, "hot in the news." Sometimes his topics precede the news. One in-

THEODORE GRANIK

stance of this occurred when Marvin McIntyre, secretary to President Roosevelt, suggested that Granik choose for a debate topic the advisability of exchanging old United States destroyers for British bases. Granik arranged the debate and later received thousands of letters from listeners favoring the exchange—all this before Roosevelt made the proposal to Congress.

Once a subject has been selected, Granik invites a proponent and an opponent to express their views. The two speakers present their sides briefly; then the panel discussion takes place, with the last half of the program being devoted to questions from the studio audience. Members of the radio and television audiences sometimes participate too by telegraphing or telephoning in their questions. The program is closed with a brief summation of each side by the guest speakers. Because the subjects of American Forum are highly controversial, the discussion frequently becomes heated and occasionally the moderator has difficulty maintaining order. The conduct on the program of Granik, who prides himself on his own impartiality, has been described by Sonia Stein of the Washington *Post* (June 19, 1949): "He keeps himself so self-effacing that the audience forgets he's there. If he smiles, winces or otherwise shows his opinions, he does it so discreetly it's not noticeable even though he sits plumb between the two participants."

Continuing his weekly Monday evening radio show on the Mutual network, Granik in the spring of 1949 began a Sunday afternoon television series of the forum for NBC. The following September the American Forum was signed by NBC for simultaneous radio and tele-

GRANIK, THEODORE—*Continued*

vision presentation from the Wardman Park Hotel in Washington, D.C. The same format was followed on the television show as was used in the original radio broadcast, and *Variety* (June 18, 1952), reviewing a show in which aspirants for the 1952 Presidential nomination, Senators Taft and Kefauver, debated, commented: "Granik kept the show moving quickly, knowing that he had plenty of good TV debate material and that unnecessary preliminaries should be avoided."

Before the *American Forum of the Air*—the oldest program of its kind—began its twenty-fifth year on the air on April 27, 1952, President Truman wrote Granik a letter saying that while many people gave "perfunctory support" to the principle of free speech, he had "the right to be proud of putting the principle into action" (New York *Times,* April 26, 1952). While Granik has received much public recognition for his program, financially he estimated that it had cost him more than $250,000 out of his private law-practice savings to carry on the show, because money paid him was not sufficient to meet expenses (*Collier's*). These expenses include an average long-distance phone bill of $2,000 a month for inviting people to participate on the show and salaries for a staff of secretaries, researchers, and clerks who, with Granik, devote as many as fifty hours a week to planning the program.

In recent years Granik has embarked on two other radio-television projects, one of them an FM radio station, WHMB, in which he invested $50,000. The second is a weekly television series, *Youth Wants to Know,* originated by Granik in 1951, on which high school students question a prominent political figure on issues of the day. Well-known people who have appeared on *Youth Wants to Know* include Mrs. Eleanor Roosevelt, Senator Joseph McCarthy, and James A. Farley.

Granik has been described by Gross as "a genial, balding six-footer with a perennially naïve expression." His wife, whom he married in June 1931, is the former Hannah Hayne; they have a son, William, and a daughter, Marian. He received an honorary LL.D. degree from St. John's University in 1943 and the Cross of the Order of the Crown from the Belgian government in 1946, for his services in helping that country procure aid from the United States after World War II.

References

Collier's 125:32 Ap 1 '50
N Y Times p10 S 15 '41
Time 37:54 Mr 24 '41
Washington (D.C.) Post p1L O 30 '49; p9B Mr 17 '52
Who's Who in America, 1952-53
Who's Who in Commerce and Industry (1951)
Who's Who in the South and Southwest (1950)

GRAVES, ALVIN C(USHMAN) Nov. 4, 1909- Physicist
Address: b. P.O. Box 1663, Los Alamos Scientific Laboratory, Los Alamos, N. Mex.; h. 4723 Sandia Dr., Los Alamos, N. Mex.

Deputy chief of all United States atomic tests since 1947 Alvin C. Graves is the head of the weapons testing division of the Los Alamos atomic energy laboratory in New Mexico and the scientific director of the Atomic Energy Commission's Nevada proving grounds. Graves, who has taken part in the United States atomic energy program since its inception in 1942, directed tests of the smaller atomic weapons in the United States and tests of the larger atomic bombs on Eniwetok Atoll in the Pacific.

Born in Washington, D.C., on November 4, 1909, Alvin Cushman Graves was the youngest of six children of Herbert C. Graves, an engineer in the Federal Governments' Coast and Geodetic Survey, who served on the United States Peace Commission after World War I. As a senior at Eastern High School in Washington, Alvin was a runner-up in the national high school oratorical contest. He studied electrical engineering at the University of Virginia and was graduated in 1931 at the head of his class with the Bachelor of Science degree. He then went north to spend a year in postgraduate study at the Massachusetts Institute of Technology, where his interest in nuclear physics was aroused by reading a book by the Italian physicist Enrico Fermi. After experiencing three years of unemployment during the depression Graves decided to quit engineering and study physics.

Graves accepted a graduate fellowship at the University of Chicago and there he met and married a fellow candidate for the Ph.D. degree, Elizabeth Riddle. Doing his doctoral research under the direction of Professor A. J. Dempster, Graves wrote as his dissertation *The Packing Fraction Difference Among Heavy Elements.* He used Dempster's double-focusing mass spectrograph to compare the packing fractions (a measure of the energy required to hold the atom together) of fourteen metals and also calculated two atomic weights, one exactly and the other more accurately than had previously been achieved by that method. After receiving his Ph.D. degree in physics in 1939 from the University of Chicago, Graves became an instructor in that subject at the University of Texas, being promoted to assistant professor in 1941 and to associate professor in 1942.

In January 1942, a few weeks after the Japanese attack on Pearl Harbor, Graves received a phone call in Texas from Arthur H. Compton in Chicago, asking him to work on an unspecified project vital to the war effort. Soon he and Mrs. Graves were engaged in research at the University of Chicago Metallurgical Laboratory. There Graves worked for about a year (1942-43) under Fermi, who was in charge of the experimental nuclear physics aspect of the atomic bomb project. The first self-sustaining chain reaction pile was built on the Stagg Field squash court that fall, and the first man-made self-sustaining nuclear chain reaction was obtained on December 2, 1942. After this Fermi was transferred to Los Alamos, New Mexico, as head of the advanced development section of the newly organized atomic bomb laboratory, where Alvin and Elizabeth Graves were also assigned and have been working since 1943. Because the Los Alamos project is carried on by the University of California as contractors for the Government, the Graves are employees of that university. Graves has seen all the atomic blasts within the United States, including the first one, in Alamogordo, New Mexico, on July 16, 1945.

It was in 1945 that Dr. Graves was promoted to be a group leader in the Los Alamos project, the next year becoming an associate division leader. Graves was severely injured by exposure to radiation in 1946, when a quantity of fissionable material was accidentally brought to a critical point. Dr. Louis Slotin, standing directly in front of Graves, probably saved the lives of his colleagues when he tore the stuff apart with his hands. Dr. Slotin died ten days later, and Graves, disabled for several months, now suffers from a gradual deterioration of the vision of his left eye, as a result of the accident. The following year Graves published his first paper since his dissertation: his and R. L. Walker's *A Method for Measuring Half-Lives* appeared in the January 1, 1947, *Physical Review* and *Spin and Magnetic Moment of Tritium*, a report of nuclear induction experiments written by Graves and others, was issued the following March. The next month *Relative Moments of H_1 and H_3*, also by Graves and colleagues, presented a determination of the ratio of triton to proton magnetic moments.

During 1947-48 Graves was deputy scientific director of the Pacific Proving Grounds Operations—the tests of atomic weapons known as Operation Sandstone. In December 1947 the Atomic Energy Commission announced that Eniwetok Atoll in the Marshall Islands, 2,500 miles southwest of Hawaii, was to be a permanent testing ground for atomic weapons, and the 145 inhabitants were to be transferred to another of the Marshalls. Five months later President Truman disclosed that tests of three atomic weapons "of improved design" had been "successful in all respects," and that 10,000 Army, Navy, and Air Force personnel had participated. The AEC annual report indicated that other successful tests of new designs in atomic weapons were run in Nevada in 1948, the year Graves was promoted to be the leader of the weapons testing division at Los Alamos.

After a year and a half of preparation, tests were conducted during April and May 1951 in which an improved type of atomic bomb, with several times the destructive power of those used against Japan in World War II, was exploded on Eniwetok Atoll in the central Pacific. Graves, as deputy commander of the task force, had charge of the scientific side of the tests which involved nearly 9,000 men of the three armed services and the Atomic Energy Commission, 110 aircraft, and about 900 measurements on 27 structures of

Wide World Photos

ALVIN C. GRAVES

various kinds. Calling the experiments "highly successful," officials of the AEC and of the Defense Department later reported that the tests had "contributed all the way across the boards" to development of a hydrogen bomb (New York *Herald Tribune,* June 14, 1951). At the same time, both AEC chairman Gordon Dean and Graves emphasized that no hydrogen-atomic bomb had been "either produced or tested." Graves told Austin Stevens of the New York *Times* (June 14, 1951) that "much useful information" had been gained in the "basic phenomena underlying the thermonuclear reactions," which would be necessary to set off a hydrogen bomb. Stevens reported that "thousands of mice, some pigs and dogs, all of which were bred on Eniwetok to fit them to the Pacific environment," had been shipped to the United States to be studied for the effects of the explosion on their "skin tissues, glands, and circulatory systems."

Before the Eniwetok tests, which were scheduled for January 1951, were made, a new 5,000-square-mile AEC proving ground, 75 miles north of Las Vegas, Nevada, known officially as the Las Vegas Bombing and Gunnery Range, was set up for operation on a permanent basis, and Graves was named its scientific director. This testing ground was designed for experiments with weapons that did not release the great explosions or require the elaborate instrumentation of the larger atomic weapons, which had been tested on Eniwetok. Working with Administrative Director Carroll L. Tyler and with a staff of about fifty scientific personnel drawn from the Los Alamos and Sandia laboratories, other AEC contractors, the Public Health Service, the Department of Defense, the Civil Defense Administration, and other Federal agencies, Graves directed in early 1951 the first series of full-scale atomic tests in the United States since

GRAVES, ALVIN C.—*Continued*

1945. According to Gordon Dean, these were "authentic nuclear detonations" but not A-bombs.

Scheduled for the fall of 1951, the second series of tests at the new proving grounds had an unfavorable beginning when the first blast failed to go off as the switch was thrown—the first time there had been a failure. On Graves's orders, links of the intricate electrical firing system were immediately disconnected and the miles of electric cables, controls, and switches were checked. By the time the failure was traced to a defective electrical circuit atop a hundred-foot steel tower, a few inches from the A-bomb, the tests had to be postponed because many of the scientists had worked for thirty hours without sleep. Three days later, however, "by far the smallest nuclear detonation ever set off" was fired at Yucca Flat as "the opening shot in a new program by the AEC to test laboratory theories developed at Los Alamos, New Mexico, with particular emphasis on the tactical use of atomic energy against troops in the field" (New York *Herald Tribune,* October 23, 1951). In the words of William L. Laurence of the New York *Times* (October 24, 1951), physicists at the annual meeting of the American Institute of Physics in Chicago regarded the test "as probably the most important development in the military application of atomic energy since the test explosion of the first atomic bomb." Noted for his caution in managing atomic tests, Graves was able to report that "not one person was injured in the twelve Nevada tests during 1951" (Bill Becker, *Saturday Evening Post,* April 19, 1952). Becker also quoted Graves's estimation that American atomic "know-how" had doubled during 1951.

The third series of tests in Nevada took place in the spring of 1952, the detonation on April 22, 1952, becoming the first such explosion to be nationally televised in the United States. In this first atomic test in the country to which press, radio, and television men were officially invited, Graves assured the newsmen that their position on News Nob, some ten miles from the bull's-eye, was safe because "in fourteen previous nuclear explosions at this Nevada testing ground the Air Force pilot delivering the atom bomb never has missed the target" (*Christian Science Monitor,* April 22, 1952). The most powerful bomb yet to be exploded anywhere, with the exception of the new weapons tested at Eniwetok, this detonation was unique in that 2,100 ground and airbourne troops came "closer to the dread area directly beneath the bomb burst than any troops have ever been" (New York *Times,* April 22, 1952) and for the first time they were advanced through the area under the burst. Hanson W. Baldwin in the New York *Times* (April 20, 1952) reported that with this test the Nevada proving ground "becomes a full-fledged indoctrination center, where men in uniform, drawn from widely different parts of the services, will be concentrated periodically to accustom them to the awesome sight of an atomic explosion and to train them how best to protect

themselves against a battlefield blast." Another series of tests at Eniwetok Atoll was announced (New York *Times,* September 10, 1952) by the Government as being scheduled for the fall of 1952 under strict security regulations.

As Dr. Graves told writer Bill Becker, each atomic test requires months of planning, and "there are more than ten thousand steps involved in getting a test to the button-pushing stage." One test may include hundreds of experiments designed to obtain and cross-check medical, military, biological, physical, and chemical data. To quote the New York *Times* (June 24, 1951): "In some cases, special instruments set close to a burst must measure events which take place within a fraction of a millionth of a second and transmit the measurements to a safe place where they can be recorded before the detecting instruments are vaporized. The data are transmitted directly by cable, or by radio links, and are recorded by high-speed oscilloscopes, magnetic tapes, photographic plates, and other means." Graves and his colleagues have, at various times, considered building a model city in which to test the effects of atomic bombing, but have abandoned the idea because, Graves told Daniel Lang (*New Yorker,* May 10, 1952), "There aren't any two cities alike," and what applies to one may not apply to another. Graves once said: "I am not in the atomic business because I like to manufacture things that kill people. I am thoroughly convinced that the reason we are not in a third world war now is because of the work the United States has done in atomic energy. Increasing our stockpile is our best safeguard for the future" (*Saturday Evening Post*).

Graves is a member of the American Physical Society, the American Institute of Physics, Sigma Xi (honorary fraternity for scientific research), and Tau Beta Pi (engineering fraternity). The Graves's two children are Marilyn Edith and Alvin Palmer. Mrs. Graves, who also holds the Ph.D. degree in physics, has patented a device for detecting fission fragments in the presence of other high-energy particles. She is a technical researcher in physics for the Los Alamos project, but she has said: "We rarely discuss our work at home" (*Saturday Evening Post*). Graves is a blond, blue-eyed six-footer. A community leader in Los Alamos, the Atomic Energy Commission city in New Mexico, he is active in the nondenominational Protestant Community Church and at his wife's urging has learned to play the cello in the local orchestra.

References

Sat Eve Post 24:32 + Ap 19 '52 pors
American Men of Science (1949)
Who Knows—And What (1949)

GRECO, JOSÉ (grĕk'o hō-sā) Dec. 23, 1918- Dancer; choreographer

Address: b. c/o L. A. Weissberger, 509 Madison Ave., New York 22; h. 4311 Digney Ave., New York 66

The American dancer and choreographer José Greco has recently received international acclaim as one of the foremost exponents of the Spanish dance. Born in Italy, he was brought to the United States at the age of ten and grew up in Brooklyn. Beginning his career as a dancer in the 1930's, he was Argentinita's last partner from 1943 until her death in 1945, when he went to Spain and danced there with the company of her sister, Pilar López, for two years. He then organized his own group of Spanish dancers, which made its debut in Barcelona in 1949 and subsequently visited European and South American capitals. In the fall of 1951 Greco's Spanish Ballet opened its first United States tour with a two months' engagement in New York City.

José Greco was born Costanzo Greco on December 23, 1918, in the Italian village of Montorio nei Frentani; his father, Paolo Emilio Greco, was Italian, his mother, Carmela (Bucci) Greco, Spanish. He has an elder sister, Norina, a soprano who sang with the Metropolitan Opera Company for several seasons. When José was seven years old, he was taken to Seville, Spain, to his mother's family; there he remained three years. In 1928 his father, who by then was in the United States, sent for his family and they settled in Brooklyn, where young Greco attended public elementary schools, the St. Clair McKelway School, and Franklyn K. Lane Junior High School. He left the high school, without graduating, at the age of fourteen to study at the Leonardo da Vinci Art School in New York with the intention of becoming a painter.

According to *Dance Magazine* (April 1945), it was as an art student that Greco first began attending dance recitals in order to observe more closely the body in motion. However, after seeing the Spanish dancer Vicente Escudero, Greco decided to concentrate thenceforth on Spanish dancing, with painting relegated to a secondary place. For two years he took dance lessons from Hélène Veola. One day, while practicing in a Broadway rehearsal studio, he was noticed by the ballet mistress of the now defunct New York Hippodrome Opera Company, with the result that she offered him a place. Accordingly, in 1937 he made his first professional appearance in the incidental dances for the opera *Carmen* at the old Hippodrome. "The now renowned Nora Kaye was the prima ballerina and I was the premier danseur," he told Rosalyn Krokover (*Musical Courier*, February 1, 1945). When the opera season ended, he joined Gloria Belmonte, assumed the professional name of Ramon Serrano, and obtained an engagement at La Conga, a New York night club. Muriel Bentley, later with the Ballet Theatre, was one of his partners for a season before he became a solo dancer. During slack periods in the entertainment field he studied more about Spanish culture and history, and taught dancing—from the samba to the Suzy-Q—at hotels and summer resorts.

The turning point in Greco's career dates from his first meeting with Argentinita, the celebrated Spanish dancer, who saw him dancing at La Conga. Later, when her partner, Federico Rey, was inducted for military service late in 1942, she invited Greco to join her

Antonio, Zaragoza

JOSÉ GRECO

small ensemble of Spanish dancers. The two dancers appeared together for the first time with the Cincinnati Symphony Orchestra in that city on January 8, 1943. Three months later, when he danced in his first Carnegie Hall recital with the group, John Martin described him in the New York *Times* as "cool in style, light, controlled and objective in approach." He was soon given featured billing and a number of solos on Argentinita's program. During the next two years Argentinita and her company toured the country, gave recitals in New York, and appeared as guest artists with the Ballet Theatre in its spring and fall seasons at the Metropolitan Opera House, at which times Greco danced leading roles in such Argentinita ballets as Ravel's *Bolero*, de Falla's *El Amor Brujo*, Granados' *Pictures of Goya*, *El Café de Chinitas*, and dances from *Carmen* and *Capriccio Espagnol*. By the time that Argentinita's group gave its last New York concert recital in February 1945, Edwin Denby wrote in the *Herald Tribune* that the "elegant and suave" Greco had become "a limpid virtuoso," and that it was "admirable" to see how Argentinita had "perfected and enlarged" the dancing of both Greco and her other male partner, Manolo Vargas. It was then that Greco was quoted as saying: "I have so many more things to learn, for I want to create, too. All my own dances are of my own creation and supervised by Argentinita. . . .I have learned unending resources of the Spanish dance since my association with this great artist."

After Argentinita's death in September 1945, her sister and partner, Pilar López, announced that she would never dance again, and Greco and Vargas joined her in escorting Argentinita's body back to Spain for burial. When, upon the continued insistence of Greco, Vargas, and cultural groups in Spain, Pilar López finally decided to return to the stage in her sister's repertoire, the two male dancers then made their Spanish debut with her in Madrid on June 7, 1946. The reorganized group, known as Ballet Español, scored an immediate success and later visited other Spanish cities. Its reper-

GRECO, JOSÉ—*Continued*

toire was augmented by several new works for which Greco was the choreographer, including *Cana y Farruca, Sentimiento, Triana, Polo,* and a new version of de Falla's *The Three-Cornered Hat.* Within a year the company was rated as "the best in the Iberian peninsula" and "the biggest money-making proposition" in the Spanish theater, according to a *Newsweek* report. Greco and Vargas, said that magazine, had "taken Spain by storm" and were "mentioned in the same breath with Escudero and Rafael Ortega." During the two years Pilar López's Ballet Español toured Spain and Portugal, Greco practiced five hours daily and spent all his free time in little known corners watching the gypsies and peasants in folk dances. "Dancing in America was for me a profession," he stated at that time, "but here in Spain it has become a religion for me. . . . Of course, I want to return home, but not until I know I can never lose what I feel I have now acquired."

While in Spain, in 1948 Greco was the choreographer of, and the principal dancer in, a ten-minute dance sequence for *Manolete,* a motion picture about bullfighters. The enthusiastic reception of this film encouraged him later that same year to form in Madrid his own company of Spanish dancers around the nucleus of the group he had assembled for the picture. As the Ballets y Bailes de España, Greco's company gave its first public performance in January 1949 at the Apollo Theatre in Barcelona, where it enjoyed an engagement of four weeks. Early February, at the Théâtre des Champs-Elysées in Paris, the troupe met with such acclaim that it remained there until the end of the month and then made a tour of other French cities. A subsequent engagement of three months in Norway, Sweden, and Denmark was followed by visits to the Netherlands, Belgium, and Switzerland.

The company's 1950 season opened in March in the Netherlands, then continued for a return engagement to Scandinavia and added Finland to the itinerary. At the end of the tour Greco was invited to appear with his group at a lecture-demonstration on Spanish dancing given by Señorita Doña Dolores de Pedroso-Sturdza, at London's Covent Garden Opera House, on December 10, 1950. This private performance, sponsored jointly by the Royal Academy of Dancing Production Club, the Spanish Embassy, and the Covent Garden Opera Trust, so impressed the critics that the British Arts Council asked the company to return to London during the Festival of Britain. To accept that commitment Greco cut short his first four-month tour of South America, where he and his group danced in Argentina, Uruguay, Chile, and Peru. The group appeared at the Sadler's Wells Theater in London on June 18, 1951, and following a month's run there returned to Oslo, Stockholm, Copenhagen, Brussels, and Amsterdam.

Upon seeing the dance sequence from *Manolete,* Lee Shubert, the Broadway producer, arranged to introduce Greco and his Spanish Ballet in New York and to sponsor the company's first tour of the United States. With Greco billed as producer, director, principal dancer, and choreographer, the troupe of thirteen dancers included Nila Amparo (Greco's wife). Accompanying the group were a guitarist, a flamenco singer, a pianist, and a small orchestra. Greco's Spanish Ballet made its North American debut at the Shubert Theater on October 1, 1951, with a program that remained the same throughout the engagement, consisting of Spanish ballets and dances of classic, folk, flamenco, and modern derivation. Of the thirteen ensemble and solo numbers on the program, five were designed by Greco, one by Carola Goya, and two were revivals from Argentinita's repertoire; the rest were authentic folk dances. The Greco works, included *El Cortijo,* a symbolic dance for four men, with music by Breton; *Rincón Flamenco,* a traditional series of dances for the entire company, set to music by Rogelio Reguera; *Old Madrid,* a quartet adapted from a *zarzuela* of the 1890's by Chueca; *Juerga,* a suite of dances in the eighteenth century style, employing music by Bautista, Chueca, and Marti; and *Cante Jondo,* a trio danced to Reguera's music. After its scheduled four weeks in New York, the company moved to a larger theater for an extended run of an additional four weeks. The company then started on a national tour.

Reviewing the company's New York debut for the *Herald Tribune,* Walter Terry described it as "the finest ensemble of Spanish dancers and musicians" he had ever seen, and praised Greco's ability to fuse the elements of a dance recital with those of a popular revue "without lowering the high standards of Spanish dance itself." As for Greco's own performance, Terry stated: "He may not be as fiery as some of his assistants, but he has intensity, graciousness, and a commanding stage presence, and to his dances he brings an expert technique and a body line which mirrors both grace and pride, essential elements in the dance of Spain. Furthermore, he is a choreographer of no mean attainments. His current show attests to this not only in the range of material but in choreographic details distinguished by inventiveness of movement sequence and by imaginativeness in stage design." Martin, of the *Times,* said: "Mr. Greco, himself, who used to be a good dancer when he was partner to Argentinita, is an even better one now. His footwork is particularly brilliant, and he moves with notable elegance." Writing for *Dance Magazine,* La Meri found Greco both "an impeccable dancer whose artistic expression lies in the purity of the neo-classic school" and "a strong and imaginative choreographer." Most significantly, she felt, he had proved, with his company composed of native Spanish and native American dancers, that "the Spanish dance is a universal art form and not merely another folk dance. . . .He has done this through courage, artistry, and tireless work, and even if this were his only contribution, it would put the dance world eternally in his debt."

On August 16, 1946, Greco married Nila Amparo, who is now one of the chief supporting dancers in his company. She was born Lucille Peters in West Virginia, of Syro-Lebanese descent, and was reared in Brooklyn. Before her marriage she was a student and a performer in the Hindu dance, having appeared with La Meri's Company and with Ruth St. Denis. She went to Madrid at the request of Pilar López and danced many of Argentinita's roles with the Ballet Español. Although Greco is a naturalized United States citizen, when he first began dancing in Spain his admirers there refused to believe he was not a native of that country—he speaks fluent Spanish (besides English without an accent). The dancer, who stands five feet nine inches tall and weighs 149 pounds, has dark brown eyes and dark hair. His political party is the Democratic, his church the Roman Catholic. He lists travel as his favorite diversion. Greco has designed most of his costumes and still keeps up his painting. "I don't care whether people think I'm a great dancer or not, that's not important," he told a Washington *Post* interviewer, "but when they admire our company . . . I feel justly proud."

References

Dance 19:6-7 Ap '45; 22:13 Jl '48 pors
Mus Courier 131:12 F 1 '45 por
N Y Daily Mirror Mag p4 Jl 6 '47
Newsweek 30:84 Jl 7 '47; 38:92-3 D 3 '51 pors
Washington (D.C.) Post p15B D 30 '51; pl Ja 13 '52

GREDE, WILLIAM J(OHN) (grā'dĭ) Feb. 24, 1897- Manufacturers' organization official

Address: b. c/o National Association of Manufacturers, 14 W. 49th St., New York 20; c/o Grede Foundries, Inc., 1320 S. 1st St., Milwaukee 1, Wis.; h. Elm Grove, Milwaukee, Wis.

At its fifty-sixth annual meeting in New York City in December 1951 the National Association of Manufacturers elected as its 1952 president William J. Grede, owner and operator of five foundries in Wisconsin and one in Michigan. The association has in 1952 a membership of around 17,000 firms throughout the United States, and is said to represent about 85 per cent of the country's manufacturing capacity.

William John Grede was born February 24, 1897, in Milwaukee, Wisconsin, the son of Henry L. and Fannie (Runkel) Grede. With his brother and two sisters William Grede was brought up in Milwaukee. He attended its local grade and high schools, and on graduation from the latter in 1914 entered the University of Wisconsin, where he met expenses by door-to-door peddling of aluminum kitchenware. His major was economics and he was house manager of Delta Upsilon and assistant manager of the Harefoot Club. By 1916, when he had cleared four hundred dollars, he was urged by his father, a retired carriage maker, to leave college and enter business. Young Grede did so by becoming in 1917 the assistant

to the president of a foundry in Decatur, Illinois. Except for his World War I service as a second lieutenant of infantry, he remained with the Decatur concern until 1920.

In 1920 the Liberty Foundry (which produced gray iron castings) in Wauwatosa, Wisconsin, was offered for sale, whereupon twenty-three-year-old Grede purchased the plant, agreeing to make a small down payment and to pay the remainder in fifteen years. Three years later (1923) the Liberty Foundry, Inc, was registered as the succeeding corporation. Expanding his holdings, in 1927 Grede became president of the Spring City Foundry Company of Waukesha, and in 1932 he was elected chairman of the board of the Milwaukee Steel Foundry Company. These enterprises were merged in 1940 as Grede Foundries, Inc., with Grede as owner as well as president. Today his business consists of six plants, five in Wisconsin and one in upper Michigan, with 1,100 employees producing some 33,000 tons of iron and steel castings yearly.

Throughout his thirty-one years as a foundry executive or owner, Grede has been a "ruggedly free businessman." The quoted phrase is from a *Time* article of December 17, 1951, which continued, "Grede has refused to bargain collectively, and has no union contracts. He has licked the C.I.O. steel workers in strikes, or has headed off organizers by wage boosts, pensions, vacations, and pay scales at the industry level." As early as 1924, said a NAM release, well before so-called "fringe benefits" became a union demand, Grede inaugurated a group-insurance plan which was expanded three years later to include sickness and accident insurance. In 1926 vacations with pay became the rule at the Liberty Foundry, and subsequently pensions were established for all employees at this and other Grede plants. Grede (who, *Time* stated, likes to call himself a "sand rat," a common foundry worker) is said to take special pride in the fact that employees who reach their fourth or fifth year at the plant rarely leave thereafter; approximately one hundred of the names on the present-day Grede payroll have been there twenty-five years or more. As chairman of a foundry industry research committee, Grede pioneered in efforts to combat silicosis in Wisconsin. He has also been influential in the development of foundry cost methods, while under his leadership the Milwaukee Foundrymen's Association initiated a cooperative research program with the University of Wisconsin.

The National Association of Manufacturers, to the board of directors of which Grede was first elected in 1946, was founded in 1895. Its main objectives is "to provide leadership in sound management practices; to assist manufacturers to appraise the significance of social, legislative, and economic trends; to improve relations between employer and employees, government and industry, and the public and business; to bring to the public and to the government the viewpoint of the manufacturers; and to promote the American capitalistic system." It is generally regarded as the voice of American business (NAM had in 1951

WILLIAM J. GREDE

about 17,000 member firms, four-fifths of which had fewer than 500 employees). NAM's policies are worked out in various committees, whose recommendations are subject to the approval of the board of directors. In the five years following his election to the board, the Wisconsin foundry owner saw service on the inter-association relations committee, as chairman of the Federal debt management committee, and as vice-chairman of the Government spending committee; and was the NAM regional vice-president for the Dakotas, Minnesota, and Wisconsin area in 1950 and 1951. The NAM national president is elected annually at the association's three-day "Congress of American Industry," cannot succeed himself, and on completion of his one-year term becomes automatically the chairman of the board.

Elected the 1952 president of NAM on December 6, 1951, the second day of the association's fifty-sixth annual convention, held in New York City, William J. Grede succeeded William H. Ruffin, a North Carolina textile executive. These congresses, at which national issues and future action are discussed as well as officers chosen, are known for their forums on economic theory and policy, at which guest speakers include prominent exponents of divergent views. In an hour-long press conference following his election as president, Grede declared that "one of the most important jobs NAM has before it for the coming year is to extend, broaden, and promote a program at grass-roots level of telling the common man and woman throughout the country what free enterprise is." He expressed his opposition to wage and price controls except for raw materials, production, and allocation relating to the rearmament effort; and while he "approved of unions under a free bargaining proposition" he "was opposed to any group that would tend to deprive the individual worker of individual

thinking and action" (*Christian Science Monitor*).

Other industry organizations in which Grede has been or is now active include the American Foundrymen's Association, the American Society for Testing Metals, the Steel Founders Society of America, the Gray Iron Founders Association (past director and treasurer), and the Gray Iron Research Institute. He is a director of the Mueller Furnace Company of Milwaukee, the Le Roi Company of West Allis, and Moe Light, Inc., at Fort Atkinson (all in Wisconsin); and vice-president as well as director of the Nye Tool and Machine Company and the Advance Spring Corporation, both of Chicago. A director and past president of the Wisconsin Manufacturers Association, past president of the Employers Association of Milwaukee, and a director of the latter city's Better Business Bureau, Grede is in addition a director of the Federal Reserve Bank of Chicago and a trustee of Carroll College at Waukesha and of Milwaukee-Downer College. The industrialist, who was an appointee of President Truman to the Labor-Management Conference of 1945, has been active for twenty-five years in Young Men's Christian Association affairs at local, State and national levels, and was a member of both the North Central and National Boards. In June 1951 he was chairman of the Milwaukee YMCA building fund campaign, and on May 25, 1952, he was elected national president of the YMCA. He has also been the Boy Scout examiner in Milwaukee County for the Foundry Merit Badges.

William J. Grede and Margaret Weiss, neighbors in their childhood, were married in 1919; they have two daughters, Janet (Mrs. Burleigh E. Jacobs, Jr.) and Betty (Mrs. Walter S. Davis, Jr.), and five grandchildren. Grede, whose hobby is amateur photography, is a member of the Milwaukee, Wisconsin, City, University and Bluemound Golf and Country clubs in Milwaukee. He is an active member and former trustee of the Wauwatosa Congregational Church. His political party is the Republican. With a height of six feet he has a weight of 155 pounds; his eyes are blue, and his hair is a graying brown.

References

N Y Herald Tribune p6 D 7 '51
Time 58:94 D 17 '51 por

Business Executives of America (1950)
Who's Who in Commerce and Industry (1951)
Who's Who in the Midwest (1949)

GREY, J(AMES) D(AVID), REV. Dec. 18, 1906- Pastor; Southern Baptist Convention president

Address: b. c/o First Baptist Church, 3436 St. Charles Ave., New Orleans 15, La.; h. 4524 S. Galvez St., New Orleans, La.

In May 1952 the Southern Baptist Convention, at the largest annual meeting in its history in Florida, re-elected the Reverend J. D. Grey as president. When first elected, in 1951, he had become at forty-four the youngest man ever to hold that post. Described as "conservative theologically," Grey, who is pastor of the First Baptist Church of New Orleans, now heads the fastest growing religious denomination in the United States, according to *Time*, and the second largest—only the Methodists being larger—in number of members.

James David Grey, one of five children of George Lindsay and Lucy Ann (Keeney) Grey, was born December 18, 1906, in Princeton, Kentucky. His father, a farmer who later became a railroad employee, moved the family to Paducah, where his son attended Tilghman High School. While there young Grey participated in dramatics, public speaking, and debating. After graduation in 1925 he attended Union University in Jackson, Tennessee, at which he selected English literature as his major subject. He was a member of the debating team for four years, president of the student body, a member of Alpha Tau Omega, and winner of the Strickland medal for his commencement oration. Upon receiving his B.A. degree in 1929, he attended the Southwestern Baptist Theological Seminary at Fort Worth, Texas, there taking the degree of Th.M. in 1932.

During his first full-time pastorate, at Vickery, Texas, in 1930, Grey preached the annual sermon for the Dallas County Baptist Association. He left Vickery in 1931 to become the pastor of the Tabernacle Baptist Church of Ennis, Texas. The following year, at the Texas Training Union Convention at Mineral Wells, Texas, he gave the consecration sermon. The minister first took part in the program of the Southern Baptist Convention in 1933. In 1934 he became the pastor of the First Church at Denton, Texas, and in the same year he was elected a member of the executive board of the Texas Baptist Convention, a position he filled until 1937.

Grey moved to his present charge, the First Church in New Orleans, Louisiana, in 1937; in the time he has been there the membership has grown from 1,561 to 3,578, and the budget has increased from $26,000 to $225,000. Elected a member of the executive board of the Louisiana Baptist Convention in 1940, he became a member of the budget control committee of the State convention in 1942. He was elected as the Louisiana member of the Home Mission Board of the Southern Baptist Convention in 1943; two years later he was chosen to preach the annual sermon at the Louisiana Baptist Convention.

When the Reverend Grey made a tour of Europe in 1947, he attended the Baptist World Alliance meeting held in Copenhagen. He served his first term as president of the Louisiana Baptist Convention in 1948; in that year, too, he became president of the Southwide Alumni Association, Southwestern Baptist Seminary, serving in the latter office for three consecutive terms. In 1949 he was re-elected president of the Louisiana Baptist Convention and was chosen as the first vice-president of the Southern Baptist Convention. He became the first speaker to be elected for

REV. J. D. GREY

the three months' series of *Baptist Hour* radio broadcasts, which were given in April, May, and June of 1949. The minister became chairman in 1950 of the committee on order of business for the Southern Baptist Convention, which was to meet in San Francisco the following year. The executive committee of Baptist World Alliance chose him as one of its members in 1950.

At the ninety-fourth session of the Southern Baptist Convention, held in San Francisco in June 1951, Grey was elected president of the convention, the youngest man ever to fill that post in the one hundred and six years of the organization's history. At this meeting the convention emphasized the Baptists' traditional stand on church autonomy in a resolution which declared that the Southern Baptists would enter into no alliance with the National Council of Churches, the World Council of Churches, or any similar organization. Another statement of principle concerned the separation of church and state: Baptist institutions were urged to accept no Federal grants under any conditions. The convention warned against marriages between Catholics and Baptists. It also decided to ignore previously set territorial restrictions, recommending that "Southern Baptist boards and agencies be free to serve as a source of blessing to any community . . . in the United States."

In May 1952 the largest annual meeting ever held of the Southern Convention took place in Miami, Florida. Over eleven thousand "messengers" (theoretically members who attend are not delegates, because the Baptist Church believes in the complete autonomy of the separate churches) were present at the session and re-elected Grey as their president. In his address he delivered a warning to political candidates: "In conscience' sake [the Baptists] cannot countenance any candidate, even

GREY, J. D., REV.—*Continued*

one of their own number, who does not make it crystal clear that he opposes any and all missions to the Vatican or to any other religious organization in the world." The president also discussed the growth of the Southern Baptists; the Convention now includes 28,289 churches with a total of 7,373,498 members.

The Southern Baptist Convention came into being in 1845, when the Southern and Northern Baptists separated over the question of slavery. The Southern Baptists are more Calvinistic in their doctrines. Since all Baptists are opposed to rigid organization or discipline, the individual churches are considered independent and autonomous entities. The Southern Baptists, however, still maintain that no individual church should be forced to abide by the decision of a group of delegates. The various Baptist Congregations are not united to form one "church" but maintain the looser grouping known as the "convention." The Southern Baptists strongly condemn the use of liquor and all gambling, protesting "unprincipled" liquor advertising and the few types of gambling considered legal, such as bingo. They comprise the second largest Protestant denomination in the United States; the total membership passed seven million in 1950 when 376,000 converts were made.

Grey has conducted revivals in most of the States of the Southern Baptist Convention and has preached in the pulpits of a number of Baptist churches outside the convention. He has contributed articles to Baptist publications and has spoken at gatherings throughout the country. The minister, who is a member of the United Fund Organization for New Orleans, traveled 20,000 miles on a tour of Southern Baptist mission work in three continents and visited briefly seventeen countries in July and August of 1952.

Also an active participant in civic affairs, he is a founder and director of the Louisiana Moral and Civic Foundation, a member of the Displaced Persons Commission for the State of Louisiana, a director of the New Orleans Chapter of the American Red Cross, and for two years he served as the chairman of the speakers' bureau of the New Orleans Community Chest. The minister is a member of the board of directors of the Boy Scouts of America, New Orleans area, and the New Orleans League for Better Hearing; he is also a member of the advisory board of the Salvation Army.

In 1938, nine years after his graduation from Union University, Grey received an honorary degree of Doctor of Divinity from that institution, the youngest graduate to be so honored by the university. He was made an honorary Doctor of Laws by Louisiana College in 1952. Governor Earle C. Clements appointed him an honorary "Kentucky Colonel" in 1950. He is a member of Kiwanis and served on the board of directors in 1946-47. The minister is an independent voter.

Grey and Lillian Tooke were married on September 16, 1927; their twin daughters are named Martha Ann and Mary Beth. With a height of six feet, he weighs 220 pounds; he has blue eyes and brown hair.

Reference

Who's Who in the Clergy, 1941-42

GRIEDER, NAOMI LANE BABSON
See Babson, N. L.

GROPIUS, WALTER (ADOLF) (grō'pĭ-us") May 18, 1883- Architect; university professor
Address: b. c/o The Architects' Collaborative, 96 Mount Auburn St., Cambridge 38, Mass.; h. Baker Bridge Rd., Lincoln, Mass.

NOTE: This biography supersedes the article which appeared in *Current Biography* in 1941.

Walter Gropius, who in 1938 became the chairman of the Department of Architecture, Graduate School of Design, Harvard University, headed "the nation's No. 1 architectural school" (in the word of *Time* magazine) until his resignation in July 1952. Under his direction Harvard architectural students began to use the "learning by doing" technique which had proved successful at the Bauhaus, the pre-Hitler school of architecture and design which Gropius had established in his native Germany. Examples of the techniques and international influence of the Bauhaus could be observed early in 1952 in the retrospective exhibition of Gropius' work shown at the Boston Institute of Contemporary Art: in architecture, furniture design, industrial design, and city planning. Other examples of his work include residences, housing developments, prefabricated houses, theaters, academic buildings, and factories, constructed in the United States, England, and Germany.

Walter Adolf Gropius was born May 18, 1883, in Berlin, Germany, of a family with a long tradition in the fields of painting and architecture. He is the son of Walter Gropius, privy surveyor at the Policy Presidency in Berlin, and of Manon (Scharnweber) Gropius. Walter Gropius attended the Leibnitz Gymnasium (secondary school) in Berlin-Charlottenburg and the Kaiserin Augusta Gymnasium in Berlin-Steglitz, where he graduated in 1903. Later in the same year he studied for a time at the Technische Hochschule in Munich. Having intended since an early age to become an architect, Gropius volunteered to work in the studio of Professors Solf and Wichards, where he remained until, for his required military training, he joined a regiment of hussars in 1904. He was made a corporal in 1905 and a vice-sergeant major the next year.

While studying at the Berlin Technische Hochschule between 1905 and 1907, Gropius executed his first independent group of buildings, workmen's houses constructed in 1906 on his uncle's estate in Pomerania. For a while afterward he traveled abroad, chiefly in Spain but also in Italy and England. On his return to Berlin in 1908, he became head assistant to Professor Peter Behrens. Prior to World War I, Gropius, who was in practice for himself from 1910 to 1914, designed a factory at Alfeld, settlements at Wittenberg and Frankfort, and other factories and residences, which were distinguished by their clean, functional lines, their freedom from applied decoration, and for the unusual materials employed. His other contributions to prewar design were furniture, interiors, and benzol-driven locomotives. Gropius was a member at this time of the Deutscher Werkbund (1911), to the Berliner Architekten-Verein (1911) and the Bund Deutscher Architekten (1912). In the year preceding the war, he received the gold medal awarded at the World Exhibition in Ghent, and in 1914, he erected a factory and offices in Cologne. Entering the reserve regiment of the Ninth Hussars in 1914 as a lieutenant, Gropius by 1916 was adjutant of the regiment. When he was discharged in November 1918, he held the Second Class Iron Cross, the Bavarian Military Medal for Merit, the Austrian Royal Distinction for Military Merit, the First Class Iron Cross, and a Mark of Distinction for wounds.

Invited in 1918 to succeed Henry van der Velde as director of the Grand Ducal Saxon School of Arts and the Grand Ducal Saxon School of Arts and Crafts and of the Grand Ducal Saxon Academy of Art, Weimar, Germany, Gropius brought about the amalgamation of the two schools under the name of Staatliches Bauhaus. "The foundation and development of the Bauhaus," Gropius has stated, "aimed at the introduction of a new educational method in art and a new artistic conception that derived development of all artistic form from the vital functions of life and from modern technical means of construction." (Books by Gropius on the Bauhaus theories are *Staatliches Bauhaus* and *The New Architecture and the Bauhaus*.) During the first years of the Bauhaus, Gropius designed the Sommerfeld Block House in Berlin and the Otte House in Zehlendorf (1922), a town theater for Jena (1923-24), a paper factory in Alfeld (1924), several tombs (1924), a warehouse in Alfeld (1924-25). Local opposition to the Bauhaus in Weimar, where it was accused of "architectural socialism," brought about the offer of funds and a building site in Dessau. There the $230,000 school designed by Gropius was dedicated December 4, 1926—one day after the title of professor had been conferred upon its designer by the Government of Anhalt. The glass-walled Bauhaus itself has been described as an impressive achievement of modern architecture. Teachers on the Bauhaus staff included names well known in the fields of painting, typography, furniture, ceramics, weaving, stage design, and other applied arts. Gropius has expressed the theory that a team can raise its integrated work to higher potentialities than the sum of the work of its members when they work separately.

After the establishment of the Bauhaus in Dessau, Gropius was commissioned by the

WALTER GROPIUS

Reich to design a 316-unit experimental housing project in Dessau-Törten (1926-28), notable, according to Henry-Russell Hitchcock in *Modern Architecture*, for making use of concrete on a mass-production scale. This was followed in 1927 by a "total theater" project and two houses for the Weissenhof Werkbund exhibition in Stuttgart. On April 1, 1928, Gropius resigned from the directorship of the Bauhaus to resume the private practice of architecture in Berlin, where he designed a number of private residences, among them the Lewin house, at Berlin-Zehlendorf; in Dessau that year he constructed shops, an apartment house, and the city employment office. Gropius, who, in Hitchcock's opinion, does his best work when dealing with problems of social importance, designed the Reich Research Settlement for Spandau (which received the first prize in 1929), the Dammerstock Siedlung near Karlsruhe in collaboration with a group of other architects (1929-30), the Berlin-Siemensstadt settlement (1929-30), and a settlement at Frankfort on Main (1929). As chairman of the committee on design of the Adler Automobile Company (1929-33), he designed bodies for Adler cars; and similar work in industrial design was done by him for the Frank Stove Factory (1931-33). From then until he left Germany in 1934, he evolved the plans for the Werkbund Exhibition in Paris and a theater in Karkov, Russia (1930), for the Berlin Building Exhibition (1931), for prefabricated houses put up at Hirsch Kupfer Company for a plan submitted in the international competition for the Palace of the Soviets (1931), and for the metal exhibition in Berlin (1934).

Gropius went into voluntary exile from Hitler's Germany in 1934, at which time the Bauhaus was used as a Nazi leader school. In England, his first country of refuge, he worked in collaboration with Maxwell Fry on several residences in London and Kent (1934-

GROPIUS, WALTER—*Continued*

36), and on the Village College built at Impington in Cambridgeshire (1936-37). The fact that plans drawn by him and Fry for a new building at Christ Church, Oxford, were never put into effect was retrospectively considered by the British *Architects' Journal* as a "great loss to Britain."

Gropius, who had visited the United States for the first time in 1928, became a permanent resident of that country in 1937, when, in collaboration with Marcel Breuer, he began three years of residential construction in Massachusetts. The architects' own houses in Lincoln, the Hagerty house in Cohasset, the Abele house in Framingham, and the Franck house in Pittsburgh were designed by Gropius and Breuer. They also did projects for the Pennsylvania State exhibition at the New York World's Fair in 1939 and for Black Mountain College in North Carolina and Wheaton College in Massachusetts.

In 1937 Gropius was named senior professor of architecture at Harvard University and in 1938 chairman of the Department of Architecture of the university's Graduate School of Design. (He and Moholy-Nagy had already established the New Bauhaus in Chicago, subsequently known as the Chicago Institute of Design.) Commissioned by the United States Government in 1941 to design a 250-unit defense housing project, Aluminum City, in New Kensington, Pennsylvania, Gropius and Breuer provided the units at a cost of $3,280 each. Subsequently Gropius designed the recreation center at Key West, Florida (1942). He has been consultant on the plan to rebuild or renovate a seven-mile-square area surrounding Michael Reese Hospital on Chicago's South Side since 1946. Two years later, as consultant to the Container Corporation of America, he helped design its Greensboro (North Carolina) plant, which *Architectural Forum* described as bearing "the mark of a sure, confident designer. . . .One of the distinguishing elements of the design is its refusal to overdramatize the architectural impact on the viewer."

Perhaps the major building done by Gropius in the United States is the $3,000,000 Harvard Graduate Center (completed in 1950), which was designed by the Architects' Collaborative, a firm in which Gropius is one of eight partners, some of whom were formerly his students. This firm is also responsible for a twenty-acre group of houses at Lexington, Massachusetts, and for a second development at Lexington of which 30 houses are finished (1952). *Architectural Review* remarked that Harvard turned to "Gropius and the Architects' Collaborative for the design after thirty years of architectural timidity." Students under Gropius also participated in the preliminary studies. The framing of the dormitories is reinforced concrete with buff-colored brick facing, and the seven dormitory units are connected by sheltered walks with a community center. "This graduate center," said the *Christian Science Monitor*, "exemplifies the enhancements which modern building and design can furnish student life for individual growth and group activity." In July 1952 Gropius resigned from his position at Harvard (*Time*, July 14, 1952).

According to *Architecture d'Aujourd'hui*, which in February 1950 devoted an entire issue to Gropius' work, Gropius in 1910 had submitted to Emil Rathenau a "Plan for the Constitution of a General Enterprise of Construction." In the year 1944 Gropius with Konrad Wachsmann had evolved a system of prefabrication which resulted shortly in the production of completely finished, factory-produced plywood panels, which could be used interchangeably for either walls or ceiling when connected by specially designed interlocking joints. These were being produced by the General Panel Corporation of New York (of which Gropius and Wachsmann were officers). As a consultant to General Clay in 1947, Gropius submitted a plan for reconstruction work in Germany to Secretary of the Army Kenneth C. Royall, which was reprinted by *Task* in 1948. Other of his suggestions on city planning—by construction of new townships along superhighways to disperse industry and population from crowded cities—were discussed in *Architectural Forum* (July 1943) and in a lecture "Urbanism," delivered to the C.I.A.M. Congress at Bridgewater, England (*Architects' Journal*, September 25, 1947).

In his book *Rebuilding Our Communities* (1946) Gropius gave the details of his city-planning and urban-decentralization projects. His earlier books were *Staatliches Bauhaus, Weimar, 1919-23* (1923), *Internationale Architektur* (1925), *Bauhausbauten in Dessau* (1930), *The New Architecture and the Bauhaus* (translation by T. M. Shand, 1935), and *The Bauhaus—1919-28* (1939). The last-named was published in connection with an exhibtion devoted to the work of the Bauhaus held by the Museum of Modern Art in New York. Another retrospective exhibition of work done by Gropius and under his influence was held at the Boston Institute of Contemporary Art early in 1952. Of the most recent exhibition, Gropius has said (according to *Newsweek*) it should "give the chronological impression that Gropius as an individual disappears. We need few stunts and more anonymity in architecture." Regarding architecture as an "interpretation of life" and as a "social art," Gropius has stated that the foremost need of the ideal architect is high human qualities. "The outward forms of modern architecture," he has also pointed out, "are not the whims of a few architects eager for innovation. They are the inevitable products of the intellectual, social, technical conditions of our time" (quoted in the *Christian Science Monitor*, January 21, 1952). (A bibliography of published materials by and about Gropius, covering the years 1919-50 was compiled by Ruth V. Cook for the American Institute of Architects in 1951.)

Prior to leaving Germany, Gropius was a member of the board of experts of the Reich Research Institute for Economy in Building (1928), an honorary member of the Kokusai-Kenchiku-Kiokai (Tokyo, 1928), a member of the Bund Deutscher Architekten Board

(1928), the Deutsches Werkbundes Board (1928), the German Academy of City Planning (1928), the Comité Permanent International des Architectes (1928), vice-president and German delegate of the International Congresses for New Building (1931). He was named corresponding member of the Sociedad de Arquitectos del Uruguay and of the Société Belge des Urbanistes et Architectes Modernistes in 1932. While he was residing in England he was elected in 1937 vice-president of the Institute of Sociology in London, and that same year, was made an honorary member of the Royal Institute of British Architects.

Honorary degrees have been bestowed upon the architect by the Technische Hochschule in Hannover (Dr. Ing., 1929), by Harvard University (M.A., 1942), and by Western Reserve University (D.Sc.). Gropius was also given honorary membership in Phi Beta Kappa in 1942 and was made a fellow of the American Academy of Arts and Sciences in 1944. "In consideration of his eminence and efficiency in creative design for industry," the Royal Society of Arts in 1948 named him "honorary royal designer for industry." Three years later, he was the first recipient of the Howard Myers Memorial Award of $500 given by the Architectural League of New York. That league also in 1951 awarded the gold medal to the Architects' Collaborative for the Harvard Graduate Center. The architect is a member of the American Institute of Architects and the American Society of Planners and Architects.

Gropius' clubs are the Thursday Evening (Boston), the Harvard (Boston), and the Harvard (New York). By his marriage in 1916 to Alma (Schindler) Mahler, Walter Gropius was the father of a daughter, Alma Manon, who died in 1935; an adopted daughter, Beate Eveline, is now Mrs. Charles Forberg. Following his divorce in 1921, on October 16, 1923, he married Ise Frank. The architect, who has a height of five feet seven inches, weighs 160 pounds; the color of his eyes is blue, of his hair, dark-brown. He names his political party as the Democratic, and riding as his chief outdoor recreation.

References

Architecture d'Aujourd'hui 20:1-116 F '50
Arts and Arch 63:18 F '46
Christian Sci Mon p9 Ja 21 '52
Harvard Alumni Bul O 14 '50
Time 59:58 Ja 21 '52
Giedion, S. Space, Time, and Architecture (1941)
Hitchcock, H. R. Modern Architecture (1929)
International Who's Who, 1951
Who's Who, 1951
Who's Who in America, 1950-51
Who's Who in Massachusetts, 1942-43
World Biography (1948)

GUILLAUME, AUGUSTIN (LEON) (gē" yōm' ô"güs"tăn' lā"ôn') July 30, 1895- French Colonial administrator
Address: Office of the Resident General, Rabat, Morocco

The present Resident General of French Morocco, General Augustin Guillaume, was assigned to the North African post in October 1951. There he is seen as functioning both as a statesman and a soldier. He must deal with the pressure of Moroccan nationalists and guard the interests of France and of her allies in the North Atlantic Treaty Organization, for which the French protectorate is particularly strategic as an air base. Guillaume, who served in both world wars, has held military and administrative posts in Morocco for many years. As a result he is regarded as having much influence with the Berber tribes who supplied fighting men to the Allies in Europe and whose opposition to the Arab ruling classes is seen as a stay to the nationalist movement of the Arab League.

Augustin Léon Guillaume was born July 30, 1895, in Guillestre, a small French town in the department of Hautes-Alpes, bordering Italy. A cadet at the military academy of France, at Saint-Cyr, he graduated in 1914 in the wartime class, which went into its first World War I engagement wearing the plumed shakos and white gloves of the cadet corps. Lieutenant Guillaume was taken prisoner, and after attempts to escape he was interned in the same prison camp as Captain Charles de Gaulle. In 1918 he received his captaincy.

After postwar duty with French occupation forces in Eastern Germany and along the Rhine, Guillaume joined the Moroccan department of native affairs. Now he began a study of the Berbers, tribesmen of northwest Africa, and of their language. Under his direction, the Berber soldiery, the "Goums," were organized as units of the French army. He left Morocco to serve briefly with a French military mission at Belgrade and for advanced study in Paris at the war and staff colleges. Back in Morocco again, he was commander of the territory of Azilal in the Casablanca department from 1934 to 1936. About this time was published his book on the role of the Berbers in the French pacification of the Central Atlas Mountain region of Morocco.

A post on the military staff of the Supreme War Council recalled Guillaume to Paris in 1936, as it did several times later also. In 1940, several months after the outbreak of World War II, he returned as a colonel to Morocco to become director of political affairs. When the Vichy Government of France capitulated to Germany in June 1940, Guillaume retained his office. Instead of cooperating with the occupation officials, however, *Paris Match* reported that he assembled a force of some 20,000 Berbers, who he led the Germans to believe were simply a police force, and secretly trained them for war duty.

Following the liberation of North Africa by the Allies in 1943, Guillaume resumed his military functions. Promoted that year to brigadier general, he was first placed in command

GEN. AUGUSTIN GUILLAUME

of the armored infantry groups which participated in the Italian campaign. In the battle to liberate France, he headed the Third Division of Algerian Infantry, which went ashore on the Mediterranean coast of France in August 1944 and took part later that year in the dislodgment of the Germans from Alsace and the capture of Stuttgart. Shortly afterward in January 1945, Guillaume's division accomplished its mission of protecting newly liberated Strasbourg from recapture by the Germans in their final counteroffensive of the war. The newspaper *l'Aurore* stated that the general was wounded during his service in World War II.

After the end of hostilities, Guillaume was assigned to Moscow as military attaché at the French Embassy, a post he filled until March 1948. That same year saw the publication of his *Pourquoi l'Armée rouge a vaincu* ("Why the Red Army Won"), chiefly an analysis of the factors of supply, organization, and morale which accomplished Russia's victory. He also wrote a book on the course of the German-Soviet war itself.

Guillaume's transfer, in succession to General Joseph-Pierre Koenig, to the post of Commander in Chief of the French zone of occupation in Germany in March 1948, placed him in an area where armies of the West and the East were close together, a situation in which his understanding of the Russians was important. Early in 1951 he became commander of General Eisenhower's NATO forces in the Central European sector. It was his duty, reported *Pathfinder*, to "forge three divisions of French youths into an army that can do its share to defend Western Europe." "Yes, we have Communists among the men," said Guillaume, "but we try to appeal to their patriotic sense. Then, of course, they are young, and we keep them busy."

On October 3, 1951, Guillaume, succeeding General Alphonse Juin, arrived in Casablanca to assume the office of the French Resident General in Morocco and Inspector General of Armed Forces in North Africa. The question of Moroccan independence, one frequently disputed since the sultanate, technically kept intact, in 1912 was divided into a French and a Spanish protectorate, had aroused disagreement between Juin and Sultan Sidi Mohammed. The latter had insisted that his Cabinet be staffed by the Istiqlal (Freedom) party, but Juin's contention that the group was subversive finally prevailed, and the Sultan dismissed the Ministers. Guillaume, too, maintained that if not actually allied to communism, the Istiqlal helped the Soviet cause by weakening the western anchor of NATO's southern flank. Speaking on a related point at the Anglo-American Press Association meeting in Paris on October 30, 1951, Guillaume asked that American State Department officials not be allowed to support the Istiqlal and thus partially undo the effect of such defensive measures of the United States in Morocco as the building of five large air bases. Since the Resident General makes decisions in all the Sultan's foreign affairs, the Moroccans had no voice in the matter, the Franco-American agreement being that "the bases shall belong to the French and must be restored to them when the two governments agree that the danger [of communist aggression] is over" (Homer Bigart in the New York *Herald Tribune*).

The importance of the Berbers (who comprise about three and a half million of French Morocco's eight and a half million inhabitants) to the Western cause has been stressed by Guillaume. Before the meeting of the 1951 United Nations General Assembly he reported in Paris on his tour of Berber villages in which he spoke to the tribesmen in their own language: he has said that among the Berbers alone he can raise 100,000 fighting men.

Guillaume, now a general of the second highest French rank, is a grand officer of the Legion of Honor and has received many military awards. Among these are the World War I Croix de Guerre, the United States Army Bronze Star, and fifteen mentions in military dispatches. "The bright-eyed rubicund general," Joan Thiriet wrote in the *Christian Science Monitor* of November 1, 1951, "speaks eight languages": the list of his linguistic accomplishments in *Paris Match* comprise, (in addition to French) German, English, Italian, Russian, Serbian, Arabic, Berber, and "l'Américain de Brooklyn."

References

L'Aurore p8 Jl 17 '51 por
Paris Match p8 No 130 S 15 '51
Pathfinder 58:25 Ap 18 '51 por
Dictionnaire Biographique Français Contemporain (1950)

HABER, HEINZ (hä′bĕr hīnts) May 15, 1913- Physicist

Address: b. c/o Institute of Transportation and Traffic Engineering, Department of Engineering, University of California, Los Angeles 24, Calif.; h. 744-C So. Bundy Dr., Los Angeles 49, Calif.

One of the initiators of the new field in medical science known as space medicine, Heinz Haber in May 1952 left his position as assistant professor of astrophysics in the United States Air Force School of Aviation Medicine, Randolph Field, Texas, to become an associate physicist in the Institute of Transportation and Traffic Engineering, University of California, Los Angeles. Since moving to the United States from his native Germany in 1946, he has carried on research about the effects of the upper atmosphere and of "free space" upon the human body and has written articles and given lectures on the subject.

On May 15, 1913, Heinz Haber was born in Mannheim, Germany, the third of four children of Karl and Maria (Saar) Haber. His father, who died in 1931, was a business executive and president of the incorporated Sugar Industry of Southern Germany. Heinz Haber has a married sister and two brothers; the older, Fritz Haber, is an aerodynamics engineer and the younger, Franz Haber, is a biochemist. Heinz attended elementary schools and the Humanistic Gymnasium in Mannheim, graduating from the latter in 1932. For his higher education he studied at the universities of Leipzig, Heidelberg, and Berlin, where he concentrated on physics and astronomy, receiving his Ph.D. degree in physics from the University of Berlin in 1939 and his Ph.D. degree in astronomy and astrophysics from the same institution in 1944.

While a student at the University of Berlin, Haber was appointed a research assistant at the Kaiser Wilhelm Institute for Physics in Berlin-Dahlem (1937-39). In 1942 he was named head of the Department of Spectroscopy at the Kaiser Wilhelm Institute for Physical Chemistry, also in Berlin-Dahlem, where he remained for the next three years. He moved to the United States in 1946 to become an assistant professor of astrophysics in the United States Air Force School of Aviation Medicine, Randolph Field, Texas. Here, in collaboration with Dr. Hubertus Strughold, former director of the German Aero-Medical Research Institute, Haber initiated the study of space medicine, an extension of aviation medicine. Developed under the sponsorship of General Harry G. Armstrong, Surgeon General, of the United States Air Force, the new science is described as the "study of the human factor involved in flights at highest altitudes and eventually in space." In May 1952 Haber joined the faculty of the University of California in Los Angeles as an associate physicist attached to the Institute of Transportation and Traffic Engineering, in the Department of Engineering.

Haber outlined the probable steps leading to travel in outer space at a meeting of forty of

HEINZ HABER

the world's leading specialists in space travel held in the spring of 1952 in San Antonio, Texas, under the sponsorship of the Randolph Field School of Aviation Medicine. Following further exploration with high-altitude rockets, he predicted, a small craft containing only instruments would be "hung in space" to circle the earth like a small moon "continuously broadcasting all manner of reports." The next experiment would require sending up test animals whose heartbeat, blood pressure, and other bodily reactions most closely approximate those of man under conditions of existence in space; these reactions would be sent to the earth by means of instruments. Finally, scientists would be ready to launch a space ship piloted by a human being.

In an article entitled "Human Body in Space," written for *Scientific American* (January 1951), Haber pointed out that the problems of space medicine could not be solved as a pilot would meet them in space, but would have to be anticipated and solved as completely as possible in advance. "Man," he explained in a *Collier's* article (March 22, 1952), "was not made to survive in the 'hostile territory of space.'" Since man cannot be redesigned, the problem of the engineers designing the space ships and the space "stations" (which must be established for re-fueling and re-launching the ships) is to provide a "highly mobile, self-contained, 'packaged' environment for space-faring man." Among the foreseeable dangers which Haber has named for the human being traveling in outer space are the absence of oxygen, the lack of atmospheric pressure, the presence of ultraviolet rays and cosmic rays, and the quality of weightlessness. With all these dangers, however, Haber has concluded that "the crews of rocket ships and

HABER, HEINZ—*Continued*

space stations, while they can never be completely protected against hazards such as meteors, will probably be safer than pedestrians crossing a busy street at a rush hour" (*Collier's*).

At the Air Force symposium on physics and medicine of the upper atmosphere, held in San Antonio, Texas, in November 1951, Haber predicted that in the future guided missiles would be used for transporting passengers to distant parts of the earth. Such an express ship, which he has called the "ionocruiser," could be shot with rocket power to a height of about twenty miles and could then turn its nose toward its destination, shut off the power, and glide there at supersonic speeds.

The author of about thirty scientific papers on optics, aviation medicine, spectroscopy, and space medicine, Haber has also written articles for popular publications like *Collier's* and *Scientific American.* He was a contributor to a handbook *Space Medicine*, edited by J. P. Marbarger (University of Illinois Press, 1951), and to *Physics and Medicine of the Upper Atmosphere* (University of New Mexico Press, 1952), of which he was also associate editor. Also in 1952 Haber contributed the chapter on space medicine to *Across the Space Frontier*, the work of six experts on various aspects of rocket travel. Reviewing this book in the New York *Times* (October 5, 1952) John Pfeiffer called it "an authoritative, clearly written and superbly illustrated preview of man's first space station and what it will mean to citizens of all nations." The book is an expanded version of articles originally appearing in *Collier's*; Haber's article "Can We Survive in Space?" was published in the March 22, 1952, issue of this magazine. The physicist has lectured before scientific societies and civic groups in a number of States.

Haber is a member of the Optical Society of America, Sigma Xi (national honorary scientific society), the American Aero-Medical Association and its auxiliary organization, the American Space-Medical Association. Co-founder of the latter, he was the principal speaker at its foundation session in 1950. With a height of six feet one inch, Haber weighs 150 pounds; he has blue-gray eyes and graying brown hair. His church affiliation is Lutheran. On February 15, 1940, he married Anneliese Huendle, a former technical research assistant; they have a son, Kai, and a daughter, Cathleen. Haber's favorite sports are tennis and swimming; for relaxation he prefers chess, reading, and writing.

HALLINAN, VINCENT (W.) 1896- Political party leader; lawyer

Address: b. c/o Progressive Party, 150 W. 46th St., New York 19; 345 Franklin St., San Francisco. Calif.; h. Ross, Marin County, Calif.

At its convention in Chicago in early July 1952, the Progressive party confirmed the se-

lection made earlier by its nominating committee of Vincent Hallinan as candidate for President of the United States. Hallinan was at that time serving a six-month jail sentence on contempt charges arising from his conduct in defending Harry Bridges in the perjury trial of 1949-50. The San Francisco lawyer, whose name has been associated with a number of well-known trials, has made speeches for reform in the judiciary system, civil rights legislation, and immediate peace in Korea.

A second cousin of the Irish revolutionist and statesman Eamon de Valera, Vincent W. Hallinan was born in San Francisco, California, in 1896, one of eight children of Patrick and Elizabeth (Sheehan) Hallinan, both Irish immigrants. Hallinan has told that his father, a San Francisco cable-car conductor, worked for fourteen hours every day of the year and that the younger children seldom saw him since he left for work while they were still asleep and returned after they had gone to bed. In an effort to better his situation his father took part in several strikes, Hallinan has also recalled; during one of these strikes he broke his right hand. Before he was in his teens the boy took a job running errands for a grocery store.

While studying for his B.A. degree at Ignatius College, a Jesuit institution which later became the University of San Francisco, Hallinan edited the college magazine, played on the basketball team, and became captain of the football team and boxing champion of the school. (Athletics have been a major interest in Hallinan's life: playing on the team which won the Pacific Coast club championship, he was dubbed the "Iron Man of Football" by Robert Ripley for playing every minute of every game in five successive seasons; when thirty-eight he helped his Rugby team win the State championship.) In his free time the young man collected funds and weapons for the use of rebels in Ireland and India.

After World War I Hallinan, who had enlisted in the United States Navy, returned to St. Ignatius College to complete his law course. He was admitted to the bar in 1921. In her book, *My Wild Irish Rogues* (1952), Mrs. Vincent Hallinan tells that her husband chose law as a career because of the opportunities it offered to fight injustice. Successful in his practice from the beginning, Hallinan won a $200,000 will contest during his first year at the San Francisco bar. He became known for his skillful oratory, his militant approach, his use of parable in presenting a problem to the jury, and his readiness to accept difficult or unpopular cases. In 1932 Hallinan was engaged to defend Frank Egan, the Public Defender of San Francisco, who was accused of the murder of a woman whose insurance beneficiary he was. The sensational case, which aroused much public indignation against the defendant, a bias that Hallinan accused the judge of sharing, brought the attorney one of several sentences for contempt of court. Among other murder trials which gave Hallinan wide publicity were the Hanford Windmill case (1925) and the Irene Mansfeldt case (1949).

For several years, as the account is given in a biographical release by the Progressive party, Hallinan "conducted a one-man crusade to eliminate a corrupt jury system which prevailed in San Francisco. He had to battle against corrupt judges, corrupt jury officials, and their supporters, the newspapers. This battle was finally won with the exposure of the Jury Commissioner as a grafter and the entire system was then renovated and corrected." During his years of practice, he is said never to have represented a corporation.

When he was requested in November 1949 to replace Richard Gladstein in defending Harry Bridges, president of the International Longshoremen's and Warehousemen's Union, Hallinan had retired from the practice of law and was engaged in writing a book on law and lawyers. He was also at this time active in opposing what he regarded as "war hysteria" and as repression of unpopular opinions and invasions of civil rights. Bridges' trial, a long and complex one, was on charges of perjury and conspiracy in denying at naturalization hearings that he had ever been a Communist. Two previous deportation hearings, in 1939 and 1941, had ended in the vindication of the Australian-born union leader. This time Government witnesses against Bridges included chairmen of his past defense committees and former members of the Communist central committee, as well as Bridges' rivals and enemies. The tone of Hallinan's defense was set by his opening statement, a two-day speech outlining the history of Bridges, his "unselfish and heroic efforts to better the conditions of labor," and the relentless campaign against him by powerful industrial and financial interests; he also accused the Government of fraud and corruption in the present case. Arguing frequently with the judge, whom he accused of bias and misconduct and repeatedly asked to disqualify himself, Hallinan was sentenced to six months' imprisonment for criminal contempt of court.

During the eighty court days of the trial, Hallinan succeeded in discrediting a number of witnesses. When Paul Crouch and Manning R. Johnson testified that Bridges attended the 1936 Communist convention, Hallinan disproved their statements by showing newspaper lists of those present and also affidavits that Bridges was attending an ILWU meeting on the West Coast at the time. On the other hand, several persons were found to have tampered with prosecution witnesses. On April 5, 1950, the defendants were convicted on all counts. In the following months Hallinan fought for not only their various appeals, but his own, and also filed a slander suit against the prosecutor, F. J. Donohue, and others—a suit dismissed by the court. On March 11 the Supreme Court upheld the contempt sentences for Hallinan and his junior partner James M. MacInnis; the following month Hallinan entered McNeil Island Federal Prison, Washington, to serve a six-month sentence.

In March 1952 the Progressive party nominating committee chose Hallinan and Charlotta Bass as the party's candidates for United States President and Vice-President

VINCENT HALLINAN

respectively, a selection later confirmed at the party's convention in Chicago, July 4-7. (When the Independent Progressive party was formed in 1947 under the leadership of Henry Wallace, Hallinan and his wife joined it because, as Mrs. Hallinan has explained, they felt it offered a policy of peace and hope for "economic freedom and equality.") Released from Federal prison on August 17, 1952, Hallinan opened his campaign the following Sunday at a peace rally in San Francisco in which he called for an end to the fighting in Korea and charged that the policies of the Democrats and Republicans were indistinguishable. In a speech in Chicago on September 6, carried over the television network of the National Broadcasting Company, the Presidential candidate urged the enactment of civil rights legislation and offered a program for immediate peace. "Peace, economic security, equality, and freedom are wrapped up in a single bundle . . . and that is why the Progressive party makes peace the No. 1 issue of 1952." Later that month he said that he expected to take enough votes from the Democrats in New York, California, and Michigan to "throw those States to Eisenhower." By holding the balance of power there, he explained, the Progressives could "force the Democrats to campaign on more liberal issues in the future." The Progressive party, which is expected to be on the ballot in thirty-two States, was assured a place on the ballot in New York State when on August 28, 1952, the American Labor Party nominated Hallinan for President.

Newspaper accounts have stated that Hallinan is a large investor in downtown San Francisco real estate; under the California community property law he is the half owner, but it is otherwise Mrs. Hallinan's property. In 1952 Hallinan is described by the New York Times as a millionaire; the scale of the family income is possibly indicated by the Bureau of Internal Revenue claim that he owes $134,000 in back income taxes for 1948, $97,000 for

HALLINAN, VINCENT—*Continued*
1949, and $108,000 for 1950 (New York *Times*,
March 20, 1952). The black-haired, blue-eyed
attorney is a man of rugged appearance; he
stands five feet ten and weighs about 180
pounds. The Hallinans have six athletic boys,
Patrick, Terence, Michael, Matthew, Conn, and
Daniel. Hallinan teaches his sons to be skeptical
of everything, including his own opinions.
Another of his attitudes that Mrs. Hallinan
discusses in her book is that the mere element
of danger is no reason for him, his wife, or
his children to hesitate to do anything interesting.

References

Frontier 1:6 Ap 1 '50 por

Hallinan, V. My Wild Irish Rogues
(1952)

HANDLIN, OSCAR Sept. 29, 1915- Educator; historian
Address: b. c/o Department of History, Harvard University, Cambridge 38, Mass.; h. 18
Agassiz St., Cambridge 40, Mass.

Oscar Handlin is the author of *The Uprooted*, which in May 1952 won for him the
Pulitzer Prize for "a distinguished book on
the history of the United States" published
during the preceding year. Dr. Handlin, an
associate professor of history at Harvard University, is also the author of *Boston's Immigrants* (1941), with his wife coauthor of *Commonwealth* (1947), compiler and editor of *This
Was America* (1949), and a frequent contributor to scholarly and general periodicals.

One of the three children (two sons and a
daughter) of immigrant parents, Joseph Handlin and the former Ida Janowitz, Oscar Handlin was born in Brooklyn, New York, on

OSCAR HANDLIN

September 29, 1915. He was brought up in
Brooklyn and is a 1931 graduate of the local
New Utrecht High School. Musically inclined,
he played in the high school orchestra at New
Utrecht. Subsequently, at Brooklyn College,
where he majored in history, his extracurricular activities included both music and athletics.
He completed the undergraduate course in
three years, taking his B.A. degree in 1934
and winning the Union League Award for
history. At Harvard University, at which he
registered for postgraduate study, he received
his M.A. degree in history in 1935. A Frederick Sheldon Traveling Fellowship enabled
him to devote a year to research in England,
France, Italy, and Ireland. For two years
(1937-39) he taught history at Brooklyn College before returning to Harvard in 1939 as
an instructor in the History Department and
as a candidate for the Ph.D. degree. He received the doctorate in the following year.

In speaking of his years at Harvard, Handlin
has stated that he worked with the professors
Samuel Eliot Morison, Frederick Merk, and
Arthur Meier Schlesinger. "The last-named,"
he explained, "directed my attention to the
subjects of social history that have since occupied much of my attention." It was Professor Schlesinger who suggested to Handlin
the subject of his doctoral dissertation, a study
of the late eighteenth and early nineteenth
century influx of immigrants to Boston which
"from a consideration of the society the immigrants found on arrival and left behind . . .
attempts to explore the basic factors influencing
their economic, physical, and intellectual adjustment." The thesis, with its documentation
simplified, was published in 1941 under the
title *Boston's Immigrants, 1790-1865; a Study
in Acculturation*. It was praised by Henry
Pratt Fairchild in the *American Sociological
Review* as "an excellent case study . . . of social assimilation," and by L. M. Hacker in the
New York *Herald Tribune* as "a monograph
. . . characterized by imagination as well as
learning." Later (in 1942) it was awarded
the J. H. Dunning prize of the American Historical Association as "the best work by a
young scholar" published during 1941. Handlin,
who was the recipient of the Brooklyn College
Alumni Award of Honor in the year following,
was promoted to an assistant professorship at
Harvard in 1944.

For three years ending in 1945 Dr. Handlin
and his wife, the former Mary Flug, were
occupied with the research for and writing of
*Commonwealth: a Study of the Role of Gov-
ernment in the American Economy, Massachusetts, 1774-1861*. One outgrowth of this
study was a paper by Handlin called "Laissez-
Faire Thought in Massachusetts, 1790-1880"
which appeared in the December 1943 supplement of the *Journal of Economic History*. A
grant from the committee of research in economic history of the Social Science Research
Council then made possible the completion, in
1945, of *Commonwealth* and its publication in
1947. Perry Miller of the New York *Times*
summed up the work as "an undogmatic, judicious survey that is in the best tradition of
empirical scholarship." Parts of *Common-*

wealth had previously appeared in the *Journal of Economic History* under the titles "Radicals and Conservatives in Massachusetts" and "Origins of the American Business Corporation." Also during the period of the preparation of *Commonwealth*. Handlin's participation in a program of study in American civilization instituted under Professor David Frederick Bowers at Princeton University, led to his writing the essay "The Immigrant in American Politics," which is included in Bowers' anthology *Foreign Influences in American Life; Essays and Critical Bibliographies* (1944).

It was in early 1947 that Dr. Handlin, who had meanwhile been transferred as an assistant professor to the newly formed Department of Social Science at Harvard, made the first of his several contributions to the Jewish cultural publication *Commentary*, writing on the subject "Democracy Needs an Open Door." (Among later *Commentary* articles by Dr. Handlin are "Our Unknown Jewish American Ancestors," "Prejudice and Capitalist Exploitation," and "Group Life Within the American Pattern.") With Mrs. Handlin he collaborated in 1948 on the B'nai B'rith Anti-Defamation League pamphlet *Danger in Discord*, and in September of the same year was called, as an expert on immigration, to testify before a United States Senate Judiciary subcommittee studying proposed revision of the immigration and nationalization laws. He argued that, far from having reached a saturation point in immigration, the United States faced "an actual population decline" and that it would thus be "economically advantageous" to liberalize the quota restrictions. In 1948 Dr. Handlin returned to the History Department at Harvard as an associate professor, and soon thereafter took the affirmative side in a debate sponsored by the American Historical Association at Boston on the subject "Is New England Withering?" His arguments and those of his opponent, Professor Howard Mumford Jones, were published in the *Atlantic Monthly* of April 1949.

The year 1949 also witnessed the publication of Handlin's compilation *This Was America*, a collection of writings by eighteenth, nineteenth, and early twentieth century Europeans who traveled in the United States and recorded their impressions of the American scene. Of that anthology T. R. Ybarra wrote in the New York *Times*: "This reader felt, after laying down the book, that he had been watching, from a good seat in the theater, a sequence of adroitly chosen . . . moving pictures." In the *Herald Tribune* Dumas Malone commented, "A major merit of this collection is its freshness and its scope. It will prove an invaluable supplement to the well-known accounts of America." One of Handlin's own observations on the United States appeared in an *Atlantic Monthly* contribution for January 1951, "Yearning for Security." In it he charged that the American college of today is "muggy with modest ambitions" and that the "little dreams" of its students "are not of wealth or fame or monumental accomplishments, but of bureaucrats' offices in government or the corporations."

Handlin's Pulitzer Prize-winning book in history, *The Uprooted; the Epic Story of the Great Migrations that Made the American People*, was published in October 1951. The award was announced May 5, 1952. Its author pointed out that, rather than write a history of immigration in America, he wished "to examine the social and personal implications of separation from the old cultures and involvement in a new, for the 35 million immigrants who form the basis of American population." The book, completion of which was facilitated by grants from the Social Science Research Council and the Clark-Milton Fund of Harvard University, has been described in the New York *Herald Tribune* as follows: "*The Uprooted* concerns the personal human side of the flood of immigration . . . from Europe after 1820. Mr. Handlin wrote of the European settlements from which the immigrants came, then followed through the hardships of their crossing, in steerage, and life that followed in the United States." Reviewing *The Uprooted* for the New York *Times*, Milton Rugoff recognized it as "history with a difference—the difference being its concern with men's hearts and souls, no less than an event." For Frances Witherspoon, who reviewed it for the *Herald Tribune*, the book (which is written with the general reading public in mind) possessed "great poignancy"; while the *New Yorker* deemed it "strong stuff, handled in a masterly and quite moving manner."

Scholarly, professional, and historical organizations to which Handlin belongs are the Colonial Society of Massachusetts, the Massachusetts Historical Society, American Jewish Historical Society, the American Association of University Professors, the American Historical Association, the Mississippi Valley Historical Association, the Economic History Association, and the Southern Historical Association. Among periodicals (other than those already mentioned) to which he has been a contributor are the *New England Quarterly*, *William and Mary Quarterly*, *American Historical Review*, *Partisan Review*, *Saturday Review*, *Journal of General Education*, and New York *Times Magazine*. Oscar and Mary (Flug) Handlin, who were married September 18, 1937, are the parents of two daughters, Joanna F. and Ruth B., and one son, David P. Dr. Handlin has a height of five feet seven inches and a weight of 190 pounds; he has brown eyes and black hair. His faith is the Jewish.

References

Commentary 3:1 Ja '47; 5:104 F '48
N Y Herald Tribune p16 My 6 '52
N Y Times p24 My 6 '52 por
Who's Who in New England (1949)

HANNAH, JOHN A(LFRED) Oct. 9, 1902- College president
Address: b. c/o Michigan State College, East Lansing, Mich.; h. Cowles House, 7 Faculty Row, East Lansing, Mich.

During the past two decades John A. Hannah has directed the growth of Michigan State Col-

HANNAH, JOHN A.—*Continued*

lege from its position as a relatively small institution to its present status as the twelfth largest in enrollment in the United States, one of the most attractive in physical plant, and one of the famed "Big Ten" in intercollegiate athletics. He is credited with originating the self-liquidating loan plan which made possible much of the expansion. Formerly a specialist in poultry science, Hannah came to the presidency of M.S.C. on July 1, 1941, from the Michigan State Board of Agriculture, on which he had been secretary since 1935.

Of Scotch and Irish ancestry, John Alfred Hannah was born October 9, 1902, in Grand Rapids, Michigan, to Wilfred Steele and Mary Ellen (Malone) Hannah. Hannah's two brothers (he also has a sister) are now engaged in the large florist and chicken hatchery businesses started by their father. After his graduation from Grand Rapids South High School in 1919, the youth entered Grand Rapids Junior College. For two years he studied law at the University of Michigan, but then, as *Newsweek* reported, "he visited a State fair and met some farmer friends who talked him into an agricultural career." Hannah enrolled in what was then the Michigan Agricultural College, from which he graduated in 1923 with the B.S. degree. Two years after his graduation, the name of the institution, the oldest land-grant college, was changed to Michigan State College of Agriculture and Applied Science, in the first move toward enlarging its sphere from exclusive concentration on farming and home economics.

Each of the eighty-three counties of the State of Michigan has an agricultural agent (the "county agent"), a home-demonstration agent, and a Four-H Club organizer, all financed partly by Federal funds and all holding semi-faculty status as extension specialists of Michigan State College. For ten years after graduating from Michigan State, Hannah was an extension specialist in poultry husbandry, giving lectures and demonstrations of improved practices, writing information bulletins and pamphlets, explaining the latest research findings, and generally assisting local poultrymen. He is still a member of the Academy of Poultry Science and of the Poultry Science Association and was a delegate to the World Poultry Science Association meetings in Ottawa in 1927, London in 1930, Rome in 1933 (as chairman of the United States delegation), Leipzig and Berlin in 1936, and Copenhagen in 1938. During the years from 1930 to 1939 Hannah was on the board of the International Baby Chick Association, of which he was president in 1934-35.

During 1933-34 Hannah worked for the United States Department of Agriculture and the NRA as NRA code administrator; on a leave of absence from Michigan State, he was managing agent of the Federal Hatchery Coordinating Committee, in St. Louis, Missouri, until 1935. In that year he returned to Michigan State as secretary of the State Board of Agriculture, the M.S.C. governing body. Upon the retirement of Robert S. Shaw from the

M.S.C. presidency, Hannah succeeded him on July 1, 1941.

As board secretary and then as president, Hannah has been regarded as "the human dynamo behind State's spectacular growth" from a 3,300-student school in 1930 to a 16,000-student liberal and applied arts college with one of the country's most impressive campuses in 1950. During the depression year of 1930, when building was at a standstill and the college was faced with decreased appropriations, he devised the self-liquidating loan plan which enabled the institution to expand its plant without cost to the State. He obtained from a Detroit bank an unsecured loan of $413,380 at 6 per cent for the construction of women's dormitories, to be repaid from the earnings of the buildings. In 1936, on the same self-liquidating basis, M.S.C. began work on nine new major buildings at a cost of about five million dollars (they are now valued at twice that sum). With 45 per cent of the funds furnished by the Public Works Administration, Hannah floated self-liquidating loans for the remainder to erect a large auditorium, health center, music and art building, field house, and other dormitories, which are being paid for by athletic receipts, concert tickets, medical fees, auditorium rentals, and the like. During Hannah's first year as president, the interest on the loan was reduced from 6 per cent to 1½ per cent through refinancing.

On the same terms President Hannah in 1946 borrowed $18,700,000, which he expects to be amortized by 1961. The new self-liquidating buildings—identified by signs reading "Constructed Without Expense to the Public"—include many dormitories, eleven low-rent apartment buildings for the faculty, a 51,000-seat stadium, hotel rooms for visitors, bowling alleys, a barbershop, cafeterias, lounges, and offices. By 1950 the M.S.C. building program had reached the $31 millions mark, of which one-third was self-liquidating and the remaining two-thirds, spent for classroom, laboratory, and library facilities, was provided by State and Federal funds. Five thousand acres remained for future expansion.

Keeping pace with its physical expansion, M.S.C. enlarged the number of its courses so that by 1950 it offered undergraduate degrees in seventy fields and graduate degrees in sixty, in addition to special short courses attended by 100,000 people a year and extension work that included publications with a yearly circulation of a million. In 1944 Hannah introduced what is called the "basic college," a curriculum under which all students are required to devote their first two years at M.S.C. to at least five of seven comprehensive courses covering broad areas. "The most significant part of the program," President Hannah pointed out in *Michigan Education Journal* (April 1945), "is the approach in each course—the subject matter is presented with the individual student as the center of interest, and all of the impacts of the field upon him and his life are explored from the center out in all directions. . . . It is hoped to sort out as early as possible those students who are not fitted for four-year specialized courses, directing them into two-year-term curricula . . . so that they may leave after two years, not as failures, but as persons who have completed the comprehensive core courses, and with training as technicians in some field." The basic college program, which has attracted many students from out of the State, is said to have wide appeal for boys not planning to enter a profession, and, reported a *Saturday Evening Post* article, "Many educators believe [it] turns out more-rounded, better-informed students than a formal curriculum." In February 1951, Hannah announced the inauguration of a year-round study program, requested by the Defense Department, which would make students available for military service or defense work a year earlier by enabling them to obtain a degree in three calendar years.

An enthusiastic sports fan and regular attendant at M.S.C. football games, Hannah was also interested in furthering the college's athletic activities. In 1939, when the University of Chicago withdrew from intercollegiate football competition, Hannah, as related by Stanley Frank in the *Saturday Evening Post*, "began taking dead aim" at membership in the "Big Ten" Western Conference, a membership which carried much prestige and added an estimated $250,000 a year to the members' gate receipts. The opportunity came when Chicago withdrew from the Big Ten in 1946. In order to win the Conference seat, in February 1949 the college suspended the 125 Jenison and Gunston athletic scholarships which, according to Stanley Frank, had "brought M.S.C. most of its outstanding performers." Michigan State College was elected to membership in the Big Ten on May 20, 1949, a year in which its football budget was $120,000 and its football receipts, after taxes, were $409,207.14. Because the conference football schedules are drawn up four years in advance, the M.S.C. Spartans will not appear in Big Ten football until 1953, but their participation in the other intercollegiate sports began immediately. In November 1951 Hannah was appointed chairman of a ten-man committee of college presidents called upon to make recommendations to the American Council of Education in connection with recent scandals in intercollegiate athletics. Among the measures advocated in the committee's report were eliminating bowl games and postseason tournaments, abolishing athletic scholarships, adopting stricter controls on recruiting players, excluding freshmen from varsity competition, and limiting the practice and playing seasons.

Hannah has received honorary doctorates from M.S.C., the University of Michigan, and the University of the Ryukyus, a "baby university" on Okinawa "adopted" by M.S.C.; and Epsilon Sigma Phi has bestowed on him its Certificate of Recognition. A member of the national committee on Boys and Girls Club Work, he has been awarded a citation for outstanding service to 4-H. In 1941-42 he served on the Michigan State Council of Defense and War Board, and he has been a director of the Lansing Community Chest since 1938. President of the Association of Land-Grant Colleges and Universities in 1948-49, he was the chair-

Michigan State College

JOHN A. HANNAH

man of its executive committee from 1949 to 1951. Hannah is active in the American Council of Education and serves on the Government's Point Four International Development Advisory Board. In the business world, he is a director of the Michigan Bell Telephone Company, was chairman of the board in 1951, and is board chairman of the Federal Reserve Bank of Chicago's Detroit Branch.

On June 22, 1938, Hannah married Sarah May Shaw, daughter of M.S.C.'s former president. Their four children are Mary Elisabeth, Robert Wilfred, Thomas Arthur, and David Harold. Hannah's religious affiliation is Episcopal; in politics he is a supporter of Republican candidate Dwight Eisenhower. The Greek-letter societies which carry his name on their rolls are Phi Kappa Phi, Sigma Delta Chi, Pi Kappa Delta, and Alpha Phi Omega. He is a Mason and a Rotarian and belongs also to the University Club of Detroit and New York, the Detroit Athletic, and the Country Club of Lansing. With a weight of 190 pounds, Hannah stands six feet one inch tall; he has blue eyes and graying black hair. *Time* said of the informal and energetic educator that when he became president of M.S.C. he ordered the removal of the door to his office so that everyone would feel free to go in for a talk.

References

Country Gentleman 11:8 Jl '41
N Y Times p66 N 27 '49
Newsweek 17:54 Je 6 '41
Sat Eve Post 223:30 O 14 '50 por
Time 55:38 Ap 10 '50 por
American Men of Science (1949)
Leaders in Education (1948)
Who's Who in America, 1952-53
Who's Who in American Education, 1951-52
World Biography (1948)

HARDING, ALLAN FRANCIS *See* Harding, Sir J.

HARDING, SIR JOHN Oct. 2, 1896- British Army officer

Address: b. c/o War Office, Whitehall, S.W. 1, London, England; h. Lower Farm, Nether Compton, Dorset, England.

General Sir John Harding was named chief of the British Imperial General Staff (equivalent to the United States Army Chief of Staff) to assume office when Sir William Slim retires from that position on November 1, 1952. Prior to receiving this three-year appointment Harding had served eighteen months as commander

British Inf. Services

GEN. SIR JOHN HARDING

of the British Army of the Rhine. Before that he had held commands in Italy, England, and the Far East. A veteran of both World Wars, he won the Military Cross in the first and three times earned the Distinguished Service Order in the second. In 1943 Harding commanded the famed "Desert Rats" in their advance from El Alamein to Tripoli; as chief of staff to General Sir Harold Alexander in Italy, he has been credited with making the plans that secured Rome's capture in June 1944. Harding became the first military Governor of the Free City of Trieste in 1946.

Francis E. and Elizabeth Ellen (Anstice) Harding gave the name Allan Francis Harding to their son, born October 2, 1896, but in 1944 he legally assumed the prename John and dropped both of his other Christian names. Reared in Compton Way, South Petherton, Somerset, where he was born, the boy completed his secondary education at the nearby Ilminster Grammar School in 1912. Later he joined the Territorial Army (the British home guard) and when World War I began in 1914,

he was called to regular army duty. The next year he received a second lieutenant's commission in the Somerset Light Infantry, with which he served with distinction in the Gallipoli and the Egyptian campaigns and gained mention in dispatches; he was wounded twice and was awarded the Military Cross. After a period of duty in the final year of World War I (1918) as a staff officer with the Egyptian Expeditionary Force, he spent several months in 1919 as an acting lieutenant colonel with the Machine Gun Corps.

In the permanent rank of first lieutenant, Harding in 1920 rejoined the Somerset Light Infantry and for three years (1922-25) was regiment adjutant. Following his advancement to captain in 1923, he was sent to the staff college, from which he was graduated in 1928. For the months December 1934 to January 1935 Harding served as a brigade major in Great Britain's unit of an international military force that had been sent to keep order during the Saar plebiscite. Breveted as major in 1935, Harding was assigned the next year to the War Office in London. A brevet lieutenant colonel by 1938, the second of his three years at Whitehall, Harding became a regular lieutenant colonel in 1939.

When World War II began Harding was stationed in India commanding the First Battalion of the Somerset Light Infantry. In October 1939 he was transferred to the Middle East as a staff officer and in the summer of 1940 he was created a Commander of the Order of the British Empire. Early in 1941 Harding was advanced to brigadier and in December of that year he was awarded the Distinguished Service Order for service in the Middle East from February to July 1941. Having been promoted to major general in January 1942, Harding the following September was named commander of the 7th Armored Division (the "Desert Rats"). He led this group in a three-month advance from El Alamein to Tripoli; then, on January 19, 1943, while observing the enemy from atop a tank, Harding was wounded severely by a shell.

Harding's next appointment was in March 1944 when he became chief of staff to General Sir Harold Alexander, commander of the British 8th Army in Italy, who later credited Harding with laying the plans which in June 1944 made the capture of Rome possible. Shortly afterward King George VI visited the Mediterranean front and June 16 created Harding a Knight Commander of the Bath in recognition of "gallant and distinguished service" in Italy. By the end of World War II, Lieutenant General Sir John Harding, who commanded the British 13th Corps during the final battles in Italy, had added two bars to his Distinguished Service Order, indicating that he had won this honor on three separate occasions. When hostilities ceased he headed the occupation forces in Venezia Giulia, subsequently being named the first military Governor of the Free City of Trieste.

As commander of the British Central Mediterranean Force (appointed in late 1946), Harding in July 1947 commuted to life imprisonment the death sentence for German Field Marshal

Albert Kesselring. Later the same year he began a two-year tour of duty in England as head general of the Southern Command, and while occupying this position he crossed the Atlantic as an army exchange lecturer under the Kermit Roosevelt Memorial Fund. In the United States he spoke at West Point, the National War College, and the Fort Leavenworth Command and General Staff School. Promoted to full general in 1949, Harding was reassigned in February of that year to overall command of the British Far East Land Forces, with headquarters in Singapore, a post which he held until being placed in command of the British Army of the Rhine in March 1951. General Harding was advanced to the rank of Knight Grand Cross of the Order of the Bath through the King's birthday honors of June 6, 1951. Foreign honors conferred on the British soldier include the United States Legion of Merit and the French Legion of Honor and the Croix de Guerre.

On May 26, 1952, the War Office announced that General Harding would succeed Field Marshal Sir William Slim on November 1, 1952, as Chief of the Imperial General Staff, an appointment said to have been recommended by Field Marshal Montgomery and widely approved in the London press. The *Observer* commented that General Harding resembled Montgomery in two respects: "He has first the very same gift for capturing the imagination of troops . . . [and] second, he has a Montgomery-like talent for reducing complex problems to their essentials." Before relinquishing his post as commanding general of the Army of the Rhine to Lieutenant General Sir Richard N. Gale, General Harding planned the British Army joint war maneuvers in Germany with Belgian and Netherlands units. On September 15, 1952, the day before the combined ground and air exercise (involving 200,000 Allied soldiers and air men) was launched, Harding explained that the purpose of the test was to show how an attack from the east could be stopped and the enemy dealt "damaging blows." In preparation for his new position, during August he had inspected Suez Canal zone military installations.

Lady Harding is the former Mary Gertrude Mabel Rooke, daughter of the late J. Wilson Rooke of Knutsford, Cheshire. The Hardings were married April 4, 1927, and have one son, John Charles. General Harding is a member of the Church of England and of the Conservative Party. The general has blue eyes and brown hair; he has only two fingers on his left hand because three were blown off during World War II. He has been described in a British Information Service release as "a short dapper figure, always neat in his dress, with a close-cropped sandy mustache, and a friendly twinkle in his eye." The article goes on to explain that "his sharp, slightly nasal speech can cut sharp and deep when he pounces upon careless, slovenly work [for] he insists on efficiency, first of all in himself." *Newsweek* has described him as an "electric little man, only slightly taller than Napoleon's supposed five feet two inches." Harding, who enjoys outdoor recreations—his favorites being hunting, shoot-ing, polo, and gardening—remarked upon hearing of his new appointment (according to *Newsweek*): "I hope I don't have to live in London."

References

N Y Herald Tribune p4 My 27 '52 por
N Y Times p12 My 27 '52 por
Newsweek 39:38+ Je 9 '52
Observer (London) Je 1 '52
Kelly's Handbok of the Titled, Landed and Official Classes (1952)
Who's Who, 1952
World Biography (1948)

HARNONCOURT, RENÉ D'   *See* D'Harnoncourt, R.

HARRISON, WILLIAM K(ELLY), JR.
Sept. 7, 1895- United States Army officer
Address: b. c/o Department of the Army, The Pentagon, Washington 25, D.C.

General William K. Harrison, Jr., who on May 19, 1952, succeeded Vice-Admiral C. Turner Joy as senior delegate of the United Nations at the truce meetings at Panmunjom, Korea, has been since December 1951 the deputy commander of the Eighth Army in that country. Harrison was graduated from West Point in 1917 and served in the cavalry until 1932, when he entered the General Staff School. After World War II, during which he was assistant commander of the 30th Infantry Division, he served under General Douglas MacArthur in the Japanese occupation from August 1946 to February 1949.

The birthplace of William Kelly Harrison, Jr., is Washington, D.C.; his birth date is September 7, 1895. The future general was graduated seventy-third in his class of 139 from the United States Military Academy on April 20, 1917, with the degree of Bachelor of Science, and commissioned a second lieutenant. (Among his classmates were Generals Matthew Ridgway, J. Lawton Collins, and Mark Clark.) He commenced his military career with the 1st Cavalry at Camp Lawrence J. Hearn, California, and at Douglas, Arizona, being promoted to first lieutenant on May 15, 1917, and temporary captain on August 5, 1917. At the end of a period of duty (August 1918-May 1919) at the Military Academy, he was sent to France, where he remained until August 1919 in order to study French. In the rank of permanent captain, dating from April 22, 1920, he visited Spain to learn that country's language. Returning then to the United States, he taught at West Point until August 1922, when he entered the Cavalry School at Fort Riley, Kansas, finishing his course in May 1923.

Harrison next reported for duty with the 7th Cavalry at Fort Bliss, Texas. At that post he remained until November 1925, when he was sent to the Philippine Islands to serve with the 26th Cavalry School at Camp Stotsenburg. His following assignment, in December 1927, took

U. S. Air Force

MAJ. GEN. WILLIAM K. HARRISON, JR.

him back to Fort Riley, to 2d Cavalry. On completing an advanced course at the Cavalry School there in June 1929, he remained as a member of the 9th Cavalry and the Cavalry Board. In August 1932 Harrison entered the Command and General Staff School at Fort Leavenworth, Kansas, becoming an instructor after being graduated in June 1934. He was promoted to major on November 1, 1932. His next training was at the Army War College from July 1937 to April 1938; and on the latter date he reported for duty with the 6th Cavalry at Fort Oglethorpe, Georgia. In July 1939 Harrison became chief of one of the sections in the War Plans Division of the General Staff of the War Department; he received the title of deputy chief of the Strategic Plans and Policy Group when the War Plans Division became the Operations Division in March 1942.

In June 1942 Harrison, given the temporary rank of brigadier general, became assistant commander of the 78th Infantry Division at Camp Butner, North Carolina. A few months later, in October, he was transferred to the 30th Infantry Division as assistant commander, continuing to head that division when in February 1944 it was sent overseas for service in England and on the Continent. The New York Herald Tribune stated that Harrison was admired by his men because he would appear in the vanguard of the fighting with a tommy gun in his hand. It was during action in France that the General was wounded. He was appointed commander of the 2d Infantry Division in Czechoslovakia, on June 2, 1945, later returned to the United States with this division, and was relieved as commanding general on September 10, 1945, to become assistant commander. In April 1946 Harrison was placed in command of the 38th Regimental Combat Team at Camp Carson, Colorado, for mountain and winter warfare training; and

he was appointed as head of Camp Carson in May 1946.

Service under General Douglas MacArthur with the occupation troops in Japan was his next assignment. He was ordered to duty in that country in August 1946 and on November 3, 1946, was appointed Executive for Administrative Affairs and Reparations at the General Headquarters of the Supreme Commander for the Allied Powers. Harrison's rank as brigadier general was approved as permanent January 24, 1948. On May 14, 1948, he became chief of the Reparations Section, in addition to being responsible for other duties. General Harrison on February 1, 1949, became chief of the Army-Airforce Troop Information and Education Division in the Office of the Chief of Staff, and he remained in that post when the group was renamed the Armed Forces Information and Education Division upon its being transferred on September 1, 1950, to the Office of the Secretary of Defense. His next orders made him commander of the 9th Infantry Training Division at Fort Dix, New Jersey. Meanwhile, on March 1, 1949, he received the temporary rank of major general, with date of rank from December 18, 1944, a grade which was made permanent on April 29, 1952.

In December 1951 General Harrison was named Deputy Commander of the Eighth Army in Korea, and on January 24, 1952, he was appointed by General Ridgway as a replacement for Major General Claude B. Ferenbaugh on the Korean Armistice Delegation under the United Nations command. In that duty he also cooperated with Major General Howard M. Turner of the Air Force on subdelegation proceedings. He retained his post as deputy commander of the Eighth Army when, on May 19, 1952, Vice-Admiral C. Turner Joy, upon leaving Korea to become superintendent of the Naval Academy, chose Harrison as his successor. Commentators remarked upon the possible underlying cause for the change—U.N. decision that little was left to be discussed at Panmunjom and that the Allied forces would stand firm on their previous proposals.

The one remaining issue before the armistice delegations was the repatriation of prisoners held by the U.N. forces. The Chinese and North Koreans had refused to accept as valid an Allied investigation which showed that a good percentage (62,000 of the 132,000 prisoners) would forcibly resist return to the Communists. The Communists maintained that the Geneva Convention (which they had not accepted) gave them the right to demand the return (by force, if necessary) of all prisoners, while Harrison opposed the use of force and the disregarding of the wishes of the prisoners. When the Chinese-North Koreans rejected a U.N. offer to allow Communist officials to participate in a joint rescreening of the prisoners following the armistice, the Allied command declared that the Communist's attitude was based upon reluctance to make it publicly known that many of their personnel would struggle against repatriation. General Harrison said that the riots on Koje Island were schemes to divert world attention from this fact. As the daily meetings did not produce a solution, in mid-June 1952 the U.N. delegation, stating that its proposal was "final and unalterable," announced it would not appear again for a meeting until June 21. As the end of the month neared, the situation remained unchanged.

General Harrison has been given the Distinguished Service Cross, Distinguished Service Medal, Legion of Merit, Silver Star, Bronze Star Medal with one Oak Leaf Cluster, and the Purple Heart. Among his decorations from foreign governments are the French Legion of Honor and Medal of Reconnaissance, as well as the Netherlands Order of Orange Nassau. He has contributed articles to military journals.

Described by the New York *Times* as "deeply religious," General Harrison, a Baptist lay evangelist, often preaches at army religious services. He frowns on the habits of drinking, smoking, and swearing. His favorite pastime in Korea is horseshoe pitching.

References

N Y Herald Tribune II p1 My 25 '52 por
N Y Times p1 My 20 '52 por
N Y World-Telegram p13 My 24 '52 por
Time 59:24 Je 2 '52 por
Who's Who in America, 1952-53

HARVEY, E(DMUND) NEWTON Nov. 25, 1887- Biologist; college professor

Address: b. c/o Biology Department, Princeton University, Princeton, N.J.; h. 48 Cleveland Lane, Princeton, N.J.

E. Newton Harvey, in 1952 president of the International Society for Cellular Biology, is known for his studies of the luminescence in living things, observed in the field and at his Princeton University laboratories. His discovery, said William L. Laurence of the New York *Times*, may lead to a new age of chemical illumination. The Princeton biologist has written three books and numerous articles on that subject, as well as other studies in biological research. His work in decompression sickness during World War II brought him a citation.

On his father's side the biologist is the grandson of Irish immigrant David Harvey, who arrived in the United States in 1808; and on his mother's, he is a direct descendant, through eight generations, of the English-born Richard Newton who settled in Massachusetts in 1638. Born in Philadelphia, Pennsylvania, on November 25, 1887, Edmund Newton Harvey is the only son of William and Althea Ann (Newton) Harvey; the other children of the family were three half-sisters. William Harvey, who was a manufacturer, died when his son was six years old. As a student at the Germantown (Pennsylvania) Academy, a preparatory school, young Harvey gave much of his spare time to collecting animals and insects and to chemical experimentation. "I was apparently born with an interest in science which showed early in life," he has remarked. After his 1905 graduation from the academy, he entered the University of Pennsylvania, where, as a biology major, he received a num-

E. NEWTON HARVEY

ber of prizes. His fraternity is Sigma Xi. After he received his Bachelor of Science degree in 1909, Harvey was enabled by scholarships to complete his graduate work in biology at Columbia University. The dissertation he submitted for the doctorate he received in 1911 was *Studies on the Permeability of Cells*.

In 1911 Harvey joined the staff of Princeton University as an instructor in physiology. Promoted to assistant professor in 1915, he held that rank for four years before becoming a full professor. In 1933 he was named Henry Fairfield Osborn Professor of Biology at Princeton, the chair he continues to hold in 1952. As visiting lecturer, Harvey has taught biology at the Massachusetts Institute of Technology (1940-41), the Instituto de Biofisica in Rio de Janeiro (1946), and in Switzerland under the auspices of the Swiss-American Foundation for Scientific Exchange (1949).

Part of Harvey's research has been concerned with cell permeability, nerve conduction, regulation in plants, ultrasonic radiation, cell surface tension, decompression sickness, wound ballistics, and brain potentials. On the last subject he worked in collaboration with A. L. Loomis and Garret A. Hobart 3d. Speaking of "an objective method of investigating activity of the brain" by electrical wave-length recordings, Harvey summarized some of their findings in *Science* magazine in an article entitled "Cerebral States During Sleep as Studied by Human Brain Potentials." Another study by Harvey, "Electrical Potentials of the Human Brain," was contributed to G. A. Baitsell's series, *Science in Progress*.

The major part of Harvey's researches has been in the field of bioluminescence—his first important contribution to this field was summarized in *Science* in 1916, "The Mechanism of Light Producing in Animals." Basing his research at that time on work done by the French

HARVEY, E. NEWTON—*Continued*

professor Raphael Dubois and others, Harvey spoke of this light-producing mechanism, luciferase.

Contributor of more than 200 papers on scientific subjects to reviews, Harvey has written for *Scientific Monthly, Nature Magazine, Scientific American, Smithsonian Report, Mentor, Scientia,* and *Natural History,* among others. He is an associate editor of the *Review of Science and Industry,* the *Biological Bulletin, Biological Abstracts,* the *Journal of Cellular and Comparative Physiology,* the *Survey of Biological Progress,* and the *Review of Scientific Instruments.* A textbook by him is *Laboratory Directions in General Physiology* (1933). He has spoken on bioluminescence in a CBS *Science Service Radio Talk.* In a contribution to W. Weaver's volume, *The Scientists Speak,* Harvey discussed the relative values of pure and practical science: "The motive is curiosity and I have one hope, that the direction of research will never suppress the innate desire to explore the unknown, no matter how unexpected the search may seem."

In 1913-14 Harvey was a member of the Carnegie Institution Expedition to the Great Barrier Reef; other travels have taken him to Europe, Japan, China, the Philippine Islands, the East Indies, Australia, India, New Zealand, the South Seas, and the West Indies. The biologist, who was engaged in scientific research for the United States Government during World War I, was a member of the subcommittee on decompression sickness of the Committee on Aviation Medicine and of the Committee on Wound Ballistics of the Committee on Medical Research during World War II; for his work on decompression sickness he received an Army's Certificate of Merit in 1948. Other honors bestowed on him are the John Price Wetherill Medal of the Franklin Institute of Philadelphia (1934) and the Rumford Medal of the American Academy of Arts and Sciences (1947), in recognition of his research in bioluminescence. The Government of Brazil in 1946 named him an officer of the Order of the Southern Cross (Ordem Nacional do Cruzeiro do Sul). In 1951 Harvey was the recipient of an honorary D.Sc. degree from Johns Hopkins University.

Harvey is president of the International Society for Cellular Biology, of which he was vice-president from 1947 to 1950. He is a trustee of the Bermuda Biological Station for Research, and a vice-president and trustee of the Marine Biological Laboratory at Woods Hole, Massachusetts. Scientific societies to which Harvey belongs are: the American Association for the Advancement of Science, the American Society of Naturalists, the American Society of Biological Chemists, the American Physiological Society, the Society of Experimental Biology and Medicine, the American Society of Zoologists, the Society of General Physiology, the Growth Society, the Society of American Bacteriologists, the Botanical Society of America, the New York Academy of Sciences, and the National Academy of Sciences. He is also a member of the National

Geographic Society, the American Association of University Professors, and the American Philosophical Society. In the National Research Council he is assigned to the committee on luminescence and deuterium, and to the committee on growth.

Professor Harvey is a Republican. His marriage to Ethel Nicholson Browne took place March 12, 1916. Mrs. Harvey and their elder son, Edmund Newton, Jr., are both listed in *American Men of Science,* she for her distinguished work in biology and he for his work in physical chemistry. The other son, Richard Bennet, is a physician. The biologist is slightly over six feet tall, weighs 190 pounds, and has gray eyes and black hair. His hobbies are tennis, travel, and music.

References

American Association for the Advancement of Science Directory (1940-48)
American Men of Science (1949)
International Who's Who, 1951
Who's Who in America, 1950-51
Who's Who in American Education, 1947-48
Who's Who in the East (1951)
World Biography (1948)

HASKELL, WILLIAM N(AFEW) Aug. 13, 1878—Aug. 13, 1952 Former Army officer; director of relief organization; following graduation from West Point in 1901 served in the Philippine Islands, the United States, and Europe; directed Allied relief programs in Russia and the Balkans after World War I; commanded New York National Guard (1926-40); retired from the Army in 1942 with rank of lieutenant general; executive director of CARE relief organization (1945-47). See *Current Biography,* 1947

Obituary

N Y Times p23 Ag 14 '52

HAVILL, EDWARD Nov. 29, 1907- Author

Address: b. c/o William Sloane Associates, Inc., 119 W. 57th St., New York 19; h. R. D. 1, Bluff Point, N. Y.

Reprinted from the *Wilson Library Bulletin,* Jan. 1952.

Edward Havill, a New York State regional novelist, believes that "the identity of a writer, if it is worth anything, must be found within the body of his work." Certainly his earliest novels, *Tell It to the Laughing Stars* (1942) and *The Low Road* (1944), were regarded as autobiographical by some critics. Virginia Kirkus called the latter "a suspiciously autobiographical portrayal which is for a limited market." Margaret Wallace in the New York *Times* regarded the other as "a first novel of unusual fervor and sincerity, written with self-conscious beauty of style and with what sometimes strikes one as deliberate eccentricity of manner. It may not be autobiographical, and probably is not so in literal detail, but the reader will find himself automatically identifying the hero Steve Lanely with the author Edward Havill." *The Pinnacle,* published early in 1951, is more detached in its portrayal of personal relations, though set in the grape-growing country which the novelist knows well from personal experience.

Edward Havill was born November 29, 1907, Rochester, New York, one of the two sons of Frederick Morse Havill, a hardware merchant of English descent—a great-grandfather was educated in England as a doctor and was one of the first physicians to settle in Rochester— and Anna Magdalen (Weingartner) Havill, of German stock. Edward graduated at nineteen from the East High School. While in school he did part-time work for the Rochester *Journal-American* and in various libraries. Some of his schoolmates were also interested in writing, notably Jerre Mangione (author of *Mount Allegro*). Inspired by Thoreau, Whitman, and Sherwood Anderson, Havill took to the woods without delay as a winter caretaker in the Adirondacks near Old Forge and a landscape gardener and vineyard worker at Tryon, North Carolina, for several years, followed by a summer on Buzzards Bay, near New Bedford, Massachusetts.

After his marriage to Anna Margaret Nasset in May 1940, Havill and his wife, who was of Dakota pioneer stock, went to Keuka Lake, Penn Yan, New York, where they built a cabin. Three boys were born here, Eric, Mark, and Steven, all of them in 1952 in grade school. The Havills lived in West Branch, Keuka, for ten years, the head of the family busy with writing, farming, vineyard-working, and house-painting.

They spent four months in Willmar, Minnesota, and Dickinson, North Dakota, harvesting and absorbing local color for Havill's historical novel, *Big Ember* (1947), which was published in England two years later and is scheduled for publication in Norway. Describing frontier life in a section of southern Minnesota, settled by a group of Norwegians in 1862, it ends with a devastating raid by the Sioux Indians. Critics praised the novel for its sincerity and authenticity. Joseph Henry Jackson wrote in the San Francisco *Chronicle:* "What makes *Big Ember* a genuinely good novel is the author's understanding of what he's getting at. . . . He has a quiet, good feeling for the great grassy sweeps, the fine black soil, the beautiful lakes of the Minnesota country." Virginia Kirkus thought it "a sincere, simple, often moving account," while a reviewer in the *New Yorker* wrote that "there is something warm and fresh in his chronicle of decent, self-reliant people taking root in a new land."

Havill's first short story was published in the English *Adelphi* in 1939. Others appeared in *Story, Harper's Bazaar*—one of these, "The Kill," was reprinted in the 1940 *O. Henry Memorial Prize Stories,* winning third prize— the *Yale Review, Mademoiselle,* and *Redbook.*

EDWARD HAVILL

Tell It to the Laughing Stars and *The Low Road* had similar settings, a farm on the shores of a northern New York lake, and similar characters, young married couples adjusting to each other and their neighbors. Of *The Low Road,* Herbert Kupferberg wrote in the New York *Herald Tribune Weekly Book Review* that "Mr. Havill conveys to the reader the beauty which Clay Treman and his wife, Karen, find in one another, in their child, and in the life they lead. . . . When it comes to describing his countryside and the people who live in it, Mr. Havill is at his best."

The Pinnacle, his latest novel, is set in the grape country of upstate New York and deals with the love of two men for the same woman. The Chicago *Tribune* found it "a rich and vital book that merits wide readership," and J. H. Jackson wrote of it in the San Francisco *Chronicle* that "Mr. Havill understands the farmer and the grape-grower, and his picture of the countryside, its hills and its vines, its gray lakes and the fishing, its woods and deer, the grapes and the wine-making and the rest— all this adds up to a regional reflection-in-fiction which is exceptionally convincing and transparently true."

Brown-haired and hazel-eyed, an inch under six feet in height and weighing 160 pounds, the writer is in fine physical trim. Besides the authors who were his first inspiration, Havill likes Dreiser, Hemingway, Steinbeck, Wolfe, Hardy, and Shakespeare. He is in 1952 writing a factual book about his life at Keuka and another novel on the Dakota settlers. Like the hero of *The Low Road,* he sometimes reminds himself that "it is easy to lose yourself in the vastness of accumulated language, if you forget the original need that began it all, the necessity and longing of life to make itself heard among the winds of chance."

HAWKINS, HARRY C(ALVIN) Mar. 25, 1894- Educator; foreign trade expert

Address: b. c/o Fletcher School of Law and Diplomacy, Tufts College, Medford 55, Mass.

In January 1952 Harry C. Hawkins, then director of the State Department's Foreign Service Institute, was named as the first appointee to the William L. Clayton chair of international finance at the Fletcher School of Law and Diplomacy at Tufts College. An international trade expert and career diplomat, he had been associated with the State Department for some twenty-five years. As chief of its

Wide World Photos
HARRY C. HAWKINS

divisions of trade agreements (1936-40) and commercial policy (1941-44), he was a key negotiator in the reciprocal trade agreements program of former Secretary of State Cordell Hull. In 1944 Hawkins became director of the Department's Office of Economic Affairs, and later that year was assigned as economic counselor to the American Embassy in London, in which position he had an important role in the formation of the International Trade Organization.

Born in Reed City, Michigan, on March 25, 1894, Harry Calvin Hawkins is one of the five children (three sons and two daughters) of Harvey W. and Nettie (Thompson) Hawkins. His father owned a general store in Reed City, where young Harry graduated from secondary school in 1912. Entering Olivet (Michigan) College, he began majoring in English but later changed to economics. As an undergraduate he played football and helped support himself by various jobs as a waiter and as a motion picture machine operator, and by working in a laundry agency. His education was interrupted by World War I, during which he served overseas as a first lieutenant in the in-

fantry from 1917 to 1919. In the latter year he returned to Olivet College, which then granted him a B.A. degree (as of 1917). He was encouraged to go on to graduate work in business administration by Robert Jackson Ray, who was at that time professor of economics and business administration and a dean at Olivet. After studying at the University of Michigan in the summer of 1919, Hawkins entered the Harvard Graduate School of Business Administration in the fall. Two years later he received his M.B.A. degree from that institution, having written his thesis on the exchange problems of Argentina, Brazil, and Chile.

Hawkins began his career in 1921 as a special agent in the Transportation Division of the Department of Commerce, in Washington, D.C. The following year he joined the faculty of the University of Virginia as an assistant professor, teaching foreign trade subjects. On October 16, 1924, he was appointed a Foreign Service officer, thus entering the Department of State. There he became a drafting officer dealing with shipping questions and working on commercial treaties. He interrupted his Federal service to accept a professorship in business administration at the University of Oregon in September 1925. Two years later he rejoined the State Department as a drafting officer, remaining there until 1930, when he again began a year of teaching at Oregon.

In August 1931 Hawkins returned to the State Department as a divisional assistant in the Treaty Division. As technical adviser to the United States delegation, he attended the International Monetary and Economic Conference in London in the summer of 1933. He was appointed assistant chief of the State Department's Division of Trade Agreements in May 1935, and on August 1 of the next year succeeded Henry F. Grady as chief of this division, which had charge of the Administration's reciprocal trade treaty program, under the leadership of Cordell Hull, then Secretary of State. After bearing the "main burden" through thirty months of negotiation, according to *Business Week*, Hawkins was "primarily responsible" for the successful concluion of the trade agreements signed with Great Britain and Canada in 1938. He was made chief of the Division of Commercail Treaties and Agreements in July 1940, and continued in the same capacity when it became the Division of Commercial Policy and Agreements in 1941. In the summer of that year he was United States participant in the first International Wheat Conference in Washington. Charged with responsibility "for matters of foreign policy involved in the negotiation of lend-lease agreements," the Division of Commercial Policy and Agreements was also charged with "supervising the formulation, negotiation, and administration of commercial treaties of the United States and international agreements affecting the commercial relations of this country; and with cooperating in the formulation of the international commercial policy of the Government." Hawkins held membership on the Board of Economic Operations of the State Department (1941-43); on the interdepartmental Committee for Reciprocity Information

(1941-44) ; and, as an alternate, on the Inter-American Financial and Economic Advisory Committee (1942-44).

Following the reorganization of the State Department, Hawkins in January 1944 was made director of its Office of Economic Affairs. This office, which included the divisions of commercial policy, financial and monetary affairs, labor relations, commodities, and petroleum, had the responsibility of initiating and coordinating policy and action in all matters pertaining to international economic affairs other than those of a wartime character. From June to September of that year he was also vice-chairman of the Executive Committee on Economic Foreign Policy. On September 12, 1944, Hawkins was assigned to the Foreign Service as economic counselor at the American Embassy in London to "assist Ambassador Winant in dealing with economic matters of a long-range character." He remained in this post for the next three years, attaining the rank of Minister in 1945.

Serving under Clair Wilcox, Hawkins was vice-chairman of the United States delegation to the London meeting, in the fall of 1946, of the Preparatory Committee, which had been established by the United Nations Economic and Social Council, to draw up the agenda for a proposed international conference on trade and employment. This committee, working on the basis of a suggested draft charter put forward by the United States, had completed at its second session in Geneva in the summer of 1947 a draft charter that was presented for consideration at the United Nations Conference on Trade and Employment, which opened in Havana, Cuba, on November 21, 1947. Hawkins attended this conference as the principal United States delegate. At its conclusion in March 1948 the text of the Havana Charter, creating the International Trade Organization (ITO) as a specialized agency of the U.N., was adopted by representatives of fifty-three nations. The charter, which Wilcox called "the most comprehensive international agreement in history," was then referred to the various governments for ratification. The ITO will come into being when the charter has been accepted by the governments of twenty countries.

It was announced in November 1947 that Hawkins had been named professor of international economic relations at the Fletcher School of Law and Diplomacy, in Medford, Massachusetts. This graduate school of international affairs is administered by Tufts College in cooperation with Harvard University. Early the next year, after Hawkins had accepted the appointment, General George C. Marshall, then Secretary of State, described Hawkins departure as "a significant loss to the Government." "Yours is a record of outstanding distinction," General Marshall's statement continued.

On December 1, 1949, Hawkins was appointed to succeed Dr. William P. Maddox as director of the State Department's Foreign Service Institute, a post he took over the following month. Established in 1947, the Institute develops educational and training policies and programs for departmental and Foreign Service personnel (from Class 6 vice-consuls up to Ambassadors), and for other Federal employees requiring instruction in the field of foreign relations. The training school gives a basic three-month orientation course required of all newly appointed Foreign Service officers before going into the field and provides intermediate, advanced, and specialized instruction for officers with many years experience in the service. According to the New York World-Telegram, more than 4,000 individuals had received instruction at the Institute by 1950—in which year it maintained a large teaching staff as well as utilizing the services of hundreds of departmental officials and nongovernmental persons as part-time lecturers and consultants. Hawkins headed the Institute for two years. Then, on January 17, 1952, it was announced that he had been named as the first appointee to the William L. Clayton chair of international finance at the Fletcher School of Law and Diplomacy. The new chair was established by the American Cotton Shippers Association and the Cotton Trade Journal. He assumed his new duties on March 1, 1952.

The international trade expert is the co-author of Merchant Shipping Industry (1925), a textbook on ocean shipping published under the pen names of H. C. Calvin and E. G. Stuart; Survey of Foreign Trade Activities of Oregon Manufacturers (1931), a pamphlet written with Lowell Angell; and Commercial Treaties and Agreements—Principles and Practice (1951), written with the assistance of Nan Grindle and four of Hawkins' students at the Fletcher School. An honorary degree has been conferred upon him by Olivet College. He holds membership in Pan Xenia, a foreign trade fraternity. On December 9, 1917, he married Ruth Dayton Spencer, who at that time was a teacher. They have two daughters, Barbara Hope and Kathryn Mather. Hawkins, who stands five feet ten and a half inches tall and weighs 168 pounds, has blue eyes and brown hair. He names his church affiliation as the Unitarian. Among his relaxations is horseback riding.

References

N Y Times p6 N 22 '47; p27 D 2 '49; p12 Ja 18 '52 pors
Biographic Register of the Department of State (1951)
Who's Who in America, 1950-51
World Biography (1948)

HAYWOOD, ALLAN S(HAW) Oct. 9, 1888- Labor union official

Address: b. c/o Congress of Industrial Organizations, 718 Jackson Place, N.W., Washington, D.C.; h. Taylor, Ill.

The national director of organization for the Congress of Industrial Organizations since 1939, English-born Allan S. Haywood was elected to the newly created post of executive vice-president of that body in 1951. Haywood, whose activity in the labor movement began when, as a boy, he worked in the mines of his

Chase News Photo.

ALLAN S. HAYWOOD

native Yorkshire, has long been closely associated with Philip Murray, president of the CIO. An official in the Illinois area of the United Mine Workers of America, Haywood has been a leader in the CIO since its inception in 1935. As the national official best known to rank and file members throughout the country, he has earned the nickname of "Mr. CIO."

Born on October 9, 1888, in a coal-mining village in Yorkshire, England, Allan Shaw Haywood is the ninth of the ten children of Arthur and Ann Haywood. Arthur Haywood and three of his elder sons were miners, and at the age of thirteen Allan also went into the pits and joined the British Miners' Federation. Five years later, in 1906, he left for America and settled in Illinois, where he continued to work in the coal mines. Bringing a union transfer card with him from England, he immediately joined the United Mine Workers of America.

For the next thirty years Haywood served in various capacities in the labor organization in Illinois. He was successively subdistrict vice-president, subdistrict president, and district executive board member of the United Mine Workers, and was vice-president of the Illinois State Federation of Labor. In 1936 he entered the larger arena of the national labor movement. For a year he was adviser to the United Rubber Workers of America, negotiating the first contract signed with a major rubber company, the Firestone Rubber Company. During that year he also was active in negotiations between the United Automobile Workers and the Dodge, Chrysler, General Motors, and Ford automobile manufacturers. When the U.A.W.A. called a strike at General Motors, Haywood was a member of the strike policy committee. Other fields in which he was to organize workers were the paper, gas, coke, chemical, department store, communications, packinghouse, and toy industries.

In 1937 the labor leader transferred the scene of his activities to New York. In May he was appointed CIO regional director for New York City. Haywood took part in negotiations between John L. Lewis' Transport Workers Union of America and the Interborough Rapid Transit subway line of New York City, the largest urban transportation system in the world. The resultant contract established the first closed shop in New York's transportation history. In the course of the next two years Haywood was also the regional director of the Steel Workers Organizing Committee, chairman of the Utility Workers Organizing Committee, and president of the New York State Industrial Union Council.

At the national convention of the CIO in 1939 Lewis appointed Haywood national director of organization, a title he still holds in 1952. With a staff of some 230 regional directors and organizers, Haywood provides assistance to member unions which need help in organizing situations, settles jurisdictional disputes between rival member unions, and is the CIO "ambassador to the general public." According to Elise Morrow, whose article on Haywood appeared in the Saturday Evening Post of November 4, 1950, he has concentrated on wages, hours, and working conditions, rather than the broader social objectives of the intellectuals, the younger CIO leaders. "To his friends," wrote Mrs. Morrow, "he is the blood and bones of the union, the trouble-shooter, the maintenance man, and the heart of its strength"; James Carey, secretary-treasurer of the CIO, once said of Haywood, "His greatest virtue is his capacity for everything." Colleagues less friendly, wrote Mrs. Morrow, say he would "compromise almost anything."

One of Haywood's major concerns in recent years has been reorganization in those fields affected by the expulsion from the CIO of several unions accused of being Communist-dominated. "Cleaning out of Communists is the first order of business for organized labor in its defense program," he has said. At the 1949 national convention, held in November, two unions were expelled on this charge, and committees were established to conduct hearings which eventually led to the expulsion of nine other unions. An estimated 800,000 workers were involved. It was part of organizational director Haywood's responsibility to allocate jurisdiction in some of the areas affected to unions remaining in the CIO, and to initiate organization in other areas. A year later Haywood announced that over 1,000,000 members had been gained since the expulsions.

The organizing of store employees has been a typical and major project. In New York, for example, several locals seceded from the CIO Retail, Wholesale and Department Store Union in 1948 over disputes involving local autonomy and charges of Left-wing domination. A year later the CIO awarded jurisdiction over department store employees to the Amalgamated Clothing Workers of America. In 1951 Haywood announced the reaffiliation with the CIO of the R. H. Macy local and the formation of a new Department Store Union

Organizing Committee, with jurisdiction over all new department store organizing, which would begin a national drive for 1,500,000 members. Other fields in which new organization has been initiated following Left-wing expulsions are insurance, where the first major gain was the winning of an election involving 6,000 agents at the John Hancock Mutual Life Insurance Company, Federal and local government employees, and electrical workers.

It has been said that if Haywood has a favorite among the unions he has helped form, it is the Communications Workers of America. Organized in forty-nine independent unions, the telephone workers called a strike in 1947, during which Haywood placed all of CIO's instrumentalities at the service of the striking employees. There followed a two-year campaign to unify all telephone workers in one collective bargaining unit, headed by Haywood as chairman of the Telephone Workers Organizing Committee. This campaign culminated in June of 1949 in the affiliation of the Communications Workers of America (representing 230,000 employees) with the CIO, whose TWOC represented another 90,000 workers in the industry. Elise Morrow suggested that Haywood's gratification at this outcome stemmed in part from his dependence on the telephone, which he uses during a large part of his working day.

The CIO official was quoted by the New York *World-Telegram* in 1950 as predicting that the trade union membership in the United States would grow to 23,000,000 in the course of the next decade. The categories which he considers the greatest source of new membership are white-collar, chemical, and farm workers, and he forecast increased organization in the depressed-wage areas of the South. Widespread unionization would affect social legislation, the organizer declared, and bring about a higher standard of living and a lower crime rate. Haywood, who frequently speaks at labor conventions, has expressed CIO's stand on a number of issues, among them labor's right to participate in formulating civil defense policy on such matters as loyalty tests, and in combating inflation, calling for "equality of sacrifice" among workers and management.

In addition to his office as director of organization, Haywood has been a vice-president of the CIO since 1942. In September 1950 he was appointed to head the Department of Industrial Union Councils. Regarded as one of the possible successors to Philip Murray as president of the CIO (he has worked with Murray since 1919), he became the first executive vice-president of that body in 1951, a move "ostensibly aimed to lift some of the burden from President Philip Murray's shoulders" (*Business Week*). (Haywood receives an annual salary of $12,500.) Another decision made at the 1951 convention was the establishment of a plan to eliminate jurisdictional disputes among unions within the CIO, the plan to consist of a rising series of arbitrational efforts by officers of the local unions, officers of the international unions, Allan Haywood, and

finally a "superarbitrator" to whose decision the unions would be committed.

Haywood was one of eleven CIO leaders who were sent to Moscow in 1945 as a goodwill delegation, following a meeting of the World Trade Union Conference in England. In 1949 he was a delegate to the meeting in London which established the International Confederation of Free Trade Unions, as opposed to the communistic World Federation of Trade Unions. On that occasion he became so encouraged by the possibility of merging the CIO and AFL that he became an active member of the joint committee established to explore the prospects, and served on it until these efforts broke down in the fall of 1951.

Other posts held by Haywood are administrator of the Union of Federal Workers (1941-44), chairman of the Paper Workers Organizing Committee (1944), member of the Union of Railroad Workers Organizing Committee (1944), member of the CIO Committee to Protect the Rights of Montgomery Ward Workers. He served as a member of the Labor Advisory Committee to the Office of Price Mobilization and as the labor member on the advisory board of the Advisory Committee to the Council of National Defense (1940).

The labor leader has been described as "a short, deep-chested man with a strong, pink face, powerful arms and an aggressive, rolling walk." He speaks with a trace of his native Yorkshire accent. He is said to be a less effective speaker before a large audience than before a small group, when he is "warm and persuasive." Married on May 31, 1909, Allan and Kate Haywood have three children, Albert, James, and Kathleen. With his home in Taylorsville, Illinois, and his office in Washington, D.C., Haywood spends a major portion of his time "on the road." He has been quoted as saying, "When you join a union and work for it, it's kind of like joining a church. You work for nothing else and you live for it."

References

N Y World-Telegram p15 D 9 '50
Sat Eve Post 22:34+ N 4 '50
Who's Who in Labor (1946)

HEALD, HENRY TOWNLEY (hēld)
Nov. 8, 1904- University administrator
Address: b. Office of the Chancellor, New York University, Washington Sq., New York 3; h. 5 Washington Sq., New York 3

Elected the ninth chancellor of New York University, to take office early in 1952, Henry Townley Heald succeeds Harry Woodburn Chase, who announced his retirement in July 1951. Heald, who was previously associated with Chicago's Illinois Institute of Technology for twenty-four years in teaching and administrative positions, is well known in the Midwest as an educator, business executive, civic leader, and practicing engineer.

One of three children (two girls and one boy) of Frederick DeForest and Nellie (Townley) Heald, Henry Townley Heald was born in Lincoln, Nebraska, on November 8, 1904.

(Continued next page)

Fabian Bachrach
HENRY TOWNLEY HEALD

His father, a noted botanist, was at that time teaching at the University of Nebraska and was subsequently engaged by the United States Department of Agriculture in research on plant pathology in Texas and Pennsylvania. For many years before his retirement he headed the Department of Plant Pathology at Washington State College, where young Heald studied civil engineering and took his B.S. degree in 1923. Employed by the United States Geological Survey in the State of Washington, Henry Heald during three summers of his college years took part in surveying projects. For a year following his graduation he worked as assistant engineer for the United States Bureau of Reclamation at Pendleton, Oregon, on the construction of the McKay Dam. He then enrolled at the University of Illinois to take courses in civil engineering for his M.Sc. degree, which was awarded to him in 1925.

Before entering upon his career as an educator, Heald filled a number of assignments in engineering: as designer in the bridge department of the Illinois Central Railroad in Chicago (1925-26), structural engineer in the bureau of design of the City of Chicago's Board of Local Improvements (1926-27), and as superintendent of construction on an apartment building at Pullman, Washington (1927). In September 1947 he joined the staff of the Armour Institute of Technology in Chicago as assistant professor of civil engineering. While in this post until 1931, he was employed by the Louisville (Kentucky) Bridge and Iron Company during the summer of 1929 and by the Walter Bates Steel Company of Gary, Indiana, during the summer of 1930. Academically, through a series of advancements to associate professor of civil engineering and assistant to the dean in 1931, to dean of freshmen in 1933, to professor of civil engineering and dean of the institute in 1934, and to presi-

dent of the Armour Research Foundation in 1936, Heald was elected acting president in 1937 and president in 1938 of the Armour Institute of Technology.

When in July 1940 the Armour Institute of Technology was consolidated with the Lewis Institute (also in Chicago) to form the Illinois Institute of Technology, Heald became president of the new institute. At this time he was also renamed head of the Armour Research Foundation—which became a part of the Illinois Institute of Technology—now regarded as one of the country's largest independent scientific research organizations, and in 1941 assumed the presidency of the Institute of Gas Technology. Since 1940, under Heald's guidance, the Illinois Institute of Technology has expanded in enrollment from 400-odd to over 7,000 students and in area from seven acres to eighty-five. With its assets quadrupled and its annual operating budget multiplied nine times, the institute acquired eleven new buildings valued at $15,000,000, while two additional buildings are under construction. The function of the institute is, in the words of Heald, the "never-ending job of pushing back the frontiers of technology and applying the new findings for the good of mankind." Heald views its goal as the achievement of "a successful partnership of science, industry, and education" (*Look*, September 12, 1950). In an interview for *Business Week* (June 18, 1949) he expressed the fear that industry was allowing government to gain control of science by failing to provide enough money for research. Later in the year 1949, at a convention of the American Gas Association, Heald stressed the need for industry-sponsored research rather than government-sponsored research, as "an ultimate source of more commodities, better service, and greater comforts for our people" (New York *Times*, October 21, 1949).

While directing the growth of the institute, the engineer-educator also led a project to clear slums near Chicago's South Side and to build a new development in this area. A registered structural engineer and professional engineer in Illinois, Heald has held a number of positions in connection with building: trustee of the Urban Land Institute since 1945 and member of its building technique and material research council since 1950, member of the board of governors of the Metropolitan Housing Council since 1946 and member of its planning committee since 1947, chairman of the South Side Planning Board since 1946, vice-chairman of the Land Clearance Commission of Chicago since 1947, president of the Citizens' Building Code Committee since 1948, and member of the advisory committee on housing research of the Housing and Home Finance Agency since 1950.

After twenty-four years at the Illinois Institute of Technology, Heald in October 1951 accepted the chancellorship of New York University, to fill a post left vacant by the retirement in July 1951 of Harry Woodburn Chase. Heald assumed office on February 2, 1952. With a student body exceeding 68,000 and a faculty of some 4,000 members, the university is the largest in the United States. Since its founding in 1831, New York University, a privately endowed institution, has expanded to include fourteen schools, colleges, and divisions in six centers of instruction in Greater New York. Chief among its fields of study are law, engineering, liberal arts, fine arts, commerce, education, medicine, dentistry, nursing, and business administration. Currently the university, completing its $5,000,000 law center, is developing in conjunction with New York's Bellevue Hospital a $30,000,000 medical center. There are plans for erecting a new Applied Science Building (on the large University Heights campus) to cost from $3,000,000 to $4,000,000, thus completing the Advanced Technology Center. Heald was formally installed as ninth chancellor of N.Y.U. at the university's 120th commencement exercises on June 11, 1952.

In World War II Heald was called upon to serve as regional adviser of Engineering Defense Training, District 15 (1940-41), regional adviser of Engineering, Science, and Management War Training, District 14 (1942-45), regional representative of the War Manpower Commission, Region 6 (1943), and member of the consultative committee on engineering of the War Manpower Commission (1942-44). A special adviser of the Bureau of Naval Personnel (1942-45) and a member of the Navy's Bureau of Personnel Advisory Committee (1945-49), he was the recipient of the Navy Award for distinguished civilian service. Among more recent posts filled by Heald in connection with national defense are as member of the advisory board of the research and development branch of the military planning division of the Office of the Quartermaster General (since 1946), member of the advisory panel of the scientific manpower mobilization committee of the General Staff (since 1947), member of the advisory board of the Chicago Ordnance District (since 1950), and member of the committee on national defense of the Chamber of Commerce of the United States (since 1951).

In Chicago Heald is a director of the First Federal Savings and Loan Association, Swift & Company, American Steel Foundries, Stewart-Warner Corporation, and Peoples Gas, Light and Coke Company. Aside from previously mentioned activities in housing, he is a member of the board of directors of the Chicago Association of Commerce and Industry, an honorary civil member of the Rotary Club, and a member of the Community Fund of Chicago, Inc.

The author of numerous articles on engineering education and related subjects, Heald in recent years has contributed "Engineer in a Post-War World" (1941) and "Wanted: A Plan for Industrial Training" (1943) to the *Journal of Engineering Education* and "Nature and Scope of Society's Accident Problem" (1946) to the *Journal of Educational Sociology*. Among the engineering associations to which he belongs are the Western Society of Engineers (president, 1945-46), Illinois Engineering Council, Engineers' Council for Professional Development, American Society of Civil Engineers, American Society of Mechanical Engineers, and the American Institute of Architects. In the field of education he maintains member-

ship in the American Society of Engineering Education (president, 1942-43), Association of Urban Universities (president, 1943-44), American Council on Education, Association of NROTC Colleges (executive committee, since 1948), George M. Pullman Educational Foundation (board of directors, since 1950), and National Commission on Accrediting (since 1950). He has filled executive positions on the National Safety Council and the National Research Council.

The recipient of many civic awards, Heald has also had three honorary degrees conferred upon him: the D. Eng. from Rose Polytechnic Institute (1942), the LL.D. from Northwestern University (1942), and the D. Eng. from Clarkson College of Technology (1948). He holds honorary membership in the Tau Beta Pi, Sigma Tau, Phi Kappa Phi, and Chi Epsilon fraternities. His clubs are the Chicago, University, Chicago Engineers', Tavern, Commercial, Economic, Wayfarers, Illinois Athletic, and Newcomen Society. He is a Mason. On August 4, 1928, Heald married Muriel Starcher of Yakima, Washington. The blue-eyed, light-haired educator stands six feet two inches tall and weighs 175 pounds. Since 1946 he has been a trustee and president of the board of the Central Church of Chicago and since 1948 the Protestant cochairman for Chicago of the National Conference of Christians and Jews.

References

Look 15:33 N 20 '51 por
N Y Herald Tribune p2 O 1 '51; p1+ O 3 '51 por
N Y Times p1+ O 3 '51 por
Time 58:97 O 15 '51 por
American Men of Science (1949)
International Who's Who, 1951
Leaders in Education (1948)
Who's Who in America, 1950-51
Who's Who in American Education, 1947-48
Who's Who in Chicago and Illinois (1950)
Who's Who in Engineering, 1948
Who's Who in the Midwest (1949)
World Biography (1948)

HENDRICKSON, ROBERT C. Aug. 12, 1898- United States Senator from New Jersey

Address: b. Senate Office Bldg., Washington 25, D.C.; h. 2300 Connecticut Ave., Washington, D.C.; 325 Cooper St., Woodbury, N.J.

Senator from New Jersey Robert C. Hendrickson was elected to the United States Congress in November 1948 for the term ending January 1955. His committee work in the Senate has been on the Committee on the District of Columbia, the Rules and Administration Committee, and the Select Committee on Small Business. The legislator achieved prominence in New Jersey politics in 1934, when he was chosen to fill an unexpired term as State Senator from Gloucester County. In 1939 and again in 1941 he was re-elected to the post; in 1940

HENDRICKSON, ROBERT C.—*Continued*

he was the unsuccessful Republican nominee for Governor. Two years later, at a joint session of the New Jersey Legislature, he was elected State treasurer, an office to which he was re-elected in 1946. In World War II Hendrickson, while an officer in American Military Government, served for seven months as Deputy Commander of Upper Austria.

The son of Daniel F. and Emma R. (Megary) Hendrickson, Robert C. Hendrickson was born in Woodbury, New Jersey, on August 12, 1898. Shortly before his graduation from Woodbury High School in June 1918, he enlisted as a private in the United States Army. His high school diploma was presented to him just previous to his departure for France, where he took part in the Aisne-Marne, St. Mihiel, Campagne, and Meuse-Argonne offensives, for which he was awarded the Medal of Verdun, Unit Citations, and Letters of Commendation. Upon his discharge from the Army, he entered the Law School of Temple University in Philadelphia, graduating with the degree of LL.B. in 1922. Admitted to the New Jersey bar in that year, he began the practice of law in Woodbury as a member of the firm of Hendrickson and Wicks.

Entering politics in 1934 when chosen to complete an unexpired term as State Senator from Gloucester County, Hendrickson four years later was re-elected to the post and the following year was named Senate Republican majority leader. After being elected president of the State Senate in 1939, he became a year later a member of the Board of Managers of the Council of State Governments. In his campaign for the Governorship against Charles E. Edison, he was defeated in the 1940 election, but in 1941 was re-elected State Senator. During his years in the New Jersey Senate he served on several important State bodies—the Social Security Commission, which set up the present Unemployment Compensation Commission, the New Jersey Commission on Tax Law Revision, and the Commission on Constitutional Revision. At a joint meeting of the New Jersey Legislature in 1942, he was named State treasurer, a post he occupied until his election to the United States Senate in 1948.

When Hendrickson volunteered for service in the Army on May 31, 1943, he was commissioned a major and was granted a leave of absence as State treasurer. In October of that year he was sent to Europe; assigned to the Mediterranean Theater of Operations, he served in North Africa, Italy (where as senior legal officer he entered Rome with the combat forces), and Upper Austria. At the end of 1944, he was promoted to lieutenant colonel, in which rank as legal officer of Lazio-Umbria, including Rome and seven surrounding provinces, he was charged with the responsibility, among other duties, of re-establishing Italian courts. His next assignment required that he assist in planning the reorganization of the government of Upper Austria, with particular regard to the operation of civil and military courts. Deputy commander of the Austrian Task Force, which flew from Italy to join General Patton's Third

Army as it crossed the Austrian border, he remained in Upper Austria for seven months, concerned with the reorganization of civil government (including police protection), the restoration of civil rights, and the care of more than 2,000,000 displaced persons. He was separated from the service on February 10, 1946. Upon being offered a post with a United States Military Government mission in October 1947, which, he said, would place him "in executive control of Bavaria for at least a year," he rejected it with the observation that "he could be more useful in this country, selling the idea that America must help in the rehabilitation of European countries" (New York *Times*, October 18, 1947).

Following his return to civilian life, Hendrickson resumed his duties as New Jersey State treasurer, to which office he was re-elected in 1946. "A holdover State treasurer," the New York *Times* reported, "he had announced that he was not a candidate for return, but the State Legislature . . . named him anyway." Soon thereafter he became vice-chairman of the Commission on the Delaware River Basin. Hendrickson, who had declined to run for the United States Senate in 1942, became the Republican nominee in 1948. He was chosen, according to the *Times* "in the role of a peacemaker when he sought to avoid a bitter intraparty primary fight and himself became the compromise candidate." At the end of his campaign he stated: "Lasting peace and genuine prosperity are the twin objectives of public policy I support. . . .I submit my candidacy to the people on a record of twenty years of public service as a State legislator, as State treasurer, as director of interstate agencies, and as a military government administrator overseas." Following his election he said: "We must strive for a period of unity and prosperity at home and peace and security abroad."

During his freshman term as a Senator, Hendrickson was appointed, in the first session of the Eighty-first Congress, to the Committee on the District of Columbia. In 1949 he voted to uphold an antifilibuster ruling and supported a revision of the cloture rule (March); he opposed a 10 per cent reduction in the Marshall Plan authorization and a measure allowing segregation in public housing (April). He cast his vote for a bill authorizing a Federal expenditure of $300 million in aid to education (May), for restricting use of the injunction to emergency strikes (June), and for a coalition revision of the Taft-Hartley Labor Law (June). He also supported the North Atlantic Security Pact, a twenty-year defensive alliance with Canada and ten Western European nations which declared that an armed attack against one or more of its signatories "shall be considered an attack against them all" and committed each signatory to take "such action as it deems necessary, including the use of armed force," to restore and safeguard the security of the North Atlantic area. In August 1949 Robert S. Allen cited Hendrickson's "yeoman service in fighting for civil rights." At a press conference held in January 1950, Hendrickson urged the Senate to "stop bluffing" and "making a political football" out of the civil rights issue and announced that he would propose a measure in the coming session designed to cut off filibusters.

In association with a group of liberal Republican Senators, Hendrickson criticized the Republican policy statement issued in February 1950 as a retreat from the party platform of 1948. "I feel that the 1948 platform was a great platform," he stated, "and that all we needed to do was to press for vigorous action in all fields covered by that platform." During the second session of the Eighty-first Congress, he was one of two Republican members (the other was Senator Margaret Chase Smith) on the Senate Rules subcommittee on privileges and elections which investigated the 1950 Maryland Senatorial election in which John Marshall Butler, Republican, defeated former Senator Millard Tydings, Democrat. Early in that session he cosponsored a bill to liberalize the Displaced Persons Act. In June he voted in support of the authorization of $45 million for the Act for International Development, the Point IV Program outlined by President Truman in his 1949 Inaugural Address, endorsed a six-month extension of rent control, and opposed draftee segregation. That month he joined a group of fellow-Republican Senators in issuing a "Declaration of Conscience" criticizing the methods of Senator Joseph R. McCarthy. In June he also sponsored a resolution advocating a five-year disarmament program "that would turn funds destined for weapons to a world program of scientific advance and reconstruction." On June 17, 1950, he voiced a warning that United States officials in Germany had failed to impress a democratic attitude on Germans and disclosed that he had cosponsored "a resolution calling for the appointment of a bipartisan commission to inquire into American foreign policy in Germany."

Among votes cast by Hendrickson in the first session of the Eighty-second Congress were those favoring a cut in government civil payrolls (June 1951) and a $250 million cut in European economic aid (August). He voted "nay" to limiting public housing to 5,000 units (June), to government operation of defense plants (June), and to a $5.5 billion tax increase (June). In the summer of 1951 he introduced a resolution intended, in his words, "to put a stop to 80 years of rambling"; it would require a Senator enjoying the privilege of the floor "to confine himself to the question under debate" (Washington *Post*, July 10, 1951). In Strasbourg, France, in November of that year he attended a conference of American and European political leaders to discuss problems of rearmament and closer ties among the nations of the free world. As chairman of the taxation subcommittee of the Select Committee on Small Business, he conducted public hearings early in 1952 to ascertain the tax problems of small business concerns. In August 1952 he was one of a group of Senators who conferred with Italian officials in Rome regarding problems connected with the influx of political refugees from behind the Iron Curtain. Hendrickson voted in the second session of the Eighty-second Congress against ending eco-

ROBERT C. HENDRICKSON

nomic controls on June 30 (May); he gave his support to a $6.7 billion foreign aid bill (May), using the Taft-Hartley Act in the steel strike (June), shelving the St. Lawrence project (June), and not granting funds for new reclamation dams (June).

The New Jersey Senator was an organizer and charter member of the Woodbury Rotary Club, of which he is now an honorary member. He is commander of the William Stokes Bonsal Post, No. 133, American Legion Department of New Jersey; in 1930 he was vice-commander of the Gloucester County American Legion. For his heroism in an attempt to rescue a friend from drowning in 1938, he was awarded medals by the American Legion and the New York Life Saving Benevolent Association. In recognition of his services during World War II he was awarded the World War II Medal, the European-African-Middle Eastern Theater Service Medal with four bronze stars, the Army Commendation Ribbon, and the Allied Military Government Medal, Fifth Army. In June 1951 Temple University conferred an honorary LL.B. degree upon him. His wife is the former Olga Bonsal, whom he married in 1919. The Hendricksons have five children—Claire (Mrs. Ivor Macfarlane), Olga (Mrs. Willard Lloyd Nyburg), Marguerite (Mrs. Donald Brewer), June, and Robert C., Jr. The legislator is a member of the Vestry of Christ Episcopal Church of Woodbury. His hobbies are chess, fishing, and boating. He describes himself as a "student of intrastate affairs and problems, and of Federal functions and operations affecting State government."

References

N Y Times p4 N 10 '37; p1 My 23 '38; p36 D 13 '38; p5 Ja 11 '39; p42 Je 3 '43; p6 F 3 '45; p7 O 18 '47; p18 N 3 '48; p1 Je 2 '50

(Continued next page)

HENDRICKSON, ROBERT C.—*Continued*
    Congressional Directory (1951)
    Who's Who in America, 1952-53
    Who's Who in United States Politics
    (1950)

HENIE, SONJA Apr. 8, 1912- Ice skater;
producer; motion picture actress
Address: h. 243 Delfern Dr., Los Angeles 24,
Calif.

> NOTE: This biography supersedes the
> article which appeared in *Current
> Biography* in 1940.

Winner of the women's figure skating championship in three successive Olympics contests
and for ten consecutive years the world's
amateur champion ice skater, Norwegian-born
Sonja Henie joined the ranks of the professionals in 1936. Thereafter a Hollywood film

Wide World Photos
SONJA HENIE

luminary for nearly a decade, she was also for
thirteen years, beginning in 1938, the star and
coproducer of the annual *Hollywood Ice Revue*.
The pioneer exponent of ballet on ice, Miss
Henie was also associated, for ten years beginning 1940, with the presentation of skating
spectacles. In 1952 she appears in her own
production, *Sonja Henie with Her 1952 Ice
Revue*.

Born in Oslo, Norway, on April 8, 1912,
Sonja Henie is the younger of the two children
of the late Hans Wilhelm Henie, and Selma
(Lochman-Nielsen) Henie. Her father, a well-
to-do wholesale fur merchant and past bicycle
champion, gave the child her first skates on
the Christmas following her sixth birthday.
Miss Henie tells in her book *Wings On My
Feet* (1940) that it was from her brother Leif

that she received her first skating instruction.
Poise and balance were developed through
skiing, while her delight in dancing as early
as her fifth year was encouraged by her
parents, who sent her to Love Krohn, a former
teacher of Anna Pavlova, for ballet lessons.
Her agility and grace on the ice were quickly
noted, and in her eighth year she won the
children's figure skating championship of Oslo.
Twelve months later Sonja was the victor in
the Junior Class C national contest. Her
formal education was placed in the charge of
private tutors, while from Oscar Holte, Norway's prominent skating instructor, she received professional coaching. She continued
her lessons with Krohn and in the summer of
her tenth year was taken by her mother to
London for the first of several courses of
instruction from the famous Russian ballerina
Karsavina.

In 1923, at the age of ten, Sonja Henie won
the national figure skating championship of
Norway; and at the beginning of the next year
(1924) was entered, mainly for the sake of
the experience, in the winter Olympic Games
at Chamonix in the French Alps. There, she
took third place in the free skating competition. This was followed in 1926 by the Scandinavian championship. A year later, in 1927,
in Oslo she won the first of ten consecutive
world figure skating championships. The following summer the young girl again visited
London, and it was at this time she first saw
Anna Pavlova dance; the experience, according
to her own account, rekindled her enthusiasm
for ballet and made her decide to introduce
choreographic design into her free skating. In
attaining this objective she was helped by the
instructor Martin Stixrud. The novelty was a
factor in her winning of the women's figure
skating championship at the next winter Olympic Games, at St. Moritz, Switzerland, early
in 1928. This first of her three Olympics
triumphs was followed later in the same year
by her retention, at London, of the world figure
skating title and again, at Budapest, Hungary,
in 1929. In New York City, where the next
world championship contest was held, Miss
Henie in January 1930 made her first "exhibition" appearance in the United States, as the
principal soloist of the New York Skating
Club's carnival *Land of the Midnight Sun* at
Madison Square Garden. A few days later
she again won the world championship, and
added another victory at Berlin in 1931. By
the beginning of the next year (1932) she was
back in the United States for the winter Olympics at Lake Placid, New York, where she
carried off the women's figure skating championship for the second time. Miss Henie
received several offers to "turn professional"
during this trip, but decided to remain an
amateur at least four years longer and seek a
third Olympics victory. She retained her world
championship at Montreal in 1932, Stockholm
in 1933, Oslo in 1934, and Vienna in 1935.
During this period she received additional
tutelage from Howard Nicholson in London
and made many exhibition appearances in the
principal cities of Europe. Her famous ice

version of Pavlova's "Dying Swan" was first presented at Milan, Italy, in 1933. As recorded in *Hvem er Hvem*, she also held the European championship during 1931-36.

Further details of Sonja Henie's amateur career—which ended with her third Olympics triumph at Garmisch-Partenkirchen in Bavaria early in 1936 and her tenth world championship at Paris a little later—are related in her autobiographical *Mitt Livs Eventyr* (published in Oslo in 1938) and in *Wings on My Feet* (1940), which includes her advice on "Skating for Fun and Competition." Within a month of her Paris triumph, Miss Henie had contracted with the Chicago promoter Arthur Wirtz to make a series of professional exhibition appearances in the United States. Her tour, which covered seventeen performances in nine cities in March and April of 1936, proved highly profitable. About this time her father (who had left his fur business in charge of his son in order to manage his daughter's affairs) arranged for her two performances at a Los Angeles rink in May 1936. The second of these was seen by Darryl F. Zanuck of Twentieth Century-Fox, who shortly afterward signed the Norwegian skating star to a five-year film contract.

Miss Henie's first film was *One in a Million*, released at the end of 1936. Bosley Crowther in reviewing the picture for the New York *Times* found the "skating queen . . . satisfactorily blonde, dimpled, and ingratiating," while in the several ice interludes she was "like a transfigured Dégas ballerina." The same reviewer thought her second film, *Thin Ice* (1937), "one of the brightest comedies of the year." Both were box-office successes, with the consequence that in 1937 their star earned over $200,000 from her film work alone. In the *Motion Picture Herald* popularity poll she rose from eighth place in 1937 to third in 1938. Later films, such as *Happy Landing* and *My Lucky Star* (1938), *Second Fiddle* (1939), *Everything Happens at Night* (1939), *Sun Valley Serenade* (1941), and *Wintertime* (1942) were likewise successful, and *Iceland* (1942) and *It's a Pleasure* (1944) somewhat less so. Meanwhile, in 1938 the former Olympics champion had embarked, in association with Wirtz, on her first *Hollywood Ice Revue*, in which she was to make annual personal appearances in leading American cities through the next twelve years. The success of a feature of the 1940 show, the presentation on ice of the ballet *Les Sylphides*, prompted Miss Henie and her partner to take over the Center Theatre in New York City as an all-the-year-round home of ice revues. Miss Henie's connection with this venture was financial and advisory; she made no personal appearances in the Center entertainments, the first of which, *It Happens on Ice*, had its première on October 9, 1940.

After a visit to her native city early in the summer of 1945, Miss Henie made an eight-week tour of American army hospitals in Europe as a USO entertainer. Returning to the United States in July, she reassembled her *Hollywood Ice Revue* company for the sequence of fall and winter tours of principal cities.

She made one new film, *The Countess of Monte Cristo*, in 1948. The Center Theatre shows, with ice ballets designed by the choreographer Catherine Littlefield, continued to flourish, the initial *It Happens on Ice* being followed by *Wintertime* (1943), *Hats Off to Ice* (1944), *Icetime* (1946), and *Howdy Mr. Ice* (1948). The series came to an end in the summer of 1950, when the theater was converted to television. Miss Henie's most recent appearance was made in the perennial *Hollywood Ice Revue* at Madison Square Garden on January 20, 1951, at which time the New York *Post* critic Vernon Rice found her "just as fresh and youthful as she was last year and the year before." In the following August her sixteen years of business association with Arthur Wirtz (which, according to *Variety*, netted the star a reputed $10,000,000) came to an end, the two being unable to reach terms for the renewal of their agreement. Miss Henie, who is known as a good businesswoman, set about organizing her own ice show. Like previous productions, Miss Henie's 1952 ice spectacle (*Sonja Henie with Her 1952 Ice Revue*), which opened in San Francisco in November 1951, was notable for its lavish costuming. A waltz and a hula were among the six ice dances performed by the star herself. "Miss Henie's ice virtuosity," commented *Variety*, "is at its peak."

By decree of King Haakon, Sonja Henie was made a Knight First Class of the Order of St. Olaf in December 1937. She has given command performances before the crowned heads of Norway, Great Britain, Belgium, and Sweden. During the Nazi occupation of Norway, the skating star, who became a United States citizen in September 1941, contributed a reported $45,000 to relief funds for her native land. Another donation was the proceeds of the opening performance of her 1952 ice revue to the Damon Runyon Cancer Fund. The blond-haired, blue-eyed skater is five feet two inches in height and weighs about 104 pounds. Her first marriage, to Daniel Reid Topping on July 4, 1940, ended in divorce in 1946. Three years later, on September 15, 1949, she became the wife of Winthrop Gardiner, Jr. A horsewoman, swimmer, and hockey player, she is also a tennis enthusiast.

References

Am Mag 124:32-3+ N '37 pors
Christian Sci Mon p6 Jl 3 '46 por
N Y Times p15 Jl 5 '40; p23 Ja 29 '51 por
N Y World-Telegram p17 Ja 25 '41 por
Newsweek 15:38 Ja 29 '40 pors; 32:86 O 25 '48 por
Read Digest 39:41-4 N '41
Time 34:51-4 Jl 17 '39 pors; 51:50-4 F 2 '48 por
Columbia Encyclopedia (1950)
Henie, S. Wings on My Feet (1940)
Hvem er Hvem? (1950)
International Motion Picture Almanac, 1950-51
Who's Who in America, 1950-51

HEUVEN GOEDHART, G(ERRIT) J(AN) VAN (hūv′ĕn gōōd′härt gĕr′ĭt yän vän) Mar. 19, 1901- United Nations official; journalist

Address: b. c/o Office of the United Nations High Commissioner for Refugees, Geneva, Switzerland

With the termination of the operations of the United Nations International Refugee Organization in January 1952, the problem of rehabilitating and resettling persons displaced by World War II and postwar events passed to the United Nations High Commissioner for Refugees, an office which began to function on January 1,

United Nations

G. J. VAN HEUVEN GOEDHART

1951, for what is expected to be a three-year period. The U.N. High Commissioner for Refugees, who was elected December 14, 1950, is Dr. G. J. van Heuven Goedhart, one-time vice-chairman of the Netherlands delegation to the General Assembly. Van Heuven Goedhart, formerly a newspaperman, was active in the Dutch underground movement during World War II and in 1944-45 served as Minister of Justice in the Netherlands Government-in-exile. From 1947 to 1950 he was a member of the upper chamber of the Netherlands parliament and a member of the Netherlands delegation to the U.N.

Born at Bussum in the Netherlands on March 19, 1901, Gerrit Jan van Heuven Goedhart is the son of Gysbert Willem and Francina (van Heuven) Goedhart (he adopted his mother's family name as a part of his own surname). The boy Gerrit was reared in his native community, some miles southeast of Amsterdam, and after completing his *gymnasium* training entered the University of Leyden, where he proceeded from the study of economics and sociology to law, and acquired his LL.D. degree in 1926. The title of his dissertation, pub-

lished during that year, may be rendered in English as *The Development of Unemployment Relief in the Netherlands.*

Upon leaving the university, van Heuven Goedhart, who had gained some experience as a newspaper reporter in 1925, joined the editorial staff of the Amsterdam *Telegraaf*, of which he was made editor in chief in 1929. A year earlier (1928) he had completed *The Development of Labor Exchange in the Netherlands,* another sociological study. In 1933 he left Amsterdam for Utrecht to become editor in chief of the *Utrechtsch Nieuwsblad,* a position he retained until the Nazi occupation of the Low Countries early in World War II. During the 1930-1940 decade, Dr. van Heuven Goedhart made numerous visits to other European countries to observe political and social trends, his impressions of Czechoslovakia appearing in book form in 1938 under the title *Unrest in the Land of Masaryk.* His *Finland as I Saw It* followed in 1940.

When the Germans overran Holland in May 1940, van Heuven Goedhart "went underground": "I was heart and soul with the Dutch Resistance Movement," he was later to write in a letter to the British weekly *New Statesman and Nation.* "I collaborated there with a group which is known as Left Wing, strictly democratic." Thus during the latter part of 1940 he became a leading contributor to the resistance publication *Wederopbouw* (Reconstruction) and was coeditor of the underground newspaper *Het Parool* from January 1942 until early in 1944 when at the request of several resistance groups he undertook a mission to England. (The mission is described in his book *The Journey of Colonel Blake,* published in 1945.) Since he had spent all of his private resources between 1940 and 1944, upon his arrival in London in April 1944, after a roundabout and hazardous journey through Belgium, France, and Spain, van Heuven Goedhart was practically penniless. His talents were quickly put to use in the post of Minister of Justice in the Netherlands Government-in-exile, to which he was named on July 12, 1944. A month later he made an important radio speech promising future punishment for collaborators with the Nazi regime and in another address during October urged his countrymen "to collect facts and note identity of German war criminals" (New York *Times*).

Having resigned as Minister of Justice in February 1945, van Heuven Goedhart returned to the Netherlands soon after the liberation and in August 1945 took over the editorship of *Het Parool,* which he established as a leading Amsterdam daily, nominally independent, but in general supporting the policies of the moderate democratic-socialist Labor party led by Premier Willem Drees. The editor was elected a Labor member of the First (upper) Chamber of the States-General in 1947 and served as such until 1950. The Labor party, which "recognizes self-determination by the peoples of overseas territories" (*Political Handbook of the World*), strongly supports the United Nations. Also in the year 1947 van Heuven Goedhart became a member of the Dutch delegation to the U.N. General Assembly. Elected to the U.N. Economic and Social Council's Subcommission on Freedom of Information and the Press, he was made chairman of that body, serving at its first and second sessions (1947, 1948). In 1948 he was head of the Netherlands delegation to the United Nations Conference on Freedom of Information and adviser of the Netherlands delegation to the seventh session of the Economic and Social Council. During the 1949 and 1950 sessions of the General Assembly he was vice-chairman of the Netherlands delegation.

In mid-1947, or at about the time van Heuven Goedhart became a delegate, the United Nations voted to establish at Geneva an International Refugee Organization for the purpose of re-establishing 1,500,000 persons uprooted through the war—this to be accomplished through maintenance of camps and assembly centers, transportation, political protection, resettlement, and other services. A four-year existence was envisioned for the IRO and an over-all expenditure exceeding $355 millions was authorized. It having become apparent that the IRO would have already resettled 1,200,000 persons by the time of its expiration on October 31, 1951, the General Assembly, in voting to set up an office of U.N. High Commissioner for Refugees as the IRO's successor, "decided to write off the relief and resettlement projects" (Mac R. Johnson in the New York *Herald Tribune*). The new High Commissioner was charged with responsibility for affording legal international protection to remaining refugees and was instructed "to promote agreements with governments to improve the position" of the refugees, to accelerate naturalizations, assist in voluntary repatriations, and to work with other organizations concerned with refugee problems. His budget was limited to $800,000 for the first year, and it was stipulated that he should "not appeal to governments for funds or make a general appeal" without the approval of the General Assembly.

For the post of High Commissioner for Refugees, the U.N. Economic and Social Council on December 14, 1950, chose van Heuven Goedhart by a 30 to 24 vote, in preference to the director-general of the outgoing IRO, J. Donald Kingsley of the United States. (This vote expressed the majority opinion that a European should be appointed to the post.) Van Heuven Goedhart, who draws a salary and allowances amounting to approximately $20,000 and has a rank equivalent to that of Assistant Secretary General, opened offices at Geneva on January 1, 1951. Funds at his disposal did not permit him to maintain field offices like those of the IRO, and the following October his operating difficulties were increased by a vote of the U.N. to cut his budget to $570,000 in the ensuing year. He tried vainly to get the cut restored and was still unsuccessful when in January 1952 the IRO (whose life had twice been extended) was terminated, leaving the High Commissioner a legacy of 5,000 still unsettled Oriental refugees in Shanghai, 150,000 in Germany and Austria, 20,000 in Italy, 15,000 in Greece, and a scattering elsewhere. The following month (February), the General Assembly voted the High Commissioner per-

mission to "approach governments and private individuals to raise a fund of $3 millions for carrying on his work" (*Christian Science Monitor*). Aid was promised by Britain, Sweden, Norway, and the Netherlands, and on August 3 announcement was made by director Paul G. Hoffman of the Ford Foundation of a grant of $2,900,000 to the U.N. Relief Emergency Fund to be spent in an attempt to find a solution to the refugee problem. "These funds," stated Hoffman, "will be administered by Dr. G. J. van Heuven Goedhart. . . .The work will be carried out by private agencies." It was further stipulated that the work "must not relieve governments of their moral responsibilities" and "must avoid direct material relief."

Honors conferred on Dr. van Heuven Goedhart include the Dutch World War II Military Cross for Merit and the chairmanship of the Court of Honor of the Resistance Movement at Amsterdam from 1946 to 1951. He was created a Knight of the Order of the Netherlands Lion in 1949. Van Heuven Goedhart and the former Erna Hauan were married in Oslo, Norway, on April 10, 1932. They have two children, Karin S. and Bergliot.

References

N Y Times p21 D 15 '50 por
U N Bul 2:664 Je 17 '47 por; 9:407-8 O 15 '50 por
International Who's Who, 1951
Who's Who in the United Nations (1951)
Wie Is Dat? 1948
World Biography (1948)

HIGGINS, ANDREW J(ACKSON) Aug. 28, 1886—Aug. 1, 1952 Shipbuilder; in early career engaged in lumber business in South; formed the Higgins Lumber and Export Company in New Orleans (1922), which became the owner of a large fleet of ships; organized Higgins Industries, Inc., (1930) to build motorboats and barges; in World War II built landing craft and other vessels for the armed services; after the war manufactured pleasure craft, camp trailers, and airplanes, and ships for the fighting in Korea. See *Current Biography,* 1943.

Obituary

N Y Times p15 Ag 2 '52

HIGHTOWER, JOHN M(ARMANN) Sept. 17, 1909- Journalist

Address: b. c/o Associated Press, Evening Star Bldg., Washington, D.C.; h. 8415 Brad Blvd., Bethesda, Md.

For his journalistic achievements in 1951 John M. Hightower, diplomatic editor of the Associated Press, in 1952 won the Pulitzer Prize, the Raymond Clapper Award, and the Sigma Delta Chi Award, the first newspaperman to be awarded all three honors in one year. Hightower, a veteran Washington correspondent for the Associated Press, who joined the A.P. in Nashville, Tennessee, in 1933, has covered

JOHN M. HIGHTOWER

the Department of State during the terms of five successive secretaries. In 1951 he reported upon and interpreted the deepening of the conflict between General MacArthur and the Truman Administration and the series of events which led up to the former's dismissal; that year he also obtained exclusive stories on the Korean armistice proceedings and Churchill's decision to visit Washington in January 1952.

John Marmann Hightower was born on September 17, 1909, in Coal Creek, Tennessee. For his early education he attended the public schools in Knoxville and then studied at the University of Tennessee for two years prior to becoming a reporter for the Knoxville *News-Sentinel*. Not long after joining the Associated Press in Nashville in 1933, he was advanced to the position of Tennessee State editor of the A.P. While he was engaged in this capacity in covering Tennessee's delegations to the Republican and Democratic national conventions in 1936, his reporting brought him to the attention of Byron Price, at that time chief of the Washington Bureau of the A.P., who had Hightower transferred in the same year to Washington, D.C.

As a news analyst for the A.P. in the nation's capital, Hightower was assigned first to the Navy Department and then, in 1943, to the State Department. In the latter post he wrote upon many of the most important diplomatic events of the time, including the Roosevelt-Churchill meeting in Quebec, the chartering of the United Nations at San Francisco, the early U.N. meetings in New York and London, and the establishment and development of the Marshall Plan and the North Atlantic Pact. He also reported on the series of con-

ferences of the Council of Foreign Ministers, in February 1947 sailing on the Swedish-American steamship *Gripsholm* with four other American journalists, to cover the meeting of the Allied powers in Moscow. In the course of his years at the State Department, Hightower has reported upon the activities of five successive Secretaries.

It was during his assignment to the Navy Department that Hightower is said to have started to develop his explanatory-interpretive method of reporting. After the entrance of the United States into World War II he began to ask why that country was seeking to wrest control from the Japanese of many seemingly unimportant small islands in the Pacific. In trying to answer this question in his own mind, he adopted a journalist approach which attempted to bring clarity to the mind of the reader and later used this method in his assignments dealing with diplomatic and international relations. His aim, he has stated, is "to strive for understanding."

The excellence of Hightower's journalism in 1951 won him in 1952 three high awards, never before received by a reporter in a single year. "For the sustained quality of his coverage of news of international affairs," he was presented with the Pulitzer Prize on May 6. At the convention of the American Society of Newspaper Editors on April 19, he won the eighth annual Raymond Clapper Memorial Award of $500 for "exceptionally meritorious" coverage of the State Department. On April 2 Sigma Delta Chi, the national journalism fraternity, conferred on Hightower its annual award for "distinguished service in the field of Washington correspondence," citing him for his "penetrating and accurate analysis of domestic and foreign affairs during the tension-filled months of 1951." Besides receiving these honors, Hightower was initiated on May 10, 1952, into the Gridiron Club, an association of Washington correspondents.

Especially mentioned for citation at the time that he was selected as a Pulitzer Prize winner was Hightower's interpretive reporting of the events leading up to the dismissal of General of the Army Douglas MacArthur. Almost two months before MacArthur's removal, the A.P. diplomatic editor in a February 14, 1951, dispatch, later described by the Association Press as a "penetrating analysis," stated: "Officials here see little chance that General Douglas MacArthur will get the power and authority he considers necessary to achieve complete victory over the Chinese Communists in Korea." The increasing conflict between MacArthur and the Truman Administration was clearly depicted by Hightower about three weeks before the General's dismissal, when the reporter revealed, "The Administration dissociated itself today from MacArthur's declaration that if the United Nations want to expand their military operations into attacks on the Chinese mainland they can destroy Red China. . . .The reasons for the Administration's sensitiveness appears to be a feeling here that MacArthur's statement had somewhat the look of an ultimatum although it was not." On March 26

Hightower reported that the dispute had "reached fever heat."

Six days prior to MacArthur's being relieved of his United Nations command, Hightower alone among journalists correctly interpreted the significance of the General's letter to House Republican leader Joseph Martin of Massachusetts, advocating the use of Chinese Nationalist troops against the Chinese Communists, a viewpoint strongly opposed by the Administration. At this time Hightower disclosed, "The latest incident has renewed speculation in some quarters of the Administration that Mr. Truman may consider removing or recalling MacArthur." He obtained the exclusive story on the event which precipitated MacArthur's dismissal, writing on April 12, 1951, "President Truman personally concluded that General MacArthur had to go as soon as he saw a copy of General MacArthur's letter to House Republican leader Martin." The A.P., on nominating Hightower for the Pulitzer Prize, said, "From the beginning, Hightower consistently pointed out the depth of the split . . . its significance and its possible eventual consequences. These consequences were pointed up with striking sharpness just before the dismissal."

Scoring a "beat" on every other newspaperman, Hightower on July 25, 1951, obtained information about the terms of the Communist compromise offer for withdrawing military forces from Korea. These terms, he reported, would not involve the withdrawal of foreign troops until after an armistice and would require that the U.N. merely promise to discuss this matter after the truce had been arranged. Hightower procured this exclusive story by personally conjecturing on the most likely Communist proposal, then asking the key officials for their opinions. Another Hightower exclusive was his dispatch stating that "General Matthew B. Ridgeway's truce instructions will permit him to make minor adjustments but no concessions in the U.N. demand that an armistice buffer zone in Korea follow the present battle line." The A.P. contrasted Hightower's "careful and cool-headed reporting under pressure" on this news event with rival dispatches which "were feverish early in the week with false hopes for a quick cease-fire." The decision of Winston Churchill to visit Washington in January 1952 was also exclusively reported by Hightower on November 11, 1951. Characterizing the A.P. newspaperman as "painstaking," the New York *Times* told that on one occasion Hightower verified an inside news item given him by a Secretary of State with two other sources before making a dispatch on this story.

Hightower is married to the former Martha Nadine Joiner of New York City and is the father of three children. The newspaperman is described as a "quiet, modest reporter" (*Time*) and is said to be so "cool and efficient under pressure" that "you can't tell by looking at him whether he is dictating a hot bulletin or a Sunday advance." Golf, gardening, and woodworking are listed as his hobbies.

Reference

N Y Times p24 My 6 '52 por

HILALY, AHMED NAGUIB (hĭ-lä'lĭ ä'măd nä'gēb) 1891- Former Premier of Egypt
Address: Cairo, Egypt

Upon taking office as Egypt's new Premier on March 2, 1952, Ahmed Naguib Hilaly, an independent politically, announced his intention to rid Egypt of corruption and reach an agreement with the British over the question of the Sudan. He was called upon by King Farouk to replace Aly Maher, whose resignation was forced by his failure to reach any agreement

Wide World Photos
AHMED NAGUIB HILALY

with the British. Hilaly, a lawyer, had held other Cabinet posts. For the third time in six months Egypt changed Premiers on June 29, 1952, when Hilaly was replaced by Hussein Sirry. He was recalled to form a new Cabinet less than a month later, but on the following day, July 23, resigned his office at the request of Major General Mohammed Naguib, who in a *coup d'état* appointed Aly Maher to the Premiership.

Ahmed Naguib Hilaly Pasha ("Pasha" is a title of honor), who was born in 1891, is reported by *Time* to be the "scion of a wealthy family." A law school graduate, he has taught that subject at Fuad University in Cairo, is said to have made a fortune in its practice, and is regarded as one of Egypt's foremost jurists. He has been a deputy and advisory local director of Barclays Bank, and has served successively as Minister of Education in the wartime Cabinet (1943) and briefly as Minister of Commerce and Industry. He gave up public office when graft in the Wafd party (the only organized political group in Egypt) was first exposed in 1943-44. At one time a Wafdist leader, Hilaly was expelled from the party in November 1951 reportedly because he

HILALY, AHMED NAGUIB—*Continued*
had accused former Minister of the Interior
Serag-el-Din of illegal wire tapping.

With the reputation of being a moderate and
"sharing none of the anti-Britishism which
characterizes the more fanatic Wafdists"
(*Time*, March 10, 1952), Hilaly was appointed
Premier by King Farouk on March 2, 1952.
He succeeded Aly Maher Pasha, who resigned
because of disagreement with King Farouk,
who wanted to come to "sensible" terms with
the British. Maher preferred, with the aid of
the Wafd party, to do "what he could with the
British," said *Time*. The Wafdists have been
charged with having no intention of making
a settlement with the British but using the
dispute to cover internal corruption.

Premier Hilaly Pasha turned his attention
first to corruption within the Government. In accordance with King Farouk's real purpose in
forming a new government (to dissolve the
Wafd party), Hilaly's first act under martial
law was to suspend the Wafdist-dominated
Parliament for thirty days. In opposing the
Wafd party the King and his Premier were
seen as risking a revolution. (*Time* magazine
has suggested that if Farouk loses his power
to the Wafdists, Egypt will be lost to the
West as a key in the Middle Eastern defense.)
In an effort to win public support in a late
election, Hilaly's next act was to postpone
the elections from May until October 1952.
This was the sixth time in Egypt's recent history that the normal process of constitutional
parliamentary government has been set aside.

In justifying what the Wafdists called an
"unconstitutional" act, the Premier stated that
Parliamentary seats were being sold and that
government posts had become the prerogative
of relatives and friends of those in office. As
part of his clean-up program he purged the
police and the army of all suspected Wafdist
sympathizers and within three days had seven
high officers relieved of their commands after
learning that two regiments would support the
Wafd in case of a "violent showdown" (*Newsweek*, March 31, 1952). He also arrested two
Wafd leaders who were responsible for the
Cairo riots of January 26, 1952. Early in
March he took other drastic action when, calling Fuad University "a rumor serpent," he
closed the institution following a student demonstration which threatened a riot if the British
were not "thrown out within twenty days"
(*Time*).

When Premier Hilaly approached the British
government with the intention of settling the
British-Egyptian treaty dispute, he asked Britain to evacuate her troops from the Suez Canal
Zone and to recognize Egyptian sovereignty
over Sudan. The British are willing to withdraw the 50,000 men stationed in the Canal
Zone within some months if Egypt adheres to
two conditions: (1) she must join a Briton-
headed Middle East Command, and (2) British technicians, military and civilian, must remain to man the canal installations until a sufficient number of Egyptians have been trained
for such duties. In an agreement that dates
from 1899, Britain and Egypt were to have
joint rule over that rich cotton area. However,

since the treaty went into effect all Sudan's
governor generals have been Britons. On April
2, 1952, Britain offered the Sudanese a limited
self-rule charter with provision for their own
Cabinet and Parliament. Early in May a new
formula was offered by the British: Britain and
Egypt, or Britain, Egypt, and representatives
of the Sudanese negotiate a settlement. If the
Sudanese are willing to recognize King Farouk
as their ruler, the British are prepared to agree
to that (New York *Times*, May 4, 1952). Early
in June Hilaly met with members of a Sudanese delegation at their third and last formal
meeting in the attempt to achieve Sudanese
independence under the Egyptian Crown. Replaced as Premier by Hussein Sirry on June 29,
1952, Hilaly was recalled to form a new Government less than a month later. On the next
day, July 23, following a *coup d'état* by Major
General Mohammed Naguib, he yielded the
Premiership to Aly Maher. Hilaly was one of
a number of prominent Egyptians arrested in
September 1952 on political charges; he was
accused of "having suspended the Constitution
for an indefinite period and of aggression
against the Council of State."

"Mild-spoken" Hilaly Pasha has been called
an able statesman. When he became Premier
he received this message from King Farouk:
"I hope that you will succeed in the great program which includes everything that I might
have asked you to do."

References

N Y Herald Tribune p1 Mr 9 '52
N Y Times p1 Mr 3 '52
Time 59:38 p38 Mr 10 '52
Who's Who in Egypt and the Middle
East, 1948

HILTON, FRANK C. Oct. 12, 1908- Veterans organization official; businessman
Address: b. c/o Hilton Brothers, Reading, Pa.

The third veteran of World War II to be
elected commander in chief of the Veterans
of Foreign Wars of the United States is Frank
C. Hilton, a businessman of Reading, Pennsylvania. Active in veterans affairs since 1946, he
assisted in the organization of a post of the
Veterans of Foreign Wars in Womelsdorf,
Pennsylvania, and later became an official in
the Pennsylvania State organization. In 1949
he was elected a junior and the following year
a senior vice-commander in chief, thus automatically stepping into the top position of the
V.F.W. for 1951-52 in succession to Charles C.
Ralls. Hilton joined the United States Army
as a private and by 1946, when he was discharged, he had been advanced to the rank of
captain.

Frank C. Hilton was born in Pittsburgh,
Pennsylvania, on October 12, 1908. There he
attended public elementary and secondary
schools. He next entered Springfield College
at Springfield, Massachusetts. At college, continuing the interest in athletics he had shown
in high school, he earned letters in football,
basketball, baseball, swimming, and boxing.
After graduating from college he went to Read-

ing, Pennsylvania, where he engaged in business and eventually became a broker in the cork products field. In 1952 he is the president of Hilton Brothers, a cork brokerage firm. For some years in Reading he coached the high school swimming team, which won several local and State championships.

In March of 1942 Hilton volunteered for service as a private in the United States Army. After a training period he was assigned to the overseas Allied Force Headquarters and saw a year of active service in the military campaign in Italy. He rose in the commissioned ranks until in 1946, when he received his honorable discharge, he held the rank of captain.

On his return to civilian life and his cork brokerage business, Hilton manifested an interest in the Veterans of Foreign Wars of the United States and was instrumental in organizing the Max W. Schaeffer Post 6558 in Womelsdorf, Pennsylvania, of which he was elected the first commander. His evident enthusiasm for the organization and success as a speaker led to his endorsement by the members of his area for a position in the State organization, and in July 1946 he was elected senior vice-commander of the Department of Pennsylvania. This election meant that in 1947 he would become commander of the department, the first veteran of World War II to hold that office. During 1950-51 he was chairman of the State organization's legislative committee and a member of its bonus committee, a group which participated in a successful campaign for the payment of a State bonus to World War II veterans.

Meanwhile Hilton has become a member in 1948 of the V.F.W's national legislative committee, and in 1949, at the Golden Jubilee Encampment, held in Miami, Florida, had been elected junior vice-commander in chief. The following year he advanced to the rank of senior vice-commander in chief, a position which carries with it automatic election to the highest rank, that of commander in chief. At the fifty-second encampment, held in New York City in September 1951, Hilton was duly elected, succeeding Charles C. Ralls.

Upon assuming the chief office in the Veterans of Foreign Wars of the United States, Hilton took command of an organization dating from 1899 and ranking as the second largest veterans organization in the United States, with a membership of over one million. The members, who are organized in 9,800 local posts in all the States of the Union, are dedicated to the preservation and strengthening of their comradeship, to the perpetuation of the memory of those American soldiers who have died in service, and to the assistance to their widows and orphans. For those dependents the V.F.W. maintains a 640-acre national farm and home in Michigan. It also has as its purpose the maintenance and extension of American institutions, including the fostering of "true patriotism" and the defense of the United States. Its interests, as classified in the *Social Work Yearbook*, are "fraternal, patriotic, historical, and educational."

The national meeting at which Hilton was elected saw the passing of resolutions on five

FRANK C. HILTON

major issues. The first of these was concerned with a defense program, seeking the establishment of Marine Corps with four full-strength combat divisions, activation of a National Security Training Corps, and control of shipments to Communist areas. The second involved domestic affairs, in which the veterans asked for a more effective economic stabilization program and statehood for Alaska and Hawaii. In the field of veterans affairs, the national convention sponsored measures providing pensions at the age of sixty-five to veterans of both world wars, aid to housing and construction of additional hospitals for veterans. Pay increases for members of the armed services were also urged, as was better housing for those in service. And lastly, the V.F.W. passed resolutions looking for a revision in the immigration laws that would "protect the political and economic rights of citizens of the United States," the death penalty for those convicted of espionage or treason, and the elimination of those sections in textbooks judged to be "objectionable from the American viewpoint."

In accepting his executive post Hilton pledged himself to further the resolutions. On September 27, 1951, he called on President Truman, himself a member of the V.F.W., to bring the veterans legislative program to the Executive's attention. He also left on Truman's desk a recommendation that Dean Acheson be removed as Secretary of State. During his term of office Hilton represents the V.F.W. on radio networks, press conferences, and legislative hearings. He attempts to meet with members of the local posts in the United States as well as those in Japan, Korea, and possibly Europe. For the 1952 membership drive, a particular concern of Hilton, the commander in chief in his regular monthly editorials in the *V.F.W. National News*, offers suggestions and incentives for activating members and gaining

HILTON, FRANK C.—*Continued*

new ones. He considers himself a "general sales manager" for the association.

The Hiltons—Mrs. Hilton is the former Viola Rogers—have a daughter named Gay Smith. Hilton is a Thirty-second Degree Mason and a member of the Moose organization. He has taken part in programs of the Rotary International and the National Grange. Active also in political groups, he was formerly chairman of the Young Republicans of Pennsylvania and vice-chairman of the Young Republican National Federation; on September 10, 1952, he was named head of the Republican National Committee's Veterans Division. He attends the Christ Episcopal Church of Reading.

References

N Y Times p5 S 1 '51
V.F.W. National News p22 O '51

HOLLAND, (GEORGE) KENNETH
May 10, 1907- Educational administrator

Address: b. c/o Institute of International Education, 857 5th Ave., New York 17; h. 28 Avon Rd., Bronxville, N.Y.

Dr. Kenneth Holland, who was elected the third president of the Institute of International Education in November 1949 and assumed office in September 1950, came to this post after many years of government service commencing with an appointment in 1933 as educational adviser to the Civilian Conservation Corps. Later he was attached to the State Department's Inter-American Office in various capacities, and more recently was head of the Department's Office of Educational Exchange and permanent United States representative to UNESCO.

George Kenneth Holland was born May 10, 1907, in Los Angeles, California, one of the two sons of Charles Alfred Holland, an electrical contractor, and Cora Effie (Spring) Holland. Young Kenneth Holland was brought up in the city of his birth, where, after high school he enrolled at Occidental College, an institution which emphasized the study of the social sciences. During two summer vacations he worked as a lifeguard, and during another was chief musician in the orchestra aboard an Orient-bound liner; during college terms his chief extracurricular interests were in the debating team and the student-body organization, of which he was president. In 1929, upon receiving his B.A. degree from Occidental, he proceeded to Princeton University to prepare for the M.A. degree, which was conferred on him in 1931. He is a member of both the Phi Beta Kappa and Tau Kappa Alpha fraternities.

The Institute of International Education, the organization of which Holland is now the director, was established in 1919. Founded by the Carnegie Endowment for International Peace at the instance of the late Stephen Pierce Duggan, it was designed "to promote international exchange of ideas in all aspects of education." It allotted and administered, among other grants, the American Field Service fellowships in international relations. One of these

was conferred on Holland. Thus, on taking his master's degree at Princeton, he was able to take a year of additional postgraduate study first at Grenoble and then at the Sorbonne in Paris. On completion of his courses in 1932, he was appointed secretary of the International Student Service, a position in which, during the year he filled it, he made studies of the youth labor camps of Europe, living in some of them. His article "German Work Camps"—one of the earliest of many he has contributed to such educational periodicals as *School and Society*, *School Life*, and the *Nation's Schools*—was published in the first-named weekly in July 1933. Three days before its appearance he wrote to the New York *Times* outlining the character of what he described as "the pre-Nazi German Voluntary Service Camps" and urging that their recreational programs be imitated in the forestry camps of the Civilian Conservation Corps. Shortly afterward Holland was appointed educational adviser to the CCC in the First Corps (New England) area and was able to put into operation many of his ideas on recreation and vocational training for unemployed youth.

When the American Council on Education established the American Youth Commission in September 1935, with Homer P. Rainey as director, Kenneth Holland was named associate director and placed in charge of the Commission's CCC study. In this connection he was asked to revisit the European labor camps. A preliminary account of his 1936 observations appeared in the *Annals of the American Academy* for November 1937 under the title "European Labor Service," and supplied the nucleus of his first book, *Youth in European Labor Camps*, published by the American Council on Education in 1939. Of this work the New York *Times* reported that it "covers a wide field with satisfactory thoroughness, even to . . . a resumé of the labor camp movement in South Africa, Australia, and Japan." Two years later (1941) the council issued two pamphlets by Holland entitled *Work Camps for College Students* and *Work Camps for High School Youth*, the latter in collaboration with George L. Bickel. These publications were prepared for the American Youth Commission, as was *Youth in the CCC* (1942), a collaboration by Holland and Frank Ernest Hill. Though a reviewer for *Survey Graphic* regarded this study as "too long," he considered it a "valuable record of a remarkable industrial experiment." S. A. Queen wrote in the *Annals of the American Academy* that it "offers to all educators and citizens with open minds some serious challenges."

Some months prior to the appearance of this book, a new phase in the career of Kenneth Holland had begun when in 1941 he was named as the chief of the education section of the Office of Inter-American Affairs. Holland was a delegate to the Inter-American Committee on Intellectual Cooperation meeting at Havana, Cuba, in the same year, and the United States delegate to the Second American Conference on Agriculture held at Mexico City in the year following. Also in 1942, he was given the title of Director of the Division of Education, and in 1943 he went to Panama City as consultant to the United States delegation to the Inter-American Conference of Ministers and Directors of Education. Holland was largely responsible for the formulation of a program whereby the Office of Inter-American Affairs provided, over a three-year period, $5,000,000 in funds for the development of new primary and secondary schools in Latin-American countries. In 1945 he became president of the Inter-American Educational Foundation, the agency set up to implement this plan, his work as such requiring him to speak at the Institute of Inter-American Affairs and at schools and colleges.

Holland, who has been credited with a prominent part in the development of the program of the United States participation in the United Nations Educational Scientific and Cultural Organization (UNESCO), served with his country's delegations to that body's conferences at London in 1945 and Paris in 1946. During 1946, also, he was acting as assistant director of the State Department's Office of International Information and Cultural Affairs, which "develops and executes international information programs of the Department and assures dissemination of media materials" (*United States Government Organization Manual*); and as such he attended the UNESCO conferences at Mexico City in 1947 and Beirut in 1948. In the latter year he was appointed director of the State Department's Office of Educational Exchange, which "develops and executes international exchange programs of the Department and assists similar activities of private agencies abroad" (*Government Manual*). At the same time he was named permanent United States representative to UNESCO and participated in its general meetings at Paris in 1949 and Florence in 1950.

On taking office in 1947 as president of the Institute of International Education, Laurence Duggan announced that in the future objectives of the institute would be "correlated" with those of UNESCO through that body's American commission. When, as a result of the sudden death of Laurence Duggan in December 1948, the post of president of the Institute of International Education became vacant, Holland was selected to fill it. His election was announced by chairman of the board George N. Shuster on November 14, 1949, but because of pending UNESCO affairs and other previous commitments he was unable to assume his new duties until September 1950. The institute had been delegated by the Ford Foundation to advise on, and administer, grants for projects involving international exchange of persons. The agreement covered grants totaling $225,000 to the Massachusetts Institute of Technology, the American Chemical Society, and the National 4-H Foundation to enable young men and women from other countries to study in, or visit, the United States; and in July further grants of $25,000 and $50,000 were received from the Commonwealth Fund and the Rockefeller Foundation respectively to "help the exchange of persons between the United States

Fabian Bachrach

KENNETH HOLLAND

and . . . other countries." (A report issued by the institute earlier in the year had set the number of foreign students in the United States at 29,813 and the number of American students abroad at around 20,000.) Holland is a member of the UNESCO Working Party on Exchange of Persons, the Inter-American Advisory Committee, the Greater New York Council for Foreign Students, the Inter-American Academy of Comparative and International Law, the Iran Foundation, and the Committee on International Policy of the National Planning Association. He is also a member of the Alliance Française, the American Association for the United Nations, the Germanistic and Pan-American Societies, the American Association of School Administrators, and the National Education Association. He holds honorary LL.D. degrees from Occidental College (1946) and Middlebury College (1951). Holland's clubs are the Cosmos in Washington and the Kenwood Country Club.

Kenneth Holland and Mary Frances Kimball were married in Lexington, Massachusetts on July 11, 1936; they are the parents of four children, Kenneth Kimball, Susan Sawyer, Marcia Spring, and Wendell Allen. Mrs. Holland, who was a student of piano and cello at the Boston Conservatory before her marriage shares enjoyment in music with her husband; for outdoor recreation he turns to swimming and tennis. Holland is an independent in politics and a Methodist in creed. He stands five feet ten inches in height and has brown eyes and graying brown hair.

References
N Y Times p21 N 15 '49
American Men in Government (1949)
America's Young Men, 1936-37
Leaders in Education (1948)
(Continued next page)

HOLLAND, KENNETH—*Continued*
Who's Who in America, 1950-51
Who's Who in Commerce and Industry (1951)
World Biography (1948)

HOMER, ARTHUR B(ARTLETT) Apr. 14, 1896- Industrialist
Address: b. c/o Beth!ehem Steel Corporation, Bethlehem, Pa.

The president of the Bethlehem Steel Corporation, the second largest steel-producing enterprise in the world, is Arthur B. Homer, who first joined the corporation's shipbuilding subsidiary in 1919. He became vice-president in charge of the shipbuilding division of the Bethlehem Steel Company in 1940 and suc-

Wide World Photos
ARTHUR B. HOMER

ceeded Eugene Gifford Grace—now chairman of the board—as president of both the Bethlehem Steel Corporation and the Bethlehem Steel Company in December 1945.

Arthur Bartlett Homer was born April 14, 1896, in Belmont, Massachusetts, a suburb of Boston, the son of Eleazer B. and Elizabeth F. (Hough) Homer. He is a graduate of Brown University, having received the Ph.B. degree there in 1917. He immediately commenced his World War I service as a Naval Reserve lieutenant and was trained at Annapolis for duty with the submarine fleet, in which he served for the duration of the conflict.

Returning to civilian life in 1919 Homer began his career in the shipbuilding and steel industry as assistant to the general superintendent of the Fore River yard of the Bethlehem Shipbuilding Corporation at Quincy,

Massachusetts. Since that year he has been associated with either that corporation or the operating Bethlehem Steel Company and the Bethlehem Steel Corporation.

The Bethlehem Steel Corporation is the holding concern for the family of companies developed from the Bethlehem Steel Company established by John Fritz in South Bethlehem, Pennsylvania, in 1899 and taken over by Charles M. Schwab in 1903. The Bethlehem Steel Corporation, within which the shipbuilding corporation was organized as a subsidiary, was incorporated in 1904. During the next fifteen years the steel-producing enterprises of Bethlehem were closely tied to the expanding needs of the shipbuilding subsidiary, both under Schwab and under Eugene Gifford Grace, who became president of the Bethlehem Steel Company in 1913 and president of the Bethlehem Steel Corporation in 1916, when Schwab moved on to the chairmanship of the board. Much of the country's World War I maritime construction program was carried out at the Fore River yard.

In 1921, after two years at Quincy, Homer was transferred to headquarters at Bethlehem to take over the management of Diesel engineering and sales. He was appointed manager of sales in New York City in 1926, and five years later—the shipbuilding corporation having become the shipbuilding division of the Bethlehem Steel Company—he was made assistant to the vice-president in charge of shipbuilding and repair. When World War II broke out in 1939, he held the post of assistant vice-president at Quincy, to which he had been appointed in 1934.

In May 1940, following the death of Samuel W. Wakeman, Homer was elected a director of the Bethlehem Steel Corporation and vice-president of the Bethlehem Steel Company's shipbuilding division. As the magazine *Fortune* was later to say, he was "handed the biggest shipbuilding job in history." This was the time (eighteen months before the United States entered the war) when the "arsenal of Democracy" was being prepared. "Shown United States plans for a two-ocean navy," reported *Fortune*, "Homer jumped the gun. Before legislation authorizing construction was passed he was ready to go." During the six years that followed, Bethlehem produced 73,000,000 tons of steel, about one-third of the armor and forgings needed for the Navy's big guns; it built 1,127 fighting and cargo vessels and converted, serviced, or repaired more than 37,000 ships (New York *Herald Tribune*). This was the "largest and most diverse" program of its kind ever executed by a private organization. According to *Fortune*, Bethlehem "practically built the Navy," while Homer is regarded by experts in the Navy as the "ablest man in the business."

Following the end of the war and the advent of the reconversion period, Eugene Grace moved up to the chairmanship of the board of the Bethlehem Steel Corporation—a post vacant since the death of Schwab in 1939—and at the same time (December 20, 1945) Homer was elected president of both the Bethlehem

Steel Company and the Bethlehem Steel Corporation. Grace continued to function as chief executive officer but thereafter "much of the day-by-day operation" was taken over by Homer (*Time*). Shipbuilding remained a "No. 1" activity, and in the following year Bethlehem constructed fifty-one ocean-going vessels and lesser craft and reconverted or repaired 4,764. In 1947 a twenty-week strike reduced the number of vessels constructed to only twenty-two.

Labor trouble continued, and early in 1948 Bethlehem followed United States Steel in yielding to the demands of the United Steel Workers of America for a third-round wage raise. Somewhat over a year later (August 1949), after a fourth-round increase had been demanded and a fact-finding board had been set up by President Truman, Homer declared that this board "appeared to be a vehicle designed to force concessions on the steel industry." The union demanded wage and welfare benefits totaling 30 cents an hour per worker, on the ground that steel productivity had risen 50 per cent since 1939, with proportionate profits to management. Homer, arguing his company's case before the board, countered with the assertion that Bethlehem's profits had lately averaged 6.3 per cent on sales as compared with 8.1 per cent in 1940, while wages had "increased at a rate far exceeding" that of productivity. In subsequent negotiations the unresolved issues eventually narrowed down mainly to the matter of pensions and other "fringe benefits," but no agreement was reached and a nation-wide strike involving 500,000 workers (77,000 of them in Bethlehem plants) began. It lasted, so far as Bethlehem was concerned, until October 31, when Philip Murray announced that an agreement had been reached with the corporation regarding pensions and social insurance.

In January 1950, in testimony before the Joint Congressional Committee on the Economic Report, Homer stated that "to keep its existing plant and equipment efficiently producing by replacing and rebuilding worn-out and obsolescent capacity, Bethlehem should, on the average, procure at least $117 millions each year," to assure which a $4-a-ton increase in steel prices was necessary. In the following June Homer announced that the Bethlehem Steel Company would embark on a $32 millions expansion and modernization program at its Johnstown (Pennsylvania) plant. He further disclosed in March 1951 that the company was starting to build up its ore supply from mines in Venezuela and was about to start a new iron ore development in Chile and to develop manganese in Brazil. During the ensuing November, in a speech to the Society of Naval Architects and Marine Engineers, he described current reports of a national steel shortage as "a distortion of the picture" and in particular criticized a cut in allocations of steel for shipbuilding through Government controls.

At the time of the breakdown of bargaining negotiations between the steel union and management, which led to the President's seizure of the steel industry in the spring of 1952, Homer was one of the negotiators and was acting as an industry spokesman. On May 4, 1952, commenting on the final breakdown of the talks, he pointed out that the companies, which had tried in earnest to reach an agreement, "could not accept" the union shop. He added that "while the Government had previously assured the industry that if a wage offer of 'a certain amount' were made, the companies would 'be taken care of' on prices," there had been no recent assurance from the White House that adequate price increases would be forthcoming (*New York Herald Tribune*).

The vice-president of the Society of Naval Architects and Marine Engineers, Homer is also a member of the American Iron and Steel Institute. He is a trustee of Brown University. His fraternity is the Alpha Delta Phi; his clubs are the University and Links in New York City. Mrs. Homer is the former Sara Yocom. The Homers were married September 14, 1922, and have one daughter, Constance (Mrs. David L. Rawls, Jr.), and two sons, Richard W. and Stephen B. The industrialist has a forty-foot yawl on which he finds his chief relaxation.

References

Fortune 33:176 Mr '46 por
N Y Times p27 D 21 '45
Time 46:78-80 D 31 '45 por

Business Executives of America (1950)
Who's Who in America, 1952-53
Who's Who in Commerce and Industry (1951)
Who's Who in the East (1951)

HOOK, SIDNEY Dec. 20, 1902- Educator; philosopher
Address: b. c/o New York University, Washington Sq., New York 3; h. 606-A 3d St., Brooklyn 15, New York

The American philosopher and educator Sidney Hook, author of *Towards the Understanding of Karl Marx* (1933), *Reason, Social Myths and Democracy* (1940), *The Hero in History* (1943), *Education for Modern Man* (1946), is known for his interpretations of John Dewey's views on metaphysics and education and for his own ideas in both fields. A member of the teaching staff of New York University since 1927, Hook is now the chairman of this institution's Graduate Division of Philosophy and Psychology. He is also the principal founder and chairman of the American Committee of Cultural Freedom, an organization to combat Russian propaganda.

Born to Isaac and Jennie (Halpern) Hook in New York City on December 20, 1902, Sidney Hook was reared in the Williamsburg section of Brooklyn and was graduated in 1919 from the Brooklyn Boys High School. He then studied philosophy under Morris R. Cohen at the College of the City of New York, where in 1922 he was awarded the Ward Medal in Logic and in 1923, on being graduated with the B.S. degree, he received the Certificate of Merit in Philosophy. In the fall of 1923 while teaching in New York City public schools, Hook

Wide World Photos

SIDNEY HOOK

began part-time postgraduate studies at Columbia University, where he obtained a scholarship in philosophy. He acquired his M.A. degree from Columbia in 1926 and after winning a university fellowship continued studying under professors John Dewey, James Montague, and Frederick Woodbridge to take his Ph.D. degree in 1927. Before completing his doctoral dissertation (*The Metaphysics of Pragmatism*, 1927) Hook had already contributed papers to *International Journal of Ethics, Monist, Open Court,* and *Archiv für Philosophie*.

In mid-1927 young Dr. Hook began the first of several seasons as a lecturer in the Columbia University summer sessions; in the fall of the same year he became an instructor in philosophy at the Washington Square College of New York University. During the 1928-29 academic year he studied abroad on a Guggenheim research fellowship at the universities of Berlin and Munich and at the Moscow Marx-Engels Institute pursuing what he has called his "active interest in the theory and practice of the working class movement." Having resumed his instructorship at the Washington Square College, he began in 1931 his still-continuing lecture series at the New School for Social Research. The next year he was promoted to assistant professor at New York University. In the introduction of his book *Towards the Understanding of Karl Marx; A Revolutionary Interpretation,* which was published in 1933, Hook pointed out: "This book is not written by an 'orthodox' Marxist." Marx himself, Hook maintained, was not an orthodox Marxist: "Orthodoxy is not only fatal to honest thinking; it invited the abandonment of the revolutionary standpoint which was central to Marx's life and thought." The work emphasizes that Marx's philosophy was not one of "retrospection" but of action. Selig Perlman, critic for the *American Political Science Re-*

view, called the book "the best presentation of the social philosophy of Karl Marx in the English language."

Hook was advanced in 1934 to associate professor and chairman of the Department of Philosophy at New York University. The following year he and Horace M. Kallen edited a critical anthology *American Philosophy—Today and Tomorrow.* Hook's next two books were *From Hegel to Marx* (1936) and *Planned Society—Yesterday, Today and Tomorrow* (1937). *John Dewey: An Intellectual Portrait,* a tribute to the most influential of Hook's mentors, appeared in 1939. In *Reason, Social Myths and Democracy* (1940) Hook pointed to the propaganda of Hitler, Mussolini, and Stalin as a threat to democracy, warning that "those who believe in democracy must distinguish intelligently . . . between honest opposition *within* the framework of the democratic process" and the totalitarian-subsidized and controlled opposition which "must be swiftly dealt with if democracy is to survive." In a review of the book the *Nation* remarked that Hook's attitude toward Marxism was "moving from heresy to apostasy."

The author of articles on determinism, materialism, and dialectical materialism in the *Encyclopaedia of the Social Sciences,* Hook also contributed articles to philosophical, sociological, and educational journals, and to the *New Republic, Nation, Current History, Saturday Review of Literature,* and the New York *Times Magazine. The Hero in History: A Study in Limitation and Possibility,* published in 1943, was termed by Jacques Barzun (in the *Nation*) as "the richest and fullest of his historico-philosophical studies." In this work Hook divides "great men" into "those who are more or less 'creatures of events' and the more positive 'extraordinary men'" (*New Yorker*) and he subjects to definite limitations the Hegelian-Spencerian theory that the nature of leadership is determined by events and that "the past has created the conditions of the present." The work won for its author in April 1945 the Butler Silver Award annually bestowed on the graduate of Columbia University who "has shown the most competence in philosophy or in educational theory, practice and administration." The citation called the book "an important contribution to the recent attempts to interpret history from the point of view of American naturalism and experimentalism."

Having studied under John Dewey, Hook became interested in modernizing teaching methods. The June 30, 1945, issue of the *Saturday Evening Post* contained his article, "The Case for Progressive Education," and a year later his book, *Education for Modern Man,* was published. The *Nation* found that the book approached "education from the point of view represented . . . by John Dewey, but in general to be defined as experimental, democratic and secular." The book's axiom, according to the reviewer, was that "education should aim to develop the powers of critical independent thought." In a twenty-two-page appendix Hook criticized the widely discussed experimental curriculum of St. John's College, Maryland, and thought the recommendations of the Harvard report and of University of Chicago Chancellor Robert M. Hutchins were "out of line with American living in the 20th Century."

The New York University Graduate School named Hook the head of its Department of Philosophy in 1948 and chairman of the Division of Philosophy and Psychology in 1949. In March of the latter year Hook organized Americans for Intellectual Freedom, a group of some two hundred scholars and cultural leaders in the arts and religion, to protest the allegedly Communist-controlled Cultural and Scientific Conference for World Peace that was then meeting in New York City. A few weeks later (April 1949) Sidney Hook and the novelist James T. Farrell, as representatives of Americans for Intellectual Freedom, attended a Paris meeting designed to counteract a concurrent Communist-sponsored Congress of Partisans for Peace. The purpose of the meeting—"to establish a world federation of intellectual freedom"—led to the organization of the American Committee of Cultural Freedom, with Professor Hook as chairman. This committee is one of nine "national communities" now affiliated with the Congress for Cultural Freedom, which assembled for the first time June 26, 1950, in the American sector of Berlin. At this session Hook spoke on "the distortion of words in Communist practice."

During 1950 Hook edited a symposium, *John Dewey: Philosopher of Science and Freedom,* in honor of that philosopher, who was then entering the tenth decade of his life. The same year witnessed the publication of Julien Steinberg's collection of essays, *Verdict of Three Decades,* in which an article by Hook that appeared in the *American Mercury* under the title "Communism and the Intellectual" was reprinted as "The Literature of Disillusion." Other recent articles by Hook are "What Shall We Do About Communist Teachers?" (*Saturday Evening Post,* September 10, 1949) and three contributions to the New York *Times Magazine,* "The Scientist in Politics" (April 9, 1950), "Why They Switch Loyalties" (November 26, 1950), and "To Counter the Big Lie: A Basic Strategy" (March 11, 1951). He wrote the review of Whittaker Chambers' book *Witness* for the New York *Times Book Review* (May 25, 1952).

Sidney Hook has been married twice, to Carrie Katz on March 31, 1924, and to Ann E. Zinken on May 25, 1935. By the earlier union he has a son, John Bertrand, and by the second, a son and a daughter, Ernest Benjamin and Susan Ann. The "ebullient, scrappy" philosopher (as *Time* has described him) is active in the International Committee for Academic Freedom, the American Philosophical Association, the American Association of University Professors (of which he is a past council member), and the John Dewey Society. "In summer," according to the *Saturday Evening Post,* "he disappears into a wild part of Vermont, where he has a grand quiet time with his wife, their . . . children, a dog, a cat, and no telephone." Gardening is his favorite recreation."

References

Sat Eve Post *222*:168 S 10 '49

Author's and Writer's Who's Who (1948-49)

Directory of American Scholars (1951)

Hook, S. Metaphysics of Pragmatism (1927) ; Towards the Understanding of Karl Marx ; A Revolutionary Interpretation (1933)

Kallen, H. & Hook, S., eds. American Philosophy Today and Tomorrow (1935)

Steinberg, J., ed. Verdict of Three Decades (1950)

Who's Who, 1951

Who's Who in America, 1952-53

Who's Who in American Jewry, 1938-39

Who's Who in Philosophy (1942)

HOOPES, DARLINGTON Sept. 11, 1896-

Socialist party leader; lawyer

Address: b. 212 N. 6th St., Reading, Pa.; c/o National Socialist Party, 303 4th Ave., New York 10; h. 1521 Greenview Ave., Reading, Pa.

Darlington Hoopes, an attorney-at-law of Reading, Pennsylvania, and former member of the State Legislature, is a leader of the Socialist party on the national level. The party's candidate for the Vice-Presidency of the United States in 1944 and the organization's national chairman since 1948, Hoopes was nominated for the Presidency of his country on June 1, 1952, thereby taking the place of Norman Thomas, who had declined to run again for the White House office.

The son of Price and Lizzie L. (Tucker) Hoopes, Darlington Hoopes was born September 11, 1896. He is a descendant of Daniel Hoopes, a Quaker who came to Pennsylvania from England on the ship *Providence* in September of 1683. Darlington Hoopes was born and reared in Harford County, Maryland, where the family had a farm; there he attended public school through the eighth grade. He then entered George School, a preparatory school in Pennsylvania, where he was a member of the debating and track teams. Upon graduation in 1913, Hoopes enrolled at the School of Agriculture at the University of Wisconsin for a year's study. While attending the university he was active in debating as a member of the Philo Mathia Debating Society.

His formal education at an end, Hoopes read law in an office and on February 14, 1921, was admitted to practice before the Supreme Court of Pennsylvania. Until 1927 he practiced law in Norristown, after which he moved his office to Reading, where he has since maintained his practice. In 1928 he was elected Assistant City Solicitor of Reading, a position which he held through 1932. Then, from 1936 to 1940 he filled the post of City Solicitor of Reading, the chief legal officer of the city. Meanwhile, from 1930 through 1936 he had served three terms in the State Legislature at Harrisburg as a member of the Pennsylvania House of Representatives, and was at

United Press

DARLINGTON HOOPES

one time voted the "most able member" of the Pennsylvania House by newsmen at the State capital.

An active member of the Socialist party, Hoopes received the nomination for Vice-president of the United States in June 1944, running on the same ticket with Norman Thomas, the party's fifth-time Presidential candidate. In 1948 he again was a candidate for the Vice-Presidential nomination, but withdrew before the voting took place at the Socialist convention held that May in Reading. At this time, however, the convention elected Hoopes national chairman of the party for the two-year term, to which he was re-elected in 1950 and again in 1952. He has been chosen a Socialist candidate for other offices as well, running for Judge and District Attorney of Berks County on several occasions and for the United States Congress from the Thirteenth Pennsylvania District in 1950. Hoopes has also contributed political .articles to the *Socialist Call*, the *Reading Labor Advocate*, and the *Progressive*.

On June 2, 1950, the Socialists held their twenty-seventh national convention in Detroit, Michigan, to decide upon certain fundamental points of party policy. In planning the Congressional platform for the fall elections, they called for universal disarmament "down to a police level under the supervision and control of a strengthened United Nations." From the outset the party was of divided opinion on the matter of participation in "hopeless" election contests. Norman Thomas led a group favoring greater emphasis on educational measures and on support to organizations having Socialist aims such as labor unions and Americans for Democratic Action, rather than spending party funds on election campaigns in which they had no chance of victory. The opposition to Thomas was led by Hoopes, who

argued that Presidential campaigns, although futile in outcome, give the party the kind of national attention that is necessary for its survival. A majority of delegates (70 to 37) to the three-day convention favored Hoopes's position, repudiating the leadership of Thomas by electing a national executive committee favoring increased political activity in which Thomas was given a minority voice. Hoopes, however, issued a laudatory statement on Thomas' long record of service to the party, a tribute that was seconded by the delegates present.

Norman Thomas having refused during the 1950 convention to become a candidate for a seventh time, Hoopes began to be considered as the next Presidential candidate. On May 5, 1952, Massachusetts Socialists at their State convention endorsed Hoopes of Pennsylvania and Miss Robin Myers of New York (the party's secretary) for the Presidential and Vice-Presidential offices. At the party's twenty-eighth national convention, held in Cleveland in the spring of 1952, Hoopes, who had been re-elected the party's national chairman on May 31, was nominated for President by acclamation on June 1, Samuel H. Friedman of New York and William A. Briggs of Los Angeles having withdrawn from the nomination. The political platform adopted by the party included opposition to military conscription and advocacy of a world-wide "peace income tax" to be contributed to the United Nations' funds for use in widening the Point Four program. Hoopes himself expressed the opinion that the major emphasis in American foreign policy should be placed on "helping the distressed people to raise their living standards to the point where the Communist appeal will become ineffective."

Since its founding in 1901, the Socialist party has been on the ballot in every national election, frequently as the chief third party in the country. In the 1948 Presidential election Thomas polled 170,000 votes. Considered radical in the early part of its history, Socialism stood for old age pensions, public ownership of banks, natural resources, basic industry, and utilities, unemployment insurance, abolition of child labor, and shorter hours with higher wages for the worker, many of which reforms were later enacted by the New Deal.

Hoopes is active in a number of local and State organizations in Pennsylvania. He has been director and chairman of the membership committee of the Reading Central Young Men's Christian Association, chairman since 1944 of the Community Race Relations Council of Reading, member of the State Executive Committee (the State Council for a Pennsylvania Fair Employment Practice Committee), and member from 1947 to 1951 of the board of directors of the Eastern Cooperatives, Inc., with offices then in New York City. He has also been interested in the work of the Boy Scouts of America and of the Playground Association of Reading.

Married since October 16, 1925, to the former Hazelette Miller, who was a YWCA secretary, Hoopes is the father of two sons and one daughter, Darlington, Jr., Rae, and Delite. For recreation he likes tennis, handball, and gardening. A Quaker, Hoopes is a trustee of the Reading-Exeter United Monthly Meeting of Friends. He is five feet, seven inches tall, weighs 160 pounds, and has hazel eyes and graying brown hair.

References

N Y Times Je 2 '52 por

Who's Who in United States Politics (1950)

HORNE, JOHN E(LMER)   Mar. 4, 1908-
United States Government official

Address: b. c/o Small Defense Plants Administration, 1337 E St., N.W., Washington 25, D.C.; h. 804 Janney's Lane, Alexandria, Va.

Small Defense Plants Administrator John E. Horne has since September 1952 headed the United States Government agency responsible for helping small plants and businesses obtain defense contracts and necessary supplies and equipment. Before being advanced to this position, Horne had served as deputy administrator of the administration from the beginning of its operations in the fall of 1951. The former Alabama teacher and one-time publishing house representative had from 1947 to 1951 been an administrative assistant to Senator John J. Sparkman of Alabama.

John Elmer Horne was born on March 4, 1908, in Clayton, Alabama, one of eleven children of John Eli and Cornelia Elizabeth (Thomas) Horne, farmers of English descent. The boy attended the Barbour County High School in Clio, Alabama, where he was a member of the football team and tennis club, manager of the baseball team, and vice-president of his senior class, graduating in 1925. At the University of Alabama in Tuscaloosa, which he later entered, he majored in history, held a history readership, and defrayed all his expenses by working at odd jobs. During his years in college he was the president of two fraternities—Pi Kappa Alpha and Phi Delta Kappa, a member of Omicron Delta Kappa and Kappa Delta Pi, vice-president of the International Relations Club, a member of the Cotillion Club, and editor of *Corolla*, the college yearbook. He also attained election to Phi Beta Kappa. Between 1928 and 1931 Horne taught history and mathematics at the high school in Columbiana, Alabama. For two years after he had received his B.A. degree in history from the University of Alabama in 1933, Horne, as a holder of a teaching fellowship, remained at this institution in the position of instructor in history. Some years later he resumed postgraduate work to take his M.A. degree in history (with a minor in school administration) in 1941 at the University of Alabama.

When he left teaching to enter the publishing field in 1935, Horne became the southeastern representative of the Macmillan Company. He was employed by this company until he joined the Row, Peterson Publishing Company

JOHN E. HORNE

in 1939 as its representative in the same territory. During World War II, in April 1943, Horne was commissioned a communications officer, with the rank of lieutenant (j.g.). A year later he was promoted to lieutenant (s.g.), a rank he held until he left active service in 1946. (In 1951 Horne became a lieutenant commander in the Naval Reserve.) Following World War II service Horne returned to his position with the Row, Peterson Publishing Company, remaining here until his appointment in 1947 as administrative assistant to the newly elected junior United States Senator from Alabama, John J. Sparkman, who, along with a number of other committee posts, in 1950 became the chairman of the Senate's Select Committee on Small Business. Following the establishment of the Small Defense Plants Administration, which began operations in the fall of 1951, Horne left his position with Sparkman to accept the post of deputy administrator of the bureau, serving under Telford Taylor. Upon the resignation of Taylor, Horne was chosen on September 12, 1952, by President Truman for the top position of chief administrator, a recess appointment pending the return of Congress in January 1953.

The SDPA was established by Congress, under an amendment to the Defense Production Act in the summer of 1951, to aid small manufacturing plants and other small businesses (with fewer than 500 employees) to obtain defense contracts and to protect the competitive position of small business in the industrial mobilization for defense. Since assuming direction of the new agency Horne has initiated a program to speed up government loans to small plants by permitting the regional offices of the agency to recommend directly loans of comparatively small amounts, thus saving time formerly spent in processing the loan application in the Washington headquar-

HORNE, JOHN E.—*Continued*

ters. Horne has also authorized some of the field representatives of the bureau to become "circuit riders" who can reach businessmen in small communities remote from the regional offices. These representatives will work with chambers of commerce, State commissions set up to aid small businesses, and civic organizations in helping owners of small plants to get their fair share of defense work.

In October 1952 when Horne visited the New York Regional Advisory Board, he stated that the SDPA had made "some progress in protecting the interests of small business, but not enough" (New York *Herald Tribune,* October 13, 1952); he further reported that as of September 26, 1952, the Reconstruction Finance Corporation had approved 189 loans recommended by the SDPA, amounting to $22,393,-258, to small firms that could not get aid from other sources. At the same time Horne also announced that his bureau had issued forty-one "certificates of competency" to defense contract bidders, under Congress' authorization for the agency to pass on the ability of any small business to perform satisfactorily on a government contract. The certificates usually are issued upon appeal made by small manufacturers whose ability to deliver is questioned by purchasing agencies. Horne said that military agencies had to accept the certificate decisions and that his office, while thus far concentrating on the military procurement program, would soon press the civilian agencies to buy as much as they could from small businesses. The SDPA head also disclosed that 196 contracts for small companies had been agreed upon under the "joint determination program" which was set up in the Defense Production Act to assure that military procurement officers would sit down with SDPA representatives to determine how many contracts should go to small businesses. In the words of the New York *Times* (October 12, 1952), the differences between the Small Defense Plants Administration and the Department of Defense, which were "at a high point" when Horne took office, were "being ironed out."

The government official is a member of the National Press Club in Washington, D.C., the University of Alabama Alumni Club, the Alabama Society Club, the Parent-Teacher Association, and the Community Chest Fund Committee. He is a Democrat and an Episcopalian. On July 27, 1938, Horne married Ruth Florence Kleinman, a former secretary; their two daughters are Linda and Susan. The blue-eyed and brown-haired administrator is five feet ten inches tall and weighs 165 pounds. He enjoys watching football and baseball matches and playing tennis and volleyball; other recreations are reading and gardening. He is a member of the American Legion, the Veterans of Foreign Wars, and AMVETS, and is a holder of a Letter of Commendation for his services in World War II.

Reference

Who's Who in American Education, 1949-50

HORNSBY, ROGERS Apr. 27, 1896-
Baseball club manager

Address: b. c/o Cincinnati Baseball Club, 307 Vine, Cincinnati, Ohio

"Perhaps the greatest right-handed hitter of all time," was the estimate, by John Drebinger of the New York *Times,* of Rogers Hornsby on the occasion of the latter's election in 1942 to the Baseball Hall of Fame. Hornsby's career as an active player, which had ended five years earlier, had covered well over twenty years, most of which were spent as second baseman and later as player-manager of the St. Louis (National League) Cardinals. In that period Hornsby amassed notable records, including the National League batting championship for seven years, the second highest lifetime batting average in the annals of baseball, and also the highest single season batting average on record in the National League. Hornsby, who at one time or another managed the Boston Braves, the Chicago Cubs, and the St. Louis Browns, returned to major league activity as manager (for the second time) of the St. Louis Browns, beginning October 1951. In July 1952 Hornsby was named manager of the Cincinnati (National League) Reds.

Rogers Hornsby was born in Winters, Texas, on April 27, 1896, the youngest of the six children of Edward Hornsby and the former Mary Dallas Rogers. His ancestry is Scottish and Irish. The father, a rancher, died while the last of his offspring was still an infant; his widow then took her four sons and two daughters first to the neighborhood of Austin and afterward, when "Rog" was four, to North Fort Worth, where the future baseball star grew up and received his education. Circumstances of the Hornsby family have been described as "modest"—during his schooldays the boy sold newspapers and held a series of part-time jobs. His interest in baseball was early aroused. "Cobb was my idol, my ideal of a ballplayer," Hornsby was to tell Harvey Breit of the New York *Times* in an interview nearly forty years later. "When I lived in Fort Worth, Cobb used to come down with his team for exhibition games. I watched him. I thought if those fellows could become real good, why couldn't I?"

Young Hornsby played ball on the neighborhood sandlots, and by the time he was fifteen was taken on by a local semiprofessional team which paid him at the rate of two dollars a game. A year later he was given a tryout by the Dallas (Texas League) club, was found promising but insufficiently experienced, and was dispatched for seasoning first to Tyler in the East Texas League and then in 1914 to the Hugo-Denison club of the Texas-Oklahoma League, as a shortstop. He played the same position with the Denison club of the Western Association in 1915.

Hornsby's minor league record shows that he batted only .232 at Hugo-Denison and improved to .277 with the Western Association. However, Bob Connery, a scout for the St. Louis Cardinals of the National League, combing the Class D circuits for prospects, thought well enough of Hornsby's speed to negotiate the purchase of his contract from Denison for $500. The young Texan's first day with the Cardinals was September 10, 1915, playing shortstop, and he hit .246 in the eighteen remaining games of the year. "I was one of the weakest hitters around," Hornsby told Harvey Breit, adding that at this time he weighed only 135 pounds. "Miller Huggins, the manager, called me in. He told me maybe he'd have to farm me out because I was too light. I didn't know what he meant except that I thought he really wanted me to work on a farm. So I did. I worked hard on the farm, and I drank a lot of milk and I got a lot of sleep. I came back weighing 160." When he did, it was to meet a turning point in his career, for at the beginning of the 1916 season one of the Cardinal coaches, noticing the now solid weight, suggested that Hornsby change his batting style and swing for distance. (Previously, Hornsby had "choked" the bat, aiming to spray short hits just beyond the infielders.) He became almost overnight a "sizzling" line-drive hitter, batting .313 in 1916 and attaining the fourth highest average in the league.

In 1917 Hornsby batted .327 for the Cardinals and achieved his first record. But it was in 1920, the year in which he became a fixture at second base, that he became famous in the baseball world; while as a fielder he made numerous errors in a new position, he led the league with a .370 batting average and went on to hold that championship for five ensuing seasons, or through 1925. "He was a savage batter," Arthur Daley of the New York Times has written. "He stood about as far back in the box as the law allowed and stepped in smartly with rhythmically level swing." The "Rajah of Swat" (or more briefly, "Rajah"), as the right-handed slugger came to be called, raised his hitting record to .397 in 1921 and to .401 in 1922, the highest National League batting average in twenty-three years. In 1922 he also created a modern league record by hitting safely in 33 consecutive games, scored the most home runs, and led National League second basemen in fielding. Two years later (1924) Hornsby established the modern National League batting record with a percentage of .424.

Hornsby had been a Cardinals infielder a little less than ten years when, on June 1, 1925, he was named manager of the club, taking over from Miller Huggins' successor, Branch Rickey, who moved into the business office. A change in leadership had been indicated—the Cardinals had ended up in sixth place in the league standings in 1924 and in the early weeks of the new season dropped into what is known in baseball slang as "the cellar." Continuing at second base, Hornsby drove his teammates up to fourth place in the remainder of 1925, himself hitting .403 and again winning the National League home run leadership as well as the first of his two "Most Valuable Player" awards. Under Hornsby's direction the Cardinals won the pennant in 1926 and went on to defeat the New York Yankees in the World Series games. This

ROGERS HORNSBY

triumph was, nevertheless, to prove the preliminary to the end of Hornsby's long association with the Cardinals. He felt that it warranted a permanent increase in salary from $40,000 to $50,000 a year. The club's owner, Sam Breadon, disagreeing, further friction developed between the two; and on December 26 Hornsby was traded to the New York Giants, in exchange for second baseman Frank Frisch.

According to Dan Daniel of the New York World-Telegram, Hornsby "was delighted to come to New York, with a possible chance to become the pilot of the Polo Grounders." (The veteran manager John McGraw was already planning to retire.) However, on occasions during 1927 when Hornsby took over direction of the team for the manager at times, they did not see eye to eye. This situation, together with a disagreement with the owner Charles Stoneham, over the use of a pinch-hitter in a certain game, resulted in Hornsby's departure by a trade in the winter of 1927-28. For New York he had batted .361 in 155 games.

In his new position, with second division Boston Braves, he was named manager May 25, 1928. While he hit .387 for Boston, antagonistic feeling between him and the players led to another change, a trade to the Chicago Cubs for five players and $200,000. With Chicago, in 1929 Hornsby had one of his best-playing seasons, hitting 40 home runs and achieving a batting percentage of .380, as well as again winning the "Most Valuable Player" award for his part in carrying the Cubs into a World Series with the Philadelphia Athletics. When Joe McCarthy resigned as manager of the Cubs on September 23, 1930, Hornsby took his place and continued therein until August 2, 1932. He finished out the year as a second baseman with his old team, the Cardinals.

(Continued next page)

HORNSBY, ROGERS—*Continued*

On July 26, 1933, Hornsby was appointed manager of the St. Louis American League team, the Browns. Though primarily a "bench" manager with the Browns, he did take the field on special occasions; thus his career as an active major league player did not actually conclude until his release by the St. Louis American League club in August 1937. In his twenty-three seasons in the majors, Hornsby had an over-all batting average of .358, a figure topped only by Ty Cobb's .367. His lifetime total of 1,582 runs batted in is exceeded only by Babe Ruth's 2,209.

In July 1938, following a brief engagement as a coach with the Baltimore Orioles of the International League, Hornsby was appointed manager of the Chattanooga (Tennessee) club in the Southern Association. The following year found him back with the Baltimore Orioles—this time as manager. Then, for one year beginning June 1940, he guided the destinies of the Oklahoma City club of the Texas League. On November 16, 1941, he took over both the field and general management of the Fort Worth team in the same league, and was so occupied in his boyhood home city when elected to the Baseball Hall of Fame in January 1942. World War II conditions caused the Texas League to suspend playing in February 1943, and for a period thereafter the "Rajah" managed the Vera Cruz team of Jorge Pasquel's Mexican League. In 1945 Hornsby undertook the direction of a baseball school established in Chicago by a local newspaper. He returned to minor league management five years later, when he assumed responsibility for the Beaumont team in the re-established Texas League. In 1951 he managed the Seattle (Washington) club of the Pacific Coast League. Both Beaumont and Seattle won pennants under Hornsby.

The St. Louis Browns, the team with which Hornsby had ended his active career as a player and from the managership of which he had been deposed in 1937, brought about his return to a major league. William Veeck, Jr., who had purchased the Browns, then deep in the "cellar" (in 1950), announced the appointment of Hornsby as manager on October 8, 1951, in succession to Zack Taylor. For a brief period early in 1952 the Browns under Hornsby led in American League standings, but by the end of May they were in a "slump." Hornsby's insistence on perfection, unremitting effort, and what some regarded as over-strict training and curfew rules, antagonized the team, with the result that on June 10 Hornsby was summarily dismissed by Veeck and succeeded as manager by Marty Marion.

Hornsby was not long unemployed, however, and when on July 28 he was named manager of the Cincinnati (National League) Reds in succession to Luke Sewell, General Manager Gabe Paul gave him what he felt to be a professional vindication: "We believe him to be the type of manager best fitted for our particular situation. . . . He is baseball through and through, and has demonstrated that winning is paramount with him." Hornsby's con-

tract with the Reds is said to run through the 1953 baseball season.

Divorced from Sarah E. Hornsby in 1923, Rogers Hornsby married Mrs. Jeannette Fennington Hine of St. Louis on February 29 of the year following, and now makes his permanent home in Chicago with his second wife. Their son, William, who has played professional baseball, is now engaged in business. A son by his first marriage, Rogers, Jr., died in an Air Force plane crash in 1949. The "Rajah" has hazel eyes and gray-brown hair; he stands five feet eleven inches in height and at the peak of his playing career weighed between 175 and 180 pounds. "He now wavers between 205 and 214," stated Harvey Breit. Baseball is his absorbing interest. "I've never been much of a mixer," Hornsby told Breit. "I don't want to go to dinner or the theater.... I care about baseball. . . . I don't know about other things."

References

Collier's 102:20+ Jl 16 '38 por; 129:16-17+ Ja 12 '52
Life 32:84-6 Mr 31 '52 pors
Lit Digest 78:55-7 S 1 '23; 82:46-8 Ag 23 '24 por; 96:57-60 F 25 '28 por
Look 16:55+ Je 17 '52 pors
N Y Herald Tribune p11 O 10 '51 por
N Y Times p25 Ja 21 '42 por; p17 Jl 19 '45; p35 O 9 '51 por; p39 O 17 '51; VI p15+ My 11 '52 por; p26 Jl 29 '52 por
N Y World-Telegram p23 O 8 '51; p29 O 9 '51
Newsweek 19:50 F 2 '42 por; 38:91 O 22 '51
Sat Eve Post 224:30+ F 9 '52 pors
Sport Life 5:16+ Ap '52 por
Time 39:58-9 F 2 '42 por; 59:57 Je 22 '52

Baseball Register (1951)
Collier's Encyclopedia (1950)
Columbia Encyclopedia (1950)
Grayson, H. They Played the Game (1945)
Horowitz, H., & Tolleris, R. Big-Time Baseball (1950)
Meany, T. W. Baseball's Greatest Hitters (1950)
Powers, J. J. A. Baseball Personalities (1949)
Sher, J. Twelve More Sport Immortals (1951)
Shoemaker, R. H. The Best in Baseball (1949)
Turkin, H., & Thompson, S. C. Official Encyclopedia of Baseball (1951)

HORSBRUGH, FLORENCE (hôs'bŭr-ō)

1889- British Minister of Education

Address: b. c/o Ministry of Education, Curzon St., London, W. 1, England; h. 19 Warwick Sq., London, S.W. 1, England; 18 E. Camus Pl., Edinburgh, Scotland

On November 2, 1951, a few days after the victory of the Conservatives in the British general election, Prime Minister Winston Churchill announced that the new Minister of Education was to be the Right Honorable Florence Horsbrugh, who was returned to Parliament in the same election. While the Minister of Education is not included in the Cabinet, Miss Horsbrugh's office is of Cabinet rank—she is the first woman to reach that rank in a Conservative Government. Before the Labor Government came into power in mid-1945, Miss Horsbrugh had sat in Parliament since 1931. For approximately six of those years (1939-45) she served as Parliamentary Secretary to the Ministry of Health, and for some months thereafter she held the same title in the Ministry of Food.

Florence Horsbrugh is a Scot, born in Edinburgh in 1889. Her father, Henry Moncrieff Horsbrugh, was a chartered accountant in the Scottish capital, and her grandfather had been sheriff-clerk of Fife, Scotland (the senior legal officer of the county), following two earlier members of the family in that office. Her mother, before she became Mrs. Horsbrugh, was Mary Stark Christie. Florence Horsbrugh was educated first at Lansdowne House, an Edinburgh school, and later at St. Hilda's, Folkestone, Kent. She did not enter a university.

At a comparatively early age Miss Horsbrugh became deeply interested in public service, especially in public health and the welfare of mothers and children. Many years later, in 1945, reported Melita Spraggs, of the *Christian Science Monitor*, she said: "I am interested in people and things. I only took up politics as a way of getting things done." She joined the Scottish Unionist (Conservative) Association and trained herself as a public speaker by appearing on Conservative platforms throughout Scotland. World War I gave her an opportunity to do practical social work, in the municipal kitchens. She was made a Member of the Order of the British Empire (M.B.E.) in 1920. With the swing to the Right in the general election of 1931, Miss Horsbrugh was chosen to represent Dundee in Parliament, the first Conservative from that contituency in a century. In the election of 1935 she topped the poll again, over a strong Liberal and over a Labor candidate who trailed her by more than 6,000 votes.

Besides public welfare, another lifelong concern of Miss Horsbrugh has been the promotion of international understanding and peace; in the years 1933, 1934, and 1935 she was a member of the United Kingdom delegation to the League of Nations Assembly, at Geneva. In November 1936 she became the first woman ever to move the address to the Throne at the opening of parliament (the only one opened by Edward VIII). In 1937 she piloted a bill designed to combat the extreme of alcoholic addiction, which became law that year as the Methylated Spirits (Sale by Retail) Act (Scotland).

As Parliamentary Secretary to the Ministry of Health, in July 1939 Miss Horsbrugh attained a junior ministerial office. The same year she was chiefly instrumental in securing the passing into law of the Adoption of Chil-

British Inf. Services

FLORENCE HORSBRUGH

dren (Regulation) Act (Scotland). One of her chief functions, according to the *Christian Science Monitor*, was "to gear up administrative machinery to soften the impact of possible war conditions on British mothers and babies." Two months after her appointment World War II did break out, and the carefully prepared plans for the evacuation of mothers and children from London and other populous centers were implemented. While many administrators were concerned in this vast operation, much credit reportedly redounded to Miss Horsbrugh for her part in carrying out smoothly the movement to country districts of 1,200,000 mothers and children without any major mishap. She became a Commander of the British Empire in the same year (1939).

Miss Horsbrugh's Parliamentary record in 1940 was marked by her close association with the Old Age and Widows' Pensions Act. She was heavily occupied during the bombing blitz of 1940-41 with constant visits to the air-raid shelters to supervise conditions there. After the raid on the engineering town of Coventry she is reported to have reached there by car before the flames had died down. (She was twice under the necessity of evacuating her own London apartment, once because of bomb damage and once because of an unexploded time bomb.) During the war the British infant mortality rate actually fell; for this some of the credit was given to Miss Horsbrugh. In 1945, the year of her appointment to the Privy Council, she was one of two British women delegates (the other being the late Ellen Wilkinson) to the San Francisco Conference on International Organization, which charted the United Nations. In May of that year she was appointed to the Ministry of Food as Parliamentary Secretary.

In the first postwar election, Miss Horsbrugh lost her seat in Parliament by some

HORSBRUGH, FLORENCE—*Continued*

7,000 votes. Now followed five years in the "political wilderness," with Miss Horsbrugh again unsuccessful in the general election of February 1950, when she contested the seat for the Scottish counties of Midlothian and Peebles. However, when a seat became vacant for Moss Side, Manchester, she came forward as a candidate; and in March she polled some 25,340 votes against her Labor opponent's 16,770 and her Liberal opponent's 2,600 (also approximate figures). In the election of October 1951 she increased her majority to nearly 11,000, polling about 27,700 votes against the Labor candidate's 16,800.

Before the close of 1951 Miss Horsbrugh felt in duty bound to warn local education authorities that, in their estimates for 1952, they were to provide for a reduction of about 5 per cent on the 1952-53 forecasts (already above those of recent years). Fears were expressed lest she should curtail the duration of children's stay at school, either by providing for their entry one year later or their leaving one year earlier. This she avoided, saying that the economies to be made should leave untouched the "essential fabric" of the educational system. The London *Sunday Express* parliamentary columnist wrote on December 16 that "she must now face the probability that the Socialists will table a motion of censure when Parliament resumes. And in that event the Liberals are likely to vote with them."

Britain's Minister of Education has received several honorary degrees—the D. Litt. from Mills College, California (1945) and the LL.D. from Edinburgh University (1947); in 1940 the Royal College of Surgeons of Edinburgh made her an honorary fellow. She belongs to the Ladies' Carlton Club. Her opinion on the place of women in the world today has been quoted: "I am one of those people who think men and women should work together." "We've got to keep alive the memory of what war means. This is something very special for women. . . .Peace must be won, just as wars must be won."

References

Christian Sci Mon Ap 20 '45
Burke's Peerage (1949)
International Who's Who, 1951
Kelly's Handbook to the Titled, Landed, and Official Classes, 1949
Who's Who, 1951

HOUTTE, JEAN VAN (hou'tĕ zhäN vän)
Mar. 17, 1907- Premier of Belgium

Address: b. c/o Office of the Premier, Brussels, Belgium; h. Boul. Saint-Michel, Brussels, Belgium

Jean van Houtte, a member of Belgium's Social Christian (Catholic) party, accepted the request of King Baudouin to form a new Cabinet on January 15, 1952, after the resignation of Joseph Pholien, the Premier since August 1950. Van Houtte, a lawyer and a former professor of economics at the universities of Liége

and Ghent, entered public life in 1944. In July 1949 he was elected to the Senate and in August 1950 accepted the portfolio of Minister of Finance in Pholien's Cabinet.

Jean van Houtte was born to Flemish parents on March 17, 1907, in Ghent, one of the principal cities in the Flemish-speaking section of Belgium. At the age of twenty-one, upon receiving his degree as Docteur en Droit (Doctor of Law) from Ghent University, he began the practice of law in Barreau and Ghent, later extending his practice to Brussels. Simultaneously he continued his studies at Ghent University in order to qualify in 1931 as a *notaire*, a position in Belgium held by comparatively few individuals and carrying with it considerable prestige and legal responsibility. In 1931 he also became a *chargé de cours* at Liége University, which is an appointment usually preliminary to that of a professorship and requires giving one or more courses at the university. In 1936 Van Houtte was promoted to the position of professor of economics at Liége University and that same year assumed a similar position at Ghent. He continued to be associated with the universities until his retirement from teaching in 1949.

While a professor, Van Houtte wrote several books and numerous articles for Belgian, Dutch, and French periodicals. Among these writings, in the field of fiscal law and taxation, were a book on the responsibilities of the government in air transportation (1940), an outline of Belgian economic history (1943), and a study of world trade (1945). One of his more recent publications dealt with war reparations and was issued in connection with a law drafted by him and passed by the legislature in October 1947, concerning the payment to Belgian citizens of war damage claims.

In 1944 Van Houtte, entering upon the first of a series of assignments in the Belgian government, became *chef de cabinet* (executive director) of the Ministry of the Interior and the next year held the same position in the Ministry of Information. His service in 1946 as a member of the Higher Board of Finance was followed in 1947 by his appointment to the presidency of the Belgian Institute of Public Finance and of the Counseil Superieur de la Famille. His next office was as member of the Belgian delegation to the meeting of the International Chamber of Commerce, held in Montreux, Switzerland, in 1947. The following year he was a member of the Legal Committee for Benelux, the economic union of Belgium, the Netherlands, and Luxembóurg. After a period as assessor for the Council of State of Belgium, to which he was named in 1948, he was elected to the Belgian Senate on July 19, 1949. He aided in the preparation of the fiscal reform bill introduced by Gaston Eyskins' Government and more recently was the author of a tax law. In August 1950, when Joseph Pholien was chosen Premier, Van Houtte accepted an appointment as Minister of Finance.

The Cabinet in which Van Houtte became Finance Minister was composed of members of the Social Christian party, in power by a narrow majority as the result of the 1950 general election. (In 1952 the party has a majority of four in the Chamber of Deputies and seven in the Senate.) Formerly called the Catholic party, the conservative Social Christian party is supported by the nobility, industrialists and businessmen, the Flemish peasants, and the Catholic labor groups. After the return of King Leopold III to Belgium in the summer of 1950 and his abdication in favor of his son, Prince Baudouin, in a move supported by some Social Christian leaders, chose Joseph Pholien to head the Government in an effort to conciliate the pro-Leopold voters of the Flemish-speaking areas of Belgium. Pholien's regime (described by a commentator for the *Christian Science Monitor* as "Rightist") continued in power until January 9, 1952, when growing dissatisfaction with the internal and international economic policies of the Government, expressed by the trade union and other elements within the party, prompted Pholien to resign. Two days later the King requested Van Houtte to form a new government and by January 15 a new Cabinet had been named. Pholien's administration having fallen because of demands that economic experts take a stronger role in Belgium's affairs, Premier Van Houtte appointed three new Cabinet members: ex-Premier Duvieusart as Economic Affairs Minister, Baron Albert Janssen as Finance Minister, and Pholien as Minister of Justice. Van Houtte himself assumed the chairmanship of its economic coordination committee. The exclusively Social Christian Cabinet thus retained most of the members of its predecessor.

In announcing the policies of his Cabinet Van Houtte stressed the maintenance of social progress and of the living standards of the population as the main tasks, to be achieved by strengthening the country's domestic, economic and, financial policies and by adapting these to the changed international situation. He expressed the desire of his Government to fulfill existing obligations under the North Atlantic Treaty Organization, welcomed the formation of a European defense community, spoke of the Schuman Plan to pool the Continent's coal and steel resources as the cornerstone of the economic structure of a new Europe, and looked forward to the final achievement of the Benelux Union—a complete economic fusion of Belgium, the Netherlands, and Luxembourg. He also declared that his Government intended to increase Belgian forces in the defense of the Belgian Congo and to continue the progressive development of this area as well as of the area of Ruanda-Urundi. At a press conference Van Houtte and his Foreign Minister, Paul van Zeeland, outlined their plan for a European federation that would embrace the Schuman Plan, the European Army, the European Payments Union, and the development of a European Customs Union. The six European nations now contributing to the European Army would be invited to join as well as the Scandinavian countries, Britain, and, ultimately, the United States.

With the announcement in February 1952 of King Baudouin's decision not to attend the

Belgian Govt. Inf. Center

JEAN VAN HOUTTE

funeral of King George VI of England, Van Houtte's Cabinet (regarded as responsible for the King's actions) was censured in the Chamber of Deputies. Van Houtte, who announced that he and Army and Air Force chiefs of staff would be present at the funeral with Belgium's Prince Albert, stated that he saw no reason for the demand that his Government resign.

The Belgian Prime Minister is described by the *Christian Science Monitor* correspondent as "scholarly." In 1928 he was awarded the Lauréat du Concours des Bourses de Voyage and in 1936 he received from Northwestern University the Charles Clarence Linthicum Foundation Prize. During the summer of 1946 he made a trip to the United States as a visiting scientist in fiscal law and taxation with the Belgian Scientific Mission on a grant awarded him by the Belgian American Educational Foundation. Van Houtte married Cécile de Stella in 1932.

Reference

Le Soir (Paris) p1 Ja 14 '52

HUME, EDGAR ERSKINE Dec. 26, 1889 —Jan. 24, 1952 United States Army officer; doctor; as lieutenant in the Medical Corps served at Fort Leavenworth (1917); commanding officer of a base hospital with the Italian Army and later with the British Expeditionary Force in World War I; in World War II became chief of Allied Military Government of the Fifth Army in the Mediterranean theater; chief surgeon, Far East Command (1949-51). See *Current Biography,* 1944.

Obituary

N Y Times p21 Ja 25 '52

HUMPHREY, HELEN F. Sept. 20, 1909—
Attorney; United States Government official
Address: b. 610 La Salle Bldg., 1028 Connecticut Ave., N.W., Washington 6, D.C.; h. 3900 16th St., N.W., Washington 11, D.C.

The former chairman of the Wage Stabilization Board's National Enforcement Commission, Helen F. Humphrey was appointed on July 30, 1952, as chairman of the recently created National Enforcement Commission, a body which has authority in cases involving regulations of the Salary Stabilization Board and

HELEN F. HUMPHREY

the Railroad and Airline Wage Board, as well as the Wage Stabilization Board. Miss Humphrey's association with the Economic Stabilization Agency, of which the enforcement commission is a part, began in March 1951 with her appointment as chief of the litigation branch of the Wage Stabilization Board. For twelve years previously she had been an attorney for the National Labor Relations Board, which she joined in 1939 upon leaving her law practice in New York City.

Helen F. Humphrey was born in Detroit, Michigan, on September 20, 1909, the daughter of D. Norman Humphrey, of English descent, and M. Isabel (Scanlan) Humphrey, of Irish-American and English descent. Her two brothers are Dr. William F. Humphrey, a geologist, and Dr. Norman D. Humphrey, a sociologist. After her graduation in 1927 from Detroit's Northwestern High School, where she had been editor of the school's weekly newspaper, Miss Humphrey entered the University of Michigan in Ann Arbor. Here, reported Flora Gill in the Washington *Post* (July 30, 1951), instead of taking courses in "political science and economics, as prospective lawyers" usually do, she chose English as her major study, writing her undergraduate thesis on the subject of Walter Pater and the life of art.

At college she held several scholarships, won a Phi Beta Kappa key, belonged to Phi Kappa Phi and Mortarboard, and received her B.A. degree *magna cum laude* in 1931.

Graduated "in depression days," Miss Humphrey obtained a $100-a-month position as a map custodian in the William L. Clements Library of Americana. In this independently endowed institution located on the Michigan campus, where she was surrounded by a valuable collection of Revolutionary War documents, she became interested in early Michigan history and wrote an article which appeared in the *Mississippi Valley Historical Review* (September 1934). "The Identity of Gladwin's Informant," as the article was entitled, maintained that Detroit had been saved during the rebellion of the Indian chief Pontiac not by a beautiful Indian girl, as had been claimed by the historian Francis Parkman, but by a young French woman. At the end of two years Miss Humphrey left her post with the Clements Library and moved East to take courses at New York University, where she was again employed in a library. "It fell to my lot to classify and catalogue the law collection," she told Flora Gill, and she therefore thought it desirable to take some courses in law. Since "one wasn't supposed to combine a professional job and a full-time course," she pursued her law studies at Brooklyn Law School rather than at New York University. Upon taking her LL.B. degree from the Brooklyn institution in 1938, Miss Humphrey engaged in private law practice in New York City for a year.

In 1939, when she heard of the opening of the Wage-Hour Division, Miss Humphrey went to Washington, D.C., and accepted employment with the National Labor Relations Board, where she remained for the next twelve years. After serving from 1939 until 1942 as a NLRB enforcement attorney in Washington, she moved to the NLRB's New York office as trial attorney, returning the following year to Washington again as enforcement attorney. In the latter capacity it was her responsibility to prepare briefs and oral arguments before various Federal courts of appeal and the United States Supreme Court. Her next assignment, from 1944 until 1946, took her to St. Louis, where she was chief law officer of the NLRB's regional office—"the only woman," Flora Gill reported, "who's ever been chief law officer with the agency." She held the same post in Philadelphia from 1946 until 1948 and in November of the latter year was transferred to New York City to head the NLRB's legal staff in a region which comprised New York, northern New Jersey, and part of Connecticut.

When the Wage Stabilization Board of the Economic Security Agency began operations, Miss Humphrey, who returned to Washington in March 1951, accepted an assignment as its chief of litigation. Leaving this position after a few months, she became in June 1951 associate general counsel of the ESA in charge of enforcement. The following month, on July 23, 1951, George W. Taylor, chairman of the WSB, announced the creation of a National Enforcement Commission for that board and named Helen Humphrey as its chairman. Granted authority over fourteen regional commissions, the national commission was to act as a final court of appeal. Employers might be penalized for granting wage increases above authorized amounts, and unions also could be punished if they assisted in circumventing regulations. The enforcement commission, reported the New York *Herald Tribune* (July 24, 1951), while concerned with correcting employers who unintentionally violated regulations, was primarily interested in those who deliberately defied them in order to attract manpower in areas where labor was in short supply; the latter risked penalties as high as $10,000 and a year's imprisonment. Miss Humphrey's associates on the three-member commission were Professor Ralph Fuchs of the University of Indiana Law School and Professor Charles O. Gregory of the University of Virginia.

Miss Humphrey occupied this post a year and then in July 1952 was appointed chairman of a newly created ESA National Enforcement Commission, which was empowered to determine tax disallowance sanctions for violations of regulations established not only by the WSB, but also by the Salary Stabilization Board and by the Railroad and Airline Wage Board. She was sworn into this office on August 8, 1952, by Roger Putnam, ESA administrator. On November 1, 1952, Miss Humphrey began the private practice of law both in Washington and in New York City.

The government attorney is a member of Phi Delta Delta (professional legal fraternity) and of the American Bar Association. She has been admitted to practice before the following bars: New York, District of Columbia, United States Supreme Court, United States Circuit Court for the Third, Eighth, and Tenth circuits, and United States District Court, Southern District, New York. She has contributed a number of papers to *Proceedings of New York University's Annual Conference on Labor*: "The Scope of Collective Bargaining under the Taft-Hartley Act: The Effect of Decisions since the Effective Date of the Act on some Aspects Thereof" (1949), "Practice and Procedure under the National Labor Relations Act" (1950), "The Duty to Bargain: Five Years under the Taft-Hartley Amendments" (1952). She also wrote "The Rights and Obligations of Strikers: From the Mackay Case to the Mackay Case: An Instance of Administrative Adaptability" for *The Record of the Association of the Bar of the State of New York* (March 1952). Miss Humphrey is a Democrat and an Episcopalian. With a height of five feet three inches, she weighs 135 pounds; she has gray hair and gray eyes.

Reference

Washington (D.C.) Post p5 Jl 30 '51 por

HUNTER, KIM Nov. 12, 1922- Actress
Address: b. c/o Warner Brothers Pictures, Inc., 321 W. 44th St., New York 18; h. 28 Grove St., New York 14

For her screen re-creation of a character in the drama *A Streetcar Named Desire*, Kim

KIM HUNTER

Hunter received the 1952 award of the Academy of Motion Picture Arts and Sciences as the best supporting actress. Miss Hunter, whose career has been about evenly divided between the stage and screen, played with stock companies from the age of seventeen until 1943, when she made her first appearance in a motion picture, *The Seventh Victim*. Other roles before the camera (as of the spring of 1952) have been in *Tender Comrade, When Strangers Marry, You Came Along, Stairway to Heaven, Deadline—U.S.A., Anything Can Happen*. Her Broadway plays have been, aside from *Streetcar, Darkness at Noon* and *The Chase*.

Kim Hunter was born Janet Cole on November 12, 1922, in Detroit, Michigan, the daughter of Donald and Grace M. (Lind) Cole. Her forebears, of English and Welsh stock, came to America before the Revolution. Her father, who was a consulting engineer until his death in 1926, came from a Baltimore family interested in amateur theatricals: her paternal grandfather belonged to a group which entertained Edwin Booth whenever he came to the Maryland city. Prior to her marriage, Mrs. Cole was a concert pianist. Janet Cole received part of her elementary schooling in her native city. After her mother's remarriage (she is now Mrs. Bliss Stebbins) the family moved to Florida, where Janet, then ten years old, continued her education at Miami Beach elementary and high schools. Following her graduation from secondary school, in which she had acted in school plays, the seventeen-year-old girl joined the stock company of Gant Gaither. She tells that she had long had the desire to act: "I was lonely growing up. My only brother was nine years older and had little time for me. So I picked friends out of books and played 'let's pretend' games, acting out their characters before a mirror."

(Continued next page)

HUNTER, KIM—*Continued*

She next joined the Theatre of the Fifteen, a repertory group of young people, in which she played ingénue roles until 1942. Then because of the war, the troupe disbanded and she obtained engagements with other stock companies in Hendersonville, North Carolina, and in Baltimore. Among the small parts she played was one of the Eskimos in *Petticoat Fever*. Other appearances during this period were in *Yes My Darling Daughter*, *Old Acquaintance*, and the *Philadelphia Story*. When one of her former directors suggested that she obtain an audition for the Pasadena Playhouse she went West and was accepted for the Playhouse's production of *Arsenic and Old Lace*.

That appearance brought her to the attention of the Hollywood film producer David O. Selznick, who at the time of signing her to a contract with Vanguard Films, changed her name. "He told me Janet Cole could be anyone," she recalled for Dee L. Katcher (*Collier's*, March 8, 1952), "but that 'Kim Hunter' had individuality and would go far as an actress." Nevertheless, because Selznick had "a line-up of actresses almost impossible to penetrate," Miss Hunter found herself among the "loan-outs" to other studios.

Accordingly it was in an RKO production that Miss Hunter made her screen debut in 1943, in *The Seventh Victim*, a "horror" picture. In her next film, *Tender Comrade* (1944), in a supporting role she portrayed a war widow doing her "best to afford a basis of credibility to the film" (Howard Barnes in the New York *Herald Tribune*). In November of the same year *When Strangers Marry* was released by Maurice and Franklin King; in a review of it in *Variety*, Miss Hunter was described as the "comparative newcomer" who "is attractive as well as immensely appealing as the distraught but loyal wife." In her next role, *You Came Along* (1945), "a boldly presumptuous fable" (New York *Times*), Miss Hunter was mentioned as appearing to good effect in a minor part.

About the time this film was being completed, the English directors Michael Powell and Emeric Pressburger were looking for someone to play the part of a WAC stationed in England for the forthcoming J. Arthur Rank production *Stairway to Heaven*. Upon Alfred Hitchcock's recommendation (he recalled some bits she had done in tests) Miss Hunter, chosen as a "typical American girl," was assigned the part. In 1945 she departed for England for the filming of the picture, which was released there as *A Matter of Life and Death* and was selected for the first royal command film performance. While in England she was also cast in *A Canterbury Tale*.

Having returned to Hollywood, Miss Hunter has told, she found herself "out of work again." A former coworker in the Theatre of the Fifteen, now directing summer stock in Stamford, Connecticut, heard that she was free and offered her the title role in *Claudia*. During that summer of 1947 she was also given a part in *Wuthering Heights*. A few years later Miss Hunter was to recall those who helped "rescue" her in gaps in employment. "People have always been so helpful," she relates. "Without outside help I'd never have got anywhere. I am shy and retiring at all the wrong moments" (Dee Katcher in *Collier's*).

While she was in the East, an agent of the Broadway producer Irene Selznick called on her. Remembering her ex-husband's enthusiastic endorsement of the young actress, Mrs. Selznick wanted Miss Hunter to read for a part in the Tennessee Williams' drama *A Streetcar Named Desire*. "I was scared stiff of Broadway," the actress has said, "but I just couldn't refuse." She began rehearsing in the role of Stella Kowalski on October 1, 1947; and the play opened on December 3. In a review in the New York *World-Telegram*, William Hawkins judged her performance "mellow and philosophical as the devoted Stella, who tries to synchronize two impossible loyalties." To Howard Barnes of the New York *Herald Tribune* she was "completely convincing and singularly engaging as the sister who settled for sex." After directing Miss Hunter in this role Elia Kazan said of her, "She is unique among actresses. She is first a person and second a member of the acting profession." *A Streetcar Named Desire* brought her the Donaldson Award (1948) and the Critics Circle Award (1948) for the best supporting actress.

The play, which ran for two and a half years on Broadway, was then bought for screen production. Kazan, assigned as director, asked for Miss Hunter (who was then in Chicago appearing in *Two Blind Mice*) to play in the screen version opposite Marlon Brando and Vivien Leigh. Her ability to fill stage and screen roles "with equal dexterity" won for her the critics' approval when the film was released in September 1951. She was described by Alton Cook of the New York *World-Telegram* as the sister who "played with all of her old torrent of pity and affection." On March 20, 1952, Miss Hunter won the award of the Academy of Motion Picture Arts and Sciences for the "best supporting role" in her portrayal of Stella in the *Streetcar*. For one of its Achievement Awards *Look* magazine chose her for "standing out in bold normality among the frenetic characters around her." She was also given the Foreign Correspondents Award (1952) for her performance in that motion picture.

Miss Hunter, who believes it is best to vary one's work, likes to alternate between the stage and screen. Her second stage role, in 1951, was in Sidney Kingsley's dramatization of Koestler's novel *Darkness at Noon*, opposite Claude Rains. Her own comment on her interpretation was: "I didn't like myself too well in that part." Her subsequent film, *Anything Can Happen*, provided a change from heavy drama to character comedy. In this adaptation of the autobiographical best seller of 1945, which tells the amusing story of the Papashvilys, Miss Hunter plays the part of Helen, the wife. Otis L. Guernsey, Jr., reviewed the film for the New York *Herald Tribune*: "Kim Hunter's portrayal . . . is not only likeable and convincing; it also comes very close to reality in a combination of appealing freshness and practical skepticism." To Bosley Crowther of the New York *Times* she was "sweet and ornamental but disturbingly unreal." Miss Hunter's "modesty" and "lack of personal vanity" (*Collier's*) makes her a "favorite" among directors.

Another screen vehicle was *Deadline—U.S.A.*, opposite Humphrey Bogart, which was released in March 1952. In the role of Bogart's estranged wife, Miss Hunter drew the opinion from Richard Brooks that the part demanded "sensitivity and an understanding sophistication. It called for an actress who could express emotions without using words to spell them out. Few actresses can do that. Kim is one of the few." *The Chase*, a melodramatic Wild West saga, produced by José Ferrer in the spring of 1952, was Miss Hunter's third stage role. In it, said *Variety*, she gave "a glowing and magnetic portrayal."

Miss Hunter is a member of the Actors Studio, a workshop for a select group of young players, started by Elia Kazan. Miss Hunter's preference for the footlights is ascribed to the fact that she is a perfectionist, said Dorothy Masters of the New York *Sunday News*. "When she's playing for the theater, there's a chance to improve on characterization." Not typed as a Hollywood "pin-up" girl, Miss Hunter was once described as having "nothing but talent." She is five feet four inches tall and weighs 115 pounds, has hazel eyes and light-brown hair. Her marriage to William Baldwin (a "nonprofessional") on February 11, 1944, terminated in divorce two years later; their daughter is named Kathryn. On December 20, 1951, she married Robert Emmett, also of the theater. According to a studio release, Miss Hunter is studying singing and dancing; she lists the waltz and polka as her favorites. Admitting record and book collecting to be her "pet extravagances," she includes Dreiser, Kafka, and Chekhov among her preferred authors. The actress, who describes herself as a liberal in political leanings, is a member of Americans for Democratic Action.

References

Collier's 129:44+ Mr 8 '52 por
N Y Post Mag p33 D 26 '46 por
N Y Times II p4 Mr 16 '52
International Motion Picture Almanac, 1950-51
Winchester's Screen Encyclopedia (1948)

IBÁÑEZ (DEL CAMPO), CARLOS
(ē-bä′nyās *thĕl* käm′pō) Nov. 3, 1877- President of Chile

Address: La Moneda, Santiago, Chile

President of an authoritarian regime in Chile from 1927 to 1931, General Carlos Ibáñez again took over the Presidency of that South American country for a six-year term on November 3, 1952, after the September election gave him a plurality of the vote and Chile's National Congress subsequently confirmed his victory. Following an early career in the army, Ibáñez in 1925 became Minister of War and later held the posts of Minister of the Interior and Vice-President before advancing to the Presidency in 1927. The Chilean political leader, who spent many years of exile in Argentina and was reportedly supported by that country's President Perón in his effort to regain power, campaigned in 1952 on a platform that favored nationalization of Chile's copper and coal industries.

Carlos Ibáñez del Campo was born in Linares, Chile, on November 3, 1877, the son of Francisco and Nieves (del Campo) Ibáñez, owners of a small ranch in southern Chile. Having finished his early studies at the Liceo of Linares, young Ibáñez in 1894 entered the Escuela Militar (military school) in Santiago. He was promoted in 1898 to the rank of ensign in the cavalry and five years later became a lieutenant. In 1903 Ibáñez went to El Salvador, where he filled the position of an instructor in that country's army for the next five years, being advanced in 1905 to the rank of colonel in the Salvadorean Army and appointed that same year as director of the Escuela Militar in El Salvador.

In 1908 Ibáñez returned to Chile as a captain in the Chilean Army, three years later rising to adjutant of cavalry inspection and then adjutant of establishments of military instruction. At the Academia de Guerra, which he entered in 1913, he became a member of the staff of the First Division, three years later attaining the post of commander of the First Division in Tacna. Transferred in 1918 to be the second commander of the cavalry of the Second Regiment, Ibáñez organized and directed the Escuela de Carabineros. He was chosen the following year as a section chief in the Ministry of War and as chief prefect of the province of Tarapacá and of its capital city, Iquique. A year after he had become the director, with the rank of major, of the Escuela de Caballeria (cavalry school), he was sent, in 1922, as the delegate from the army to the Concurso Hipico in Rio de Janeiro. Ibáñez remained at the cavalry school until 1924 when he was assigned as a military attaché to the Chilean legation in Paris. Back in Chile in September 1924, he took part in the revolution that month and subsequently joined the military junta which co-operated with the government junta. In January 1925 he participated in another revolution, through which he was named Minister of War, a post he held for the next two years.

Soon after announcing his candidacy for the Presidency of Chile on September 25, 1926, Ibáñez withdrew in favor of Dr. Emiliano Figueroa, who subsequently became the country's chief executive. Ibáñez was made premier of Chile and, with strong army backing, forced Figueroa to suspend the country's constitutional guarantees (*Saturday Evening Post*, November 28, 1931). In 1927 he became Minister of the Interior and Vice-President and upon Figueroa's resignation on May 27, 1927, assumed the office of President. In an

Wide World Photos

GEN. CARLOS IBÁÑEZ

election held shortly thereafter he was confirmed as President by a majority of 98 per cent of the votes cast.

Known as "The Horse" and as Chile's "Iron Man," Ibáñez during his four years (1927-31) as chief executive attempted to reduce governmental inefficiency and to further material progress by abolishing sinecures and graft and by initiating a large-scale plan of public works, encouraging aviation, constructing roads, and Americanizing the telephone system. His regime reorganized the public education system, instituted better hygienic methods in hospitals, enacted advanced labor laws, and started an agrarian reform program. Ibáñez also sponsored the Cosach-Chilean nitrate monopoly and encouraged formation of the Central Bank of Chile. In harmony with his policy of absolute rule (according to the *Saturday Evening Post*), he censored the Chilean press and purchased the newspaper *La Nacion* as an outlet for his views. *Time* reported that he disposed of congressmen who did not agree with him by banishing them to penal colonies and once threatened to send the entire Supreme Court into exile. He was thought to favor the interests of the middle class at the expense of all others.

While Chile's economic conditions remained favorable, Ibáñez received strong support from the people, but in 1929, with the advent of a world-wide depression, dissatisfaction spread and two attempts were made to assassinate the President. A revolt, touched off in August 1931 by National University students in Santiago over the forced resignation of cabinet leader Pedro Blanquier, was aided by a coalition of liberals and reactionaries. As the unrest grew Ibáñez resigned, he said, to prevent civil war and then spent a short period in jail, where he declared that his downfall had come about because of an "indefatigable campaign of falsehoods coupled with the world economic crisis" (*Saturday Evening Post*). A few weeks after his resignation he went into exile in Argentina, leaving with the rank of general. The years of Ibáñez' exile in Argentina were broken at intervals by attempted coups in which he hoped to regain power in Chile. On July 12, 1932, one year after Ibáñez had left Chile, Alejandro Loza was arrested on charges of taking part in a plot to bring Ibáñez back. When the general himself returned to Chile on July 6, he was welcomed by President Davila. Shortly afterward, on July 29, he left for Argentina to serve as Chile's Ambassador to that country for a time. After a revolt had deposed President Davila, Ibáñez offered to resign the Ambassadorship on the grounds that this appointment might have been one of the reasons for the uprising, but his resignation was refused.

In another plot to overthrow the government, on January 8, 1934, letters were found that seemed to link Ibáñez with the Chilean conspirators. The following April the general was named as the manager of a large ranch west of Bahía Blanca, Argentina, where he remained until he again returned to Chile on May 10, 1937, to announce his candidacy for the Presidency. Maintaining that a change in policy was needed, Ibáñez stated that social reform must be instituted if the conservatives were not to be destroyed by a revolution. Among his supporters were members of the Chilean Nazi party, who staged a revolt on September 5, 1938, in the hope that it would assist him in his Presidential aspirations. Ibáñez, who was arrested but later absolved of any complicity in the plot, withdrew his name from the campaign and returned to Argentina. In 1942 he again ran for the Chilean Presidency, again received Nazi backing, and again was defeated. For six years Ibáñez remained out of public life until he and retired General Romon Vergara were arrested on November 1, 1948, on charges of conspiracy against the state through a proposed revolt that was said to be directed from Argentina and synchronized with other Latin American uprisings. The next month the former President was acquitted of the charges brought against him and in 1949 was elected to the Chilean Senate.

On a visit to Argentine President Juan D. Perón, Ibáñez in Buenos Aires announced his candidacy for President of Chile in the 1952 election. The general's platform, nationalistic in spirit, contained promises of economic relief for the "shirtless ones" of Chile. His campaign was aided by at least two circumstances: one, the moderate and the relatively democratic forces split and each was backing a separate candidate; two, the Radical party then in power had been unable to control inflation and unemployment, so that under Radical President Gabriel González Videla the cost of living, *Time* reported, had increased 150 per cent in the last five years. Ibáñez' supporters spread a slogan designed to appeal especially to Chilean women, who were voting for a President for the first time: "How much did you pay for bread when Ibáñez was President and how much do you pay now?" Ibáñez himself promised to reduce the price of milk from its 8 pesos and 40 centavos a bottle to the 40 centavos it had cost when he was President before. Adopting a broom as his campaign symbol, Ibáñez promised to clear away a burdensome bureaucratic structure that had been built up during the Radicals' fourteen years in control of the government. On election day, September 4, 1952, the general received a purality of 47 per cent of the votes; his closest contender, Liberal Arturo Matte, gained 26 per cent. Since a candidate who does not receive a clear majority must be certified by the congress, on October 24 Chile's National Congress confirmed by a vote of 132 to 12 the election of Ibáñez as President for a six-year term beginning November 3.

The election of Ibáñez aroused much speculation in the United States press regarding the possible effect of his return to power on relations between the United States and Chile. Among issues of concern were his association with former Nazis, his friendship with Perón, and his campaign promise to nationalize Chile's copper mines, which are owned largely by United States companies. The general's own statements on domestic and foreign policy were described as vague and contradictory. One view of Ibáñez' intentions was given in the *Christian Science Monitor* (October 25, 1952): "Most observers believe that General Ibáñez is more interested in redeeming his domestic reputation . . . than in becoming a junior partner with General Perón in a nebulous continental crusade against 'Wall Street imperialism.'"

Ibáñez is a member of the Club Hípico, Club Militar, Paperchase Club, and the Automóvil Club. He has received the following decorations: Grand Cross, Légion d'Honneur (France); Order of the British Empire; St. Olaf (Norway); White Eagle (Poland); Order of Merit (Austria); Mérito Militar (Spain); St. Maurice (Italy); Golden Tassel (China); Sol del Perú; Chrysanthemum (Japan); Order of Mohammed Ali (Egypt); Libertador (Venezuela), and the Medal First Class, Abdón Calderón and Del Mérito (Ecuador). Ibáñez is a former president of the Alianza Popular Libertadora.

While in El Salvador, Ibáñez married a native of that country, Rosa Quiroz, who died in 1918; they had two children, Rosa and Carlos. The President in 1927 married his present wife, the former Graciela Letelier Velasco. Their children are Margarita, Graciela, Ricardo, Francisco, Nieves, and Gloria. *Time* (September 15, 1952) remarked that Ibáñez possessed "perhaps the most forbidding air of personal *digniad* in all Latin America." Isaac Morcosson in the *Saturday Evening Post* wrote that "his whole manner suggested quiet forcefullness."

References

Bul Pan Am Union 61:741-2 Ag '27
Sat Eve Post 204:16-17+ N 28 '31
Diccionario Biografico de Chile (1944)
International Who's Who, 1935
Who's Who in Latin America (1940); Pt 4 (1947)
World Biography (1948)

IBARRA, JOSÉ MARÍA VELASCO *See* Velasco Ibarra, J. M.

ICKES, HAROLD L(E CLAIRE) Mar. 15, 1874—Feb. 3, 1952 Former Secretary of the Interior; reporter with Chicago newspapers (1897-1900); began practicing law in 1907; in the course of active career in reform politics worked with Republicans, Bull Moose party, independent Republicans, LaFollette Progressives, and New Deal Democrats; Secretary of the Interior in Cabinets of Roosevelt and Truman (1933-46); author of a number of books on American politics and of the syndicated newspaper column *Man to Man*. See *Current Biography*, 1941.

Obituary

N Y Times p1+ F 4 '52

INGRAM, JONAS H(OWARD) Oct. 15, 1886—Sept. 10, 1952 Retired United States naval officer; football official; commissioned ensign in the United States Navy (1909); Annapolis head football coach (1914-17) and director of athletics and football (1926-30); in 1930's directed Navy public relations and commanded New York Naval Shipyard in Brooklyn; promoted in 1944 to Commander in Chief of the Atlantic Fleet with the rank of full admiral; retired from the Navy in 1947 and became commissioner of the All-America Football Conference (1947-49); vice-president of the Reynolds Metals Company. See *Current Biography*, 1947.

Obituary

N Y Times p31 S 11 '52

IRWIN, HELEN G. Women's organization official

Address: b. c/o National Federation of Business and Professional Women's Clubs, Inc., 1819 Broadway, New York 23; c/o Equitable Life Insurance Company of Iowa, Des Moines, Ia.; h. 917 Locust St., Des Moines, Ia.

Helen G. Irwin is the first business woman in seventeen years to be chosen president of the National Federation of Business and Professional Women's Club, Inc., an organization of about 160,000 members in 2,700 clubs located in every State in the United States, in Hawaii, Alaska, and the District of Columbia. On her election to the presidency on July 2, 1952, after twenty-seven years in an official capacity in the federation, she succeeded Judge Sarah T. Hughes, who had served since 1950. Concurrently with holding her present office in the women's organization, Miss Irwin is employed by the Equitable Life Insurance Company of Iowa as supervisor of the preparation of legal documents.

Born in Savannah, Georgia, the daughter of missionary parents, Helen Irwin believed at an early age that she wanted to be a missionary. Her childhood and education were divided between her native Savannah and Richmond, Vir-

HELEN G. IRWIN

ginia, where her parents settled. After graduating from high school in 1920, Helen Irwin took a position as secretary to a firm of lawyers in Des Moines, Iowa. Five years later, in 1925, she accepted an offer on the secretarial staff of the president of. the Equitable Life Insurance Company of Iowa, in Des Moines. She found this gave her a chance to express her missionary spirit by helping to increase the company's personal service to policyholders. Her interest in this field recognized, she was transferred in 1927 to the unit of the. company set up to handle the expanded service, shortly afterward being made its supervisor. In 1950 Miss Irwin was promoted to the executive position of registrar of the company, in which she was given charge of the preparation of legal documents in connection with life insurance.

Helen Irwin's career as a clubwoman began in 1925, the same year that she joined the Equitable Life Insurance Company of Iowa. Aware of a need to unify the efforts to advance the interests of employed women in her community, she became a member of the local organization in Des Moines of the National Federation of Business and Professional Women's Clubs. She served this club in a number of official capacities, acting at intervals as chairman on membership, on legislation, on news service, and on public affairs; she was also parliamentarian. In the State organization, known as the Iowa Federation of Business and Professional Women's Clubs, she held the positions of treasurer, vice-president, and president, retaining the last-named office for two years. While president of the Iowa federation, in which she was responsible for inaugurating and supervising the district organization, she served as a member of the National Federation's board of directors.

Appointed chairman of the national candidate data committee of the National Federation of Business and Professional Women's

Clubs in 1941, Helen Irwin remained in this position five years. From 1946 to 1948 she was national chairman of legislation in this organization. Her advance in the National Federation was rapid: in 1948 she was elected third vice-president for a term of two years. In endorsing her candidacy "for any national office," the Iowa State group said: "Helen Irwin is deliberate, careful, and fair in all her decisions. She is fearless in her support of principles she believes to be right" (*Independent Woman*, March 1948).

In July 1950 Miss Irwin was made first vice-president of the National Federation of Business and Professional Women's Clubs, at the organization's biennial convention in San Francisco. At this convention, the federation authorized its State and local clubs to plan for full membership of women in all phases of civil defense and economic and military mobilization. It adopted resolutions prohibiting night work for women and urged that the principle of equal pay for equal work be incorporated in the International Labor Organization convention. It agreed to become a member of the "All American Conference to Combat Communism." In the cause of international understanding and world peace, the executive committee established a World Friendship Fund "to help members of the International Federation of Business and Professional Women to come to the United States to advance themselves professionally" (*Independent Woman*, September 1951). Approval was given to establishing a UNESCO fund to be raised from scholarship gifts from member clubs. From its original purpose, adopted by the organization at the time of its founding in 1919, to advance the interests of women themselves, the National Federation of Business and Professional Women's Clubs had widened its outlook to include the international horizon, with emphasis on what contributions women can make throughout the world. It grew to comprise in 1952 some 160,000 members in 2,700 clubs in the United States, Hawaii, and Alaska.

During the second term that she held the vice-presidency of the National Federation, Helen Irwin assisted the organization in a nation-wide hunt to aid the United States Civil Service in recruiting trained women for the professional and clerical personnel in Federal agencies. She also helped launch a project to speed the recruitment of young women for the women's armed services. Also in the course of her tenure as vice-president the national steering committee of the federation, on March 5, 1952, voted to support companion bills in Congress to permit women to have the same rank and privileges as men in all medical branches of the armed services. Mainly through efforts of the National Federation of Business and Professional Women's Clubs. a law was passed in April 1952 giving Hawaiian women the privilege of serving on juries.

As a leader of the United States group, Helen Irwin attended a four-day conference in June 1952 of the International Federation of Business and Professional Women. Here were discussed problems with which Miss Irwin as a business woman was well acquainted, such as questions relating to the economic, educational, legal, and social status of women. In his greetings to the opening meeting of the conference Governor Dewey of New York noted: "Throughout the United States, the Business and Professional Women's Clubs form a ready and willing companionship to help all women develop better opportunities, better economic conditions, better community lives. . . .It is in the many non-governmental organizations, brought together not through fear of war but in pursuit of common interests that the truest world understanding and unity will be created." President Truman's message to the conference named as one of the main objectives of the United States group the task of urging the Government to include more qualified women in all international meetings, with greater representation in the Secretariat of the United Nations.

In an acceptance speech in July 1952 following her election as president of the National Federation of Business and Professional Women's Clubs in succession to Judge Sarah T. Hughes, Helen Irwin said: "I am confident that this Federation will grow in strength and power and that it will serve our members, our country, and our world in the interests of all humanity. . . .Each woman in our organization is a leader in her own right" (*Independent Woman*, August 1952). At the convention which elected her, the National Federation re-endorsed the Equal Rights Amendment to the United States Constitution which would give women the same privileges, responsibilities, and status as men, provide men and women with equal pay for equal work, and remove all discriminations on the basis of sex or marital status. In contrast to this endorsement, the Federation voted not to include in its legislative program the registration and drafting of women. Regarding this vote Miss Irwin remonstrated: "If you want equal rights and equal opportunity, then, please, I plead with you, reconsider this question" (*New York Times*, July 4, 1952). Against the protests of the States of Washington and Georgia, as reported by the *Christian Science Monitor* (July 3, 1952), the National Federation voted to eliminate support of conservation, but to retain it as a study and educational program to save natural wealth in the United States. On other national issues the federation at its July 1952 convention tabled a bill in favor of universal military training and went on record as opposing compulsory Government-controlled health insurance and medical care. It voted down an amendment in the Armed Services Act to permit women to stay on reserve status after the birth of children and on the same date endorsed the Bricker amendment requiring full vote of both Houses of Congress to ratify treaties.

Speaking of the economic status of the average man and woman in the United States, as quoted by the New York *Times* (July 3, 1952), Helen Irwin stated: "The demand now is for two pay envelopes. Our economy is so geared that it is no longer a matter of women working for pin money. . . .If we are going to pay the Government debt, everyone must work." She urged more women to go into the "critical shortage" fields in industry and added that women, as the "new secret weapon" in America's defense, require that industry "raise its sights about the advancement of women." Over the National Broadcasting Company's network on July 5, 1952, Miss Irwin stressed the economic value of women in increasing America's wealth. "I urge those who are designing the world of tomorrow," she said, "to be equally alert to remember that women, too, are people, and must be employed so that they can pay taxes and help lighten our great national debt, and to remember that women have resources that have never been tapped." She further emphasized the economic ramparts to which women can contribute in an article entitled "Women Vital to Nation's Economy" in the September 28-October 4 issue of *National Business Women's Week*: "We must make sure there are jobs enough to go around and that the Federal, State, and local governments set an example of good management and thrift to our people. We must work to keep America economically free."

Helen Irwin is honorary president of the Iowa Federation of Professional and Business Women's Clubs. Since 1940, she has been a member of the Iowa Council for Better Education and the Iowa Legislative Council, both made up of men and women's service organizations. She is also a member of the Council of the Civil Service League of America and of the Iowa Council of Republican Women. Her other organization memberships include the Order of the Eastern Star and the White Shrine. Her church affiliation is Presbyterian. The National Federation's president has been described as "a handsome woman, always well-groomed, with an excellent platform presence and a warm personality that makes friendships easily." In 1951 Miss Irwin, whose favorite hobby is traveling, received a plaque from the United Air Lines recognizing her 200,000 miles of air travel. She also collects miniatures in her spare time.

References

Independent Woman 27:79 Mr '48; 29: 76 Mr '50; 31:225 Ag '52

IRWIN, ROBERT B(ENJAMIN) June 2, 1883—Dec. 12, 1951 Official of organization for the blind; educator; lost his sight as a child; became superintendent of classes for the blind in Cleveland public schools (1909); appointed director of the bureau of research and education of the American Foundation for the Blind, Inc., (1923) and executive director of the foundation (1929); noted as organizer of special educational facilities, legislative measures, and vocational rehabilitation for the blind. See *Current Biography*, 1948 .

Obituary

N Y Times p34 D 13 '51

JAGENDORF, MORITZ (ADOLF) (yä' gĕn-dôrf) Aug. 24, 1888- Author; dentist
Address: b. 150 E. 39th St., New York 16; h. 260 Riverside Dr., New York 25; Carmel, N.Y.

Reprinted from the *Wilson Library Bulletin,* Dec. 1952.

Some of the rollicking spirit and gusto of the folk tales which Moritz Jagendorf collects in anthologies for young and adult readers alike is reflected in the life of this author-editor. A former dramatic director, a prolific writer, an energetic researcher, and a part-time practicing dentist in New York, Jagendorf writes of himself: "I love work. The more I work, the more I live. Sleep is a waste of time. If

Conway

MORITZ JAGENDORF

people would devote more time to literature and the art of eating, they wouldn't have time for war and murder."

Moritz Adolf Jagendorf, born in Austria on August 24, 1888, is the son of an artist, Samuel Gétzel Jagendorf and Augusta (Füss) Jagendorf. His childhood in the university town of Bukovina, Czernowitz, was dominated by an early and passionate interest in the theater and the circus. Once he ran away from home to join the circus, but he was brought back ignominiously two days later.

At thirteen he came to the United States and entered the New York public schools where his ambitious plans to produce Shakespearean tragedy rather disconcerted his teachers. When he was ready for college, he spent a year at the Yale Law School. Here he distinguished himself in fencing and wrote what he calls a "Dostoevskian" novel which was read, with some encouraging comment, by Professor William Lyon Phelps. Jagendorf then returned to New York to study at Columbia University.

Thanks to a persistent inability to pass a course in plane geometry (which he took five times), he never got the degree in drama and literature for which he was working. He did manage to pick up a D.D.S. degree in 1916, but he has never allowed his dental practice to interfere with his literary career.

While at Columbia, Jagendorf took an active part in dramatics. In his sophomore year he made an adaptation of the medieval French farce *Pierre Pathelin,* which is still bringing in royalties. With the encouragement of Professors Brander Matthews, and George Odell, Jagendorf embarked upon a theatrical career. He worked first as an agent and translator at the Century Theatre. Then, as director of the Free Theatre, he produced, among other plays, some of the works of Lord Dunsany, with whom he became friends. Jagendorf also directed plays in the Children's Playhouse and worked for a while with the famous Washington Square Players.

Writing proved to be the more powerful attraction, however, and Jagendorf began to devote most of his time to it. During the 1920's and 1930's he published many collections of plays, puppet shows, and pantomimes for children and young people. Meanwhile a long-standing interest in folklore led Jagendorf into the work for which he is best known today— the retelling, for young readers, of popular legends and tales.

He has drawn on material from the Old World and the New World. *Tyll Ulenspiegel's Merry Pranks* (1938), for example, introduced his young American readers to the immortal rascal of European legend. A reviewer in the New York *Herald Tribune* pointed out that this was "something more than a child's book the 'pranks' belong to literary history and appeal to the love of mischief and sympathy for a good-natured joker that lies in everybody's breast." Anne T. Eaton described it in the New York *Times* as "an outstanding book for which boys and girls and their elders will be grateful."

Similarly, in *The Merry Men of Gotham* (1951), Jagendorf retold eighteen of the popular legends of "Old England," and the *Saturday Review of Literature* commented: "Old as they are, they have in them the humor that is latent in all of us. . . ." He plans five more books of European folk stories and began collecting material for them in a recent trip abroad.

Jagendorf's work in American folklore is equally ambitious in scope. In preparation are collections of tales from the southern, southwestern, northwestern and western States. He has already canvassed the New England area in *New England Bean Pot* (1948), the Middle Atlantic states in *Upstate, Downstate* (1949), and New York's Catskill region in *The Marvelous Adventures of Johnny Caesar Cicero Darling* (1949).

Reviewers have been impressed with the vigor and simplicity of Jagendorf's style. The *Library Journal,* in its comments on *Johnny Darling,* referred to the author as a "matchless storyteller." B. A. Botkin, well-known folklorist, has said of Jagendorf that ". . . he loves a

good tale as he loves a good wine, for its body
and flavor. . . . He knows that stories are
not made but grow, and never stop growing."

When not writing or keeping his dentist
office hours, Jagendorf works on his farm in
Carmel, New York, where he raises cattle. He
is president of the New York State Folklore
Society and vice-president of the International
Folklore Congress. Among his favorite recrea-
tions are fencing, traveling, and eating fine food
(he cites membership in Les Amis d'Escoffier).
Jagendorf is married to the former Sophie
Sokolsky, who assists him in his research work,
and their two children are André-Tridon and
Merna-Paula.

RENÉE JEANMAIRE

JEANMAIRE, RENÉE (zhäN-mâr' rē-nā')
Apr. 29, 1924- Dancer
Address: b. c/o RKO Radio Pictures, Inc.,
Los Angeles, Calif.

When Renée Jeanmaire made her first appearance in the United States in 1949 as the
leading ballerina of Les Ballets de Paris in
Roland Petit's ballet version of *Carmen*, she
won immediate critical and public applause for
her dramatic interpretation of the role. The
following year the young French dancer, who
had been a member of Les Ballets des Champs-
Élysées before joining Petit's Ballets de Paris
in 1948, attained further success in the title role
of *La Croqueuse de Diamants*, another Petit
ballet, which pictured a fantastic Parisian underworld. After signing a motion picture contract with Howard Hughes, she went to Hollywood, where she was "loaned" to Samuel Goldwyn to costar in his film production of the life
of Hans Christian Andersen. Critics have acclaimed Miss Jeanmaire for her acting and her
ability to project her enthusiasm as well as for
her dancing; she has been called "one of the
supreme personalities of the stage."

Born in Paris on April 29, 1924, Renée
Jeanmaire is the daughter of Marcel Jeanmaire,
owner of a Paris chromium factory. When she
was nine years old she entered the Paris Opera
Ballet School and while there appeared with
the children's ballet corps from the school in
the French film *La Mort du Cygne*. At the
school she also met Roland Petit and when she
left the Paris Opera Ballet at the age of seventeen, she appeared in some of the young
choreographer's early ballets. After spending
several seasons with the de Basil and de Cuevas
Russian ballets, she became an original member of Les Ballets de Champs-Élysées, a company formed in October 1945 by Petit and
other young dancers. She left this group in
early 1948 to join Petit's newly organized company known as Les Ballets de Paris de Roland
Petit, a troupe of fifteen dancers, each a soloist. Following a successful engagement in Paris,
Les Ballets de Paris made a tour of Western
Europe, appearing for the first time in February
1949 in London, where three new ballets by the
head of the company were presented at the
Princess Theatre. Miss Jeanmaire starred in
Carmen, a choreographic version of the opera,
which was so well received that it was given
at every performance and played to standing

room only during the London run. In the summer of 1949 the troupe's presentation of the
new ballet in Paris played to full houses for a
record three months.

Les Ballets de Paris, brought to the United
States by Arthur Lesser in association with
the Shuberts, gave its first performance in New
York on October 6, 1949, at the Winter Garden Theater. Petit's interpretation of *Carmen*,
which is performed to Bizet's music with some
additions and which departs from the score to
add a seduction scene, was received with enthusiastic notices from the reviewers. Walter
Terry of the New York *Herald Tribune* (October 7, 1949) said of Miss Jeanmaire, "Her
Carmen is a remarkable, if not very profound,
characterization . . . her movements are rich in
dynamic color and the shifts of her emotional
interests, the degrees of intensity with which
she meets varying incidents are clearly revealed
in her actions." In his review in the New
York *World-Telegram* (October 7, 1949) Louis
Biancolli observed, "Renée Jeanmaire's Carmen
is one of the most amazing portrayals of the
modern stage. Using almost strictly classical
technique, abetted by a shrewd sense of subtly
graded pantomine, she manages to depict the
whole tantalizing personality of Don Jose's
femme fatale." Other critics commented on the
effect of her exaggerated eye make-up and
cropped hair in creating a "sensual and bold"
Carmen. After giving 118 performances in
New York, the troupe visited other Eastern
cities and Canada with its production of *Carmen*.

Following a six-month period of recovery
from a leg injury and operation, Miss Jeanmaire on September 25, 1950, appeared in a
new ballet by Petit called *La Croqueuse de
Diamants* (*The Diamond Cruncher*), which had
its premier in Paris. Les Ballets de Paris returned to New York on October 8 for its first
performance at the National Theater, where

JEANMAIRE, RENÉE—*Continued*

the dancer reappeared in her familiar interpretation of Carmen some weeks later. On October 31 *La Croqueuse de Diamants* had its first presentation in New York. The ballet, a fantasy which tells of a woman who has an insatiable appetite for diamonds (as food) much to the despair of her underworld associates and who is eventually reformed by a delivery boy, was an innovation in that the principals sang and spoke as well as danced. Some critics felt that the introduction of song gave the ballet a "musical comedy quality," while others referred to its "operatic touch." Dancing the title role, Miss Jeanmaire also sang, reportedly in a manner modeled after that of the French *chanteuse* Edith Piaf, "Je suis la croqueuse de diamants." The *New Yorker* (November 11, 1950) critic found, "The tiny and fascinating Renée Jeanmaire has the central part, and, performing with tremendous charm, she reveals herself to be a highly talented comedienne"; the writer of the *Musical America* review (November 15, 1950) commented, "She dances, mimes, and sings with an intensity that makes the most fantastic episodes seem wholly natural . . . and she tosses off the technically difficult solos and duets with the utmost ease." In discussing types of dancers, Arnold L. Haskell in *How to Enjoy Ballet* named Miss Jeanmaire as an example of dancers who defy classification.

At the conclusion of an eight-week engagement in New York, Les Ballet de Paris went on a tour of the United States, and upon the company's reaching the Pacific coast in February 1951, some of its members were signed by Howard Hughes to make a motion picture version of *Carmen*. With the postponement of this production, however, the members of the troupe were dismissed, with the exception of Miss Jeanmaire and Petit, whom Hughes signed to individual contracts. In the early part of 1952 Samuel Goldwyn, planning a motion picture called *Hans Christian Andersen*, a fantasy based upon imaginary incidents in the life of the nineteenth century Danish storyteller, sought to bring dancer Moira Shearer from England to costar with Danny Kaye and Farley Granger in his $4 million Technicolor film. Since Miss Shearer was unable to fulfill this commitment, Goldwyn decided to replace her with Renée Jeanmaire, whom he accordingly borrowed from Howard Hughes. Her comment on the decision of the Goldwyn studios to introduce her to motion picture audiences as simply Jeanmaire, ignoring her first name in the tradition of Pavlova, was said to be that the American public would continue to call her Jean Mary no matter what names were added or subtracted.

In the forthcoming Goldwyn production, scheduled for release in late 1952, Miss Jeanmaire will have her first straight acting part and will sing a duet with Danny Kaye as well as dance in four ballet sequences. Petit was signed by Goldwyn to stage the ballets and An-

toni Clavé, who designed the much praised sets for *Carmen*, worked with Richard Day to provide settings for the picture. Miss Jeanmaire's role in *Hans Christian Andersen* is that of a ballerina married to her ballet director. Andersen writes her a love letter in the form of the folk tale "The Little Mermaid," and while not perceiving the underlying meaning of the letter, she is intrigued by the story and insists that her husband stage it as a ballet. Performed by Miss Jeanmaire, Petit, and a troupe of twenty dancers, this ballet, which is the climax of the film, lasts about seventeen minutes on the screen and cost a reported $400,000 to film. It has been described by publicity releases as "the most impressive single production number Goldwyn has staged in his entire career."

A biographic sketch of Miss Jeanmaire from the Goldwyn studios characterized her as lively and witty and as very serious in her attitude toward dancing. She was quoted as saying, "There is nothing interesting about me personally. But when people see me dance, they understand me. That is the important thing." The brown-eyed dancer is five feet tall and weighs 100 pounds. Her black hair is worn short, "a poodle cut without curls" which inspired a Parisian trend to the short "hairdo" when she won popularity in her native city.

References

N Y Times II p3 Je 29 '52
Silver Screen 22:30 S '52 pors
Chujoy, A. ed. Dance Encyclopedia (1949)

JOHNSON, DAVID M(OFFAT) Apr. 30, 1902- Canadian Representative to the United Nations

Address: c/o Canadian Delegation to the United Nations, 620 5th Ave., New York 20

The Permanent Representative of Canada to the United Nations is David M. Johnson, who took up that assignment in 1951, at the close of two years in the post of Canadian High Commissioner to Pakistan. The latter appointment had followed his service as Acting High Commissioner in Dublin. His previous Government positions in Canada's capital had been in the Department of Finance and the Department of External Affairs. By profession he is a lawyer.

David Moffat Johnson was born April 30, 1902, in Lachine, in the Canadian Province of Quebec. He is the son of William Steele Johnson. After attending the Lachine High School, in 1919 he entered McGill University in Montreal, where he received first-class honors in mathematics and physics upon his graduation in 1923 with the Bachelor of Arts degree. At this time Johnson, the quarter-mile champion runner of Canada, was named as one of his country's contestants in the 1924 Olympics, held in Paris, in which he placed fourth in the quarter-mile competition. From 1923 to 1926 the young

Canadian studied for his second Bachelor of Arts degree at Oxford University, completing his work there with honors in jurisprudence. From Oxford Johnson also received the degree of Bachelor of Civil Law.

Entering the practice of law in 1926, Johnson was associated for the succeeding ten years with the Montreal firm of Stairs, Dixon and Claxton. In Ottawa for the ensuing decade he was in Government service, engaged by the Department of Finance as solicitor to the Treasury. Temporarily posted in 1941 to the Department of External Affairs, he was assigned to the Office of the High Commissioner for Canada in London, where he held the post of attaché until joining the Canadian Army in August 1943 for World War II service.

Johnson served as a gunner in Europe and later was stationed at the Second Canadian Corps Headquarters before being demobilized with the rank of captain in September 1945. From then until 1947 he was again with the Department of Finance in the Canadian capital. On January 27, 1947, he rejoined the Department of External Affairs with the grade of foreign service officer 6, in which capacity he was named chief of the American and Far Eastern Division, holding that post in 1947-48. During the same period he was secretary of the Canadian section of the Permanent Joint Board on Defense, which had been set up some years earlier by the United States and Canada to study problems relating to the defense of the northern part of the Western Hemisphere. Appointed Acting High Commissioner for Canada in Ireland in February 1949, Johnson filled that post in Dublin until the following December, when he was sent to Karachi as Canadian High Commissioner to the Government of Pakistan.

While serving as High Commissioner in Pakistan, Johnson attended the meeting of Commonwealth Foreign Ministers in Colombo, Ceylon, where in January 1950 was projected a fourteen-nation cooperative development scheme for South-East Asia. He also represented Canada at another 1950 meeting of the standing committee of the Commonwealth Consultative Committee on South and South-East Asia, also held at Colombo. When, in February 1951, delegates of the nations involved were completing their conference on the projected five-billion-dollar, six-year public works development for the area, Johnson, in behalf of Canada, offered $25 millions for the first year's operating expenses. "The wording of Canada's offer of $25 millions," reported Robert Trumbull of the New York Times, "was interpreted by observers as a gentle hint to the United States that completion of the South Asian plan depended in large measure upon Washington's contribution." Johnson himself said: "I wish to say that the Canadian Government very fully appreciates the constitutional and administrative difficulties of the United States which make it impossible for its representative to make a full and binding statement at this time. On the other hand, the Canadian Government has felt

Canadian Nat. Film Bd.

DAVID M. JOHNSON

from the beginning that its own contribution of dollars could not be considered entirely apart from the aid that might come from the United States." Estimates by the participating nations of India, Pakistan, Ceylon, other British Commonwealth nations in South-East Asia, and Viet-Nam (the sole "outside" nation invited as of that time) called for more than $2 billions to supplement their financial contributions.

In late September 1951 the Canadian Department of External Affairs announced Johnson's appointment to succeed Herbert Norman (former Acting Canadian Permanent Representative) as the Permanent Representative of Canada to the United Nations. "Mr. Johnson," said an official press release, "will take over his new duties at the beginning of the forthcoming session of the General Assembly and will be a member of the Canadian Delegation to the General Assembly in Paris." In the monthly alphabetical rotation of each country in various bodies of the United Nations, Johnson's first assignment was that of chairman, for the month of March, of the newly formed Disarmament Commission, successor to the defunct United Nations Atomic Energy Commission. At the initial meeting Johnson delivered "a warning against dreams of sudden achievement," said John G. Rogers of the New York Herald Tribune. Under discussion at that time were Soviet charges that the United States had employed germ warfare in Korea, accusations which were ruled "out of order" by chairman Johnson, who was upheld by an 11-to-1 vote of the commission. A subsequent ruling by the chairman limited discussion to arms elimination or reduction, barring specific charges by the delegates.

Reference

World Diplomatic Directory, 1951

JOHNSON, JOSEPH T(RAVIS) May 28, 1894- Bankers association officer

Address: b. c/o Investment Bankers Association of America, 33 S. Clark St., Chicago 3, Ill.; c/o The Milwaukee Company, 207 E. Michigan St., Milwaukee 2, Wis.; h. 1260 N. Prospect Ave., Milwaukee, Wis.

The 1,100 delegates at the November 1951 convention of the Investment Bankers Association of America elected Joseph T. Johnson, Milwaukee investment banker, to its presidency. Frequently a member of the committees of the association, Johnson had been particularly prominent in its public education committee, of which he was chairman. Under his presidency it is believed that the association will strongly emphasize the development of infor-

Fabian Bachrach
JOSEPH T. JOHNSON

mational services to the public. In the securities business since the 1920's, Johnson had previously been an agent of the Bureau of Internal Revenue and head of its Wisconsin Division.

Born in Laurens, South Carolina, on May 28, 1894, Joseph Travis Johnson is the son of Joseph Travis and Sarah (Anderson) Johnson. From 1910 to 1912 he attended Wofford College in Spartanburg and, in 1914, George Washington University in Washington, D.C. The following year Johnson entered Federal service as an internal revenue agent, and soon afterward the United States Treasury Department sent him to Milwaukee in the same capacity. In 1920 Johnson was placed in charge of the Wisconsin Division of the Bureau of Internal Revenue, a position which he filled for two years.

Johnson entered the banking business on January 1, 1923, when he joined the Second

Ward Securities Company of Milwaukee, an investment banking concern. Three years later he became the manager of its bond department. In 1928 the company merged with the First Wisconsin National Bank, thus leaving Johnson free to join others in the formation of the Milwaukee Company the following year. Vice-president of the Milwaukee Company until 1934, Johnson at that time became its president, an office he continues to hold in 1952. The Milwaukee Company, a member of the Midwest Stock Exchange, maintains Wisconsin branches in Madison and Wausau, and others in Chicago and St. Paul.

In the meantime, Johnson had become active in the Investment Bankers Association of America, which is composed of individuals, partnerships, and corporations engaged in that field of banking. The I.B.A., which was founded in 1912, was formed (states the preamble of its constitution) "In order that investment bankers may the better serve both those who purchase and those who sell securities, through which the necessary funds are raised for the operation and expansion of business activities and for the carrying on of public functions, and may thus contribute to the increase in national wealth and its wide diffusion; and in order that they may aid in these directions through mutual cooperation, through the maintenance of high standards of service, through self-regulation and through the support of appropriate legislation."

In 1934 Johnson served on the Investment Bankers conference committee; and at other times thereafter he was a member of a number of national committees of the I.B.A. As representative of the Central States group, he held office from 1945 to 1948 on the association's board of governors, and, in the latter year he was elected a vice-president of the I.B.A. It was in 1948, too, that Johnson, as head of a special committee, brought to the association's attention the need for a public relations campaign concerning the activities of the securities business. This led to the formation of a public education committee, of which he was chairman from 1948 to 1951. "Through the public education committee," declared Laurence M. Marks, the then president of the I.B.A., "member firms have been stimulated to join the campaign designed to improve public understanding of our business. Mr. Johnson and his committe have done a splendid job with a difficult assignment, and we can expect an extension of the progress made under his leadership."

On October 25, 1951, the I.B.A. board of governors nominated Joseph T. Johnson to succeed in the presidency, a nomination tantamount to election, which was confirmed on November 30, at the I.B.A. convention held in Hollywood, Florida. In his inaugural address Johnson called for cooperation among various groups in the United States: "As equal partners, government, labor and business can face the future with some measure of equanimity; as reluctant allies, their efforts will be spent in petty squabbles behind the lines." (This conviction, said the New York *World-Telegram*, was the result of recent travels Johnson had made in Europe and the Orient, which had made him believe that "America is the present hope of mankind.") The new I.B.A. president, referring to his previous efforts as spokesman in behalf of the group, also declared: "Our business would stand in higher public esteem today, if during the past generation, or even during the last ten or twenty years, we had steadfastly pursued an intelligent and comprehensive program of informing the public about our business."

At the 1951 convention the I.B.A.'s various committees voiced their opposition to municipal financing of industrial buildings for rental (and subsequently voted to by-pass such bonds issued by municipalities); advocated a ceiling on taxes, and supported the return of the Federal Reserve Banking System to its original status as an agency independent of the Executive branch of the Government. Under Johnson, said C. Norman Stabler, financial editor of the New York *Herald Tribune*, the I.B.A. could be expected to intensify its campaign of education, begun the previous year, such as the issuance of a motion picture on investment banking processes, making a portable exhibit ("Money Tells Its Own Story") available to member firms and other organizations, publication of five monographs on securities based on material gathered by the Wharton School of Finance. Another objective of such a program under Johnson's leadership, reported *Business Week*, "will be to broaden greatly the number of people who are shareholders in American industry."

From 1929 to 1940 Johnson was a member of the Public Debt Commission of the City of Milwaukee. For a number of years interested in flying, upon his election to the board of directors of Northwest Airlines in 1939 he began the custom of flying on each first flight of newly extended routes of that line. He is also a director of the National Thrift Committee, Inc. The Wisconsin banker's political preference is Republican, he is a member of the Methodist Church, and his fraternity is Delta Tau Delta.

Johnson has memberships in clubs in several parts of the country—the Milwaukee, the Wisconsin, the Milwaukee Country, the Minneapolis, and the Chicago; in New York his clubs are the India House and the University. On July 5, 1917, he married Ruth Hennessey. Cooking, said *Business Week*, is Johnson's "avocation."

References

Bsns W p121 D 1 '51
Fortune 44:118 D '51 por
Who's Who in America, 1950-51
Who's Who in Commerce and Industry (1951)
Who's Who in the Midwest (1949)

KAHMANN, (MABLE) CHESLEY Jan. 27, 1901- Author

Address: b. c/o Random House, Inc., 457 Madison Ave., New York 22; h. "Lambs' Quarters," Great Meadows, N.J.

Reprinted from the *Wilson Library Bulletin*, Nov. 1952.

That every experience is grist for an author's mill is amply proved by Chesley Kahmann's work. Her books and stories have the authenticity that comes from thorough knowledge of her chosen fields. Although she has written some adult fiction and some stories for boys, she has claimed for her own two unusual spheres—Puerto Rico, of which she was the first

CHESLEY KAHMANN

and remains the only exponent in fiction for older girls; and gypsy life, with its mystery and romance appealing so strongly to teenagers.

Both sides of the family of Chesley Kahmann (who was born Mable Chesley) were pre-Revolutionary Americans, and both grandfathers trekked to Minnesota in covered wagons. Her mother, named Minnesota Mable Norton "because that State seemed the most beautiful place in the world," graduated from Hamline University in St. Paul and "could translate Horace and Livy to her dying day." Her father, Orin Gilbert Chesley, was president of several hail insurance companies in Iowa, to which State the family had moved before her birth, in Des Moines, on January 27, 1901.

She had pet ponies from the age of six, her father teaching her, her brother Ralph, and her sister Lucile, first to ride bareback, and then to saddle the pony themselves. One cream-colored beauty with black mane and tail was five-gaited and so good at playing dead, marching to music, and kneeling, that he was bid for by a circus and later was celebrated in her story

KAHMANN, CHESLEY—*Continued*

Gypsy Luck, run as a serial, "The Cream Colored Pony," in *Story Parade,* and picked up by CBS for its program, *Tales from Far and Near.*

After graduating from Des Moines High School, she attended Ohio Wesleyan University, majoring in English and receiving her B.A. degree in 1922. Her interest turned to gypsy life as a result of graduate work at Columbia University, where she took her M.A. degree in 1923. The research for her thesis on gypsy characters and gypsy lore in English literature gave her such an insight into their traits that her stories of gypsy life are written from a gypsy point of view, and the Gypsy Lore Society of England has complimented her because the backgrounds, psychology, and characterizations ring true.

Similarly, her stories of Puerto Rico adopt the standpoint of a Puerto Rican girl and have been praised by islanders for their sincerity and fidelity. She wrote not as an outsider but as an active participant in their life. While heading the English department in the Ponce High School, she lived with a Puerto Rican family, learning their habits, their speech, their personalities, eating rice and beans twice a day, and often being the only North American at their festivities.

Mrs. Kahmann has had eleven books published. Six have been Junior Literary Guild selections, and many of her magazine serials and stories have been included in anthologies and literary readers.

Although the first story she wrote was *Gypsy Luck,* this was her fifth book to be published (1937). It was preceded by *Felita,* a Puerto Rican story (1932); *Carmen, Silent Partner* (1934); *Tara, Daughter of the Gypsies* (1935); and *Raquel, a Girl of Puerto Rico* (1936)—all for older girls. Both *Gypsy Luck* and *Felita* have been reprinted recently. *Lupe and the Senorita* (1938) is another teen-age story, but in *Jasper the Gypsy Dog* (1938) and *Sinfi and the Little Gypsy Goat* (1940) she reached a younger audience.

For boys from nine to twelve she wrote *XDY and the Soap Box Derby* (1941). Accompanying her husband, George Ames Kahmann, editor of *News & Views* for General Motors Acceptance Corporation, to the national soap box derby at Akron, Ohio, she was in close touch with the youthful contestants, absorbed local color and details and tied them in with a boys' club—XDY—she had created for a series of short stories in *Child Life.*

Her most recent books for girls return to the gypsy theme. *Gypsy Goes to College* (1941) develops the conflicts that arise when a care-free gypsy girl enters a conservative midwest college, rooming with a very proper American girl whose life she could not understand, and hedged in by rules. "What would this do to the gypsy and to her roommate?" Mrs. Kahmann asked herself. The book is the answer. In her other gypsy stories she had shown them living independent lives, in their own world. Now she questions whether gypsies have a responsibility as Americans.

Gypsy Melody (1949) pursues this further, telling of a talented girl violinist who wishes to remain a gypsy, while her gypsy lover feels they should cooperate with the "Cajos." The *Journal of the Gypsy Lore Society* commends it for "sympathetic understanding of gypsy ways and gypsy feelings . . . among the very few stories about Gypsies with any real knowledge of the subject."

Mrs. Kahmann, her husband, and daughter Chesley (called "Lee") live on a farm on a hill above Great Meadows, New Jersey. A lively person, with brown hair and gray eyes, she sandwiches her writing in with home chores, sheep raising, and handcrafts, often putting in ten hours a day at her typewriter, but "getting a lot of fun out of it." She is now writing a book about gypsies for boys of intermediate age.

KANIN, GARSON (kā′nǐn) Nov. 24, 1912-
Stage and motion picture director; playwright
Address: b. 30 E. 60th St., New York 22;
h. 242 E. 49th St., New York 17

> Note: This biography supersedes the article which appeared in *Current Biography* in 1941.

Almost all phases of the theater, considered in its widest sense, have engaged the talents of Garson Kanin. From a career in the mid-30's on the legitimate stage in New York as an actor and director, he went to Hollywood to write scripts and direct motion pictures, *A Man to Remember* (1936) and *My Favorite Wife* (1940) being among his notable early films. *Born Yesterday,* a highly acclaimed play written by Kanin and directed by him in its 1946 Broadway production, was followed by a number of motion pictures, including *A Double Life* (1948) and *Pat and Mike* (1952), of which he was coauthor with his wife, Ruth Gordon. In 1950 the Metropolitan Opera Company employed him to direct and refurbish Johann Strauss's opera *Die Fledermaus.*

Garson Kanin was born on November 24, 1912, in Rochester, New York, the son of David and Sadie (Levine) Kanin. When the boy was about twelve years old, his family moved to Brooklyn, New York, where his father was employed as a builder. Upon leaving James Madison High School after two years' attendance, young Kanin held jobs as a messenger for Western Union and as a salesman in a store. Using the knowledge of music he had acquired in his earlier study of the saxophone and clarinet, he in time found a position with a jazz band. Later he played as a comedian in vaudeville and performed various small parts in radio programs (among them *The March of Time*) and in summer theaters, mainly in the Catskill Mountains resorts in New York.

In preparation for a professional acting career, Kanin took a two-year course at New York's American Academy of Dramatic Arts, where at a later period he reportedly became a member of the faculty. In 1933, the year of his graduation from the academy, he was given his first Broadway role, in *Little Ol' Boy.* During the following years the plays in which he appeared comprised *Spring Song* (1934), *Ladies Money, Three Men on a Horse* (1935), *The Body Beautiful* (1935), *Boy Meets Girl* (1935), and *Star Spangled* (1936). While none of his roles were starring parts, his acting attracted some critical notice, John Anderson in the New York *Evening Journal* making this comment on his performance in *Boy Meets Girl*: "Garson Kanin works wonders with the musical kidding." The association which at this time he developed with theatrical producer George Abbott (as recounted some years later by Kanin in an interview with a New York *World-Telegram* reporter) was attributed to the young actor's practice of sitting at an empty desk in Abbott's office with sufficient regularity to become an accustomed sight. From 1935 to 1937 Kanin assisted Abbott in the directorial work on *Three Men on a Horse, Boy Meets Girl, Brother Rat,* and *Room Service.* For Abbott he also directed *Hitch Your Wagon* (1936) and *Too Many Heroes* (1937).

As a director on the production staff of Samuel Goldwyn, Kanin went to Hollywood in 1937. His contract shortly terminated by agreement, Kanin, who had made no pictures with Goldwyn, moved to RKO, where he was first given the task of producing a low-budget film, *A Man to Remember* (1938). This unpretentious motion picture, the story of a small-town doctor rated a failure, made a favorable impression on critics, calling forth the observation of the New York *Herald Tribune* reviewer, "Mr. Kanin . . . makes an auspicious start as a director. He has given the show pace and fluency, while wisely avoiding sheer camera trickery."

There followed in 1938 Kanin's direction of *Next Time I Marry* and a year later his *A Great Man Votes,* starring John Barrymore, and *Bachelor Mother,* with Ginger Rogers. In 1940 release was made of *My Favorite Wife,* a burlesque skit about bigamy which director Kanin "built up with clockwork timing, a gallery of marvelous characterizations, and priceless spontaneity of humor" (*Friday,* May 24, 1940). Discussing Kanin's work on another 1940 film, *They Knew What They Wanted* (starring Carole Lombard and Charles Laughton), the *Christian Science Monitor* critic remarked, "Kanin's direction is thoroughly efficient, but lacks the distinction which has characterized many of his pictures." A seventh film for RKO, *Tom, Dick and Harry,* in which Kanin directed Ginger Rogers and Burgess Meredith in the leading roles, was highly praised for the wit and fantasy with which it told the story of a hare-brained girl engaged at the same time to three men.

When Kanin entered the Army in 1941, he was stationed for a time with the Training Film Laboratory at Fort Monmouth, New Jersey, as a private in the Signal Corps. He then saw a period of service (1942-43) as a sergeant in the Air Force. In 1943 he became a captain in the Office of Strategic Services attached to the Supreme Headquarters, Allied Expeditionary Force in Europe. It was in this position that, together with the British Carol Reed, he compiled out of

GARSON KANIN

official military films *The True Glory,* which was named best film of 1945 by the National Board of Review.

Back on Broadway in 1946, Kanin directed *The Rugged Path,* written by Robert Sherwood and starring Spencer Tracy. Later that same year, on February 4, 1946, *Born Yesterday,* written and directed by Kanin, opened on Broadway. This farce, about a junk dealer who engages in wholesale corruption in wartime Washington until he is brought to a downfall by his naïve girl friend's awakening to morality, was to run on Broadway for 1,642 performances (at its closing the sixth longest run) and to have additional presentations by road companies and in a number of foreign countries. For *Born Yesterday,* generally regarded as his most successful work, Kanin received the Donaldson awards for the best first play and the best direction of the 1945-46 season and the Sidney Howard Memorial (shared with Arthur Laurents). Describing the feelings his varied relations to this play inspired in him, Kanin told a Boston *Sunday Post* writer: "The task has inspired an interesting excursion into schizophrenia. The playwright and the director fulfill two completely different functions in the theater. The playwright's world is one of imagination, the director's one of reality."

Beginning a period of collaboration with his wife Ruth Gordon (widow of Gregory Kelly), whom he married on December 4, 1942, Kanin directed her play *Years Ago* (1946), starring Fredric March and Florence Eldridge. Later Kanin and his wife together wrote the scenarios for Universal International's *A Double Life* (1948) and Metro-Goldwyn-Mayer's *Adam's Rib* (1949); for the latter the authors received an Academy of Motion Pictures Arts and Sciences Award nomination and the Box Office Blue Ribbon Award. Two motion pictures released in 1952 for which they wrote the story were *The Marrying Kind* for Columbia and

KANIN, GARSON—*Continued*

MGM's *Pat and Mike*, a comedy about a lady athlete and a sports promoter starring Spencer Tracy and Katharine Hepburn.

Meanwhile, for presentation on Broadway, Kanin directed *How I Wonder* (1947) and *The Leading Lady* (1948). He was both writer and director of *Smile of the World* (1949) and *The Rat Race* (1950), neither of which enjoyed success at the box office or a warm reception from the critics. Of the latter play, dealing with a young saxophone player, Kanin said, "This is very close to the source material. I feel that I was able to present it from truth. From the point of view of stagecraft, this is a great advance for me. I think I made a wider use of the magic of the theater" (New York *Post*, January 8, 1950). *The Live Wire*, written and directed by Kanin in 1950, was regarded by Howard Barnes as "tired and tiresome"; while Brooks Atkinson found it "too random and unsubstantial for complete enjoyment," noting, however, "Kanin knows how to orchestrate a gag by timing it shrewdly, and how to weave a gag throughout a performance, like a theme in a piece of music."

Stepping into a new field, in 1950 Kanin was called upon to assist the Metropolitan Opera Company in its English-language revival of Johann Strauss's *Die Fledermaus*. The company's director, Rudolf Bing, had selected this work, last presented by the Metropolitan in 1905, as one which might draw to the opera house that audience which was accustomed only to plays and musical comedies. Kanin's contribution was to refurbish the dialogue, revise the plot to some extent (while leaving the music untouched), and direct the entire performance. Critical response to his contribution was mixed, Arthur Bronson, as an example, saying in *Variety*, "Kanin's book and especially [Howard] Dietz's lyrics were excellent fun, with many cute colloquialisms and double entendres. But Kanin's staging was heavy-handed." The popular success of *Die Fledermaus* was such that a special company was organized to present the new version on a thirty-week tour of the United States and Canada.

As one equally familiar with the stage and screen, Kanin has on occasion drawn comparisons between the two media. For *Theatre Arts* (September 1941) he summed up: "Making the transition from stage to screen requires only a physical adjustment." He noted the limitations of Hollywood—censorship, big business dominance, an atmosphere hostile to creativity—but said, "these are things that can be changed—every day." On Kanin's work as a movie director Lewis Jacobs in *Theatre Arts* (March 1941) commented: "The focus of Garson Kanin's efforts is to tell a story well . . . Kanin seeks to achieve his aim through minute attention to acting, situation, dialogue, with a minor stress on camera and cutting. Convinced that the film is an interpretive medium, he insists that the camera must never interfere with the illusion of actuality, and he has an abhorrence of moving the camera."

Kanin is a member of the Screen Directors Guild, the Writer's Guild, the Dramatist Guild, the Academy of Motion Picture Arts and Sciences, and the American Veterans Committee. With a height of five feet seven and one half inches, he weighs 130 pounds; he has brown hair and blue eyes. The director-playwright has been pictured by a New York *News* reporter "as a quiet talker . . . the inner force that has driven him to success is scarcely visible in his relaxed moments."

References

Friday 1:19 My 24 '40 por
Life 7:27-8 Jl 3 '39
N Y News p80+ D 15 '46 pors
N Y World-Telegram p37 O 12 '40
Pageant 4:138-43 Mr '49 por
Theatre Arts 25:225-6+ Mr '41; 25: 640-4 S '41
International Motion Picture Almanac, 1950-51
International World Who's Who (1949)
Who's Who in America, 1952-53

KARFIOL, BERNARD May 6, 1886—Aug. 16, 1952 Figure and landscape painter noted for his romantic vision of subject; studied five years (1901-06) in Paris, the first year under Jean Paul Laurens; as exponent of French postimpressionistic style, exhibited at the Armory Show of modernistic painting in New York (1913); beginning 1933 showed most of his work at the Downtown Gallery in New York; one of the earliest representatives of the modernist movement in the United States. See *Current Biography*, 1947.

Obituary

N Y Times Ag 17 '52

KARSH, YOUSUF (yōo'sōof) Dec. 23, 1908- Portrait photographer

Address: b. Arcade Bldg., 130 Sparks St., Ottawa, Ontario, Canada; h. "Little Wings," Prescott Highway, Ottawa, Ontario, Canada

The man whose name appears under many of the best-known photographic portraits of internationally important personages, Yousuf Karsh, first drew general attention by a picture he made of Winston Churchill in 1941. From his studio in Ottawa, Canada, Karsh has traveled to the chief cities of Europe and America to make portraits of leading figures in western civilization which have received wide reproduction in many of the world's foremost magazines, including *The Illustrated London News* and *Life*. In 1946 a selection of seventy-five was published in his book *Faces of Destiny*.

Yousuf Karsh was born December 23, 1908, in Mardin in the mountains of Armenia. With the memory of the Turkish massacres of 1915-18 strong in their minds, the family sent Yousuf at the age of fifteen to Canada, where his uncle, A. G. Nakash, had a photographic studio in Sherbrooke, Quebec. The boy, whose grandfather had been an engraver (his father was in the import-export business), took a

great interest in his uncle's work. He was
eager that the friends he had left in Mardin
should understand the new world in which he
was living and saw in photography a means
of telling them about it. Finding that the
youth had a talent for the art and that his interest in it was serious, Nakash took him to
Boston to study under a friend, John Garo,
also of Armenian birth. The six months
Karsh was to have remained there became
three years. Writing in the foreword to *Faces
of Destiny* of the meaning of this period to his
later work, Karsh emphasized the intellectual
and aesthetic stimulation of the atmosphere of
Garo's studio, crediting it with forming his
standards.

At the end of this period of apprenticeship
and study Karsh returned to Canada and opened
a studio of his own in Ottawa in 1933. His
work soon became well known in the capital
city, particular attention having been drawn by
his portraits of the Governor General of Canada, the Earl of Bessborough, and of Lady
Bessborough. In 1935 he was commissioned
to do official Canadian Government portraiture.
He was also appointed official photographer to
the Drama Festivals, an annual event of the
Canadian amateur theater. To his experience
in this capacity, in which he watched and shot
scenes from numerous plays, Karsh has attributed the distinctive treatment of backgrounds in his portraits. It also led him to
experiment with lighting effects and to develop
his own system, an important element in his
mature photographic technique.

Since Ottawa in wartime was visited by
many of the world's great figures, in 1941
came the opportunity for the picture that was
to make Karsh internationally known. Given
the chance through the aid of the late Prime
Minister W. L. Mackenzie King to photograph Winston Churchill when the latter, fati-
gued after addressing the Canadian Parliament,
was smoking a cigar, Karsh obtained the expression of aroused and obstinate anger he
wanted to catch by snatching away Churchill's
cigar. The resulting portrait was highly acclaimed and received widespread reproduction
as a symbol of Britain's fighting spirit.

The success of the Churchill portrait led to
an arrangement for Karsh to spend two
months in England photographing celebrities.
On this mission, which though unofficial had
the blessing of the Canadian Wartime Information Board and the Department of External Affairs he took with him approximately 750 pounds of photographic equipment
in anticipation of British wartime shortages.
Among the sixty personalities who faced his
camera were Their Majesties the King and
Queen and the Princess Elizabeth; Lord
Wavell, then Viceroy of India; Montagu Norman, Governor of the Bank of England;
United States Ambassador Winant; Lord
Beaverbrook; the Right Honorable Clement
Attlee; George Bernard Shaw; H. G. Wells.
A copy of each of the portraits became the
property of the Canadian Government for its
records. Published in the leading magazines
of many countries, the pictures made on this

Karsh

YOUSUF KARSH

British trip brought Karsh international recognition. For a commission from *Life* magazine
for a series of portraits of United States
leaders, Karsh made studies of Charles Evans
Hughes, Bernard Baruch, Harold Ickes, General Eisenhower, John L. Lewis, Mrs. Eleanor
Roosevelt, among others. Another *Life* assignment took the photographer to the United
Nations Conference at San Francisco in 1945.

In 1946 a selection of seventy-five portraits
by Karsh with his notes on the subjects was
published under the title *Faces of Destiny*.
Commenting on the book in the New York
Herald Tribune, Richard F. Crandall ranked
the portraitist with such photographers as
Steichen and Stieglitz. The reviewer remarked
on the contrast between Karsh's simple backgrounds and the "effects" of English photographer Cecil Beaton; he also noted the Canadian's frequent use of his subjects' hands as
elements of composition. "Hands," Karsh has
been quoted as saying, "give a more complete
expression of character than the face alone.
They also allow for more artistic composition
in a picture." In a survey of the work of the
"photographic virtuoso" in *Popular Photography* magazine Bruce Downes wrote: "Karsh
has a well-nigh unerring instinct for pictorial
composition in which we find the head placement in relation to the hands and surroundings
just right, and this arrangement of the parts
is enhanced further by intuitively fine placement of the strong highlight accents." He
went on to observe that the Canadian photographer's lighting method emphasized texture
and produced an "agreeable luminosity."

The tendency of his work to carry a greater
weight of interpretation than the simply personal is what characterizes it. In the foreword to *Faces of Destiny* Karsh pointed out
that it has been his aim to record his sitters
both as personalities and as figures in history.

(Continued next page)

KARSH, YOUSUF—*Continued*

Part of the portraitist's technique consists in his ability to induce his subjects, by soothing or provocative conversation, to fall into characteristic, unselfconscious poses. A not infrequent reaction to the results obtained was expressed by Lord Beaverbrook, who on seeing his proofs said, "Karsh, you have immortalized me."

Taking as his theme men of peace, in the summer of 1949 Karsh made portraits of Pope Pius XII, Jean Sibelius, Richard Strauss, Bertrand Russell, Jean Cocteau, and many other well-known European men of arts and letters. The following year he entered the field of industrial photography when he made for Atlas Steels, Ltd., Wellington, Ontario, a series of studies of industrial workers, emphasizing their skill and craftsmanship on the job, their pride in their skill. He later undertook further industrial work for Ford of Canada, Ltd. The much sought-after photographer, who has a library of sittings numbering over 11,000 (with about 20 negatives for each sitting), keeps cameras and equipment in Ottawa, London, Paris, and New York. He always uses a white camera, considering the regulation black to be depressing; his focusing cloth, which varies in color with his mood, is frequently a rich red velvet lined with gold satin. When traveling on commissions, he takes 250 pounds as his minimum in photographic equipment, including camera, spotlights, and floodlights. A group of Karsh's portraits forms part of the permanent collection of the Brooklyn Museum Department of Photography; of Eastman House, Inc., Rochester, New York; and the Museum of Modern Art, New York City. Prints for the permanent collections of the Art Institute of Chicago and the Huntington Library, San Marino, California, are in course of preparation (1952).

In acknowledgement of his contribution to Canadian art and culture, in January 1947 the Canadian Government invited Karsh to become one of its chosen citizens and to accept one of the first Canadian Citizenship Certificates. The Armenian-born photographer has been described by a writer for *Macleans Magazine* (September 1, 1942) as "a gentle little man," with "enough of an accent to be interesting, but not difficult." (His native language is Arabic.) His head, which is bald on top, is outlined by a thick roll of curly black hair; his eyes are brown. Conversational skill and audacity, accompanied by a winning smile, have been called essential ingredients of his success. He is short, slight, and quick in his movements. In 1939 he married Solange Gauthier, a woman of French birth who had lived in Canada from childhood. She and Karsh met in connection with an Ottawa Drama League production in which she was acting. Since their marriage Mrs. Karsh frequently has posed for her husband's photographic compositions other than portraits. The couple has a modern home on the Rideau River, a few miles outside Ottawa. There, gardening and tennis are the photographer's recreations; he did the landscaping for the three acres on which their home is set.

References

N Y Post Mag p27 Mr 18 '47
Nat Home Mo 17:18 My '46
Macleans Mag 55:19 S 1 '42; 57:5 F 1
   '44; 62:8 N 15 '49
Pop Photography 16:19 My '47
Read Digest 51:67 N '47

KAYE, DANNY Jan. 18, 1913- Comedian; actor

Address: b. c/o Samuel Goldwyn Productions, Inc., 1041 N. Formosa, Los Angeles, Calif.; Box 750, Beverly Hills, Calif.; h. 1103 San Ysidro Dr., Beverly Hills, Calif.; 550 Park Ave., New York 21

NOTE: This biography supersedes the article which appeared in *Current Biography* in 1941.

Since his early Broadway successes in *Lady in the Dark* (1940) and *Let's Face It* (1941), Danny Kaye through his widely praised performances in motion pictures and in his own variety shows has become one of the world's highest paid comedians. Best known to American moviegoers for his patter and for his portrayals of several characters in the same film, he starred in *The Secret Life of Walter Mitty* (1947) and *The Inspector General* (1949), among other pictures. His most recent screen appearance is in the title role of Samuel Goldwyn's *Hans Christian Andersen*. Kaye is also popular in Great Britain, where he has made personal appearances for the past five seasons.

Born David Daniel Kominski on January 18, 1913, in Brooklyn, New York, Danny Kaye was the youngest child of Jacob Kominski, a tailor, and Clara (Nemerovsky) Kominski, who had immigrated to the United States from Russia. As a child while he reportedly never thought of becoming a performer, he enjoyed entertaining anyone who would watch him, and in New York City Public School 149 he took part in a minstrel show. At Thomas Jefferson High School in the same city the youth preferred athletics such as pole-vaulting, handball, and swimming to acting. He relinquished his early interest in becoming a surgeon because family finances prohibited his going to college.

After three and a half years of high school David Kominski and another boy ran away to Florida, starting their journey, it is said, with $1.50 and returning with a $7 profit earned by Danny's singing to his friend's guitar playing. The youth next found work as a soda fountain clerk and then as an office worker in an insurance company, where after ten months he was promoted to the position of an automobile appraiser. The story is told that a mistake on his part which cost the company thousands of dollars discouraged the young man's ambitions in the world of business. He turned to entertaining at private parties in a "song, dance, and funny-saying" performance called *Red and Blackie*, which he presented with a friend. The broadcast of their harmony act over station

WBBC, Brooklyn, led to summer work as "toomlers"—creators of tumult or all-round entertainers in the Borscht Circuit summer hotels and camps in the Catskill Mountains. During the winters of his four years as a "toomler," Kaye lived on his summer earnings (which rose to $1,000 a season) and tried without success to interest a Broadway producer in his abilities.

In 1933 the redheaded entertainer joined the dancing act of Dave Harvey and Kathleen Young. At the opening performance of *The Three Terpsichoreans* in Utica, New York, in the fall of that year, Kominski, through an accident on the stage in which he lost his balance, according to report, aroused much laughter from the audience. The incident was written into the routine and the young man was given billing under his chosen name Danny Kaye. When the team reached Detroit, A. B. Marcus (producer of an annual revue that toured "wherever no one else did") tried to engage Harvey and Young without Kaye, but when they refused Marcus signed the three to a contract for the price of two.

For five months Marcus' *La Vie Paree* gave forty-one one-night engagements in a tour of the United States and then sailed for the Orient in February 1934. By that time Danny Kaye was singing, dancing, "monologuing," playing "straight," and learning the skill of changing costumes quickly. Confronted with non-English-speaking audiences, he developed his face-making techniques, pantomiming, and "scat" singing—the expressive presentation of gibberish with an occasional recognizable word to emphasize a point. Because of the unpredictability of Japanese, Chinese, Malayan, and Siamese stagehands, Kaye learned to perform without props and to invent "stage business" on the spur of the moment. When the lights went out during an Osaka typhoon, Kaye sat on the edge of the stage and sang every song he knew, spotlighting himself by flashlights that he held in each hand.

Back in the United States in 1936, Danny Kaye resumed his search for bookings. He acted as master of ceremonies for one night in a Baltimore night club, became a foil in an act of Nick Long, Jr., and toured for eight weeks with Abe Lyman. When Henry Sherek, owner of a cabaret in London's Dorchester Hotel, tried to engage Kaye, he found the comedian under contract to Long and so booked the entire act. At the opening of the show at the Dorchester—on the night of the Munich crisis—Danny Kaye met an unresponsive audience. One bright spot in his eight weeks in London in 1938 was an appearance at a Sunday band concert in Guildford, at which, according to bandleader Jack Jackson, "he was colossal" (D. Richards, *The Life Story of Danny Kaye*, 1949). A role in *Sunday Night Varieties* in New York—which lasted one performance—led Kaye to a summer engagement at Max Liebman's Camp Tamiment in the Pennsylvania hills, where he rehearsed from 10 A.M. to 6 P.M. with pianist-composer Sylvia Fine. Kaye soon discovered that in his childhood he had lived in the same neighborhood as Miss Fine and had attended the same schools without

Wide World Photos

DANNY KAYE

having met her. The sophisticated comedy of Miss Fine's satire was ideally suited to Danny Kaye's delivery, and at Tamiment together they worked out some of Kaye's perennially popular numbers, including "Anatole of Paris", "Stanislavsky," and "Pavlova."

At the close of the season, Miss Fine and Liebman put their best numbers into one show —*The Straw Hat Revue*, which opened on Broadway in September 1939, with Imogene Coca. Kaye, appearing in ten of the sketches, received the following comments from the New York *World-Telegram* reviewer: "Danny Kaye worked hard and well last evening in any number of capacities," while the *Sun* critic noted "some of the customers laughing so hard at Danny Kaye that the tears streamed from their eyes." With the closing of the show after ten weeks, the comedian went on a vacation to Florida, where in Fort Lauderdale on January 3, 1940, he married Sylvia Fine. Reviewers, admirers, and Kaye himself feel that his success is due in large measure to the witty and distinctive material written for him (with Max Liebman's collaboration) by Miss Fine, who serves also as his personal director, coach, critic, and occasionally as his accompanist.

One month after his marriage, Danny Kaye secured a $250-a-week engagement at the New York night club La Martinique. After playwright Moss Hart saw the entertainer in his 65-minute act, he wrote a part for him in *Lady in the Dark*. Kaye, who is said to need an audience in order to be his funniest, did so poorly at rehearsals that only Moss Hart's insistence—and coaching—kept him in the show. On opening night at the end of 1940, Kaye scored a hit when he rattled off in thirty-eight seconds the names of fifty Russian composers strung together by Ira Gershwin for the tongue-twisting effect. A short time later Kaye received billing under the show's star, Gertrude

KAYE, DANNY—*Continued*

Lawrence, and a raise in salary to $500 a week. In addition to giving eight weekly stage performances, Kaye returned to La Martinique for another engagement, which was reported to be so popular that $50 tips for ringside tables became common and his salary was raised to $2,000 weekly. When Kaye's act opened next at New York City's Paramount Theatre, it was held over for five weeks of five shows a day.

Leaving *Lady in the Dark* in 1941, Kaye accepted the lead in the musical comedy, *Let's Face It*, in which he sang numbers prepared especially for him in addition to Cole Porter's songs. Richard Watts, Jr., reviewing the play for the New York *Herald Tribune* commented: "The oncoming Danny Kaye is brilliantly funny and has one exceptional comic number. . . One strange thing about the score is that the most striking number has not been contributed by Mr. Porter at all. It is something called 'Melody in F,' and it is the work of Sylvia Fine and Max Liebman. The narrative of the career of a selectee, it is done in what I can only describe as triple-talk. At least, it seems to go a step beyond mere double-talk, in that it doesn't even pretend to be using words."

After the United States entered World War II Kaye sold for the government $1 million worth of bonds in six months by appearing in benefits and war bond rallies. Rejected by the Army because of a back ailment, he devoted his efforts to performing in two-hour shows with his friend Leo Durocher at Army camps and hospitals in the South Pacific; later he made USO tours in Europe and on the Korean front.

It was in 1944 that Kaye appeared in his first feature motion picture, Samuel Goldwyn's *Up In Arms*, about which Howard Barnes wrote in the New York *Herald Tribune*: "The chief distinction of *Up In Arms* is that it brings Danny Kaye's talents to the screen. He is superbly funny in the dither and double-talk ditties that made him famous on the stage." The following year Kaye played two roles (a prim scholar and the ghost of his contrary brother) in *Wonder Man*, the first of four motion pictures in which he portrayed several different characters in the same film. Of his starring role in *The Kid From Brooklyn* (1946), Howard Barnes wrote: "Those who may have supposed that Kaye was something of a one-man vaudeville act will be surprised to discover that he is a very accomplished actor in his newest film assignment." He gave his second multiple-role performance in *The Secret Life of Walter Mitty* (1947), playing a meek commuter and the six varied heroes of his daydreams. The New York *Herald Tribune* critic remarked, Kaye was "as triumphant as ever in his odd excursions of clowning."

On his next picture, *A Song Is Born* (1948), comments were less favorable, with Archer Winston of the New York *Post* making a typical observation, "Danny Kaye stands for a mad kinetic hilarity of word and movement, and you keep waiting for him to break out with it and he never does." The year 1949 saw Kaye returning to his multiple roles, this time as an arrogant Prussian, an elegant Frenchman,

a brisk Briton, and a bewildered yokel in *The Inspector General*. Howard Barnes found that Kaye "has never been better. He has never had more captivating material." And Bosley Crowther wrote in the New York *Times* that "especially in his performance of the several musical turns that are carefully spotted throughout the picture does Mr. Kaye sparkle and shine." From this picture, of which Sylvia Fine was associate producer, the Kayes reportedly earned $310,000 plus a percentage of the profits. Again playing multiple-roles in *On the Riviera* (1950), he portrayed a suave French industrialist and a brash American entertainer. The *Christian Science Monitor* thought that in this picture "the many faceted talents of comedian Danny Kaye have never been more flamboyantly mirrored."

From his recordings of "scat," patter, songs, and children's stories Kaye is reported to earn an estimated $50,000 a year. In early 1945 he entered the field of radio entertainment with a "package" show (with Harry James and Eve Arden) at $17,500 a week. This program, on which he appeared for a year, held fifth place in the *Radio Daily* popularity poll. In personal appearances, the medium of entertainment that Kaye prefers, he has scored great successes during his five annual seasons in Great Britain, beginning in 1948. "For the first time in living memory the staid British Isles were indulging in a type of worshipful hysteria . . . which affected young and old of both sexes . . . [and] all classes" (*Life*). Britons sent him 100,000 letters in a week; the royal family went to see him; he was entertained by Shaw, complimented by Churchill, presented with a cane by Sir Harry Lauder, cast in wax by Bernard Tussaud. On Kaye's fifth annual visit (in 1952) he added a tour of provincial music halls which drew an estimated 80,000 patrons. Ed Sullivan (New York *Sunday News*, August 31, 1952) stated that "Danny Kaye registered the greatest success any American— or British— act ever has scored at the Palladium."

Kaye went to Canada also in 1950 as the first single performer to be starred at the Canadian National Exhibition, where the 24,000-seat grandstand was sold out during each of his fourteen appearances, giving Kaye earnings of about $70,000. Later in New York he played to half a million people in three weeks. When he performed in September 1952 at the Curran Theatre in San Francisco, *Variety* noted, "Danny Kaye, heading what has become popularly known in and out of the trade as a Palladium-type show . . . [displayed] the same remarkable ability to hold and excite an audience for an almost interminable period as the late and great Al Jolson."

In January 1951 Kaye, who had parted company with Samuel Goldwyn in 1947, was signed again by the producer to a two-picture contract. One picture is to be a sequel to *The Secret Life of Walter Mitty*. The other film, expected to be released in late 1952, is the $4 million Technicolor production, *Hans Christian Andersen*, a fantasy based upon a fictitious incident in the life of the Danish writer of fairy tales. Some protest appeared in the Danish press and other quarters to having the national hero portrayed by a comedian, but when Kaye visited Denmark in the summer of 1952 to publicize his picture, he was reportedly well received by the people of that country.

Kaye is a 160-pound six footer with reddish-blond hair and blue eyes. He has a daughter named Dena. "The paradox he presents," to quote John Mason Brown, "is that a force so explosive can be contained in so seemingly . . . refined . . . and dapper a man." His clubs are the Lambs and a British equivalent; his religion is Jewish. For recreation he plays golf and tennis and watches baseball.

References

Am Mag 139:40 F '45
Collier's 107:18 Ap 12 '41 por; 123:30 My 14 '49 por
France Illus 5:186 Ag 20 '49
Life 26:47+ Je 13 '49 pors
N Y Herald Tribune IV p1 Jl 22 '51 por
N Y Post p3 My 22 '41 por; p5 D 31 '50 por; p5 Jl 29 '51 por
N Y Sun p26 F 6 '41
N Y Times IX p1 F 9 '41
Newsweek 25:82 Ja 15 '45 por
PM p51 Mr 23 '41 pors
Sat Eve Post 222:30 Je 10 '50 por
Theatre Arts 25:435 Je '41 por
Time 45:48 Ja 15 '45 por; 47:63 Mr 11 '46 pors
International Motion Picture Almanac, 1951-52
Richards, D. The Life Story of Danny Kaye (1949)
Shulman, M. How to Be a Celebrity (1950)
Who's Who, 1952
Who's Who in America, 1952-53
Who's Who in the Theatre, 1952
World Biography (1948)

KERSTEN, CHARLES J. May 26, 1902- United States Representative from Wisconsin

Address: b. House Office Bldg., Washington 25, D.C.; 231 W. Wisconsin Ave., Milwaukee 3, Wis.; h. 516 E. Day Ave., Milwaukee, Wis.

Charles J. Kersten, Republican Representative from the Fifth District of Wisconsin, was elected to the Eightieth Congress in 1946, to the Eighty-second Congress in 1950, and to the Eighty-third Congress in 1952. During his first term in the House of Representatives he was a member of the Merchant Marine and Fisheries Committee and chairman of the education and labor subcommittee, which investigated Communist affiliation in labor unions. In the first session of the Eighty-second Congress the Milwaukee lawyer sponsored legislation appropriating money to aid underground movements in Communist countries.

The son of Charles H. and Nora (Gillespie) Kersten, Charles J. Kersten was born in Chicago, Illinois, on May 26, 1902. He was graduated in 1925 with the degree of LL.B. from the Marquette University College of Law in Milwaukee, Wisconsin. For a year after leaving college he traveled and studied in Europe and the Near East. In Milwaukee in 1928, Kersten, who had been admitted to the Wisconsin bar in 1925, began practicing law as a member of the firm Kersten and McKinnon. In 1934 he was chosen First Assistant District Attorney of Milwaukee County, a post which he occupied until 1943.

As a candidate of the Republican party in 1946, Kersten was elected to the Eightieth Congress from the Fifth Wisconsin District to represent some 390,000 people in one of the two districts of Milwaukee County. Soon after he took his seat in the House of Representatives, Kersten in February 1947 voted in favor of a bill to establish a two-term limit of office for the President of the United States. During the same month he approved the $31.5 billions Federal budget (thus indicating a wish to return to prewar levels of appropriations) and also cast his vote for legislation banning portal-to-portal pay suits. In May, upon the President's informing Congress that the housing shortage was still acute, Kersten voted in favor of a rent control extension bill. The Congressman joined in June an unsuccessful attempt to override Truman's veto of a tax reduction bill, and when the tax bill was placed before the House in revised form in July, Kersten's vote helped override the second Presidential veto. Kersten supported the Taft-Hartley labor legislation over Truman's veto (June), an anti-poll tax bill (July), the Greek-Turkish Aid bill (May), and the *Voice of America* bill (June).

During the first session of the Eightieth Congress the Wisconsin legislator envinced a strong interest in international affairs. Named chairman of a subcommittee to visit Russia in September 1947 to study education and labor conditions, he requested permission of the Soviet Government to make a tour of that country. When the visas were not granted by Soviet officials, he wrote to Secretary of State George C. Marshall asking the "immediate removal of all excess Russian nationals" from the United States. In November 1947, upon returning from a tour of Europe, he urged the reconstruction of Germany and the termination of the denazification program as soon as possible. He described the European economy as "now very sick," and stated that "to abandon Europe to the Russian police state would be historical fatalism."

Kersten aided the passage of the Knutson tax reduction bill, which was placed before the second session of the Eightieth Congress in February 1948. This legislation, closely similar to that which Truman had vetoed during the previous session of Congress, was passed over the President's veto in April. The Wisconsin Republican voted against repealing oleomargarine taxes (April) and in the same month expressed himself in favor of the tidelands oil bill giving States ownership of resources

CHARLES J. KERSTEN

under waters within their boundaries. Kersten affirmed legislation (May) which established heavy penalties for subversive activities designed to "establish in the United States a totalitarian dictatorship under the domination or control of a foreign government or organization." On three measures in June of that year he expressed himself in favor of action to admit a limited number of displaced persons to the United States; opposed the President's veto of a social security bill which Truman said was a "piecemeal" attack on the old age insurance program; and supported the Wolcott Housing bill, which provided for Federal aid in constructing 500,000 low-rent housing units over the following five-year period.

During the Eightieth Congress Kersten was a member of the Merchant Marine and Fisheries Committee. He and Representative Carroll D. Kearns of Pennsylvania comprised in 1947 and 1948 a two-man House education and labor subcommittee which in March 1947 investigated Communist membership of two top officials of Local 248 of the United Automobile Workers. In 1948 this subcommittee continued its investigations, threatening to initiate contempt proceedings against witnesses who refused to answer questions. On December 20, 1948, Kersten claimed to have established definite proof of Communist control of the CIO Electrical Workers Union. Victor Riesel, New York *Post* columnist, reported that the subcommittee had found pro-Soviet feeling in the course of an investigation of military bases in Alaska.

Failing to obtain re-election in 1948, Kersten went back to his law practice in Milwaukee for two years. Returned by his district to the House of Representatives in January 1951 for the Eighty-second Congress, that month he voted in favor of restoring to the Rules Committee the power to block legislation by preventing bills from reaching the floor. He voted in favor of: an extension of the military draft (April), a bill prohibiting the government from building defense plants (April), a cut of $350 millions in European economic aid (August), and a $7.5 billions foreign aid bill (August). Kersten sponsored an amendment to the Mutual Security Act, passed in the closing days of the 1951 session, which allocated $100 millions to aid escapees within and without the Soviet Union. "My amendment," he explained, "contemplates the possibility of aiding the underground organizations that may now exist and may come into existence in the future." Andrei A. Gromyko, acting Russian Foreign Minister, charged that Kersten's amendment "represents unparalleled violation of the standards of international law." Earlier in this session of the Eighty-second Congress Kersten had protested on the floor of the House that the trials of William N. Oatis in Czechoslovakia and Archbishop Josef Groesz of Hungary were typical Communistic injustices of a "macabre" nature, and had urged the United States to break off relations with those countries.

In March 1952, in the second session of the Eighty-second Congress, Kersten voted in favor of a $6.2 billions mutual security bill, and in favor of cutting economic aid to Europe by $615 millions. He affirmed in April legislation placing a $46 billions ceiling on military spending, and in the same month cast his vote against a bill raising old age benefits and liberalizing retirement aspects of the social security program. Kersten became spokesman for more than one hundred Republican Representatives in January 1952 in asking Secretary of State Dean Acheson to investigate Soviet genocide; in February he called for the United States to break relations with all Communist regimes to prevent diplomats from engaging in spying; and in March recommended in a speech that the United States adopt a foreign policy aimed at freeing all of the countries now under Soviet domination. Kersten won election to the Eighty-third Congress on November 4, 1952.

Representative Kersten is a member of the Coast Guard Reserve, the Milwaukee Athletic Club, and the Wisconsin and Milwaukee bar associations. Married to Mary Edith McKinnon of Antigo, Wisconsin, he is the father of one daughter, Mary Callista, and four sons, Edmund Campion, George Patrick, Kenan John, and Kevin. The legislator, who belongs to the Knights of Columbus, is a member of the Catholic Church.

References

Biographical Directory of the American Congress, 1774-1949 (1950)
Congressional Directory (1951)
Who's Who in America, 1952-53
Who's Who in United States Politics (1950)

KILGALLEN, DOROTHY July 3, 1913-
Columnist; radio and television personality

Address: b. c/o New York Journal-American,
220 South St., New York 2; c/o Mutual Broadcasting System, 1440 Broadway, New York 18;
h. 630 Park Ave., New York 21

KOLLMAR, DICK Dec. 31, 1910- Actor;
producer

Address: b. c/o Mutual Broadcasting System,
1440 Broadway, New York 18; h. 630 Park
Ave., New York 21

Principals on the morning husband-and-wife
broadcast show *Breakfast With Dorothy and
Dick*, Dorothy Kilgallen and Dick Kollmar
reach a wide radio audience. As Broadway columnist for the New York *Journal-American*
Miss Kilgallen comes in contact with celebrities
of stage, screen, and society, and the life of
that circle provides them with a stock of material. This they supplement with comments on
general affairs and incidents of their home life
for the morning program. Her articles and
fiction appear in forty-five newspapers of the
King Features Syndicate. Kollmar is a radio
and stage actor, having first attracted general
attention when he played one of the leading
roles in *Knickerbocker Holiday* (1938). As a
Broadway producer he was associated with
such hits as *By Jupiter, Early to Bed, Are
You With It?*

A daughter of the well-known International
News Service journalist James Lawrence (Jim)
Kilgallen, Dorothy Mae Kilgallen was born
to him and Mary Jane (Ahern) Kilgallen in
Chicago, Illinois, on July 3, 1913. While their
father was making a name as a newspaperman
in Chicago and Indianapolis, Dorothy and her
sister Eleanor attended grade schools in those
two cities; they continued their education in
Brooklyn when Kilgallen's career with Hearst's
INS took the family to New York. After
graduating from Erasmus Hall High School
there, Dorothy went to the College of New
Rochelle (New York).

In the summer of 1931, after her freshman
year at New Rochelle, Miss Kilgallen took a
job as a cub reporter with the New York
Evening Journal, intending to work only during the vacation. However, after two weeks
on the paper, which, the assistant city editor
told her, was "a flamboyant, human-interest type
of newspaper," a story on a child in a hospital
won the girl reporter a by-line. Thereupon she
decided to make journalism her career and to
start on it immediately, not returning to college;
by the time she was twenty years old, her by-
line was familiar to readers of the *Evening
Journal*. The assignment that was to bring her
fame as a newspaperwoman came in 1936, when
her paper sent her on a round-the-world flight
in competition with reporters from other papers.
Using commercial routes, Miss Kilgallen made
the trip in twenty-four days, twelve hours, and
fifty-two minutes. Her comments, cabled back
from points en route, were front-page copy.
The account of the exploit, in *Girl Around
the World*, published in 1937, was described by
M. P. Hazen of the Boston *Transcript* as "a

Bruno of Hollywood
DOROTHY KILGALLEN

rapid-fire, factual, action narrative." In November of that year Miss Kilgallen went to
Hollywood to report on the motion picture
studios and stars for the *Journal-American* (the
two Hearst New York papers, the *American*
and the *Evening Journal*, had merged under that
name in June 1937), and to appear in the motion picture *Winner Take All*.

In 1938 the *Journal-American* gave Miss
Kilgallen what Carol Hughes in a *Coronet*
article "Dorothy Kilgallen: Star Reporter"
called "one of the toughest but one of the most
coveted jobs in journalism" by making her its
Broadway columnist. An invasion of what until that time had been considered an exclusively
male field, Miss Kilgallen's *Voice of Broadway*
column won the admiration of veterans in the
line, including Walter Winchell, and soon began
to appear in twenty-four out-of-town newspapers. (By 1950 her six columns per week were
being distributed to forty-five papers in the
King Features Syndicate.) In addition to this
daily piece, Miss Kilgallen covered many big
news stories such as the coronation of George
VI, the Hauptmann trial, Franklin D. Roosevelt's first campaign, and the Philadelphia convention at which Truman was nominated for
President. She also writes features for the
Journal-American Saturday Home Magazine;
national magazines in which articles and fiction
by the journalist have appeared include *Collier's, Nation's Business*, and *Reader's Digest*.

The newspaperwoman entered radio in 1941
with a *Voice of Broadway* series, broadcast
Saturday mornings over the Columbia Broadcasting System's network. "Crisp and sparkling," said a *Newsweek* review of the chat
program. In 1947 she was heard on *Star Time*,
a daily fifteen-minute morning show over the
American Broadcasting Company stations, which
Variety noted "rates an above-par score . . . by
virtue of Miss Kilgallen's newsbeats, expert de-

Bruno of Hollywood

DICK KOLLMAR

livery, and nicely worded interviews." She is best known in radio, however, for her daily (except Saturday) program *Breakfast With Dorothy and Dick*, which she began to broadcast in 1945 with her husband, actor and Broadway producer Dick Kollmar, five years after their marriage.

Richard Tompkins Kollmar was born December 31, 1910, to John and Christine L. (Smith) Kollmar, in Ridgewood, New Jersey, where his father was an architect. One of his great-great-grandfathers, Daniel D. Tompkins, was Governor of New York for ten years, and Vice-President under James Monroe. Young Kollmar attended the Ridgewood grade schools and later was a student at St. Bernard's School (1927-29). He received the B.A. degree from Tusculum College (Tennessee) in 1933. While at Tusculum he was editor of the college paper, took part in dramatics, sang in the glee club, and was leader (as well as drummer and singer) of a band called Moby Dick and His Ten Whalers. At Yale, where he enrolled in 1933 with the thought of earning the Master of Fine Arts degree, he became particularly interested in dramatics, studying for a year at Professor Baker's "47" Workshop. This led to his appearance in 1934 in summer stock at Whitefield, New Hampshire, as Pierre in *The Two Orphans*.

That fall Kollmar did not return to Yale, but went to New York, hoping to get on the stage. Agents there, however, advised him to try radio instead. His first success came when he was given a part in a serial, *Bill Batchelor*. In the radio career which followed, he was heard in *Gang Busters*, *Grand Central Station*, *Palmolive Beauty Box Theatre*, *Pretty Kitty Kelly*, *Life Can Be Beautiful*, etc. He has "doubled" for voices of famous singers. The first show in which Kollmar sang as himself

(his voice has been described as "a resonant bass-baritone") was *Dreams of Long Ago*, a Sunday morning program of Southern songs.

That program proved to be Kollmar's big opportunity, for the enthusiasm of his sponsor for his singing led to his introduction to an actor's agent. The agent in turn took him to audition for Kurt Weill, the composer of *Knickerbocker Holiday*, a musical comedy then being cast for the 1938-39 Broadway season, and to see Joshua Logan, director of the Playwrights Producing Company, which was handling the show. The result was that Kollmar was given the leading juvenile role of Brom Broeck in the production. The fact that unknown actor Kollmar was getting feature billing in his first Broadway role created something of a sensation in theatrical circles. It also led to his meeting, in January 1939, with Broadway columnist Dorothy Kilgallen. They were married on April 6, 1940.

Kollmar's success in *Knickerbocker Holiday* was followed by roles in *Too Many Girls* (1939-40), *Crazy With the Heat* (1941), *Early To Bed* (1943). (His part of El Magnifico in *Early To Bed* has been cited by Kollmar as his favorite.) In 1942 the actor also became a producer when he was associated with Dwight Deere Wiman and Richard Rodgers in the production of *By Jupiter*. He was producer and director, as well as star, of the long-run musical comedy *Early To Bed* the next year. *Dream With Music* (1944; book by Dorothy Kilgallen, Sidney Sheldon, and Ben Roberts), *Are You With It?* (1945-46), and *Windy City* (1946) followed. (The last-named did not play on Broadway.) In 1948 Kollmar appeared in the motion picture *Close-Up*. Television claimed him in 1949 as master of ceremonies for *Broadway Spotlight*, replacing Danton Walker; two other TV commitments were *Manhattan Sketchbook* (1949) and *Talent Search* (1950). Kollmar directed the redecoration of Larue, "the newest sensation" among Manhattan's fashionable dine-and-dance places.

Heard every morning except Saturday, *Breakfast With Dorothy and Dick* was initiated in 1945. The program is broadcast direct from the Kollmar apartment, the microphones being set on a table among breakfast dishes. Its popularity is commonly attributed to the intimate atmosphere—the couple chat naturally about family incidents, plays they have attended, parties they have been to, people they know. The product being advertised is brought into the conversation. On Sunday morning programs their two children, Dickie (named after his father) and Jill-Ellen, are heard from time to time. Informal, as well as unrehearsed, the show takes shape from notes they jot down in the course of their days—at lunch at the Waldorf, at the theater, the opera, the Stork Club. When they made a trip to Europe in the summer of 1951, their program was transcribed from the Continental setting. Miss Kilgallen, formerly on TV's *Leave It To The Girls*, now appears on *What's My Line?*; Kollmar is heard on radio's *Behind the Story*.

After their morning radio stint their schedules diverge. Kollmar usually rests for a few hours, while his wife, who reads six newspapers a day, sets to work on her mail and her column. She is aided by two secretaries with three telephones, one of whose tasks is to check on the numerous "tips" sent in for the columnist's use. Usually she must finish by one o'clock in order to lunch with a celebrity. She may take a nap in the afternoon, followed by time with the children, often spent in the park. Husband and wife dine out together about three times a week, attending all first nights and regularly covering several night clubs; they return home about 3 A.M.

The Kollmars are alike in their religion (Catholic) and politics (independent). Slim, with dark brown hair, fair complexion, and blue-gray eyes, Dorothy is called "Dresden-dollish." The gowns she wears before the TV camera are described as "gorgeous." Kollmar is five feet eleven inches tall, is of medium weight, and has brown eyes and brown hair. The Kollmar home has been called one of the show places of New York—"a mixture of our mutual tastes, brainstorms, whims, and caprices" is her comment.

References

> Brooklyn (N.Y.) Daily Eagle D 11 '38
> Coronet 28:53 Je '50
> Cosmopolitan 129:66+ S '50
> N Y Herald Tribune N 6 '38; p17 Ap 24 '46
> N Y Post Mag p9 Jl 10 '43; p3 Jl 27 '46 por
> New Yorker 22:50 Ag 10 '46
> Newark Evening N N 19 '45
> Newsweek 17:67 Ap 14 '41
> American Women (1939)
> Variety Radio Directory, 1940-41
> Who's Who in America, 1950-51
> Who's Who in the East (1951)
> Who's Who in the Theatre (1947)
> Women of Achievement (1940)

KILLION, GEORGE (LEONARD) Apr. 15, 1901- Business executive

Address: b. c/o American President Lines, 311 California St., San Francisco 4, Calif.; h. 1012 Ashmount Ave., Oakland 10, Calif.

President of the American President Lines since 1947, George Killion has helped direct this company to its present status as one of the United States' widest reaching maritime ventures, with a global fleet of some thirty passenger and cargo vessels. Since August 1938 APL has operated under the United States Maritime Administration (formerly the Maritime Commission), which at that time reorganized and took control of the then debt-ridden Dollar Steamship Company. Killion, who was formerly a newspaper reporter and public relations official, had also served as a finance director for the State of California and as treasurer of the Democratic National Committee, before assuming his present position.

George Leonard Killion was born at Steamboat Springs, Colorado, on April 15, 1901, to James Abraham and Lydia Jane (Harris) Killion. His father, a rancher and druggist, was a native of Springfield, Illinois; his mother

came originally from Chattanooga, Tennessee. After one year (1920-21) as a student at the University of Southern California and another (1921-22) at the University of California, George Killion in 1922 joined the staff of the San Diego (California) *Sun* as a waterfront reporter and during the ensuing eight years worked as a reporter, city editor, managing editor, and editorial writer on daily papers in San Diego, Los Angeles, and Sacramento. In 1930 Killion gave up the editorship of the Sacramento *Bee* to establish his own public relations firm in Oakland, California, the city which has since been his permanent place of residence. As owner and director of this enterprise, he handled tax returns, other financial work, and political campaigns until 1935, when he became an executive of the Safeway Stores, with headquarters in Oakland. For the next four years he served that large grocery and foodstore chain as consultant on public relations, advertising, and business development, and also (according to *Time*) as its lobbyist in the California capital.

When Culbert Levy Olson became Governor of California in January 1939, he appointed Killion as his secretary and as the Commissioner of San Francisco's Golden Gate Exposition. During his years as a Sacramento newspaperman and later as a political campaign manager, Killion had become friendly with Olson (the one-time "End Poverty in California" leader who defeated the Socialist Upton Sinclair for re-election as Governor in 1938 to become California's first Democratic chief executive in forty years). In 1940 Killion was promoted to the post of State director of finance, taking over all financial, budget, and business affairs of the California government, while further serving as chairman of the State Board of Control and of the State Lands Commission and as a member of the Toll Bridge Authority, the State Teachers Retirement Board, the State Employees Retirement Board, and the Water Authority. "As California director of finance," *Time* has reported, "Killion helped the State out of a $60 million hole by getting bankers to lower their interest rates on the debt from five per cent to one per cent." He "soon won a name for raising and handling funds" and "by the time he left the job, California was well into the black."

With the defeat of Olson for re-election to the Governorship in 1942 by Republican Earl Warren, Killion relinquished his position as finance director early the following year. Commissioned a major in the United States Army shortly thereafter, Killion in 1943 was assigned to the staff of the Allied Military Government but later that year was detached to become a special assistant to the Petroleum Administrator for War in Washington, D.C. He resumed political party work during the 1944 Presidential campaign as assistant to the treasurer of the Democratic National Committee, Edwin W. Pauley, a fellow-resident of California and an old friend. Killion was serving as national financial director of the committee when, in the spring of the following year, Pauley resigned as treasurer to become United States representative on the Interna-

Palmer Pictures

GEORGE KILLION

tional Reparations Commission. Chairman Robert E. Hannegan on May 1, 1945, named Killion treasurer of the Democratic Committee and he served as such until August 1947, when he was elected to the presidency and to the board of directors of the American President Lines.

American President Lines was organized in 1938 as successor to the Dollar Steamship Lines, Inc., of Delaware. Started in 1893 by the northwestern lumber magnate Captain Robert Dollar as a small Pacific Coast shipping concern, the Dollar Line developed into an important Trans-Pacific cargo enterprise, later carrying passengers and mail. After World War I numerous surplus vessels were obtained from the United States Government and the company's operations were extended around the world. "The steamship line prospered in the twenties," Business Week (October 7, 1950) related. "But the depression hit it hard. Though the Dollars had bought most of their ships from the Federal government's wartime Shipping Board at bargain-basement prices, they were heavily in debt to the board."

By 1937—when the Shipping Board was supplanted by the United States Maritime Commission—the Dollar Line was in "desperate condition." The following year on August 15, 1938, R. Stanley Dollar, the founder's son, signed an agreement whereby 92 per cent of the steamship company's Class B voting stock was surrendered to the Commission, while the Robert Dollar Company sold its shipping assets and transferred its personnel to a new company which was to be known as American President Lines. However, the Dollar family retained a majority of 32,000 shares of preferred stock and it was to become the key point of subsequent litigation whether or not actual title to the transferred common stock was vested in the government agency.

American President Lines having prospered during World War II, by 1943 all its indebtedness was paid off, and when in 1945 the commission advertised to sell APL to the highest bidder, Dollar succeeded in stopping the sale by suing to recover his common stock, which he claimed had merely been pledged as collateral for his debts. The matter was still in the courts when on August 13, 1947, Killion took over the presidency of APL in succession to Henry F. Grady. His election to this $25,000-a-year position by a vote of the stockholders was looked upon by some as "tantamount to a political appointment" because the Commission held more than 90 per cent of the stock (New York World-Telegram, August 13, 1947). Business Week later reported: "Anyone who thought Killion would collect his $25,000 and keep quiet was in for a rude shock. Declaring that APL had grown complacent under government operation, he ruthlessly streamlined the organization. His cost-cutting program has apparently been successful. Though APL's revenues in 1949 declined $8 million from 1948, the net profit increased $1.7 million."

In June 1950 when the APL liner President Jackson was launched, George Killion reported that it was the first of three sister ships under construction for APL's round-the-world service. He pointed out that in addition to being passenger ships and possible troop carriers, the three ships would be valuable cargo carriers, adding that they would be followed by four other slightly smaller ships that were in the planning stage. By the end of 1951 the American President Lines—with two regular route systems, one between San Francisco and the Orient and the other around the world—was showing a profit of approximately $3 million on gross revenue of $53 million, while the luxury-cruise business was growing apace. Killion had instituted many ideas for "making sea voyages memorable for each passenger," including "flying home newspapers to foreign ports of call, stationery in each cabin printed with the passenger's name, a personal letter at the end of each cruise to each passenger" (New York Herald Tribune, October 9, 1950). By August 1952 Killion was able to report that in the last five years the American President Lines had increased its fleet of vessels by more than 100 per cent, its corporate net worth by nearly 50 per cent, and its net current assets by 65 per cent (New York Times, August 16, 1952). He added: "During the critical period since the outbreak of the Korean conflict, the company has maintained a high level of commercial cargo and passenger service to unaffected areas in the Far East and to the many ports on its round-the-world trade routes, at the same time meeting its full responsibility to the public interest in the national and world emergency created by the action in Korea."

After a seven-year legal effort on the part of Dollar to recover control of the American President Lines, an agreement was reached in June 1952 by which the stock would be sold to the highest bidder, the Government and the Dollar interests then evenly dividing the proceeds of the sale. On October 28, 1952, a syndicate known as A.P.L. Associates, Inc., received controlling stock of the lines with its bid of $18,360,000. It was indicated at that time that Killion would be retained as president.

A founder member of the American Society of Traffic and Transportation and a board member of the American Bureau of Shipping, Killion also belongs to the American Arbitration Association, the Navy League of the United States, and the Newcomen Society of England. Other affiliations are the Stock Exchange and Commercial Club of San Francisco, the Commonwealth Club of California, and the Propeller Club of the United States. He married Grace Ludora Harris on December 25, 1922, and they have one son, James Leonard. As reported by the New York *Herald Tribune*, the APL president's hobby is "building a library of biographical and historical material, devoted chiefly to American statesmen."

References

Bsns W p42+ O 7 '50 por; p33 Je 21 '52
N Y Herald Tribune p25 O 9 '50 por
Time 50:82 Ag 25 '47 por; 53:23 Je 6
'49 por
Business Executives of America (1951)
Who's Who in America, 1952-53
Who's Who in Commerce and Industry
(1951)

KIMBLE, GEORGE H(ERBERT) T(INLEY) Aug. 2, 1908- Geographer, meteorologist

Address: b. c/o American Geographical Society, 156th St. & Broadway, New York 32; h. Warren Lane, Alpine, N.J.

The American Geographical Society, which is celebrating its centennial in 1952, has been directed since 1950 by George H. T. Kimble, who came to this organization in New York City from the faculty of the University of McGill in Montreal. The British-born geographer taught at the University of Reading and the University College of Hull in England in the 1930's and as a member of the meteorological service of the British Navy was engaged throughout World War II in forecasting the climatic feasibility of various invasion projects. Dr. Kimble is the author of a number of articles and books on geography.

Born on August 2, 1908, in London, England, George Herbert Tinley Kimble is the elder of two sons of John Herbert and Minnie Jane (Dickerson) Kimble, whom he has described as "hard-working people of middle-class origin zealous in the cause of education and religion." His brother, thirteen years younger, whom he helped to educate, now heads the department of adult education at the University College of the Gold Coast in West Africa. George attended the Eastbourne Grammar School of London, where, he recalls, his geography master, W. J. Stacey, imbued his pupils with a lively interest in the subject he taught. At King's College in London Kimble took his B.A. degree with first class honors in geography in 1929, his A.K.C. (divinity) degree in 1930, and his M.A. degree

in 1931. (Some years later he completed work for the Ph.D. degree in geography, awarded *summa cum laude* by the University of Montreal, Canada, in 1948.) After he had left King's College, Kimble lectured in geography at the University College of Hull until 1936, when he joined the staff of the University of Reading, also in the capacity of lecturer in geography.

With the outbreak of World War II about three years later, Kimble volunteered for duty in the British Naval Meteorological Service. Entering the service in 1939 with the rank of lieutenant, he spent five years "in back rooms" doing research which he has described as being exciting because he knew it was valuable. His first assignment was to study the movement of the Doldrum Belt in the tropics with the objective of planning naval maneuvers there. Later he became one of a group of researchers engaged in the study of wind and wave conditions governing weather on the beaches of continental Europe. Before the Tehran conference Kimble prepared a graph, to be used at that meeting by Winston Churchill, which gave the weather conditions for each day of the year on "Omaha Beach." (This report helped determine the date of the D-Day invasion by the Allied forces.) A short time before D-Day, his researches having been turned toward the Pacific theater of war, Kimble was sent around the world to contact agencies having skill in forecasting beach conditions. While he was in Canada in the course of this trip, the Vice-Chancellor of McGill University conferred with him about a projected department of geography at that institution. Several weeks later, in Nairobi, Africa, he received a telegram asking him to join the McGill faculty. Following his release from the British Navy in 1945 (in the rank of lieutenant commander) Kimble went to McGill as professor of geography, chairman of the newly established department of geography, director of the meteorological observatory, and commanding officer of the university's Naval Training Division. Two notable achievements of his work there were the founding of the McGill Summer School of Geography located at Stanstead, Quebec, and the establishment of an Arctic Research Center.

In 1950 the American Geographical Society of New York, the oldest organization of its kind in the United States, invited Kimble to become its director, a post he assumed in June of that year in succession to Dr. John Kirtland Wright, who retired from the directorship after eleven years of service. The purpose of the American Geographical Society, founded in 1852, is "to collect and disseminate geographical information by discussions, lectures, and publications; to establish in the chief city of the United States a place where may be obtained accurate information on every part of the globe; and to encourage such exploring expeditions as seem likely to result in valuable discoveries in geography and the related sciences" (*Geographical Review*, June 1950). Principal objectives of the organization at the present time are the revision of the Millionth Map of Hispanic America, judged by the *Britannica Book of the Year* (1952) to be "the best integrated and most accurate map of that conti-

Blackstone Studios

GEORGE H. T. KIMBLE

nent," the preparation of an *Atlas of Disease* containing about twenty-five maps showing world distribution of all major diseases, and the prosecution of glaciological research in Alaska (the Juneau Ice Field Research Project). This project, directed by the society under contract to the Office of Naval Research and in cooperation with the Army, Air Force, and the United States Forest Service, is primarily an investigation of Arctic climatic conditions and glacier fluctuations over a number of years.

Among other activities of the society are lectures and special research publications for its members, publication of the scholarly quarterly *Geographical Review* and the more topical monthly *Focus*, and maintenance of one of the largest geographical libraries in the world and the largest collection of maps in the United States. The association's map collection, containing some 220,000 maps, as reported in the New York *Herald Tribune*, was used by the War Department in both world wars. At its centennial celebration in August 1952 the American Geographical Society awarded medals to five of the world's leading geographers. Also celebrating the society's centenary, the International Geographical Union, of which Kimble is secretary-treasurer, held its seventeenth International Congress in Washington in August, the first to convene in this country since 1904.

Regarding his field of interest Kimble has said, "Geography isn't what it used to be," observing that when the American Geographical Society was founded "half of the world was still unexplored," whereas today "there is scarcely a peak that has not been scaled, or a tribe that has not been filmed and psychoanalyzed." More than the rapid advance in knowledge, however, he emphasized a change in outlook, an increased interest in social use of the findings of the geographer. In his inaugural address at McGill University, where his department was classed with the social sciences, he described modern geography as being "primarily concerned with viewing the earth as the home of human communities and cultures, and with examining the way in which man has shaped the habitable parts for his own ends, and has himself been influenced in the process" (*Canadian Geographic Journal*, November 1945). Pointing out that the geographer is to a large extent dependent upon other sciences for his material, he has defined the science as "the systematic study of the relations of peoples to their physical environment and a consideration of the ways in which those relations may be stabilized so as to ensure that the earth abides and that man does not perish from its face" (*The Role of Geography in the Modern World*).

Chosen to deliver the three Rushton Lectures at Birmingham Southern College in February 1952, Kimble spoke on the strength of the earth, the perseverance of man, and the resilience of society. In the course of these lectures he discussed the increasing shortage in the world's natural resources and the need for man to "learn to live within the means offered by this environment." Kimble has contributed papers to several journals, including *Geographical Magazine*, *Scientific American*, *Geographical Journal*, the *Canadian Geographical Journal*, the *Geographical Review*, and the *Bulletin of the American Meteorological Society*. He is the author of *Geography of the Middle Ages* (1938), which has been called a "fine example of integrative thinking on a recondite subject"; *The World's Open Spaces* (1939), an investigation of the world's possible areas for resettlement of Germany's Hitler-persecuted Jews; *The Weather*, written in collaboration with Raymond Bush, first published in England in 1943 and in the United States in 1946, in a paper-bound edition which has sold over 200,000 copies; and *A Military Geography of Canada* (1949). In 1937 he translated and edited, for the Hakluyt Society of England (founded in 1846 for the purpose of publishing rare and unprinted accounts of voyages), *Esmeraldo de Situ Orbis*, an account of African travel by an early Portuguese explorer Duarte Pacheco Pereira. *The Shepherd of Banbury*, published in 1941 by Reading University, is Kimble's annotation of twenty-four ancient pieces of weather lore.

In addition to holding the office of secretary-treasurer of the International Geographical Union (since May 1949), Kimble is a member of the United States National Committee of that body; a fellow of the Royal Geographical Society and of the Royal Meteorological Society; and a member of the Association of American Geographers and of the History of Science Society. On July 20, 1936, Kimble married the former Dorothy Stevens Berry; they have a son, Stephen, and a daughter, Gillian. Kimble has hazel eyes and dark brown hair, stands six feet one-half inch tall, and weighs 165 pounds. His recreations are music and gardening. He is a member of the Century Club and attends the Riverside Church.

References

Can Geog J 35:178 sup 9 O '47
Geog R 40:1-3 Ja '50 por
Nature 164:1033 D 17 '49
Directory of American Scholars (1951)
International Who's Who, 1950
Who's Who, 1952
Who's Who in America, 1952-53
World Biography (1948)

KING, CECIL R(HODES) Jan. 13, 1898-
United States Representative from California
Address: b. House Office Bldg., Washington
25, D.C.

Cecil R. King, Democratic Representative
from the Seventeenth District of California,
was first elected to the United States Congress
in 1942. For approximately six years (as of
1952) he has been a member of the important
House Ways and Means Committee, of whose
special subcommittee he was made chairman
in March 1951 in the investigation of the administration of the Internal Revenue Bureau.
Before going to Washington, King had for a
decade represented Los Angeles in the California State Assembly.

Cecil Rhodes King was born January 13,
1898, in Youngstown, Niagara County, New
York, and has been a resident of California
since his tenth year. After being educated in
the public schools of Los Angeles, he served
in 1917-18 as a World War I infantry soldier
in the Canadian Expeditionary Force. For
twenty-three years beginning in 1919 he was
engaged in business in southern California.
King won his first legislative seat in 1932,
when he was elected to the California Assembly
as a Democrat from Los Angeles. Serving for
nearly a decade, he eventually became Democratic floor leader and his party's State chairman.

The death of United States Representative
Lee Edward Geyer of the Seventeenth California District in late 1941 created a vacancy,
and at a special election on August 25, 1942,
King was chosen to fill out the brief remainder
of Geyer's term in the Seventy-seventh Congress. He was sworn in on October 12, cast
his first vote (in favor of the anti-poll tax
bill), and four days later called "Yea" to the
teen-age draft bill. The date of his first election to the House of Representatives was also
the date of the California primaries, and King
(as permitted by the State law) sought renomination by both the Democratic and Republican parties. He was victorious in both party
primaries. Returned to the Seventy-eighth
(1943) Congress in the November balloting,
King has been re-elected in similar circumstances to the Seventy-ninth, Eightieth, Eighty-
first, and Eighty-second Congresses. His District, which comprises Los Angeles County
Assembly Districts 46, 66, 67, and 68, had a
1940 population of 392,616. It has been
described as "highly prosperous and indus-
trialized."

During the two sessions of the Seventy-
eighth Congress (1943 and 1944) Representa-

Wide World Photos
CECIL R. KING

tive King served on five committees—Civil
Service, Expenditures in Executive Affairs,
Merchant Marine and Fisheries, Patents, and
Rivers and Harbors; from the floor of the
House, however, he spoke but rarely. The
chief legislative proposals he sponsored were
bills to extend construction of Marine hospitals and to empower the Reconstruction Finance Corporation to underwrite bank loans
up to $1,000 to returning servicemen (October
1943). King's voting record in the same Congress supported the Administration on all major
issues, while his affirmations of the Fulbright
Resolution (September 1943) and authorization
of UNRRA (January 1944) underscored an
international consciousness. As a Californian,
he was also mindful of Pacific Coast interests,
voting in favor of raising OPA ceilings on oil
(June 1944) and protesting that established
Eastern steel companies were trying to "kill
off" a new steel plant to be operated by Henry
Kaiser at Fontana, California (August). His
reputation, then as later, was that of a "reliable party man" (*United States News*) and
a "hard worker" and "one of the quietest of
Congressmen" (Peter Edson in the New York
World-Telegram).

King's record brought him advancement to
the important Ways and Means Committee in
the Seventy-ninth Congress (1945-46), whereupon he was relieved of his lesser assignments.
On February 13, 1945, as an early end to
World War II seemed probable, the California
Democrat sponsored a bill to create an investigating committee to recommend legislation to
help the Pacific Coast States reconvert to
peacetime economy; and six days later he came
forward with a resolution (subsequently passed
in the House by voice vote) to authorize the
United States to join its Allies in tracking

KING, CECIL R.—*Continued*

down war criminals by "all means available in addition to treaties of extradition." (The purpose was to prevent such criminals from taking asylum in neutral countries.) Among King's significant votes in the Seventy-ninth Congress were those he cast against a permanent House Un-American Activities Committee (1945) and in favor of the three and three-quarter billion-dollar loan to Great Britain (1946).

Having been the second to last Democrat in the Ways and Means Committee in point of seniority, King lost his place in that body in the Republican-controlled Eightieth Congress (1947-48) and returned to Merchant Marine and Fisheries. In that Congress he cast votes against limiting the presidency to two terms and against banning portal-to-portal pay suits (February 1947) and in favor of Greek-Turkish aid (May). In the fall of 1947 he went to Greece for a three-month visit in which he "shook off the guides furnished him by the Greek Government and wandered through the provinces with his own interpreter" (*New York Times*). King regained his place on the Ways and Means Committee when his party again acquired control of the House in January 1949, and is in 1952 the ninth Democrat in rank on that body.

In the first session (1949) of the Eighty-first Congress, the Representative from California voted to extend rent controls (March), to repeal Federal taxes on oleomargarine (April), and to enact the Administration's long range housing bill (June); he supported Marshall Plan extension and opposed a 50 per cent cut in European arms aid. In the second session (1950) he favored economic aid to Korea and Formosa (February), but not the Lodge-Gossett Constitutional Amendment to abolish the electoral college (July). He also voted (September) against overriding President Truman's veto of the bill requiring any Communists to register. In April of 1949, speaking as chairman of the California delegation in Congress, King assailed the British film quota and financial regulations as having "the obvious purpose . . . to drive American motion pictures from the British market," and obtained a pledge from Secretary of State Dean Acheson that the State Department would do everything "within the bounds of propriety" to remedy the situation. In March 1950 King brought to the attention of fellow party members on the Ways and Means Committee a suggestion by John A. Kennedy of the San Diego *Journal* that the Government raise revenue through fees for broadcasting, export, and other licenses; and in January 1951 he sponsored a bill (passed by the House) to allow motorists under certain conditions to deduct State gasoline taxes on their Federal income tax returns. During the first session of the Eighty-second Congress (1951) King opposed restoring former powers to the Rules Committee (January) and the guarantee of so-called "reasonable profits" under all price ceilings (July). Also, in July he voted in favor of the tidelands oil bill, which would give coastal States a clear title to the submerged littoral oilfields.

It was in sequence to his appointment (March 1951) as chairman of a House Ways and Means Committee special subcommittee on Administration of the Internal Revenue laws that Congressman King became, toward the end of the year, a front-page figure in national news. Testimony at hearings of the Senate Crime Investigating (Kefauver) Committee and other sources had pointed to widespread tax evasion by racketeers and gangsters and the possibility of collusion with venal officials. The House decided to investigate, and on March 9 an appropriation of $50,000 was approved to initiate an inquiry by Representative King and colleagues. Chairman King promptly stated that the inquiry would cover "all tax enforcement policies," and about ten days later the subcommittee took its first public action by releasing a list of 121 "allegedly prominent underworld figures" prepared by the Bureau of Internal Revenue. During the summer, also, employees of the Bureau were sent questionnaires regarding their sources of income, and a "selected group" was interrogated. The results were (in King's words) "disturbing" and tended "to indicate that there may have been in the making an organized plot to corrupt collectors in several districts."

Formal hearings by the King subcommittee, begun October 3, 1951, were preceded by the announcement of a code of procedure which Arthur Krock of the New York *Times* considered "very fair and enlightened indeed." It defined and limited the circumstances in which hearings could be held in public; assured witnesses at any public hearing of the right to cross-examine others giving testimony relating to them; forbade the release of "any report or statement of misconduct by any person under investigation" until after said person should have had "reasonable opportunity" to enter a reply; and banned any subcommittee or staff member from accepting pay for articles or speeches about the work of the subcommittee. In ensuing weeks the subcommittee conducted investigations in New York, Boston, San Francisco, St. Louis, Nashville, Detroit, and elsewhere—investigations which were "accompanied by resignations, suspensions and indictments at top personnel levels" (New York *Times*). The resulting scandals led to demands in some quarters for the resignation of Attorney General J. Howard McGrath and the determination of President Truman to institute a general "housecleaning." On November 4, 1952, King was elected to the Eighty-third Congress.

Representative King, who is married and has one child, is described in the *United States News* as "a man of much aloof dignity . . . handsome, remote."

References

N Y Herald Tribune II p1 D 9 '51 por
U S News 30:38+ Ap 6 '51 por

Biographical Directory of the American
   Congress, 1774-1949 (1950)
Congressional Directory (1951)
Who's Who in America, 1950-51
Who's Who in the West (1949)
Who's Who in United States Politics
   (1950)

KIRBY, ROLLIN Sept. 4, 1875—May 8 1952 Cartoonist; author; turned from painting early in his career to illustrating for magazines; became newspaper cartoonist successively for a number of New York papers: *Mail, Sun, World, World-Telegram*, and *Post*; after 1942 did cartoons for *Look* and the New York *Times Magazine*; writer of verse, short stories, and editorials for magazines; three-time winner of the Pulitzer Prize for his cartoons— 1921, 1924, and 1928. See *Current Biography*, 1944.

Obituary

N Y Times p21 My 10 '52

KIRSTEIN, LINCOLN (EDWARD) (kûr' stēn) May 4, 1907- Ballet company director; author

Address: b. c/o New York City Center of Music and Drama, Inc., 130 W. 56th St., New York 19; h. 128 E. 19th St., New York 3

On October 1, 1952, Lincoln Kirstein was named managing director of the New York City Center of Music and Drama, a privately sponsored, nonprofit corporation that provides cultural entertainment at popular prices in the municipally owned City Center Theater. As scholar, impresario, and writer, Kirstein has pioneered for the development of ballet in the United States. He helped establish and is now director of the School of American Ballet, and since 1948 he has served as general director of the New York City Ballet, one of the City Center's three units. A founder and editor of the *Hound & Horn* (1927-34), he has also written extensively on painting, sculpture, and photography.

Lincoln Edward Kirstein was born in Rochester, New York, on May 4, 1907, one of the three children of Louis Edward and Rose (Stein) Kirstein. His paternal grandfather had followed Carl Schurz to the United States from Germany in 1848; his father, a nationally known Jewish philanthropist, was for many years vice-president and later chairman of the board of William Filene's Sons, one of Boston's largest department stores. After attending New Preparatory School in Cambridge, Massachusetts, young Kirstein entered Harvard College in 1926. As an undergraduate, he helped found and was an editor of the *Hound & Horn*, a literary and critical journal that first appeared in 1927. He was also a cofounder of the Harvard Society for Contemporary Art. By 1930, the year that he received his B.S. degree, the *Hound & Horn* had earned the reputation of being "the most serious magazine printed in America." In 1933 he became sole editor of the quarterly, which was forced to cease publication in the fall of the following year. Kirstein had, in the meanwhile, published a novel, *Flesh Is Heir* (1932); his volume of poems, *Low Ceiling*, appeared three years later.

Interested in the ballet since early youth, Kirstein saw Anna Pavlova during her American tours and for the first time, in 1924, attended performances of Serge Diaghilev's Russian Ballet, in London. "Ballet became an

LINCOLN KIRSTEIN

obsession with me," he has explained. "Far more than the ordinary influence or attractions of Harvard, the ballet seemed my real education. As time passed, I was increasingly magnetized towards some direct participation with it." When he was twenty-five years old, Kirstein took ballet lessons with Michel Fokine, afterward, in 1934, writing a monograph on that famous choreographer's work. He also assisted Madame Romola Nijinsky in collecting material for the biography of her husband, the celebrated dancer. Through his research for this undertaking in the documents of the Imperial Ballet School, in St. Petersburg, Kirstein became increasingly preoccupied with the idea of establishing a school in the United States similar to the Russian school. While visiting London in the summer of 1933, he was introduced by Madame Nijinsky to George Balanchine, who had studied at the Imperial Ballet School and had served as choreographer of the Diaghilev company from 1924 to 1919. With the financial assistance of Edward M. M. Warburg, one of his former Harvard classmates, Kirstein was able to persuade Balanchine to give up his work in Europe, come to the United States, and found a school and ballet company.

The School of American Ballet was opened in New York in January 1934, with Balanchine as artistic director and Kirstein as director of the division of theatrical sciences. According to the prospectus, the aim of the school was "to preserve and further the tradition of classical theatrical dancing in order to provide adequate material for the growth of a new national art in America." The school's producing company, known as the American Ballet, made its initial appearances in Hartford, Connecticut, in December 1934, and played a two week's engagement in New York the following March. Kirstein wrote the libretto for *Transcendence*, one of the four new ballets Balan-

KIRSTEIN, LINCOLN—*Continued*

chine created for the group. In the fall of 1935 the American Ballet was engaged as the official ballet company for the Metropolitan Opera, to provide opera ballets and present its own repertory. While with the Metropolitan Opera, Balanchine staged a controversial production of Gluck's *Orpheus* (1936); the next year the American Ballet commissioned Igor Stravinsky to compose *Jeu de Cartes*, which was premiered at the Metropolitan in a program devoted to three Stravinsky ballets choreographed by Balanchine. The American Ballet's association with the Metropolitan Opera was terminated in the spring of 1938.

Meanwhile, in the summer of 1936, Kirstein organized the Ballet Caravan, an ensemble of twelve dancers recruited from the American Ballet and its school. The function of this experimental group, which Kirstein directed, was to provide an opportunity of expression to young American choreographers, dancers, composers, and scenic designers. From 1936 to 1939, Ballet Caravan toured the United States and visited Cuba and Canada; in 1940 the company played an extended engagement at the Ford Pavilion of the New York World's Fair. The group's repertory was supplied by its own member-dancers, chiefly Lew Christensen, Eugene Loring, and William Dollar. Kirstein himself devised the librettos for *Harlequin for President, Pocahontas, Yankee Clipper, Filling Station, Charade, City Portrait,* and *Billy the Kid*—this last work being regarded by many critics as the finest ballet on an American theme. At the invitation of the Coordinator of Inter-American Affairs of the United States State Department, Kirstein in the spring of 1941 merged the Ballet Caravan with the remnants of the American Ballet for a good-will tour of South America. Among the new ballets mounted for this occasion were *Juke-Box* and *Time-Table,* both with librettos by Kirstein. When the five-month tour ended in October 1941, the performing company, of which he had served as director general, was disbanded.

In 1940 Kirstein became director of the School of American Ballet, a post he still holds. During that same year he gave his private collection of over 5,000 dance documents and dance books to the Museum of Modern Art, in New York, to form the nucleus of an American archives of the dance. As the museum's consultant on Latin-American art (1941-43), he went to South America in 1942 to purchase art works under the terms of the museum's Inter-American Fund. When these were later displayed at the museum, he wrote the catalogue for the exhibit, *Latin-American Collection of the Museum of Modern Art* (1943). Kirstein joined the Army in 1943, and while stationed at Fort Belvoir, with the Corps of Engineers, he spent some time studying the history of American battle art. This research resulted in an exhibition at the National Gallery of Art, in Washington, and his book, *American Battle Painting: 1776-1918* (1944). Later sent overseas and attached to the Arts, Monuments, and Archives Section of the Third

Army, he was one of those who discovered the art treasures the Germans had hidden in the salt mines.

Following his discharge from the Army, Kirstein joined with Balanchine to found the Ballet Society, a nonprofit membership organization for the encouragement of the lyric theater by the production of new works. Drawing upon the students and graduates of the School of American Ballet for its performing company, Ballet Society emphasized the planned collaboration of independent easel-painters and progressive choreographers and musicians, "employing the full use of advance-guard ideas, methods, and materials." Its staff included Balanchine as artistic director and Kirstein as secretary. The group, which made its debut in New York in November 1946, during the first two seasons offered ten new ballets and five revivals to its regular subscription audience. The society's most notable achievement was the world première, in April 1948, of Stravinsky's *Orpheus,* with choreography by Balanchine, a work which critics hailed as a "contemporary masterpiece."

Under the name of the New York City Ballet, Ballet Society provided the official ballet for the New York City Opera Company's fall season in 1948 at the City Center Theater. The group was so well received that the theater's management arranged for it to become a production branch of the City Center and to give several independent seasons of ballet each year. Between 1948 and 1952 the New York City Ballet Company, with Balanchine as artistic director and Kirstein as general director, has played eleven seasons at the City Center. Within this short space of time, in the opinion of John Martin (New York *Times*), the group raised the standards of the ballet "to artistic heights that had never before been attained in America, or indeed, in many other parts of the world." In the summer of 1950, the company appeared for six weeks at London's Covent Garden Opera House, and in 1952 it scored an unprecedented success during a five-month spring and summer tour of seven European countries (including Germany, where it was presented under the auspices of the United States State Department at West Berlin's Arts Festival). Many leading dancers have left other companies to join the group, and its repertory has been constantly augmented by new ballets staged by Balanchine, Jerome Robbins (the associate artistic director), Frederick Ashton, Antony Tudor, and other choreographers.

It was announced on October 1, 1952, that Kirstein had been unanimously elected to the newly created post of managing director of the New York City Center of Music and Drama. This nonprofit organization was incorporated under the State educational laws in 1943, with Mayor LaGuardia as president and Newbold Morris as chairman of the board. Its purpose is to sponsor cultural entertainment at popular prices in the New York City Center Theater, formerly known as Mecca Temple. Acquiring the building through tax foreclosure, the city leases it to the corporation at a low rent; business organizations, trade unions, and artistically minded individuals contribute toward meeting the City Center's operating expenses. A member of the board of directors since May 1952, Kirstein in his new post formulates and executes policies of the board and co-ordinates the activities of the center's three units—the New York City Opera Company, the New York City Drama Company, and the New York City Ballet Company. He serves without salary.

Founder and one of the editors of *Dance Index*, a scholarly dance periodical published from 1942 to 1948, Kirstein is the author of *Dance: A Short History of Classic Theatrical Dancing* (1935). This work was followed in 1938 by *Blast at Ballet* and the next year by *Ballet Alphabet*. More recently he collaborated on *The Classic Ballet: Basic Technique and Terminology* (1952). In the field of fine arts he has written the text for *Murals by American Painters and Photographers* (1932, with Julien Levy); *Gaston Lachaise* (1935); *Walker Evans—American Photographs* (1938); *William Rimmer* (1946); *The Photography of Henri Cartier Bresson* (1947, with Beaumont Newhall); *The Drawings of Pavel Tchlitchew* (1947); *The Sculpture of Elie Nadelman* (1948); and *Elie Nadelman Drawings* (1949). He has contributed articles to a number of magazines, and from 1949 to 1952 served as art critic of the *New Republic*.

"Of all contemporary Americans," states the *Dance Encyclopedia*, "Kirstein has done most for the development of ballet in the United States." John Martin wrote of him in *World Book of Modern Ballet*: "The acuteness of his vision for the art [of ballet] has given him his extraordinarily disinterested approach to it together with a self-effacement that is unique in the field. . . .He has persisted indomitably in the pursuit of his central ideal, which is the realization for the classic ballet tradition of its highest potentialities in terms of an American theater art." On April 7, 1941, Kirstein married Fidelma Cadmus, the sister of the painter Paul Cadmus. The ballet company director stands over six feet tall, has dark eyes and short-cropped dark hair, and wears gold-rimmed glasses. He has been described as a "militant perfectionist, belligerently convinced of the things he believes in," and one friend commented that his life "passes in ceaseless activity because he daily devises new projects to work on." According to *Newsweek*, Kirstein's purpose in life has always been to "do the things nobody else would do." That, he explains, "is the only reason I exist."

References

Ballet 12:33-6 Ja '52; 12:40-7 F '52
Dance 3:15 Je '37
N Y Times p31 O 2 '52; II p16 O 26 '52 por
Newsweek 32:95 O 25 '48
Amberg, G. Ballet in America (1949)
America's Young Men (1936-37)
Chujoy, A. ed. Dance Encyclopedia (1949)
Kirstein, L. Blast at Ballet (1938)

Who's Who, 1952
Who's Who in America, 1952-53
Who's Who in American Art, 1940-47
Who's Who in American Jewry, 1938-39

KNIGHT, O(RIE) A(LBERT) Sept. 24, 1902- Labor union official

Address: b. c/o Oil Workers International Union, 1840 California St., Denver 2, Colo.

The year 1952 marks the twelfth year of O. A. Knight's presidency of the Oil Workers International Union, a CIO affiliate with a membership of 100,000 refinery and pipeline workers in the United States and Canada. Knight was one of the early organizers in this field, helping to create AFL locals before the establishment of the CIO. In the spring of 1952 he was the foremost leader in the first nation-wide strike in the United States oil industry, involving twenty-two AFL, CIO, and independent unions. A vice-president of the CIO, he has been prominent in opposing Communist-dominated unions in that organization.

Orie Albert Knight was born September 24, 1902, in New Hampton, Iowa, where his father, William Leonard Knight, was a livestock dealer. His mother's maiden name was Clara Mae Ransome. With his high school education completed, Knight began to work in oil refineries, becoming a "stillman," which is described in a union release as "the most highly skilled refinery operative."

While in the employ of the Shell Oil Company, from 1926 to 1937, Knight in 1933 helped organize the workers in its East Chicago (Indiana) refinery. Later he became one of the founders of the American Federation of Labor local number 210 in Hammond, Indiana, an affiliate of what was then known as the International Association of Oil Field, Gas Well and Refinery Workers, which became the Oil Workers International Union in 1936. At that time Knight was elected a member of the Congress of Industrial Organizations' newly formed international executive council, to represent district 6 of the union. Resigning from this office in 1937, Knight as CIO staff representative devoted the following three years to organizing the California and mid-continent oil workers.

The locals of the International Association of Oil Field, Gas Well and Refinery Workers of America were organized in 1917 (as reported in *Trade Union Publications*) and affiliated with the AFL the following year. When the union under the leadership of then President Fremming supported John L. Lewis at the 1935 AFL convention and subsequently participated in the formation of the CIO, it invited suspension by the AFL in 1936 and revocation of its AFL charter in 1938, following a number of jurisdictional strikes. As a CIO affiliate the union in 1937 adopted the name of Oil Workers International Union. Knight, who had been a member of the organization since 1933, was elected its president in 1940, attaining re-election, stated a union release, every ensuing year "by direct referendum vote of the mem-

Shelburne Studios, Inc.

O. A. KNIGHT

bership." At two of the major refineries difficulty in securing recognition of the union led to strikes in 1939 and 1941, with the latter being settled by the National Labor Relations Board. From 1938 to 1941 the *CIO News* published a special oil workers edition. In a test case involving the union during the August 1947 transition between the Wagner Act and the Taft-Hartley Act, Knight testified before a United States District Court that the union's financial statements had been filed voluntarily with the Labor Department for some time, that the union constitution excluded Communist members or officers, and that the union operated autonomously and not under CIO direction.

After World War II, Knight's union secured an 18 per cent wage increase in the first round negotiations, reported *United States News,* after a 1945 strike and Government seizure of the oil properties; the 1946 second-round agreement was based on a cost-of-living bonus. Knight, pointed out the same publication, preferred a straight wage increase to this basis in the third-round negotiations of 1948. Knight's offer to arbitrate the wage issue was refused by the employers, reported *Business Week,* prior to the eventual settlement. In the fourth round, Knight's emphasis was on the institution of a $100-a-month pension plan for workers retiring at the age of sixty-five and on the re-establishment of the 36-hour week in effect before the war, with, however, maintenance of the current wage level. With other CIO, AFL, and independent unions, the O.W.I.U. met in convention in 1950 to discuss better pension plans, the one issue under joint consideration. At this same March 1950 convention Knight voiced his union's determination to continue "to compete and shoot against the independents and the AFL. . . .We earnestly believe the O.W.I.U-CIO to be the most soundly constructed union."

The sixth-round demands of Knight's union, put forth in the fall of 1951, called for a $2-a-day increase, amounting roughly to 12.5 per cent, as well as fringe benefits such as premium wages for night work. (*Time* estimated that the current rate of $2.03 an hour makes the oil industry workers among the highest paid in the United States.) This demand for increases in excess of wages previously allowed by Wage Stabilization Board was supported by representatives of the union's 100,000 members and by those of 150,000 additional oil workers belonging to AFL and independent unions, all of whom pledged mutual support at a joint meeting in St. Louis in November. These and other unions, twenty-two in all, in April 1952 went on a nation-wide strike following the collapse of Government mediation attempts to obtain the demanded increase of twenty-five cents per hour, plus higher rates for night work. Altogether, about seventy companies were affected—refineries, distribution plants, and pipelines—California refineries being unaffected in order to maintain supplies for the Korean front. Civilian aviation services both in America and England were reduced. By May 22 scattered settlements, all of which called for a 15-cent hourly wage increase, had been reached, affecting some 60,000 of the 90,000 striking oil workers.

Elected to a vice-presidency of the CIO in 1947, Knight was re-elected to that office in the conventions of the succeeding years. It was Knight who at the 1949 convention urged adoption of President Philip Murray's report condemning the Left-wing leadership of certain CIO affiliates. In 1950 Knight was named head of a CIO committee to investigate Communist influence in CIO unions, and it was on the basis of reports made by this group that in 1950 the International Longshoremen's and Warehousemen's Union (led by Harry Bridges) and one other union were expelled from the CIO, bringing to eleven the number of CIO affiliates expelled since the convention first met. Several times Knight has been named the CIO's fraternal delegate to meetings of the Confederation of Latin American Workers (CTAL), at one of which in 1948 he presented a defense of the European Recovery Program. He is a member of the CIO committee on Latin American affairs.

Knight, who has served on War Labor Board panels, in June 1951 was named deputy administrator of the National Production Authority (headed by Manly Fleischmann), which plans the over-all mobilization effort. (*Business Week* has observed that Knight's appointment was opposed in AFL circles.) In 1947 Knight was a member of the Committee for the Marshall Plan to Aid European Recovery. He is a member of the board of directors of the American Arbitration Association. The union president has received a human relations award from B'nai B'rith, "for his record of achievement in helping to make Denver a better place in which to live." (The union's headquarters were transferred to that city in 1949 from Fort Worth, Texas, said the *Christian Science Monitor,* "because of what its official history calls the oppressive and antiunion attitude of Texas.") Knight divides his time between Washington and Denver, where he has his home; his wife is the former Evelyn Luella Dokken, whom he married January 30, 1925. The *Christian Science Monitor* described Knight as "an aggressive and intelligent organizer." *Time* reported that the "wiry" labor leader is known as "Jack" among his associates.

Reference

Who's Who in Labor (1946)

KOLLMAR, DICK *See* Kilgallen, D., and Kollmar, D.

KOLLMAR, RICHARD TOMPKINS *See* Kilgallen, D., and Kollmar, D.

KOLLMAR, MRS. RICHARD TOMPKINS *See* Kilgallen, D.

KOLLONTAY, ALEXANDRA (MIKHAILOVNA) Apr. 1, 1872—Mar. 9, 1952 Soviet diplomat; as refugee from Czarist Russia lectured on socialism in the United States and Europe (1908-17); after Russian Revolution was appointed the first Soviet Commissar of Welfare; became Minister to Norway (1923), Minister to Mexico (1926), Minister to Sweden (1930), Ambassador to Sweden (1943); retired in 1945; was awarded Order of Lenin (1933); author of books on feminism and communism. See *Current Biography*, 1943.

Obituary

N Y Times p27 Mr 12 '52

KOTSCHNIG, WALTER M(ARIA) (kŏch′nĭk) Apr. 9, 1901- United States Government official

Address: b. c/o Department of State, Washington 25, D.C.; h. 108 E. Bradley Lane, Chevy Chase 16, Md.

A leading specialist in international organization, Walter M. Kotschnig is a permanent member of the United States delegation to the United Nations and the director of the Department of State's Office of the United Nations Economic and Social Council. Kotschnig, who was born in Austria, traveled extensively in the United States as a representative of the International Student Service and of the League of Nations before he became a resident of this country in 1936. Following a period of teaching at Smith and Mt. Holyoke colleges, he joined the State Department in 1944. He has written widely on subjects related to education and international relations.

Walter Maria Kotschnig was born on April 9, 1901, in Judenburg, Austria, the son of Ignaz and Therese (Huber) Kotschnig, of Austrian peasant stock. His father is a school teacher and a musician; his one sister also became a teacher. Walter was reared in Austria, Germany, and the Netherlands. At the *Realgymnasium* in Graz, from which he graduated in 1919, he headed one of the first student governments established in Austria. In 1920 he entered the University of Graz, later enrolling at the University of Kiel in Germany. He received a full scholarship throughout the period of his university studies and supported himself by varied employment such as tutoring, farm work, and service as an attendant in a state hospital.

In his undergraduate days Kotschnig was an active member of the World Student Christian Federation. A short while before his graduation he contracted tuberculosis—"Starved and ill as I was after the first World War," he has said, "my life was saved by American relief activities in Austria and friends in the Netherlands. This taught me the importance of international cooperation and set the pattern for my life work." Of his attitudes in these years and the influences which determined his choice of a career, Kotschnig has further stated, "Ever since my earlier student days I have been opposed to totalitarianism of every kind, beginning with a street fight against Communists in Graz. Throughout my life I have been devoted to the promotion of improved international relations."

After leaving the University of Kiel with the Ph.D. degree in political science in 1924, Kotschnig served as a first assistant at the Institute of World Economics in Kiel. In 1925 he went to Geneva as the Secretary General of the International Student Service (devoted to university relief work and the promotion of international studies), a position which enabled him to visit the United States for a three-month lecture tour in 1926. Beginning in 1934 he worked in London and Geneva on the staff of the League of Nations as Director of the High Commission for Refugees from Germany, dealing with resettlement problems. Kotschnig, whose activities had brought him frequently to the United States, moved to this country with his family in 1936 and became an American citizen in 1942. For seven years beginning in 1937 he taught at Smith and Mt. Holyoke colleges in Massachusetts as Professor of Comparative Education. During this period, in which he was also engaged in research, he taught at summer sessions at Harvard University and the University of Minnesota.

As a specialist on international organization, Kotschnig entered the United States Government service in 1944, becoming acting chief in 1945 and chief in 1947 of the Division of International Organizational Affairs of the State Department. In his State Department post he took part in preparations for the United Nations from its inception, at the Dumbarton Oaks Conference held in Washington in 1944 and at the San Francisco Conference in 1945. As secretary of the delegation from the United States, Kotschnig attended the London conference for the establishment of the United Nations Economic and Social Council in 1945; the following year he served as Acting Executive Secretary to the Preparatory Commission of UNESCO, also meeting in London. Subse-

WALTER M. KOTSCHNIG

quently he attended the UNESCO General Conference meetings in Paris (1946) and in Mexico City (1947). He represented the United States at two sessions of the International Labor Organization General Conference (Paris, 1945, and Geneva, 1949) and at two meetings of the Governing Body of the ILO (Geneva, 1949). In 1946 he became associate executive secretary and consultant of the U.N. Subcommission of Economic Reconstruction of Devastated Areas, in which capacity he investigated the extent of war damages in Czechoslovakia and in Poland. Later he attended the U.N. Conference on Technical Assistance in New York in 1950 as an alternate delegate and signed the final act of that conference in behalf of the United States. In the same year Kotschnig served as an adviser to the United States delegation to the U.N. General Assembly. In the State Department his post since 1949 has been director of the Office of United Nations Economic and Social Affairs.

Since 1946 Kotschnig has attended thirteen of the fourteen sessions of the Economic and Social Council, as adviser to the United States representative and, for the last five sessions, as deputy representative. Among the important decisions made by that body in which he has had a share are the establishment of a permanent agency to aid children and the rejection of the World Trade Union Federation's proposal to consider whether rearmament was cutting workers' living standards in western countries. Speaking for the United States, in August 1951 he opposed a proposed U.N. pact on freedom of information, for which he said the United States believed the times were not propitious. (When attempts were made the following year to write treaties in this field, Kotschnig maintained that lack of agreement in concepts about freedom of information and the press would make U.N. efforts futile at present. The differences in ideas, he noted, existed not only be-

tween the Soviet Union and the United States, but also among noncommunist nations.) In March 1951 Kotschnig introduced a proposal that the Economic and Social Council investigate slave labor throughout the world, and in June 1952 he turned over to the committee carrying on this investigation evidence gathered by the United States State Department which he said proved that "slavery of a type and on a scale the world has never before known" existed in the Soviet Union. In a speech before ECOSOC in July 1952 he compared the living standards of the United States and those of the Soviet Union.

During the period of his work with the International Student Service, Kotschnig and his wife edited *The University In A Changing World; A Symposium* (1932), described by the New York *Evening Post* as dealing with "the predicament of the modern university in the modern world, in each country according to its own peculiar post-bellum lunacy." Kotschnig's second book, *Unemployment in the Learned Professions; an International Study of Occupational and Educational Planning* (1937), concerned the overcrowding of the world's universities and the growing unemployment of their graduates. The *New Statesman and Nation* found, "It is difficult to exaggerate the importance of this careful and illuminating book," and the New York *Times* commented, "Dr. Kotschnig, in bringing together a great mass of new facts in a readable and stimulating manner, has presented students of social planning with a thought-provoking situation." His best known work, *Slaves Need No Leaders*, which appeared in 1943, was subtitled "an answer to the fascist challenge to education." The book discusses problems of re-education in fascist countries, calls for broader educational opportunities in the United States and for stronger Federal support of education, and condemns indoctrination in education, whether for democracy or any other political or economic system. Harry Hansen, writing in the New York *World-Telegram*, called the book "one of the best calls to battle for educators that [he had] seen," and *School Review* characterized it as "a professional publication of crucial importance, which must not be neglected." Paul Hagen, reviewing the work in *Books*, thought it "impressionistic and historically not documented," but "full of challenging ideas and opinions." Kotschnig is also the author of some fifty to sixty articles on problems of international relations, economics, politics, and education, written in English, French, and German, many of which have been translated into other languages.

The statesman is a trustee of the Institute of International Education (New York) and a member of the American Section of the International Institute of Administrative Sciences. He has been awarded the St. Sava Order of Yugoslavia (1926) and the Officers Cross, Civil Service Order of Bulgaria (1929). In 1945 he received an honorary LL.D. degree from Rockford College, Illinois. Kotschnig's travels have included all but two European countries, the forty-eight States, South America, India, Burma, Thailand, and Japan. He has commented,

"In my travels in recent years I have been guided by the idea that American foreign policy can only be effective if it is based on a full understanding of what makes other countries tick."

Dr. Kotschnig is five feet eleven inches tall, weighs 180 pounds, and is blue-eyed and blond. His religious affiliation is with the Society of Friends (Quakers). On December 10, 1924, he married Elined Prys of Talgarth, Wales, a psychological consultant. Their three children are Enid Maria Ileana, Christopher Hans Owen, and John Walter. One son, Christopher, is a member of the Secretariat of the International Labor Organization. Kotschnig's recreations are reading, gardening, and mountaineering.

References

N Y Daily News II p4 Jl 20 '52
Who's Who in America, 1952-53
Who's Who in the United Nations (1951)

Wide World Photos

JOSEPH KRAMM

KRAMM, JOSEPH 1908- Playwright; stage director; actor

Address: b. c/o Leah Salisbury, 234 W. 44th St., New York 36

The 1952 Pulitzer Prize for the most distinguished original American play of the season went to playwright Joseph Kramm for *The Shrike*. A psychological melodrama set in the mental ward of a municipal hospital, this is the ninth play he has written but is the first to be produced. Kramm began his career in the theater in 1929 as an actor in Eva Le Gallienne's Civic Repertory Theatre, and subsequently appeared on Broadway in *L'Aiglon*, *Bury the Dead*, and revivals of *Processional* and *Liliom*. Since 1946 he has been directing plays for summer theaters and for the Experimental Theatre of the American National Theatre and Academy in New York.

Joseph Kramm was born in South Philadelphia, Pennsylvania, in 1908 and attended public schools in that city. "My father was a druggist who felt that his store was a prison and spent a good deal of his time sitting in the prescription laboratory in the back, writing poetry," Kramm told a *New Yorker* interviewer. "My mother taught me poetry, which she insisted on my reciting before large gatherings. . . .I suppose my interest in acting dates from that." While an undergraduate at the University of Pennsylvania, young Kramm was active in off-campus little theater groups, and reportedly almost was failed in his junior year because he devoted too much time to acting. Following his graduation in 1928, he got a job as a copy boy on the Philadelphia *Inquirer* and soon rose to the rewrite desk of that paper. He also was a rewrite man on the Philadelphia *Record*.

In 1929 Kramm auditioned for Eva Le Gallienne's company at the old Civic Repertory Theatre on Fourteenth Street in New York. Accepted as an apprentice actor, he played a variety of minor roles in more than thirty plays presented by the group. Among the roles in which he appeared were Voznesensky in Tolstoy's *The Living Corpse* (1929), Friar John in *Romeo and Juliet* (1930), Keller in Giraudoux's *Siegfried* (1930), The Sergeant in Schnitzler's *The Green Cockatoo* (1930), a Guest in *Camille* (1931), the Plain-Clothes Policeman in Molnar's *Liliom* (1932), David Garrick in *Dear Jane* (1932), and The Dodo in *Alice in Wonderland* (1932). After the Civic Repertory Theatre was disbanded, he acted the parts of Foresti and The First Conspirator in Rostand's *L'Aiglon*, which opened on Broadway in November 1934 with Miss Le Gallienne and Ethel Barrymore in the starring roles.

The year 1936 saw Kramm playing The Third Soldier in the Actors' Repertory Company's original Broadway production of Irwin Shaw's antiwar drama, *Bury the Dead*. As Jake Psinski, the agitator, in John Howard Lawson's *Processional*, which the WPA Federal Theater Project revived in October 1937, Kramm (said the New York *Herald Tribune* critic) was "a very vigorous figure and true to life." The following year he was a member of the Group Theatre's second company for its London production of Clifford Odets' *Golden Boy*. In January 1940 he was seen on Broadway as Senator Talbot in *The Man Who Killed Lincoln*, by Elmer Harris and Philip Van Doren Stern. Two months later, when Burgess Meredith and Ingrid Bergman costarred in a revival of *Liliom*, Kramm played the role of Linzman in that production. He next had the role of Malachi in the Playwrights' Company production of Maxwell Anderson's Biblical drama, *Journey to Jerusalem*, which opened in October 1940. He again appeared with Miss Le Gallienne in Thomas Job's murder melodrama, *Uncle Harry*, which ran on Broadway from May 1942 to May 1943. Between acting commitments Kramm did some teaching,

KRAMM, JOSEPH—*Continued*

worked as a guide on sight-seeing busses, and once did research for a historical project.

When the United States entered World War II Kramm studied radio engineering and received a first-class FCC license. He worked during the day as a control-room engineer at radio station WNEW in New York, while he was appearing in *Uncle Harry* at night. Later he entered the army and became a cryptographic technician, coding and decoding messages for the Signal Corps. Kramm saw service as a cryptographer with a Signal Corps Batallion in Europe, where he took part in the Battle of the Bulge. After V-E Day he was sent from the European theater to the Philippines. By the time of his discharge, he had served three years in the Army and had won five campaign stars.

In the years following the war, Kramm turned his attention to directing—for two seasons he was at the summer theater in Sayville, Long Island. One of his notable productions there was a new treatment he made of Eugene O'Neill's *Anna Christie*, which was first put on in August 1947. By converting the second and third acts into two scenes of a new second act, he condensed the original four acts of the play into three. Reviewing this version for the New York *Post*, Vernon Rice said it was "completely satisfying" and "brought distinction to the summer season." Kramm himself took the part of Chris in this production. He staged his version of *Anna Christie* in November 1947 for the Equity Library Theater in New York, and again in July 1948 for the Theater Guild at the Westport (Connecticut) Country Playhouse, when June Havoc played the title role. That same summer Kramm also met José Ferrer, whom he directed in the Hecht-MacArthur comedy, *Twentieth Century*, at the Olney (Maryland) Theater. It was with Richard Harrity's one-act drama, *Hope Is the Thing with Feathers*, that Kramm's directorial efforts were first seen on Broadway. Presented without sets, costuming, or realistic props, this was one of a trio of short plays offered in April 1948 by a small group of professional actors known as the Six O'Clock Theater, under the aegis of the Experimental Theatre of the American National Theatre and Academy (ANTA). Various critics praised Kramm's direction as "acute", "perceptive," and "superb." A year later he staged Jack Balch's *Me, the Sleeper* for the off-Broadway invitational series of ANTA's Experimental Theatre.

Meanwhile, Kramm had written eight plays, none of which were produced. With the intention of collaborating on a play about the mismanagement and lack of facilities in mental hospitals, he and a psychiatrist friend studied one of the city hospitals for several months. Although this project did not materialize, Kramm made use of his research in writing *The Shrike*, his ninth play, which he began in late December 1949 and completed in eight weeks. This drama tells the story of an unemployed stage director, who, finding himself a prisoner in the psychiatric ward of a municipal hospital after an attempted suicide, has no chance of being released except by putting himself permanently in the custody of his possessive wife—the predatory "shrike" of the title. José Ferrer was given the first opportunity of reading the finished script and in May 1950 he took an option on it. However, other commitments making it impossible for him to schedule an early production of the play, he gave up his rights three months later. The producing team of Richard Aldrich and Richard Myers then held the option until the spring of 1951, when Ferrer acquired it again, but relinquished it to producer Jed Harris in June. Harris spent five months planning his production and then dropped his option because of casting difficulties. In December Ferrer took over the play for the third time, placed it in immediate rehearsal, and within five weeks *The Shrike* opened on Broadway on January 15, 1952. (In addition to producing the play in association with Milton Baron, Ferrer also directed it and costarred with Judith Evelyn.)

The Shrike drew highly favorable notices from nearly all the first-string critics of the daily New York press. It was rated "the best drama the season has given us so far," by Robert Coleman (*Mirror*), who called Kramm "the most promising new playwright." "An interesting, original, and exciting first play," was the judgment of Brooks Atkinson (*Times*). To John Chapman (*News*) it seemed "a psychological thriller of the first order"; that critic also praised the economy of Kramm's writing. Richard Watts, Jr. (*Post*) felt that the author had written his play with such "passionate conviction" that it took on "an almost frightening credibility," with an "enormous" emotional impact. Less enthusiasm was expressed by John Mason Brown (*Saturday Review*): he thought that the play lacked "literary subtleties" and failed to be more than "an interesting and unusual melodrama." This opinion was shared by George Jean Nathan (*Theatre Arts*), who believed that although the play had "some occasional melodramatic force," it was, on the whole, "too literally written and too arbitrary to be convincing."

On May 5, 1952, announcement of the Pulitzer Prize winners revealed that Kramm had received the $500 award in drama for *The Shrike*. It was the first drama to win the prize since Arthur Miller's *Death of a Salesman* received the award in 1949: *South Pacific*, a musical, was the prize winner in 1950, and no drama prize was given in 1951. Commenting on the award in a review of *The Shrike* in book form, Henry Hewes observed in the *Saturday Review* that it "might be disputed by those who expect more literary quality in a prize-winner"; but he said further that the play, "which in its finest moments is a stripping bare of our society's norms," filled the Pulitzer requirement—"an original American play which shall represent the educational value and power of the stage, preferably dealing with American life." In June *The Shrike* received *Billboard*'s Donaldson Award as the best play of the 1951-52 season. Because of Ferrer's film commitments, the play closed on May 31, after 161 performances.

Another play by Kramm, *The Gypsies Wore High Hats*, was bought in March 1952 by Aldrich and Myers. Adapted from an unpublished novel, *The Neighbors Needn't Know*, by Sylvia Golden, this domestic comedy tells of an upper-class Hungarian and his difficulties in adjusting himself to the American striving for economic security. It is scheduled for try-outs in the summer.

At the time *The Shrike* opened, Kramm had been directing TV commercials and supervising a daytime television show for an advertising agency. He is in mid-1952 a teacher of acting in the American Theatre Wing's Professional School. The playwright's wife is Isabel Bonner, an actress, whom he first met when they were in the cast of *Processional* and who played the role of a doctor in *The Shrike*. Of medium height, Kramm is of stocky build; the *New Yorker* has described him—"brown eyes, a mild expression, a bold profile, and dark, wavy hair parted in the middle." One of his diversions is to play records, and he likes to cook. "Everyone asks me how success feels," he recently told a *Theatre Arts* interviewer, "but I don't feel anything at all. The only real thrill I've had is in the actual creating."

References

N Y Herald Tribune IV p3 Ja 13 '52;
    p16 My 6 '52 por
N Y Sunday News II p3 Ja 27 '52
N Y Times II p1 F 24 '52; p24 My 6
    '52 por
N Y World-Telegram p21 Ja 16 '52 por
New Yorker 27:26-7 F 9 '52
Sat R 35:35-6 F 16 '52 por

KRASNA, NORMAN Nov. 7, 1909- Motion picture writer, producer, director; playwright

Address· b. RKO-Radio Studios, 780 Gower St., Los Angeles 38, Calif.

One of Hollywood's best-known and most successful screen writers, Norman Krasna has written stories and screen plays for more than twenty-five films, including *Richest Girl in the World*, *Fury*, *Bachelor Mother*, *The Devil and Miss Jones*, and *Princess O'Rourke* —the latter picture winning him an Academy Award for the best original screen play of 1943. He has also served as a writer-producer and director, and is the author of such popular stage plays as *Small Miracle*, *Dear Ruth*, and *John Loves Mary*. Krasna, a former newspaperman and motion picture press agent, joined with Jerry Wald in 1950 to form a major independent producing unit at RKO-Radio Studios. Two years later, in May 1952, Krasna sold his interests in Wald-Krasna Productions to Wald.

Born in the Corona section of Queens, Greater New York, on November 7, 1909, Norman Krasna is the son of Benjamin and Beatrice (Mannison) Krasna. His mother wanted him to become a lawyer: hence, following his graduation from high school, he attended the night law school of St. John's University in Brooklyn. During the day he worked as a clerk at $18 a week in Macy's department store. After studying law for two years, he decided to turn to journalism as a career. He persuaded Louis Weitzenkorn, then Sunday editor of the old New York *World*, to give him a job as a copy boy in the city room of that paper, where he ran errands for such notables as Alexander Woollcott, St. John Ervine, Quinn Martin, and Alison Smith. From them he learned something about the theater, and eventually, in 1928, he was promoted to assistant dramatic editor and film critic. When Weitzenkorn left the *World* for the New York *Evening Graphic*, Krasna accompanied him and in 1929 became its dramatic editor and critic—shortly before Jerry Wald began working for that tabloid as a radio columnist.

When Krasna left the *Graphic* he joined the New York staff of the *Exhibitors Herald-World*, a film trade paper for which he wrote a column entitled *Sound Box*. This, in turn, led to a position in Hollywood at $50 a week as an assistant to the director of publicity at Warner Brothers. His experiences there provided him with the material for his initial dramatic effort, *Louder, Please*, which opened on Broadway in November 1931 with Lee Tracy and ran for 68 performances.

Krasna was next engaged by Columbia Pictures for its writing staff. Working on four films for that studio, he first wrote the original story and collaborated with Jo Swerling on the scenario and dialogue for *Hollywood Speaks* (1932). This was followed by the adaptation of *That's My Boy* (1932), the screen play for *Parole Girl* (1933), and the story and dialogue for the Bert Wheeler-Robert Woolsey comedy, *So This Is Africa* (1933). Released from his Columbia contract, Krasna went to Metro-Goldwyn-Mayer to collaborate with Herman J. Mankiewicz on the original story for *Meet the Baron* (1933)—a comedy that marked the screen debut of radio star Jack Pearl—and then to Universal to assist director Eddie Buzzell with the adaptation and dialogue for *Love, Honor, and Oh, Baby* (1933), starring Slim Summerville and ZaSu Pitts. His first important success, however, was the original story and screen play for *Richest Girl in the World*, an RKO picture, starring Miriam Hopkins and Joel McCrea, which was nominated for the Academy Award in 1934. The New York *Herald Tribune*'s Richard Watts, Jr., found the film "managed in a mood of calm, urbane and high spirited humor . . . always pleasantly mannered and quite disarming in its bantering gaiety." For the same studio Krasna and Don Hartman wrote the original story for *Romance in Manhattan* (1934), with Ginger Rogers and Francis Lederer. By that time the twenty-four-year-old screen writer was being hailed as "the Boy Wonder" of Hollywood.

Krasna's second play, *Small Miracle*, opened on Broadway in September 1934 for a run of 117 performances. It was described by Burns Mantle (New York *Daily News*) as "a taut little melodrama, giving graphic cross sections of city life within the space of an evening spent in the lounge of a theater while a play was going on." In 1935 Krasna adapted *Small*

NORMAN KRASNA

Miracle for the screen; it was released by Paramount under the title *Four Hours to Kill!* with Richard Barthelmess. Krasna remained at Paramount to collaborate with Vincent Lawrence and Herbert Field on the screen play of *Hands Across the Table* (1935), with Carole Lombard and Fred MacMurray in the starring roles and Ernst Lubitsch supervising the production. André Sennwald (New York *Times*) praised it as "an uproariously funny romantic comedy, with a brilliant screen play." The following year Krasna collaborated with Alice Duer Miller and John Lee Mahin on the MGM production *Wife Versus Secretary*, starring Clark Gable and Jean Harlow. But his most noteworthy achievement up to that time was the original story for another MGM picture, *Fury* (1936), the first American film directed by Fritz Land, with Spencer Tracy and Sylvia Sydney in the leading roles. Reviewing this "grim and purposeful" story of mob hysteria and attempted lynching, Frank S. Nugent of the New York *Times* rated it as "the finest original drama" the screen had provided during that year.

Warner Brothers next secured Krasna's services to collaborate with Groucho Marx on the story and script for *The King and the Chorus Girl* (1937). He then went to Universal to write the original story for *As Good As Married* (1937), with John Boles and Doris Noland. That same year Krasna became a writer-producer, at a reported salary of $1,200 a week, for MGM. His first assignment was *The Big City* (1937), starring Luise Rainer and Tracy. Howard Barnes wrote of this film in the *Herald Tribune*: "It would seem that Krasna, the producer, was being very tolerant with Krasna, the writer, when the latter's original story was put in the works. . . . [It] has resisted all efforts to mold it to a distinctive screen outline." Krasna's second

production, *The First Hundred Years* (1938), with Robert Montgomery and Virginia Bruce, was also based on one of his original stories. More enthusiastically received by the critics was *Three Loves Has Nancy* (1938), a "screwball comedy" with Janet Gaynor and Montgomery, which Krasna produced but did not write. Also released in 1938 was the Paramount film, *You and Me*, with George Raft and Miss Sydney. Although based on an original story by Krasna and directed by Lang, it did not repeat the success of *Fury*.

The year 1939 saw Krasna at RKO preparing the screen play for *Bachelor Mother*, starring David Niven and Miss Rogers. Critic Nugent thought this film "a merry comedy . . . all new and brightly shining and full of the most unexpected nonsense." Krasna was signed by Universal the following year to write the scenario of *It's a Date*, a picture for Deanna Durbin that the *Variety* reviewer believed "excellent in all-round craftsmanship." Back at RKO in 1941, Krasna did the original story and screen play for *Mr. and Mrs. Smith*—Alfred Hitchcock's first American comedy, starring Montgomery and Miss Lombard. To Kate Cameron (New York *Daily News*), the story seemed "thin and tenuous," but she felt that Hitchcock's direction had made it into "an interesting screen exhibit." RKO also released *The Devil and Miss Jones* (1941), an independent production which Krasna and Frank Ross, as coproducers, made for $600,000. Based on an original story and play by Krasna about "the richest man in the world" who becomes a labor spy in his own department store only to discover that "strikers are people," this film was written especially for the talents of the leading players—Jean Arthur, Charles Coburn, and Robert Cummings. Critics unanimously acclaimed it as one of the year's best comedies. Returning to Universal, Krasna wrote the original movie play for René Clair's first Hollywood production, *The Flame of New Orleans* (1941), a romantic comedy with a historical setting, starring Marlene Dietrich, and then collaborated with Leo Townsend on the scenario for another Deanna Durbin vehicle, *It Started with Eve* (1941).

In November 1941 Frank Ross produced Krasna's third play, *The Man with Blonde Hair*, a melodrama about a fugitive Nazi prisoner of war who learns tolerance and human decency from a Jewish family on the Lower East Side, which Krasna himself staged. "Mr. Krasna's battle with his plot is desperate and clever, but he never quite succeeds in making it come true," was the verdict of Brooks Atkinson (New York *Times*). The play was withdrawn at the close of its first week on Broadway. Krasna's initial directing assignment for the screen was the Warner Brothers film, *Princess O'Rourke*, starring Olivia de Havilland, Cummings, and Coburn. Bosley Crowther (*Times*) considered it "a thoroughly delightful film . . . in the best tradition of American screen comedy." This story (of an American pilot who falls in love with a girl and then discovers she is a refugee princess of European royalty) won for Krasna the Academy Award for the best original screen play of 1943. Later that same year he joined the Army Air Force's first motion picture unit. The next Hollywood film for which he wrote the original story was *Bride by Mistake* (1944), an RKO picture with Laraine Day and Alan Marshal. This was followed by the original screen play for the Paramount production *Practically Yours* (1944), a "zippy, witty farce" with Claudette Colbert and MacMurray.

Krasna's outstanding Broadway hit to date (as of May 1952) has been *Dear Ruth*, which opened in December 1944 and ran for 683 performances. According to Lewis Nichols (*Times*), this "delightful" farce was probably "the comedy to end all comedies of juvenile misunderstanding." Almost as popular was *John Loves Mary*, a farce dealing with the marital mix-ups of two returning GI's, which opened in February 1947 and lasted for 423 performances. Louis Kronenberger observed in *PM* that the author was "a trained popular psychologist in the field of laughter . . . a dealer in slick prefabricated parts in the field of construction." Both of these comedies were sold to Hollywood for large sums, and Jerry Wald produced *John Loves Mary* for Warner Brothers. Again collaborating with Groucho Marx, Krasna wrote *Time for Elizabeth* and directed this family comedy about the problems of retirement. It opened on Broadway in September 1948 and closed within a week. In 1950 Krasna wrote, directed, and produced *The Big Hangover*, an MGM film starring Van Johnson and Elizabeth Taylor, which Otis L. Guernsey, Jr. (*Herald Tribune*) described as "a curious, cloudy mixture of farce, sociology, and romance."

It was announced in June 1950 that Krasna and the producer Jerry Wald had formed an independent producing unit, Wald-Krasna Productions, with Krasna as its vice-president and treasurer. Two months later an agreement was reached with Howard Hughes, managing director of RKO, whereby this semiautonomous unit would produce twelve pictures a year for RKO during the next five years. In addition to weekly salaries of $2,700 each, Krasna and Wald were also to receive half of net profits on each of their films. At that time they announced the titles of eight original stories they had conceived or written themselves for future production. Their schedule was delayed, however, while they supervised the completion, editing, and polishing of some twenty RKO features. The first four films produced by the team were *The Blue Veil* (1951), *Behave Yourself* (1951), *Clash by Night* (1952), and *This Man Is Mine* (1952). Differences with Hughes over the degree of autonomy for the producing were reported in November 1951, but the following January it was revealed that under a one-year extension of their contract Krasna and Wald would make eight pictures for RKO in 1952. Wald was then designated as the executive producer of the unit, while Krasna became a writer-director and was scheduled to direct two of the films—one based on an original story by him, the other an adaptation of a story by another author. It was announced in May 1952 that Wald had completed arrangements to buy out the interest of Krasna in

Wald-Krasna Productions. Krasna was expected to return to free-lance writing and directing.

For about ten years Krasna was married to actress Ruth Frazee. Their marriage was dissolved in 1950. On December 7, 1951, he married Mrs. Erle Galbraith Jolson, the widow of Al Jolson. The "tall, lanky, and bespectacled" writer-producer-director is said to be "restless and outspoken."

References

Lit Digest 119:10 Ja 5 '35 por
N Y Herald Tribune O 28 '34
N Y Morning Telegraph p2 Ap 27 '41
N Y Post O 5 '39
N Y World-Telegram Je 26 '37; F 27 '42

International Motion Picture Almanac (1950-51)
Who's Who in American Jewry (1938-39)

LA CAVA, GREGORY Mar. 10, 1892—Mar. 1, 1952 Motion picture director; after attending art school worked as a cartoonist for New York newspapers, headed animated cartoon department of William Randolph Hearst Enterprises; went to Hollywood in 1922 to write and direct two-reel comedies; directed *Saturday's Children* (1927), *Gabriel Over the White House* (1933), *My Man Godfrey* (1936), *Stage Door* (1937), *Living in a Big Way* (1947), and others. See *Current Biography*, 1941.

Obituary

N Y Times p92 Mr 2 '52

LAGERKVIST, PÄR (FABIAN) May 23, 1891- Author

Address: b. c/o Random House, Inc., 457 Madison Ave., New York 22; c/o Albert Bonniers Förlag, 605 Madison Ave., New York 22; h. Lidingö, Sweden

On November 15, 1951, it was announced that the Swedish Academy had awarded the 1951 Nobel Prize for literature to one of its own members, Pär Lagerkvist. Equally distinguished as a dramatist, poet, and novelist, Lagerkvist has written more than thirty-five books and is generally regarded as the foremost literary figure to have emerged in Sweden since World War I. Two of his novels have been published in English translations in the United States: *The Dwarf* (1945) and *Barabbas* (1951).

Pär Fabian Lagerkvist was born in Växjö, a small town in the southern Swedish district of Småland, on May 23, 1891. He is the youngest of the seven children of Anders Johan and Johanna (Blad) Lagerquist, whose ancestors had been farmers. His father worked as a linesman at the Växjö railway station. For several years prior to passing his matriculation examination in his native town in 1910, young Lagerkvist was influenced by certain radical trends and movements, mostly as a reaction

PÄR LAGERKVIST

against the religious and conservative background of his home. Early interested in literature, he studied humanistic subjects at the University of Uppsala during 1911 and 1912. His literary debut dates from 1912, when some of his poems appeared in the Socialist paper, *Storm Klockan*, and his first book, *Människor* ("People"), a *novella*, was published. This was followed in 1913 by *Två sagor om livet* ("Two Tales About Life"). In contrast to the fiery vigor of his first poems, these two prose works are said to be characterized by a certain *fin de siècle* attitude toward life.

Visiting Paris in 1913, Lagerkvist came under the influence of the Fauvist, cubist, and "naïvist" movements in modern painting. While there he wrote *Ordkonst och bildkonst* ("The Art of Words and the Pictorial Arts"), a critical essay in which he contrasted the "decadence of modern fiction" with the "vitality of modern art." Attracted both by the intellectual discipline of the cubists and by archaic and primitive vitality in the arts, he wanted to see the same force and power permeate literature. He turned against naturalistic writing, called for a more sober and severe artistry, and held up as models various folk tales, legends, and fables from many different countries and periods. These theories he applied to his own work in *Motiv* (1914, "Motifs"), including poems and prose pieces, and *Järn och människor* (1915, "Iron and Men"), a volume of short stories. But it was with a collection of poems entitled *Ångest* (1916, "Anguish") that he emerged as an author of rank. The poems in this book, which has been called the first expressionistic work in Swedish literature, are noted for their originality, suggestive choice of words, and individual imagery.

According to Holger Ahlenius (*American-Scandinavian Review*, December 1940), two central experiences form the point of departure

for Lagerkvist's work: the conflict between the Christian and the scientific-deterministic views of life (he called himself "a religious atheist") and the tragedy of World War I. During most of the war he lived in Denmark, of which period Ahlenius characterized his writings as "one single cry of despair over the bestiality of man." It was at this time that Lagerkvist centered his attention on the theater. His first play, *Sista människan* (1917, "The Last Man"), has been described as an apocalyptic vision of the extinction of human life on earth. The following year he published *Teater*, a volume containing three one-act plays, under the collective title *Den svåra stunden* ("The Difficult Hour"), in which the dreams and visions of the moment of death are portrayed. In an introductory essay, Lagerkvist stated that the contemporary dramatist could ignore the older realistic traditions of Ibsen but not the later symbolic plays of Strindberg; it is through the common influence of Strindberg that Lagerkvist's dramatic writings have been linked with those of the German expressionists. The most successful of his early plays, *Himlens hemlighet* ("The Secret of Heaven"), was included along with stories and poems, in the volume *Kaos* (1919, "Chaos"). This "cosmic fantasy drama" presented a brutal and hopeless vision of life upon earth where love is only a fleeting dream. In 1919 Lagerkvist served as theater critic for the Stockholm newspaper *Svenska Dagbladet*, but thereafter he devoted himself entirely to his creative writing.

During the 1920's Lagerkvist spent a great deal of time in France and Italy. It was then that his earlier pessimism gradually yielded to a more positive view of life, which Ahlenius has described as "love, sublimated into a Christian-Platonic mysticism." Among his poetic works of this period are *Den lyckliges väg* (1921, "The Happy Man's Way"), which showed a development in the line of simplicity and directness; and *Hjärtatssånger* (1926, "Songs of the Heart"), a volume of love lyrics. In the field of prose fiction, he published the long story, *Det eviga leendet* (1920, "The Eternal Smile"), and *Onda sagor* (1924, "Evil Tales"). Two works of major importance in his development are *Gäst hos verkligheten* (1925, "Guest of Reality"), which tells the story of his boyhood, and *Det besegrade liv* (1927, "Life Conquered"), a volume of philosophical meditations and reflections. Writing in the *American-Swedish Monthly* (November 1951), Alrik Gustafson said that these two autobiographical documents affirmed Lagerkvist's faith "in the indestructible spirit of man" and in "the ultimate triumph of good over evil," providing the point of departure for all his later creative work. This faith first found expression in *Den osynlige* (1923, "The Invisible One"), which was constructed like a medieval morality play with all the actors embodying certain powers in life. Lagerkvist's next play, *Han som fick leva om sitt liv* (1928, "He Who Was Permitted to Live his Life Over Again"), is said to introduce a new phase in his dramatic writing, in which he adopted a more realistic technique and a simpler, everyday language.

With the growing threat of force and violence in Europe during the 1930's, Lagerkvist brought the focus of his art to bear more directly upon contemporary political and social developments. According to Gustafson, he became "the most eloquent and rigidly uncompromising Swedish critic of totalitarianism," defending the values of a "heroic humanitarian idealism." His most famous condemnation of spiritual tyranny and the modern cult of violence was the macabre satire, *Bödeln* ("The Hangman"), originally written as a long story in 1933 and dramatized the following year. Successful productions of this powerful play in 1934 made it "the most talked-of theatrical event of the decade" in Scandinavia, and it was also given in London in October 1935. Less sensational was *Konungen* (1932, "The King"), a symbolic drama about social revolution with an Oriental fairy-tale background. Two later ideological plays are said to reveal Lagerkvist's art as a dramatist in its "most finished and satisfying form": *Mannen utan själ* (1936, "The Man Without a Soul"), a study of a political terrorist who through love is converted to humanitarian ideals; and *Seger i mörker* (1939, Victory in the Dark"), which centers on the struggle between a democratic statesman and his twin brother, a corrupt demagogue. During this decade appeared two books of Lagerkvist's poetry: *Vid lägereld* (1932, "By the Campfire") and *Genius* (1937). He also published two collections of short stories and prose sketches, *Kämpande ande* (1930, "The Spirit in Arms") and *I den tiden*, ("In That Time"); a volume of philosophical studies defending the values of the classical and Biblical tradition, *Den knutna näven* (1934, "The Clenched Fist"); and an important essay, *Den befriade människan* (1939, "Liberated Man").

The year 1940 saw the publication of a volume of Lagerkvist's poems, *Sång och strid* ("Song and Struggle"), many of which dealt with the tragedy brought on by the German invasion of Norway and Denmark. This was followed in 1941 by *Midsommardröm på fattighuset* ("A Midsummer Dream in the Poorhouse"), a play depicting the small world of humble goodness and beauty, and the next year by another collection of poems, *Hemmet och stjärnan* ("The Home and the Star"). His best-known work of this decade, however, was *Dvärgen* (1944, "The Dwarf"), an allegorical novel of Renaissance Italy as seen through the eyes of a malevolent court dwarf. When the English translation appeared in 1945, critics compared Lagerkvist's "savage insight" into the evil will of man to that of Jonathan Swift, and praised the book's "strange and disturbing beauty." More recently, Lagerkvist has published two "profound" problem plays, *De vises sten* (1947, "The Philosopher's Stone"), and *Låt människan leva* (1949, "Let Man Live"). The latter drama presents a number of historic and imaginary characters—Christ, Socrates, Bruno, Joan of Arc, a World War II underground figure, and an American Negro—all of whom are bound together by their common fate as victims of intolerance and inhumanity.

The outstanding literary event in Sweden in 1950 was the publication of Lagerkvist's *Barabbas,* a novel about a condemned thief whose place Christ takes on the Cross. "Beyond all possibility of doubt, a remarkable book," was the opinion of André Gide, and other European critics hailed it as the culminating achievement of Lagerkvist's career. After *Barabbas* was brought out in the United States in October 1951, Graham Bates wrote in the *Saturday Review of Literature* that the book combined "the utmost physical realism with an intensity of spiritual conflict not often equalled in the retelling of Biblical tales." Charles J. Rolo, in the *Atlantic Monthly*, termed it "nothing short of a masterpiece." Harvey Breit, of the New York *Times*, thought that the author had taken "a complex moral theme" and realized it "with a craftsman's complete mastery and simplicity," joining together "an elaborate, moral vision and austere poetic style." Within a year *Barabbas* had been translated into nine languages; a film version is scheduled for production in Sweden in 1952. In addition to *The Dwarf* and *Barabbas*, several other works by Lagerkvist have been translated into English: *Guest of Reality* (a volume also comprising *The Eternal Smile* and *The Hangman*) was published in England in 1936; and two of his plays, *The Man Without a Soul* and *Let Man Live*, have been included in *Scandinavian Plays of the Twentieth Century*, in the first series (1944) and third series (1951) respectively.

"If Swedish literature after 1914 may be expressed by a single name, that name must without question be Pär Lagerkvist," a Scandinavian critic has recently said. According to Ahlenius, Lagerkvist "introduces a new period in Swedish literature and is besides the only dramatist of rank in his generation." Swedish critics also consider him as one of the most important poets in the language. Eskil Sundström has stated that Lagerkvist is, in outlook, "more of a European than any other Swedish author," and Lucien Maury has observed that had he written in a language more easily accessible to Western readers, he would much sooner have been acclaimed as "one of the leaders of our time." In the opinion of Gustafson, all of Lagerkvist's work reveals a basic concern with "the profound ethical and metaphysical problems of human existence," and he considers its central quality to be "the magnificent fusion of the purely speculative instinct and the intense artistic vision." Within the last decade, Gustafson continues, Lagerkvist has been recognized outside his own country as "among the most incisive and powerful literary figures on the present-day European scene."

Lagerkvist was elected one of the eighteen "Immortals" of the Swedish Academy of Literature in 1940, inheriting the chair vacated upon the death of Verner von Heidenstam. It is this group which annually awards the Nobel Prize for literature. In 1950 the authors' associations of Sweden, Norway, Denmark, and Finland suggested Lagerkvist as a candidate for the prize. However, the held-over 1949 award went to William Faulkner and the 1950 prize was bestowed on Bertrand Russell. Ac-

LAGERKVIST, PÄR—*Continued*

cording to reports, Lagerkvist was the chief runner-up to Faulkner in the balloting, but cast his own vote in favor of the American novelist. On November 15, 1951, it was announced that the 1951 Nobel literary prize had been awarded to Lagerkvist "for the artistic power and deep-rooted independence he demonstrates in his writings in seeking an answer to the eternal questions of humanity." King Gustaf VI formally presented the $32,000 prize to the author at a ceremony in Stockholm on December 10.

One of Sweden's most coveted literary prizes, awarded by the Samfundet De Nio, was bestowed upon Lagerkvist in 1928. He received an honorary Ph.D. degree in 1941 from the University of Gothenburg. His first marriage, to Karen Dagmar Johanne Sörensen of Denmark, took place in 1918, and was dissolved seven years later. In 1925 he married Elaine Luella Hallberg, the widow of the noted Swedish painter, Gösta Sandels. Since 1930 he has lived with his family in Lidingö, a small island community outside Stockholm, but his love for travel frequently takes him to the Mediterranean countries in the summers. The Swedish author, who is said to be dignified, shy, and "somewhat remote," has consistently shunned publicity and is almost never seen at public functions. Asked for a statement by the press after winning the Nobel Prize, he replied: "I have no particular message; it is all in my books."

References

Am Scand R 28:301-08 D '40
Am-Swedish M 45:11 N '51
Christian Sci Mon p5 N 15 '51
N Y Herald Tribune p12 N 16 '51 por; II p1 N 18 '51 por
N Y Times p1+ N 16 '51 por
N Y Times Book R p4 N 25 '51 por
Bonniers Konversations Lexikon vol 8 (1947)
Clark, B. H. and Freedley, G. (ed) History of Modern Drama (1947)
Fredén, G. Pär Lagerkvist (1934)
Hörnström, E. Pär Lagerkvist (1946)
International Who's Who, 1951
International World Who's Who (1949)
Scandinavian Plays of the Twentieth Century 1st series (1944) 3d series (1951)
Smith, H. ed. Columbia Dictionary of Modern European Literature (1947)
Svenska Män och Kvinnor (1948)
Vem är Det, 1951
World Biography (1948)

LAHR, BERT Aug. 13, 1895- Comedian
Address: c/o Lambs Club, 128 W. 44th St., New York 18

"A clown of monumental dignity," Bert Lahr, who in the summer of 1951 opened in the revue *Two on the Aisle*, has been a familiar theatrical personality since 1927, when he made his first appearance in a Broadway musical comedy.

Before that he was a successful "funnyman" in burlesque and vaudeville. In the twenty-five years (as of 1951) since his beginning in musicals, the comedian has starred in a total of fourteen Broadway productions, has appeared in motion picture versions of several of them, has played comic roles in other Hollywood productions, and has been a guest star on radio and television shows. In the 1946-47 theatrical season he played a dramatic role, as Skid in the revival of the play *Burlesque*.

Bert Lahr was born Irving Lahrheim in the Yorkville section (a predominantly German community) of New York City on August 13, 1895, son of a house decorator who had come from Germany. After leaving school at the age of fifteen, reported *Time* (October 1, 1951), he worked at odd jobs as errand boy and stockroom clerk until he had an opportunity to join a child vaudeville troupe presenting a "school" act. For the next three years he toured the United States in vaudeville, learning the techniques of older comedians and appearing in such acts as "Nine Crazy Kids", "Boys and Girls of Avenue B" (in which he replaced Jack Pearl on the West Coast), and "College Days." Back in the East the eighteen-year-old comedian joined the Columbia Burlesque Circuit, at a starting salary of $35 a week, with a troupe called the Roseland Girls. Lahr worked now to perfect his "Dutch" dialect and to develop his interpretation of the popular burlesque "Dutch" character type which had fascinated him as a boy. Eventually he was promoted to chief comedian of the show and when he left the troupe after seven years, he was earning a weekly $165, a top salary at that time among burlesque entertainers.

Lahr's years in burlesque formed the basis of his subsequent comic creations. An interview by Lucius Beebe, carried in the New York *Herald Tribune* (January 5, 1947), quoted Lahr's comment on the burlesque theater of that early era: "Burlesque as we knew it then was at once universal and a respected occupation. . . .Our shows were clean; the strip tease was unknown and the sort of humor that passes as currency on whatever vaudeville and burlesque stages still survive wouldn't have been tolerated by actors, managers, or patrons either." Considering himself "the last of a once mighty race," Lahr is quoted as believing "there are other survivors from the old burlesque days . . . but they've all grown rich and gone to Hollywood and probably forgotten the technique of being terrible on the stage. It sits easily on me."

In 1919, after serving in World War I as an enlisted man in the Navy, Lahr, with his future wife, Mercedes Delpino, formed the vaudeville team of Lahr and Mercedes, in which he played the character of the "Dutch cop" and used his burlesque routine. His opportunity to appear in a Broadway musical review came in November 1927 with the inclusion of that act in *Delmar's Revels*, which played for four months and which Lahr considers his "only real flop." The next year he was chosen to play the role of Gink Schiner, the prize fighter in *Hold Everything*. The musical, which ran for 413 performances, was a hit and Lahr the comedy "find" of the season. He is reported by *Theatre Arts* still to remember the thrill he had the day after the show opened when he read a New York *Journal* headline: "New Comedy King Born." "He played the Palace three times in six months with his old cop act at $4,500 a week," noted the *Time* article.

Thereafter Lahr was a regular star in stage productions. In 1930 he appeared in *Flying High*, two years later in *Hot-Cha*, and later that same year (1932) in George White's *Music Hall Varieties*. In August 1934 he opened in *Life Begins at 8:40* and the next year was seen in *The George White Scandals*. He was associated with Beatrice Lillie in *The Show is On*, which began its run in December 1936. Three years later he costarred with Ethel Merman in *Du Barry was a Lady* and in December 1944 began an engagement in the Billy Rose extravaganza, *Seven Lively Arts*, which ran 198 performances. In the winter of 1949 he replaced the comedian of *Make Mine Manhattan* for the last few weeks of its run, taking over most of the original sketches and adding some of his own routines, including his woodchopping scene which he had originally performed for *The Show is On* and which *Life* considered "one of Lahr's greatest moments."

The comedian's current (1951-52) starring vehicle is *Two on the Aisle*, which opened in July 1951. In skits calling for nineteen costume changes, he appears as Captain Universe of the Space Brigade, a baseball player, a paper "picker-upper" in the park, a clown, a gaucho, Siegfried, and Queen Victoria, among other roles.

The criticis' approval of Lahr's talents in *Two on the Aisle* is representative of the opinion expressed through the years. Ward Morehouse of the New York *World-Telegram*, finding the production as a whole a "lively and funny revue," wrote that Lahr's "mournful physiognomy, which can suddenly take on the brightness of the morning sunlight" was a "welcome sight. . . .He is a superior mountebank, a comedian who learned many a trick on the old Burlesque Wheel and who has since thought up a few of his own. . . .Let the living theater keep and cherish him." The judgment of Brooks Atkinson of the New York *Times* was: "Mr. Lahr is the sort of expansive clown who can fill a theater with wonderful nonsense without crouching behind a microphone or assaulting the audience with a murderous drumfire of wisecracks. He has the special genius of a theater performer. . . .He radiates a kind of genial though lunatic good nature. His voice has range, volume, and color." From *Time* magazine: "Lahr remains among the best of the old-time funnymen. . . . He has a nice comic face. . . .He has a showman's sixth sense; his antics have authority. Best of all, he can lose his head splendidly when all about him are stodgily keeping theirs." A less favorable review came from Otis L. Guernsey, Jr. of the New York *Herald Tribune*, who found the revue had "a few good but undeveloped comedy ideas and music to

Wide World Photos

BERT LAHR

match. . . .Lahr is a durable clown who can fill in gaps with his private collection of personality sight gags or strange vocal noises, but the timing of these skits seems to be way off." Less than a month after the production opened, Lahr and Dolores Gray, the costar in *Two on the Aisle*, received the Show-of-the-Month Club's annual award for outstanding performances in a musical comedy.

The only dramatic role (aside from the lead in a road company's production of *Harvey*) that Lahr has played thus far was in the revival of the legitimate stage play *Burlesque*, the story of Skid, the burlesque comic who makes his way to Broadway stardom but fails to stay there. After perfecting the role for two seasons at summer theaters, he opened on Broadway on December 25, 1946. Well-received by critics and public alike, *Burlesque* ran for more than a year in New York City and later was seen in the theaters of the East, Midwest, and West Coast. Brooks Atkinson commented on Lahr's appearance in a dramatic play in the January 5, 1947, issue of the New York *Times*. "Apart from his broad leers and uproarious bellows as a low comic, he has a respect for the stage . . . he plays character with instinctive tastes . . . [and] makes his roistering way through three acts like a human being. . . .He has two qualities that are essential to the low comedian and priceless on the more attentuated dramatic stage—exuberance and heart." Louis Kronenberger's review for *PM* read in part: "Mr. Lahr has long been one of our best comics and in *Burlesque* he shows that he can be a sound character actor as well." The New York *World-Telegram* critic wrote that the actor's performance was "ingenious and amusing."

In addition to his stage engagements Lahr has appeared in twenty-six motion pictures. His first film role was in *Faint Heart* in 1931, the

LAHR, BERT—*Continued*

year he played in the MGM version of the musical *Flying High.* The comedian was subsequently seen in *Mr. Broadway* (1933), *Hizzoner* (1934) *Merry-go-Round of 1938* and *Love and Hisses* (both produced in 1937), *Josette* and *Just Around the Corner* (1938), *Zara* (1939), and in *The Wizard of Oz* (1939), in which he portrayed the Cowardly Lion. In 1942 he appeared in three cinemas—*Du Barry was a Lady, Sing Your Worries Away,* and *Ship Ahoy.* The year 1944 saw him at work in the film *Meet the People,* and his most recent screen appearance was in *Mr. Universe,* a comedy about wrestling, filmed for the most part in New York City in 1950.

Lahr has been a frequent guest on radio shows. With the advent of television, he believed that his talents as a comedian could be more readily appreciated than on the radio. Television audiences have seen him in his wood-chopping skit and in the role of Skid in a TV version of *Burlesque.* In 1950 Lahr signed an exclusive three-year television contract with the Columbia Broadcasting System. A televised spectacle was Macy's 1951 Thanksgiving Day parade, of which Lahr was the grand marshal as Captain Universe.

The actor's wife is the former Mildred Schroeder, who had been a show girl. Married on February 11, 1940, he has a son, John, and a daughter, Jane. Lahr has another son, Herbert, by his first wife, who was Mercedes Delpino, his former vaudeville partner; their marriage was annulled in 1939. Reportedly a good businessman, Lahr has made sound investments in the course of years. The offstage Lahr is described as quiet and untheatrical; he likes fishing and usually takes his golf clubs with him when he is on tour.

References

N Y Herald Tribune IV p1 D 31 '44
Time 58:46 O 1 '51
International Motion Picture Almanac, 1950-51
Treadwell, B. Fifty Years of American Comedy (1951)
Who's Who in the Theatre (1947)

LANGER, WILLIAM Sept. 30, 1886-
United States Senator from North Dakota
Address: b. Senate Office Bldg., Washington 25, D.C.; h. Wheatland, R.F.D. 1, N.D.

North Dakota's senior United States Senator, former Governor William Langer, who was first elected to the upper house in Washington in 1940, was re-elected in 1946 and again in November 1952. He is a Republican, but has frequently differed with party leaders on outstanding issues. In the matter of foreign relations Langer is known as one of the country's most outspoken isolationists.

The son of Frank J. and Mary (Weber) Langer, William Langer was born September 30, 1886, on his parents' farm near Everest, in what was then the Dakota Territory. He was

about three years old when North Dakota was admitted to the Union as the thirty-ninth State, and not yet four when his father became a member of the first State legislature. The boy received his elementary education in a district school and completed it at the nearby town of Casselton where (states the *Congressional Directory*) his "first teacher was Alice Rutledge, a cousin of the sweetheart of Abraham Lincoln." The same source of information also tells that at the age of fifteen he was a hired hand on a neighbor's farm, "where as a result of his ability to handle large crews of men he was appointed foreman."

Langer continued his education at the Casselton High School, and on graduation proceeded to Grand Forks to study in the law department of the University of North Dakota; he passed the State bar examination at the early age of eighteen, and received his LL.B. in 1906. Too young to practice his profession, he enrolled as an undergraduate at Columbia University, New York, where he won the Roelker medal (which is awarded to the most outstanding student), was president and valedictorian of his class, and was voted (reported the *Literary Digest*) "the biggest politician, noisiest student, most popular man, and the one most likely to succeed." Langer received the B.A. degree from Columbia in 1910.

Having become eligible on his twenty-first birthday to practice in North Dakota, Langer refused an offer from a leading New York law firm and in 1911 hung out his shingle in Mandan, in North Dakota's Morton County, across the Missouri River from Bismarck, the State capital. Soon active politically, he was elected State's Attorney for Morton County for the two-year term beginning 1914 and "got a runaway start . . . by nailing the North Dakota railroads for a $1,250,000 judgment for failure to pay rentals on leased sites" (Lemuel F. Parton in the New York *Sun*). The case, which was fought up to the North Dakota Supreme Court, brought Langer State-wide celebrity just as the Nonpartisan League, a newly formed farmers' political organization, was in process of getting control of the Republican party in the State. The league backed Langer for the Attorney General's office, to which he was elected in November 1916, at the same time Lynn J. Frazier was elected Governor.

Langer, who also served the State Council of Defense as legal adviser during World War I, was re-elected Attorney General in 1918, and in the year following was "credited with having much to do with the establishment and maintenance of the Bank of North Dakota, a State-operated financial institution" (Louis H. Cook in the *Saturday Evening Post*). Subsequent bitterness between Frazier and Langer resulted in a contest between the two for the regular Republican nomination for Governor at the State primaries of 1920. Langer won the party nomination, but the Nonpartisan League supported Frazier as an independent, and Langer was defeated in November. (His views on the league's record in its first five years may be found in *The Nonpartisan League, Its*

Birth, Activities and Leaders, which he wrote at the time of that campaign.)

For the next twelve years Langer held no elective office, but occupied three appointive posts after Frazier in 1923 became United States Senator: he was a member of the State Parole Board and State Board of Equalization for eight years and president of the State Board of Health for four. He further served, in 1924, on the State's Robert M. La Follette-for-President campaign committee—he had similarly supported the Wisconsin Senator's presidential aspirations in 1912 and 1916 and had been comanager of the North Dakota Hiram Johnson-for-President campaign in 1920. Meanwhile his law practice, which he had established in Bismarck in 1916, flourished to such extent that in the period between the stock market crash of 1929 and the election of 1932 Langer was in a position to reorganize the somewhat fading Nonpartisan League. Re-entering the political lists in 1932, he emerged as the only Republican Governor elected in a State which supported Franklin D. Roosevelt as President. (As a result of the same election Gerald P. Nye, Republican, joined Lynn Frazier in the United States Senate.)

Langer was inaugurated in January 1933. He remained in office until July 17, 1934, when he was removed by the Supreme Court of North Dakota (*Biographical Directory of the American Congress*). The charge on which he was convicted, states *Who's Who in Law,* was "conspiracy to obstruct the orderly operation of an Act of Congress"; specifically, for soliciting political contributions from Federal employees. Langer appealed the verdict and challenged the impartiality of the Federal Judge who had imposed a fine and sentence—the biographical entry in the *Congressional Directory* states that the Senator is the "only person ever arrested in any English-speaking country for filing an affidavit of prejudice against a judge." On May 1935 the United States Circuit Court of Appeals reversed the decision on the grounds that the prosecution had failed to prove "overt acts" of political solicitation and that such solicitation "is not a matter of concern to the Federal Government unless some lawful government function was thereby obstructed." As a result Langer again ran for the governorship and was re-elected, for the 1937-39 term. (An account of his career through 1937 is given in *The Fighting Governor,* a biography by Langer's Columbia classmate John M. Holzworth.)

In the 1940 campaign Governor Langer sought the United States Senate seat occupied by Lynn Frazier, and was successful in the November 5 election, polling 40 per cent of the total ballots in a three-cornered contest. When Langer was presented to the Seventy-seventh Congress on January 3, 1941, he was confronted with a petition by eight North Dakota voters that he not be seated. On the motion of Senator Alben Barkley of Kentucky Langer was temporarily seated "without prejudice," and the petition was referred to the Elections and Privileges Committee for action. A subcommittee headed by Senator Scott Lucas of Illinois conducted a probe of Langer's record

WILLIAM LANGER

in North Dakota, and in December 1941 the committee voted 13 to 3 to recommend that Langer be barred (New York *Times,* December 19, 1941). When the issue came to the Senate floor early in 1942, the Senators, after three weeks of debate, voted 52 to 30 to permit Langer to retain his seat.

During the 1941 session of the Seventy-seventh Congress the junior Senator from North Dakota (who served on the Civil Service, Indian Affairs, Judiciary, Post Offices and Post Roads, and Printing committees) reflected the isolationist sentiment of his area by opposing passage of the lend-lease bill (March), transfer of Axis ships to Britain (May), and extension of selective service (August). In the second session (1942) he fought the "Little Steel" wage formula, and during the Seventy-eighth Congress (1943-44) opposed extension of the Reciprocal Trade Agreements Act, was one of two Republican Senators to vote against the Ruml "pay-as-you-go" tax plan, and conducted what has been described as a "one-man fight" against repeal of the "informer" statute. On the supporting side he joined Senator McCarran of Nevada in urging statehood for Alaska (April 1943) and also fought for pay increases for postal workers and servicemen. In November 1944 Langer was the only Senator to oppose confirmation of Edward R. Stettinius, Jr., as Secretary of State. During February of 1945 the North Dakotan (now the senior Senator, Nye having failed of re-election) joined the Democrats and eight Republicans to confirm Henry A. Wallace as Secretary of Commerce. In international matters Langer continued strongly isolationist. He voted against the Bretton Woods monetary agreement (November 1945) and the $3,750,-000,000 loan to Great Britain (May 1946) and was one of two Senators who opposed ratification of the United Nations charter.

On November 5, 1946 (when he was re-elected for the Senate term ending January 3, 1953) he carried all of North Dakota's fifty-

LANGER, WILLIAM—*Continued*

three counties. In the Republican-controlled Eightieth Congress he became chairman of the Civil Service Committee (later merged with the Post Office Committee), where he continued to press for better pay for postal employees, and was also the second Republican in rank on the Judiciary Committee, of which Senator Wiley of Wisconsin was the head. During 1947 he opposed Greek-Turkish aid (May), and differed with the majority of his party colleagues in voting against a ban on portal-to-portal pay suits (March) and against the Taft-Hartley Act (May). Outstanding in his record in the Eighty-first Congress were the votes he cast against the Barkley antifilibuster ruling (March 1949), the North Atlantic Security Pact (July), and linking of wage and price controls (August 1950). The Senator's assignments in the Eighty-second Congress (1951-52) are to the Judiciary, and the Post Office and Civil Service committees. He voted during 1951 against universal military training (March) and the President's plan to reorganize the Reconstruction Finance Corporation (April); and in favor of cutting economic aid to Europe by $500,000,000 (August). On the final day of the year Langer sent a telegram to the pastor of the Old North Church in Boston requesting that two lanterns be hung in the belfry to warn Americans of the approaching visit of British Prime Minister Winston Churchill. The Senator from North Dakota was re-elected on November 4, 1952.

Mrs. William Langer, who has been her husband's political lieutenant, is the former Lydia Cady of New York City. The couple, who had met at a concert while Langer was studying at Columbia, were married February 26, 1918. They are the parents of four daughters, Emma Bulkley (Mrs. J. Peter Schaeffer), Lydia Cady (Mrs. D. King Irwin), Marv Erskine (Mrs. Franklyn Gokey), and Cornelia Lyndon. "Big Bill," as he is called in North Dakota, is six feet in height and weighs a good 200 pounds; he has been described as "natty of dress."

References

Life 12:28+ Ap 6 '42 pors
Lit Digest 118:5 Jl 28 '34 por; 123-9 Ja 16 '37 por; 124:6+ Ag 21 '37
N Y Post p4 D 31 '48
N Y Sun p13 N 4 '41
Newsweek 4:6-7 Jl 28 '34 por; 11:12 Je 27 '38 por; 19:30 Mr 30 '42 por
Sat Eve Post 213:29+ Je 7 '41 por
Time 55:18 Mr 20 '50 por
Biographical Directory of the American Congress, 1774-1949 (1950)
Columbia Encyclopedia (1950)
Congressional Directory (1951)
Holzworth, J. M. The Fighting Governor (1938)
International Who's Who, 1951
Who's Who in America, 1950-51
Who's Who in Law, 1937
Who's Who in the Midwest (1949)
Who's Who in United States Politics (1950)
World Biography (1948)

LATTRE DE TASSIGNY, JEAN (JO-SEPH MARIE GABRIEL) DE Feb. 2, 1889—Jan. 11, 1952 French Army officer; before World War II commanded 151st Infantry at Metz; commander of Fourteenth Division of Infantry (1940); commander in chief in Tunisia (1941-42); commander of the First French Army (1944); inspector general of French Army (1945-48); commander of Land Forces of Western Europe (1948-50); High Commissioner and commander of the French forces in Indo-China (beginning 1950). See *Current Biography*, 1945.

Obituary

N Y Times p3 Ja 12 '52

LAURITZEN, JONREED July 22, 1902- Author

Address: b. c/o Doubleday & Company, 575 Madison Ave., New York 22; h. Tumurru Ranch, Ariz.

Reprinted from the *Wilson Library Bulletin*, Nov. 1952.

"My life has been one of quiet adventure and rather lonely striving to achieve some beauty and significance in expression." So Jonreed Lauritzen, regional novelist of the Southwest, epitomizes his autobiography and his literary credo. In his three published novels, *Arrows into the Sun*, *Song before Sunrise*, and *The Rose and the Flame*, the adventure has often been more thunderous than "quiet," and the highly favorable critical response to his books tends to cancel out some of the "lonely striving" he speaks of. But essentially Lauritzen's life and works bear him out—simple, rugged, intensely poetic, like the Arizona country where he grew up and still lives.

One of a family of what he calls "inveterate pioneers," Jonreed Lauritzen was born in the Mormon town of Richfield, Utah, on July 22, 1902, the seventh of ten children. His father, Jacob Marinus Lauritzen, was Danish, and his mother, Annie Gardener, of Scotch-Irish descent. Of his childhood he recalls a series of moves around the Southwest until, when he was seven, his family settled at Tumurru, a ranch near Short Creek, Arizona, where his father set about reclaiming the land and raising cattle.

Lauritzen's mother, a poet and writer on religious subjects herself, was the first to encourage his creative ambitions. She gave him his earliest education, instilling in him a reverence for literature which he carried with him even as he did his chores on the family ranch. Because of his taste for books and his disinclination for bronco-busting and the more strenuous duties of ranch life, Jonreed became his father's shepherd, reading perhaps more industriously than watching the sheep. His formal education was limited to a year at Dixie College in St. George, Utah, and some art school training in California, and he was inevitably drawn back to the ranch in Arizona. There in 1931 he married Verda Judd, a schoolteacher.

A painstaking craftsman in his writing Lauritzen wrote and rewrote a number of short stories, a play, and three novels, without submitting any of them for publication. It was his fourth novel, *Arrows into the Sun*, which launched him in print when the forty-eight pages of it that he brought to a writers' conference in Boulder, Colorado, first caught the eye of a publisher. Published in 1942, *Arrows into the Sun* is set in the Navaho country about the Grand Canyon in the 1800's. The hero is a part-Navaho, part-white boy who struggles for his white heritage in a setting of violence and social upheaval, finding his place at last with the aid of a beautiful Mormon girl. The reviewers were almost unanimous in hailing this as an extraordinarily promising first novel. What impressed them most was Lauritzen's intimate and reverent knowledge of the West. No "horse opera," *Arrows into the Sun* captured all the flavor of the frontier West, but did so poetically and imaginatively. Soon after the publication of his first novel, Lauritzen took a field job with the Department of the Interior and traveled some 12,000 miles through the West and Southwest, thus further steeping himself in the scenery and lore which was to be the background of his later work.

Song before Sunrise was published in 1948. This time Lauritzen went back to the Spanish occupation of New Mexico for his setting and tells a strangely poetic story against a background of blood-and-thunder action. Some reviewers felt that Lauritzen was too heavy-handed and that the novel suffered from an involved plot and a cluttering-up of violent incidents. But J. H. Jackson, writing in the San Francisco *Chronicle*, saw real merit in the book: "Altogether, Mr. Lauritzen writes as a poet might, and with a degree of thoughtfulness which transforms a story of action and violence into a novel in which the philosophical overtones are always present. His eye for the beauty of the strange desert-and-canyon country is sharp, and his sense of the oneness of things is quick and sure."

With *The Rose and the Flame* (1951) Lauritzen firmly established himself as a writer of exciting historical romance of the old West. The novel is set in 1680, and its theme is the conflict between the Spanish and the Indians for the possession of the land. Once again Lauritzen reveals his mastery of his setting if, to be sure, he still has a weaker grasp on matters of plot and characterization. Paul Engle wrote in the Chicago *Tribune*: "It is the Navajo material which is probably the finest section of the novel, coming with a clean force into a narrative which often suffers from superficiality of characterization and too easy division of men and women into good and bad." The novel was especially praised for its lusty vividness and "swashbuckling vigor," one reviewer suggesting that "devotees of Sabatini will gulp it down."

Lauritzen, who is a handsome, rugged-looking man, his wife, and their seven children live at Tumurru in a house he built himself with the stones from the near-by hills. With the canyons of the Colorado on two sides, a desert

JONREED LAURITZEN

to the west, and high cliffs to the north, Lauritzen has ideal surroundings for the solitude and contemplation he enjoys. He is currently at work on a new novel based on the Coronado Expedition in 1540 and a juvenile book with a Navaho setting.

LAWRENCE, ERNEST O(RLANDO)
Aug. 8, 1901- Physicist; university professor
Address: b. c/o Radiation Laboratory, University of California, Berkeley 4, Calif.; h. 111 Tamalpais Road, Berkeley 4, Calif.

NOTE: This biography supersedes the article which appeared in *Current Biography* in 1940.

Professor Ernest O. Lawrence, the 1939 Nobel Prize winner for physics and the director of the Radiation Laboratory of the University of California, is noted for his research in the structure and transmutation of the atom and in the application of physics to biology and medicine. His atom-smashing cyclotron has been called "as useful in research as the microscope." One of the top-ranking scientists called upon by the United States Government for work on wartime projects, he was a key figure in the development of the atomic bomb.

The elder of two sons of Carl Gustavus and Gunda Regina (Jacobson) Lawrence (both of whom were of Norwegian descent), Ernest Orlando Lawrence was born August 8, 1901, in Canton, South Dakota, where his father was superintendent of schools. Some years afterward Carl Lawrence became the State superintendent of public instruction; later he headed several teachers' colleges, retiring in 1939 as president of South Dakota's Northern State Teachers College. The other son, John, now

Wide World Photos
ERNEST O. LAWRENCE

heads medical physics research at the University of California.

After study in 1918-19 at St. Olaf's College in Northfield, Minnesota, Ernest Lawrence returned to South Dakota and was graduated from the State university in 1922. Lawrence's M.A. degree was granted by the University of Minnesota, and following a year (1923-24) of study at the University of Chicago, he entered Yale as a doctoral candidate. After receiving his Ph.D. degree in 1925, Lawrence was enabled, by a postdoctoral fellowship of the National Research Council, to remain at Yale for two more additional years. His doctoral dissertation, directed by Professor W. F. G. Swann, was on photoelectric effect in potassium vapor, as a function of the frequency of light. Most of Lawrence's early papers dealt with ionization, which can be described as energizing or electrifying atoms by either adding or removing electrons; the usual method is to chip an electron off the atom's outer shell by striking it with a high-speed particle. According to the *National Cyclopædia of American Biography*, Lawrence's measurement of the ionization potential of the mercury atom was the most accurate determination of an ionization potential that had been made.

After a year as assistant professor of physics at Yale, twenty-seven-year-old Lawrence joined the University of California at Berkeley in 1928, with the rank of associate professor. In 1929 he conceived the idea of the cyclotron. From well-known formulas of electromagnetic theory, he calculated that, when a charged particles moves in a magnetic field, the length of its path always increases in proportion to its speed, so that it always takes the same length of time to complete a semicircular path. The essential idea of the cyclotron is, under these circumstances, to give the passing ions an electrical "kick" to speed them up, each time they

pass a certain cross line. Thus they are made to whirl faster and faster, to reach exceptionally high speeds and high voltage, without the use of high-voltage current, as a child on a swing picks up high speed by means of many properly timed small pushes.

In a note in *Science* in 1930 Ernest O. Lawrence and M. Stanley Livingston predicted that, by the use of successive small accelerations from alternating current, 5,000-volt potentials would accelerate protons to a speed equal to that obtainable from a 500,000-volt charge. So much interest was aroused that Lawrence was asked to demonstrate the device to the first Western meeting of the National Academy of Science in September 1930. For the demonstration Lawrence used a tiny vacuum chamber only four inches in diameter (made of window glass, brass, and sealing wax) placed between the poles of a magnet that was likewise a miniature compared with present day cyclotron magnets. This crude apparatus was placed on a chair and the various wires were held by a clothes tree found handily nearby for the demonstration. Despite its crudeness, it did show the correctness of the cyclotron resonance principle and served to introduce to the scientific world a machine that has become one of its most powerful tools. Scientists were excited by the prospect of a research tool that made it possible to smash atoms and transmute elements without the use of methods both hazardous and forbiddingly expensive.

Lawrence, who became a full professor at twenty-nine, performed all or most of his basic research and development of the cyclotron in collaboration with Livingston, a graduate student who remained at Berkeley until 1934 as an instructor and research associate and is now a physics professor at the Massachusetts Institute of Technology. While a series of Lawrence-Livingston papers reported new achievements with the cyclotron, Professor Lawrence coauthored with N. E. Edlefson, a series of research reports in the field of photoionization (charging particles by means of light), and also contributed to other reports. He founded the Radiation Laboratory at the University of California to house his cyclotrons in 1932, and in 1936 became the director of what is now a large institution.

Because the size of a cyclotron determines maximum energy that can be reached, Lawrence and his colleagues built successively larger models; and with each increase in size, technical problems and the cost increased. Lawrence's early cyclotrons were built inexpensively. With a magnet of pole faces eleven inches in diameter, he and Livingston reported in 1932, a current of a billionth of an ampere of 1,220,000-volt protons was produced in a tube to which not more than 4,000 volts were applied. When Lawrence asked the scientific philanthropist Dr. Frederick G. Cottrell for help in raising $500 to finance the building of a larger cyclotron, Cottrell advised him to ask for $5,000, which he said was "easier to get" (quoted by Howard W. Blakeslee). Thus advised, Lawrence succeeded in raising $10,000, and in 1933 constructed a cyclotron approximately three feet in diameter with an 80-ton electromagnet. The magnet was given to him by the Federal Telegraph Company which had abandoned plans for using it in China.

Aware of the possible dangers of radiation, Lawrence called upon his brother, then connected with the Yale School of Medicine, to look into the question of necessary safeguards. Dr. John Lawrence's experiments with mice indicated that neutron rays produced by the cyclotron were 3.8 times as lethal as X rays— but also 5.1 times as effective in destroying tumors. This evidence of the cyclotron's great medical and biological usefulness and the value of radioactive isotopes as tracers enabled Lawrence to raise the money to build a 60-inch cyclotron with a 225-ton magnet in 1938, and to obtain more than a million dollars from the Rockefeller Foundation for the purpose of constructing still another magnet five times the size of the largest then in existence. The Lawrence brothers worked together on medical-physical research; John was appointed to the university medical school staff in 1937 and was made director of the Donner medical physics laboratory in 1941, and Ernest became a consultant to the Institute of Cancer Research at Columbia in 1935.

Working with the 225-ton cyclotron, Lawrence and others effected transmutation of elements, created radioactive isotopes, and produced currents of 16,000,000-volt deuterons and 32,000,000-volt alphas. In September 1941 the director announced "the first man-made cosmic ray"—a current of 96,000,000-volt carbon ions, four times more powerful than the highest-energy currents obtained up to that time. Two years earlier the California scientist had been awarded the 1939 Nobel Prize for physics, which included a money award of about $45,000. "It goes without saying," said the recipient, "that it is the laboratory that is honored. I share this honor with my coworkers, past and present."

Lawrence was one of six top-ranking scientists appointed in 1941 "to evaluate the importance of the uranium [atomic energy] program and to recommend the level of expenditure at which the problem should be investigated" (in the words of the Smyth report). After the Japanese attack on Pearl Harbor, when the Office of Scientific Research and Development was organized for all-out work on the uranium fission bomb, Lawrence was one of three program chiefs, the others being A. H. Compton and H. C. Urey. Lawrence had already started work on his electromagnetic method of separating the chemically identical isotopes, U-235 and U-238; the day before Pearl Harbor, he had reported that he was able to deposit in one hour one microgram (a millionth of a gram) of U-235 from which a large portion of the U-238 had been removed, this being the largest amount of purified uranium 235 that had been produced. To do this, the 37-inch cyclotron was converted to a new isotope separation device, later to become known as a calutron. Lawrence's 184-inch magnet, scheduled for completion in 1943, was rushed to completion by May 1942 and was immediately put to use in extending the isotope separation work to larger units. The results of

this work were so promising that in November of that year General Groves authorized the building of the $350,000,000 Oak Ridge project, a large-scale application of the Berkeley electromagnetic separation method. Altogether, six Lawrence cyclotrons were used for research and pilot plant purposes in the atomic energy program.

Upon completion of the calutron development project at the radiation laboratory, the 184-inch magnet was restored to its originally planned use on November 1, 1946, and, Lawrence reported, produced deuterons of energies up to 200,000,000 electron-volts, and alpha particles up to 400,000,000 electron-volts. In early 1948 the first artificially created (or man-made) mesons were made by bombarding carbon with the alpha particle beam of the big cyclotron. With this discovery it became possible to study these particles, previously found only in cosmic rays, under controlled laboratory conditions. In the spring it was announced that the Atomic Energy Commission would finance the construction of a 110-foot, nine million-dollar, heavy particle synchrotron called the bevatron. This giant accelerator to be built at the radiation laboratory will weigh more than ten thousand tons and is of a radically new design; its magnet will be a massive hollow ring enclosing a ringed shaped vacuum chamber. Lawrence served the Government as one of four scientific advisers to the postwar committee on atomic energy, as adviser to the Knolls Atomic Power Laboratory from 1946, and as a member of the Board of Foreign Scholarships under the Fulbright Act.

Since his graduate student days at Yale Lawrence had made a hobby of television, and as early as 1925 had built an all-electronic system in his spare time. As reported in articles in the Washington *Post* (September 23, 1951) and *Time* (October 13, 1951), Lawrence devised a TV tube of his own in his garage workshop, to help answer his children's questions. The result of his "tinkering" was a tube in the production of which Paramount Pictures Corporation is reportedly interested. It is said to be "amazingly" simple, and inexpensive to manufacture, capable of receiving any known kind of TV broadcast and of switching itself automatically from one kind to another. First mentioned at FCC hearings on color television in May 1950, the Lawrence tube was demonstrated in September 1951.

Lawrence, who is a contributor to the *Proceedings of the National Academy of Sciences* and *Physical Review*, has received many honors: the D.Sc. degree from the University of North Dakota (1936), Princeton (1937), Yale (1937), Stevens Institute (1937), Harvard (1941), Rutgers (1941), the University of Chicago (1941), McGill University (1946) and the universities of British Columbia (1947), Southern California (1949) and San Francisco (1949); the LL.D. from the University of Michigan (1938) and the University of Pennsylvania (1942). He holds, among other awards, the Elliott Cresson Medal of Franklin Institute (1937), Comstock prize of the National Academy of Sciences (1937), Hughes Medal of the British Royal Society (1937),

LAWRENCE, ERNEST O.—*Continued*
Holley Medal of the American Society of Mechanical Engineers (1942), and a medal of the Association of Graduate Engineers of the University of Liège, Belgium (1947). For services on the Manhattan Project he was decorated with the Medal for Merit in 1946. A fellow of the American Physical Society, the American Association for the Advancement of Science, and the American Academy of Arts and Sciences, he is also a member of the National Academy of Sciences, the Newcomen Society, and the American Philosophical Society. Other organizations with which he has been associated include the U.S.S.R. Academy of Sciences (honorary member, 1943), the Royal Society of Edinburgh (honorary fellow, 1946), and the Royal Irish Academy (1948). He was made a member of the board of trustees of the Carnegie Institution of Washington in 1944.

The physicist's fraternities are Phi Beta Kappa, Sigma Xi, and Gamma Alpha, and his social clubs are the University Faculty and the Bohemian (honorary member of the latter). In May 1932 he married Mary Kimberly Blumer, daughter of the emeritus dean at Yale Medical School; their children are John Eric, Margaret Bradley, Mary Kimberly, Robert Don, Barbara Hundale, and Susan. Lawrence, who is a tall, broad-shouldered man with reddish hair, is described as "very easy to talk to." His recreations are boating, tennis, ice skating, and music.

References

    Am Scand R 28:60 Mr 1 '40
    Nature 145:852 Je 1 '40; 147:22 Ja '41
    Sci Digest 25:63 Ap 1 '49
    American Men of Science (1949)
    Columbia Encyclopedia (1950)
    International Who's Who, 1951
    Jaffe, B.   Men of Science in America (1944)
    National Cyclopædia of American Biography Current vol G, 1943-46
    Shapley, H. and others Treasury of Science (1946)
    10 Eventful Years (1947)
    Who's Who, 1951
    Who's Who in America, 1950-51
    Who's Who in Engineering, 1948
    Who's Who in the West (1949)
    World Biography (1948)

LAWRENCE, GERTRUDE July 4, 1901—
Sept. 6, 1952 Actress
Address: b. 36 W. 44th St., New York 36

> *Bulletin:* Gertrude Lawrence died on September 6, 1952.

> *From September 1952 issue:*
> NOTE: This biography supersedes the article which appeared in *Current Biography* in 1940.

In the spring of 1951 Gertrude Lawrence, the English-born actress known to theater and motion pictures audiences on both sides of the Atlantic, received another starring role, in the Rodgers and Hammerstein musical drama *The King and I*. Her appearance in this prize-winning production marks her fortieth year in the theater (she had first appeared as a child, in 1911) as dancer, singer, comedienne, and dramatic actress, in revues, musical comedies, motion pictures, and light as well as serious dramas. In 1924 Miss Lawrence made her debut on the American stage and since then has alternated her commitments between England and the United States in such productions as *Private Lives, Tonight at 8:30, Susan and God, Skylark, Lady in the Dark,* and *Pygmalion.* In 1950 she made her American screen debut in *The Glass Menagerie;* and the following year she joined the faculty of Columbia University as a director of the School of Dramatic Arts.

Gertrude Lawrence was born in London, England, on July 4, 1901, the only child of Arthur Lawrence Klasen, an English resident of Danish birth, and Alice Louise (Banks) Klasen, who was Irish. She was given the name Gertrud Alexandra Dagmar Lawrence Klasen. From both her parents Miss Lawrence inherited a talent for the stage—her father (whose professional name was Lawrence) was a singer and her mother an actress. Before she was able to record any impressions of her father her parents were divorced, and it was only as an adolescent that Miss Lawrence became acquainted with her father. Meanwhile (Miss Lawrence tells in *A Star Danced,* her autobiography) her mother had bit parts in minor London productions, the earnings from which eked out the fluctuating income of her stepfather, whom her mother had married while Gertrude was still a young child. At the age of six, while on a holiday with her family at Brighton, she was in the audience at a beach show. When the manager invited anyone to entertain the crowd, Gertrude (at the urging of her mother and stepfather) sang and danced for the applauding spectators and received a sovereign from the manager.

Her next opportunity came in 1910, when she sang in the children's chorus of the Christmas play *Babes in the Woods*—a production in which her mother also had a small part. The girl began to study dancing with Madam Espinosa and acting with Italia Conti. It was at the studio of the latter teacher (who had offered to give the talented child free lessons) that she met Noel Coward, a young pupil like herself. At the same time the aspiring actress studied at the Convent of Sacré Coeur in Streatham. In 1911, with her appearance as one of a hundred child choristers in Max Reinhardt's London production of *The Miracle,* she felt her career was definitely launched. She recounts that a fortune telling machine predicted stardom for her, and that she forthwith had cards printed to announce "Little Gertie Lawrence" (she took her parents' stage name), child actress and danseuse. While still underage she joined Arthur Lawrence, her father, in a joint contract for tours of the provinces in variety sketches; whereupon followed engagements as principal dancer in several productions.

In June 1916 Miss Lawrence was engaged as principal dancer and understudy for a vaudeville production in London. The next year she had a similar part in *Some*, this time as Beatrice Lillie's understudy. Miss Lawrence's chance to win the critics' attention came when Miss Lillie was out of the show for two months because of a broken leg. In 1918 Miss Lawrence again was a principal dancer and Miss Lillie's understudy, so that when the star left to marry, Miss Lawrence was given the part. Thereafter she was a stellar performer in several musical revues and in 1920 was the leading lady at Murray's Club, in London's first cabaret entertainment.

Miss Lawrence was a recognized comedienne, dancer, and singer by 1924, the year of her debut on the American stage, playing with Beatrice Lillie in *André Charlot's Revue of 1924*. The critics and audiences liked her "true and clear" voice, the "magical lightness" of her dancing, and her "style and sophistication." Particularly noteworthy was her singing in the number called "Limehouse Blues." The unusually successful revue remained in New York for almost a year before going on a tour of twenty weeks through the United States.

In 1926 the English actress was chosen by Ira and George Gershwin to star in their musical, *Oh, Kay*, both for the New York production and in the next year for the London one. Following several other musicals, in the fall of 1929 Miss Lawrence made her first appearance in America in a play—*Candle-Light*, in which, one critic felt, she had occasional moments of overacting. In 1930 she established herself as a star of sophisticated light comedy when she costarred with Noel Coward in *Private Lives*, a play Coward had written especially for her. After a three-month run in London the play moved on to New York, where in January 1931 it began a six-month run. Of the many approving critics, two in New York (in the *Times* and *World*) wrote of Miss Lawrence: "[She] plays with rapidity and humor. Her ruddy beauty, her supple grace, and the russet drawl in her voice keep you interested in the slightly wind-blown affairs of a scanty comedy"; "Miss Lawrence is a comedienne of glowing and ripened gifts."

Miss Lawrence returned to England in the fall of 1931 and for the five ensuing years appeared in a number of successful plays—*Can the Leopard?* (1931); *Behold We Live* (1932); *This Inconstancy* and *Nymph Errant* (1933); *The Winding Journey* and *Moonlight is Silver* (1934); *Hervey House* (1935). During that period Miss Lawrence also appeared in British films. The first, *The Battle of Paris*, was made in 1929 and others included *Aren't We All?*, *Rembrandt*, and *Men are Not Gods*. In 1936 she again costarred with Coward, in his series of one-act plays, *Tonight at 8:30*, which was presented both in England and America. While reviewers were not too favorable toward the production, *Theatre Arts* commented on Miss Lawrence's good support in the epigrammatic dialogue with her "spirited playing."

The actress next accepted the leading role in John Golden's *Susan and God*. The New York

Maurice Seymour
GERTRUDE LAWRENCE

Times critic's opinion was: "[She] is all animation; she is all expression and eloquence." From the New York *World-Telegram*: "The vividness of her lines was given expression by her every gesture . . . by the raising of an eyebrow, the flick of a wrist. Her performance will be long remembered." John Mason Brown called her interpretation "the most complete and scintillating performance of her career." After two successful seasons in *Susan and God* Miss Lawrence had another personal triumph in *Skylark*, which opened in 1939. For her work in this play she was awarded the New York Academy gold medal for the "best performance of the year," and from the Comedia Matinee Club she won recognition for "the most outstanding theatrical performance of the year." In 1941 came one of Miss Lawrence's most successful vehicles for her singing, dancing, and acting talents—*Lady in the Dark*, which ran for three years on Broadway and was on tour from New England to California. The *New Yorker's* Wolcott Gibbs wrote: "In a careless word, she is superb, where prone on her consultant's [her psychoanalyst's] sofa, running over her symptoms, or merrily singing a fine, tough song."

In the spring of 1944 Miss Lawrence returned to England in order to become a member of ENSA (Entertainment National Service Association), an organization for British troops similar to the USO. Her unit was among the first to cross to Normandy in order to entertain soldiers in France, Belgium, and Holland. Miss Lawrence then returned to the United States, and in 1945 became a member of the USO, touring the Pacific area with her own company. Her other wartime activities were with the British War Relief Society and sponsorship of the program that brought the children of the British Actors Orphanage to the United States during the Battle of Britain. She was also a

LAWRENCE, GERTRUDE—*Continued*

staff assistant of the American Red Cross and a colonel in the United States Auxiliary Ambulance Corps.

At the end of World War II Miss Lawrence began a three-year engagement in a revival of Bernard Shaw's *Pygmalion*. This revival ran longer in New York than any other production of the play and on its coast-to-coast tour, which included Canada and Mexico, it had equal success. The New York *Sun* reviewer wrote that Miss Lawrence "builds up the part beautifully, blending its comic and tragic aspects skillfully, and bringing the play to a superb climax." The New York *Times* critic commented that Miss Lawrence knows "how to wring the fun from Mr. Shaw's lines, and in her scene in the home of Professor Higgins' mother, she is just about perfect." "Her performance," wrote the *PM* critic, "is a remarkable one . . . for the sincerity and skill with which she illumines every facet of Shaw's heroine."

The year 1948 found her in London, in *September Tide*. At the conclusion of its run in August of 1949, Miss Lawrence returned to the United States to star in the film version of Tennessee Williams' play *The Glass Menagerie*. Some critics felt that Miss Lawrence's American screen debut was poor medium for her talents, the New York *Herald Tribune* reviewer commenting, "Miss Lawrence's performance flickers with the vitality and virtuosity of a fine and experienced actress, but, like the play itself, she seems to be operating bravely in an unsuitable element." The *New Yorker* critic observed that "as the mother, Gertrude Lawrence has an actress's field day, pouring on the old plantation dialect as if she had almost forgotten the sound of Bow bells." In October 1949 she played in a television drama, *Biography*, by S. N. Behrman. One critic called her "typically vivacious and captivating" and the New York *World-Telegram* critic wrote: "I liked her elegance, her high gloss, and superb assurance."

After appearances at summer playhouses in New England, Miss Lawrence prepared for the role of the English schoolteacher for the children of the King of Siam, in the Rodgers and Hammerstein musical play *The King and I*. Opening in New York City on March 29, 1951, the production was immediately recognized as one likely to run for at least two years before making tours in the United States and England. Writing of the star, the New York *World-Telegram* critic commented: "Miss Lawrence, who has always been synonymous with glamour to me, disdains all her deft tricks and knowing enchantment, to play most simply as Anna. She is warm and human, and her natural humor keeps her from seeming to nag." *Variety* described her performance as the "dominant element in drive, authority, versatility, and personal magnetism."

Miss Lawrence considers her role in *The King and I* the most satisfying one of her career. In an interview with William Hawkins, printed in the New York *World-Telegram*, she spoke of her singular success as an actress,

remembering that in the United States she had never had a failure. "I must have a lucky star," she is reported as saying. "I've never been a great dancer, but I'm light on my feet, and I've never been a great singer, but I know how to put over a song." According to a *Collier's* article, the actress has always striven for versatility, succeeding in the arts of singing, dancing, and acting. In September 1951 she was appointed one of the directors of the School of Dramatic Arts at Columbia University. In this capacity she works (also in 1952) with a group of advanced students in the theory and practice of acting, reviewing with them dramatic scenes from various plays and assisting them in the analysis of characters and the creation of roles. She is turning her salary into a scholarship fund for the most promising members of the class.

While Miss Lawrence was still a relatively minor actress in London she was married to Francis Gordon-Howley, a theatrical director, and by him had one child, Pamela. The marriage was dissolved in 1927, and on her birthday in 1940 she and Richard S. Aldrich were married; he is a Broadway producer and the owner of several summer theaters on Cape Cod. They had met when Miss Lawrence made her debut in summer stock in *Skylark* in his Cape Playhouse. The actress has been described as "tall, somewhat angular, yet lithe and graceful, with a winning smile." She enjoys swimming and gardening. Her clubs are the Tavern Club of Chicago, the Press Club of San Francisco, and the Cosmopolitan Club of New York. In 1948 she received the honorary degree of Doctor of Fine Arts from Ithaca University.

References

Am Theatre Mag 1:56-7 Mr '40 por
Collier's 105:11 F 10 '40 por; 113:71-2 Mr 11 '44 por
Forum 100:238-9 N '38
Lit Digest 123:22 My 15 '37 por
N Y Herald Tribune p17 F 16 '40 por; p7 Jl 4 '40 por
Theatre Arts 23:714-16 O '39 por
Time 34:36 O 23 '39 por
International Motion Picture Almanac, 1951-52
Lawrence, G. A Star Danced (1945)
Who's Who, 1952
Who's Who in America, 1952-53
Who's Who in the Theatre (1951)
World Biography (1948)

LAYTON, MRS. ROY F(RANCIS) Girl Scout official

Address: b. c/o Girl Scouts of the U.S.A., 155 E. 44th St., New York 17; h. 686 Rollingwood Dr., Chevy Chase, Md.

At the biennial convention of the Girl Scouts of the United States of America in October 1951 Mrs. Roy F. Layton was elected national president for a two-year term. Active in Girl Scout work on both the local and national levels for more than a decade, Mrs. Layton had served from 1947 to 1951 as chairman of the national personnel department committee and as a member of the national board of directors. The Girl Scouts of the U.S.A. is a voluntary, nonsectarian, nonpolitical organization whose purpose is to help girls of all races and creeds learn and practice good citizenship.

The future Mrs. Layton was born Olivia Cameron Higgins in Buffalo, New York, around the turn of the century. Her parents, William J. and Gertrude (Cameron) Higgins, who were born in Canada, later became naturalized United States citizens. Her father worked for the Western Union Telegraph Company in Buffalo and in New York City for fifty-two years. The family moved to Glen Ridge, New Jersey, when Olivia was ten years old; she graduated from the public high school there. It is told that her parents were somewhat strict: they did not allow her to join the Girl Scouts in Glen Ridge, because the local troop went on hikes in the woods and did "hazardous" things like camping out. With the intention of becoming a teacher, Miss Higgins studied education and the liberal arts at Teachers College, Columbia University, which granted her a Bachelor of Science degree in 1919. For a period of eight years after her graduation she was secretary to George D. Pegram, then dean of the School of Mines, Engineering, and Chemistry at Columbia, and she also worked (1932-35) for Professor Wesley C. Mitchell, a Columbia economist.

In October 15, 1927, Miss Higgins was married to Roy Francis Layton, who had taught physics at Columbia while working for his Ph.D. degree in physical chemistry. After their marriage her husband was an engineer for the Western Electric Company in New Jersey and Chicago. During her residence in the latter city Mrs. Layton worked on the staff of the Elizabeth McCormick Memorial Fund. Later they moved to Milburn, New Jersey, when Layton assumed the position of secretary and chief chemist of the Lusteroid Container Company, in nearby Maplewood. While living in Milburn, Mrs. Layton was coeditor of the *Township Tattler,* a newspaper for men and women in war service (1942-45); chairman of the Milburn Red Cross Canteen (1943-45); and chairman of the nursing committee (1944-47) and vice-president (1947-48) of the Milburn Neighborhood House. The following year, when her husband was appointed an analyst at the Applied Physics Laboratory, in Silver Spring, Maryland, they moved to Chevy Chase. (In 1951 Layton was serving as operations analyst with the United States Air Force.)

Mrs. Layton's association with the Girl Scouts dates from 1938, when she first joined the Milburn Township Girl Scout Council, "After once starting, I found that I just couldn't leave it alone," the Washington (D.C.) *Post* has quoted her as saying. She served successively on the Milburn council as registrar (1939-41); commissioner—the highest office in the council (1941-43); treasurer (1943-45); and as a member of its nominating-membership committee (1945-47). These local Girl Scout councils, of which there were 1,437 in 1951, are composed of men and women

MRS. ROY F. LAYTON

drawn from diverse social, business, educational, and religious groups. They are responsible for obtaining and training suitable troop leaders, for financing and interpreting the work of scouting, and for maintaining national standards in the community. Since moving to Chevy Chase in 1949, Mrs. Layton has been a member at large of the District of Columbia Girl Scout Council. On the national level of the Girl Scout organization, she was named a member of the personnel department committee in 1943, and four years later was appointed chairman of that committee, which develops the training and standards for voluntary and professional Girl Scout workers. She also held membership on the national committee for the Edith Macy Training School Girl Scout adult education center (near Pleasantville, New York) and on the national convention program committee in 1947, 1949, and 1951. Since 1947 she has been a member of the national board of directors of the Girl Scouts, which, together with its executive committee and national staff, carries on the work of the national organization between the biennial conventions of the national council.

The thirty-first national convention of the Girl Scouts opened in Boston, Massachusetts, on October 15, 1951; its theme was "Girl Scouts—a Growing Force for Freedom." Delegates from local councils in every state in the Union, Hawaii, Alaska, Puerto Rico, and representatives from fourteen foreign countries made this convention the largest ever held by the organization. During the course of the meetings it was reported that membership in the Girl Scouts had reached an all-time peak of 1,770,000 on June 30, 1951, including 20,000 men serving on local councils and 410,000 women leaders. Among the topics discussed was the necessity for expanding the Girl Scout

LAYTON, MRS. ROY F.—*Continued*

movement to complete geographical coverage of the United States by 1960. At the closing session on October 18, Mrs. Layton was elected national president for a two-year term. She succeeds Mrs. C. Vaughan Ferguson, who became president in March 1946 and was reelected in 1947 and again in 1949. According to a newspaper report, Mrs. Layton was a little reluctant at first to accept the nomination as the Girl Scouts' national president, having always worked more behind the scenes in the organization—"doing difficult and challenging jobs that didn't have much glory attached to them."

An unsalaried officer, the national president of the Girl Scouts guides the making of the organization's policies, while a paid national executive director administers these policies. (Miss Dorothy C. Stratton, wartime head of the SPARS, assumed the latter post at the beginning of 1951.) As active head of the entire organization, Mrs. Layton, among other duties, assists in securing funds for its support, coordinates the work of all national committees, presides at the semiannual meetings of the national board of directors, and travels extensively throughout the country to speak at regional and area conferences. Concerning her new post, she reported that tentative plans call for getting more volunteers to help the organization "cope with the ever-growing numbers of girls." "We also plan to work hard," she said, "on the application of our program to civil defense efforts. We are cooperating as much as possible with local defense activities." The local level of Girl Scouting is her major interest, and she hopes, through her administration, to strengthen the local councils · through more valuable services from the national organization.

The Girl Scouts of the United States of America (until 1947 known as Girl Scouts, Incorporated) was founded in Savannah, Georgia, by Mrs. Juliette Low, in March 1912. She brought the idea of Girl Scouting from England, where her friends, the late Lord Baden-Powell and his sister, Miss Agnes Baden-Powell, had first established the Boy Scout and Girl Guide movements several years earlier. The United States organization is a member, together with similar organizations from thirty other countries, of the World Association of Girl Guides and Girl Scouts, and close liaison is maintained with these groups in all parts of the world. Girl Scouting is based on the Girl Scout Promise and Laws, a simple code which girls can practice in everyday living. In 1951 it comprised 82,370 troops in every State and possession of the United States. Members of these troops (consisting of from sixteen to thirty-two girls) elect their own officers and plan and carry out activities under the guidance of adult volunteer leaders. The program embraces eleven major fields: agriculture, homemaking, arts and crafts, health and safety, literature and dramatics, out-of-doors, music and dancing, sports and games, community life, nature, and international friendship. Member-

ship is open to all girls from seven through seventeen years of age.

Aside from the Girl Scouts, Mrs. Layton's interests include work agencies in the fields of child care, family welfare, and related social services. She was a member of the College Club of the Oranges (New Jersey) from 1940 to 1948. The Girl Scout official, who has green eyes and gray hair, stands five feet five inches tall and weighs 128 pounds. In personality she has been described as "poised and rather quiet, but informal and good-humored." One of her favorite hobbies is collecting antiques. Since her marriage she has traveled extensively in Europe and the Western Hemisphere.

Reference

Washington (D.C.) Post p6B O 30 '51

LEBRUN, (FEDE)RICO (lĕ-brŭn' fĕ"dĕ-rē'kō) Dec. 10, 1900- Artist

Address: b. c/o Jepson Art Institute, 5703 W. Adams St., Los Angeles 16, Calif.; h. 5488 Rodeo Rd., Los Angeles 16, Calif.

The Award of Merit of the American Academy of Arts and Letters was granted in April 1952 to the California artist Rico Lebrun, who is best known for his group of paintings and drawings on the theme of the Crucifixion. Born and educated in Italy, Lebrun came to the United States as a designer of stained glass in 1924 and later established himself as a successful commercial artist. During the 1930's he executed murals for the WPA Federal Art Project and was awarded a Guggenheim Fellowship for two successive years. He achieved national prominence in the next ten years for his drawings, paintings, and ballet designs, and won a number of prizes. Since 1947 he has served on the faculty of the Jepson Art Institute in Los Angeles, of which he was director in 1951 and 1952.

Born in Naples, Italy, on December 10, 1900, Federico Lebrun is one of the three children (two sons and one daughter) of Eduardo and Assunta (Carione) Lebrun. His father, an Italian railroad official, was of French descent, while his mother was of Spanish descent. Young Federico (who later shortened his name to Rico) attended the National Technical School (graduated 1914) and the National Technical Institute in Naples (graduated 1917). Although trained for a career in banking, he began drawing and painting by himself at an early age and at one time even seriously considered becoming a writer. During World War I he served in the Italian Army. From 1919 to 1921 he studied at the Industrial Institute and attended night classes in drawing at the Naples Academy of Fine Arts. In Naples and also in Florence he worked with the fresco painters Albino and Cambi.

Lebrun began his career as a designer in a stained-glass window factory in Naples. In 1924 the Pittsburgh Plate Glass Company bought this Italian factory and its patents and moved its key personnel to Springfield, Illinois, to establish a branch factory there. Despite the fact that he knew no English, Lebrun accepted the guarantee of a year's work in the United States teaching glassmakers. After that year he moved from Springfield to New York City in 1925 and there worked in a number of fields before becoming a very successful fashion illustrator and advertising artist. This success, however, did not divert him from his ambition to devote himself wholly to his painting. In the early 1930's he went back to Italy with his savings to study intensively the frescoes of Signorelli during a long stay in Orvieto. Returning to New York, he was commissioned by the Sections of Fine Arts of the Public Buildings Administration to execute a mural (now reportedly destroyed) for the annex of the New York City Post Office. He was awarded a Guggenheim Fellowship in 1936, which was renewed the following year. During 1936-37 he conducted classes in life drawing, mural design, and fresco painting at the Art Students' League in New York. Then, late in 1938 he settled in Southern California, where he taught advanced drawing and composition and fresco and mural painting at the Chouinard Art Institute in Los Angeles (1938-39). During the year 1940 he was a teacher and lecturer at the Walt Disney Studios in Hollywood.

It was Lebrun's drawings that first won him wide recognition. By the early 1940's he had earned the reputation as "one of the most finished draftsmen of the younger generation." Among his most noted drawings were *Woman Looking Up* and *Figure in Dust Storm* (1936); *Thus He Died* (1939); *Seated Clown, Migration to Nowhere, Birds in the Sky,* and *The Ragged One* (1941). A number of his drawings were studies of beggars, clowns, cripples, and street musicians—one reviewer defined the central theme of Lebrun's work at this time as "abject or devastated people—the poor of Europe." Less well known were such oil paintings of this period as *Slaughter House* and *Bather* (1940); *Sirocco* and *A Penny* (1941); and *Bull Ring* (1943), which was bought by the Metropolitan Museum of Art. Critics found Lebrun's style "under the spell of the Renaissance masters" and frequently classed him among the painters of the neobaroque and neoromantic traditions.

The first important exhibitions of his work were held on the West Coast, but early in 1942 he was one of the eighteen artists represented in the exhibit, "Americans 1942," at the Museum of Modern Art in New York. His first one-man show in New York was an exhibition of drawings at the Julien Levy Gallery in January 1944. During the academic year 1942-43 Lebrun taught at the Newcomb College for Women at Tulane University in New Orleans, and for the first two months of 1945 he served as visiting instructor in drawing and painting at the Colorado Springs Fine Arts Center. From 1945-46 he was artist-in-residence at the Santa Barbara (California) Museum of Art, lecturing at that museum in the latter year.

Ann Rosener

RICO LEBRUN

According to Jules Langsner (*Art News*), the year 1944 marked a new stage in Lebrun's development as a painter, after which he "attained the full power of maturity." Breaking away from the "firm grip of his classical training," the artist "began to make increasing use of the psychological possibilities of the dramatic gesture." It was in 1947, the year that he joined the faculty of the Jepson Art Institute in Los Angeles (of which he was director in 1951-52), that Lebrun began on the series of paintings and drawings treating the theme of the Crucifixion, a project that engaged his attention almost exclusively for the next three years. The works in this cycle comprise numerous versions of the Magdalene and the women of the Crucifixion, Roman soldiers and horsemen, the carpenters and ladders of the Cross, mob scenes, the Massacre of the Innocents, the traditional rooster, Golgotha heads; and studies of devastated machines and modern weapons, studies of armored creatures such as the turtle and armadillo (for use in the soldiers' armor), and studies of the Cross itself. Lebrun has stated that his choice of the Crucifixion theme and related subjects was prompted by "the constantly repeated history of man's blindness and inhumanity," while the principal purpose guiding the actual organization and execution of the cycle was to see it adapted to filming. (A twenty-minute "art film" of the entire project was eventually made.) When eight paintings from the cycle were shown at New York at Jacques Seligmann's in the spring of 1950, Alfred M. Frankfurter wrote in *Art News*: "[They] constitute the most important exhibition of a living American artist's new work in this reviewer's memory."

The culmination of Lebrun's Crucifixion cycle is a triptych, sixteen feet high and twenty-six feet across, depicting the *Deposi-*

LEBRUN, RICO—*Continued*

tion of Christ on the central panel, *Sleeping Soldier with Screaming Rooster* on the left, and *Mob with Centurion* to the right. In this triptych, which was completed in six weeks in 1950, Lebrun employed a limited or monochromatic color scheme, both for the purpose of preparing the material for the camera and because he felt the black-and-white range "a most potent carrier of visual shock." This triptych had its first public showing at the Los Angeles County Museum in December 1950 in an exhibition consisting of 41 paintings and 160 drawings on the Crucifixion theme. "What the show compellingly demonstrates," said Langsner, "is the validity of Lebrun's conviction that painting achieves transcendent power when it encompasses timeless human drama by means of the enduring human figure." The exhibition, Langsner thought, pointed toward "a revived visual eloquence," accomplished "not through the anecdotal picture, but rather by forcing to the utmost those plastic means accessible to the contemporary artist." In March 1951, when the triptych went on display at New York's Museum of Modern Art, Emily Genauer (*Herald Tribune*) felt it was "an extraordinarily moving and powerful work," and Ralph M. Pearson (*Art Digest*) believed it challenged "many an old master of European art." Other critics found it to be similar in many respects to Picasso's *Guernica* mural. Two months later a group of "Paintings and Drawings Towards the Crucifixion Triptych" was shown at the Seligmann Gallery. "For sledge-hammer strength nothing seen here this winter comes faintly near them," was the opinion of Henry McBride (*Art News*).

In recent years Lebrun's paintings have received a number of national prizes and awards. His *Vertical Composition* won the Norman Wait Harris Silver Medal and the first prize of $500 at the Chicago Art Institute's fifty-eighth annual American exhibition, "Abstract and Surrealist Art," in 1947. The following year his painting *Burnt Spinner* was awarded the $500 first prize at the Los Angeles County Museum's second local annual. In 1949, at the second Illinois National Exhibition of Contemporary Painting, sponsored by the State university, his *Mocking Soldier* received a purchase prize of $1,500. During the summer of 1950 Lebrun was one of the six painters whose work was selected to represent the United States at the twenty-fifth "Biennale" in Venice. Later that same year his *Centurion's Horse* was awarded the $2,500 second prize in the national competition, "American Painting Today," held by the Metropolitan Museum. On April 23, 1952, it was announced that Lebrun had been granted the 1952 Award of Merit of the American Academy of Arts and Letters. This award, which is made annually for outstanding attainments by a non-member of the Academy, carries with it a prize of $1,000. The two painters who have previously won the award are Charles E. Burchfield (1942) and Andrew Wyeth (1947).

"My painter's language is founded on the belief of a traditional function of art," Lebrun has said; "that is, to communicate, through dramatic presentation, a legend, a story. . . . My inclination is to be a maker of images, a storyteller, and not a specialist in private charades. . . . In dealing with ideas, vision and techniques for the task of communicating to the many, I hope for the day when a few of us, by using contemporary techniques (the camera, animation, the hand-made montage), will finally correlate some of the facts of contemporary vision, and collectively, even anonymously, say what we feel about the world around us."

In his introduction to the catalogue of Lebrun's 1950 exhibition at Seligmann's, W. R. Valentiner wrote: "The first impression created by the recent paintings of Rico Lebrun is of broad, intensely dramatic conceptions of monumental character, such as are rarely to be found in American art." Further: "It was a long road which stretched behind until the artist reached this point, long and cumbersome because he had to carry with him the burden of a rich European tradition. He is at home in Italian Gothic and Renaissance art, in French and German primitivism; he has studied the Baroque masters as well as the great painters of our time. He knows Paolo Uccello and Piero della Francesca, Dürer and Grunewald, Greco, Caravaggio, and Tiepolo, and recognizes the importance of Picasso, Henry Moore, and Miró. But to know and appreciate their art meant to balance accounts with them. Only after he had assimilated and digested these influences could he create a new, original style. Now that this process has been accomplished, the flood, repressed for many years, bursts out with doubled force into a remarkably rich and rapid production."

The California painter has designed the scenery and costumes for Antonia Cobos' *The Mute Wife,* which was first offered by the Ballet International in 1944, and for Carmelita Maracci's *Circo de España,* premiered by the Ballet Theater in the spring of 1951. Paintings and drawings by Lebrun are represented in the collections of the Museum of Modern Art, Whitney Museum of American Art, Munson-Williams-Proctor Institute, Rhode Island School of Design, Boston Museum of Fine Arts, Fogg Art Museum of Harvard University, Addison Gallery at Phillips Andover Academy, St. Paul Gallery and School of Art, W. R. Nelson Gallery of Art, Mills College Art Gallery, Los Angeles County Museum, de Young Memorial Museum, Santa Barbara Museum of Art, and the University of Hawaii, as well as in private collections. He is national vice-president of Artists Equity Association and a member of the United Scenic Artists Union. On July 19, 1948, he married Constance Johnson, of Pasadena; he has a stepson, David Hovey. The artist, who is five feet seven inches tall and weighs 150 pounds, has brown eyes and black hair. For recreation he likes hunting and fishing.

References

Art Digest 19:31 D 15 '44; 25:6-7 My 1 '51 por

Art N 49:36-9 D '50
Cincinnati Mus Assn Newsnotes N
    1 [3] Ap '42
Mag Art 31:718 D '38
N Y Times II p11 D 24 '50
Pacific Art R 1 no 3-4:8-13 Winter '41-
    '42

Los Angeles County Museum Paintings
    and Drawings of the Crucifixion
    Catalogue of Lebrun Exhibition (1950)
Miller, D. C. ed Americans:1942
Soby, J. T., & D. C. Miller Romantic
    Painting in America (1943)
Wight, F. S. Milestones of American
    Painting in Our Century (1949)

LEE, CANADA May 3, 1907—May 9, 1952
Negro actor; was a violinist, jockey, and prize
fighter before beginning career on stage; first
appeared in WPA production *Brother Mose*;
played role of Bigger Thomas in *Native Son*;
appeared also in *Anna Lucasta*, *The Tempest*,
and *Set My People Free*, among other stage
plays, and in motion pictures *Lifeboat* and *Cry,
the Beloved Country*. See *Current Biography*,
1944.

Obituary

N Y Times p21 My 10 '52

LEE, LAURENCE F(REDERICK) Nov.
16, 1888- Insurance executive; business association official

Address: b. c/o Chamber of Commerce of the
United States, Washington 6, D.C.; c/o Occi-
dental Life Insurance Company, Raleigh, N.C.;
Peninsular Life Insurance Company, Jackson-
ville, Fla.; h. 3903 Ortega Blvd., Jacksonville,
Fla.

The president of the United States Chamber
of Commerce for the one-year term beginning
May 1, 1952, is Laurence F. Lee, president of
the Occidental Life Insurance Company of
Raleigh, North Carolina, and of the Peninsular
Life Insurance Company of Jacksonville, Florida. Lee entered the life insurance field after a
career in law, in the course of which he was
retained as counsel by banks and insurance
companies.

Eldest of the sons of Frederick William and
Maud (Armstrong) Lee, Laurence Frederick
Lee was the first white boy born in the western
part of Colfax County on the Colorado border
of what was then the Territory of New Mexico. The date was November 16, 1888, the
closest neighbor was twenty miles distant, and
the area was at the time the scene of a typical
frontier settlers' feud known as the Maxwell
Land Grant War. Young Lee became an expert horseman and learned to take cover at
the approach of suspicious strangers to the
family's log cabin home. Before he reached
school age the family had moved to Albuquerque. There Laurence attended public elementary and secondary schools. In his free time
he sold newspapers or worked from time to time
as a call boy for engine crews in the local

LAURENCE F. LEE

yards of the Atchison, Topeka and Santa Fe
Railroad. At the University of New Mexico
(also at Albuquerque) he completed the requirements for the B.A. degree in three years.
His extracurricular activities included the business management of several college publications,
coaching athletics, and the presidency of the
student body. Also, in preparation for his degree (which he received in 1910) he wrote a
thesis on the tenets and practices of the Brotherhood of the Penitentes, a lay order of the
Southwest.

During summer vacations Lee turned to the
selling of insurance as a means of meeting
college expenses. It was as a result of expeditions to mining camps in search of prospects
that he gave up an early ambition to become
a mining engineer. "The bleakness and monotony of mining camp life emphasized itself upon
his mind," stated a United States Chamber of
Commerce release, and "he shifted his target to
a law career." The winning of a State oratorical contest made it possible for him to go
East after his graduation from the University
of New Mexico in 1910 and to enroll for a
special three-year course at the Yale University Law School, where again he met expenses
by selling insurance. He qualified for admission
to the New Mexico bar at the end of his second year, but returned East to complete his
training. Accordingly, he did not begin his
fifteen years of law practice at Albuquerque
until 1913, when he obtained his LL.B. degree
from Yale. At first Lee hung out a "solitary
shingle," but in 1914 he married Eileen Mc-
Millan, and several years after that he
formed with his father-in-law the partnership
of McMillen and Lee, which was later expanded to become the firm of McMillen, Lee,
Ryan and Johnson.

Lee was retained as general counsel by the
Albuquerque First Savings Bank and Trust
Company, the first trust company chartered in

LEE, LAURENCE F.—*Continued*

New Mexico; later he was general counsel for the First National Bank and the Albuquerque Gas and Electric Company, as well as for the Occidental Life Insurance Company, of which he was elected vice-president after some time. (Subsequently Lee became, and still remains, vice-president of the Fernandez Company, the ranching enterprise headed by his brother Floyd.) In 1926 the Occidental Company transferred its headquarters from Albuquerque to Raleigh, North Carolina; and two years later, on election as president of the company, Lee moved to Raleigh. There (according to an article written for the *Eastern Underwriter* by John A. Park, publisher of the Raleigh *Times*) his reputation was that of "a blunt, plain-spoken, hardheaded businessman" who was "conspicuously civic-minded and generous in his private dealings." Lee and his family were residents of Raleigh until 1934, when Occidental acquired control of the Peninsular Life Insurance Company, and they established their home in Jacksonville, Florida.

As president of both the Occidental and Peninsular companies the former Albuquerque lawyer heads what *Business Week* has described as "a couple of firms that fall considerably short of what is usually thought of as Big Business," but which were "big enough to make Lee an important member of his industry." As such he became one of the organizers and earlier directors of the Institute of Life Insurance, considered the "public relations voice" of the industry; and in 1940, when the Temporary National Economic Committee was set up by Congress to investigate "concentration of economic power," he began to serve on the committee of five which represented 151 insurance concerns at committee hearings. Their report (which emphasized both the financial safety record of the insurance companies throughout the depression and the basically competitive nature of their business) received special attention in the insurance world. In 1944 he was elected president of the American Life Convention, an international organization of American and Canadian companies. A year later Lee was elected to the board of directors of the United States Chamber of Commerce and later was called upon to serve on President Truman's Loyalty Review Board and the Gordon Gray "dollar gap" committee. He became vice-president of the United States Chamber of Commerce in 1949.

The United States Chamber of Commerce was established in 1912 in response to a "call on businessmen" by President William Howard Taft to "form a national organization that would bring government a uniform business view" (*Business Week*). Today it is composed of 3,200 organization members—local, State and regional chambers of commerce and other trade and industrial associations. Sometimes called "the trade associations' trade association," the national chamber claims to speak for about 1,300,000 businessmen and differs from the National Association of Manufacturers in that its scope of membership is considerably broader while the influence of small business on its policy making is regarded as greater. The president is elected to a one-year term, and then he is eligible to become chairman of the board the following year and chairman of the executive committee the third year. On April 30, 1952, the final day of the fortieth annual convention, Laurence Lee was chosen to serve for the year 1952-53 as the national organization's twenty-fourth president. (Dechard A. Hulcy, his predecessor, became chairman of the board.) Lee has taken a year's leave of absence from the Occidental and Peninsular companies.

A policy statement adopted by the 2,500 delegates urged the termination of emergency wage and price controls, omitted a previous endorsement of universal military training, and supported passage of a Constitutional amendment to limit Federal taxation. In a separate vote on President Truman's seizure of the steel industry, the delegates adopted a resolution declaring that failure to challenge such action would be "to condone assumption of powers which can nullify the American concept of due process of law."

Organizations of which Lee is a member are the American Bar Association, the American Life Convention, the Association of Life Insurance Counsels, the Life Insurance Association of America, and the American Service Bureau. His fraternities are Pi Kappa Alpha and Phi Delta Phi, while his clubs are the Yale and Lawyers' in New York City, the Union League in Chicago, the Carolina Country, the Timaquana Country in Jacksonville, and the Florida Yacht in Jacksonville. The marriage of Laurence F. Lee and Eileen McMillen took place on September 16, 1914. They have two daughters, Elizabeth (Mrs. Lawrence A. Long) and Florence Odie (Mrs. J. B. Headley) and one son, Laurence Frederick, Jr., now vice-president and treasurer of the Peninsular Life Insurance Company. The life insurance company president has been described in a Chamber of Commerce release as "trimly set and on the tallish order."

References

Bsns W p104-06 My 3 '52 pors
East Underw 41:32 D 6 '40 por
Newsweek 39:76-9 My 5 '52 por
Business Executives of America (1950)
Poor's Register of Directors & Executives (1952)
Who's Who in America, 1952-53
Who's Who in Commerce and Industry (1951)
Who's Who in the South and Southwest (1950)

LEIGHTON, MARGARET (CARVER)
Dec. 20, 1896-   Author

Address: b. c/o Houghton Mifflin Company, 2 Park St., Boston, Mass.; h. 226 Palisades Ave., Santa Monica, Calif.

Reprinted from the *Wilson Library Bulletin*, Oct. 1952.

The writing of really distinguished historical fiction for teen-age readers is as rare as it is welcome. In Margaret Leighton's *Judith of France* (1948) and in her latest book, *The Sword and the Compass* (1951), reviewers have found a combination of lively style, excellent taste, and real historical interest.

Mrs. Leighton was born in Oberlin, Ohio, December 20, 1896, the daughter of Thomas Nixon Carver and Flora Frazee (Kirkendall) Carver. Both parents were of pre-Revolutionary stock which had gradually migrated from the east coast to the west, and Mrs. Leighton recalls many summer trips in her childhood to California and to Iowa to visit relatives. Her father's career brought the family east, however, first to Ohio, where he was professor of economics at Oberlin College, then to Harvard. Most of her schooling was in Massachusetts, except for a brief period in Paris and another in Lausanne. She took her B.A. degree in 1918 at Radcliffe College, majoring in social ethics, economics, and philosophy. An important influence on her writing ambitions was her friendship in college with the author Rachel Field, who later encouraged her to write children's stories.

In 1921, Margaret Carver married James Herbert Leighton, then a graduate student at the Harvard School of Business Administration. The next years were crowded ones for her, and, in her own words, ". . . my family rather swamped my literary efforts—four children in six years were enough, together with my attractive and energetic husband, to fill my life." The Leightons lived for ten years in Westfield, New Jersey, and in 1934, when her husband took a job in Washington, D.C., they moved to Ballston, Virginia, where they lived in an old house she later described in her book, *The Secret of the Old House* (1941).

After her husband's death in 1935, Mrs. Leighton moved with her four children to California, where her parents had settled. Here she began writing. "I live in a house covered with vines on a quiet street in Santa Monica, so near the edge of the cliffs overlooking the Pacific Ocean that we can hear the waves breaking on the sand—that is, whenever we are quiet enough to listen. Our household consists of my father and mother, who recently celebrated their sixty-third wedding anniversary, and the three small daughters of my son Jim, and myself. . . . My younger son comes home from his job on week ends, and my married daughters are not too far away to drop in frequently. So . . . we have plenty of excitement and activity."

Mrs. Leighton's first short story was published in the *Portal* in 1937. Since then she has had an active career, publishing stories and articles in a number of children's magazines, including *Boys Today, Child Life,* and the *American Girl.* Her books include a collection of ten short plays on the American epic, *Junior High School Plays* (1938), and novels which fall into two groups—first, adventure stories set in the contemporary scene, and second, historical fiction. The action of *The Singing Cave* (1945), for example, takes place on a ranch in southern California where a young

MARGARET LEIGHTON

western boy and a girl from New York spend an exciting summer. Virginia Kirkus found it "a fast-moving and well-written story," while May Lamberton Becker praised it for "combining attractions of a mystery with those of a ranch story." It was a Junior Literary Guild selection.

Her historical fiction ranges in subject matter from medieval France to early colonial America. Following the ancient dictum that it is the function of literature to teach as well as to delight, Mrs. Leighton is a careful scholar. In *Twelve Bright Trumpets* (1942), a collection of stories for older boys and girls, she described the life, manners, and customs of the Middle Ages. A similar background is the scene for *Judith of France,* a novel based on the life of the great-granddaughter of Charlemagne, which Ellen Buell of the New York *Times* called ". . . a distinguished piece of fiction for the transitional reading period of older girls." A. M. Jordan, in the *Horn Book,* commented, "This romantic young novel moves swiftly, giving vivid life to the ninth century in France and England."

Set partly in the American scene is the life story of the swashbuckling Captain John Smith told in *The Sword and the Compass.* In this volume (which is, incidentally, illustrated by her son James) Mrs. Leighton traces the hero's life from his birth in a small English village, his adventures in Turkey, where he was captured and sold as a slave, and his greatest adventure with the Jamestown colony in America.

Mrs. Leighton is currently at work in the fall of 1952 on another biography of an historical figure—Frederick the Great, for the Real People Series. Aside from her writing, she reports, her time is filled with "the usual occupations" of a housewife, mother, and grandmother. Her favorite reading at the moment is Joyce Cary and she has special admiration for Hope Muntz' novel of the last days of Saxon England, *The Golden Warrior.*

(Continued next page)

LEIGHTON, MARGARET—*Continued*

Blue-eyed and gray-haired, Mrs. Leighton is a Republican and a member of the California Writers' Guild, Author's League, and International P.E.N.

LEMONNIER, ANDRÉ (GEORGES)
(lĕ-mô"nyā' äʀ"drā' zhôrzh) 1896- French Naval officer

Address: b. c/o Supreme Headquarters, Allied Powers in Europe, Rocquencourt, France; h. "Les Lierres," 1 rue Pierre-Bourdon, Marly-le-roi, Seine-et-Oise, France

The international naval units of the Supreme Headquarters of the Allied Powers in Europe are under the supervision of French Admiral André Lemonnier, deputy naval commander to General Matthew B. Ridgway, Supreme Allied Commander in Europe. A combatant with the French Navy in both World War I and World War II, Lemonnier has received the Croix de

French Embassy Inf. Div.
VICE-ADM. ANDRÉ LEMONNIER

Guerre and the Legion of Honor from his Government. During the struggle for the liberation of France in the early 1940's, he succeeded in putting the French Merchant Marine back into commission and commanded the Free French naval units which joined the Allies in the liberation of Metropolitan France.

Born in 1896, André Georges Lemonnier was only seventeen when he became a combatant in the French naval forces of World War I on an aviso. The young man, who was planning to enter the Naval Academy, was assigned to the Marines, with which he fought in the Dardanelles and on the Macedonian front from 1914 to 1918, service which brought him two citations. Subsequently, upon his graduation from the War Naval School in which he stood

first in his class, Lemonnier held a number of commands, including those of a submarine (he is a specialist in submarine warfare), a torpedo boat, a destroyer, and a cruiser. One of his ships was the *Georges-Leygues.*

With the outbreak of World War II, Lemonnier joined the defense of Paris as commander of naval antiaircraft batteries named to defend the French capital, and, with the same units, saw duty in the fighting of 1939-40 in Belgium. Following the occupation of France by the Nazis, Lemonnier rallied to the French forces which, after the landing of the Allies in North Africa in November 1942, were continuing the fight for the liberation of their motherland, from overseas. It was he who put the French Merchant Marine back into operation in 1942, by gathering all the French commercial vessels to be found in North African ports and restoring them to a navigable state so that they could contribute to the Allied war effort. Directing the Merchant Marine Offices of the Free French forces "with rare competence and energy," stated a French Information Service press release, Admiral Lemonnier "in that particularly delicate post displayed excellent qualities as an organizer."

Named Chief of Staff and Commander in Chief of the Free French Navy on August 12, 1943, Lemonnier had under his command 300,000 tons of shipping, 3,000 officers, and 50,000 sailors, comprising both maritime and aeronaval elements. In a press conference given at that time, Lemonnier said, "We are conscious of the immense services which the Allies have rendered us by permitting us to reconstitute our Navy. Besides, our Navy does not constitute a separate unity, but fights along with the Allies in different fields of operation. . . .Despite our losses at Toulon, where more than half of the French fleet was destroyed, the situation of our Navy is less serious than it would appear to be." During 1943 he commanded the debarkation operations of the French in Corsica and in 1943-44 was a member of the French Committee for National Defense in Algiers. In 1944 he also commanded the French Maritime forces during the debarkation in Provence, where he himself landed near Fréjus with American Secretary of the Navy Forrestal, Vice-Admiral Hewitt, and General Patch. George Sessions Perry, describing in the *Saturday Evening Post* the reaction of liberated French citizens to the sight of a French admiral in a jeep with the Americans, quoted Secretary Forrestal as saying jocosely, "By electioneering real hard, we could elect Admiral Lemonnier Mayor of St. Raphael in the next election!" Upon the liberation of France in 1945, Lemonnier was made chief of the French Naval Staff, a post which he held until 1947; he was in 1950 appointed director of the Institut des Hautes Etudes de Défense Nationale. Lemonnier has also served as director of research in the Ministry of Defense and is a member of the French Higher Council of War.

On April 3, 1951, Vice-Admiral Lemonnier was chosen by General Eisenhower as Deputy Naval Commander of SHAPE (Supreme Headquarters of the Allied Powers in Europe).

"His chief tasks," reported the New York *Herald Tribune* (April 3, 1951), "will be to advise General Eisenhower on the best use of naval forces for defense of Europe, represent him in dealing with naval authorities of the twelve Atlantic states, and guide training of the combined land, sea, and air forces." As deputy naval commander, observed the New York *Times Magazine,* Lemonnier formed part of the military team that the Supreme Allied Commander "leads in the drive to weld an efficient and powerful multi-nation force for the security of the free world." SHAPE is the military arm of the North Atlantic Treaty Organization, formulated in a treaty signed by twelve nations in Washington, D.C., on April 4, 1949, and effective August 24, 1949. Implementation of NATO came about through bilateral agreements drawn up between the United States and each respective nation desiring military aid (Greece and Turkey subsequently became signatories). In December 1950 the NATO council convoked in Brussels came to an accord on the establishment of an "integrated force under centralized control and command" (*Encyclopedia Americana Yearbook,* 1952), which later became known as SHAPE. When General Eisenhower resigned from the post of Supreme Allied Commander for Europe in 1952 in order to become a candidate for the Presidency of the United States, he was succeeded by General Matthew B. Ridgway. On July 4, 1951, Lemonnier was appointed commandant for the first year of a projected NATO College to open in Paris in November for the purpose of training military and civilian leaders and to study all issues pertaining to the mutual defense system. Headed by Lemonnier, a group from the college in early September 1952 made a study of military conditions in Norway.

From the French Government Lemonnier has received the Croix de Guerre (1914-18 and 1939-45), l'Ordre du Mérite Maritime, and the Légion d'Honneur (Grand Officier, September 5, 1945). The Belgian Government has honored him with the Croix de Guerre Belge and the Ordre de la Couronne Belge (Grand Officier); the Government of the United States has named him a commander of the Legion of Merit, and the Government of Great Britain, a Knight Commander of the Order of Bath. The French admiral is a resident of Marly-le-roi, a suburb of Paris in the Seine and Oise department. Admiral and Madame Lemonnier (who was born Mademoiselle Lecerf) are the parents of five children: Claire, Claude, Rose, Anne, and Lise.

References

Climat N 2 '50
International Who's Who, 1952
World Biography (1948)

LETOURNEAU, JEAN (lĕ-tōōr″nō′ zhäN)
Sept. 18, 1907- French Cabinet Minister
Address: b. c/o Office of Minister Resident in Indo-China, Saigon, Indo-China

French military and political responsibilities in Indo-China are under the supervision of Jean Letourneau, who since 1950 has been Minister in charge of the Associated States of Indo-China and since the death of Jean de Lattre de Tassigny in 1952, Minister Resident in Indo-China with duties formerly performed by the French High Commissioner. Letourneau has conducted much of France's negotiations with the three autonomous States of Indo-China and with the United States for military aid in that region. A member of the French Assembly, Letourneau has also held a number of cabinet posts in Ministries of the Provisional and the Fourth Republics. His activity in the Resistance movement during the occupation of France brought him the Resistance medal with rosette.

Jean Letourneau was born September 18, 1907, in Le Lude, Sarthe, the son of Emmanuel and Juliette (Réveil) Letourneau. After receiving his Litt.B. degree from the Collège St. Louis in Le Mans, capital of the Department of the Sarthe, he continued his studies in Paris, where he was awarded his *licence* in law by the Faculty of Law. For a time thereafter he was prominent in the Catholic youth movement, which was also the training ground for other Christian Democrats, such as Georges Bidault and François de Menthon. Prior to World War II Letourneau was a member of the executive committee of the Parti Démocrate Populaire, described by *Encyclopédie Politique* as "favorable to conciliative methods and to the League of Nations" in external affairs, and in domestic matters "to trade unionism, collective bargaining, and a protective legislation for the wage earners." During that period Letourneau served on the editorial board of the magazine *Politique* and wrote frequently on foreign policy for the newspaper *l'Aube.* In 1938 he entered the employ of Société Générale in Paris. Later he became chief accountant of the Paris branch of the Central Hanover Bank and Trust Company of New York. A short time before World War II he was named managing director of the Compagnie Française des Charbonnages de Dakar in Paris.

After the signing of the Franco-German Armistice in 1940, Letourneau participated with Estienne d'Orves in the earliest resistance movement against the invader. In 1941 with François de Menthon in the South, he joined the Liberté movement. In collaboration with Georges Bidault, after 1941, he continued his clandestine work, while with Pierre Henri Teitgen and Francisque Gay, he prepared the reorganization of the French press to be undertaken after the war. Upon the Liberation of France in 1944, Letourneau was named Director of the Press Division of the Ministry of Information, retaining that post until the close of 1945. In November 1944 he became a member of the executive committee of the Mouvement Républicain Populaire, in some respects successor to the prewar P.D.P. Running on the MRP ticket Letourneau was elected Deputy from the Sarthe Department to the First Constituant Assembly on October 21, 1945, and to the Second, on June 2, 1946. Under the new Constitution of the Fourth Republic, he was

French Embassy Inf. Div.

JEAN LETOURNEAU

elected to the National Assembly on November 10, 1946, and re-elected on June 17, 1951.

In the successive Governments of the Provisional and of the Fourth Republic, Letourneau held a number of Cabinet positions. From January 27 to June 11, 1946, he was Minister of Post, Telegraph, and Telephone in the Cabinet of Félix Gouin, an assignment which he again held in the Cabinet of Georges Bidault from June 24 to November 28, 1946. Under Paul Ramadier, from January 22 to November 19, 1947, he was first Minister of Commerce, then Minister of Reconstruction and Urbanism. With the return of Bidault to power, Letourneau on October 28, 1949, again entered his Cabinet as Minister of France Overseas, retaining that portfolio until June 24, 1950. In that capacity, during May 1950, he criticized American State Department officials' demands for autonomous government in French African possessions. He was then Minister of Information in the brief Queuille Cabinet of July 1950. Named Minister in charge of the Associated States of Indo-China on July 12, 1950, Letourneau later was given the title of Minister Resident in Saigon in charge of the Associated States of Indo-China when he was appointed on April 1, 1952, to succeed the recently deceased High Commissioner Jean de Lattre de Tassigny in directing French military and civil affairs.

In October 1950 Letourneau was dispatched by Premier René Pléven on a special study mission to Indo-China, where he made a survey of the political situation, while General Alphonse-Pierre Juin did the same for the military. Conferences between Letourneau and Bao Dai, Chief of State of Viet-Nam, the following month resulted in an agreement for the French to finance a three-division Viet-Namese army,

with partial financing of the force to come from the Viet-Namese themselves. The filing of Letourneau's report with the French Cabinet in mid-November led to a decision to increase French naval and aviation action in the war area; and a subsequent Cabinet decision made him military as well as political arbiter in Indo-China, with direct access to Defense Minister Jules Moch for manpower and material. In a far-reaching policy statement late in November, Letourneau said that accords reached with the Indo-Chinese the previous year would be implemented "even more in their spirit than in their letter and with maximum of liberalism" and that French administrative facilities in Indo-China would be transferred to the three Indo-Chinese States of Viet-Nam, Cambodia, and Laos at the beginning of the new year; his statement was affirmed by a resolution of the National Assembly. With de Lattre de Tassigny, then Commander in Chief of the French forces in Indo-China and High Commissioner, Letourneau returned there early in 1951 to make another survey. For the first five months of 1951, he reported in May of that year, United States aid in artillery, aviation, and supplies had greatly helped the French offensive. At the end of the year, however, he characterized subsequent United States aid as "disappointing," since the supplies agreed upon at a September conference in Washington had not yet been forthcoming. When the French Assembly voted military credits for Indo-China at the end of December 1951, Letourneau stated that an armistice would not be sought with United Nations intervention, adding, "We shall not cease our efforts to put an end to the war but on terms which will respect the rights of Indo-China's populations, the rights of the free world, and the rights of France."

Arriving in Saigon in January 1952, Letourneau expressed fear of a Chinese Communist invasion of Indo-China; he also declared that France would take no unilateral action toward a settlement with the insurgent Indo-Chinese Communists, but would act in coordination with the three Indo-China States of the French Union. After a February conference with Bao Dai, Letourneau and the other consultants agreed that new top-ranking leaders, preferably to be drawn from among the Viet-Namese themselves, would be needed. By this means, he said in March, France would be able to have sufficient officers for her European commitments, while at the same time she could continue the fight in Indo-China. He also countered criticism of French censorship of the press in the war region by asserting that all of the liberty of information that could be permitted by military security had been allowed.

When he took up the post of Minister Resident in Indo-China in April 1952, Letourneau confronted unrest in Cambodia, where there was agitation against French supremacy in judicial, military, and economic matters. He returned to Paris late in May to participate with other French Cabinet members in defense discussions with United States Secretary of State Dean Acheson, devoted to increasing American military aid to France. Continuance of these discussions was carried on by Letourneau on a visit to Washington early in June, on the heels of a statement by Acheson to a Senate ccmmittee that the United States would not be able to give any aid in actual manpower to the French in Indo-China. With this Letourneau, reported the New York *Times*, expressed himself as substantially in agreement, save in the event of a Chinese Communist invasion of Indo-China, because "the very appearance of foreign troops in Indo-China might incite the Chinese to send their 'volunteers.'" In that case, he said in an interview with *France-Amerique*, France would seek United Nations intervention. As a result of the Letourneau talks, noted the New York *Herald Tribune*, United States military aid to Indo-China would probably be increased in the forthcoming two years, so that France would be freer to fulfill her obligations toward the North Atlantic Treaty Organization.

As president of the French delegation to the International Conference on Freedom of Information, held in Geneva in 1948 under United Nations sponsorship, Letourneau presented a discussion of the official French attitude toward that subject, which was reprinted in *Vital Speeches*, June 15, 1948. He also called for the formation of an International Information Council connected with the Economic and Social Council to issue international press accreditation cards and to review and correct errors in the press. In 1948-49 Letourneau was president of the French delegation to the Joint Committee for a French-Italian Customs Union. He was France's representative in 1949 to the Fourth United Nations General Assembly. Letourneau, who holds the Resistance medal with rosette, is a Chevalier of the French Legion of Honor. By marriage, on April 30, 1936, to Françoise Dhellemmes, he has three daughters.

References

Dictionnaire Biographique Français Contemporain (1950)
World Biography (1948)

LEVANT, OSCAR Dec. 27, 1906- Musician; actor; radio personality

Address: b. c/o Columbia Artists Management, Inc., 113 W. 57th St., New York 19; h. 180 W. 58th St., New York 19

NOTE: This biography supersedes the article which appeared in *Current Biography* in 1940.

Bringing to the world of entertainment a musical virtuosity combined with "brash humor" and verbal ingenuity, Oscar Levant has become well known to American audiences through his performances in radio, television, motion pictures, and on the concert stage. He first won wide public attention as the expert in music on the radio program *Information Please*, on which he made his initial appearance in 1938, and in 1940 gained further popularity as the author of the best-selling book *A Smattering of Ignorance*. Among the screen successes in which he had a role are *Rhapsody in Blue*, *Humoresque*, and *An American in Paris*. A

OSCAR LEVANT

concert pianist acclaimed in particular for his interpretation of the music of George Gershwin, Levant has appeared as soloist with a number of major orchestras in the United States.

Oscar Levant was born in Pittsburgh, Pennsylvania, on December 27, 1906, the son of Max and Annie (Radin) Levant. His father owned a small jewelry and watch-repair shop in the front of the house in which the family lived. Oscar was the youngest of four sons, all of whom studied a musical instrument, Harry and Howard the violin and Benjamin and Oscar the piano, while the girls of the family became pupils of the ballet. Practicing in an attic converted into a studio, over his father's store, the boy is said to have developed much of the musical technique and memory which later made him famous. While a student in the Pittsburgh public schools, he worked for a period on Saturdays as a shoe salesman and in his free time organized a band which played at school dances. Following his father's death, young Levant left the Forbes High School in his junior year to study music in New York City. To support himself, for a time he earned a dollar an hour playing the piano for children's ballet classes. Outside of work he attended recitals to which he was given free passes and studied piano with Sigismund Stojowski.

During the years that Levant was preparing himself as a concert pianist, he secured employment with several small dance bands. About the year 1923 he played the piano at a roadhouse, the Mikado Inn at Harmon-on-Hudson; then he worked for his brother Harry, who was conductor at the New York Winter Garden Theatre. At one time in the early part of his career he reportedly played in the orchestra for the stage production *Ladies First*. After a period as a member of a three-piece luncheon orchestra at the Hotel Ambassador, he joined

LEVANT, OSCAR—*Continued*

Dave Bernie's band at Ciro's night club. From Ciro's he went to London with Rudie Wiedoeft's band. In 1928 he played the piano in the speakeasy scene of Arthur Hopkin's stage success *Burlesque* and then went to Hollywood to act in Paramount's screen version of the play entitled *The Dance of Life* (1929). For about two years before returning to Broadway he remained in Hollywood composing music for motion pictures (one of which was *Street Girl*) and working as assistant to a producer of Western films. At this time he also wrote various musical compositions, including a piano concerto, two string quartets, a nocturne, and several popular songs, among these the successful "Lady Play Your Mandolin."

Upon meeting George Gershwin in 1929 Levant became that composer's devoted friend and admirer. As described by Maurice Zolotow in the *Saturday Evening Post* (October 21, 1950), this meeting had a paralyzing effect on the musical creativeness of Levant, who, reported Zolotow, played only Gershwin's music. To Levant, however, has been attributed the music and lyrics of the motion picture *In Person*, which was released in 1935. About a year after the death of Gershwin, Levant in the summer of 1938 met a young radio producer, Dan Golenpaul, who invited him to be a guest on the new program *Information Please*, on which Clifton Fadiman, John Kieran, and Franklin P. Adams appeared. His musical knowledge and original wit having made his performance on the program a success, Levant became one of the regular experts of the show, with which he remained until 1942. Audiences were especially impressed by his musical memory which enabled him to play an entire composition after hearing a fragment of its theme. He was also seen in motion picture versions of this quiz program.

Returning to Hollywood in 1940 after conducting the orchestra for the Broadway success *The American Way* in 1939, Levant resumed his motion picture career when he played a part modeled on his own personality in the Bing Crosby film *Rhythm on the River*. The next year he was cast in the role of the leftist columnist in the screen version of Clare Boothe's comedy *Kiss the Boys Goodbye* (1941). This was followed in 1945 by *Rhapsody in Blue*, the story of George Gershwin, in which Levant acted his "real life role" and recorded the title piece and *Concerto in F*, in addition to serving as adviser to the producer on little-known aspects of his friend's personality. On his performance in this film E. C. Sherburne of the *Christian Science Monitor* commented, "Carrying over well to the screen is Mr. Levant's style of brash humor which brought him wide popularity in *Information Please* radio programs. He is the chief custodian of the fun in this picture." Eileen Creelman wrote in the New York *Sun*, "His acid, smart-alecky remarks are one of the hits of the film"; while the *Variety* critic found, "He has the meatiest, brittlest lines and whams over the titular 'Rhapsody in Blue' with virtu-

osity and authority as befits a real-life confidant of the late composer."

Since 1945 Levant has been seen in a number of roles that accord with his own temperament, in *Humoresque* (1947), *Romance on the High Seas* (1948), *The Barkleys of Broadway* (1949), and *An American in Paris* (1951), which won an award of the Academy of Motion Pictures Arts and Sciences. In her review of *Barkleys of Broadway* Eileen Creelman remarked, "Levant's piano playing is far from small. His snarling comedy and his playing of the piano are equally entertaining." William K. Zinsser of the New York *Herald Tribune* observed that he "plays Gershwin with his usual impeccable touch." In the summer of 1952 Levant signed with Metro-Goldwyn-Mayer to act the part of a Broadway playwright in *The Bandwagon*, a musical film starring Fred Astaire.

Meanwhile on radio in October 1947 Levant began playing the piano and acting as a foil for Al Jolson on the *Kraft Music Hall*, a National Broadcasting Company program on which he was heard for two seasons. In 1949 he made the first of a series of regular appearances over television on the NBC *Who Said That?* For two performances in 1951 he was starred on the television quiz program *General Electric House Party* over the Columbia Broadcasting System, a short-lived replacement for the Fred Waring show.

Levant, who studied composition under Arnold Schönenberg from 1935 to 1937, has had his music played by the Boston Symphony (which introduced his *Overture 1912* and *Dirge*) and by the symphony orchestras of Cleveland, St. Louis, Rochester, Pittsburgh, Minneapolis, Brooklyn, and the National Broadcasting Company. It was his success on *Information Please* that led to demands for his appearance as a concert pianist and to his success in this field. After a year of work refurbishing his technique, he began giving concerts in 1942. Levant has appeared as soloist with the New York Philharmonic, Philadelphia Orchestra, Pittsburgh Symphony, Los Angeles Symphony, Detroit Symphony, and with other important orchestras in the United States. His annual Gershwin concert at the Lewisohn Stadium in New York draws an audience that often exceeds the seating capacity of the stadium by several thousand. In his *Program of Piano Music with Comments* he frequently appears as pianist-raconteur in solo recitals, offering no printed program but announcing the numbers as he goes along. For Columbia Masterworks he has recorded over a hundred classical compositions including the Khachaturian Piano Concerto (recorded with the New York Philharmonic Symphony) and works by Debussy, Chopin, Gershwin, Tschaikovsky, Beethoven, and Grieg. "Levant has a sonorous tone," Maurice Zolotow has written, "an exciting percussive technique, and a mastery of handling tricky rhythms and polyrhythmic effects in modern music."

As an author Levant has contributed articles on musical subjects to *Good Housekeeping, Harpers, Town and Country, Vogue,* and the *Saturday Review of Literature*. His book on music and musicians, *A Smattering of Ignorance* (1940), is filled with anecdotes about himself and his musical friends, including a tribute to Gershwin in the chapter characteristically entitled "My Life: or The Story of George Gershwin." The book is at the same time a compendium of serious comments on music, such as a defense of American music and a discussion of writing music for the screen. "An informal, racy, chatty book," was *Cue*'s description, "crammed with venomous anecdotes and acidly dogmatic judgments."

The "fabulous quality" of Levant's personality has given rise to many stories about his eccentric living habits, impudent wit, sullen manner, and the predominantly Freudian terminology of his conversation. He married a dancer named Barbara Smith on January 5, 1932; they were divorced shortly afterward. On December 1, 1939, he married the Hollywood actress June Gale. Their three daughters are Marcia Ann, Lorna, and Amanda. While not an athlete himself, Levant is an ardent baseball fan, his boyhood ambition having reportedly been to play professionally. The musician is medium tall and has a husky build, curly black hair, and large dark eyes.

References

N Y Herald Tribune p12 Mr 30 '41
N Y World-Telegram p7 Ag 24 '40
Sat Eve Post 223:24 O 21 '50
International Motion Picture Almanac, 1950-51
Who's Who in America, 1952-53

LEVI, CARLO (lä'vē) Nov. 29, 1902- Author; painter
Address: Via Dua Macelli 47, Rome, Italy

The Italian author, painter, and political journalist Carlo Levi is best known in the United States for his prize-winning *Christ Stopped at Eboli*, published in Italy in 1945 and in the United States in 1947. The book is the story of Levi's year (1935-36) of exile in a remote village in the Southern Italian province of Lucania, to which he was sent by the Fascist government for his wartime leadership in the resistance movement. Since his student days, Levi had crusaded against Fascism and the totalitarian state, during and after the war becoming an anti-Fascist editor and writer. Before this he had received his M.D. degree, but except for his year in exile did not practice medicine because he preferred to paint. He is also the author of two other books that have been translated into English and published in the United States—the philosophical essay *Of Fear and Freedom* (1950) and the novel *The Watch* (1951).

Carlo Levi was born November 29, 1902, in the North Italian industrial city of Turin, to Ercole and Annetta (Treves) Levi. His father, a merchant, was also an amateur painter; his mother was a sister of Claudio Treves, a Socialist Party leader who had opposed Mussolini since the early days of Fascism. With his brothers and his sister Luisa (who later became a practicing physician), Carlo was brought up in his native city, where he became actively interested in politics as early as his fifteenth year. In 1922, while a student at the University of Turin Medical School, he joined the anti-Fascist "underground" and became a contributor to a political review founded and edited by his close friend, Piero Gobetti, who was later killed by the Fascists. About this same time, Levi began seriously to take up painting, following in his early work the neoclassic style.

When he received his M D degree in 1924 from the University of Turin, he stayed for a short while at this institution as a medical assistant, engaged for some time in scientific and biological research. Then, according to an autobiographical sketch in the New York *Herald Tribune* (October 7, 1951), he "suddenly abandoned the practice of medicine in order to devote himself to painting." As a painter (stated *Art News*) he had by 1925 reacted against his earlier style and had become a postimpressionist. Equally effective in portraiture, landscape, and still life, he developed what a *Herald Tribune* art critic later described as "a determined quality in his painting, a directness which he relates to nature with considerable manual force." After a year of military service (1925-26), Levi, devoting his full time to painting, soon found his work winning recognition; he held successful one-man exhibits in Turin, Milan, Rome, Genoa, London, and Paris during the five years beginning in 1929.

In 1928 Levi took up residence in Paris, where two years later he helped to found the secret anti-Fascist Italian Action Party, three years later becoming a cofounder and the director of the new "underground" publication *Giustizia e Libertà* (*Justice and Liberty*). Levi returned to Italy in 1933, where he was twice jailed for anti-Fascist activity. In 1934, since nothing could be proved against him, he was released after a few months in a Turin prison; in 1935 he was sent to the notorious Regina Coeli prison in Rome, for opposing Mussolini's projected invasion of Ethiopia.

From that prison he was exiled in August 1935 to the isolated malaria-infested village of Gagliano in the southern Italian province of Lucania, for supposedly a three-year term. There he not only painted some of his best-known pictures but also amassed the material for his most famous literary work, *Cristo si è fermato ad Eboli* (*Christ Stopped at Eboli*), which was not written until almost nine years later. He spent less than one full year at Gagliano—a period which, he later told Mary Braggiotti (New York *Post*, June 19, 1947), "had more influence on his painting than any other period of his life, including the war." During this time, however, Levi was not left exclusively to his painting, for when he saw how many peasants were dying because of improper medical treatment, he became their doctor; and when the Fascists ordered him to desist, the peasants protected him and he treated them in secret. This year in exile was the only time he ever formally practiced medicine (Mary Braggiotti). Early in the summer of 1936 Levi was set free when Mussolini celebrated the capture of the Ethiopian capital of Addis

F. A. Russo, Inc.

CARLO LEVI

Ababa by declaring an amnesty for political prisoners.

Having gone to France in 1939, Levi was staying in a place overlooking the harbor of Saint Nazaire when World II began in September 1939. There and then he began to write, without (he has said) "any thought of publication," the eight chapters which were later to form the book *Paura della Libertà* (*Of Fear and Freedom*) and which were conceived as an introduction to a longer work describing "the contemporary crisis in its entirety" and proceeding to "a critical analysis of ideologies" and Levi's own views on the state and liberty, aesthetics, and religion. Levi was forced to interrupt his writing and return to Paris in December 1939. With the capture of the French capital, Levi fled to Cannes, taking his unfinished manuscript with him. Then in 1941, after Italy entered the war on the side of Germany, he went back in secret to his native land. "Levi was clapped into jail for two months after his arrival in Florence," Mary Braggiotti has related. "Thereafter he lived underground—that is, knocking on the doors of anti-Fascists in the dead of night and asking if he could sleep in their houses." During 1943-44 Levi was a leader of the resistance movement in the province of Tuscany, and the following year (1944-45) he undertook the editorship of the daily *Nazione del Popolo* (*The People's Nation*), issued in Florence as the organ of the National Liberation Committee. After the war, Levi served for about a year (1945-46) as the chief editor of *Italia Liberà* (*Free Italy*), the Action Party daily paper published in Rome.

Levi wrote his internationally admired *Cristo si è fermato ad Eboli*—recollections of his 1935-36 political exile in the village of Gagliano—during his "underground" existence in Florence between December 1943 and July 1944. He got the title of the book from the peasants who had told him: "We're not Christians—Christ stopped short of here, at Eboli." Levi in the introduction goes on to explain, "'Christian,' in their way of speaking, means 'human being.'" The book, vivid in its character studies of the inhabitants of a primitive, superstition-ridden community and powerful in its implicit condemnation of the totalitarian state, was published in Italy late in 1945, won the first Arianna Mondadori del Corriere Lombardo Prize, and "consistently topped Italy's best-seller lists" (*Newsweek*). When in April 1947 an English translation by Frances Frenaye was published in New York as *Christ Stopped at Eboli,* it was received with unqualified enthusiasm. Alfred Kazin, writing in the New York *Herald Tribune* Sunday book section (April 20, 1947), called it "the work of a gifted writer with a great sense of style and a happy ability to unite life to politics," while Professor Paolo Milano in the New York *Times* (April 20, 1947) found "the remarkable quality of the book . . . shown first in its portraits. . . . The downtrodden heroes . . . are the peasants. They are not picaresque or Tolstoyan . . . but timeless, speechless—as if they were animals, but burdened with a human consciousness of their lot." Milano explained that the book "has been called in turn a diary, an album of sketches, a novelette, a sociological study and a political essay. It has more than a trait of each genre; yet it remains as hard to classify as every beautiful book, or as the man who wrote this one."

Concurrent with the publication of the American edition of *Christ Stopped at Eboli* in the spring of 1947, Carlo Levi made his first trip to the United States, a two-and-a-half month tour under the sponsorship of the American Society for Cultural Relations With Italy. Shortly after his arrival, he told a New York *World-Telegram* reporter (April 11, 1947) that he had come to "gain support for a cultural rebirth in Italy . . . to get all the . . . necessities that are a part of rebuilding the educational side of life." By profession a painter, "ranking," in the opinion of Milano, "with the very best of his generation," Levi the next month exhibited a number of his paintings at the Wildenstein Galleries in New York City. At that time art critic Howard Devree (New York *Times,* May 18, 1947) observed, "Levi is a colorist and his impasto landscapes have strange swirling strength.... Monotypes of figures, executed in an original technique, perhaps owe something to Pompeiian wall paintings, yet they are modern and forceful."

Three years later (1950) came the publication in the United States of Adolphe Gourevitch's translation of Levi's book *Of Fear and Freedom*, eight chapters of which had been published in 1946 in Turin as *Paura della Libertà*. This received diverse criticisms in the United States. The *New Yorker* reviewer, calling it a "really sustained metaphysical prose poem, sharply didactic and humming with thoughts, conceits, and twists in logic," thought that "the book is remarkable because, for all its probing into the murky regions of man's mind and soul, it is as clear as spring water." Albert Guerard in the *Nation* found that "while each sentence is marvelously clear, each paragraph, each chapter, and the whole book are shimmering in a luminous haze, 'dark with excess of light.'"

The following year (June 1951) Levi's *The Watch* appeared in an English translation in the United States, after a 1948 publication in Italy as *L'Orologio.* This novel, based on modern life in Rome after World War II and concerned with the philosophical problems of time, evoked both favorable and unfavorable criticism. To Irwin Edman in the New York *Herald Tribune* (June 24, 1951), *The Watch* had "some of the virtue of *Christ Stopped at Eboli,* but only some and only spasmodically." The New York *Times* critic, Paolo Milano (June 24, 1951), said: "I love *The Watch.* I find it a broader and deeper book than *Christ Stopped at Eboli.*" *Time* (June 25, 1951) commented that "here and there, *The Watch* has patches of writing as good as anything in *Eboli.* But its pace is slowed by tedious, pointless speeches on Italian politics."

Since his visit to the United States Levi has contributed a number of articles to the New York *Times Sunday Magazine,* among them "Eboli Revisited" (March 13, 1949) and "Italy Fights the Battle of Illiteracy" (November 6, 1949); at home in Italy he regularly produces articles and drawings for *L'Italia Socialista* and other newspapers and periodicals. Outside of trips to exhibit his paintings in foreign countries, Levi, since the war, has lived in Rome, where he has a studio on the top floor of a "magnificent old seventeen century place" from which he can see the whole city (autobiographical sketch in New York *Herald Tribune*). In this residence, which he described in *The Watch,* he keeps a cat, a turtle, and a ping pong table which he uses "either as a drawing-board or for sport"; but he has not brought himself to keep here the owl which he portrayed on the cover of the Italian edition of *The Watch.* This owl, named Graziadio, has been painted so often by Levi that it has become the artist's signature.

Levi, who once told Mary Braggiotti that he preferred "painting to anything else," later wrote in the New York *Herald Tribune*: "Of the many enterprises I have undertaken in my life I consider only two to be fundamental; painting and writing." Consequently, he divides his time between the two, rising late to paint during the afternoon, reserving his writing for the night "when the darkness and silence induce a sense of solitude." The artist enjoys trying strange foods and likes good wine in small amounts. For reading he chooses the classics. Mary Braggiotti described him as "a stocky man of medium height with wild brown hair, civilized vital blue eyes and a quiet manner of expression," while the *Saturday Review of Literature* commented that he could be "sharply witty or expansively jolly."

References

Art News 46:21+ Je '47 por
N Y Herald Tribune Book R p27 O 7 '51
N Y Post Mag p35 Je 19 '47 por
N Y Times VII p4+ My 11 '47 por
N Y World-Telegram p12 Ap 11 '47
Sat R Lit 34:8 Je 30 '51 por
Chi è? (1948)
Columbia Encyclopedia (1950)
Enciclopedia Italiana (1949)
International Who's Who, 1952
Levi, C. Christ Stopped at Eboli (1947); Of Fear and Freedom (1950)
World Biography (1948)

LEVIERO, ANTHONY H(ARRY) (lĕ vēr'ō) Nov. 24, 1905- Journalist
Address: b. c/o New York Times Washington Bureau, 711 Albee Bldg., Washington 5, D.C.; h. 2445 Porter St., N.W., Washington 8, D.C.

The Pulitzer Prize for "distinguished national reporting" during 1951, awarded May 5, 1952, went to Anthony H. Leviero, a member of the Washington bureau of the New York *Times* and at present that newspaper's White House correspondent. The award recognized Leviero's "achievement in securing a record of the talks between President Truman and General MacArthur on Wake Island in October 1950" and the published account which appeared in the *Times* of April 21, 1951. When called to active World War II service from his work as a *Times* reporter, Leviero became a military intelligence officer and is credited with suggesting the name "Rangers" for the American counterpart of the British Commandoes. Later in the war he was chief of the publications branch of the Military Intelligence Division of the War Department General Staff. He joined the Washington bureau of the New York *Times* in September 1945.

Anthony Harry Leviero is a native of Brooklyn, New York, born November 24, 1905, and one of the six children (four boys and two girls) of Anthony Faustino Leviero, a masonry contractor, and Thomasina (Lepore) Leviero. After completing his grade schooling in Brooklyn, he began, at the age of fourteen and a half, to earn his own living, starting as an office boy and working up to clerk and auditor in maritime insurance and shipping concerns.

"I was always bookish," states Leviero (who was a student at the Alexander Hamilton High School during a part of this period, but did not graduate), "and turned to newspaper work as a result." This change in occupation occurred in 1926 when, aged twenty, he joined the New York *American* as a copy boy for a weekly wage of ten dollars. Following a period as a night police reporter for that paper in the Bronx, Leviero in 1928 became a general reporter for the Bronx *Home News* at thirty-five dollars a week. His connection with the New York *Times* started in 1929, and for the

ANTHONY H. LEVIERO

next twelve years his duties with that paper included coverage of courts and general assignments. At intervals during these early reportorial years he also took courses at Columbia University and the College of the City of New York.

Young Leviero had enlisted in the 106th Infantry regiment of the New York National Guard as early as April 1923 and twelve years later (January 1935) was commissioned a second lieutenant in the Military Intelligence Reserve. Called to active duty on March 1, 1941, as a first lieutenant, he was assigned to emergency duty with the War Department in Washington, and while there was called upon to suggest a suitable name for the new American fighting unit to be trained along the lines of the British Commandoes. Leviero's suggestion was "Rangers," which was adopted. "To me the term somehow had come to mean a sort of land freebooter, a reckless fellow who likes a scrape," he has stated. "It seemed to have a swashbuckle flavor." Soon afterward Leviero was advanced to captain in the Army of the United States and was sent to the European Theater of Operations as an intelligence officer (G-2); in 1942-43 he served in the same capacity first with the Eastern Assault Force and then at Allied Field Headquarters in North Africa. Leviero then went back to Washington in June 1944 to become chief of the publications branch of the Military Intelligence Division of the War Department General Staff and was so occupied until August 1945. At the time of his discharge he had the rank of lieutenant colonel in the General Staff Corps. On March 20, 1946, after his return to civilian life, Leviero received a War Department citation for "conspicuous service in expediting the Allied victory," the commendation referring specifically to his service in

"directing, editing and production of more than 5,000,000 copies of periodicals, monographs, and manuals on enemy activities for all echelons of the United States and Allied forces."

Returned to Reserve status from the General Staff Corps, Leviero ended his active service on November 28, 1945. He had meanwhile rejoined the New York *Times* and was assigned (September) to the Washington bureau. In addition to regular capital news coverage, he contributed to the paper's Sunday magazine section the articles "Army a la Mode" (May 26, 1946), "Blueprint for a Greater Washington" (June 9, 1946), and "Air War Across the Pole" (December 14, 1947), among others. He became the *Times* White House correspondent and in the course of that assignment wrote a series of articles for the Sunday magazine with such titles as "Press and President: No Holds Barred" (August 21, 1949), "Harry Truman: Musician and Music Lover" (June 18, 1950), and "How the President Makes Decisions" (October 8, 1950). Also (to quote from his notebook) he followed the Chief Executive "on a ski lift, train, airplane, seaplane tender, destroyer, crash boat, bus, jeep, ferry, and by foot" in the course of cross-country tours, political campaigning, and other Presidential activities. Leviero was one of the correspondents who accompanied the President to Wake Island for his historic conference with General Douglas MacArthur in October 1950. Somewhat less than a month later, on the afternoon of November 1, he was in an office at the White House at the time of the attempted assassination of Truman by two members of the Puerto Rican Nationalist party. He hurried to the scene at nearby Blair House, where the shooting happened, and wrote the lead story of the occurrence.

Leviero was the White House correspondent from November 1947 to March 1951, when he was given a roving assignment for a year to explore any phase of Washington affairs that promised to make news. On April 19, 1951, Leviero watched on television in the Washington Bureau office as General MacArthur delivered his message to Congress and heard MacArthur, who had been relieved of his Tokyo command, criticize the President's Far East policy as being "blind to reality." He recalled his own impression that the two had been in substantial agreement at the time of the Wake Island meeting. According to the account by Meyer Berger in *The Story of the New York Times*, Leviero decided that it might be well to ascertain what really had happened at the meeting. He therefore applied to three Administration sources for access to the official reports. The following morning one of these sources brought out the records for Leviero at a secret meeting but permitted him to take only such notes as he would need "to give the sense of these reports" and enjoined him not to quote anything directly. Leviero prepared a four-column story for the next morning's (April 21) *Times* in which he reported the General's assurance that victory would be achieved in Korea by Thanksgiving, his belief that the Chinese would not intervene, and his conviction that it would be possible to release the 2d Division for duty in Europe by January 1951. Other newspapers and syndicates later hinted that the Administration had used Leviero to "plant" the story in the press, to which suggestion Leviero replied: "No member of the President's staff ever volunteered to give me any kind of story. If I got exclusives, it was only by asking the right questions at the right time." Subsequently Leviero became the *Times* White House correspondent again.

The New York *Times* correspondent wrote for his newspaper (December 1951) a series of articles on American psychological warfare against the Soviet Union. Later, for the April 1952 issue of *Nation's Business,* he wrote a piece entitled "Two Can Play at Sabotage," which stressed the role played by the *Voice of America,* the German-staffed RIAS (Radio in the American Sector), and the Central Intelligence Agency in guiding undercover operations behind the Iron Curtain. The Pulitzer Prize awarded Leviero on May 5, 1952, for "distinguished national reporting," was specifically given for "his achievement in securing a record" of the Wake Island talks. It was one of several journalism awards for reporting annually bestowed, in accordance with the will of Joseph Pulitzer, by the trustees of Columbia University on recommendation of the advisory board of the university's School of Journalism. Prizes of $1,000 are given for local, national telegraphic, international telegraphic, international, and national reporting; and each is presented "for a distinguished example of a reporter's work during the [preceding] year, the test being strict accuracy, terseness, the preference being given to news stories prepared under the pressure of edition time, that rebound to the credit of the profession of journalism."

A New York *Times* colleague once described Anthony Leviero as a "quiet, bespectacled" newsman who "has none of the vices of the movie reporter, doesn't even smoke." "Bushy-browed, diligent" are adjectives applied to him by *Time.* The Pulitzer Prize winner has brown eyes and brown hair, is five feet eight inches in height and 157 pounds in weight. He married Fay Harrison, a newspaperwoman, on August 29, 1936. They have a child, Toni Harrison. The journalist is a Catholic; his political party is the Democratic. In Washington he belongs to the National Press Club. A member of the Audubon Society, he speaks of bird watching, as well as photography and fishing, as his recreation.

References

N Y Herald Tribune p16 My 6 '52
N Y Times IV p2 Ag 30 '42 por; p24 My 6 '52 por
Time 59:47 My 12 '52 por

LINDEMANN, FREDERICK ALEXANDER, 1ST BARON CHERWELL *See* Cherwell, F.A.L., 1st Baron

LINLITHGOW, VICTOR ALEXANDER JOHN HOPE, 2D MARQUESS OF Sept. 24, 1887—Jan. 5, 1952 Former Viceroy of India; entered British government service as member of agricultural committees; Civil Lord of the Admiralty (1922-24); chairman of the Royal Commission on Indian Agriculture (1926-28); chairman of the Joint Select Committee on Indian Constitutional Reform (1933); Viceroy and Governor-General of India (1936-43); chairman of the Midland Bank. See *Current Biography,* 1942.

Obituary

N Y Times p92 Ja 6 '52

LITVINOV, MAXIM (MAXIMOVITCH) July 17, 1876—Dec. 31, 1951 Russian Communist leader and diplomat; represented the U.S.S.R. in England for a short period after the Russian Revolution; during the 1920's headed Russian delegates to disarmament commissions and negotiated nonaggression pacts with a number of European nations; People's Commissar for Foreign Affairs (1930-39); Ambassador to the United States (1941-43); Deputy Minister of Foreign Affairs (1946). See *Current Biography,* 1941.

Obituary

N Y Times p1 Ja 2 '52

LLOYD, (JOHN) SELWYN (BROOKE) July 28, 1904- British Minister of State *Address:* b. c/o Foreign Office, London, S.W.1, England; h. 32 Queens Rd., Hoylake, Cheshire, England

The Right Honorable Selwyn Lloyd, who was named Minister of State in the British Foreign Office following the return of Winston Churchill to power in October 1951, ranks next to Foreign Secretary Anthony Eden in the conduct of Britain's international relations. He was Eden's deputy through the greater part of the United Nations General Assembly session at Paris from November 1951 to February 1952. In 1945 Lloyd, who had just completed six years' service in World War II, won his first seat in Parliament as the Conservative member for a Cheshire division. A barrister, he became a King's Counsel in 1947.

John Selwyn Brooke Lloyd, son of J. W. Lloyd, a physician, was born July 28, 1904, in Liverpool, England, across the Mersey River from the division of Cheshire which he now represents in the House of Commons. He prepared at Fettes College in Edinburgh for Magdalene College, Cambridge, where he was a leader in debating and president of the University Union in 1927. After taking an honors degree in classics and history, he proceeded to London to read law at Gray's Inn, was called to the bar in 1930, and returned to Liverpool to practice on the Northern Circuit. In Hoylake, in the Wirral peninsula between the Mersey and Dee estuaries, where he lives, he sought election to the Urban District Council and became its chairman in 1936. Then at the

British Inf. Services

SELWYN LLOYD

age of thirty-two, he was the youngest chairman that local body had ever had.

As a junior barrister Lloyd had built up a "considerable reputation" in pleading insurance cases before the threat of World War II caused him to join the Territorial Army (equivalent to the National Guard in the United States) in June 1939. Commissioned a second lieutenant in the Royal Horse Artillery, he was promoted to captain in January 1940, to major in the following July, to lieutenant colonel in 1942, and to full colonel in 1943, when he was invested with the Order of the British Empire and assigned as General Staff Officer at the headquarters of the 2d Army. Advanced in 1944 to brigadier—he was one of the few Territorials to reach that rank—Lloyd made a "D-Day" landing in Normandy and was mentioned in dispatches. He was elevated to the rank of Commander of the Order of the British Empire (C.B.E.) in 1945, and after the war received the degree of Commander in the American Legion of Merit in 1946. He also earned the Territorial Decoration. Today he is honorary colonel of the 349th Light Anti-Aircraft Regiment, Territorial Army.

In January 1945, while still in military service, Lloyd was adopted as prospective Conservative candidate for Parliament by the Wirral division of Cheshire, the incumbent member having decided not to seek re-election. Demobilized in May after Germany had surrendered, Lloyd returned to the Merseyside to begin campaigning. The three-cornered contest in the Wirral in July 1945 resulted in the election of Lloyd to the House of Commons by 42,544 votes to 25,919 for the Labor candidate and 14,302 for the Liberal. His constituency is normally Conservative (it "went Tory" by nearly 35,000 in 1931 and by nearly 26,000 in 1935), but the fact that Lloyd obtained a clear majority at a time when the country at large

was supporting Labor was of special interest to his defeated party's leadership.

The M.P. made his maiden speech in Commons on February 12, 1946, when he assailed the Labor-sponsored trade disputes and trade unions bill as one in which it was "possible to detect . . . the totalitarian bias of the Government" (London *Times*). He had also spoken on financial subjects and on the cotton trade—he criticized the Attlee Government's centralized pooling scheme for cotton. Meanwhile, he had reopened his barrister's practice in Liverpool. In May 1947 he "took silk" (that is, became a King's Counsel and is now a Queen's Counsel) and for the ensuing sixteen months was heard more frequently in the London courts. Lloyd was appointed recorder of Wigan in September 1948, in which capacity he was for the next three years the sole judge in that Lancashire manufacturing town's separate Court of Quarter Sessions. In Parliament he continued to be "devastating in debate" (*Time*) and was frequently called upon to "wind up" for the Opposition, especially on financial and economic matters. Lloyd also began, fairly early in his Commons career, what he himself has called "two and a half years of really hard labor" as a member of a Parliamentary committee to study the "thorny" question of leasehold reform.

Selwyn Lloyd's official connection with foreign affairs may be considered to have started in July 1948, when he was named as a substitute delegate to the first meeting, at Strasbourg in 1949, of the Consultative Assembly of the Council of Europe. In September he was a Conservative delegate to the thirty-eighth Conference of the Interparliamentary Union at Stockholm. Another of his activities outside the House of Commons was as a member of the committee set up in 1949 under Lord Beveridge to study the organization of the British Broadcasting Corporation. In that connection he visited the United States and Canada to study their radio and television systems (stated a release by the British Central Office of Information), came home to write a minority report in which he advocated the ending of the BBC's monopoly, the admission of sponsored programs, and the development of local stations. Returned to Commons by Wirral in the election of February 1950 (but still a member of the minority), Lloyd made a mark in the new Parliament as one of what the *Manchester Guardian* has characterized as a "band of zealots ready to prolong debate indefinitely and capable of doing so with argument that could not be dismissed as mere word spinning." At the Conservative party conference at Blackpool in the late summer of 1950 he made, in a few minutes, such a lucid explanation of the problem of leasehold reform that in the following December he was given the honor of opening debate for the Opposition on the leasehold property bill. (Opening debate is traditionally the prerogative of the "front bench," which is occupied by the party leaders and members who have held ministerial rank.)

With the return of the Conservatives to power in October 1951 the expectation was general that Selwyn Lloyd, as one of the outstanding "Young Turks" of the Conservative party, would be moved up to the front bench through some appointment carrying ministerial rank. The first backbencher to be advanced, Lloyd was on November 3, 1951, appointed to the post of Minister of State for Foreign Affairs, an office which had been held in the Labor Government successively by Hector McNeil and Kenneth Younger. The Minister of State is right-hand man to the Foreign Secretary and his deputy at conferences and in Parliament. While not a member of the Cabinet, he holds Cabinet rank. Thus, a few days after the announcement of his appointment, Lloyd was on his way to Paris with Foreign Secretary Anthony Eden and soon afterward took over the direction of the British delegation to the United Nations General Assembly, meeting in the French capital. At a session of the Political and Security Committee on November 22, 1951, he called on the Soviet Union for "good will" toward Western proposals for disarmament, and later was spokesman for the West in urging Western and Soviet leaders to meet behind closed doors to work out a disarmament plan.

In mid-January, in response to Andrei Vishinsky's presentation of a peace plan, Lloyd, again speaking for the West, stated that he welcomed the submission of the Soviet proposals, but was skeptical as to the outcome. "It is not wise to raise false hopes," he explained, because, he feared, when the Soviet points were analyzed for exact meaning, "great gulfs of disagreement" might continue to exist. Thomas J. Hamilton of the New York *Times* felt that Lloyd had "said the right thing when, without of course committing his Government, he gave the Soviet proposals a warm welcome in the hopes that they would prove real concessions." On January 28, 1952, in reply to a speech by Vishinsky, Lloyd declared that in case "aggression" in Southeast Asia was "in contemplation by the Chinese Communist Government or the Soviet Union or both, it should be clearly understood that the United Kingdom Government associates itself" with a statement made a few minutes earlier by the United States delegate John Sherman Cooper: Any such aggression would be viewed as "a matter of direct and grave concern" requiring "the most urgent and earnest consideration by the United Nations."

Lloyd is vice-chairman of the House of Commons branch of the British Legion, as well as deputy chairman of the Inns of Court Conservative and Unionist Association. His London club is the Carlton. Miss Elizabeth Marshall, also of Cheshire, became Mrs. Selwyn Lloyd on March 29, 1951. Described by the *Manchester Guardian* as having "a neat mind and a neat, keen manner," Lloyd is further characterized by *Time* as typifying "the millions of middle-class young Britons who went through the war . . . and desperately want to build an improving life for themselves and contribute to the progress of their countrymen."

References

Life 31:32 N 5 '51 por
Manchester Guardian p6 O 31 '51
Time 53:30 O 22 '51 por
Who's Who, 1951
World Biography (1948)

LLOYD, WESLEY P(ARKINSON) June 16, 1904- University professor
Address: b. c/o Guidance and Welfare Institute, Supreme Command Allied Powers, Tokyo, Japan; c/o Brigham Young University, Provo, Utah; h. 1171 Cedar Ave., Provo, Utah

A step toward the democratization of Japan was taken early in 1951 when the Ministry of Education of the Tokyo government requested the Allied occupation authorities to sponsor what is now known as the Japanese Universities Welfare and Guidance Institute. The director of this organization, which consists of

Wide World Photos
WESLEY P. LLOYD

five other leading American experts in student counseling and vocational guidance, is Dr. Wesley P. Lloyd, chairman of the Department of Philosophy of Education at Brigham Young University since 1939 and dean of students since the creation of that post in 1945.

Born in Ogden, Utah, on June 16, 1904, Wesley Parkinson Lloyd is one of the six children of Charles Edward and Lucy (Parkinson) Lloyd, who were of Welsh and English descent. The couple reared the four sons and two daughters in the faith of the Church of Jesus Christ of Latter-day Saints. Young Wesley spent most of his boyhood in or near the town of St. Anthony in southeastern Idaho, where the elder Lloyd was engaged in ranching and the real estate business. He attended the St. Anthony High School for two years (1918-20) and completed his secondary school education at the Latter-day Saints High School in Salt Lake

LLOYD, WESLEY P.—*Continued*

City, where he was prominent in athletics and debating. Graduated in 1922, he entered Brigham Young University at Provo. There he majored in the social sciences, participated in athletics, debating and other student activities, and had a part-time job as a salesman in a shoe store.

In his choice of a lifework he was, he says, greatly influenced by his parents and by two members of the Brigham Young faculty: on taking his B.S. degree in 1927 he chose education as his career. Lloyd's first appointment was as instructor in social sciences and athletics coach at the Midway High School at Rexburg, Idaho; but he was soon transferred to the Edmunds High School in the same town, and became its principal in 1927. In 1930 he was made principal of the Latter-day Saints Seminary at Grace, Idaho, and a year later was assigned to the same post at the seminary in Oakley, Idaho. Among the functions of both these institutions was the provision of formal training for young Mormon missionaries before leaving for their fields of labor.

In the fall of 1932 the young seminary principal returned to Brigham Young University to work for the M.Sc. degree in sociology which he received in 1934. A two-year scholarship enabled him to proceed to the University of Chicago for further postgraduate study. After teaching education at Brigham Young during the summer of 1935, he returned to the University of Chicago where, beginning in the following year, a fellowship at that institution's School of Divinity enabled him to complete the requirements for the Ph.D. degree in education and religion in 1937. His doctoral dissertation, entitled *The Rise and Development of Lay Leadership in the Latter-day Saints Movement*, stresses the value of the mission as "a practical training school for the lay leaders."

Wesley Lloyd now returned to Brigham Young University in the dual capacity of assistant professor of philosophy of education and acting dean of men. He became dean of men as well as an associate professor in 1938, and in 1939 was made a full professor and chairman of the Philosophy of Education Department. The following year (1940) saw the appearance of his *Learning to Live* and his appointment to a one-year term on the general board of the Young Men's Mutual Improvement Association (a Latter-day Saints organization) and to membership in the national committee on student orientation of the National Association of Deans and Advisers of Men. In the 1941-42 wartime years he was a member of the Defense Council of Utah County (in which Provo is located) and then, as now, served as bishop (voluntary pastor) of the Provo Seventh Ward. His article entitled "Character for Our Times" appeared in the October 1941 issue of *National Parent-Teacher*.

With the beginning of the 1945-46 academic year Lloyd became dean of students at Brigham Young University, this post (he states) having been created as part of a "new plan for higher education" which "centered . . . in

a study of the student and his needs." He was "charged with the administrative responsibility of directing an area of university life to be known as the Special Services and with the supervision of special committees responsible for such matters as admission and credits, attendance and scholarships, athletics, counseling for both men and women, health service, and student employment, housing, loans, organizations, and publications. (Its aim and first year's attainment are outlined in Dean Lloyd's paper "Administration of Student Personnel Service" in the *Association of American Colleges Bulletin* for December 1946.) The educator was elected to the presidency of the Utah Conference on Higher Education for the year 1946-47 and of the National Association of Deans and Advisers to Men for 1950-51. Other organizations in which Dr. Lloyd has been or is active include the Academic Council of the Western Personnel Institute, National Association of Student Personnel Administrators (president, 1949-50), the National Education and National Youth associations, and the Utah Academy of Arts and Letters. As chairman of the Field House fund committee at Brigham Young University, Lloyd was given much credit for raising funds for a million-dollar building on the campus.

The latest phase of Dr. Lloyd's career began with the announcement, in June 1951, of his appointment as director of the Japanese Universities Guidance and Welfare Institute, an organization sponsored by the Supreme Command of the Allied Powers at the request of the Japanese government's Ministry of Education. The idea is the outgrowth of a series of postwar visits by Japanese educators to American colleges, and the purpose of the Institute has been defined as "to help reorganize Japanese university life and to promote democratic relationships between faculty members and students." More precisely, as Lloyd explained to Fred M. Hechinger of the New York *Herald Tribune* just before he left for the Orient, the problem is that "the Japanese system of higher education, following closely on German academic lines, has long suffered from lack of personal cooperation between professor and student. . . . Under the old lecture method, with an almost unbridged gulf between lecturer and class, unquestioning acceptance of authority and superior wisdom had strengthened the Japanese national trait of passive subservience," while at the same time "little attention was paid to the student's individuality or his personal and career problems." The special aims of the institute will accordingly include "the development of student organizations and activities (both in class and extra-curricular), the administration and philosophy of guidance services and the use of occupational information; and the place of women in higher education and in a democratic society." The institute, which began to function September 1, 1951, has a staff of six and is assisted with technical advice by the American Council on Education and a committee of educators under the chairmanship of Dean E. G. Williamson of the University of Minnesota. At the universities of Tokyo, Kyoto, and Fukuoka, the institute established three major stations to deal with the three types of Japanese universities: national, prefecture, and independent. Some 240 faculty members from these universities are expected to devote full time to work with the institute.

Wesley P. Lloyd and Lillie Murdock first met as fellow undergraduates at Brigham Young University. They were married December 30, 1927, and are the parents of two sons, Kent and Gary. The educator has a height of six feet, a weight of 185 pounds, green eyes, and brown hair. He belongs to the Timpanogas Knife and Fork Club, of which he was president during 1949-50. Among his recreations are basketball, hiking, and reading.

References

Leaders in Education (1948)
Who's Who in America, 1950-51
Who's Who in American Education, 1947-48
Who's Who in the West (1951)

LLOYD-GEORGE, GWILYM (gwĭl'ŭm) Dec. 4, 1894- British Minister of Food

Address: b. c/o Ministry of Food, Dean Bradley House, Horseferry Rd., London, S.W.1, England; h. 231 St. James Court, Buckingham Gate, London, S.W.1, England

When the British Conservative party came to power in October 1951, Major the Right Honorable Gwilym Lloyd-George was appointed Minister of Food, with the duty of controlling the purchase and distribution of various foods in the light of import restrictions, rationing, and other difficulties in world markets. A Liberal, elected for Newcastle North with Conservative support, Lloyd-George previously had held two minor ministerial posts as Parliamentary secretary and then had served as Minister of Fuel and Power in the wartime Coalition Government from 1942 to 1945.

Gwilym Lloyd-George was born in Criccieth, North Wales, Great Britain, December 4, 1894, the second son of David Lloyd George, World War I Prime Minister, and of Margaret (Owen) Lloyd George, daughter of Richard Owen of Criccieth. (The original name was George, but the Lloyd was invariably used with it. When three months before his death in 1945, David Lloyd George was created Earl Lloyd-George of Dwyfor, the family name remained as before, but the peer's title was spelled with the hyphen. Subsequently Gwilym elected to add the hyphen to his family name, lining it up with the title.) He was educated at Eastbourne College and at Jesus College, Cambridge, where he read for the Mechanical Science Tripos (engineering), but his schooling was interrupted by World War I. He joined the Royal Artillery in 1914 and served in France throughout the war until 1918, being mentioned in dispatches and reaching the rank of major.

In 1922 (the year his father's Coalition was broken up by the celebrated "Carlton Club meeting" of the Conservative party), Gwilym Lloyd-George was elected to Parliament as a Liberal member for Pembrokeshire, Wales; in 1924 he was appointed assistant to the Liberal Whip in the House of Commons. After losing his seat in the House the latter year, he stayed out of active politics for the next five years while he worked as a director of various companies. In 1929 he returned to Parliament, again for Pembroke, and remained there until 1950, when he was displaced by only 129 votes out of a total of 50,000 cast. In the election of 1951 he stood for Newcastle North as a Liberal-Conservative and was elected, although the Conservative vote was split by a rival candidate.

Lloyd-George began his ministerial career as Parliamentary secretary to the Board of Trade in the National Government formed by Ramsay MacDonald in 1931, but he did not perform this function for long, resigning on a point of principle. Reappointed to the same office in 1939, he retained it until 1941, when Winston Churchill appointed him as Parliamentary secretary to the Ministry of Food. At the end of a year there he was promoted, in 1942, to full ministerial status as Minister of Fuel and Power, serving in that capacity until 1945. Announcement of his new appointment was made in June 1942, when the Government published a White Paper telling that it had taken over the British coal industry and had drawn up a plan for consumer rationing. At the time Lloyd-George took office, there was a deficit of 11 million tons of coal, but a year later the Minister announced that the coal "gap" had been closed (New York *Times*, April 15, 1943). Two months after this announcement, however, he disclosed, during a debate in the House of Commons on the Government's efforts to step up coal production, that 4½ per cent of the miners, who absented themselves from work unnecessarily, were costing the country 8 million tons yearly.

By the following October Lloyd-George disclosed a plan to conscript men for mines on the same basis as for the armed forces. And two months later Labor Minister Ernest Bevin announced that for the first time in Britain's industrial history ballots would be drawn to determine which young men between the ages of 17 and 25 years would be drafted as the first contingent of perhaps 30,000 new miners. The spring of 1944 witnessed a widespread wave of strikes in the coal fields in which the veteran miners—not the new draftees—participated. By July of that year Lloyd-George made public statistics on the decline of the British coal industry since 1938, stating that "coal strikes this year have cost Britain more than 2 million tons in the first quarter alone" (New York *Times*, July 9, 1944).

During Labor's tenure of office, from 1945 to 1950, Lloyd-George served only as a member of Parliament. In January 1946, when House of Commons' members were debating the Labor Government's legislation to put the entire coal industry under full public ownership, Lloyd-George led the Conservative attack on the measure. He stated that "he had kept an open mind on the question and was not convinced that nationalization would solve Britain's coal problem. It would drag the industry in to

British Inf. Services

GWILYM LLOYD-GEORGE

politics, he said, with no adequate safeguards as to how the nationalized coal mines would be run" (New York *Herald Tribune*, January 31, 1946).

With the Conservative accession to power in October 1951 Lloyd-George, who had lost his seat in 1950, was returned as a Liberal (with Conservative support) for Newcastle North (Newcastle-upon-Tyne), with a majority of 6,925 over his Labor opponent. At that time the London *Daily Telegraph* cited him as a possible successor to Colonel Clifton Brown in the Speakership of the House of Commons, while the London *Evening News* described him as "an acknowledged authority on parliamentary procedure." The post to which he was assigned, however, was Minister of Food.

Assuming his new office shortly before Christmas, Lloyd-George announced a reduction in the meat ration and a refusal to grant the usual Christmas food bonus. This move was at once described by the Labor opposition as a "Scrooge-like" procedure, while Conservatives argued that this step had been necessitated by Labor's previous handling of the food situation. On December 21, 1951, Lloyd-George signed a multilateral agreement with Commonwealth sugar exporters to run to the end of 1959, designed to secure (according to the London *Daily Telegraph*) "the orderly marketing of Commonwealth sugar up to 2,375,000 tons a year." In February 1952 he announced the price decontrol of soap, semolina, cocoa, drinking chocolate, and flour confectionery and the next month he was reported in the London *Sunday Times* as saying that the food outlook was "not rosy," but that, "once the overriding problem of the adverse balance of trade has been solved and the country is solvent and secure, the food problem can, and will be, tackled comprehensively and successfully."

In the summer of 1952 the House of Commons expressed confidence in the Conservative Government's food policy by defeating a Laborite motion by 301 votes to 274. Denying during this debate that the food problem had become more acute since the Conservatives took office, Lloyd-George maintained that "food prices soared above wages even more rapidly during the last year that the Labor Government was in power" (New York *Times*, July 1, 1952). In accordance with the Government's policy of reducing subsidies on foods that had been sold below cost to the consumer for many years, Lloyd-George in September told the British that the price of butter, margarine, fats, cheese, sugar, and bacon would go up. As of that month all of these products in addition to tea were rationed, as were meat, eggs, chocolates, and candy. In early October 1952 the Government announced that tea rationing would be discontinued.

Lloyd-George is the only Welsh-speaking Minister in the Conservative Government. Calling him an "easy and persuasive speaker," the *London Daily Telegraph* reported in November 1951 that Lloyd-George had dealt with a string of twenty-four questions and had "answered all with good humor." Delos W. Lovelace in the New York *Sun* described the Minister in 1944 as "smooth faced, smooth-haired, stocky, and with eyebrows that break at an angle as sharp as a sergeant's stripes." Writing before the elder Lloyd George's death, Lovelace said that Gwilym, his sister (Lady Megan), and their father, "M.P.'s all, lock hands in a political threesome [which was sometimes called the] . . . United Liberal party. They certainly are, especially where the senior Lloyd George is concerned. Say a word against his long-gone but still talked-of Prime Ministership and both Gwilym and Megan are after you hot and heavy."

On June 14, 1921, Lloyd-George married Edna Gwenfron, a Welsh woman and daughter of David Jones of Gwynfa, Denbigh; they have two sons, David and William. The Minister is a member of the London Welsh Rugby Club, the Boodle's Club, and the Manchester Reform Club, of which he was president in 1944. He enjoys grouse-shooting and in his younger days liked to play cricket and Rugby football.

References

N Y Sun p18 Ap 11 '44
Burke's Peerage (1949)
Who's Who, 1952

LOCKE, EDWIN A(LLEN), JR. June 8, 1910- United States Government official; banker

Address: b. c/o Department of State, Washington 25, D.C.; c/o Chase National Bank, 18 Pine St., New York 15; h. 1150 5th Ave., New York 28

Edwin A. Locke, Jr., is the special diplomatic official named by President Truman in November 1951 to administer $160 millions in American economic and technical aid to eight countries of the Near East. Locke in the years of World War II served the nation in a series of administrative and confidential capacities, most notably as executive assistant to Chairman Donald Nelson of the War Production Board and as personal representative of the President in China. His new official title is "Special Representative of the Secretary of State to Coordinate Economic and Technical Assistance in the Near East" and carries with it the personal rank of Ambassador. Before his appointment to this post, he was a vice-president of the Chase National Bank of New York City.

Born in Boston, Massachusetts, on June 8, 1910, Edwin Allen Locke, Jr., is one of the four children of Dr. Edwin Allen Locke and the former Elizabeth Gilmor Ferguson. Young Locke attended the Country Day School at Newton, a suburb of Boston, and after graduation therefrom in 1927 enrolled for an additional year of preparation for college at Phillips Academy (Exeter, New Hampshire) before proceeding to Harvard University, where he took his B.A. degree *cum laude* in June 1932. He entered the employ of the Chase National Bank in the following September, spent a year working in various departments at the bank's main office in New York City, and in 1933 was assigned to the Paris branch. Next, after several months at the London branch beginning 1935, he returned to the main office in New York City in April 1936. Four years later he was granted leave of absence to begin a period of national and wartime service which was to extend until the end of 1946.

Locke's first governmental appointment, effective in November of 1940, was to the office of the Coordinator of Purchases of the Advisory Commission to the Council of National Defense, under Donald M. Nelson. Two months later (January 1941), when the Office of Production Management was set up at Washington, Locke was made Assistant Deputy Director of the Priorities Division, and as such was principally occupied with problems relating to lend-lease for Great Britain and the Soviet Union.

In October 1941, when Donald Nelson became Executive Director of the newly created Supply Priorities and Allocation Board, he made Locke his deputy chief staff officer; then, in January 1942, when Nelson was elevated to the chairmanship of the War Production Board, he named Locke his executive assistant. For a short while thereafter Locke's work was mainly concerned with priority privileges for Canadian manufacturers. In the following May, as the result of Allied shipping losses to submarine attacks, a committee of experts was set up by the WPB to study the possibility of large-scale development of cargo planes; with this body Locke also worked. Its first report, completed in six weeks, spurred the manufacture and successful use of the C-46 and kindred aircraft. Locke gave a comprehensive survey of the problem in his address "Cargo Planes," which was delivered at the Maryland Academy of Science in Baltimore on August 5, 1942, and published in the September 9 issue of *Vital Speeches*. Other addresses made by Locke in this period were to the Canadian Club of Montreal on "The United War Effort of Canada and

EDWIN A. LOCKE, JR.

the United States" (June 29, 1942) and to the Canadian Club of Toronto on "North American War Production" (October 5, 1942). Reportedly Locke became acquainted with Truman when the WPB had dealings with the Senate War Contracts Investigating Committee, then headed by Senator Truman.

As executive assistant to Donald Nelson, Locke accompanied the War Production Board chairman on an official visit to Canada in July 1943, and later in the same year (September and October) went with his chief on a Presidential mission to Great Britain, North Africa, and Russia. In August and September of the following year Nelson and Locke were engaged in another Presidential mission—this time to the Soviet Union, China, Australia, and New Zealand. Nelson's reports to President Roosevelt early in October 1944 resulted in his appointment as personal representative of the President to foreign countries and as head of an American production mission to Nationalist China. Again he chose Locke as his executive assistant, and in November the two, with a staff of assistants, were in Chungking. There, at the request of Generalissimo Chiang Kai-shek's Minister of Economic Affairs, Locke (reported *Time*) "laid in a supply of head towels and midnight oil" and within four days had drafted an "organic law" for a Chinese War Production Board which, five months later, was "functioning smoothly" and "was more streamlined and less hampered by red tape than Washington's WPB had ever been. It brought Chinese industry and government together for the first time."

Shortly after the death of President Roosevelt in April 1945, Donald Nelson submitted his resignation. It was accepted on May 12 by President Truman, who at the same time announced the appointment of Locke as Nelson's successor as personal representative of the

LOCKE, EDWIN A., JR.—*Continued*

President to foreign countries. "I want you to assume responsibility for and direction of the (China) mission until arrangements are completed to wind it up," the President told Locke in his letter of notification; Locke was further authorized to accept appointment as economic adviser to Chungking. The mission of about twenty American industrial specialists continued to maintain (in the words of an official White House release) "close collaboration with the Chinese Government," and following the surrender of Japan gave aid to that government "in dealing with initial problems of reconversion and industrial revival."

On September 29, 1945, accordingly, President Truman announced that he was sending Locke again to China to conclude the work of the war mission and to discuss the ways in which the industrial experience of the United States could be best utilized to aid sound peacetime economic reconstruction and development. Locke would (stated the official news release) "give particular attention to the immediate situation confronting the Chinese as a result of China's acquisition of large industries in Manchuria and other liberated provinces." On March 19, 1946, Truman named Locke as his special assistant and assigned him, among other duties, to work on governmental reorganization plans. Late in December, however, Locke resigned this post to return (January 1, 1947) to the Chase National Bank as a newly elected vice-president.

When Locke left the White House staff at the end of 1946, President Truman told his outgoing special assistant in a letter: "You must not be surprised if from time to time I call upon you for advice and assistance." An important call came on November 13, 1951, when the President announced that Locke had been appointed special representative of the Secretary of State to coordinate economic and technical assistance in the Near East and that he had that day approved for Locke the personal rank of Ambassador. The appointment was seen as hastened by the need to withstand Communist pressures and to offset in the Moslem world the adverse effects on Western prestige of the ousting of the Anglo-Iranian Oil Company from Iran, the renouncement by Egypt of her treaty with Britain, and anti-French and anti-American demonstrations in Morocco. The assistance program was made possible by Congress' approval of $160 millions for Egypt, Israel, Jordan, Saudi Arabia, Syria, Lebanon, Iraq, and Yemen (excluding Iran) as part of the Mutual Security Act passed in October 1951.

The New York *Times* editorial opinion (November 15, 1951) was that the fund was inadequate. "At first sight," stated this newspaper, "it seems as if it ought to be easy to spend $160,000,000 in a region of eight or nine countries where needs are limitless and all the wealth of the United States could do no more than alleviate an unfathomable misery. In reality nothing could be harder. . . .The amount of money is so small in relation to the needs that it has aroused resentment, rather than gratitude." A New York *Herald Tribune* editorial was likewise pessimistic, but declared that "there can be nothing but applause for the appointment" of Locke, who was sworn into office on November 15, 1951. Locke, whose headquarters are at Beirut, Lebanon, told newsmen that he expected his assignment to last "at least two years." Before his departure for his post on December 9 he stated at a press conference that the disposition of the aid would be decided only after careful surveys since the relations among the nations involved are delicate. The greater part of the funds may be used to stimulate agricultural and industrial productivity in accordance with the Point Four approach. "What Point Four is after," Locke said in an interview for the New York *Post*, "is to improve the lot of the ordinary fellow." The Ambassador was named by President Truman on January 17, 1952, to represent the United States on the Advisory Commission of the United Nations Relief and Works Agency for Palestine refugees in the Near East; his appointment was confirmed by the Senate the following month.

Locke is a director of the Munson Steamship Line. Among the organizations in which he has been active in the postwar period are American Youth Hostels (treasurer), the National Multiple Sclerosis Society (treasurer), and the China Medical Board (trustee). He was New York City chairman of the Planned Parenthood Campaign in 1948. Mrs. Locke is the former Dorothy Q. Clark, who for a time was a volunteer worker on courier duty for the Frontier Nursing Service ("nurses on horseback") in the Kentucky mountains. The Lockes, who were married June 16, 1934, have one daughter, Elizabeth Eliane, and two sons, Edwin Allen 3d and Benjamin Clark. "Amiable, energetic, lithe" are adjectives applied to the official; he is an even six feet in height, weighs about 160 pounds, and has hazel eyes and brown hair. He is an Episcopalian and a Democrat. His two New York clubs are the Harvard and the Racquet and Tennis, his Washington club is the Metropolitan.

References

Bsns W p20 My 19 '45 por
Christian Sci Mon p9 D 11 '51
N Y Herald Tribune p1 N 14 '51 por;
II p1 N 18 '51 por
N Y Post p2 Mag N 25 '51 por
N Y Times p1 N 14 '51 por
N Y World-Telegram p15 N 17 '51 por
The Chase p10 Jl '45
Business Executives of America (1950)
International Who's Who, 1951
Who's Who in America, 1950-51
Who's Who in Commerce and Industry (1951)
World Biography (1948)

LORD, MARY STIMSON PILLSBURY

See Lord, Mrs. O. B.

LORD, MRS. OSWALD B(ATES) Nov. 14, 1904- Organization official

Address: b. c/o Citizens for Eisenhower-Nixon, 51 E. 47th St., New York 17; h. 770 Park Ave., New York 21

Prominent for twenty-five years as a volunteer worker in the fields of public health and social welfare, Mrs. Oswald B. Lord in March 1952 was elected president of the National Health Council. Concurrently she holds the posts of chairman of the United States Committee for the United Nations International Children's Emergency Fund and, since August 1952, of cochairman of Citizens for Eisenhower-Nixon. Among earlier positions filled by Mrs. Lord were the presidency of the New York Junior League, national chairmanship of the New York World's Fair National Advisory Committee on Women's Participation, and chairmanship of the Civilian Advisory Committee of the Women's Army Corps.

Born in Minneapolis, Minnesota, on November 14, 1904, the daughter of Charles Stimson and Nelle Pendleton (Winston) Pillsbury, Mary Stimson Pillsbury Lord was the granddaughter of Charles Alfred Pillsbury, flour merchant. Her great-grandfather was Colonel John Harrington Stevens, one of the founders of Minneapolis. After attending St. Timothy's School in Catonsville, Maryland, she entered Smith College in Holyoke, Massachusetts. Here she first became interested in social work when she volunteered to care for children of sick or working mothers. Upon graduating with the B.A. degree (*cum laude*, with special honors in French) from Smith in 1927, she returned to Minneapolis to spend two years training as a social worker with the Family Welfare Association. She was married to Oswald Bates Lord, a textile merchant, in December 1929 and the following month they moved to New York City.

After her marriage Mrs. Lord continued her volunteer social welfare work. Attributing this to her education, she has said: "If one's intellectual interests have been stimulated at college, as mine were at Smith, one cannot settle down into an inactive life . . . lying in bed until noon and worrying about nothing but the dinner party that's coming off" (New York *Herald Tribune*, February 19, 1940). For five years, beginning in 1930, she was a voluntary case worker for the Charity Organization Society, now known as the Community Service Society, in New York City. During her term (1936-38) as president of the Junior League of New York, she sponsored the experimental "housekeeper service" to take care of families in which a mother's long illness might otherwise entail breaking up the home and placing the children in an institution. From 1939 to 1943 she served as vice-president and director of East Side Settlement House in New York City.

The 1940 New York World's Fair brought Mrs. Lord two other posts—chairman of the National Advisory Committee on Women's Participation in the Fair and director of the hospitality program. During this same period, as vice-president of the Woman's City Club, she

MRS. OSWALD B. LORD

frequently attended meetings of the City Council. In 1941 she accepted the chairmanship of the Citizens' Health Committee of the New York City Department of Health, joined the Nursing Committee of the Henry Street Visiting Nurses, and became cochairman, with Marshall Field, of the New York City Defense Recreation Committee. Another defense post came her way on September 27, 1941, when Mayor La Guardia appointed Mrs. Lord assistant director of Civilian Defense for the Second Corps Area, comprising New York, New Jersey, and Delaware. In accepting this position, which she held until 1943, Mrs. Lord said: "I believe my work as cochairman of the New York City Defense Recreation Committee and my job as chairman of the National Advisory Committee on Women's Participation in the World's Fair will help me most. . . .As a case worker I visited many homes. I think I know something of housewives' everyday problems—the rising cost of living, sons drafted, or husbands called to out-of-town defense jobs" (New York *Post*, September 31, 1941). It was her task to help co-ordinate the work of women's organizations through volunteer offices of Civilian Defense.

Chairman of the Women's Council of the Greater New York Fund in 1943, Mrs. Lord was also during that year chairman of the Women's Activities of the National War Fund, a federation of voluntary Federal relief agencies which placed all the recognized war charities under one office and offered specialized welfare and casework services for children, the aged, and the disabled victims of the war. In an article, "Voluntary Agencies' Role in Europe" (*Survey*, August 1945), Mrs. Lord, describing the fund as essential in building world peace, stated that "substantial peace depends on quick return of mental and physical health to stricken Europe." Another fund of which Mrs. Lord

LORD, MRS. OSWALD B.—*Continued*

was chairman in 1943 was the Women's Division, New York War Fund.

The War Department in September 1944 appointed Mrs. Lord national chairman of the Civilian Advisory Committee for the Second Service Command of the Women's Army Corps to aid in WAC recruiting. She organized the Fifth Avenue WAC recruiting station in New York City and in May 1945 toured overseas WAC installations to study the needs of more than 7,000 WACs in England and France, 1,600 in the Mediterranean area, and 500 in the Middle East. She recommended to the War Department that those WACs who had acquired sufficient points for discharge should have an equal opportunity with the servicemen to return home. In 1946 Mrs. Lord served as secretary of the Board of Community Chests and also as assistant pre-convention manager of the "Donovan for Senator" campaign.

Upon the organization in January 1948 of the United States Committee for the International Children's Emergency Fund, Mrs. Lord was elected its chairman. "This committee, made up of seventy prominent educators, religious, political and labor leaders and the heads of women's clubs and business organizations, was formed . . . to acquaint the public with the work which the Children's Fund is doing to help supply medicines, clothes and food to millions of children in Europe and the Far East" (New York *Times*, March 7, 1949). Mrs. Lord said the United States committee "would concentrate on 'promoting' the work that the Fund is doing by a year-round effort to inform the public where its dollars are being spent." The United States so far has contributed the largest amount to this fund—$75 millions. During August 1948 Mrs. Lord toured European countries, including a few behind the Iron Curtain, to ascertain how the food supplied by the International Children's Emergency Fund was being distributed. She inspected homes, hospitals, schools, orphanages, and day camps in Poland, Czechoslovakia, Austria, Hungary, Yugoslavia, France, and Germany and presented a report, "Consider These Children," to President Truman at a White House Ceremony on November 16, 1949. In it she stated that the fund had provided "food, clothing, and medical care for more than 6,000,000 children in many parts of the world" (New York *Herald Tribune*, November 17, 1949). Mrs. Lord has since expressed the hope that more people in the United States would become familiar with the fund because "it is one of such agencies in the world that is above politics. It goes a long way toward maintaining peace because of the nature of the work it does, the close relationship its member countries have with one another and voluntary governmental gifts."

With her election on March 14, 1952, as president of the National Health Council, Mrs. Lord became the leader of an organization comprising forty-two national voluntary health and welfare associations, professional societies, and official agencies and citizens groups interested in health. Two major functions of the council, organized in 1921, are to encourage the de-

velopment of local health councils (of which some 1,300 have been established) and more adequate local health services, and to provide public health information through the National Health Library in New York City. In 1951 the council established the Citizens' Committee for the World Health Organization, representing a conviction expressed at its thirty-second annual meeting "that health security can effectively be achieved through international pooling of knowledge and skills under international direction." When Mrs. Lord was elected president she stressed the need for streamlining public health education methods and has since emphasized the council's goal of establishing more local health units.

After the Republican political convention in July 1952, Mrs. Lord was appointed cochairman, with Walter Williams of Seattle, of Citizens for Eisenhower-Nixon, the successor of 2,900 volunteer clubs organized by Mrs. Lord and Mr. Williams to bring about the nomination of General Eisenhower for President of the United States. While co-ordinating the activities of the citizens' group with those of the National Republican Committee to promote the election of General Eisenhower, Mrs. Lord has emphasized securing the votes and the contributions of "independents, dissident Democrats, and new voters" who are unwilling to work through the regular Republican party channels (New York *Times*, August 4, 1952). She first met Eisenhower in Frankfort, Germany, soon after VE-Day, while she was touring Europe as an adviser to the WACs. As reported by Robert Farrington of the Washington *Post* (August 21, 1952) the general and Mrs. Lord later "worked together in Washington on legislation which made the WAC part of the Army, rather than an auxiliary."

Among the articles written by Mrs. Lord in which she has voiced her opinions on human relations is "My Hope for Race Relations" (*Opportunity*, January 1949). In this she said, "I feel that every one of us has a great and serious responsibility to see that relationships in our own local community are of the best." After being appointed adviser to the housing committee of the Secretary of Defense in 1950, Mrs. Lord expressed her ideas about the close relationship between housing and the security of the family in an article, "Today's Crisis and Tomorrow's Families" (*Journal of Social Hygiene*, March 1951): "I am proud to have a part in the program to safeguard our stronghold . . . the family. Some of the important problems to which we must give our best efforts are those of recreation, housing, and health."

The Federal Government in 1943 awarded Mrs. Lord an Office of Civilian Defense ribbon for 5,000 hours of volunteer service; the American Woman's Association in May 1946 named her "woman of the month;" General Omar Bradley in 1948 presented her with a citation; and *Parents Magazine* in March 1950 honored her among the "Friends of Children." Mrs. Lord is a member of the honorary society Phi Beta Kappa and of the advisory committee of the Institute of Applied Arts and Sciences of the State University of New York in Brooklyn. Of the institute she has said: "It has shown a good example to the rest of the country of how young people could be trained, and it has encouraged them to learn in a constructive way." She is a member of the National Advisory Board for Women in the Armed Services, the New York Woman's Council, the Cosmopolitan Club, the National Women's Republican Club, the Colonial Dames of New York, the Woman's City Club, the board of directors of the Metropolitan Opera Guild, and the board of trustees of Smith College. Her church affiliation is Congregational.

Mrs. Lord is the mother of two sons, Charles and Winston Lord. In the Washington *Post* (July 10, 1952) Christine Sadler described her as "one who makes decisions quickly and remains in good humor. She dresses simply, usually in dark print dresses and small matching hats." Mrs. Lord has dark-blue eyes and black hair, and is five feet seven inches tall. Her hobby is photography.

References

N Y Times p25 S 28 '41 por
Who's Who in America, 1952-53

HARRY J. LOYND

LOYND, HARRY J. Feb. 12, 1898- Drug company official

Address: b. c/o Parke Davis & Company, Joseph Campau Ave., Detroit 32, Mich.; h. 610 Neff Rd., Grosse Pointe 30, Mich.

Harry J. Loynd became the president of Parke, Davis & Company, the Detroit manufacturer of pharmaceuticals, on April 3, 1951. He had joined the company as a salesman in 1931, became vice-president in charge of domestic and Canadian sales in 1945, and was elected to the board of directors in 1946. Parke, Davis & Company, which the New York *Times* has called the world's largest maker of pharmaceuticals, manufactures about 1,400 products, many of which were developed in its own laboratories.

Born February 12, 1898, in a one-room log cabin in Springville, Utah, Harry J. Loynd is one of the five sons of Joseph S. and Amelia (Allsworth) Loynd. For the greater part of his seventy-four years of life, the elder Loynd was a field man for the American Beet Sugar Company. Until Harry was seven years old the family lived in his birthplace; and as his father's position made it necessary, in 1905 the Loynds moved to Colorado, residing for brief periods at Lamar, Rocky Ford, and Manzanola (where Harry attended public school through the fifth grade) before going to Fowler, where he completed his elementary and secondary schooling. There he was initiated into the retail drug business by working in a local drug store after school hours. His extra-curricular high school activities were baseball, football, and basketball, and he was a member of the 1916 Fowler High School debating team which won the Colorado State championship.

Following his graduation from high school, Loynd entered the University of Utah. "To get by the first two months," stated a biographical sketch supplied by Parke, Davis & Com-

pany, "he worked in a cafeteria from 5 P.M. until 1 A.M. nightly." Subsequently, he found other jobs, firing boilers, waiting on table, washing dishes in a dormitory, and doing janitor work in the university medical laboratory. Loynd was a sophomore when, in 1918, he joined the Navy for World War I service as a seaman, third class. He was sent on several training cruises in the Pacific and was attending a school for commissioned officers at Mare Island, San Francisco, when he received his discharge in February 1919. The future executive then worked fourteen hours daily in a bakery at $17 a week before returning in the fall to the University of Utah to specialize in accounting, business administration, and business law. He was elected to Beta Theta Pi and was on the baseball team for two years. Receiving the B.S. degree, he graduated in 1922.

During his last three years at the university Loynd supported himself by working a regular shift in one of the 196 stores of the Owl Drug Company chain. The president, W. M. Berg, was impressed by his "vitality, judgment and experience," and in April 1922 offered him the position of manager of an Owl store in San Francisco. Loynd accepted, and later in 1922 was transferred to a larger store at Oakland, where his salary was $60 a week. In February 1925, having meanwhile qualified (in 1923) as a registered pharmacist, Loynd was sent to Portland, Oregon, to manage two Owl stores; two more years passed, and he returned to Salt Lake City to be city manager in charge of three stores. Loynd's final employment with the Owl chain was as manager, beginning April 1931, of a large downtown store in San Francisco.

Harry Loynd, having come to the conclusion that he had advanced as far as he could in the Owl organization, took an annual salary cut of $5,000 to join the sales force of Parke, Davis

LOYND, HARRY J.—*Continued*

& Company, the old Detroit drug manufacturer. He began his association with the company on July 15, 1931, working out of the Kansas City office as a sales and medical service representative for Utah and southeastern Nevada. Four years later (1935) he won a national Parke, Davis sales contest, and in September was promoted to field manager for the Southwest area. On July 1, 1942, Loynd, having been transferred in the meantime to the home office at Detroit, was advanced to assistant domestic sales manager; on June 5, 1944, he was appointed assistant to Dr. Alexander William Lescohier. who had become president of Parke, Davis in 1938. Loynd was made vice-president in charge of domestic and Canadian sales and promotion on June 23, 1945, and was elected to the Parke, Davis board of directors in the year following.

Parke, Davis & Company, incorporated in 1876 (fourteen years after its founding) declared its first dividend in 1878 and since that time has not missed a quarterly payment. By 1931 it had long been recognized as one of the world's principal drug houses, in 1951 being described by the New York *Times* as the world's largest ($90,000,000) company of its kind. It manufactures more than 1,400 different chemical, pharmaceutical, and biological products and employs nearly 9,000 people in its plant and laboratories.

While record high earnings were reported by Parke, Davis for 1946 (*Barron's Weekly*, July 18, 1949), a decline in sales was noted in 1947. More progressive sales methods were accordingly initiated under Loynd. In 1949 the company enjoyed the most prosperous year in its history, with net sales of $86,786,490. These figures were topped in 1950, when sales mounted to $105,707,659, an increase of 21.8 per cent. The gain was explained by Dr. Lescohier in his annual report as in part a reflection of "the increasing availability of our new antibiotic drug, Chloromycetin, and its widespread acceptance and use by the medical profession."

The election of Harry Loynd as the seventh president of Parke, Davis & Company on April 3, 1951 (twenty years after joining the firm), followed the retirement of Dr. Lescohier from the office after thirteen years incumbency and his elevation to chairmanship of the board. At the same time Loynd replaced Lescohier as the fourth member of the executive committee of the corporation, which has 22,531 stockholders, none of whom own as much as 4 per cent of the shares outstanding.

Harry J. Loynd and Myrtle Williams met while fellow employees in an Owl drugstore in Salt Lake City. They were married March 22, 1923, and now reside in Grosse Pointe, Michigan, with their adopted daughter, Sandra. The Parke, Davis president, who votes Republican, is a member of the Detroit Club and the Essex Golf and Country Club. His golf score frequently gets into the 70's, while other outdoor diversions he enjoys are duck and pheasant hunting and angling for trout and sailfish. He "more than holds his own at bridge and poker,"

reported a company release. Loynd is five feet ten inches in height, weighs 195 pounds, and is said to have "an ever-present sense of humor."

References

N Y Times III p3 S 2 '51 por
Business Executives of America (1950)
Who's Who in America, 1950-51
Who's Who in Commerce and Industry (1951)
Who's Who in the Midwest (1949)

LUNDEBERG, HARRY 1901-   Labor leader

Address: b. c/o Seafarers International Union of North America, 450 Harrison St., San Francisco 5, Calif.; Sailors Union of the Pacific, 450 Harrison St., San Francisco 5, Calif.

Secretary-treasurer of the Sailors Union of the Pacific, AFL, since 1936 and president of the Seafarers International Union, AFL, since organizing it in 1938, Harry Lundeberg has been described by the *Christian Science Monitor* as one of the most powerful men in American labor. He rose to prominence during the 1934 West Coast maritime strike, at which time he was closely associated with Harry Bridges, leader of the CIO maritime unions, but Lundeberg's syndicalist views soon caused him to break with Bridges. The rivalry between the CIO unions led by Bridges and the AFL groups under Lundeberg was counted an important factor in the 1946 maritime strike and was considered a "stumbling block" in negotiating the 1952 maritime strike.

Harry Lundeberg was born in 1901 in Oslo, Norway, the son of Karl and Allette (Koffeld) Lundeberg. As a child Harry became acquainted with two different theories of labor movements because his mother headed the Norwegian Labor party, which sought to attain its goals through political action, while his father was a syndicalist who believed that labor should employ only economic measures—mainly the strike—to achieve its ends. Lundeberg's acceptance of syndicalism played a major part in shaping his career. Following his graduation from grammar school, at the age of fourteen he began working on "square rigger" sailing ships—the only place a man can really learn the sea, he has said—being employed all over the world on the ships of nine different nations. During his years at sea, Lundeberg, in the words of *United States News*, "lived and loved the tough life of the forecastle hand. But he disliked and rebelled at some of the conditions imposed upon himself and his shipmates." He joined unions whenever possible, becoming a member of Norwegian and British maritime unions, a British syndicalist union, and a Spanish union with syndicalist leanings, and also affiliating for a time with the Industrial Workers of the World.

An unsuccessful strike in 1921, along with an increase in the labor supply and a decrease in available ships, reduced job opportunities by 50 per cent. When Lundeberg, who had been affected by the decline in employment, landed at Seattle in 1923, he decided to sail from then on from that port, changing his union membership in 1926 from the Australian Seamen's Union to the Sailors Union of the Pacific and applying in 1928 for his first United States citizenship papers. With worsening conditions during the depression, Lundeberg, after nineteen years as a seaman, came on land to live in 1934—the year of the West Coast waterfront strike in which he rose to prominence from his union's rank and file and became an associate of West Coast labor leader Harry Bridges. "Always active in union matters, energetic and courageous" (*United States News*), after that strike Lundeberg was elected business agent in Seattle in 1935 and with the backing of Bridges became first president of the Maritime Federation of the Pacific, which staged a successful strike in 1936. Lundeberg, reportedly because of his syndicalist views, shortly afterward broke with Bridges and resigned as federation president to become in 1936 secretary-treasurer of the Sailors Union of the Pacific (SUP).

The following year the United States Maritime Commission under Joseph P. Kennedy reported to Congress that conditions in the maritime industry were "deplorable," citing labor trouble as a contributing factor. The commission advocated machinery to provide for a sixty-day wait after a union vote to strike, during which a proposed mediation board would seek to settle the difficulty. Fearful of Federal regulation, Lundeberg opposed this suggestion: "It would rob us of the right to strike when a strike would be most effective. You've got to pick your time to strike . . . you don't want to wait around a couple of months, while the bosses get ready for you." By 1938 tension between Bridges' longshoremen and Lundeberg's seamen led to riots, in one of which Lundeberg's jaw was broken with a baseball bat. During that same year Lundeberg founded and became first president of the Seafarers International Union of North America.

The year 1946 was to witness what the press at the time termed "the worst strike in American maritime history." "The dominant theme in the events leading up to the strike—besides the basic drive for higher wages—was the intense rivalry between the CIO and AFL maritime unions" (New York *Times*, September 15, 1946). "The brotherhoods compete in proselytizing workers; they vie in winning higher wage scales for their members." That year collective bargaining between two AFL unions and one independent union, represented by Lundeberg, and shipowners of the Pacific, East, and Gulf Coasts resulted in an agreement giving West Coast seamen $22.50-a-month wage increases and East and Gulf Coast workers $27.50-a-month increases. However, this agreement was contingent upon the National Wage Stabilization Board's approval, which would have permitted the private shipowners to make up for their increased labor costs by raising shipping charges and would have necessitated an increase to the sailors of the CIO, as well as eventual raises for other industrial workers. When the NWSB disapproved certain of the

Wide World Photos

HARRY LUNDEBERG

wage agreements, Lundeberg on September 6, 1946, called a strike which longshoremen, radiomen, masters, mates, pilots, and machinists in repair yards promised to support. By the end of a week about 1,500 American ships were unable to move, 500,000 men were unemployed, and shipping from every United States port was stopped. The strike was settled in late September when the Maritime Commission awarded $27.50-a-month wage increases to all seamen and Director of the Office of War Mobilization and Reconversion John R. Steelman succeeded in getting an amendment to the Federal wage regulations.

In a speech the following year Lundeberg stated that he would call a nation-wide strike if the Taft-Hartley Act were interpreted by shipowners as a basis for eliminating the sailors' central hiring hall, considered by some as a form of the closed shop. After talking with Senator Robert A. Taft in September, Lundeberg commented, "Mr. Taft was much impressed by our arguments and stated he would give serious consideration to recommending to Congress to revise the law to permit the hiring hall and closed shop" (*Christian Science Monitor*, September 24, 1947). The labor leader contended that the prohibiting of the hiring hall would permit "'raiding' by Joseph Curran's National Maritime Union (CIO), as well as the hiring of known Communists." On the other hand since Lundeberg had done a "rather thorough job of eliminating Communists" from his union, he argued that the hiring of SUP sailors would be in keeping with the anti-communist provisions of the Taft-Hartley Act. When the new contract was made it included a union hiring hall, which Lundeberg said was equivalent to the closed shop.

On November 29, 1949, a two-year contract was signed with the shipowners containing a welfare plan which Lundeberg referred to as

LUNDEBERG, HARRY—*Continued*

"the first pension agreement in the maritime industry" (New York *Times*, November 26, 1949). The companies agreed to contribute twenty-five cents a man per payroll day, with no contributions by the union, to a fund for building a home for retired and crippled seamen. Further gains were made in September 1951 when, on the eve of a strike, the shipowners increased overtime pay and basic wage scales, along with raising the welfare contribution to fifty cents. Another union victory came on July 29, 1952, when a sixty-three day strike was ended with the union receiving, according to Lundeberg, not only its original demands in full, but extra gains including a wage increase of 5 per cent, subject to WSB approval, and a clause enabling the union to reopen the contract on fifteen days notice. Besides causing losses of $20 million, this strike threatened to destroy California's $300 million fruit crop which could not be canned because the supply of sugar was cut off; it also threatened for a time to cripple the Alaska defense construction program by prohibiting twenty-seven Alaska Steamship Company vessels from leaving United States ports with their construction cargos.

As reported by the New York *Times* (July 28, 1952) the chief stumbling block in negotiations had been a jurisdictional conflict between the Lundeberg and the Bridges unions, which both claimed the right to handle ship stores because of agreements with the maritime association. Frederick Woltman stated in the New York *World-Telegram* (July 26, 1952) that Harry Bridges had launched "what's probably his final bid to bring all West Coast shipping under Communist control. He's reviving his once powerful Maritime Federation of the Pacific with the announced intention of raiding the 'rank and file' of the West Coast maritime unions." Woltman said Bridges was making a "desperate move" to destroy Harry Lundeberg, who, as quoted by *Time* (June 14, 1948), had called Communists "enemies of the working class."

Lundeberg has served as vice-president of the California State Federation of Labor, as an officer in the AFL Maritime Trades Council, and as the editor of the *West Coast Sailors*. The labor leader, who speaks with a Scandinavian accent, signed in 1947 as an able seaman aboard the *Marine Jumper*, a converted United States troop transport, so that he could make a trip to Oslo to visit his family, whom he had not seen in thirty years. He is six feet two inches tall and has thinning blond hair and blue eyes.

References

Bsns W p26 N 20 '37 por
Christian Sci Mon Mag p2 O 4 '47 por
Fortune 16:123-8+ S '37 por; 34:151 N '46 por
U S News 21:81 S 20 '46 por
Who's Who in Labor (1946)

LYSENKO, T(ROFIM) D(ENISOVICH)

(lĭs-yĕn'kŭ trŭ-fēm' dyĭ-nyĕ'sŭ-vĭch) Sept. 29, 1898- Agricultural biologist
Address: b. c/o Institute of Genetics, B. Kaluzhskaya 33, Moscow, U.S.S.R.

The leading scientist and administrator in agriculture in the Soviet Union T. D. Lysenko is president of the Lenin All-Union Academy of Agricultural Sciences, director of the Institute of Genetics of the Soviet Academy of Sciences, and vice-president of Supreme Soviet. As an exponent of the theory that environment rather than heredity determines the characteristics of organisms, the Russian biologist is regarded as a key figure in the Mitchurin-Mendel controversy in genetics, which has become an issue in the ideological conflict between the Soviet Union and the West. The theories in Lysenko's books *Heredity and Its Variability* and *The Science of Biology Today* predominate in the teaching of biology in his country.

The son of Denis Nikanorovich Lysenko, a peasant, Trofim Denisovich Lysenko was born in the Ukrainian town of Karlovka on September 29, 1898. When he had completed his studies at Kiev Agricultural Institute in 1925, Lysenko joined the staff of the Ganja (now Kirovobad) Experimental Station in the Caucasus, where he was engaged in agricultural research until 1928. On his father's farm in 1929 he conducted his first successful test in "vernalized" grain and soon afterward became known for "yarovization" or "vernalization," a process of moistening and refrigerating wheat grains whereby he claimed that he was able to impart the characteristics of winter wheat to spring wheat and to increase yields by 40 per cent. Lysenko, who has often been compared with Luther Burbank, has also been credited with developing a new method of pruning cotton plants and with evolving new varieties of cotton.

Since 1929 millions of acres of farm land in the Soviet Union have been planted with vernalized wheat. "Lysenko's method of applying scientific control to the germinating stages of seeds," stated a writer in the New York *Post* (June 23, 1943), "has been reported to have produced as many as five crops of spring wheat a year, to have made semitropical crops bloom in the arctic cold of Siberia and the food crops of the north flourish in the hot and arid regions of Central Asia." Having thus seemed to solve the problem of recurring famines in Russia, he was widely acclaimed in his own country (outside the Soviet Union plant breeders, using his method and data, were unable to duplicate his results). He first gained attention of biologists in other countries through the efforts of Nikolai I. Vavilov, then Russia's leading geneticist, who in 1932 spoke favorably of Lysenko's work at the International Congress on Genetics at Cornell University in New York.

After the death in 1935 of Ivan V. Michurin, a Soviet geneticist who had criticized Vavilov's work because of what he regarded as its inadequate stress on environment, Lysenko came into prominence as a foremost adherent of the doctrine that characteristics acquired through environment can be inherited. Like Michurin, Lysenko denies the Mendel-Morgan theory, "which maintains," as Julian Huxley has expressed it, "that heredity depends on a system of material particles, the genes, hereditary variation on the *mutation* of genes, and evolution on the automatic process of *natural selection.*" In denouncing this theory, which has been generally accepted since 1911 when the American biologist Thomas Hunt Morgan published the results of his researches on genes, Lysenko asserts that the gene does not exist, that changes in organisms result from differences in environment, and that these changes, or acquired characteristics, can be and are transmitted to succeeding generations. Thus he believes it possible to "disestablish" a plant's heredity and artificially introduce variations which will be passed on to its offspring, by changing the surroundings in which it develops. He and his followers hold that by these means they have "shattered the heredity" of tomatoes, wheat, barley, and potatoes.

Lysenko's views, which conform to Communist doctrine regarding the all-important role of environment in determining the basic characteristics of organisms, whether plants, animals, or human beings, won increasing official support. (Georgi M. Malenkov in particular has been mentioned as being impressed with Lysenko's work and theories.) In 1937 Lysenko was appointed a deputy to the Supreme Soviet and in that year also became director of the Institute of Selection and Genetics in Odessa. Meanwhile, in 1936, the Russian Communist Party organ, *Under the Red Banner*, sponsored a debate between Lysenko and Vavilov, and in 1939 at another public controversy Lysenko emerged as the victor. It was around this time, as related by H. J. Muller in the *Saturday Review of Literature* (December 4, 1948), that Lysenko was appointed president of the Lenin All-Union Academy of Agricultural Sciences and head of the Institute of Plant Production, positions previously held by Vavilov. In 1942 Lysenko was called upon to serve on the Soviet Commission on Nazi Crimes in Russia.

In the summer of 1948, from July 31 until August 7, the Lenin All-Union Academy of Agricultural Sciences presented a debate on genetics that drew international attention. As president of the Academy, Lysenko delivered the opening address, in which he restated his belief that the characteristics of organisms can be changed by experimentation and hybridization and again assailed the Mendel-Morgan laws of heredity as "an alien foreign bourgeois biology"; he also, stated the New York *Times*, attacked by name those Russian geneticists who adhered to and taught the Western theories. Several of these geneticists, including I. I. Shmalhausen, B. M. Zavadovsky, N. P. Dubinin, and A. R. Zhebrak, opposed him vigorously, Zavadovsky charging him with misrepresenting the views of those he attacked and with basing his own theories on insufficient experimental evidence. At the end of the debate Lysenko announced that his address had been approved by the Central Committee of the Communist Party. The academy then adopted a resolution, the New York *Times* further reported, "calling for the rewriting of university textbooks and the revision of courses in biology and related sciences so as to remove all traces of foreign geneticists' views and to bring all teaching in conformance with the Lysenko-Michurin position." The following month (September 1948) on the occasion of his fiftieth birthday, Lysenko received the Order of Lenin in recognition of his contributions to agriculture.

The validity of Lysenko's views has been both supported and contradicted by experiments conducted in the United States. Professor Tracy M. Sonneborn, of Indiana University, stated in September 1948 that he had demonstrated that environmental factors can change the nature of single-celled organisms and that the changes are inherited (*Newsweek*, September 6, 1948). Experiments at Columbia University showed, according to William L. Laurence of the New York *Times*, "that certain micro-organisms that appeared to have changed as a result of a changed environment actually had inherited those changes before the environment had been altered." Lysenko, who was awarded a first Stalin prize in April 1949 for his work in agrobiology, announced in December of that year that Soviet agronomists had succeeded in transforming wheat into rye by planting wheat in areas unsuitable to it. He credited this feat, which has been described as equivalent to changing a cat into a dog, to "Stalinist teaching on gradual, concealed, unnoticeable, quantitative changes that result in quick, qualitative, basic changes" (quoted by the New York *Times*, December 16, 1949).

An early book by Lysenko, *The Vernalization of Agricultural Plants*, of which in 1943 over 1,300,000 copies had been printed, has been translated into sixteen languages and dialects. His *Heredity and Its Variability*, written in 1943, was translated into English in 1946; and his address before the Lenin Academy in July 1948 appeared in English in that same year as *The Science of Biology Today*. Lysenko's teachings were said by Muller in 1948 to be "widely disseminated" in the Soviet zone of Germany and his *Heredity and Its Variability* to be distributed in a Spanish translation in South American countries. In a despatch to *Commonweal* in May 1952 Gunnar D. Kumlien reported: "Lysenko's theories on heredity form a large part of Communist cultural propaganda in Italy today. . . . In many countries in Europe where the Communists are strong the Lysenko propaganda is increasing intensively." Besides occupying the posts mentioned, Lysenko is vice-president of the Supreme Soviet, deputy chairman of the Council of the Union of the Supreme Council of the U.S.S.R., a member of the praesidium of the Soviet Academy of Sciences, and director of four agricultural research stations. He holds, in addition to the awards cited, the title of Hero of Socialist Labor.

(Continued next page)

LYSENKO, T. D.—*Continued*

References

N Y Times II p6 Ag 22 '48; p12 Ag 25 '48
Sat R Lit 29:28-32 Mr 9 '46 por
Columbia Encyclopedia, 1950
International Who's Who, 1951
World Biography (1948)

MCCARTHY, LEIGHTON (GOLDIE)
Dec. 15, 1869—Oct. 4, 1952 First Canadian Ambassador to the United States; lawyer; industrialist; Liberal member of Canadian Parliament (1898-1908); left politics in 1908 to enter law corporation practice; board chairman of Canada Life Assurance Company and of the National Trust Company; largely instrumental in establishing Aluminum Company of Canada and the Union Carbide Company of Canada; named Canadian Minister to Washington in 1941; became Canada's first Ambassador to the United States (1943-45); trustee of the Warm Springs Foundation. See *Current Biography*, 1942.

Obituary

N Y Times p25 O 6 '52

MCCONNELL, F(OWLER) B(EERY)
Dec. 4, 1894- Business executive
Address: b. c/o Sears, Roebuck & Company, 925 S. Homan Ave., Chicago, Ill.; h. 700 Ardsley Rd., Winnetka, Ill.

F. B. McConnell, president of Sears, Roebuck and Company, which is known as America's largest retailer of general merchandise, is a veteran of more than thirty-five years of service with his company. From his first job

Fabian Bachrach
F. B. MCCONNELL

as stockman, through a variety of retailing and managerial posts, he has gained wide experience in the many phases of Sears's operations. "A capable and experienced administrator," in the judgment of *Fortune*, McConnell administers a corporation which sells more than two billion dollars' worth of goods annually to the consumer through its familiar mail-order catalogue and, in increasing volume since 1945, through its chain of over six hundred retail stores in the United States.

Fowler Beery McConnell was born in Upper Sandusky, Ohio, on December 4, 1894. He is the son of Robert N. McConnell, a physician (whose ancestors emigrated from the north of Ireland and settled in Pennsylvania in 1750), and of Leefe (Beery) McConnell. Young McConnell spent his early years in Upper Sandusky and graduated from high school there in 1912. Then he proceeded to the University of Chicago and received a Ph.B. degree in 1916. In college he played varsity football and baseball and was elected to Delta Tau Delta fraternity.

In November 1916 McConnell began work at Sears as a stockman, when his work entailed physical handling of merchandise. He has been with the company ever since, except for a two-year period from 1917 to 1919, during which he served as a captain in the army in World War I, spending nine months overseas with the AEF. In May 1919, when he returned from military service, he became an assistant buyer. Three years later, in August 1922, he was a merchandizing department manager in a branch house, and in January 1926 he became merchandizing superintendent. During this period McConnell's major concern was in the inauguration of Sears's retail stores, the first of which was opened in 1925, thirty-three years after the company was founded.

In January 1930 McConnell was moved to Philadelphia as manager of the branch mail order plant in that city. Transferred a year later to Atlanta, he was designated Southern territorial officer of the company. There he acted as representative of the president, supervising all mail-order plants and retail stores within the area.

Although it is the general policy of Sears, Roebuck to decentralize wherever possible, giving a greater measure of autonomy to the local managers, there was a temporary movement toward centralization of management in 1932 when the territorial offices were abolished for a short time. McConnell therefore returned to Chicago in May 1932 as assistant to the vice-president in charge of retail administration.

McConnell's responsibilities were enlarged to include supervision of all personnel activities in 1935 when he was appointed secretary of the company and assistant to the president. This was the first time, Boris Emmet and John E. Jeuck point out in their history of Sears, *Catalogues and Counters* (1950), that the personnel function was given high executive status. Under McConnell's administration Sears has developed its personnel management to the point where, the same authors report, employee morale is generally high and labor relations are peaceful. This has been achieved through extensive personnel studies, testing programs, reserve-group training for executive posts, profit-sharing and pension plans, and similar measures. In describing a series of questionnaires and interviews conducted by the company to survey employee morale, McConnell stated that these "are directed toward building a dynamic cooperative organization which will maintain a high level of morale and enthusiasm, tap the human resources of men and women at all levels, stimulate the growth of individuals and achieve the purposes of the company because it meets the human requirements of its people."

McConnell continued his steady rise in the Sears, Roebuck organization. In April 1938 he became vice-president in charge of retail administration and a member of the board of directors. In March 1946, thirty years after joining the company, McConnell was elected its president.

In the office of president, McConnell works directly under the chairman of the board of directors, General Robert E. Wood, who has been the top executive at Sears since 1924. Wood, reported *Fortune*, "has long realized that operational decentralization is one of the facts of big business life." Emmet and Jeuck point out that as a result of his long association with General Wood, McConnell has acquired much of Wood's business philosophy, and his election to the presidency, they write, "reflected the degree to which his own administrative skill and competence developed" under the decentralized management "which he epitomized as retail administrator."

In 1946, when McConnell took office, a writer in *Business Week* commented that he would have the task of bettering the 1945 sales record of more than one billion dollars. By 1948 Sears reported sales at two billion "and still growing." Since the end of World War II Sears has embarked on a program of expansion. Inventories were increased, new retail stores were opened, and older ones were enlarged and modernized. The 1947 annual stockholders' report announced the building of new stores in Mexico City, Rio de Janeiro, and in São Paulo, Brazil. In 1952 sixteen retail stores are operating in Mexico, Central and South America. *Business Week* reported in April 1952 that in the postwar period Sears, Roebuck sales rose 154 per cent. In the fiscal year ending January 31, 1952, profits were 212 per cent greater than they were in 1946. In 1948 Sears employed 150,000 in its 632 retail stores (from the large department-store type to small auto accessory stores with some "hard" lines), 11 mail-order plants, and 341 order offices; millions of copies of its catalogues are distributed annually.

McConnell holds directorships in the Harris Trust and Savings Bank and in the Allstate Insurance Company. In 1949 the University of Denver awarded him an honorary LL.D. degree, and he is a trustee of the University of Chicago. On January 21, 1926, he married Lucille Larson; they have two daughters, Marilyn and Judith, and two sons, John and Fowler B., Jr. McConnell's clubs are the Exmoor, Old Elm, Chicago, and Commercial. A large

man, he is six feet three inches tall and weighs 250 pounds; he has gray hair and blue eyes. His political allegiance is Republican, and he attends a Presbyterian church.

References

Bsns W p83 Ap 6 '46 por
Fortune 38:86 Ag '48
Mag of Wall St p263 Je 3 '50
Emmet, B., & Jeuck, J. E. Catalogues and Counters (1950)
Who's Who in America, 1952-53
Who's Who in Commerce and Industry (1951)

MCCORMICK, LYNDE DUPUY August 12, 1895- United States naval officer

Address: b. c/o Department of the Navy, Washington 25, D.C.; h. "Clermont," Berryville, Va.

One of the United States Navy's four full admirals, Lynde Dupuy McCormick, on January 30, 1952, was appointed Supreme Allied Commander of the Atlantic, the North Atlantic Treaty Organization post paralleling that of General Dwight D. Eisenhower in Europe. McCormick, who saw service in both world wars, has commanded battleships and submarines, and has served as War Plans Officer for the Pacific Fleet and as Assistant Chief of Naval Operations for Logistics Plans. In August 1951 he became Commander of the Atlantic Fleet of the United States Navy.

The son of a naval officer, Lynde Dupuy McCormick was born in Annapolis, Maryland, the seat of the United States Naval Academy, August 12, 1895. His parents were Rear Admiral Albert Montgomery Dupuy McCormick and Edith Lynde (Abbot) McCormick. Young McCormick was educated at St. John's Preparatory School and College at Annapolis until his appointment by President William Howard Taft to the United States Naval Academy in 1911. As a midshipman he played lacrosse and soccer, and as a first classman was business manager of the *Lucky Bag*. As second in a class of 183 he was graduated with the B.S. degree and an ensign's commission in June 1915.

Ensign McCormick's first assignment was to the battleship U.S.S. *Wyoming*, in which he served while she operated with the British Grand Fleet during World War I and attended the surrender of the German High Fleet in the North Sea. From the *Wyoming* in April 1919 he went to the staff of Commander Division 4, United States Fleet, serving as aide and flag lieutenant until June, when he was assigned to the U.S.S. *South Carolina*. There he remained until September, when he became aide and flag lieutenant on the U.S.S. *Birmingham*, flagship for Commander Destroyer Squadron 4 of the Pacific Fleet; in December 1920 he was transferred to the destroyer U.S.S. *Buchanan*, where he remained eight months.

In August 1921 the young officer took command of the U.S.S. *Kennedy*, but it was only for a few months: in October 1921 he became an instructor in the Department of Navigation at the Naval Academy. McCormick taught un-

ADM. LYNDE DUPUY MCCORMICK

til June 1923, when he became a student himself, this time at the Submarine School in New London, Connecticut. The instruction was followed by service until June 1924 in the submarine S-31, operating with Submarine Division 16 in the Pacific. After brief service with the S-37 and the submarine tender *Canopus,* he took command in August 1924 of the R-10 at Honolulu, a command he retained until June 1926. There followed two years of duty in the executive department at the Naval Academy in Annapolis. In August 1928 he went to sea again for almost three years as a commander of the submarine V-2, operating with Submarine Division 20 as a fleet submarine.

McCormick returned to the Naval Academy, as aide to the Superintendent in May 1931, to remain there three years. His next assignment, in June 1934, was as navigator of the U.S.S. *Marblehead,* and in April 1936 he assumed command of the U.S.S. *Neches.* In June 1937 he left that command to take the senior course in the Naval War College, Newport, Rhode Island. The course completed in May 1938, he remained for a year on the staff of the college.

In June 1939, three months before the outbreak of World War II in Europe, his official duty became operations officer on the staff of Commander, Battleships, Battle Force, U.S.S. *West Virginia,* Flagship. The following January he took over the same post on the staff of the Commander of the Battle Force on the flagship U.S.S. *California.* Later, in February 1941, he reported for duty as assistant war plans officer on the staff of the Commander in Chief, Pacific Fleet, and was in that post at the time of the Japanese attack on Pearl Harbor.

Appointed war plans officer for Admiral Chester W. Nimitz in April 1942, McCormick served in that capacity during the battles of the Coral Sea, Midway, and Guadalcanal. By July 15, 1942, he had advanced to the rank of rear admiral. It was for "exceptionally meritorious conduct in the performance of outstanding services to the Government of the United States as War Plans Officer on the Staff of the Commander in Chief, Pacific Fleet and Pacific Ocean Areas, from February 1, 1941, to January 14, 1943," that he received the award of the Legion of Merit. Detached from Nimitz' staff in February, 1943, the Rear Admiral took command of the U.S.S. *South Dakota,* which operated first in the Atlantic Area, and later with the British Home Fleet in northern European waters.

In the fall of 1943 McCormick went to Washington for detail (from October 1943 to March 1945) as Assistant Chief of Naval Operations for Logistics Plans, in the Office of the Chief of Naval Operations in the Navy Department. At the same time he became Chairman of the Joint Logistics Committee of the Joint Chiefs of Staff, in that post accompanying Admiral King to the second Quebec and Yalta conferences. For his work in logistics he was awarded a Gold Star in lieu of another Legion of Merit, and a letter of commendation reading, in part: "For exceptionally meritorious conduct in the performance of outstanding services. . . .His mastery of the relationship between strategy and logistics and his understanding of the process of procuring and distributing critcal items have been important factors in meeting the needs of area and Fleet Commanders. In a field in which the magnitude and complexity of the problems were without precedent in the history of the Navy, he has displayed conspicuous ability and brilliant leadership."

In March 1945 Rear Admiral McCormick became Commander of Battleship Division 3, and while in this command saw action as Task Group Commander for two months at the battle of Okinawa. This service also brought him a Gold Star for his Legion of Merit: "For exceptionally meritorious conduct in the performance of outstanding services to the Government of the United States as Commander of a Battleship Division, of a Task Group, and of a Fire Support Unit, in action against enemy Japanese forces on Okinawa, Ryukyu Islands, from March through May 1945." The naval officer also took part in the initial occupation of Japan, until in November 1945; he was then ordered to duty as Chief of Staff and Aide to Admiral John H. Towers, Commander in Chief, Pacific Fleet and Pacific Ocean Areas. The following month he was named Deputy Commander in Chief, Pacific Fleet and Pacific Ocean Areas, and shortly thereafter, on February 13, 1946, was advanced to the temporary rank of vice-admiral.

At the end of December 1946 Admiral Towers announced the creation of a "unique" joint command in the central Pacific, to coordinate central Pacific defenses. The top level staff would include Admiral Towers, an Army general, an Air Force general, and Vice-Admiral McCormick. The Vice-Admiral served in this command about a month: in February 1947 he left to become Commander, Battleships-Cruisers, Atlantic Fleet, a post he was to hold through November 1948. (In January 1948 the Commander led a mission to Buenos Aires aboard the heavy cruiser *Albany* as part of efforts to establish cordial relations with the Argentine military.) His next post, as Commandant, Twelfth Naval District, with headquarters at San Francisco, was assigned December 8, 1948, and at that time he reverted to his permanent rank of rear admiral.

In the rank of vice-admiral, on April 3, 1950, McCormick reported as Vice-Chief of Naval Operations, Navy Department, the second highest post in the Navy, the only man above him in command being Admiral Forrest P. Sherman. When legal limits in rank were lifted because of the declared national emergency, McCormick was nominated by President Truman to the rank of admiral, thus giving him equal rank with officers of the other services in similar positions. His nomination was confirmed by the Senate as of December 22, 1950.

Upon Admiral Sherman's death in Europe while on a Western defense mission in July 1951, Vice-Admiral McCormick took over that mission temporarily. Then, Admiral William M. Fechteler was named to that post on August 1, 1951, while Admiral McCormick was assigned Fechteler's post as Commander of the Atlantic Fleet. This was the Admiral's first fleet command. The following month, at a ceremony recommissioning the aircraft carrier *Wasp*, Admiral McCormick said at a press conference: "The size of the atomic bomb has been reduced and its availability increased." It was assumed that atomic bombs had been developed small enough to be carried by the light bombers on aircraft carriers. The Admiral also stated that he planned to pursue with no changes the policy established by his predecessor as head of the Atlantic Fleet. In September, also, Admiral McCormick commanded in the Atlantic the first major fleet exercises since the outbreak of the Korean War.

Meanwhile, reports from Washington indicated that Admiral McCormick would be named head of the twelve-nation North Atlantic Treaty Organization's entire Atlantic Command, despite Prime Minister Winston Churchill's insistence that the naval post go to a British Admiral. However, in talks with President Truman in January 1952 the Prime Minister agreed to the naming of an American. According to the New York *Times* and other newspapers (January 19, 1952) President Truman had planned to recommend to the United States, British and French Chiefs of Staff (who compose the Standing Group of the alliance) that Admiral McCormick be named to the post, which would be equal with and separate from General Dwight D. Eisenhower's command in Europe. On January 30 the joint announcement of the United States and Britain gave McCormick the top command of the entire Atlantic. He assumed his new command on April 10, 1952, with the opening of his headquarters in Norfolk, Virginia. Two deputies will serve under him.

In addition to the Legion of Merit with two Gold Stars, the Admiral is entitled to wear the Victory Medal, Grand Fleet Clasp (U.S.S. Wyoming), the American Defense Service Medal, the European-African-Middle Eastern Campaign Medal, the Asiatic-Pacific Campaign Medal, the American Campaign Medal, and the World War II Victory Medal. The Admiral, whose home address is Berryville, Virginia, married Lillian Addison Sprigg on October 2, 1920. Their children are Lynde Dupuy, and James Jatt 2d. (A third son, Montrose Graham, is deceased.) The Admiral's clubs are the Jett, Army and Navy, and the Army-Navy Country Club (in Washington).

References

N Y Herald Tribune p2 Jl 23 '51
N Y Times p30 N 6 '49 por p4 Ja 19 '52
U S News 31:48 Ag 10 '51 por
Washington (D.C.) Post p3 Jl 23 '51 por

Who's Who in America, 1950-51

MCDANIEL, GLEN Mar. 21, 1912- Association president; lawyer
Address: b. 30 Rockefeller Plaza, New York 20; h. 1165 5th Ave., New York 29

The fifteenth president and first full-time salaried chief executive of the Radio-Television Manufacturers Association is Glen McDaniel, who assumed that post in April 1951 and in June 1952 announced his resignation. Associated with the New York law firm of Sullivan and Cromwell for six years prior to entering the United States Navy in World War II, McDaniel as a Naval officer was chiefly concerned with legal and procurement problems. In 1946 he became vice-president and general counsel of RCA Communications, Inc., and two years later vice-president of the Radio Corporation of America.

Born in Seymour, Texas, on March 21, 1912, Glen McDaniel is the son of John Otho and Mary Burnet (Kerr) McDaniel. After graduating from the local high school in 1928, McDaniel entered Southern Methodist University at Dallas, where he took his Bachelor of Arts degree in 1932 and his Master of Arts degree the following year. From 1933 to 1936, he was a student in law at Columbia University, which awarded him his Bachelor of Laws degree in 1936. At Columbia McDaniel was in the forefront of student activities, serving as president of his class in the first and second years, as president of the student body, and as editor of the *Columbia Law Review*. Upon his graduation from Columbia the young attorney was invited to join the staff of the large law firm of Sullivan and Cromwell in New York City, with which he remained until 1942. During this period, reported a biographical release of the Radio-Television Manufacturers Association, he specialized "in litigation involving corporate reorganization and proceedings before regulatory commissions in Washington."

In March 1942 the lawyer was named civilian special counsel to Under Secretary of the Navy Forrestal, to devote himself to aircraft pro-

Moss Photo.

GLEN MCDANIEL

curement problems. Entering the United States Navy two months later as a lieutenant (j.g.), McDaniel served until October 1945, when he was discharged with the rank of lieutenant commander. His work during this period as assistant counsel for the Bureau of Aeronautics of the Navy Department and counsel for the Bureau of Aeronautics General Representative, Eastern District, brought him a citation and commendation ribbon from Secretary Forrestal. In 1945-46 he was chairman of the Navy Board of Contract Appeals, conducting hearings on appeals made by Navy contractors against decisions rendered by chiefs of Naval bureaus, on the basis of which hearings McDaniel wrote his opinions.

Returning to civilian law practice in January 1946, Glen McDaniel at that time became vice-president and general counsel of RCA Communications, Inc., a position which required him to represent the firm in proceedings before the Federal Communications Commission and to conduct negotiations with the Departments of War, Navy, and State. In July 1948 he was named vice-president of the Radio Corporation of America. That year he was representative of RCA at the Brussels conference of the International Telegraph Consultative Committee.

On April 1, 1951, Glen McDaniel succeeded Robert Sprague as president of the Radio-Television Manufacturers Association, the fifteenth incumbent of that post and the first to hold it on a full-time, paid basis. Originally founded in 1924 as the Radio Manufacturers Association "to promote the best interests of the radio and electronics industry," the group in its early years had marshaled opposition to proposed Federal and State taxes on radios and to attempts to ban automobile radios as an accident hazard. Through its efforts, too, higher freight and express rates for radio

parts and equipment were combated. Besides stimulating the sales of radios, the R.M.A. encouraged technical innovations to reduce the cost of producing radios. Production of civilian radios was suspended during World War II. When civilian production was resumed, the R.M.A. pressed for, and won, price increases on radios and the decontrol of radio prices. About this time its name was changed to the Radio-Television Manufacturers Association, with headquarters in Washington, D.C.

Noting that television production had risen from about 6,500 sets in 1946 to more than seven million in 1950, McDaniel in a New York *World-Telegram* article (April 9, 1951) predicted a rise in the industry's production costs and hailed a Federal Communications Commission suggestion to increase television service in ultra-high frequencies. On behalf of the industry McDaniel in June appealed for a relaxing of credit restrictions because of lowered output and increased unemployment; when the appeal was granted by the Federal Reserve Board a more encouraging outlook for television manufacturers was noted. Since technicians for servicing sets were scarce, McDaniel at the end of the year announced a training program under R.T.M.A. auspices to encourage servicing instruction on a nation-wide basis in vocational schools, to be supplemented—where the schools had no such courses —by a course prepared by the Radio Corporation of America Institute.

An all-over survey of the radio and television industry's prospects early in 1952 found McDaniel, according to the New York *Herald Tribune*, declaring that 1952 production levels would probably be below that of the preceding year. With augmented military production in view, McDaniel said, the industry could "step up employment and absorb much of the idle plant capacity that plagued the industry in mid-1951." (This would be chiefly in electronic equipment for the armed services.) On June 29, 1952, McDaniel announced his resignation as president of the Radio-Television Manufacturers Association.

The association president is a member of the Bar Association of the City of New York. His clubs are the Carmel Country and the Rockefeller Center Luncheon. In religion McDaniel is a Presbyterian. On March 4, 1942, Dorothy Sandlin, a soprano of the concert and opera stages, became his wife.

References

Business Executives of America (1950)
Who's Who in America, 1951-52
Who's Who in Commerce and Industry (1951)

MCDANIEL, HATTIE June 10, 1898— Oct. 26, 1952 Radio, television, motion picture actress; started career as singer; made motion picture debut in 1931, appearing in some 300 films; became first member of Negro race to receive the Academy of Motion Picture Arts and Sciences Award, for her performance as Mammy in *Gone With the Wind*

(1940); later moved to radio on the Eddie Cantor show and *Amos 'n' Andy;* became star of *Beulah* show on radio and television. See *Current Biography,* 1940.

Obituary

N Y Times p27 O 27 '52

MCGRANERY, JAMES P(ATRICK) July 8, 1895- United States Attorney General; judge

Address: b. c/o Department of Justice, Washington 25, D.C.; h. Hotel Warwick, Philadelphia, Pa.

To take over the duties of Attorney General of the United States from J. Howard McGrath, President Harry S. Truman on April 3, 1952, nominated Federal Judge James P. McGranery of the Eastern District of Pennsylvania. Judge McGranery is no stranger to the Justice Department. Prior to his appointment to the Federal bench in 1946, he had served for three years as Assistant to the Attorney General. From 1937 to 1943 Democrat McGranery represented the Second Pennsylvania District in the United States House of Representatives.

A native and lifelong resident of Philadelphia, James Patrick McGranery was born July 8, 1895, in the Pennsylvania city to Patrick and Bridget (Gallagher) McGranery, who came to this country from County Donegal in Ireland. Devout Roman Catholics, they sent their son to local parochial schools. Before completing his secondary education he worked for a while in the printing plant of the Curtis Publishing Company and today still carries a membership card of the Philadelphia Electrotypers and Finishers Union. When the United States entered World War I in 1917, McGranery joined the Army. Commissioned in the Air Force, he served as a balloon observation pilot and later also saw duty as an adjutant of the 111th Infantry. Upon being demobilized in 1919, he obtained the prerequisites at Maher Preparatory School for entrance to Temple University in his native city.

While still a student at Temple (stated a biographical sketch in *Time*) McGranery became active as a Democrat in South Philadelphia ward politics. When he graduated from the Temple University Law School and was admitted to the Pennsylvania bar in 1928, he began four years of membership in the Democratic State Committee and managed the Presidential campaign of Governor Alfred E. Smith of New York in the area. Defeated in his own first attempt to win a public office—as court clerk—he began legal practice as junior partner of the firm of Masterson & McGranery and "as a young lawyer . . . represented cops and the city's firemen's union" (*Time*). He campaigned unsuccessfully for election as a district attorney in 1931 and for Representative of the Second Pennsylvania District to the United States Congress in 1934. In 1934 McGranery was appointed chairman of the Registration

Wide World Photos

JAMES P. MCGRANERY

Committee of the City of Philadelphia by Pennsylvania's Democratic Governor, George H. Earle, and two years later he ran again for Congress in the Second Pennsylvania District comprising six Philadelphia wards. This time he was successful, defeating his Republican opponent by 65,779 to 41,267. McGranery was re-elected in 1938, 1940, and 1942.

In approximately seven years in the Seventy-fifth to Seventy-eighth Congresses, McGranery served successively on the House Banking and Currency, Interstate and Foreign Commerce, and Ways and Means committees. His voting record was generally that of a stanch New Dealer and party "regular." In his first two years his "Yeas" were for President Roosevelt's Supreme Court retirement bill and the Wagner housing bill (1937) and the wage-hour bill (1938). During June 1939 Representative McGranery caused a mild sensation by predicting that from seventy to seventy-five members of Congress would boycott a reception for the King and Queen of England unless the State Department moved for immediate release of the Irish revolutionary Séan Russell, who had been arrested in Michigan for illegal entry. In November 1939 and again in 1940 McGranery's vote was recorded against passage of the Hatch Act, he supported the Administration on lend-lease and the institution of price controls in 1941, and opposed the Smith antistrike bill in the same year. In July 1943 McGranery sponsored extension of the Guffey Coal Act before the House Rules Committee after continuation had been tabled by the Ways and Means Committee. Another vote of that year was his opposition to the Hobbs antiracketeering bill.

During his second term in Congress (1939-40) McGranery was sponsored by Pennsylvania's Senator Joseph F. Guffey for appointment as judge of the United States District Court for Eastern Pennsylvania in succession

MCGRANERY, JAMES P.—*Continued*

to President Roosevelt's recess appointee, Guy K. Bard. The expectation was that Bard would be given one of the new Federal judgeships about to be created, thus making way for Mc-Granery, but opposition to this maneuver developed in the Senate.

Three years later (October 7, 1943) President Roosevelt nominated McGranery to be Assistant to the Attorney General. Confirmed by the Senate, he resigned his seat in Congress on November 17, and for the next three years, under Attorney General Francis F. Biddle and his successor Tom Clark, had supervision over all major units of the Department of Justice and United States attorneys and marshals. He was chief liaison officer with Congress and other Departments and agencies.

During the World War II years he also handled reviews of the findings of the Board of Appeals under the Selective Service Act. (His paper entitled *The Department of Justice and the War* appeared in the *Pennsylvania Bar Association Quarterly* for October 1944.) As to the degree of McGranery's connection in 1945-46 with the outcome of the *Amerasia* case (resulting from the discovery by the FBI of "top secret" documents in the office of that periodical), there have been varying estimates. Frederick Woltman of the New York *World-Telegram* was of the opinion that the case should be scrutinized with special attention to McGranery's part in it. *Time*, on the other hand, reported that "McGranery was not involved in the controversial prosecution." McGranery himself declared in testimony before a House of Representatives investigating committee that "what blew up the case" was an illegal entry by the FBI. In March 1946 he received from the President a Medal for Merit for his wartime service with the Department of Justice.

Named by President Truman as the United States Federal Court Judge for the Eastern District of Pennsylvania, McGranery resigned as Assistant to the Attorney General on October 4, 1946. His appointment unanimously confirmed by the Senate, he was sworn in as judge five days later. In the course of about five and a half years on the Federal bench, from time to time McGranery was reportedly considered for Cabinet or high party posts, but "each time . . . was sidetracked by protests from other segments of the badly divided Democratic party in Pennsylvania" (Oliver Pilat in the New York *Post*). Offices in connection with which he was mentioned were Postmaster General, Chairman of the Democratic National Committee, and Attorney General. As a judge, McGranery made headlines in 1949 by refusing to let Representative Earl Chudoff, a Philadelphia Democrat, appear as a defense attorney in his court on the ground that no Congressman had the right to represent a client in a Federal proceeding; and in 1950 he presided over the espionage trial of Harry Gold.

Announcement that President Truman had chosen Judge McGranery to succeed J. Howard McGrath as Attorney General of the United States was made at the press conference on April 3, 1952. (McGrath's resignation had followed closely on his own dismissal of Newbold Morris, the special assistant named two months earlier to conduct an investigation of corrupt practices in government.) Interviewed in his chambers in Philadelphia the same day, McGranery announced that his job would be "to restore the faith of the American people in the Government of the United States" and that it would be done "completely by the Department of Justice." This was interpreted as meaning that neither Morris nor any other special assistant from outside the Department would spearhead the investigation. The assumption was confirmed on the following day when McGranery conferred with the President in Washington and afterward stated that the Morris office would be "dismantled quickly" and that he would rely on the FBI to ferret out possible malfeasance. "The first order of business," he told the press, "is to find out if a clean-up is needed and where." In Congress, meanwhile, Representative Harold H. Velde, an Illinois Republican who had formerly been an FBI agent, questioned McGranery's connection with the *Amerasia* case; and on April 6 Senator Pat McCarran of Nevada, chairman of the Senate Judiciary Committee (the Committee which would approve his appointment before the Senate would vote) revealed that he had called on the FBI for a report on McGranery's record. Upon confirmation of his appointment by the Senate, he took his oath of office as the Attorney General of the United States on May 27, 1952.

Judge McGranery is active as a Roman Catholic layman. He is a trustee of Immaculata College and a member of the advisory council of Villanova College, which awarded him an honorary Doctor of Laws degree in 1949; he is also a member of the advisory board of the Law School of Temple University. At the Vatican in April 1950 Pope Pius conferred on him the insignia of Knight Commander of the Order of St. Gregory the Great; and in May of the next year the Pope appointed him a Private Chamberlain of the Cape and Sword. Also, in 1951 Judge McGranery received an honorary Doctor of Humanities degree from LaSalle College in Philadelphia.

A member of the Pennsylvania Bar Association and the American Bar Association, McGranery also belongs to the American Judicature Society and is an honorary member of the Association of Immigration and Nationality Lawyers of the United States. Other memberships of his are in the American Legion, the Pennsylvania Society, the American Catholic Historical Society, and the Friendly Sons of St. Patrick; his fraternity is the Phi Alpha Delta, and his clubs are the Philopatrian Literary Institute in Philadelphia and the Manhattan in New York City. Mrs. McGranery, the former Regina T. Clark, is, like her husband, a lawyer and was at one time a special deputy to the Attorney General of Pennsylvania. The couple, who were married November 29, 1939, have two sons, James Patrick, Jr., and Clark, and a daughter, Regina. Five feet ten inches in height, he weighs 165 pounds.

James Patrick McGranery has blue-gray eyes, graying black hair and a ruddy complexion; he is described in *Time* as an "affable, self-assured, vigorous speaker with an infectious smile," while Oliver Pilat has noted that he is "always gregarious" and "a great storyteller." He used to enjoy horseback riding and golf.

References

Christian Sci Mon p12 Ap 4 '52
N Y Herald Tribune II p2 Ap 6 '52 por
N Y Post Mag p2 Ap 6 '52 por
N Y Times p1 Ap 4 '52 por
N Y World-Telegram p13 Ap 5 '52
Newsweek 39:27 Ap 14 '52 por
Time 59:22 Ap 14 '52 por
U S News 32:52 Ap 11 '52
Washington (D.C.) Post p4 Ap 4 '52; p4B Ap 5 '52 por; p13B Ap 8 '52
American Catholic Who's Who, 1952-53
Biographical Directory of the American Congress, 1774-1949 (1950)
Congressional Directory (1937)
Who's Who in America, 1950-51
Who's Who in the Nation's Capital, 1938-39
Who's Who in United States Politics (1950)
World Biography (1948)

MACK, NILA (nī′lä) Radio writer-director-producer

Address: b. c/o Columbia Broadcasting System, Inc., 485 Madison Ave., New York 22; h. 55 W. 53rd St., New York 19

For almost a quarter of a century Nila Mack has been writing, directing, and producing one of radio's oldest children's programs, *Let's Pretend,* heard every Saturday morning over the nation-wide network of the Columbia Broadcasting System. Her original adaptations have won her numerous awards from educational and social groups as outstanding contributions to the field of radio entertainment for children. Using the fairy tales of such well-known authors as Hans Christian Andersen, Andrew Lang, and the Grimm brothers, Miss Mack has adapted some 200 of these classics for radio dramatization; to play all the roles in the fantasies she has trained and directed two generations of child actors, many of whom have gone on to professional radio, stage, and screen careers. Immediately before becoming the director of *Let's Pretend* in 1930, Miss Mack had been a program director for a small local station. Her earlier work in the field of entertainment included several years in vaudeville and the legitimate theater.

Nila Mack is a native of Arkansas City, Kansas, and the only daughter of a railroad engineer and a dancing teacher. Her family name, which had been MacLoughlin when her ancestors arrived in the United States from Scotland, was shortened to Mac and later became Mack. When young Nila was still a student at the local grammar school, her father, who had had the honor of running the

NILA MACK

first train on the Sante Fe Railroad over the tracks into "Indian territory," met his death as the result of a train accident in which his actions had saved the lives of the passengers. After the death of her father, her mother opened a dancing school, where young Nila played the piano for the matinee classes as well as for private lessons, using her earnings to pay for her own theatrical training. By the time she was a student in the city's high school she had become the pianist for the local open-air motion picture theater which from time to time was also used as the stage for touring dramatic companies. While still living in Arkansas City, Miss Mack also participated in regional entertainments, showing talent as an actress, dancer, and singer. Competing in the cake-walking contests held at that time, she won 208 cakes.

From high school, Miss Mack entered Ferry Hall, a girls' finishing school in Lake Forest, Illinois, here meeting part of her tuition costs from her earnings as an entertainer. After completing the course at Ferry Hall, she went to Boston, Massachusetts, for further training in dancing, voice, and French. It was at this time, when she was sixteen years old, that she was offered her first professional engagement— as leading lady in a Western repertory company, at a salary of $25.00 a week. With her mother, who had closed the family home in order to accompany her daughter, she traveled throughout the United States. In the course of the tour Miss Mack met Roy Briant, an actor with the company, who was to become her husband a few years later. At Metropolis, Illinois, the stage troupe, in which both Briant and Miss Mack were by then playing leading roles, ran out of funds and engagements. Miss Mack, her mother, and Briant decided to establish a second theater in the town, Briant to act as manager, Miss Mack to play the piano, and Miss Mack's mother to sell tickets.

(Continued next page)

MACK, NILA—*Continued*

Since this venture did not prosper, Miss Mack and Briant joined another touring company, and after their marriage in St. Anthony, Idaho, enjoyed considerable success as husband and wife romantic leading players.

Just before the beginning of World War 1 the couple settled in Chicago, where Briant worked as a writer for Paramount Pictures and Miss Mack became a member of the theatrical company organized by the famous actress, Alla Nazimova. For six years Miss Mack remained with the Nazimova company, in which she had a role in the film, *War Brides*, starring Madame Nazimova. As Miss Mack was preparing for a Broadway role, she was called to Los Angeles to be with her ill husband, who shortly afterward died. Some time later she returned to the stage as a vaudeville trouper, writing the lyrics for her numbers. During the seventy-five weeks that she appeared with Tom Wise, she also wrote scenarios for movie shorts. In 1927 she played in that year's Broadway production of *Fair and Warmer*; she was also a member of the cast for Ibsen's *The Doll's House*. Then becoming interested in the expanding field of radio, Miss Mack joined the Columbia Broadcasting System as an actress and took part in the *Radio Guild* productions, which became the basis for the successful experimental program later known as *The Columbia Workshop*. On the radio she also had roles in *Nit-Wits* and *Night Club Romances*. These New York engagements came to an end when Miss Mack returned to Arkansas City in order to take care of her mother. There she found employment as program director for the local radio station and learned the many phases of radio production. In 1930 CBS asked her to return to New York to direct its children's program *The Adventures of Helen and Mary*, which under her supervision became known as *Let's Pretend*. This program, CBS Radio Network's oldest continuous dramatic series and Miss Mack's major radio effort, on September 27, 1952, celebrated its twenty-second anniversary.

Describing her early work with the children's program, Miss Mack, in an interview in the New York *World-Telegram* (September 18, 1952), recalled: "We were deep in the depression when this began. Children's entertainment was at a low ebb. I remembered fairy stories that filled me with wonder when I was very young. I figured that if these lively pieces with a message at their hearts had meant so much to me, other children would like them, too." With this point of view, Miss Mack began to adapt the classic stories of the Grimm brothers, Hans Christian Andersen, Andrew Lang, and the *Arabian Nights* for radio presentation, modifying them, where necessary, to emphasize honor, service in a good cause, courtesy, and kindness. Her scripts plainly speak against racial prejudice and she wrote an original allegorical drama, *Castles of Hatred*, to dispel the idea that all stepmothers are cruel. Unlike many programs for children, Miss Mack's productions make no effort to compete with what *Newsweek* has called "the bang-bang cliff hangers which set the little ones' glands to working

overtime just before supper." Instead, her dramatizations, which are carried every Saturday morning over the network of CBS, are filled with "kings and queens and princes who ride talking horses through enchanted forests." The author does not present scripts which maintain a condition of suspense at the end because she believes that each story should be completed each week, with "blood and thunder" in the middle, perhaps, but everything coming out right in the end, the villains having received their due punishment.

Another innovation on *Let's Pretend* is Miss Mack's use of children rather than adults to enact all the roles, since it is her conviction that fantasy and the elements needed to produce the effects of magic and unreality are best achieved through the use of child actors who can transmit the childlike wonder of fairy tales to an audience of children. Thus, Miss Mack instituted auditions for talented boys and girls ranging in age from five to sixteen, coached them in microphone technique, and gradually built a repertory company of veteran actors who could rotate in the playing of starring, featured, and minor roles, with emphasis placed on the total production, rather than on the performances of individual actors. As soon as a child is able to read scripts Miss Mack begins to train him in radio acting; in her twenty-two years with children she has trained such successful performers as Nancy Kelly of the stage and screen, Rosalyn Silber of the radio program, *The Goldbergs*, and several of the boys who played the first roles in the stage and cinema productions of *The Dead End Kids*.

Since *Let's Pretend* was established it has won more than forty awards as the "best children's program in radio." These acclamations have come from the poll of radio editors in the New York *World-Telegram, Motion Picture Daily,* and *Radio Day,* from the Women's Press Club of New York City, the Women's National Radio Committee, and the Illinois Federation of Women's Clubs. In 1943 *Let's Pretend* won the George Foster Peabody Award, sometimes called the Pulitzer Prize of radio; it was voted the "most effective commercial program developed by a national network" by the College of the City of New York and "the national program contributing most to education and public interest" by the American Schools and Colleges Association.

While each week a different Saturday morning drama is presented, there are a few perennials which are repeated each year. Among these are *Cinderella, Goldilocks,* and *Little Red Riding Hood,* which in 1951 were given in modern musical comedy versions, and Miss Mack's original *House of the World,* an allegory of Good Will's triumph over Intolerance, Greed, Selfishness, and Poverty, which since 1933 has been presented every year during the Christmas season. The radio writer and producer has written several children's stories for magazines, a book titled *Animal Allies,* and an illustrated story book based on the popular radio dramas. Recordings of the favorite fantasies from *Let's Pretend* have also been made.

Time magazine (September 8, 1952) related that Miss Mack is convinced that children today, in spite of the new models for heroes being offered them, still like to hear about giants, witches, and fairy godmothers. She is quoted as saying: "I'll back seven league boots and magic wands any time against six-shooters and space ships." Miss Mack keeps two Siamese cats, Sapphire and Tsing Fooey, in her midtown Manhattan terrace apartment.

References

> Newsweek 21:108 Je 28 '43
> Time 60:85 S 8 '52
> Variety 163:34 Ag 21 '46

MACKAY, JOHN A(LEXANDER), REV.
(mȧ-kī') May 17, 1889- Theologian

Address: b. c/o Princeton Theological Seminary, Princeton, N.J.; h. 86 Mercer St., Princeton, N.J.

The third president of Princeton Theological Seminary, the oldest Presbyterian theological school in the United States, is the Reverend Dr. John A. Mackay, who has served as president and professor of ecumenics there since 1936. For a number of years prior to that time he was an educational missionary in Peru, and later lectured and wrote for the South American Federation of YMCA's. He has held office as secretary (1932-36) and president (1944-51) of the Board of Foreign Missions of the Presbyterian Church, U.S.A. Since 1948 Dr. Mackay has been chairman of the International Missionary Council and a member of the Central Committee of the World Council of Churches.

Born in Inverness, Scotland, on May 17, 1889, John Alexander Mackay is the son of Duncan and Isabella (Macdonald) Mackay. According to *Newsweek*, he decided at the age of fourteen to become a minister. Of this he has written in the *Christian Century*: "At the time of my conversion as a high school boy . . . I caught from St. Paul in his letter to the Ephesians a vision of Christ as the center and meaning of all things." Mackay obtained his M.A. degree, with first class honors in philosophy, from the University of Aberdeen in 1912, and also attended theological schools of the Free Presbyterian Church of Scotland, in Inverness (1910-11), and in Wick (1912-13). Going to the United States in 1913 as a Fullerton scholar in philosophy, he pursued further studies at Princeton Theological Seminary, which awarded him a B.D. degree two years later. As Gelston-Winthrop fellow in didactic and polemic theology, he spent the year 1915-16 studying Spanish literature at the University of Madrid. It was at this time that he first met Miguel de Unamuno, the Spanish philosopher, whose personality and work were the subject of Mackay's dissertation. In *The Other Spanish Christ* he described Unamuno: "[He was] the man who had opened up for me the secrets of the Spanish soul, and whose writings had stirred my mind more than those of any contemporary thinker."

Returning to Scotland, Mackay was ordained a Presbyterian minister in Inverness on August 1, 1916. Later that year he was sent

Wide World Photos
REV. JOHN A. MACKAY

as an educational missionary of the Free Church of Scotland to Lima, Peru, where he founded the Anglo-Peruvian College and was its principal until 1925. Under his leadership this secondary school became one of the outstanding Protestant institutions in Latin America. The National University of San Marcos, in Lima, conferred a Litt. D. degree upon Dr. Mackay in 1918—reportedly the first it had ever given to a foreigner—and seven years later appointed him to the chairs of metaphysics and the history of modern philosophy. In 1925 he moved to Montevideo, Uruguay, accepting an invitation from the South America Federation of the Young Men's Christian Associations to lecture under its auspices in various university centers throughout the continent. Dr. Mackay studied at the University of Bonn, Germany, in 1930—the year that Karl Barth, the Swiss theologian, began teaching there. In response to a request from a group of Mexican intellectuals that he concentrate his evangelist YMCA activities in that country, Dr. Mackay next lived in Mexico City during 1930-32. He returned to the United States in the latter year to become a secretary (with special responsibility for the work carried on in Latin America) of the Board of Foreign Missions of the Presbyterian Church, U.S.A., a position he held for four years. In December 1944 he was elected to succeed the Reverend Dr. Paul C. Johnston as president of the board, in which office he continued until June 1951. From 1944 to 1946 he was also chairman of the Council of Theological Education of the Presbyterian Church, U.S.A.

On May 18, 1936, it was announced by the board of trustees of Princeton Theological Seminary that Dr. Mackay had been elected the third president of that institution. (During the nineteenth century—it was founded in 1812—no presidential appointments were made, the senior

MACKAY, JOHN A., REV.—*Continued*
member of the faculty having acted as administrative head.) He officially accepted the post early the next month, succeeding the Reverend Dr. J. Ross Stevenson, who resigned after serving as the seminary's head since 1914. Dr. Mackay assumed his new duties at the opening of the fall term in 1936 and was formally installed February 2, 1937—the year that the Seminary celebrated the 125th anniversary of its founding. In his inaugural address, "The Restoration of Theology," he stated that the churches "must return to theology or they will perish. . . .We are living in a time when only the emergence and dominance of a great theology will produce a great philosophy on the one hand and a great religion on the other." He felt that "world view" was needed, not only to give unity and direction to the educational programs of the universities, but also "to give meaning and unity to life and thought in general." According to an interview reported in the New York *Times*, he outlined plans to reorganize the seminary's curriculum in accordance with this philosophy of religious education, placing greater emphasis on graduate work and such subjects as religion, theology, and philosophy, and developing studies in Christian ecumenics. Three months after Dr. Mackay's installation, plans were announced for a drive to raise over two million dollars to provide for the seminary's general needs and for modernization of its plant and equipment; these plans were based on a survey made by the new president.

The seminary which Dr. Mackay heads is the oldest Presbyterian theological school in the United States. The proposal which led to its foundation took definite form in 1809; its plan was adopted by the General Assembly of the Presbyterian Church in 1811; and the school was established in Princeton in 1812 and its first session began in August of that year with three students and one instructor. Since then nearly 10,000 students have been enrolled, coming from all parts of the United States and from many foreign countries. At the 1950 commencement 119 degrees were awarded—the largest number in the institution's history, and in 1951 there were 403 students in attendance. Academic reciprocity between the seminary and Princeton University secure for students of either institution admission to the courses of the other without additional tuition. Under Dr. Mackay's guidance the seminary instituted in 1940 a course of study leading to the degree of D.Theol.; organized the annual summer sessions of the Princeton Institute of Theology to provide instruction, inspiration, and fellowship for ministers and laymen belonging to many different denominations; and established in 1944 the graduate School of Christian Education, which confers the degree of Master of Religious Education and admits a selected group of young women. The seminary campus, enlarged in 1943 by the acquisition of the land and buildings belonging to the Hun Preparatory School, by 1951 covered thirty acres and the plant comprised twelve buildings. Construction was begun in that year on a new $900,000 Student Center.

In addition to his teaching duties at Princeton Theological Seminary, where he has been professor of ecumenics since 1937, Mackay has delivered series of lectures at a number of other institutions. He was Merrick lecturer at Ohio Wesleyan University (1932); James Sprunt lecturer at Union Theological Seminary, in Richmond, Virginia (1940); Lyman Coleman lecturer at Lafayette College (1941); Otts Foundation lecturer at Davidson College (1942); Chancellor's lecturer at Queen's University, in Kingston, Canada (1945); Charles F. Deems lecturer at New York University (1945); Moore lecturer at San Francisco Theological Seminary (1945); N. A. Powell lecturer at the Canadian School of Missions (1946); Croall Foundation lecturer at New College, Edinburgh University (1948); Gary lecturer at the Southern Baptist Theological Seminary, in Louisville (1948); and Fondern lecturer at Southern Methodist University, in Dallas (1949). In 1941 he was made a member of the advisory council of the department of philosophy at Princeton University.

Since January 1, 1948, when he succeeded Bishop James Chamberlain Baker, Dr. Mackay has served as chairman of the International Missionary Council (I.M.C.), an international body composed of various national missionary organizations and Christian Councils. A prominent figure in the ecumenical movement, the churchman attended the Jerusalem meeting of the I.M.C. in 1928, and was chairman of the Commission on the Universal Church and the World of Nations at the Oxford Conference on Church, Community, and State in 1937. From 1946 to 1948 a member of the provisional committee of the World Council of Churches, he was present at the first General Assembly of that organization, held in Amsterdam in August 1948. Since then he has held membership on its Central Committee, and attended the committee's first annual meeting at Chichester, England, in July 1949. Immediately thereafter he went to Buenos Aires as guest speaker at the Inter-American Evangelical Conference, sponsored by the Committee on Cooperation in Latin America and the Evangelical Councils of Central and South America. In December of that year, as chairman of the joint committee of the World Council and the I.M.C., he attended the East Asian Conference held under the auspices of the two groups in Bangkok, Thailand. During the summer of 1951 he visited Europe to study for the I.M.C. the status of Protestants in five predominantly Roman Catholic countries.

A frequent contributor to the *Missionary Review*, *International Review of Missions*, New York *Times Magazine*, *Christian Century*, and other periodicals, the clergyman served also as editor of *Theology Today* (1944-51) and is now chairman of its editorial council. His first two books were written in Spanish and published in South America: "*. . . Mas Yo os Digo*" (1927) and *El Sentido de la Vida* (1931). Of his next volume, *The Other Spanish Christ; a Study in the Spiritual History of Spain and South America* (1933), W. W.

Sweet stated in the *Christian Century* that it was "the best book in English" for "those who desire to understand contemporary religion in South America." This was followed in 1935 by *That Other America.* According to N. F. S. Ferré (*Journal of Religion*), Mackay's *A Preface to Christian Theology* (1941) made "available simply and beautifully, the best both in the attitude and in the insight of a new age." *Heritage and Destiny* (1943), which, in the opinion of H. P. Van Dusen (*Crozer Quarterly*), laid bare "the contradictions and frustrations of the contemporary scene" and found their resolution "through profounder apprehension of the classic Christian views of God, of man, and of community." More recently (1950) *Christianity on the Frontier* appeared. Reviewing this collection of essays for the *Christian Science Monitor*, Neil Martin said they indicated that the author saw "as clearly as any man today the present dangers to freedom."

Honorary D.D. degrees have been conferred upon the seminary president by Princeton University (1937), Aberdeen University (1939), Debrecen University in Hungary (1939), and Presbyterian College in Montreal, Canada (1942); the LL. D. by Ohio Wesleyan University (1937) and Albright College (1938); and the L.H.D. by Boston University and Lafayette College (both 1939). Elected an honorary fellow of Stanford University in 1941, he is a trustee of Waynesburg (Pennsylvania) College and served as president of the board of trustees of Mackenzie College, in São Paulo, Brazil, in 1948. Organizations in which he holds memberships include the American Association of Theological Schools (president, 1948-50); British and Foreign Bible Society (honorary foreign member); and the American Theological Society. Dr. Mackay was a founding member and one of the two vice-presidents of Protestants and Other Americans United for Separation of Church and State, a national organization which was formed in January 1948. He belongs to the Nassau Club in Princeton. On August 16, 1916, John Mackay married Jane Logan Wells; they have four children: Isobel Elizabeth, Duncan Alexander Duff, Elena Florence, and Ruth. A New York *Times* interviewer once described the theologian as "vigorous and earnest . . . with a bit of native Scottish burr in his speech." His favorite recreations are listed as walking and motoring.

References

Christian Cent 56:873-5 Jl 12 '39; 76: 888-890 Jl 27 '49
London Q R 173:5-6 Ja '48
N Y Times p26 My 19 '36; VIII p12 F 21 '37; p12 D 22 '44 pors
Newsweek 7:37 Je 13 '36
Directory of American Scholars, 1942
Leaders in Education (1948)
Religious Leaders of America, 1941-42
Who's Who, 1951
Who's Who in America, 1950-51
Who's Who in American Education, 1947-48
Who's Who in Philosophy (1942)
World Biography (1948)

MCKELDIN, THEODORE R(OOSE-VELT) Nov. 20, 1900- Governor of Maryland; lawyer

Address: b. State House, Annapolis, Md.; h. Government House, Annapolis, Md.

"Mr. Republican" of Maryland, reputedly his party's most effective speaker and best vote-getter in the State, Theodore R. McKeldin was elected Governor in 1950 by the largest majority in Maryland's history. He had some years earlier been called from his law practice to fill a four-year term as mayor of Baltimore (1943-47), the city's first Republican mayor in twelve years. At the Republican National Convention in July 1952 it was McKeldin who placed in nomination the name of Dwight D. Eisenhower for President of the United States.

Theodore Roosevelt McKeldin was born in South Baltimore, Maryland, on November 20, 1900, one of eleven children of James Alfred and Dora (Grief) McKeldin. His father, the son of a Scotch-Irish immigrant from Belfast, was successively a stonemason and a policeman. His mother was brought to this country as a baby by her parents, who left Germany because of their opposition to militarism. It was from his mother, related Edward F. Ryan in the Washington *Post*, that young McKeldin learned "his one hobby, work." After graduating from grammar school at the age of fourteen he took a job in a bank as an office boy at five dollars a week. With his mother's encouragement he took high school courses at night, but his lack of a regular high school education, he has said, checked his ambition to become a preacher. On his first vacation from his bank job he obtained work as a grave digger to earn extra money. He attended night classes until receiving the LL.B. degree in 1925 from the University of Maryland Law School, where he won the Gold Honor Key. Many years later (in 1947) McKeldin studied economics at Johns Hopkins University

Soon after he was admitted to the bar, he entered politics by campaigning for William F. Broening, candidate for mayor of Baltimore. When Broening was elected in 1927, he named McKeldin as his executive secretary. Four years later, upon the termination of his secretaryship, McKeldin turned to private law practice. His office, situated on the eighteenth floor of a Baltimore skyscraper, afforded him an inspiring view of the city. "From here," he pointed out to an interviewer, "you see the very basis for the greatness of Baltimore, its magnificent harbor. . . .Over there on Sparrows Point are the steel plants, the largest on the Eastern Seaboard. . . .Here is where the great masses of people in East Baltimore and South Baltimore live and it's a challenge to you to see that their conditions in life are improved." In 1939 he was unsuccessful in his campaign to be elected Mayor of Baltimore. Three years later he made the first of several bids for the governorship. "Nobody would run," he has told, "and I considered it a joke that I should aspire to that high office. But the campaign was going by default, and I considered that a disgrace. So I waited until 11:55 P.M. (with a midnight deadline) and then when no one else filed, I

THEODORE R. MCKELDIN

did." Again he was defeated. "He polished up his oratory," the New York *Sun* reported, ran for mayor a second time in 1943, and scored an upset victory. According to his own estimate, twice as many Democrats as Republicans voted for him. As mayor, his associates stated, he demonstrated a talent for concentrated serious effort. "I have been a champion of minority groups," McKeldin has said, "and during my term as mayor of Baltimore, I appointed the first Negro assistant city solicitor and made numerous other appointments of that nature."

Having lost again in his campaign for the Governorship in 1946, McKeldin, on the expiration of his term as mayor the following year, returned once more to private law practice. He entered his third gubernatorial race in 1950. An "irrepressible vote-chaser," as he has been described, with a vivid oratorical style, he conducted an intense and vigorous campaign, spending little time at his headquarters, preferring to appear before the electorate as much as possible. He based his campaign chiefly on opposition to the sales tax instituted by his predecessor and opponent, Democratic Governor William Preston Lane, Jr., promising to work for its "eventual elimination." A three-to-one Democratic registration notwithstanding, McKeldin was elected by an unprecedented majority and became the fourth Republican governor in the history of the State. The Southern High School of Baltimore sent him a class ring, school letter, diploma, and a complete set of grades, the lowest of which was 93. "From meager beginnings in South Baltimore," as the New York *Times* put it, "the one-time boy orator had vaulted all the way to the State's highest honor." In his inaugural address, delivered January 10, 1951, the new Governor stressed civilian defense as Maryland's foremost problem and the need to adopt "a policy of rigid economy."

On the basis of his experience as mayor of Baltimore, where, he said, he "worked perfectly with a Democratic city council," he was confident that he would be able to cooperate with a Democratic Legislature. Soon after he took office, however, the Legislature overrode two gubernatorial vetoes—the first time that this had happened in Maryland in fifty years—and by May 1951 he had vetoed sixty bills. He made his views known on various local and national issues in a series of speeches in 1951 and 1952. Addressing the Baltimore Advertising Club in April 1951, he sharply criticized the practice of lobbying in Annapolis by State department heads. "I intend to do whatever is in my power at future sessions of the Legislature," he stated in part, "to stop this practice. Proper legislation should stand on its own virtues. Improper legislation should die of its own ills." At the annual Conference of County Commissioners in September 1951, he expressed his belief that Federal and State governments had "grown too big," and advocated "more home rule for the counties of Maryland." Opening the annual convention of the Maryland State Teachers Association the following month, he denounced "the smear technique," "the big lie," and "the sly innuendo," which he said constituted the greatest menace to personal liberty in the United States. "There is a deplorable intolerance which characterizes much of our so-called public discussion," he added. "It is conducted not on the level of a debate; it descends to name calling and mud slinging."

At the Southern Governors Conference in November 1951, McKeldin, the only Republican Governor present, surprised many of his conservative colleagues, the *Christian Science Monitor* reported, "with outspoken advocacy of many of the social reforms of the New Deal and Fair Deal." He urged that no "Dixiecrat" or any other splinter party be set up in the South, remarking that Republican chances of winning several Southern States in 1952 would be improved if there were no splinter party to appeal to those Democrats who were dissatisfied with the Truman Administration. McKeldin was the main speaker at the Lincoln Day Dinner of the National Republican Club on February 12, 1952, in New York, on which occasion he attacked corruption in the Democratic Administration and predicted: "The plundering potentates of the Potomac and the pusillanimous parasites of the palace guard are having their last ride on the merry-go-round of privilege and pelf."

On a European tour in the spring of 1952, the Maryland chief executive visited General Eisenhower in Paris and discussed with him the possibility that Maryland's twenty-six Republican convention delegates would vote for him. "If I don't get the nomination on the first ballot," McKeldin afterward told reporters in reference to his own "favorite son" candidacy, "we will decide who the delegation will vote for. I always follow the leadership of Governor Dewey, and Dewey, as you know, is backing Eisenhower." This statement, he explained subsequently, was an expression of personal preference only; the delegation would be unpledged and entirely free to vote its own choice. On July 7, 1952, at the opening of the Republican National Convention, McKeldin was chosen to place General Eisenhower in nomination for President. By accepting the assignment, he at once put an end to his own nominal candidacy. One of his most recent official acts was the dedication on July 30, 1952, of the new $45 millions Chesapeake Bay Bridge, which connects Maryland's Eastern Shore with the "mainland." He hailed the bridge, which was projected by his predecessor, as a symbol of America and of industrial progress.

McKeldin has been a director of South Baltimore General Hospital, member of the board of the Council of Social Agencies of Baltimore, member of the Real Estate Board, chairman of the Board of the Baltimore Civic Opera Company, second president of the Junior Association of Commerce. Other organizations to which he belongs are the American and Maryland bar associations, German Society, Maryland Historical Society, Hibernian Society, St. Andrews Society, Elks, Odd Fellows, Tall Cedars of Lebanon, Order of the Eastern Star, Order of Amaranth, the Kiwanis Club, the Advertising Club, and the Trial Table Law Club. He is a 32d degree Mason, a Knight Templar, and a Shriner. His Greek letter societies are Sigma Phi Epsilon, Phi Theta Pi, and Tau Kappa Alpha. McKeldin holds honorary LL.D. degrees from Rider College, University of Maryland, Morgan College, Washington College, Beaver College, Hanover College, Eastern Nazarene College, and Westminster College, and an honorary D.Lit. degree from Indiana Central College. He formerly taught at the University of Baltimore Law School, the Baltimore College of Commerce, and Forest Park Evening School. With Dr. John C. Krantz he wrote *The Art of Eloquence*.

Maryland's Governor, whose church is the Episcopal, has been a Sunday school teacher and is said to be "so thoroughly at home in the pulpit" that he has frequently been invited to preach, without regard to sect. He married the former Honolulu Claire Manzer on October 17, 1924; they have two children—Theodore Roosevelt, Jr., and Claire Whitney. McKeldin is six feet two and one half inches tall and weighs about 210 pounds; he has brown hair and blue eyes.

References

N Y Sun p16 Jl 15 '46
N Y Times p13 Jl 8 '52
Washington (D.C.) Post p3B O 29 '50; p14 N 15 '50 por; p1 Ja 10 '51; p1B Ja 11 '51

MACKENZIE, C(HALMERS) J(ACK)
July 10, 1888- Canadian Government official; civil engineer

Address: b. c/o Atomic Energy Control Board, Ottawa, Ontario, Canada; h. 210 Buena Vista Rd., Rockcliffe, Ottawa, Ontario, Canada

The wartime and postwar atomic energy research carried on by Canada has been directed by C. J. Mackenzie, who became president of the Atomic Energy Control Board of Canada

Capital Press Service

C. J. MACKENZIE

in 1948 and who in 1952 is head of Atomic Energy of Canada, Ltd., the crown company formed to develop industrial uses of atomic energy. From 1939 to 1952 Mackenzie was successively acting president and president of the National Research Council of Canada. Prior to that he was dean of the Faculty of Engineering at the University of Saskatchewan and a consulting engineer on major projects.

Chalmers Jack Mackenzie was born July 10, 1888, to James and Janet (Campbell) Mackenzie. For his early education he attended schools in his native town, St. Stephen, New Brunswick, Canada. A year after receiving his Bachelor of Engineering degree from Dalhousie (Halifax) University in 1909, he began to practice as consulting engineer as a member of the Edmonton (Canada) partnership of Maxwell and Mackenzie, with which he was associated for five years. In 1914 Mackenzie took his master's degree in civil engineering at Harvard University. From 1916 to 1918 he saw World War I duty overseas with the 54th Canadian Infantry Battalion, a service for which he was awarded the Military Cross in the latter year.

Upon his return to Canada, Mackenzie in 1918 was invited to become professor of civil engineering at the University of Saskatchewan. There he was named Dean of the College of Engineering three years later. During this period (1921-39) Mackenzie engaged in engineering practice as a consultant on a number of municipal and structural engineering projects, including the design and construction of two reinforced concrete bridges in Saskatchewan.

In October 1939 Mackenzie was appointed acting president of the National Research Council of Canada, of which he was named president in 1944. Under the supervision of the NRC, said Herbert Nichols of the *Christian Science*

MACKENZIE, C. J.—*Continued*

Monitor, are hydraulic, construction, and aeronautic research laboratories, radar laboratories, and regional laboratories in Saskatchewan and Nova Scotia, as well as other projects in universities and institutions subsidized by the NRC. Fifty postdoctoral fellowships are given annually by the Council to both Canadian and foreign researchers for study in its laboratories. Among the projects under way in 1950 were research on conversion of heat from the earth and on artificial rainfall, river control, and cold weather lubricants.

A great part of the Council's postwar research has been concerned with atomic energy developments, the Council having taken over administration of the Atomic Energy Project at Chalk River, Ontario, in February 1947. Responsibility for this enterprise has rested chiefly with Mackenzie, who was appointed president of the Atomic Energy Control Board of Canada in 1948. Early in the previous year he had announced for the Council that Canada had succeeded in obtaining small stockpiles of plutonium through heavy water reaction—the research on which Canadian scientists were engaged during World War II, while United States researchers concentrated on obtaining a similar result from graphite.

In 1947, too, Mackenzie estimated that twenty years' work would be needed to develop atomic energy as an economical substitute for other power, with the first five-year period limited to purely experimental research. Of Canada's determination to concentrate on peacetime uses of atomic energy, Mackenzie said: "We can't afford to concern ourselves with any possible atomic arms race. . . .We think of atomic energy as possibly the biggest scientific field of all time, and all the plutonium and allied fission products we can produce will quickly be used up here at home for fundamental physical, chemical, and biological research" (*Christian Science Monitor*). With radioactive isotopes, Mackenzie told a press conference in late 1947, Canada expected to develop new agricultural methods (particularly in the use of fertilizers); it was also announced that Canada was offering isotopes for the use of medical researchers.

In a plea for a more liberal exchange of atomic information between the United States and Canada, Mackenzie in 1951 revealed that Canada had developed a presumably faster atom-splitting reactor than any known to be used by the Americans, stated Frank Carey of the Washington *Post*. Because of the McMahon Act passed by the United States Congress in 1946, the flow of atomic information from the United States to Canada was cut off. Of this stoppage Mackenzie remarked: "There's nothing about the atomic bomb that would help our research, but our research might help makers of the bomb." When Great Britain, Canada, and the United States agreed in early 1952 to exchange vital metals, the question was reopened, with the result that by the end of January resumption of the exchange of information again began, made possible by an amendment to the McMahon Act.

With the formation of Atomic Energy of Canada, Ltd., a crown company, the Chalk River plant passed under its control in April 1952. According to the Canadian weekly *Saturday Night*, Mackenzie, while retaining the presidency of the Atomic Energy Control Board, would be relieved of the administrative duties connected with the National Research Council of Canada in order to serve as head of the new crown company. Besides supervising the construction of a new thirty-million-dollar reactor at Chalk River, Atomic Energy of Canada under Mackenzie would develop industrial uses of atomic energy. "Mackenzie will have to pick the projects that pay off," said *Saturday Night*.

Engineer Mackenzie has performed other services for his Government: he has been a member of the Council for Scientific and Industrial Research (since 1935), of the Defense Research Board, of the Inventions Board (1940-49), the Army Technical Development Board (1942), and chairman of the War Technical and Scientific Development Committee (1942). He was chairman of the Saskatoon City Planning Commission (1928-39) and chairman of the Saskatoon City Hospital Board (1937-39).

Professional societies to which Mackenzie belongs are the Engineering Institute of Canada (of which he was president in 1941) and the Saskatchewan Association of Professional Engineers. He is a fellow of the Royal Society and of the Royal Society of Canada, a director since 1937 of the Canadian Geographic Society; and an honorary fellow of the Royal College of Physicians and Surgeons. The Canadian engineer has received the Plummer Medal and the Sir John Kennedy Medal of the Engineering Institute of Canada, the United States Medal of Merit (1947), and the French Legion of Honor (1947). Honorary degrees bestowed upon Mackenzie are: the LL.D. by Dalhousie University (1941), Western Ontario University (1943), Queen's College (1944), Algiers University (1944), Saskatchewan University (1945); D. Eng. by Toronto University (1944); D.Sc. by McGill University (1941), Laval College (1946), Cambridge University (1946), University of British Columbia (1947), and Princeton University (1949). The citation accompanying the last-named read, in part: "In an hour of peril by wise authority and astute political insight, he inspired the research agencies of Canada, Great Britain and the United States to a united effort indispensable for victory. . . .He preserved an undefended boundary opinion between his country and our own, where essential ideas crossed back and forth in the business of freedom."

Mackenzie, who has written articles for a number of technical publications, has also contributed to the *Trades Labor Journal*, the *Financial Post*, the *Independent Canadian*, the *Canadian Banker*, and *Canadian Business*. In Ottawa he belongs to the Rideau Club and the Royal Ottawa Golf Club. Married to Genevieve Gallon in 1924, Mackenzie is the father of one son, Peter, and two daughters, Sylvia and Eleanor. The sports he prefers are golf and curling.

References

International Who's Who, 1951
Who's Who, 1951
Who's Who in America, 1952-53
Who's Who in Canada, 1949-50
World Biography (1948)

MCKINNEY, FRANK E(DWARD) June
16, 1904- Political party official; bank executive
Address: b. c/o Fidelity Trust Co., 123 E.
Market St., Indianapolis, Ind.; h. 4906 N.
Meridian St., Indianapolis, Ind.

On November 1, 1951, Frank E. McKinney
became the new chairman of the Democratic
National Committee, succeeding William M.
Boyle, Jr., who resigned. McKinney, an Indianapolis banker and former owner of the
Pittsburgh Pirates, had previously held one
elective office and had been active in the Democratic party's organization in Indiana. He was
replaced as Democratic National Committee
chairman by Stephen A. Mitchell on August 10,
1952.

Born in Indianapolis, Indiana, on June 16,
1904, Francis Edward McKinney (who later
adopted his present first name) is the son of
Roscoe A. and Anna (Moss) McKinney. His
grandfather, who came as a young man to the
United States from Ireland, fought in the
Union Army in the Civil War; his father was
the chief of the Indianapolis fire department.
In his secondary school education McKinney
went as far as the sophomore year at the
Sacred Heart High School. He was reported
by the New York *World-Telegram* to have
decided not to study for the Roman Catholic
priesthood as his father wished, but to enter
the banking field.

Beginning in 1919 as a runner for the Meyer-
Kiser Bank in Indianapolis, reportedly at a
salary of $3.25 a week, he next got employ-
ment as a bookkeeper in People's State Bank in
the same city. He now began to study at night
at the University of Indiana Extension Division
and to take the correspondence courses of the
La Salle Institute of Accounting and the
American Institute of Banking. By 1933 he
was the bank's assistant cashier.

Meanwhile, through his friendship with Owen
J. Bush, the manager of the Indianapolis Indians baseball club, McKinney had the opportunity of becoming a candidate for the office
of treasurer of Marion County, which includes
Indianapolis. In 1934 he was elected to that
public office, to which he was re-elected
for another two-year term. At that time the
county treasurer was awarded a percentage of
collections of delinquent tax accounts with the
result that, as improved business conditions
after the depression brought in many tax ar-
rears, McKinney began to receive an annual
income of about $35,000 (according to a re-
lease from the Democratic National Committee). It was about this time, too, that Mc-
Kinney was able to acquire a large block of
stock of the Fidelity Trust Company for
$100,000. Seeing an opportunity to get back
into banking, he borrowed enough money for

Hessler Studio
FRANK E. MCKINNEY

the purchase of the stock, a loan he paid in
the course of his four years as county treasurer. Becoming president of Fidelity Trust in
1934, he expanded the commercial banking operation at Fidelity Trust, which in 1941 purchased the Marion County Bank. The New
York *Times* reported that the assets of the
company had increased from $2,000,000 in 1935
to $25,000,000 in 1951. Among his other busi-
ness interests were the ownership of Station
WISH in Indianapolis and a directorship of
the Bush-Freezle Sporting Goods Company.

The Indianian had been a baseball fan ever
since he was manager of the semiprofessional
team at high school in the early 1920's. In
1938 he and Owen Bush bought the Louisville
Colonels, an American Association team. After
he and his associates sold the Colonels to the
Boston Red Sox, in 1941 they bought the Indianapolis Indians. His biggest venture in
baseball was the purchase, in 1946, of the National League Pittsburgh Pirates in association
with three other men, one of whom was Bing
Crosby. According to the release from the
Democratic headquarters, the club built up a
farm system and developed into a "valuable,
profitable" baseball property. Later McKinney,
the club president, sold his stock in the Pittsburgh enterprise to two of his associates, and
in September 1951 disposed of his Indianapolis
baseball holdings.

During World War II McKinney entered the
United States Army as major and was advanced
to lieutenant colonel and afterward in 1944 to
colonel in the Advance Payment and Loan
Branch of the Army Finance Division, in an
operation involving loans to war contractors,
and upon release from the Army in 1945 he
was chosen assistant to Robert Hinckley, then
in charge of war contract renegotiations. Recalled to public service in 1949 to become a
member of the President's Military Housing

MCKINNEY, FRANK E.—*Continued*
Committee, he is credited with showing the Army how to cut the cost of military housing in Alaska.

In October 1951 William M. Boyle, Democratic National Committee chairman, resigned after it was charged he had used political influence to induce the Reconstruction Finance Corporation to grant a loan to a company which had formerly employed him as attorney. President Truman now had the task of selecting a successor from among the thirty persons considered eligible. Prominent in Democratic politics largely through services performed without title, McKinney had also held party offices from time to time: treasurer of the Indianapolis and Marion County Democratic Committees in the late 1920's and early 1930's, subtreasurer of the Democratic National Committee for Indiana in 1936, and vice-chairman of the Democratic National Finance Committee in 1940. More recent posts were as treasurer of the Indiana Democratic State Central Committee and as subtreasurer of the National Committee for Indiana.

Sponsored by Frank M. McHale, an important figure in politics and business in Indiana, and recommended by the President, McKinney was unanimously elected chairman of the Democratic National Committee on November 1, 1951. On learning of his nomination he disposed of a large stock ownership in the United States Pipe Line Company, which was then applying to the Petroleum Administration for Defense for the allocation of some 100,000 tons of steel. This step he took to free himself from suspicion of using his prospective position to influence a government agency in behalf of any business in which he held an interest. At this time, too, McKinney withdrew from several other business affiliations, retaining the presidency of the Fidelity Trust Company, the treasurership of the Universal Broadcasting Company, directorship in the Indiana Bell Telephone Company, and some real estate interests in Indianapolis.

In his acceptance address McKinney announced that no salaried employees of the committee might accept money in exchange for exerting influence, that the circumstances in which each employee had been engaged would be investigated, and that, except for salaries, he himself would have to approve all disbursements of funds until a new budget was drawn up. Approval was given to his proposal that an eleven-member executive committee be selected from among the national committeemen to meet frequently to advise and assist the chairman. McKinney also stated that he would not accept the $35,000-a-year chairmanship salary, a post he said he would hold for one year. On the day after McKinney's election, President Truman announced that he favored the new chairman's advice that the collectors of internal revenue be chosen by civil service examination instead of by Presidential appointment. "We will get to the core of corruption [in Government] and weed it out whenever we find it," was one of several statements McKinney made as he pressed for the punishing

of wrongdoing among Federal employees. In connection with the announcement of an unusually large profit he and McHale had made in a stock transaction in the now defunct Empire Tractor Corporation, McKinney said he had made both lucrative and unprofitable investments, that he had nothing to conceal—"All of them were ethical and honest." Soon after Governor Adlai E. Stevenson became the Democratic candidate for President, he appointed Stephen A. Mitchell to succeed McKinney on August 10, 1952, as chairman of the Democratic National Committee.

Frank McKinney married Margaret K. Warner on November 24, 1932; their four children are named Claire, Robert, Frank Edward, Jr., and Margaret Kathleen. The party leader belongs to the Indianapolis Athletic Club, the Highland Golf and Country clubs, the Elks, the Kiwanis, the American Legion, and Forty and Eight. A Catholic, he is a member of the Sovereign Order Knights of Malta and of the Indianapolis Knights of Columbus, and holds an honorary Ph.D. degree from St. Francis College of Loretto, Pennsylvania. His church is the St. Thomas Aquinas Catholic Church. Broad-shouldered McKinney, who has black hair and brown eyes, is five feet nine and a half inches tall and weighs 183 pounds; he has been described as a "polished, ruggedly good-looking family man."

References

> Christian Sci Mon p9 N 27 '51 por
> N Y Herald Tribune II p1 N 4 '51 por
> N Y Times p21 N 1 '51
> N Y World-Telegram p12 O 31 '51; p15
>   N 3 '51 por
> Sat Eve Post 220:20+ My 8 '48 por
> U S News 31:56 N 9 '51 por
> Washington (D.C.) Post p1 O 30 '51
> Who's Who in Commerce and Industry
>   (1951)
> Who's Who in the Midwest (1949)

MCMAHON, (JAMES O')BRIEN Oct. 6, 1903—July 28, 1952 United States Senator from Connecticut; lawyer; became special assistant to the Attorney General of the United States in 1933 and Assistant Attorney General in 1935; elected to the United States Senate in 1944 and re-elected in 1950; Chairman of the Joint Committee on Atomic Energy and member of the Committee on Foreign Relations; author of the McMahon Act for the Control of Atomic Energy. See *Current Biography,* 1945.

Obituary

> N Y Times p1+ Jl 29 '52

MCMILLAN, EDWIN M(ATTISON)
Sept. 18, 1907- Physicist; university professor
Address: b. c/o Radiation Laboratory, University of California, Berkeley 4, Calif.

Edwin M. McMillan, who shared the 1951 Nobel Prize in chemistry with Glenn T. Seaborg, is the codiscoverer of plutonium, the first heavier-than-uranium element, which made it easier and less costly to produce atomic bombs. Among his other achievements at the Radiation Laboratory of the University of California, with which he has been associated since 1934, was to increase the power of the cyclotron (the atom-smasher), and thus make possible the first man-made cosmic rays. During World War II the California physicist was engaged in atomic research for the United States Government.

The son of Edwin Harbaugh and Anna Marie (Mattison) McMillan, Edwin Mattison McMillan was born September 18, 1907, in Redondo Beach, California. When he was one year old the family moved to Pasadena, where the father practiced medicine until his retirement in 1951. Young Edwin attended local public schools. Interested in physics as far back as he can remember (said a University of California release) as a boy McMillan built "all of the standard gadgets, including high-frequency coils," and began at an early age to attend the weekly public lectures at the nearby California Institute of Technology. After graduation from Pasadena High School, he became a student at the California Institute of Technology, where his abilities were recognized by election to the scientific research honor society Sigma Xi, and the engineering honor society Tau Beta Pi. His major was physics.

While still an undergraduate, McMillan collaborated with Linus Pauling (who at that time was an assistant professor) on published X-ray studies of alloys of lead and thallium. After receiving his B.S. degree in 1928, McMillan remained at Cal Tech for his master's degree; then he went East to study for his doctorate at Princeton. A number of McMillan's experiments were done without collaborators during this period, among them those reported in *Electric Field Giving Uniform Deflecting Force on a Molecular Beam*. After receiving the Ph.D. degree in 1932 he spent two years at the University of California at Berkeley on a National Research Council fellowship. At Berkeley he joined the science honor society for graduate students, Gamma Alpha. In 1934, when Ernest O. Lawrence organized the new Radiation Laboratory, McMillan was appointed to its staff with the title of research associate. He has been connected with that laboratory ever since, being named an instructor in physics the next year, assistant professor the ensuing year, associate professor in 1941, and full professor in 1946. At the university McMillan is described as an outstanding teacher.

Edwin McMillan, who took part in the development and use of Lawrence's atom-smashing cyclotron, concerned himself also with a relatively wide range of questions. The nearly sixty published papers and reports which bear his name include some dealing with the sun, measurement of the charge on electrons, the production of X-rays by electrons, and several investigations which employed spectroscopic methods. The bulk of his work deals with artificial and natural radioactivity and particle

Univ. of California
EDWIN M. MCMILLAN

bombardment. Some of his notes in journals report findings of immediate practical usefulness in designing instruments. Together with laboratory director Lawrence he transmuted aluminum and nitrogen by bombarding them with deuterons; with M. Stanley Livingston (coinventor of the cyclotron) he produced radioactive oxygen; and by himself he reported on gamma rays accompanying artificial nuclear disintegration, on long-lasting artificial radioactivity, and on the results of activating uranium by bombarding it with beams of neutrons. In 1940 he was one of a group which used radio sulphur as a tracer in investigating the body's use of thiamine.

Before World War II McMillan had started upon what William L. Laurence of the New York *Times* called a "postscript to Genesis" by creating the first man-made chemical element. At the time it was believed by the leading scientists that element 93, if it could be found, would have characteristics similar to those of manganese and rhenium. Chemical analysis of a product which McMillan had inadvertently produced while bombarding uranium oxide with neutrons in the sixty-inch cyclotron showed that it did not act like rhenium but like the "rare earth" elements in the middle of the periodic table. Despite this evidence McMillan was convinced that the new substance was not produced by fission but by transmutation, and he resumed work on it early in 1940. With a visiting scientist, Philip H. Abelson, he repeated the experiments, this time using one of the rare earths as a "carrier." Thus they were able quickly to separate the new element from the target uranium and identify its distinctive chemical characteristics. McMillan named this first heavier-than-uranium element neptunium after the planet Neptune, next after Uranus.

(Continued next page)

MCMILLAN, EDWIN M.—*Continued*

In his subsequent undertaking, a search for element 94, McMillan bombarded the uranium with deuterons, heavier subatomic "bullets," and found a distinct pattern of radioactivity in the results. So little of a new element is created in each transmutation, however, that many repetitions are required to collect the one-millionth of a gram necessary for satisfactory radiochemical microanalysis. Not enough of element 94 had been produced when, in November 1940, McMillan was called into defense work, to help organize the first research on radar. All his work on element 94 he turned over to Glenn Seaborg, who, with Joseph W. Kennedy and Arthur C. Wahl, completed the experiments. The resulting element, which Seaborg named plutonium (following the same planetary analogy) became the eventual atomic-bomb explosive.

Meanwhile, until August 1941 McMillan was in charge of the field testing of the country's first airborne microwave radar. Then he was assigned to organize the Navy sonar development project at San Diego, California, from which his Berkeley colleague J. Robert Oppenheimer took him to help organize the Los Alamos atomic energy laboratory. McMillan was in charge of the early development of the Hiroshima-type bomb and later worked on the Nagasaki-type bomb. Also, he prepared the first seven chapters (on terminology) of the book, *Lecture Series in Nuclear Physics*, written in 1943 and published by the United States Government in late 1947. McMillan, who was an assistant professor when he left Berkeley for his wartime duties, was promoted twice *in absentia* and returned as a full professor.

In the September 1945 *Physical Review* a note by McMillan was headed *The Synchrotron—A Proposed High-Energy Particle Accelerator*; in it he outlined the plan for the first real improvement in atom-smashing since the invention of the cyclotron fifteen years earlier. The cyclotron, which speeds up particles to very high energies by giving them an encouraging electrical shove each time they pass a certain spot, will not work at energies higher than about 100 million electron-volts. After that the particles gain mass as they gain speed and arrive at the electrical pulse just in time to be slowed down. McMillan's idea was to overcome this by changing the particles' path for them, which, he wrote, "can be done by varying either the magnetic field or the frequency. . . .The similarity of this behavior to that of a synchronous motor suggested the name of the device." The theory, "phase stability," on which McMillan based the synchrotron later proved to have been independently proposed earlier (in 1944) by the Russian scientist V. Veksler (said Daniel Wilkes, science writer for the University of California).

The new Berkeley cyclotron, with a 4,000-ton, 184-inch electromagnet, was converted into a synchrocyclotron with frequency modulation achieved by a variable condenser consisting of a rotating spoked wheel. (The system had first been tried out on Lawrence's old 37-inch cyclotron, and McMillan had also in

October 1945 begun construction of an electron synchrotron, which was completed in 1948 and now operates at an energy of 322,000,000 electron-volts or 322 "mev.") Using FM, the 184-incher was able to work on electric power of only some 15,000 volts, about one-fourteenth of the voltage originally planned. With this, it easily accelerated heavy deuterons to 200 mev and alpha particles to 400 mev. For the first time, physicists were able in 1948 to reach high enough energies to create mesons. In 1950 McMillan, with J. M. Peterson and R. S. White, reported his work in *Production of Mesons by X-rays*, and in that year, too, McMillan published *The Origin of Cosmic Rays*. At that time a nine-million-dollar synchrotron designed to accelerate protons to 6.4 billion electron volts (called the bevatron) was under construction at Berkeley with Atomic Energy Commission support.

In May 1951 the Research Corporation presented its $2,500 Scientific Award to Edwin McMillan, with a citation stating, in part: "His contributions, as an individual and in collaboration with others, constitute distinct milestones in scientific progress, each in itself eminently worthy of high recognition." McMillan was, however, little known to the public when he and Glenn Seaborg were announced as cowinners of the 1951 Nobel Prize in chemistry. The value of the Swedish money prize to be shared by the Californians was given as $32,517, or about $16,260 each.

On June 7, 1941, McMillan, a doctor's son, married a doctor's daughter, Elsie Walford Blumer, a sister of Mrs. Ernest O. Lawrence and daughter of the former dean of the Yale University School of Medicine. A "handy man" about the house, Edwin McMillan also enjoys gardening on Sundays. In his youth he climbed the Matterhorn, and he hopes to resume camping and mountain climbing when his children, Ann, David, and Stephen, are old enough to go along. Visitors to the physicist's office are likely to find there some interesting mineral specimens which he had picked up while hiking. McMillan has been honored by election to the National Academy of Science, and is a fellow of the American Physical Society. He is a member of the Faculty Club at Berkeley.

References

N Y Times p1 N 16 '51
Newsweek 27:60 My 13 '46
American Men of Science (1949)
Who's Who in America, 1950-51

MACVEAGH, LINCOLN (măk-vā') Oct. 1, 1890- United States Ambassador to Spain
Address: b. c/o United States Embassy, Madrid, Spain; h. New Canaan, Conn.

NOTE: This biography supersedes the article which appeared in *Current Biography* in 1941.

In his nineteenth year of diplomatic service, Lincoln MacVeagh in March 1952 assumed the post of United States Ambassador to Spain, to which he had been appointed the previous

January by President Truman. Formerly a New York publisher, MacVeagh left the presidency of Dial Press, Inc., of which he was the founder, to become Minister of Greece in 1933. He has since been accredited as his country's envoy to Iceland, the Union of South Africa, Yugoslavia, again to Greece, and to Portugal.

Lincoln MacVeagh was born October 1, 1890, in Narragansett Pier, Rhode Island, the second of six sons of Charles and Fanny Davenport (Rogers) MacVeagh. Charles MacVeagh, general solicitor and assistant general counsel of the United States Steel Corporation, was President Coolidge's Ambassador to Japan. A direct descendant of Thomas Rogers, the eighteenth signer of the Mayflower Pact, Lincoln MacVeagh represents the third consecutive generation of his family in high-level Government service. His grandfather, Wayne MacVeagh, a Philadelphia lawyer, was Attorney General in James Garfield's Cabinet and Minister to Turkey and Italy; and Franklin MacVeagh of Chicago, a brother of Wayne, was President Taft's Secretary of the Treasury. Lincoln MacVeagh's great-grandmother, Margaret Lincoln, was a cousin of the Civil War President.

After graduation in 1909 from Groton School (Massachusetts), where in the course of his six-year attendance he won the Greek Prize, MacVeagh entered Harvard University. In the winter of 1912-13, having completed the four-year course in three years, he was employed as secretary to the director of the Boston Art Museum. While at Harvard, from which he received the B.A. degree *magna cum laude* in 1913, MacVeagh was a holder of a John Harvard scholarship, was an editor of the Harvard *Advocate*, and a member of Phi Beta Kappa Society. In Paris during 1913-14 he studied philosophy and foreign languages at the Sorbonne, and then returned to work as a clerk with the United States Steel Products Company for one year. In 1915 he began his career in publishing by joining Henry Holt & Company of New York in the position of salesman, which required his visiting colleges and universities throughout the country.

In the American Expeditionary Force during World War I, he took part in the fighting on the Artois front and in the St. Mihiel and Meuse-Argonne areas as an aide to the commanding general of the 80th division and of the 9th and 6th Army Corps; later he was assigned to the historical section of the general staff. MacVeagh, who advanced from lieutenant of infantry to captain and then to major, was cited by General Pershing in April 1919 for "exceptionally meritorious services."

Resuming his activities in publishing after the war, MacVeagh became a director of Henry Holt & Company. A major project which he undertook at that time was the editing and revising of *Champlin's Encyclopedia for Young Folks*, giving his particular attention to the volumes on biography, history, literature, art, and mythology. He maintained a constant interest in classical language and literature, often reading Homer in the original while he commuted from his Connecticut home to his New

LINCOLN MACVEAGH

York office. In December 1923 MacVeagh left the Holt publishing house to become the founder and president of the Dial Press, Inc. At the same time he filled the positions of secretary and treasurer of the Dial Publishing Company, publisher of the *Dial* magazine. Under MacVeagh's direction the new company discovered a number of writers who afterward achieved wide recognition. It also published scholarly works like Denis Saurat's *Blake and Modern Thought*, A. E. Taylor's *Plato*, and Herman Finer's *Theory and Practice of Modern Government*. Another publication of the Dial Press was an anthology compiled by MacVeagh, *Poetry from the Bible* (1925).

MacVeagh's linguistic accomplishments in German, French, Spanish, Latin, and Greek were mentioned when, in 1933, President Roosevelt appointed him United States Minister Plenipotentiary to Greece, a country he had visited a number of times. *Time* (March 24, 1947) reported that in Athens MacVeagh "followed the presentation of his credentials with a speech in classical Greek which few of his hearers understood, but all applauded." A major problem presented itself to the new Minister almost immediately, for the United States was at that time attempting to win the extradition from Greece of financier Samuel Insull. After the close of the incident the Paris *Herald*, in its leading editorial of March 23, 1934, commented: "The bright spot of the Insull episode in Greece has been the temperate, dignified, and firm behavior of the American Minister at Athens, Mr. Lincoln MacVeagh. . . .It was only the calming hand of the American Minister which prevented the inflamed Insull incident from becoming virulent." MacVeagh's dispatches from Greece to Washington, D.C., during this early period of his diplomatic career were regarded as "classics" in the State Department files for their humor, re-

MACVEAGH, LINCOLN—*Continued*
ported the *United States News* (November 8, 1940).

Leaving Athens in 1941 when the German army overran Greece, MacVeagh returned to the United States via Berlin, Switzerland, and Spain. He was then appointed the first United States Minister to Iceland. There he was called upon to make decisions requiring diplomatic skill: by international agreement, sovereignty and normal economic life were to be maintained while strategic centers of Iceland were occupied by United States troops. During his stay in Iceland the Minister negotiated the agreements leading to the construction of the Keflavik airfield, which was vital to the operation of the Northern Ferry Command. In 1942 he left Iceland to take up a new assignment as Minister to the Union of South Africa. In this mission MacVeagh also served as the American member of the South African Supply Council, an Allied group which helped arrange for the procurement of such vital resources as chrome and coal from South Africa for the Allied war effort. MacVeagh also coordinated the American wartime agencies in South Africa with such success that he was specially commended by the Department of State. In the following year (1943) he was transferred to Cairo to be Ambassador near the exiled Greek and Yugoslav governments, and then returned to Athens as Ambassador to Greece in 1944.

MacVeagh early became aware of the danger of supporting partisan or extreme Left-wing movements in the Balkans, and his secret testimony before the Foreign Relations Committee of both houses of Congress in the spring of 1947 was considered an important factor in the initiation of what has become known as the Truman Doctrine. In 1950 the President commended MacVeagh for his foresight in recognizing the part Greece was likely to play in postwar developments. The Ambassador also urged the postwar Greek government to pursue a democratic course, to undertake internal reforms, and to follow a "better and broader" amnesty policy. Because of his contribution to Greek recovery and stabilization MacVeagh was called "a specialist in enlightening other people regarding their own interests" by the Athens correspondent of the *Christian Science Monitor.*

After the death of Mrs. MacVeagh (the former Margaret Charlton Lewis) in Athens in September 1947, the diplomat was granted a leave of absence for reasons of health. On his recovery he was appointed Ambassador to Portugal in 1948. In this post he was instrumental in securing Portugal's admittance to the Atlantic Pact group of nations; and he negotiated and signed the treaties effecting her inclusion in the Marshall Plan and her participation in the Mutual Defense Assistance program and the Azores Defense Agreement of 1951.

After spending three years in Lisbon, MacVeagh was nominated by President Truman on January 29, 1952, to succeed Stanton Griffis as United States Ambassador to Spain. His ap-

pointment having been confirmed by the Senate in February, MacVeagh presented his credentials in Madrid on March 27, 1952, to take up his first task of negotiating agreements regarding American use of Spanish naval and military bases, and the allocation of $100 millions voted by Congress in 1951 for technical, economic, and military aid to Spain. The formal American proposal to Spain was reported by the New York *Times* (April 12, 1952) as being virtually completed in the form of a Mutual Security Agency agreement. It was expected that the United States would provide facilities for training Spanish personnel and would build new installations and enlarge existing ones for storing oil, munitions, and spare parts. In the event of war it is thought that Spain would be expected to extend the use of her facilities to the United States and its allies against a common aggressor. American aid would be directed toward improving Spain's agricultural yield and transportation and storage facilities. For these transactions, the Washington *Post* (January 28, 1952) wrote in an editorial, MacVeagh "comports exactly with the requirements of representation in Spain."

Throughout his diplomatic career MacVeagh has taken a particular interest in the training of younger men in foreign service and is said to be proud of the number of Foreign Service officers of top ranks who were at one time or another members of his official family. Several of his interests were the result of his long residence in Greece. In 1937 he and Mrs. MacVeagh wrote *Greek Journey*, a book for children aged eleven to thirteen. The story, told with frequent references to mythology, art, and ancient history, takes its four chief characters on a tour through modern Greece in the family Ford; it received commendation in the *Library Journal* and the New York *Herald Tribune*. For years MacVeagh conducted excavations beneath the eastern face of the Acropolis and made archeological contributions to the National Museum in Athens.

In the course of the years that he was the United States envoy to Greece, MacVeagh was made honorary citizen of Athens, an honorary fellow of the Athens Archeological Association, a member of the Order of George the First, and a trustee of the American School of Classical Studies. The Greek Government honored him by having a bust of him made by the Greek sculptor Constantine Papachristopoulo, and the University of Athens awarded him an honorary Ph.D. degree. He is also the recipient of the Order of the Falcon, bestowed on him by the Icelandic Government in 1942. MacVeagh belongs to the Council of Foreign Relations, American Archeological Association, the Stuart Club of Edinburgh (Scotland), the Society of Mayflower Descendants, and the American Legion. His clubs are the Century and University in New York, the Country Club of New Canaan (Connecticut), the Jefferson Islands Club of Maryland, and the P.E.N. Club. He attends the Episcopal Church.

The MacVeaghs were married on August 17, 1917, and their one daughter, Margaret Ewen, is the wife of Samuel E. Thorne, a member of the Yale University Law School faculty. The diplomat is a man of medium height, with gray hair and brown eyes. He enjoys horseback riding, swimming, and playing tennis and squash; his hobbies are chiefly classical archeology, chess, and reading history.

References

N Y Herald Tribune II p3 Mr 23 '47 por; p4 Ja 30 '52 por; II p1 Mr 23 '52 por
N Y Times p6 Ag 1 '41
N Y World-Telegram p1 Ja 21 '41 por
Newsweek 39:22 F 4 '52
Time 46:20+ Mr 24 '47
U S News 9:36 N 8 '40 por; p40 F 8 '52 por
International Who's Who (1951)
National Cyclopædia of American Biography Current vol F, 1939-42
Who's Who in America, 1952-53
World Biography (1948)

MACY, EDITH DEWING *See* Macy, Mrs. E. W.

MACY, MRS. EDWARD W(ARREN)
Young women's organization official

Address: b. c/o National Board of the Young Women's Christian Association, 600 Lexington Ave., New York 22; h. 128 Willow St., Brooklyn 2, N.Y.

As president of the Young Women's Christian Association of the United States and chairman of the executive committee of the association's national board, Mrs. Edward W. Macy directs an organization which serves more than three million women and girls in the United States. Before her election to this top administrative post in May 1952 for a three-year term, Mrs. Macy had for fifteen years filled a number of offices in the YWCA, from adult education chairman of the Brooklyn YWCA to vice-president of the national board, in which she pursued the YWCA aim of helping young women achieve "physical health, mental growth, and the moral strength derived from a Christian way of life." As president Mrs. Macy is also a member of the World's YWCA Council, the executive body of the international organization, which includes thirty-six national YWCA's and provides recreational and educational facilities for women and girls in sixty-five countries.

Mrs. Macy was born Edith Dewing in London, England. After receiving her education in English schools, she came with relatives to the United States in 1911. In August 1914 she was married to Edward Warren Macy, an executive in the social welfare field.

Drawn into community work by her interest in the care and development of children and young people, Mrs. Macy from 1924 to 1930 held the presidency of the Parent-Teachers Association at the Friends Seminary in New York. In the 1930's she became active in the League of Women Voters and was made chairman of the league's committees on city and State government and child welfare. With the city group she worked on a survey of children's courts and delinquency; while chairman of the State group she directed local league committees in studies of local needs in child welfare legislation. Also during this period Mrs. Macy became a member of the board and of the executive committee of the Brooklyn Maternity Center, which tried to reduce the mortality rate in childbirth and gave courses to parents on the care of infants.

Shortly after the Macys moved to Brooklyn in 1933, Mrs. Macy was asked by an acquaintance to accept membership on a Brooklyn YWCA committee. She was assured that her duties would take no more than a day a month. Once in the YWCA Mrs. Macy became much interested in the adult education program, an important part of the YWCA's work, begun in the 1870's when the emphasis was on vocational training. From 1934 to 1941, during which period Mrs. Macy was chairman of the adult education committee of the Central Branch of the YWCA in Brooklyn, she helped organize both vocational training and leisure-time activity classes. To Mrs. Macy the accomplishment that gave her the most pleasure was also her most significant work: the establishment of a school to train urgently needed practical nurses and the successful drive to secure State legislation for standards and certification of these nurses. A school for beauticians was also organized at the Brooklyn YWCA in this period.

While still engaged in local YWCA activities, Mrs. Macy was introduced to the problems of YWCA administration on the national level in 1938 upon her election to the national board, the body that unifies the autonomous YWCA branches in the United States and links them to the equally independent YWCA's in foreign countries. Mrs. Macy was one of the sixty "resident" members (those living in commuting distance of New York City) who met once a month; the full board of 120 members met twice a year. During these years, from 1938 to 1941, she was chairman of the YWCA's national service division (now called the community division), which provided an advisory service for more than 400 community associations. In World War II, when the YWCA became one of the six national agencies to make up the United Service Organizations and as such operated 250 clubs for military and industrial personnel, Mrs. Macy was the first chairman of the YWCA's USO division and was also named a member of the executive committee of the board of directors of the National USO. Later, from 1945 to 1948, Mrs. Macy headed the board's interpretation and support committee (now called the committee for national support), which sough financial contributions by interpreting YWCA accomplishments and objectives to members and friends.

At the end of the war Mrs. Macy turned her attention to the work for world rehabilitation, being appointed the only woman member on the clothing allocation committee and later on the food allocation committee, both of the President's War Relief Control Board. Here

Pach Bros.

MRS. EDWARD W. MACY

she helped determine how the food and clothing collected in two nation-wide drives should be distributed in Europe and Asia. In the YWCA she served as chairman in 1947-48 of the national executive committee of the Round-the-World Reconstruction Fund, which by early 1949 had raised $2,244,470 to help carry on the work of the YWCA's in thirty war-torn nations.

The interracial policies of the YWCA have been of special interest to Mrs. Macy, who at the 1946 convention headed the committee that wrote the YWCA's Interracial Charter. While recognizing the right of local associations to determine their own interracial policies, the convention accepted the Charter's statement of general principles that "fellowship without barriers of race" was the YWCA goal and pledged "to continue to pioneer in an interracial experience that shall be increasingly democratic and Christian." The resolution noted that women of minority races formed "more than one-tenth of the association constituency."

At the 1949 YWCA convention in San Francisco Mrs. Macy was elected one of the six vice-presidents of the National Board. Three years later at the next convention, in Chicago, she was nominated for president and on May 7, 1952, was elected to that office, succeeding Mrs. Arthur Forrest Anderson. In her acceptance speech before the 2,700 delegates Mrs. Macy spoke of "new opportunities and responsibilities for women of Christian purpose in this topsy-turvy world." A foremost item on her three-year presidential agenda is the centennial celebration in 1955, in connection with which a drive was started to increase and strengthen membership, to "tell the Y's story" over the world, and to raise funds to continue its work. Mrs. Macy heads an organization comprising 1,049 local associations in 435 cities, towns, and villages and on 614 university and college cam-

puses; 75 per cent of the members are under twenty-five years old. The national board, as explained in YWCA publications, "recruits, trains, and places local, national, international leadership; organizes conferences, advises and consults with local associations and YWCA's overseas on program and purpose; gives financial aid to YWCA's overseas and to the World's YWCA on behalf of the YWCA's of the United States." To achieve its purpose of building a fellowship of young women devoted to realizing in everyday life the Christian ideals of personal and social living, the YWCA maintains residences for women and provides opportunities in education and recreation.

Medium in build, Mrs. Macy is five feet six inches tall; she has blue eyes, gray hair, and a ready smile. She used to play tennis; now she prefers sailing, gardening, and reading. Her clubs are the Civitas, Ihpentonga, and Brooklyn. She is an Episcopalian. The Macy son, Edward A., is employed by the State Department. The death of Mrs. Macy's only daughter, Molly E. Macy, gave her additional reason, she has said, to want to work in the service of young women.

References

N Y Herald Tribune p7 My 7 '52 por
N Y Times p23 My 7 '52 por
YWCA Magazine 46·3 Je '52 por
Who's Who in America, 1952-53

MAGGIOLO, WALTER A(NDREW) (mä-jōl'ō) June 26, 1908- Federal mediator
Address: b. c/o Federal Mediation and Conciliation Service, Washington 25, D.C.; h. 15 E. 31st St., Brooklyn 26, N.Y.

Walter A. Maggiolo, who was appointed general counsel of the Federal Mediation and Conciliation Service in March 1952, has been active in labor-employer relations for fifteen years. From 1939 to 1943 he was trial attorney for the New York State Labor Relations Board, and in 1943 he became a commissioner of conciliation of the United States Conciliation Service. Named acting general counsel of the Federation Mediation and Conciliation Service in December 1951, he was appointed general counsel and assistant to the director four months later.

The son of Charles and Alice Virginia (Rovere) Maggiolo, Walter Andrew Maggiolo was born in the Bronx, New York City, on June 26, 1908. (He has a brother, Henry L. Maggiolo, an arbitrator.) Walter Maggiolo attended Xavier High School in New York City, taking part in the debating society and playing basketball and baseball. Upon graduating in 1926 he enrolled at Holy Cross College, Worcester, Massachusetts, to major in philosophy. There he joined the debating and Metropolitan clubs and participated in intermural athletics and track. In 1930 he received the B.A. degree *cum laude* from Holy Cross. Studies on the graduate level took him to Harvard Law School, from which he obtained the LL.B. degree in 1933. Subsequently, he took other postgraduate studies at Columbia University,

New York University, and St. John's University. It was while he was at college, Maggiolo has said, that he first felt an interest in labor-management relations.

Maggiolo practiced as an attorney in New York City from 1933 until 1939. "In my first year practicing law," he says, "I was called in as a private mediator in a protracted strike in Brooklyn. The distrust, enmities, and complete failure of the parties to try to understand each other's problems and their disregard of the human relations problems and values which underlay the dispute persuaded me that this was a challenging field to which I could and should make a contribution."

He began his public service in 1939 when he became trial attorney for the New York State Labor Relations Board. Concurrently, he became engaged in teaching labor law and industrial relations, and has since been associated with the faculties of Holy Cross College, the School of Industrial and Labor Relations of Cornell University, and the Graduate School of Social Service of Fordham University. He has also been a lecturer or a member of the faculties of Crown Heights School of Industrial Relations, the Xavier Institute of Industrial Relations, and the St. James Labor School. He was cofounder of the first Catholic colored labor school in the United States.

In 1943 Maggiolo received his appointment as a commissioner of conciliation in the United States Conciliation Service. His task was to help bring about peaceable negotiations in disputes between labor and management through the orderly process of collective bargaining. Two years later he became regional representative of the Service in New England, at which time he originated the clinic method of teaching grievance problems in industrial relations. After 1945 he was the Commissioner of Conciliation in New York City.

Maggiolo has participated in the settlement of many labor disputes of national significance since 1945. In 1949 he served as Federal mediator in the threatened milk strike in the New York metropolitan area. At that time a three-State milk delivery strike was set for October 24, 1949, which would have stopped milk delivery to 11,000,000 customers in New York City, Long Island, Westchester, and parts of New Jersey and Connecticut. In reporting on the matter, the New York *Times* (October 26, 1949) quoted Maggiolo as saying: "More than 60 issues in the dispute were explored and resolved, after 60 hours of continuous negotiations. . . . This is the first time since 1941 that a basis for agreement was voluntarily reached across the table through negotiation." The *Times* further stated that the settlement, which included a pension and welfare fund financed by a contribution by employers (ten cents per hour) but no wage increases, was regarded by all parties as industry-wide in its influence.

In 1951 Maggiolo became acting general counsel for the Federal Mediation and Conciliation Service. On August 22, 1947, under the Labor Management Relations Act of that year, the Federal Mediation and Conciliation Service had been created to take over the functions of the older Service. The FMCS

Mario Rosel

WALTER A. MAGGIOLO

endeavors to promote the settlement of labor disputes by conciliation and mediation rather than by strikes, lockouts, and forms of coercion. As acting general counsel Maggiolo participated in the steel dispute of 1951-52, which involved 700,000 steel workers and the major steel producers of the United States.

Following his appointment on March 10, 1952, as general counsel of the Federal Mediation and Conciliation Service by the director of this government agency, Cyrus S. Ching, Maggiolo participated in the settlement of the telephone dispute of April 1952. He was the leader of the team of Federal mediators working in New York to bring about a satisfactory agreement between Western Electric Company and Communications Workers of America (CIO). According to the New York *Times* (April 26, 1952), "Agreement was announced after a twenty-two-hour session. . . . Walter A. Maggiolo finally brought the parties together. . . . Workers in twenty-nine cities in twenty-one states received wage increases of from 11 to 16 cents an hour."

Other major labor disputes in which Maggiolo has mediated were the strike in the non-ferrous industry (1945), the maritime dispute (1946), the telephone dispute (1948), the Wall Street strike (1949), the telephone dispute (1950), the New York *World-Telegram* strike (1951), and the Ohio Power Company strike (1951). Articles he has written on labor-industry relations include "The Professional Employee and the Taft-Hartley Act" and "Cases and Materials for Grievance Clinics."

The Crusader Award for Outstanding Contribution to the Field of Education in Labor and Industrial Relations was given to Maggiolo in 1945 by his alma mater, Holy Cross College. His memberships in organizations and clubs comprise the American Bar Association, the Brooklyn Bar Association, the Catholic Law-

MAGGIOLO, WALTER A.—*Continued*

yers Guild, the American Management Association, the American Catholic Sociological Society, the American Arbitration Association, the Industrial Relations Society, the Royal Arcanum, the Knights of Columbus, the Harvard and Holy Cross alumni associations. His political affiliation is Democratic and his religious faith is the Roman Catholic.

In an article in *This Week* entitled "Strike Doctor," Maggiolo was described by Philip Harkins as a man who "talks softly and doesn't carry a big stick"; the mediator was quoted as saying, "When disputes are settled, a conciliator feels pretty good. He feels that he's helped keep the big machine rolling. And that's something." Maggiolo, who weighs 185 pounds, stands about five feet eleven inches in height, and has brown eyes and black hair. His hobbies, he says, are tennis, golf, bowling, photography, public speaking, and teaching.

References

Sign Je '52
This Week p8 Je 16 '46
American Catholic Who's Who (1952-53)

MAGLOIRE, PAUL E(UGÈNE) (mä″glwär′ pôl ü″zhân′) July 19, 1907- President of Haiti

Address: Presidential Palace, Port-au-Prince, Haiti

The President of Haiti, Colonel Paul E. Magloire, was elected to that office on October 8, 1950, in the country's first popular presidential election. In the course of a career almost exclusively military, he twice before had held

Wide World Photos
PAUL E. MAGLOIRE

office in the Haitian Government, both times chiefly as a member of a military junta ruling after a bloodless revolution. President Magloire has proposed a program of rural, industrial, and social development for the Caribbean republic.

The son of Eugène François and Philomene (Mathieu) Magloire, Paul Eugène Magloire was born July 19, 1907, in Cap-Haitien, the second largest city in Haiti. At about the age of twenty-two Magloire was a teacher for a short period (in 1929-30) at the Lycée Philippe Guerrier in Cap-Haitien. Later as a graduate of the military academy at Port-au-Prince, the republic's capital, he entered upon his military career. In 1931 he received his first commission, as second lieutenant, and in 1933 became a first lieutenant. From assistant district commander at Cap-Haitien in 1935, he was promoted in 1938 to district commander, with a simultaneous advance in rank to captain. (The following year he received the LL.B. degree from the law college in Port-au-Prince.)

The army officer was then transferred (in 1941) to the capital to occupy the post of district commander of the national penitentiary and later, in 1944, to serve for a time as chief of the capital city police force. The latter year, in which he was also made a major, saw him appointed departmental commander of the military forces at the national palace, where he remained until 1948. In 1946 his present rank of colonel had been attained.

Stationed at the national capital and in close contact with government figures, Magloire was introduced to political affairs during the presidency of Elie Lescot, who had been elected in 1941. On April 20, 1944, Lescot's term in office had been extended by the National Assembly to May 15, 1951. Some time afterward charges were made that this extension was improper and that the president had often been tyrannical. With a small group of army officers who led a bloodless revolt, Magloire on January 11, 1946, helped persuade Lescot to resign and go into exile. Thereupon governmental power was assumed by a three-man military junta (the Executive Military Committee) with Magloire one of the members, Antoine Levelt the other, and Colonel Frank Lavaud the presiding officer. On the election by the National Assembly of Dumarsais Estimé to the presidency on August 16, 1946, the junta resigned.

Under Estimé's regime conditions in Haiti were at first calm. In January 1949, however, the government claimed to have unearthed a plot (which was reportedly aided by the Dominican Republic) to oust the President, and later that year, in November, Estimé declared a state of siege, banned several political parties, and instituted a censorship. After a period of protest strikes and political agitation, the Cabinet on May 7, 1950, resigned, because the Senate, opposing Estimé, rejected a proposed constitutional amendment to allow him to seek re-election in 1952 on the expiration of his mandate. On that day there were short-lived disorders; they ended when the same military junta which had ruled in 1946 assumed power again, with Magloire in charge of administration, and compelled the President to resign. Subsequently, in the new Cabinet, in which Magloire was Minister of the Interior briefly, but from which he resigned on August 6, 1950, leaving Antoine Levelt the only military member.

The National Assembly members, elected in October, proceeded to amend the constitution to provide for choosing the President by popular suffrage rather than by majority vote of assembly. Magloire's candidacy for the office was opposed by a supporter of Estimé, Fénelon J. Alphonse, an architect and engineer, who, however, withdrew from the contest on the stated grounds that the election was farcical. In his statement after the balloting of October 8, 1950, Magloire, winner of 99 per cent of the votes, named restoration of national unity as the chief concern of his administration. (*Newsweek*, October 23, 1950, noted that the Haitian leader "seems even to have transcended the rivalry between the Negro masses and the mulatto aristocracy which is the traditional dividing line in Haitian politics.") On December 6, 1950, he was inaugurated for a six-year term as the thirtieth president of Haiti and the thirty-third head of state, excluding temporary military dictators, since the liberation from France in 1804 and the establishment of the largely Negro republic.

Haiti, which occupies the western third of the Caribbean island of Hispaniola, has over 3,000,000 French patois-speaking inhabitants in its 10,700 square miles of territory (of which some 8,000 are mountainous), and produces sisal, sugar, coffee, and cotton for export. To remedy the low subsistence level caused by overcrowding and exclusive reliance on agriculture in a country with limited arable land, Magloire proposes to improve soil utilization and to establish food-processing and other industries. Early in his administration the Haitian Government took measures to stimulate the advancement of agriculture by permitting duty-free importation of tools and fertilizers, and by borrowing $10,000,000 from the Export-Import Bank to continue work on its $19,700,000 Artibonite Valley agricultural development. To encourage foreign investment in Hatian industry, the Government has offered exemptions from licenses and taxes for a number of years. A message from President Magloire, published as a full-page advertisement in the New York *Times* (January 3, 1951, and January 4, 1952), pointed out the advantages of Haiti's low labor costs and stabilized currency.

Additional efforts by Magloire to remedy the backwardness of his country include giving much aid to public education (one tenth—$2,000,000—of the budget is devoted to this) and to sanitation work. A long-standing problem in Haiti's foreign affairs, its oft-times hostile relations with the Dominican Republic, which occupies the eastern two-thirds of Hispaniola, has also had his attention. Brought together by the Organization of American States, Magloire and Trujillo, the President of the neighboring Caucasian and Spanish-speaking state, concluded an agreement in February 1951 to establish tariff concessions, promote commerce, fight communism on Hispaniola, and support hemispheric solidarity.

The President of Haiti and the former Yolette Leconte have four children. In the *Saturday Evening Post* of November 17, 1951, Joe Alex Morris described Magloire as "a tall, husky and soft-voiced military man," and *Pathfinder* on October 4, 1950, gave the characterization of "strong, silent, and with a reputation for action." He has received the Haitian decoration Honneur et Mérite and is a member and former president of the Club Militaire and a member of the Cercle Bellevue.

References

N Y Herald Tribune p10 O 10 '50
Travel Guide to Haiti (1951?)
Who's Who in Latin America, Pt 7 (1951)

MAGSAYSAY, RAMÓN (mŏg-sī-sī rä-mŏn') Aug. 31, 1907- Philippine Secretary of National Defense
Address: c/o Camp Murphy, Luzon, Philippine Islands

Secretary of National Defense of the Republic of the Philippines since 1950 Ramón Magsaysay is credited with revitalizing his country's army and constabulary, giving the nation its first honest election in years, and reducing the revolutionary communist "People's Liberation Army," the Huks, from a major threat to a "continuing nuisance." After World War II, in which he had fought in the Philippine Army, Magsaysay was elected on April 23, 1946, to his country's House of Representatives, where he held membership in a number of important committees. The New York *Times* has called him "easily the Philippines' most generally popular national figure."

The son of blacksmith Exequiel Magsaysay, Ramón Magsaysay, who was born in Iba, Zambales Province, Luzon, on August 31, 1907, has called himself a mixture of Tagalog, Ilokano (two of the chief native peoples of the Philippines), Chinese, and Spanish. (The Tagalog name, Magsaysay, may be translated as "explain, explain.") Ramón attended the Castillejes Elementary School and the Zambales Academy, a private high school in San Narciso, before entering the University of the Philippines in 1927, where he became an athlete. By working as a chauffeur he was able to support himself while he attended the university's college of liberal arts (1927-31) and its college of engineering (1927-29), and then the Institute of Commerce of José Rizal College (1928-32).

Having advanced from the positions of automechanic and shop superintendent in the transportation department of the estate of Teodoro R. Yangco, Magsaysay was the company's branch manager by the time the United States entered World War II in December 1941. When the United States Army requisitioned his 110 trucks, manager Magsaysay went with them, at his own request, to work in the motor pool of the 31st Infantry, 31st Division. The

Signal Corps, AFP

RAMÓN MAGSAYSAY

trucks were lost on Bataan, but Magsaysay escaped to the hills. Shortly before the surrender of Bataan in 1942, Magsaysay joined other Filipino and American officers and civilians in organizing the Western Luzon Guerrilla Forces, in which he was commissioned a captain on April 5, 1942, serving as G-1 and supply officer in this fugitive army. For three years Captain Magsaysay was headquarters commander in Sawang, San Marcelino, Zambales, under Colonel Gyles Merrill of Texas. According to Gretta Palmer (*American Weekly*, March 30, 1952), Magsaysay, with a price of $50,000 on his head, once disguised himself as a farmer and strolled into the Japanese Army post in Lingaen to borrow a cigarette.

The years of guerrilla warfare against the Japanese occupation provided Magsaysay with a knowledge of tactics, such as importing bloodhounds, offering paroles to enemies, and posting and paying large rewards for captives, which he was later to use against the Huks. On January 12, 1945, Captain Magsaysay was made commanding officer of the Zambales Military District, comprising more than 12,000 guerrillas; four days later his men stormed the San Marcelino airfield to destroy twenty enemy aircraft and a powerful Japanese radio station. On General MacArthur's orders, Magsaysay's guerrillas cleared the Zambales coast of all Japanese soldiers so successfully that American troops encountered no resistance when they landed there on January 29, 1945. Later the captain led his guerrillas in support of the 38th Division at the Battle of Zigzag Pass.

On February 4, 1945, Ramón Magsaysay was appointed by the United States Army as the military governor of Zambales, a post he held until MacArthur turned the liberated province over to the civilian government of the Philippine Commonwealth. Magsaysay, then a major, was honorably discharged from the army

in February 1946 and ran for Congress—"mainly," according to William L. Worden (*Saturday Evening Post*, January 12, 1952), "because he could not stomach the fact that all the other candidates in his province had been collaborators" with the Japanese. Elected Representative from Zambales in April 1946 by a 3,000-vote margin over his nearest rival, Magsaysay, a Liberal, was appointed chairman of the House Committee on National Defense, serving also on the committees of rehabilitation and reconstruction, public works, franchises, national companies, railroads, pensions, and guerrilla affairs. Two years later (April 1948) President Manuel Roxas appointed Congressman Magsaysay to head the Veterans' Mission to Washington, D.C., where he successfully lobbied for passage of the Roger's Bill, giving extensive benefits to Filipino veterans. Magsaysay, who was voted one of the five best Assemblymen of the four-year term by the House Press Club, was re-elected in November 1949 by a more than 7,000-vote margin.

Retaining his post as chairman of the national defense committee, the Representative from Zambales was appointed also to the appropriations and to the internal government and privileges committees. In April 1950 Magsaysay was again sent to Washington, this time on a one-man mission to secure more American military aid for his country. That year he rose in the Philippine House to make an attack on his own party, the Liberals, then in power, in which he demanded a real fight against the revolutionary communist Hukbalahaps or Huks (short for "People's Liberation Army"), who were terrorizing the Luzon countryside and threatening the capital itself, and called for a reform of the evil social conditions which had produced the Huks. In this chaotic situation, Magsaysay took some direct action: in the words of *Time* (November 26, 1951), "when politicians kept him from buying Quonset huts he needed as schoolhouses for Zambales, he gathered some of his wartime guerrillas, raided a surplus dump, and made off with 140 huts. Later he paid for them—50 centavos (25¢) apiece, the price he figured the profiteer who owned them had paid in the first place." With the support of Manila newspapers and the approval of American advisers, President Elpidio Quirino three times offered Magsaysay the post of Secretary of National Defense, which he finally accepted.

Shortly after taking the oath of office on September 1, 1950, Magsaysay called a staff meeting. When told that two weeks would be required to move a battalion against the Huks, Secretary Magsaysay announced, "If the army doesn't move in three hours, there will be a court-martial"—and the army moved (*American Weekly*). Magsaysay took over the army—described by Time (November 26, 1951) as "a demoralized, politics-racked conglomeration that couldn't fight its way out of a bamboo hut with a howitzer"—while thousands of communist revolutionaries were rampaging in a dozen provinces, with the support of villagers who looked to them for relief from oppressive landlords and from a constabulary that was said to prey on the people rather than to protect them. To remove the Defense Department from the atmosphere of politics, Magsaysay changed the location of its headquarters from downtown Manila to Camp Murphy, in the suburbs. To a leader known to be gathering forces for a revolt, Magsaysay said, "Give me ninety days. If I haven't done anything by then, go ahead" (*Saturday Evening Post*).

Within eighty-three days, Magsaysay had retired three generals and had discharged or demoted many other officers for inefficiency, failure to lead their troops into battle, or lack of attention to the needs of their men. He gave the 18,000 enlisted men better food, quarters, and pay, took them off the drill field, reorganized them into Scout Ranger battalions, and sent them into the jungles and paddies with the command, "Kill Huks." In April 1951 the Philippine Constabulary, then semi-independent, and feared by the people almost as much as the Huks, was taken into the Defense Department, where Magsaysay outlawed its rackets and severely punished corruption and maltreatment of civilians. When his private airplane was unable to land at army outposts he wanted to visit, Magsaysay went by car or by water buffalo cart to check on conditions and sometimes even join in fighting. Borrowing tricks from the Huks, he too occasionally dressed his fighters in women's clothes and disrupted Huk communications with false messages and forged letters. Magsaysay sent civil officers to the villages to tell the people about the reforms and ask for their support. From a $500,000 fund contributed by businessmen and landowners, he paid large rewards (as high as $50,000) for information leading to the capture of Huk leaders. One month after Magsaysay took office, this policy led to the arrest and conviction of twenty-nine top Communist leaders, including six officials of the Philippine Politboro, some labor leaders, professors, and a diplomat.

The Defense Department encouraged voluntary surrenders by giving Huks medical treatment, parole, as well as homes on new farms, carved for them out of the Mindanao jungle by Magsaysay's Economic Development Corps, which has built farmhouses, schools, hospitals, electrical power plants, and other facilities. Magsaysay's program for rehabilitation of the communists also offered vocational training to those serving jail sentences and loans to aid in establishing small businesses. Nurseries were provided for young Huk children picked up by the army in raids of Huk camps. To counteract the communist philosophical indoctrination, Magsaysay arranged for lectures to be given to captured and surrendered Huks on the errors in Marxist ideology. In the November 1951 elections, when the Huks tried to enforce a boycott by threatening to kill anyone who voted, Magsaysay ordered his 40,000-man army, some 4,500 ROTC cadets, and about 5,500 reserves to police the land, thus permitting four million Filipinos to vote and give the opposition Nacionalistas a decisive victory. An aftermath of the policing was the filing of murder charges against a number of Liberal officials, including a governor, three mayors, two police chiefs, and one entire local police force. In the summer of 1952 Magsaysay took on the additional responsibility of initiating a program to subdue the unconquered Moro (Moslem) outlaws, reportedly second only to the Huks in defying Manila's rule. Magsaysay also has forces fighting under the United Nations command in Korea.

While on a short visit to the United States in June 1952, Magsaysay was presented with the United States Legion of Merit with rank of commander by Army Secretary Frank Pace, Jr., for "exceptionally meritorious service" in his present cabinet post. He also received an honorary Doctor of Laws degree from Fordham University in New York. The following October Magsaysay attended a conference in Manila between United States and Philippine representatives to decide on measures for strengthening the internal and external security of the Islands and for defending Southeast Asia.

Magsaysay has reorganized the Manila railroad and is chairman of the board of the Philippine Air Lines. He has been described as a highly energetic man and a leader who "has won an unchallenged reputation for honesty" (*Time*, November 26, 1951). On July 10, 1933, he married Luz Banzon, of Bataan; their children are two daughters, Teresita and Milagres, and a son, Ramón, Jr. Standing five feet eleven inches tall, Magsaysay is said to tower over most of his countrymen. As a hobby the former mechanic likes to repair engines.

References

Am W p10 Mr 30 '52 por
N Y World-Telegram p2 Je 11 '52 por
Sat Eve Post 224:26 Ja 12 '52 pors
Time 57:28 Ap 9 '51 por; 58:33 N 26 '51 por
Washington (D.C.) Post p7B Jl 20 '52 por

MAHER, ALY (mä'hĕr ăl'ĭ) 1882- Former Premier of Egypt

Address: h. 36 rue Mohammed Mazhar Pasha, Zamalek, Cairo, Egypt

When the incumbent Egyptian Cabinet was unable to control the anti-British riots in Cairo early in 1952, King Farouk dismissed Premier Nahas, of the Wafd party, and called upon Aly Maher Pasha, an Independent, to establish a new Government. Maher, who had been Premier in 1936 and 1939, thus returned to power for the third time. The British, who had caused him to be interned during World War II for allegedly pro-Axis sympathies, welcomed his appointment because, reported *Time*, they considered him "the strongest man in sight." After being succeeded by Ahmed Naguib Hilaly in March 1952, Maher was recalled as Premier in July 1952, following the *coup d'état* of Major General Mohammed Naguib, who himself replaced Maher on September 7. Maher, a jurist, has served in the Egyptian Senate and has held other Cabinet posts.

Aly Maher Pasha ("Pasha" is an honorary title) was born in 1882 in Cairo, the son of

Wide World Photos

ALY MAHER

Mohamed Maher Pasha, onetime Under Secretary of War in the Egyptian Government, who was removed from his post by the Earl of Cromer, then British Consul General in Egypt, as "an obstacle to harmonious cooperation" between the Khedive and the British. Another son, Ahmed Maher Pasha, was also to be Premier of Egypt, in 1944. Admitted to the bar in 1905 after studying at the Khedive School of Law, Aly Maher became a judge two years later.

Following anti-British outbreaks in Egypt in 1919, Britain dispatched an investigating mission under Lord Milner to that country in December. In June of 1920 an Egyptian delegation, of which Aly Maher was a member, was sent to London for parleys on recommendations made by the Milner mission. This resulted in the drafting of the Milner-Zaghlul agreement, securing Egypt's independence in 1922 in return for her assumption of certain obligations. Subsequently Maher was named, in 1923, dean of law and professor of public international law. Entering the Egyptian Parliament (1924) he received the post of Under Secretary of State for Education in that year, and in the succeeding year, that of Minister of Education. Maher, who left the Ministry of Education in 1926, returned to the Cabinet in 1928 as Minister of Finance, a post he held until the succeeding year. From 1930 to 1932 he was a member of the Senate and Minister of Justice.

At the time of King Fuad's last illness late in 1935, there was confusion as to whether Royal orders came from the King or from the Controller of the Royal Estates. This led the British Resident to suggest the restoration of the office of Chief of the Royal Cabinet (reported *Americana Annual*, 1935), to which Maher was appointed. At the King's express will, Maher replaced Nessim Pasha as Premier, Minister of the Interior, and Minister of For-

eign Affairs in January 1936, shortly after an outbreak of student rioting. Heading a "nonparty" Cabinet until elections were held under the 1935 Constitution in May 1936, Maher stepped out of office when Nahas Pasha, leader of the victorious Wafd party, succeeded him. Fuad had died the preceding month, leaving the succession to his minor son Farouk, and the rule to a regency, which ceased when Farouk came of age in July 1937. At that time Aly Maher was named the young King's political adviser, and in the same year he again took over the post of Chief of the Royal Cabinet. As a member of the Egyptian delegation, Maher returned to London in 1939 for the Palestine Conference.

For the seven years from 1939 to 1946, Aly Maher Pasha was again a member of the Egyptian Senate. Once more called upon to head the Government after the resignation of Mohammed Mahmud Pasha in mid-August 1939, Aly Maher succeeded in forming a Cabinet six days later by enlisting the support of the Saadists; the Liberals, however, refused to join the Government. Maher's announced policy was that of improving the living conditions of the peasants and workers. With the outbreak of World War II, Maher Pasha, Military Governor of Egypt as well as Premier, attempted to maintain his country's neutrality, refusing to declare war on the Axis and limiting action to the severance of diplomatic relations with Germany. Italy's declaration of war on Egypt found him reluctant to send what he considered inadequate Egyptian forces into battle, and even after the Italians bombed the border town of Solum, he hoped to refrain from active participation in the war. "The Premier argued that this had been provoked by the British," recalled the New York *Times*, "who had bombed Italian positions in Libya from Egyptian bases, and that the incident could be settled through diplomatic channels."

On June 23, 1940, Maher was obliged to resign because of this stand and was succeeded by Hussein Sabry Pasha. Upon the return of Mustapha el-Nahas Pasha to power, Maher Pasha was placed under house arrest in April 1942 "for reasons relating to the safety and security of the State," remaining in custody until his brother, Ahmed Maher, became Premier in 1944. After his return to political life in November 1945, Maher (said the New York *Herald Tribune*) asserted that "the Arab world must have friendly relations with Britain." The ensuing year found him among those opposed to the Anglo-Egyptian treaty drafted by Sidky Pasha and Ernest Bevin.

Unrest in Egypt, over the issues of British forces in the Suez Canal Zone and the Sudan (two questions covered by the 1936 treaty) mounted toward the end of 1951. On January 26, 1952, riots broke out in Cairo and other Egyptian cities: presumably well organized, the rioters were frequently joined by the police sent to control them. Declaring martial law the following day, the King dismissed Premier Nahas for "failing to maintain security and order" and called upon Maher to form a new

Cabinet. Assuming the multiple posts of Premier, Foreign Minister, Minister of the Army, Navy, and Radio and Military Governor, Maher formed a Cabinet composed of "independents." The Cabinet received the "overwhelming" support of the Egyptian Parliament, including that of deputies belonging to Nahas' nationalist Wafd Party. In its January 28 session, martial law was extended for two months. Asserting his intention to press for British evacuation from the Canal Zone and the union of the Sudan with Egypt, Maher stated to the Chamber of Deputies, "I assure you that these aspirations are not born in 1952, but in 1919 since Egypt united in demanding them. This is not a new policy but the people's policy, and that of all governments that preceded me."

Britain's Foreign Secretary Anthony Eden offered to enter into negotiations with Egypt for settlement of the disputes arising from the 1936 treaty, with the proviso that Egypt accept the Middle East defense project sponsored by the United States, France, Turkey, and Britain, to be organized under the United Nations guarantee for regional defense pacts. (A similar proposal, made to Nahas, was rejected by him.) "We are ready to consider any understanding Mr. Eden might propose," was Maher's statement to the press soon after interviewing the Ambassadors of the four nations calling for the pact. Subsequently both the British and the Egyptian Governments indicated a desire to wait for more settled conditions in Egypt before resuming negotiations, while early in February Eden voiced a hope for negotiations solely between those two nations (as signatories to the 1936 treaty) toward an agreement which would eventually be international. The Washington *Post* suggested that, in this case, Egyptian and British troops would both police the Suez Canal Zone. Maher's comment was: "It is my wish that a healthy atmosphere for a better understanding prevail between Egypt and all the powers of the free world. The Middle East Command and the inter-Arab security pact will be matters for discussions with the Egyptian national front." Since economic conditions of Egypt had been one of the major factors in the January riots, Maher, as a measure against what he called "the horrors of the high cost of living," asked his Ministers and Under Secretaries on February 1 to organize a new economic program, for which they would be personally responsible. The Premier urged a reduction in governmental costs, a more equitable allotment of ration cards and rationed articles, a halt of profiteering on rice (a staple of the Egyptian diet), and consideration of limitations on the importation of luxury goods. He also ordered that only one car be placed at the disposal of officials. On February 12 he announced that youth would be trained to "fulfill the country's aims." This, he explained, was not intended as a militant anti-British drive, but to divert teen-agers into "orderly government-controlled service."

In a dispute over a proposal to dissolve Parliament, Maher, resigned his Premiership on March 1, 1952, and was succeeded by Ahmed Naguib Hilaly. The following July he was recalled as Premier by Major General Mohammed Naguib, who had seized the Government on July 23, 1952. Since Maher was thought by Naguib and his followers to be overly cautious in his approach to an announced program of reform, he was replaced by Naguib on September 7.

Aly Maher has received an honorary doctorate from the Fuad I University, of which he is a member of the board. His treatise, *Public International Law*, was published in Arabic in 1923-24. Decorations given to Maher by the Egyptian Government are the Grand Cross of the Order of the Nile (1925), the Grand Cross of the Mohamed Aly Order (1936), and the Fuad I Gold Chain (1938). The Grand Crosses of the following foreign orders have also been awarded to him: the Order of Leopold II (1925), the Order of Leopold (1936), the Finnish White Rose Order (1936), the Ethiopian Holy Trinity Order (1936), the Dutch Order of Orange-Nassau (1938), the Order of the German Eagle (1938), the Greek Order of George I (1938), the Iranian Crown Order (1938), the French Legion of Honor (1938), the Order of Al Somow from the Caliphite-Government of Maghrab (1939), the Greek Order of the Saviour (1939), and the Italian Order of Sts. Maurice and Lazarus (1939). The Egyptian Premier is a director of the National Bank of Egypt. He holds the presidency of the Fuad I Society for the Protection of Orphans and Foundlings, of the Fuad I Federation of First Aid Societies, the Association of Social Studies, and the Moslem Benevolence Society. The Premier's club are the Mahamed Aly, the Gezira Sporting Club, the Royal Egyptian Hunting Club, and the Royal Automobile Club of Egypt. Ali Maher Pasha, whom *Time* described as "one of the richest men in Egypt," resides in Zamalek, an island in the Nile near Cairo.

References

Manchester Guardian p3 Ja 28 '52; p7 Ja 29 '52
N Y Herald Tribune p2 Ja 28 '52
N Y Times p3 Ja 28 '52
N Y World-Telegram p12 Ja 28 '52
Time 59:17 F 4 '52

International Who's Who, 1951
Who's Who in Egypt and the Middle East, 1949
World Biography (1948)

MALENKOV, GEORGI M(AXIMILIAN-OVICH) (mŭ'lĕn-kŏf gyĭ-ôr'gyû-ĭ mŭk" syĕm-ĕl'yän-ô-vyĭch) Jan. 8, 1902- Russian Government official
Address: Moscow, U.S.S.R.

The secretary of the Central Committee of the Communist party and member of the Politburo, Georgi M. Malenkov is one of the Soviet leaders closest to Premier Joseph Stalin—his deputy in the Orgburo (organization bureau), one of his five Deputy Premiers, and his recently proclaimed coadviser. A member of

Wide World Photos

GEORGI M. MALENKOV

Stalin's five-man War Cabinet, Malenkov early in World War II was made responsible for increasing the production of tanks and airplanes; and after the war he was prominent in organizing the Cominform, of which he is considered the head. Speculation as to the probable successor of Stalin as Premier of the Soviet Union has lately pointed to Malenkov rather than Viacheslav Molotov or Lavrenti P. Beria.

Georgi Maximilianovich Malenkov is a native of the Cossack country, in the Urals, having been born in Orenburg (now Chkalov), near the southeast border of Russia-in-Europe, on January 8, 1902. In the spring of 1919, when he was seventeen, he volunteered for service in the Bolshevik Army, and within some months was made political commissar of a squadron in the Army of Turkestan. He served through the 1919-20 campaign against the White leader General Kolchak; rose to brigade commissar; joined the Communist party in 1920; and a year later, at the age of nineteen, was named political commissar with the Turkestan and Eastern Army.

The Civil War over, Malenkov entered a higher technical school at Moscow to complete an interrupted education and was graduated in 1925. During his three or four years of study at this institution, where he was also indoctrinated in Marxism, the future Deputy Premier served as secretary of the Bolshevik Students' Organization, and as such aroused the interest of the Central Committee of the Communist party. For five years, beginning in 1925, he was engaged in responsible work in the Committee, and at some time during this period was also appointed to the personal secretariat of

Stalin. Edgar Snow in a *Saturday Evening Post* article (May 19, 1952) suggested that Malenkov's advancement at this time was due to the influence of Lazar Kaganovitch, who recognized the young man's administrative ability and recommended him to Stalin.

In 1930 Malenkov was named head of the Orgburo (organization bureau) of the Moscow Committee of the party, and after another four years was advanced to head of the Department of Leading Party Organizations in the Central Committee. His thorough knowledge of the records of party personnel, remarked the New York *World-Telegram*, is said to have played a vital part in the "purge trials" of the 1930's. "Andrei Vishinsky, as prosecutor, got all the publicity," wrote correspondent Andrew Tully, but Malenkov "provided Mr. Vishinsky with his evidence."

Malenkov was elected head of the Cadre Administration of the Central Committee, Secretary to the Committee, and a member of the Central Orgburo in 1939. He was fulfilling these duties when, in February 1941, he made at a general conference of the Communist party the speech which first brought his name and personality to the attention of the outside world. In the address he assailed bureaucratic incompetence and bungling in the industrial effort, with the result that a number of prominent commissars, including Madame Molotov, were either retired or demoted. The day after this speech Malenkov was appointed an alternate or "candidate" member of the Politburo, and soon after the German invasion of the U.S.S.R. in the following June became one of the five members of the Committee of State Defense, or War Cabinet (other members were Stalin, Molotov, Beria, and Andrei A. Zhdanov).

Placed in charge of aircraft and tank production, Malenkov through a strict priority system made Russian tank power equal to that of the Germans on the Russian front. In two years he raised the annual output of fighter planes to 40,000, an administrative achievement which won for him the Hammer and Sickle Gold Medal, the Order of Lenin and the title of Hero of Socialist Labor. By August 1943 the Nazi invaders (partly in consequence of a Soviet air victory near Kursk) were in retreat, and Malenkov became the leading member of a Committee for Economic Rehabilitation of Liberated Districts, responsible for the political and economic rebuilding of the areas devastated by the Germans. On February 8, 1946, he said in a speech: 'The war is over and now we must roll up our sleeves and set about healing the wounds. . . .We who follow the Marxist teaching must study our contemporary experience . . . and stop living by old formulas."

A month later Malenkov became one of the twelve full members of the Politburo and in October was named one of the eight vice-chairmen of the Council of Ministers, or Deputy Premiers of the U.S.S.R. Later, because of the opposition of a number of elder Bolsheviks and Politburo members (it has been suggested), Malenkov lost his secretaryship of the Central Committee, was dropped from fourth to ninth place in Politburo precedence, and "found himself stuck in a secondary role in the Agricultural Administration" (*Time*). This lasted until September 1947, when the old Communist International was revived as the Communist Information Bureau (Cominform) to combat the Marshall Plan and unite efforts to spread Communism throughout the world. The Cominform has been regarded as the creation of Zhdanov, but the special abilities of Malenkov were considered indispensable to its successful launching. He thus had a prominent role in organizational meetings in Warsaw, Budapest, and elsewhere. In the words of Edgar Snow, he is in 1952 "the real boss of the Cominform" and the director of "a vast army of foreign propagandists and political workers." Malenkov, who represents the Klinskii district of Moscow in the Supreme Soviet, is a former member of the Presidium.

By July 1948 Malenkov, who had meanwhile recommended such popular measures as the ending of food rationing in the Soviet Union and the revaluation of the ruble, had regained the secretaryship of the Central Committee; and after the death of Zhdanov later in the year, he was made Stalin's deputy in the Orgburo. In this post, wrote Edgar Snow "he can make or break officials in every branch of the state. He is the executive—acting for Stalin—who transmits all Politburo directives." Within a year the name of Malenkov began to figure prominently in speculation as to Stalin's eventual successor as party leader. Others mentioned as Stalin's heirs include Molotov and Beria, the latter the head of the secret police (MVD). Joseph and Stewart Alsop (as well as other commentators) found the strongest evidence of Malenkov's new rise in the fact that he was chosen on November 7, 1949, to deliver the annual speech commemorating the Bolshevik revolution, an honor which at the two preceding anniversaries had been conferred first on Zdhanov and then on Molotov. This was the speech in which Malenkov accused the United States of planning "to create through violence and new wars a world American empire" and predicted that "should the imperialist unleash a third world war, this war will be the grave . . . for the whole of world capitalism."

A little over a month after this address Malenkov, in a special *Pravda* article honoring Stalin's seventieth birthday, "emphatically recalled . . . Stalin's declaration that capitalism and socialism could live together peacefully" (New York *Times*); and this, together with his place of honor at Stalin's left hand at the birthday festivities, was taken as further indication of his preferred position. Significant also was the awarding to Malenkov, on his own fiftieth birthday on January 8, 1952, of the Order of Lenin for the second time and in the message of greeting from the Central Committee, which described him as "a true pupil of Lenin and a coadviser of Comrade Stalin." In August 1952 it was announced that Malenkov had been chosen to deliver the report for the Central Committee at the meeting of the All-Union Congress of the Communist party the following October.

Dark-haired, blue-eyed Malenkov is about five feet seven inches tall and weighs approximately 250 pounds. In a New York *Times* article Edward Crankshaw wrote of his "black, arching eyebrows," sharp nose, and his smile, which "has the look of spontaneous joviality." To this *Time* adds the suggestion that "if he does not drink heavily, he obviously eats well; a favorite snack is French pastry. He smokes an expensive brand of Russian cigarettes." He has reportedly been married twice, the second time to Elena Krushchev.

References

Bsns W p22-4 My 15 '48 por
Christian Sci Mon p9 Ja 15 '48
Life 11:18 Jl 14 '41 por; 27:24 Jl 4 '49 pors
N Y Herald Tribune II p1 N 20 '49; p22 Ja 10 '52; Mag p4 Ap 13 '52
N Y Times p3 Je 23 '49; p28 Ja 10 '52
N Y Times Mag p8-9+ F 2 '47 por; p10-11 Ap 4 '48 por; p6 Je 19 '49 pors; p7+ Mr 13 '49 por
N Y World-Telegram p11 Ja 12 '52; p13 Ap 26 '52 pors
Newsweek 39:41 Ja 21 '52
Sat Eve Post 217:39+ Mr 24 '45 por; 219:15-17+ Mr 22 '47 por; 224:29+ My 17 '52 por
Scholastic 59:13 Ja 23 '52 por
Spec 187:811-12 D 14 '51
Time 55:25-27 Mr 20 '50 por; 59:29 Ja 21 '52 por
U S News 27:42-3 D 9 '49 por
Washington (D.C.) Post p2B Ja 21 '51 por

Duranty, W. Stalin & Co. (1949)
Robinson, D. The 100 Most Important People in the World Today (1952)
Slavonic Encyclopaedia (1949)
World Biography (1948)

MALONEY, WALTER E(DWARD) May 5, 1911- Marine association official; lawyer

Address: b. c/o American Merchant Marine Institute, Inc., 11 Broadway, New York 4; h. 28 Rose Ave., Madison, N.J.

Chief attorney during the last decade for the American Merchant Marine Institute, Inc., Walter E. Maloney in February 1952 was elected president of this ship owners' trade association. Maloney, who was employed from 1939 to 1941 by the City of New York as an assistant corporation counsel, has practiced law since 1936, except for two years during World War II when he served as a lieutenant in the United States Coast Guard Reserve. After the war (1946) he became a member of the Wall Street law firm of Burns, Currie & Rich, which represented the A.M.M.I.

Walter Edward Maloney was born on May 5, 1911, in Phillipsburg, New Jersey, to Michael E. and Mary Huston (Cooper) Maloney. The boy spent his early years in this town, attending local grade schools and the Phillipsburg High School. At that time a teacher, his father is now (1952) principal of the high school that Walter attended. During his high school years young Maloney was a member of the baseball team, the president of his class, and valedic-

Parker Studio
WALTER E. MALONEY

torian. Upon his graduation in 1929, he entered Lafayette College in Easton, Pennsylvania, to major in government and history; another interest was law. As an undergraduate he managed the varsity basketball team and joined Kappa Sigma fraternity, the Interfraternity Society, and the Maroon Key club, an honorary group. In 1933 when he received his B.A. degree *cum laude*, he was awarded a scholarship to the Columbia University School of Law. Here Maloney studied from 1933 to 1936, working summers as a clerk in law offices.

In the same year (1936) in which he was granted his LL.B. degree at Columbia, Maloney was admitted to the bar and began the general practice of law in New York City. Three years later he temporarily gave up his private work in law to fill the position of assistant corporation counsel for the City of New York (1939-41). In 1942 Maloney was chosen chief attorney for the American Merchant Marine Institute, a post he held until his unanimous election as president of this association in February 1952. His career with the A.M.M.I. was halted for two years (1943-45) during World War II when he served as lieutenant in the United States Coast Guard Reserve. After the war (1946) Maloney became a member of Burns, Currie & Rich, the Wall Street firm which handled legal work for the A.M.M.I. As the institute's legal representative, Maloney was an adviser to management committees that negotiated collective bargaining agreements with CIO and AFL maritime unions covering shipping from the Atlantic and Gulf coasts. He also represented the A.M.M.I. in the establishment of post-war and Korean emergency shipping matters, appearing for the industry before Congressional Committees, the Federal Maritime Board, and its predecessor, the Maritime Commission.

After the outbreak of war in Korea, Maloney headed the A.M.M.I.'s committee which decided how privately owned ships of the American merchant marine could be made available for military service in the Pacific. Later, he represented the shipping industry in negotiations with the National Shipping Authority for a contract, under which private companies operate government-owned merchant vessels withdrawn from lay-up. In 1949 Maloney, again as the shipping industry's representative, "played an important role," reported the New York *Herald Tribune*, "in the successful effort of the shipping and stevedoring industries for legislation halting overtime-on-overtime suits under the wages and hours law that threatened to bankrupt the latter industry."

When Maloney assumed the presidency of the A.M.M.I. in February 1952, he succeeded Frank J. Taylor, who had been the chief executive of the trade association since 1938, the year the A.M.M.I. was incorporated. Before that date, the group, founded in 1905, had been known as the American Steamship Owners Association. In 1952 the institute represents 70 per cent of the nation's private shipping companies, handling more than eight million gross tons of American shipping. Companies owning and operating tankers, passenger liners, and cargo ships are members of the A.M.M.I., which represents their interests in disputes and in wage and hour agreements with employees and labor groups, in negotiations with government agencies, in legislation affecting the maritime industry, and in relations with the public.

Three months after becoming president, Maloney took a prominent part in the Maritime Day celebrations, which each May honor the American merchant marine's contribution to this nation's economy and defense. Also in May 1952 negotiations were begun between Atlantic and Gulf Coasts ship operators and members of the National Maritime Union, CIO, for a 15 per cent across-the-board wage increase for unlicensed sea-going personnel. The lawyer, as chairman of the employers' group, conducted the hearings, under terms of an agreement which provided for wage and overtime rate reviews at six-month intervals. The next month Maloney, again as chairman of the employers' committee, opened hearings on a request by the National Organization of Masters, Mates, and Pilots, AFL, for wage increases and higher welfare fund payments from East and Gulf Coast shipowners. (Involved in the discussions are forty-eight steamship lines under contract to the labor group; results of the negotiations, however, are expected to establish wage and welfare fund patterns for the other 130 companies under contract to the union.) As chairman of the Merchant Marine Committee of the Whole, which comprises six maritime organizations, Maloney attended conferences in Washington in April 1952 between his committee and government agencies concerned with shipping. Afterward he announced that private ship companies had been assured that they would get "maximum consideration in the assignment of export cargoes" and that government-owned ships would not be used as "rate-breakers."

The A.M.M.I. executive has blue eyes and brown hair; he weighs 180 pounds and is six feet one inch tall. On June 26, 1937, he married Mary C. Reynolds, a former secretary, who bore him two sons, James Michael and Thomas Reynolds. Maloney is a Roman Catholic and a Republican. He belongs to the American Bureau of Shipping, the United States Maritime Law Association, the Propeller Club of the United States, the New York City Downtown Athletic Club, the Morris County Golf Club (Convent, New Jersey), the Shongum Club (Dover, New Jersey), and the American Legion.

References

N Y Herald Tribune p27 F 6 '52
N Y Times p55 F 6 '52

MANNING, HARRY 1897- Merchant marine commander

Address: b. c/o United States Lines, 1 Broadway, New York 4

To command the new S.S. *United States*, largest and most luxurious of American passenger vessels, the United States Lines in March 1952 assigned Harry Manning, who is the commodore of its merchant fleet. Perhaps the best known of contemporary American mercantile shipmasters, Commander Manning first attracted widespread notice in January 1929, when as chief officer of the old S.S. *America* under Captain George Fried, he commanded the lifeboat which rescued the crew of an Italian freighter the S.S. *Florida*. A seaman or ship's officer since 1914, Manning has commanded many vessels, including the new *America*, of which he was master from 1946 to 1948. In August 1952 he relinquished command of the *United States*, a month after the ship, leaving New York on July 3, had broken speed records on her maiden voyage across the Atlantic Ocean.

Harry Manning, born in 1897 in New York City, is the only son of William E. Manning, who was engaged in the export business, and Anna M. Manning. When he left high school at the age of sixteen he was enrolled in a merchant marine academy. Trained on the New York State schoolship *Newport*, he shipped aboard the bark *Dirigo* as an able seaman in 1914. Subsequently he entered the service of the old Isthmian Line as a third officer, and during World War I was second officer on the Atlantic Transport liner S.S. *Minnewaska*, then taken over as a troopship.

Emerging from the war as a first lieutenant in the United States Naval Reserve, he entered in July 1921 the employ of the United States Lines, that name having been given to a group of former German-owned ships which were put into operation under the American flag by the United States Shipping Board. From the rank of second officer on the S.S. *George Washington* he had risen to senior first officer when transferred to the S.S. *Leviathan* in 1923. He served as chief officer aboard a number of other vessels, including the *Republic*, the *President Harding*, the *President Arthur*, and

HARRY MANNING

the *President Roosevelt* before receiving his first temporary command in 1928, taking over the *President Roosevelt* from Captain George Fried, who had been reassigned to the *America*, the former *Amerika* of Hamburg registry. Manning was master of the *President Roosevelt* for four transatlantic round trips in 1928 and was at the time the youngest captain of a passenger vessel on the seas.

In January 1929 Manning was back with Captain Fried as chief officer of the *America*. He commanded the lifeboat which (in the words of a New York *Times* account) "negotiated gale-lashed Atlantic seas to rescue from certain death the entire thirty-two man crew of the Italian freighter *Florida*." For this feat, which was subsequently cited in a United States Navy textbook as a model of rescue operations, Manning on the return of the *America* to New York shared with Captain Fried the honor of a ticker-tape parade along Broadway, and on the *America*'s next voyage served as acting captain. The following year (1930) the United States Lines fleet was purchased by the International Mercantile Marine Company, which had operated the White Star Line and other fleets of British registry before being reorganized as a wholly American concern and disposing of its foreign flag vessels.

Under the new ownership Manning was assigned to the S.S. *American Trader* in 1931. In May 1932, however, he was chief officer of the *President Roosevelt* under Fried when the transatlantic flier Lou Reichers was forced down in heavy weather off Ireland. Manning commanded the lifeboat which rescued Reichers. This achievement, together with the *Florida* rescue, brought him American and foreign

MANNING, HARRY—*Continued*

honors: the United States gold medal for lifesaving, the Navy and Marine Corps gold medal, the Lifesaving Benevolent Association gold medal, the New York State Conspicuous Service Cross, the New York City medal for heroism, the Italian Government medal for lifesaving, and the title of *chevalier* in the French Order of Maritime Merit.

In July 1934 Manning left the maritime service to take an executive position with the National Ordnance and Forge Company, but by September he was back with the United States Lines as chief officer of the S.S. *Manhattan*. He was made captain of the S.S. *American Traveler* in October 1935, of the *America* in December of the same year, and of the S.S. *American Banker* in September 1936. Through the aviatrix Amelia Earhart Putnam, one of his passengers during his command of the *President Roosevelt* in 1928, Manning had become interested in flying, and in September 1930 had qualified for a private pilot's license. Early in 1937 he took leave of absence from the United States Lines to become navigator and radio operator for Amelia Earhart Putnam on her first attempt at a globe-circling flight. Following an accident in a take-off at Honolulu, Captain Manning had to return to his ship before repairs on the plane were completed. Manning himself gave up flying as an avocation in 1938, when a crash of his private plane in Long Island almost cost him his life.

Manning was made master of the S.S. *President Roosevelt* in March 1939. In the year following, as commander of the S.S. *Washington*, he won what has been described as "America's first argument with a German submarine" in World War II. "An enemy craft halted the *Washington* with 1,000 passengers aboard in July 1940," stated a United States Lines release, "and signaled its intention to torpedo the vessel. While passengers were being put into lifeboats by the crew Manning stood by the blinker flashing forceful messages to the captain of the submarine who finally thought better of his plan." In July 1941 the *Washington* was converted into a Navy transport and renamed the U.S.S. *Mount Vernon*; Manning, called from reserve to active duty as lieutenant commander, remained with the vessel as navigator, and early in the following year participated in the evacuation of war refugees from Singapore. Subsequently he commanded the Maritime Service training ship *American Navigator*. His final World War II duty was as superintendent of the United States Maritime Service Radio Training Station at Hoffman Island, New York, beginning January 1944. Manning's present rank in the Naval Reserve, that of captain, dates from February 1947.

Released from active duty with the Navy in September 1944, Manning rejoined the United States Lines and in 1946, when the *Washington* was returned to her owners, resumed command. In September 1946 the announcement was made by John M. Franklin, president of the United States Lines, that Manning had been named commodore of the company's fleet and had

been assigned as master of the new 33,500-ton *America*, namesake of Captain Fried's famous craft. The new *America*, construction of which had actually been completed in 1940, had been used during the war as a transport; now reconditioned, she was the most luxurious as well as the largest and speediest United States passenger vessel afloat. She was scheduled to begin her maiden voyage from New York to Europe on October 17, 1946, but just before sailing time the Masters, Mates and Pilots Association demanded that Captain Manning join that union. "I will starve first," Manning replied. A strike delayed the departure of the *America* until November 14, on the trip which broke the American (though not the British) speed record for an eastbound Atlantic crossing. Manning continued as captain of the *America* until 1948, when he was assigned to supervise the construction of the new S.S. *United States* at the yards of the Newport News (Virginia) Shipbuilding and Dry Dock Company. This luxury liner, well over three years in the making, has a gross tonnage of 52,000, a length of 990 feet, and accommodation for approximately 2,000 passengers; she was practically completed when, on March 6, 1952, the announcement was made that Captain Manning has been appointed her commander. On her maiden voyage across the Atlantic, the *United States*, which left New York for England on July 3, 1952, broke previous records with an average speed of 35.59 knots an hour. A month later it was announced that Manning would turn over his post as master of the new ship to Captain John W. Andersen.

Harry Manning and Florence Isabella Trowbridge Heaton, an aviatrix, were married on January 29, 1940; the union later terminated in divorce. The blue-eyed captain, ruddy, stocky, and athletic, has been called a good boxer and tennis player. He is five feet seven and one half inches tall and weighs 160 pounds. Of taciturn temperament, he is rarely seen to smile: "A uniform and a smile don't go together," he has been quoted as saying. Two of his recreations are reading Shakespeare and playing the piano.

References

N Y Herald Tribune III p5 O 20 '46 por
N Y Sun p28 N 13 '46
N Y Times p2 Ja 25 '29 por; p33 Jl 4 '34 por; p16 S 27 '36 por; p39 Ja 30 '40; p55 S 25 '46 por; p39 F 17 '47; p55 Mr 12 '52 por
Sat Eve Post 220:18-19+ F 28 '48 pors
Washington (D.C.) Post p2 F 27 '48 por

MANSFIELD, MICHAEL J(OSEPH)
Mar. 16, 1903- United States Representative from Montana; Senator-elect from Montana
Address: b. c/o House Office Bldg., Washington 25, D.C.; h. Missoula, Mont.

The Democratic Representative of Montana's First Congressional District, Michael J. (Mike) Mansfield, is the only member of Congress to have served in the Army, the

Navy, and the Marine Corps. Previous to his election in 1943 he was a miner, a mining engineer, and from 1933 to 1942 a professor of history and political science at the Montana State University. A member of the House Foreign Affairs Committee since the Seventy-eighth Congress, Mansfield was President Roosevelt's investigator in China in 1944 and a Congressional delegate to the United Nations General Assembly in 1951-52. The Representative won a seat in the Senate in the 1952 elections.

Michael Joseph Mansfield was born in New York City on March 16, 1903, son of Patrick and Josephine (O'Brien) Mansfield. When the boy was three years old the family moved to Great Falls, Montana, where he attended local public schools. At the time of World War I he left school before completing the eighth grade to join the navy in February 1918. After ten months' service overseas, he enlisted in 1919 as a private in the army; then, from 1920 to 1922 as a Marine private first class he saw duty in the Philippines, Japan, Siberia, and China.

For eight years after leaving the armed forces, Mansfield worked as a miner and mining engineer in Montana copper mines. Since he had not attended high school, he was required to pass entrance examinations in secondary school subjects before being admitted to college. In 1927 he enrolled at the Montana School of Mines for a year's study and then entered Montana State University, where he graduated with the Bachelor of Arts degree in 1933. Remaining there as an instructor of history and political science, Mansfield also completed requirements for the Master of Arts degree, awarded by that university in 1934. Subsequently he extended his graduate studies in summer school classes at the University of California at Berkeley, in 1936 and 1937. He advanced at the Montana university to full professor of Latin American and Far Eastern history. He became a charter member of the American Federation of Teachers.

It was as a Representative of the First Montana District (comprising seventeen counties with a population of almost a quarter of a million people) that Mansfield, replacing Jeannette Rankin, entered the Seventy-eighth Congress in 1943. He cast votes at that time for lend-lease and for authorization of the United Nations Relief and Rehabilitation Administration; against the tax bill veto by President Roosevelt, and against the soldier vote bill, which was a compromise measure allowing servicemen to use a Federal ballot only if State authorities certified that it would be legal under various State election laws. Just after Mansfield's freshman term in Congress, President Roosevelt called upon the Montana Democrat to make a tour of inspection of conditions in China. Mansfield, who knows the Chinese language, returned to Washington three months later, in January 1945, with a 7,000-word account of his findings in which he reported malnutrition among soldiers, disunity among the people, and the unpopularity of the Kuomintang. The estimate given by Mansfield

MICHAEL J. MANSFIELD

of the strength of Chinese Communists, whom he regarded as "more agrarian reformers than revolutionaries," was the highest made by any observer up to that time. In favor of the United States support of Chiang Kai-shek, Mansfield stated, "Chiang is the one man who can make Chinese unity and independence a reality" (quoted by *Time*, January 22, 1945).

In the Seventy-ninth Congress Mansfield voted in favor of a health service for United States employees, the United Nations implementation bill, an extension of the trade agreements act, an increase in fourth class postal rates, an anti-poll tax bill, an extension of price control, Federal aid to States on school lunches, a housing subsidy, and exemption of fathers and teenagers from the draft. He voted against the taxation of Civil Service annuities, the Revenue Act of 1945, the court review of OPA actions, and the creation of an Un-American Activities Committee. He submitted bills to increase pensions for World War I disabled veterans, to exempt veterans from certain taxes to help them buy homes, and to implement the creation of an Alaskan International Highway Commission. In the Eightieth Congress Mansfield supported the displaced persons bill, the Greek-Turkish aid bill, an anti-inflation bill, the European Recovery Program, and the Mundt-Nixon anti-Communist bill; he opposed a constitutional amendment to limit Presidential tenure, the Taft-Hartley bill, a 15 per cent rent increase, and a peacetime draft. He offered bills for a revision of the United Nations Charter, another recommending that personal income taxes be lowered, and an amendment to the aid bills to China, Greece, and Turkey, which would strike out the military aid.

Near the conclusion of his third consecutive term in Congress, on November 1, 1949, Mansfield was offered an appointment by President Truman as Assistant Secretary of State for

MANSFIELD, MICHAEL J.—*Continued*

Public Affairs, which would have put the Montana Congressman in charge of the *Voice of America* and other international information services. In declining the appointment, Mansfield explained, "It is my first duty to remain in Congress to continue to work for the development of Montana's resources and the betterment of our people, both of which have always been close to my heart." He also said that by remaining in Congress and a member of the House Foreign Affairs Committee, he could continue to uphold President Truman's foreign policy.

Mansfield's voting record in the Eighty-first Congress shows him in favor of an anti-poll tax bill, a minimum wage of seventy-five cents an hour, and social security increased coverage, Korean aid, and extension of rent control; and against flexible support of agricultural prices and a 50 per cent cut in European arms aid. He introduced an amendment to the Yugoslavian aid bill requiring the State Department to report every three months on the degree of Yugoslavia's compliance with aid terms, including the right of the United States to supervise food distribution. In the subsequent Congress — the Eighty-second — Mansfield voted "Yea" to the India emergency food aid act, the defense production act, and draft extension-universal military training bill; and "Nay" to an increase in taxes and a cut in economic aid for the Mutual Security Act countries. He was one of a bipartisan group of eight members of the House which introduced a bill favoring a Pacific Pact and Far Eastern Recovery Program (to parallel the programs in Europe), implemented by an organization for Far Eastern economic cooperation.

In 1951 Mansfield headed a group of seventy-five Representatives who urged doubling the size of the Marine Corps and granting it increased weight on the Joint Chiefs of Staff. Much of the group's program for the Marines' expansion, which was sponsored in the Senate by Paul H. Douglas, has since been implemented. Mansfield also offered a solution that year to the dispute between the Federal Government and various States over the control of marginal seacoast areas and the natural resources found there; the Montana Representative suggested that the Government assume control of the tidelands but pledge all revenue from submerged oil to a long-range program of aid to States in public education. Although not accepted by Congress, Mansfield's plan was called by the press "a realistic and equitable" suggestion for administration "in the interest of the American people."

As a delegate to the United Nations General Assembly session which opened in Paris in November 1951, Mansfield "slugged it out orally" with Andrei Vishinsky, Soviet Foreign Minister, over the United States Mutual Security Act and the imprisonment of four American fliers in Hungary. The Mutual Security Act, on which the Montana legislator worked in Congressional committee meetings, appropriates up to $100 millions to aid anti-Communist refugees and help them form armed units in support of the North Atlantic Treaty Organization. When Vishinsky charged before the U.N. Political and Security Committee in December 1951 that the act was aggressive, Mansfield was spokesman for the United States, and at the request of President Truman he returned to Paris in January 1952 to answer Vishinsky before the plenary Assembly. By a vote of 42 to 5 (with eleven nations abstaining) the U.N. rejected a Soviet demand that the United States be found guilty of "aggressive intervention." Later in January at the opening meeting in Geneva of a three-member U.N. Prisoner of War Commission, Mansfield proposed that an inquiry be conducted inside the Soviet Union on the fate of missing prisoners of World War II.

In addition to serving on the House Foreign Affairs Committee, Mansfield is a member of a Select Committee to Conduct a Study and Investigation of the Problems of Small Business, and in 1950 he headed a House special committee to investigate campaign expenditures. On February 8, 1952, he stated that he would seek nomination for a Montana Senatorial seat; after his victory in the July primary, he defeated Senator Zales N. Ecton, Republican, in the 1952 election. Mansfield, who was once described as "a dark, pipe-smoking fellow," married Maureen Hayes on September 13, 1932; they have one daughter, Anne.

References

N Y Post p25 O 20 '44
N Y Sun p16 Ja 23 '45
Nation 156:295 F 27 '43
PM p10 Mr 8 '43
Washington (D.C.) Post p3B F 10 '52
Biographical Directory of the American Congress, 1774-1949 (1950)
Congressional Directory (1952)
Who's Who in America, 1950-51

MANSFIELD, MIKE *See* Mansfield, M. J.

MARCIANO, ROCKY (mär-sĭ-*a*'nō) Sept. 1, 1924- Boxer

Address: b. c/o Al Weill, 1579 Broadway, New York 19

The winner in all forty-four of the bouts in which he has participated since his first professional appearance in July 1948, boxer Rocky Marciano became the world heavyweight champion when he defeated Jersey Joe Walcott on September 23, 1952. The new champion, whose pugilistic style and power have sometimes been compared with those of Jack Dempsey, ended the ring career of former champion Joe Louis with a knockout in October 1951. Following his defeat of Louis, Marciano scored another important knockout victory over Lee Savold in February 1952.

The real name of the heavyweight fighter now professionally known as Rocky Marciano, is Rocco Francis Marchegiano. Born in Brockton, Massachusetts, on September 1, 1924, he is the eldest of the three sons of Pirrino and Lena (Piccento) Marchegiano, who also had three daughters. The elder Marchegiano, an immigrant from Italy, had fought with the American Expeditionary Force in World War I and had been so severely gassed that he was able to work in the Brockton shoe factories only intermittently. In his grade school days the athletic interest of the future prize fighter was centered on baseball; but later, on entering high school with a weight of 150 pounds, he fixed his sights on the gridiron. "I made the Brockton High team as a freshman," he recently told the New York *World-Telegram* sportswriter Lester Bromberg. "I played every game. I could play center or full back. My coach, E. Marion Roberts, was sure I could wind up with a scholarship to Boston College or Fordham."

However, during young Marciano's sophomore year his mother's brother, John Piccento, suggested that it was time the boy got a job: "He'd done a lot for us," Marciano told Bromberg. "That was enough for me." He consequently went to work as a dishwasher in a diner. Among the other jobs he had before induction into the army for World War II service were as a mixer in a candy factory, a deliverer of beer for a brewery, a gardener, and, finally as a benchworker in a local shoe factory.

It was his uncle, too, who gave the boy his first instruction in boxing, after young Rocco had lost his first "kid's fight." "Learn to hit with both hands, Rocco, learn to use the left as well as the right," was the uncle's admonition (as quoted by Tim Cohane in an article in *Look*). The boy then defeated his adversary and in another "scrap," at the age of twelve he discovered the efficacy of the overhand right swing which he calls the "Susie-Que." It was not until after his call to war duty on March 4, 1943, that Marciano "really got interested in boxing" and then chiefly because at the induction center at Ford Devens, Massachusetts, he "discovered that the winning of a recreation-period bout would get him a three-day pass" (Tim Cohane). From Devens the future pugilist went to other camps for basic and specialized training, and then overseas with the newly activated 150th Combat Engineers.

While stationed in Wales during 1945 Marciano won the gratitude of his outfit by silencing a bragging Australian in a village pub, and shortly afterward, in a quickly arranged bout, used the "Susie-Que" to knock out the bully of his own company. After the end of the war, while on duty at Fort Lewis, Washington, he fought in a number of Junior Amateur Athletic Union boxing matches. He returned to civilian life in late 1947.

Marciano's first job after going back to Brockton was with a road construction gang. He was looking forward, however, to a career in professional baseball. With his closest friend, Al Colombo, he became a star of a local team known as the Brockton Pros, and in the spring of 1948 was given a three-week tryout at the Fayetteville (North Carolina) farm of the Chicago Cubs. Rejection at the end of this period because of fielding weakness resulting from a wartime injury convinced him

ROCKY MARCIANO

that he had no future on the professional diamond. Thus, on the advice of Colombo, he started to prepare himself for a pugilistic career. "Uncle John Piccento encouraged the idea," Cohane reported. "Rocky had thirty amateur fights, won all but three. Colombo trained and seconded him. His manager was Gene Caggiano, a Brockton mechanic."

Rocky Marciano fought his first professional bout in Providence, Rhode Island, on July 12, 1948, knocking out Harry Balzerian in the first round of a match arranged under the indirect auspices of the New York promoter Al Weill. Weill told A. J. Liebling of the *New Yorker* in 1951 that, hearing of the prowess of the Massachusetts amateur boxer, he had sent for him and had tried him in a gymnasium fight with a young heavyweight. The result was so promising that Weill turned him over to a promoter in Providence. After his fifth professional bout in the New England area Marciano was taken in hand by Charles Goldman, Weill's trainer, and in a series of "soft" contests gradually improved his fighting style. In his first appearance in New York at Madison Square Garden at the beginning of December 1949, Marciano knocked out Pat Richards in the second round, and later in the same month defeated Carmine Vingo in the sixth round.

The knockout of Vingo was Marciano's twenty-second in twenty-four straight victories as a professional heavyweight, but it was generally acknowledged that he had yet to face first-rate opposition. In his next fight he was matched with Roland LaStarza, described as "a clever, cautious fighter," who had remained undefeated in thirty-seven matches. Marciano won a split decision over LaStarza at the Garden, a verdict not universally approved. "The fight crowd," Howard Cohn has written in *Collier's*, "labeled Marciano clumsy and was

MARCIANO, ROCKY—*Continued*

so unimpressed that he went into the ring a heavy underdog in his next major fight—a July 12, 1951, bout with Rex Layne." The latter, a rising, hard-hitting young heavyweight from Utah, had recently won a ten-round decision over the next world champion, Jersey Joe Walcott. Marciano trained intensively under Goldman for three weeks; then, "following instructions perfectly, he crowded the favored Layne, backed him up, wore him out. In the sixth, Layne went down" (Tim Cohane).

Three months later Marciano was matched with Joe Louis, the former world champion, who, after retiring from the ring, was endeavoring to make a comeback. They met in New York on October 26, 1951, and at the end of the eighth round Louis was on his knees, after a blow "solidly hooked" to the left jaw. The sequel was told by Marciano to Bob Brumby of *Sports Stars*: "After I knocked Joe down with a left hook I set him up with another one. Then I let go with my right. The punch made all my dreams come true. But it was the saddest punch of my life. How else could I feel seeing such a great ex-champion and one of the finest sportsmen that ever lived lying there on the canvas?"

The knockout of Louis was Marciano's thirty-third in a series of thirty-eight straight victories, and was at Philadelphia followed on February 13, 1952, by a seventh-round technical knockout of Lee Savold. "The victory," said J. B. Dawson of the New York *Times*, "kept Marciano among the three top heavyweights, assuring his position as the outstanding challenger after Jersey Joe Walcott defends his title against Ezzard Charles." From the Savold fight Rocky went on to knock out Bernie Reynolds at Providence on May 12, and Harry (Kid) Matthews of Seattle at the Yankee Stadium in New York City on July 28, ending the latter contest with two solid left blows in the second round. About a month later it was announced that Marciano and Walcott would fight for the heavyweight championship at Philadelphia on September 23, 1952. (Earlier in August Weill had announced that he was giving up his International Boxing Office position to devote his full time to managing Marciano.) By a knockout in the thirteenth round Marciano won the match against Walcott and thus became the first white heavyweight to hold the title since 1937.

Marciano, whose height is five feet ten and a half inches, weighed in for his bout with Matthews at 187½ pounds. "Out of the ring," Bob Brumby has written, "Rocky is a gentle fellow. . . .The one love of his life has been his wife, the former Barbara Cousens, whose books he carried home from grade school." Mrs. Marciano, who is of Irish descent, is the daughter of a retired Brockton police officer; her marriage to the heavyweight challenger took place on December 31, 1950. The Marcianos are Roman Catholics.

References

Collier's 129:60-61 Je 7 '52 pors
Look 16:70-72 Ja 15 '52 pors
N Y Herald Tribune p33 Mr 23 '50

N Y World-Telegram p32 O 31 '51 por; p27 N 1 '51 por; p29 N 20 '51 pors; p23 N 21 '51 por; p3 Jl 31 '52 por
New Yorker 27:102+ N 17 '51
Parade p7 Ja 21 '52 por
Sports Stars 4:14-16 My '52 pors

MARKEL, LESTER Jan. 9, 1894- Newspaper editor

Address: b. c/o New York Times, 229 W. 43d St., New York 18; h. 135 Central Park West, New York 23

The Sunday editor of the New York *Times* and chairman of the executive board of the International Press Institute is Lester Markel, who began his career as a reporter and served as a city editor and assistant managing editor of the old New York *Tribune* before he came to his present post with the *Times* in 1923. Under his direction the Sunday *Times* has expanded to include an enlarged and improved *Magazine* and *Book Review* and a new section, the *News of the Week in Review*. Circulation of the Sunday paper in 1952 is about 1,100,000; it has readers in more than 11,000 cities and towns in the United States. Founded in May 1951 after Markel had proposed such an organization at a meeting of the American Society of Newspaper Editors, the International Press Institute in 1952 has members in thirty-two countries who are concerned with the problems of news gathering and news dissemination in the free world.

Born in New York City on January 9, 1894, Lester Markel is one of the three sons of Jacob Leo and Lillian (Hecht) Markel. His father, Russian-born, had been graduated from the gymnasium in Hamburg, Germany, and three years later, in 1881, had immigrated to the United States. In his adopted country he was a senior member of the Markel Brothers' banking firm from 1881 to 1926, when he organized and became president of the Merchants Bank of New York. Young Markel attended Townsend Harris High School, a New York City secondary school for boys of superior ability. In 1912 he studied at the College of the City of New York and the following year entered Columbia University School of Journalism, which was at that time an undergraduate division. Here Markel received his Bachelor of Letters degree in 1914, while working as "legman," sportswriter, and linotype operator for the now defunct Bronx *Northside News*.

Upon graduating the twenty-year-old reporter obtained a position on Ogden Reid's New York *Tribune*, which has since become part of the New York *Herald Tribune*. The next year, 1915, he was advanced to night city editor, later became night editor, and in 1919 was named assistant managing editor of the *Tribune*. Four years later, in 1923, Adolph Ochs, then publisher of the New York *Times*, asked Markel to confer with him: the story is told that the two men met in Atlantic City one winter day and discussed plans for a reorganization of the *Times*'s Sunday supplements during a three-hour ride on the boardwalk in side-by-side rolling chairs. Impressed by Markel's ideas, as related by Meyer Berger in *The Story of the New York Times*, Ochs at the end of the ride hired the young man as Sunday editor of the *Times*, to succeed Ralph Graves.

In his new position Markel inherited a staff of three editors, a secretary, an office boy, and what *Time* magazine (March 8, 1948) has described as "a skinny magazine with stodgy make-up and a grabbag of features." During the following years this organization was to develop into a staff of eighty-four, responsible for weekly issues of a greatly expanded New York *Times Magazine*, often reaching its press limit of eighty pages, and such additional Sunday sections as the *News of the Week in Review*, an expanded *Book Review*, and a drama section of from twenty-four to forty pages of articles on drama and other arts, travel, and hobbies. Markel conceived of the Sunday sections as bringing to readers the setting and significance of the news in greater detail and coherence than was possible in the usually disjointed daily news stories.

For the enlarged New York *Times Magazine*, Markel, in an attempt to anticipate happenings, ordered background articles from *Times* correspondents all over the world on the basis of where he believed important news would be breaking. About 90 per cent of the material in the *Magazine* continues to originate in such assignments from Markel and his editors. The incorporation of the *Times* rotogravure section into the *Magazine*—a mechanical change proposed by Markel—was, as Berger reported, postponed because of a newsprint shortage until February 1942. As the new *Magazine* flourished, the Sunday circulation of the *Times* rose until in April 1946 it passed the million mark and in 1950 this section of the paper was third in the United States in advertising lineage covered, being topped only by the *Saturday Evening Post* and *Life*. Meanwhile, the Sunday *Book Review* section was expanded to an average of thirty-two pages of reviews, "literary letters" from abroad, news of books and publishers, and interviews with noted authors, with Christmas and spring issues of as many as eighty pages. *Time* magazine (October 24, 1949) described it as "an oasis of prosperity, if not brilliance" in the book-reviewing business, a "news book review." Other features added to the various Sunday sections were science news notes in 1931, an education page in 1942, crossword puzzles in 1942, and news of home furnishings in 1943. Without "stooping to comics or sex," *Time* magazine (March 8, 1948) pointed out, the Sunday *Times* had doubled its circulation in twenty-five years under Markel's direction.

In 1943 Markel and James Reston, *Times* diplomatic correspondent, worked out the format for an overseas weekly tabloid for the armed forces, a "condensed *News of the Week in Review*," without advertising. Plastic plates were flown to Iran in August 1943, as told by Berger, and the first edition was printed there for the Persian Gulf Command. Sold through the Army Exchange Service, the weekly was available on sixteen war fronts before the end of World War II. After the war in several

LESTER MARKEL

public addresses and in magazine articles and books, Markel expressed concern over the fact that Americans were not well informed; barely 25 per cent of the voting population, he stated repeatedly, showed any knowledge of foreign issues.

Disturbed over the problem of how to develop well-informed opinion at home and abroad, Markel noted that he had found meetings of the American Society of Newspaper Editors of great value in gaining an understanding of points of view in other parts of the nation. "I felt that if the idea of the A.S.N.E. could be translated into international terms, there might evolve an organization with large potentialities for world peace," he later explained. With this thought he proposed at the April 1949 meeting of the A.S.N.E. the formation of an international press institute to further understanding among editors and consequently among peoples, and also to study such problems as infringements on freedom of the press and barriers to the flow of news across national boundaries. The following September fifteen foreign editors met with Markel in New York to discuss the proposal, and in May 1951 the International Press Institute was formally established, to be financed for its first three years by grants of $150,000 and $120,000 from the Ford and the Rockefeller foundations, respectively. The understanding was that if it proved successful, the members would take over its support thereafter. When the organization's secretariat was established in Zurich, Switzerland, Markel was named chairman of the executive board.

By 1952 the International Press Institute had a membership of 582 editors in thirty-four countries, with a national committee in each member nation to serve as a link between it and the secretariat in Zurich. Markel announced in April 1952 that research work was "well under way." One project was a survey of coverage and presentation of news from and about Russia.

(Continued next page)

MARKEL, LESTER—*Continued*

For another project, the study of news of the United States published abroad, the Ford Foundation had granted $225,000. If the United States were to understand other nations, Markel held, the manner in which news was gathered in those countries and presented in the United States and, conversely, the manner in which United States news was reported abroad were of "prime concern." At the institute's first international assembly, in Paris in May 1952, the result of a survey of editors on the reporting of world affairs was made known; the survey had revealed, according to the institute, "a growing tendency in democratic as well as nondemocratic countries to restrict the free gathering of legitimate news."

To *The Newspaper, Its Making and Its Meaning* (1945), by members of the staff of the New York *Times*, Markel contributed the chapter, "Interpretation of the News and the Sunday Newspaper." For *While You Were Gone* (1946), a compilation of essays reporting on wartime life in the United States for the benefit of returning servicemen, he wrote the chapter "The Newspaper." Markel also edited and was one of nine contributors to a symposium, *Public Opinion and Foreign Policy* (1949). His articles for the New York *Times Magazine* have included a number on public opinion and foreign affairs and two studies of President Harry S. Truman. "European Ledger: Tangibles-Intangibles," a January 1952 survey of European feeling toward the United States, was written after a trip to Europe, and "Report on a Stirring Human Adventure," in November 1950, recounted the editor's impressions after his first visit to Israel. A frequent speaker on current affairs at women's clubs and schools, he has also participated occasionally in New York *Times* lecture courses for New York City school teachers. Citing him as "editor, educator, and crusader," the New School for Social Research in January 1952 conferred on Markel the honorary degree of Doctor of Letters.

Time magazine has described Markel's temperament as "executive, hard-riding"; beginning his day at 6 A.M., he runs himself and his staff "on a tight, merciless schedule." New York *Times* correspondents in Washington or London sometimes hear from him four or five times a day. Of his insistence to authors that they rewrite, Markel has said, "I have a reputation for being tough on them. I'm tougher on myself; I often rewrite a piece four times." The editor's wife, whom he married on April 3, 1917, is the former Meta Edman, sister of Irwin Edman, the philosopher. The Markels have one daughter, Helen. For relaxation the editor enjoys gardening at his country home in New Jersey. He has brown eyes and black hair and is five feet eight and one-half inches tall.

References

N Y Herald Tribune p8 Ap 16 '51
N Y Times p24 S 19 '50; p28 Ja 30 '52; p27 Ap 17 '52; p6 Ap 19 '52
Time 49:71 Mr 3 '47; 51:45-6+ Mr 8 '48; 54:84 O 24 '49

Berger, Meyer　The Story of the New York Times, 1851-1951 (1951)
The Newspaper, Its Making and Its Meaning (1945)
Who's Who in America, 1952-53
Who's Who in American Jewry, 1938-39
Who's Who in New York, 1938

MATHEWSON, LEMUEL　Mar. 29, 1899-
United States Army officer

Address: b. c/o United States Office of Military Government for Germany, Berlin, Germany; United States Department of Defense, The Pentagon, Washington 25, D.C.

As an officer in the United States Army for more than three decades, Major General Lemuel Mathewson, who became United States Commandant in Berlin on February 1, 1951, has seen duty in the Philippine Islands, in a number of military posts in the United States, and in the European theater in World War II. For several years he taught at the United States Military Academy, West Point, and at Fort Sill, Oklahoma. During the early phases of World War II he was a member of the War Department General Staff in Washington, D.C., and later was placed in command of the artillery of the 18th Airborne Corps in Europe. Prior to his appointment to succeed Major General Maxwell D. Taylor in Berlin, Mathewson was a member of the European Command Headquarters in Heidelberg, Germany.

Lemuel Mathewson was born in Bath, New York, on March 29, 1899. Subsequent to his enlistment in the United States Army in 1918, he was accepted as a student at the United States Military Academy in West Point, New York. Upon graduating with the B.S. degree in 1922, he received on June 13 of that year a commission as second lieutenant of infantry in the regular Army. His first two and a half years of service were spent at Camp Furlong, New Mexico, and at Camp Stephen D. Little, Nogales, Arizona, at both posts as company officer and platoon commander of the 25th Infantry. In 1925 he began a two-year period of duty as company officer and as commander of the 24th Brigade, stationed in the Philippine Islands. When he returned to the United States, he was transferred from the infantry to the field artillery and assigned as battery reconnaissance officer at Fort Sill, Oklahoma, where he completed the battery officers' course at the Field Artillery School.

Following a year of study at the Centre de Estudies Historices in Madrid in 1930-31, Mathewson was recalled to the United States to teach Spanish at the Military Academy in West Point. Here he remained until 1936 when he was assigned to Fort Benning, Georgia, as battery commander of the 83d Field Artillery. Two years later he studied at the Command and General Staff School, at Fort Leavenworth, Kansas, and at the end of his training was assigned in September 1939 as an instructor in the Department of Tactics and Communication. Between November 1940 and June 1941 Mathewson was stationed in Washington, D.C., as a member of the plans section in the War

Plans Division of the War Department General Staff. In July 1941 he was assigned to the Latin American Theater Group, eventually becoming chief of the group after attaining the rank of lieutenant colonel (temporary) in December 1941. For his services here Mathewson was awarded the Legion of Merit, the citation stressing his share in establishing United States bases in the Central American countries as well as in other Latin American countries embraced by the Caribbean Defense Command. His work with the Latin American Theater Group also involved development of cooperative agreements with Mexico and with Brazil, the latter country granting the United States full military use of air bases in Northeast Brazil. The citation read in part: "His achievements have been an outstanding contribution, not only to the defense of the Western Hemisphere, but also to the foundation of a sound and enduring policy of military cooperation between Latin American Republics and the United States of America."

Transferred to the office of the Military Aide to the President, Mathewson filled this position until the early months of 1944, when he went overseas as assistant artillery officer of the 7th Corps in the European theater. In December 1944 he assumed command of the artillery of the 18th Airborne Corps, with which unit he remained for the rest of the war. The first postwar assignment of Mathewson, who was made brigadier general in April 1945, was to the Canal Zone, where he was chief of staff of the Caribbean Defense Command. Three years later, on November 1, 1948, he became Coordinator of the Inter-American Defense Board in Washington, D.C. In the spring of 1949 he moved to the position of artillery commander for the 11th Airborne Division at Camp Campbell, Kentucky. He was serving at European Command Headquarters in Heidelberg, Germany, when it was announced on January 15, 1951, that he had been named the successor to Major General Maxwell D. Taylor as United States Commandant in Berlin, to assume office on February 1, 1951. He was shortly afterward promoted to major general.

As the chief military officer for the United States forces in the American zone of Germany and in the four-power controlled city of Berlin, Mathewson has been involved in the many clashes between the Western Allies and the Soviet Government that have arisen in connection with their occupation of the divided capital city. Soon after assuming his command, Mathewson imposed an economic blockade against East Germany in response to earlier restrictions placed by the Soviet authorities on goods exported from West Berlin. Later in the year, he participated in the Allied protest against the seizure by East German authorities of the hamlet of Steinstuecken, a small Berlin suburb described by the New York *Herald Tribune* as "legally a part of West Germany, but physically inside the Soviet Zone." After threats of countermeasures by the three Western Allies, the suburb was returned to its previous status. Tension again mounted during the early summer of 1952 when more than forty notes and protests were exchanged over a period of

MAJ. GEN. LEMUEL MATHEWSON

seven weeks between the Soviet authorities and the three Western Allies.

One of the sharpest protest actions from Mathewson came as the result of the kidnapping of an anti-Communist official from West Berlin into the Soviet zone of Germany. In his note to the Soviet Control Commission, Mathewson wrote: "I have been shocked not only by the outrageousness of this crime but by the evidence of collusion of persons under Soviet control. . . .Personal freedom and safety for individuals are basic principles of the policy of the United States Government guaranteed to residents of the areas of which it holds responsibility. I must warn you that I regard this act . . . as intolerable and one which must be rectified" (quoted by the New York *Herald Tribune*). In retaliation for the kidnapping, a blockade of all roads leading into the surrounding Russian zone was imposed, thus turning the Allied sectors into a "virtual armed camp." When the Soviet authorities requested the curtailment of the movements of United States troops in Berlin, Mathewson replied: "Americans have traditionally enjoyed a brand of freedom which in itself leaves no room for application of such 'measures' as you are presumably suggesting." Later, however, Mathewson did request his staff and the members of the American community to stop making purchases in the East German stores. In a report from Berlin in *Look* magazine (July 15, 1952), Mathewson was quoted as saying: "We are going to have to live with this situation for a long time, so we'd better all develop the kind of patience and fortitude the Berliners are showing." The peril in Berlin, Mathewson in September 1952 told a New York *Times* reporter, was as critical as it had ever been, including the time of the Soviet blockade in 1948-49.

(Continued next page)

MATHEWSON, LEMUEL—*Continued*

Major General Mathewson in addition to his Legion of Merit award, holds an Oak Leaf Cluster (for "outstanding services" during the six-month period from June to December 1944) a second Oak Leaf Cluster, and the Bronze Star Medal. His foreign decorations are the French Legion of Honor, the Belgium Croix de Guerre, and the Mexican Order of the Aztec Eagle.

Reference

Who's Who in America, 1952-53

MATHIAS, ROBERT BRUCE (m*ȧ*-thī'*ǎs*)
Nov. 17, 1930- Athlete
Address: h. 790 E. King St., Tulare, Calif.

Robert Bruce Mathias, the young Californian who won the decathlon championship in the 1948 Olympic Games at London, repeated this achievement at Helsinki, Finland, four years later. He holds the distinction of being the sole athlete in modern Olympics history to win the decathlon at two meets. Winner also of the 1949 James E. Sullivan Memorial Trophy for extraordinary athletic achievement, Mathias is currently majoring in physical education at Stanford University, where his four-year course will end in the summer of 1953. Mathias also has a notable record in high school and college football and in track competition, and in the view of some sportswriters takes precedence over Jim Thorpe as America's most versatile all-time, all-round athlete.

Distinction in amateur sport is a tradition in the family of Robert Bruce Mathias, who was born in Tulare, California, on November 17, 1930, the second child in a family of three boys and one girl. The father, Dr. Charlie Milfred Mathias, a physician and surgeon of

ROBERT BRUCE MATHIAS

Scotch-Irish-English ancestry, had been an "All-State" football (tackle) player at the University of Oklahoma, where his future wife, Lillian Harris, who is of Scandinavian and English descent, was also a student. Their eldest son, Charles Eugene, now a hospital administrator, was an outstanding high school football player before a concussion forced his withdrawal from the gridiron; and both James Paul, their third son, and their daughter, Patricia Louise, have shown high athletic promise: the son has competed in the National Decathlon and the daughter excels in swimming.

Robert ("Bob") Mathias displayed what has been described as "an amazing sense of coordination" almost from infancy, and although he suffered from anemia in early childhood he was demanding acceptance by his elder brother and the latter's friends in their baseball games when not yet six years old. ("So Robert . . . made the team even then. We knew we had an athlete on our hands," Mrs. Mathias has said, as quoted in a *Time* article.) The Mathias backyard at Tulare was in use as a track "morning, afternoon and night," and by the time the second Mathias boy was twelve and a half years old he was able to take a high jump of five feet and six inches. He was then in the last year of grade school.

At the Tulare High School, where he became senior class president, Bob Mathias was a member of the basketball team for the four years (1944-48) with a scoring average of 18 points a game during the final season. As a football fullback over a period of three years he has been described (by Margery Miller in the *Christian Science Monitor*) as "brilliant," while *Time* noted that in high school track he won 40 first places and broke 21 records. He became a California Interscholastic Federation discus and shotput champion in 1947, won also at high hurdles, tied for second place in the high jump, and brought the Tulare team home first in the final lap of the relay race. It was at this point, according to most accounts, that Virgil Jackson, the Tulare High School track coach, realized that he had an Olympic "prospect." Applying to the Amateur Athletic Union, he obtained the necessary information as to qualification and rules and concluded (stated *Time*) that the decathlon "was just the thing for Bob's versatile talents." (The decathlon, most grueling of Olympic contests, comprises ten events—high jump, 100-meter dash, broad jump, shot-put, 400-meter run, 110-meter hurdles, discus throwing, pole vault, javelin throwing, and 1,500-meter run—the athlete's place being determined by the aggregate of points. Jackson set young Mathias to perfecting his form in hurdling, jumping, and running, and with the aid of a track manual guided him to the mastery of such sports as pole vaulting and javelin throwing, which the youth had not attempted before.

As a part of his plan Jackson entered Mathias, then seventeen, in the annual Pacific Coast games at Pasadena, California, in the early summer of 1948. There, after three weeks of practice, Mathias threw the javelin 171 feet and pole-vaulted 11 feet 6 inches, taking first place in the contest with comparative ease. Two weeks later he was participating in the National Decathlon and Olympics tryout at Bloomfield, New Jersey, where he outpointed the three-time national champion, Irving Mondschein, by a good margin. At the subsequent 1948 summer Olympic games in Wembley Stadium near London, Mathias placed third on the first day of the decathlon; but the end of the third day (August 5) found him the winner with 7,139 points. ("In rain, on a track covered with water . . . in fading light, and finally under floodlights, it was an amazing achievement," said Allison Danzig in the New York *Times*.) The victory was scored over competitors from nineteen countries, with Mathias bettering the unofficial records established by Jim Thorpe at Stockholm in 1912 in all events except the 100-meter dash and 1,500-meter run.

In his scholastic record at Tulare High School Mathias had not matched his athletic record and had failed to pass college entrance examinations. Accordingly, after his return from London the young champion was enrolled at the Kiski School in Salzburg, Pennsylvania. He was there when in January 1949 he was chosen by A.A.U. officials to receive the James E. Sullivan Memorial Trophy, which is presented annually to the "amateur athlete who, by performance, example and good influence, did most to advance the cause of good sportsmanship during the year." He also received the honorary degree of chevalier in the Order of DeMolay and a citation by the American Legion for good citizenship, both in 1949. Completing his course at the Kiski School, Mathias passed the entrance examination for Stanford University, where he has since been majoring in physical education. At Stanford he abandoned an early resolution to compete only in decathlon-type sports and joined the football team, soon becoming an outstanding fullback. He ran 96 yards for a touchdown against Southern California in November 1951 and was a member of Stanford's Rose Bowl team on January 1, 1952.

With an eye on the 1952 Olympics, Mathias neglected no opportunities to maintain and perfect his form through decathlon competition. In Tulare in the summer of 1949 he had already won the National Decathlon for the second time, and has gone on to capture the Scandinavian championship at Oslo, Norway. On July 1, 1950, again at Tulare, he won the National Decathlon for the third time, scoring 8,042 points to pass the Olympics record and the world record of 7,900, which had been scored by Glenn Morris in Berlin in 1936. In August of the same year (1950) Mathias won the Swiss National Decathlon at Berne with 7,312 points; then, at Tulare in July 1952, he took the American National Decathlon championship for the fourth time, a feat never before performed. At the Olympic Games in Helsinki less than four weeks later (July 26) he achieved the unprecedented feat of winning the decathlon for the second time, scoring 7,887 points, 62 in excess of his own world record. His javelin throw was a little over 194 feet.

Once again Mathias eclipsed Jim Thorpe's 1912 achievement. There has been debate among sportswriters and others as to whether Thorpe or Mathias should be recognized as the greatest all-round athlete.

After his graduation in June 1953, Mathias will be called for two and a half years' service in the Marine Corps. (He is now a member of the Marine Reserve.) At Stanford he belongs to the Phi Gamma Delta fraternity and the Letterman's Club. He has blue eyes and brown hair, is six feet three inches tall, and weighs 204 pounds. Among his interests he lists photography, travel, music (he plays the piano), and his collection of records. He is active in DeMolay and the Young Men's Christian Association, and attends the Methodist Church. Now twenty-one years old, he plans to vote Republican in the November 1952 election.

References

Christian Sci Mon II p15 S 12 '51 por; p15 Ag 12 '52 por
Collier's 122:6 O 9 '48 por
Fortnight 12:16-17 My 12 '52 por
Life 27:27-31 Jl 11 '49 pors; 31:147-8 D 3 '51 pors; 33:90-91 Ag 11 '52 pors
N Y Times p36 Jl 6 '50 por; p26 Jl 7 '52 por
N Y World-Telegram p32 N 13 '51
Newsweek 33:68-9 Ja 17 '49 por; 40:58 Jl 14 '52
Scholastic 53:16-17 S 4 '48 pors
Sport 6:101+ Ap '49 pors; 13:34+ Ag '52 pors
Sport Life 5:55 Ap '52 por
Time 52:59 Ag 16 '48 por; 60:44 Jl 14 '52 por; 60:69+ Jl 28 '52 pors

MATTHEWS, FRANCIS P(ATRICK) Mar. 15, 1887—Oct. 18, 1952 Ambassador to Ireland; former Secretary of Navy; lawyer and corporation executive; was appointed counsel for Reconstruction Finance Corporation in Nebraska and Wyoming (1933-49); as a leading Roman Catholic layman was Supreme Knight of Knights of Columbus (1939-45); became director of finance department, United States Chamber of Commerce (1941); member of President Truman's Committee on Civil Rights (1946-47); Secretary of Navy (1949-51); was appointed United States Ambassador to Ireland (1951); partner in Matthews, Kelly Matthew & Delehent of Omaha and president of radio station WOW in Omaha. See *Current Biography*, 1949.

Obituary

N Y Times p88 O 19 '52

MATTHEWS, W(ILMOT) DONALD July 2, 1906- Minister in the Canadian Embassy

Address: b. c/o Canadian Embassy, 1746 Massachusetts Ave., N.W., Washington, D.C.

An important role in the official relations between Canada and the United States is filled by W. Donald Matthews, who has held the

MATTHEWS, W. DONALD—*Continued*

rank of Minister in the Canadian Embassy at Washington since November 1949 and frequently deputizes for Ambassador Hume Wrong in international negotiations. Turning from his career as a lawyer and stockbroker, Matthews became supervisor of Canada's Foreign Exchange Control Board in 1939 and later was appointed chief administrative officer in the Department of External Affairs at Ottawa in 1943 and Assistant Under Secretary of the Department in 1948.

Wilmot Donald Matthews, the son of Wilmot L. and Annabel M. (Osler) Matthews, was born in Toronto, Ontario, on July 2, 1906. He was a member of the class of 1923 at Ridley College, a preparatory school at St. Catharines in his native province. After graduation he attended the Royal Military College in Kingston, Ontario, before enrolling at the University of Toronto in 1925. Here he majored in history and was elected president of the Historical Club as well as a member of the Kappa Alpha fraternity.

On receiving his Bachelor of Arts degree in 1929, Matthews joined the Dominion of Canada's recently instituted independent diplomatic service to be assigned as an attaché at the Legation at Washington, D.C., which had been established two years earlier with Vincent Massey as Minister. The first secretary at that time was the present-day Canadian Ambassador to the United States, the Honorable Hume Wrong, who had preceded Matthews at both Ridley College and the University of Toronto. After one year in Washington, however, Matthews decided to fit himself for the legal profession and so returned to Toronto to read law with the firm of Blake, Lash, Anglin and Cassels, at the same time taking the law course at the Osgoode Hall Law School. He was admitted to the bar in 1933 and for the next four years practiced as a barrister with the Toronto partnership of Armstrong and Sinclair.

In 1937 Matthews turned to the stockbroking business, becoming a partner in the Toronto firm of Wills, Bickle and Cayley, and was so occupied when, as a consequence of Canada's entrance into World War II, the Foreign Exchange Control Board was set up on September 16, 1939. Matthews left his brokerage business to become supervisor of the FECB, which was described in the 1941 volume of *Canada Year Book* as "an administrative body [established] to exercise continuous control over transactions that require licenses or permits" and to the authority of which "all transactions between residents of Canada and other countries" were subject. Thus from his office at Ottawa during the next three and a half years, Matthews was directly concerned with the official rate of exchange, flow of currency in and out of the Dominion of Canada, and conditions of settlement of international trading accounts.

Hume Wrong meanwhile had been named Assistant Under Secretary in the Department of External Affairs, and in April 1943 Matthews joined the department as Wrong's special assistant and chief administrative officer. A few months later (November) Canada

reached reciprocal diplomatic agreements with the United States, the Soviet Union, China, and Brazil by virtue of which her missions to the capitals of those countries were elevated to embassy rank and the consular service was greatly extended. In 1945, accordingly, Matthews, whose duties of chief administrative officer covered supervision of personnel, made what an official External Affairs Department publication describes as an "extensive inspection tour of Canadian missions in Europe." In October of that year he also accompanied Prime Minister Mackenzie King to London for general discussions with British leaders. Matthews' superior, Hume Wrong, had been advanced to Associate Secretary for External Affairs some time earlier and in September 1946 was named Canadian Ambassador Extraordinary and Plenipotentiary to the United States.

Matthews was promoted to Assistant Under Secretary for External Affairs in April 1947, soon after Lester Pearson (now head of the Department) became Under Secretary. The growing importance of Canadian-American relations in the matter of collective security presumably had much to do with the posting of Matthews, in May 1949, as counselor at the Canadian Embassy in Washington. Six months later (November 10) Matthews was promoted to the rank of Minister in the Washington Embassy, at which time the announcement was made that an additional duty would be to "act as deputy to Ambassador Hume Wrong in the sterling-dollar consultations that are expected to be continued between the American, British and Canadian Governments." He also assisted Ambassador Wrong in facilitating the negotiation of such international agreements as the Niagara River Power Treaty and the Canada Military Assistance Pact, which regulates the purchase of arms in either country by its neighbor.

The Niagara River Power Treaty, signed by United States Secretary of State Dean Acheson and Ambassador Wrong in February 1950, supersedes several earlier agreements dating back to 1909 and covering the projected joint construction of a canal for ocean-going vessels linking Lakes Erie and Ontario, together with a large-scale electric power generation project. Both the canal (St. Lawrence Waterway) and the power development had been strongly supported by American Presidents since William Howard Taft as well as by Canada, but had failed of ratification by the United States Congress. The new treaty again failed of ratification by Congress in the late spring of 1952, at which time Canada herself decided to begin construction of the waterway. However, the power development on the St. Lawrence (in which the State of New York wished to participate) would remain a joint project with Canada and a body chosen by the United States sharing an estimated cost of $400 millions. Cost of the waterway, to be assumed by Canada alone, was calculated at $250 millions. Minister Matthews, in a radio interview on June 1, 1952, predicted that the seaway would take from four and one half to five years to complete, and that it would thus be impossible to "look forward to the shipment of goods through the new canal before 1958." He emphasized (stated a United Press dispatch) that "Canada did not propose to develop the navigation without United States help because it wanted 'sole control of the seaways'" and insisted that his country's "first preference still would be to have a joint Canadian-United States development of this international waterway."

Mrs. W. Donald Matthews is the former Janet L. McCullough, of Galt, Ontario. The couple, who were married August 1, 1931, have five children—Jennifer A., Wilmot L., Robert O., Donald L., John E. The Canadian Minister's clubs are the Toronto and University in his native city and the Rideau in Ottawa. Fishing is mentioned as his favorite outdoor recreation.

References

Canadian Who's Who, 1948
International World Who's Who (1949)
World Diplomatic Directory (1951)

EWING W. MAYS

MAYS, EWING W(OODROW) Jan. 10, 1918- Veterans' organization official

Address: b. c/o Disabled American Veterans, 1423 E. McMillan St., Cincinnati 6, Ohio; h. 4006 Lakeview Rd., North Little Rock, Ark.

One of the principal ex-servicemen's organizations in the United States, the Disabled American Veterans, held its thirtieth annual convention at Milwaukee, Wisconsin, in August 1951, and at that time elected Ewing W. Mays of Little Rock, Arkansas, as its national commander for the term 1951-52. Commander Mays, who is an abstracter in the office of the Arkansas State Land Commission, has been active in the D.A.V. since 1946. He is a double amputee, having lost his legs while serving with the First Rangers Battalion in Sicily in 1943.

Ewing Woodrow Mays, the only child of Claude J. and Mary Elizabeth (King) Mays, was born January 10, 1918, in Lake City, Arkansas. He comes, he says, from a family of "two-fisted fighters." His father was a soldier, and young Mays throughout his boyhood looked forward to a military career. Accordingly, in 1937 on graduation from the Central High School at Caraway, Arkansas (where he played in the band and was active in sports), he enlisted in the Army. First assigned, at the age of nineteen, to the 2d United States Cavalry at Fort Riley, Kansas, he spent nearly four peacetime years at this post and at Fort Clark, Texas, as cook, cavalryman, and expert rifleman, and rose to the grade of staff sergeant. In 1941 he was transferred to the 8th Armored Division at Fort Knox, Kentucky, and subsequently (after the United States entered World War II) was attached to the 20th Armored as weapon instructor and administrative noncommissioned officer. From Fort Knox he was sent to Camp Campbell, Kentucky, as acting first sergeant

of Company B, Combat Supply Battalion. Sergeant Mays was stationed at Camp Patrick Henry, Virginia, when on May 9, 1943, he was sent overseas and shortly thereafter was transferred to duty with the now famous 1st Rangers Battalion.

The Rangers, modeled on the famous British Commandos, were composed of volunteers from American troops stationed in the British Isles, and were originally activated on June 9, 1942. Their commanding officer was Colonel "Bill" Darby of Fort Smith, Arkansas, who, while still in training with the British Commandos in Scotland, put in a request for his fellow Arkansan, Sergeant Mays. Mays served through the North African campaign, spearheaded with his fellow Rangers the Allied landings in Sicily, and was about to participate in the invasion of the Italian mainland when, at Messina, he was shot down by 210-millimeter fire from an enemy shore battery across the Messina Straits. In an interview with Sergeant Mays published in the *Arkansas Democrat* of September 23, 1951, Fay Williams reported Mays's own account of this turning point in his life in which he lost both his legs. Out of 2,000 Rangers, only 199 returned to the United States; Mays is one of the 64 of these survivors to wear the Purple Heart.

Back in the United States six months after he became a casualty, Mays was for the next twenty-one months a patient at the McCloskey General Hospital in Texas. Although Mays is a double amputee, his knees had been saved, and through learning the mastery of artificial limbs at McCloskey today he is able to play such games as golf and croquet, to drive his car, and to march in parades. "As he slowly recovered he appeared on various radio shows—*Army Hour*, *Vox Pop*, and local programs," stated a bio-

MAYS, EWING W.—*Continued*

graphical sketch prepared by the Disabled American Veterans. "He took an active part in the fourth, fifth, and sixth war loan drives, selling over a million dollars' worth of bonds. At the same time he did recruiting work for defense plants with marked success." Mays received his final discharge from the hospital and from the Army in May 1945, and three months later started work as a land abstracter in the office of the Arkansas State Land Commission at Little Rock. Shortly thereafter, also, he began attending night classes at the Arkansas Law School in preparation for a degree as title attorney.

It was in 1946, the year following his discharge, that Mays joined the Disabled American Veterans, the organization originally chartered by Congress in 1920 as the Disabled American Veterans of the World War, and comprised of "veterans . . . who served honorably in time of war in the Armed Forces of the United States and who became wounded, gassed, injured or disabled as a result of that service." The purpose of the organization (the name of which was modified to cover World War II service) is to render to those who come within the scope of its charter free aid through hospitalization, liaison, insurance claims, rehabilitation by employment, counseling, vocational training, and other means. While since 1946 it has derived considerable revenue through the sale of identification tags, its work is in the main supported by voluntary contributions and the proceeds of fund drives. As adjutant of North Little Rock Chapter No. 7— he has made his home in the Lakewood development across the Arkansas River from the State capital—it fell to Mays to organize an auxiliary and to help put on two benefit balls and launch a Forget-Me-Not Drive. He was later elected commander of the chapter. An effective public speaker, Mays was also in demand for addresses in and outside the State; and in 1948, after serving as department treasurer and legislative committeeman, he was elected to a one-year term as national second junior vice-commander. He became first junior vice-commander for 1949-50 and in 1950-51 served his district as national executive committeeman.

The national commander of the D.A.V. holds office for one year and cannot succeed himself. At the organization's thirtieth annual convention at Milwaukee, Wisconsin, Mays was, on August 17, 1951, chosen for that post. In Arkansas the honor to a native son was recognized through a gubernatorial proclamation setting aside August 31, as "Ewing Mays Day." The young national commander was granted a leave of absence from the State Land Office in order that he might make an automobile tour designed to take him to D.A.V. chapters and veterans' service offices in every State of the Union. One objective of the trip was to arouse public sentiment against curtailment of the veterans' rehabilitation program, while another was to increase D.A.V. enrollment, which in 1949-50 stood at 141,361 members in approximately 1,500 chapters. "A quarter of a million members is my aim," Mays told Fay Williams

just before starting on his tour, which took him first to New York City and later to Washington, D.C., where he called on President Truman and invited him to address the next D.A.V. convention, in August 1952, when Mays's term expires.

The veterans' leader has long been active as a Mason, a Knight of Pythias, and a member and officer of the International Civilian Club of Little Rock. He is a Democrat and a Baptist. Mays is six feet in height and 205 pounds in weight, and has brown hair and blue eyes. His marriage to Zelma Fay Dial took place on June 18, 1944, while he was a patient in the Texas hospital. They have two daughters, Sherry Fay and Sheila Kay, and one son, Ewing, Jr. Mays and his wife, a former music teacher, enjoy musical entertainment; he also likes fishing and hunting and is known for his cooking specialties.

Reference

Arkansas Democrat (Little Rock) Mag p1+ S 23 '51 pors

MEHTA, G(AGANVIHARI) L(ALLU-BHAI) (mä'tä gŭ-găn"vē-hä'rē là-lū'bī) April 15, 1900- Indian Ambassador to the United States

Address: b. c/o Embassy of India, 2107 Massachusetts Ave., N.W., Washington, D.C.; h. 2700 Macomb Ave., N.W., Washington, D.C.

On July 12, 1952, G. L. Mehta was appointed to replace B. R. Sen as Ambassador from the Republic of India to the United States and to Mexico. The new Ambassador has spent nearly all his life in the service of his country, having held among other positions the presidency of the Indian Tariff Board, membership in the National Planning Commission, and the chairmanship of the Tariff Commission, and having represented India at a number of international economic conferences. Because his administrative experience has been primarily in the fields of business and finance, rather than in politics and diplomacy, his Ambassadorial appointment was regarded as showing, the New York *Times* commented in an editorial, that "India undoubtedly realizes that the economic relationship between the United States and the new South Asian democracy is of the utmost importance." Mehta presented his credentials in Washington on September 25, 1952.

Gaganvihari Lallubhai Mehta was born in Ahmedabad, India, on April 15, 1900, the son of Sir Lallubhai Samaldas and Shrimati Satyavati B. Divatia. Mehta's family had for a long time taken an active part in Indian political affairs: his grandfather and his uncle were Diwans (chief ministers) in the state of Bhavnagar in Saurashtra (western India), and his father, Sir Lallubhai, was revenue commissioner for Bhavnagar, an office which he resigned to settle in Bombay. Here Sir Lallubhai became prominent in civil affairs and was a member of the old Bombay Legislative Council and then of the Council of State. Also active in Indian industrial movements, he is credited with having done pioneer work in the establishment of enterprises in shipping, electricity, and banking, and with being a founder of the Indian cooperative movement. Mehta's eldest brother, V. L. Mehta, also a leader in the cooperative movement and rural industries, was Finance Minister of Bombay from 1946 to 1952 and is now member of the Finance Commission appointed by the Government of India. Another brother is in business, and his sister (now deceased) was a well-known writer in Gujerati, a vernacular language.

For his secondary school and undergraduate college education, Mehta attended the New High School in Bombay and Elphinstone College of the University of Bombay, from which he received his B.A. degree, with honors in history and economics, in 1921. His extrascholastic interests were debating in the Economic and Historical Society, writing for the college magazine, and playing tennis. Proceeding to the London School of Economics and Political Science, Mehta studied under the late professors L. T. Hobhouse, Graham Wallas, Harold J. Laski, and others for a postgraduate diploma in sociology. In June 1928, at the Bombay School of Economics and Sociology, Mehta took his M.A. degree (first class), for which he submitted the thesis *The Social Thought of Bertrand Russell*.

On his return to India in 1923 from study in England Mehta joined the staff of the Bombay *Chronicle*, a leading nationalist newspaper, as assistant editor. Although two years later he gave up journalism for a business career, he has continued his literary interests and has produced two collections of humorous writings published in his native land—*From Wrong Angles* (1934) and *Perversities* (1942). He is also the author of *Equality of Trading Rights* and of a booklet on Gandhism called *The Conscience of a Nation* (1932).

After Mehta joined the Scindia Steam Navigation Company in 1925 as executive officer, he was stationed first in Rangoon. Then in 1928 he became manager of the Calcutta office, relinquishing this post in 1947 upon his appointment as president of the Indian Tariff Board. During the years of his association with the Scindia Company, Mehta had also been engaged in public relations work for both government and private firms. Interested in the development of the Indian Chamber of Commerce in Calcutta, he helped establish the Indian Chemical Manufacturers' Association, represented the Indian Chamber on such bodies as the Commissioners for the Port of Calcutta, became a member of several of its technical committees (light houses, pilotage) connected with shipping, and served as its president for the year 1939-40. In 1937 he attended the Biennial Congress of the International Chamber of Commerce in Berlin, where he addressed the group on the problem of the economic development of backward countries.

Mehta's work with the Federation of Chambers of Commerce and Industry, "the apex body of all Indian commercial bodies," of which he became president in 1942, took on special international significance during World War II, when, faced with the possibility of a

G. L. MEHTA

Japanese invasion, India was also in the throes of its nationalist struggle to attain independence from Great Britain. In March 1943 Mehta addressed the federation's national convention, criticizing British political and business practices and expressing the fear that American lend-lease policies might boomerang upon India. "In India," he said, "the program of defense, civil or military, is not broadly based on popular will. The demand for application to India of principles for whose vindication the United Nations claim to be waging this war—for immediate recognition of India's status as a free national unit—has remained unheeded." He emphasized that Indian commercial organizations "are an integral part of the national movement and are in full accord with the essentials of the national demand for full sovereignty." In an article published a year later in the *Annals of the American Academy of Political Science*, he wrote: "Indian commercial interests have realized all too keenly that the solution of India's economic problems is indissolubly bound up with the achievement of political independence and national emancipation."

During World War II years Mehta was in touch with Louis Johnson and William Phillips, President Roosevelt's representatives in India, and with the Supply Mission under Dr. Henry F. Grady, which went to India in 1942. He made his first visit to the United States in 1944 as deputy leader of the Indian delegation to the International Business Conference held in Rye, New York, at which Mehta was on the sectional committees for private enterprise and on transport, including shipping and aviation. While in the United States for this meeting, he made several addresses on the political situation in India and visited the shipyard of the Bethlehem Steel Works in Baltimore and the Massachusetts Institute of Technology and Harvard University in Cambridge. In 1947 Mehta attended the Inter-

MEHTA, G. L.—*Continued*

national Conference on Trade and Employment held in Geneva, the meeting at which steps were taken that led to the writing of the Havana Charter for the International Trade Organization. In the same year he also was a member of the International Labor Organization's Committee on Inland Transport and a member of the Indian delegation to the Congress of the International Chamber of Commerce in Montreaux, Switzerland, where he addressed a plenary session on the needs of underdeveloped areas.

Upon his return to India later in 1947, Mehta was elected to the Constituent Assembly which was drafting the Indian Constitution. In 1947 he became president of the Tariff Board, which in the two and one half years of his term investigated cases of more than thirty industries that applied for protection or other assistance and also determined the prices of controlled commodities like cotton textiles, steel, pig iron, paper, and superphosphate. Other governmental positions held by Mehta at about this time were memberships in the All-India Council of Technical Education (1945 and 1950), the governing body of the Council of Scientific and Industrial Research (1947-52), general council of the Indian Standards Institute (1950), and the court and the council of the Indian Institute of Science, Bangalore.

When India became a republic in 1950, Mehta was appointed a member of the National Planning Commission, set up by Prime Minister Jawaharlal Nehru, and was put in charge of the division concerned with industry, trade, and transport. This post Mehta held until August 1952 when he prepared to assume his duties as Ambassador to the United States and to Mexico. The Indian statesman had also been chairman of the Import Control Inquiry Committee (1950), of the Nuffield Foundation Indian Advisory Committee (1950-52), of the Tariff Commission (January to August, 1952); and member of the council of the Indian Statistical Institute in Calcutta and of the Banaras Hindu University. Mehta was associated as director with the Chaparmukh-Silghat Railway Company, Ltd., Indian Starch Productions, Ltd., Textile Machinery Corporation, Ltd., and Standard Pharmaceutical Work, Ltd.

Mehta's appointment on July 12, 1952, as Ambassador from India to the United States, in succession to B. R. Sen, was regarded as an indication of Prime Minister Nehru's interest in "closer ties between New Delhi and Washington in the economic sphere" (New York *Times*). Because of Mehta's experience in Indian economic development, he will come to Washington, the newspaper reported, "as one of the foremost experts" on the serious economic problems of his overpopulated and still underdeveloped country. The new Ambassador formally took office on September 25, 1952.

Mehta was married on December 3, 1924, to Shrimati Saudamini Ramanbhai, a graduate of Bombay State University and an active worker in Indian social welfare and educational groups. They have three daughters, Mrs. S. K. Dhar,

Uma, and Aparna. The Ambassador belongs to the Rotary Club in Calcutta, Bombay, and New Delhi, the Radio Club, Bombay, and to the Indian Council of World Affairs in New Delhi. His recreations are watching cricket and tennis and reading and writing.

References

N Y Times p14 Jl 13 '52

Nalanda Year Book and Who's Who in India and Pakistan, 1950-51

World Biography (1948)

MERRILL, ROBERT June 4, 1919- Singer
Address: b. c/o Metropolitan Opera Association, Inc., 147 W. 39th St., New York 18; c/o National Concert & Artists Corp., 711 5th Ave., New York 22; h. 76-22 169th St., Kew Gardens, N.Y.

The American-born, American-trained baritone Robert Merrill made his debut with the Metropolitan Opera Company in December 1945 as the elder Germont in *La Traviata*, a role he later repeated in a radio concert under Toscanini. He has also been admired for his interpretations of Escamillo in *Carmen*, Figaro in *The Barber of Seville*, and several other standard operatic roles, as well as for his 1950-51 re-creation of the part of Rodrigo in Verdi's less familiar *Don Carlos*. Merrill, who has been described in *Time* as "one of the Met's best baritones," is also a well-established radio and television soloist and enjoys success as a recording artist of popular and operatic music.

Born June 4, 1919, in Brooklyn, New York, Robert Merrill is the son of Abraham Merrill, a now retired shoe dealer, and the former Lillian Balaban. His Russian-born mother, who had had an operatic and concert career in Poland before her marriage, guided him in the early stages of his musical training. When young Merrill (who first sang in public at the age of twelve on a local radio program) developed into what has been described as "a remarkable boy soprano," Mrs. Merrill did not press her son's vocal training or seek to divert an ambition then centered on becoming a crooner like Bing Crosby. Instead, she grounded him in harmony, theory, and sight reading, and postponed voice coaching until he was sixteen, when his voice had become a baritone. "There were differences of opinion between us—to put it mildly—when the practice time conflicted with ball games," Merrill has remarked in an article in *Étude* for June 1947. The story is told that it was not until two years later, when he was taken to a Metropolitan Opera performance of *Il Trovatore*, that he was inspired to prepare for a musical career. Arrangements were made for him to take singing lessons from Samuel Margolies, with whom he has studied ever since.

To pay for these lessons young Merrill, who had graduated from the New Utrecht High School in 1935, worked during the winters in his father's store, and during the summers earned extra money as a pitcher for the Kings Team, a semiprofessional baseball club. He also sang aboard Caribbean cruise ships and at summer resorts in the Catskills and Adirondacks. "Certainly singing in a summer hotel is a far cry from singing on an operatic stage," Merrill commented in *Etude*, "but it has the advantage of teaching the young performer to face audiences." One such engagement was at Grossinger's Hotel in the Catskills, where he became acquainted with his present personal manager, Moe Gale, who arranged a Sunday appearance for the young baritone as featured soloist with H. Leopold Spitalny's orchestra on a coast-to-coast radio program. A National Broadcasting Company contract resulted; and later, after the conductor Erno Rapee had heard a "ghost voice" recording Merrill had made of "The Star Spangled Banner" for Fox Movietone News, the young singer was engaged for a nine-week season at the Radio City Music Hall. Merrill also made radio appearances on the *Song of Your Life* show and with Mark Warnow's orchestra, and eventually, in 1943, Dr. Frank Black of NBC sent him on a concert tour which brought him a contract for three performances a week on Spitalny's *Serenade to America* program.

Merrill made his first try for an operatic engagement on New Year's Day of 1939, when he entered the preliminaries of the fourth annual *Metropolitan Auditions of the Air*. He failed to reach the finals, but aroused the interest of the conductor Wilfred Pelletier, who encouraged him to persist. It was not until 1943, however, that Merrill again felt himself "ripe for the stage," and sought specialized coaching from the late Angelo Canarutto, who taught him the roles of Germont in *La Traviata* and Tonio in *I Pagliacci*; Renato Bellini who worked with him on Amonasro in *Aïda*; and Armando Agnini who drilled him in *mise en scène*. Merrill made his operatic debut at Trenton, New Jersey, in the fall of 1944, singing Amonasro in *Aïda*. Soon afterward he repeated the role in a Connecticut Opera Association production at Worcester, Massachusetts, and also sang Tonio in *I Pagliacci* in the same city. Later, at Detroit, he added Germont in *La Traviata* to his repertoire.

November 1944 found Merrill again a contestant in a Metropolitan radio audition, now called *The Metropolitan Presents*. He passed the preliminaries on November 26 with a rendition of the Figaro aria in *The Barber of Seville;* in the finals his enthusiastically received singing of Iago's "Credo" from Verdi's *Otello* brought him, on April 1, 1945, a first prize shared with the tenor Thomas Hayward, and the award of a Metropolitan contract. Before his debut at the Metropolitan Merrill returned to Trenton to make his first stage appearance as Valentine in *Faust*, and at Dayton, Ohio, in May he sang Escamillo in *Carmen*. His recording (with Jeannette MacDonald) of four numbers from Sigmund Romberg's operetta *Up in Central Park* resulted in a Victor contract to "run the gamut of all types on song" on Red Seal records, and in a number of radio and concert engagements. Merrill's debut at the Metropolitan on December 15, 1945, as the elder Germont in *La Traviata* followed a 1944-45 tour of twenty American cities,

James J. Kriegsmann

ROBERT MERRILL

where he sang such operatic numbers as the Brindisi from the Ambroise Thomas *Hamlet* and the "Vision Fugitive" from Massenet's *Hérodiade*. The critic Robert A. Hague wrote of his performance: "Mr. Merrill displayed a rich vigorous baritone, ample in volume, effortlessly and surely produced."

Of his second Metropolitan role (the toreador in *Carmen* on January 7, 1946) Irving Kolodin observed in the New York *Sun* that the young man "had the qualities to become an imposing Escamillo"; and in summing up the Metropolitan season, Olin Downes of the New York *Times* commented that in Merrill the organization had found "a baritone with a beautiful voice and a real concept of *bel canto*." In May, after the opera season was over, Merrill made two appearances at the Carnegie "Pops" Concerts, and at the end of the month received the honor of being selected to sing at a joint service by both Houses of Congress in memory of President Franklin D. Roosevelt. At the service, which took place on July 1, 1946, Merrill sang the deceased President's favorite hymn "Eternal Father, Strong to Save" and "The Lord's Prayer."

Beginning June 2, 1946, Merrill was engaged as featured soloist on the Sunday afternoon *RCA-Victor Show*, and during the same summer he made many additional discs, both popular and classical, for Red Seal Records. His rendition of the aria "Ah dite alla giovine" from *La Traviata* won an Annual Recorded Award as one of the best classical records of the year. Additional prestige in musical circles resulted from his interpretation (on December 1 and 8, 1946) in the famous two-part broadcast concert version of the same opera with the NBC orchestra under Arturo Toscanini. (Irving Kolodin called Merrill's "Di provenza" "magnificent.") The following year (1947) Merrill's vogue as a popular-type singer reached new heights with his recording of the "Whiffenpoof Song," which sold 700,000 copies.

(Continued next page)

MERRILL, ROBERT—*Continued*

Meanwhile, on November 15, 1947, Merrill had made his first Metropolitan appearance as Figaro in *The Barber of Seville*, blending "rich tones with nimble patter" (New York *Herald Tribune*), and followed this on December 11 with his first Count di Luna in *Il Trovatore*. Among other roles in the Metropolitan repertoire of Merrill, who has the reputation of having "worked hard to polish his natural rich baritone" and "noticeably improved each season," (*Newsweek*), are Sir Henry Ashton in *Lucia di Lammermoor*, and the High Priest in *Samson et Dalila,* which he first sang in November 1949. The baritone began television appearances with NBC's *Saturday Night Revue* in 1949 and continued on the same program, renamed *Your Show of Shows*, in 1950.

Following the retirement of Edward Johnson as managerial director of the Metropolitan Opera Association, his successor, Rudolf Bing, chose for the inauguration of his first season, beginning December 6, 1950, a freshly staged and directed revival of Verdi's rarely performed *Don Carlos*. In this production, Merrill, who was cast as Rodrigo, seemed to Virgil Thomson of the New York *Herald Tribune* "in every way elegant." Olin Downes was likewise impressed by the baritone's "admirably intelligent and sonorous singing." Toward the close of the season in February 1951, Merrill, who during the previous summer had signed a motion picture contract with Paramount Pictures, was summoned to Hollywood. Faced with a conflict of contracts, the baritone asked impresario Bing to release him from his obligation to take part in the Metropolitan's annual spring tour. Bing refused as a matter of principle and, when Merrill did not appear for the regular spring tour, Bing charged the singer with breach of contract and declared that he was no longer a member of the company. In Hollywood the singer was cast in the film version of the rural comedy *Aaron Slick from Punkin Crick*. A visit to Europe during the following summer to entertain servicemen gave Merrill an opportunity to talk with Bing at the Salzburg Festival. In January 1952, after receiving Merrill's expression of regret, Bing announced that the baritone had been restored to the Metropolitan roster and would join the company in time for the 1952 spring tour.

Some thirty or more single records or albums of Merrill's renditions have been made, ranging in character from popular songs, through folk melodies and spirituals, to operatic selections. The baritone's recorded death scene from *Thaïs* is a favorite of the critic David Hall, while Irving Kolodin has written that Merrill's "Nemico della patria" from Giordano's *Andrea Chenier* "summons the power and beauty of sound in his remarkable voice for a performance of overwhelming richness."

Merrill is a member of the American Federation of Radio Artists and the American Guild of Musical Artists, and is honorary chairman of the Brooklyn Orchestral Society, which he helped found. Described as handsome, he has brown curly hair and brown eyes, stands five feet ten and a half inches tall, and weighs 172

pounds. On March 30, 1952, Merrill married Roberta Peters, a soprano of the Metropolitan Opera; the couple was divorced on June 26, 1952. The baritone, whose favorite opera is said to be *The Barber of Seville*, has a record library of some 1,000 rare discs and a collection of operatic costumes worn by famous singers. His sport is golf.

References

Etude 65:315+ Je '47 por
Mus Courier 133:3 Ja 15 '47 por; 138:3 O 15 '48 por
N Y Herald Tribune p11 Ap 2 '45 por
N Y Post Mag p47 Ap 11 '47 pors; p3 Jl 2 '50 por
N Y Times p32 Ap 2 '45 por
Newsweek 36:65 Jl 3 '50
Opera N 9:8-9 Ap 2 '45 por; 10:11-12 D 10 '45 pors
Scholastic 52:27 F 2 '48 por
Victor Record R 7:7 Ap '45 por
Musicians' International Directory and Biographical Record (1949-50)
Saleski, G. Famous Musicians of Jewish Origin (1949)
Who is Who in Music (1951)
Who's Who in America, 1950-51

MEYER, K(ARL) F(RIEDRICH) May 19, 1884- University professor; pathologist

Address: b. c/o George Williams Hooper Foundation, University of California Medical Center, San Francisco 22, Calif.; h. 1779 22d Ave., San Francisco 22, Calif.

A 1951 Lasker Award of the American Public Health Association was awarded to K. F. Meyer, director of the Hooper Foundation of the University of California Medical Center, for his major role in the control of food poisoning, psittacosis, and plague. It was Meyer who developed the flash sterilization method of canning, proved that parrot fever could be spread by numerous species of birds and animals, showed that plague infests many varieties of wildlife, and, with coworkers, developed the antiplague serum.

Born May 19, 1884, in Basel, Switzerland, Karl Friedrich Meyer is a descendant of the Zum Pfeil von Buerens, an old Junker family whose printed genealogy dates back to the fourteenth century. His father, Theodor Meyer, was a tobacco merchant with an international trade, and his mother, Sophie (Lichtenhahn) Meyer, was a schoolteacher. Young Karl Friedrich and his two sisters were reared in Basel, where the boy attended secondary school. As a child, he recalls, he was fascinated by pictures showing scenes of the Black Death, the plague of the fourteenth century. At the age of sixteen, while skinning a hare, young Meyer found abscesses under the skin, an experience which made a deep impression on him. After completing the classical European education and receiving his B.A. degree from the University of Zurich in 1905, he studied veterinary medicine, in which he was granted his doctorate by Zurich in 1909. The future pathologist had also taken courses in 1905-06 at the University of Munich, Germany, and had had further training at the universities of Berlin and Paris and the Bern Institute for the Study of Infectious Diseases. His 106-page study of one kind of bacterial disease of the intestines, was published in the institute's journal in 1909. Fifteen years later Dr. Meyer was to add a Ph.D. degree in zoology to his list of earned degrees.

Before the granting of his first doctorate, Meyer was in South Africa in 1908 as pathologist in the Transvaal Department of Agriculture at Ondersteport. Hundreds of thousands of cattle had died from East Coast fever, and Meyer found the continent, in his words, a research "gold mine. The animals were huge reservoirs of disease. . . .We used horses instead of guinea pigs," he tells. "Horses were cheaper." The young Swiss performed autopsies on thousands of animals. With the help of twenty Kaffir assistants, he carried on experiments and showed that cattle could be protected against the deadly tick-borne fever by intraperitoneal inoculation with the spleen of sick cattle. (Some of this work he reported in a paper published in 1909 in the Berlin *Journal of Infectious Diseases* and the Edinburgh and London *Journal of Comparative Pathology and Therapy.*) According to Paul de Kruif (in a *Reader's Digest* article, "Champion Among Microbe Hunters") Meyer resigned this position rather than allow his chief, newly returned from Europe, to take the credit for the achievement.

Twenty-six-year-old Meyer, now internationally known, in 1910 accepted an assistant professorship of pathology and bacteriology at the University of Pennsylvania School of Veterinary Medicine; he has remained in the United States, of which he became a citizen in 1922. To demonstrate his skill, Meyer once made a bet (which he won) with his Pennsylvania colleagues that he could perform an autopsy on an elephant, unassisted and dressed in formal dinner clothes, without soiling his shirt front. After one year he was advanced two ranks to full professor and was appointed director of the Pennsylvania Livestock Sanitary Board's laboratory and experimental farm. In 1913 the pathologist moved to the Pacific Coast to become professor of bacteriology and protozoology at the University of California. Two years later, in order to have more opportunity for research, Meyer joined the university's George Williams Hooper Foundation in San Francisco, with the lower rank of associate professor of tropical medicine.

At that time the foundation had small funds; thus while Dr. Meyer had his own laboratory, he had little equipment and no assistants. He made researches in typhoid fever, but failed to find the carrier. During the influenza epidemic (in which the pathologist nearly died) he predicted the existence of the "flu" virus, but lacked the means to work on the theory. Verifying his suspicion that unpasteurized milk from inspected dairy herds was contaminated with the contagious abortion microbe, he tramped the pastures of San Francisco

Univ. of California

K. F. MEYER

Bay area and proved his point. Meyer developed a skin test for the presence of microbe, but later told a medical society meeting, "Gentlemen, my test turns out to be the poorest of several that have been proposed." In the words of Paul de Kruif, "Karl Meyer was bursting with energy and bacteriologic know-how with no place to go." In 1920 he began his consultant association with the California State Department of Public Health and the Southern Pacific Railway, and the following year became acting director of the Hooper Foundation and professor of research medicine at the university. He completed the requirements for a Ph.D. degree in zoology at the University of Zurich, granted in July 1924, when he was forty. His thesis was on "bacterial symbiosis" in certain mollusks (he was interested in some mollusks, too, from the viewpoint of their healthfulness as food). The year Meyer received his doctorate he was advanced from acting director to director of the Hooper Foundation and was appointed professor of bacteriology both at the university medical school in San Francisco and at the university proper, across the bay in Berkeley. Both these professorships he retained until 1948, when he became professor of experimental pathology at Berkeley. Meyer's book, *Practical Bacteriology*, was published in 1925.

One of Dr. Meyer's most important research opportunities came when an outbreak of botulism in the World War I period was traced to California-canned olives. Asked to help save the olive-canners from threatened embargoes and possible ruin, the pathologist pointed out that other foods might well be poisoned, but stated that he lacked laboratory evidence to be of help. The head of Calpac, one of the world's largest canning companies, set up the research budget Meyer required at the Hooper Founda-

MEYER, K. F.—*Continued*

tion, and in 1926 the professor became director of the research laboratory maintained by the National Canners Association. (The association provided funds to a number of universities for research.) Before that many thousand tests showed that the botulinus bacilli, found everywhere, existed in California in a particularly deadly spore form which could be destroyed only by boiling for six hours, which would have destroyed the food as well. Within three years Dr. Meyer and his associate developed the flash sterilization technique, in which food is sterilized for sixty seconds at 260°, then sealed into presterilized cans. Canneries installed "fakeproof" recording instruments, and at the cost of hundreds of thousands of dollars yearly had every pack supervised and inspected by State health department inspectors. Since 1925, except for one outbreak of botulinus poisoning traced to an unscrupulous canner, botulism from commercially canned food has been virtually wiped out.

In 1930 Dr. Meyer received reports of a sleeping sickness among horses in the San Joaquin Valley. When laboratory experiments found nothing, the pathologist and an assistant went into the field, where Meyer destroyed a sick horse and removed the brain. He and his assistants were able to grow the trapped virus in chick embryos, thus making possible a vaccine which Lederle Laboratories produced and which saved the lives of horses throughout the country. As Meyer predicted, encephalitis spread to humans and was shown to be mosquito-borne.

During this period Meyer found that a baffling form of pneumonia was the same disease as psittacosis, or parrot fever, the incidence of which had caused the United States to forbid the importation of parrot-family birds except for research purposes. As a result 25,000 parrots, parakeets, and macaws in pet shops and aviaries were destroyed in one year. Ten years of research on psittacosis by Meyer and his coworkers showed, however, that the disease has been found in some fifty species, including canaries, chickens, ducks, pigeons, and sea gulls, and Meyer has accordingly renamed it ornithosis. (A paper by Meyer, H. Karrer, and B. Eddie appeared in the July-August 1950 *Journal of Infectious Diseases.*) Actually, Meyer had also worked with the disease in mice. Once, because someone had failed to adjust an electric heater, two hundred infected parakeets and five hundred infected mice died overnight; Meyer and his assistant, Dr. Bernice Eddie, worked until late performing autopsies on the seven hundred birds and mice and inoculating new specimens, thus recovering every virus strain. Dr. Meyer himself caught psittacosis pneumonia; this he dismisses as his own fault. His analysis of two hundred and sixty human cases of ornithosis between 1945 and 1950 showed that only a few were due to infection from psittacines, and as a result the restrictions on parrots were lifted in the United States. In May 1951 Meyer and Dr. Eddie reported on human carriers of the disease.

Meyer was appointed consultant to the Secretary of War on tropical medicine in 1942, the year he began his service as an Army consultant on epidemic diseases. During World War II he and his coworkers developed for the armed forces a serum against plague, made by injecting rabbits with living but nonvirulent plague bacilli. ("Plague," in its modern medical sense, is caused by *Bacillus pestis* in several forms, of which the bubonic and pulmonary are the most common.) Next Meyer developed a therapy which combined the plague vaccine with sulfadiazine for protection and which proved successful in China, where expensive drugs and vaccines were not available. By using streptomycin and destroying rodents by means of new poisons, he believed by 1947 that plague can finally be "obliterated from all closely inhabited areas on the face of the earth." After the war he continued to be on call for public health "detective work," to edit three journals (*Acta Tropica, Journal of Infectious Diseases,* and *Journal of Immunology*), and to submit research papers to medical journals in other parts of the world. Among subjects of his more recent papers are plague immunity, leptospirosis, botulism from infected wounds, brucellosis immunity, diagnosis of virus infection, disinfection of mail, and what Meyer called "global strategy in preventive medicine."

Since 1931 Meyer has been selected to deliver eleven (as of 1951) honorary lectures in universities in the United States. His honorary degrees are the M.D. from the College of Medical Evangelists at Los Angeles (1936) and Zurich University (1937), the LL.D. from the University of Southern California (1946), and the D.V.M. from Zurich (1949). From the American Public Health Association he received the Sedgwick Memorial Medal in November 1946 and the Lasker Award in October 1951. Meyer was also awarded the James D. Bruce Medal in preventive medicine by the American College of Physicians in 1949, and was honored by the American Academy of Tuberculosis Physicians in June 1950. Among the numerous professional organizations (listed in *Who's Who in America*) with which Meyer is affiliated as an officer, member, or fellow are the American Academy of Arts and Sciences, American Association of Pathologists and Bacteriologists, American Society of Tropical Medicine, and American Public Health Association. He is a member of the National Foundation for Infantile Paralysis committees on virus research and on epidemics and public health, of the national medical and health advisory committee of the American Red Cross, and of the U. S. Army epidemiological board; and is a general consultant of the California State Board of Public Health. His Greek-letter societies are Sigma Theta, Sigma Xi, Delta Omega, Phi Sigma, and Alpha Omega Alpha; his clubs, the Commonwealth and The Family.

Meyer and Mary Elizabeth Lindsay, of Philadelphia, who were married July 16, 1913, have a daughter, Charlotte (Mrs. Bartley P. Cardon). Five feet eleven inches in height, he weighs 190 pounds; he is gray-haired and gray-eyed. He is described as "an outdoor scientist living in a state of permanent outdoor emergency." When he climbs mountains nowadays it is likely to be more in line of duty than for recreation. He names philately as a hobby.

References

Am J of Public Health 36:1453-6 D '46
Read Digest 56:35-40 Je '50 por
Scholastic 59:4 O 24 '51 por
Sci Mo 64:76-9 Ja '47
American Men of Science (1949)
Who's Who in America, 1950-51
Who's Who in the West (1951)
World Biography (1948)

MIDDLECOFF, (EMMETT) CARY Jan. 6, 1921- Golfer; dentist

Address: Peabody Hotel, Memphis, Tenn.

One of the leading purse-winners in professional golf in the United States is former dentist Cary Middlecoff, who in 1947 left the amateur ranks for the professional. Holder of Memphis and Tennessee State amateur championships, Middlecoff was the first amateur to win the North and South Open, in 1945, while he was still a captain in the United States Army. Subsequently he took a number of other major golf titles, including the National Open in 1949.

Born January 6, 1921, in Halls, Tennessee, Emmett Cary Middlecoff is one of four sons of Dr. Herman F. and Lucille (Hutchinson) Middlecoff. The father, by profession a dentist and by avocation a golfer, taught his son the game when the boy was seven: Cary Middlecoff has recalled for Frank Waldman of the Christian Science Monitor, "I used to go out with the other kids my age and shoot six or seven holes once a week. By the time I was fourteen I was playing 54 holes a day. But it wasn't till I was around seventeen that I got serious about the game." Unlike a number of other golfers, Middlecoff did not work as a caddy—his father, champion of the Chickasaw Golf Club, allowed him to charge purchases at the club's pro shop.

Winning a junior club championship in 1937, young Middlecoff went on the following year to capture the Memphis High School Championship, to which he later added the Memphis City Championship and the Tennessee State Championship. He was graduated from Christian Brothers College, a secondary school in Memphis, in 1938. Like his father and two uncles, Cary Middlecoff decided to enter the profession of dentistry, with the result that after first attending the University of Mississippi, he completed his work for the D.D.S. degree at the University of Tennessee in 1944. His college fraternities are Kappa Alpha and Psi Omega.

Receiving his commission as a second lieutenant soon afterward, Middlecoff practiced dentistry in the Army Dental Corps for eighteen months, reported Bill Fay in Collier's, before hospitalization for an eye injury kept him on the inactive list during a nine-month convalescence. Toward the end of this period he began to "brush up" on his golf so that he was able to enter the 1945 North and South Open and emerge as its winner, the first amateur ever to take that title. Following his discharge from the army with the rank of captain, Middlecoff practiced dentistry with his father, who encouraged him not only to continue playing golf, but to keep on in tournament play. In 1947 Middlecoff rejected an opportunity to play with the American Walker Cup team, instead entering the professional ranks. His first tournament that year, the Jacksonville Open, found him in a three-way tie for twelfth place and netted him prize money of $260; it remained for his third professional tournament, the Charlotte (North Carolina) Open of 1947, to bring him into first place, for a purse of $2,000. Fay of Collier's gave Middlecoff's 1947 total winnings as $6,119 and those for 1948 as $16,821.

Time has itemized Middlecoff's showings in the 1948-49 winter circuit as a win in the Rio Grande Valley Open, a second place in the St. Petersburg Open, a first in the Miami Four-ball (with partner Jim Ferrier), and a second in the Virginia Beach Specialists Tournament, for $900 prize money. After taking the Jacksonville Open first place with a 274 total in March 1949, Middlecoff fell to third in the Augusta Masters the following month. In May he defeated South African Bobby Locke by a two-stroke lead for a 72-hole total of 265 in the Greenbrier Open, only to lose to the same player later that month in the Goodall Round Robin, played on the Wykagyl course. At the Medinah (Illinois) National Open in June, Middlecoff, said Al Laney of the New York Herald Tribune, "won his title in a most difficult way," sitting "in the press room for an agonizing hour" while Sammy Snead and Clayton Heafner played off, until his one-stroke victory was confirmed by a tally of 286 for the seventy-two holes. Of this victory, Lawrence Robinson of the New York World-Telegram observed, recalling doubts about the advisability of Middlecoff's turning pro, "It is amazing how Cary improved his game. He straightened out his drives, and at Medinah, down one of the narrowest tree-lined layouts in America, his driving gave him the winning edge, although his most important improvement, was learning to 'soften' his irons."

In a hole-by-hole tie in the play-off of the Detroit Motor City Open at the end of June, Middlecoff came through even with Lloyd Mangrum, the two golfers sharing both the first and second prize money, bringing them each $2,250. "Today's winning," said a writer in the New York Times, "boosted Middlecoff into the No. 1 spot among the nation's golf money earners." Ascribing his succeeding victory to improved putting, Middlecoff in July again defeated Sammy Snead, to take the Reading (Pennsylvania) Open, with a $2,600 first prize.

Middlecoff did not place first again in a tournament until the February 1950 Houston Open, according to the New York Times, when his 72-hole 277 brought him $2,000. He then

CARY MIDDLECOFF

repeated his Jacksonville Open victory of the previous year in March, with another first prize of $2,000, using the putter he had painted black for good luck. (To achieve better putting, he uses a putter he has finished off himself to meet his own requirements.) Middlecoff went down to "Dutch" Harrison in the April Wilmington (North Carolina) Open. He rounded off his big wins of 1950 at the St. Louis Open in September by defeating "Porky" Oliver in an extra-hole play-off, to take the $2,600 first prize with a crucial twenty-foot putt.

Middlecoff, who had not retained the National Open Championship in 1950, came in second to Byron Nelson in the January 1951 Bing Crosby Tournament at Pebble Beach, California, and later that month won the Lakewood Park Open at California's Long Beach course—13 under par for a total of 271. He was top man again at the Colonial National Invitation played in Fort Worth, Texas, in May, and at the All-American Pro tournament at Chicago in August, before dropping to second in the Fort Wayne Open later that month. In mid-September Middlecoff "recovered remarkably on the last nine holes" (New York *Herald Tribune*) to win the Eastern Open title on Baltimore's Mount Pleasant course. For the second successive year he took the St. Louis Open title in October, tallying 269 for seventy-two holes and prize money of $2,400. "Middlecoff was in trouble frequently, but he had the strokes when things looked worst," said the New York *Times*. A three-way tie for the lead in the Kansas City Open forced Middlecoff into a play-off in October.

After playing in the Phoenix (Arizona) Open in January 1952, Middlecoff the following month lost in the Tucson Open only to come through later in February with first place in the El Paso Open, scoring 269 on seventy-

two holes for first money of $2,000. In ensuing big tournaments at St. Petersburg, he placed third in March, and at the Palm Beach round robin on the Wykagyl course in New Rochelle, New York, in May, he placed second. At the close of May, defending his title in the Colonial National Invitation tournament in Fort Worth, Middlecoff dropped to sixth place. On July 13 he won the $2,400 first prize in the St. Paul Open and on August 18 the $2,400 first prize in the Kansas City Open. As of mid-1952 Middlecoff was the winner of twenty-six major Professional Golfers' Association Championships.

Middlecoff's golf style has been described by Lawrence Robinson of the New York *World-Telegram*: "A tall fellow, he stands well over the ball, pivots almost mechanically, and throws that face in square and hard." The golfer himself, who is the author of *Golf Doctor* (1950), summed up his fairways philosophy for Frank Waldman of the *Christian Science Monitor*: "I believe that the proper mental attitude is easily 50 per cent of the game. By that I mean being able to leave your game on the eighteenth green, not take it home with you and replay it that night in bed. Another part of what I call the proper mental attitude toward golf is the ability not to become upset over a poor shot, a poor hole or a poor round." Middlecoff appeared in the motion picture biography of Ben Hogan's life, *Follow the Sun*. The Memphis golfer, who is six feet two inches tall with a weight of 185 pounds, has brown hair and brown eyes and has been described by *Newsweek* as "darkly good-looking." He belongs to the Professional Golfers' Association and the Memphis Country Club. His church is the Christian. A partial influence on his decision to turn professional was his marriage on March 4, 1947, to Edith Lorraine Buck, an airline stewardess, who accompanies him on the tournament circuit.

References

Christian Sci Mon p14 Ap 30 '47
Collier's 124:50 Ag 27 '49
Newsweek 33:77 Mr 28 '49
Sports Stars 4:69 Ag '51
Time 53:77-8 Ap 25 '49
Professional Golfers' Association. Official PGA Tournament Record (1951)

MILLER, IRVING Dec. 24, 1903- Rabbi; organization official

Address: b. c/o Zionist Organization of America, 41 E. 42d St., New York 17; 111 Irving Pl., Woodmere, L.I., N.Y.; h. 975 Allen Lane, Woodmere, L.I., N.Y.

Irving Miller, rabbi of the Sons of Israel congregation of Woodmere, Long Island, was elected to succeed Benjamin G. Browdy as president of the Zionist Organization of America at its annual convention in June 1952. Prominent in Jewish religious and public affairs for more than a quarter of a century, he has ministered to congregations in Ohio, Massachusetts, and New York and has been secretary general of the World Jewish Congress, vice-president of the Zionist Organization of America, and president of the American Jewish Congress. During World War II he undertook many important missions on behalf of European Jewry and had a leading role in discussions of Jewish postwar problems with representatives of Allied governments in London.

From his native city of Kaunas, Lithuania, Irving Miller, who was born on December 24, 1903, to Abraham and Tillie (Lemanowitz) Miller, was brought to the United States at the age of nine. He attended the College of the City of New York from 1921 until 1924 and then pursued theological studies at Yeshiva College in New York, becoming a rabbi in 1926. During the academic year 1926-27 he took courses at the University of Pittsburg and in 1932 he completed requirements for the B.S. degree at Columbia University. Meanwhile in 1926 he had became rabbi of Temple Emanuel in Youngstown, Ohio, and in 1928 of Temple Beth El in Chelsea, Massachusetts. Two years later he went to New York as rabbi of the congregation Shaaray Tefila in Far Rockaway, Long Island, where he remained until being named to his present ministry in 1946 as rabbi of the Sons of Israel congregation in Woodmere, Long Island.

A delegate to the founding session of the World Jewish Congress in Geneva in 1936, Rabbi Miller also served later as secretary general of the organization from 1942 until 1945. In that capacity, which engaged him in many assignments in behalf of European Jews threatened by Nazism, he spent three months during 1943 in London, urging "an earnest and effective effort to save the Jews in Europe from total destruction" and endeavoring particularly to raise funds for the settlement of Jewish children from Axis-controlled countries in Palestine. On his return from England in June 1943, he revealed that he had discussed the Jewish problem with forty-five leading statesmen of the United Nations and that several neutral countries had initiated discussions with Germany for the release of large numbers of Jewish children in Occupied Europe. On the darker side, however, he said he had left London "depressed by the growing anti-Semitism evident among representatives of governments in exile." As a member of the executive committee of the World Jewish Congress, he attended the Paris Peace Conference in 1946.

For more than twenty-five years Rabbi Miller has belonged to the Zionist Organization of America, serving as a member of its national executive committee since 1936 and as chairman of its national administrative council from 1946 until 1948. He was elected to the actions committee of the World Zionist Congress in 1939 and re-elected in 1946. On his return in 1947 from a meeting of the actions committee in Basle, Switzerland, he denounced the British White Paper on Palestine of 1937, stating: "Great Britain virtually severed the partnership with the Jewish people in rebuilding the Jewish national home and thus brought an end to an era in the history of our movement" (New York Times, January

Hal Harrison

IRVING MILLER

26, 1947). Later that year, in November 1947, he assailed England again for what he termed "direct sabotage" of the United Nations partition plan for Palestine. "There is still time," he said, "for wiser heads in Britain to change this policy and to cooperate gracefully in bringing out a new order of peace and good will in Palestine" (New York Times, November 24, 1947).

The rabbi has also been associated for a number of years with the American Jewish Congress, having been elected chairman of the executive committee of the Congress in 1942, chairman of its postwar reconstruction committee the following year, and having served on its national executive committee from 1945 until 1949. On November 13, 1949, he was unanimously elected president of the congress to succeed its founder and first president, the late Rabbi Stephen S. Wise. After his election, the New York Times reported, he pledged the congress to increased effort for development of cultural and spiritual bonds with Israel, for advancement in civil rights in the United States, for arousing American opinion to the threat of a renascent German nationalism, and for intensified appreciation of Jewish traditions. Addressing the national executive committee of the American Jewish Congress in January 1950, he criticized Congressional inaction on civil rights, in contrast to anti-discrimination measures passed by various States and localities. The following month he advocated in another public address: "Rather than spending our energies on 'anticrusades,' we should be pooling our resources and strengths for a positive campaign to ensure better health, better housing and better educational facilities for the people of this country and for the ending of all forms of racial discrimination and segregation in our midst" (New York Times, February 12, 1950).

MILLER, IRVING—Continued

The establishment of the state of Israel led many Jews to doubt the further need for Zionism, which had been founded to accomplish precisely that end. In answer to this question, Rabbi Miller suggested in June 1950, at the seventh annual Conference of the Manhattan Region of the Zionist Organization of America, that the movement had a new role to play. Rejecting the concept that Zionism should be merely an instrument to aid Israel, he pointed out that it must now place primary emphasis on the unity of Jewish people and on the continuity of Jewish tradition everywhere. Following the expiration of his term as president, the rabbi affirmed in January 1952 that the American Jewish Congress had "a total program for the creative Jewish survival of American Jews, a program of positive identification with the Jewish people everywhere and of integration into the general culture of America."

At its fifty-fifth annual convention, in New York in June 1952, the Zionist Organization of America elected Rabbi Miller as its president for a one-year term, in succession to Benjamin G. Browdy. Miller had campaigned chiefly on a program advocating close ties with the general Zionist party in Israel, the second largest party there, which emphasizes private enterprise and opposes the administration of Prime Minister David Ben-Gurion. After his election, Miller stated that under his leadership the organization would "facilitate a climate encouraging freedom of expression" and would become "the chief American instrument for aiding Israel." Zionists must participate "to the fullest," he added, "in all phases of Jewish communal life and thus ensure a creative and meaningful future for Judaism in America" (New York *Times*, June 17, 1952). In August 1952 at a meeting of the administrative council of the Z.O.A. he outlined a general program providing for economic aid to Israel, the promotion of Jewish language and education in the United States, and the creation of a national commission on Israel and the Middle East "aimed at the reactivation of Zionist membership in the area of public opinion." At the same time he asked the American Government "to bend every effort to bring about direct negotiations between the Arab states and Israel for an early, peaceful settlement of their disputes and to grant military assistance to Israel under the Mutual Security Act" (in the words of the New York *Herald Tribune*). Observing that friendship for Israel was a "cornerstone" of United States foreign policy, he predicted that this policy would be continued by whichever party won in the November election.

At the request of Prime Minister Ben-Gurion, Miller in early October 1952 flew to Tel Aviv to discuss problems of mutual concern to the United States and Israel. On his departure for London after two weeks in Israel, the Z.O.A. president said that he had pursuaded Ben-Gurion to abandon his proposal for the formation of an over-all Zionist federation in the United States and to give his support instead to a strengthening of the American Zionist Council.

Rabbi Miller has been a member of B'nai Brith, a vice-president of the Zionist Organization of America, a national executive committeeman of the United Jewish Appeal, and associate chairman of the United Jewish Appeal in New York. He married Florence Ashinsky on June 29, 1927. The Millers have two children, Naomi Joan and David Paul.

References

N Y Times p6 N 14 '49 por
Who's Who in America, 1952-53
Who's Who in American Jewry, 1926

MILLES, CARL (WILHELM EMIL)
(mĭl'lĕs) June 23, 1875- Sculptor
Address: b. c/o Cranbrook Academy of Art, Bloomfield Hills, Mich.

NOTE: This biography supersedes the article which appeared in *Current Biography* in 1940.

Swedish-born Carl Milles, who has been described as "the most competent of living sculptors in the important task of harmonizing sculpture with its architectural setting," is director of the Department of Sculpture at the Cranbrook Academy of Art in Michigan. His work, consisting chiefly of monuments, heroic figures, and fountains, is represented in the principal cities of Europe and the United States and has won for him numerous awards and honors. Often referred to as a tireless worker, by 1946 he had produced more than 100 major works, many of them fountain groups comprising ten or more large figures. In September 1952 he was engaged in designing a symbol for the National Arts Foundation—whose advisory committee on sculpture he heads—to represent "all the arts and man's desire for greater self-understanding through the arts."

The second child and eldest son of Major August Emil (or Mille) and Valborg Maria (Tisell) Anderson, Carl Wilhelm Emil Milles was born in Lagga, Stockholm, Sweden, on June 23, 1875. His father, who had fought in the French army during the Franco-Prussian War, was so popular in the vicinity that his nickname was adopted as a surname for his children, who were generally known as "Mille's children." Carl, whose mother died when he was four years old, was a delicate and rebellious child with a deep love of nature. When he was sent to the Jacob School in Stockholm at the age of ten, to compensate for his lost fields and forests he developed a fondness for ships and wharves that led him at the age of fourteen to try to run away to sea. As a disciplinary measure, and also because the boy had shown unusual manual skill since early years, his father apprenticed him to a cabinetmaker. After working hours, young Milles attended evening classes in the Technical School (1895-97) and won a scholarship in the more advanced grade, where he received instruction in carving and ornamental modeling. It was at this time that he decided to become a sculptor. In 1897 he won the Swedish Arts and Crafts Society Prize of 200 kronor, and with this modest prize (the equivalent of $50), he set out for Chile, where he hoped to earn a living teaching Swedish gymnastics in a school directed by a family friend.

On his journey to Chile, which he never reached, Milles stopped off at Paris and was so delighted with that city that he remained there for seven years. Here he found a few odd jobs: he worked for a firm of Italian ornament makers, was a waiter in a restaurant, and was employed by a coffinmaker who allowed him to sleep in the shop. He attended classes at the Academy Colarossi, took a thorough course in anatomy and life drawing, and visited the Jardin des Plantes to study plant forms and make sketches of animals. By 1900 his work was gaining recognition: his marble *Hylas* received honorable mention at the Salon des Artistes Français, and his study of an adolescent girl won a silver medal at the Paris World Exposition. Within two years of his arrival in Paris, his work was exhibited at the École des Beaux Arts, where he studied from 1898 until 1900. One of his groups, however, was rejected: "One day there was a knock on his door," S. J. Woolf related in the New York *Times* (June 13, 1943). "A little man with a large beard stood on the threshold saying he wanted to meet Milles the sculptor, for he had fought to have the group accepted for exhibition. The visitor was Rodin." Soon afterward the great French sculptor employed Milles for a time in 1900 as an assistant in his studio in Meudon. In Morton Dauwen Zabel's opinion, once Milles "had learned the lesson of Rodin's monumental style, he recognized his weakness in the epic and purely plastic orders of imagination early enough to draw away from that master and thus to save his own talent from the brutality of massive force that afflicted most of Rodin's disciples" (*Nation*, March 22, 1941).

In his native country recognition came to Milles when he was awarded fourth place for the monument to Sten Sture in Uppsala, Sweden, an award later changed to first place on demand of the student body. Because of disagreements and lack of funds, the completion of the monument was postponed until 1925, but Milles' reputation in Sweden was established. Between 1902 and 1904 he made a notable series of animal groups and shortly before leaving Paris completed sculptured designs for the new Dramatic Theater in Stockholm. From Paris he went to Munich, where he married a young Austrian court painter. Soon after his marriage, the years of strain and overwork in Paris resulted in a long period of illness for the sculptor. In 1908, having returned to Sweden to settle near Stockholm, he began to build his famous villa near Lidingö, which was to house his rapidly accumulating works and to become known throughout Sweden both for its exceptional charm and its embodiment of his art theories. His achievements were honored in 1914 by a special exhibition of his works in Malmö. Between the years 1914 and 1916 he carved *Susanna* (a fountain in black granite) and in

Wide World Photos

CARL MILLES

1916 executed a second *Susanna* (a fountain in bronze), both of which stand in the gardens of the villa in Lidingö. A change having taken place in his concepts about art, Milles in 1917 felt impelled to destroy part of his earlier work, which he by then regarded as academic. His sculptures of the ensuing period are marked by greater individualism and unconventionality. "True art," he has since said, "must flow from the heart, but it must be a happy mixture of heart and head. The trouble with much of the work of the present day is that it is all head and no heart. It is metaphysical instead of the expression of an emotion. Too much thought and not enough feeling will not produce a work of art" (New York *Times,* June 13, 1943).

As professor of modeling in the Royal Academy of Art in Stockholm, a position which he accepted in 1920, Milles found himself increasingly at odds with the academic world around him because of his new stylistic development. Gaining an ever-increasing recognition in Sweden and abroad, in 1923 his new works were given a prominent place in the Tercentenary Exhibition in Gothenburg, and three years later his sculptures were exhibited at the Tate Gallery in London—his first showing outside of Sweden. Among the projects undertaken by Milles in the 1920's were his *Europa Fountain* in Halmstad; his *Rudbeckius* monument, a massive Gothic figure with a chubby sprite perched humorously on its shoulder; and his bronze *Folkunga Fountain,* a figure of Folke Filbyter on his horse. The last-named work, completed in 1927, stands in the market-place in Linköping in central Sweden. Another well-known piece of this period is the bronze *Diana Fountain,* finished by Milles in 1928, which stands in the courtyard of the Swedish Match Company in Stockholm.

At the invitation of Holabird and Root, a Chicago architectural firm, Milles made his first

MILLES, CARL—*Continued*

visit to the United States in 1929 to design a fountain for its Michigan Square Building on the same theme as his *Diana Fountain*. In that year he accepted a post at the Cranbrook Academy of Art in Michigan, with the provision that he be able to spend his summers in Sweden. He has been associated with Cranbrook ever since and in 1931 took up permanent residence in Michigan. At Cranbrook, where he has come to enjoy, as one writer put it, "the rank of a minor deity," Milles as director of the Department of Sculpture is not required to hold formal classes, but criticizes finished designs submitted by his students, and conducts informal discussions at his home. His first years in the United States were occupied with the completion of his *Orpheus Fountain*, commissioned in 1926, which was set up in Stockholm. He held the first American exhibition of his work in 1932 at the Brooklyn Museum of Art and has since exhibited at galleries and museums in Boston, Baltimore, and New York. In 1939 he was awarded a prize at San Francisco's Golden Gate Exposition. Two of his statues, the monumental and savage *Astronomer* and the highly stylized *Pony Express,* were shown at the New York World's Fair. Also in the late 1930's Milles began work on a project which was to take twelve years to complete— the $250,000 *Fountain of Faith* for the National Memorial Park in Falls Church, Virginia (unveiled in October 1952). A group of thirty-eight figures "stands in a polished, dark granite pool, each statue set on a slender stalk above water level, so that they seem to drift and float across the calm water" (*Time,* October 20, 1952). The figures were drawn from Milles' memories of departed friends.

The work for which Milles is probably best known in the United States is his huge *Meeting of the Waters,* which brought about "an art storm in the Missouri metropolis," as *Newsweek* reported, when it was erected on Aloe Plaza in St. Louis in 1940. The nineteen heroic nude figures, which depict the meeting of the Mississippi with his bride the Missouri, who is attended by a troop of playful naiads and tritons, was deplored by the board of aldermen as a "convocation of Nordic monsters." When the work, intended as a memorial to a former president of the board of aldermen, was unveiled, Milles in his dedication speech admonished the "boys and girls in the pool" to "behave well . . . enjoy life but remember that at every sunrise you have to be here." Early in 1941 Milles completed a wood-carved mural for the Time and Life Building in New York's Rockefeller Center. *Art Digest* described the mural in these words: "The carving, which is more than eleven feet high, depicts a mounted woodsman pausing in a forest to listen to the song of a bird. . . .The woodsman is flanked by figures of a faun which appears to be annoyed by the intruder and a nymph which, in contrast, appears greatly interested. The idea for the work, Milles reported, grew out of a line written by Johann Gotfried Seume in 1804: 'Where song is, pause and listen; evil people have no song.'" For the courtyard of Des

Moines' new Art Center, Milles designed a larger-than-life *Pegasus*—a bronze stallion with the rider soaring above it. The sculptor was quoted by *Time* (July 18, 1949) as explaining, "Greek and other artists always depicted Pegasus with the rider on his back, while I visualize the poet flying independently . . . both animal and man having expressions of longing for something, we don't know what."

The American Academy of Arts and Letters awarded its medal of merit and a prize of $1,000 to Milles in May 1943. This honor is given annually "to a highly outstanding person in America (not a member of the academy. . .) representing either painting, sculpture, fiction, poetry or drama." Shortly after the award was made, Edward Alden Jewell wrote of Milles' large-scale works: "If not of uniform excellence, these at any rate embrace some superb creations, richly imaginative, plastically magnificent." S. J. Woolf termed Milles "one of the few great sculptors of the present day," adding, "He is unique because in this period of artistic fads he is modern without a trace of modernism. . . .The work of no other contemporary sculptor combines such a happy balance of architectural stability and romance and lightness." In his review of Meyric R. Rogers' *Carl Milles: An Interpretation of His Work* (1940), Zabel commented that the sculptor is an artist "of vigorous energies, high spirit, and remarkably fluent and graceful invention, an enthusiast with taste, and a folk craftsman of instinctive sophistication who possesses a genuine aptitude for bringing the eccentricity of the present imagination and the archaism of the studio out of their traditional confines into the public uses of the park, the garden, and the modern city." A contributor to *Architectural Forum,* while noting the eclectic character of Milles' work, stated that "the strongest strain and the most consistent is Swedish, reflecting the temperament of his native land in its qualities of homeliness and energetic strength coupled with the sly humor and stark tragedy of folk legends."

To celebrate his seventieth birthday in 1945, the Art Institute of Chicago exhibited a group of Milles' works, including his *Monument to Genius,* a tragic and powerful winged figure reminiscent of his demonic *Orpheus.* In January 1947 Milles was elected a lifetime member of the National Institute of Arts and Letters, an organization limited to 250 distinguished American artists. The American National Art Foundation appointed him chairman of its advisory committee on sculpture and commissioned him to design a symbol for the foundation. At the same time he disclosed that he had modeled a monument at the request of the United Nations. At the end of 1951 he was chosen a member of the American Academy of Arts and Letters. In September 1952 arrangements were made for Milles to discuss art matters with President Truman and with the presidential candidates of both parties.

Milles' work is represented in the major cities of Europe and the United States, including Stockholm, Göteborg (*Poseidon Fountain*), Malmö, Berlin, Hamburg, Moscow, Venice,

London (*Pavlova Fountain*), Worcester, Chicago, New York, St. Paul, St. Louis, and Wilmington (*Delaware Monument*). The sculptor is a member of the Swedish Academy of Science and an honorary member of the American Institute of Architects, the National Sculpture Society of New York, the American League of Architects, the Vienna Architectural Verein, the Edinburgh Academy of Art, and the Royal Academy of London. He holds the decoration of the French Légion d'Honneur and honorary doctorates from several European and American universities, including the degree of L.H.D. from Yale, and has been awarded gold medals by the Architectural League of New York and by the Architectural Association of New York. His club in New York is the Century.

The sculptor, who became a naturalized citizen of the United States in 1945, has given his home in Stockholm, with its hundreds of pieces of sculpture and paintings, to the Swedish Government to use as a museum. Milles married Olga Louis Granner in 1905. His stocky build and long white hair give him an impressive appearance.

References

Apollo 20:31-4 Jl '40
Arch Forum 84:92-6 Je '46 por
Art Digest 21:27 Ag 1 '43 por
Artwork winter '40
Life 8:110-12 Je 10 '40 por
Mag Art 31:422-4 Jl '38; 31:599 O '38
Newsweek 15:31-2 My 6 '40; 37:82 Ja 22 '51
N Y Times VI p14 Je 13 '43 por; p23 Ja 3 '47
Parnassus 6:7-9 Ja '34
Studio 90:3-9 Jl '25
Time 31:31 Je 6 '38; 52:51-2 Jl 19 '48 por
Baeckström, A. F. E. Carl Milles, the Swedish Sculptor (1935)
Casson, S. Twentieth Century Sculptors (1930)
International Who's Who, 1952
Rogers, M. R. Carl Milles: An Interpretation of His Work (1940)
Vem Är Det, 1949
Verneuil, M. P. Carl Milles (1929)
Who's Who in America, 1952-53
Who's Who in American Art, 1940-47

MILLIKAN, ROBERT A(NDREWS)
Mar. 22, 1868- Physicist; educator
Address: b. c/o California Institute of Technology, Pasadena 4, Calif.; h. 1640 Oak Grove Ave., San Marino 9, Calif.

NOTE: This biography supersedes the article which appeared in *Current Biography* in 1940.

"There can be few among living leaders of scientific thought and action," Sir Henry Dale once wrote in the London *Times*, "whose careers have included so rich a variety of experience and activity as that of Robert A. Millikan." Awarded the 1923 Nobel Prize in physics for his work on light and electricity, Dr. Millikan, who was formerly head of the California Institute of Technology, is noted also for his work in other fields of physics and for his authorship of textbooks in his field.

Robert Andrews Millikan was born March 22, 1868, in Morrison, Illinois, the second son of the Reverend Silas Franklin Millikan, a Congregational minister, and Mary Jane (Andrews) Millikan, a former dean of women at Olivet College; he had two brothers and three younger sisters. Robert's grandparents, of Scotch-Irish and English extraction, were New Englanders who pioneered in settling the Middle West; one grandfather was active in the underground railroad which helped escaped slaves to reach Canada. The boy was reared in several Mississippi River communities and attended school in Maquoketa, Iowa. There he led a largely rural existence, helping with the farm chores, and from the age of fourteen working ten-hour days during summers for a dollar a day in a local barrelhead factory. He assumed responsibility for his own expenses except board and room and later worked his way through college and helped pay for the education of the younger children.

In high school Millikan gave little attention to science, except for mathematics, in which he did well. Graduated in 1885, the youth learned shorthand and worked as a court reporter before entering the preparatory department of Oberlin College in the fall of 1886. Because of his excellent physical development, Millikan was appointed assistant to the Oberlin gymnasium director, a position he held throughout his college years. At the end of Millikan's second year (during which he took one twelve-week course in physics and found it "a complete loss") his Greek professor was given charge of the preparatory department and asked Millikan to teach elementary physics. Accepting the job for the sake of the salary, the youth spent the summer mastering Avery's *Elements of Physics*.

Beginning in his junior year, Millikan taught physics at Oberlin, and after graduating with the B.A. degree in 1891, he remained as tutor of that subject at $600 a year. Studying alone and with little guidance, he earned his M.A. degree in 1893 by mastering Sylvanus P. Thomson's *Dynamo Electric Machinery*. One day he read his own name in the list of recipients of the newly created Columbia graduate fellowships—the Oberlin professors had secured a fellowship in physics for the young man without his knowledge. Thus, in 1893-95 Robert A. Millikan was the only graduate student in physics at Columbia. After one semester the fellowship went to a student of Michael Pupin, from which time dated Pupin's interest in Millikan, who remained at the university while he earned some money as a tutor.

Millikan's doctoral research on the polarization of light emitted by incandescent surfaces was sponsored by Professor Ogden N. Rood. Having secured permission from the director of the United States Mint in New York, Millikan measured the polarization of light emitted by large pots of molten gold and silver. The

ROBERT A. MILLIKAN

thesis was published in the new *Physical Review*. After Millikan's Ph.D. degree was awarded in early 1895, Pupin insisted that he go to Germany for further study; and, not finding another position, Dr. Millikan accepted Pupin's loan of $300 (he insisted on paying 7 per cent interest) for the purpose. Before leaving, Millikan had agreed to return to Oberlin at $1,600 a year. However, while he was attending the universities of Berlin and Göttingen (1895-96), he received an invitation from A. A. Michelson, the future first Nobel Prize winner, under whom Millikan had spent the 1894 summer quarter at the University of Chicago, to become an assistant in physics at $800 a year. Obtaining his release from the commitment to Oberlin, Millikan accepted the latter because of the research opportunities it offered. Michelson agreed to raise the salary to $900, and to allow Millikan to devote half his twelve-hour working day to his own research.

During his early years at the University of Chicago, from 1896 to 1908, Millikan, as he tells in his autobiography, spent half his working time organizing his courses and preparing textbooks. After translating Paul Drude's *Physik des Aethers* (1897) from the German, Millikan, by then associate professor in physics, set about writing textbooks at the four different levels for which they were needed. All his turn-of-the-century texts are used today in revised editions; one, published in 1903, sold for thirty-five years before revision. Besides developing a new kind of science education, in which laboratory work and quizzes, rather than lectures, carried the thread of the course, Millikan devoted time to simplifying methods and equipment so that beginning physics could be taught in schools with small laboratories. From 1908, too, Millikan was responsible for the assignment of all thesis problems and the

direction of all graduate student research in physics at Chicago.

Millikan's research produced few publishable results during his first fourteen years at Chicago. His first full-scale theoretical contribution, in 1897, could not be published because Drude himself anticipated it. Years of research on the free expansion of gases led to no theory, but later the equipment and methods Millikan had developed for the purpose were used by his students (H. W. Moody in 1912, Margaret Shields in 1917) in establishing the validity of the quantum theory. Similarly, the full value of Millikan's turn-of-the-century work on electrical discharge effects in very high vacuum was not evident for another fifteen years. In 1903 he found the photoelectric emission from metals to be completely independent of temperature, but five years' work did not suffice to produce consistently duplicable results, and in 1908 Millikan laid aside his writing to devote more time to an attempt to isolate and measure the fundamental electrical unit, the charge on one electron.

In what has been called "one of the cleverest as well as one of the most important achievements of modern scientific endeavor," Millikan developed the method of holding one microscopic drop of liquid in mid-air with an electric field, causing it to become charged by exposing it to X rays and radium, and determining the charge on the drop by measuring the direction and amount in which it moved. Presented at a meeting in Winnipeg in September 1909, Millikan's proof that all electrons have the same charge attracted world-wide attention, and following its presentation the forty-two-year-old physicist was made a full professor at Chicago. Nearly all Millikan's free time until the summer of 1912 was spent in refining his measurement of the electronic charge, which is smaller than one two-billionth of an absolute electrostatic unit. For this achievement, in April 1913 he was awarded the National Academy of Sciences' Comstock Prize.

The three years following Millikan's return from Europe in October 1912 he spent in testing the validity of the photoelectric stopping-potential equation which had been advanced in 1905 by Einstein. Using complex precision equipment under high vacuum, Millikan obtained the complete verification of the equation, and in the process made the first direct photoelectric determination of Planck's constant.

An unsolicited Rumford Fund grant in 1916 (when Millikan was president of the American Physical Society) provided funds for his hot-spark spectroscopic work at high vacuum with Ira S. Bowen (an extension of his work of 1903-08), which helped to bridge the gap between X rays and ultraviolet light and furnished the chief basis for the important concepts of the "stripped atom" and the "spinning electron." In that year, too, Millikan began a ten-year period as an expert witness in patent litigation. During World War I he was vice-chairman and physics division chairman of the National Research Council formed to mobilize United States scientists before that country was drawn into the war. He took a major part in developing antisubmarine devices, evolved new methods of manufacturing and organizing production of the indispensable optical glass, was in charge of meteorological services from August 1917 to January 1919, and headed the Signal Corps Science and Research Division with the rank of lieutenant colonel. His part in developing balloons to carry propaganda more than a thousand miles led to his interest in cosmic ray investigation. In 1922, at Kelly Field, Texas, Millikan and his student Bowen sent balloons carrying his special ultrasensitive seven-ounce electroscope to a height of ten miles. (For many years the terms "Millikan rays" and "cosmic rays" were used synonymously.)

In 1921 Millikan left Chicago to be director of the Norman Bridge Laboratory and chairman of the executive council (equivalent to president) at the then small California Institute of Technology. There, he felt, a good balance was maintained between science and engineering, and some study of the humanities was required of every undergraduate each year. In 1922 Millikan went to Belgium as the first American exchange professor, and from that year until 1932 he represented the United States on the League of Nations Committee for Intellectual Cooperation. To Millikan is given much of the credit for the present high standing of California Institute of Technology. Associates recall how he attracted leading professors to low-salaried positions by glowing descriptions of the Pasadena climate and "traveled far and wide" raising funds. In 1923 he was named the Nobel Prize winner in physics. The award, including a money grant of about $45,000, was conferred on him for measuring the charge on the electron and for his achievements in the photoelectric effect.

From 1919 Millikan worked on the difficult experimental problem of the behavior of "field currents," and, finally, in 1928 he and Charles C. Lauritsen established by experiment the laws governing them. Millikan also pursued earlier research interests, such as his work with Bowen on the spectroscopic properties of light atoms in all stages of "stripping." Important contributions not previously mentioned include Millikan's study of the Brownian movements in gases and his correction of the Stokes law of fall, both of which were incidental to obtaining refined measurement of the electronic charge. Perhaps the greatest research interest of his later years lay in cosmic rays, to study which he and his assistants carried equipment up the highest North American mountains, climbed the Bolivian Andes in 1926 to eliminate the effects of the Milky Way, visited Tasmania in 1939, and followed that with three months in India. The work of Millikan and others, including his Nobel-laureate student Carl D. Anderson, is recounted in Millikan's 642-page book *Electrons* (+ *and* —), *Protons, Photons, Neutrons and Cosmic Rays* (revised edition, 1947). After his retirement in 1946, at the age of seventy-eight, the scientist continued to work twelve-hour days; his autobiography, which appeared in 1950, was described in the *Saturday Review of Literature* as "one of the

most entertaining and significant scientific testaments." Professor emeritus Millikan is now vice-chairman of the board of trustees of the California Institute of Technology and chairman of the board of the nearby Huntington Library and Art Gallery.

The physicist has been awarded twenty-five honorary degrees, the Hughes medal, Royal Society of Great Britain (1923); Faraday medal, London Chemical Society (1924); Matteucci medal, Socicta Italiana della Scienza (1925); Messel medal, British Society of Chemical Industry (1928); Edison medal (American Institute of Electrical Engineers); Oersted medal of the American Association of Physics Teachers (1940). He is also the recipient of the gold medals of the Society of Arts and Sciences, American Society of Mechanical Engineers, Radiological Society of North America, Roosevelt Memorial Association, Franklin Institute, and Indian Association for the Cultivation of Science. He is a commander of the Legion of Honor, received the Chinese Order of Jade in 1940, is a past president of the American Association for the Advancement of Science, and an honorary or corresponding member of many foreign academies, among them the Pontifical Academy of Science. His clubs are the Sunset, the California, and the Twilight.

On April 10, 1902, Robert Millikan married Greta Irvin Blanchard, who had majored in Greek at the University of Chicago; she is a director of several organizations, including the Southern California Symphony and the Visiting Nurses Association. Of the Millikans' three sons, Clark Blanchard is a professor of aeronautics at Caltech, Max Franklin a professor of economics at Massachusetts Institute of Technology, and Glenn Allen at the time of his death in 1947 was head of a medical school department of physiology. The white-haired, blue-eyed physicist is five feet six inches tall and weighs 160 pounds. He is described as seeming far younger than his years. He campaigned actively for Republican Presidential candidates except Harding. In church affiliation he is a Congregationalist who has spoken and written on religion.

References

Chem Digest 9:2 Jl '50 por
Newsweek 35:54 My 8 '50 por
American Men of Science (1949)
Bridges, T. C., & Tiltman, H. H. Master Minds of Modern Science (1934)
Columbia University Encyclopedia (1950)
Encyclopædia Britannica (1949)
Fisher, D. F. American Portraits (1946)
Hylander, C. J. American Scientists (1935)
Jaffe, B. Outposts of Science (1935)
Law, F. H. Modern Great Americans (1926)
Lotz, P. H. ed. Vocations and Professions (1940)
MacCallum, T. W., & Taylor, S. The Nobel Prize-Winners (1938)
(Continued next page)

MILLIKAN, ROBERT A.—*Continued*

Millikan, R. A. The Autobiography of Robert A. Millikan (1950)
National Cyclopædia of American Biography Current vol A (1926)
Who's Who, 1951
Who's Who in America, 1951-52
Who's Who in California, 1942-43
Woolf, S. J. Drawn from Life (1932)
World Biography (1948)

MITCHELL, HOWARD (BUNDY) Mar. 11, 1911- Orchestra conductor

Address: b. c/o National Symphony Orchestra, 1727 K St., N.W., Washington, D.C.; h. 4400 Fessenden St., N.W., Washington, D.C.

Howard Mitchell became conductor and musical director of the National Symphony Orchestra of Washington, D.C., in November 1948, succeeding the orchestra's founder, the late Dr. Hans Kindler, who at that time retired. About eight years after joining the orchestra as first cellist in 1933, Mitchell began conducting in 1941 and was advanced to the post of assistant conductor and later associate conductor. Following three successful seasons on the podium, he was re-engaged in February 1952 for another three-year period.

Into a family of six children Howard Bundy Mitchell was born March 11, 1911, in Lyons, Nebraska, but was brought up in Sioux City, Iowa, to which his father, Cheever Mitchell, moved to follow his occupation as a barber. All of the five Mitchell boys and their sister were musical and were encouraged by their parents to develop their talents. Howard, grounded in piano by his mother, the former Vera Bundy, also became a trumpeter and sang in a choir while attending the Sioux City Central High School. His extracurricular activities were not,

Fabian Bachrach
HOWARD MITCHELL

however, all musical: he created something of a local sensation by winning the Sioux City golf championship at the age of fifteen. While in high school Mitchell began taking lessons on the violoncello, and after six months his proficiency was such that he won first place in a State-wide competition for a scholarship at the Peabody Conservatory in Baltimore, Maryland. In concentrating on music after his graduation from high school in 1928 Howard Mitchell was greatly influenced by his elder brothers Lucien and Lloyd, the former now a violinist with the San Francisco Symphony and the latter head of the department of piano at the Pennsylvania State Teachers College.

At the Peabody Conservatory in 1928-29 Howard Mitchell studied cello under Felix Salmond and was also one of a trio which presented musical interludes over the Baltimore radio station WFBR. The trio's violinist was a fellow Peabody student named Alma Metcalf, who two years later became Mrs. Mitchell. Mitchell took first cello prize in the Federation of Music Clubs National Competition at Boston, Massachusetts (1929) and a scholarship at the Curtis Institute at Philadelphia, where he was an honor graduate in 1935. At Curtis he was one of a class of six cellists, all of whom have attained fame. "Part of their class work there," Sonia Stein wrote in the Washington *Post,* "included tearing each other's work apart after two-hour recitals by each student."

The young Midwesterner's promise as a student at Curtis attracted the attention of Dr. Hans Kindler, conductor of the National Symphony Orchestra, which he had organized in 1931 at Washington, D.C. Kindler, himself a violoncello virtuoso, engaged Mitchell as his first cellist in 1933 and thereafter, in addition to performing in the ensemble, the latter made occasional appearances as a soloist, both in the regular winter series of the orchestra in Constitution Hall and at the free summer concerts on the Potomac inaugurated in 1935.

"It was in 1941," Sam Stavisky stated in a Washington *Post* biographical sketch, "that Howard Mitchell first switched from bow to baton—at the suggestion of 'Pat' Hayes, the concert promoter, who was at that time arranging for a summer 'pops' at Riverside Stadium, and in the pattern set by the Boston Symphony Orchestra culled the ranks for likely podium prospects." Mitchell's "first appearance with the baton won warm approval." In 1944 he became commentator at, and conductor of, the children's concerts of the National Symphony, and two years later (1946) was advanced to assistant conductor in the orchestra's regular season. On February 23, 1947, when Hans Kindler became ill Mitchell was called to the Constitution Hall podium on a few hours' notice. "Mitchell's performance thrilled the audience," Stavisky reported; and, when a subsequent operation kept Dr. Kindler from activity for several weeks, Mitchell conducted other concerts in Washington and Baltimore and on tour. He was made associate conductor of the National Symphony early in 1948 and led the whole series of Watergate summer concerts during that year.

The resignation of Dr. Kindler brought the announcement on November 30, 1948, that Howard Mitchell had been made full director of the National Symphony. Frank Jelleff, first vice-president of the organization, commented that the 37-year-old appointee, one of the youngest conductors of a major orchestra in the United States, was "recognized by musicians as a very fine musical scholar . . . very popular with his men." Mitchell immediately announced plans to increase the number of concerts in Washington and to present as guests a number of well-known conductors and soloists. In the following October his contract was renewed, at an increased salary, through the summer of 1952. When the orchestra began its first full season under Mitchell's direction on October 26, 1949, he conducted the opening concert from the first cellist's desk, leaving the podium empty in what *Musical America* called "eloquent testimony to Hans Kindler's memory." Mitchell also reseated the ensemble according to the arrangement developed by Leopold Stokowski, Frederick Stock, and Arturo Toscanini, and improved rehearsal methods. When he himself conducted he always tried to follow scrupulously the composer's intent: "He is giving the National Symphony a new and hitherto unknown sense of making music as the composer set it down," stated the Washington critic Paul Hume in December 1949. "He is demanding and showing the way to technical polish such as the resident orchestra has not previously displayed."

In his first full season as maestro of the Washington orchestra, Mitchell had among his guest conductors Sir Thomas Beecham, George Szell, Ernest Ansermet, and Dimitri Mitropoulos; the soloists included Margaret Truman, Jorge Bolet, and Ruggiero Ricci. The 1950 summer program at Watergate was highlighted by a performance of Tchaikovsky's "1812" overture with a cannonade from four 75-mm. howitzers which were brought from Fort Myer.

The National Symphony opened its twentieth season in October 1950, said *Musical America*, "with a concert that gave every promise of a brilliant season. In the six succeeding concerts the orchestra, under Howard Mitchell's direction, has fulfilled this promise with solid vigorous playing that has a new cohesion, resonance, and clarity. The programs have been commendably well rounded and frequently exploratory." In that season Mitchell devoted much attention to creating the Junior National Symphony, an organization of about one hundred high school students in or near the capital; they gave their first concert at Constitution Hall on May 7, 1951. The season ended with the National as the only major symphony in the country to show an increase in subscriptions. Also, in 1951 Mitchell was engaged to give advanced courses in conducting at both the Catholic University of America and the Navy School of Music.

The National Symphony began its 1951-52 season with the cellist Gregor Piatigorsky inaugurating a year which (the Washington *Post* commented editorially) should "gladden the hearts of music lovers": soloists and conductors were also to include such other celebrities as William Kapell, Artur Rubinstein, Jascha Heifetz, Sir Thomas Beecham, and Leopold Stokowski. Announcement that Mitchell had been re-engaged as director until 1955 was made on February 19, 1952. Gordon Reid, president of the Orchestra Association, commented on Mitchell's "enthusiasm and artistic understanding," while the conductor expressed himelf as "particularly happy" about the granting to his musicians of what he called "the best contract, longest and highest scale, in the history of the orchestra." Mitchell is a member of Locals 161 and 77 of the American Federation of Musicians. He was awarded an honorary Doctor of Music degree by American University (Washington) in June 1950 and in the following year received a citation from the National Conference of Christians and Jews.

Howard Mitchell and Alma Metcalf were married June 2, 1931, and have five children— Lorraine, Glenn, Martha, Gerard and Andrew— all of whom give evidence of musical talent. Their father, who is 5 feet 11 inches in height and 165 pounds in weight, has hazel eyes and black hair. Sam Stavisky has described him as "slim, handsome . . . thin-faced." Mitchell mentions golf and fishing as favorite recreations, and is a member of the Kenwood Country Club. A convert to the Catholic faith in 1930, he belongs to the Holy Name Society.

References

> Time 53:77-8 Mr 21 '49 por
> Washington (D.C.) Post p2 D 1 '48;
>   pls O 16 '49 pors; p11 F 20 '52 por
> American Catholic Who's Who, 1952-53
> Who is Who in Music (1951)
> Who's Who in the South and Southwest
>   (1950)

MITCHELL, STEPHEN A(RNOLD)
March 3, 1903- Political party official, lawyer
Address: b. c/o Democratic National Committee, 1200 18th St., N.W., Washington 6, D.C.; c/o Mitchell, Conway and Bane, 141 W. Jackson Blvd., Chicago, Ill.; h. 422 W. Briar Pl., Chicago, Ill.

The Chicago lawyer and "political amateur" Stephen A. Mitchell was chosen by Presidential candidate Adlai E. Stevenson on August 8, 1952, to become chairman of the Democratic National Committee in succession to Frank E. McKinney. A few years earlier Mitchell, who had been interested in reform movements, helped Stevenson enter politics and win his campaign for Governor of Illinois. During World War II Mitchell was employed by the Lend Lease Administration as Chief of its French Division and later by the Department of State as adviser on French economic affairs. In March 1952 he was named chief counsel of the House Judiciary Subcommittee investigating alleged corruption in the Federal Department of Justice.

The son of Stephen Arnold and Dorothy Norton (Higgins) Mitchell, Stephen Arnold Mitchell was born on March 3, 1903, in Rock Valley, Iowa, about fifty miles north of Sioux

STEPHEN A. MITCHELL

City, Iowa. His Irish forebears migrated to the Midwest around 1850; Mitchell's father was a dairyman with a small banking business. The boy attended the public and parochial schools in Rock Valley and in Hood River, Oregon, where his family lived from 1913 to 1917. When the Mitchells moved to a farm near Eagle River, Iowa, he attended the Creighton University preparatory school, in Omaha, Nebraska. During these years Stephen helped his father with work on the family farm in the summer, milking cows and delivering milk in town, and after his graduation from preparatory school in 1921, he ran the farm for one year. He also held a position in Waterloo, Iowa, in the early 1920's as assistant credit manager of the Paul Davis Dry Goods Company.

When he had completed his pre-law course at Creighton University in Omaha in 1926, Mitchell, who was at that time employed as credit and sales manager for the General Motors Acceptance Corporation, moved to Washington, D.C. Here at night he attended the School of Law of Georgetown University until receiving his LL.B. degree in 1928. He then went to New York City, where he worked in legal and executive capacities for General Motors until 1932. From 1932 to 1942 he was associated with the law firm of Taylor, Miller, Busch & Boyden in Chicago, becoming a partner in 1936.

In the period of World War II Mitchell began his contribution to national defense as chairman of the speakers bureau of the Illinois War Savings Staff for 1941 and 1942. He returned to Washington in 1942 to serve for two years as chief of the French Division of the Lend Lease Administration. During 1944 and

1945 he was occupied with duties in Washington and Paris as the adviser on French economic affairs for the United States Department of State. Upon the conclusion of the war in 1945 he returned to Chicago, practicing law for five years as a partner in the law firm of Bishop, Mitchell, and Burdett. He then (in 1950) became a partner in the firm of Mitchell, Conway and Bane. Among the clients of Mitchell, whose law practice was estimated by *Life* magazine to bring him $50,000 yearly, are Britton I. Budd, head of Public Service of Northern Illinois, and Cardinal Stritch. When, in March 1952, he was chosen as chief counsel of the House Judiciary Subcommittee investigating charges of corruption in the Justice Department of the Federal Government, Mitchell immediately submitted an exhaustive audit of the cases handled by his law concern. He worked with Representative Frank L. Chelf, head of the subcommittee, and James McGranery, the new Attorney General, in the dismissal of personnel and in the reorganization of the department, conducting, according to the New York *Post*, a "quiet, thoroughgoing" investigation, without seeking publicity.

On August 8, 1952, Adlai E. Stevenson, Governor of Illinois and Democratic candidate for the President of the United States, chose Mitchell as Chairman of the Democratic National Committee to succeed Frank E. McKinney. Stevenson and Mitchell, both members of the Chicago bar, had been intimate friends for about fifteen years prior to 1952, having met in 1937 at the time they were members of the William Allen White Committee to Defend America by Aiding the Allies. In 1947, when new candidates were being sought by the Democratic party in Illinois, Mitchell and two friends aided Stevenson's entrance into politics by forming a "Stevenson for Senator" group. Later, a turn in party politics caused Paul Douglas to become Senator, while Stevenson received the gubernatorial nomination. Mitchell himself has never run for a public office, but has been influential in reform movements within the Democratic party in Illinois and was a supporter of Mayor Martin Kennelly of Chicago. For a time in 1947 he was interested in becoming a candidate for the office of district attorney, but was opposed by Jack Arvey, the Democratic "boss" of Illinois.

In departing from the tradition of the Democratic party, which in the past twenty years has had a professional politician as its national chairman, Stevenson is said to have selected Mitchell because of the desirability of countering Republican charges of corruption and G.O.P. demands for a "change" (James Reston in the New York *Times*). Political observers pointed in this connection to Mitchell's role in the investigation of the Department of Justice and the fact that he was not associated with the Truman Administration. While many problems of Stevenson's campaign are handled by Wilson W. Wyatt, his "personal manager," Mitchell has among other responsibilities the scheduling of radio and television time, administering the treasury of the party, and raising funds. "Most important," wrote William V.

Shannon in the New York *Post*, "he will be a listening post for the complaints and suggestions of local party leaders. . . .He intends to move quickly in time available to him to revitalize the loose coalition which is the real source of Democratic voting strength. That coalition includes labor union members, Negroes and members of other minorities, independent-minded-League-of-Women-Voters type liberals, and young people."

One of Mitchell's first problems, in the view of some political reporters, concerned Stevenson's policy of "dissociating" (*Newsweek*) himself from the Truman Administration, while simultaneously remaining friendly with it. At a news conference on August 20 the national chairman said that President Truman would be continually consulted about campaign problems and gave the impression that the President's help would be welcome in the organization field. Emphasizing the unity between the old and new elements in the Democratic party, the incoming official stated that he did not intend "to preside over the liquidation of the Democratic party." The Chicago lawyer also announced that a series of regional meetings would be held during Stevenson's speaking tours of the country to enable State politicians and local nominees to become personally acquainted with the Presidential candidate. In his address on August 28 in New York before 300 members of the Democratic State committee, Mitchell described himself (as reported by the New York *Times*) as "a politically minded individual who believed strongly in party discipline and regularity and who subscribed to the doctrine that the fruits of victory should go to the party workers laboring in the vineyards."

A prominent Catholic layman, Mitchell is a director of the Catholic Charities of Chicago. The Democratic chairman is also a director of DePaul University and vice-chairman of the board of lay trustees. He is a member of the Tavern Club and the Union League Club in Chicago and the Metropolitan Club in Washington, D.C. Mitchell married Evelyn Josephine Miller of Waterloo, Iowa, on February 16, 1931, while she was studying for the M.A. degree in education at Columbia University. Their two oldest sons, Stephen Arnold, Jr., and Michael William, in 1952 are attending college, while their youngest son, John Anthony, is in preparatory school. Mitchell has a ranch at Ranchos de Tatos, New Mexico, where he goes for relaxation. He is slender, stands six feet tall, and has blue eyes. His associates, the New York *Post* reported, regard him as "hard-working, methodical, and decisive with a quiet sense of humor."

References

Life 33:133+ S 13 '52
N Y Post Mag p7 Ag 17 '52 por
N Y Times p1 Ag 9 '52 por
N Y World-Telegram p2 Ag 9 '52
Washington (D.C.) Post p1 Ag 9 '52 por
Who's Who in the Midwest (1952)
Who's Who in United States Politics (1952)

MITROPOULOS, DIMITRI (mē-trô′pōō-lôs) Feb. 18, 1896- Orchestra conductor
Address: b. c/o The Philharmonic-Symphony Society of New York, 113 W 57th St., New York 19

> NOTE: This biography supersedes the article which appeared in *Current Biography* in 1941.

Dimitri Mitropoulos, the musical director of the New York Philharmonic-Symphony Orchestra, first visited the United States in 1936 as a guest conductor in Boston, remained to lead the Minneapolis Symphony Orchestra for twelve years, filled a series of guest engagements with his present orchestra in 1940-43 and 1947-49, and shared the podium with Leopold Stokowski in 1949-50. Appointed musical director for the latter season, he is now under contract to the Philharmonic-Symphony through the spring of 1953. Mitropoulos, who excels in the interpretation of nineteenth and twentieth century scores, is also a pianist of distinction. He is the composer of an opera, a Concerto Grosso, and several sonatas and songs.

Of Greek parentage, Dimitri Mitropoulos was born in Athens on February 18, 1896. His father, Jean Mitropoulos, a leather merchant, was the son of a priest of the Greek Orthodox Church and the nephew of an archbishop. Dimitri's mother was Angeliki (Anagnostopoulos) Mitropoulos. His parents, who enjoyed concerts and the opera, arranged for their son to begin piano lessons at the age of seven. By his twelfth year, when he graduated from elementary school, the musical bent of the boy was so clear that the elder Mitropoulos abandoned his own hope of making a marine officer of him and consented to his enrollment at the Odeion, the conservatory at Athens. There during the next six years Dimitri studied piano and composition, and played percussion instruments in the Odeion orchestra. He began composing at the age of fourteen, principally for the theater, and was soon supplying background music for the tragedies of Sophocles and Euripides. His first teachers were a German, Ludwig Wassenhoven, who taught him piano, and a Belgian, Armand Marsick, who taught him composition.

Throughout his conservatory years Mitropoulos expected eventually to enter a monastic order—two of his elder relatives were monks at Mount Athos. However, when he was informed that he would have to leave all musical instruments behind, he decided not to become a monk.

After brief service as a drummer in the Balkan War the youth entered the University of Athens where, in his final year, he composed, at the age of twenty-three, his opera, *Soeur Béatrice*, which is based on the play of that name by Maurice Maeterlinck. This "Debussyesque" work was performed at the Odeion in 1919 and was heard by Saint-Saens, who wrote a laudatory review for a Paris newspaper and offered to take Mitropoulos to the French capital for further study. However, a Belgian concert violinist, César Thomson, had already arranged to send the young man

DIMITRI MITROPOULOS

to Brussels, where in the 1929-30 season he studied organ and composition.

From Brussels the young Greek musician proceeded (on a scholarship from the city of Athens) to Berlin, where he was introduced by the pianist Egon Petri to the composer-pianist Ferruccio Busoni, professor in composition at the Academie der Tonkunste. Mitropoulos was accepted as a member of Busoni's five-member class, though the sonata of his own composition that he played when applying for admission was criticized as having "too much passion." Busoni, whose idol was Mozart, taught his young Greek pupil to find in the works of that composer "the purity and form through which music speaks" (Mitropoulos regards the Italian as the greatest of his masters.) The eventual outcome of their association was to turn Mitropoulos away from composition as his chief musical aim. "From what Busoni told me," he has declared, "I lost all respect for myself as a composer. . . .I listened to Busoni, absorbed his knowledge, and ended up as a re-creator instead of a creator." Before abandoning compositon entirely, Mitropoulos wrote some additional sonatas, a number of songs, a Concerto Grosso, and an orchestral piece entitled "La Mise au Tombeau du Christ."

During the early months of his study with Busoni, Mitropoulos acted as piano accompanist for various artists and, at the Schauspielhaus, played piano and organ and conducted incidental music. After three years (1921-24) as assistant conductor of the Berlin Staatsoper he was named to the vacant post of conductor of the Athens Symphony and director of the Odeion. The international reputation of Mitropoulos may be said to date from his debut as guest conductor with the Berlin Philharmonic in March 1930, when he substituted for soloist Egon Petri in performing Piano Concerto No. 3 of Prokofieff while simultaneously conducting the orchestra from the keyboard. The feat "made music news across the Continent." Mitropoulos repeated his Prokofieff performance at his Paris debut with the Orchestra Symphonique in February 1932, and subsequently in London and other capitals. He toured the principal Italian cities in 1933, 1934, 1935, and 1936, and from 1934 to 1937 conducted a three-month season at Monte Carlo. Other guest appearances took him to Liverpool, Nantes, Bordeaux, Leningrad, and Moscow.

It was Serge Koussevitzky, musical director of the Boston Symphony Orchestra, who invited Mitropoulos to Boston as a guest conductor for two weeks beginning January 20, 1936. His performance—marked by an "illuminating" reading of the rarely played *Sinfonia Domestica* of Richard Strauss—resulted in 1937 in guest appearances with the Cleveland and Minneapolis orchestras. Mitropoulos was invited in the fall of 1937 to become permanent head of the Minneapolis Symphony in succession to Eugene Ormandy.

When Dimitri Mitropoulos made his bow to a New York Philharmonic-Symphony audience at Carnegie Hall on December 19, 1940, he chose the Strauss *Sinfonia Domestica* to conclude his first concert in a month's guest conductorship. Olin Downes wrote in the New York *Times* that he made that work so "incredibly exciting" that "the subscribers . . . did everything except steal the goalposts." Virgil Thomson of the New York *Herald Tribune* wanted to "hear what he does *with* or *to* Mozart, Schubert, Debussy" before undertaking to "chalk up a complete score" on the conductor, though he conceded that "Mr. Mitropoulos is obviously a great orchestral technician." Mitropoulos was invited to return in the 1941-42 and 1942-43 seasons, took part in the centennial celebration of the old Philharmonic Orchestra in the latter season, and on January 5, 1943, gave the first New York performance of his celebrated rendition of the Prokofieff Third Piano Concerto. He did not appear with the Philharmonic between 1943 and 1947, but he brought his own Minneapolis Orchestra to Carnegie Hall for regular annual performances. He was guest conductor at Mexico City, Chicago, Hollywood, Rochester, and elsewhere, and in 1945 became the permanent conductor of the summer concerts in Robin Hood Dell at Philadelphia. Two years later the Greek conductor established permanent residence in the United States, of which he became a citizen in 1946.

In the next twelve years Mitropoulos developed the Minneapolis orchestra "into one of the most notable ensembles of the country" (Howard Taubman in the New York *Times*). At the outset he announced that at least three programs a season would be devoted to "intellectual concerts" featuring music of a modernistic character, such as the works of Gustav Mahler, Arnold Schönberg, and Paul Hindemith. (Mitropoulos won the Mahler Medal of Honor for 1940 for "his efforts to create greater interest in and appreciation of" that composer's scores in this country.) Of numerous recordings made by the Minneapolis Orchestra under Mitropoulos' direction, that of Mahler's First Symphony is perhaps the most universally admired; also praised are discs of the *Fantasia on a Theme by Tallis* by Ralph Vaughan-Williams, the *Portsmouth Point* overture by William Walton, and Rachmaninoff's Second Symphony.

Artur Rodzinski, conductor of the Philharmonic-Symphony left that organization early in 1947, and for the next two seasons the orchestra's podium was occupied by guest conductors. Mitropoulos was called in to direct part of the orchestra's 1947 spring tour and to lead it for four weeks and eight weeks, respectively, in the 1947-48 and 1948-49 seasons. Toward the end of that period Mitropoulos and Leopold Stokowski were invited under a new policy to share a regular conductor's responsibilities during the ensuing year and the title of "musical adviser" to the society. Mitropoulos resigned his Minneapolis post to accept this appointment and conducted the New York orchestra for ten weeks in 1949-50. Stokowski had meanwhile decided that other plans would render impossible his continuance as "musical adviser," and in December 1949 the announcement was made that Mitropoulos had been appointed full musical director for the 1950-51 season. One year later his contract was renewed to cover 1951-52 and 1952-53.

Prior to the opening of the regular 1950-51 season Mitropoulos took the New York orchestra to the Roxy Theatre for a two weeks' engagement of four performances a day between showings of a feature film. ("It's the music that counts, the time or place doesn't matter," said the conductor.) The experiment proved so successful in bringing good music to a large new audience that a return engagement was arranged for the following year. A highlight of the previous season had been a concert-form performance, under Mitropoulos, of Richard Strauss's opera *Elektra*, the reception of which led Mitropoulos to schedule three more concert-operas for 1950-51, as well as to give the first performance in the United States (October 26, 1950) of the "Christus Symphony" of the modern Greek composer Harilaos Perpessa. The first two "theater pieces," Darius Milhaud's *Les Choéphores* and Ravel's one-act opera bouffe *L'Heure Espagnole*, were given for the first time on the same evening (November 17, 1950) and made a deep impression. A triumph for the musician was the revival on April 12, 1951, of Alban Berg's atonal opera *Wozzeck*, an event that to Olin Downes "left no doubt that as an interpretative artist Mr. Mitropoulos is the modernist par excellence." The Philharmonic-Symphony's *Wozzeck* performance has been recorded for a Columbia album. Other admired Columbia records by Mitropoulos with the New York Philharmonic-Symphony are Khachaturian's Concerto for Piano and Orchestra (with Oscar Levant as soloist) and Roger Sessions' Second Symphony.

In the summer of 1951 Mitropoulos took the orchestra to Edinburgh for fourteen performances in the Festival of Britain celebrations;

then, on October 11 he inaugurated at New York's Carnegie Hall the Philharmonic's 110th year, with a program which incorporated a concert performance of the one-act "theatrical capriccio" entitled *Arlecchino*, the work of Busoni. A month later (November 15) he introduced Arnold Schönberg's musical monodrama *Erwartung* to New York in a concert-form presentation, while for later in the season he scheduled performances of Monteverdi's *Orfeo* and Mendelssohn's oratorio *Elijah*. Mitropoulos conducts without baton or score. Of dispensing (like Toscanini) with a score he has said: "That you can do, if you are willing to pay the price. In effort it means one hour expanded to long hours of preparation, but after the effort you are in complete control of your people."

Among many honors that have been conferred on Dimitri Mitropoulos are an honorary degree from Aanatolia College at Salonika (1948) and the decoration of the French Legion of Honor (1951). Of his recreations and personal regimen, Dorle Jarmel has written: "His chief diversion is mountain climbing. . . .He lives quietly in a hotel very near Carnegie Hall. He works very hard. His diet is usually Spartan in its simplicity. . . .His leisure hours at home are spent in reading the works of his favorite philosophers, Plato, Socrates, Nietzsche, Kierkegaard, or the Greek dramatists." His ascetic life has been remarked upon by several writers. In Minneapolis he was known for his philanthropy in helping college students meet their expenses and making gifts to struggling composers.

References

Life 20:57-8+ F 18 '46 pors
Lit Digest 123:28-9 Mr 20 '37
Mus Am 71:3 Ja 1 '51; 71:15 Ap 1 '51 por
N Y Herald Tribune p23 S 20 '50 por; IV p2 D 9 '51
N Y Times IX p7 D 22 '40; p26+ O 8 '50 pors; II p7 O 7 '51
New Yorker 16:14 Ja 11 '41; 26:33-40+ Ap 15 '50 por
Time 25:54 F 10 '36 por; 33:39 Ap 24 '39 por; 35:34-5 Ja 6 '41
Baker, T. ed. Biographical Dictionary of Musicians (1940)
Beard, A. E. S. Our Foreign-Born Citizens (1946)
Brooks, D. International Gallery of Conductors (1951)
Ewen, D. ed. Living Musicians (1940)
National Cyclopædia of American Biography, Current vol G (1943-46)
Thompson, O. ed. International Cyclopaedia of Music and Musicians (1939)
Who is Who in Music, 1951
Who's Who, 1951
Who's Who in America, 1950-51
Who's Who in Central and East-Europe, 1935-36
Who's Who in the Midwest (1949)
Wier, A. E. ed. Macmillan Encyclopaedia of Music and Musicians (1938)
World Biography (1948)

MONTESSORI, MARIA Aug. 31, 1870—May 6, 1952 Italian educator and physician; founder of a method of education for children stressing freedom of self-expression, self-education, and sense training; founder and principal of the Orthophrenic School for mentally defective children (1898); opened the first Montessori School, in Rome (1907); founded schools and gave courses in her method in several European countries and India; author of a number of books on education. See *Current Biography,* 1940.

Obituary

N Y Times p27 My 7 '52

MONTGOMERY, ELIZABETH RIDER
July 12, 1902- Author
Address: b. c/o Dodd, Mead & Company, 432 4th Ave., New York 16; h. 4801 Beach Dr., Seattle 6, Wash.

Reprinted from the *Wilson Library Bulletin,* May 1952.

Many enthusiastic young teachers are dismayed with some of the tools they must use. Often they find that the textbooks, particularly for beginners, are outdated, inadequate, or badly suited to the group under their immediate charge. One such teacher did something about it. Elizabeth Rider, as she was then, found herself faced with the necessity of introducing first-graders to reading by means of a thoroughly unsatisfactory primer. She promptly set about writing a new one that would better meet the needs of her class. This direct action launched her upon a long and successful career as author of school textbooks and later of trade juveniles as well.

Elizabeth Rider Montgomery was born July 12, 1902 in Huaraz, Peru, where her parents,

ELIZABETH RIDER MONTGOMERY

Charles Q. Rider and Lula (Tralle) Rider, were Baptist missionaries. When she was a year old the family returned to the United States, and young Elizabeth grew up in Independence, Missouri. After graduating as valedictorian of her high school class, she went on to Western Washington College of Education in Bellingham, Washington, and then had a term at the University of Southern California in Los Angeles.

It was as a teacher in the Los Angeles schools that she conceived the idea of writing a better primer than the ones in use there. She had already shown a literary bent in childhood, winning various essay prizes before and during her high school course. The primer, published in 1940, brought her the post of staff writer for the textbook publishing house of Scott, Foresman. From 1940 to 1948 she turned out nine primary textbooks. At the same time she was working on other juveniles for general reading, three of them for the very young age group. They were: *Sally Does It* (coauthor with Dorothy Baruch, 1940); *Bonnie's Baby Brother* (1942); and *Keys to Nature's Secrets* (1946).

Mrs. Montgomery has also written a number of children's plays, notably "Old Pipes and the Dryad," which won a prize in a national contest in 1948; and "Noel's Ark," prize winner in the YMHA 1951 competition. She was script writer for the Girl Scouts radio show broadcast from Los Angeles in the 1945-46 season. A play, *All Kinds of People,* was published in 1950.

In 1944 Mrs. Montgomery published the first book in her teen-age series, "The Story behind Great—." Of the first one, *The Story behind Great Inventions,* Virginia Kirkus said: "Excellent content material for social studies, and should appeal tremendously to students whose special interest is science, stimulating interest in further research." The Topeka *Daily Capital* said: "These dramatic tales explain the story of all the great inventions, from the invention of printing down to the present day. . . . In addition to entertainment the book is highly educational." *The Story behind Great Medical Discoveries* (1945) was a Junior Literary Guild selection. H. H. Lent, reviewing it in the New York *Times,* commented, "The forty-three episodes in the book hold the suspense and excitement of a mystery story, richly rewarding the reader with their human interest and their inspiring portrayal of how the world's great medical challenges have been met."

In 1947 came *The Story behind Great Books.* A. M. Wetherell in *Library Journal* reported: "Interesting information which will add to book reviews in the upper grades." Vincent Starrett wrote in the Chicago *Tribune*: "An excellent telling for young people of the circumstances in which certain famous tales were created. . . . Told in a way young people will like, and her enthusiasm will lead them to the volumes themselves." *The Story behind Great Stories* (1947) impressed *Booklist* as "rather superficial, but . . . useful when a few facts about one of these authors are requested." B. W. Bell in *Library Journal* said: "The unusual and interesting information . . . is needed for young people and teachers who do not have time for personal research." *The Story behind Modern Books* (1949) brought the following comments. L. S. Bechtel in the New York *Herald Tribune*: "A young reader may well find this book a good introduction to titles he has missed. . . .It is also a good book for young would-be writers, for it shows vividly the variety of inspiration, of ways of working, of the kinds of lives of many authors." Elizabeth Hodges in the New York *Times*: "Though some of the sketches are quite superficial, the book for the most part gives interesting and valuable information."

Mrs. Montgomery now lives in Seattle with her husband (Norman Athol Montgomery) and two children, a daughter of seventeen and a son of twelve (in 1952). She says she never can resist any job that has to do with children or young people. She has done active P.T.A. and Girl Scouts work, serving at one time as a cub scout den mother, and is superintendent of the junior department at her children's Sunday school. She does considerable public speaking, chiefly at schools and libraries. She has just finished a junior novel for older girls and a child's history of the State of Washington, and is in 1952 at work on a new book. She lists her recreations as water-color painting, rug making, folk dancing, and playing the cello.

Mrs. Montgomery loves her work, and says confidently, "I have far too many ideas; if I wrote steadily for ten years I could not exhaust the supply of ideas in my notebook. And the trouble is, more come all the time. I never get through with one book without having something else started."

MONTGOMERY, JAMES SHERA, REV.
Oct. 17, 1864—June 30, 1952 Former Chaplain of the United States House of Representatives; Methodist Episcopal minister; after ordination in 1893 held pastorates in Toledo and Minneapolis; pastor in Washington, D.C., of the Metropolitan Memorial Methodist Church (1911-16, 1926-33) and Calvary Methodist Church (1916-26); Chaplain of the House of Representatives (1921-50); Chaplain emeritus (since 1950). See *Current Biography*, 1948.

Obituary

N Y Times p23 Jl 1 '52

MOORE, MARIANNE (CRAIG) Nov. 15, 1887- Poet
Address: b. c/o Macmillan Company, 60 5th Ave., New York 11; h. 260 Cumberland St., Brooklyn 5, N.Y.

A poet of foremost standing in twentieth century American literature, Marianne Moore is the author of seven volumes of poetry, the first of which, *Poems,* appeared in 1921. Among notable recent awards that have been presented to Miss Moore in recognition of the high quality of her writing are the Bollingen Prize in Poetry and the 1952 Pulitzer Prize for

George Platt Lynes
MARIANNE MOORE

her *Collected Poems* (1951). Poet T. S. Eliot has praised her work "as part of the small body of durable poetry written in our time . . . in which original sensibility and alert intelligence and deep feeling have been engaged in maintaining the life of the English language."

Marianne Craig Moore was born in Kirkwood, near St. Louis, Missouri, on November 15, 1887, the daughter of John Milton Moore, an engineer, and Mary (Warner) Moore. Her brother John Warner Moore, who for forty years has been a chaplain in the Navy, is in 1952 Chaplain of the Gunnery School, Washington, Connecticut. She spent her early childhood in the home of her maternal grandfather, the Reverend John R. Warner, who was pastor of the First Presbyterian Church of Kirkwood. In Carlisle, Pennsylvania, to which the family later moved, Marianne Moore and her brother attended Metzger elementary school. For her high school education she entered the Metzger School for girls, where later her mother taught English. Miss Moore has spoken of an interest in ethics and aesthetics as a determining influence on her lifework. As a young girl, while not caring for "poetry" or thinking of writing as a career, she was devoted to books.

Prepared by her mother for the Bryn Mawr College entrance examinations in English, Marianne Moore enrolled at Bryn Mawr in 1905. "Most of my time," she has said, "was spent in the biology laboratory despite my interest in English and language courses, for which I seemed not to have an aptitude." After leaving college with her B.A. degree in 1909, she studied at the Carlisle Commercial College, graduated in 1910, and for three and a half years (1911-15) was in charge of the commercial department of the United States Indian School in Carlisle. Here her pupils included James Thorpe and various members of "that astonishing group of Indian athletics"

MOORE, MARIANNE—*Continued*

(*Newsweek*, December 24, 1951). While her brother was Pastor of Ogden Memorial Church of Chatham, New Jersey, Miss Moore and her mother lived in Chatham. They later lived in New York City, where Miss Moore was an assistant in the Hudson Park Branch of the New York Public Library from 1921 to 1925.

Miss Moore first saw her poems in print in Bryn Mawr College publications. In 1915 some of her work appeared in Harriet Monroe's *Poetry* magazine (Chicago) and in *The Egoist*, a London magazine in which much of the early work of the Imagist group was published. In 1921 H.D. (Hilda Doolittle) and Bryher (Winifred Ellerman) assembled and had printed for her (without her knowledge) a volume, *Poems*, at the Egoist Press, London. Some of these early poems, with additions, were later printed under her supervision in *Observations*, which upon publication in the United States in 1925 won the Dial Award as an outstanding contribution to American literature. Reviewing this volume in the *Nation* (March 18, 1925), Edwin Seaver noted: "In respect to her work Miss Moore hews to an ideology that is aristocratic and severe and pure. Against the commonplace and the easy her subtlety of sarcasm is devastating. Herself a modernist . . . she is yet austerely conservative, gifted with an instinctive taste and the wit to prove its supremacy." The inspiration of *Observations* was Miss Moore's reading and conversation of her friends, as shown by the notes that she appended to her book. In 1925 Miss Moore was invited to join the staff of *The Dial*, "a journal of art and letters," in the opinion of *Newsweek* the best literary magazine in American history. She served as acting editor and later as editor until the magazine was discontinued in 1929. She and her mother then moved to Brooklyn, where she still lives.

With the publication in 1935 of *Selected Poems*, Miss Moore, who had earlier (1933) won the Helen Haire Levinson Prize, was awarded the Ernest Hartsock Memorial Prize. Reviewing *Selected Poems*, G. N. Shuster said (*Commonweal*, June 7, 1935) that the poetry of Miss Moore was "verse really very much like the satires of [the seventeenth century poet John] Donne, and yet characterized by the keen archery of a modern American woman. . . .The sole difficulty is that to many all this 'precision' will seem heartless as Aristotle and not much more beguiling." The New York *Times* critic found, "The effect she produces is always positive and exhilarating." *Selected Poems* was followed in 1936 by *The Pangolin and Other Verse*. A year after receiving the Shelley Memorial Award from the Poetry Society of America, Marianne Moore, in 1941, produced *What Are Years*, a volume of fifteen poems, some of which had appeared earlier in American and British periodicals. The poem from which the book took its title, "What Are Years?" was described by Malcolm Cowley (*New Republic*, November 10, 1941) as "a celebration of human freedom in bondage that rightly comes first in the book. It is among the noblest lyrics of our time." The *New*

Yorker acclaimed Miss Moore's work as "an almost incredible phenomenon to appear in the amorphous culture of our country and day. For it is a book which could be produced, it would seem, only at an advanced point of civilization. It bears the indisputable marks of high style."

Upon the appearance in 1944 of *Nevertheless*, all six poems of which had been published previously in periodicals, Miss Moore was awarded the Contemporary Poetry's Patrons' Prize and the Harriet Monroe Poetry Award of $500, presented by the University of Chicago. (She was the second American to receive the latter award, the first having been Muriel Rukeyser.) In his comment on *Nevertheless* a critic for the New York *Sun* observed, "The deliberate skill with which she serenely records the movements of such disparate subjects as the weasel, an elephant, or the human mind in phrases composed all of sinew, woven into lines of clean-cut beauty will continue to astound her faithful readers." Oscar Williams regarded "In Distrust of Merits" as "one of the finest war poems we have by a first-line poet" (*New Republic*, October 23, 1944). In April 1945 Miss Moore was granted a John Simon Guggenheim Fellowship for creative writing in the field of poetry and in May 1946 received a joint grant of $1,000 from the American Academy of Arts and Letters and the National Institute of Arts and Letters "in recognition of the wit and wisdom she has . . . imprisoned in poems of the rarest distinction." The following year she was elected a member of the National Institute of Arts and Letters, an organization devoted to the furtherance of creative work, which has a life membership limited to 250 American artists, writers, and composers designated as creative artists whose works are most likely to achieve permanence in American culture.

For *Collected Poems* (1951), which comprises most of the poems she has published since her first volume in 1921, Marianne Moore on January 11, 1952, received the Bollingen Prize in Poetry of the Yale University Library. Members of the 1952 Bollingen Committee making the selection were W. H. Auden, chairman; Leonard Bacon, Louise Bogan, and Richard Eberhart, poets; and Malcolm Cowley, critic. In accepting the National Book Award for Poetry, conferred upon her in January 1952 for *Collected Poems*, Miss Moore said: "To be trusted is an ennobling experience; and poetry is a peerless proficiency of the imagination. I prize it, but am myself an observer; I see no reason for calling my work poetry except that there is no other category in which to put it." She expressed her thoughts about what poetry is by quoting from Wallace Stevens' *The Necessary Angel*—he "puts his finger on this thing poetry . . . where he refers to 'a violence within that protects us from a violence without.'" In poetry, she further explained, "understatement is emphasis. In poetry metaphor substitutes compactness for confusion and says the fish moves 'on winglike foot.' It also says—and for 'it' I had better say Confucius—'If there be a knife of resentment in the heart, the mind will not attain precision.'

That is to say, poetry watches life with affection" (quoted by the *Christian Science Monitor*, February 7, 1952). In May of the same year she won the 1952 Pulitzer Prize of $500 awarded for a distinguished volume of verse published in 1951 by an American author. (Among other winners of the Pulitzer Prize in poetry in recent years have been Carl Sandburg, Gwendolyn Brooks, Peter Viereck, and W. H. Auden.) A recent poem by Marianne Moore, "Then the Ermine," appeared in *Poetry* magazine, October 1952. The poet is at present engaged in translating the fables of La Fontaine.

Characterized by wit, brevity, precision, restraint, objectivity, and an epigrammatic quality, Miss Moore's poems have been described as "definitions, encyclopedia articles set to music," in which acute observations about plant life and about creatures like whales, zebras, sea and land unicorns, jerboas, cats, peacocks, and cockroaches concern people and human virtues and weaknesses. "She is a naturalist without pedantry," Louise Bogan has written of her, "and a moralist without harshness." While she has at times been compared with the Imagists, her poems are generally regarded as being too highly individual to be classed with any poetic school. Some critics have called her "esoteric"; *Twentieth Century Authors* (1942) expresses the view that when her poems are hard to understand, they are so "not because they are obscure but because they are so compact." A skillful craftsman, "she succeeds in that most difficult of all metrical performances: sustaining a steady rhythm, while continually varying the line length" (Paul Engle, Chicago *Sunday Tribune*, January 20, 1952).

Besides writing poetry, Miss Moore has contributed a number of book reviews and critical articles to periodicals. Two of her essays, "Henry James as a Characteristic American" (*Hound & Horn*, April-June 1934) and "The Poetry of Wallace Stevens" (*Poetry*, February 1937), have been reprinted in M. D. Zabel's *Literary Opinion in America* (1937, 1951), in which a discussion of Miss Moore's work also appears. During the summer of 1942 she taught composition at Cummington School, Massachusetts; she has addressed groups of students at Bryn Mawr, Vassar, Harvard, and other colleges and universities. She has taken part in the New York Public Library series of poets' readings and in such seminars as that conducted by Harry Levin at Harvard in 1950 with a distinguished group of poets and critics, including John Crowe Ransom, Robert Penn Warren, Kenneth Burke, and Stephen Spender. She received an honorary Litt. D. degree from Wilson College (1949), from Mount Holyoke College (1950), from the University of Rochester (1951), and from Dickinson College (1952).

A "staunch Brooklynite," Marianne Moore was in June 1952 chosen one of twelve Brooklyn residents to receive the annual "Youth Oscar" awards of Youth United for a Better Tomorrow, a social agency aiding eight Brooklyn settlement houses and awarding the "Oscars" to serve as inspiration to the 15,000 young persons enrolled in the settlement houses. For a time Marianne Moore collected contributions for the Red Cross in the apartment house in which she lives. With a height of five feet three and one-half inches, she weighs 127 pounds; her eyes are blue-gray and her hair is gray (originally reddish brown). Miss Moore is a member of the Presbyterian Church. She votes independently. Among her favorite authors are Chaucer, Spencer, Sir Thomas Browne, Samuel Johnson, Molière, and Thomas Hardy. She has enjoyed tennis from childhood and takes an interest in drawing, dancing, music, lectures, the theater, photography, printing, animals, typography, and documentary films.

References

Bryn Mawr Alumnae Bulletin spring 1952
N Y Herald Tribune p10 Ja 12 '52 por
N Y Times p16 Ja 12 '52 por; p24 My 6 '52 por
N Y World-Telegram Ap 24 '45
Newsweek 38:69-71 D 24 '51 por
American Women, 1939-40
Living Authors (1937)
Who's Who in America, 1952-53
Who's Who in New York, 1952
Twentieth Century Authors (1942)

MOOREHEAD, AGNES Dec. 6, 1906- Actress

Address: b c/o Orson Welles Productions, Hollywood, Calif.

Agnes Moorehead, who in 1951-52 toured the United States and England with the First Drama Quartette as Donna Ana in the highly acclaimed reading of Bernard Shaw's *Don Juan in Hell*, has distinguished herself in a variety of roles in radio, motion pictures, and the theater. A "character actress in the best sense of the term," she has never been typed, and her repertory ranges from comedy to tragedy: old ladies to young girls, villainesses to heroines— all roles played, in the verdict of the reviewers, with conviction, depth, and success. She is known to radio audiences especially for her performance in *Sorry, Wrong Number*, which she first gave on the *Suspense* program in 1943 and has since repeated on the air a number of times. Among her recent motion pictures are *The Blue Veil* and *Showboat*.

A native of Clinton, Massachusetts, where she was born December 6, 1906, Agnes Robertson Moorehead, principally Irish in ancestry, is the daughter of John Henderson Moorehead, a Presbyterian minister, and Mary Mildred (McCauley) Moorehead. Agnes attended school in Reedsburg, Wisconsin, where her father had a pastorate. Then she proceeded to Muskingum College in Ohio (an institution founded by her uncle). Some years later she went to the University of Wisconsin for graduate work in English and public speaking, leading to the Master of Arts degree, stated a Columbia Broadcasting System release.

Miss Moorehead has told that she made her first "public appearance" at the age of three, singing "The Lord Is My Shepherd" on a church program. As a young girl she looked

AGNES MOOREHEAD

toward a career in the theater. While her first position was as teacher of public speaking and English at the high school of Soldiers Grove, Wisconsin, she also coached the drama group in the town. Meanwhile she had her radio debut as a singer in the then infant medium in 1923 over stations KSO and KMOX in St. Louis, in which city for three seasons she appeared as a dancer and singer with the Municipal Opera Company at its annual festivals in Forest Park.

When Miss Moorehead had earned enough money for her expenses, she went to New York, where she enrolled in the American Academy of Dramatic Arts and began serious training for the stage. She was also a teacher of dramatics at the Dalton School in that city. An honor student at the academy, she had roles in several Broadway plays—in the Theater Guild's productions of *Marco's Millions*, *Scarlet Pages* with Elsie Ferguson, *All the King's Horses*, *Soldiers and Women* with Violet Heming, and *Candlelight* with Gertrude Lawrence. Her rise in the legitimate theater was halted, however, by the depression which followed the stock market crash of 1929. With Broadway offering no opportunity, she turned again to radio. Among the numerous programs on which she appeared were *The March of Time*, *Cavalcade of America*, comedy shows with Phil Baker, Fred Allen, and Bob Hope, and a daytime serial in which she played "Joyce Jordan, Girl Interne." To radio listeners she was usually anonymous, but in 1939 when she appeared on *Cavalcade of America* as Marie Dressler in a dramatized biography of that star, *Variety* commented: "In the 'ugly duckling' leading role, Agnes Moorehead turned in a superb performance, steadily changing from a diffident, youthful-voiced tyro to the celebrated and assured, but huge-hearted old woman."

Meanwhile Miss Moorehead had come to the attention of Orson Welles, the young organizer

and director of the Mercury Players, of which company she became a member. When Welles went to Hollywood in 1941 to produce *Citizen Kane* she went along to play Kane's mother, a small but "memorable bit" in the picture. Her roles in this and subsequent Welles film productions—*The Magnificent Ambersons* (1942) and *Journey into Fear* (1942)—she characterized (in a New York *Herald Tribune* interview) as "gloom parts," but they served to establish her reputation as a tragedienne of the first order. For her portrayal of the neurotic spinster aunt in *The Magnificent Ambersons* she received the New York Film Critics' Award in 1942 as the best actress of the year and she was also nominated for an award of the Academy of Motion Picture Arts and Sciences. Howard Barnes of the New York *Herald Tribune* spoke of her "brilliant and thoughtful" performance.

Miss Moorehead's career in Hollywood became as varied as her radio work. She played a Chinese peasant in *Dragon Seed* (1944), a glamorous French aristocrat in *Mrs. Parkington* (for which she was again nominated for an Academy Award, in 1944), the aunt of the deaf-mute in *Johnny Belinda* (another Academy Award nomination, in 1948), and a woman of well past one hundred years in *The Lost Moment* (1947), a screen adaptation of Henry James's *The Aspern Papers*. For that role the application of make-up required five hours. While the result was grotesque, one reviewer, Cecelia Ager of *PM*, said of Miss Moorehead that her "eloquent voice . . . all by itself achieves a distinguished, complete characterization that no amount of make-up can quite snuff out."

She played also a number of smaller parts before the camera: in 1943 in *The Youngest Profession* and *Government Girl*; in 1944 in *The Seventh Cross*, *Jane Eyre*, *Since You Went Away*, and *Tomorrow the World*; in 1945 in *Keep Your Powder Dry*, *Our Vines Have Tender Grapes*, and *Her Highness and the Bellboy*. In 1947 she appeared in *Dark Passage* and in the role of a German refugee scientist in *The Beginning or the End*, a semi-documentary picture about the atom bomb. In 1948 she was seen in her first Western film, *Stations West*; in the motion picture based on Wilkie Collins' mystery story, *The Woman in White*; and in *Summer Holiday*, a musical version of Eugene O'Neill's *Ah, Wilderness!* in which she was Cousin Lilly. In 1949 she appeared in *The Great Sinner* and as Ma Stratton in the *Stratton Story*. Her most recent films are *Showboat* (she was Parthy Ann, Captain Andy's nagging wife), *Caged*, *The Blue Veil*, *Fourteen Hours*, *Black Jack*, and *Adventures of Captain Fabian*. In all, as of 1952, Miss Moorehead has played in about thirty motion pictures.

At the same time Agnes Moorehead continued her radio work, in "homey" comedy as Cora Dithers in *Blondie* and as Marilly, housekeeper for Lionel Barrymore, in the *Mayor of the Town* series. She was heard frequently with Orson Welles in *Ceiling Unlimited* and *Hello Americans* on CBS. In a 1942 radio performance of *The Man Who Came to Dinner,* she played two roles, "jumping effortlessly," said *PM,* "from the part of a teen-aged ingénue to that of a batty old-maid aunt." In May 1943 she was heard on the radio program *Suspense* in the "harrowing" dramatic monologue called *Sorry, Wrong Number.* In the role of a bedridden invalid who accidentally overhears a murder plot on the telephone and with growing horror and hysteria realizes that she herself is the intended victim, Miss Moorehead gave a performance that, in the words of *Variety,* "has rarely, if ever been equaled on the air. From the woman's first faltering lines, through the scenes of growing dread to the final moments of gibbering semidelirium, it was a blood-chilling performance of a brilliantly agonizing script." The program was repeated five times betwen 1943 and 1947 and was recorded for Decca, becoming so popular on wax that in 1948 Miss Moorehead tried to restrain disc jockeys from playing the record. (It was also made into a motion picture in 1948 with Barbara Stanwyck in the leading part.) For the CBS Documentary Unit's hour-long program *The Sunny Side of the Atom,* presented in July 1947, Miss Moorehead, as narrator, impersonated the CBS reporter who did the research for this exposition of atomic energy.

Early in 1951 Miss Moorehead returned to the theater with the First Drama Quartette reading the brilliant but rarely produced *Don Juan in Hell,* which is the third act of Bernard Shaw's play *Man and Superman.* With Charles Laughton as the Devil, Charles Boyer as the Don, and Sir Cedric Hardwicke as the Commander, Miss Moorehead participated in a unique theatrical venture. After its first presentation in February 1951 in Stockton, California, the reading was given at Constitution Hall in Washington, D.C., and received so favorable a response that the Quartette began a tour that took it from Oakland, California, to Duluth, Chicago, New Orleans, New York, and to England. They played a series of one-night stands in high schools, churches, synagogues, concert halls to "capacity" audiences.

As Donna Ana, in a mauve satin gown with her red hair arranged high on her head, Miss Moorehead was, to quote critic Walter F. Kerr, "striking to watch." Many spectators were surprised to learn, said H. L. Monk in the St. Louis *Globe-Democrat,* that she "is not as old as the characters she creates on the screen and is considerably more attractive." Reviewing the performance in the New York *World-Telegram,* William Hawkins wrote, "The actress has the crisp, clean elegance of a lily. She falls into exquisite poses and moves like a self-appointed queen, to give the play its chief visual attraction." In April 1952, when the Quartette was giving its third series of performances in New York City, the New York Drama Critics Circle voted to cite *Don Juan in Hell* as "a distinguished and original contribution to the theater" in the balloting session for the 1951-52 season.

Miss Moorehead was married on June 6, 1930, to John Griffith Lee, an actor, from whom she was divorced June 11, 1952. She has

an adopted son, Sean. One of her major interests is her 320-acre farm in Ohio, where—usually "by remote control" because of her acting schedule—she raises crops and livestock. This property was a Western Reserve land grant to her great-grandparents who came from England. The blue-eyed actress stands five feet six inches tall and is of slender build. She is a member of Lambda Alpha Lambda, Delta Gamma, and Phi Beta, and has an honorary Doctor of Literature degree, conferred on her in 1947 by Muskingum College.

References

N Y Sun Je 24 '33
Newsweek 29:54 F 3 '47

International Motion Picture Almanac, 1950-51
Who's Who in America, 1950-51
Who's Who in the West (1949)
Winchester's Screen Encyclopedia (1948)

MORANO, ALBERT PAUL Jan. 18, 1908- United States Representative from Connecticut
Address: b. Old House Office Bldg., Washington 25, D.C.; h. Indian Harbor, Greenwich, Conn.

Albert Paul Morano, one of the Republicans elected in November 1950 to the United States House of Representatives, entered the Eighty-second Congress as the Representative from the Fourth District of Connecticut. He had served a political apprenticeship as secretary, in 1939, to the late Dr. Albert E. Austin, Representative in the Seventy-sixth Congress; and again as secretary, from 1943 to 1946, to former Congresswoman Clare Boothe Luce. Immediately preceding his election to Congress, from January 1947 to August 1950 Morano was a member of the Connecticut State Unemployment Commission, acting as its chairman during the last seven months of his term with it. The Representative was re-elected to Congress in November 1952.

Albert Paul Morano was born to Anthony and Clementina (Belmonte) Morano on January 18, 1908, in Paterson, New Jersey. His father had served in the Bersaglieri, the infantry corps of the Italian Army famed for its marksmanship and known by the distinctive plume of feathers on the felt hats. The Morano family, in which there were four sons and three daughters, moved from New Jersey to Greenwich, Connecticut, where the future legislator attended high school. In January 1939 Morano became secretary to Dr. Albert E. Austin, a Greenwich physician, who was elected to the Seventy-sixth Congress. He remained with Austin until the latter, candidate for re-election, was defeated (1940). When Clare Boothe Luce, stepdaughter of Austin, began her first term in 1943 as United States Representative from Greenwich, Morano became her secretary and again observed national legislative affairs. His association with the Congresswoman continued until Mrs. Luce completed her service in the Seventy-ninth Congress at the end of 1946. Mrs. Luce, reported a columnist in the New York *Sun,* summed up her estimate of his

Wide World Photos

ALBERT PAUL MORANO

efficiency in these words: "I wouldn't swap Al Morano for all the 906 secretaries and assistants on the White House staff."

Immediately afterward, in January 1947, Morano was named to the Connecticut State Unemployment Commission, to represent the Fourth Congressional District of the State. During the last seven months of his more than three and a half years with the commission, Morano was chairman of the organization, which has the responsibility of administering the State unemployment insurance law. In the fall of 1950, a few months after terminating his work with the Commission, he was elected on the Republican party's ticket to represent the Fourth District in the Eighty-second Congress. His constituency, comprising a population of over 400,000, is the County of Fairfield, which is generally regarded as a high-income suburban region.

One of Morano's first acts on taking his seat in Congress in January 1951 was to ask for the return of Bernard Baruch to Government service to assist in stemming inflationary tendencies. In the same month he signed a statement with thirteen other Republican "freshmen" Representatives, pledging the signers to support with "vigorous action" a number of domestic and foreign legislative programs. These included the restoration of Congress as a policy-making body of the Government, reduction of Government nondefense spending, end of the "drift into State socialism," and a consistent foreign policy, with no shipments to the Iron Curtain countries. In January he also asked the House Committee on Taxation to consider exempting the Metropolitan Opera Association from the 20 per cent Federal admission tax, and the next month offered a bill granting the same exemption privileges to concert perfor-

mances. After this suggestion had been favorably passed on by the House, Morano, who on this occasion described himself as "an ardent lover of the opera," appeared before the Senate Finance Committee in August to urge the upper legislative group to endorse the House action. (Subsequently, symphony orchestras, nonprofit opera companies, and similar groups were exempted from payment of the tax.) At the same session he asked for removal of the 10 per cent excise tax on electric shavers. Another bill which Morano offered for consideration during the first session would make discrimination against workers over forty-five years of age an unfair employment practice.

Morano joined with forty-one other Republican first-time Representatives in signing a petition demanding the removal of Secretary of State Acheson, and later proposed Clare Boothe Luce as the Secretary's successor. He urged in September 1951 that the terms of the Italian Peace Treaty be liberalized to permit Italian rearmament to enable Italy to contribute fully to European defense. In key legislative issues Morano was generally in agreement with his party. He voted for the Trade Agreements Extension Act of 1951, which, although it continued to permit the President to enter into foreign trade agreements, reduced his power by requiring a full report to Congress on controversial issues. He was with the House majority when he voted against granting the President power to make temporary reorganizations of government agencies and with it again when he favored the Draft Extension-Universal Military Training bill of April and the $7½ billions foreign aid bill of August. He voted for the defense production bill, for a cut of $10 millions in reclamation funds, a cut in government civil payrolls, a cut of $350 millions in European economic aid, and an amendment to the Federal Security Agency appropriations which limited the hiring program of the agency to 25 per cent of vacancies occurring in 1952. He was against the revenue act of 1951 which increased individual and corporate income taxes, the legislation continuing rent controls, and import controls on fats and oils. While other Republican members from Connecticut voted against the bill to provide FHA mortgage insurance for the construction of housing in defense areas, Morano favored the program.

Another issue of concern to Congressman Morano was the morale of the men at Camp Pickett, Virginia, where soldiers of the Forty-third National Guard Division, many of whom are residents of Connecticut, were stationed. After visiting the post, Morano wrote to Defense Secretary Marshall, placing the blame for low morale among the soldiers on the Defense Department and on the commanding general of the division. As the result of a complaint from a constituent, Morano in October 1951 asked the Federal Communications Commission to remedy a situation in which a "disc jockey" is at present free "to malign individuals over the public airways without any record or transcript—with no restraining authority exercised to insure good taste and absence of malevolent rancor." In the Eighty-second Congress the

Connecticut Republican has been on the House Administration Committee and on the Board of Visitors to the Coast Guard Academy.

On February 27, 1952, Morano received an appointment within the Republican party organization as assistant to national chairman Guy G. Gabrielson. With the title of director of the Italian-American Section of the Ethnic Origins Division for the Presidential Campaign, he will help elect Republicans to the Senate and House from States with large Italian-American populations. Morano retained his seat in the House in the November 1952 elections.

The Connecticut Representative is five feet seven inches in height, weighs 175 pounds, has brown eyes and gray hair. A Catholic, he is a member of the Knights of Columbus. He married Millicent Greco in March 1933 and has a son, Anthony Albert, and a daughter, Clare Ann. A sport the legislator enjoys is baseball.

Reference

Congressional Directory (1951)

MORGAN, ANNE (TRACY) July 25, 1873—Jan. 29, 1952 Philanthropist; social worker; active in behalf of war relief in France, international good will, opportunities for women; helped organize the American Ambulance Service in World War I and the Committee for the Devastated Regions of France; in World War II founded the Committee for Civilian Relief in France; was made commander of the French Legion of Honor (1932); president of the American Woman's Association in New York (1929-43). See *Current Biography*, 1946.

Obituary

N Y Times p25 Ja 30 '52

MORRIS, NEWBOLD Feb. 2, 1902- Lawyer

Address: b. 1337 E St., N.W., Washington, D.C.; c/o Lovejoy, Morris, Wasson & Huppuch, 52 Wall St., New York 5; h. 340 E. 72d St., New York 21

Appointed a special assistant to the United States Attorney General on February 1, 1952, Newbold Morris was the man selected by President Truman and Attorney General J. Howard McGrath to conduct an investigation of corrupt practices in government and to recommend remedial legislation. Two months later Morris was dismissed from this position by Attorney General McGrath, who resigned from his own office the same day. A lawyer by profession Morris, who has described himself as a "Lincoln Republican," has a long record in municipal administration, having served as president of the New York City Council for eight years (1937-45) under Mayor Fiorello H. La Guardia. On numerous occasions he officiated as acting mayor, and was twice a candidate for the office of mayor.

Eldest in a family of three boys, Newbold Morris (who long ago dropped his first name, Augustus) is a direct descendant of Richard

Wide World Photos
NEWBOLD MORRIS

Morris, one of Oliver Cromwell's Roundhead officers, who came to New York in the middle of the seventeenth century and purchased from the Indians that part of the Bronx which became known as Morrisania; later Morrises were famous in colonial and early Federal history. Newbold Morris' father, for whom he was named, served as a lieutenant colonel on the staff of General John J. Pershing in World War I, was a probate lawyer, and a Republican county committeeman. His mother, nee Helen Schermerhorn Kingsland, was a granddaughter of Ambrose Kingsland, a "Reform" mayor of New York in the 1850's. Born in New York City on February 2, 1902, Newbold Morris, like his younger brothers, George Lewis Kingsland and Stephanus Van Cortlandt, was brought up in a brownstone house in Manhattan. Since the family was well-to-do, young Newbold was sent to private elementary schools in New York and Massachusetts before preparing for college at Groton School. He considers his headmaster at Groton, the Reverend Endicott Peabody, to have been one of the two "great influences" on his character and outlook (the other was to be Fiorello H. La Guardia).

From Groton he went to Yale University, where he was elected to the Alpha Delta Phi and Scroll and Key Society; he also rowed against Harvard on the freshman crew in 1921, though impaired health was later to prevent him from winning his varsity letter. Other athletic activities of his at college were tennis and skating. Morris was graduated with the B.A. degree in 1925 and received his LL.B. degree from the Yale Law School in 1928. He is a member of the Phi Delta Phi law fraternity and a fellow of Branford College.

(Continued next page)

MORRIS, NEWBOLD—*Continued*

In the summer of 1928 Newbold Morris attended the Republican National Convention, where, reported *PM,* he was "somewhat bewildered" to find the committeemen who had voted against inclusion of a prohibition-repeal plank in the party platform gathered around a large cocktail shaker. The year following his departure from Yale saw him joining his father's old law firm of Morris & McVeigh and taking over his father's place on the Republican county committee. The part played by the gangster "Dutch" Schultz in the defeat of Republican Walter S. Mack for the State Senate aroused Morris' ire against corruption in government, and in 1930 he entered into active campaigning as a district captain in the Fifteenth Assembly and Aldermanic District of Manhattan. Soon afterward he became treasurer of the Fifteenth District Republican Club, and in 1933 was elected the club's president.

Early in the summer of 1933 Adolf A. Berle, Jr., then City Chamberlain, brought together Morris and former Congressman Fiorello H. La Guardia at a dinner. "La Guardia just took me over completely that first night," Morris has been quoted as saying (*PM*). "He was the most vital person I had ever met in politics." Morris subsequently helped to unify factions of the anti-Tammany groups, with the result that La Guardia was chosen the Fusion candidate for Mayor. Victorious in the November 1933 election, La Guardia appointed Morris an assistant corporation counsel; as such the latter worked with the 1934 New York City Charter Commission on the framing of the new charter which a few years later was to give the city a substantial degree of "home rule" or semiautonomy within the State. He was also sent to the State Capitol to assist in promoting the interests of the charter, and was so occupied when in the summer of 1934 Joseph Clark Baldwin, alderman for the strongly Republican Fifteenth District, resigned to run for the State Senate. Morris was appointed to the vacancy, was elected in the following November, and was re-elected in 1935. In 1936, however, when he became the Republican candidate for president of the Board of Aldermen, he was defeated by his Democratic opponent.

In the following year (1937) the new city charter became law, and the old Board of Aldermen was superseded by a new City Council. Morris was nominated by the Republican, American Labor, Fusion, and Progressive parties for president of the Council and won in the November election by a plurality of 235,000. Giving up his law practice, he took office on January 1, 1938. "It wasn't long," Murray Davis was later to write in the New York *World-Telegram,* "before the professional Republican politicians began to wonder just what political Frankenstein they had wrought. He wouldn't take orders from political leaders. He wouldn't even appoint clubhouse loafers to traditional sinecure jobs. . . . His administration economies sent them reeling," especially when he cut his own budget from $70,000 to $40,000 a year. His loyalty to La Guardia

(who gave up his Republican enrollment in favor of the American Labor party) and his close association with Adolf Berle, a founder of the Liberal party, did not endear him to the G.O.P. "regulars." Neither did his sympathy with the Roosevelt social relief policy, or his endorsement of such New Deal measures as the Social Security Act. (When later told that he "sounded a lot" like a New Dealer himself, Morris was quoted by Oliver Pilat in the New York *Post* as replying: "If you speak of the New Deal as an ideal, I believe I am one. If you speak of the New Deal as a political party, of course I am not.")

Morris was re-elected president of the City Council in 1941. He also took over from La Guardia the gavel at the meetings of the Board of Estimate, and as a member of that board was largely responsible for the successful unification of the city's subway systems. He also worked on reorganization of pension funds, establishment of a free port on Staten Island, and revision of the rules of the Board of Estimate. In 1943, when the municipality was obliged to take over the Mecca Temple on West 55th Street in default of taxes, Morris was largely responsible for converting the building into the New York City Center of Music and Drama, known for presentations of ballets and operas. Morris was chairman of the New York City War Council through the World War II period, and on numerous occasions served as acting mayor during La Guardia's absences.

Morris entered two contests for the office of mayor of the City of New York. The first was in 1945, when he was the nominee of the so-called "No Deal" party, hastily formed by the supporters of La Guardia after the outgoing mayor expressed dissatisfaction with the candidacies of both Judge Jonah Goldstein (Republican - Liberal - Fusion) and William O'Dwyer (Democrat). Morris was defeated by O'Dwyer in November. The name of Morris (who had meanwhile returned to private law practice as partner of the firm now known as Lovejoy, Morris, Wasson & Huppuch) appeared on the ballot again, in 1949, as Liberal-Fusion candidate, but again he lost to O'Dwyer. "Long before the Senate Crime Investigating Committee appeared on the scene," reported Mary Hornaday in the *Christian Science Monitor,* "Mr. Morris was publishing information about New York gangsters." In his campaign speeches of 1949 he named one gangster as "the real boss of the city." The following year (1950) Morris was active in behalf of the successful candidacy of Rudolph Halley, counsel to the Kefauver Committee, for the presidency of the City Council.

As a practicing lawyer, Morris (with his partners) was called upon in 1948 to help set up the China International Foundation, to assist Chinese students stranded in the United States and to provide scholarships for American students of Sinology. The foundation, of which Morris became chairman, was involved early in 1952 in a Senate subcommittee investigation of sales of war surplus materials at exorbitant prices. Morris denied any personal gain in the foundation's purchase of a number of war-surplus tankers.

On February 1, 1952, announcement was made that President Truman had appointed Morris as a special assistant to Attorney General J. Howard McGrath to investigate "misconduct by employees of the Federal government" and to "make recommendations to strengthen the integrity and efficiency of the entire administration of government functions." Accepting this new responsibility on the eve of his fiftieth birthday, Morris described himself an an "Abraham Lincoln Republican," stressed that his work would be "nonpartisan and nonpolitical," said that his first field of investigation would be the Justice Department itself. His personal qualities and good faith were generally recognized by the press—"We New Yorkers have known him long and favorably as . . . always a warmhearted independent on virtue's side," stated a New York *Herald Tribune* editorial. His arrival in Washington to direct the investigation of corruption drew mixed reactions from Congressmen and political observers, some of whom were skeptical that he would have a free hand in investigating the Justice Department.

On March 18, 1952, the Senate Judiciary Committee opposed granting to Morris the subpoena powers that Truman had requested be given him. Meanwhile the corruption investigator had begun his inquiry by preparing a questionnaire, sixteen pages long, regarding sources of income and expenditures. Intending to start with the Department of Justice, Morris on March 18, 1952, delivered there 596 copies of the questionnaire to be distributed among officials of that department. McGrath, who objected to Morris' methods in investigating corruption, refused to distribute the questionnaires and on April 3, 1952, dismissed Morris from office. On the same day, at the request of President Truman, McGrath resigned as Attorney General. Just before his departure from Washington, Morris stated that he would leave recommendations for measures to stop corrupt practices in government, but expressed doubt that the Administration would act on his suggestions. "Official Washington doesn't want to be cleaned up," the press quoted him as saying.

The marriage on August 1, 1942, of Newbold Morris and Mrs. Constance (Hand) Jordan was Morris' second; his first, to Margaret Copley Thaw on September 5, 1925, had ended in divorce in 1940. He has two children, Peter and Newbold, Jr., by the earlier union; and two, Lewis Hand and Frances Learned, by the latter. His church is the Episcopal; his lodges are the Masons, the Elks, and the Knight of Pythias. Gray-eyed Morris, who has a height of six feet two and a half inches, has been described by Richard Rovere in the *New Yorker* as a "gregarious, enthusiastic man" with a "boyish" face. The winner of the Middle Atlantic amateur figure-skating championship in 1935, he still exercises on the ice and is also considered a competent tennis player. He smokes a pipe, drinks in moderation, and enjoys pinochle, the theater, and music.

References

Christian Sci Mon p12 F 4 '52
Cue 18:13+ O 8 '49 por
Life 19:29-35 O 29 '45 por
N Y Herald Tribune p1 Ag 2 '42; II p3 O 21 '45 por
N Y Journal-American p2 N 4 '45 por
N Y Post p3 Mr 30 '43 pors; p12 Ap 8 '43; p33 Ag 8 '45 por; p31 Jl 25 '49 por
N Y Sun p22 Je 20 '45
N Y Times p12+ N 3 '37 por; IV p2 S 18 '38 por; p6 F 2 '52
N Y World-Telegram p6 N 1 '45 por; p4 F 2 '52
New Yorker 16:15+ Ja 18 '41; 20:28-32+ O 28 '44 por; 20:28-32+ N 4 '44 por
Newsweek 39:25+ F 11 '52 por
PM p3-6 Ap 11 '43 pors; p9 Ag 6 '45 por
Time 59:20 F 11 '52 por
U S News 32:51 F 22 '52 pors
Washington (D.C.) Post p1 F 2 '52
Who's Who in America, 1950-51
Who's Who in Law, 1937
Who's Who in New York, 1947
World Biography (1948)

MORRISON, WILLIAM SHEPHERD

Aug. 10, 1893- Speaker of the British House of Commons

Address: b. c/o House of Commons, London, England; 1 Tanfield Court, Temple, London E.C.4, England; h. The Manor House, Withington, Gloucestershire, England

The new Speaker of the British House of Commons, elected at the opening assembly of Parliament on October 31, 1951, is the Right Honorable William Shepherd Morrison, Conservative member from Gloucestershire since 1929. Speaker Morrison held Cabinet offices under Prime Ministers Baldwin, Chamberlain, and Churchill from 1936 to 1945, during part of which time he served as Britain's first Minister of Food and as wartime Postmaster General. He is a barrister by profession and became a King's Counsel in 1934.

Descended from a long line of clansmen in the Outer Hebrides but himself a native of the Scottish mainland, William Shepherd Morrison was born August 10, 1893, in western Argyll. His father, John Morrison of Torinturk, was a gentleman farmer; his mother's maiden name was Marion McVicar; and lingually he is equally at home in English and the Gaelic of his childhood countryside. Completing his secondary schooling at George Watson's College in Edinburgh, he matriculated at Edinburgh University, but after his first two undergraduate years enlisted as a gunner for World War I service and was at the French front by November 1914. Wounded and mentioned three times in dispatches, he won the Military Cross for valor in action in 1915, and held the rank of captain in the Royal Field Artillery when he returned to civilian life four years later. He resumed his studies at

British Inf. Services
WILLIAM SHEPHERD MORRISON

Edinburgh, where he became president of the Union (debating society) and senior president of the Students' Representative Council in 1920.

Having taken his Master of Arts degree at Edinburgh—he was later also to receive honorary LL.D. degrees from both Edinburgh and Leeds universities—Morrison proceeded to London to read for the bar; and when in 1922 the Liberal leader David Lloyd George was succeeded as Prime Minister by Andrew Bonar Law, the young Scotsman was appointed private secretary to the Solicitor General in the new Conservative Cabinet, Sir Thomas Inskip, later the first Viscount Caldecote. Morrison was called to the bar of the Inner Temple in 1923, and at the general election of the same year made his first try for a seat in the House of Commons in the Western Isles (Outer Hebrides) Division of Inverness-shire and Ross and Cromarty. This was traditionally a Liberal constituency, but Morrison partly perhaps because he was of local ancestry, lost only by 3,158 votes to 3,391. He recontested the West-Isles division at the election of October 1924, lost for a second time, but was reappointed as private secretary to Inskip, who again became Solicitor General in the new Cabinet of Prime Minister Stanley Baldwin. Morrison continued as Inskip's private secretary when Inskip was made Attorney General in 1927. At some point early in his career Morrison became for a time Commissioner of Crown Lands.

In the general election of May 1929, Morrison was the Conservative candidate in the Cirencester and Tewkesbury Division of Gloucestershire and this time was victorious, topping the combined vote for his Liberal and Labor opponents. Inskip was defeated, but returned to Parliament through a by-election; he again became Attorney General in the Baldwin cabinet, and for the four years beginning 1931

Morrison served as his Parliamentary private secretary or deputy in the House of Commons. "He became," stated a British Information Services release, "a prominent personality among back-benchers," and from 1932 to 1935 was chairman of the influential Conservative Private Members' Committee. At this period, too, he began six years (1931-36) of membership in the Medical Research Council and the Industrial Health Research Board, and became increasingly known as an authority on industrial and agricultural problems and planning. (His article "Industrial Society and Conservative Principles" appeared in the *English Review* for June 1933.) "He has always been a planner and coordinator," the journalist Augustus Muir was later to point out, adding that "his work at the English bar increased his native capacity for the swift grasping of detail and the sifting of data." Successful as a barrister, Morrison "took silk" (that is, became a King's Counsel) in 1934. Continuing his professional as well as his Parliamentary career, he served in 1935-36 as recorder, or chief magistrate, of the large Staffordshire iron-foundry town of Walsall.

Morrison was appointed Financial Secretary of the Treasury in 1935. During the following year he went to Geneva to represent his country in the League of Nations and served both as a member of the League's Economic and Financial Committee and as the first chairman of the International Committee established in London to enforce nonintervention in the Spanish Civil War. His first Cabinet appointment came in late October 1936, when in an extensive reshuffling of portfolios by Prime Minister Baldwin he was made Minister of Agriculture and Fisheries in place of Walter Elliott. Morrison retained this post—which carried with it membership in the Privy Council and the title of Right Honorable—when Neville Chamberlain succeeded Baldwin as Premier in May 1937. In January 1939, when Lord Chatfield took over the recently created post of Minister of Co-ordination of Defense, Morrison was redesignated Chancellor of the Duchy of Lancaster, a position with Cabinet rank but without specific duties, with the understanding that he would be Lord Chatfield's spokesman in the House of Commons and would assist him "on the economic aspects of the defense program" (New York *Times*). He was also placed in charge of the Food Defense and Plans Department of the Board of Trade, and is credited with building up a reserve of food stocks against the threat of war. On September 4, 1939, following the outbreak of World War II, he was appointed Minister of Food, taking part in the initial planning of the new and expanding Ministry, which was to become a vast organization. As Food Minister he put into effect Britain's wartime rationing regulations and price-fixing policy for essential foodstuffs and home produce.

Early in April 1940 Morrison was transferred from the Food Ministry to the Postmaster Generalship, a move which prompted the head of the London bureau of the New York *Times* to remark that Morrison had had "one of the saddest careers in politics, always getting the dirtiest jobs." The Ministry of Agriculture, it was pointed out, had long been "a graveyard of British political reputations," while as Minister of Food he had been "set up as a general target." At one time Morrison was forced to direct operations from a sickbed in the basement of the blitzed General Post Office. His Ministry was praised for the efficiency with which service was maintained under the bombings.

At the beginning of 1943 Morrison took over the new post of Minister of Town and Country Planning (with authority in England and Wales though not in Scotland) and was said to regard the challenge thus presented as both great and welcome. "We have got to see," he told Augustus Muir, "that our land of England and Wales is used much better than it has been used in the past. . . . And what problems it raises—the location of industries and workers' homes; the safeguarding of good agricultural land; the redeveloping and modernizing of the towns and cities; the preservation of the coastline . . . and so on." His direction of this task was, however, cut short after two years by the overthrow of the Conservative government in the general election of July 1945, though he himself was returned to Parliament by his Gloucestershire constituency. He was again re-elected by the Cirencester and Tewkesbury Division in February 1950; served as chairman of the Conservative Party's Parliamentary Committee on National Insurance, Education, and Pensions in the Parliament of 1950-51; and was re-elected to the House of Commons in October 1951.

When the new Parliament assembled on October 31, 1951—with the Conservatives under Winston Churchill becoming the majority party by 321 seats to Labor's 294—the senior Conservative member of the Commons rose to move "that the Right Honorable W. S. Morrison do take the chair of this House as Speaker." The Speaker of the Commons, unlike that of the United States House of Representatives, is expected to maintain a strictly impartial attitude—he is traditionally "free from all party ties during his tenure of the chair"—and to officiate as a moderator rather than as a political leader. Because of this his authority is even greater than that of the Speaker of the House of Representatives, the rules of the Commons empowering "the Chair to accept or refuse the cloture, to check irrelevance and tedius repetition, to quell disturbances, to reprimand and, if may be, to commit offenders." Only members known to be of the highest integrity are ever suggested for the chair; a nominee is ordinarily ascertained in advance to be acceptable to all parties, and his election is traditionally unanimous. However, although the Speaker does not participate in debate on bills or motions, he has the deciding vote in the case of a tie; and this fact, in view of the very slim Conservative majority, may have been a consideration in Labor's challenge of Morrison's election. Morrison was installed as Speaker by 318 votes to 251 for James Milner, the Opposition's choice.

The office of Speaker, notable for the traditions and ceremony connected with it, commands much deference from Members of Parliament, who are required to bow to him on entering or leaving the House, while by authority of a 1919 Order in Council he ranks in social precedence "next after the Prime Minister and the Lord President of the Council and . . . before all peers of the realm except the archbishops" (*Encyclopædia Britannica*). Morrison's salary (according to *Time*) is £5,000 ($14,000), and upon retirement he will be given a peerage.

On his election as Speaker, Morrison, in accordance with custom, resigned from all industrial and commercial concerns with which he was formerly associated, among them the London Tin Corporation and the Midland Counties Electric Supply Company. His clubs are the Carlton, Cirencester Golf, and the Caledonian. Mrs. Morrison, nee Katherine Allison Swan is, like her husband, a barrister. They were married April 22, 1924, and have four sons, John William, Alasdair Andrew Orr, Nial Ranald, and Godfrey Donald. Augustus Muir has described Morrison as a "practical visionary" who "plays the violin, has written mystical and macabre short stories and some Scots verse of quality." He has contributed to *English Review, Manchester Guardian, Scots Magazine, Saturday Review*, and *Week End Review*. The *Manchester Guardian* has commented on his "simple dignity," while elsewhere he has been characterized as "tall . . . with prominent dark eyes" and as possessed of a "resonant voice."

References

Great Britain and the East 47:832 D 10 '36 por
Time 58:30 N 12 '51 por
Authors' and Writers' Who's Who (1948-49)
Burke's Peerage (1948)
International Who's Who, 1951
Who's Who, 1951
World Biography (1948)

MUNIZ, JOÃO CARLOS (moo-nēz' zhwoun kär'lōs) Mar. 31, 1893- Brazilian representative to the United Nations

Address. c/o Brazilian Delegation to the United Nations, 350 5th Ave., New York 1; h. 1115 5th Ave., New York 28

The fourth largest of United Nations members in respect to area and the seventh largest in population, Brazil has been called the unofficial leader of the Latin American states in the world organization. Head of the Brazilian Permanent Delegation to the United Nations is Ambassador João Carlos Muniz, a career diplomat who has served his country in consulates and embassies in the United States and Europe, and in its Ministry of Foreign Affairs as assistant to former Foreign Minister Oswaldo Aranha.

João Carlos Muniz was born in Brazil's inland state of Mato Grosso, in the capital city,

JOÃO CARLOS MUNIZ

Cuiabá, on March 31, 1893. His parents were Polydoro Antunes and Anna Virginia (Costa Marques) Muniz. Young Muniz attended the Colégio Anchieta, a secondary school in Rio de Janeiro, graduating in 1908. Then, at the University of Rio de Janeiro, he studied juridical and social sciences, and in 1913 received the degree of Bachelor of Laws. He was later (1923), while a consul in New York, to earn the Doctor of Juristic Science degree at New York University.

Upon entering Brazil's diplomatic service in 1918 Muniz was assigned to New York as consul for a period of eight years. In October 1925 came his first experience in the work of a world organization—he served in Washington as secretary of the Brazilian delegation to the Conference of Interparliamentary Union. His next diplomatic assignment was as consul in Chicago (1926-28). In the spring of 1928 he attended the Pan American Conference, the sixth international conference of American states, at Havana, as secretary of the Brazilian delegation.

During those years as consul in the two largest cities of the United States Muniz also represented Brazil at a number of international trade conferences, one of his specialties became economic affairs. These were the Convention of Associated Advertising Clubs of the World in Houston, Texas, in 1925; the Bankers Conference in Philadelphia in 1926; the Coffee Roasters Convention in West Baden, Indiana, in 1926, and again in Chicago in 1927, as a representative of the Brazilian Coffee Institute; and the Conference on Commercial Aviation in Washington in 1927.

Stationed in England from 1929 to 1931 Muniz was consul in London. Other consular posts followed: from 1931 to 1933 he was consul in Baltimore and the next year held the same post in Warsaw, Poland; he was briefly

consul and consul general at Geneva in 1934, the year he was also commissioned to study coffee raising in Central America. Later that year, advanced to minister counselor, he served in Washington during 1934-35 as commercial counselor in the Brazilian Embassy. His next post was consul general from 1935 to 1938 at Geneva, where he also acted as observer for Brazil at the League of Nations. In the course of the three years in Geneva Muniz was also representative of Brazil on the governing board of the International Labor Office.

The diplomat returned to his nation's capital in 1937 to become chief of staff for the Minister of Foreign Affairs, Oswaldo Aranha, who espoused a policy of close cooperation with the United States; this was during the dictatorship regime of President Getulio Vargas. While in this post Muniz, whose rank was minister plenipotentiary, was one of two foreign office aids to accompany Aranha to Washington in 1939 in response to an invitation from President Franklin Roosevelt to President Vargas for a conference. On the assumption that "all friendly peoples have to fear Germany," the conferees, according to *Newsweek* (February 20, 1939) discussed money and arms aid to Brazil from the United States and methods of cutting Nazi trade in Brazil.

From 1938 to 1941, while executive assistant to Aranha, Muniz was also chairman of the Brazilian Council on Immigration and Colonization. This was during the period when President Vargas was engaged in a campaign of "Brazilianization," to counteract Fascist domination of German, Japanese, and Italian minorities in Brazil. In this period Muniz was also chief pro tem of economic services in the Ministry of Foreign Affairs and member of the efficiency commission of the ministry (1938); member of the committee on the agenda for the eighth Pan American Conference (1938); and director of the federal council of foreign trade (1939-40).

Muniz again went abroad in 1941, as Minister Plenipotentiary to Havana, Cuba, the year he attended the second Pan American Conference of National Committees of Intellectual Cooperation at Havana. The following year (1942) he began a three-year period as Ambassador to Ecuador. President Vargas selected Ambassador Muniz in May 1943 to head the Brazilian Commission to the Hot Springs (Arkansas) Conference on Food and Agriculture. The New York *Times* reported (May 16, 1943) that the delegation would be instructed to say that Brazil would put its vast food resources at the disposal of the United Nations, to share in the burden of feeding the postwar world (Brazil had entered World War II in 1942), and that Brazil was planning long-range planting, with the assistance from the United States of experts, agricultural machinery, seeds, and credit.

When Muniz returned to Rio de Janeiro in 1945 it was as chief of the Diplomatic and Consular Department and Secretary General of the Ministry of Foreign Affairs. The next year the diplomat, who had by that time participated in several inter-American conferences, was named to represent Brazil on the governing board of the Pan American Union in Washington. The *Bulletin of the Pan American Union* welcomed the appointment with the comment that he had "a deep knowledge of social, economic, and cultural affairs throughout the Americas." Muniz held this post for only slightly more than a year, for in August 1947 he was named head of the Brazilian Permanent Delegation to the United Nations in New York, succeeding Dr. Oswaldo Aranha.

The Brazilian diplomat's first assignment in the United Nations came in 1946, when he served as a delegate to the second part of the first General Assembly; and he continued to represent Brazil at General Assembly meetings, the second through the fifth (1947-50). When Brazil was elected to the Security Council for 1946-47, he was his country's representative on that body, and again joined the Security Council in 1951 when Brazil was re-elected for a two-year term. In the same month of his appointment as head of his delegation, August 1947, Muniz took an active part in Security Council deliberations on the dispute between Egypt and Great Britain over the presence of British troops in the Nile Valley and British rule in the Sudan. Muniz offered a resolution to send the case back to the disputants for new negotiations on the ground that appeals to the Security Council should be restricted to questions presenting an immediate threat to peace. Security Council intervention should be considered a last resort, when traditional methods of settlement had been exhausted, he said, arguing that recourse to an international agency had the disadvantage in some cases of tending "to accentuate divergencies. That is why it should not be allowed as a form of pressure or threat to bring about or to influence negotiations." His resolution was supported by China, the United States, Belgium, and France. According to the New York *Times*, he had "raised in effect the unsolved problem of defining the stage at which a dispute becomes a threat to security."

Muniz was active in May 1949 in pressing for a resolution sponsored by Brazil, Colombia, Peru, and Bolivia to rescind the U.N. recommendation against sending ambassadors and ministers to Spain; this move was finally successful in November 1950. Interested in cutting "bureaucracy" for economy reasons, in November 1949 Muniz, in an address to a joint session of the Economic, Social and Budgetary Committees on budget problems of the U.N. pointed out that U.N. expenditures had risen from $43 millions in 1947 to $220 millions in 1949, and suggested that delegations refrain from presenting new projects unless they were urgent. A few months later at its first meeting (in January 1950) the fifteen-nation Interim Committee, the so-called "Little Assembly," charged with preparatory work between sessions of the General Assembly, elected Muniz chairman. On accepting the chairmanship Muniz commented that the Soviet boycott (the Soviet delegates had walked out in protest against continued membership in the U.N. of Nation-

alist China) had "somewhat hampered" the usefulness of the committee. The Interim Committee, in effect, was unable to take any conclusive action before the September Paris meeting of the General Assembly; issues before it were passed on to the Assembly without recommendations.

From 1948 to 1950 Muniz was a member of the U.N. Economic and Social Council, and in February 1950 presided at a council discussion of current and long-range problems of the world economy. Muniz urged, as a solution to Europe's dollar-gap problem, that aid in dollars be channeled to underdeveloped countries, such as those in Latin America, to enable those nations to purchase consumer goods from Europe; in addition he suggested increased exports of capital to Latin America in the form of government loans or private investments, and more importing of Latin American raw materials to be used for stockpiling.

At the first session of Brazil's second two-year term on the Security Council in January 1951, Ambassador Muniz according to the New York *Times,* got into a "sharp tangle" with the Soviet delegate when he held that peace would be based on whether the Soviet Union was willing to "renounce its policy of fostering social revolution in other countries." In June of that year *World Government News* named Ambassador Muniz recipient of its award for 1950-51 for advocating at the council's opening session, an eventual world federation, as the "best approach to world order." Muniz meanwhile had been named chairman of the twelve-power U.N. Collective Measures Committee, set up to carry out the Acheson plan for maintaining armed forces for possible employment with U.N. troops in Korea. He was re-elected chairman of that committee in April 1952; and as chairman of the Security Council for October, Muniz presided during the dispute between Great Britain and Iran over British-operated oil fields in Iran.

A member of the United Nations Disarmament Commission, the Brazilian in May 1952 placed blame for that group's lack of progress on the Soviet Union, charging that it demanded immediate agreement on absolute goals "perhaps knowing beforehand that such goals were not obtainable," and used the commission as a sounding board for propaganda. Muniz again questioned the motives of the Soviet representative in July 1952 when the Soviet Union opposed an investigation by the Red Cross of Communist charges of bacteriological warfare in Korea.

The diplomat married Yvonne Germaine Guidain of Paris on October 15, 1926. Their two daughters are Thereza Regina (the Marchioness de Belmonte de la Vega Real of Spain) and Silvia Maria (Mrs. Fernando Pedro Mihanovich of Argentina). The family's faith is Roman Catholic. His club memberships include the Instituto dos Advogados in Rio de Janeiro and the Metropolitan Club in New York, and he is a member of the Phi Delta

MUNIZ, JOÃO CARLOS—*Continued*

Phi. Ambassador Muniz is said to be a "voracious reader of political philosophy."

References

Bul Pan Am Union 80:249 My '46
N Y Herald Tribune II p1 O 7 '51 por;
    p50 Mr 31 '52 por
World Government News 9:9-10 Je '51
    por
Who's Who in America, 1952-53
Who's Who in Latin America pt 6
    (1946-51)
Who's Who in the United Nations
    (1951)
World Biography (1948)

MURRAY, PHILIP May 25, 1886-Nov. 9, 1952 Labor union president; began work in coal mines of his native Scotland at the age of ten; came to United States (1902); worked in Pennsylvania coal pits; elected president of local United Mine Workers union (1904), member of executive board of U.M.W. (1912); vice-president of international executive board of U.M.W. (1919-40); participated with John L. Lewis in founding Committee for Industrial Organization (later Congress of Industrial Organizations) in 1935; as vice-president of CIO, directed Steel Workers Organizing Committee (1936); first and only president of United Steelworkers of America beginning 1937; president of CIO beginning 1940. See *Current Biography*, 1949.

Obituary

N Y Times p1+ N 10 '52

NAGUIB, MOHAMMED (nă-gēb') Feb. 20, 1901- Premier of Egypt; Army officer

Address: Cairo, Egypt

Major General Mohammed Naguib, the fifty-one-year-old Commander in Chief of the Egyptian armed forces, who led the July 23, 1952, *coup d'état* which brought about the abdication of King Farouk, assumed the Premiership of Egypt and the post of Minister of War and Marine on the following September 7. As Premier he succeeded Aly Maher, his own nominee for the position six weeks earlier, who had been regarded as "too cautious" in pushing forward an announced program of purging existing political parties of corrupt elements and the breaking up of large estates for redistribution to the peasantry. Naguib, who achieved some recognition in his own country through his part in the Egyptian campaign against Israel in 1948, was unknown outside the Middle East before his recent assumption of political power.

The new Premier and "strong man" of Egypt comes from soldier stock; his Sudanese grandfather on his mother's side was a lieutenant colonel in the Egyptian Army and died with the British General Charles Gordon in the siege of Khartoum in 1885; while his father, Captain Youssef Naguib, was a veteran of the subsequent successful expedition under General Kitchener to liberate the Sudan from the Mahdi. The eldest of three sons in a family of nine children, Mohammed Naguib was born at Khartoum on February 20, 1901; he spent his boyhood at Wad Medani, where his father was stationed as a District Commissioner. At the local Moslem school, he excelled in football, while in studies he easily led his fellow pupils. District Commissioner Naguib envisioned a career in teaching or the law for his eldest son, but the boy had other ambitions. "One night while his roommates slept," as related in an article in *Time*, "he sneaked out of school and made his way on foot and by paddle steamer to Cairo, 1,000 miles away." There he presented himself to the Royal Military Academy, where he so impressed the admissions board with his zeal and brilliance that he was before long accepted as a student.

Having completed the scheduled two-and-a-half year course at the academy in nine months, Naguib received his commission as a second lieutenant of infantry at the age of nineteen. A dispatch to the New York *Times* has stressed that Naguib's "formative years were . . . spent in a period when British military ascendancy over Egypt [a British protectorate since 1914] was complete, but when Egyptian nationalism, under Mohammed Zaghlul Pasha, founder of the Wafdist party, was developing rapidly." Naguib had been an officer for less than three years when, on February 28, 1922, pressure by the nationalists caused Britain to declare Egypt "an independent, sovereign state," at the same time reserving the right to station troops therein for the defense of the country and of the Suez Canal.

In the period between the two world wars, Naguib rose gradually through grades, but saw no field action. Since his military duties were light, to occupy his mind he took courses (for which he holds degrees in law and political economy) at Fuad I University and also taught himself to speak German, French, Italian, and English. His country being technically neutral in World War II, Naguib passed most of the period from 1939 to 1945 at an administrative job in the Adjutant General's office; thus it was not until May 1948, when Egypt launched her expedition against the new state of Israel, that he saw military action. While reportedly opposed to invading Palestine because he believed that the Egyptian Army was not prepared for a desert campaign, he led a machine gun and infantry regiment in the Sinai desert, was three times seriously wounded and once left for dead upon the battlefield. For his heroism in the fight against Israel he was awarded the Fuad I Star. Naguib's experiences in the Israel campaign made him a crusader for reform. "While fighting upon the burning sands of the desert," he was subsequently to tell David Duncan of *Life*, "we learned that the enemy was lurking not only in the night before us, but was also entrenched in our cities behind us—traitors of our own blood. Weapons were delivered to our troops, but minus vital parts. . . .Medical supplies for our wounded, and they were many, came through to us in pitiful quantities. Many items of field equipment desperately needed by fighting men never arrived at all."

Now a national hero, Naguib, who went into the campaign a brigadier and emerged a major general, was made chief of the frontier administration and was so occupied when in 1950 details of the Israel war supply transactions became known, revealing corruption extending into the palace of King Farouk. For personally assailing the "unbearable corruption," he was demoted to command of the Infantry Training School in Cairo. This was, however, a "key position . . . to establish good relations with the rising generation of officers" (New York *Times*), and as a result a reform-minded organization calling itself Dobbat el Ahrar (Free Officers) came into being. "Except for myself," Naguib later told David Duncan, "there was no man involved who held rank higher than lieutenant colonel. . . .None had any connection with any political party or religious group." The next important development occurred during the early part of 1952, when the Free Officers were successful in electing Naguib president of the Cairo Officers Club over Commander in Chief Haidar Pasha, a palace favorite. King Farouk declared the election invalid, dissolved the general committee of the club, and shortly afterward, when a new Premier, Hussein Sirry Pasha, tried to form a Cabinet, vetoed the latter's choice of Naguib as Minister of War and Marine. With the appointment by Sirry's successor, Ahmed El Hilaly Pasha, of Farouk's brother-in-law to the cabinet post, Naguib, who had hitherto been "reluctant to move against the King," now agreed to take the leadership in a *coup d'état* which had been under discussion ever since the Cairo Officers' Club incident.

The tactics of the July 1952 coup (Naguib's own account of which appeared in *Life*, August 25, 1952) were said by some reporters to be planned by an advisory board of former German army officers. Early in the morning on July 23, the Egyptian Free Officers "moved into Cairo with big field guns and tanks and cordoned off the palace and communications facilities" (*Time*), and by 11:30 A.M. Naguib broadcast that he was in "complete control." Premier Hilaly had meanwhile resigned, and King Farouk, at the insistence of the newly proclaimed Army Commander in Chief Naguib, called on Ali Maher, leader of an offshoot of the Wafdist party and "a wealthy conservative with a good record as a reformer," to form a government. Three days later (July 26) Farouk abdicated in favor of his infant son, who was proclaimed King Ahmed Fuad II, and was permitted to leave for Italy with his queen and children. Naguib had meanwhile proclaimed an intention to "leave politics to the politicians," but his hand was detected in the action of the Cabinet in abolishing the Egyptian peerage on July 30 and in the Maher Government's proposed land reform legislation for the wholesale expropriation of private lands," wrote Michael Clark of the New York *Times*. "No individual, endowment or company would be allowed to hold more than 200 acres of farm land. The surplus would be expropriated by the

Wide World Photos

MAJ. GEN. MOHAMMED NAGUIB

state and distributed among the landless poor and peasants holding less than two acres." At the same time General Naguib personally announced that elections for a new Egyptian Parliament would be held in February 1953, provided that political parties had meanwhile been purged of "corrupt elements."

Because of Premier Maher's desire to proceed with caution, by the beginning of September it was rumored that friction between the Army and the civilian government had become such that Maher's resignation was imminent. That resignation was submitted on September 7, at which time General Naguib formed a Cabinet with himself as Premier (Egypt's seventh Premier since January 1952) and Minister of War and Marine. "It was the first time in contemporary Egyptian history," the New York *Times* pointed out, "that an army general had occupied the Premier's chair." After jailing former aides of King Farouk and leaders of the powerful Wafdist party, Naguib on September 9 proclaimed a "quarantine" of existing political parties for one month, during which time they would be required to satisfy the Interior Minister as to their aims, resources, and organization, or face dissolution. On the same day the Cabinet, comprising fifteen civilian experts, adopted the army's land reform program, which was sent to the Regency Council for promulgation. Later in September Naguib requested the Royal Egyptian Medical Association to undertake a study of the British National Health Scheme in order to make proposals for a national health plan in Egypt. In foreign affairs the Premier has publicly expressed himself in favor of military and economic cooperation with Western nations. Political observers have pointed out a parallel situation between

NAGUIB, MOHAMMED—*Continued*

Kemal Ataturk of Turkey and Naguib in seizing the government for purposes of reform, noting, however, that Naguib lacks a political party to support his measures.

Premier Naguib, whose own faith is the Moslem, is on record as favoring complete freedom of worship. He is married and has three sons, Farouk, Youssef, and Ali; his one daughter is deceased. The General stands five feet six inches tall. He was characterized by L. S. Chakales in the Washington *Post* as a man who "likes people" and thinks they are "intelligent, patriotic, and instinctively good." His home life is described by the same writer as "simple . . . almost Spartan."

References

Life 33:103+ Ag 25 '52 pors
N Y Herald Tribune p60 S 7 '52
N Y Times p3 Jl 24 '52
Newsweek 40:38 Ag 1 '52 por; 40:32+ Ag 25 '52
Pathfinder 57:30 Ag 6 '52 por
Time 60:25-6 Ag 4 '52; 60:35-9 S 8 '52 pors
Washington (D.C.) Post p3B Ag 24 '52 por

NUCKOLS, WILLIAM P(RESTON) Apr. 13, 1905- United States Air Force officer

Address: b. c/o Department of the Air Force, The Pentagon, Washington 25, D.C.

The official spokesman for the United Nations delegation in armistice conferences with North Korean and Chinese Communists at Panmunjom, Korea, from mid-1951 to July 1952, as well as the Allied briefing officer for newspaper correspondents at the headquarters of General Matthew Ridgway, was Brigadier

U. S. Air Force

BRIG. GEN. WILLIAM P. NUCKOLS

General William P. Nuckols of the United States Air Force. Following a newspaper career, three years of service in the Army Air Corps, and four years in the public relations field in civilian life, he was recalled to active duty in 1938. During World War II he saw service in Europe. His duty in the Orient dates from the summer of 1950, when he was ordered to Tokyo as public information officer of the Far East Air Forces. It was to this post that he returned upon his departure from Korea in the summer of 1952.

William Preston Nuckols was born in Atlantic City, New Jersey, on April 13, 1905. Upon completing secondary school he attended Swarthmore College and the University of Virginia Law School. Entering the newspaper field, he was employed successively as a reporter, special writer, as an editor on daily papers in Richmond, Virginia, in his native Atlantic City, and in Miami, Florida.

Nuckols was twenty-six years old when, in June 1931, he first entered the Army Air Corps as a cadet. Graduated from flying school a year later with a pilot's rating and a second lieutenant's commission in the Air Reserve, he was assigned to France Field in the Panama Canal Zone for duty both as pilot and as public relations officer of a bombardment squadron. He was relieved from active duty in June 1934, and for nearly four years thereafter was engaged in publicity work in New York City, helping among other things to promote the New York World's Fair.

The rearmament program and expansion of the Army Air Forces brought his recall to active duty in March 1938 and his assignment to Randolph Field in Texas, where he was instrumental in establishing and conducting a public relations program for attracting cadets. He was promoted to first lieutenant (temporary) in March 1939 and to captain (temporary) in February 1941.

Still occupied with public relations at Randolph Field when the Pearl Harbor attack brought the United States into World War II, Captain Nuckols was made a major (temporary) in February 1942 and a lieutenant colonel (temporary) in the following July. His advancement to colonel (temporary) came on December 12, 1942, with his reassignment to the Pentagon in Washington, D.C., as Deputy Director of the War Department Bureau of Public Relations for Air. Transferred to the European theater of operations in September 1943, Colonel Nuckols served under Lieutenant General Hoyt S. Vandenberg as a member of the Plans Division of the Allied Expeditionary Air Force, which was charged with coordinating the air effort in the coming invasion of France. Then, just before the Normandy landings in June 1944, he was named chief of the AEAF information division and air member of the SHAEF public relations staff. His final duty in Europe, beginning in September 1944, was as public relations officer of General Vandenberg's 9th Air Force. For his World War II service Nuckols has been awarded the Legion of Merit and the Bronze Star Medal. He is rated as a senior pilot.

Returned to the United States in August 1945, Colonel Nuckols became director of the Air Force School of Public Relations at Orlando, Florida. Deciding to remain in the service after the war, he received his first regular commission as captain (permanent) in July 1946. Promoted to major (permanent) in the following April, he held that rank when, on July 26, 1947, the Air Force became a separate service within the new Department of Defense. Two months later (September) Nuckols was again assigned to Washington, this time as deputy director of the Air Information Division, Directorate of Public Relations, Office of the Secretary of the Air Force; and in January 1948 he became director of the division. Promoted to colonel (permanent) in April, he was named Special Assistant to the Director of Public Relations in February 1949. Relieved of this duty in August, he entered the Air War College at Maxwell Air Force base in Alabama, and on graduation in July 1950 was appointed public information officer with the Far East Air Force at Tokyo, Japan. Nuckols was made a brigadier general (temporary) on October 4, 1950.

In his earlier Air Force public relations assignments the name of the newly promoted brigadier general had been comparatively little known beyond press and military circles. This, however, changed after his appointment late in July 1951 as Deputy Chief of Information of the United Nations Command and official briefing officer for United Nations correspondents covering armistice negotiations near Kaesong, Korea. "Until General Nuckols took over this job in the peace train," stated a New York Times dispatch from Tokyo, "a series of army officers had served in that capacity. It was a job no one wanted and it was assigned to General Nuckols as a last resort to try to patch up . . . quarrels betwen the press and the Army Public Information Office." The dispatch reported that Nuckols had already "managed quite skillfully as a mediator" in his "paradoxical" tasks of "persuading United Nations delegates to make news available to the press and to persuade the correspondents to desist from prying too closely into the details of the conference." His routine in a sixteen-hour working day which carried him from camp to conference room and back again was described. "At the close of the meetings," said the Times, "he fences off the correspondents, runs interference for the photographers, and then returns to the camp with the delegates. Here it is decided what can be made available to the press and what must be withheld."

A "good phrasemaker," Brigadier General Nuckols received praise in mid-August (1951) for his definition of the United Nations delegation's attitude as "'patient' toward Communist stubbornness, 'firm' in insistence on a sound defense line, 'reasonable' toward any feasible adjustment of the line, 'persistent' in pressing toward a realistic military armistice." ("Four Good Words" was the heading of a New York Times editorial.) Nuckols remained at Kaesong until the end of the same month, when he was reassigned to the Japanese Peace Conference at San Francisco; but he was back in Korea when the armistice talks, which had meanwhile been broken off, were resumed at Panmunjom on October 25, 1951. In July 1952 he left Korea to return to Tokyo as public information officer of the Far East Air Forces.

William P. Nuckols and Alice Browne of Karnes City, Texas, were married in 1933. The General is described in the New York Times as "tall . . . with a casual manner and a slight stammer."

References

N Y Herald Tribune II p1 S 2 '51 por
N Y Times p4 Ag 1 '51 por

NYROP, DONALD W(ILLIAM) (nĭ′rŏp)
Apr. 1, 1912- United States Government official; lawyer

Address: h. 3436 Martha Custis Dr., Alexandria, Va.

Active in civil and military aviation for more than a decade, Donald W. Nyrop became Chairman of the Civil Aeronautics Board in April of 1951, and at the end of that year President Truman reappointed him to that "top policymaking agency in aeronautics." His resignation from his post as chairman of the CAB was announced on October 15, 1952. The aviation executive began his Federal service in 1939 as an attorney for the Civil Aeronautics Authority, and during World War II was an Army officer in the Air Transport Command. In 1948 he was a Deputy Administrator for the Civil Aeronautics Administration, the agency in the Department of Commerce which carries out the policies and regulations of the Civil Aeronautics Board. In September 1950 Nyrop became the chief executive of the CAA, remaining in this position until his selection as Chairman of the CAB in 1951.

Born in Elgin, Nebraska, on April 1, 1912, Donald William Nyrop is the son of William A. and Nellie (Wylie) Nyrop. He completed his undergraduate studies at Doane College in Nebraska in 1934, receiving in that year the B.A. degree. He then left his native State for the District of Columbia, where he studied law at George Washington University. Five years later, in 1939, he was granted the LL.B. degree; the year previous he had been admitted to practice in the District of Columbia.

Nyrop's career in the Government began in 1939 when he became an attorney in the General Counsel's office of the Civil Aeronautics Authority and the Civil Aeronautics Board. At the end of two years, in January of 1942, he became executive officer to the Chairman of the CAB. He entered upon three and a quarter years of World War II duty in September 1942, joining the United States Army Air Forces as executive operations officer in the Air Transport Command. Upon his release from active military duty with the rank of lieutenant colonel in January of 1946, he was awarded the Legion of Merit medal.

Nyrop now became a representative of the United States Airlines and was a specialist in international policy matters for the Air Transportation Association. In 1946 and again in

DONALD W. NYROP

1947 he was a member of the official United States delegation to the International Civil Aviation Organization Assembly. The next year, in August 1948, he returned to Government service by accepting the position of Deputy Administrator in charge of operations for the Civil Aeronautics Administration. In September 1950 he became the Administrator. About six months later President Truman nominated him to the post of Chairman of the Civil Aeronautics Board, an appointment confirmed by the United States Senate on April 17, 1951. He was reappointed by President Truman in December 1951.

The Government agency with which Nyrop was associated dates back to 1938, when the Civil Aeronautics Act was passed to create an independent agency composed of the Civil Aeronautics Authority, with five members, the Administrator, and the Air Safety Board, with three members. Later the Reorganization Act of 1939 changed the name of the policy-making group to the Civil Aeronautics Board, with power to make rules, prescribe regulations and standards, and to investigate and adjudicate independently of the Secretary of Commerce. Certain functions of the aeronautics authority were transferred to the Civil Aeronautics Administration, the head of that organization working under the direction and supervision of the Secretary of Commerce. The five members of the Board are appointed by the President with Senate approval, one member being designated annually as chairman and another as vice-chairman. All members serve for a period of six years.

The four chief functions of the Board which Nyrop headed are the regulation of economic aspects of air carrier operations, such as the fixing of rates for passenger and air mail service; the promulgation of safety standards and civil air regulations; the investigation of aircraft accidents; and cooperation in estab-

lishing and developing international air transportation. In the language of the *United States Government Organization Manual*, the Civil Aeronautics Administration "encourages and fosters the development of civil aeronautics and air commerce; encourages the establishment of civil airways, landing areas, and other air navigation aids and facilities; . . . makes provisions for the control and protection of air traffic; . . . maintains and operates the Washington National Airport; . . . has under construction two airports in Alaska; . . . and also enforces the civil air regulations prescribed by the Civil Aeronautics Board." In connection with the last-named function, the agency examines and inspects airmen and aircraft, issues safety certificates, and registers aircraft. Programs to aid in the construction of airports and to increase the training of air personnel are also carried on by the CAA. All civil aviation defense production requirements are collected and processed by the Administration, which maintains nine regional offices.

Nyrop's first report as Civil Aeronautics Administrator, issued in December of 1950, stated that civil flying during that year had played an important role in the nation's economy. Scheduled airlines in the United States had carried a total of 18,828,000 paying passengers and had flown them a total distance of 460,453,000 miles, with only four accidents. He further reported that more than half of the 92,650 civil aircraft in the country had been used in business and agriculture. Referring to this last use, Nyrop predicted an increased use of planes for such agricultural operations as dusting, spraying, seeding, and fertilizing from the air, especially in the quantity production of major crops. During 1950 about 5,000 planes, operated by almost 2,000 firms and individuals, had been used for these purposes. While Administrator of the CAA Nyrop concerned himself with assisting civil aviation to "make a maximum contribution to national defense," as he phrased it in an article for *Skyway*, "with a minimum of dislocation and restriction on the industry." To that end he authorized the issuance of defense-order ratings, which would help the airlines obtain necessary parts and electronic devices, and from the National Production Authority he received assurances that the materials would be available.

Soon after Nyrop assumed the chairmanship of the CAB, a change in the program of subsidy payments to airlines was announced. Formerly payments for air mail service were combined with a Government subsidy system and the whole charged to the Post Office Department. Following the recommendations of the Hoover Commission, the Board announced its intention to separate the payments, so that subsidy money, openly appropriated by Congress from tax funds, could be clearly distinguished from payments for carrying the mails. The change was expected to result in an estimated saving of $6 millions yearly. Nyrop, who called the change an "administrative separation," said (in the words of the New York *Times*) that it was "one of the Board's most important actions of the last thirteen years."

Public awareness of the CAB in 1952 has centered around its investigations and rulings made in connection with several major air crashes, particularly in the vicinity of the Newark (New Jersey) airport. As a result of CAB action, the Newark airport was partially closed, all overseas flights to and from La Guardia Airport on Long Island were eliminated, and domestic flights were reduced by 226 flights a day. Later the CAB charged the airline whose plane had crashed over Elizabeth, New Jersey, in December 1951, with overloading and failure to train pilots properly in emergency procedures and also found the company which had overhauled the plane's engine guilty of faulty mechanical work. In addition, the CAB, acting jointly with the CAA, tightened the operating procedures and regulations for the nonscheduled airlines. Investigation had demonstrated to the Board the "inadequate" operating procedures of some of these lines and "carelessness" in the selection and training of pilots. The new regulations, already in effect for the scheduled lines, are expected to promote greater safety both for passengers as well as for residents in areas adjacent to airports. Nyrop resigned from the chairmanship of the CAB on October 15, 1952, his resignation to become effective on November 1.

The former CAB chairman is a member of the Society for the Advancement of Management. He married Grace Cary on April 17, 1941, and has one child, Nancy.

References

N Y Times p8 Mr 20 '51
N Y World-Telegram p13 F 16 '52
Who's Who in America, 1952-53

O'NEILL, J(OHN) E(DWARD) Oct. 21, 1892- Automobile association official; rancher; business executive

Address: b. P.O. Box 1832, Fresno, Calif.; c/o American Automobile Association, 17th St. & Pennsylvania Ave., Washington 6, D.C.; h. 3406 Huntington Blvd., Fresno, Calif.

For thirty-five years a member of the American Automobile Association, J. E. O'Neill of California was elected in October 1951 to the presidency of the half-century-old organization of motorists. Before entering upon that office he had been a member of the board of directors and president of the California State Automobile Association and a director, member of the executive committee, and senior vice-president of the national organization. O'Neill, a cotton grower and cattleman, is the founder, vice-president, and director of the Producers Cotton Oil Company of Fresno, California, and a member of the board of directors of three general farming and livestock corporations.

John Edward O'Neill was born in Pendleton, Ontario, Canada, on October 21, 1892, one of seven children in the family of Andrew and Catherine (Brownrigg) O'Neill. His grandparents were immigrants to Canada—his two grandfathers came from County Cork, Ireland, one grandmother from Scotland, and the other

Gladser Studio

J. E. O'NEILL

from France. His family, which, as he phrases it, were "poor but of proud pioneer stock," had a farm near Ottawa, where the boy spent his early years. On the completion of his elementary schooling he began to work. Saving enough from his earnings to pay for a course in shorthand and typewriting, he was able in 1910 to get a position as a stenographer in the Canadian Parliament at a weekly salary of seven dollars. A year later he obtained employment with the Ottawa Hide and Leather Company.

In 1914 the twenty-two-year-old Canadian left for the United States, going to Calexico, in the Imperial Valley of Southern California. O'Neill recalled that experience for *Today*, the publication of the American Automobile Association: "As I stepped down off the train, feeling just like an Eastern dude, I wanted more than anything else to be taken for a Westerner. I spent $9.50 for a big old cowboy hat; though it was most of my money [he had arrived with $17.50], that hat was well worth it."

O'Neill soon found a job as office boy and stenographer for the Pacific Cotton Company. In his free time he studied accounting and, on a part-time basis, kept books for several other firms. In 1917, after suggesting a system for revising the bookkeeping of a large produce shipping company in the Imperial Valley, he was employed by the firm, first as timekeeper and later as superintendent. He remained with the shipping firm five years. In 1917 O'Neill acquired some land of his own and not long afterward brought his parents and five brothers from Canada to California. When he lost his farm in the early depression years (1920-21), he moved to Los Angeles. Later, in 1926, he was able to return to agriculture, this time in the San Joaquin Valley, where experiments in the growing of cotton on irrigated soil were just beginning. He developed a cotton farm in the western part of Fresno County, devising

O'NEILL, J. E.—*Continued*

new methods of irrigation and producing cotton on the once-barren land. In 1930 he was one of the principal organizers of the Producers Cotton Oil Company, which consists of a brokerage house, advisory service company, and cotton seed oil milling and ginning division. In 1952 O'Neill is vice-president and a member of the board of directors of the company.

In the course of the years since 1930 O'Neill has established other farms and ranches in the San Joaquin Valley, marketing the products through the J. E. O'Neill, Inc., the O'Neill Farms, Inc., and the A. M. O'Neill & Sons, Inc. In 1952 O'Neill is the president and director of the first two companies, and vice-president and director of the last-named. His holdings on the west side of the valley amount to 5,000 acres, and on the east side he owns 10,000 acres of ranch land with approximately 10,000 head of cattle.

Soon after establishing himself in the Imperial Valley, O'Neill became a member of the Automobile Club of Southern California and, later, of the California State Automobile Association. In 1939 he was elected a member of the board of directors of the State group, and two years later was elected a director of the American Automobile Association, the national organization. He became president of the State body in 1945 and a member of the executive committee of the A.A.A. in 1947. In 1949 he was elected senior vice-president of the national organization and also served as chairman of the traffic safety committee. In October of 1951 O'Neill was chosen to fill the nonsalaried post of president of the A.A.A.

The American Automobile Association was founded in Chicago in 1902 by nine `pioneer automobile clubs, for the purpose of protecting and advancing interests and needs of owners of automobiles. As motor travel increased (in 1952 there are approximately 52,000,000 registered motor vehicles in the United States), district and State clubs were formed as affiliates of the national association. In 1952 there is a total membership of 3,500,000 in 750 affiliated clubs paying fees ranging from five dollars to twenty dollars a year for emergency road service, road maps, and information about lodgings for tourists, restaurants, and other motoring services. In 1951 a total of almost $35 millions was paid in fees to the local clubs (which contribute 25 cents a member to the national club) to cover the cost of such services. Some 35,000 repair and tow trucks, under contract to the local clubs, traveled in 1951 a distance of 10,000,000 miles to answer emergency calls from members. The A.A.A. conducts a youth safety program, a course in driving for high school students, and maintains ten field reporters who check on road conditions, hotel accommodations, motor courts, and eating places. On its fiftieth anniversary, which was observed in March 1952, in Chicago, the A.A.A. became the subject of a United States postage stamp.

The white-haired rancher has blue eyes, **stands five feet seven inches tall,** and weighs 175 pounds. He is a member of the West Side Land Owners Association (which is cooperating with the Federal government in long-range irrigation projects), is chairman of the Fresno County Agricultural Conservation Association, and is the president and a member of the board of directors of the 21st District Agricultural Association. O'Neill's clubs are the Rotary, the Sunnyside Country, and the Sequoia. He is a Democrat. A communicant of the Catholic Church, he belongs to the Knights of Columbus and wears the papal decoration of St. Gregory the Great, which was bestowed upon him in 1949 by Pope Pius XII. In January of 1918 the Californian married Hughina M. Brunet (now deceased), by whom he has a daughter, Virginia Patricia (Mrs. C. J. Heflin) and two sons, John Edward, Jr., and Dennis Hugh. His marriage to his second wife, Paloma (who was a schoolteacher), took place July 4, 1932; their children are Margaret Catherine and Edwin Randle. Two of his favorite diversions are riding and giving Western-style barbecues at which he serves O'Neill-labeled beef.

Reference

Today p3-4 O 25 '51

OURSLER, FULTON Jan. 22, 1893—May 24, 1952 Writer, editor; edited *Metropolitan* magazine (1923), *Liberty* magazine (1931-42); became vice-president and editorial director of Macfadden Publications in 1941, and a senior editor of the *Reader's Digest* in 1944; writer of plays, motion picture scenarios, novels, short stories, magazine articles, and newspaper columns; noted for popular treatment of religious subjects as in *The Greatest Story Ever Told* (1949). See *Current Biography*, 1942.

Obituary

N Y Times p92 My 25 '52

PACKER, FRED L(ITTLE) Jan. 4, 1886- Cartoonist

Address: b. c/o New York Daily Mirror, 235 E. 45th St., New York 17; h. 216 Lakeview Ave. E., Brightwaters, N.Y.

The selection of the Pulitzer Prize awards in May 1952 for distinguished achievement during the preceding year brought the $1,000 award for editorial cartooning to Fred L. Packer, of the New York *Daily Mirror*. His winning cartoon, as described by *Time*, "lampooned Truman's confusing press conference remarks about the press handling of classified information." Associated for twenty years with the *Mirror*, to which he came as a protégé of Arthur Brisbane, Packer had previously worked for the same editor on the New York *Journal* and the New York *American*. Except for a twelve-year period (1919-31), when he was engaged in commercial and advertising art, Packer has devoted the major part of his career to newspaper work, having entered the field on the Los Angeles *Examiner* and the San Francisco *Call-Post*. His cartoons and posters for the World War II defense effort earned him citations from the Treasury Department and War Production Board.

Fred Little Packer was born in a suburban section of Los Angeles, California, on January 4, 1886. His mother, the former Elizabeth Little, was a daughter of Martha Little, who had come to California in a covered wagon. Jacob W. Packer, his father, arrived on the Pacific Coast in the late 1860's from his birthplace in Ohio; he was the propagator of a number of rare varieties of roses. (Besides Fred, the Packers had one other son, Glen J. Packer, three years his elder, who was associated with the sheriff's office in Los Angeles prior to his death in 1947.) After attending the Los Angeles public schools, young Packer studied at the Los Angeles School of Art and Design in 1902-03. In 1904 and 1905 he was a student at the Chicago Art Institute, where he was a member of the theatrical group and played center on the students' football team. Of his early influences Packer has said that he was greatly encouraged by the late F. M. Townsend, a patent attorney and friend of the family, and later by E. D. Coblentz, a Hearst executive.

When his studies at the Chicago Art Institute were completed, Packer in 1906 joined the staff of the Los Angeles *Examiner* as an artist, supplying drawings for the Sunday supplements. Some of his sketches were of courtroom scenes. A New York *Daily Mirror* biographical piece on Packer recorded that he left the *Examiner* in 1907 to work for the San Francisco *Call*. When the *Call* was succeeded by the *Call-Post*, Packer became art director of that paper, a position he has held from 1913 to 1918. The next year Packer left Los Angeles for New York, where he worked until 1931 as a commercial artist, doing book and magazine illustration as well as art work for leading advertisers. Among the advertisers who retained him were Vivadue, Kellogg's, Procter & Gamble, Congoleum, Cliquot Club, White Rose, and J. C. Penney.

The artist returned to newspaper work in 1932 as cartoonist on the New York *Journal* and New York *American*. "His editorial cartoons caught the eye of the late Arthur Brisbane," said the *Mirror* biography. "After the death of Winsor McKay," Packer told, "I did most of the Sunday editorial cartoons for Arthur Brisbane." When Brisbane took over the editorship of the New York *Daily Mirror* in 1933, he moved his preferred cartoonist from the *Journal* staff to the *Mirror*, with which Packer continues to be associated in 1952.

When the annual Pulitzer Prizes were decided upon on May 5, 1952, it was announced that Fred L. Packer would receive the $1,000 prize for cartooning done during 1951. Although the award takes into consideration the artist's entire output for the year, the specific cartoon for which Packer was cited had appeared on October 6, 1951, in the New York *Daily Mirror*. Captioned "Your editors ought to have more sense than to print what I say!" the cartoon showed President Truman "lecturing" the Washington press corps. It had been occasioned by the President's recent criticism of newspaper releases on United States mili-

FRED L. PACKER

tary supplies and installations, information which, it subsequently developed, had been approved by the various Government agencies involved. The Pulitzer Prize committee citation accompanying the award read in part: "For a distinguished example of a cartoonist's work in a United States newspaper . . . the determining qualities being that the cartoon shall embody an idea made clearly apparent, shall show good drawing and striking pictorial effect, and shall be intended to be helpful to some commendable cause of public importance."

Some time earlier Packer had been awarded citations from the Treasury Department and the War Production Board for the cartoons and posters he supplied for their drives during World War II. From 1942 to 1946 Packer was vice-president of Victory Builders, the organization that prepared colored posters for war industries, intended to spur production. Other work Packer has executed, for the American Red Cross and the American Cancer Society, has brought him special recognition.

Packer's political party is the Republican, and his church is the Presbyterian. He is founder and president of the South Shore Arts Association of Long Island, New York. A resident of the Long Island community of Brightwaters, Packer lives there with his family—his wife, the former Mrs. Lillian Pabst Wilson, and his stepdaughter, Marjorie. The Packers' marriage took place on February 14, 1941. Standing six feet one inch tall, the cartoonist weighs 178 pounds. His hair is light in color, his eyes are blue. He likes to relax with a mystery or adventure story; or when he is not at his drawing board, he may turn to painting or color photography.

References

N Y Daily Mirror p2 My 6 '52
N Y Times p24 My 6 '52
Who's Who in America, 1952-53

PADOVER, SAUL K(USSIEL) (păd'
ōv-ĕr kōōs'ĕl) Apr. 13, 1905- Educator; historian

Address: b. c/o New School for Social Research,
66 W. 12th St., New York 11; h. 161 W. 54th St.,
New York 19

Dean of the School of Politics of the New
School for Social Research Dr. Saul K. Padover is a widely recognized authority on the
political thought of Thomas Jefferson and author of several books about this early American.

SAUL K. PADOVER

Apart from his work in education, historical
research, and writing, Padover from 1939 to
1943 held the position of assistant to the
United States Secretary of the Interior and in
the winter of 1944-45 was a member of a special team of investigators sent to Germany by
the Office of Strategic Services to gather information for formulating United States occupation policy. Before joining the graduate faculty of the New School in 1949, Padover was
for two years an editorial writer for the newspaper *PM*.

Born in Austria on April 13, 1905, Saul
Kussiel Padover is the son of Keva and Fanny
(Goldmann) Padover. His father, an American
citizen, was descended from Jewish forebears
living in Padua (or Padova), Italy, from which
the name "Padover" was taken. From Austria,
where the family had moved early in the nineteenth century, they migrated to Memphis, Tennessee, around the year 1890. The maternal
branch of Saul K. Padover's family were
farmer-squires in Austria who lived for 150
years on land originally granted the family by
Emperor Joseph II. Saul and his older brother
were raised by their mother in Vienna until
1920, when their father sent for the family to
join him in the United States. In Detroit,
Michigan, Saul attended grammar school and

Northeastern High School, from which he was
graduated in 1925. As a high school student he
edited the school paper, was president of his
class, and played tennis and rode a bicycle for
exercise.

While specializing in history and English at
Wayne University in Detroit, Padover edited
the university literary magazine, wrote a signed
column in the school's paper, and was a member
of the journalistic fraternity. Upon being
awarded the B.A. degree *cum laude* in 1928, he
attended graduate classes at Yale University
during the year 1928-29. At the University of
Chicago he took his M.A. degree in 1930, having
submitted a thesis entitled *The Homestead
Strike*, and his Ph.D. degree in 1932, for which
he wrote the dissertation *Prince Kaunitz and
the First Partition of Poland*. His advanced
education was financed by a university fellowship (1930-32), a professorship in history at
the West Virginia State College (summers of
1930 and 1931), and a research assistantship at
the University of Chicago (1932). From 1933
to 1936 he was employed as a research associate in history at the University of California
and in the summer of 1935 as a lecturer in history. Studying under a Guggenheim Fellowship
he was engaged in research during 1936-37 in
the archives of Paris, Vienna, and London.

Padover joined the staff of the United States
Department of the Interior in 1938 as personal
and confidential assistant to Secretary Harold
L. Ickes. While holding this position until
1943, he was made consultant in 1942 to the
Office of Facts and Figures and in November
1942 became director of the department's Research Unit on Territorial Policy, which post
he filled until November 1943. Meanwhile, in
1943 and 1944, he went to London as the principal political analyst of the Federal Communications Commission. As an intelligence officer
with the assimilated rank of lieutenant colonel,
he entered the Office of Strategic Services in
1944, being attached to the Psychological Warfare Department of the First, Third, and
Ninth Armies of the United States. Padover,
who landed at Normandy shortly after D-Day,
was in the center of fighting through the French
and German campaigns; after the breakthrough
at the Rhine he and his group were often a
considerable distance ahead of the American
Army. In the winter of 1944-45, working for
the O.S.S. with two other American civilians,
Dr. Paul Robinson Sweet of Bates College and
Lewis F. Gittler of the Office of War Information, Padover interrogated a large number of
German civilians in order to obtain information upon which the American Military Government could base its policies. His work led to
a transformation of the denazification activities
of the AMG, since his report on Aachen,
strongly relied upon by General Dwight D.
Eisenhower in the formation of policy, was
one of the influences behind Eisenhower's removal of General George S. Patton from
Munich, after the latter had made his muchpublicized statement that there was as little difference between Nazis and non-Nazis as there
was between Democrats and Republicans in the
United States. In presenting Padover with the
Citation for the Bronze Star Medal, President

Truman praised the social scientist for his "distinguished and meritorious services," for producing "interrogation reports of great value," and for obtaining "at considerable risk" information upon which important policies were based.

Speaking in New York City in October 1945 at the *Herald Tribune* Forum on Current Problems, Padover, who in that year was the recipient of a Rockefeller Fellowship, urged a combination of military occupation and self-government on local levels in Germany as the optimum solution for problems in the occupation of that country. Padover went to Germany in 1946 on a mission as consultant to the United States War Department. From 1946 to 1948 he wrote a signed column for the New York City newspaper *PM*, also serving this publication as foreign correspondent. In an article about the Soviet Union for *PM* he stated in 1947, "It is a tragedy that, in the name of socialism, a self-chosen elite should deprive men of . . . rights without which there can be neither popular culture nor human dignity." Returning to the field of education in 1948, Padover was engaged for the next two years in research and consultation at the Hoover Institute of Stanford University in California. During 1949 he gave a course at the Sorbonne University in Paris as Visiting Professor of American Politics. His association with the New School for Social Research began in 1947 with his appointment as a lecturer, from which position he was advanced to professor in the graduate faculty in 1949 and to Dean of the School of Politics in 1950.

An authority on the political theories of Thomas Jefferson, Padover has produced a number of books on this subject, with another currently scheduled for publication. The author became interested in this early American when studying at the University of Chicago under Professor William E. Dodd, the noted historian, who inspired Padover to specialize in American history, with emphasis on the Jeffersonian period. *Thomas Jefferson on Democracy* (1939), which Padover edited, is a collection of excerpts from Jefferson letters and writings expressing his social and political concepts. In the opinion of the *Saturday Review of Literature*, "The book is expert, skillfully arranged, logical . . . will prove a stimulating surprise to those who think Jefferson somehow belongs to the eighteenth century." President Roosevelt kept a copy of this work on his desk for frequent reference and once presented a copy to Harold Laski with the inscription, "I think you will like this as I did: a fine sample of Jefferson at his best." On Padover's biography, *Thomas Jefferson*, the critic for *American Historical Review* commented, "This volume, containing little, if anything, new to the student of Jefferson, is one of the most attractive and readable studies in compact form of its highly versatile and interesting subject." Other of Padover's publications about Jefferson are *The Complete Jefferson* (1943), *Jefferson and the National Capital* (1945), and *A Jefferson Profile*. "Secretary Ickes and I," Padover has said, "were responsible for the inscription in the Jefferson Monument in Washington: 'I have sworn upon the

altar of the Almighty eternal hostility to tyranny over the mind of man.' " These words, selected by Padover, were delivered to President Roosevelt in a covering letter by Ickes.

An early book by Padover, *Let the Day Perish* (1932), is an account of the persecutions suffered by the Polish Jews in World War I and the years immediately afterward. "The attitude of the author," the Chicago *Daily Tribune* found, "is passionately partisan. . . . There is no mellowness. . . . The style is direct, picturesque, and honest." *The Life and Death of Louis XVI* (1939) was described by the New York *Times* as "a full-length biography of the unfortunate Louis that possesses an added value from the fact that it is almost entirely based on archive material." *Forum's* critic observed, "This is an extraordinarily good piece of historical revaluation—and remarkably effective writing as well." Reviewing Padover's *Experiment in Germany; the Story of an American Intelligence Officer* (1946), Arthur M. Schlesinger, Jr., remarked in the New York *Times* that it "has great life and gusto. But it has the defects of gusto—that is, a sentimentality which is often pat and sometimes embarrassing. . . . But if you indulge Padover's excesses, you will get the benefits of that excess—that is, a warm-hearted, fast, and colorful picture of the Goetterdaemmerung." Other books by Padover are *The Revolutionary Emperor: Joseph the Second* (1934); *Secret Diplomacy; A Record of Espionage and Double-Dealing* (1937, with J. W. Thompson); *Wilson's Ideals* (1942, editor); *Liberty and Property: the Basic Writings of James Madison* (editor); *La Vie Politique des Etats-Unis; France: Setting or Rising Star*; and *Psychological Warfare*. He has written four chapters in J. W. Thompson's *The Medieval Library* (1930) and has contributed articles to the *United Nations World, American Scholar, New Republic, Nation, Saturday Review of Literature, American Mercury, Science Digest, Reader's Digest, Reporter, Public Opinion Quarterly,* and New York *Times Book Review*.

Padover was the recipient of the Commonwealth Silver Medal from the Commonwealth Club of San Francisco (1935), the United States Army's European Theatre ribbon with five battle stars, and the Wayne University Alumni Award in May 1952. In 1947 he was made Chevalier of the Legion of Honor of the French Republic. Padover is a member of the Society of American Historians and a regular lecturer at the Ethical Culture Society and the Foreign Policy Association. Each year he is a discussion leader for the Quaker International Summer Seminars in Europe. Other affiliations are with the Institut International d'Histoire Politique et Constitutionelle, Society of American Historians, and the Jewish Academy of Arts and Sciences. He was a member of the National Archives Council in 1944 (alternate for the Secretary of the Interior). On March 7, 1942, Padover married Irina Raben, now deceased. He is five feet six inches tall and weighs 155 pounds; he has black hair and "snapping" brown eyes. Reading and shopping are his recreations.

(Continued next page)

PADOVER, SAUL K.—*Continued*

References

Chelsea News p4 My 4 '50
PM p17 My 21 '46 por
Lerner, D. Sykewar (1950)
Who's Who in America, 1952-53
Who's Who in the East (1951)
World Biography (1948)

P A I G E ,   L E R O Y   (R O B E R T) Sept. 1904(?)- Baseball player
Address: b. c/o St. Louis Browns, 2911 N. Grand, St. Louis, Mo.

Leroy ("Satchel") Paige, the principal relief pitcher of the St. Louis Browns in the 1951 and 1952 baseball seasons and an appointee to the American League team in the All-Star Game of the latter year, is one of the oldest players currently active in the major leagues. Prominent in Negro organized baseball for well over twenty years before the color barrier in the major teams was breached by Jackie Robinson of the Brooklyn Dodgers in 1946, Satchel Paige in his prime threw a "blazing" fast ball and was admired by Joe DiMaggio and Grover Cleveland Alexander, star performers themselves. By the time Paige broke into the major leagues with the Cleveland Indians in 1948 his speed had slowed down, but control, shrewdness of judgment, and a wide assortment of deliveries made him still a formidable adversary, particularly as a relief player. He was released by Cleveland in February 1950, and in July of the year following went to the St. Louis Browns. Used chiefly in relief in the first half of the 1952 season, he won six games and lost four.

The birthplace of Leroy Robert Paige is Mobile, Alabama. His birth date, as suggested by Ted Shane (in *True*, October 1948, in which the writer refers to World War II draft registration and the pitcher's mother), is September 1904; he was the sixth of eight children born to the Paiges. He has told that he "started out as a pitcher" while still a child— "I tossed stones at tin cans all day long." As a youth, he played sandlot ball in Mobile and combined the earning of a living and the strengthening of his pitching arm by delivering ice and working as a porter at the Union Station. When or where he made his debut as a professional ballplayer is not definitely established. The team most generally mentioned is the Birmingham (Alabama) Black Barons and the year 1927. The Negro pitcher is said to have acquired his nickname "Satchel" (a contraction of "Satchelfoot" and a reference to his outsize feet) at Chattanooga. Another Negro team with which he played early in his career was the New Orleans Pelicans.

Negro organized baseball had been established in 1920 with the founding at Kansas City, Missouri, of the Negro National League. A year later the Negro Eastern League came into being and the two organizations—which began playing their own World Series in 1924 —continued to operate until 1932, when the

depression brought about their disintegration. While detailed rosters were not retained, Paige is mentioned as pitching for the Chattanooga Lookouts in 1925, the Birmingham Barons in 1928, and subsequently for the Baltimore Black Sox, the Chicago American Giants, and the Pittsburgh Crawfords, on whose rolls he remained for seven years. In 1933 he pitched 42 games, winning 31 and losing 4, and at one time had a winning streak of 21 consecutive games and 62 scoreless innings. Another of his notable seasons was 1934, in which he played for a Bismarck (North Dakota) team which won 104 out of the 105 games in which it participated. "And I pitched in every game, I guess," Paige has been quoted as saying in the New York *Times*. "I know there was one month when I started twenty-nine games." The regular season over, he defeated Dizzy Dean by a 1-to-0 margin in an exhibition contest which lasted thirteen innings. His future major league employer, Bill Veeck, was a spectator who remarked, "It's the best I've ever seen."

Not long after Paige's accomplishment of this feat, the president of the Dominican Republic, Rafael Trujillo, decided (in the words of sportswriter Tom Meany) "to organize an all-Negro team to dominate winter ball in Latin America." He signed Paige along with Josh Gibson and other Negro stars, and for a number of winters thereafter Satchel pitched in Venezuela, Mexico, Cuba, Puerto Rico, Colombia, and elsewhere. At this period he is said to have been paid $500 for every game in which he appeared on the mound. Meanwhile, he was accustomed to spending the summers in the United States with various teams such as the Homestead (Pennsylvania) Greys and the Kansas City Black Monarchs, and playing exhibition contests. It was in one of these, in California in 1937, that he won praise from Joe DiMaggio as the best pitcher he had ever faced. The war threat and the revival of organized Negro baseball in the form of the Negro American and National Leagues combined in 1941 to cause Paige to leave Latin America. Rejoining the Kansas City Monarchs, he helped to pitch that team to victory in the Negro World Series of 1942. Four years later he again "helped the Monarchs to win the league pennant, allowing only two runs in ninety-three innings and running a streak of scoreless innings to sixty-four" (New York *Times*). In the course of his long career in Negro baseball, Paige has pitched a number of no-hit and one-hit games and has tied the record of Bob Feller of the Cleveland Indians in striking out eighteen batters in a single game.

By 1946, when the engagement of Jackie Robinson by the Brooklyn Dodgers broke down the color barrier in the major league, Satch Paige had seen his best years, and his celebrated fast ball was slowing. For a while there was little interest shown in bringing the famous Negro hurler into baseball's "big time." In the fall of the year following, however, he defeated the Cleveland Indians' Bob Feller by 8 to 0 in an exhibition game at Los Angeles, striking out sixteen batters. The interest of Veeck, the Indians' owner, in the Negro moundsman was revived; and in July 1948, when the Indians were driving toward a probable pennant under the management of Lou Boudreau, Veeck decided to offer Paige a contract. Paige was thus the seventh player of his race to don a major league uniform. In his first American League game on August 13 of the same year, Paige scattered nine hits to defeat the Chicago White Sox by 5 to 0; then exactly a week later he hurled a three-hitter against the same team for another "shut out." During the remainder of the regular season Paige won four more games while losing one, for an earned run average of 2.47; and in the fourth game of the ensuing World Series against the Boston Braves allowed no hits in two-thirds of an inning. The following season (1949), however, "Old Satch" was troubled by a stomach disorder. Used mainly in relief, he lost seven games while winning four. Veeck sold his interest in the Indians in the same year, and in February 1950 the new owners gave Paige his release. "He did the job asked of him in bringing up six victories toward the pennant in 1948," General Manager Hank Greenberg was quoted as saying. "We want to release him now so he can make his own plans for the 1950 season."

With his release by the Cleveland team, Paige rejoined the Kansas City Monarchs. "Paige pitched 62 games around the nation in 1950," stated the magazine *Baseball*, "and was on the same type of extensive junket . . . when Veeck re-entered big league baseball with the Browns." The pitcher's ailment had meanwhile responded to treatment, and in July 1951, when Veeck purchased the St. Louis American League team, he summoned the "ageless" Negro back to the major league as a relief pitcher. During the remainder of the 1951 season Paige made twenty-three mound appearances for the St. Louis Browns and won three games while losing four, but the supporting team was weak. Extensive trading greatly strengthened the Browns in the ensuing winter, and in the first half of the 1952 season Paige won six important games for Manager Rogers Hornsby and his successor Marty Marion while losing four. Named by the American League manager Casey Stengel to represent the Browns in the All-Star Game played against the National League at Philadelphia on July 9, Paige had one of the great disappointments of his career when the contest was halted by rain at the end of the fifth inning—Stengel had promised "Satch" that he could pitch the eighth inning.

Although he has in recent years added a curve, a slider, and a "hesitation pitch" to his deliveries, Paige still finds his fast ball his most effective stock in trade. "He delivers it with all the motions of a windmill," a United Press writer has said. "He stands on one foot, and cranks up into weird contortions in his wind-up. The other foot is cocked high, and many batters claim that Paige's pitching effectiveness stems from that brandished leg which obscures the ball and even the rest of the park." He is a right-handed pitcher and batter.

St. Louis Browns

LEROY PAIGE

The veteran ballplayer, who has been married more than once, is the father of three young children by the former La Homa Brown, whom he married on August 18, 1942. Gun collecting is mentioned as his principal hobby; an article in *Esquire* added that the "fabulous flinger" is also "more than an ordinary connoisseur of antique silverware and china." Paige, who is six feet three inches in height and weighs 180 pounds, has attributed his success in keeping in good physical trim to the taking of steaming hot baths before and after each game. "He likes to sing and dance," Lemuel Parton once wrote of him, "always takes a big guitar with him wherever he goes."

References

Baseball Stars 1:68 N 2 '50 por
Christian Sci Mon II p8 Jl 23 '51 por
Esquire 20:123 Jl '43
Life 10:90-1 Je 2 '41 pors; 25:49-50+ Jl 26 '48 pors
N Y Sun p34 S 23 '41
N Y Times p26 Jl 8 '48; VI p24 S 18 '48 por; p24 Jl 2 '52
N Y World-Telegram p20 Je 27 '52
Newsweek 28:82 S 30 '46; 32:66 Ag 9 '48
Read Digest 54:39-42 Je '49
Sat Eve Post 213:20+ Jl 27 '40 pors
Time 35:44 Je 3 '40 por; 52:56+ Jl 19 '48 por
Washington (D.C.) Post p2C F 10 '52
Baseball Register (1951)
Lewis, L. It Takes All Kinds (1947)
Turkin, H., and Thompson, S. C. Official Encyclopaedia of Baseball, Jubilee Edition (1951)

(Continued next page)

PAIGE, LEROY—*Continued*

> Who's Who in Colored America, 1950
> Who's Who in the Major Leagues (1949)

PAIGE, SATCHEL *See* Paige, L. R.

PATON, ALAN (pā'tŭn) Jan. 11, 1903-
Author

Address: b. c/o Charles Scribner's Sons, 597 5th Ave., New York 17; h. Southport Anerley, Natal, South Africa

With the writing of *Cry, the Beloved Country*, which was published in 1948, the literary talent of Alan Paton was given expression after he had been occupied for twenty-five years as an educator and public official. From 1925 to 1935 he taught, first in a native school

Lensk

ALAN PATON

at Ixopo, South Africa, and then at Pietermaritzburg College, and since 1935 he has been known as South Africa's expert on penal reform. His novel was adapted for the stage as *Lost in the Stars* in 1949 and for the motion picture under the original title in 1952.

The eldest of the four children of James and Eunice Warder (James) Paton, English settlers in South Africa, Alan Paton was born in Pietermaritzburg, South Africa, on January 11, 1903. His father, a civil servant, and his mother, a teacher, were both deeply religious, an influence strongly felt in his writings. For his high school education he attended Martzburg College School until the year 1918. Although an excellent student in English and mathematics, with a poetic talent as well, Paton chose the sciences as his major study at the University of Natal, from which he

graduated in 1922 with the degree of Bachelor of Science. In his years at college he took part in a wide variety of activities: he became student president and was sent to Europe to represent the University of Natal at an international students conference. He continued to write verse, was active in dramatic and religious organizations, and as an athlete was the five-mile winner of his year. In his university years, Paton has told, he and his friends explored the whole province of Natal on foot, walking thirty miles a day over rough country.

A few years after graduating the young man received his B.Ed. degree from the same university, and in 1924 he went to Ixopo to teach in a Zulu school. (It was Ixopo and the surrounding country that he used for much of the setting of his novel.) From Ixopo he returned to Pietermaritzburg as a school teacher in 1928 to remain there for seven years. For a time he wrote poems and he completed and discarded two novels, but finally he put aside literature altogether for his interest in social problems. Toc H, a South African organization similar to the American Kiwanis and Rotarian clubs, began to take more of Paton's time and he became engrossed in the problems of the underprivileged and in South Africa's racial question.

In 1935 Paton went to Johannesburg to become principal of Diepkloof Reformatory, where he earned a reputation as "the man who pulled up barbed wire fence and planted geraniums." When he took over, the institution had recently been transferred from the Department of Prisons to the Department of Education. He thus had the task of re-educating the staff, who were trained under the old system, as well as the care of the 650 young African inmates of the reformatory. The new principal established the system of graduated freedom, which meant complete control of a youth on arrival followed by lessening restraint as he earned the right to it, until many prisoners were given almost complete freedom. This system also afforded the staff an opportunity to observe an inmate's reaction to liberty in preparation for his eventual release from Diepkloof. The advent of World War II prevented the realization of some of Paton's reforms, but he continued to serve as best he could under the existing conditions, often undertaking manual labor by the side of his charges.

For many years Paton channeled his mastery of language into speaking and writing on social problems of the day, so that he was accepted as an authoritative and objective interpreter of South Africa. While he wanted to turn his attention to more creative activity, he could not find the time without abandoning his educational career, and that he was reluctant to do. For ten years (1938-47) he served as vice-chairman of Toc H and from 1940 to 1945 as chairman of the YMCA-Toc H War Services. He had tried in 1939 to enlist in the army, but the Department of Education, feeling that his services at Diepkloof would be more valuable, refused to release him.

At the end of the war Paton sold his insurance policies to raise money, his wife took a position to support the family, and in 1946 he set out on what was to have been a tour of penal institutions in Scandinavia, Great Britain, the United States, and Canada. On a train from Stockholm to Trondheim, he says, "the creative energy that had dammed up in me broke." Upon reaching Trondheim he began work on *Cry, the Beloved Country*. However, he continued to study penal practice while he wrote in Gothenburg, London, on board the S.S. *Queen Elizabeth*, in New York, Washington, D.C. (where, he has said, he was influenced by the spirit of Abraham Lincoln), Texas, and Arizona. He completed the manuscript in December 1947 in San Francisco. Almost a year later it was published, and since that time it has sold more copies in South Africa than any other book with the exception of the Bible, has become a best seller in the United States, and has been translated into twelve languages.

Cry, the Beloved Country is the story of Stephen Kumalo, a Zulu parson from Ixopo, in search of a sister, who has disappeared, and his son, who has murdered a white man. He loses his faith, but in the end he recovers it and wins the friendship of the murdered man's father. The novel received an enthusiastic reception from the book reviewers. "A beautiful and profoundly moving story . . . steeped in sadness and grief but radiant with hope and compassion," was Orville Prescott's opinion of it (New York *Times*). Comparing it with one of the few other books which have come out of South Africa, Olive Schreiner's *The Story of an African Farm* (1883), James Stern of the *New Republic* found *Cry, the Beloved Country* "the more profound, compassionate, dramatic and important book . . . probably . . . one of the best novels of our time. In the magic, symbolic Zulu idiom of its prose, it is without doubt one of the most beautifully written." In the San Francisco *Chronicle* Edith James called it "a book which presents a clear and compassionate picture of one land and yet is universal in its basic theme." Daniel A. Poling, writing in the *Christian Herald*: "I find it one of the most distinguished [novels] of any period in my reading life. There is a fire in it that runs like a flame across the wide veld. There is hidden passion that comes into the vast open of human hunger for a homeland."

A year after the publication of *Cry, the Beloved Country*, Alan Paton returned to New York City for the opening, on October 30, 1949, of *Lost in the Stars*, a musical play based on the novel, with words by Maxwell Anderson and music by Kurt Weill, and Todd Duncan in the leading role. The production had a long run on Broadway and on tour. "It would not be impossible to quarrel with some of the hasty treatment the authors have applied to Mr. Paton's perfectly composed novel," Brooks Atkinson wrote in the New York *Times*. "Probably, *Cry, the Beloved Country* should not be translated into a drama. But it has been, and into a drama that is illuminating and memorable." In January 1952 the novel appeared in still another form, this time a screen version under the original title. Paton wrote the script

himself and assisted in the production, and Canada Lee starred in the picture, which was filmed in South Africa. "Out of Alan Paton's beautiful and profound narrative," said Bosley Crowther in the New York *Times*, "Zoltan Korda, with Mr. Paton by his side, has made a motion picture of comparable beauty and power." In the New York *World-Telegram* Alton Cook called *Cry, the Beloved Country* "a passionately eloquent movie. . . .Alan Paton himself put all the qualities of his novel into his equally deep-spoken screen play."

Since the publication of his novel Paton has written a number of articles for the *Saturday Review of Literature, Christian Century*, and the New York *Herald Tribune*. In these shorter pieces, as in his book, he shows his concern for the problems of South Africa and, by extension, of the world and his conviction that they can only be solved by spiritual means. He said in the *Christian Century* of March 8, 1950: "It may be necessary for men to face suffering and death in their attempts to achieve [a just multiracial community in South Africa]. But it will not be their suffering and death that achieve it; it will be men's apprehension of the great obedience that called these things forth, their apprehension of the great Power which called for such obedience." Paton is now (1952) working on a biography of Jan Hendrik Hofmeyr, a notable South African liberal who served as Deputy Prime Minister under Field Marshal Jan Christiaan Smuts.

In February 1952 the novelist admitted that he was in a state of distress over national and international affairs. With his wife he went to a community of colored tubercular patients in the countryside near Durban City, South Africa. He plans to live there for at least a year doing manual labor as he did at Diepkloof to improve the accommodations for the 600 patients. When Paton left the Union Education Department in 1948, it was decided to call the first industrial school in South Africa for African boys, the Alan Paton School. The writer is president of the Convocation of the University of Natal, president of the Transvaal Association of Non-European Boys' Clubs, and honorary commissioner of Toc H in South Africa.

Mrs. Paton is the former Doris Olive Francis; they were married July 2, 1928, and have two sons, David Francis and Jonathan Stewart. The brown-haired, gray-eyed South African weighs 155 pounds and is five feet eight inches tall. His church is the Anglican. He was described by Emma Bugbee in the New York *Herald Tribune* as "typically British in appearance and manner," is said to have humor and wit, which have not shown themselves in his writings. "You must understand," he says, "that when I wrote that book, I didn't see much to laugh at. But I want to write another with some laughter in it." Paton's recreations are reading, bird-watching, and traveling.

References

Life 27:149 N 14 '49 por
N Y Herald Tribune p13 O 20 '49 por; IV p1 Ja 20 '52
Washington (D.C.) Post p7B Ja 29 '50

PATTERSON, ROBERT P(ORTER) Feb. 12, 1891—Jan. 22, 1952 Former United States Secretary of War; member of law firm of Webb, Patterson & Hadley from 1920 until his appointment in 1930 as judge of the United States District Court for Southern New York; was promoted to judge of Second Circuit Court of Appeals in 1939; was named Assistant Secretary of War in 1940 and a few months later Under Secretary of War; Secretary of War from 1945 to 1947. See *Current Biography,* 1941.

Obituary

N Y Times p20 Ja 23 '52

PAYNE, FREDERICK G. July 24, 1900- Governor of Maine; United States Senator-elect from Maine.

Address: b. State House, Augusta, Me; h. Blaine House, Augusta, Me.

Frederick G. Payne, Republican Governor of the State of Maine since January 1949, was elected to the United States Senate on September 9, 1952, after winning the primary contest over Senator Owen Brewster the previous June. From a career in business as an executive of a large New England theater chain, Payne entered public life with his election as Mayor of Augusta, Maine, in 1935. Five years later he became State Budget Officer and Finance Commissioner, a post he held until he resigned to join the United States Army Air Force in 1942. Maine's newly chosen Senator is generally identified with the progressive wing of the Republican party.

The son of Frederick G. and Nellie (Smart) Payne, Frederick G. Payne was born on July 24, 1900, in Lewiston, Maine, where he attended public schools and was graduated from the Jordan High School. As a youth he worked as a newsboy, grocery clerk, theater usher, and dishwasher. Payne studied at the Bentley School of Accounting and Finance in Boston and taught accounting for a while before joining the Maine & New Hampshire Theatres, Company, operator of 132 New England theaters, in which he became chief disbursing agent, handling about $10 million annually. Payne has stated that the late William P. Gray, who was the general manager of this company, and Senator Wallace H. White of Lewiston both influenced his later choice of a career.

On January 1, 1935, Payne took office as Mayor of Augusta, the capital city of Maine, a post which he occupied for six years, being re-elected twice. At this time he was also an efficiency expert for the State Liquor Commission and an industrial consultant for the Central Maine Power Company, largest public utility in the State. After his defeat by 2,429 votes in his attempt to gain the Republican nomination for Governor of Maine in 1940, he was appointed State Budget Officer and Finance Commissioner. Payne resigned this position in 1942 to become a captain in the United States Army Air Force, rising by the end of the war to the post of lieutenant colonel

in the fiscal and budget division. In the years immediately following the war, he served as an executive for the Waldoboro Garage and the Tri-County Farm Equipment company in Rockland and Waldoboro.

Having been successful in his second attempt to win the Republican gubernatorial nomination, Payne was elected Governor of Maine on September 13, 1948, by a vote of 145,956 to 76,554. Shortly after his inauguration in January 1949, he stated that new deposits of manganese discovered in Aroostock County, Maine, could be used in United States steel production to make up for the loss of supply of ore from Russia. During his Governorship Payne was active in promoting manganese ore mining in Aroostock County; this ore has not as yet been exploited commercially because of its low grade. At the same time that he urged the exploitation of the Maine deposits, he suggested that a possible source of power for this work could come from reviving the Passamaquoddy tidal power project. This plan for harnessing the tides of Passamoquoddy Bay had been initiated by President Franklin D. Roosevelt, but after about $7 million had been expended for preparatory work it was abandoned when Congress refused to make further grants. Payne's proposal, developed in conjunction with the Maine Congressional delegation in Washington, was to revive the project under the joint auspices of the United States and Canada. He told a joint international commission investigating the feasibility of the project that "the future economic stability of northern New England and Canada" depended on the renewal of this undertaking (New York *Times,* August 23, 1949).

In July 1949 when United States Secretary of Commerce Charles Sawyer conducted an economic survey of New England, Payne concurred with the Governors of other States in this region in proposing the repeal of wartime excise taxes and the easing of plant depreciation rulings. The same year Governor Payne became one of the corporators of the Development Credit Corporation of Maine, which was organized to supply risk capital to small businessmen.

Unopposed for renomination as Governor in 1950, Payne on September 11 was re-elected to this post, in the eighth straight Republican sweep of major Maine offices. Payne's margin of 50,000 out of a total of 240,000 votes cast was a decrease from the margin of 69,000 in his first gubernatorial election. Seeking re-election mainly on the record of his two-year term, Payne was opposed by Democrat Earl S. Grant, a Portland educator, who had contended that the State's functions were being conducted in an unbusinesslike way, and by State's Rights Democrat Leland B. Currier, a Litchfield lumberman, who had urged private development of Maine's water power resources.

One of the first problems Payne faced during his second term was the choice between running the State at a deficit or increasing taxes. For several years Maine had had a financial deficit, but a $7 million surplus, acquired during World War II, had been used to remedy the situation. In 1951, when the surplus had been expended, John H. Fenton in the New York *Times* (January 1, 1951) made the following comment: "Two years ago Governor Payne warned Maine's ninety-fourth Legislature that any increase in State services would have to be met by increased taxes. He managed to hold these at a minimum, but rising costs of labor and materials during the year while the Legislature was absent from the State House at Augusta have brought a new crisis." Seeking to avert this crisis, Payne, while submitting a record-breaking $57.9 million budget, sought to raise about $12 million by urging passage of a 2 per cent sales tax on all purchases except consumer food. This levy, he said, would raise enough additional funds to enable the State to repeal "antiquated" property and tobacco taxes. In 1951 the 2 per cent sales tax was adopted.

Soon after he had begun his second term, Governor Payne launched a drive against gambling in his State. He acquired the funds for the investigation, headed by State Attorney General Alexander LaFleur, from the State's contingent fund by vote of his council "on faith for a project" for which he promised an eventual and full accounting. In this way he avoided the publicity which would have ensued from a legislative grant, thereby enabling the investigation to function more effectively. On the national scene in 1951, Payne was appointed in May by President Truman to a one-year term on the Civil Defense Advisory Council, a consultative body for the Federal Civil Defense Administration.

The next year, on February 27, 1952, Payne announced that he would seek the Republican nomination for the United States Senate in the primary election that June. In doing so, Payne, a comparative neophyte in politics who represented a liberal viewpoint among Maine Republicans, was opposing Senator Owen Brewster, an Old Guard Republican for thirty-five years, who was seeking the Senatorial nomination for a third term. The State meeting of the Maine Republicans on March 27 to select delegates to the National Republican Convention in July constituted the first test of strength between the two aspirants: Senator Brewster supported Senator Robert A. Taft, a close friend and Harvard Law School associate, for United States President, while Payne had been chairman of the original Maine committee for General Dwight D. Eisenhower and resigned this post only upon entering the Senatorial primary race. Nine of Maine's sixteen delegates were committed to support Eisenhower—a move which was interpreted as being favorable to Payne—five were pledged to Taft, and two delegates remained uncommitted.

The primary battle evoked charges and countercharges of graft, influence peddling, and corruption on the part of both contestants, and was, in the words of the New York *Times* (June 15, 1952), "one of the bitterest in Maine history." During the primary campaign there was a State legislative investigation of Maine's

Dora Clark Tash

FREDERICK G. PAYNE

$20 million-a-year liquor monopoly, in which Senator Brewster and Governor Payne were named by witnesses at the hearing who made countercharges involving claims of political influence in liquor deals in the State Liquor Commission. Payne won the primary election on June 16 by 3,356 votes and later (October 23, 1952) was cleared by the Kennebec County Grand Jury of any wrongdoing in the Liquor Commission scandal. His exoneration was disclosed in indictments lodged against two other men which charged them with conspiring to spread what they knew to be "falsehoods" that Governor Payne had taken money from various sources corruptly. On September 9, 1952, in the Maine Republicans' ninth consecutive sweep of the State, Payne was the victor in a three-man contest for the United States Senate in the nation's first general election of this year. Winning with 59 per cent of the votes, Payne achieved a victory that had been denied seven previous Maine Governors who had tried to attain membership in the national Congress directly from the State capital. Payne takes his seat in the Eighty-third Congress in January 1953.

Payne married Mrs. Ella R. Marshall (the former Ella Hodgdon) of Waldoboro on February 27, 1944. They have two children, Putnam and Thomas Lee. Payne is a member of the Congregational Church. His hobbies are fishing and boating. He has brown hair and brown eyes, is six feet one inch tall and weighs 192 pounds.

References

N Y Herald Tribune II p1 Je 22 '52 por
N Y Times p11 Je 18 '52
N Y World-Telegram p13 Je 21 '52 por
Who's Who in United States Politics (1952)

PAZ, HIPOLITO JESUS (päs ē-pō'lē-tō hā-sōōs') Jan. 9, 1917- Argentine Ambassador to the United States
Address: Embassy of the Argentine Republic, 1815 Q St., N.W., Washington, D.C.

The Argentine Ambassador to the United States, Hipólito Jesús Paz, in the summer of 1951 succeeded Ambassador Jeronimo Remorino, who in turn was appointed to Paz's previous post as Foreign Minister of Argen-

Wide World Photos
HIPOLITO JESUS PAZ

tina. Since the establishment of the Perón regime in 1943, Paz, a former law professor and attorney, held a number of government positions before becoming Minister of Foreign Affairs in August 1949.

Hipólito Jesús Paz was born January 9, 1917, in Buenos Aires, Argentina, the youngest of five children of Dr. Jesús Hipólito Paz and Ana Rosa Gutiérrez. Paz's father is a well-known law professor whose opinion is sought on questions of interpretation of the Argentine Constitution. Young Paz received his legal education at the School of Law and Social Sciences of the University of Buenos Aires. The Buenos Aires newspaper *La Prensa*, in summarizing his scholastic career, stated that, in addition to the Mitre Prize for his paper on legal and constitutional organization written in 1938 and the Eduardo F. Justo Award, he won both the university prize and the Virgilio Teden Uriburu Award in 1939. As candidate for the degree of Doctor of Jurisprudence he wrote a thesis on the relation between civil and criminal law.

Shortly after his graduation Paz became associate professor of criminal law at the University of Buenos Aires, joining his father who was at the time associate professor of law and social sciences. He was also active as a member of the Institute of Criminal Law and as a partner in the family law firm with his father and elder brother, Jesús H. Paz, Jr. A change in the course of his career occurred some time after June 1943, when Juan Perón and a group of nationalist army officers brought about the ousting of President Ramón Castillo and the reorganization of the Argentine government. The new administration appointed Paz the Director General of Penal Institutions of Buenos Aires Province, a position from which he subsequently resigned to take the post of legal adviser to the Ministry of Justice and Public Instruction. Still later, when this department was reorganized as the Ministry of Education, Dr. Paz was formally named its chief adviser.

Upon the resignation of Foreign Minister Juan A. Bramuglia in August 1949, Perón named Paz to the vacant post, taking into account, reported the *Christian Science Monitor*, Paz's "party loyalty and ranking" in making the assignment. In their comments on the appointment, political observers expected that Perón would take a firmer hand in establishing policy, with Paz as his spokesman. The New York *La Prensa* observed that Paz is an intimate of Argentine leaders friendly to North America, such as Dr. José Arce and the former Ambassador to Washington, Dr. Oscar Ivanissevich. That newspaper also remarked that it was generally believed that Paz would concentrate his efforts on the measures necessary to improve relations, and to stimulate commerce, between the two countries. Less optimistic, the London *Economist* expressed a British point of view that there was little probability that this "injection of new blood" into Perón's Cabinet would disclose further possibilities for Anglo-Argentine amity or contribute to the implementation of the commercial pact which had been recently concluded at the time.

Foreign Minister Paz himself indicated that he was replacing a man, not a policy. His remarks, addressed to the diplomatic corps a few days after his appointment, were reported by *La Prensa* in Buenos Aires: "I want only to say to you that in the position in which Providence has placed me, I aspire wholeheartedly to follow the policy which General Perón embodies, and which is traditional in the history of my country; the policy of cordial friendship, of open arms, of the tightening of ties and of cooperation with all countries in order to collaborate in the work for peace and friendship."

Shortly after the outbreak of the Korean War Paz cabled the United Nations that Argentina intended to fulfill her commitments as a member of the United Nations and that the Argentine Government expected to be asked to consult directly with the unified command. This expression of policy was qualified the next day by a further statement by Paz that before Argentine troops could be ordered to Korea, the action must be approved by the congress in compliance with the Argentine constitution. *Time* and the United States press in general viewed the second statement as a direct result of the strong isolationist and nationalist feelings of the Argentine population expressed in peace demonstrations held in Buenos Aires, the capital, and in Rosario, Argentina's second largest city.

Visiting the United States for the first time in March 1951, Paz attended a meeting of the Organization of the American States in Washington, D.C., a conference of Pan American Foreign Ministers held to plan measures for the defense of the Western Hemisphere against Russian encroachments and Communist infiltration. Paz's approach to the conference was that it would place him in a position of having to speak with words of "double valence," a term which is understood to mean that the Minister would always be addressing his own government and people as well as members of the meeting. With the delegates from Mexico and Guatemala, Paz expressed himself in opposition to the original wording of the Resolution on Collective Defense—the most controversial issue raised at the meeting—which included a pledge of support for any military activity of the United Nations against aggression. After the addition of amendments leaving to the discretion of each country the determination of its "national self-defense" and its ability to supply troops, Paz announced that he would vote for the revised resolution.

The hemisphere conference, occurring as it did directly after the suppression of the independent Buenos Aires newspaper, *La Prensa*, called upon Paz to meet the criticism, official and unofficial, which was directed against his government for its action. He maintained that *La Prensa* had been forced to cease publication by a labor dispute, that the case was now under legislative investigation, and that it was a purely domestic affair. Beyond hewing to the policy already laid down by the Perón government in this matter, Paz made the point that Argentina would sign again—despite the *La Prensa* issue—her commitments as to free access to information incorporated in the Chapultepec agreement of 1945. At the same conference Paz reasserted Argentina's claim to the British-occupied Falkland Islands near Antarctica.

In late June 1951 Buenos Aires announced an exchange of assignments: Remorino was appointed Foreign Minister of Argentina and Paz took his place as Ambassador to the United States. (According to *Time*, Paz had taken a liking to the United States while he attended the conference of Foreign Ministers and had asked Perón for the Washington assignment.) He presented his credentials to President Truman on August 28, when, reported the New York *Times*, most of the ceremony "dealt with 'ideals' and 'bilateral cooperation' between the two Western Hemisphere nations." Paz was head of the Argentine delegation at the San Francisco Japanese peace treaty conference (September 1951), and head of the Argentina delegation to the Fourth General Assembly of the United Nations, in Paris (1952).

Paz, who is married and has two daughters, Patricia and Carmen, has been described as amiable and brilliant. The author of a volume of short stories entitled "The Abyss," he has also written detective stories and three volumes on the Argentine government. According to *Time*, among his favorite authors are Faulkner and Dos Passos.

References

Time 58:31 Jl 9 '51
Washington (D.C.) Post p3B Jl 4 '51
Quien es Quien en La Argentina, 1947
Who's Who in Latin America Pt V (1950)

PERLMAN, PHILIP B(ENJAMIN) Mar. 5, 1890- Solicitor General of the United States
Address: h. Shoreham Hotel, Washington, D.C.

As Solicitor General of the United States—an office ranked by lawyers as the highest that can be held by a practicing lawyer—Philip B. Perlman was in charge of the preparation and presentation of the lawsuits of the Government. His record of cases argued before the Supreme Court was unprecedented, both in the number argued by Perlman personally and in the proportion of cases won. For some twenty years before going to Washington in 1947 as Solicitor General, Perlman conducted a law practice in Baltimore, Maryland, where he had earlier been State Assistant Attorney General (1918-20), Secretary of State of Maryland (1920-23), and City Solicitor of Baltimore (1923-26). Perlman left his post as Solicitor General on August 15, 1952, and was shortly afterward, in September 1952, appointed by President Truman as chairman of a special Commission on Immigration and Naturalization.

Born in Baltimore, Maryland, on March 5, 1890, Philip Benjamin Perlman is the son of Benjamin and Rose (Nathan) Perlman. After attending City College (one of Baltimore's high schools for boys) during 1904-08, the youth began to work as a reporter for the Baltimore *American* while studying law at Johns Hopkins University. He continued to report news for the *American* and later for the *Star* until he joined the staff of the new *Evening Sun*, one of the city's three "Sunpapers." A year before Perlman received his LL.B. degree from the University of Maryland in 1912, he was admitted to the bar of that State on June 24, 1911. The young attorney continued with his newspaper career, however, and in 1913 became city editor of the Baltimore *Evening Sun*, where one of his colleagues was H. L. Mencken, then editor of the *Sunday Sun*.

In 1917 the twenty-seven-year-old city editor resigned that position to become an assistant to Albert C. Ritchie, the State Attorney General, and the following year he was made one of two assistant attorneys general. In the absence of Ritchie for a period during World War II when he served as counsel to President Wilson's War Industries Board, Perlman shared with Acting Attorney General Ogle Marbury the responsibility for the legal affairs of the State of Maryland. The two attorneys argued all the State's cases before the Maryland Court of Appeals at a time when, as Marbury has recalled, "Mr. Perlman had been actively practicing only about a year" (*American Bar Association Journal*, October 1947).

(Continued next page)

PHILIP B. PERLMAN

Marbury and Perlman were partners in private law practice in 1920-23, years during which Ritchie, then Governor, had Perlman as his Secretary of State and Marbury as chairman of the State Board of Prison Control. The year 1923 saw the publication of Perlman's compilation of the debates of the Maryland Constitutional Convention of 1867.

From 1923 to 1926 Philip Perlman was City Solicitor of Baltimore, an appointive post in which he prepared and argued all the city's important cases before the Appellate Court. The first zoning ordinances were prepared by him, and, according to Judge Marbury, he "fought them through adverse decisions of the courts until they were finally approved and put into force." While maintaining his own law office, to which he had returned in 1926, he was called upon by mayors and governors for service on commissions during the next twenty years. In 1926 he was a member of the Baltimore Efficiency and Economy Commission and in 1927 of the Zoning Committee. Four years later he was appointed to the Mayor's Unemployment Relief Commission, and in 1937 Perlman, a patron of the arts, was on the Mayor's Commission on Art Education. In 1933, too, he served on the State Water Resources Commission. The Baltimorean was a delegate to the Democratic National Convention which nominated Franklin D. Roosevelt to run against President Hoover in 1932, was functioning in the same capacity when Roosevelt was nominated for a third term in 1940, and helped write the platform of Harry Truman in 1948.

Consulted by Maryland governors on legislative matters, Perlman drafted a number of laws, including the first State merit system law, the constitutional amendment reducing by half the number of elections held in the State, and other administration measures. As chairman of the State Bar Association's committee on laws, Perlman worked to secure the passage of endorsed measures through the State legislature. His private law clients included large corporations, among them the Baltimore and Ohio Railroad, the Automatic Voting Machine Corporation, Montgomery Ward, the Doughnut Corporation of America, the United Railways of Baltimore; and during the years from 1938 to 1946 Perlman was general counsel of the Baltimore Housing Authority. His former partner, Ogle Marbury, said of Perlman in 1947, "His practice was not confined to such clients as these. Only recently he successfully represented in the Court of Appeals of Maryland several Baltimore city firemen who were threatened with premature retirement." Perlman is reported to have argued more cases before the State's highest court than any other lawyer, and to have done so with "an excellent record of success."

On January 31, 1947, President Truman appointed Philip B. Perlman Solicitor General of the United States in succession to J. Howard McGrath, who had been elected Senator. While the Perlman appointment (reported the New York *Times* of July 22, 1947) was endorsed unanimously by the Baltimore City Council, the Maryland legislature, and the State's Congressional delegation, and favored by both parties, his Senate confirmation was delayed for six months by Senator Homer Ferguson, head of the judiciary subcommittee, who was reported to believe that Perlman was the Democratic boss of Maryland.

Perlman entered upon his new office in time to prepare the Department cases for the Supreme Court's 1947-48 term, in which he personally argued twelve cases and won eight. In 1948-49 he won eleven of his twelve cases, and in 1949-50 all the litigation in which he appeared was successful, a record unprecedented both for activity and success. As of May 1952, Perlman has appeared for the Government sixty-one times, and ten of the decisions have gone against him. His most far-reaching victories, some observers believe, are those against racial discriminatory practices. In December 1947 Attorney General Tom C. Clark and Solicitor General Perlman submitted what has been called "a historic brief" against racial restrictive covenants on real estate. Intervening as a friend of the court (*amicus curiae*) in appeals by private individuals from decisions in St. Louis, Detroit, and Washington, D.C., Perlman argued that such restrictions hampered the work of Government agencies, lowered national prestige, and injured the general welfare by working heavy hardship on millions of citizens. The Supreme Court's 6-to-0 decision in May 1949 was that such covenants, being "repugnant to the law," were not enforceable by the courts. The Clark-Perlman brief, admired for its thoroughness, clarity, and human interest, was published as a 104-page book in 1948, under the title *Prejudice and Property*. It was Perlman who, in a December 1949 speech, announced that no new FHA mortgage insurance would be granted to housing restricted on the basis of race, creed, or color.

Normally it is the Solicitor General's task to defend a Federal agency that is brought into the Supreme Court, but in October 1949 Perlman took the unusual step of filing a brief supporting the plaintiff in a railroad segregation case in which the Interstate Commerce Commission was codefendant. "We think it altogether creditable," commented the Washington *Post*, "that the Government's weight should be thrown into the scales in the interest of justice rather than in the interest of a mistaken Governmental position." The Justice Department also joined in the Sweatt and McLaurin cases which challenged the "separate but equal" doctrine of 1896, on which racial segregation was based. Perlman argued that separate facilities were never in fact equal and that segregation "is in itself a negation of . . . citizenship." This view the Court upheld in the transportation case. In the case on schools the Court held unanimously in June 1950 that segregation facilities, to be constitutional, must be proved equal. Thus, commented Arthur Krock, "Mr. Perlman got the Supreme Court to put a price-tag on it which may have the same effect" as forbidding it.

Perlman appeared for the Government in clearing the Federal title to the oil fields in the marginal sea outside the low-water mark. He argued several cases involving the National Labor Relations Board, in one of which the validity of the Taft-Hartley Act requirement of non-Communist oaths from union officials was upheld. He also argued against review of the conviction of Hideki Tojo and ten other Japanese war criminals and opposed appeals by Alger Hiss and Gerhart Eisler. In other cases he defended the right of the Attorney General to list groups as subversive without hearings or explanation; opposed the appeal of the eleven convicted Communist leaders on any ground except that of the validity of the Smith Act; presented the antitrust case to require five large motion picture companies to dispose of their theater chains; upheld the legality of the rent control law; opposed review of the FCC order settling on the CBS color television system.

At one point in the Dollar-American President Lines case, Perlman, with Secretary of Commerce Sawyer and other officials, was cited for contempt of court. In another case he failed in an attempt to have the Court review the constitutionality of the Georgia county-unit system of voting. In January 1952 Perlman declined appointment to a Presidential "clean-up" commission on the ground that such an investigation should be headed by someone outside the Administration. In May-June 1952 Perlman, who was Acting Attorney General as well as Solicitor General, had the task of defending Truman's seizure of the steel mills to prevent a steel strike. In answer to the case against the President argued by John William Davis, counsel of the United States Steel Corporation, Perlman maintained that the Executive's action was justified by "inherent powers" which he had the right to exercise in times of national emergency. The Supreme Court upheld the ruling of Federal Judge David A. Pine that the seizure was illegal. Soon after Perlman's resignation as Solicitor General became effective on August 15, 1952, President Truman, in September 1952, appointed him chairman of a special Commission on Immigration and Naturalization.

The attorney is a member of the American, Federal, Maryland, Baltimore, and District of Columbia bar associations and the Maryland chapter of the legal fraternity Order of the Coif. He is a past president and board member of the Baltimore Symphony Orchestra, vice-president of the board of the Walters Art Gallery, on the boards of the Baltimore Museum of Art, the Municipal (Peale) Museum, and the Maryland Art Institute. Perlman is also on the board of the Associated Jewish Charities. He is a member of the National Press Club in Washington, and in Baltimore belongs to the University and Metropolitan clubs and to the Elkridge-Harford Hunt.

References

Am Bar Assn J 33:1008 O '47 por
N Y Herald Tribune II p1 My 11 '52
  por; p12 F 1 '47 por
Time 59:25 My 26 '52 por
Who's Who in America, 1952-53
Who's Who in the South and Southwest
  (1950)

PERÓN, (MARIA) EVA (DUARTE) DE
May 7, 1919—July 26, 1952 Wife of President Juan Perón of Argentina; appeared as an actress in motion pictures and on the radio before her marriage in 1945; was interested in labor reforms, woman's suffrage, and charitable activities; founded the Eva Perón Foundation, a social welfare organization; was considered a powerful political influence on the Perón Administration. See *Current Biography,* 1949.

Obituary

N Y Times p1+ Jl 27 '52

PETIT, ROLAND (pĕ"tē' rô"län') 1924-
Choreographer; dancer

Address: b. c/o Samuel Goldwyn Productions, Inc., 7210 Santa Monica Blvd., Hollywood 28, Calif.

Choreographer and dancer Roland Petit is generally considered to be the foremost figure to have emerged in French ballet during the last decade. Trained at the ballet school of the Paris Opéra, he was a cofounder of Les Ballets des Champs-Élysées in 1945, and subsequently served as that company's chief choreographer, maître de ballet, and premier danseur. In January 1948 he left this group to form his own company, Les Ballets de Paris de Roland Petit, in May 1948 and has since made successful American tours in the fall and winter of 1949-50 and 1950-51. When Petit went to Hollywood in 1951 to stage the ballets for the film *Hans Christian Andersen*, the group was temporarily disbanded. Among his outstanding ballets are

PETIT, ROLAND—*Continued*

Les Forains, Les Amours de Jupiter, Le Jeune Homme et la Mort, Les Demoiselles de la Nuit, Carmen, and *La Croqueuse de Diamants.*

Roland Petit was born in the Paris suburb of Villemomble in 1924. His French father, Edmond Petit, owns a small bistro in the market quarter of Paris, while his Italian mother runs a shop that sells ballet slippers. As a young boy Roland Petit liked very much to clown and mime for the patrons of his father's cafe. When he was ten years old he entered the ballet school of the Paris Opéra, where he studied under Gustave Ricaux and later worked with Serge Lifar, chief choreographer, maître de ballet, and premier danseur étoile of the Opéra Ballet. At the age of sixteen Petit was accepted into the corps de ballet at the opera, and in January 1943 he advanced to the rank of "premier sujet" in Lifar's production of de Falla's *L'Amour Sorcier,* dancing opposite Térésina in the role originally created by Vicente Escudero. Meanwhile, beginning in 1941 and continuing throughout the Nazi occupation, Petit gave annual recitals in Paris. His partner was Janine Charrat, who at the age of twelve in 1936 had appeared prominently in the film *La Mort du Cygne* (English title *Ballerina*). Their choreographic talents both attracted the attention of the celebrated poet, Jean Cocteau, who designed the décor for one of their most successful dances, *Orphée* (1943). The program of their Salle Pleyel recital in the spring of 1944 included *Paul et Virginie* as well as *La Jeune Fille Endorme* and *Guignol.*

At the end of the summer of 1944, shortly after the Liberation of Paris, Petit left the Opéra Ballet to strike out on an independent career. Several months later the ballet critic Irène Lidova and the impresario Claude Giraud organized an important series of recitals called the "Vendredis de la Danse," to exhibit the talents of the younger generation of French dancers who had grown up during the occupation. The first of these Friday recitals took place at the Théâtre Sarah-Bernhardt on December 1, 1944. During the course of the ten subsequent performances, Petit was the partner of Nina Vyroubova in fragments from *Giselle* and created for her a new ballet, *Le Rossignol et la Rose,* after a story by Oscar Wilde, with music by Schumann. Excited by the potentialities of these young dancers, Bérard, Sauguet, and Boris Kochno (who had served as Serge Diaghilev's secretary, adviser, and librettist in the 1920's) offered to collaborate with Petit on *Les Forains,* a ballet about a group of strolling circus players. It was given its première on March 2, 1945, as a special evening devoted to ballet, whose program also included *Les Deux Pigeons, Guernica,* and *Mephisto Valse.* The extraordinary success of *Les Forains,* which was hailed as the first important contribution to French ballet since the occupation, encouraged Petit to prepare, with the financial assistance of his father, another evening of ballet in June. For this occasion he choreographed *Le Rendez-vous,* a realistic ballet by Jacques Prévert about the street life of Paris, and *Le Poète,* a short divertissement

Impressed by the popular response to these undertakings, Roger Eudes, then director of the Théâtre des Champs-Élysées, put his theater at the disposal of the group of young dancers presided over by Petit for a Paris season in October 1945. It was at this time that the eighteen dancers became a permanent company and adopted the name of Les Ballets des Champs-Élysées. Eudes was its managing director, Kochno artistic director, and Petit chief choreographer, maître de ballet, and premier danseur. In October Petit staged *Le Déjeuner sur L'Herbe,* a pastoral ballet by Lidova, danced to Lanner waltzes; and two months later he produced *La Fiancée du Diable,* a romantic period ballet by Kochno, with a score by Jean Hubeau based on themes from Paganini's *Caprices.* During the next two years Les Ballets des Champs-Élysées toured the Continent, visited London twice, and was scheduled to make its American debut in the spring of 1947 (at which time Petit first visited New York), but negotiations broke down and the engagement was canceled. Wherever the company appeared it won acclaim for its creative activity, the youth and freshness of its dancers, and its "chic and elegant style." Many critics pointed out that this company alone was continuing the Diaghilev tradition of artistic experiment and innovation.

According to Richard Buckle (*Ballet Annual*), Petit's "most ambitious and important creation" for Les Ballets des Champs-Élysées was *Les Amours de Jupiter* (March 1946), based on episodes from Ovid's *Metamorphoses,* with music by Jacques. However, the work by Petit that aroused the most controversy was *Le Jeune Homme et la Mort,* a dramatic ballet which Cocteau devised for Jean Babilée and Nathalie Philippart. Petit rehearsed the two dancers to jazz, carefully timed, in order to obtain the atmosphere Cocteau felt essential to the theme; only on the night of its première, in June 1946, did Cocteau reveal that the work would actually be danced to Bach's Passacaglia in C Minor. *Le Jeune Homme et la Mort* won such plaudits from the critics as "an absolute tour de force", "a magnificent piece of theater," "a masterpiece which compares with the greatest creative work to be seen in ballet today." This was followed in December 1946 by *Le Bal des Blanchisseuses,* a humorous ballet Petit choreographed as a vehicle for the acrobatic dancer, Danielle Darmance, with music by Vernon Duke. Less successful was *Les Treize Danses* (November 1947), a series of divertissements in the setting of a Venetian carnival, danced to Grétry's music, with décor by Christian Dior.

In January 1948 Petit left Les Ballets des Champs-Élysées to organize his own company. He spent the next five months preparing a new repertoire, with the assistance of Janine Charrat, and enlisting as his artistic collaborators some of the foremost French writers, composers, and painters. Known as Les Ballets de Paris de Roland Petit, this troupe of fifteen young dancers—each a soloist—was first presented to the public at the Théâtre Marigny on May 22, 1948. For the occasion Petit created what a number of critics consider one of his most noteworthy achievements—*Les Demoiselles de la Nuit*, a fantasy by Jean Anouilh. Margot Fonteyn appeared as a guest artist in the leading role of this ballet. Also on the opening night program was Petit's *Que le Diable l'emporte!* a comic ballet with a score by Manuel Rosenthal. At the conclusion of its very successful Paris engagement, the new group toured Western Europe and in February 1949 appeared in London for the first time. That month three ballets by Petit were given their world premières: *L'Oeuf à la Coque*, a satirical revue sketch, featuring Colette Marchand, with music by Maurice Thiriet and décor by Lepri; *Pas d'Action*, an abstract composition danced on an empty stage to music from Wagner's *Tristan*; and a freely adapted choreographic version of Bizet's *Carmen*, starring Renée Jeanmaire.

Overnight *Carmen* became a *succès de scandale*, and it was given at every performance for the remainder of the London season. This success was repeated in Paris during the summer of 1949 when the group played to capacity audiences for over three months—a record for ballet in that city. Reviewing *Carmen* for the Paris *Herald Tribune*, one critic found it "the most exciting new ballet in a long time . . . that rare and wonderful thing—a complete fusion of music, dance, and décor." The unprecedented popularity of this work prompted Arthur Lesser, in association with the Shuberts, to bring Les Ballets de Paris to the United States. Its New York debut took place on October 6, 1949, in a single bill featuring *Carmen*, which received such enthusiastic notices from the critics that it ran there for 118 performances, after which the group visited other Eastern cities and Canada. When the tour ended in March 1950, Petit was invited to London by the Sadler's Wells Ballet to create a new work for that company—*Ballabile* (May 1950), a suite of dances to Chabrier's music. According to the *Dancing Times*, this ballet was "extremely acrobatic" and at times "very clever." For the third Paris season of Les Ballets de Paris in the summer of 1950, Petit produced *Les Chaises Musicales*, a series of group dances suggested by the parlor game of musical chairs, with music by Georges Auric; and later that season he staged and also helped Alfred Adam devise the scenario and Jean-Michel Damase write the songs for *La Croqueuse de Diamants*, a sophisticated fantasy.

These two new works were given their first American performances in the fall of 1950 when Les Ballets de Paris returned for a second Broadway engagement. *La Croqueuse de Diamants* scored an immediate hit with both dance and drama critics, who agreed that in the work Petit had succeeded in combining musical comedy and ballet idioms to create a distinct new theater form, which blended song, pantomime, and various dance styles. After playing in New York for eight weeks, Les Ballets de Paris visited the Pacific Coast and the tour ended there in February 1951, after certain members of the group were signed by Howard Hughes to appear in a film version of *Carmen*.

ROLAND PETIT

However, this project was postponed in the summer, and all the dancers dismissed, with the exception of Petit and Mlle. Jeanmaire, who remained in Hollywood under contract. In October 1951 Petit replaced George Balanchine as the choreographer for Samuel Goldwyn's $4,000,000 Technicolor musical *Hans Christian Andersen*, starring Danny Kaye. Later Mlle. Jeanmaire was called in to take Moira Shearer's place as the leading ballerina in this film, which is scheduled for release in November 1952.

It has frequently been stated that Petit is the first outstanding French choreographer since Marius Petipa and the golden era of French ballet in the nineteenth century. Pierre Michaut (in *Le Ballet Contemporain*) called him "the 'scout' of the avant-garde . . . the most eminent figure in young French ballet," while Audrey Williamson (in *Ballet Renaissance*) wrote: "Petit is the outstanding example of precocious French genius, and if he does not burn out his flame early through overwork— a real danger—he should take the leading place in world ballet in the future." Regarding Petit's ability as a dancer, Richard Buckle (in *Ballet Annual*) said: "He has a fine classical technique and excellent line; his sense of showmanship is as evident in his own performances as it is in the skill with which he presents other dancers to advantage in his creations." Among the roles that Petit has created in his own ballets are the Conjurer in *Les Forains*; the Young Man in *Le Rendez-vous*; the Vagabond in *Le Déjeuner sur L'Herbe*; the Devil in *La Fiancée du Diable*; Jupiter in *Les Amours de Jupiter*; the Butcher Boy in *Le Bal des Blanchisseuses*; the Lover in *Les Demoiselles de la Nuit*; Don José in *Carmen*; and the Delivery Boy in *La Croqueuse de Diamants*. In ballets by other choreographers he has appeared as the Toreador in *Los Caprichos*, James in *La Sylphide*, the Prince in

PETIT, ROLAND—*Continued*

Lac des Cygnes, the Sailor in *'Adame Miroir*, and the Hussar in *Le Beau Danube*.

"Of distinguished appearance," the French choreographer is tall and has brown eyes and black hair. Descriptions of his personality emphasize his restlessness, ambition, and "passionate energy" for work. Going to the movies is his favorite form of recreation, and it is reportedly his ambition one day to make a film "really worthy of ballet." He prefers to leave analyses of the dance to the ballet critics, but he believes that ballet is a language which anyone can understand. "People seem to have the idea that it's an intellectual thing that is for a certain elite class. That's not true. If my maid is not touched by it, it isn't successful ballet."

Reference

Dance Ap '47; My '51 pors
Formes et Couleurs No. 3 70-4 '44 pors
N Y World-Telegram N 29 '49
Vogue 105 :125 Je '45

Chujoy, A. ed. Dance Encyclopedia (1949)
Haskell, A. L. ed. Ballet Annuals 1946, 1947, 1949
Michaut, P. Le Ballet Contemporain (1950)

PINAY, ANTOINE (pē″nā′ äɴ″twâɴ′) Dec. 30, 1891- Premier of France

Address: c/o Presidence du Conseil, Hotel de Matignon, Paris 7, France

At the request of President Auriol, a French Cabinet was formed in March 1952 by Antoine Pinay, member of the National Assembly and

French Embassy Inf. Div.
ANTOINE PINAY

leather manufacturer from the Midi. Successor to the recently fallen Faure Ministry, the Pinay Cabinet was the first moderately conservative one to appear on the French political scene since the beginning of the Fourth Republic; this slightly Rightist tendency brought the new Premier unexpected support from insurgent Gaullists. Long active in local politics as Mayor of his town, Pinay appeared in national politics before World War II as a member of the Chamber of Deputies and of the Senate, and afterward as a member of the Constituent Assembly and of the National Assembly. In the series of Cabinets between September 1948 and February 1952, he held the portfolio of Minister of Public Works, Transportation, and Tourism.

Antoine Pinay was born December 30, 1891, in Saint-Symphorien-sur-Coise, a town of the Department of the Rhône. He attended the Marist Fathers' school at Saint-Chamond. Upon being graduated Pinay entered a tannery business in Saint-Chamond, in the Department of the Loire. Active in groups devoted to his industry's interests, Pinay has been vice-president of the sole-leather division of the General Association of Leather and Hide Manufacturers (Syndicat Général des Cuirs et Peaux) and honorary president of the Association of the Rhône Leather and Hide Industry (Syndicat de l'Industrie des Cuirs et Peaux du Rhône). Serving as a noncommissioned officer in the artillery during World War I, Pinay, who was wounded, received the Croix de Guerre and the Médaille Militaire.

Pinay, reported Lansing Warren of the New York *Times*, "is said to have entered politics largely against his will, for he considered himself as strictly a businessman." His first elective office was that of Mayor of Saint-Chamond (1932). Subsequently he was a general councilor of the Department of the Loire. At the time of the heavy vote for the Popular Front of Léon Blum in 1936, Pinay, running on the ticket of the Independent Radical party, was one of the few moderates returned to the Chamber of Deputies. In the ensuing elections of 1938 he was returned to the French Senate, and it was as a Senator that he joined some 560 other members of the French Parliament two years later in voting extraordinary powers to Marshal Pétain following the collapse of France. After the Liberation, declared Warren, "the Communists violently attacked him for having been appointed member of the National Council of the Petainist regime." Pinay retained his post as Mayor of Saint-Chamond throughout the World War II years: "Pinay managed to avoid collaborationist charges by his excellent record as wartime Mayor," noted *Time*. To this Lansing Warren added: "He stood up against the Nazis, and the workers remember this and have since kept him as their Mayor."

Antoine Pinay returned to the national political scene in 1946, first with his election to the second Constituent Assembly of that year, and then to the first National Assembly under the new Constitution of the Fourth Republic. Under the revised electoral system of 1951, Pinay was re-elected to the National Assembly as an associate of the Independent Republican group.

The first Cabinet post held by Pinay was that of Secretary of State for Economic Affairs under Henri Queuille, from September 11, 1948, to October 5, 1949. From the investiture of the first Pleven Cabinet on July 12, 1950, until the fall of the Faure Cabinet on February 29, 1952, Pinay remained in the several successive ministries as Minister of Public Works, Transportation and Tourism. His chief task while incumbent of this post was the projected reorganization of the French National Railroads (La Société Nationale des Chemins de Fer). Interested in coordinating facilities for rail and road transportation, Pinay in November 1951 came to the United States to study the American solution of such transport coordination problems.

With the fall of the Faure Cabinet over its proposal to raise taxes and the subsequent inability of former Premiers Reynaud and Pleven to assemble new ministries, Pinay was requested by Premier Auriol to form a Government. Wishing specialists (regardless of political connections) for his Government, Pinay sought support among the Rightist and Centrist parties with proposals for a "political truce" to enable stabilization of the nation's economy, a tax amnesty, and an eventual reform of the Constitution. By an unexpected revolt of twenty-seven Gaullist deputies (their Rally of the French People had heretofore refused to support any Government which their leader did not head), and with votes from other Center and Right groups, Pinay was confirmed as Premier on March 6, 1952, by 324 to 206 votes, the Socialists and the Communists abstaining. Speaking on his program before the National Assembly, Pinay said: "The remedies proposed to you are neither of the Left or of the Right. They are the technical steps that should be taken in an atmosphere of political truce." Despite opposition to Robert Schuman, Pinay retained him as Foreign Minister in the seventeen-member Cabinet which was approved by a simple majority of 290 to 101 on March 11 (the Gaullists and Socialists abstained; a single Gaullist deputy and the Communists comprised the opposition). "Premier Pinay failed in his aim to have the Cabinet composed mainly of experts and technicians," said Lansing Warren, who pointed out, however, that the conservative compositon of his ministry had had a favorable reaction on the Bourse and in financial circles.

Pinay immediately attacked the financial crisis by obtaining a $100,000,000 credit for France from the European Payments Union, thus preventing the necessity of drawing upon the Bank of France's gold reserves before scheduled gold repayments by Germany were made in May. (The latter sum was visualized as partial repayment for the E.P.U. loan.) At the same time the Premier reached an agreement with the Bank of France to postpone for two months the reimbursement of 25 billion francs borrowed by the Government from the bank in February. Further measures taken by Pinay were the freezing of rates charged by national utilities and services and the issuance of new short-term, low denomination government bonds. To reduce consumer prices, Pinay brought about the reduction of milk prices to the usual summer level, with the expectation that this would act similarly on other dairy product prices; and simultaneously released a 1,000 tons of government-held butter toward the same end. He and his Cabinet then planned to consider the problem of tax evasion and of the repatriation of French capital placed abroad, with a probable amnesty for tax delinquents and to hoarders, but heavy penalties for future evasions. On March 22 he presented 1952 budget estimates, which provided for 110 billion francs' ($314 millions) reduction in Governmental expenses and an unchanged amount of 1 trillion ($4 billions) in national defense expenditures. Editorials in the United States commented on his wisdom in balancing the budget without imposing new taxes, the measure that caused Faure's downfall.

In 1949 Pinay became president of the General Council of the Loire, a position he retains in 1952. *Time* has described Pinay as having "near-crinkly" hair, a long thin face, and a small mustache. The French Premier is married and has three children—Pierre, Geneviève, and Odette—and several grandchildren.

References

N Y Herald Tribune II p1 Mr 9 '52
Time 59:28 Mr 17 '52

PINE, DAVID A(NDREW) Sept. 22, 1891-
Judge

Address: b. c/o United States District Court, Washington, D.C.; h. 1625 Nicholson St., N.W., Washington, D.C.

As a judge of the District Court of the United States for the District of Columbia, which heard the case of the steel owners against Government seizure of their plants, David A. Pine ruled on April 29, 1952, that the Presidential order authorizing the emergency measure was unconstitutional and granted the steel mills a temporary injunction against the seizure. His decision was described by the New York *Times* as "the most precise and firmest restraints on Executive power that have been stated by a Federal court in our history." Before 1940, when Pine was appointed to the Federal bench by President Roosevelt, he had served in the Department of Justice at various times as clerk, as special assistant to the United States Attorney General and as chief assistant to, and himself, the United States Attorney for the District of Columbia. He was not attached to a Government office for thirteen years, during which period he maintained his own law office in the nation's capital.

David Andrew Pine is a native of Washington, D.C., having been born in that city on September 22, 1891, to David Emery and Charlotte (McCormick) Pine. His father, who was a lawyer in Washington, died when young Pine was still a schoolboy. Subsequently, leaving high school, the youth took a job as a clerk in the office of a railroad. He continued his education at night, however, completing his high school studies and a course in a business

DAVID A. PINE

college before becoming a student at Georgetown University Law School.

During his college years he earned his expenses by working as a secretary to a general in the War College and later as law clerk to Attorney General James C. McReynolds. In 1913, upon receiving his LL.B. degree from Georgetown University, he was admitted to the District of Columbia bar. The next year (1913-14), while attending postgraduate classes at the university, he entered the employ of the Justice Department as a confidential clerk to United States Attorney General Thomas W. Gregory. There he remained until 1916. When he left Government service to join the Army in 1917, he had reached the rank of assistant attorney.

During World War I Pine, who entered the Army as a first lieutenant and left as a captain, served in the Provost Marshal's office. In 1919 he returned to the Justice Department as special assistant to the United States Attorney General, an appointment involving a number of Federal cases concerning water and mineral rights in the Western States. Having left the Federal employ in 1921, Pine engaged in private law practice in Washington until 1934, for part of this time (1925-29) as a member of the firm of Easby-Smith, Pine and Hill. He handled cases for labor unions as well as management groups. In 1934 he accepted the appointment as chief assistant to the United States Attorney for the District of Columbia, from which post he was advanced four years later to United States District Attorney for the District of Columbia. In his two years in this office, reported the *United States News* (May 9, 1952), Pine revealed himself to be "an aggressive prosecuting officer, bearing down heavily on Washington's gambling racketeers, exposed corruption in the United States Marshal's Office, and sent a Congressman and his son to

jail for conspiring to sell a West Point appointment."

When a vacancy occurred in 1940 on the bench of the United States District Court for the District of Columbia, the Federal Bar Association, which usually submits to the President the names of three or four candidates for the judgeship, suggested only Pine for the appointment. On April 2, 1940, he became one of fifteen judges of that District Court.

In the twelve years (as of 1952) that Pine has been a Federal judge, a number of the cases which he tried, each dealing with questions of individual freedom, received wide notice. In 1945 he was one of three judges who found eight Hollywood writers and producers guilty of contempt of Congress for refusing to tell the House Committee whether they were members of the Communist party. Another case, tried in 1948, involved a treason charge against an American-born woman who broadcast for the German radio during World War II; Pine ruled that insufficient evidence prevented treason proceedings. In May of 1950 he imposed the maximum sentence of a year in prison and a $1,000 fine on Eugene Dennis, secretary of the Communist party in the United States, for contempt of Congress in refusing to testify before the House Committee on Un-American Activities.

The case involving the powers of the President in peacetime, on which Pine was called upon to render the decision, began on April 8, 1952, when President Truman ordered the Secretary of Commerce to seize the seven-billion-dollar steel industry and to operate the plants of 92 companies for the Federal Government as a means of preventing a strike by 650,000 members of the United Steelworkers of America (CIO). Refusal of the steel owners to accept the wage recommendations of the Wage Stabilization Board unless they were coupled with increases in steel prices, the threatened walkout of steel workers as a result of this breakdown in negotiations, and the strategic importance of steel in national defense programs were the three issues which led to the Presidential order. On the appeal from the steel owners for a temporary injunction against the seizure, Judge Pine ruled on April 29, 1952, that the act was unconstitutional and therefore illegal and issued an order restoring the industry to its private owners. However, a United States Court of Appeals stayed the order pending a Supreme Court review, which opened on May 12, 1952. Of seventy seizures of private companies executed by Presidential order since 1941, this was the first to be questioned on the Constitutional powers of the President.

In judging the steel seizure an unconstitutional act, Pine became, in the words of the *United States News*, "the first modern jurist to draw a line firmly limiting the powers of the President in time of peace." He ruled that the President has no more authority to assume powers not granted by the Constitution than have Congress and the courts, however grave the emergency. The Federal judge found in his decision that "there is no express grant of power in the Constitution authorizing the President to direct this seizure. There is no grant of power from which it reasonably can be implied. There is no enactment of Congress authorizing it." Nor did Pine find in the Constitution any "residuum of power" or "inherent" powers permitting the President to order the seizure of private property. He concluded his decision: "I believe that the contemplated strike, if it came, with all its awful results, would be less injurious to the public than the injury which would flow from a timorous judicial recognition that there is some basis for this claim to unlimited and unrestrained executive power. . . .Such recognition would undermine public confidence in the very edifice of government as it is known under the Constitution."

Judge Pine is the author of *Judicial Control of Executive by Mandamus and Injunction* (1923). He is a member of the American Bar Association, Federal Bar Association, the Lawyers Club, and the Barristers Club, for which last-named organization he once served as president. He belongs to the Democratic party and names his church as the Episcopal. His club in Washington is the Metropolitan. On August 23, 1916, he married Elizabeth Bradshaw. In former years he, his wife, and their one child, Elizabeth (Pine) Dayton, enjoyed horseback riding together. One of his other diversions is reading novels. The jurist has been described as "a slightly stooped man with iron-gray hair and a dry humor."

References

N Y Herald Tribune p13 Ap 30 '52; II pl My 4 '52 por
N Y Mirror p10 My 1 '52 por
N Y Times p57 Ap 27 '52
U S News 32:73 My 9 '52 por
Who's Who in America, 1952-53
Who's Who in Law, 1937
Who's Who in the South and Southwest (1950)
World Biography (1948)

POINDEXTER, JOSEPH B(OYD) Apr. 14, 1869—Dec. 3, 1951 Former Governor of Hawaii; practiced law in Montana (1892-1917); judge of the United States District Court in Hawaii (1917-24); entered private law practice in Honolulu (1924); one-time president of the Bar Association of Hawaii and member of the Democratic Territorial Central Committee; Governor of Hawaii (1934-42). See *Current Biography*, 1942.

Obituary

N Y Times p33 D 4 '51

POOLE, DEWITT C(LINTON) Oct. 28, 1885—Sept. 3, 1952 Organization official; educator; served twenty years in United States consular and diplomatic posts (1910-30); chairman of the advisory board of Princeton's School of Public and International Affairs (1930-48); director of the Foreign Nationalities Branch of the Office of Strategic Services (1941-45); first president of the National Committee for a Free Europe (1949-51) and vice-chairman (1951); president of the Free Europe University in Exile (1951-52). See *Current Biography*, 1950.

Obituary

N Y Times p27 S 4 '52

POPOVIC, VLADIMIR (pō'pō-vĕch vlăd-ē'mēr) Jan. 27, 1914 Ambassador from Yugoslavia to the United States
Address: b. c/o Embassy of the Republic of Yugoslavia, 1520 16th St., Washington, D.C.; h. 2221 R St., N.W., Washington, D.C.

The Ambassador of the Federal People's Republic of Yugoslavia to the United States is Vladimir Popovic, who was assigned to the Washington post in 1950, when Yugoslavia leaned toward friendlier relations with the Western powers. A former deputy Foreign Minister of Yugoslavia, Popovic has been described by the New York *Times* "as perhaps the most influential figure in the Yugoslav Foreign Office after Dr. Edvard Kardelj, the Foreign Minster." From 1945 until the Cominform denunciation of Yugoslavia in 1948, Popovic was his country's ambassador to the Soviet Union. He has also served on delegations to the United Nations General Assembly and to the Paris Peace Conference (1946). During World War II he was a leader of his country's Partisans.

The son of Luka and Stana (Jovanovic) Popovic, Vladimir Popovic was born January 27, 1914, in Cetinje, a town in the mountainous Montenegrin province of what is today part of Yugoslavia. After spending his childhood and youth in Cetinje, Popovic in 1932 entered the School of Medicine of the University of Belgrade, from which he received his medical degree five years later. Shortly after his graduation Popovic was chosen by his former fellow students to represent them as their delegate to the World Students Congress, held in Paris in 1937. It was in that city, *Time* reported, that the young Yugoslavian, who had in 1932 joined the Yugoslav Communist party, met Tito (Josip Broz) in 1938, when the latter had just become secretary of the Yugoslav Communist party. Shortly thereafter, in the rank of captain in the Spanish Republican Army, Popovic saw duty as a medical officer with the Loyalist forces from 1937 to the end of the Spanish Civil War in 1939.

Following the invasion of Yugoslavia by German forces at the beginning of World War II, Popovic in 1941 became a leader of the Peoples' Liberation Movement in Croatia. The Nazis, seeking to prove they were being supported in occupied areas, erroneously reported two years later that he was one of two Yugoslavian leaders who had gone over to the Germans (*Time*, June 21, 1943). Popovic, in 1944 advanced to the rank of major general, was placed in command of the Third Army Corps of the Peoples' Liberation Army in Bosnia. Under the leadership of Marshal Tito, the Liberation forces—more popularly known as the

Wide World Photos

VLADIMIR POPOVIC

Partisans—had fought not only against the Axis invaders, but against the native Chetnik army of General Draja Mikhailovitch. Until 1945, when the Yugoslav struggle for liberation was achieved with the aid of Soviet forces, Popovic was also a member of the Supreme Headquarters of the Peoples' Liberation Army and Partisan Units of Yugoslavia.

A kingdom since its establishment in 1919 (after the collapse of the Dual Monarchy), Yugoslavia became the Federal People's Republic of Yugoslavia on November 29, 1945. At that time the provisional government set up by Tito the previous March, under a mandate from King Peter permitting him to form a regency council, was confirmed by the early November elections for the Constituent Assembly. As a delegate from what was then the provisional government of Yugoslavia, with Marshal Tito as its Premier, Popovic was sent to Bulgaria early in 1945 to be Yugoslavian political and military representative there, with the rank of lieutenant general. On May 2, 1945, he was named Yugoslavia's first Communist Ambassador to the Soviet Union. Shortly afterward, speaking of the relations between his country's Communist Government and that of the Soviet Union, Popovic commented: "I believe that we shall meet with full understanding in official circles in Moscow and that the U.S.S.R. will support all our justified aspirations" (*Time*, May 28, 1945). A year later (May 1946) Tito, Popovic, and other Yugoslav representatives reached an agreement in Moscow with the Soviet government on foreign trade, economic cooperation, and armament supplies for Yugoslavia; both countries were in accord on the exchange of commodities and certain raw materials. On July 25, 1947, Popovic was signatory to another such agreement, for the 1947-48 period, said *Keesing's Contemporary Archives*. At a December 1947

meeting of diplomats called in Moscow to protest against the U.S.S.R.'s newly established diplomatic exchange rate for the ruble, Popovic defended the Russian revaluation of its currency. He served as Ambassador to the Soviet Union until the condemnation by the Communist Bureau of Information (Cominform) of the Communist regime in Yugoslavia, in 1948.

Besides denouncing the organization and composition of the Yugoslav Communist party, the Cominform resolution denounced its leaders, among whom Tito and Popovic, with others, were named as "spies" and "enemies of the working and peasant class . . . who do not translate the will of the peoples of Yugoslavia but that of the Anglo-American imperialists" (*Archives Internationales*). Premier Tito's intransigeance before Cominform pressure, which at home brought about national unity behind Tito, caused the Soviet Union and its satellites to impose on Yugoslavia an economic blockade, which in turn led that country to look to the Western powers for economic aid. As first Deputy Minister of Foreign Affairs from 1948 to 1950 under Foreign Minister Edvard Kardelj, Popovic, who was elected to the Central Committee of the Yugoslav Communist party in 1948, was one of the Yugoslav diplomats occupied with the transition of his country's policy during a period when relations with the Soviet Union continued to deteriorate.

For five successive years, from 1946 to 1950, Popovic was a member of the Yugoslavian delegation to the United Nations General Assembly. At the first meeting of the General Assembly held in London in January 1946 and at the Peace Conference held in Paris from August to October of that year, he served on the delegations which put forward Yugoslavia's claims to the territories of Trieste, Venezia Giulia, and Gorizia; and which denounced the draft treaty with Italy as "a violation of the fundamental principles" upheld in World War II. At a U. N. General Assembly meeting in New York on October 16, 1947, Popovic attacked the "Little Assembly" plan put forward by American delegate John Foster Dulles and Australian delegate Evatt. Until the split between Yugoslavia and the Soviet Union in 1948-49, the Yugoslavian U.N. delegation had voted with the Soviet bloc—a situation which had changed by the time Popovic became chief of the delegation attending the second part of the third General Assembly in the autumn of 1949. With United States support, the Yugoslavian delegation succeeded that October in obtaining election of its country to the Security Council, to a seat contested by Czechoslovakia, which remained in the Soviet orbit. Soviet-Yugoslav relations reached so low a point in 1950 that the Yugoslav delegation to the U.N. General Assembly demanded assurances of Western military aid in the event that Yugoslavia were attacked.

On March 30, 1950, it was announced that Vladimir Popovic had been named Yugoslav Ambassador to the United States, to succeed Sava Kosanovic, who was recalled to Belgrade to fill a Cabinet post. *United States News* considered his appointment an indication that Tito "wants very much to further friendly relations with the United States." Upon his arrival in the United States in May, Popovic stated in an interview for the New York *Herald Tribune*: "It is the wish of Yugoslavia to maintain the broadest possible and lasting cooperation based on respect of Yugoslavian independence and sovereignty." He further said that his country wanted no "bloc system whatsoever" since "blocs lead to war." Threatened by famine in the second half of 1950, following crop failures, Yugoslavia was granted a $15,000,000 loan by the United States in August "for essential purposes." Shortly afterward Ambassador Popovic returned to Belgrade to discuss financing of food purchases in the United States and on his return, presented a formal request for an estimated $105,000,000 in food products to United States Secretary of State Dean Acheson, who showed himself to be favorable to such a grant, subject to legislative action. (In November 1950, $38,000,000 in food supplies went to Yugoslavia for the use of its armed forces.) A request for military aid submitted to Acheson by Popovic in June 1951 "was accompanied by indications that Mr. Popovic did not believe any immediate crisis in the Balkans was pending," noted a New York *Herald Tribune* editorial, "but that the continuing pressure of the Soviet bloc on its former member made the strengthening of the Yugoslav Army imperative." The following month, the United States, Great Britain, and France agreed to give Yugoslavia $50,000,000 in economic aid. On November 7, 1952, at the sixth congress of the Yugoslav Communist party (Federation of Communists of Yugoslav), Popovic was elected a member of the party's central committee.

The Yugoslav Ambassador's wife is the former Vjera Radimir, whom he met during World War II and married in Paris in 1946. In 1941, reported *Time*, she had been captured and tortured by the Nazis, who wanted to know the whereabouts of Popovic. Mme. Popovic takes an interest in the fostering of Yugoslav cultural relations with other countries. Both she and the Ambassador enjoy tennis, skiing, and swimming. Another sport of Popovic's is hunting, an enthusiasm he shares with Marshal Tito, often his companion on shooting trips in Serbia. Six feet three inches tall, Popovic has been described by Elizabeth Maguire of the Washington *Post* as having a "rather dynamic and forceful make-up."

References

N Y Herald Tribune p13 My 16 '50
N Y Times p7 Mr 31 '50
U N Bul 6:440 My 1 '49
Washington (D.C.) Post p7S Je 11 '50 por

Who's Who in America, 1950-51
Who's Who in the United Nations (1951)
World Biography (1948)

PORTER, MRS. ELIZABETH K(ERR)

May 21, 1894- Organization official; nurse
Address: b. c/o Frances Payne Bolton School of Nursing, Western Reserve University, 2063 Adelbert Rd., Cleveland, Ohio; h. 2554 Derbyshire Rd., Cleveland Heights, Cleveland, Ohio

As president of the American Nurses' Association, Mrs. Elizabeth K. Porter is the leader of 175,000 nurses, who comprise the only national nursing organization made up entirely of registered professional nurses. First elected to the presidency in 1950 by the association's house of delegates in San Francisco, Mrs. Porter was re-elected to this office on June 20, 1952. Since 1935 she has been active in the teaching of nurses and in the work of State and national organizations promoting the welfare of nurses. She has been professor of nursing and director of programs in nursing education at the Frances Payne Bolton School of Nursing at Western Reserve University since 1949.

Born on May 21, 1894, in Pittsburgh, Pennsylvania, Elizabeth Kerr Porter was the first child of Richard and Catherine (Anderson) Kerr, who had two other daughters and two sons. As a young girl, Elizabeth studied piano and came to love music. At Fifth Avenue High School in Pittsburgh she prepared for a teaching career but upon graduating in 1911 took a position as a stenographer for two years. After her marriage in 1914 to Eugene Vandergrift Porter, she studied piano at the Bingham Studio in Bellevue, Pennsylvania, where she later (following the death of her husband in 1921) taught music for five years. In 1926, she has said, she decided that she did not have "sufficient talent for music as a career but only as an avocation." Mrs. Porter, whose two closest friends were nurses, soon began to see nursing as a career that offered "great possibilities for a very interesting life with real meaning and usefulness."

Consequently, Mrs. Porter in 1927 entered Western Pennsylvania Hospital School of Nursing in Pittsburgh. After graduating from this school in 1930, she continued her studies in nursing education at Teachers College, Columbia University, from which she received her B.S. degree in 1935 and certificate to teach in schools of nursing. In 1936 she obtained the M.S. degree in education from the University of Pennsylvania and in 1946 the Ed.D. degree in educational administration from the same university.

While she was working for her degrees, Mrs. Porter held the position of teaching supervisor at Western Pennsylvania Hospital (1930-35). Between 1933 and 1935 she was also a part-time lecturer in nursing at Margaret Morrison Carnegie College in Pittsburgh. In 1935 she accepted an appointment as assistant professor of nursing education at the University of Pennsylvania, while at the same time lecturing in nursing education at Johns Hopkins University. Expressing her views on nursing-education needs in a speech, "Principles Underlying Postgraduate Education," at the forty-fifth annual convention of the National League for Nursing Education (New Orleans, 1939), she said: "The American people as a whole have faith that education can take them where they want to go. The impact of all this is felt in all systems of education, and nowhere more forcibly than in our own [nursing] field. Our continued progress is dependent upon oppor-

Chase News Photo.
MRS. ELIZABETH K. PORTER

tunities for research and experimentation." In the course of World War II (1943-44) Mrs. Porter was coordinator of a central teaching program at the University of Pennsylvania in which four schools of nursing participated to speed up the preparation of nurses for war service. She was promoted from assistant professor to associate professor, then to full professor of nursing education at the University of Pennsylvania between the years 1940 and 1949.

Leaving the University of Pennsylvania in 1949, Mrs. Porter became a professor of nursing and the director of advanced programs in nursing education at the Frances Payne Bolton School of Nursing, Western Reserve University. The following year she was elected president of the American Nurses' Association by its house of delegates at San Francisco. From an organization of a few hundred nurses in 1896, known then as the Nurses' Association Alumnae of United States and Canada, the association has grown to a body of approximately 175,000. (In 1899 Canada was dropped from the name when the organization was incorporated in New York State, where representatives of two nations were prohibited.) The association took its present name in 1911 when the basis of membership was changed from nurses' alumnae groups to State nurses' associations. From its early interest in such nursing problems as educational standards and State registration, the organization has widened its scope to include questions relating to the distribution and nature of nursing services. The A.N.A.'s over-all purpose is to promote high standards in nursing and to advance the welfare of individual nurses. Since 1900 it has been a member of the International Council of Nurses, and since 1909 it has cooperated with the American Red Cross. Working closely with Federal government nursing services, the asso-

ciation promoted the bill which gave full rank to members of the Army nurse corps. In 1946 it recommended that all State and district nurse associations eliminate membership bans on Negro nurses, and since 1948 the organization has permitted Negro nurses to become direct members of the national body in States that prohibit their membership in local groups.

During Mrs. Porter's presidency in 1950, the American Nurses' Association began a five-year study to see how nursing tasks could be more effectively distributed among nurses, auxiliary helpers, and other workers. In July of the same year at a Chicago conference of secretaries of nurses' associations, Mrs. Porter urged more professional nurse representatives on hospital advisory committees. "Only twenty-two States have professional nurse representatives on their State hospital advisory committees, although nursing care is the major service provided by hospitals. Nurses have failed to assert their rightful position of leadership in matters in which they enjoy highly qualified competence and experience" (New York *Times*, July 10, 1950).

With Mrs. Porter presiding, on January 23, 1951, the American Nurses' Association advisory council took a unanimous stand against the proposed Equal Rights Amendment before Congress, holding that this amendment would eliminate legislation that protects women as homemakers and workers. In June of the same year Mrs. Porter testified in Washington before the House and the Senate Banking and Currency Committees on the question of economic controls to prevent inflation. The New York *Times* (June 2, 1951) quoted her as saying: "Efforts to maintain an adequate nurse force will be seriously jeopardized if our national Government fails to correct economic imbalances and inequities that impose special burdens on nurses and fixed-income workers." Bernard Baruch was reported by the *American Journal of Nursing* (August 1951) as replying to Mrs. Porter: "You have spoken not only for the nursing profession, but for the people you serve, and indeed for the whole country."

Early in 1952 Mrs. Porter denounced the organized pressure on nurses to oppose the Truman Administration's proposal for compulsory national health insurance, stating that "it is not up to other groups to tell nurses what to do" (New York *World-Telegram*, January 22, 1952). This same year she also emphasized the importance of the A.N.A.'s "no-strike" policy which assigned the bargaining rights of individual nurses to State nurses' associations. "There is no intention," she said, "of altering the basic 'no-strike' policy [adopted in 1950], because under no circumstances would the national leaders approve strikes which might jeopardize patients. What needs to be stressed is the obligation of State nursing associations to advise groups whose conditions seem intolerable and to help them negotiate with their employers before strike action becomes necessary" (New York *Herald Tribune*, January 22, 1952).

At the Atlantic City convention the A.N.A. house of delegates on June 20, 1952, re-elected Mrs. Porter president. At the same time they expanded the organization and accepted a new platform, including cooperation with the Federal Civil Defense Administration and the Department of National Defense in promoting health care in times of emergency, advancement of State nursing practice laws to protect the public, improvement of employment conditions for nurses and legislation to expand their educational facilities, and continuing support of the United Nations and its agency the World Health Organization through the International Council of Nurses. The association's individual sections were increased to comprise general duty nurses, industrial nurses, private duty nurses, institutional administrative nurses, educational administrators, consultants and teachers, and special group sections. The house of delegates of the expanded American Nurses' Association endorsed a selective service for nurses in the event of a national emergency, approved a resolution for efforts to achieve a commission status for men nurses in the armed services, and called for a forty-hour week for nurses, without reduction in present salaries, providing for two consecutive days off and time and one-half for overtime.

In an article, "The Economic Security Program and the Profession of Nursing," written for the *American Journal of Nursing* (December 1948), Mrs. Porter stated: "The nursing profession stands on the threshold of revolutionary changes both in our system of nursing education and in our system of nursing service. . . .The economic security program means that the nursing profession is gradually shifting to a new status in employer-employee relations. Like other groups, nurses are moving from the authoritarian relationship to one that involves greater democratic participation in policy development. In a word, the economic security program will promote justice between nurses and employers." Among other articles written by Mrs. Porter are "A Realistic No-strike Policy" and "Salute to the Future" (*American Journal of Nursing*, September 1951 and August 1952 respectively).

Mrs. Porter is a member of the honorary education society Pi Lamda Theta, the Joint Commission for Improvement of Patient Care, the Inter-Association Committee on Health, the board of directors of the International Council of Nurses, and the Board of National Health Council. Some of her positions during the 1935-50 period were secretary of the Pennsylvania League of Nursing Education, a member of the board of directors of the Philadelphia League of Nursing Education, the chairman of the economic security committee of the Pennsylvania State Nurses' Association, a member of the board of directors of the American Nurses' Association, the executive director of the former joint committee of the Pennsylvania State Nurses' Association and the Hospital Association of Pennsylvania on Personnel Policies and Practices, and a member of the Nursing Council of Metropolitan Philadelphia.

Her friends in the national nursing organizations refer to Mrs. Porter as "an idealist." She has brown eyes and reddish-brown hair and is five feet seven and one-half inches tall.

Her hobbies are reading, "good" movies, concerts, and forum lectures; her favorite pastime was chess playing until, as she put it, she was unable to find a partner for the game. She has said of her work: "There are changes going on in the field of nursing, and it gives me great happiness to be in a position where I have a feeling of participation in bringing some of these changes about."

PORTER, MRS. EUGENE VANDER-GRIFT *See* Porter, Mrs. E. K.

PRIEST, IVY (MAUDE) BAKER Sept. 7, 1905- Political organization official; Treasurer of the United States-designate
Address: b. c/o Republican National Committee, 923 15th St., N.W., Washington 5, D.C; h. Bountiful, Utah

Soon after his victory in the November 1952 election, President-elect Dwight D. Eisenhower, designated Mrs. Ivy Baker Priest as the next Treasurer of the United States.

IVY BAKER PRIEST

In the Presidential campaign, as assistant chairman in charge of the women's division of the Republican National Committee, she had the task of securing a large number of votes from women for General Eisenhower and other Republican candidates. Mrs. Priest, who was appointed on August 15, 1952, by national committee chairman, Arthur E. Summerfield, to succeed Mrs. Gilford Mayes in that position, entered politics in 1932 when she began organizational work with the Young Republicans. Formerly a member of the Utah State Republican Committee, she has also been, since 1944, a member of the Republican National Committee. In 1950 she was the Republican

PRIEST, IVY BAKER—*Continued*

candidate from Utah for election to the United States Congress.

Born September 7, 1905, in Kimberley, Utah, Ivy Maude Baker Priest was the oldest of seven children of Orange Decatur and Clara (Fearnley) Baker. She attended the elementary schools in Kimberley and high school in Bingham, Utah, where her father was a miner. As reported by the *Christian Science Monitor* (September 8, 1952), Mrs. Clara Baker, who was much interested in politics, earned the title of "Mrs. Republican" in Bingham. In encouraging women to vote, on election day she had her ten-year-old daughter go to the polls after school to take care of babies and do errands for women voters.

When she had graduated from high school, Ivy Maude Baker sought to continue her education by taking extension courses at the University of Utah. Her father having become ill, she found it necessary to discontinue her studies in order to contribute to the family resources by going to work. Her first position was as telephone operator, from which she advanced to supervisor. Her interests soon drew her into the field of merchandising; while in this occupation, she also taught evening school classes in American history and citizenship. On December 7, 1935, she married Roy Fletcher Priest, a wholesale furniture dealer.

From her first work in party politics with the Young Republicans in 1932, Mrs. Priest rose to the presidency of the Utah State Young Republican Organization (1934-36) and to the directorship of the Young Republican Western States Organization (1936-40). During the years 1940-1944 she was a member of the Utah State Republican Committee and in 1944 she became a member of the Republican National Committee for Utah, after first serving on its executive committee. While engaged in these political activities, Mrs. Priest was from 1937 to 1939 president of the Utah State Women's Legislative Council. During the next few years she played an important part in establishing the Youth Center for Davis County, Salt Lake City, and was a leader in the movement which resulted in the first minimum wage law for working women in Utah. Her interest in the public affairs and welfare of the West led her to serve as vice-president and secretary of the Republican organization of eleven Western States. Since 1945 she has been vice-president and director of the women's division of the Utah Safety Council.

A delegate of the National Committee on Women from Utah, Mrs. Priest in June 1948 attended the Republican party convention in Philadelphia. At this convention, for the first time a woman was chosen to become chairman of the subcommittee of the strategic resolutions committee (New York *Times*, June 20, 1948). This was a move in the direction toward which Mrs. Priest has stated she believed women should go—toward more elective and governmental positions. She has said, as quoted by the New York *Times*, that there were "many women qualified for any appointive post, in-cluding one in the Cabinet, as well as for elective office."

After running unsuccessfully as Republican candidate for Utah's Second Congressional District to the United States House of Representatives in September 1950, Mrs. Priest became the Republican party's national committeewoman. She led the so-called "Young Turk" forces that campaigned for General Eisenhower before his nomination for the Presidency on the Republican ticket. At the Chicago convention in the summer of 1952 she was one of the people who tried to open the convention credential committee meetings to televison. On August 15, 1952, Mrs. Priest was appointed by Arthur E. Summerfield, chairman of the Republican National Committee, to succeed Mrs. Gilford Mayes as assistant in charge of the women's division of the National Committee. Her opponent and counterpart in the Democratic party is Mrs. India Edwards; each is endeavoring to win the women voters for her party. When Mrs. Priest took over her post, she predicted that the votes of millions of women, now exceeding men in the United States, would put General Dwight D. Eisenhower in the White House in November 1952. "Women," she said, "are going to the polls this year because, first of all, they want peace, and, second, they want a change for the better" (New York *Times*, August 21, 1952). For both reasons, she stated, they would vote for and elect General Eisenhower.

In her office as assistant to Summerfield, Mrs. Priest had the responsibility of coordinating the efforts of all the various women's organizations working in the campaign for the victory of the Eisenhower-Nixon ticket. "From all over the country," the New York *Times* (August 21, 1952) quoted her as saying, "we've been getting requests from women's clubs and groups asking for information about the issues and how to get out the vote. Our big job will be to see that this information gets the widest possible distribution." The organization in which Mrs. Priest holds office, the Republican National Committee, had been authorized at the Republican National Convention in Philadelphia in June 1856 for the purpose of conducting the national convention every four years and of aiding in the election of the Republican Presidential candidate and other Republican candidates for national office nominated at the convention. It has the responsibility of raising funds for the Presidential election campaign and of promoting the interests of the Republican party through publications and press and radio releases. Mrs. Priest announced in August 1952 a campaign project employing visual aid presentation of political issues, including such films as *Who? Me? Or What Taxes Are Doing to the Average American Family*, which were to be shown on portable projectors.

Mrs. Priest came to her position with the Republican National Committee in Washington directly following a meeting with fourteen prominent Republican women leaders and General Eisenhower in Denver, Colorado. At this meeting, she stated that she found the Presidential nominee uncommunicative regarding plans to put women in high office, if he were elected: "General Eisenhower was well aware of the increasing role women must play in election campaigns, but declared he had given no commitments about putting them in high office" (New York *Times*, August 21, 1952). Speaking of the General's qualifications for office, she said: "In General Eisenhower we have a candidate who knows the horrors of war and is trained in the best way to bring one to swift conclusion. Moreover, people have confidence in General Eisenhower because of his 'admirable administrative ability.'" On the need for a change in government, Mrs. Priest has commented: "Women know that inflation has riddled their household budgets, and the best cure would be the all-out attack of a Republican administration on waste in government and public expenditures" (New York *Times*, August 21, 1952). With two other top-ranking women on the Republican National Committee, Mrs. Priest in September 1952 attended the convention of the National Federation of Women Republican Clubs in St. Louis, where she spoke on women's part in the Presidential campaign and also appeared in place of Summerfield, who at this time was on Eisenhower's campaign train. After the convention she planned to make a campaign tour on which she would speak in Lansing (Michigan), Topeka (Kansas), and Oklahoma City.

In reference to the appointment of Mrs. Priest to the committee post, Summerfield stated on August 15, 1952: "The 1952 election is one of the most vital to women in our history, and no one knows this better than Ivy Priest. The significance of her appointment lies in the realization of Dwight D. Eisenhower, Senator Nixon, and the entire Republican organization that women will play a greater role in this election than ever before. . . . As a housewife, mother, and experienced political worker . . . Mrs. Priest knows organization work as well as anyone in politics today." On November 25, 1952, President-elect Eisenhower announced that after his inauguration in January 1953 he would appoint Mrs. Priest Treasurer of the United States.

Mrs. Priest is the mother of four children: Patricia Ann, Peggy Louise (deceased), Nancy Ellen, and Roy Baker. She holds membership in the General Federation of Women's Clubs and the American Red Cross, and was chairman of the Junior Red Cross of Davis County from 1938 to 1940. Her religious affiliation is the Church of Jesus Christ of the Latter-day Saints. She is tall and trim with brown eyes and dark hair.

References

N Y Times p12 Ag 16 '52; p13 Ag 21 '52
Who's Who in America, 1952-53

PRIEST, MRS. ROY F(LETCHER) *See* Priest, I. M. B.

PUSEY, MERLO J(OHN) (pū'-zĭ) Feb. 3, 1902- Author; editor
Address: b. c/o Washington Post, 1515 L St., N.W., Washington 5, D.C.; h. 5209 Albemarle St., Washington 16, D.C.

Merlo J. Pusey, associate editor of the Washington (D.C.) *Post* and author of several articles and books on various aspects of public administration, was awarded the Pulitzer Prize for his biography, *Charles Evans Hughes,* in 1952. This two-volume work on the late Supreme Court Justice, the result of six years of research including many personal interviews with Chief Justice Hughes himself, was chosen for the $500 prize as being "the best American biography teaching patriotic and unselfish service to the people."

Merlo John Pusey was born on February 3, 1902, on a farm at Woodruff, Utah, one of eight sons of John Sidney and Nellie (Quibell) Pusey, both of English ancestry. The elder Pusey was a merchant and postmaster in the ranching community during his son's boyhood and later became employed in a wholesale house in Salt Lake City. Merlo Pusey attended school in the winter, helping after school in his father's country store, and spent his summers in the hayfields. For a time he also worked as a railroad hand in the neighboring town of Evanston, Wyoming. His early proficiency in writing was encouraged by one of his teachers.

His highest ambition as a boy, however, was to become a cabinetmaker, an ambition which was to be changed after he enrolled at the Latter-day Saints University in Salt Lake City in 1919. While completing his secondary schooling at this institution Pusey became an active member of the debating team. Here again he was given encouragement in his writing. He considers the most decisive event in making journalism his career to have been his election to the editorship of the school paper, the *Gold and Blue*, a post which he held during the year 1921-22.

After graduation from high school in 1922, Pusey obtained work on the *Deseret News*, a daily newspaper in Salt Lake City. There he held the successive positions of proofreader, cub reporter, reporter on regular assignments, and, from 1926 to 1928, assistant city editor. Once established as a reporter on the *Deseret News*, he had begun to take some courses at the University of Utah (in the same city), where he majored in English. Pusey, who continued his newspaper work during his years at the university, was elected to Phi Kappa Phi Society and awarded the B.A. degree with high honors in 1928.

In Washington, D.C., to which he moved after graduation, Pusey procured temporary work reading copy for the Washington *Daily News*. After two months, in November of 1928, he obtained a position as editorial writer for the Washington *Post*, on the staff of which he is still employed. During the

Harris & Ewing

MERLO J. PUSEY

depression years 1931 to 1933, he supplemented his "diminished income" by filling a part-time position with the Senate Finance Committee; his title was expert for the majority. Later on, from 1939 to 1942, he taught evening classes in journalism at George Washington University. Then, in 1945 he was promoted to associate editor of the Washington *Post*, his present position.

Shortly after becoming established in Washington, Pusey began writing magazine articles on housing and other public topics; among them were "Our Housing Hodgepodge" (*Harper's Magazine*, June 6, 1936), "Reclaiming Our Slums" (*Yale Review*, June 1939), "Washington: A National Disgrace" (*Forum* December 1939), and "Problem of Presidential Succession" (*Congressional Digest*, January 1947). He is also the author of two pamphlets, *The District Crisis* (about the government of the District of Columbia) and *Turning on the Light* (about the matter of Congressional investigations). For several years he also wrote a weekly column for the *Post*.

A problem of particular concern to Pusey during the Roosevelt Administration was the possible consequence of increased power in the Executive branch of the Government under the New Deal. On May 9, 1937, he addressed a meeting (in Philadelphia) of the Middle States Association of History and Social Science Teachers to the effect that an extension of Presidential powers would be a move in the direction of dictatorship and that the removal of judicial review would be revolutionary.

His first book, *The Supreme Court Crisis* (1937), was written in "twenty-two nights of toil" during the dispute caused by President Roosevelt's attempt to reorganize the Supreme Court. The book, completed before the defeat of the measure in Congress and prepared in cooperation with Senate opponents of the bill, presents the point of view that the President's court reorganization plan was an attempt to "pack" the Supreme Court with New Deal supporters. Pusey's case for the preservation of the court, commented the *Christian Science Monitor* critic, is given "with exceptional compactness and logical force." During the late 1930's and early 1940's Pusey was working on a book about Washington, which, because of the paper shortage and the war, was not published. He next devoted two and a half years to the writing of *Big Government: Can We Control It?* (1945), which traces the origins and developments of trends toward "dangerous and unwieldy bigness" in the Federal Government, most notably in the Executive branch, evaluates the significance of these trends for society, and advocates a program of reforms.

In the autumn of 1945 when Pusey began to write *Charles Evans Hughes*, he was able to benefit from the direct aid of the retired Chief Justice himself, having approached Hughes on the subject at about the time the Justice was completing his biographical notes. After several interviews Hughes turned these notes over to Pusey and granted him exclusive access to his personal and public papers as well. The interviews also continued, so that during the last three years of the Chief Justice's life (1945-48) Pusey was able to discuss with him in detail all of the major and many minor events of his career. He was able also to consult many of Hughes's friends, fellow workers, and critics, and had the cooperation of the Hughes family after the Chief Justice's death.

The resultant two-volume biography, published in 1951, renders in its eight hundred pages, including twenty-eight cartoons and twenty-seven photographs, an account of the personal and public life of the former Supreme Court Justice set against the background of contemporary American history. "A lively, warm, and stirring story," was the observation of O. J. Roberts in the New York *Herald Tribune*. H. H. Bernt noted in *Library Journal*: "[Hughes's] weaknesses and mistakes are played down, and some will criticize the work on this account. . . .Sustained interest and readability throughout lengthy work shows experienced hand of journalist." For the contribution to American thought and letters made with *Charles Evans Hughes*, Pusey received the Pulitzer Prize for biography, announced on May 5, 1952, as well as the honorary degree of Doctor of Letters from the Brigham Young University and the Bancroft Award in American history, diplomacy, and international relations.

Pusey has associated himself with a number of organizations directed toward the advancement of various aspects of public welfare. Until 1945 he was for some years a member of the advisory committee to the District of Columbia Juvenile Court and is in 1952 a member of the Board of the Social Hygiene Society of Washington. He has been connected with the home rule movement of the District of Columbia and with the charter movement in Montgomery County, Maryland. He also maintains membership in the American Political Science Association and the American Association for the Advancement of Science, as well as in the National Conference of Editorial Writers, the National Press Club, and The Inquirendo (former president).

The family of the journalist consists of his wife, Dorothy (Richards) Pusey, a former teacher, whom he married on September 5, 1928, and their three sons, Conway Richards, David Richards, and John Richards. Since residing in Washington he has taken several trips to the West Coast and most of the States, vacations in Canada, and a European tour with his wife in 1937. His political affiliation is with the Republican party, and he belongs to the Church of Jesus Christ of Latter day Saints. He is five feet ten inches tall, weighs 175 pounds, and has brown eyes and dark-brown hair. Aside from reading, he enjoys hiking in the mountains, gardening, and golf.

References

N Y Herald Tribune p6 My 6 '52
N Y Times p24 My 6 '52
Washington (D.C.) Post p1 My 6 '52
Who's Who in America, 1952-53

Hausmann-Steiger

ROGER L. PUTNAM

PUTNAM, ROGER L(OWELL) Dec. 19, 1893- United States Government official; manufacturer

Address: b. c/o Economic Stabilization Agency, 811 Vermont Ave., N.W., Washington 25, D.C.; c/o Package Machinery Company, West Chestnut St., East Longmeadow, Mass.; h. 216 Central St., Springfield 5, Mass.

On December 1, 1951, Roger L. Putnam took office as Administrator of the Economic Stabilization Agency, a post which Eric Johnston, his predecessor, called "the toughest, and yet most stimulating" in the mobilization setup. This appointment gives Putnam jurisdiction over the wage-price control programs with which the Administration is combating inflation. Former Mayor of Springfield, Massachusetts, for three terms (1937-43), he was the unsuccessful Democratic candidate for the governorship of that State in 1942. During both world wars he served in the Navy, and from 1944 to 1946 he was deputy director of the Office of Contract Settlement, in Washington. Putnam has been president of the Package Machinery Company, near Springfield, for more than eighteen years. In November 1952 Putnam announced that he would soon retire as head of the ESA.

Born in Boston on December 19, 1893, Roger Lowell Putnam is descended from two of Massachusetts' most distinguished families: the Lowells, who left England for Newbury in 1639; and the Putnams, who settled in Salem before 1641. His parents had two other sons and two daughters. His father, William Lowell Putnam, was a member of a Boston law firm and a director of many corporations, most of them in New England. Roger's mother, Elizabeth (Lowell) Putnam, was a sister of Amy Lowell, the poetess, and of A. Lawrence Lowell,

president of Harvard University from 1909 to 1933. For many years a leader among the Republican women of the State, she was the first woman to be elected president of the Massachusetts electoral college.

After receiving his preparatory education at Noble and Greenough School in Boston (1905-11), Roger Putnam entered Harvard College to major in mathematics. As an undergraduate he won a scholarship in 1914, served on the *Advocate* board (treasurer, 1914), and was a member of the Memorial Society. His clubs were the Yacht, Nobles, Institute of 1770, Hasty Pudding, Iroquois, and Fly. Obtaining his B.A. degree, *magna cum laude*, from Harvard in 1915, he spent the next year studying mechanical engineering at the Massachusetts Institute of Technology. He began his career in the summer of 1916 with the New London (Connecticut) Engine and Ship Company, working seventy-two hours a week on diesel engines. The following year he took a position with the Multibestos Company, in Walpole, Massachusetts, where he was later made assistant plant superintendent. When the United States entered World War I he enlisted in the Navy, graduated from the Cadet School at Harvard, and served as an ensign on the U.S.S. *Mississippi* during a West Indies cruise. Because of his training in mathematics, he was later transferred to the Indian Head (Maryland) Naval Proving Ground as assistant experimental officer. Following his discharge in 1919 with the rank of lieutenant (j.g.), he went to work as a salesman for the Package Machinery Company, in Springfield, Massachusetts, of which his father was then president. In 1921, when the senior Putnam became chairman of the firm's board of directors, his son was promoted to vice-president and secretary. Six years later Roger Putnam was elected president, a post he has held since that time

PUTNAM, ROGER L.—*Continued*
except for the period from 1942 to 1948, when
he was chairman of the board.

The firm which Putnam heads was incorporated in 1919 to succeed the Package Machinery Company, which had been organized
six years earlier as a consolidation of five companies. It manufactures about eighty models
of automatic wrapping and bottle-hooding machines. The company was one of the first concerns in the New England area to institute
profit-sharing and life-insurance plans for its
employees. According to the New York *Post*,
the profit-sharing program, which was adopted
in 1926, operates so that every employee receives the earnings from four shares of stock
for each year of service with the firm; and
all employees are given, without cost to them,
life insurance equal to $100 for each year of
service up to twenty years. During the depression, Putnam "poured in money to develop new
machinery," according to *Time*, and "kept employment at a high level by going on a five-
day week." In 1949 the firm merged with the
Frank D. Palmer Company, of Chicago, and
acquired from General Mills, Inc., the Palmer
carton-forming and tray lock business. By
1951 the Package Machinery Company employed some 800 workers at its East Longmeadow plant (near Springfield) and had
branch sales offices in nine United States cities
as well as in Toronto and Mexico City. *Moody's
Manual* reported that the firm's net sales in
1950 totaled $4,823,545 and its net income was
$101,370.

Although his family's political affiliations
were largely Republican, Putnam registered as
a Democrat in 1932—he has described himself
as "a consistent, liberal Democrat." During the
early 1930's he served on the commission that
drew up the present Massachusetts unemployment laws, and in 1936 he was named to the
advisory board of the State Commissioner of
Education. On November 2, 1937, Putnam,
running on the Democratic ticket, was elected
Mayor of Springfield—the third largest city in
the State. Re-elected in 1939 and again in 1941,
he thus became the first Mayor in the city's
history to serve a third term. It is his conviction that "unless businessmen will take an
active part in government, particularly local
government, they will get the kind of government they love to kick about." In 1940 he attracted nation-wide attention by devising the
so-called "Springfield Plan" to help break the
bottleneck caused by the shortage of skilled
mechanics and machinists in the rearmament
program. Under this system the city trained
unemployed men in machine-shop practice to
fill specific jobs in the local defense industries.
He gained further notice the following year
by sponsoring a series of local conferences between high school students and businessmen for
the purpose of developing "a better understanding of the problems and policies of free business enterprise and their relation to American
democracy." In the September 1942 State
primaries, Putnam topped former Lieutenant
Governor Francis E. Kelly by more than
22,000 votes to win the Democratic nomination

for Governor. However, in the November 3
elections, Leverett Saltonstall, then incumbent
Republican Governor (in 1951 United States
Senator), defeated him by a plurality of
128,137 votes.

During World War II Putnam served from
April 1943 to September 1944 as a lieutenant
commander in the United States Naval Reserve.
Appointed director of research and development of the Amphibious Force of the Atlantic
Fleet, he was in 1943 attached to the London
staff of Rear Admiral Alan G. Kirk, then
head of the Navy task force in Europe, and
participated in the Normandy invasion in June
1944. The next year Putnam went to Washington, D.C., as deputy director of the Office
of Contract Settlement, which had been created
in July 1944 to provide for the settlement of
claims arising from terminated war contracts.
In September 1946 President Truman nominated him as director of that Office, which was
abolished three months later. More recently,
Putnam has served as a member of the advisory board of the Reconstruction Finance
Corporation.

On November 26, 1951, President Truman
selected Putnam for appointment as Administrator of the Economic Stabilization Agency, effective December 1. He is the third official
and first Democrat to head the ESA since the
agency was established in September 1950 under the authority of the Defense Production
Act of that year, for the purpose of controlling
inflation and maintaining the stabilization of
the national economy. (His predecessors were
Eric Johnston and Dr. Alan Valentine.) Among
the functions of the ESA Administrator are
"to plan and develop both short- and long-
range price and wage stabilization policies and
measures and to create the necessary organization for their administration," and "to establish
price ceilings and stabilize wages and salaries
where necessary." Considered one of the key
figures in the Government today, he ranks just
below the Director of Defense Mobilization
(in 1951 Charles E. Wilson), and has supervisory jurisdiction over the activities of the
Office of Price Stabilization (headed in 1951
by Michael V. DiSalle) and the Wage and
Salary Stabilization Boards. Putnam took office December 1. Since his appointment to
the $17,500-a-year post was made while Con-
gress was in recess, it is subject to Senate
confirmation in January 1952.

At his first press conference Putnam called
his new position "a tough job which needs a
tough man," and said he had set a limit of six
months on his term of service. Describing the
economic stability of the United States as a
staff upon which the whole free world depends,
he explained that it was his job "to keep this
staff strong so that we in America may be
the guiding light of freedom everywhere." According to the New York *Times*, the post is
classed by Washington officials as "one of the
most unpopular in the defense setup," Putnam
takes over "at a time when increasing governmental expenditures, mostly for defense . . .
are creating new pressures on the general
price level, and thus leading to new demands
for wage increases by organized labor." Com-

menting in the New York *Times*, Charles E. Egan said that Putnam's task was made "doubly difficult," because he has the "responsibility for keeping the whole economy on an even keel," while his direct powers are limited. "He cannot dictate restrictions to be imposed on installment buying and consumer credits in general, nor can he initiate savings campaigns that might help to siphon off excess buying power and thus ease inflationary pressures."

One of the first tasks of the new Economic Stabilizer was to deal with the wage increase demands of the United Steel Workers in their negotiations for a 1952 wage contract. In an effort to hold to the formula policy of the Wage Stabilization Board, Putnam advised the steelworkers in mid-December 1951 that increases in excess of those allowed by the policy would not be approved. At the same time he told the president of United States Steel that the corporation could not raise ceiling prices on steel to offset a wage boost. "As calamitous as a steel strike might be," Putnam observed, in reference to a strike threatened for January 1, "runing our stabilization program would be even worse." Soon after the Republican victory in the 1952 Presidential election, it was announced that Putnam would resign as head of ESA; his resignation was expected to become effective before January 1, 1953.

Following his appointment as ESA chief, Putnam had announced he would retain the presidency of the Package Machinery Company. In Springfield he is also a director of the Van Norman Machine Tool Company, Perkins Machine and Gear Company, American Bosch Corporation, Third National Bank and Trust Company, and Future Springfield, Inc. Putnam has resigned as the chairman of the Springfield Centennial (1852-1952) Committee, and as chairman of the board of trustees of the Soldiers' Home in Holyoke, Massachusetts. He is chairman of the Springfield chapter of the American Red Cross; a director of the Springfield Library Association and a member of the city's committee on the Museum of Fine Arts; treasurer of the Petersham (Massachusetts) Memorial Library; a director of the American Management Association, New York; a director of both the Massachusetts branch of the United World Federalists; and a director of the New England Council, having done much labor relations work for the latter group. Since 1927 the sole trustee of the Lowell Observatory, in Flagstaff, Arizona (built by his uncle, Percival Lowell), Putnam is also a member of the visiting committee of the Harvard Observatory, the American Astronomical Society, the Astronomical Society of the Pacific, and a fellow of the American Association for the Advancement of Science. Other organizations in which he holds membership include the Kiwanis Club, the Elks, the Knights of Columbus, and Delta Psi. He belongs to the Harvard clubs in Boston and New York City, the Colony Club in Springfield, and the Army and Navy Club in Washington, D.C.

An honorary LL.D. degree was bestowed upon Putnam by Boston College in 1949. On October 19, 1919, he married Caroline Piatt Jenkins, of Charles County, Maryland; they have six children: Caroline (a nun), Roger Lowell, Jr., William Lowell, Anna Lowell Finnerty, Mary Compton (Putnam) Post, and Michael Courtney Jenkins. A descendant of Charles Carroll of Carrollton, one of the first gentlemen of Catholic Maryland and a signer of the Declaration of Independence, Mrs. Putnam is the founder and president of Catholic Scholarships for Negroes, a member of the Springfield Housing Authority, and a director of the South End Community House in that city. She received one of the two James J. Hoey Awards for Interracial Justice in September 1951. The new ESA head entered the Roman Catholic Church, the faith of his wife, while serving with the Navy during World War II. The gray-eyed, brown-haired ESA Administrator, who is five feet ten inches in height and weighs 190 pounds, has been described as "stocky in build, but quick-moving both in person and speech." According to *Time*, he "does not smoke; weaves [twine] belts which he gives to friends; dabbles in astronomy for fun; and saws wood to keep in trim." He names forestry as his special interest.

References

Christian Sci Mon p3 N 27 '51 por
N Y Herald Tribune p1+ N 27 '51 por; II p1 D 2 '51 por
N Y Post Mag p2 D 2 '51 por
N Y Sun p17 Je 27 '41
N Y Times p1+ N 27 '51 por
N Y World-Telegram p5 Je 10 '40 por
Time 40:22-3 S 28 '42 por; 58:27 D 10 '51 por
America's Young Men, 1936-37
American Catholic Who's Who, 1950-51
Business Executives of America (1950)
Who's Who in America, 1950-51
Who's Who in Commerce and Industry (1951)
Who's Who in Massachusetts (1940-41)
Who's Who in New England (1949)
World Biography (1948)

QUO TAI-CHI 1889—Feb. 29, 1952 Chinese diplomat; attached to president's office and later to the Ministry of Foreign Affairs in China (1921-32); appointed Minister to Great Britain (1932), Ambassador to Great Britain (1935); became Minister of Foreign Affairs in Nationalist Government (1941), chairman of the foreign affairs committee of the Supreme National Defense Council (1942), and permanent representative to the Security Council of the United Nations (1946). See *Current Biography*, 1946.

Obituary

N Y Times p15 Mr 1 '52

RABAUT, LOUIS CHARLES (rǎ'bō)
Dec. 5, 1886- United States Representative
from Michigan
Address: b. c/o House Office Bldg., Washington 25, D.C.; h. 1015 Three Mile Dr., Grosse
Pointe Park, Mich.

A member of Congress from 1935 through
1946 and elected again in 1948, Representative
Louis Charles Rabaut of the Fourteenth Michigan District is known as both a New Deal
and a Fair Deal Democrat. As a prominent figure in the House Appropriations Committee he

Wide World Photos
LOUIS CHARLES RABAUT

has traveled in Europe and South America, on
occasion to make inspections of Foreign Service
offices in connection with his duties as chairman
of the subcommittee on appropriations for the
Departments of State, Commerce, and Justice,
and the Judiciary. Rabaut was a practicing
lawyer in Detroit before his election to Congress.

A native of Detroit, Michigan, and a lifelong
resident of that city or its suburbs, Louis
Charles Rabaut is one of the several children
of Louis Aloysius and Clara Lenau (Reid)
Rabaut. His birth date is December 5, 1886.
After attending Catholic parochial schools the
future Congressman entered Detroit College,
where he took his B.A. degree in 1909. In
1912 he received his law degree from Detroit
College of Law, his M.A. degree from the
University of Detroit, and was admittted to the
Michigan bar. He established a legal practice
in Detroit, and later was active also in the
building business, becoming president of the
Standard Homes Investment Corporation in
1926. Rabaut served from 1925 to 1928 as a
trustee of the village of Grosse Pointe, the
Detroit suburban community where he is today
a voter. Defeated in 1932 in his first candidacy for election to Congress from Michi-

gan's Fourteenth District (which at the present
time covers Wards 18, 19 and 21 of the city of
Detroit and the townships of Gratiot and
Grosse Pointe in Wayne County), he was successful in 1934, and has been returned at all
subsequent biennial elections except that of
1946.

Rabaut campaigned on a New Deal platform,
was carried into Washington on the wave of
national endorsement of President Franklin D.
Roosevelt's first two years of administration,
and was later to say that "when F.D.R. was
alive" he had "followed his principles from the
word go." His few important departures were
to be in connection with certain agricultural appropriations and with defense policy and aid
to the Allies in the period shortly before the
Pearl Harbor attack. Seated in the Seventy-
fourth Congress on January 3, 1935, he voted
during his first year as a legislator in favor
of enactment of such measures as the Social
Security Act (April), the Eccles Banking Bill
(May), and continuance of the National Recovery Administration (June); and against the
Guffey-Snyder coal bill (August). Also during
his freshman term in Congress, Rabaut made
the first of four official overseas trips, attending the inauguration of the Philippine Commonwealth as a guest of the new government.
In the following year he was a delegate to the
Democratic National Convention at Cleveland,
and also in 1936 he received from the Veterans
of Foreign Wars a special citation for his
services as chairman of the Michigan Congressional Committee.

During the 1937 session of the Seventy-fifth
Congress, Rabaut cast pro-Administration votes
for the Supreme Court Retirement Bill (February) and the Wagner Housing Bill (August), and opposed imposition of a peacetime
munitions exportation embargo (March). In
March he also defended Michigan Governor
Murphy's handling of the sit-down strike in
the Chrysler plant at Detroit, and in April he
voted against Federal investigation of sit-down
strikes. In the first session of the Seventy-
sixth Congress (1939) he was recorded as opposed to enactment of the Hatch Pernicious
Political Activities Bill and, as the Representative of an urban area, opposed the Administration on the current policy of farm parity
payments.

During the summer of the same year Rabaut
was (with Representatives Hamilton Fish of
New York, Dewey Short of Missouri, Harold
Knutson of Minnesota, and Thomas McMillan
of South Carolina) one of a five-man bipartisan
Congressional delegation to the Interparliamentary Union at Oslo, Norway, and was still in
Europe when World War II broke out. Returning an isolationist in viewpoint, he voted in
1940 in favor of continuance of the mandatory
arms embargo and against the conscription bill.
The Detroit Congressman was a delegate to
the 1940 Democratic National Convention at
Chicago, where (in the words of Delos Lovelace of the New York *Sun*) he "did his bit"
in an unusual way to make the convention a
success. Rabaut, who has a gift for melody,
when "buttonholed for a convention song . . .
squared away with an experimental finger tum-

tumming up and down the piano and by nightfall had turned out not one song but two."

Comparatively early in his Congressional career Rabaut was assigned to the House Appropriations Committee and in due course became acting chairman and then chairman of the subcommittee on appropriations for the Departments of State, Commerce, and Justice, and the Judiciary. As such he was made chairman of the first official Congressional committee to inspect Foreign Service offices in Central and South America and to study the effects of our cultural relations program south of Mexico. In a two months' tour beginning August 1941, Rabaut and his committee visited seventeen countries and returned with augmented faith in the value of the Reciprocal Trade Agreements Act and the "good neighbor" policy in general. (Subsequent observations by Rabaut on the subject of "Latin America, its People, Resources, Problems, and Share in the War" were to appear as "extension of remarks" in the *Congressional Record* for June 30, 1942, and were later reprinted in pamphlet form.) Meanwhile, Rabaut had voted against the lend-lease bill (February 1941), repeal of the ban on arming merchant ships (October), and the establishment of price controls (November); but after his country became a belligerent in World War II he moved rapidly toward the "one world" viewpoint and voted in favor of the Fulbright Resolution in September 1943 and the authorization of UNRRA in January of the year following. Also in 1944, Rabaut was the recipient of the annual award of the International Economic Council for "outstanding devotion to world trade."

In August 1945, the hostilities in Europe having ended, he headed, at the invitation of Secretary of State Stettinius, a six-member Congressional group to inspect Foreign Service establishments and other Federal activities in Great Britain and several other countries. His tour took him to Rome, where he was twice granted audiences with Pope Pius, and later to Spain, which he was quoted as describing as "a country which economically and spiritually has been better preserved than any other . . . in Europe."

Over a period of years from 1941 onward Rabaut was active in Congress on behalf of the St. Lawrence Seaway Project—authorization of which would be of great benefit to Detroit—and throughout World War II was concerned with safeguarding the interests of labor. In February 1942, for instance, he had sponsored a bill to grant the President authority to distribute about $300,000,000 in assistance to workers displaced by the defense effort. Similarly in 1946, he opposed the guaranteeing of so-called "reasonable profits" in OPA ceiling prices (April) and voted "Nay" on overriding President Truman's veto of the Case Strike Control bill (June). The Michigan Democrat opposed the continuation of the Un-American Activities Committee on a permanent basis. When he lost his seat in the November 1946 election to Republican Harold Youngblood in a very close contest, he blamed his defeat on what he regarded as a campaign of "vilification"

by newspapers allegedly doing the bidding of the National Association of Manufacturers. "They called me a Communist," he protested to writer Cornelius Vanderbilt, "although they know that . . . I have been a good Catholic all my life."

After two years of law practice in Detroit, Rabaut defeated Youngblood in November 1948 and in the following January resumed his seat in Congress and his membership, though not his seniority, in the House Appropriations Committee. He was again re-elected by the Fourteenth Michigan District in 1950. Noteworthy in Rabaut's voting record in the Eighty-first and Eighty-second Congresses have been his approval of Marshall Plan extension (April 1949), the Administration's long-range housing bill (June 1949), economic aid to Korea and Formosa (February 1950), and universal military training (April 1951); and his opposition to the Lodge-Gossett constitutional amendment limiting the Presidency to two terms. In the Eighty-first Congress, Rabaut became a member of the Appropriations Committee's Subcommittees of Deficiencies and Army Civil Functions. He further serves on the Joint Commission on Renovation of the Executive Mansion. Rabaut was re-elected to the House on November 4, 1952.

Louis Charles Rabaut and Stella Marie Petz were married June 28, 1911; they are the parents of three sons, one of whom is a priest, and six daughters, three of whom are nuns. The sons are the Reverend Francis Dermott, S.J., Louis 3d, and Vincent, who is a Naval Reserve Officer. The daughters are Marie Celeste (Sister Mary Palmyre), Mary Jane (Mrs. August John Amato), Carolyn (Mrs. Jules De Porre), Joan Marie, Stella Marie (Sister Stella Maris), and Sister Martha. The Michigan legislator has been described by Delos Lovelace as "chunky, silver-haired, natty." His avocation is singing, in which, when a young man, he was offered opportunities for a professional career.

References

N Y Post Mag p48 Ja 3 '47
N Y Sun p14 Ag 14 '45
American Catholic Who's Who, 1950-51
Biographical Directory of the American Congress, 1774-1949 (1950)
Congressional Directory (1951)
International World Who's Who (1949)
Who's Who in America, 1950-51
Who's Who in Detroit, 1935-36
Who's Who in the Midwest (1949)
Who's Who in United States Politics (1950)

RACKMIL, MILTON R. Feb. 12, 1903- Business executive

Address: b. c/o Decca Records, Inc., 50 W. 57th St., New York 19; c/o Universal Pictures Co., Inc., 445 Park Ave., New York 22; h. 140 Riverside Dr., New York 24

One of the founders in 1934 of Decca Records, Inc., and its president since 1949, Milton R. Rackmil in July 1952 assumed the additional

MILTON R. RACKMIL

position of president of Universal Pictures Company, Inc., following Decca's acquisition of controlling interest in the motion picture concern. Under Rackmil's presidency Decca Records, an American pioneer in marketing low-priced discs, has become the third largest record producer in the United States; Universal Pictures under his leadership has announced plans to add to its regular production of feature pictures the making of films for television.

Milton R. Rackmil, the eldest of three children of Isaac and Fanny (Laver) Rackmil, was born February 12, 1903, in New York City. His father had come from the Balkans to follow his trade as a carpenter in Brooklyn, where Milton and his younger brother and sister were reared. Here the boy attended public grade and high schools and a Hebrew religious school, which he has said instilled in him the habits of methodical study and of systematic reading. As a young boy he earned pocket money by selling chewing gum, newspapers, and magazines, and by shining shoes; later, in high school days, he worked evenings and on Saturdays in a shoe store, where he showed his flair for salesmanship on his first day of employment by winning a prize of one dollar for the biggest sales total of the day. While in his next position as a $30-a-week bookkeeper for a jobber, he enrolled in 1920 in the evening school of New York University to study accounting. Because of university regulations, Rackmil gave up his bookkeeping job and accepted a $12-a-week wage as an apprentice in a certified public accountant's office. In 1924 he received his Bachelor of Commercial Science degree from New York University and two years later passed his C.P.A. examination.

Upon setting himself up in business, Rackmil accepted as his first major client a bankruptcy lawyer, for whom the young C.P.A. performed work which he later credited with developing in him a "diagnostic sense to detect the exact

spot in a financial operation that spelled the difference between success and failure." Rackmil continued as a C.P.A. until through a friend he secured a position with Warner Brothers, the motion picture producers. Shortly afterward, Warner bought the Brunswick Radio Corporation and Rackmil in 1929 was made assistant comptroller of Brunswick, soon becoming chief comptroller, a position he held until 1931, when Warner Brothers sold Brunswick to American Records (a subsidiary of Consolidated Industries Films, now Republic Pictures). The new owners in 1932 named Rackmil general manager of the Scranton, Pennsylvania, plant, which post he held for two years.

Meanwhile (1931) Jack Kapp, Brunswick's production manager, had been sent to England to negotiate an agreement with E. R. Lewis, head of "the English record concern known as Decca, which had featured cheap records much used on portable phonographs in the First World War" (New York *Times*). Lewis had been interested in acquiring a subsidiary in the United States and had proposed purchasing the Brunswick stock held by American Records, but the negotiations were dropped when the stockholders raised their price. In the spring of 1934—the year in which the record industry reached a low ebb—Kapp, Rackmil, and E. R. Stevens decided to start an American Decca company, with capital supplied by Lewis. Rackmil later recalled for a *Variety* reporter (July 30, 1952): "The heads of our company and of other record companies were ready to throw up their hands. They thought their business had reached its peak and was on its way out with the development of radio. 'Why should anyone buy records,' they asked, 'when by flicking a switch people could get all the music they wanted for free?'" On August 4, 1934, Decca Records, Inc., was launched with Kapp as president, Stevens as vice-president, and Rackmil as treasurer.

The initial product of Decca Records, Inc., and the foundation of its eventual success, was a thirty-five cent record with a hit tune on each side. The firm at first went through a difficult period, which began when 200,000 "pressings" ordered by the company turned out to be unsatisfactory. Rackmil later explained to Alfred Russel of the New York *World-Telegram*: "It put the firm in a hole. Its initial capital of about $250,000 evaporated. From then on caution was the word. . . .RCA-Victor and Columbia Records could have killed us off easy in those days." Deciding to exploit the popularity of radio stars, Decca engaged Bing Crosby among the first, later signing contracts with Guy Lombardo, Al Jolson, the Mills Brothers, Danny Kaye, Ted Lewis, the Andrews Sisters, and Ethel Waters.

By 1937, the year in which Rackmil was elected a vice-president, while continuing as treasurer, the company's profits netted $80,000. In 1938 Kapp and his associates bought up the shares which had been held by the English Decca company; the following year their profits rose to $394,000. Decca took over the Brunswick Radio Corporation in 1941, acquiring the Brunswick "label" along with some

6,000 titles; two years later Decca bought the World Broadcasting System, Inc., and began issuing transcribed radio shows to tie in with music publishing. The company reached its all-time high in 1946, when it made a net profit of $1,984,000, selling that year close to 400,000,000 records. In the middle of that year (July 28) Rackmil was elected executive vice-president and became a member of the board of directors. After the war the company built additional plants to speed up distribution and began the manufacture of discs for children and of albums of Broadway musical shows (including *Oklahoma* and *Carousel*) with the original casts.

When Decca president Jack Kapp died on March 25, 1949, Milton R. Rackmil was elected to succeed him in office. The first in his series of changes, innovations, and expansions came the following August with Decca's announcement that it would make available its entire catalogue of 650 albums on long-playing, unbreakable, microgroove discs that made 33⅓ revolutions a minute. Two months later (according to *Variety*, October 12, 1949) "apparently prompted by the solid sales success of its hottest albums on long-playing microgroove discs, Decca Records got back into the race for new Broadway show music. . . .Decca for sometime hadn't been anxious to grab original cast rights to shows, letting Columbia Records collar them without an argument." At this time Decca secured the recording rights to *Lost in the Stars.* In August 1950 Decca disclosed plans to enter the field of serious music with the release of the new Decca Gold Label Series, devoted to symphonies, concertos, chamber music, operas, songs, and choral music. The following December Decca announced that Rackmil in accordance with the company's expansion policy had successfully concluded two transactions: First he had arranged for the purchase of all outstanding common stock in the Compo Company of Canada and had been named its board chairman. Secondly, he had concluded an agreement with the Deutsche Grammaphon company of Germany whereby the latter firm gave Decca the exclusive rights to its entire catalogue for distribution in the United States, its possessions, and Canada, while the German company acquired sole rights to Decca's catalogue in Germany, Austria, and Norway.

During the fall of 1951 Decca Records began buying stock in Universal Pictures Company, Inc., producers of feature films for theater showing under the name Universal-International. By July 1952, when Milton Rackmil was elected to the Universal directorate, Decca had acquired voting control of Universal by its purchase of large blocks of stock from top holders, including the J. Arthur Rank interests of London. On July 15, 1952, Rackmil was elected president of Universal, with Nate J. Blumberg, president since 1938, becoming chairman of the board. Rackmil's contract as president of Universal (as reported by *Variety*, August 13, 1952) was for seven years at an annual salary of $80,000, plus expenses and offices in Hollywood and New York City. He remained president of Decca Records.

A few weeks after he became Universal president, Rackmil told *Variety* (July 30, 1952) that the plan of merging Universal and Decca was off but the two companies would "work together in instances where they complement each other." The trade weekly went on to report that Rackmil was "high on telefilm production," and that he saw an "inevitable marriage" of television movies and theatrical film production at the major film studios. "Rackmil made the point that radio had actually promoted the sale of discs by building new stars, familiarizing millions of people with music and offering a ready means of plugging new tunes. He sees video similarly offering the opportunity to exploit" motion pictures and build stars. Rackmil also announced at this time that Universal's subsidiary, United World Films, was preparing three series of television films and had four finished in the initial round. In August 1952 Rackmil announced that Universal would use Technicolor in all but ten of the thirty-six pictures scheduled for production in the fiscal year beginning in November and that the studio would continue its highly profitable policy of engaging a select number of top-name stars on a profit-participation basis. As reported by the New York *Times* (August 29, 1952), Universal in 1950 had introduced a new policy in picture making by being the first to arrange agreements with stars who in exchange for working for a fraction of their normal salaries received a percentage in their pictures' earnings.

Rackmil married Marie Stevelman on November 3, 1928, and they have one daughter, Marlene, now Mrs. Martin Philip Salkin. He is a member of the Free and Accepted Masons and of the Aldecress Country Club. His faith is the Jewish. In recognition of his service to the record industry, he has been named to head the Record Industry Association of America.

References

N Y World-Telegram p19 Ja 13 '51 por
Newsweek 40:69 Jl 28 '52 por

Business Executives of America (1950)
Who's Who in America, 1952-53

RADHAKRISHNAN, SIR SARVEPALLI

(rä'dŭ-krĭsh'nŭn sŭr've-pŭl'lĭ) Sept. 5, 1888-
Indian statesman; philosopher

Address: h. Edward Eliots Rd., Mylapore, Madras, India

The Hindu idealist philosopher Sir Sarvepalli Radhakrishnan, who was named India's Ambassador to the Soviet Union in 1949, resigned his diplomatic post, effective April 18, 1952, to become the Congress party's candidate for Vice-President of India, for which office he was duly chosen in the following May election. Author of a number of important books on Indian and Western philosophies, Radhakrishnan has also held professorships in philosophy at Mysore University, Calcutta University, and Oxford University; has served as Vice-Chancellor of Andhra University and Benares Hindu

SIR SARVEPALLI RADHAKRISHNAN

University; and has lectured in leading universities in the United States. Other contributions made by Sir Sarvepalli to cultural understanding among nations have been his work as member of the International Committee on Intellectual Cooperation of the League of Nations (1931-39) and as head of the Indian delegation to UNESCO (1946-50).

Sarvepalli Radhakrishnan was born September 5, 1888, in Tiruttani in the Chittoor District of the Madras Presidency in southern India. Though his parents were Telugu Brahmins who held the conventional Hindu religious beliefs, their second son was enrolled in a German mission school at nearby Tirupati when he was eight years old, and after five years there and four more (1901-05) at Voorhees College in Vellore, he entered Madras Christian College. "I became familiar not only with the teaching of the New Testament," Radhakrishnan points out in his widely quoted short autobiography *My Search for Truth*, "but with the criticisms leveled by Christian missionaries on Hindu beliefs and practices." "Deeply hurt" by that criticism, he made a study of Hinduism to "find out what is living and what is dead in it" and so chose ethics of the *Vedanta* as the subject of the thesis required for the M.A. degree in philosophy, which he received in 1909. The promise in his work was seen by Principal Hobbs of the Madras Presidency College and led to the appointment of the young Brahman as a lecturer for the Provincial Education Service at one hundred rupees a month. Two years later (1911) Radhakrishnan was appointed assistant professor of philosophy at Madras Presidency College. He was advanced to a full professor in 1916.

The following year twenty-nine-year-old Radhakrishnan was transferred to the Arts College at Rajahmundry (Madras) as a lecturer in philosophy, and one year later (1918) was named professor of philosophy at the University of Mysore. There in the course of the next three years he completed his first two important books, *The Philosophy of Rabindranath Tagore* (1918) and *The Reign of Religion in Contemporary Philosophy* (1920), the latter a critique of current western theories (Bergson and others) from the point of view of Absolute Idealism. In his biographical introduction to one of Radhakrishnan's books, D. S. Sarma records that *The Reign of Religion in Contemporary Philosophy* made the author well known in the philosophical world and attracted the attention of Sir Ashutosh Mukherjee, Vice-Chancellor of Calcutta University, who offered him the King George V professorship of philosophy. It was at Calcutta that Radhakrishnan completed the first volume (published in 1923) of his comprehensive *Indian Philosophy* (in the "Library of Philosophy" series), this first volume covering, among other matters, the philosophy of the *Vedas* and the *Upanishads* and the ethical idealism of the Buddhists.

In 1926, when Professor Radhakrishnan was invited to deliver the annual Upton Lectures at Manchester College, Oxford University, he chose Hinduism as his topic. "His first appearance on the international scene was, therefore, in the role of an interpreter," Humayun Kabir has pointed out in the magazine *March of India*. "He interpreted India to the West and there were few better qualified to perform this task." The Upton lectures concluded, Radhakrishnan made his first visit to the United States and during August 1926 delivered at the University of Chicago the year's Haskell Lectures in Comparative Religion.

Radhakrishnan's Upton lectures were published in London in 1927 as *The Hindu View of Life*, and in the same year his *Indian Philosophy* was completed with a second volume, which includes an account of the six Brahmanical systems. Vincent Sheean has called this work "a pillar of Sanskrit scholarship" with which "there is no other, even in Germany, to compare." (The scholar contributed the article on that subject to the fourteenth and subsequent editions of *Encyclopaedia Britannica*.) *The Religion We Need* followed in 1928, and *Kalki, or the Future of Civilization* in 1929. In the autumn of the latter year Radhakrishnan returned to Oxford to reoccupy the Upton Chair of Comparative Religion at Manchester College (his *East and West in Religion*, published in 1933, is based on the first of his 1929 Upton lectures), and in 1929 also was called upon to give the Hibbert Lectures (published three years later under the title *An Idealistic View of Life*). Dr. Sarma considers this "the most important of Radhakrishnan's books, for it is here that we have his original contribution to . . . religious thought"; while C. E. M. Joad, who reviewed the work for the *Spectator*, regarded it as "one of the most profoundly moving religious books of our time."

Sir Sarvepalli Radhakrishnan—he received a knighthood from George V in June 1931—became Vice-Chancellor of Andhra University at Waltair on his return to India later in the year. After five years at Waltair, Sarvepalli was named to the newly created Spalding Professorship of Eastern Religions and Ethics at Oxford in 1936; also resuming his chair in philosophy at Calcutta, he divided his time between these two appointments until the outbreak of World War II prevented his annual voyage to England. During 1938 Sir Sarvepalli was invited by the British Academy to deliver its annual "Master Mind" lecture, and his discourse, published in 1939 under the title of *Gautama, the Buddha*, brought its author the distinction of being the first Indian to be elected to fellowship in the Academy. In 1939, too, Radhakrishnan edited and supplied the introduction to *Mahatma Gandhi; Essays and Reflections on His Life and Work*, which was presented to Gandhi on his seventieth birthday; while in the same year his Spalding lectures, demonstrating the influence of the *Upanishads* on European idealist philosophers from Plato onward, were published under the title *Eastern Religion and Western Thought*. Radhakrishnan, who received the M.A. and Litt.D. degrees from Oxford, as well as numerous honorary degrees from other universities, is a fellow of All Souls College, Oxford.

Sir Sarvepalli accepted in 1939 the Vice-Chancellorship of Benares Hindu University, which made him the effective head of that institution. Two years later (1941) he took over in addition the Sir Sayaji Rao Chair of Indian Culture and Civilization at Benares and at the same time ended his twenty-year occupancy of the King George V professorship at Calcutta. He returned there as a visiting professor in the following year, however, to deliver the Kamala Lectures published in 1947 under the title *Religion and Society*. In 1944 Radhakrishnan was called by the Chiang Kai-shek Nationalist Chinese Government to Chungking to give a series of twelve lectures which appeared in book form in the same year as *India and China*; and two years later (1946) he again visited the United States to lecture under the auspices of the Watumull Foundation at fourteen universities, including Harvard, Yale, Michigan, and Cornell on "the Indian view on subjects such as Indian culture, international relations . . . and the meaning of religion" (*Newsweek*). Radhakrishnan resigned as Vice-Chancellor of the Benares University in January 1948 in order to accept the chairmanship of the Indian Universities Commission of the new Indian Government and to prepare for the press his translations of the *Bhagavadgita* and the *Dhammapada* issued in 1948 and 1949, respectively. At his sixtieth birthday Sir Sarvepalli was honored by the presentation of a collection of essays on his work and influence by Dean W. R. Inge, Professor L. P. Jacks, and others. These were published in London in 1951 under the title *Radhakrishnan: Comparative Studies in Philosophy*.

The Indian philosopher's direct connection with international affairs dates from 1931, when he was named to membership in the Committee of Intellectual Cooperation of the League of Nations and attended sessions at Geneva until 1939. In 1946, after the United Nations had been formed, he became the leader of the Indian delegation to the Educational, Scientific and Cultural Organization (UNESCO) and a member of the latter's executive board. He was elected vice-chairman of UNESCO in 1948 and chairman in 1949. Meanwhile, beginning in 1947 he also sat as a member of the Indian Assembly which drafted the present Constitution of India, adopted on November 26, 1949. That he was not a member of the Assembly on that historic date was due to his appointment by Premier Jawaharlal Nehru on the previous July 12 as India's first Ambassador to the Soviet Union. Near the close of his nearly three years in Moscow, on April 5, 1952, Sir Sarvepalli had what he called "a very frank discussion" with the Soviet Premier, in which he spoke to Stalin about democracy as practiced in India. It is the Indian's conviction that "there is no outstanding problem now dividing the world which could not be settled by discussion and negotiation," and that "every effort should be made to get top people together."

Radhakrishnan's retirement as Ambassador a few days later was brought about by his nomination (on March 24) by the working committee of the Congress (Nehru) party as its candidate for Vice-President of India; his nomination followed provincial and national parliamentary elections which were held between October 1951 and February 1952 and which returned the Government of Premier Nehru to power under the continuing presidency of Dr. Rajendra Prasad. The principal function of the Vice-President of India (who is elected by the two chambers of the Assembly) is to preside over the upper chamber of the national legislature. Radhakrishnan was duly elected to this office in May 1952. At opening session of the seventh general conference of UNESCO, which took place in November 1952, the Indian statesman was chosen conference president.

Sir Sarvepalli is an honorary fellow of the Royal Asiatic Society of Bengal. He and his wife, Siva Kamamma, are the parents of one son and five daughters. "He likes solitude, books, dreaming, traveling . . . giving his grandchildren a good time. . . .He is pithy, polished, and precise in speech," said D. B. Dhanapala. C. E. M. Joad in his book *Counter Attack from the East, the Philosophy of Radhakrishnan* also comments on Radhakrishnan's "beautifully modulated voice," his "keen, alert face," and his "spare, straight figure."

References

March of India 2:2-5 N-D '49 por
N Y Herald Tribune p8 O 8 '49
Newsweek 27:81 Ap 1 '46 por
Author's and Writer's Who's Who (1948-49)
Brown, E. A. ed. Eminent Indians (1947)
Ferm, V. T. A. ed. Religion in Transition (1937)

(Continued next page)

RADHAKRISHNAN, SIR SARVEPALLI
—Continued

Indian and Pakistan Year Book and Who's Who, 1950

Inge, W. R., and others Radhakrishnan (1951)

International Who's Who, 1951

Joad, C. E. M. Counter Attack from the East (1933)

Radhakrishnan, S. Great Indians (1949)

Who's Who, 1951

Who's Who in India, 1946-47

Who's Who in Philosophy (1942)

World Biography (1948)

RANDALL, CLARENCE B(ELDEN)
Mar. 5, 1891- Industrialist

Address: b. c/o Inland Steel Company, 38 S Dearborn St., Chicago, Ill.; h. 700 Blackthorn Rd., Winnetka, Ill.

On December 21, 1951, Clarence B. Randall was appointed chief executive officer of the Inland Steel Company, after having been president of that company for more than two years. An official of the company since 1925, he has held the positions of assistant vice-president and vice-president. Randall, who has been a leading spokesman for the steel industry in its disputes with the United Steelworkers of America and the United States Government, has been described by *Fortune* as "a notably articulate businessman."

The son of Oscar Smith and Esther Clara (Belden) Randall, Clarence Belden Randall was born in Newark Valley, New York, on March 5, 1891. His merchant father was descended from John Randall, a native of England who settled in 1600 in Westerly, Rhode Island. Clarence Randall attended Wyoming Seminary in Pennsylvania from 1906 to 1908, after which he entered Harvard College; he was graduated in 1912 with the B.A. degree. In 1915 he received the LL.B. degree from Harvard Law School and was admitted to the Michigan bar. In the same year he commenced practicing law in Ishpeming, Michigan, in association with William P. Belden.

Commissioned a first lieutenant in the infantry on August 15, 1917, Randall first served in World War I as an aide-de-camp at headquarters in the 169th Infantry Brigade. He arrived in France in August 1918, to be stationed at the headquarters of the 35th Division of the American Expeditionary Force. His promotion to the rank of captain is dated February 27, 1919, and his discharge April 29, 1919. Returning to Ishpeming, from September 1, 1919, to August 1, 1925, he was a member of the law firm of Berg, Clancey and Randall.

On August 1, 1925, Randall joined the Inland Steel Company of Chicago, as assistant vice-president in charge of raw materials. He was appointed vice-president on May 1, 1930, and continued in that post until 1948. In the meantime he had been made a director on September 30, 1935. As vice-president he organized the production and transportation of the raw materials used in the company's manu-

facturing operations, chiefly iron ore, coal, and limestone. In the course of these years at Inland, Randall formed and became president of the Inland Lime & Stone Company, a subsidiary. He developed a large limestone operation at Port Inland in northern Michigan, as well as the Greenwood mine, a new deposit of hard iron ore. Through his efforts the Inland Steel Company acquired the Morris, Sherwood & Iroquois mines. Randall took over the developed Inland's large coal mines at Wheelwright, Kentucky, and expanded the company's steamship operations on the Great Lakes.

On April 27, 1949, when Randall succeeded Wilfred Sykes as president, the Inland Steel Company was ranked eighth in size in the United States, as measured by its capacity on January 1, 1949. *Standard & Poor's* in 1952 listed Inland as the seventh largest steel producer in America. This corporation manufactures nearly all types of rolled and finished steel, with the exception of wire and pipe, selling its products principally to the construction industries, railroads, automotive industries, and to users of farm equipment, industrial machinery, and metal containers. It usually employs over 25,000 workers. The company spent $20,193,849 in 1950 for improvements and expansion, and for bettering its raw material position, thereby bringing the total of capital expenditures since the beginning of 1946 to over $116,000,000. By July 1, 1950, the ingot capacity of the open hearth furnaces was increased from 3,400,000 to 3,750,000 tons. Additional increases in ingot capacity were scheduled for completion by early 1952.

In June 1948 Randall presented an article in the *Atlantic Monthly*, in which he surveyed the iron resources of the United States, disagreeing with current reports that the country's ore deposits were becoming exhausted, and presenting an optimistic viewpoint on the iron reserves. In the summer of 1948 he was invited by Paul G. Hoffman to serve as steel consultant for the Economic Cooperation Administration in Paris. Interviewed by *Business Week*, Randall, regarded as one of the best-informed American industrialists on this subject, said that the expansion of Western Europe's steel production was vital to Europe's self-sufficiency after the end of the Marshall Plan, and praised the ECA for its efforts in this direction. Concerning the Schuman Plan to unify European steel production, Randall stated in another article in the *Atlantic Monthly* (October 1951) that this proposal might "weaken Europe by laying the dead hand of socialism and bureaucracy across its basic industry," without safeguards to maintain a vigorous private enterprise.

Randall in 1949 came into conflict with the United Steelworkers of America (CIO), which is headed by Philip Murray. In August 1949 the Inland Steel Company executive condemned the appointment of a Presidential fact-finding board in a dispute between the union and the steel industry as an "industrial revolution" presaging either socialism or the corporate state, and the end of collective bargaining. He charged that Murray had a political alliance with the Government which gave him "power to induce the President of the United States to take extralegal action at his request." When Truman's fact-finding board in September 1949 recommended that the steel corporation pay the full cost of workers' pensions and social insurance, Randall opposed the suggestion, calling it a "very dangerous new principle" to permit any person to be fully relieved of the duty of providing for the future welfare of himself and his family. (Philip Murray maintained that steel company executives received noncontributary retirement benefits and that the same program should be applied to the employees.)

On December 21, 1951, Randall was appointed chief executive officer of the Inland Steel Company in the midst of protracted and controversial wage negotiations between the steel corporations and the U.S.W.A. The Wage Stabilization Board's recommendations in March 1952 for wage increases were rejected by the companies on the ground that such increases would necessitate rises in the price of steel. The WSB contended that its proposed wage increases could be absorbed by profits, plus the $2 to $3 a ton price increases the corporations would be entitled to under the Capehart amendment. Efforts to achieve an agreement having failed, on the evening of April 8, 1952, President Truman ordered the seizure of most of the country's steel plants to prevent a nationwide strike. The following night, in a radio talk Randall, as spokesman for 92 companies, denounced the seizure as an "evil deed" which "discharged a political debt to the CIO," declaring that Truman had "transgressed his oath of office . . . abused the power which is temporarily his . . . seized the private property of one million people without the slightest shadow of legal right." He charged that the public members of the WSB had at various times been on the payrolls of the CIO and AFL, and stated that the President's speech was a "shocking distortion of facts." In mid-May 1952 the United States Supreme Court was deliberating on the legality of the seizure of the steel mills.

Randall has been characterized by the New York *Herald Tribune* as "an effective, immensely convincing spokesman." In magazine articles he has asserted that "socialism is a failure" on the basis of the current conditions in England; that the free enterprise system is not, however, a "hunting license," but carries with it a responsibility for the public welfare. "Production is not an end in life,"he has written, but is a 'tool" which helps man to "live the good life." Randall's social philosophy has been described by *Fortune* as a type of "humane conservatism," without traces of Midwestern isolationism. In 1938 he and Roger N. Baldwin (director of the American Civil Liberties Union) lectured under the Godkin Foundation at Harvard, each giving in two lectures his point of view on labor-management relations—civil liberties, picketing, strikes, etc. The lectures were later published by Harvard under the title *Civil Liberties and Industrial Conflict*, concerning which the reviewer for *Commonweal* wrote: "Each presents a clear, temperate, and highly readable statement." The *New Republic*'s opinion was: "Very lively es-

Wide World Photos

CLARENCE B. RANDALL

says. . . .Frank, provocative, a labor must."

In 1933 the Iron and Steel Institute awarded Randall a medal for the best paper presented before that organization. He was chairman of the trades and industries division of the Chicago Community Fund Campaign in 1934-35, and from 1930 to 1936 was president of the Board of Education of Winnetka, Illinois. He has been a trustee of the University of Chicago since 1936 and was a trustee of Wellesley College during 1946-49. In 1944 he was general chairman of the Chicago Community and War Fund Campaign, and in 1944-45 was director of the National War Fund. He has served the Chicago National History Museum as a trustee since 1946, and is an Associate in the American Ornithologists Union. A member of the Harvard Alumni Association, he was president of that body in 1949; and since 1947 he has been a member of the Harvard board of overseers. In 1937-38 he was president of the Associated Harvard Clubs. He has been a member of the National Industrial Conference Board since 1946; he is also a member of the Business Advisory Council. Randall was formerly a director and a national vice-president of the National Association of Manufacturers and a director of the United Charities. Other memberships comprise Phi Beta Kappa Associates, Phi Beta Kappa, and Delta Upsilon. Randall's clubs are the Commercial, Chicago, University, Mid-Day, and Indian Hill Country, as well as the Union Club of New York City and Club Interalliee of Paris. Honorary degrees conferred on Randall are the D.Eng. by the Michigan College of Mining and Technology (1947), the LL.D. by Northeastern University (1948), and the D.E. by Rose Polytechnic Institute (1952).

Randall married Emily Fitch Phelps on August 18, 1917; they are the parents of two children, Mary Fitch and Miranda Belden. The

RANDALL, CLARENCE B.—*Continued*
industrialist is an Episcopalian and a vestryman
of Christ Church. In political allegiance he is
a Republican. Finding enjoyment in the outdoors, he is an eager amateur ornithologist and
devotes much time to taking colored motion
pictures of wild birds.

References

> Am Bar Assn J 35:435-6 My '49 por
> Fortune 42:12-13 N '50 por
> Sat Eve Post 225:32 D 6 '52
>
> Business Executives of America (1950)
> International Who's Who, 1950
> National Cyclopædia of American Biog-
> raphy Current vol F, 1939-42
> Who's Who in America, 1952-53

REID, HELEN ROGERS Nov. 23, 1882-
Newspaper publisher
Address: b. c/o New York Herald Tribune,
Inc., 230 W. 41st St., New York 36; h. 834
5th Ave., New York 21

> NOTE: This biography supersedes
> the article which appeared in
> *Current Biography* in 1941.

As president of the New York Herald
Tribune, Inc., Helen Rogers Reid heads one of
the great newspapers in the United States.
Mrs. Reid, who was elected to that office upon
the death of her husband, Ogden Mills Reid,
in 1947, has spent more than thirty years in
various aspects of the active management of
the daily morning newspaper, which, as the
Tribune, was founded by Horace Greeley in
1841. Among the foremost interests of Mrs.
Reid, once a leader in the woman suffrage movement, is the advancement of women in professional and business fields. For her achievements in journalism she has been honored by
many universities and civic and professional
groups.

Helen Rogers Reid, whose five sisters and
five brothers were older than herself, was born
November 23, 1882, in Appleton, Wisconsin, to
Benjamin Talbot and Sarah Louise (Johnson)
Rogers. Benjamin Rogers had been the proprietor of a store in a northern Michigan mining town before moving to Appleton, the site of
Lawrence College, the institution he wished his
children to attend. He died when his youngest
child was three years old. For part of her
elementary education Helen Rogers attended a
local public school; and from her eleventh to
her sixteenth year she was a student at Grafton
Hall, a boarding School in Fond du Lac, of
which her brother, the Reverend Benjamin
Talbot Rogers (later the bishop's chaplain at
the Cathedral of St. John the Divine in New
York City) was headmaster.

For her college education she went to New
York, there entering Barnard College in 1899
with the intention of becoming a teacher of
Greek. After some years of study in the classical language, she chose zoology as her second
major. By assisting in the bursar's office, helping to manage the dormitory, and tutoring, the
young student was able to earn funds for part

of her expenses. Chosen business manager of
the *Mortarboard* (Barnard's yearbook) in her
senior year, she directed the financing of the
publication so well that it was the first one
managed by a Barnard girl not to show a
deficit. She received the Bachelor of Arts degree in 1903.

Instead of becoming a teacher Miss Rogers
secured the position of social secretary to Mrs.
Whitelaw Reid, the wife of the publisher of the
New York *Tribune*. The newspaper owner,
who on two occasions had been special representative of the President of the United States
to Britain, was in 1905 appointed Ambassador
to the Court of St. James. Thus Miss Rogers
alternately lived abroad and in the United
States during the eight years she was Mrs.
Reid's social secretary. It was to the only son
of the Reids, Ogden Mills Reid, that Miss
Rogers was married in Wisconsin on March
14, 1911. The Reid heir had joined the staff
of his father's newspaper upon graduating from
Yale University Law School in 1907 and was
the managing editor at the time of Ambassador Reid's death in 1912, when he inherited
the newspaper property and became its editor.

During the first six years of her married
life Mrs. Ogden Reid devoted her time largely
to homemaking, with the woman suffrage
movement her chief "outside" interest. "When
I was at Barnard, working my way through,
the necessity for complete independence of
women was borne in on me," said Mrs. Reid
(quoted in *Today*, July 11, 1936). She felt
that not only did the world need women's direct contribution to public affairs, "but that
woman needs suffrage for her own spiritual
and intellectual development." As treasurer of
the New York State organization for the suffrage campaign, Mrs. Reid was chiefly responsible for raising $500,000 for the cause. "Win-
ning the battle in New York in 1917," she declared, "was winning the battle nationally two
years later." At the time of World War I
she saw to it that the 800-acre Reid estate,
"Ophir Hall," was sown with alfalfa, corn, and
oats, and became a producing farm.

In 1918 Mrs. Reid's career in the newspaper publishing field began when she became
a solicitor of advertising for the New York
Tribune, in which $15 millions of the Reid
fortune had reportedly been invested since 1898.
"Come down to the office," *Time* quoted Ogden
Reid as saying to his wife, "and work the
paper's success out with me." At that time,
reported Mona Gardner in a *Saturday Evening
Post* article on Mrs. Reid, "the ink was still
red on the *Tribune* ledgers." The first two
industries Mrs. Reid "tackled" in her initial
efforts to sell display advertising space were
department stores and automobile manufacturers. Aside from the prestige of the Reid name,
several writers have commented, she was
equipped with an acute business sense and persuasive argument when she called on her prospects.

At the end of two months Mrs. Reid was
appointed advertising director of the *Tribune*,
which in the course of the subsequent year
showed a doubling in advertising lineage. With

her enlarged corps of salesmen she would meet weekly to review their progress, aim at new prospects, and stimulate selling efforts with "pep" talks and prizes. In 1922 Mrs. Reid's titles were advertising director of the newspaper and vice-president of the company, offices she retained after the Reid interests bought Frank A. Munsey's New York *Herald* in 1924 and merged the two papers as the New York *Herald Tribune*. Twenty-three years later, upon the death of Ogden Reid in January 1947, Mrs. Reid became president of the newspaper property.

While Mrs. Reid's official province during her husband's lifetime was advertising, every department of the newspaper was said to have come under her scrutiny. She was considered a "dominant factor," said *Today*, in the decisions to syndicate Colonel House's memoirs, to purchase the New York rights to the Woodrow Wilson letters, and to engage several well-known columnists. "She encouraged her husband," wrote Mona Gardner in the *Saturday Evening Post*, "to have stop-watch tests made of various type faces to find the one most quickly read and the one producing the least eyestrain. Their linotype machines are fed with a special metal formula which gives sharp clear edges." (The *Herald Tribune* has received nineteen national awards for typographical excellence).

The newspaper's Forum on Current Problems was launched in 1930 by Mrs. Reid and Mrs. Willaim Brown Meloney, the editor of *This Week*, the *Herald Tribune*'s Sunday magazine. An annual event which had its beginning in the interest of women's clubs in current events, it draws large audiences to the Waldorf-Astoria Hotel ballroom to hear famous speakers discuss a wide range of topics of the day. It has been called the projection of the Reid credo for the paper—"intelligent, dispassionate presentation of world news and issues." With the assistance of other members of the staff, Mrs. Reid has been responsible for planning the forum programs and for obtaining the speakers, who include statesmen, scientists, scholars, generals, with one or two "glamour" names. Another project of special interest to Mrs. Reid is the newspaper's Fresh Air Fund, which makes it possible for thousands of underprivileged city children to spend some weeks in the country during the summer.

A firm believer in full opportunity for women in all fields of employment, Mrs. Reid gives good space in the paper to the reporting of the achievements of her sex, to discussions of careers, clubs, news, and women's interests generally. In the *Herald Tribune*'s Home Institute she sponsored the first experimental newspaper kitchen in America. During World War II she advocated the drafting of women: "I am glad to see women in industry," she said. "Their families will be better for it. I want to see fathers back in the home, a more equal division of work, sharing of domestic responsibility." Her own wartime assignment was to the Advisory Committee on Women in the Services.

Chase-Statler

HELEN ROGERS REID

Independent Republican under Ogden Reid's editorship, the New York *Herald Tribune* retains that political stand under Mrs. Reid. At the close of the 1951 forum she announced that the newspaper would support General Eisenhower for the Presidency in 1952. In the politically charged debate over the recall of General MacArthur by President Truman, the *Herald Tribune*, together with the New York *Times* and *Christian Science Monitor*, was judged the fairest by a poll conducted by the *Saturday Review of Literature*. While hewing to the line of objective news reporting, the *Herald Tribune*'s style of writing has been described as lively and warm, as distinguished from the more rigid impersonality of most of the country's newspapers (Kenneth Stewart and John Tebbel in their *Makers of Modern Journalism*).

The one-hundred-year-old morning newspaper has a daily (Monday through Friday) circulation of more than 343,000; a Saturday circulation of nearly 262,000, and a Sunday press run of about 596,000. The Paris edition of the *Herald Tribune*, which was started in 1924, has since 1935 been known as the New York *Herald Tribune European Edition*. Its publication was suspended for a time during World War II; the first edition after the liberation of Paris appeared on December 22, 1944. As head of the Reid Foundation, Inc., Mrs. Reid directs the awarding of fellowships, for travel and study abroad, to journalists of other papers.

Many organizations have honored Helen Rogers Reid. In 1935 she received the medal of award at the Friendship dinner of the American Women's Association "for professional achievement, public service, and personality." The Cuban Red Cross decorated her with the Comendador Cross of the Order of Honor and Merit for her "helpful understanding of world

REID, HELEN ROGERS—*Continued*

problems and friendliness toward Latin America." Mrs. Reid was elected to the post of first vice-president in 1943 of the New York Newspaper Women's Club. At the annual dinner of the Hundred Year Association of New York, an organization of 150 business institutions with more than a century of unbroken existence in New York, she was awarded a gold medal in 1946 for services in behalf of the welfare and prestige of the city. The 1949-50 seal of the Council Against Intolerance in America was presented to her for "outstanding service in the cause of tolerance and equality." She was selected by the editors of the *Book of Knowledge* as one of twelve women who are "inspiring examples of intelligence and accomplishment"; she was one of four women elected fellows of the American Academy of Arts and Sciences in 1950; and in 1951 was one of ten outstanding women in industry, communications, labor, and the professions in New York State. In the spring of 1952 she received one of that year's "Woman of Achievement" awards from the New York alumnae chapter of Theta Sigma Phi, national journalism sorority.

Of the universities which conferred honorary degrees on Mrs. Reid, Miami (Oxford, Ohio) University was the first when it awarded her the degree of Doctor of Letters in 1931. Other honorary degrees bestowed upon Mrs. Reid comprise the Doctor of Humanities, Rollins College, 1933; Doctor of Laws, Oglethorpe University, 1935; Doctor of More Humane Letters, Syracuse University, 1941; Doctor of Humane Letters, Lafayette University, 1941; Doctor of Humane Letters, New York University, 1944; Doctor of Laws, University of Toronto, 1947; Doctor of Laws, Smith College, 1948; Doctor of Letters, Columbia University, 1949; Doctor of Humane Letters, Yale University, 1950; and Doctor of Letters, Bates College, 1951.

The two sons born to Ogden Reid and Mrs. Reid continue the family tradition of active participation in the affairs of the New York *Herald Tribune*. The elder son, Whitelaw, who served as a naval aviator in World War II, has been the vice-president and editor of that newspaper since 1947; and her other son, Ogden, a paratroop officer during the war, joined the news staff of the *Herald Tribune* in 1950. (A daughter, Elisabeth, the second child born to the Reids, died in childhood.) Mrs. Reid, who is a trustee of Barnard College, holds memberships in the Colony Club, Women's University Club, Women's City Club, New York Newspaper Women's Club, and River Club (all in New York), and in the University Women's Club in Paris. Her church is the Episcopal. She is slender, has a height of five feet one inch; her eyes are green, her hair is gray. Fond of outdoor sports, she swims, plays tennis, shoots, and sails her own sloop. "She has a literal, orderly, and direct mind," wrote Mona Gardner. "She is easily and eagerly absorbed by all relevant minutiae." *Newsweek* described her quiet, gracious manner as characterized by a crisp efficiency.

References

Ed & Pub p24 F 25 '33 por
Fortune 12:88 S '35 por
Ind Woman 14:337+ O '35
Ladies Home J 53:50 Jl '36
Look 7:20 Ap 20 '43 por
New York Woman p11-13 D 23 '36
Newsweek 6:19 N 23 '35 por; 7:19 Je 13 '36 por; N 11 '46
Sat Eve Post 216:9-11+ My 6; 18-19+ My 13 '44
Time 46:72 N 12 '45
Today p8-10 Jl 11 '36
American Women, 1939-40
Stewart, K., and Tebbel, J. Makers of Modern Journalism (1952)
Who's Who in America, 1950-51
Who's Who in Commerce and Industry (1951)
World Biography (1948)

REID, MRS. OGDEN MILLS *See* Reid, H. R.

REYNOLDS, ALBERT PIERCE *See* Reynolds, Allie

REYNOLDS, ALLIE Feb. 10, 1919- Baseball player

Address: b. c/o New York Yankees, 745 5th Ave., New York 22; h. 2709 Cashion Pl., Oklahoma City, Okla.

One of baseball's outstanding present-day pitchers, Allie Reynolds of the New York Yankees established an American League record in 1951 by pitching two no-run, no-hit games in the same season, an achievement for which he received the Sid Mercer award as the "Player of the Year." Reynolds, a right-handed fast hurler, has been in professional baseball since 1939. He played on the Cleveland Indians team before joining the Yankees in 1947.

Allie (Albert Pierce) Reynolds, who is of mixed Irish, Indian, and English ancestry, is a native of Bethany, Oklahoma, and one of three sons born to David C. and Mary S. (Brooks) Reynolds. His date of birth is February 10, 1919. His father, who was a member of the Creek tribe, is a preacher in the Church of the Nazarene and would have liked his son to enter a religious calling. At the Oklahoma Agricultural and Mechanical College, however, where the youth enrolled on an athletic scholarship after graduating from Capitol Hill High School, Oklahoma City, in 1934, his interests were concentrated on sports. In 1942 Reynolds, whose name appeared on the dean's honor list, was awarded the B.S. degree.

Reynolds started out as a track man. To improve his physique, since he weighed only 140 pounds at that time, he turned first to discus and javelin throwing and then to football, building up his poundage to 200 while on the varsity gridiron team. "I liked football best of all," he told a New York *Sun* sportswriter some years later, "except for spring practice. I cut spring drill to play baseball, in a fraternity league. Otherwise I might have gone into pro ball with the Cleveland Rams of the gridiron." While the Rams did claim Reynolds in a college player "draft," he decided in favor of the summertime sport. "I thought baseball . . . better adapted to long-time earning possibilities when a guy got out of college," he told the *Sun* writer. "I went to Cleveland after all—but with the baseball side of their organization."

After he had become the property of the Cleveland (American League) Baseball Club in 1939, the pitcher spent nearly four full seasons in minor leagues before joining the Cleveland team. "I was supposed to be a strike-out pitcher, as a converted javelin-thrower," Reynolds has remarked; and in his first year as a professional player (with the Springfield, Ohio, club of the Class "C" Middle Atlantic League) he struck out a total of 140 opposing batters in 155 innings, winning eleven games and losing eight. This record brought his advancement to the Cedar Rapids, Iowa, club of the Class "B" Triple-L League, where he won twelve games and lost seven in 1940. During the following year with Cedar Rapids he balanced ten wins with ten losses, but some of his defeats were due to poor fielding support, and in the spring of 1942 he was moved up to the Wilkes-Barre, Pennsylvania, club of the Class "A" Eastern League. Here he won eighteen games as against seven losses. He led the league in strike-outs (193) and earned run average (1.56) before being called to Cleveland for a major league trial in September 1942.

Making good by not yielding an earned run in five innings of relief pitching, Reynolds was retained by the Cleveland Indians and in the ensuing 1943 season led the American League in strike-outs (151) though losing twelve games to eleven won. After he passed the pre-induction physical examination for the Navy in May of the following year, he dropped to 84 in his strike-out record for 1944. He was deferred, however, and finished the season at Cleveland. He was then stationed at the Oklahoma City Air Technical Command. In February 1945, as the result of a head injury incurred while playing basketball for the Command team, he was reclassified as a 4-F. In the next season with Cleveland, while he reached a new high of 247 innings pitched (with eighteen wins and twelve losses) he showed erratic control, yielding 130 bases on balls, the League record for that year. In the spring of 1946, after winning his first game, he lost five straight before winning another; then he lost four more before hitting a winning streak of six in a row. He finished out the season as "one of the most dependable hurlers of the Cleveland staff" (New York *Herald Tribune*), but the team had serious infield weaknesses. On October 19, 1946, accordingly, he was traded to the New York Yankees for infielders Joe Gordon and Eddie Bockman.

In his first season (1947) with New York, the "Chief" or "Wahoo" (as Reynolds was nicknamed because of his Indian blood) won

New York Yankees
ALLIE REYNOLDS

nineteen games as against eight losses—his best major league pitching percentage (.704) up to that time. The Yankees won the pennant that year, and in the subsequent World Series with the Brooklyn Dodgers Reynolds defeated Vic Lombardi by a ten-to-one score. Reynolds won sixteen games and lost seven in 1948 and racked up a seventeen-to-six record in 1949; his earned run average in the latter year was a comparatively high 4.00, and several victories were saved for him by the relief pitching of Joe Page. Reynolds completed only four games in the regular 1949 season; but he redeemed himself in the World Series against Brooklyn, pitching on October 5 what Grantland Rice described in the New York *Sun* as "the greatest game of a long career—as perfect a masterpiece as one would care to see." He beat Don Newcombe in what Rice thought "could have been a no-hit game with any luck," yielding only two hits and striking out nine Dodgers. In 1950 Reynolds won sixteen games for the Yankees as against twelve losses and struck out 160 batters. He pitched three innings and yielded only one hit in the all-star game of that year, and in the World Series with the Philadelphia National League team beat Robin Roberts by a three-to-one score.

"Early this spring," wrote Lou Miller in the New York *World-Telegram* in the midsummer of 1951, "it appeared the Oklahoma A. and M. alumnus . . . was near the end of his career. He was bothered by elbow chips, missed most of the preseason conditioning, and didn't start a game until the campaign was several weeks gone." Gradually, however, he "worked out the kinks" and in a night contest with Cleveland on July 12, realized the dream of every moundsman by pitching a no-run, no-hit game. He "walked" only two players, won by 2-to-0 over

REYNOLDS, ALLIE—*Continued*

Bob Feller, defied the baseball superstition that it is fatal to mention the possibility of achieving the so-called "perfect game" until the final batter has been retired. "I could see the scoreboard like everybody else," Reynolds said after the contest had ended. "In the seventh inning I told Yogi Berra [the catcher] I didn't want to throw any fast balls, because I had a no-hitter going."

Ten weeks later (September 28) Reynolds pitched his second no-hit, no-run game against the Boston Red Sox in the first part of a double-header, thus providing the opportunity for Vic Raschi to make certain the pennant for the Yankees in the nightcap. His feat of pitching two "no hitters" in the same season established an American League record and has been matched or bettered in the rival National League only by Johnny Vander Meer of the Cincinnati Reds, who pitched two such games in successive mound appearances in 1939. In his second no-hit game, in which he defeated Mel Parnell, Reynolds issued four "walks" and struck out nine. The pitcher's regular season record in 1951 was seventeen wins and eight losses, with an earned run average of 3.05, the fifth best in the league. In the 1951 World Series with the New York Giants, Reynolds lost the first game to Dave Koslo, but came back in the fourth when his team scored 6 to the Giants' 2.

The New York chapter of the Baseball Writers' Association on December 29, 1951, named Reynolds as the "Player of the Year" and the recipient of the Sid Mercer Memorial Award. The latter was formally presented to him on February 3, 1952, a day after he received the Hickok Award as the outstanding "professional athlete of the year," and a diamond-studded belt. He also was given a pay raise—his salary is now said to be about $35,000—for the 1952 season.

Allie Reynolds and Dale Earlene Jones were married July 7, 1935, and have two sons. Their home is in Oklahoma City, where in the winter months the baseball player is engaged in the importing business. Brown-eyed, black-haired Reynolds, who is an even six feet in height and weighs about 200 pounds, names hunting and golf as his favorite outdoor relaxation. He belongs to the Masonic Lodge; his political party is the Democratic and his church is the Methodist.

References

N Y Herald Tribune III p1 D 30 '51 por
N Y Sun p27 O 6 '49
N Y Times V p1 D 30 '51 por
N Y World-Telegram p19 Jl 13 '51
Baseball Register (1951)
Turkin, H., & Thompson, S. C. Official Encyclopedia of Baseball (1951)
Who's Who in Baseball (1952)

RICKENBACKER, EDDIE *See* Rickenbacker, E. V.

RICKENBACKER, EDWARD VERNON (rĭk′ĕn-băk″ẽr) Oct. 8, 1890- Airline executive

Address: b. c/o Eastern Air Lines, Inc., 10 Rockefeller Plaza, New York 20; h. Rickenbacker Ranch, Hunt, Texas.

NOTE: This biography supersedes the article which appeared in *Current Biography* in 1940.

The president of Eastern Air Lines, Inc., Edward Vernon ("Eddie") Rickenbacker, has made substantially his whole career in the automobile and aviation fields. In his early adventuresome life he had narrow escapes from death as an automobile racer and as a World War I ace combat pilot; and he was saved after being adrift three weeks on a rubber raft following a plane crash over the Pacific while on World War II duty. Following some years in the automobile industry, which he had entered in 1921, he was on the staff of several plane manufacturing companies. In 1938 Rickenbacker became president and general manager of Eastern Air Lines, which in 1951 stated that it would be the first airline to use planes capable of being equipped immediately with jet engines when such engines become available a few years hence.

The third of eight children (five boys and three girls) of William and Elizabeth (Barcler) Rickenbacker, both of Swiss birth, Edward Vernon Rickenbacker was born Edward Rickenbacher in Columbia, Ohio, on October 8, 1890. The spelling of his family name was changed at the time of World War I, *Time*'s article (April 17, 1950) on Rickenbacker explained; at that time, too, he took the middle name of Vernon. During the life of his father (a building contractor) young Eddie, according to his biographer, Hans Christian Adamson, was extraordinarily high-spirited. The death of his father when the boy was eleven years had a sobering effect: as the family's mainstay, he took a job in a glass factory working twelve hours daily six days a week for $3.50. Subsequently he found employment at ever increasing wages, in a brewery, a shoe factory, a stonecutter's yard, and in the Pennsylvania Railroad's locomotive shops. While employed in 1906 at the Frazer-Miller Air Cooled Car Company in Columbus, young Rickenbacker studied combustion engines in a mechanical engineering course he took from the International Correspondence School. As the engineer for the Columbus Buggy Company in late 1907, he engaged in experimental work on automobiles.

Automobile racing, in which Rickenbacker had first taken part as Lee Frazer's mechanic in the 1907 Vanderbilt Cup races held in Garden City, Long Island, soon came to occupy much of his time. During the same period (1909-14) in which Rickenbacker was engaged in devising a way to keep the water from boiling out of engines in hot climates and selling cars in Texas and Omaha, he entered many races, frequently winning. The team of Lee Frazer and Rickenbacker entered the first 500-mile automobile race, which was held on May

31, 1911, at the Indianapolis Speedway, but finished eleventh. Rickenbacker, though a regular entrant, was never to win this classic competition. At Daytona Beach, Florida, he did, however, establish a new automobile speed record of 134 miles per hour while riding a Blitzen Benz. In 1914, Rickenbacker (then teamed with Oldfield in racing Maxwell cars) was rated sixth among United States speed champions by the American Automotive Association; his standing rose to fifth in 1915 and to third in his last racing year, 1916. Rickenbacker was in England preparing a racing team for the Sunbeam Motor Company when the United States was drawn into World War I.

Organization of American automobile racers and mechanics into a flying corps was urged by Rickenbacker early in 1917. While his plan was not accepted, when the United States entered World War I he was determined to get into military aviation. He enlisted in the army on May 25, 1917. Upon arriving in France as a sergeant on General Pershing's motor car staff, he was assigned to drive the car of Colonel William Mitchell, who was famous as an aviation enthusiast. Though twenty-seven years old at the time and hence two years over age (Rickenbacker recounts) partly with Mitchell's help he was assigned to the Primary Flying School at Tours on August 25. Transferred to the Issoudun field as engineering officer in September, Rickenbacker (then a lieutenant) persuaded his superior to release him so that he might attend a gunnery school at Cazeaux, France. Ultimately he went to a combat assignment with the 94th Aero Pursuit Squadron, which later adopted the hat-in-the-ring insignia and became the first American aero unit to participate actively on the Western Front.

In command of the squadron's Flight One, Rickenbacker in the spring of 1918 scored his first victories against the "flying circus" led by the German ace Richthofen. By the war's end the 94th had surpassed all other United States pursuit units, with sixty-nine enemy craft to its credit. Of these, twenty-six (twenty-two planes and four balloons) were shot down by Rickenbacker, who had been promoted to captain and made squadron commander in September. For his most spectacular exploit, a single-handed attack on September 25, 1918, against seven German planes, two of which he downed, he was awarded the Congressional Medal of Honor some years later. Other honors he received were the Croix de Guerre, with four palms; the French Legion of Honor, and the Distinguished Service Cross, with nine oak leaves. Rickenbacker's last duty overseas was to take his squadron to the occupation headquarters at Coblenz. He has described his war experiences in *Fighting the Flying Circus* (1919), which the New York *Times* found "bubbling with the spirit of youth and adventure."

Back in the United States, Eddie Rickenbacker returned to the automobile business, this time as a manufacturer. His Detroit company, the Rickenbacker Motor Company, previ-

Budd

EDWARD VERNON RICKENBACKER

ously operating but not formally organized until 1921, presented its three models at the New York automobile show in January 1922. The line embodied safety features found in racing models. The company was not successful, however, and Rickenbacker, the vice-president and director of sales, resigned from the company in 1926. The next year he bought the controlling interest in the Indianapolis Speedway for $700,000, and in November 1945 he sold the famous motor course for a reported $750,000 (New York *Times*).

Later, Rickenbacker became assistant sales manager in charge of the La Salle division of Cadillac Motors. In 1929 he was associated with Fokker Aircraft Corporation, builder and operator of planes. Next he joined the American Airways, Inc., of which he was vice-president. Following a year as assistant to the president of the Aviation Corporation of America, he moved in 1933 to North American Aviation, Inc., where he became vice-president. In 1935 he began his association with Eastern Air Lines, Inc., just purchased by General Motors, as its general manager and vice-president. When General Motors disposed of its holdings in Eastern Air Lines in 1938, Rickenbacker was made president, general manager, and director of the line.

After the fall of France to the invading German forces in May 1940, Rickenbacker was at first opposed to United States intervention in the European conflict and made a number of speeches expressing his views on the war. To protect America, he urged in an article in *Look* (August 27, 1940), a force of 250,000 military airplanes was needed. At other times he spoke of establishing long-range bomber bases and of building up military air power by training pilots in commercial flying. By June 1941, however, he said that the United States

RICKENBACKER, EDWARD VERNON
—*Continued*

had in effect been in the war for a year and acknowledged the necessity of defeating Hitler.

When the United States entered World War II, Rickenbacker's technical knowledge led Secretary of War Henry Stimson to send him on missions to inspect American air bases abroad. On his second mission, which took him to the Pacific area, the plane on which he flew out of Hawaii missed its destination, and on October 24, 1942, was forced down some 600 miles north of Samoa. Seven men survived the ordeal of twenty-three days on small rafts during which they were able to catch some fish and they drank rain water. Rickenbacker and the two others on his raft were picked up by a Navy helicopter on November 12 and flown (Rickenbacker strapped to a wing of the small plane) to a hospital. After a two-week rest he went to Guadalcanal. Other missions took him to Asia, North Africa, Iceland, Greenland, and the Aleutians. Having seen the fighting men on a number of fronts, Rickenbacker made several speeches in the United States on what he considered a sluggishness on the part of workers at home to do their utmost in the war effort.

In *Seven Came Through*, published in 1943, Rickenbacker tells the story of the Pacific rescue besides facts about the mission and his conclusions on the future of American aviation. Critics commented particularly on the personality of the author as he revealed himself. "This is really the story of . . . a strong man, strong in disaster, a fighter for what he believes in and what he intensely feels, whoever may disagree" (from the New York *Times*); "His forthrightness and his sincerity are implicit in every passage, although the last thing Rickenbacker pretends to be is a hero or a superman" (from the New York *Herald Tribune*). The flier was the subject of a motion picture, *Captain Eddie*, which was released immediately after the war.

Before the end of the war, Rickenbacker had proposed a program of civil airline expansion to absorb thousands of men who had been trained to fly and to service military craft. He had urged several times that all first-class mail be carried by air and much freight as well. Eastern Air Line's own postwar expansion was reported to have earned it a profit each year, even in years when other airlines were showing losses. So successful were Eastern's operations that Rickenbacker requested the Civil Aeronautics Board's permission in 1947 to reduce the line's fares by 10 per cent, but was refused. He has also attacked "coddling" of airlines by subsidies except in cases where service is supplied to regions with scant populations.

Rickenbacker announced in July 1951 that Eastern would spend $100,000,000 to purchase 72 Super-Constellations and Martin 4-0-4s (New York *Times*, July 18, 1951). The airline's monthly passenger capacity would be made almost double the 1951 figure of 320,000. Through a changeover that can be made without altering the structure of the aircraft, these Super-Constellations—the first went into oper-

ation in December 1951—will be equipped with turbo-jet and jet propulsion motors as soon as these are released for civilian craft. With this future equipment an airliner will have a speed of 400 miles an hour. On July 18, 1952, the directors of Colonial Airlines announced their acceptance of the terms of a merger offered by Eastern Airlines and submitted by Rickenbacker in June. Acceptance of this proposal was subject to approval by the companies' stockholders. The Eastern Airlines executive, who is also a director of Foremost Diaries, Inc., Jacksonville, Florida, was chosen as the outstanding leader in business by a 1951 survey conducted by *Forbes* magazine.

The list of his posts in organizations includes chairmanship of the Will Rogers Memorial Fund and of the Aeronautic Division of the Greater New York Fund in 1943, the presidency of the Army Air Forces Aid Society, and trusteeship of Ithaca (New York) College and Asheville (North Carolina) School for Boys. A member of the executive board of the National Council of Boy Scouts of America, he received that organization's highest award, the Silver Buffalo award in 1944. For 1943 he received the American Educational award, given by the Associated Exhibitors of the National Education Association. He is the recipient also of the Medal for Merit, and the International Benjamin Franklin Society's gold medal for 1951 in testimony of outstanding Americanism.

Rickenbacker has been awarded the honorary degree of Doctor of Aeronautical Science by Pennsylvania Military College (1938), John Brown University of Siloam Springs, Arkansas, (1940), and the University of Miami (1941); the Doctor of Science degree by the University of Tampa (1942) and Westminster College of New Wilmington, Pennsylvania, (1944); the Doctor of Humane Letters degree by University Foundations and American Theological Seminary, Wilmington, Delaware, (1943); the LL.D. degree by Oklahoma City University (1944) and Capital University, Columbus, Ohio (1945), and the College of South Jersey (1948); and the D. Eng. by Lehigh University, Pennsylvania (1948). Among the clubs to which he has belonged are the Early Birds, Elks, St. Andrew's Golf (Mount Hope, New York), Lotos (New York), Detroit Athletic, Quiet Birdmen, Saints and Sinners, and Siwanoy Country. Other of his clubs are the Links, Twenty-Nine, and Question. He was chairman of the sports committee for the New York World's Fair.

Rickenbacker and Mrs. Adelaide Frost Durant were married on September 16, 1922, and have two sons, David E. and William F. Captain Rickenbacker (who prefers that title although he was made an honorary colonel in the Air Force Reserve in August 1950 for his promotion of safety in civil and military aviation) stands six feet two inches tall and weighs about 175 pounds. Rickenbacker's faith in the efficacy of prayer has often been commented upon; for three years he served on the board of sponsors of the World Council of Christian Education, which awarded him a scroll in 1948.

References

Aero Digest 32:78 My '38 por
Am Mag 137:17+ Je '44
Bsns W p17 Mr 12 '38 por
Life 14:19-26+ Ja 25; 78-9+ F 1; 94:
  100+ F 8 '43
N Y Herald Tribune p34 N 15 '42; p25
  F1 51por; p10 Ap 6 '51 por
N Y Sun p2 O 24 '43 por
N Y Times p13 F 28 '41
Scribner's Commentator 10:45-52 Je '41
  por
Time 31:60+ Mr 14 '38; 55:24-7 Ap 17
  '50 por
Adamson, H. C. Eddie Rickenbacker
  (1946)
Blue Book of American Aviation (1942)
Business Executives of America (1950)
Columbia Encyclopedia (1950)
Rickenbacker, E. V. Fighting the Fly-
  ing Circus (1919); Seven Came
  Through (1943)
Whittaker, J. C. We Thought We
  Heard the Angels Sing (1944)
Who's Who, 1951
Who's Who in America, 1950-51
Who's Who in Aviation, 1942-43
Who's Who in New York, 1947
Who's Who in the East (1951)
World Biography (1948)

ROBINSON, BOARDMAN Sept. 6, 1876—
Sept 5, 1952 Political cartoonist; painter; book
illustrator; teacher; cartoonist for the *Morning
Telegraph* in New York (1907-10) and for
the New York *Tribune* (1910-14); his work
compared with that of the French cartoonist
Honoré Daumier; in early 1920's became interested in mural decoration; resident art instructor at the Fountain Valley School and
director of the Colorado Springs Fine Arts
Center (1930-47); in 1946 held a retrospective
exhibition (1904-46) at Kraushaar Gallery,
New York. See *Current Biography*, 1941.

Obituary

N Y Times p84 S 7 '52

ROOT, OREN June 13, 1911- Lawyer; organization official

Address: b. c/o Hatch, Root, Barrett, Cohen &
Knapp, 25 Broad St., New York 4

> NOTE: This article supersedes
> the article which appeared in
> *Current Biography* in 1940.

For nearly two years, from the time of its
establishment in September 1950 until July
1952, the National Association for Mental
Health was under the presidency of Oren Root,
the New York attorney and liberal Republican
who set in motion the 1940-41 campaign to win
the Presidency of the United States for Wendell L. Willkie. Since his discharge from the
Navy after World War II, Root has been engaged in political activity and in the practice
of law, and was the Republican-City Fusion

OREN ROOT

candidate for President of the Borough of
Manhattan in the New York City municipal
election of 1949.

One of two children (a boy and a girl) of
Oren and Aida (de Acosta) Root, Oren Root
was born in New York City on June 13, 1911.
His father was for many years the president
of the Hudson and Manhattan tube railway
linking New York and New Jersey, and his
granduncle was Elihu Root, Secretary of
State under President Theodore Roosevelt and
subsequently president of The Hague Tribunal
and a winner of the Nobel Peace Prize. After
passing his early childhood in New York City,
the junior Oren prepared for Princeton University at St. Paul's School in Concord, New
Hampshire. On graduation from Princeton as
a Bachelor of Arts in 1933, he enrolled at the
University of Virginia Law School, where he
received the LL.B. degree in 1936.

Having completed his professional training
young Root joined the staff of the New York
City law firm of Davis, Polk, Wardwell, Gar-
diner & Reed, was admitted to the New York
bar two years later (1938), and until the
spring of 1940 was chiefly occupied in "handling the legal affairs of some of the charitable
organizations represented by the firm, drawing
wills and occasionally appearing in court"
(Floyd Taylor in the New York *World-Telegram*.

Outside the office he had campaigned for
the re-election of Fiorello La Guardia as
Mayor of New York City in 1937 and for the
election of Thomas E. Dewey as Governor in
1938, and had served as a Republican committeeman for New York County in 1939. Impressed by Wendell L. Willkie's ideas in the
article "We, the People," which appeared in the
April 1940 issue of *Fortune*, Root hurried to
Town Hall to hear Willkie lecture and made
up his mind that the speaker was Presidential
timber. The same night Root drafted an ex-

ROOT, OREN—*Continued*

perimental "declaration of support" for Willkie, a thousand copies of which were printed at his own expense (without Willkie's knowledge) and mailed for signature to recent alumni of Yale, Princeton, and Harvard. "I sent out the declarations very naively—never dreaming that I would receive the response I did," Root told Floyd Taylor about two months later, the response having meanwhile received further impetus from a political advertisement in the New York *Herald Tribune*.

When Root used the address of his law firm in soliciting support for Willkie, telephone calls, letters, and personal visits from volunteer workers came in such numbers that the routine law work was disturbed. Root consequently withdrew from the firm and carried on his campaign from office space contributed by the realtor Douglas Elliman. Russell Davenport, the managing editor of *Fortune*, also thought Willkie should be President and likewise gave up his position. As a result of their work and popular support Willkie was nominated at the Republican National Convention in July 1940. Through the ensuing campaign Root served as chairman of the Associated Willkie Clubs of America. Willkie lost the November election to President Franklin D. Roosevelt by about 5,000,000, but received 6,000,000 more votes than had the Republican candidate, Alfred M. Landon in 1936.

For his work as organizer of the Willkie clubs, Root was named in January 1941 to receive the United States Junior Chamber of Commerce Distinguished Award and cited by the Young Men's Board of Trade as "New York City's outstanding young man of the year" for 1940. A few weeks afterward he joined three former associates in the new law firm of Hatch, McLean, Root and Hinch, but his actual practice there lasted only until April 1941, when he was called to active duty with the United States Navy, about eight months before the attack on Pearl Harbor. (Root had been commissioned an ensign in the Supply Corps of the Naval Reserve as early as February 1939.) While on home service, as aide to the Navy Purchasing Officer in Manhattan, and advanced to a lieutenancy, Root made an address, "The Beliefs We Fight For," (delivered to the Associated Industries of New York State in February 1942 and later reprinted in *Vital Speeches*) and contributed the article "Do We Need a Political Realignment?" to *Commonweal* for April 15, 1942. Subsequently he was reassigned to the staff of Commander Fourth Fleet, in the rank of lieutenant commander, and still later was a member of the staff of Commander, Task Force 122, participating in the 1944 Normandy landings. Root's decorations for World War II service are two Navy Commendation Ribbons, the Brazilian Order of the Southern Cross, and the Croix de Guerre of France.

Released from active service, Root resumed the practice of law early in 1946 as a partner in the firm of Hatch, Root and Barrett (now Hatch, Root, Barrett, Cohen and Knapp). In political circles he won reappointment to the New York County Republican Committee and

was elected vice-president of the New York Young Republicans Club. He wrote for the New York *Times* of June 9 an article entitled "Youth Will Not Permit Another 1920," in which he predicted that returning servicemen would look for leadership in the liberal Republican movement headed by Harold Stassen, Wayne Morse, and others. In June 1948 Root was approved by a citizens' committee as an acceptable candidate for United States Representative from the 18th District of New York; though not nominated he took an active part in the ensuing campaign and also contributed to the September issue of the *Atlantic Monthly* an article, "The Republican Revival." In 1949 he was the Republican-City Fusion candidate for the office of president of the Borough of Manhattan in that year's municipal campaign, but lost the election in November to Robert F. Wagner, Jr., his Democratic-Labor opponent.

Another phase in the career of Oren Root began on September 15, 1950, when announcement was made of his election as full-time president of the newly certified National Association for Mental Health, a consolidation of three previously independent voluntary organizations. These were the National Committee for Mental Hygiene, founded in 1909; the National Health Foundation, started in 1946 by a group of wartime conscientious objectors who had served as emergency personnel in State mental hospitals; and the Psychiatric Foundation, launched in 1946 under the auspices of the American Psychiatric Association and the American Neurological Association. Commenting on the merger and the choice of a layman as its head, the New York *Herald Tribune* pointed out that the consolidation of the three inevitably overlapping organizations would "provide a fresh intensity and scope to the whole drive against mental disturbances"; the paper also commented, "The choice of Oren Root as president gives assurance of the vigor and effectiveness with which the association's activities are to be prosecuted." A little less than two months later, in his first speech as president, Root announced the objectives as twofold: to conduct an educational program "so that every person in the United States can be reached and helped to understand a few central truths about mental health, as is now being done with physical health," and "to see to it that mental health facilities are available to everyone who needs them and at a price he can afford to pay, whether it is a mental hospital or child guidance."

In his first annual report (November 1951) as president of the National Association for Mental Health, Root expressed the belief that "under all the circumstances the first year was an enormously successful one." Nearly $700,-000 had been contributed or pledged to the association, which had already participated in the formation of nine State and fifty-nine community societies. As the American branch of the World Federation for Mental Health, the association was sponsoring the fourth International Congress on Mental Health, meeting in Mexico City in December 1951. Another project the association had helped to sponsor and finance was a program of hospital inspection and rating conducted by the central inspection board of the American Psychiatric Association. The organization had also conducted researches into the causes of dementia praecox and had discovered "very good evidence" that this condition "is not merely a psychological deviation but rather that it involves deeply rooted deficiencies in metabolism, endocrine balances, and body chemistry." In May 1952, at the opening of a "Mental Health Week" proclaimed by Governor Thomas E. Dewey and Mayor Vincent R. Impellitteri for New York State and City, Root issued an additional report, partly based on the experience of State hospitals, in which it was revealed that the incidence of recovery from schizophrenia had already risen to 55 per cent. This report also disclosed that one person out of every sixteen in the United States is afflicted with mental or personality disturbances and that the number of patients in mental hospitals has risen 20 per cent since 1940. Root explained, however, that this did not mean that mental illness was "on the rise," but that more people were availing themselves of an increasing number of mental hospitals. He resigned as president of the association on July 1, 1952.

Root is a director of Freedom House and of the National Urban League and a trustee of Bard College at Annandale-on-Hudson. A Roman Catholic, Root is also a director of Catholic Scholarships for Negroes and of the National Conference of Christians and Jews. His service organizations are the Catholic War Veterans and the American Veterans Committee; his fraternities, the Delta Psi and Phi Delta Phi. On February 15, 1947, Oren Root married Daphne Skouras, daughter of Spyros Skouras, president of the Twentieth Century-Fox Film Corporation. The couple are now the parents of three children. The blue-eyed lawyer is six feet two inches in height. He has been characterized in the New Yorker as "affable" and "effervescent."

References

Life 9:78 S 30 '40 por
N Y Sun p3 Je 8 '40 por
N Y World-Telegram p4 Je 8 '40 por
New Yorker 16:10-11 Je 8 '40; 17:12-13 Mr 8 '41
Newsweek 15:31 My 13 '40
American Catholic Who's Who, 1952-53
Who's Who in America, 1952-53
Who's Who in United States Politics (1952)

ROOTH, IVAR (rōōt ēʹvär) Nov. 2, 1888- Monetary fund official
Address: b. c/o International Monetary Fund, 1818 H St., N.W., Washington 25, D.C.; h. 3200 Rowland Pl., Washington 8, D.C.

As managing director of the International Monetary Fund, Ivar Rooth since June 1951 has headed this organization established under the Bretton Woods agreement of 1944 "to promote world trade by insuring stability of exchange rates." For nearly twenty years Rooth had been governor of the Central Bank of

Sweden from which he resigned in 1948 because of a difference in policy dealing with inflationary problems. The Scandinavian lawyer was serving as head of an International Bank mission to Iraq when he was elected on April 10, 1951, to the five-year term of his present post, in succession to Camille Gutt of Belgium, the fund's original director.

Ivar Rooth was born in Stockholm, Sweden, on November 2, 1888, the son of Otto and Ellen (Hertzman) Rooth. After five years (1906-11) of undergraduate and graduate work in general subjects, economics, and law at Uppsala University in Sweden, he received the LL.B. degree in 1911; he then proceeded to the University of Berlin in Germany for an additional year of specialized study. Having returned to his native city to practice law, Rooth was engaged in 1914 as a solicitor by the Handelsbank (Commercial Bank) of Stockholm and the following year was made head of the bank's commercial credit department. From 1916 to 1919 Rooth was occupied with legal work for the Handelsbank; then for nine years beginning in 1920 he was the assistant manager and counsel for the Stockholm Mortgage Bank. He was appointed counsel and assessor of the eighteenth district of Stockholm in 1921.

In 1929, the first year of the world depression, Ivar Rooth was named governor of the Sveriges Riksbank (Central Bank of Sweden), a post bearing some resemblance to the chairmanship of the Federal Reserve Board in the United States. He held this position for nearly twenty years, during fourteen of which (1931-33 and 1937-49) he served also as director of the Bank of International Settlements in Basel, Switzerland, which began to function in 1930 to handle "all reparation transactions arising from the operation of the Young Plan" (*Encyclopedia Britannica*), later being used as a general clearing house for the banks of Europe. Rooth further undertook in 1944 the duties of attorney for the Swedish Post Office Savings Bank for four years, serving the state Pension Fund in a similar capacity from 1946 to the end of 1948.

In a move that has been described as a "protest against what he considered the inflationary policy" of Sweden's Socialist Government, Rooth in December 1948 resigned as head of the Central Bank (effective at the beginning of the new year). Writing about the resignation later John Elliott in the New York *Herald Tribune* (March 4, 1951) explained: "Specifically Mr. Rooth objected to the government's policy of pegging the long-term interest rate at 3 per cent, a policy that had led between 1946 and 1948 to large bond purchases by the central bank." Rooth was opposed in his stand by the cabinet, which "feared that higher interest rates would lead to higher rents and finally to demands for higher wages," and also by a majority of his own board of directors, who sided with the government. This did not stop Rooth from continuing to insist that "the creation of new bank reserves necessitated by the government's policy led in itself to inflationary pressures." Elliott went on to explain that "time has vindicated Mr. Rooth." Increased inflation early in 1950 forced the Swed-

Wide World Photos

IVAR ROOTH

ish Government to reverse its monetary policy and by July, "for the first time since the war, the Riksbank withdrew its support from the government bond market. As a result the quotation of the 1934 government loan which had been pegged by the bank at 99 fell at once to 95 and later became stabilized at about 94—a rise in the effective yield from 3.05 to 3.22 per cent."

After his resignation Rooth spent his time studying, writing, and lecturing on fiscal matters until he was chosen in February 1951 by the International Bank for Reconstruction and Development to head its mission to Iraq in connection with that country's application for development loans. A year later the Rooth mission recommended to the Iraqi Government the expenditure of $470 million of oil royalty revenue on a five-year plan of irrigation, public health, education, and industrial and agricultural development. Rooth was still engaged in the three-month survey of Iraq when on April 10, 1951, he was elected by the board of directors of the International Monetary Fund to the five-year term as managing director of the fund and as chairman of the executive board.

The International Monetary Fund, like its sister agency the International Bank for Reconstruction and Development, was authorized under the Bretton Woods Agreement of July 1944 and was established at Washington, D.C., on December 27, 1945, as a specialized agency of the United Nations. Fifty-four nations are now (in 1952) members of the more than $8 billion fund, whose purpose has been defined as follows: "To promote international monetary cooperation and expansion of international trade; to promote exchange stability; to assist in establishment of multilateral system of payments in respect of current transactions between members" (*Information Please Almanac*). Ex-

plaining the operation of the fund, Elizabeth Maguire in the Washington *Post* (August 5, 1951) pointed out that the voting strength of the member nations is determined by the size of their contribution to the fund. The United States casts about 30 per cent of the votes, having contributed about 30 per cent of the fund's capital of $8,130,000,000.

Under the chairmanship of Camille Gutt, former Finance Minister of Belgium, the International Monetary Fund began stabilization operations on March 1, 1947. When Gutt left that post in 1951, a Washington *Post* editor (May 16, 1951) commented: "To Mr. Gutt the standstill attitude of the nations must have been irksome. . . . .Soviet Russia turned its back on cooperation. . . . .Even the countries of the West failed to unite back of the mandate which they had given to the Monetary Fund. Led by Great Britain, they contracted regional or autarchic obsessions, and, where the Monetary Fund was concerned, were interested only in seeing that the organization was kept in its place, rather than allowed to grow into an instrument of world economy."

At the time that Rooth was named to succeed Camille Gutt, Sweden was not yet a member nation of the fund, although she had filed application for membership. His appointment was not barred, however, since the articles of the agency did not require that the managing director be chosen from a member country. In his first address as managing director on September 11, 1951, the Swedish financier told member countries that the fund "sought removal or modification of exchange restrictions and other discriminatory practices 'before the vested interests they create become an impassable obstacle to a freer flow of international trade and payments,'" and the fund proposed to "use part of its $8 billion in gold and currency to underwrite risks" taken by its member nations "in removing or relaxing restrictions on trade and payments" (in the words of New York *Times*, September 12, 1951). Great Britain immediately advised the fund that it saw little opportunity of relaxing restrictions in either 1952 or 1953 in view of the demands made by the defense effort. The United States, on the other hand, stated that the fund had no choice but to "stick to its initial objective of pressing for an end to these trade-hampering restrictions as quickly as possible" (New York *Herald Tribune*, September 13, 1951). Because of this basic disagreement it seemed at the time to Felix Belair, Jr., of the New York *Times* that the whole future of the fund "was placed in doubt."

A crisis having been averted, in February 1952 the fund formulated a new policy for the advancement of funds which required that a country pay back any drawing within from three to five years. The first transaction under the new policy was a $30 million loan to Australia on April 30, 1952. In his first annual report as IMF managing director (presented to the joint annual meeting of the International Bank and the Monetary Fund in Mexico City on September 4, 1952) Rooth stressed that the funds facilities could be put to greater use.

He also charged that international trade had suffered because of "far too severe" barriers set up by the United States on exports to dollar markets. An increase in exports to such markets he regarded as necessary to restoring a balance in international payments. He suggested that the United States trading policy be based upon a consideration of its position as a "country with a wide variety of exports which find eager markets in all parts of the world" (New York *Times*, September 5, 1952).

By his first marriage Ivar Rooth has two sons, Lars and Gösta, and a daughter, Mrs. Elsa Amboldt. On July 19, 1931, he married Ingrid Margareta Söderlind; they have a daughter, Ellen. His favorite sport is sailing; "all the Rooths are good sailors," his wife has told Elizabeth Maguire of the Washington *Post*. This same writer has described Rooth as a slightly built man with a pleasant manner.

References

N Y Times p10 Ap 11 '51 por
Washington (D.C.) Post p48 Ag 5 '51 por
International Who's Who, 1952
Vem är Det, 1951
World Biography (1948)

ROSENBACH, A(BRAHAM) S(IMON) W(OLF) July 22, 1876—July 1, 1952 Bibliophile; author; bibliographer; considered world's foremost dealer and collector of rare books; handled transactions involving from $60 millions to $80 millions through the Rosenbach Company in New York and Philadelphia; helped build the libraries of Henry E. Huntington, J. Pierpont Morgan, and John D. Rockefeller, Jr.; author of *Unpublishable Memoirs* (1917) and *Books and Bidders* (1927), among other writings. See *Current Biography*, 1946.

Obituary

N Y Times p1+ Jl 3 '52

ROSENFIELD, HARRY N(ATHAN) Aug. 17, 1911- United States Government official

Address: h. 3600 38th St., N.W., Washington 16, D.C.

As Commissioner of the United States Displaced Persons Commission, Harry N. Rosenfield, assisted by a staff of 2,500 workers, helped to organize and direct the admission of 400,744 displaced persons and refugees into the United States, as of late 1951. He was appointed to the post by President Truman in August 1948. Soon after the commission ended its work in August 1952, Rosenfield, in September, was named executive director of the President's new Commission on Immigration and Naturalization. From 1942-1948, while with the Federal Security Agency, he cooperated in the reorganization of the United States Office of Education, in addition to handling Federal grants and helping draft legislation for basic

HARRY N. ROSENFIELD

educational programs of the United States Government. An expert on the legal aspects of education, Rosenfield has frequently represented the Government in educational meetings and conventions. He taught at New York University's School of Education from 1938 to 1942, and for seven and one-half years prior to 1942 served with the Board of Education of New York City.

Born in New York City on August 17, 1911, Harry Nathan Rosenfield is the son of Max and Anna F. (Kutchai) Rosenfield. He has a sister and one brother. Their father, a manufacturer of women's dresses, was the organizer and first president of the Dress Manufacturers' Association. Harry attended Townsend Harris Hall High School in New York City, where he was the president of several clubs, sports editor of the high school paper *Arista*, and a member of the soccer team. He chose philosophy and psychology as his major subjects at the City College of New York, and was deeply influenced, he stated in later years, by the rigorous thinking and devotion to truth of the philosopher Professor Morris R. Cohen. At college Rosenfield was several years elected president of his class, was student chairman of the faculty-student curriculum committee, assistant in the library, member of the football and wrestling teams (he received a letter for athletics), and joined Tau Alpha Omega. After receiving his B.A. degree from C.C.N.Y. in 1931, he attended Columbia Law School, which granted him an LL.B. degree in 1934, the same year in which he was admitted to the bar.

Rosenfield became legal assistant to Fiorello H. La Guardia in 1933 (after the latter had been defeated in re-election to Congress) and continued as part of his "brain trust" upon La Guardia's election to the New York City mayoralty. Rosenfield has said of La Guardia: "His burning passion for the public interest

ROSENFIELD, HARRY N.—*Continued*

and deep conviction about honesty in public life left a deep mark upon my thinking and future career." In 1933 and 1934 Rosenfield was consultant to the American Civil Liberties Union, and in 1934 he became special counsel to the Senate committee investigating the munitions industry, serving as codrafter of a bill introduced by Senator Gerald P. Nye to curb war profits. In the same year, Rosenfield was a member of the counsel staff of the New York City Charter Revision Committee. As secretary, from 1935 to 1942, to Dr. Alberto C. Bonaschi, Commissioner of the New York City Board of Education, and to the chairman of the Teachers Retirement Board of that city, Rosenfield became concerned with the entire range of educational policy, administration and supervision, personnel, school building construction, school finance, and public relations.

The educator was an instructor at the School of Law of New York University from 1939 to 1942, in which year he was awarded the degree of Doctor of Juridical Science by N.Y.U.'s Law School. During that same period he was also a research associate at the university's Center for Safety Education and lectured from 1938 to 1942 on administration and supervision at the N.Y.U. School of Education. Rosenfield was principal attorney to the Federal Security Agency, Washington, D.C., during 1942-44, serving as counsel to the United States Office of Education and to Howard University. From 1944 to 1948 he was assistant to the Federal Security Administrator, of which agency the Office of Education is a constituent organization. In that post he developed educational programs, handled Federal grants, made and supported budgets for the Office of Education, and helped draft basic educational legislation for the Federal government. He also assisted at this time in the complete reorganization of the Office of Education. Another aspect of Rosenfield's work with which the Federal Security Agency was concerned was Howard University and Gallaudet College for the Deaf, which were established by Acts of Congress. In the year 1948 the educator was a member of the American Delegation to the United Nations Economic and Social Council, in Geneva, Switzerland, serving as chairman of the Human Rights Committee.

In August 1948 President Truman appointed Rosenfield the Commissioner of the United States Displaced Persons Commission. The task of this body consisted of working with public and voluntary agencies in the United States to assure DP's employment and housing upon arrival in that country. When such assurance was given, a preliminary selection was made by members of the Commission in European DP camps, followed by a legal examination of the person's record, along with a loyalty check, after which the consular officers issued visas for the United States. Reporting directly to the President, Rosenfield represented the United States at international conferences, and worked in close relation with two U.N. organizations and fifteen European governments. His work as Commissioner

brought him in close policy connection with five other major departments of the United States Government, and with international, national, and private welfare, religious, civil, and educational organizations. The New York *Times* reported that his Commission had been instrumental in bringing 100,000 DP's to the United States in the first year of its existence and 200,000 in twenty-five months. The final total of displaced persons and refugees who entered the United States with the help of Rosenfield and his staff of 2,500 workers was 400,744 (as of late 1951).

In January 1952, returning from Germany and Austria, where the work of the Commission was nearing completion, Rosenfield expressed concern over two remaining refugee problems in Europe: millions of refugees in Germany, Austria, and Italy who were uprooted by the Axis defeat; and refugees from Communist-controlled countries, who escaped into Western Germany and Austria at the rate of about 20,000 a month from East Germany and 1,600 a month from other Soviet-dominated areas. He called for a series of free universities in Europe, to train escapees for leadership in their countries in the event of the collapse of Communist regimes. The Commissioner declared that in the world today there are sixty million persons who are either refugees or individuals who cannot be supported by their national economies. In a speech on March 3, 1952, he urged the passage of legislation to "abolish the evil effects of the national origins and quota law," and to admit 100,000 immigrants a year into the United States for the following three years. He also emphasized the necessity for international efforts to facilitate migration from overpopulated areas to underdeveloped lands. His speech was the prelude to heated Congressional dispute over immigration legislation. The Displaced Persons Commission having ended its work on August 31, 1952, Rosenfield was free to accept the appointment as executive director of the President's Commission on Immigration and Naturalization, to which he was named in mid-September. This commission, set up by the President on September 4, has the function of studying and evaluating United States policies on immigration and naturalization and of making a report on them before the end of the year 1952.

Rosenfield has represented the United States Government in a number of conventions and negotiations with major educational organizations, and has helped draft legislation for various Federal educational programs. In January 1952 he was chairman of the panel session of the National Commission for UNESCO. His organization memberships include: the board of directors of the American Organization of Rehabilitation through Training Federation, the Committee on European Jewish Cultural Reconstruction, the National Lawyers Guild, National Education Association, Association of Public School Business Officials, American Society for Public Administration, International Juridical Association, and the C.C.N.Y. Alumni Association. From 1936 to 1942 Rosenfield held the honorary position of secretary of the Conference on Jewish Relations. He is an honorary member of Kappa Phi Kappa educational fraternity and in 1950 received the Founders' Award from the Association of Immigration and Nationality Lawyers.

Rosenfield has contributed about 200 educational, general, and school law articles to major educational and legal journals and has served in editorial capacities on a number of publications: as a member of the board of editors of the *Nation's Schools*, school law editor of *Legal Notes on Local Government*, and contributing editor of *Encyclopedia of Modern Education*. His own book, *Liability for School Accidents*, and the book *Education for Safe Living*, to which he contributed, were chosen by the National Education Association as among the sixty best educational works of 1940 and 1942, respectively. On June 25, 1936, Rosenfield married Dr. Leonora Cohen, the daughter of Professor Morris R. Cohen. A scholar and author, she is at present (1952) assistant professor of French at the University of Maryland. They have a daughter, Marianne Joan. A member of the Adirondack Mountain Club, Rosenfield names as his favorite recreations mountain climbing and canoeing. He is six feet one inch tall and has brown eyes and brown hair. A New York *Post* interviewer has described him as a "big, dark man with the build of a football player."

References

N Y Post Mag p33 S 27 '48 por
Leaders in Education (1948)
Who's Who in American Education, 1947-48
Who's Who in American Jewry, 1938-39

ROSS, HAROLD W(ALLACE) Nov. 6, 1892—Dec. 6, 1951 Magazine editor; in early career a reporter for the Salt Lake City *Tribune* (1906-08), Sacramento (California) *Union* (1911), Panama (Republic) *Star and Herald* (1912), and San Francisco *Call* (1917); editor of the World War I AEF *Stars and Stripes* (1917-19), *American Legion Weekly* (1921-23), *Judge* (1924); a founder and the editor of the *New Yorker* magazine, which first appeared in 1925. See *Current Biography*, 1943.

Obituary

N Y Times p1+ D 7 '51

ROSS, NANCY WILSON Nov. 22, 1907- Author

Address: b. c/o Random House, Inc., 457 Madison Ave., New York 22; h. Old Westbury, N.Y.

Reprinted from the *Wilson Library Bulletin*, Sept. 1952.

In her native American Northwest, in Europe, and in the Orient, Nancy Wilson Ross has been an interested observer of the cultures of various peoples. "I am always drawn toward the strange and exceptional, and then spend a good deal of creative energy trying to reinterpret it after more familiar thought patterns," she writes. Her travels have taken her to China, Japan, Korea, and Mexico, as well as Europe and Africa, and she has collected and written about Oriental and modern art. And, since she has been "exposed to psychoanalysis," she also finds absorbing the inner workings of people's minds. *I, My Ancestor* (1949), her most recent novel, deals with a man's recovery from a nervous breakdown, helped by a New York phychiatrist and his own father, who lives on a Puget Sound island.

Nancy Wilson Ross was born in Olympia, Washington, November 22, 1907, the daughter of Robert James Wilson, of Scotch-Irish descent, and Lydia May (Giles) Wilson. Mrs. Wilson's family were transplanted New Englanders; her father was a pioneer lumberman. Soon after receiving her B.A. degree at the University of Oregon, Nancy Wilson came to New York. In 1931-32 she was in Germany (Dessau and Anhalt), a student at the Bauhaus, a school of modern art and architecture which was later closed by Hitler as being "dangerously international." Here she met Paul Klee, the famous Swiss-German painter. (In 1951 she was a contributor to *Five Essays on Paul Klee*, edited by Merle Armitage.)

Disturbed by what she saw in Germany, she wrote an article, "German Main Street," which appeared in the *Saturday Evening Post* for October 22, 1932. Prophesying Hitler's rise, it drew a remarkable quantity of fan mail and was also charged with stirring up anti-German feeling. After returning from Europe she crossed America four times in a trailer, covering the country quite thoroughly and observing manners, customs, and ways of life, especially among Indians of the Northwest and Southwest. Their cultural patterns, arts, and religion have always fascinated her, and she has attended many of their seasonal dances and rituals.

Also in 1932, her first novel, *Friday to Monday*, was published. Her first marriage, to Charles Walton Ross, Jr., ended in divorce, but she has retained the name for her professional signature. In 1937-38 she did graduate work at the University of Chicago. A second novel, *Take the Lightning* (1940), dealt with a marital triangle in a college faculty. The *New Republic* praised its "fine flair for dialogue and good descriptions of small-town college life." Edith H. Walton in the New York *Times* called it a civilized and provocative story, though sometimes burdened with a mannered style and lush verbiage. A work of nonfiction, *Farthest Reach: Oregon and Washington* (1941), lays surprisingly little stress on lumbering, considering the author's background. Stewart Holbrook thought the book suffered from inadequate reporting, but *Time* called it "one of the best books written about the Northwest." *Westward the Women* (1944) was made up of stories of the women of all classes who helped build the Northwest, from missionaries and doctors to captives and dollar-a-dance girls—this last a section "presented with dis-

Dorothy Wilding
NANCY WILSON ROSS

cernment and humor," according to Mari Sandoz in the *Times*.

In 1942 Mrs. Ross married Stanley Preston Young, novelist and dramatist and now partner in the publishing house of Farrar, Straus and Young. They live in Old Westbury, Long Island, New York, in a large old house, "Applegreen," originally built for a trainer in the Whitney racing stables. As special correspondent assigned to the Air Corps during the war, Nancy Ross flew thousands of miles over the European front and North Africa, and received a War Department citation in 1945 "for outstanding and conspicuous service as war correspondent" in the European theater of war. Her *The WAVES; the Story of the Girls in Blue* (1945) was "a sober account, not without touches of humor," of the training and organization of the women's branch of the United States Naval Reserve.

The Left Hand Is the Dreamer (1947), the author's best-known novel, has been published in fourteen countries and was a selection of the Book Find Club, as well as an alternate selection of the Book-of-the-Month Club. It is the story of a married couple in a small town in upstate New York whose monotonous life is interrupted when Fredericka, the wife, has an affair with an Austrian refugee doctor. Virginia Kirkus thought it an "attractively, intelligently contoured story of family relationships"; to Orville Prescott in the *Yale Review* it seemed "clever, interesting, but more impressive for its sincerity of purpose than for its results." James Stern, reviewing *I, My Ancestor* in the *Times*, described that novel as "serious, sincere, and well written"; but thought it missed complete success by being overambitious.

Nancy Ross has contributed to *Story, New Yorker,* and *Harper's Bazaar. Time's Corner,* her new novel, will be published in the fall of 1952. She swims and plays tennis; is a member of the Cosmopolitan and Pen and Brush clubs in New York; and her preferred authors are Virginia Woolf, Proust, the older Russian novelists, and Suzuki. She is a Presbyterian, brown-haired, brown-eyed, of medium height, with an "outdoor glow."

RUIZ CORTINES, ADOLFO (roō-ēs' kôr-tē'nās ä-dôl'fō) Dec. 30, 1891- President of Mexico

Address: b. c/o Party of Revolutionary Institutions, Calle San Cosme, Mexico City, Mexico

In the July 6, 1952, election Adolfo Ruiz Cortines was chosen as President of Mexico, to succeed Miquel Alemán for a six-year term. Ruiz Cortines, who was formerly Secretary of the Interior, resigned his post in the Cabinet of President Alemán in 1951 to become the candidate of the Party of Revolutionary Institutions, which has dominated Mexican politics for about twenty-five years. The veteran public servant, one-time Governor of the State of Veracruz, is expected to adhere to the program of public works projects, increased industrialization, and development of closer cooperation with the United States which has formed the policy of the present administration. Ruiz Cortines was inaugurated in December 1952.

Adolfo Ruiz Cortines was born in Veracruz, Mexico, on December 30, 1891, the son of Adolfo Ruiz Tejeda and María Cortines, both of Spanish ancestry. His father, a customs broker in Veracruz, died shortly before the boy was born. With his one sister, Ruiz Cortines was reared in his native city, where he received his education at Escuela Pastoral and the Instituto Veracruzano. From a position as an accountant in a private business in Veracruz (reportedly in a clothing store), he entered the field of politics during the Mexican Revolution of 1910-20, in which in 1914 he served as army paymaster, later leaving the army with the rank of major.

An early government post held by Ruiz Cortines from 1932 to 1935 was that of chief of the Bureau of Statistics in the Secretariat of National Economy. His career fostered by a leading political figure of that time, Alfonso Robles Dominguez (reported Marion Wilhelm of the *Christian Science Monitor*), he advanced to chief clerk of the Federal District Government, which post he filled from 1935 to 1937. He was later elected to represent the State of Veracruz in the national Congress for the 1937-40 term. About this time, stated *Time* magazine, he became aide to Miguel Alemán, whose career Ruiz Cortines' was in part to parallel. At the end of a 4-year term as chief clerk of the Secretariat of the Interior in 1944, he became in December of that year the Governor of the State of Veracruz, which office he resigned three years later to accept the appointment of Secretary of the Interior in the Cabinet of President Alemán.

As Secretary of the Interior, the office from which Alemán had advanced to the Presidency, Ruiz Cortines held an important post in the Mexican Government, one variously denoted as head of the Cabinet and Secretary of the Government. His responsibilities covered all matters dealing with citizenship, supervision of the police, and control of state and local governments through the power of the national government to intervene in regional affairs. By the authority of his Secretariat the Communist party was denied registry and thus prevented from appearing on the 1952 ballot. After four years in this position, in which he was considered to have acted as the "right-hand man" of President Alemán, Ruiz Cortines was nominated in October 1951 to be the candidate of the Partido Revolucionario Institutional (PRI) for President in the July 1952 election.

Now a moderate or middle-of-the-road party, the PRI, which under various names has controlled Mexican politics for a quarter of a century, is the descendant of the party that overthrew the administration of Porfirio Diaz (1911), ordered the closing of the churches and expropriation of foreign-owned oil properties, and advanced the most progressive contemporary labor legislation. It then grew from the National Revolutionary Party of 1928, a consolidation of a number of state groups, into the expanded Party of Revolutionary Institutions, which in 1938 was organized through a proposal of President Lazaro Cárdenas to include soldiers, farmers, and workers. Upon nomination of Ruiz Cortines as the PRI candidate, editorial comment in United States newspapers pointed to the Mexican statesman's record of party loyalty and thus to the likelihood of his continuing the policy of the Alemán Administration of encouraging cordial relations with the United States, carrying out the industrialization of the basically agricultural country, expanding educational facilities and public works projects, and opposing the nationalization of coal, power, and banking advocated by Leftist groups.

Challenging the Presidential aspirations of Ruiz Cortines were General Miguel Henriquez Guzman, the military candidate of the Confederation of Peoples' Parties; Gonzalez Luna, leader of the Right-wing, Catholic-supported National Action party; and Lombardo Toledano, a self-styled "Marxist without a party." Among the notable commitments of Ruiz Cortines' campaign were his promise to introduce legislation for equal rights for women, who do not now have nation-wide suffrage in Mexico, and his indication of readiness to welcome more cooperative relations between church and state. Regarded by political observers as an unusual candidate because of his reputation for undisputed personal honesty and his modest manner of living, the PRI nominee was frequently quoted during the course of his campaign as having said while Secretary of the Interior, "I was poor as a boy, and still am. I have always tried to live on my salary." Newspaper commentators also called attention to Ruiz Cortines' concern for the rights of

ADOLFO RUIZ CORTINES

man and his advocacy of the freedom of the press to criticize the government.

In one of the most peaceful elections in Mexican history (followed, however, by a day of rioting and charges of fraud voiced by General Guzman and his supporters), Ruiz Cortines, on July 6, 1952, was chosen President by an unofficial estimate of 70 to 80 per cent of the nearly five million ballots cast. The new President, the second civilian to be elected to the office since Francisco Madero in 1913, was inaugurated on December 1, 1952, for a six-year term, after which he is prohibited by the constitution from succeeding himself.

By his marriage to Maria Izaguirre de Ruiz Cortines, the President of Mexico is the father of one son, Adolfo Ruiz. Ruiz Cortines has dark-brown eyes and dark-brown graying hair; he stands five feet seven and one half inches tall and weighs about 155 pounds. He was baptized a Catholic. "No orator," the Christian Science Monitor observed of him, "he speaks publicly and privately almost in a whisper, without gestures. But his words and manner disclose a man who cannot be fooled or panicked." As a young man he played baseball as a recreation; his pastime now is games of dominoes and reading history, biography, and science.

References

Christian Sci Mon p5 O 2 '51; p9 N 17 '51
N Y Herald Tribune II p1 Jl 6 '52 por
Time 58:43 O 22 '51 por; 60:36 Jl 14 '52 por

RUNBECK, MARGARET LEE Jan. 25, 1910- Author

Address: b. c/o Harold Matson, 30 Rockefeller Plaza, New York 20; h. 615 N. Alta Dr., Beverly Hills, Calif.

Reprinted from the *Wilson Library Bulletin*, Feb. 1952.

Just before her thirteenth birthday Margaret Lee Runbeck appeared in print as winner of a prize contest sponsored by a Washington, D.C., newspaper. The editor was amazed to find his winner a child, but was talked into letting her write a weekly human interest column for one

MARGARET LEE RUNBECK

of his feature pages. For over two years the column ran under the by-line *The Scribe*.

Miss Runbeck was born January 25, 1910, in Des Moines, Iowa. Her father, William Benjamin Runbeck, was of Swedish extraction. Her mother, Jessie Dee (Griffith) Runbeck, traced Welsh ancestry back to 1490. (The family had come to America in 1680 and settled at Harper's Ferry, Virginia.) After attending Eastern High School in Washington, Margaret majored in literature at the University of Chicago; in her sophomore year she won the David Blair McLaughlin award for excellence in prose. (John Gunther won second prize that year.) She took extension courses at George Washington and Boston universities.

Her adult writing career began in Boston, where she worked for Hearst newspapers and for the *Christian Science Monitor*. Later she was advertising manager for one of Boston's largest department stores but wrote fiction after office hours. When her stories sold nationally, she bought a small house in Massachusetts and wrote as a full-time breadwinner. There were dark periods, as there are for most writers.

There was even a time when a dollar looked like a fortune. When in 1947 she purchased a Beverly Hills house, the hard work of many years was justified. Signal recognition by fellow craftsmen came in 1951: Theta Sigma Phi, the national honorary journalism fraternity, acclaimed her the "Headliner of the Year."

More than 250 of Miss Runbeck's stories and articles have been published in the *Saturday Evening Post, Good Housekeeping, Collier's, Reader's Digest*, etc. Her first book, *Our Miss Boo* (illustrated by Peggy Bacon and published in 1942), caused May Lamberton Becker to comment. "The more a reviewer enjoys this book, the more his review is likely to misrepresent it. . . . It puts anyone who ever had or wanted a child into a state that sounds sentimental when described. Whereas the book is nothing of the kind. It is an act of love, of clear-eyed love." Millicent Taylor went on record in the *Christian Science Monitor* with, "You will hunt up excuses to read it aloud to somebody you care about. Like little Miss Boo herself, it must be shared."

The Great Answer (1944) tells of fighting men and women, and even some children, who have turned to God in the midst of danger and of how they were answered.

Hope of the Earth (1947—choice of the People's Book Club) moved the *Christian Science Monitor's* reviewer to declare: "Seldom does a modern novel provide a theme based on man's need of spiritual truths as they may be gained through loving the Bible. Now Miss Runbeck has written a story of pioneer America that holds the reader's interest, while it never ceases to stress this truth. . . . Parts of the book may seem too heavily weighted with background; some loose ends in the plot are not too skillfully tied up; and there is a certain amount of oversimplification of both characterization and setting. But those who . . . find in the construction some of the faults of a comparatively new writer of full-length fiction may gladly forgive them for the sake of a clean novel with a high purpose." The *Wisconsin Library Bulletin's* appraiser was not in entire agreement: "Highly idealistic, with a background of pioneer reality. Somewhat long drawn out and devious towards the end, with scenes to which conservative readers will object."

The title *Answer Without Ceasing* (1948) was derived from the letter of a young marine who had written: "The Bible says 'pray without ceasing.' When you do that, you have answer without ceasing." Of *Pink Magic* (1949), a short novel, the New York *Herald Tribune's* David Tilden remarked that he thought the book would be relished by youngsters as well as their elders.

Miss Runbeck in early 1952 finished another novel, *A Hungry Man Dreams*. In 1948, an article in the *Independent Woman* announced: "During Margaret Lee Runbeck's twelve years of fiction writing not one of her books has sold less than 50,000 copies; some have sold a great many more." Her articles and short stories have brought a fan mail comparable to that received by the most popular of the motion picture celebrities.

A member of the International P.E.N., the Pen and Brush in New York, and an honorary member of the local California Woman's Press Association, Miss Runbeck finds recreation in painting as well as in going to Europe every year if possible. She confided recently that she is "a Republican *now*," a Protestant, that her eyes are blue, her hair brown, her height five feet four inches, and her weight "too much." She is a visibly happy personality, and her writing radiates happiness.

About her profession she says, "set up a daily minimum stint for yourself. Make this *less* than you know you can do so that you need never fail it. Half the battle is in writing whether you want to or not. Don't put off writing because the conditions are not favorable."

SABATH, ADOLPH J(OACHIM) Apr. 4, 1866—Nov. 6, 1952 United States Democratic Representative from Illinois; native of Czechoslovakia; began law practice in Chicago (1893); justice of the peace (1895-97); as a police magistrate, helped establish juvenile court and parole system for first offenders (1897-1907); elected to Congress in 1906 and re-elected to each subsequent Congress; chairman of the Rules Committee since 1938, except during Republican Eightieth Congress; served on Immigration and Foreign Affairs Committees; as champion of New Deal legislation, introduced several labor, relief, and social welfare measures; re-elected two days before his death to his twenty-fourth term in Congress. See *Current Biography*, 1946.

Obituary

N Y Times p14 N 7 '52

SALAZAR, ANTÓNIO DE OLIVEIRA (să-lá-zàr′ ăɴɴ-tô′nyoo̅ dá ō-lē-vā′ē-rá) Apr. 28, 1889- Premier of Portugal

Address: Lisbon, Portugal

> NOTE: This biography supersedes the article which appeared in *Current Biography* in 1941.

António de Oliveira Salazar, who has been termed a "mild" dictator, has been Premier of Portugal since 1932 and upon the death of President António Oscar de Fragoso Carmona in 1951 he also became the Acting President of his country. He is regarded as the chief author of the constitution of 1933, under which Portugal as a "unitary corporative" state instituted a regimented economy. With her strategic coastal position on the Iberian Peninsula, her nearby islands in the Atlantic, and her colonies in Africa and Asia, Portugal is considered an important member of the North Atlantic Treaty Organization.

Born April 28, 1889, near the village of Santa Comba Dão in Portugal's Beira province, António de Oliveira Salazar is the youngest of the five children of António de Oliveira and

ANTÓNIO DE OLIVEIRA SALAZAR

Maria do Resgate Salazar. His peasant parents—his father has been described as a small-scale farmer and an innkeeper, and his mother as a woman of high intelligence—were ambitious for their offspring and sent their four daughters and their only son to literate neighbors for lessons until the opening of a village school in 1899. This the future statesman attended one year, after which he qualified, at the age of eleven, for admission to the Jesuit seminary at nearby Viseu. His mother called him "the little priest" (*Time*), and he did take preliminary orders on graduation from the seminary in 1908. Two subsequent years as prefect of students at the attached Via Sacra College convinced him, however, that his vocation was education rather than the priesthood.

In the summer of 1910 Salazar entered the Universty of Coimbra for the course of the Faculty of Letters. On receiving his bachelor's degree in 1914 (states Luiz Teixeira in his *Profile of Salazar*) he was appointed to the teaching staff, and two years later (1916) he published two monographs, one on the gold standard, another on agriculture, which established him as one of Portugal's recognized young economists. From assistant lecturer in the economic sciences he advanced to full professor in 1916, and a year and a half later received his doctorate in law.

Salazar had entered the University of Coimbra as a student in the year of the deposition of King Manuel II as King of Portugal and some few months before the abolition (June 19, 1911) of the monarchy and the introduction of a democratic form of government. Though republican in structure, it was largely modeled on the parliamentary system of Portugal's longtime ally, Great Britain. The political and economic confusion and the frequent changes of government which followed convinced the future Premier that the British system was not

SALAZAR, ANTÓNIO DE OLIVEIRA—
Continued

applicable to Portugal. Deeply religious, he became a leader of a party dedicated to implementing the social principles put forth in the encyclical *Rerum Novarum* of Pope Leo XIII. Several years later, having meantime written and spoken on political, social, religious, and economic topics, he played a leading role in forming a new Portuguese Catholic Centre party and in 1921 was one of three Catholic deputies elected to the Cortes, the Parliament.

A single meeting persuaded him that further attendance was futile, and he returned to his academic chair at Coimbra for another four to five years, or until May 1926, when a military coup placed the Generals Gomes da Costa and António Oscar de Fragoso Carmona in control of the government. They found the treasury empty and called on Dr. Salazar for aid. Sworn in as Minister of Finance he spent two days studying the fiscal problem but demanded a completely free hand in executing his contemplated recommendations. This refused by the generals, Salazar returned to Coimbra after only five days in office.

In November 1926 General Gomes da Costa was ousted by General Carmona, who made himself Acting President and Premier. Elected President for a regular seven-year term in March 1928 (and re-elected in 1935, 1942 and 1949), Carmona again called Salazar to the Finance Ministry and this time gave him full control of the national purse strings. Installed in April, Salazar announced that "his ministry was going to tax everything it could find and everybody who had any income at all, but that each year in the future these taxes would be lightened" (Henry J. Taylor in the *Saturday Evening Post*). He also cut the government payrolls to a minimum, and after one year succeeded in balancing the budget for the first time since the overthrow of the monarchy. Salazar assumed, in addition, the post of Colonial Minister *ad interim* in 1930, and in the depression year of 1932 liquidated the last of Portugal's foreign debt and sent the escudo to a premium on the exchanges.

Salazar succeeded Carmona as Premier in November 1932, and shortly thereafter drafted a new constitution which was adopted by plebiscite on March 19 of the following year and remains the fundamental law of the land. The document, inspired by the *Rerum Novarum* of Pope Leo XIII and the *Quadragesimo Anno* of Pius XI, created a "unitary and corporative state" which Anne O'Hare McCormick of the New York *Times* has characterized as "not a one-party state but a state without parties." It is, she explained, "unlike any other in having a two-chamber Parliament consisting of a political assembly which is not divided on partisan lines but is supposed to represent national union, and a Corporative Assembly, which does not divide on lines of special interests and is supposed to reconcile conflicting claims of capital and labor, producers and consumers, trades and professions."

Under the 1933 constitution the President appoints the Prime Minister, who in turn appoints the Cabinet, which is not responsible to the Assembly. Thus, in his dual role of Premier and Finance Minister, Salazar became the *de facto* dictator of Portugal and, before giving up the Finance Ministry in 1940, initiated by decree such measures as a workmen's compensation law, a form of social security, and public works projects. In 1936 he became Minister of War *ad interim* and Minister of Foreign Affairs, and in the latter capacity broke off relations with Republican Spain and maintained close understanding with Generalissimo Franco of Spain. During World War II Portugal aided the anti-Axis cause by granting the use of the Azores Islands for naval and air bases to Great Britain in 1943 and the United States in 1944. Salazar justified his country's technical neutrality in a widely translated speech to the National Assembly on May 18, 1945. "It is at times," he declared, "a great favor to be quiet . . . and it cannot be denied that it served a positive interest of the Allied nations for us not to have become involved in the conflict."

In a 1946 article entitled "How Bad Is the Best?" *Time* stressed that Salazar had up to that time been kept in power largely through his dominance of the army, suppression of individual rights, a secret police and a "youth movement" built on Hitlerian lines. In an article in the *United Nations World*, however, André Visson pointed out that "under Salazar's constitution no one is sent to jail for nonsupport of the government" which "in nonpolitical walks of life . . . interferes little more than ours."

It was not until 1945 that Salazar relaxed a rigid censorship of the press and announced a free election in which opposition candidates would be permitted. A *Movimento Unidade Democrática* (M.U.D.), composed of democratic, liberal, and Left-wing groups, took form and showed such potential strength that the Government resorted to repressive measures with the consequence that the M.U.D. instructed their members to abstain from voting. Three years later (1948) the M.U.D. was outlawed on the grounds that it was a Communist front.

While Portugal is not a member of the United Nations, in November 1948 Salazar told C. L. Sulzberger of the New York *Times* that "the salvation of Portugal, Western Europe, and the Occidental world lies in the formation of a true Atlantic bloc." The country eventually joined the North Atlantic Treaty Organization, with Salazar repeatedly pressing for the inclusion of Spain in the defense pact. Portugal was host to a NATO conference which opened in Lisbon on February 16, 1952. On April 15, following a two-day meeting between Salazar of Portugal and Generalissimo Franco of Spain, the two leaders announced "agreement on the basic premise that the Iberian Peninsula is a single and indivisible strategic bloc, which 'implies the adoption of adequate measures to carry out a policy for the defense of both countries within the general framework of Western defense'" (New York *Times*). Salazar became Acting President of Portugal, as well as Premier, upon the death of General Carmona on April 18, 1951.

The Portuguese statesman has received two honorary degrees from foreign universities, the D.C.L. from Oxford and the LL.D. from Fordham. He has been decorated with the grand cross of many orders by his own country as well as Britain, Belgium, Poland, Hungary, Italy, Spain, Brazil, Chile, and Colombia. Among his several books, *Doctrine and Action; Internal and Foreign Policy of the New Portugal, 1928-1939* has been translated into nine languages, including English. Devout and austere, he has not married, but adopted two little girls some years ago. He is small in stature and has graying hair. Disliking publicity and parades, he rarely grants interviews. "To many in Portugal," remarked Mrs. McCormick, "he is no more than a name. But it is not shyness that makes him shun the limelight. Inaccessible as he is, he talks freely and fluently in private conversation, and his speeches are eloquent and persuasive. He has a twinkling sense of humor and a ready smile that lights up his rather melancholy features."

References

Cath Digest 4:8-11 O '40; 6:82-7 My '42
Christian Sci Mon Mag p1-2 F 9 '38 por
Commonweal 26:317-19 Jl 28 '37; 39:37 O 29 '43
Life 9:66-7+ Jl 29 '40 pors
N Y Sun p21 Je 12 '41
N Y Times p14 Mr 1 '52
Nation 163:91-3 Jl 27 '46; 168:306 Mr 12 '49
Newsweek 17:31 Ja 20 '41 por; 22:23-4 O 25 '43 por
PM p8 O 13 '43
Sat Eve Post 214:18-19+ Ag 30 '41 pors; 217:9-10+ Ag 18 '44 pors
Scholastic 43:9 O 11 '43
Time 48:28-30+ Jl 22 '46 por
U N World 6:24-6+ Ap '52 pors
U S News 31:32 Ag 24 '51 por
Bainville, J. Dictators (1936)
Carr, A. Juggernaut (1939)
Derrick, M. Portugal of Salazar (1938)
Egerton, F. C. C. Salazar, Rebuilder of Portugal (1943)
Ferro, A. Salazar: Portugal and Her Leader (1939)
Overseas Press Club of America. Men Who Make Your World (1949)
Teixeira, L. Profile of Salazar (1944)
Who's Who in America, 1951-52
World Biography (1948)

SANDYS, (EDWIN) DUNCAN (sănds) Jan. 24, 1908- British Minister of Supply

Address: b. c/o Ministry of Supply, London, W.C. 2, England; h. 86 Vincent Sq., London, S.W. 1, England

To the Right Honorable Duncan Sandys, Minister of Supply in the Conservative Government elected in October 1951, has been assigned the task of denationalizing Great Britain's iron and steel industry. Sandys, a son-in-law of Prime Minister Churchill, was first elected to Parliament in 1935 as member for the London constituency of Norwood; he now represents Streatham, also a part of the metropolitan area. In 1944-45 he held the post of Minister of Works in Churchill's wartime Cabinet.

Born January 24, 1908, Edwin Duncan Sandys is the only son of the late Captain George John Sandys of the King's Rifles and a grandson of James Sandys, a Gloucestershire country gentleman; his mother, nee Mildred Cameron, of Scottish extraction, was the daughter of Duncan Cameron of Christchurch, New Zealand. George Sandys was for eight years (1910-18) the member of Parliament (Conservative) for the Wells Division of Somerset. Duncan Sandys, who was educated at Eton and Magdalen College, Oxford, first chose diplomacy as his career.

In 1930, after leaving Oxford with the Master of Arts degree, he entered the Foreign Office. Posted to the British Embassy in Berlin, he was there attached for the greater part of the next three years, during which time he also traveled in Russia and made a report to the Foreign Office on conditions in that country. In 1933 he was the Foreign Office representative in negotiations for commercial treaties with Denmark, Sweden, Norway, Finland, and the Soviet Union, and in the same year was a member of the British delegation to the World Economic Conference in London.

When Duncan Sandys resigned from the diplomatic service in September 1933, it was with the intention of making politics his vocation. He read law at the Inner Temple and later became a member of the national executive of the League of Industry, an association of manufacturers. In February 1935, when the appointment to the judiciary of Sir Walter Greeves-Lord, Member of Parliament for the Norwood Division of Lambeth, necessitated a by-election in that South London constituency, Sandys was named by the local Conservative organization as their candidate. He ran as a National Conservative, that is, as a supporter of the coalition government of Ramsay MacDonald. At the election on March 14, 1935, he was chosen by 16,147 votes to 12,799 for the Laborite candidate and 2,698 for Richard Findlay, Independent Conservative candidate. Campaigning for Findlay were Winston Churchill's son, Randolph, and eldest daughter, Diana, whose marriage to John Bailey had recently been terminated by divorce. A few months later (September 16, 1935) Sandys and the former Miss Churchill were married.

Through the remainder of the existing Parliament the new member for Norwood supported the policies of the National Government. After the general election of November 15, 1935 (in which he was returned as a regular Conservative) he came increasingly to share the viewpoint of his father-in-law, whose differences with the Conservative Prime Minister Stanley Baldwin had widened, particularly after the abdication of King Edward VIII in 1936. A frequent speaker on international affairs and a leading critic of the Government's failure to take a firm stand against Mussolini, Sandys soon became known as Churchill's "voice among the backbenchers" (*Time*). He was also in-

British Inf. Services

DUNCAN SANDYS

dignant at what he considered the neglect, by
Baldwin and his successor Neville Chamber-
lain, of adequate preparedness for defense, and
in 1937 he set a personal example by joining
Britain's equivalent to the National Guard, the
Territorial Army.

Commissioned a second lieutenant of the
Royal Artillery, Sandys was assigned to the
51st (London) Anti-Aircraft Brigade. His
observation and experience therein led to his
concern over delay in rebuilding Britain's
armed strength and to his submitting a formal
question in Commons in 1938 as to alleged
inadequacies of antiaircraft defense. As an
artillery officer Sandys served in 1940 with the
British Expeditionary Force to Norway, the
ill-fated "too little and too late" operation,
failure of which sent Neville Chamberlain into
retirement and made Winston Churchill the new
Prime Minister. By early 1941 Sandys had
risen to the rank of lieutenant colonel, but in
April of that year his active military service
was ended by an automobile accident.

Sandy's war service continued in his posts
as financial secretary to the War Office, to
which he was named the following July, and as
chairman of the Intergovernmental Council for
Empire Prisoners of War, a post which he
held during 1942-43. From 1941 to 1943
he was finance member of the Army Council.
Leaving the War Office at the end of the year,
he became Parliamentary Secretary (spokesman in the Commons) of the Ministry of Supply (1943-44). Because of his special knowledge of antiaircraft warfare he was also made
chairman of the war Cabinet's committee for
defense against German "V" weapons, and saw
the eighty-day flying-bomb blitz launched
by the Nazis in June 1944.

The devastation caused by the robot bombs
was a factor in the elevation of Sandys to
Cabinet rank in the following November. At
that time he received his appointment as Minister of Works in succession to Lord Wynd-
ham Portal, a member of the House of Peers.
As Prime Minister Churchill explained to Lord
Portal, "the housing situation in regard to prefabricated dwellings and bomb damage" had
become so pressing that it was desirable that
"the Minister actually responsible" for the rebuilding be a member of the House of Commons; thus he could personally "make the necessary statements and explanations." Sandys
served as Minister of Works (an office which
carried with it the title of Right Honorable and
a seat in the Privy Council) and also as chairman of the Bomb Damage Repairs Executive
until the defeat of the Conservatives in the
general election of July 26, 1945, and the advent of the Labor Government of Clement
Attlee.

From the summer of 1945 to early in 1950
Duncan Sandys was out of Parliament, for he
lost his Norwood constituency to his Labor
opponent by 2,023 votes. In 1947 the former
Minister of Works accepted several nonpolitical
appointments, including a membership on the
general advisory council of the British Broadcasting Corporation and of a directorship of
the Ashanti Goldfields Corporation. Of special
importance was his acceptance, in December
1947, of the chairmanship of the international
executive of the European Movement, an organization of which Winston Churchill was
president. In this capacity Sandys called an international economic conference at Brussels
early in 1949, and in the following September
recommended to the European Consultative Assembly meeting at Strasbourg the creation of
a "supranational political authority" to unite
the western nations.

As the general election of February 1950
approached, Sandys was the Conservative candidate for the Streatham Division of Wands-
worth (another South London constituency).
He was returned to Parliament by about 10,000
votes, and by May was leading the Opposition
attack on the record of Minister of Health
Aneurin Bevan, to whose department the
housing program had been transferred. As a
delegate to the Council of Europe, Sandys in
August was the author of a twenty-point draft
plan for the creation of a European army and
European defense ministry. At the Council
meeting in Paris in May 1951 he urged a joint
declaration "that no further expansion of the
area of the Soviet domination in Europe can
be tolerated, and in particular that any attack
upon Yugoslavia will be treated by the Western powers as an attack upon themselves."
In the Commons debate on the Iranian oil crisis
in the following month he proposed that "Britain secure the southern half of Iran by occupying it with British troops and permit Russia
to take the northern part of the country," rather
than invite an economic collapse which would
probably result in Russian occupation of the
entire country (New York *Herald Tribune*).

Following the return of the Conservatives to power after the general election of October 1951, Prime Minister Churchill appointed Duncan Sandys to the post of Minister of Supply. The position is not of Cabinet rank, but is considered of major immediate importance since one of the Conservative campaign pledges was to restore the iron and steel industry (nationalized by the Labor Government in the previous February) to private control. Primary responsibility for steering the necessary legislation through Parliament would devolve upon the Supply Minister, who (the *Christian Science Monitor* predicted) would have "a tough job on his hands." When, on November 12, Sandys outlined the Government's intention to supplant the existing Iron and Steel Corporation with a new Government-management-consumers board "to regulate the industry after its restoration to private ownership," the Government was upheld by a narrow margin of thirty-nine votes. A further crisis, also surmounted by a small margin, occurred in February 1952 when Steven J. L. Hardie, chairman of the Iron and Steel Corporation, resigned in protest against the Government's decision to permit an $11.20 increase per ton in the price of steel.

The tall (six-foot), red-haired Sandys is considered an excellent orator; off the floor of the House, however, he is inclined to shyness. He "has few friends, but those he does have are very close to him," *Newsweek* has stated. His clubs are the Carlton, Buck's, and Army and Navy. Duncan and Diana Sandys are the parents of one son and two daughters.

References

London Times p14 F 19 '35
N Y Herald Tribune II p3 Ag 13 '44 por
N Y Sun p16 Ja 9 '45
Newsweek 12:18 Jl 11 '38 por; 24:63-5
    D 4 '44 por
Time 32:16-17 Jl 11 '38 por
International Who's Who (1951)
Kelly's Handbook to the Titled, Landed
    and Official Classes, 1951
Who's Who (1951)
World Biography (1948)

SANTAYANA, GEORGE Dec. 16, 1863 —Sept. 26, 1952 Spanish-American philosopher; poet; novelist; critic; as one of the most eminent philosophers of modern times, known for his "critical realism"; went to United States from his native Spain at the age of nine; taught philosophy at Harvard (1889-1912); author of first poems *Sonnets and Other Verses* (1894) and early philosophical works *The Sense of Beauty* (1896) and *The Life of Reason* (1905); left United States in 1912 to spend rest of his life in Oxford and Rome; came to attention of general public with publication of best-selling novel *The Last Puritan* (1936) and two-volume autobiography *Persons and Places* (1944-45). See *Current Biography*, 1944.

Obituary

N Y Times p1+ S 28 '52

SARGEANT, HOWLAND H(ILL) July 13, 1911- United States Government official
Address: b. c/o Office of Assistant Secretary of State for Public Affairs, Department of State, Washington 25, D.C.

Howland H. Sargeant, chief representative of the United States to the United Nations Educational, Scientific and Cultural Organization, became Assistant Secretary of State for Public Affairs, in charge of the *Voice of America* and other Government information programs, in March 1952, succeeding Edward W. Barrett. Before joining the State Department as Deputy Assistant Secretary in 1947, Sargeant had been for two years (1944-46) chairman of the Technical-Industrial Intelligence Commission of the United States Joint Chiefs of Staff. In earlier Government positions he was associated with the Federal Home Loan Bank Board and with the Office of Alien Property Custodian.

The son of M. Motley and Grace E. Howland) Sargeant, Howland Hill Sargeant was born in New Bedford, Massachusetts, on July 13, 1911. He took his B.A. degree at Dartmouth College, graduating *summa cum laude* in 1932. Winner of a Rhodes Scholarship, he studied literature and economics at Oxford University, England, which awarded him a B.A. degree in 1934. The following year he entered Government service as assistant to the chairman of the Federal Home Loan Bank Board, for which two years later he assumed the editorship of the *Federal Home Loan Bank Review*. When he was named executive secretary of the National Science Fund of the National Academy of Sciences, he left the Government, reported *Time* (February 4, 1952), "to plan a new type of scientific foundation" for that academy. Following the outbreak of the war, Sargeant in 1942 accepted an appointment as chief of the division of patent administration of the Office of Alien Property Custodian, a post that he occupied for the next five years. For part of this same period (1944-46) he was chairman of the Technical-Industrial Commission of the Joint Chiefs of Staff.

Joining the Department of State in 1947, Sargeant became deputy chairman of the Interdepartmental Committee on Scientific and Cultural Cooperation and Deputy Assistant Secretary for Public Affairs. The Assistant Secretary for Public Affairs, who at that time was William Benton (later the post was held by George V. Allen and from 1950 to 1952 by Edward W. Barrett), is responsible for the functions of the UNESCO relations staff, the office of public affairs, the international educational exchange program, the program planning and evaluation staff, the office of international information, and the office of educational exchange. These offices and staffs embrace, in the words of *United States News*, "the Government's information services abroad, student exchanges, the printing of books and pamphlets and the preparation of motion pictures," and the *Voice of America*, "which broadcasts United States 'cold war' propaganda in 46 languages." Sargeant has spoken frequently before various bodies on the aims and achievements of his section of the State De-

HOWLAND H. SARGEANT

partment. "Soviet papers have been compelled by the *Voice*," he told the Inland Press Association of Chicago in February 1950, "to publish important international news and verbatim texts of highly important international agreements which otherwise would have been suppressed or distorted. . . .It is impossible to overestimate the importance of such *Voice* feats in telling the Soviet peoples the facts about the free nations and forcing the official Soviet press to confirm them." Writing in *Theatre Arts* in March 1951, in celebration of International Theatre Month, he stated that the United States must "challenge the minds and hearts of men to find ways of *waging peace*. One phase of this undertaking is in the field of cultural relations. Here is the task of UNESCO —building the defenses of peace in the *minds* of men."

While heading the United States delegation to the fifth general conference of the International Commission for UNESCO, held at Florence, Italy, from May 22 to June 16, 1950, Sargeant suggested to the conference that UNESCO should "focus its program for peace on Germany," as the New York *Times* reported. In his recommendation that increased help in education and communications be given to Germany in order to direct the German people toward international cooperation, he emphasized that "all Germans—and not only a courageous few—should recognize their responsibility in the protection of individual rights and the processes of justice among men and nations" (quoted by the New York *Times*, May 25, 1950). At a later session of the conference he cosponsored a resolution reaffirming UNESCO's "all-out concern for the preservation of peace."

A year later, in June 1951, Sargeant, who again led the United States delegation, was chosen president of UNESCO's sixth general conference, held in Paris. Addressing a plenary

session of the conference, he urged an accelerated effort in carrying out the chief points of UNESCO's program that had "primary and urgent objectives," such as education and technical aid. At a press conference following the final session, Sargeant and Dr. Jaime Torres Bodet, UNESCO's director general, summarized the most significant achievements of the meeting. "They cited first the decision to spend $20 million over the next twelve years for the establishment of a world network of six instruction centers . . . to train specialists to combat illiteracy" (New York *Times*, July 12, 1951). They pointed out also that the conference had consolidated a number of UNESCO projects for promoting free and compulsory education, had provided for the expansion in 1952 of a survey "to determine the extent to which the cultural pattern in backward areas has been upset by industrialization," and had drawn up plans for writing over a period of five years a scientific and cultural history of mankind.

Following the resignation of Edward W. Barrett in January 1952, President Truman nominated Sargeant as Assistant Secretary of State for Public Affairs. The Senate having approved the nomination the next month, Sargeant was sworn into office on March 6. Meanwhile he had revealed to the general session of the third national conference of the United States National Commission for UNESCO, held in New York in January 1952, that Russia and its satellites were spending more than fifteen times as much as the United States on its international information program. He recommended, among several countermeasures, "that American publishers promote the publication and sale in underdeveloped countries of American books 'competent to present an adequate, honest view of American life, as well as to explode the tissues of lies being woven by Soviet propaganda'" (New York *Herald Tribune*, January 30, 1952). He suggested also that foreign journalists be permitted to work temporarily on American newspapers and that "private groups in key communities throughout the country take on the task of seeing to it that foreign visitors are properly integrated into community life."

In New York in March 1952 Sargeant addressed the American Committee for Cultural Freedom, an association of American intellectual leaders affiliated with the international Congress of Cultural Freedom, which was founded in West Berlin on June 25, 1950, with the object of encouraging "the defense of existing freedoms, the reconquest of lost freedoms and the creation of new freedoms." He stated that the Russians were making a major propaganda effort through cultural means to win India's intellectuals to communism and had apparently marked Japan and Southeast Asia for similar campaigns. To combat Russian efforts in propaganda warfare, he urged, the United States should send to foreign countries its highest achievements in literature, art, music, the dance, and drama—"not that we may boast its excellence but in order that we may show as clearly as we can the fullness and intensity with which we share a common human cultural heritage."

In reference to attacks on UNESCO as attempting to undermine patriotism by promoting world government, Sargeant in October 1952 told the United States National Commissior for UNESCO that the organization shoulа turn its attention to combating "ideological racketeering." The following month at the UNESCO conference in Paris he was again the chief United States representative.

The accomplishments of the Office of the Assistant Secretary for Public Affairs were outlined by Sargeant in May 1952 in an address before the Massachusetts School of Home Economics. "Today," he noted, "the *Voice of America* is broadcasting in 46 different languages. It reaches an audience estimated at something like 300 million. Our press materials daily go to an estimated 10,000 foreign newspapers with a readership of more than 100 million. The 91 million copies of periodicals and pamphlets which we expect to publish by the end of June will be made available to some 900 million readers. Last year our films reached an audience of about 450 million persons in 86 different countries" (*Department of State Bulletin*, May 19, 1952).

For distinguished service to UNESCO, Sargeant and his wife, the motion picture actress Myrna Loy, who is a member of the United States National Commission for UNESCO, were awarded citations in January 1952 by Fairleigh Dickinson College. Sargeant's first marriage, to Sarah Howard Ward, ended in divorce in June 1947; he married his present wife in June 1951. The Government official is a member of Phi Beta Kappa, the honorary scholastic fraternity, Kappa Kappa Kappa, the Association of American Rhodes Scholars, the American Association for the Advancement of Science, and Sphinx. His faith is the Protestant. *Time* has said of him: "Sargeant combines a first-rate mind with a folksy manner that is effective at appropriations time on Capitol Hill."

References

    N Y Herald Tribune p5 Mr 7 '52 por
    N Y Times p6 Ja 24 '52 por
    Newsweek 39:22 F 4 '52 por
    Time 59:11 F 4 '52 por
    U S News 32:412 F 1 '52 por
    Who's Who in America, 1952-53
    Who's Who in the South and Southwest
      (1952)

SAUNDERS, HILARY A(IDAN) ST. GEORGE Jan. 14, 1898—Dec. 16, 1951 British historian and novelist; member of the Secretariat of the League of Nations (1920-37); librarian of the House of Commons (1946-50); author of the *Battle of Britain* (1941) and other official publications about World War II, *Green Beret* (1949), *Red Beret* (1950); since 1924 coauthor, with the late John Palmer under the pen name of Francis Beeding, of *The Seven Sleepers* (1925), *Eleven*

Were Brave (1941), and numerous other novels. See *Current Biography*, 1943.

Obituary

    N Y Times p31 D 18 '51

SAVITT, DICK *See* Savitt, R.

SAVITT, RICHARD Mar. 4, 1927- Tennis player

Address: b. c/o United States Lawn Tennis Association, 120 Broadway, New York 5; h. 500 S. Centre St., East Orange, N.J.

Among outstanding young tennis stars in the United States is Richard (Dick) Savitt of New Jersey, second-ranking player of the country in 1952. The previous year Savitt was simultaneously holder of the Australian and the Wimbledon singles titles, as well as of a number of United States titles. He has also been a member of the United States Davis Cup team.

Richard Savitt was born March 4, 1927, in Bayonne, New Jersey, to Morris and Kate (Hoberman) Savitt. His father is the owner of a food brokerage firm. As a boy Savitt was interested in football, baseball, basketball, and hockey; of tennis he said (from *Time*), "I didn't like it. Tennis is considered sissy by some people here in America." When he was about thirteen he began to work at the Berkeley Tennis Club in Orange as a ballboy, which gave him an opportunity to see some of the major American players in action. "It was terrific," he recalled for Margery Miller of the *Christian Science Monitor*. "It was nothing like the tennis I had seen. The game they played demanded everything of them and it was a pleasure to watch them try to give it."

With persistence Dick Savitt was able to obtain his father's permission to join the local tennis club, where, says Margery Miller, "he began the only kind of tennis lessons he has ever taken: watching and remembering. . . . He analyzed each player—good points and bad. . . .In his spare time he played all the tennis he could, trying to make the right moves and avoid the wrong ones." After winning a local junior tournament in the summer of 1940, Savitt entered the New Jersey Public Parks tournament, only to lose out in the first round.

The youth had little interest in tennis for some years after his family moved to El Paso, Texas, in 1943. For a time he preferred basketball, serving in 1945 as cocaptain and forward on the El Paso High School team, which brought him a nomination as all-State choice. A year in the United States Navy followed his graduation from high school. Stationed at Memphis, Tennessee, Savitt played on the fifth-ranking Navy basketball team. In 1946 he entered the freshman class at Cornell University, from which he was graduated four years later with a Bachelor of Arts degrees in economics. At Cornell, in the colder climate of central New York State, Savitt found little time for tennis practice except on the indoor

Wide World Photos

RICHARD SAVITT

courts at the local armory, "competing," he remembers, "with ROTC tanks rumbling around." As a freshman he was on the varsity basketball team. Later he was to captain the tennis team. With a national tennis ranking of twenty-six in 1947, Savitt held the same place the following year, and after winning the Eastern Intercollegiate tennis tournament in 1949, skipped ten places to secure the sixteenth national ranking.

During the 1950 tennis season, Savitt was to be found playing in most of the chief Eastern seaboard tournaments, taking the New York State championship from Don McNeill in July, and playing as well in the Merion (Pennsylvania) Cricket Club, Newport (Rhode Island), Spring Lake (New Jersey), Longwood (Massachusetts) Cricket Club and other tournaments. By winning through to the semifinals of the United States Nationals early in the fall, Savitt earned sixth place in the national rankings. By that time, besides the Intercollegiate and New York State championships, the New Jersey player also held the Pennsylvania Eastern Clay Court and Brooklyn titles.

Toward the end of 1950 and at the beginning of 1951, Savitt joined national champion Art Larsen for a three-month tennis tour of Australia. There Savitt became the third American in forty-three years to win the Australian singles championship by a five-set victory over Frank Sedgman (2-6, 7-5, 1-6, 6-3, 6-4) and a four-set defeat of Ken McGregor (6-3, 2-6, 6-3, 6-1) in January 1951. Shortly after his return to the United States, Savitt departed for the second lap of his first foreign tournament tour in Egypt, Italy, and other European countries. At the International match held in Paris that June Savitt and his partner, Gardnar Mulloy, went down before the Sedgman-McGregor

team in the French doubles finals. Savitt redeemed his position early in July at Wimbledon, where, said the New York *Times*, "he established himself as the world's No. 1 amateur player" with his victory over McGregor in the men's singles. Savitt's three winning sets (6-4, 6-4, 6-4) made him the fifth consecutive American to hold the Wimbledon title, and the first since Don Budge in 1938 to be simultaneous Wimbledon and Australian title holder.

Because he was tired and "over-tennised" upon his return home, Savitt refused to play in the National Claycourt championship match, which led to a demand for his suspension from the United States Lawn Tennis Association, a demand refused by its officials. He reappeared on the courts in late July to give the United States a lead in the first round of the Davis Cup American Zone elimination play, before losing in the first week of the following month in the finals of the Eastern Grass Court championship at the Orange (New Jersey) Lawn Tennis Club. In the drawings at the end of August, Savitt was named top-seeded player of the United States—above defending champion Larsen—for the national tennis championships, in which, however, he lost to Victor Seixas in the semifinals at Forest Hills. The majority of sports observers agreed that under normal circumstances Savitt, who was playing despite an infected leg, would probably have won. Savitt completed the 1951 season as a member of the United States Davis Cup team sent to Australia in December to meet the contenders there. Because Savitt won through the earlier rounds of the tournament, there was consternation when Captain Frank Shields named Ted Shroeder instead of Savitt to play in the finals, a choice which commentators considered responsible for the subsequent United States singles defeat.

Savitt was again the center of controversy when the U.S.L.T.A. drew up its January 1952 ratings of the previous year's players: his record was defended by Don McNeill, U.S.L.T.A. president Kingman, and Gardnar Mulloy as the outstanding American score of the year; but, by what Gayle Talbot of the Washington *Post* called "an unprecedented proxy vote of the delegates," Savitt was named to second place, and Seixas to first. Savitt, in the meanwhile, was the losing defender of his Australian national championship, playing, he maintained, at a disadvantage when opponent Ken McGregor was allowed to wear spiked shoes in the rainy courts. The winning semifinals score in the Adelaide January match was 6-4, 6-4, 3-6, and 6-4. Subsequently, Savitt won the National Indoor championship (February), lost the Franco-American exhibition (March), won the Kingston (Jamaica) International (March), and lost the Havana (Cuba) International (April). With Seixas, Savitt was named in May as one of the official U.S.L.T.A. players for the 1952 Wimbleton competition. He was defeated in the French tennis championship matches in Paris in May, but in August won the Canadian men's singles title at the Canadian lawn tennis championships.

Frank Shields has said of the New Jersey star, "Savitt is by far the greatest back-court player in the world. He has the biggest serve in the world and the best backhand in the world." A similar opinion was expressed by *Time*'s tennis commentator: "He is necessarily slower-footed than a smaller man and he develops too much momentum, after he gets under way, to change direction quickly. . . . What he has got is a simple, overpowering attack, a smashing serve, and deep-hard-hit ground strokes that keep his opponent scrambling in the back court, on the defensive." Sportswriters point out that by persistence and constant practice and correction of his game, Savitt has overcome the handicaps of his height (six feet three inches) and weight (185 pounds) to emerge as one of the outstanding young American champions. *Time* has described him as "a swarthy, black-haired young man with deep-set eyes and powerful slightly hunched shoulders . . . the picture of intent, unsmiling concentration."

References

Sport Life 5:15 Ag '52
Time 58:62 Ag 27 '51

SCHOEPPEL, ANDREW F. (shĕp'pĕl) Nov. 23, 1894- United States Senator from Kansas

Address: b. Senate Office Bldg., Washington 25, D.C.; h. Hillcrest Apts., Wichita, Kansas

The Republican senior Senator from Kansas, Andrew F. Schoeppel, was elected on November 2, 1948, to succeed retiring Senator Arthur Capper. Schoeppel began his political career in Ness City, Kansas, where he engaged in law practice and was elected Mayor. During 1943-47 he was Governor of Kansas for two terms, and for three years (1943-45) he held the chairmanship of the Interstate Oil Compact Commission of the United States.

Andrew F. Schoeppel, son of George J. and Anna (Phillip) Schoeppel, was born on a farm near Claflin, Kansas, on November 23, 1894. After attending the Ness County grammar school and Ransom High School, from which he graduated in 1915, he enrolled at the University of Kansas in 1916. When the United States entered World War I he left school to enlist in the Naval Reserve Flying Force. Some time after the end of the war he studied at the University of Nebraska Law School. In 1922, the year in which he received his LL.B. degree, the law student won two distinctions in another field: he played end on the Nebraska football team that defeated the famous "Four Horsemen" of Notre Dame and won honorable mention on Walter Camp's All-American Team.

Admitted to the Kansas bar on February 3, 1923, Schoeppel established a law practice in Ness City with the firm of Peters & Schoeppel, which in 1939 became Schoeppel & Smyth. He first entered local politics as city attorney, served as attorney of Ness County, and was elected Mayor of Ness City. From February 1939 until his resignation in May 1942, he filled

Wide World Photos
ANDREW F. SCHOEPPEL

the position of chairman of the Corporation Commission of the State of Kansas. Schoeppel entered a larger political arena when he won the Republican nomination for Governor of Kansas in 1942. Raymond Moley, writing in *Newsweek* before the election, observed that it "looks like an easy victory" for the "clean-cut and respected lawyer from a small city in Western Kansas." At the time of his re-election two years later, Schoeppel "piled up the largest vote of any candidate" in what proved to be a Republican landslide for the State. Shortly after becoming Governor (March 1943), Schoeppel received national notice when he signed a labor control bill which required licensing of union agents and the issuance of financial reports by unions and prohibited sit-down strikes and jurisdictional disputes. Later Schoeppel attacked the problem of farm production by appointing a Farm Labor Commission and conducting a survey of manpower, farm tool, and equipment shortages.

The State prohibition law of Kansas, often a source of political dispute, was the basis for a grand jury investigation during Schoeppel's term of office. In November 1945 the Governor publicly questioned the "good faith" of Federal liquor authorities who made occasional raids on illegal liquor deposits but, Schoeppel maintained, did not cooperate with the State in enforcing the local liquor laws. A Federal grand jury report, made public on October 8, 1946, charged State officials "including the executive head

SCHOEPPEL, ANDREW F.—*Continued*
of the State" with failure to enforce the law.
State prohibition was repealed in 1948.

Concurrent with three years of his governorship, Schoeppel was chairman of the Interstate Oil Compact Commission of the United States, a body approved by Congress in 1935 and ratified (by 1945) by sixteen States (originally twelve had been members) to deal with mutual problems regarding the gas and oil industries which do not fall under either Federal or State control.

At the close of his second term as Governor, Schoeppel returned to private law practice in Wichita, Kansas, as a member of the firm of Foulston, Siefkin, Schoeppel, Bartlett & Powers. He is still a member of this firm, which specializes in corporation, insurance, oil, gas, and real property law, and numbers among its clients some twenty insurance companies and many large oil, gas, and other industrial companies.

In 1948 Schoeppel "ran away with" the primaries for the Republican nomination for the Senate and in November defeated the Democratic nominee by a vote of 393,412 to 305,987 to become a member of the Eighty-first Congress. He thus succeeded to the Senatorial seat which had been held for thirty years by the veteran legislator Arthur Capper. During his first session in Congress he was appointed to the Committee of the District of Columbia. Since 1950 he has been a member of the Banking and Currency Committee and the Select Committee on Small Business, and throughout his term he has served on the Committee on Expenditures in the Executive Department. In June 1950 he replaced Senator Joseph R. McCarthy on a subcommittee of the Committee on Expenditures in the Executive Department which was investigating charges of misconduct among State Department employees.

The Kansas Senator's record has been, in the main, one of adherence to party policies. During the first session of 1949 he voted against an antifilibuster bill, for State option on rent control, and against an extension of the trade agreements act. With the majority of the Senate he favored the North Atlantic Security Pact, but during the same session he voted for a bill which would withhold the United States commitment of arms for Western Europe, for a bill which would decrease European arms aid by 50 per cent, and against the foreign military aid bill. He favored a bill passed in August 1950 which tied wage controls to price controls and in September voted with the majority to override a veto of the Communist control bill. Also in the second session of the Eighty-first Congress, he was paired against Federal rent control extension, was paired against an increase in Marshall Plan expenditure, and was announced for a $100 million loan to Spain. During 1951 he voted against the extension of universal military training, against sending American troops to Europe, and against Government operation of defense plants.

A supporter of measures to reduce government spending, Schoeppel in 1951 voted for cuts in government civil and publicity payrolls, for a cut in reclamation funds (though not for a cut in the river-harbor funds), for a cut in United States armed forces funds to $55 billion, and for a reduction in economic aid to Europe. He opposed the $5.5 billion tax increase measure. Speaking at the sixty-third annual Lincoln Day dinner of the Republican Party in New York City in 1949, the Senator said: "There is no magic in the financial aspects of the Federal Government. There may be a lot of monkey business, but no magic." One of the few times he broke party lines was in June 1950, when he was one of only two Republican Senators to vote for the conference report on a bill lessening a penalty provision in the Hatch "clean politics" bill. In February 1951 Schoeppel proposed a 44- to 48-hour workweek (without overtime pay, for both Federal and civilian employees) to solve a manpower shortage problem. In September 1951 he urged scrapping of the Government's meat control program. Schoeppel has indicated that he will give his support to the candidacy of Senator Robert A. Taft for the Republican Presidential nomination of 1952.

The Senator is a Thirty-second Degree Mason, a Shriner, a Knight Commander of the Court of Honor, and a member of the American Legion and the Forty-and-Eight. He was awarded an honorary LL.D. degree by Baker University at Baldwin, Kansas, in 1946. His college fraternity is Sigma Nu, and he has been elected to the Phi Alpha Delta honorary law society. He belongs to the Southwestern Kansas, the Kansas, and the American bar associations, and is a member of Ness City Lions and Rotary clubs, and the Innocents, a men's honorary society. He has served as precinct committeeman and county chairman of his party organization, has been on the Ness Ctiy School Board, and is a past president of the Chamber of Commerce. His church is the Methodist. The Senator and Mrs. Schoeppel, the former Marie Thomsen of Tilden, Nebraska, were married on June 2, 1924. He has been described as a big, "burly" man, with "tousled" gray hair.

References

Congressional Directory (1951)
Martindale - Hubbell Law Directory
    (1951)
International Who's Who, 1951
Who's Who in America, 1950-51
Who's Who in United States Politics
    (1950)

SCHUMACHER, KURT Oct. 13, 1895—
Aug. 20, 1952 German political leader; served in the Reichstag (1930); having publicly attacked Nazism, went into hiding when the Nazis came into power (1932); spent ten years in concentration camps (1933-43); as chairman of the Social Democratic party since the end of World War II, headed the opposition to Chancellor Konrad Adenauer's Christian Democrats; outspoken opponent of communism and

a lifelong Socialist. See *Current Biography*, 1948.

Obituary

N Y Times Ag 21 '52

SCHWEBEL, STEPHEN M(YRON)

(shwā'b'l) Mar. 10, 1929- Organization official

Address: b. c/o World Federation of United Nations Associations, 45 E. 65th St., New York 21; h. 915 West End Ave., New York 25

Stephen M. Schwebel, who represents the World Federation of United Nations Associations at the United Nations, was appointed in April 1952 to direct the International Seminar on Economic and Social Problems, which was held in New York from June 11 to 14. Schwebel, whose interest in the United Nations dates from his senior year at high school, founded and later became president of the United Nations Council of Harvard. The author of articles on international affairs and of a text on the United Nation's Secretary-General, Schwebel has also participated in national radio forums and lecture tours.

A native of New York City, Stephen Myron Schwebel was born there on March 10, 1929. He and his older brother are the sons of Victor and Pauline (Pfeffer) Schwebel; both parents are of Austro-Hungarian ancestry. Schwebel's maternal grandfather, Jacob Pfeffer, was a journalist, and his father is president of Safeway Petroleum Corporation. After attending elementary school in New York, Schwebel registered at James Madison High School for his secondary education. There he was an editor of the newspaper and president of the World Affairs Club. In his senior year he was appointed the first national president of United Nations Youth and in this capacity toured the Eastern States organizing other U.N.Y. chapters. In March 1946, as U.N.Y.'s representative, he spoke at the first New York *Herald Tribune* Forum on the topic "The World We Want."

Upon his graduation from high school in June 1946, Schwebel won four college scholarships. Among them was the Pulitzer Scholarship from Columbia University for study at the college of the student's choice. Schwebel selected Harvard University, where he took his major in government. In June 1950, when he received his B.A. degree from that university, he was graduated *magna cum laude* with highest honors in government and was elected to membership in Phi Beta Kappa. A Frank Knox Memorial Fellow, he attended Trinity College at Cambridge University, England, during the year 1950-51 to take courses in international law. Schwebel is continuing his studies at Yale University as a candidate for the LL.B. degree.

In his freshman term Schwebel founded the Harvard United Nations Council and served as its chairman for 1946-48. The council was organized in order to acquaint Bostonians with the activities of the United Nations. In a further attempt to bring about better interna-

STEPHEN M. SCHWEBEL

tional understanding of the activities of the U.N., Schwebel, together with Paul L. Wright, a fellow Harvard man, launched a series of radio news analyses, *This World This Week*. For two years (1947-49) the program was broadcast every Sunday over station WHDH from Boston. According to *Pic* magazine, Schwebel was a "top radio news analyst at nineteen."

Another of Schwebel's extracurricula activities at Harvard was the national chairmanship of the Collegiate Council for the United Nations, a post he held from 1948 to 1950. In an attempt to strengthen public support of the U.N., the council has established 153 chapters on college campuses in 42 States. In March 1947 Schwebel was chosen representative to the United Nations Educational, Scientific and Cultural Organization's national conference in Philadelphia. As the first spokesman for youth at a United States national conference of UNESCO, he conducted a "one-man" lobby for three days, securing three seats for representatives of student and youth organizations on the national commission for UNESCO. In the same year (1947) he appeared as a speaker on a coast-to-coast NBC broadcast in observance of U.N. Week. In 1948 and again in 1949 Schwebel appeared before the Senate Committee on Foreign Relations to present the views of the Collegiate Council on the North Atlantic Treaty, and to submit proposals for strengthening the U.N. charter.

In September 1948 Schwebel, then in his junior year at Harvard, was a member of the United Nations delegation to the Third Plenary Assembly of the World Federation of United Nations Associations, held in Geneva, Switzerland. Upon his return from Europe he made on September 23, 1948, a report on this conference in a coast-to-coast broadcast over CBS entitled "Peace Is the People's Business."

(Continued next page)

SCHWEBEL, STEPHEN M.—*Continued*

In August of the same year he took part in series of weekly broadcasts beamed to Europe, Africa, and behind the "Iron Curtain." For thirty-nine consecutive Saturdays Schwebel participated in discussions concerned with proposals and developments in European economic reconstruction. These programs were presented through the facilities of the Worldwide Broadcasting Foundation and in cooperation with the United Nations Council of Harvard.

According to a report in the Brooklyn *Eagle*, Schwebel has "probably done more than any young man in this country in strengthening public support of the United Nations." From March 1949 to June 1950 he was a member of the national board of directors and the executive committee of the American Association for the U.N. He was also a member of the Commission to Study the Organization of Peace and in 1951 was named a member of the commission's drafting committee. Schwebel served as well as an administrative aide in the executive office of Secretary-General Trygve Lie during the summer of 1949. In 1950 he was again representative of the World Federation of United Nations Associations meeting in Geneva.

In April 1950, shortly before his graduation from Harvard, Schwebel was appointed director of the American Office of the World Federation of United Nations Associations. This federation is recognized as a consultative agency with official status in the world organization. That year he was also elected for a term of one year as world president of the International Student Movement for the U.N., on the executive committee of which he had served, representing the United States, since 1948. The movement is composed of the U.N. student associations of twenty countries and is affiliated with World Federation of United Nations Associations. In 1951 he was a member of the United States delegation to the federation's Stockholm meeting. As consultant to the economic and social council of the World Federation of United Nations Associations, Schwebel was chosen in April 1952 to direct a program of seminars for foreign, and a limited number of American, students in the United States. Organized under the auspices of the W.F.U.N.A. and the Collegiate Council of the U.N., the seminar held in New York during June 11-14 was designed to acquaint the students with the economic and social areas of the United Nations.

Schwebel, who has been a speaker on local and national radio forums, appeared as a guest with Jinx Falkenburg and Tex McCrary, Martha Deane, and Margaret Arlen. He has written articles for the *British Yearbook of International Law*, *American Association for United Nations Quarterly*, *United Nations on the Campus*, and the *Harvard Advocate*. His book *The Secretary-General of the United Nations; his Political Powers and Practice* was published by the Harvard University Press in 1952. The study is based, in part, on interviews with Trygve Lie, other U.N. figures, and the two former Secretaries-General

of the League of Nations. *Rotarian Magazine* commented on the book: "An excellent historical study. . . .This work is marked by its thoroughness, with full scholarly documentation; by its historical perspective; by its concrete treatment of personalities and its acute analysis—free from bias or distortion—of specific situations and actions."

In addition to the other awards, Schwebel is the recipient of the Richard Perkins Parker Award and the Chase Prize, both awarded by Harvard. The Chase Prize is for the best thesis on a subject relating to the promotion of peace. He is a member of the Harvard Club in New York City. Schwebel is five feet eight inches tall, weighs 135 pounds, and has blue eyes and brown hair. He is a member of the Jewish faith. Concert going, rowing, and cycling are listed as his favorite recreations.

References

Christian Sci Mon p9 Je 14 '52
N Y Herald Tribune p21 Mr 24 '52

SCOGGIN, MARGARET C(LARA)
(skŏg′ĭn) Apr. 14, 1905- Librarian
Address: b. c/o New York Public Library, 127 E. 58th St., New York 22; h. 440 W. 34th St., New York 1

The New York Public Library's Superintendent for Work with Young People and with Schools, Margaret C. Scoggin, has been a member of the library staff since 1926, holding among other positions that of organizer and first librarian of the Nathan Straus Branch for Children and Young People. Editor of a number of anthologies for teen-age readers, she is also editor of a column of book reviews for *Horn Book* magazine and conducts a weekly radio program of book discussion for young people. As representative of the American Library Association and the Rockefeller Foundation, Miss Scoggin had a part in the organizing of the International Youth Library in Munich in the summer of 1949. She was also chairman of A.L.A.'s international relations committee, which was partly responsible for establishing the CARE-UNESCO Children's Book Fund.

A Midwesterner descended from Scotch, English, and Irish forebears, Margaret Clara Scoggin was born to Alfred Polk and Margaret Ellen (Bright) Scoggin in Columbia, Missouri, on April 14, 1905. "I come from a family which wandered through North Carolina, Virginia, Mississippi, Georgia, and Tennessee," she relates. "The men were lawyers, ministers, and doctors and followed pioneer trails with books, Bibles, or medicines in their saddlebags." Her early recollections were of the library of her older brother, a professor of Greek, Latin, and Sanskrit at the University of Missouri in Columbia. At the Columbia High School, from which she received her diploma in 1922, Margaret Scoggin helped edit the school newspaper in her junior year and the school magazine in her senior year. With English and classical studies as her major courses, she attended Radcliffe College (Massachusetts) from 1922 to 1926, winning election to Phi Beta Kappa honor society and graduating *magna cum laude* with the B.A. degree. She earned part of her college expenses by working in an office and teaching English to foreigners at Denison House (in Boston), a university settlement house where she lived during her last year at Radcliffe. In later years she took graduate courses in library science at the School of Librarianship of London University (1929-30) and the School of Library Service of Columbia University (1938-41).

Desiring to live in New York City after leaving college, Miss Scoggin answered an advertisement of the New York Public Library for summer substitutes, with the result that in July 1926 she was assigned as library assistant to the Mott Haven Branch. At this branch and at the Seward Park and Harlem branches, she was occupied from 1926 to 1929 in general library operations and received some training in reference service. Through Mabel Williams, a pioneer in library work with older children, she became interested in the special field of literature for young people in their teens. In 1930 she was appointed librarian in charge of school and reference work at the George Brace Branch of the New York Public Library, here responsible for selecting books for teen-agers, making contacts with schools, and supervising work connected with the reference collection.

After five years in her next position, that of librarian in charge of work with vocational and industrial high schools (1935-40), Miss Scoggin was named organizer and branch librarian of the Nathan Straus Branch for Children and Young People, which she describes as one of the first libraries with an adult department for the use of people under twenty-one years. A training and demonstration center for library service to that age group, this branch is an agency for selection of books of use and interest to young people and offers such programs as film forums and record concerts. In 1947, as reported by *Newsweek*, the library made available 10,000 volumes to approximately 2,000 young people, some seventy-five of whom formed a club through which their reviews of books, after being discussed in round-table conferences, were duplicated in monthly collections called "Circulatin' the News" and distributed to publishers and librarians. In *People Are Our Business* Beryl Williams gives an account of other features of this young people's library set up by Miss Scoggin.

As official representative of the American Library Association and the Rockefeller Foundation, Margaret Scoggin took part in the organizing and opening of the International Youth Library in Munich, Germany, from May to September 1949. She returned to New York to become assistant to the Public Library's Superintendent of Work with Schools and Young People. Two years later (1951), advanced to the position of superintendent, she was made responsible for all young people's librarians in the New York Public Library, with supervision over book selections for young people; for public library contacts with schools in Manhattan, Richmond, and the Bronx; and for young people's activities in the branch libraries.

MARGARET C. SCOGGIN

Concurrently with fulfilling her responsibilities in the public library, Miss Scoggin since 1938 has held the post of instructor in the Department of Library Science at St. John's University (Brooklyn), and since 1946 has been moderator of *Young Book Reviewers*, a weekly radio program of book discussions by teen-agers heard over station WMCA in New York. This program in 1949 was awarded the Ohio State University first prize as the best radio program for out-of-school listening and in 1952 was given two honorable mentions for programs in this classification. She has also written book reviews for the New York *Herald Tribune* and since 1948 has edited *Outlook Tower* in the *Horn Book* magazine, a column of reviews of adult books for young people and comments on young people's reading. "There is no such thing as a 'suitable' book for teen-agers," *Publishers' Weekly* quoted Miss Scoggin as saying. "It is a matter of finding the book that is suitable for the individual reader, and that is what keeps the work interesting." Young people, she has observed, have become "at least two years older mentally" than they were when she began her work with them twenty-four years ago. Other of her achievements in the field of young people's reading are four anthologies of stories for teen-agers that she has edited: *Chucklebait* (1945), *The Lure of Danger* (1947), *More Chucklebait* (1949), and *The Edge of Danger* (1951). With Christine Gilbert and Ruth Strange, she is coeditor of *Gateways to Readable Books* (1952), a bibliography of books for slow readers. Her articles on librarianship, books for teen-agers, and related subjects include "Plan Directory of Young People's Librarians," *American Library Association Bulletin* (October 1940); "Young People's Reading Interests Not Materially Changed in Wartime," *Library Journal* (September 15, 1943); "Guiding the Teen-Age Reader in the Public Library," *Catholic Library World* (April 1945);

SCOGGIN, MARGARET C.—*Continued*

"Young Book Reviewers Broadcast," *Top of the News* (September 1948); and "UNESCO-CARE Children's Book Fund Program," *American Library Association Bulletin* (December 1950).

Among incidental activities of Miss Scoggin in the field of literature for teen-agers have been her contributions as reader for the Young People's Literary Guild, judge for the New York *Herald Tribune* Children's Spring Book Festival, adviser for the Teen-Age Book Club, and leader of a summer workshop for librarians at Albany. For "outstanding service" in the world of books she was the recipient on February 15, 1952, of the Constance Lindsay Skinner Award, given annually by the Women's National Book Association. "My own experience with libraries and books here and abroad have proved to me that to be a librarian is not to sit behind a desk and hand out books," Miss Scoggin said in accepting the tribute. "To be a librarian is to be a citizen of the world."

Margaret Scoggin, who has long been a member of the American Library Association, has been especially interested in that organization's Association of Young People's Librarians and also in the work of the A.L.A.'s international relations board in increasing professional contacts among librarians throughout the world. As chairman of the A.L.A.'s international relations committee, composed of school, children's, and young people's librarians, she had a part in promoting the establishment of the UNESCO-CARE Children's Book Fund, whereby packages of selected American children's books may be sent to child-serving institutions in countries all over the world. Other organizations of which she is a member are the New York State Library Association, New York Library Club, Women's National Book Association, Booksellers' League, English Speaking Union, and American Federation of Radio Artists.

The brown-eyed, gray-haired librarian weighs 135 pounds and is five feet seven inches in height. She names her political affiliation as Democratic, but adds that she votes independently. In her free time she enjoys traveling, photography, and gardening, the latter in "an amateurish sort of way." Also fond of bicycling, in the summer of 1938 she was leader of a group of people who bicycled through the Scandinavian countries on a youth hostel trip.

References

Horn Book 28:85 Ap '52
Lib J 77:406 Mr 1 '52
Pub Weekly 161:1190-91 Mr 8 '52
Williams, B. People Are Our Business (1947)

SEARS, ROBERT R(ICHARDSON) Aug. 31, 1908- University professor; psychologist
Address: b. c/o Laboratory of Human Development, Harvard University, Cambridge 38, Mass.

Professor of education and child psychology at the Harvard University Graduate School of Education, Robert R. Sears also became the director of the university's Laboratory of Human Development in 1949. Previously he had been associated with the University of Illinois (1932-36), Yale University (1936-42), and the University of Iowa (1942-49); at the last-named he directed the Child Welfare Research Station. On June 30, 1952, it was announced that Sears in the summer of 1953 would become professor and head of the psychology department at Stanford University.

Robert Richardson Sears was born August 31, 1908, in Palo Alto, California, the son of Jesse Brundage and Stella (Richardson) Sears. His parents are descended from early American families of English origin who had moved westward in the nineteenth century from Connecticut and Virginia. As a young man Jesse Brundage Sears settled in California, where he entered the educational field, in time becoming a professor of education at Stanford University and the author of works in his specialty. Robert R. Sears has one brother, who is a physician.

At the Palo Alto Union High School, which Sears attended until 1925, his extrascholastic activities were dramatics, athletics, and editorial work on the school paper and the annual. As an undergraduate at Stanford University, he majored in psychology and English and continued his literary interests. He was an editor of the Stanford literary magazine, a member of the English Club (of which he was elected president in his senior year), and an actor in several plays at the college and in local little theater groups. While at Stanford, from which he received his B.A. degree in 1929, he was influenced by psychologists Lewis M. Terman and Paul R. Farnsworth, the latter of whom he feels was largely responsible for his choice of career. In 1929 Sears went East to pursue graduate study in psychology at Yale University, where he was appointed the Blossom fellow in neuroanatomy for the year 1931-32 and awarded the Ph.D. degree in 1932. His doctoral dissertation is entitled "Effect of Optic Lobe Ablation on the Visuo-Motor Behavior of Goldfish." At Yale he studied principally under psychologist Clark L. Hull, to whom he attributes the specific direction of his later interests.

Upon completion of his study at Yale in 1932, Sears took the position of instructor of psychology at the University of Illinois, where he remained through the spring of 1936, after having been promoted to an associateship in 1935. During the period of his employment at the University of Illinois, he held the additional position of clinical psychologist at the Institute for Juvenile Research in Chicago. In the autumn of 1936 he returned to Yale as research assistant professor in the Institute of Human Relations. The following year he was made assistant professor of psychology and in 1942 was promoted to the rank of associate professor. As visiting lecturer in psychology he spent the spring of 1937 at Wesleyan University; and as assistant professor of psychology he was at Stanford University for the summer of 1941.

Sears left Yale in 1942 to enter upon the position of professor of child psychology and director of the Child Welfare Research Station at the University of Iowa. In the latter capacity he spoke before a Senate labor and public welfare subcommittee in Washington, D.C., on May 11, 1949, arguing in favor of the national child research bill on the ground that the costs of juvenile delinquency, alcoholism, broken homes, and the like, resulting from inadequate early training, are far higher than the provision of adequate funds for research into the solution of these problems would be. A further outcome of his work at Iowa was a report on the behavior of forty-two children in an Iowa preschool group given varying degrees of discipline in the home. This report formed the basis for a symposium, "Permissiveness Versus Rigidity in Relation to Child Rearing, Personality, and Culture," which was held in New York City on December 28, 1949. After resigning his post at Iowa in 1949, Sears became professor of education and child psychology in the Graduate School of Education at Harvard University, as well as the director of the Harvard Laboratory of Human Development.

In the summer of 1949 Sears became president-elect of the American Psychological Association, a title he held for the year 1949-50 until his automatic advancement to president for the year 1950-51. (During 1945-50 he had served on its board of directors.) At the association's annual meeting at Chicago in September 1951, he discussed two studies made on dependency in children indicating a correlation between independence and adequate affection given in the home; and he delivered his presidential address, "A Theoretical Framework for Personality and Social Behavior," in which he stressed the need for the psychological study of people in pairs, as for example parents and children, husbands and wives, and employers and employees; the behavioral laws relating to these diads appear to be congruent with, but somewhat different from, those relating to individual human beings.

Sears has been a member of the Social Science Research Council since 1945 and has served as vice-chairman of its board of directors. In the National Research Council he has been active in the division of anthropology and psychology; he was also the chairman of the committee on child development for the period from 1948 to 1950. Formerly a member of the Midwestern Psychological Association, Sears shifted his membership to the Eastern Psychological Association after joining the Harvard faculty. He is a member of the American Orthopsychiatric Association, of the National Association for Nursery Education, of the Society for Research in Child Development (of which he was director in 1947). He serves also as consultant for the United States Public Health Service and the United States Children's Bureau, and during World War II engaged in psychological research for the Army Air Force, as a civilian with the National

ROBERT R. SEARS

Defense Research Committee in the Office of Scientific Research and Development. It was announced in the summer of 1952 that Sears had accepted an appointment from Stanford University as professor of psychology (effective July 1, 1953) and as head of the psychology department (effective September 1, 1953).

Sears has done work in the areas of conditioned reflexes, frustration and aggression, personality development in childhood, projective doll play, and parent-child relationships. He has been a frequent contributor of articles to psychological, psychiatric, and child development journals, among them *Child Development* and *American Sociological Review*. He also edited the *Iowa Studies in Child Welfare*; is a coauthor with John Dollard and others of *Frustration and Aggression* (1939), a publication of the Yale University Institute of Human Relations; and is author of *Survey of Objective Studies of Psychoanalytic Concepts*; a *Report Prepared for the Committee on Social Adjustment* (1943).

The psychologist, who was elected to Sigma Xi, was given an honorary M.A. degree by Harvard in 1950. Politically he is an independent, and his religious affiliation is with the Congregational Church. On June 25, 1932, he married Pauline Kirkpatrick Snedden, a clinical psychologist and research associate at Harvard. They are the parents of two children, David O'Keefe and Nancy Louise. The brown-haired, blue-eyed professor has a height of six feet two inches and a weight of 175 pounds. As a hobby he collects Chinese stamps, and for recreation he swims, plays popular music on the piano, and reads detective stories.

References

American Men of Science (1949)
Who's Who in America, 1952-53

SEIXAS, E(LIAS) VICTOR, JR. (să'-shŭs) Aug. 30, 1923- Tennis player
Address: b. c/o E. V. Seixas, Sr., 1834 Vineyard St., Philadelphia 30, Pa.; h. 1121 N. 66th St., Philadelphia 31, Pa.

Ranked first among American tennis players in 1952 by the United States Lawn Tennis Association is E. Victor Seixas, Jr., of Philadelphia, who rose to that position from eighth place, the place he held the previous year. He has played in a number of tournaments both

Wide World Photos
E. VICTOR SEIXAS, JR.

at home and abroad, visiting Australia in late 1951 as a member of the Davis Cup team. During World War II Seixas served with the Army Air Force.

Elias Victor Seixas, Jr., was born in Philadelphia, Pennsylvania, on August 30, 1923. The senior Seixas, who is of Portuguese descent, was born in Brazil and brought to the United States at the age of six. His wife, the former Anna Victoria Moon, is of Irish origin. Victor, their only son, was reared in Philadelphia, where his father had established a wholesale plumbing and heating supply business. From 1937 to 1941 Victor Seixas was a student at the William Penn Charter School in Philadelphia, from which he was graduated *cum laude*, having been a member of the Trident Honor Society there. He also received five letters in sports.

In October 1942 Seixas enlisted in the United States Army Air Force, in which as a pilot he held the rank of first lieutenant. Until his separation from the service in August 1946, Seixas spent nine months as a flight instructor and served in the Pacific theater of operations, where for a year and a half he did test flying. Upon his return to civilian life he entered the University of North Carolina, choosing a major in business administration, which brought

him a Bachelor of Science degree in commerce in 1949. Chi Psi fraternity, of which he was a member, awarded him a scholarship and elected him its president in 1949. Seixas was also a member of the Golden Fleece Honor Society. Another elective office he held was that of vice-president of the junior class. For his contribution to sports at the university, he received the Patterson medal bestowed annually upon the outstanding senior athlete: he had been a member of the varsity basketball team for two years and a member of the varsity tennis team for three, serving as its captain for two years. Tennis was a game he had played, said a newspaper account, "since he was as tall as the net."

For a number of years Seixas had been prominent in amateur tennis tournaments, but it was not until after he entered the family business as a salesman that he discovered a marked improvement in his game. "All tennis and no work sometimes made me a dull boy in past competition," was his explanation, as quoted in the *Christian Science Monitor*. "But when I had the business to occupy me, I looked forward to the limited time I had for tennis. . . .I wasn't tired of the game when I got out there on the courts."

At Wimbledon, England, in July 1950, said the New York *Times*, "Seixas led the star-spangled parade" of amateur American net stars into the quarter-finals by defeating the remaining Australian singles contender, Jack Bromwich. Seixas was victor in the Coral Beach (Bermuda) invitation tournament the following March, downing Straight Clark of California with a 6-0, 6-2, 6-3 score in the singles, and joining with Tony Vincent to win the men's doubles. Eighth ranking United States player in 1951, Seixas in July eliminated Gardnar Mulloy, the fourth ranking player from the semifinals of the Spring Lake (New Jersey) invitational, to meet William Talbert in the finals. "Seixas kept ahead with such brilliance and aggressiveness," said Allison Danzig of the New York *Times*, "that Mulloy could not get into the clear." Participating in the American Zone semifinals of the Davis Cup elimination, Seixas "moved to set point twice before smashing down the sideline for the winning point" of his 6-3, 8-6, 6-1 victory over Mario Llamos of Mexico, in a match held at the Westchester (New York) Country Club in August 1951. Although Seixas won through to the semifinals of the National Tennis Championships at Forest Hills early the ensuing month and entered the finals by defeating Richard Savitt, he himself lost the national net crown in the deciding match to Australia's Frank Sedgman.

As a member of the United States Davis Cup squad, Seixas visited Australia in late 1951 to participate in the play-offs. While he was there, Seixas in November subjected Sedgman to an unexpected defeat in the semifinals of the New South Wales championship tournaments. "His play here has been sensational," a New York *Herald Tribune* dispatch said of Seixas. "An expert volleyer and a daring net player, Seixas stormed the net at every occasion. Although he made only 46 placements to 42 for Sedgman, the slim Philadelphian made his shots when they counted." Seixas on November 24 captured the New South Wales title with his defeat of Mervyn Rose, in a two-hour match that resulted in a score of 4-6, 9-7, 4-6, 7-5, and 6-3. Australian tennis critics soon after attempted to unnerve Seixas, contended the American press, by charging him with habitual foot-faulting, which the Philadelphia player denied. He proceeded to eliminate all possibility of further criticism by standing a good foot behind the baseline, a position which "added tremendous power to his serve." With Ted Schroeder, Seixas was chosen by United States team captain Frank Shields to represent that country in the Davis Cup singles matches, in the semifinals of which Seixas again defeated Mervyn Rose. On the fifth and deciding finals match, against Frank Sedgman, which saw the Philadelphia player's defeat, Seixas later commented: "What I needed against him was a couple of extra arms and legs." He also said: "I thought I was playing as well as I ever did. Everything was working as I hoped it would except for my service, which wasn't too hot. I thought right to the end that I would win because I didn't believe anybody could keep up the kind of tennis Frank was playing. But he did."

In the tentative national rankings drawn up in December 1951, Seixas was named second by the United States Lawn Tennis Association, below Tony Trabert, a classification that was changed the following month. After a stormy meeting of representatives from all parts of the country and over the protests of Frank Shields, Seixas was named to the first place, followed by Dick Savitt in the second and Tony Trabert in third. Seixas began the 1952 season at Miami Beach, Florida, in the April fourth annual Good Neighbor tournament, where he lost in the finals to Gardnar Mulloy. During the two preceding weeks he had won the Miami Invitation and the Everglades Club tournaments. After playing in an international tournament sponsored by the Cuban Lawn Tennis Association in mid-April, Seixas participated in the Coral Beach invitational at Hamilton, Bermuda, playing in three events: the men's singles and doubles, and the mixed doubles. On September 6, 1952, Seixas was named playing captain of the United States Davis Cup team for the interzone round and was later team captain in the challenge round with Australia in December.

Victor Seixas is a member of the Merion Cricket Club and of the Cynwyd Club, both in Philadelphia. His religion is the Presbyterian. On October 22, 1949, he married Dolly Ann Dunaway. The tennis ace has blue eyes and brown hair; his height is six feet one inch and his weight 175 pounds.

SEN, B(INAY) R(ANJAN) (sĕn bē-noi' rŭn'ján) Jan. 1, 1898- Diplomat

Address: b. c/o Embassy of India, Rome, Italy

B. R. Sen, former Ambassador from India to the United States, left Washington in mid-September 1952 to become India's Ambassador in Rome with concurrent accreditation to Italy and Yugoslavia. This was the position held by Sen before he assumed the Ambassadorial post in Washington in November 1951 in succession to Madame Vijaya Lakshmi Pandit, who resigned to become a candidate for the Indian Parliament. Among the assignments that he has filled in the course of his thirty-year career in India's civil and diplomatic service have been those of the director-general of food, the director of civil evacuation, India's representative to the United Nations Security Council, and Minister to the United States from 1947 to 1950. Holding a political philosophy similar to that of India's Prime Minister Nehru, Sen has said that his country should maintain strict neutrality in the struggle between Communism and the Western world.

Binay Ranjan Sen, the son of Dr. K. M. Sen, was born January 1, 1898. After completing his education at Calcutta University in India and at Oxford University in England, he entered India's civil service in 1922 and held a number of administrative and secretariat posts in the Bengal Government. He was the Government's secretary to the political and appointment departments and the press officer from 1931 to 1934. In 1937 Sen became a district magistrate in Minapore and held this job until 1940, when he was made the Revenue Secretary to the government of Bengal. During the last year of his three years as secretary, he also served as the Director of Civil Evacuation for Bengal and as the Relief Commissioner (1942-43).

After two years (1943-45) as the Director-General of Food, Sen became the Secretary to the Department of Agriculture. In February 1947 he was appointed India's first Counselor and Minister plenipotentiary to the United States, serving that same year also as a member of the Indian delegation to the United Nations General Assembly and as the representative from India to the United Nations Security Council. The official headed the Indian delegation to the Economic and Social Council of the United Nations in 1949, the conference of the Food and Agricultural Organization also in that year, and the council of the Food and Agricultural Organization in 1950. In March of 1950 the Indian diplomat accepted the appointment as his country's Ambassador to Italy and Yugoslavia.

Upon the resignation of Madame Vijaya Lakshmi Pandit as India's Ambassador to the United States to run for Parliament, Sen arrived on November 26, 1951, in Washington to fill the post. In presenting his credentials to President Truman the official stated that India would look to the United States for economic aid to carry out its five-year development plan. In his first public address as Ambassador, given before the English-Speaking Union of the United States, Sen stated that his country would welcome the investment of foreign capital in Indian industries. Citing the recently concluded agreement with Standard Vacuum Oil Company as an example to be followed, he said there would be no government interference with company operations. He pointed out that

Chase News Photo.

B. R. SEN

because both India and the United States desire democracy and have no territorial ambitions, they can meet on common ground. " Since we agree about the basic ideas and goals for the peoples of both our countries," he continued, "there is every reason why India and America should always continue to respect, admire and understand each other" (New York *Times*, January 26, 1952).

At the April 24, 1952, National Institute of the Social Sciences meeting, Sen expressed hopes that the United States would supply $1 billion for India's domestic development. Since Indian foreign policy is the same as that of the United States in the matter of resisting aggression, he stated, India would not remain neutral in the event of aggression. Two months later at a Chicago Council on Foreign Relations luncheon, the Ambassador said, "The one thing we want most from the United States is that it understand India is a democratic country, and that we are trying to build up a democracy" (*Christian Science Monitor*, June 2, 1952). Granting a likeness in basic ideals, he further observed, there should be no objection to different methods of achieving those ideals: "We want freedom of expression and thought, just as you do in the United States." The official also told of the gratitude of the Indian people for the help they have received from the United States.

In a speech before the Colgate University Foreign Policy Conference in July 1952, Sen explained that India wished to keep away from the East-West struggle: "We believe that with cultivation of a little more tolerance of both sides, coexistence still is possible and must be worked for. We feel that by taking sides we will only hasten this march to death." Charging that the cold war had turned the United Nations into a "forum for international name-calling," Sen said that a total war now would destroy the attempts in Asia to build a democratic order.

Sen told Dorothy Schiff of the New York *Post* (August 10, 1952) that Asiatics are more concerned at present with their own problems of daily life than with problems arising out of East-West tension. They want to stay out of world conflict because they believe a long period of peace is essential to achieve their two main objectives—freeing themselves from foreign domination and raising their living standards. The Ambassador, however, feared that the outcome of the present universal tension would be war, although, he added, his country believed that this calamity could be avoided if the solution of problems was sought in a spirit of tolerance and compromise. A week after the Schiff interview Sen said India would not attend any conference of Pacific countries which did not include Communist China. He explained that India prefers to work through the United Nations, because it fears that an organization without China would develop into a regional bloc.

On July 12, 1952, it was announced that Sen would be succeeded as Ambassador in Washington by Gaganvihari L. Mehta, and in the following September Sen left the United States for Rome to resume his former duties as Ambassador to Italy and Yugoslavia.

Two articles that Sen has written for the *Annals of the American Academy of Political and Social Sciences* are "An Asian Views World Government" (July 1949) and "Nationalism and the Asian Awakening" (July 1952). He and Chiroprova Chatterjee were married in 1931; they have three daughters, Nandini, Ayesha, and Urmila. The Indian envoy is a member of the Imperial Gymkhana at Delhi and of the Calcutta club in India. Dorothy Schiff described him in the New York *Post* as "reserved, serious, dignified, reminding [one] a little of Nehru," while Alfred Friendly of the Washington *Post* (July 20, 1952) found him "a movie-handsome and ordinarily grave man."

References

Indian and Pakistan Yearbook and Who's Who, 1950
Indian Yearbok, 1951
Who's Who, 1952

SENANAYAKE, DON STEPHEN Oct. 20, 1884—Mar. 22, 1952 Prime Minister of Ceylon; was elected to the Legislative Council of the British Crown Colony of Ceylon in 1922; was elected to Council of State and appointed Minister of Agriculture and Lands in 1931; became vice-chairman of the Board of Ministers and leader of the Council of State in 1942; first Prime Minister, Minister of Defense, and Minister of External Affairs of Ceylon since 1947; leader of the United National party. See *Current Biography*, 1950.

Obituary

N Y Times p93 Mr 23 '52

SENANAYAKE, DUDLEY (SHELTON)

(sĕn-ăn-ĭ'ă-kĕ) June 19, 1911- Prime Minister of Ceylon

Address: The Temple Trees, Colombo 3, Ceylon

Following the death in March 1952 of the first Prime Minister of the Dominion of Ceylon, the Honorable Don Stephen Senanayake, his son Dudley Senanayake was named to succeed him as Prime Minister and also as Minister of Defense and External Affairs. The younger Senanayake, inheriting the leadership of the United National party, which derives its principal support from the Singhalese-Buddhist segment of the population, was confirmed in office through decisive victory in a general election held two months later. Dudley Senanayake, who had been Minister of Agriculture and Lands in his father's Cabinet, is a graduate of Cambridge University, a member of the British bar, and an anti-Communist and proponent of cooperation with the West in international matters. Ceylon, formerly a British Crown Colony, attained Dominion status in February 1948.

Dudley Shelton Senanayake is a Singhalese by race, the descendant of what has been described as a "feudal landed family" devoted to the Buddhist faith. His father, Don Stephen Senanayake, had not yet embarked on a political career and was occupied as a rubber and coconut planter when his wife, nee Emily Maud Dunuwille, gave birth on June 19, 1911, to the elder of their two sons. (Dudley Senanayake's younger brother is now a Colombo businessman.) The boy was one year old when the island of Ceylon, a British Crown Colony since 1833, began its modern constitutional development with the formation of a reformed Legislative Council and eleven years old when the elder Senanayake became the member for the Negombo District in the Legislative Council which had been granted augmented powers under a new constitution approved in 1920. Like his father, Dudley Senanayake was educated at St. Thomas' College at Mount Lavinia, Ceylon, and also like his parent made distinguished records in both studies and sports. He won "colors" in cricket, football, and boxing, as well as the Victoria Gold Medal awarded to the best all-around athlete, and in his final years was the senior prefect of the school. At Corpus Christi College, Cambridge, England, where he was enrolled in 1929 after passing the Cambridge University entrance examinations with honors, he won "blues" at cricket, soccer, and boxing. On passing the National Science Tripos examinations at Cambridge he proceeded to London to read law at the Middle Temple and was called to the bar in 1934. An article in the Ceylonese Government publication *Sri Lanka* remarked that as a student he "developed a gift of lucid speech quite unexpected in one who shone at cricket, football, boxing, tennis, polo, and athletics, while taking his scientific and legal examinations in his stride."

In 1931, while Dudley Sananayake was a Cambridge undergraduate, the new Donoughmore Constitution for Ceylon went into effect, with control over most local matters passing to a State Council, the majority of the members

DUDLEY SENANAYAKE

of which were elective. The elder Senanayake was chosen by the Council to be Minister of Agriculture and Lands, and within two years effected passage of the Land Development Ordinance, a measure which greatly improved the condition of agricultural workers. The Agriculture Minister's policies had the sympathy of his elder son, who returned to Ceylon in 1934 to practice law at Colombo; and when two years later elections for a new State Council were held, he contested and won the Dedigama seat, becoming at the age of twenty-four the council's youngest member. As it turned out, this new State Council was to be the last; for in 1937, the working of the Donoughmore Constitution having been found unsatisfactory, Governor Sir Andrew Caldecott recommended the appointment of a commission to study the question of reorganization. Before any effective steps were taken, however, World War II broke out; and it was not until late in 1944 that the British government set up under the chairmanship of the first Baron Soulbury a commission to draft a new constitution. The Soulbury Constitution—under which the State Council was to be replaced by a bicameral Parliament with a House of Representatives of 95 elected members and six members nominated by the Governor General of Ceylon and a Senate of 30 to be half-elected and half-appointed—became a political reality on December 10, 1947, when the Ceylon Independence Act passed by the British Parliament received the royal approval of King George VI. On February 8, 1948, accordingly, Ceylon entered on full-fledged Dominion status within the British Commonwealth of Nations.

Ceylon (or Lanka, in the ancient Brahminical nomenclature preferred by a majority of the inhabitants) has an area of 25,330 square miles and a population of somewhat over 7,000,000, about 68 per cent of whom are Singhalese

SENANAYAKE, DUDLEY—*Continued*
Buddhists, the remainder mainly Tamil Hindus, Moslem Moors, and Eurasians. (There are only about 5,000 Europeans.) Political alignments tend to follow race and creed; in elections for the new Parliament held in August and September 1947, the United National party headed by the Singhalese-Buddhist Don Stephen Senanayake captured 49 of the 95 seats in the first House of Representatives, and on ratification of the Independence Act in December its leader was called upon by the Governor General (representing the Crown) to form a government. (The elder Senanayake thus became Ceylon's first Prime Minister and also at this time assumed the portfolio of the Minister of Defense and External Affairs.) Dudley Senanayake took over his father's former post of Minister of Agriculture and Lands and as such (stated *Newsweek*) "made a dramatic start at reclaiming two thirds of the island's area now uncultivated," one method being through "rebuilding of the irrigation lakes, called 'tanks,' that stand beside the ghostly ruins of vast 1,000 year-old cities in grassy clearings of the jungle." *Sri Lanka* pointed to the colonization schemes at Kantalai, Alai, Huruluwewa, Attanagala, and Ridi Bendi Ela, and to the Gal Oya Valley Scheme as major important projects undertaken during his period of office, and reported that in the field of agrarian legislation he was "responsible for the passing" of the Soil Conservation Act and the Paddy Lands Bill. In 1951 both father and son paid a visit to Australia and New Zealand for the purpose of studying firsthand the agricultural policies and practices of those two countries.

Brain injuries resulting from a fall from a bolting horse caused the death of Premier Don Stephen Senanayake on March 22, 1952. Four days later (March 26) the Governor General of Ceylon, Lord Soulbury, acting on pledges of "wholehearted support and cooperation" by nineteen members of the United National party in the House of Representatives, called on Dudley Senanayake to form a Cabinet of Ministers to carry on the Government. The new head of the state, at the age of forty-one the youngest Prime Minister in the British Commonwealth, in his broadcast to the nation on the evening of the same day pledged himself to fulfillment of his father's "vision . . . of a sturdy, healthy and prosperous Ceylonese nation." Upon dissolving Parliament a week later (April 3) and calling a general election for May 22, Senanayake said, "I feel it is my duty to obtain a mandate from the people at the earliest opportunity."

By strict enforcement of certain nationality laws applying to persons of Indian and Pakistani origin, the Ceylon Government incurred the charge of discriminating against some 200,-000 Indian settlers on the tea and rubber plantations. As reported by New York *Times* correspondent Robert Trumbull on April 24, Senanayake's party, the avowedly anti-Communist United National, was "not eager to have the Indians vote because Communist trade unionism has been strong among this depressed com-munity." Only about 8,000 Hindus qualified to vote and the Indian Congress (Tamil) party put up no candidates. In a House of Representatives augmented to 101 members, the United Nationalists won 54 seats, while the Communist representation dropped from 5 to 3. "We never expected such a rout of the Left," Senanayake said on March 31. "The people realized they must go all out for stability at this time, and the issue I put before the electorate was stability versus chaos." He pledged continued cooperation with the British Commonwealth and the West. In his new Cabinet, announced June 2, 1952, Dudley Senanayake took over the position of the Minister of Defense and External Affairs as well as the Prime Ministership. He had earlier promised a re-examination of what was characterized in the New York *Times* as Ceylon's controversial policy on rubber, which had permitted the shipment of nearly 15,000 long tons of this strategic commodity to Communist China. Then in July 1952 he told the House of Representatives that Ceylon was sending a mission to Peiping to negotiate a trade pact with China to sell rubber in exchange for rice.

Dudley Senanayake's mother, known as one of her country's most active social workers, remains as *doyenne* of the Prime Minister's official residence at Colombo. Ceylon's leader, described by Robert Trumbull as "sturdily built," is said to be an habitual pipe-smoker and a golfing enthusiast. His religion is Buddhism.

References

> Christian Sci Mon p1 Mr 26 '52
> Newsweek 39:41 Je 9 '52
> Sri Lanka (Ceylon) vol 1 No 23 '52
> International Who's Who, 1952

SFORZA, CARLO, COUNT Sept. 25, 1873 —Sept 4, 1952 Italian statesman; author; educator; entered the diplomatic service of Italy as Minister to China (1911); while Foreign Minister (1920-21) acquired fame by negotiating the Rapallo Treaty with Yugoslavia; after the Fascist revolution (1922), denounced Benito Mussolini's Government and that year was exiled from Italy; returned to his country when Italy surrendered to the Allies (1943); as Minister of Foreign Affairs (1947-51) worked in behalf of European unification. See *Current Biography*, 1942.

Obituary

> N Y Times p1+ S 5 '52

SHAFER, PAUL W(ERNTZ) Apr. 27, 1893- United States Representative from Michigan
Address: b. c/o House Office Bldg., Washington 25, D.C.; h. 38 Woolnough St., Battle Creek, Mich.

Since 1937 the Third Michigan District, which comprises the south-central counties of the State, has been represented in the United States Congress by Paul W. Shafer of Battle

Creek, a former newspaper publisher and editor and municipal judge. Representative Shafer, a Republican, has served on the House Armed Services Committee since 1939 and in defense and foreign relations matters has reflected an isolationist point of view. On domestic issues he has usually voted with the conservative wing of his party.

Paul Werntz Shafer, born to John McClellan and Sarah C. (Werntz) Shafer on April 27, 1893, is a native of Elkhart, Indiana, and was brought up in Three Rivers, Michigan, about twenty miles distant. When he had completed his education in the Three Rivers public schools and at the Ferris Institute in Big Rapids, he returned to Indiana to become a reporter on an Elkhart newspaper. After World War I, in which he served with the Indiana State Militia (1917-18), Shafer moved to Battle Creek, Michigan, his present home, to continue newspaper work. Later he became both editor and publisher of the Bronson *Journal*, a small-town weekly circulating in Branch County, about thirty-five miles from Battle Creek.

During his newspaper days Shafer took a correspondence course in law from the Blackstone Institute in Chicago. He was admitted to the Michigan bar and was elected municipal judge of Battle Creek in 1929 and was re-elected in 1933. He was chairman of the Republican Committee of Calhoun County (where Battle Creek is located) during the 1934 campaign and had much to do with the election of Henry M. Kimball, a Republican from Kalamazoo, as United States Congressman for the Third Michigan District. Upon the death of Representative Kimball in October 1935, his uncompleted term was finished by Vernon W. Mason, a Battle Creek lawyer. In the 1936 primaries Representative Mason was defeated for nomination for a full term by Judge Shafer, who led his Democratic opponent by 4,718 votes in the November election. He has represented the Third Michigan District (comprising Branch, Calhoun, Eaton, Hillsdale, and Kalamazoo counties) continuously ever since.

Seated in the Seventy-fifth Congress on January 3, 1937, the newcomer from Michigan was assigned to the Invalid Pensions, Post Office and Post Roads, and District of Columbia committees; in the following June in connection with the last-named he proposed, as a revenue-raising measure, a levy on liquor consigned to the nation's capital for private consumption. The Representative of a district containing at least two important manufacturing cities, Kalamazoo and Battle Creek, Shafer assailed plans for a Government-aided cooperative tractor plant in the area, while the general pattern on his conservative and anti-New Deal thinking was indicated during his freshman year by his opposition to President Roosevelt's Supreme Court retirement bill, renewal of the Reciprocal Tariff Act, and passage of the Wagner housing bill. Also in the first session of the Seventy-fifth Congress he voted in support of an investigation of sit-down strikes and the embargo on the shipment of munitions abroad.

The Michigan Republican continued on the District of Columbia Committee through the

Wide World Photos
PAUL W. SHAFER

Seventy-sixth Congress, but dropped his other assignments on nomination, in January 1939, to the House Military Affairs Committee. As a member of the latter body he opposed, early as the middle of the following month, a favorable report on the May bill to enlarge the Army Air Force, challenging statements by Ambassadors Joseph Kennedy and William C. Bullitt by saying: "Nobody knows whether Hitler and Mussolini intend to make war." A year later he urged an end to the Army-Navy athletics rivalry as detrimental to the defense effort; and in May 1940—after his return from a 25,000-mile air trip with a joint Senate-House committee inspecting army equipment— he published in the *American Mercury* an article entitled "Local Politics: Menace to Defense," assailing "pork barrel" conditions in construction and procurement. Shafer supported the Hatch clean-politics bill in the following July, and voted against conscription in September; while early in the Seventy-seventh Congress he fought against passage of the Lend-Lease Act. In June 1941 he had inserted in the *Congressional Record* a rebuttal to Clarence K. Streit's "Union Now" proposition and later in 1941 called "Nay" on repeal of the ban on the arming of merchant vessels. In the same session of the Seventy-seventh Congress Shafer was recorded as opposed to the setting up of price controls and in favor of the Smith antistrike bill.

During the years of United States participation in World War II Representative Shafer was active in opposition to what he regarded as limitation of the free disseminaton of news. Thus, in January 1943 he sponsored a resolution charging that the Justice Department's antitrust suit against the Associated Press confronted "the United States with a most serious assault upon all the freedoms granted to its peoples"; and in the next month he assailed

SHAFER, PAUL W.—*Continued*

War Production Board plans to reduce the newsprint quota as "an insidious movement by long-haired theorists to destroy the press." In the same year Shafer supported the Hobbs antiracketeering bill, the Carlson-Ruml pay-as-you-go income tax program, and the Fulbright Resolution. He also voted to override the Presidential veto of the antistrike bill and charged that plans to "streamline" the War Department had "in reality intent to convert that great Department into a New Deal political organization."

In December 1944, with other Military Affairs Committee members, Shafer toured the European war fronts and returned with the conviction that Army censorship of news dispatches was presenting an optimistic impression of the progress of the war. He had already voted against authorization of UNRRA (November) and in the following March, when President Roosevelt asserted that "as a matter of decency" the American people should accept with good will current and future food rationing in order to help feed peoples abroad, commented that "decency, like charity, begins at home." He favored in 1945 a proposal for a permanent committee on Un-American Activities. In July 1946, shortly before departing on a Military Affairs Committee inspection trip to Alaska, the Pacific, and the Far East, Shafer cast his vote against the $3.75 billions loan to Great Britain. Other votes of his in 1946 were recorded for draft extension to 1947 and against draft exemption for teen-agers.

In 1947 Shafer gave his support to a measure providing a two-term limit for the Presidency and to the anti-poll tax bill. As chairman of an armed services subcommittee on mobilization, Shafer in February 1948 sponsored "a bill to strengthen national security and common defense by providing for the maintenance of an adequate American-made rubber-producing industry, and for other purposes" (the preamble of the bill). Shafer, who during the Eightieth Congress voted in favor of the Taft-Hartley Act and against Greek-Turkish aid and extension of rent controls, opposed extension of the Marshall Plan and the Administration's long-range housing bill in the Eighty-first. In June 1949 he demanded that President Truman suspend Major General Harry H. Vaughan as his military aide pending investigation of the General's alleged "implication" in the "five-percenters" scandals. In the second session of the Eighty-first Congress he opposed the Korea-Formosa economic aid bill and favored a cut in Federal spending by $600 millions.

Just after the opening of the Eighty-second Congress (January 1951) Shafer went on record as endorsing President Hoover's proposal to make America the "Gibraltar" of the free world by declaring that "this third world war, which is so close upon us, cannot be from our viewpoint a war for survival of any particular nation other than our own." During the same Congress he opposed draft extension and universal military training, voted against the $7.5 billions foreign assistance bill, supported a $350 millions cut in economic aid to Europe, and favored both the tidelands oil bill and the

guaranteeing of "reasonable profits" under all price ceilings. Early in 1952, Shafer denounced the pending United Nations Covenant on Human Rights as "providing Utopians with an opportunity to play at socialism" and warned that "the sponsors of these schemes are playing for keeps." Later in the second session of the Eighty-second Congress (April 1952) he sponsored "with reluctance and regret" because of his "genuine friendship and esteem" for President Truman, an impeachment resolution charging, among other offenses, that in taking over the steel industry the Chief Executive had seized private property "without due process of law." Shafer was elected to the Eighty-third Congress on November 4, 1952.

Paul W. Shafer and Ila P. Mack were married October 31, 1917. His church is the Presbyterian. He belongs to Delta Sigma Epsilon fraternity and to the National Press Club in Washington; he is also an honorary member of the Veterans of Foreign Wars, an Elk and a Lion (former district governor, 1932-33), and a Thirty-second Degree Mason and past potentate of the Saladin Temple Shrine. Another membership of the legislator (who is an amateur magician) is in the Guild of Former Pipe Organ Pumpers of the Royal Order of Jesters.

References

Biographical Directory of the American Congress, 1774-1949 (1950)
Congressional Directory (1952)
Who's Who in America, 1952-53

SHAPIRO, HARRY L(IONEL) Mar. 19, 1902- Anthropologist; educator

Address: b. c/o American Museum of Natural History, Central Park West at 79th St., New York 24; h. 26 E. 91st St., New York 28.

For almost thirty years Harry L. Shapiro, an authority in the field of physical anthropology, has studied such questions as the effects of inbreeding on populations, the results of world migrations, and the influence of environment on race, in many parts of the world, including little-known islands in the Central and South Pacific, the West Indies, Hawaii, Alaska, Canada, and Europe. Since 1942 he has been curator of physical anthropology and chairman of the department of anthropology at the American Museum of Natural History in New York City, where he had previously served as an assistant curator of anthropology (1926-31) and as an associate curator (1931-41). He is also a professor of anthropology at Columbia University, an appointment he received in 1943.

Born on March 19, 1902, in Boston, Massachusetts, Harry Lionel Shapiro is one of two sons of Jacob and Rose (Clemens) Shapiro. Reared in his native city, he was graduated from the Boston Latin School in 1919; whereupon he entered Harvard University. Here he won the Detur Prize and the John Harvard Scholarship, chose crew and the glee club as his extracurricular activities, and in 1923 received his B.A. degree *magna cum laude.* During 1923-24, as a recipient of the Bishop Museum Fellowship at Yale University, Shapiro did anthropological research in the Norfolk Islands in the South Pacific, later publishing an article "Romance of the Norfolk Islanders" (*Scientific American*, September 1926). In 1925 he received his M.A. degree in anthropology from Harvard University and began working for his doctor's degree in this field. After a year (1925-26) as a tutor at Harvard and a recipient of the Thaw Fellowship, Shapiro in 1926 received his Ph.D. degree in anthropology from Harvard University.

Beginning his professional career in 1926 as assistant curator of anthropology at the American Museum of Natural History in New York City, Shapiro the following year did field work in anthropology in Santo Domingo in the West Indies. In 1929 he was appointed a consultant in physical anthropology at the Presbyterian Hospital in New York City, and in 1930 he was chosen a foreign corresponding member (a position he still holds) of the international Italian Committee, organized in Italy for the study of population problems. Spending 1929-30 on the Polynesian Islands in the Central Pacific to conduct population studies, Shapiro reported finding natives here of partly Caucasian origin and later published this in an article "Distribution of Blood Groups in Polynesia" (*American Journal of Physical Anthropology*, March 1940). In 1930 he went to Quebec to study the French population, afterward writing "French Population of Canada," which appeared in the American Museum of Natural History publication *Natural History* in July 1932.

From 1930 to 1935 Shapiro was a research professor of physical anthropology at the University of Hawaii, which had invited him to study Chinese-Hawaiian population hybrids and Japanese peoples in Hawaii. To have a genetic control, he investigated not only immigrants of these races to Hawaii but also their relatives remaining in China and Japan, and found several physical variations which demonstrated that the immigrants to Hawaii, born in China or Japan, differed from their relatives in the native country and that their children, in turn, differed from them. In his article in *Scientific Monthly* (August 1937), "Quality in Human Populations," Shapiro concluded that populations might alter their physical characterics by a change in environment. "What then," he has asked, "does race offer us for the assessment of physical quality? Nothing." He has stated that physical quality should be measured by efficiency.

In the position of associate curator of anthropology at the American Museum of Natural History, to which he was promoted in 1931, Shapiro spent the next few years studying the inhabitants of Pitcairn Island in the South Pacific, who had descended from six mutinous sailors from the H.M.S. *Bounty*. He compiled what geneticists of the United States Department of Agriculture termed "the most extensive record of human experiment in cross-matching between two races and their consequent close inbreeding through six generations" (New York *Times*, November 8, 1936). Some

HARRY L. SHAPIRO

years later, on November 23, 1941, he described this colony on the WABC-CBS radio program *This is the Life*. The results of his research conflicted with common beliefs about cousin marriages and their offspring, his evidence having shown that close inbreeding did not necessarily produce a decline in physical and mental vigor in the offspring. He discovered that accurate and complete records of marriages, births, and deaths had been kept by the islanders since almost 1790 when the mutineers settled there with the nine Polynesian women who came with them from Tahiti. "Their medical record is good," Shapiro stated, "and the islanders are robust and healthy despite frequent cousin, nephew-aunt, and niece-uncle marriages."

During 1941 Shapiro did field research in anthropology at Point Hope, Alaska, where Dr. F. G. Rainey, also on the American Museum of Natural History staff, had previously located the remains of a prehistoric town, a discovery that strengthened the theory that the first settlers in North America had come from Asia by way of the Bering Strait. Shapiro made a summer's excavation and study on the site of the prehistoric town, whose builders and culture had disappeared 2,000 years earlier, and concluded that its maximum population had approached 3,000 settlers living in about 800 buildings constructed along five avenues. He stated that the settlers, called *Ipiutak*, differed from present-day Eskimos because their implements were not the same and because they paid more attention to hunting land animals.

In 1942 Shapiro was promoted to his present post as curator of physical anthropology and chairman of the department of anthropology of the American Museum of Natural History. The following year he accepted a professorship in the department of anthropology at Columbia University, another appointment he

SHAPIRO, HARRY L.—*Continued*

retains. The results of his anthropological studies of Latin Americans were published in an article, "Ethnic Patterns in Latin America" (*The Scientific Monthly*, November 1945), based on a paper which he had read before the Conference on Inter-American Affairs at the University of Pennsylvania Museum on November 17, 1944. Pointing out that, contrary to popular belief, Latin American groups showed marked variations, he said: "In conflict with the fairly common belief that most Latin American countries are predominantly Spanish or Portuguese, a number of them are largely Indian, and there are still others where the Negro population far outweighs the European or Indian contingents."

During World War II Shapiro became a civilian consultant to the quartermaster general's office of the American Graves Registration Command, a post he still holds. In 1946, following a law enacted by Congress that all war dead must be brought back to the United States, Shapiro went to Europe, where he set up the present system of anatomical identification for difficult cases where no other means were available. His services are now requested primarily when difficult cases are brought into New York. After the war for a year (1947-48), Shapiro went to Puerto Rico to make a biological survey of the population, the results of which are now being prepared for publication.

When in 1952 Shapiro became involved in the Communist press charge that Americans had stolen ancient Peking Man bones from China in December 1941 and had brought them to the American Museum of Natural History in New York, he denied the statements made by Dr. Yang Chien-kien (New York *Times*, January 4, 1952). The bones disappeared, with several conflicting accounts of their loss, after United States marines had failed to smuggle them out of Peking, China.

In the field of scientific writing, Shapiro was formerly associate editor of the *American Journal of Physical Anthropology*, the official organ of the American Anthropological Association, and is now chairman of the scientific publications committee of the American Museum of Natural History. He himself has written numerous articles on aspects of race, population problems, and effects of world migrations. In an article, "Magic of the Mask" (New York *Times Magazine*, April 15, 1951), he stated that the mask was among the oldest items in our present culture—perhaps 50,000 years old—dating back to the Upper Paleolithic Era. "The mask," he said, "identifies, symbolizes, and clarifies. It is not meant, except secondarily, to conceal." He expressed the belief, somewhat facetiously, that modern man should make more use of the mask, especially in international relations and conferences.

In an article entitled "Man—500,000 Years from Now" (*Natural History*, November-December, 1933), he expressed his theory about the evolutionary changes modern man was undergoing. He said he believed man's brain would probably continue "to increase in size and complexity," although there were "some indications that the quality of the brain may improve without a concomitant increase in size." *Homo futurus*, he prophesied, would be taller than his present counterpart, have a more rounded head, a smaller face, and fewer and smaller teeth. He also commented that "it is conceivable, even inevitable, in the future society of which man will be a part, that the population will be mated as carefully as the animal breeder now controls his stock."

Shapiro has written two books. The first, *Heritage of the Bounty*, a story of Pitcairn Island in the South Pacific through six generations, appeared in 1936 and was called "a fascinating volume of considerable scientific value but entirely free from pedantry and dullness" (*Manchester Guardian*, July 28, 1936). The *Saturday Review of Literature* (August 15, 1936) termed it "a complete and scholarly book, with the added merit of possessing more warmth and human insight than some less scientific works on the subject." Three years later came the publication of Shapiro's *Migration and Environment* (1939), a study of the physical characteristics of the Japanese immigrants to Hawaii and the effects of environment on their descendants. About this book the *American Anthropologist* reviewer (October 1939) said: "This is an important piece of work and it has been carefully and conscientiously carried out." The critic in the *Geographical Review* (July 1939) commented: "This is not an easy work to read, but the author is an honest scholar and, within limits, an exceptional sociological and geographical craftsman."

For the National Research Council Shapiro served in 1950 on the panel of appraisers of the *Handbook on Biological Data*, in 1948-49 on its Pacific committee of anthropological sciences, and during 1947 and 1934-36 on its fellowships board. In 1947 he was appointed a member of the board of directors of the Association of American Indian Affairs. For the year 1939 Shapiro was chairman of the anthropological section of the New York Academy of Science. Since 1927 he has been an associate of the Bishop Museum in Honolulu. Organizations of which Shapiro is a member include the National Academy of Sciences, the American Anthropological Association (president 1948), the American Association of Physical Anthropologists (secretary 1935-39; vice-president 1941-42), the American Ethnological Society (president 1942-43), the American Association for the Advancement of Science, the American Eugenics Society, the American Society of Human Genetics, and UNESCO's Special Committee on Race and Culture. His club is the Harvard Club of New York City.

On June 26, 1938, Shapiro married Janice Sandler, an artist; their children are Thomas Clemens, Harriet Rose, and James Ernest. Shapiro is six feet two inches tall, weighs 180 pounds, and has blue eyes and brown hair. He enjoys reading, music, gardening, and country life generally.

References

American Men of Science (1949)
Directory of American Scholars (1951)
International Dictionary of Anthropologists (1950)
Who's Who in America, 1952-53
Who's Who in New York (1947)
World Biography (1948)

SHAPLEY, HARLOW (shăp' lē) Nov. 2, 1885- Astronomer; educator
Address b. c/o Department of Astronomy, Harvard University, Cambridge 38, Mass.

NOTE: This biography supersedes the article which appeared in *Current Biography* in 1941.

Known particularly for his investigation in the fields of Cepheid variables and globular clusters which led to a new understanding of the structure of the universe, Harlow Shapley is said by astronomer Otto Struve to have "created a revolution in scientific thought . . . analogous to the revolution set off by Copernicus." For thirty years, beginning in 1921, Shapley was professor of astronomy at Harvard University, director of the Harvard College Observatory, and supervisor of observatories in Cambridge and Oak Ridge, Massachusetts, and in New Mexico, Colorado, and South Africa. It was announced in November 1951 that he would retire the following fall from his administrative duties to give his full time to research and teaching. The astronomer is well known as an advocate of international cooperation in politics, science, and culture.

Born in Nashville, Missouri, on November 2, 1885, Harlow Shapley is the son of Willis Harlow Shapley, a teacher who died during his son's boyhood, and Sarah (Stowell) Shapley, who was descended from early settlers in Massachusetts. His younger brother John Shapley, author and educator, is associate director of the Iranian Institute in New York City. During his school days at Carthage Academy, the boy earned money running errands, and after graduation he became a reporter for the Chanute (Kansas) *Daily Sun* to save money for a college education. By the time young Shapley entered the University of Missouri as a twenty-year-old freshman, he had risen to be the city editor.

While a student at the University of Missouri Shapley wrote a paper entitled "Astronomy in Horace with Forty-six References to His Works," which was published in *Popular Astronomy*. During his sophomore year he was appointed assistant to the Laws Observatory director, F. H. Seares. He received his B.A. degree from Missouri in 1910 and his M.A. degree in 1911. The "high precision" of Shapley's photographs of eclipsing variable stars having attracted the attention of the director of the Princeton Observatory, Henry Norris Russell, in 1912 the Missourian was awarded a Princeton fellowship. Working with Russell, Shapley completed requirements for his Ph.D. degree within a year. His doctoral dissertation, a 176-page discussion of the orbits and dimensions of ninety eclipsing binary stars, was evaluated by astronomer Otto Struve as "the most significant single contribution toward our understanding of the physical characteristics of very close double stars."

Shortly after his marriage on April 15, 1914, to Martha Betz, a student of astronomy and a mathematician, Shapley became a staff astronomer at the Mount Wilson Observatory in California. The couple collaborated on *A Study of the Light Curve of XX Cygni*. During his seven years (1914-21) at Mount Wilson, Harlow Shapley applied himself to the study of Cepheid variables, stars whose periodic changes in brightness cannot be attributed to eclipses. He established that there are changes in their temperatures, spectra, and surfaces, and concluded in 1914 that they were actually pulsating. Shapley also showed that the heavier and brighter Cepheids had longer pulsation periods, a relationship which, according to George Gamow, played a very important role in stellar astronomy. This work led the discoverer to a new and superior method of determining stellar distances by measuring the period and apparent brightness of a Cepheid, thus enabling determination of distance down to the very limit of detectability of the Cepheid variable. Shapley demonstrated that our galactic system, the Milky Way, was some thousand times larger than had previously been supposed—he estimated its over-all size at 200,000 light-years (light travels six trillion miles in one year) and placed its center at a spot in Sagittarius, now known by astronomers as Shapley Center. Earth, he showed, was on the outer fringe of the system. Applying his method to the spiral nebulae (clouds of stardust), Shapley arrived at some 100 million light-years as the greatest diameter of the universe. New observations some years later, as reported by Shapley in September 1952, indicated that the diameter of the Milky Way was "150,000 light years, with a central, comparatively hard core, including the earth, of 100,000 light years" (in the words of the New York *Herald Tribune*, September 9, 1952).

Investigating the transparency of space and the velocity of light—essential to determining stellar distances—Shapley found that there was no refraction of light in space. Nineteen papers written by Shapley in his first two years at Mount Wilson were gathered into *Studies Based on the Colors and Magnitudes in Stellar Clusters*. In 1918 he showed that our sun was a star in such a cluster. Happening to notice that ants moved fastest on the hottest days, the astronomer was led also to investigate ant physiology and to work out a published theory on the relation of ant speed to temperature. (Shapley is in 1952 president of Worcester Foundation for Experimental Biology and retains membership in other biological and botanical societies.)

In 1921, at the age of thirty-six, Harlow Shapley was appointed to succeed E. C. Pickering as director of the Harvard College Observatory and Paine Professor of Practical Astronomy. This observatory included stations in Massachusetts, Colorado, New Mexico, and

HARLOW SHAPLEY

Bloemfontein, South Africa. Shapley continued his predecessor's policy of concentrating on large-scale projects, such as the classification of hundreds of thousands of stellar spectra (which reveal the chemical composition of the stars) and the cataloguing of external galaxies, part of a vast census of some 500,000 heavenly bodies. The director also encouraged individual research in astronomy and astrophysics: in the opinion of Struve, "as an administrator, he has set a new high in the quantity and quality of the research work of his observatories."

Dr. Shapley's early papers appeared in the *Astrophysical Journal*; in recent years his work has been published mainly in the *National Academy of Science Proceedings*, in *Science*, and in *Nature*. Of his continuing stream of papers under the title *Galactic and Extragalactic Studies*, the first ten were collected into one volume in 1940. Apart from research papers and magazine articles, Shapley has written and edited a number of books. With H. E. Howarth he prepared in 1929 *Source Book in Astronomy* (containing excerpts from the writings of scientists from Copernicus to G. H. Darwin), on which a reviewer for *World Tomorrow* commented, "Will prove delightful and informative—an unbeatable combination." Other books are *Star Clusters* (1930) and *Flights from Chaos; A Survey of Material Systems from Atoms to Galaxies* (1930). Assisted by Samuel Rapport and Helen Wright, he edited *Treasury of Science* (1943). The critic for the *New Yorker* found this anthology "a brilliant compilation of fascinating reading, but it is not a coherent or logically organized course in science and should not pretend to be. It is merely a first rate collection of interesting and, in most cases, very competently written expository essays on half a hundred topics." He also edited *Readings in Physical Sciences* (1948).

Since 1920 Shapley, who has been called "a witty, articulate, sometimes impassioned speaker," has done much lecturing in the United States and other countries: he was the Hale lecturer before the National Academy of Sciences in 1920, exchange lecturer at Belgian universities in 1926, Halley lecturer at Oxford University in 1928, and Darwin lecturer before the Royal Astronomical Society in 1934. The many offices he holds in scientific associations have required him to travel abroad frequently and he has helped set up observatories and libraries in foreign countries, especially in Mexico and India.

Since the outbreak of World War II (in which he was connected with the Office of Scientific Research and Development), Shapley has devoted much time to public affairs, taking the lead among American scientists in organizing the United Nations Educational, Scientific and Cultural Organization. Shapley made news in another way in 1944, when his letter criticizing radio commercials was sent to all NBC stations by the network president. In 1945 he was one of the few Americans permitted to visit Russia (for the Soviet Academy of Science Jubilee). Shapley retained a more favorable attitude toward the Soviet Union than became popular in the light of postwar developments and in 1947 attacked the Truman Doctrine of strengthening Greece and Turkey against communism as being "commercial gravy for the few at the potential expense of the blood of the many" (quoted in the New York *Times*, April 11, 1947). The previous November, subpoenaed by the House Un-American Activities Committee for questioning about the election activities of the Independent Citizens Committee of the Arts, Sciences, and Professions, he had clashed with Congressman Rankin during a closed-door cross-examination. A month later, when Shapley was elected president of the American Association for the Advancement of Science for 1947, the election was regarded by many as a gesture affirming the scientists' faith in Shapley.

Professor Shapley was chairman of the National Council of the Arts, Sciences, and Professions, the political group which in March 1949 held at the Waldorf-Astoria an international Cultural and Scientific Conference for World Peace, denounced by the State Department as a sounding-board for Communist propaganda. Shapley denied that charge and in his address criticized the tactics of both sides in the East-West conflict. In 1950 he was one of five persons named as Communists by Senator McCarthy who were completely exonerated by a vote of the Tydings Senate foreign relations subcommittee. Having reached the compulsory retirement age for Harvard administrators, sixty-six, Shapley announced in November 1951 that he would retire the following fall as observatory director, but would continue his research and teaching.

An honorary national academician of twelve foreign countries, Shapley is also trustee of institutions ranging from Princeton University and Massachusetts Institute of Technology to a girls' school in Damascus and research foundations in India and Central Africa. He has held a number of presidencies and chairmanships, including those of the American Academy of Arts and Sciences (1939-44), Sigma Xi, Astronomical League, Science Service (which publishes *Science News Letter*), Science Clubs of America, World Wide Broadcasting Foundation, National Science Fund, Nebular Commission (1932-46), International Observatory Commission, and Clusters Commission. He has been a member of the National Academy of the Natural Research Council and vice-president of the American Philosophical Society. Among the honors conferred on the astronomer are the Draper Medal of the National Academy of Sciences (1926), a medal from the Society of Arts and Sciences (1931), a gold medal from the Royal Astronomical Society, the Rumford Medal of the Association of Arts and Sciences (1933), the Janssen Prix from the Astronomical Society of France (1933), the Bruce Medal of the Pacific Astronomical Society (1939), the Pope Pius XI Prize (1941), medals from two scientific societies in India (1947), and two Mexican decorations. Shapley also holds honorary doctorates from some fourteen universities, among them, the universities of Copenhagen, Delhi, Hawaii, and Michoacan (Mexico).

The blue-eyed, sandy-haired astronomer and his wife, Martha Betz Shapley, have a daughter, Mildred Louise, and four sons, Willis Harlow, Alan Horace, Lloyd Stowell, and Carl Betz. Shapley's clubs are the Century and Harvard in New York and the St. Botolph, Saturday, and Examiner in Boston. Carlton Brown in *Science Illustrated* has described him as "a tireless practitioner of the internationalism he preaches." In discussing religion Shapley has said, "Most astronomers are agnostics. . . . Scientists cannot have faith. Ours is a perpetual inquiry; any acceptance of faith—in a scientific or a metaphysical or an aesthetic sense—brings inquiry to a halt."

References

Am Mag 117:46 Je '34 por
Mentor 9:30 O '21
Nature 133:694 My 5 '34
Newsweek 29:56 Ja 20 '47
Pop Sci 138:104 Ap '41
Sat R Lit 13:10 Ja 18 '36
Science 54:486 N 18 '21; 105:163 F 14 '47
Science Illus 4:40 Ja '49
Sci Mo 64:189 Mr '47
Time 26:28 Jl 29 '35 pors
American Men of Science (1949)
Fisher, D. F. American Portraits (1946)
International Who's Who, 1952
Macpherson, H. C. Makers of Astronomy (1933)
National Cyclopædia of American Biography Current vol C (1930)
Who's Who, 1952
Who's Who in America, 1952-53
Who's Who in American Education, 1947-48
World Biography (1948)

SHAY, EDITH Nov. 29, 1894- Author
SHAY, FRANK Apr. 8, 1888- Author
Address: b. c/o Houghton Mifflin Company, 2 Park St., Boston 7, Mass.; h. Mill Hill Rd., Wellfleet, Mass.

Reprinted from the *Wilson Library Bulletin*, June 1952.

Cape Cod has been the scene of more literary and artistic activity than perhaps any other area its size in the United States. Prominent among those who came as summer visitors but who stayed to become all-year-rounders ("livias," as the Cape Cod natives call them, possibly a corruption of *live-heres*), is the writing team of Edith and Frank Shay. Cape Cod, specifically Provincetown, was the scene of their marriage in 1930 and ever since has served as inspiration, source of material for their work and, simply, as home.

EDITH SHAY
FRANK SHAY

In 1951 they paid their tribute to their adopted region by collaborating on *Sand in Their Shoes: A Cape Cod Reader,* an anthology of writings on the Cape ranging from an eyewitness description written in 1602 to the comments of Alexander Woollcott. Harry Sylvester, writing in the New York *Times,* found the book "extraordinarily rich," while H. B. Ellis of the *Christian Science Monitor* commented enthusiastically, "To those who truly have the Cape's 'sand in their shoes' . . . this book will be a compendium of pleasure."

Mrs. Shay was born Edith Foley in Manistique, Michigan, November 29, 1894, the daughter of Reuben Pratt Foley and Frances Edith (Jones) Foley. Shortly after her birth, her parents moved to Winter Park, Florida, where she grew up and was educated. Summers were spent in Charlevoix, Michigan. "Perhaps because both places were so lovely," Mrs. Shay writes, "I've always taken . . . great pleasure in the beauty of the visible world."

In 1915 Edith Foley took her B.A. degree at Wellesley, where she had majored in English and philosophy, edited the Wellesley magazine, and won a Durante scholarship. Always

SHAY, EDITH, AND SHAY, FRANK
—Continued

interested in writing, she joined the staff of McClurg's in Chicago, turning out advertising copy and selling books. Before long she was busy writing her own stories and books. These include about thirty pieces of light fiction published in pulps and slicks under a pseudonym which she prefers to keep secret; several pieces published in *The New Yorker* under the name Edith Shay; *Collecting Hooked Rugs* (1927), in collaboration with Elizabeth Waugh; and in collaboration with her close friend, the late Katharine Smith Dos Passos, *The Private Adventures of Captain Shaw* (1945), a lively story of the adventures of a young New England skipper in France at the height of the Reign of Terror. Several reviewers pointed out that the authors were most successful in their portrait of eighteenth century Cape Cod, the *New Yorker* commenting, "If Jane Austen had written about Cape Codders, this is surely the way she would have done it." C. V. Terry in the New York *Times* was somewhat less impressed: "Their pictures of Cape Cod . . . are truly lovely, but their book is cluttered with the oddments of history, and they lack the storyteller's skill to dramatize the material." The novel was a Book League of America selection for 1945.

Mrs. Shay relaxes at swimming, playing poker, and primarily reading. Her tastes range widely from Dostoevsky and Tolstoy through Trollope, Twain, Dos Passos, Hemingway, and Faulkner. Lately she has found herself preferring biography to fiction, liking "the old-fashioned biographies which begin, 'On November eight, a lowering day in 1744, there was born in the old manse at . . . .'"

The husband-partner in this writing team, Frank Shay, was born in East Orange, New Jersey, April 8, 1888. He traces his ancestry back to the famous Daniel who in 1786-87 led Shay's rebellion of the farmers against the oppressions of maritime Massachusetts. Frank Shay's education took the form of practical experience in the bookselling field. He left school at fourteen, but he was already a veteran bookseller, having started at the age of twelve in second-hand paper westerns, Nick Carters, and the like. In 1912 he was manager of Schulte's Book Store in New York and in 1915 he transferred to the famous Washington Square Book Shop, "one of the city's most stimulating stores." Settled thus in the heart of Greenwich Village during the days of its liveliest past, Shay played an active part in Village activities. In his bookshop the Washington Square Players, later to develop into the Theatre Guild, were started and the Provincetown Players made their New York debut.

After a period of military service in World War I, Shay returned to New York to open Frank Shay's Book Shop—"far more distinguished for its clientele than for its sales." Meanwhile, and all during his career as a bookseller, he conducted small publishing ventures, introducing Eugene O'Neill, Susan Glaspell, and Edna St. Vincent Millay to the reading public.

Since 1920, when Shay's first book, *The Bibliography of Walt Whitman* was published, he has been writing and editing steadily. His best-known works include: *Here's Audacity! Tales of American Legendary Heroes* (1930), *Incredible Pizarro, Conqueror of Peru* (1931), *Judge Lynch: His First Hundred Years* (1936), *The Best Men Are Cooks* (1941), *American Sea Songs and Chanteys from the Days of Iron Men and Wooden Ships* (1948), and *A Sailor's Treasury* (1951).

The Shays, both Democrats, make their home in Wellfleet, Massachusetts, where they have, it is said, "been instrumental in attracting a group of colonists so prominent in artistic and literary circles that it has become a sandy Parnassus."

SHELLY, WARNER S(WOYER) May 22, 1901- Advertising agency executive
Address: b. c/o N. W. Ayer & Son, Inc., West Washington Sq., Philadelphia 6, Pa.; h. Farnum St., Beverly, N.J.

On October 19, 1951, Warner S. Shelley was elected the fourth president of N. W. Ayer & Son, Inc., the oldest and one of the largest advertising agencies in the United States. The post came to him after he had been with the agency for twenty-nine years as production man, service representative, and, for fourteen of those years, as a vice-president. Before joining Ayer's in 1923, Shelly had studied engineering and law and had worked in the Hudson Tubes on engineering maintenance.

The son of Oswin W. Shelly and Anne Elizabeth (Swoyer) Shelly, Warner Swoyer Shelly was born May 22, 1901, in Catskill, New York. Since his father's occupation as an architect and contractor kept the family moving frequently from one city to another, the boy attended schools in Paterson and Hoboken (New Jersey), in New York City, and in Philadelphia. In 1918 he was graduated from the Stevens School (in Hoboken), which he had attended for college preparatory studies in engineering. After spending several months in the Students' Army Training Corps in 1918, Shelly entered the University of Pennsylvania, where for two years he studied engineering with the intention of becoming an aeronautical engineer. He has told that extracurricular activities and work outside of school, such as waiting on table at a fraternity house and tending furnaces, occupied more of his time than studying. He played freshman football in 1918, varsity lacrosse in 1919 and 1920, and was a member of the Mask and Wig Club and Delta Tau Delta. As a result of all these activities, according to an article on Shelly in the December 1951 issue of *Advertising Agency*, he was dismissed from college because of low grades in his sophomore year in the spring of 1920.

Shelly decided, after this experience at the University of Pennsylvania, that a large part of his academic troubles had been caused by a lack of interest in engineering. More drawn to the business field, he decided to study law because he felt that this was a good point from which to survey the commercial world as a whole. During his first two years in college, however, his father had lost money, so that young Shelly could no longer count on family help in continuing his education. Having therefore to earn some money for about a year before entering law school, he did surveying work at Camp Eustis, Virginia, during the summer of 1920, and after that in an engineering assignment for the Hudson and Manhattan Railroad Company in the Hudson Tubes in New York City. He began as an inspector in the river, checking against possible damage to the tunnel walls from the outside. Later he was promoted to chief of a tunnel crew doing maintenance work inside the tunnels.

Deciding in 1921 to resume college studies, Shelly enrolled this time at Fordham University in New York City, where he was permitted to enter law school without a college degree. At the same time he continued his job in the Hudson tunnels, at which he worked mostly at night. During the second year of the three-year law course, he became acquainted with the N. W. Ayer & Son organization through a friend from the University of Pennsylvania who was employed by the agency. When Shelly was offered a position he accepted it and discontinued his law studies. The position with Ayer's paid less than he was earning in the tunnels, but, said Shelly, as quoted by *Advertising Agency*, "I decided that future prospects must be good if Ayer thought it was offering me something better than I already had."

For his first three months with the agency, beginning May 21, 1923, Shelly worked in the registry section checking newspaper insertions and was then transferred to the business department, from which several young men employed there at the time have risen to important positions in advertising. At the end of two years in that department, where he had his first experience as a production man, he was assigned as a service representative to both the Philadelphia and New York offices to handle dealings with clients, a facet of advertising with which Shelly has been chiefly concerned ever since. Appointed a vice-president of N. W. Ayer & Son in 1938, he was put in charge of the client service department in New York City and in 1940 was given various executive responsibilities in New York and Philadelphia. In the summer of 1951 he was elected to the board of directors, just a few months before his election on October 23, 1951, to the presidency of the company. When he became president his predecessor, H. A. Batten, was elected chairman of the board of directors and chief executive officer.

When N. W. Ayer & Son was founded in 1869, advertising men were little more than newspaper space peddlers, and Ayer was one of the early innovators in the business. The agency introduced the idea of market research, employed the first full-time copywriter and the first art director, and handled the first sponsored radio and television broadcasts. Ayer's is prominent in business advertising, prepares about 50 per cent of the advertising placed by

WARNER S. SHELLY

private schools and camps, and for a number of years before, during, and after World War II handled the United States Army and Air Force recruiting advertisements. The firm also publishes *Ayer's Directory of Newspapers and Periodicals*, a standard reference work. With the growth in advertising functions the company has also grown physically until at the present time it has offices in Philadelphia, New York, Boston, Chicago, Detroit, San Francisco, Hollywood, and Honolulu.

In recent years Shelly has spent much of his time traveling between these offices and visiting clients, some as far away as De Beers Consolidated Mines, Ltd., in South Africa. During 1951 alone his travels totaled 50,000 miles by plane. As president of Ayer he plans to continue making business trips and his interest in the problems of the client. He plans, too, to continue handling matters with the same "personal touch" as in the past: he answers his own telephone and is accessible to any employee who wishes to see him. In an article in *Printers' Ink* (November 2, 1951) he was quoted: "If our porter has a problem and thinks I'm the only one who can solve it for him, then I make it my business to find time to discuss it with him."

Shelly married Katharine Seckel in 1931. His church affiliation is Episcopal and his political stand is independent. His principal recreation, besides music, is golf: in 1951 he was club champion of the Pine Valley Golf Club in Pine Valley, New Jersey, of which he is also a director. Other clubs to which he belongs are the Racquet Club in Philadelphia, and the Riverton Country Club in Riverton, New Jersey.

References

Adv Age 22:53 D 3 '51
Adv Agency 44:61 D '51
Printers' Ink 237:108 N 2 '51

SHEPHERD, LEMUEL C(ORNICK), JR. Feb. 10, 1896- United States Marine officer

Address: b. Headquarters, United States Marine Corps, Department of the Navy, Washington 25, D.C.

For the years 1952-55 the United States Marine Corps will be under the command of General Lemuel C. Shepherd, the twentieth commandant of the "Leathernecks," to succeed General Clifton B. Cates. In recognition of his record in World War I and World War II, as well as his service in China and Haiti between the wars, General Shepherd has received some thirty decorations from the United States and other governments.

The only son of Lemuel Cornick Shepherd (a physician) and Emma Lucretia (Cartwright) Shepherd (who also had two daughters), Lemuel Cornick Shepherd, Jr., was born February 10, 1896, in Norfolk, Virginia, a State in which his family had long been settled. He was educated at the Norfolk Academy and at the Virginia Military Institute in Lexington. Shortly after graduation from the latter with a B.S. degree, Shepherd was commissioned a second lieutenant in the United States Marine Corps on April 11, 1917, and reported for duty next month, May 19, at the Marine Barracks in Port Royal, South Carolina. Sent to France on combat duty the following month, he was wounded three times in action: twice at Belleau Wood in 1918 during the Aisne-Marne defensive of the Fifth Marine Regiment of Chateau Thierry and with the same regiment in October of that year in the Meuse-Argonne offensive. With the Navy Cross which he received for his work at Belleau Wood came this citation: "He declined medical treatment after being wounded and continued courageously to lead his men." Shepherd's war service also included fighting in the St. Mihiel offensive and in the Toulon-Troyons defensive sector as well as duty, until July 1919, with the Army of Occupation in Germany. In the course of the two succeeding years he returned to Europe twice for temporary tours of duty in France to aid in the drafting of relief maps of World War I battlefields.

While holding the post of aide-de-camp to the Commandant of the Marine Corps in 1920-22, Shepherd was also junior aide-de-camp to President Harding at the White House. After a period of temporary duty in Rio de Janeiro at the Brazilian Exposition while serving in the U.S.S. *Nevada*, he was assigned to command the Marine detachment of the U.S.S. *Idaho*, a post which he held until 1925. His succeeding command was of the Sea School Detachment at the Marine Barracks in Norfolk, Virginia. In 1927 he returned to foreign duty as regimental adjutant of the Fourth Marines, attached to the Third Marine Brigade in China, with which he remained for two years before returning to the United States in March 1929. The fall of that year found him at the Marine Corps Schools taking the field officers' course. Upon graduating in 1930 Shepherd joined the Gendarmerie d'Haiti at

Dartiguenave Barracks for four years of service as the district and department commander. Back in Washington by 1934, he became the executive officer and registrar of the Marine Corps Institute.

When Shepherd graduated in May 1937 from the Naval War College at Newport, Rhode Island, where he had been studying since 1936, he took over the command of the second battalion of the Fifth Marine Regiment, part of the First Marine Brigade assigned to the Fleet Marine Force. Posted to the Marine Corps Schools at Quantico, Virginia, in June 1939, Shepherd was director of the correspondence school, chief of the operations section, in charge of the candidates class, assistant commandant and commandant of the Marine Corps Schools. *Time* (November 19, 1951) reported that he was also commanding officer at one time of the Marine Guard to President Roosevelt at Warm Springs, Georgia. Shepherd's promotions were as follows: first lieutenant (August 1917), captain (July 1918), major (April 1932), lieutenant colonel (July 1935), colonel (August 1940), brigadier general (July 1943), major general (September 1944), Lieutenant General (June 1950), and General (January 1952).

Four months after the United States entered World War II, in March 1942 Shepherd was placed in command of the Ninth Marine Regiment, which joined the Third Marine Division in the Pacific (January 1943). As assistant division commander of the First Marine Division, he went into action with that division through the Cape Gloucester operation on New Britain from December 1943 until March 1944. For this he was awarded the Legion of Merit decoration. He was again in action with his men, securing a beachhead in the first few hours of operation during the July and August 1944 invasion of Guam, where he commanded the First Provisional Marine Brigade. The Distinguished Service Medal was given him for his part in this action. From the brigade General Shepherd subsequently organized the Sixth Marine Division, training it at Guadalcanal. Securing the Yontan airfield on Okinawa in one day—two days ahead of schedule—Shepherd's Sixth Division was able to join the street fighting to wipe out opposition in Naha, the capital. From Okinawa (April-June 1945) the Sixth was sent to China in October 1945, where Shepherd, acting in behalf of Generalissimo Chiang Kai-shek, received the surrender of Japanese forces in the Tsingtao area.

His command of the Sixth having ended in December 1945, Major General Shepherd in March 1946 took over the Troop Training Command of the amphibious forces of the Atlantic fleet, at Little Creek, Virginia. That October, at the twenty-third annual convention of the Marine Corps League in Atlantic City, Shepherd pleaded for the maintenance of sufficient armed forces in peacetime. On November 1, 1946, he entered the post of assistant to the commandant of the Marine Corps and Chief of Staff at the headquarters of the Marine Corps, where he remained until becoming commandant, in April 1948, of the Marine Corps Schools at Quantico.

During June of 1950 Major General Shepherd was appointed commanding general of the fleet Marine force of the Pacific, based at Pearl Harbor, an assignment which put him in line for advancement to the rank of lieutenant general. The Korean War, in which his forces had an early part, took him to Korea a number of times. During the Inchon landing he was a member of General MacArthur's personal staff. In September of 1950 he was flown by helicopter to the liberation of Kimpo Airfield in Korea (subsequently, in May 1951, he was to praise the use of helicopters for transportation of troops to combat areas). During the December 1950 retreat of the Marines from the Changjin Reservoir area, Shepherd lauded their spirit and the efficiency of the Marine air coverage. He was, too, said Hanson W. Baldwin of the New York *Times*, in August 1951, one of the high-ranking officers to feel concern about interservice rivalries.

Upon the expiration of the term of office of General Clifton B. Cates, Lieutenant General Shepherd was named by the President to take over on January 1, 1952, as the Commandant of the Marine Corps. Since the Marine Corps is allowed only one full four-star general, Shepherd will hold that rank during his four-year term of office. Established by Act of Congress in 1775, the Marine Corps is an integral part of the Naval Establishment. The National Security Act of 1947 confirmed its position as a service and also assigned as its mission to provide land, combat, and service forces of combined arms with supporting aviation; to serve with the fleet in seizure or defense of advanced naval bases; to develop amphibious operations in cooperation with the Army and Air Forces; to provide security and police detachments for the protection of naval property; and to perform any other duties designated by the President (*Americana Annual*). Shepherd, as commandant, states the *United States Government Organization Manual,* will be "charged with and is responsible for the procurement, discharge, education, training, discipline, and distribution of the officers and enlisted personnel of the Marine Corps, including the Reserve." Under his supervision are the divisions of administration, plans and policies, public information, aviation, reserve, recruiting and inspection, and the departments of personnel and supply. Shepherd, who took the oath of office on December 21, 1951, said soon after his appointment that he would continue the effort to have a Marine officer named to the Joint Chief of Staff. On June 28, 1952, President Truman signed a bill which, in the words of the New York *Times,* gave "the United States Marines three-divisional organization and coequal status for the corps commandant with the other Joint Chiefs of Staff where corps interests are directly concerned," thus abolishing the Marine Corps dependency upon the Navy.

Among the thirty-odd decorations and medals General Shepherd has received are the Distinguished Service Cross (Army), and an Oak Leaf Cluster in lieu of a second Legion of Merit. For his World War I service he was

GEN. LEMUEL C. SHEPHERD, JR.

awarded the Purple Heart with two Oak Leaf Clusters, the World War I Victory Medal with four bronze stars and defensive sector clasp, the Silver Star with one Oak Leaf Cluster, and the Occupation of Germany medal. Between the two world wars he was awarded the Expeditionary Medal with one bronze star (for his service in China and Haiti), the Yangtze Service Medal, the American Defense Medal, the American Campaign medal. For his World War II achievements Shepherd was given the Bronze Star and a Presidential Unit Citation with one bronze star (for Okinawa), the Navy Unit Commendation with one bronze star (Guam and Cape Gloucester), the Asiatic-Pacific Campaign medal with four bronze stars, the China Service Medal, the World War II Victory Medal, and the Navy Occupation Medal. Foreign decorations which have been awarded to Shepherd are the Croix de Guerre with Gilt Star and Fourragère (France), the Silver Medal for Bravery (Montenegro), the Order of Honor and Merit, and the Distinguished Service Medal (Haiti), the Order of Cloud and Banner, second grade (China), the Bronze plaque with special commemorative diploma (Brazil).

Married to Virginia Tunstall Driver on December 30, 1922, Shepherd is the father of two sons, Lemuel C. 3d and Wilson Elliott Driver, both Marine Corps officers, and a daughter, Virginia Cartwright (Mrs. James B. Ord). Since Shepherd sometimes works 18 hours a day, his wife, reported *Pathfinder,* once "had an orderly set an alarm clock to remind him when to eat." The General (who is an Episcopalian) installed a church bell recaptured from the Japanese in World War II in a Guam military cemetery "in memory" (as quoted by the New York *Times*) "of the men of all faiths who gave their lives" there. Five feet nine inches tall and weighing about 160 pounds, General Shepherd is frequently called

SHEPHERD, LEMUEL C., JR.—*Continued*
athletic-looking. A former polo player, he
continues riding and jumping horses, and occasional fox hunting. Swimming is another recreation he enjoys, as well as underwater spear-
fishing.

References

N Y Herald Tribune p11 N 6 '51 por
N Y Times p7 N 6 '51 por
N Y World-Telegram p15 N 10 '51 por
Pathfinder 58:21 N 28 '51 por
Time 58:25 N 19 '51 por
Washington (D.C.) Post p1 N 6 '51;
p10S N 11 '51; p7B D 23 '51 por
Who's Who in America, 1950-51
Who's Who in the South and Southwest
(1950)
World Biography (1948)

SHORT, JOSEPH (HUDSON, JR.) Feb.
11, 1904—Sept. 18, 1952 White House press
secretary; began newspaper career in 1925 as
reporter on Jackson (Mississippi) *Daily News;*
Washington correspondent for nineteen years
for Associated Press (1931-41), Chicago *Sun*
(1941-43), Baltimore *Sun* (1943-50); president
of National Press Club (1948); appointed December 1950 to succeed Charles G. Ross as
President Truman's press secretary; life-long
Democrat who vigorously defended White
House policies. See *Current Biography,* 1951.

Obituary

N Y Times p1+ S 19 '52

SHULMAN, HARRY (shōōl'măn) Mar. 14,
1903- Labor-management arbitrator; college
professor

Address: b. c/o Yale University Law School,
New Haven, Conn.; h. 1100 Ridge Rd., Hamden, Conn.

As chairman of the United States Wage
Stabilization Board's special panel for the 1951-
52 steel dispute, Harry Shulman is a key figure
in the determination of wages for industrial
workers. Active in labor-management disputes
since 1942, when he served as the chairman of
a War Labor Board panel, Shulman became
in 1943 the permanent arbitrator for the Ford
Motor Company, having been sought for the
post by the United Automobile Workers (CIO)
and the Ford company as a result of his accomplishments in earlier negotiations between the
two groups. Shulman, who joined the law faculty at Yale University in 1930, has held the
chair of Sterling Professor of Law since 1940.

Born in Krugloye, Russia, on March 14,
1903, Harry Shulman is the son of Simon and
Tille (Klebanoff) Shulman. His father died
shortly after the family went to Providence,
Rhode Island, in 1912, and the nine-year-old
Harry, together with two brothers and two
sisters, had to earn money for the family's
support; the boy's contribution came from selling newspapers, which he continued to do
through his college undergraduate years. In

his first year (1920-21) at Brown University
Shulman became a naturalized American citizen. At Brown he was elected to Phi Beta
Kappa, received awards for debating and essay
writing, and completed his course requirements
in three years to graduate with a B.A. degree
in 1923. He earned his way through Harvard
Law School by washing dishes and tutoring,
acquiring the LL.B. degree in 1926. Aided by
a fellowship, he spent another year at Harvard,
to become Doctor of Juridical Science. After
practicing law in 1928 and 1929 with a small
Wall Street concern, Shulman received a 1929-
30 appointment as law clerk to Justice Louis
D. Brandeis of the United States Supreme
Court.

Shulman became an instructor at Yale University Law School in 1930, rising to assistant
professor in 1931, associate professor in 1933,
and to a full professor in 1937. He occupied
the chair of Lines Professor of Law in 1939
and in the following year became Sterling Pro-
fesor of Law at Yale. During the 1951-52
semester he taught courses in torts and labor
law and led a seminar on labor relations.

While associate professor at Yale, Harry
Shulman served from 1934 to 1936 as counsel for the United States Railroad Retirement
Board. During the years 1937-39 he was a
reporter for the American Law Institute Re-
statement of Torts (Unfair Competition and
Labor Disputes); in 1940 and 1941 he was a
member of the United States Attorney General's committee on administrative procedure;
and in 1941 and 1942 he was a member of the
United States Enemy Alien Hearing Board
for Connecticut.

As the chairman of a War Labor Board
panel, Shulman in 1942 handled negotiations for
a second contract between Henry Ford and the
United Automobile Workers. Both company
and union chose him in 1943 as permanent
arbitrator. He early earned the reputation of
dealing severely with both the company and
workers. Shortly after becoming "umpire" he
concluded that the Ford Motor Company expected too high a degree of perfection from its
employees and that it had failed to take into
account the grave personal consequences of
discharging workers; on the other hand he
also condemned one of the U.A.W. stoppages
as "a flagrant violation of the contract . . .
totally irresponsible" and told the union to exercise more discipline. In disputes over job clas-
sifications and overtime, his decisions resulted
in Ford's making additional annual payments
of millions of dollars. On another occasion, he
ruled that Ford was not required to pay for the
twenty-minute lunch period of 70,000 employees.
A dispute that was given much publicity was
known as "The Case of the Woman in the
Bright Red Slacks": it involved a Ford worker
who was docked a half-hour's pay because her
attire reportedly distracted the men. Dr.
Shulman decided that the money had to be paid
to her.

As umpire at Ford, Harry Shulman is the
last resort for many kinds of grievances which
have not been settled by the regular worker-
management dispute machinery. According to

Fortune, his opinions are "characterized by such reasonableness and understanding that they almost constitute a new sort of industrial common law." Shulman's task is actually to harmonize the differences of viewpoint before they become disputes. His aim, he has stated, is the establishment of permanent friendly relations between company and union: "I try to teach—to change attitudes rather than merely decide each individual case. Each dispute is transitory; it's what's in the mind of the parties that lasts." Shulman was also chosen as conciliator in 1944 between Bendix Products Division and the U.A.W., as well as between Borg Warner, Warner Gear Division, and the U.A.W.; in 1946 he was the arbitrator between Singer the Sewing Machine Company and the United Electrical, Radio and Machine Workers of America (CIO). In an assignment for the Federal Government Shulman in 1942 was the public member of the War Labor Board in a disagreement between the Wilson-Jones Company and the United Paper, Novelty and Toy Workers International Union (CIO). In 1945, as War Labor Board Arbitrator, he investigated the dismissal of forty-one employees after a strike at the Wright Aeronautical Corporation. President Truman appointed him chairman of a board of inquiry on a threatened maritime strike in 1948, which involved 150,000 men who were seeking raises and the right to conduct union hiring halls.

Among other disputes between companies and unions that the Yale jurist has arbitrated are: R. H. Macy & Company, Inc., and the Retail, Wholesale and Department Store Union (Local 1-S, CIO) in 1947; New Jersey Bell Telephone Company and the Communications Workers of America (New Jersey Traffic Division 55) in 1948; and Capitol Transit Company and the Amalgamated Association of Street, Electric Railway and Motor Coach Employees of America (Division 689, AFL) in 1949.

In February 1952, as chairman of the panel of the Wage Stabilization Board which investigated the dispute between Wright and the U.A.W., Shulman recommended wage increases averaging 14.4 per cent an hour for the 11,500 workers at two Wright Aeronautical plants in New Jersey. This recommendation followed an earlier report by the Yale professor in which, as head of the copper panel of the WSB, he advocated an hourly fifteen-cent increase for copper and brass workers. Shulman's recommendations on the Wright and copper panels were regarded as indicative of what his stand might be in the 1951-52 steel dispute, in which he was chairman of another WSB panel. President Truman had averted a steel strike by referring the negotiations to the WSB, which in turn set up a six-man panel, headed by Harry Shulman, to investigate the controversy. The most important issue, that of the union's demand for a general increase of fifteen cents an hour, plus an average of three and a half cents for widening job differentials, had added significance because the decision on steel sets the pattern for wages in other industries. On the basis of Shulman's recommendation in the cop-

United Press Photo.

HARRY SHULMAN

per case, *United States News* predicted on February 15, 1952, that 1952 industrial wages would probably rise to meet increased living costs, and that extra increments, possibly four cents an hour, would be added for productivity. This would mean wage increases up to fifteen cents an hour in some industries, along with possible "fringe" benefits, such as vacation and pension arrangements. Another important issue under consideration in the steel dispute was labor's demand that the Government induce employers to accept a union shop, a step which would result in a major victory for organized labor and an increase of millions of new members in its ranks.

Harry Shulman has written numerous articles for legal periodicals and is the author of *Opinions of the Umpire* (1945). In collaboration with his friend and former Harvard professor, Felix Frankfurter, he wrote *Cases on Federal Jurisdiction and Procedure* (1937). In 1937, with Charles E. Clark, he presented the result of their investigations into procedures in certain trial courts under the title *Study of Law Administration in Connecticut.* Shulman collaborated with Fleming James, Jr., on *Cases on Torts* (1942), and was the coauthor, with Neil W. Chamberlain, of *Cases on Labor Relations* (1949).

Shulman is a member of the bars of the States of Rhode Island and New York and has been admitted to practice before the United States Supreme Court. He has served as special conciliator for the United States Conciliation Service, as president of the *Yale Law Journal,* chairman of the Connecticut State Labor Relations Board, and as member, since 1947, of the Council of the American Law Institute. He holds an honorary M.A. degree from Yale, conferred in 1937. Shulman married Rea Karrel on July 10, 1927, and has one son, Stephen Neal. The arbitrator weighs 154

SHULMAN, HARRY—*Continued*

pounds, is five feet eight inches in height, and
has dark-brown hair. A comment on his personality came from Robert A. Bedolis, who
wrote in the New York *Herald Tribune*:
"Friends insist that Dr. Shulman's surface calm
and receptivity denote real humility and maintain that this is not inconsistent with his capacity to deliberate, make a sharp decision, and
stick to it."

References

Fortune 33:170+ Mr '46
N Y Herald Tribune II p3 F 17 '52
Nation's Bsns 35:47-9+ Ag '47 por
Newsweek 28:72-3 S 30 '46 por
Who's Who in America, 1950-51
Who's Who in New England (1949)
World Biography (1948)

SIMMONS, JEAN Jan. 31, 1929- Actress

Address: b. c/o RKO Radio Pictures, Inc.,
Hollywood, Calif.

When Jean Simmons arrived in Hollywood
in September 1950 to launch her American film
career she had appeared in seventeen British
motion pictures and was best known for her
role of Ophelia in Laurence Olivier's film production of *Hamlet*. The twenty-one-year-old
actress was judged Britain's most popular star
for 1950, held four international film awards,
and was fourth among the top ten British stars
in the *Motion Picture Herald* Fame Poll.

Jean Merilyn Simmons, the youngest of four
children in a family of moderate means, was
born January 31, 1929, in Crouch Hill, London.
She was reared in Golders Green, a London
suburb, where she attended the Orange Hill
School for Girls. Her grandfather, a music hall
performer, did not wish his children to go on

Wide World Photos
JEAN SIMMONS

the stage; her father, a teacher, died before
Jean's film career began. During the early part
of World War II, along with many London
children, Jean Simmons was evacuated to
Somerset. At the age of fourteen she returned
to the city and was enrolled in the Aida Foster
School of Dancing, where, after two weeks, a
film talent scout noticed her and asked her to
audition for the role of Margaret Lockwood's
sister in Gainsborough's *Give Us the Moon*.
After the audition, director Val Guest selected
her from among two hundred contestants he
had seen, and she made her initial appearance
before the cameras in 1942.

During the next two years Jean Simmons
played such minor parts as Sally in *Mr. Emmanuel*, the harpist in *Caesar and Cleopatra* (a
Pascal film) and the singer in *The Way to the
Stars* (Two Cities), and continued with her
dancing studies. She had just earned her
teacher's license at sixteen when her first big
opportunity in films arrived, with the offer of
the part of young Estella, in *Great Expectations*. Commenting on the joint portrayal of
Miss Simmons and Valerie Hobson, who acted
the role of the grown-up Estella, Howard
Barnes wrote in the New York *Herald Tribune*, "It is rare indeed that child actors and veterans have matched performances so perfectly
that the transition from boy and girl to man
and woman is completely believable. Mistress
Simmons, in particular, turns in a job of artful
make-believe which makes her future performing something eagerly to await." In this production she attracted both a British and American following.

Success as Estella led to a series of bigger
roles. In the first of these, *Black Narcissus*
(produced and directed by Michael Powell and
Emeric Pressburger for Archers), a psychological study of the physical and spiritual de-
bilitation of a group of Protestant nuns in the
Himalayas, Miss Simmons portrayed the speechless, seductive girl named Kanchi. Following
Black Narcissus she appeared in *Hungry Hill*
and *Uncle Silas* (Two Cities) and *The Woman
in the Hall* (Wessex). Laurence Olivier, who
had noticed Jean Simmons in *Great Expectations*, early in 1947 began to think of her for
the part of Ophelia in his forthcoming production of *Hamlet*. After talking the idea over
with David Lean, Olivier obtained her release
from J. Arthur Rank, who had scheduled her
for many minor pictures. When they started
work on the film, Miss Simmons told Olivier
that she had disliked Shakespeare at school,
but hoped to change her mind. Molly Terraine,
who worked with her closely, and Olivier succeeded in winning her interest as they explained
Hamlet line by line. In his critical opinion
about her Ophelia, Howard Barnes wrote:
"Jean Simmons is extraordinarily enchanting
and touching as Ophelia. Starting at low pitch
she builds to the famous mad scene with authority and eloquence." From *Time*: "She has
an oblique, individual beauty and a trained
dancer's continuous grace. . . .Compared with
most of the members of the cast, she is obviously just a talented beginner. But she is
the only person in the picture who gives every

one of her lines the bloom of poetry and the immediacy of ordinary life." Her performance in *Hamlet* brought her the highest motion picture awards of Italy, Belgium, Switzerland, and Ireland. The film which followed, a melodrama called *Sacrifice*, was also made for Rank.

Her next outstanding picture, after the Shakespeare film, was *So Long at the Fair*, in which the actress portrayed Victoria "charmingly and persuasively." As the distraught sister in this revival of the Paris Hotel mystery of 1889, "Jean Simmons gives a characterization of the wide-eyed and winsome lass seeking the key to an enigma that is not only plausible but gives the role beauty and dignity as well" (New York *Times*). Another reviewer calls her an "intensely feminine but admirably resourceful heroine." Another starring role took her on her first trip abroad, to the Fiji Islands, for Frank Launder-Sidney Gilliat Technicolor, to play the part of a castaway in *The Blue Lagoon*. In this story of two English children marooned on a remote Pacific island, Jean Simmons was described by Eileen Creelman in the New York *Sun* as "a highly photogenic figure." As of 1951, Miss Simmons has had one role on the stage, in 1949 with an English company which toured in Tolstoi's *Power of Darkness*.

When *Trio* (1950), a collection of three Somerset Maugham stories, was released, Jean Simmons' photograph appeared on the cover of *Life*, which selected it as the motion picture of the week: "Most ambitious of the trio is *Sanatorium*, a sentimentally macabre tale of crossed lives and loves among tuberculars. Its chief asset is the pretty face of Jean Simmons." After *Trio* Miss Simmons appeared in *Cage of Gold* as a painter who finds herself in a matrimonial dilemma. In *Adam and Evalyn*, which followed, she played her role with "bubbling youth" and was "altogether charming." Costarring with Trevor Howard (son of Leslie Howard), she was given the role of an unbalanced French girl suspected of murder in *Clouded Yellow*.

In the fall of 1950 the actress visited the United States for a personal appearance in connection with *Trio*, and several weeks later returned to that country under commitment to RKO to star in Gabriel Pascal's production of Bernard Shaw's *Androcles and the Lion*. Before the film went into production, managing director Howard Hughes acquired Rank's contract and signed Miss Simmons with RKO. At a rehearsal she said she was as much in awe of Shaw as she had been of Shakespeare; Gabriel Pascal, whom Shaw chose as cinematic interpreter, overcame her anxiety. On completion of this motion picture, in which Miss Simmons played Lavinia, she was considered for the part of Rowena in *Ivanhoe*. In July 1951 Miss Simmons entered into negotiations with RKO on a three-year contract; these negotiations were not completed. In an out-of-court settlement in July 1952 the actress won a complete release from RKO.

Jean Simmons was married on December 20, 1950, to British actor Stewart Granger, in Tuscon, Arizona. The Grangers live in Bel-Air, near Beverly Hills, where the actress golfs, plays tennis, and enjoys her garden and swimming pool. Her favorite indoor games are backgammon and rummy, her favorite spectator sport is baseball. She is five feet four and a half inches tall, weighs 118, has hazel eyes and short-cut auburn hair.

References

Cue 17:11 Jl 24 '48
N Y Herald Tribune p1-V N 19 '50
N Y Post Mag p5 Ja 14 '51
Parade p13 N 26 '50
Time 51:54-6 Je 28 '48 por
British Film Annual, 1949
International Motion Picture Almanac, 1950-51
Winchester's Screen Encyclopedia (1948)

SLEEPER, RUTH Mar. 17, 1899- Organization official; nurse
Address: b. c/o School of Nursing, Massachusetts General Hospital, Boston, Mass. h. 32 Fruit St., Boston, Mass.

On June 20, 1952, Ruth Sleeper was elected the first president of the new National League for Nursing, an organization of about 25,000 registered nurses and lay members, which was formed during the June 1952 Biennial Nursing Convention with the purpose of improving nursing education and services. To her office she brought more than twenty-five years of nursing-education experience as a teacher and as an administrator of national and international health service organizations. Since 1946 she has been director of the school of nursing and nursing service at the Massachusetts General Hospital, Boston.

Ruth Sleeper was born on March 17, 1899, in Manchester, New Hampshire, the daughter of Sherburn Tilton and Ella Mary (Taber) Sleeper. After graduating from high school, she attended Simmons College in Boston for two years and then the Massachusetts General Hospital Training School for Nurses, where she received a diploma in 1922. Continuing her studies in nursing education at Teachers College, Columbia University, she obtained her B.S. degree from this institution in 1925 and her M.A. degree in 1935.

At the same time that she was studying for her degrees, Miss Sleeper was working in her chosen field of nursing education. During the 1922-23 period she was an assistant in nursing theory at the Massachusetts General Hospital Training School for Nurses, while from 1923 to 1927 she was instructor in science and for a time acting superintendent of nurses at the Peter Bent Brigham Hospital School of Nursing in Boston. In 1927 she went to Cleveland, Ohio, as an instructor in anatomy and physiology at Western Reserve University School of Nursing, where she remained for five years. Returning in 1933 to the Massachusetts General Hospital as assistant superintendent of nurses and assistant principal of the school of nursing, she served in this joint capacity until 1946.

(Continued next page)

RUTH SLEEPER

Ruth Sleeper's work in nursing education attracted the attention of the National League of Nursing Education, which appointed her chairman of its instructors' section and then chairman of its curriculum committee in 1939. The League was the outgrowth of the American Society of Superintendents of Training Schools for Nurses, organized in 1893 to establish standards in nursing education. When the society changed its name in 1912 to the National League of Nursing Education, it also extended membership to headworkers in social, educational, and preventive nursing. Thirty years later the league opened its membership ranks to non-nurses who were interested in the education of nurses and allowed these laymen to serve on the board of directors. Working closely with the American Nurses' Association (whose membership is limited to registered professional nurses) league representatives have served as civilian consultants to the Army, Navy, and Air Force nurse corps and have participated in such meetings as the Mid-century White House Conference on Children and Youth, the National Conference on International Economic and Social Development, and the Conference on Women in National Defense.

In 1941 Miss Sleeper was elected a member of the board of directors of the National League of Nursing Education. The next year as chairman of its committee on educational problems in wartime, she conducted a survey on the adjustment of nursing school programs to the war emergency. At that time she called for "a sound program of instruction in nursing schools in spite of the emergency and the shortage of qualified nurses and nurse instructors" (*American Journal of Nursing,* July 1942). Later she said the committee's greatest contribution was the "publication of fourteen bulletins relating to nursing school problems of war years, sent to every State-accredited [nursing] school in the country, as well as a series

of institutes conducted with the Association of Collegiate Schools of Nursing on problems of the collegiate school" (*American Journal of Nursing,* October 1946).

The United States Public Health Service, Nursing Education Unit, in 1942 appointed Miss Sleeper a special consultant. Two years later the unit requested her to take a leave of absence from the Massachusetts General Hospital to study South Carolina nursing schools and "advise on plans for wartime expansion and strengthening of educational facilities to meet urgent need for new student nurses" (*American Journal of Nursing,* May 1944). While making this study she helped plan a new school of nursing at the University of South Carolina.

The year 1944 brought Ruth Sleeper the presidency of the National League of Nursing Education, an office she held for four years. Under her leadership, the league amended its certificate of incorporation in 1946 and changed its stated purpose from defining and maintaining "in schools of nursing throughout the country minimum standards for admission and graduation" to advancing "educational aims and standards in nursing" (*American Journal of Nursing,* July 1952). Miss Sleeper became in 1946 the director of the School of Nursing and Nursing Service at the Massachusetts General Hospital. Convinced that the hospital school of nursing curriculum was not keeping up with the trends in social and medical sciences, she introduced a new program, which cut the course of study from thirty-six to twenty-eight months and introduced an eight-month internship. She described this experimental plan in the article "We Study Our Basic Program" (*American Journal of Nursing,* November 1951).

On June 20, 1952, in Atlantic City, Ruth Sleeper was elected president of the National League for Nursing, formed at the 1952 Biennial Nursing Convention by a merger of the National League of Nursing Education, the National Organization for Public Health Nursing, and the Association of Collegiate Schools of Nursing. (The public health group had been established in 1912 to expand community nursing services and to improve standards of public health nursing; the schools' association had been formed in 1932 to develop nursing education on a professional and collegiate level.) The new National League for Nursing has two divisions: that of nursing education, which comprises a department of diploma and associate degree programs and a department of baccalaureate and higher degree programs; and the division of nursing services, which consists of a department of public health nursing and a department of hospital nursing. The membership, open to both individuals and agencies, includes registered professional nurses, laymen who are interested in improving nursing standards or services, visiting nurse associations, health departments, and nursing services in industries, hospitals, and other institutions. Approving in principle the inclusion of qualified practical nurses as members, the league assigned a committee to work with practical nurses' associations on this question of membership and report in a year.

In accepting the N.L.N. presidential nomination in June 1952, Miss Sleeper said: "The NLN really is a 'community-centered' organization where the points of view of nurses and other citizens, both as individuals and as representatives of community health and educational agencies, will be pooled to bring about co-ordinated action in nursing for the common good." On the same day Ruth Sleeper was elected president, the National League for Nursing and the American Nurses' Association formed a co-ordinating council, which plans to sponsor a national student nurse council, "the first in nursing history," according to the New York *Times* (June 21, 1952). In the following month the N.L.N. sent twenty-eight nurses to Texas to help man immunization clinics where more than 12,000 children received injections of gamma globulin blood fraction in the hope that it would retard or prevent paralysis in the current polio epidemic.

Among Miss Sleeper's articles in the *American Journal of Nursing* are "One World—One Objective for Nursing Education" (July 1942) and "The Curriculum in the Emergency" (September 1947). As chairman of the committee on education of the International Council of Nurses, she was invited on March 25, 1952, along with nursing leaders from other countries to attend a World Health Organization Conference in Geneva, Switzerland, to discuss nursing education. According to Miss Sleeper's article "What Kind of Nurse?" (*American Journal of Nursing*, July 1952), the delegates concluded "that the kind of professional nurse needed in all parts of the world is one who is prepared, through general and professional education within her social structure to share as a member of the health team in the care of the sick, the prevention of disease, and the promotion of health." Ruth Sleeper is chairman of the Joint Commission for the Improvement of the Care of the Patient, an organization consisting of several national groups interested in improving health services. She also has served as a member of the Childrens' Bureau nursing advisory committee on maternal and child health services (1945-48), as chairman of the Nursing Advisory Council of the Veterans Administration (1946), and as a member of the American Red Cross advisory board on health services (1946-48). Her sororities are Pi Lamda Theta and Kappa Delta Pi. Her political party is the Republican and her church is the Universalist.

Mary M. Roberts, editor emeritus of the *American Journal of Nursing*, has said of Miss Sleeper: "She knows nursing thoroughly and has always maintained a very great interest in the patient and his bedside care as well as in the education of the nurse. She is a wholesome and well-balanced person." Among her friends and colleagues she is "famous for her smile." Her complexion is fair, and she is of medium height. She enjoys water color painting and change ringing.

References

Leaders in Education (1948)
Who's Who in America, 1952-53
Who's Who in New England (1949)

SLOAN, GEORGE A(RTHUR) May 30, 1893- Business and organization executive
Address: b. 14 Wall St., N.Y. 5; Chrysler Bldg., 405 Lexington Ave., N.Y. 17; h. 340 Park Ave., N.Y. 22; Vineyard Lane, Greenwich, Conn.

In both the music and business worlds George A. Sloan holds key positions. As a member and later as chairman of the board of the Metropolitan Opera Association he has organized successful fund campaigns which have made it possible for the opera to remain open through the war and through a postwar period of high operating costs. As chairman of the United States council of the International Chamber of Commerce Sloan has been a spokesman for American business in matters involving international economics. A director of several leading American corporations, Sloan is also president of the Nutrition Foundation, Inc., which is supported by leaders of the food industry.

George Arthur Sloan is one of the six children born to Paul Lowe and Anne (Joy) Sloan, of Nashville, Tennessee. He was born May 30, 1893, in that city, where his father was a merchant and civic leader. Among his forebears was Thomas Sloan, a Revolutionary War soldier of Scotch-Irish ancestry. "As a boy in Tennessee," Sloan once told an interviewer for *Opera News* (November 4, 1940), "I gave up the piano lessons of Professor Will Haury for the lure of baseball, football, and the old swimming hole. At Vanderbilt University, my alma mater, I tried out for the Glee Club, but never got beyond the first audition." He took courses in law which, though he did not intend to practice that profession, he thought would be useful in business. After graduating from Vanderbilt with the degree of Bachelor of Laws in 1915, he was admitted to the Tennessee bar. He then became associated with his father in a mercantile business.

During World War I, after schooling at the First Officers Training Camp at Fort Oglethorpe, Georgia, where he was commissioned a first lieutenant of infantry, young Sloan went overseas with the 2d Division. Afterward he was promoted to captain and at his discharge was commissioned a major in the Officers Reserve Corps. (He has also been commissioned a lieutenant colonel in the Georgia National Guard, and a colonel in the Tennessee National Guard.) After the war, from 1919 to 1922 Sloan served as assistant to the chairman of the American National Red Cross in Washington, D.C. As acting director of foreign operations of that organization Sloan was concerned with Chinese famine relief, the repatriation of war prisoners from Siberia, and medical relief to Russia.

When Sloan left Washington in 1922 it was to become secretary of the Copper and Brass Research Institute. Assisting Walker D. Hines in organizing the Cotton-Textile Institute in 1926, he remained with the institute until 1935, first as secretary, and after 1932, when Hines retired, as chairman and president. According to S. J. Woolf (New York *Times Magazine*, October 13, 1940), as president of the institute,

GEORGE A. SLOAN

Sloan "helped to obtain a shorter work week for the workers in the mills and to abolish night work for women and minors." In July 1933 Sloan became chairman of the Cotton Textile Code Authority, which submitted the first code under the National Recovery Administration. For the March 1934 *Atlantic Monthly*, Sloan prepared a report ("First Flight of the Blue Eagle") on the code in operation. His conclusion was that it was "yet too early" to determine whether NRA would be successful. "But those of us who dare not contemplate its failure place our hope in the fearless and able leadership that has so far characterized its administration, in . . . recognition of the partnership relation between government and industry . . . and finally in wholehearted . . . cooperation on the part of labor as well as management." Sloan had worked with the Government previously, in 1931-32, as a member of President Hoover's committee on unemployment relief. Appointed by General Hugh Johnson of the NRA as chairman of the Consumer Goods Industries Committee, from 1935 to 1942 he also was a member of the Business Advisory Council for the Department of Commerce.

The executive's business interests came to include such posts as director and member of the finance committee of the United States Steel Corporation and director of Goodyear Tire and Rubber Company, Middle South Utilities, Inc., and the Great American Insurance Company. From October 1944 to June 1950, when he resigned because of the "press of duties in New York," he was chairman of the board and publisher of the magazine *Farm and Ranch-Southern Agriculturist*. In early 1951 he was elected president of the Blue Ridge Mutual Fund, Inc., a newly organized investment trust resulting from the merger of Central States Electric Corporation and the Blue Ridge Corporation. He is a former director of the Southern Railway System and Bankers Trust Company.

In the nonsalaried post of New York City's Commissioner of Commerce, to which he was appointed by Mayor LaGuardia in June 1940, and in this capacity as chairman of the Mayor's Business Advisory Committee, Sloan worked closely during World War II with the War Production Board to handle production problems in the New York area. Assisted by an advisory committee of fifty-one business, industrial, and labor leaders, he carried out plans to attract business and industry to the city. By August 1943 Sloan was able to make an optimistic report—unemployment was the lowest in many years and New York had gained 479 new manufacturing plants in the first six months of the year; in addition hundreds of plants had obtained war contracts. Sloan's other posts during World War II included the chairmanship of the New York National Defense Exposition in 1941 and membership on the executive committee of the New York Council of Defense, 1941-45.

A member since 1945 of the board of trustees of the United States council of the International Chamber of Commerce (the businessman's international body), in December 1950 Sloan was elected chairman of the council for a two-year term, succeeding H. J. Heinz 2d. In the new post, according to *Business Week* (December 16, 1950), Sloan would "work with International Chamber of Commerce members all over the world, stimulating trade and smoothing the way toward international business understanding." At the first meeting of the council's executive committee in January 1951, the group recommended an extension of the Reciprocal Trade Agreements Act for not less than three years. In February Sloan was one of a group of council officials who made proposals for the creation of an international board to allocate essential raw materials among democratic nations. He suggested that the Economic Cooperation Administration serve as a central agency for distributing supplies and military equipment to members of the North Atlantic Treaty Organization. In an address in March, Sloan proposed that the ECA be put in charge of whatever new aid programs Congress might approve. When President Truman designated the Secretary of State to apportion foreign aid funds, Sloan protested that Truman had "made worse an already confused situation in the field of foreign economic policy." (New York *Times*, April 21, 1951). Sloan later proposed that the major part of funds for foreign economic development should come from private sources rather than Government grants.

In June 1951 Sloan left for Lisbon, Portugal, as head of the United States delegation to the thirteenth biennial Congress of the International Chamber of Commerce, composed of 591 delegates from twenty-eight countries. Sloan said the American delegation of sixty business executives would press for three points: the conclusion of peace treaties with Japan and Western Germany, support of the technical assistance program in President Truman's Point Four plan, and the encouragement of foreign investment by making treaties to forbid double taxation on income earned abroad. In Lisbon Sloan also appealed for steps toward re-establishing a stable international monetary standard, and charged that the United Nations Economic Commission for Europe was advocating measures that "could only spell disaster to the free world." On his return from the conference, in a CBS radio talk in August 1951, Sloan stated that the *Voice of America* and other information services abroad had "been too timid . . in explaining the true meaning and gains of free competitive enterprise in the United States."

When asked in November 1938 to serve on the Metropolitan Opera Association board, Sloan, although a long-time lover of the opera, is said to have hesitated. "I wondered if mere enjoyment of music warranted my acceptance," he later explained. On the theory that his experience with business problems and public relations might enable him to help the New York opera, he took the post. In the spring of 1940 Sloan was named chairman of a fund committee to raise $1,000,000 to permit the Metropolitan Opera Association to purchase and renovate the opera house, then owned by sixty-three stockholders who maintained thirty-five boxes in the house. The campaign brought net proceeds of $1,300,000, one-third from the opera's radio audience. In September 1940 he was elected president of the Metropolitan Opera Association, succeeding the late Paul D. Cravath. Sloan, who is also an honorary member of the Metropolitan Opera Club, received in 1940 the annual award of the National Committee for Music Appreciation.

Heading the Metropolitan Opera's drive for $300,000 in December 1943 (to tide the Opera through the war emergency, which had stopped its usually profitable spring tour), Sloan based his appeal partly on the world situation. "Although the lamps have gone out in the great opera houses abroad, we will keep the lamp lit at the Metropolitan Opera." Contributions from all over the nation brought the fund drive to a successful conclusion in March 1944 when a sum of $318,793 was reached. In February 1946 Sloan succeeded Cornelius N. Bliss as chairman of the board of the Metropolitan. One of his early tasks was to negotiate with the American Guild of Musical Artists concerning the right of the Metropolitan to determine the number and competence of chorus members without the consent of the Guild. In February 1949 Sloan announced a new campaign, this time for $250,000 for new productions for the 1949-50 season. The Metropolitan hoped that by the time the 1950-51 season opened the 20 per cent Federal admissions tax would be repealed; when this did not eventuate Sloan wrote to the more than 7,000 opera subscribers requesting voluntary contributions amounting to 20 per cent of their ticket prices. In November 1950 Sloan revealed that in the 1949-50 season the opera had incurred a deficit of $430,502 despite "virtually capacity houses." Only exemption from the admissions tax would solve the opera's "serious financial problem," Sloan said. Meanwhile, to meet opera expenses

for the new season under the management of Rudolf Bing, Sloan opened a campaign for $750,000 during the opera radio broadcast of December 30, 1950. Sloan, who was re-elected chairman of the board of the Metropolitan Opera Association in May 1951, also appealed to committees of both Houses of Congress, warning that if the amusement tax on nonprofit musical organizations were not repealed, the Metropolitan would have to cease functioning. The tax was repealed in time for the opening of the 1951-52 season in November, allowing the Metropolitan, whose operating deficit for 1950-51 was $462,491, to raise its prices 20 per cent without a change in the cost of tickets to the opera audience. In November 1951 it was announced the $750,000 goal of that year's drive had been realized.

The executive is also president of the Nutrition Foundation, Inc., organized in 1941 by leaders of the food industry with Dr. Karl Compton as chairman. By 1951 the food industry had contributed $4,000,000 to the foundation to be used in the form of grants for research in nutrition at universities and medical centers in the United States and Canada. He is also a trustee of the Milbank Memorial Fund, the America-Italy Society, the Institute for the Crippled and Disabled, as well as director of New York's Christodora House. In the educational field his affiliations are: member of the board of trustees of Vanderbilt University, life member of the Corporation of the Massachusetts Institute of Technology, fellow of the American Academy of Arts and Sciences, member of the American Academy of Political Science, and vice-president of the National Institute of Social Sciences. He is also a member at present of the advisory council of the Southern Research Institute of Birmingham (Alabama) and past president (1943-44) of the New York Southern Society. Sloan, who holds an honorary LL.D. degree from the University of Chattanooga (1945) and one from New York University (1951), was presented with the Cross of a Chevalier of the French Legion of Honor in July 1950 for his efforts to promote music and to develop Franco-American business relations. He was awarded the Phi Beta Kappa key in 1949.

Mrs. George A. Sloan is the former Florence Lincoln Rockefeller, whom he married on November 30, 1929; their two daughters are Florence Lincoln and Anne. His church is Christ Church (Episcopal) of Greenwich, Connecticut, and he belongs to a number of social clubs in New York and Connecticut. A tall man, he has been described as "athletic-looking," with light-blue eyes, white hair, and a tanned complexion. *Cue* wrote of him as "affable, not in the least standoffish." While one means of relaxation is a game of golf, he has said, "To me music brings a certain rest and freedom from care."

References

Christian Sci Mon II p9 F 28 '51 por
N Y Herald Tribune p35 My 9 '51 por
N Y Sun p10 S 12 '40 por; p6 F 26 '44
N Y Times Mag p11+ O 13 '50 por
Opera N 5:10 N 4 '40

(Continued next page)

SLOAN, GEORGE A.—*Continued*

National Cyclopædia of American Biography Current vol D (1934)
Who's Who in America, 1950-51
Who's Who in Commerce and Industry (1951)
Who's Who in the East (1951)

SMITH, IDA B. WISE July 3, 1871—Feb. 16, 1952 Former president of the Woman's Christian Temperance Union; taught in Iowa public schools for fourteen years, beginning in late 1880's; later operated a store in Iowa; became Iowa State president of the W.C.T.U. (1913) and national vice-president (1919); held post of national president of the W.C.T.U. (1933-44) and again of Iowa State president (1944-46); active in other women's organizations and public affairs. See *Current Biography*, 1943.

Obituary

N Y Times p85 F 17 '52

SMITH, JOHN L. Aug. 27, 1913- Veterans organization official
Address: b. c/o Amvets National Headquarters, 724 9th St., N.W., Washington, D.C.

Elected national commander of the American Veterans of World War II (Amvets) at the seventh annual convention on September 2, 1951, John L. Smith took office for the year 1951-52 the following month in succession to Harold J. Russell. In 1947 Smith, a veteran of the Navy who served in the war aboard troop transport ships, began to be active in the Amvet organization in Ohio. For three years prior to World War II he was employed as a tally clerk in the United States House of Representatives. After the war he was a member of the Ohio General Assembly for two years before becoming managing director of the United Truck Owners of America, Inc.

John L. Smith was born in Barberton, a suburb of Akron, Ohio, on August 27, 1913. He attended the Barberton elementary schools and was graduated from the town's Central High School. There he was active in athletics, especially in swimming. Upon completion of his secondary schooling, Smith was selected by his Congressman as an alternate appointee to the United States Naval Academy. He enrolled, however, at George Washington University in Washington, D.C., where he studied for three years before entering the National University of Law in the same city. Smith received his LL.B. degree and later pursued postgraduate studies in law at Akron University of Law.

While studying in Washington Smith attended classes at night and worked in the United States Capitol in the daytime except for one year. At the age of eighteen he took his first position, that of elevator operator in the Capitol, a job which gave him the opportunity to become acquainted with many members of the Senate and the House of Representatives.

Within the next few years Smith held a variety of positions at the Capitol—during one summer he helped to repair the roof of the Capitol. Smith's employment as a clerk in the Senate Post Office was followed by the successive appointments as sergeant and lieutenant in the United States Capitol police force, assistant superintendent in the folding room of the House and assistant in the House document room. During this period in Washington Smith was also associated with Democratic Representative Dow W. Harter from Ohio, serving as a field secretary and as manager of Harter's 1938 and 1940 campaigns.

As tally clerk in the House of Representatives for three years, Smith had the duties of tallying the roll calls taken by the clerk, preparing the daily calendar of all legislation that came to the floor from the various committees, and issuing official roll calls to members of the House. Among the high points of his work were the recording of the controversial one-vote margin on the extension of the draft in 1940 and the tallying of the votes on the declarations of war passed after the Pearl Harbor attack in 1941.

Smith's employment at the United States Capitol was terminated by the outbreak of World War II, when early in 1942 he applied for a commission in the Navy and entered a seven weeks' training program as a member of the first class of indoctrination to be established by the Navy at Princeton University. Commissioned an ensign, he was assigned to duty aboard ship as commander of a gun crew. Smith was on active duty for three years, during which time he was promoted to the rank of lieutenant, s.g. His entire sea duty was spent in troop transports sailing to all theaters of war. On his first cruise, which lasted ten months and circled the globe, his ship sailed alone, but later in the war it became a part of the convoys bearing men and materials across the Atlantic. After his three years of active duty, Smith spent seventeen months in a Navy hospital before being retired from the service in 1947.

Following his discharge from the Navy in 1947, Smith, becoming interested in the politics of his home State, ran successfully as the Democratic candidate for the Ohio General Assembly in the 1948 primary and election. While in the legislature, he coauthored a uniform weight law governing highway transportation, a slum clearance bill, a civil service reclassification measure, and a bill authorizing the appointment of an Amvet to each county's Soldiers and Sailors Relief Commission in Ohio on an equal appointment basis with other veterans organizations. Another legislative achievement was his coauthorship of the Ohio Turnpike Law, under which the State plans to build a 247-mile super-highway link with the Pennsylvania turnpike.

At the end of his two-year term on the Ohio General Assembly, from 1948 through 1950, Smith did not seek re-election. Upon leaving the State Assembly he was named managing director of the United Truck Owners of America, Inc., with headquarters at Akron, an organization comprising most of the truck operators in thirty-seven States. In the same year he was also elected chairman of the Conference of Motor Carrier Interests in Ohio. In 1952 he is on a leave of absence from his United Truck Owners position.

After his return to Ohio in 1947, Smith had become interested in American Veterans of World War II, known by the abbreviated name, Amvets. He was one of the founders of the Amvet post in Barberton and was elected department vice-commander of the same post. Then, when the State commandership was vacated by the recall to active military duty of commander William Carlin of Findlay, Smith was elected by the State executive committee to replace him. As Amvets commander in Ohio, Smith was a strong advocate of civil defense through working for, and helping to write, a resolution at the Governor's Conference on Civil Defense which was instrumental in the passage of civil defense legislation by the Assembly; and through directing the program for Ohio Amvets which produced surveys and enrolled volunteer workers in every community. Smith was retained in the State commandership by acclamation at the Ohio department convention in 1951, just prior to his election as national commander.

On September 2, 1951, in the closing session of the Amvets seventh annual convention, held at Boston, Massachusetts, Smith was elected national commander of Amvets, succeeding Harold J. Russell (the handless veteran who starred in the motion picture *The Best Years of Our Lives*). Smith was elected on the second ballot by a wide margin from a field of four candidates. He took office for the one-year term on October 1, 1951.

Amvets, the largest World War II veterans organization, was formally constituted in December 1944. It has three major aims: "To promote peace, to preserve America's way of life, and to help veterans help themselves." Toward the attainment of these ends, the organization supports such programs as are designed to procure more and cheaper housing, better social security, proper aid to veterans, adequate national defense. It maintains a national service department for the handling of legitimate claims of disabled veterans and a national peace and preparedness committee for decisions on international questions. On September 1, 1951, the Amvets approved the national executive committee's decision to affiliate the 250,000 members of the Amvets with the International Federation of War Veterans Organizations. As national commander of Amvets, Smith has introduced certain original programs in addition to administering the regular projects of the organization. Speaking before city Amvet leaders in the Waldorf-Astoria Hotel in New York on September 29, 1951, he announced his intention of presenting a proposal to President Truman that the post of Secretary of Civil Defense be established as a permanent part of the Defense Department, coequal with the Army, Navy, and Air Force. On February 21, 1952, Smith began a program termed "Operation Friendship" for the purchase and distribution of ten million rubber balls by Ameri-

Chase News Photo.

JOHN L. SMITH

can to European children in the North Atlantic Treaty Organization nations in Europe, a project which Smith says is "designed to create for posterity the harmonious world which we may never know."

John L. Smith married Elizabeth Tolson, whom he had met in Washington, where she was holding the position of a supervisor in the Government's General Accounting Office. They now have three sons, John Michael, James Daniel, and Robert Anthony.

SPEIDEL, HANS (spī'dĕl häns) 1897-
German military expert
Address: b. c/o Federal Republic of Germany, Bonn, Germany

A leading figure in the rebuilding of a new West German Army is Dr. Hans Speidel, once a lieutenant general in the Wehrmacht, chief of staff to Field Marshal Erwin Rommel in France, and a participant in the July 1944 anti-Hitler plot. After the formation of Chancellor Konrad Adenauer's Federal Republic Government, Speidel, while teaching modern history at Tübingen University, became chief adviser to the Chancellor on matters of German rearmament. He has since been prominent in the negotiations with Allied representatives over the part to be taken by Germany in the North Atlantic Treaty Organization.

Hans Speidel, a native of the town of Metzingen, Württemberg, in southern Germany, was born in 1897, son of a forester and professor at the University of Tübingen. His brother, Wilhelm Speidel, who also followed a military career, became a lieutenant general in the Luftwaffe. At the beginning of World War I Hans Speidel, having completed his studies at a *Gymnasium*, volunteered in the German Army as an ensign (a junior rank in the officers'

HANS SPEIDEL

classification) and fought with the Grenadier Regiment of King Karl of Württemberg. Progressing through military grades, he served first as a leader of small groups and of a company, later as a adjutant of a battalion and then of a regiment, in the combat areas of the Argonnes, Flanders, the Somme, Verdun, and the Meuse.

As an officer in the small post-Versailles Reichwehr, Speidel advanced in his knowledge of military tactics and studied history and economics at the University of Tübingen, where he took his Ph.D. degree in 1925. Upon his appointment in 1930 to the General Staff, he was assigned to the Third Division, known as Frankreich-Referat. Three years later, in the fall of 1933, he went to Paris as assistant to the military attaché at the German Embassy, a position which enabled him to travel to Italy, Switzerland, and Spain and brought him into contact with the point of view of military leaders of Western Europe. In the period immediately preceding World War II Speidel, who left his Paris post in October 1935, was put in charge of the Western intelligence division of the German General Staff as head of a section called Fremede Heere West. Accompanying Lieutenant Colonel Ludwig Beck, who was later one of the leaders in the conspiracy against Hitler, Speidel in 1937 visited the French General Staff on a mission to promote friendly relations between Germany and France. During these prewar years he contributed to the *Frankfurter Zeitung* and the *Allgemeinen Schweizer Militärzeitung*.

In World War II Speidel advanced from a General Staff officer of a division to that of an army corps and later to that of a group of armies (*Heeresgruppe*). While chief of staff for the commander in chief in France, he drafted the terms of surrender imposed on the French at the Hotel Crillon in 1940. In the

spring of 1942 he became chief of the General Staff of an army corps and then of an army on the Eastern front. In the course of filling his next assignment as chief of the General Staff of Field Marshal Erwin Rommel's Army Group B in northern France, and later in the same capacity on the staffs of Kluge and Model, Lieutenant General Speidel (his rank was comparable to that of a major general in the United States Army) sabotaged Hitler's order in 1944 to defend Paris against Allied invasion, a command which would have resulted in destruction of the city. "Speidel was not a Nazi," stated Drew Middleton of the New York *Times* (November 18, 1951), "and he is one of the few surviving professional soldiers who opposed Hitler's plans almost from the outset." Arrested as a suspect in the bomb plot against Hitler of July 20, 1944, he was taken to a Gestapo prison in Berlin, from which he escaped several months later, early in 1945, afterward remaining in hiding until liberated by the French at the end of the war. When Speidel appeared at the war crimes trials in Nuremberg, his role was that of a witness, not a defendant.

Through an appointment made by the Württemberg-Hohenzollern state in January 1948, Dr. Speidel was enabled to undertake research work in current history; the following year he joined the staff of Leibniz College and also the philosophic faculty of the University of Tübingen as a lecturer in history. In the following years, after becoming military councilor to the new German Government at Bonn, he continued to hold those academic posts. Late in 1948, before the formation of the Federal Republic of Germany, as Konrad Adenauer later revealed, Speidel was called upon to prepare a paper for the future Chancellor on the European defense situation and its relationship to Germany. He was subsequently appointed Adenauer's chief adviser on military affairs, collaborating with the former chief of operations for the German General Staff, Adolph Heusinger, under Theodor Blank, a trade union official and now head of the Security Office, in shaping initial military policy and setting in motion the machinery toward rebuilding West German forces.

As Western nations felt increasing concern about the possibility of Russian aggression in Europe, meetings of the Allied-German Committee were held in Bonn in the winter of 1951 to discuss problems of German rearmament. According to a report in the *Christian Science Monitor,* at this time the views of Speidel, a member of the German delegation to the committee, on the lines of Russian action in the event of an attack by that nation were that Russia would launch an offensive in the Middle East and a second assault through Germany toward the Atlantic Coast. In his opinion an Allied force of twenty divisions would be required to withstand a Russian attack in Western Europe. Speidel and Heusinger in a discussion of technical questions also argued that the smallest possible unit for the German Army was a division, as against the suggested combat team. In the summer of 1951, during which he again, in July, attended talks with the United States High Commissioner on the German contribution to Western European defense, Speidel prepared a forty-page memorandum suggesting a German Army of 250,000 men, including six corps of two divisions with each division numbering 12,000 soldiers (New York *Times*, October 3, 1951). With Theodor Blank he was present as a Bonn representative at negotiations in Paris on a European Army project to be submitted to the Council of the North Atlantic Treaty Organization. These negotiations, according to the New York *Times*, resulted in the French agreement to permit West Germany to re-create divisions in its army. Speidel was one of the chief authors of a plan, reported in January 1952, for a West German army (to be modeled after the United States Army) of an available 1,250,000 men between the ages of eighteen and twenty-one.

In his analysis of Speidel's stand on Germany's part in Western European defense, Drew Middleton said that while the general hoped for the formation of a German national army under the command of General Dwight Eisenhower, he was ready, in view of Continental opposition, to back a European army plan. Speidel's memoirs, the first by a World War II German officer to be published in the United States, *Invasion 1944*, appeared in Germany in 1949 and was later translated into French, Swedish, and English. An exposition from the German point of view of the events in the 1944 Normandy crisis, it "is more than a battle report," commented the New York *Herald Tribune* critic. "It is an absorbing account of the duel between Rommel and Hitler." Truman Smith, retired colonel of the United States Army, who wrote the introduction to the American edition (1950) of *Invasion 1944*, regards Speidel as probably the only person alive who can tell the story of this personal conflict. "Extraordinarily interesting," was the *New Yorker*'s observation on Speidel's book.

With his wife and three children Speidel lives in the town of Freudenstadt in the Black Forest. The tall, gray-haired general has been described by *Time* as an "easy, convincing debater and brilliant strategist," and by Drew Middleton as an "amiable and sometimes gay companion."

References

Christian Science Mon II p9 Mr 29 '51
N Y Times Mag p17 N 18 '51
Newsweek 37:37 F 5 '51
Time 59:25 Ja 28 '52

SPENCE, BRENT Dec. 24, 1874- United States Representative from Kentucky

Address: b. House Office Bldg., Washington 25, D.C.; h. Fort Thomas, Ky.

Brent Spence, the Democratic Representative from Kentucky, was elected to his first term in the House of Representatives in 1930 and since then (as of 1952) has been re-

Wide World Photos
BRENT SPENCE

elected for each term. He has been chairman of the House Committee on Banking and Currency since 1943 (except during the Republican-controlled Eightieth Congress). In favor of housing projects, price controls, and minimum wage laws, the Representative has usually voted for Administration programs. Before his election to Congress he was a lawyer, a State senator, and a city solicitor in Kentucky.

Born December 24, 1874, in Newport, Kentucky, Brent Spence is the son of Philip Brent and Virginia (Berry) Spence. His family has lived in the Kentucky district which he now represents since the days of the Revolutionary War. Upon his graduation from the Law School of the University of Cincinnati in 1895, he was admitted to the Kentucky bar and began practicing law the same year at Newport. He often represented municipalities in suits against public utilities and is quoted as saying that he did not "get along very well" with the utility companies.

Elected to the Kentucky State Senate in 1904, Spence served until 1908. He became the city solicitor for Newport in 1916 and held this office eight years. In 1928 he endorsed Al Smith and ran for Congress but was defeated, thus becoming, the Representative has said, the only Democrat to be defeated for Congress in that district. Two years later a successful candidate, he was elected as Representative to the Seventy-second Congress from the Sixth District of Kentucky.

During the last year of President Hoover's Administration Spence cast votes in favor of the moratorium bill of 1932, the establishment of the Reconstruction Finance Corporation,

SPENCE, BRENT—*Continued*

Philippine independence, and full payment of the bonus to veterans of World War I. Since the advent of a Democratic Administration under President Roosevelt in 1933 the Congressman (who was re-elected as a Representative at large from Kentucky) has supported most New Deal and Fair Deal measures. In the first session of the Seventy-third Congress he voted for the passage of the farm relief bill (March), the National Industrial Recovery Act (May), the arms embargo resolution (April), and the $500 millions job relief bill (April).

Spence voted "yea" on the following measures introduced in the House in the second session of the Seventy-third Congress: the gold reserve bill (January), the Bankhead cotton bill and the reciprocal tariff bill (March), and the Stock Exchange control bill (May). In 1934 he was re-elected to Congress, representing this time the Fifth District of Kentucky, a district usually in agreement with New Deal and Fair Deal policies, partly industrial and unionized, partly agricultural, with tobacco as the chief crop. The Representative cast his vote for the social security bill (April) and the Eccles banking bill (May) in 1935; and against the bill to drop old age pensions and increase relief payments (April). The next year he supported the compromise neutrality resolution (February) and the Ritter impeachment resolution (March); but voted in opposition to the bill which proposed the placing of postmasters under the Civil Service system (June). He favored, at the first session of the Seventy-fifth Congress, the extension of the Reciprocal Tariff Act in February and the Wagner housing bill in August. The Congressman cast a negative vote in March on the attempt to impose a peacetime munitions embargo in June on the bill to require Congressmen to pay income tax.

In 1938 Spence recorded a "yea" vote for the naval expansion bill (March) and the bill providing for minimum wages and maximum hours (May); and opposed the war plebiscite discharge motion (January). Other measures of the Seventy-sixth Congress receiving his support were the bill on farm parity payments (March), the arms embargo amendments (June), and the Government reorganization act (March). He voted "nay" to the Townsend old age pension plan in June. The Kentuckian was against the passage of an antilynching bill which was presented to the second session of the Seventy-sixth Congress in January and also registered a negative vote on the amendments to the Labor Act which would affect the NLRB (June) and on the bill to continue a mandatory arms embargo (November). He was in favor of the passage of the conscription bill (September) and the extension of the Trade Agreement Act (February). In 1941 he approved the following measures: the price control bill (November), the lend lease bill (February), and the $7 billions appropriation for lend lease (March). At the second session of the Seventy-seventh Congress he expressed himself in

favor of the conference report on the price control bill (January), the organization of the Women's Auxiliary Army Corps (March), and an anti-poll tax bill (October).

When Alabama's Representative Henry B. Steagall, chairman of the Banking and Currency Committee of the House, died in November 1943, Spence succeeded in the chairmanship, which has under its jurisdiction such matters as price control and housing legislation. In the first session of the Seventy-eighth Congress, the Representative from Kentucky recorded "yea" votes on the extension of the Trade Agreement Act and the passage of an anti-poll tax bill in May; and "nay" votes on the extension of the Dies Committee (February), the Hobbs antiracketeering bill (which unions feared could be used against members voting for strikes), the Ruml pay-as-you-go tax plan (May), and the bill to cut the appropriation of the OPA by $35 millions. In the following year he voted for the UNRRA authorization (January); against a legislative ban on food subsidies (February), a bill instituting a probe of the Montgomery Ward seizure (May), and against a motion to freeze social security tax at 1 per cent.

On February 15, 1945, Spence introduced in the House the Bretton Woods bill, which authorized the United States to contribute to the stabilization fund and to subscribe to the capitalization of the proposed international bank. On the following June 5 the Representative read a letter sent to him by President Truman urging the immediate adoption of the Bretton Woods plan and stating, "You and Mr. Wolcott (ranking Republican on the committee). . .have demonstrated a high degree of statesmanship and nonpartisanship of which America can be proud." Legislation increasing the lending authority and extending the life of the Export-Import Bank was introduced by Spence on June 18, 1945. The Kentucky Congressman voted affirmatively on the continuation of the RFC subsidy program in June 1945 and the Government reorganization bill and the bill to cut taxes, both in October 1945. He voted "nay" on a bill to set up a permanent Committee on Un-American Activities in January of the same year. Spence and Mike Monroney of Oklahoma made unsuccessful efforts on the floor of the House in 1946 to save the price controls bill from restricting amendments. After the veto of the bill by President Truman on June 29 Spence proposed an extension of the Office of Price Administration until July 20, during which time an attempt would be made to work out a bill acceptable to the President. The Kentucky Representative then met in conference with members of the House and Senate to work out a satisfactory bill.

Early in 1946 Spence pressed for acceptance of a provision in an Administration bill which authorized a $400 millions subsidy for housing for veterans; the measure was subsequently passed. He was also a strong supporter of the loan of $3.75 billions to Britain, regarding it, reported *United States News*, as "a sort of fundamental peace treaty." Spence's voting record in this second session of the Seventy-ninth Congress showed him supporting the conference report on the full employment bill (February) and the report on the emergency housing bill (May). He voted negatively on the bills to shelve atomic energy controls (July) and to allow reasonable profits in OPA ceilings (April). With the election of a Republican Congress, Spence lost the chairmanship of the Banking and Currency Committee to Jesse P. Wolcott, ranking Republican member of the committee. The Kentucky Representative voted in 1947 for restoring the cuts which had been made in reclamation funds (April), for the Greek-Turkish aid bill (May), the anti-poll tax bill (July), and for the *Voice of America* bill (June). He voted "nay" on the constitutional amendment to limit the Presidency to two terms (February). Spence favored the repeal of Federal margarine taxes (April), the subversive activities control bill (May), and the displaced persons bill (June) offered in the second session of the Eightieth Congress. He voted against the rent control extension bill (March), the tidelands oil bill (April), and against overriding the railroad antitrust exemption veto.

Upon resuming his post as chairman of the Banking and Currency Committee in 1949, Spence introduced the Administration rent control bill in the House and led the fight for its adoption. After the passage of the measure he became a member of the conference which met to reconcile the House and Senate bills. The long-range housing bill sponsored by Spence provided for the construction by public housing authorities of over a million low-rent housing units and loans and grants to local communities to aid in slum clearance. This much contested bill was passed by a vote of 228 to 185. The votes of the legislator in the Eighty-first Congress were recorded as follows: he favored the extension of the Marshall Plan (April); opposed striking out the public housing section in the long-range housing bill (June) and cutting European arms aid 50 per cent (August).

The Spence bill, introduced in the House by the Representative on January 6, 1950, aimed to make Government-guaranteed building loans available for the construction of moderately priced housing units. This would enable middle income families who were not eligible for the housing developments to secure adequate living quarters. The bill was passed by the House with the portion dealing with the medium priced units eliminated. In April Spence introduced a compromise rent control bill which would extend the controls for six months to January 1, 1951, and allow another six-month extension to any municipality which requested it; this bill was passed. In the second session of the Eighty-first Congress the Representative voted against an FEPC bill which contained no provisions for its enforcement (February) and a bill to cut Federal spending by $600 millions. He voted affirmatively to override the Communist control bill veto.

Spence commented favorably on the price-wage "freeze" effected in January 1951, stating that "something had to be done to control inflation." He went to work on a new economic controls law in June to replace the Defense Production Act, which was due to expire shortly. The new act relaxed credit restrictions, limited price rollbacks, and added rent controls to the bill previously in effect. In the Congress of 1951 Spence voted "yea" on the universal military training bill (April), the wheat loan to India (May), and the $7.5 billions foreign assistance bill (August). He cast negative votes on the tidelands oil bill, the bill to limit public housing, the proposed $350 millions cut on economic aid to Europe, and the measure to cut the Government civil payroll. In the second session of the Eighty-second Congress Spence served as floor manager for the Defense Production Act, urging its passage, despite the fact that amendments had been adopted which would weaken price and wage controls. A compromise bill was passed on June 29 which extended wage and price controls to April 30, 1953. In May the Representative voted for the mutual security bill and in favor of raising old age benefits. He opposed measures to shelve military training and to limit public housing (March) and to cut economic aid for Europe by $615 millions (May). Spence was re-elected to Congress in the November 1952 election.

In 1920 Spence married Ida Billerman, who is now deceased. He is a member of the Elks, the Masons, and the Knights of Pythias; he names his church as the Episcopal. Called "a bulky, cordial Kentuckian" by the *United States News*, he was further described in the same magazine as "one of the quiet, hardworking members of Congress who. . .unpretentiously leave their imprint on national legislation."

References

U S News 21:73 Jl 19 '46 por

Biographical Directory of the American Congress, 1774-1949 (1950)
Congressional Directory (1952)
Who's Who in America, 1952-53
Who's Who in the South and Southwest (1950)
Who's Who in United States Politics (1950)

SPERRY, WILLARD L(EAROYD) Apr. 5, 1882- University dean

Address: b. c/o School of Divinity, Harvard University, Cambridge, Mass.; h. 11 Francis Ave., Cambridge, Mass.

For thirty years Willard L. Sperry, formerly the pastor of two Congregational churches, has been Dean of the School of Divinity at Harvard University, where he remains past retirement age in 1952 to assist in the projected expansion of that school. Author of a number of books and articles on theological and moral issues, Dean Sperry has also lectured on those subjects

WILLARD L. SPERRY

both in the United States and England. He is one of a number of scholars who worked on the revision of the Old Testament (completed in October 1951) for the Revised Standard Version of the Holy Bible.

Willard Learoyd Sperry was born April 5, 1882, in Peabody, Massachusetts, the son of Willard Gardner and Henrietta (Learoyd) Sperry. "My father before me was also a New England Congregational minister," Dean Sperry has told. With a Bachelor of Arts degree from Olivet (Michigan) College received in 1903, young Sperry was enabled by a Rhodes scholarship to continue his studies in England, at Queen's College, Oxford University. There he received first class honors in theology in 1907. Two years later, having returned to the United States, he earned a Master of Arts degree at Yale University. From 1908, when he was ordained in the Congregational ministry, until 1913, Sperry was assistant pastor of the First Congregational Church in Fall River, Massachusetts, of which he became pastor the latter year. In 1912 he had completed the work toward his second Master of Arts degree, bestowed upon him by Oxford. Called to the Central Congregational Church in Boston, in 1914, Sperry filled the pastorate there until 1922. During much of the same period he was lecturer and professor of practical theology at Andover Theological Seminary (1917-25).

In 1921 Sperry was invited to become a member of the Board of Preachers of Harvard University, of which body he became chairman in 1929. A year later he was named Dean of the Harvard Divinity School, where in 1952 he is completing his thirtieth year of service. At the same time (1922) he was appointed professor of practical theology and, in 1929, Plummer professor of Christian morals. Under the constitution of the divinity school, which was established in 1816, it is required that "every

encouragement be given to the serious, impartial, and unbiased investigation of Christian truth, and that no assent to the peculiarities of any denomination of Christians be required either of the students or the professors or instructors." Affiliated with the School of Divinity are the Episcopal Theological School at Harvard, the Boston University School of Theology, the Andover Newton Theological School, and the Tufts College School of Religion. In 1951-52 there are 115 students registered at the Harvard School of Divinity. Dean Sperry in 1952 is remaining at the Divinity School beyond the normal age of retirement in order to assist in plans for its expansion, by means of a $5,000,000 fund-raising drive, into an interdenominational religious center for an augmented student body of three hundred students. This "revitalization" of the Harvard Divinity School, said the New York *Times*, would be for "the general purpose of strengthening religious education in the United States." A 1947 Harvard report on the need for a larger divinity school called attention to the "shortage of well-educated ministers" and to the "entirely new fields opening up requiring the services of men trained both in religious learning and Christian sociology."

Dean Sperry's contributions to religious, philosophical, and popular publications over a period of more than thirty-five years show the range of his interests. Declaring in the *Atlantic Monthly* in 1921 that the "modern minister sees himself as a kind of permanent beater for unending drives," Sperry appealed for clergymen to be freed from philanthropic duties and "allowed to preach religion in something of its totality." Two years later, in an article entitled "The Democratic Theory and Religion," written for *Outlook*, he observed, "It is the community of experience in life's deepest struggles and aspirations that makes of religion an aspect of democracy and of democracy the best organized expression of religion." In "The New Ascetism" (*Atlantic Monthly*, January 1933) Sperry treated the contemporary intellectual asceticism resting upon the scientific "conviction that the mind is sound and can know the truth," but warned "only as he [modern man] learns to distinguish between the necessary suffering given in the order of nature and the unnecessary suffering invited by the arts can he escape from this newest form of the old ascetic delusion." A later article of Dean Sperry's for *Fortune* was "Our Moral Chaos," in which he considered the relationship of modern science to religion and the value of scientific methods to religion, for "modern science sets before itself in nontheological terms exactly the same ideal and requires of itself exactly the same kind of stern moral discipline." An article in the *American Mercury* of April 1946 was entitled "What's Wrong with the Clergy"; this analysis cited the declining intellectual standards of many divinity schools in comparison with those of other professional schools; the unwillingness of young men interested in the ministry to accept the required strict orthodoxy at variance with twentieth century viewpoints; the lack of intellectual freedom permitted clergymen; the stronger appeal of the sciences; and the too hasty preparation of sermons.

After the end of World War II, Dr. Sperry wrote for the *Virginia Quarterly Review* "War's Impact on Religion," in which he said that the conflict "revived the concern for a more personal religion. . . .It may well be that these years will lead immature believers to an understanding of God more mature than that which was the convention in less troubled times." In "The Case against Mercy Killing" (*American Mercury*, March 1950), Dean Sperry pointed out that euthanasia might often be used on economic rather than medical grounds against the aged and feeble, and further stated that legalized "mercy" killing would involve a revision of the ethics of the medical profession. In 1951, writing for the *Virginia Quarterly Review*, he called attention in "The Decline of Conscience" to "the lowering of standards of private morals" in modern times and to an analagous lowering of standards on a greater scale, as in relation to the atomic bomb. Other articles by Dean Sperry are to be found in *Christian Century, Atlantic Monthly, Century, Contemporary Review, Living Age, Christendom*, the *Harvard Theological Review, Spectator, Journal of Religion, Hibbert Journal*, and the "Rice Institute Pamphlets." Essays by him have been included in several collections: *Classics of Religious Devotion*; in N. Wilder's compilation, *Liberal Learning and Religion* ("Worship in an Academic Community"); in the Garvin lectures collection, *Man's Destiny in Eternity*; and in G. P. Butler's *Best Sermons*, "Opportunity and Adversity" (1946), "The Virtue of Compassion" (1947), and the "Value of the Individual" (1949-50).

The Harvard theologian is also author of a number of books, of which the first, *Disciplines of Liberty*; *The Faith and Conduct of the Christian Freeman* was published in 1921. Henry Sloane Coffin, reviewing it for the *Literary Review*, thought the essays both "enlightening and refreshing." A later book, *Signs of These Times* (1929), was reviewed by C. H. Moehlman for *Christian Century*: "As a homilectical source book, *Signs of These Times* will find its way into the library of the minister who has not lost all intellectual curiosity." The New York *Times*'s review of Sperry's *What You Owe Your Child* (1935) commented, "Mr. Sperry is modern in his viewpoint and broadly tolerant in matters of belief." A subsequent work of Sperry's, written for Harvard's studies in English, *Wordsworth's Anticlimax*, called forth a number of appreciative reviews which characterized it as "penetrating", "lucid," "persuasive." The *Christian Science Monitor* found it "an admirably judicious little book." *Strangers and Pilgrims*; *Studies in Classics of Christian Devotion* (1939) was called by W. Norman Pittenger in *Living Church* "the best devotional guide book of this year and of several years." In 1949 A. Wilder wrote of *Jesus Then and Now* for *Christian Century*: "The book represents a rich and seasoned vindication of the liberal tradition with respect both to Jesus and the Church, but also betrays areas where the conversation with neoorthodoxy can be fruitful for both sides."

Dr. Sperry's *Ethical Basis of Medical Practice* was mentioned in the *United States Quarterly Booklist*: "That a divinity school dean should have produced such a study speaks both for the author's breadth of concern and for the intimate connections between the vocations of physician and pastor." Other books by Sperry are *Reality in Worship* (1925); *The Paradox of Religion* (1927); *Yes, But—the Bankruptcy of Apologetics* (1931); *We Prophesy in Part* (1938); *Summer Yesterdays in Maine*; *Memories of Boyhood Vacation Days* (1941); and *Those of the Way* (1945). The *Nontheological Factors in the Making and Unmaking of Church Unions* is a study that was assigned to him by the World Conference on Faith and Order in 1937. A series of volumes on religion in the postwar world published by the Harvard University Press in 1945 was edited by Sperry; its four volumes comprise *Religion and Education, Religion and Our Divided Denominations* (to which Sperry contributed a chapter), *Religion and Racial Tensions*, and *Religion of Soldier and Sailor*.

Together with Dr. Luther A. Weigle, chairman of the Standard Bible Committee, and twenty other scholars, Dr. Sperry was engaged for a number of years on the revision of the Old Testament for the Revised Standard Version of the Holy Bible, which will be published on September 30, 1952. The revised Old Testament, completed in October 1951, is reported to have involved three times as much translation as the New Testament, which was published in 1946. Actual work on revision for this 1952 edition of the Bible, the fifth authorized version in English, was begun in 1937.

On several occasions Sperry has been invited to deliver lecture series; these have been at Union Theological Seminary, at Bangor Seminary, and the Gates lectures of 1924 at Grinnell College. In 1927, in England, he was Upton lecturer at Manchester College, Hibbert lecturer, and Essex Hall lecturer in London; and in 1930 Haskell lecturer at Oberlin College. At the Yale Divinity School in 1938 he delivered the Lyman Beecher lectures, "We Prophesy in Part," in which series Edgar De Witt Jones (*Royalty of the Pulpit*, 1951) noted his vigorous approach to the subject and his emphatic plea for Christian unity. Sperry frequently appears in the pulpit at Harvard's Chapel services and has also preached at leading American colleges and universities.

During 1927-31 Dr. Sperry was dean of the National Council on Religion in Higher Education, of which he was vice-president in 1934, and was trustee of Vassar College from 1943 to 1946. He has received several doctorates in divinity from Yale (1922), Amherst (1923), Brown (1928), and Williams (1935); and the Doctor of Theology degree from Harvard (1941). Boston University has bestowed an honorary D. Litt. degree upon him (1939). He was made a fellow of the American Academy of Arts and Sciences in 1927. In New York Dean Sperry's club is the Century, in Cam-

SPERRY, WILLARD L.—*Continued*

bridge the Faculty. By his marriage on December 15, 1908, to Muriel Bennett, he is the father of one daughter, Henrietta (Mrs. R. M. Wilson). For outdoor recreation Dean Sperry prefers fishing (one of his *Atlantic* pieces told of the making and caulking of a New England fishing dory) ; indoors he may relax by playing bridge or reading detective stories.

References

> Directory of American Scholars (1951)
> Jones, E. D. Royalty of the Pulpit (1951)
> Leaders in Education (1948)
> Who's Who, 1951
> Who's Who in America, 1950-51

STEELMAN, JOHN R(OY) June 23, 1900- United States Government official

Address: b. The White House Office, Washington, D.C.

> NOTE: This biography supersedes the article which appeared in *Current Biography* in 1941.

The first and thus far only occupant of the position of Assistant to the President of the United States is Dr. John R. Steelman, who was named to this post by President Harry S. Truman on December 12, 1946, after having served for the previous six months as Director of the Office of War Mobilization and Reconversion. Steelman had been a professor of economics in an Alabama college before he entered government work in 1934 as a member of the United States Conciliation Service. Three years later he became director of the service, continuing as such until 1944. Dr. Steelman has served also as acting chairman of the National Security Resources Board and chairman of the President's Scientific Research Board and of the President's Special Commission on Higher Education. For nearly six months in 1952 he was head of the United States defense mobilization. He has been prominent in negotiating settlements of labor disputes in the railroad, steel, and coal industries.

John Roy Steelman was born in a logger's cabin in Thornton, Arkansas, on June 23, 1900, one of five children (four sons and a daughter) of Ples Cydney and Martha Ann (Richardson) Steelman. Spending his early years on a small cotton farm, the boy would rise at dawn to do his chores before going to elementary school. He finished his high school education with honor grades, and then at the age of eighteen joined the Army for World War I duty, serving during the final months of hostilities and being discharged with a corporal's stripes. "Mustered out of uniform, he turned once again to the problem of acquiring an education," wrote Ben H. Miller in the Baltimore *Sun* (December 1, 1940). "The only practical work he knew was farming, and his husky six-foot-plus body made it easy for him to get jobs as a field hand, as a logger in the cypress swamps, in a variety of manual capacities . . . but it was necessary to follow the geographical

drift of seasonal employment. So Steelman became from time to time what he describes as a 'blanket-stiff,' a hobo riding the rods or the box cars from Arkansas as far West as the fields of Oregon."

With the money he saved from such employment, he was able to enter Henderson-Brown College in Arkadelphia, Arkansas, where he was voted the "best all-round student." Having received his B.A. degree at Henderson-Brown in 1922 he attended Vanderbilt University in Nashville, Tennessee, for both his M.A. degree in sociology in 1924 and his Ph.B. degree in social ethics and practical sociology a year later. During his years at Vanderbilt, Steelman supported himself by selling insurance and maps. Following a period of study at Peabody College in Nashville, he went to Harvard as an instructor and graduate student in 1926 and afterward took his doctorate in sociology and economics from the University of North Carolina in 1928, for which he submitted the dissertation *Mob Violence in the South*.

As a professor of sociology and economics Dr. Steelman joined the faculty of Alabama College in Montevallo. When, in the summer of 1934, Secretary of Labor Frances Perkins delivered the commencement address at the college, Steelman had just finished mediating an industrial dispute in Mobile, and Miss Perkins was so impressed by the result that before the year was out she had made him a Commissioner of Conciliation. The United States Conciliation Service had been established in 1913 by President William Howard Taft to mediate industrial disputes "at the request of one or both parties involved." (It was superseded in 1947 by the present Federal Mediation and Conciliation Service.) In 1937 Steelman accepted the appointment as Director of the Conciliation Service and by 1940 he personally had helped settle a hotel strike in Washington, D.C., an aluminum dispute in Utah, a strike at the Vultee Aircraft Corporation plant in California, another in International Harvester Company plants, and one at the Allis-Chalmers works in Milwaukee.

A notable industrial decision of Steelman came on December 2, 1941, when, as the public representative on a three-man board set up by President Franklin D. Roosevelt, he sided with John L. Lewis of the United Mine Workers against Benjamin Fairless of the United States Steel Corporation and cast the deciding vote which granted the union shop to the United Mine Workers. Steelman submitted his resignation as Director of the Conciliation Service in July 1944; no action, however, was taken on it until November 6, just after the re-election of President Roosevelt for a fourth term. Upon leaving the post, Steelman expressed satisfaction that under his administration the service had grown from handling 1,287 cases yearly to 25,000 (during the 1943-44 fiscal year) and that 95 per cent of these cases had been settled without strikes (New York *Times*, November 7, 1944).

In New York City, to which he then moved, Steelman opened offices as a public relations consultant and continued as such until shortly after the death of President Roosevelt in April

1945. When Harry S. Truman assumed the Presidency, Steelman returned to Washington as an adviser to Secretary of Labor Lewis B. Schwellenbach and within a short time was named special assistant to the president himself. As such, Steelman played a leading part in settling the railway strike on May 25, 1946. On the following June 14 he succeeded John W. Snyder as Director of the Office of War Mobilization and Reconversion upon Snyder's becoming Secretary of the Treasury. Later that same month Steelman assumed in addition, but on a temporary basis, the responsibilities of Director of Economic Stabilization.

On December 12, 1946, President Truman issued an executive order consolidating various wartime agencies and boards and dissolving others, including the Office of War Mobilization and Reconversion. Simultaneously he announced the appointment of John R. Steelman to the new post of Assistant to the President of the United States, with the specific function of "co-ordinating Federal agency programs and policies." In view of the outcome of the recent coal crisis, many Washington commentators assumed at the time that Steelman's new appointment was a means of removing him from the labor scene and putting him in a post where his new obligations would be largely nominal. But Arthur Krock, writing in the New York *Times* a few days later, correctly forecast that the Assistant to the President would prove just what the name implied. Thus "when the President went away on his election campaign in 1948, he left Steelman in the White House to keep the wheels of Government rolling" (*Pageant*, January 1952).

Serving meanwhile as chairman of both the President's Scientific Research Board and of the President's Special Commission on Higher Education, Steelman in 1948 became liaison officer for the Interdepartmental Committee on Scientific Research and Development. Steelman was offered, but declined, the post of Secretary of Labor, following the death of Lewis Schwellenbach. However, on December 10, 1948, he did accept an additional appointment as acting chairman of the National Security Resources Board, a post he filled until April 1950.

Another nation-wide railroad-strike threat, this time invoked by the Brotherhood of Railroad Trainmen to secure a forty-hour week and pay increases was halted by Government seizure of the railroads on August 25, 1950. Steelman, became active in efforts to settle the dispute and on the following December 21 he obtained from representatives of the trainmen and four other railroad brotherhoods their signatures on a "memorandum of agreement" calling for a 23-cent-an-hour pay boost, a cost-of-living escalator clause, a forty-hour work week to be instituted at a future date, and a three-year moratorium on new wage and rule demands. Two of the unions voted to reject the demands, and the settlement was not effected. In May 1951 the trainmen agreed to slightly modified terms on most issues, but differences with other brotherhoods remained unsolved. Meanwhile a report of the Senate Labor Committee was critical of some phases of the settle-

Wide World Photos
JOHN R. STEELMAN

ment efforts. In January 1952 Secretary of Labor Tobin was asked to step in. Later, in his capacity as Assistant to the President, Steelman on May 21, 1952, was successful in bringing about a final settlement. "The wage raises," wrote Joseph A. Loftus in the New York *Times* (May 22, 1952) "were about the same as those agreed to by the union chiefs in December 1950."

On March 30, 1952, Charles E. Wilson resigned as director of the Office of Defense Mobilization in protest against Administration support of a Wage Stabilization Board recommendation. The WSB had suggested an 18-cent-an-hour pay increase for workers in the steel industry, without compensating authority to the steel companies to raise prices. President Truman immediately appointed Steelman acting director of the ODM, while allowing him to retain his post as Assistant to the President. At the same time the President promised the companies such price increases as might be "equitable." No agreement was reached, however, and at the beginning of April the Government seized the steel industry under alleged "inherent" Presidential emergency powers—an action subsequently declared unconstitutional by the Supreme Court. When the steel mills were returned to the operators, the United Steel Workers of America went on strike. Steelman continued negotiations in his White House office until July 24 when the 52-day-old strike was settled, with the workers agreeing to a 16-cent-an-hour pay increase and the companies to a $5.20-a-ton increase in the price of steel. With the steel emergency past, President Truman announced the appointment of Henry J. Fowler as Director of Defense Mobilization on September 6, 1952, leaving Dr. Steelman once again free to devote full attention to his duties as assistant to the Chief Executive.

(Continued next page)

STEELMAN, JOHN R.—*Continued*

Steelman has received honorary LL.D. degrees from Alfred University (New York), from Hendrix College (Arkansas), as well as from the University of Redlands (California). A member of the American Sociological Society, he has also been president of Arkansas State Society in the nation's capital. He is a 32d degree Mason and a Methodist. Steelman was awarded the Gold Medal of the American Arbitration Association in 1950 for outstanding service in labor relations. Preferring golf as an outdoor sport, he belongs to the Columbia Country Club and the Burning Tree Club. Steelman met his future wife, Emma Zimmerman of St. Louis, at a union convention while she was a secretary with the Building and Construction Trades Council; they were married on October 7, 1939. With a height of more than six feet, Steelman weighs about 215 pounds and has blue eyes and graying brown hair.

References

Am Mag 148:30-1+ O '49 por
Baltimore Sun Mag p1 D 1 '40 por
Bsns W p24-5 F 18 '50 por
Chem & Eng N 26:244+ Ja 26 '48 por
N Y Herald Tribune II p1 Ap 13 '52 por
N Y Post p5 Ap 2 '41 por
N Y Sun p23 F 6 '40; p28 Mr 28 '41
New Republic 115:625-6 N 11 '46 por
Newsweek 28:25 S 2 '46 por; 34:17 Ag 15 '49 por
Pageant 7:74-5 Ja '52 por
Scholastic 48:11 F 4 '46
U S News 19:88+ N 9 '45 por; 20:71 Je 21 '46 por
Washington (D.C.) Post p2 Mr 9 '48 por; p28 Ag 26 '51
American Men in Government (1949)
International Who's Who, 1951
International World Who's Who (1949)
National Cyclopædia of American Biography Current vol E, 1943-46
Ten Eventful Years (1947)
Who's Who in America, 1952-53
Who's Who in Commerce and Industry (1951)
Who's Who in the Nation's Capital, 1938-39
Who's Who in United States Politics (1950)
World Biography (1948)

STEVENS, GEORGE (COOPER) 1905-
Motion picture director

Address: b. c/o Paramount Pictures Corporation, Hollywood 38, Calif.

A number of Hollywood's outstanding films, both dramas and comedies, are associated with the name of director-producer George Stevens. As the youngest director in Hollywood, in 1935 he directed the screening of *Alice Adams*. This was followed by such foremost musicals and comedies as *Vivacious Lady* (1938), *Woman of the Year* (1942), *The Talk of the Town* (1942), and *The More the Merrier* (1943).

After three years as head of a Special Motion Picture Unit of the United States Army Signal Corps in six combat areas during World War II, Stevens returned to Hollywood to make the highly successful film version of *I Remember Mama*. Subsequently he directed *A Place in the Sun*, a screen adaptation of Theodore Dreiser's *American Tragedy*, which was named the outstanding picture of 1951 by the National Board of Review of Motion Pictures and for which he won an Academy of Motion Picture Arts and Sciences award.

George Cooper Stevens was born in 1905 in Oakland, California, to Landers Stevens, head of a Pacific Coast stock company and a Shakespearean actor, and his actress wife, Georgia (Cooper) Stevens. His maternal grandmother, Georgia Woodthorpe, had been known to San Francisco theatergoers in the Gold Rush days; and his paternal grandfather, James Stevens, was a prominent San Francisco lawyer of the same period. The late Ashton Stevens, famous drama critic in Chicago for many years, was his uncle. At the age of five, George Stevens appeared on the stage for the first time at San Francisco's Alcazar Theatre, in a cast of which Nance O'Neill was the star. After attending a Sonoma (California) high school for a year he acted for a time in juvenile roles with his father's company, for which he was also stage manager, before going to Hollywood in 1921. Then only seventeen, Stevens began to work as a cameraman, first as assistant, then as second cameraman, and finally chief cameraman, with the result, commented *Time*, that he became "one of the best cameramen in motion pictures." Making two-reel movies, Stevens absorbed the conventional technique of "shooting off the cuff," which he still employs, stated *Time*. During this period, in which he filmed about sixty Laurel and Hardy shorts, he also worked as a gag-writer for a time.

In 1929, when he was twenty-five, George Stevens was given a director's job by Hal Roach, for whom he made a number of "shorts" of the "custard pie comedy" variety. From these he advanced to minor feature films —*The Cohens and the Kelleys in Trouble* (1933) for Universal; *Bachelor Bait* and *Kentucky Kernels* (1934) for RKO; and for the same studio, *Laddie* and *The Nitwits* (1935). When RKO signed Katharine Hepburn for the title role in Booth Tarkington's *Alice Adams* in 1935, she insisted upon having Stevens as her director. In the summer of 1932, upon the release of that story of a small-town girl's disastrous heart affair, *Time* remarked, "The direction of George Stevens, who at thirty is the youngest important director in Hollywood, is almost flawless." Stevens continued to make pictures under RKO auspices for the next few years, completing *Annie Oakley* in 1935, *Swing Time* in 1936, *Quality Street* and *A Damsel in Distress* in 1937.

The first picture that Stevens produced as well as directed was the 1938 Ginger Rogers and James Stewart comedy, *Vivacious Lady*, which "added much to Stevens' stature," said a Paramount press release. The following year he directed Douglas Fairbanks, Jr., Cary Grant, and Victor McLaglen in *Gunga Din,* which was based on Kipling's poem. "The preposterous story," said *Newsweek,* "is smartly directed by George Stevens." His last picture for RKO was the drama *Vigil in the Night,* based on an A. J. Cronin story and starring Carole Lombard; this received unfavorable reviews for the most part.

Returning to light comedy films with the 1941 *Penny Serenade,* with Cary Grant and Irene Dunne in the leads, Stevens made the first of four successive hits. Again he was called as director by Katharine Hepburn for MGM's *Woman of the Year;* the result was a picture chosen by Bosley Crowther of the New York *Times* as one of ten best films of 1942: "This racy and topical high comedy was in the fine tradition of good, bright screen fun. It was witty, tart, and faintly satiric—and had everything that makes for gaiety." Howard Barnes of the New York *Herald Tribune* complimented Stevens on his "beguiling simplicity" in the direction and his "shrewd understanding of cinematic values." Equally successful was the same year's Columbia production, *The Talk of the Town,* which costarred Jean Arthur, Ronald Colman, and Cary Grant. "George Stevens has directed it with the slyness of a first-rate comedy man," observed Crowther. "No opportunities for comment by the camera have got by Mr. Stevens." The same reviewer was enthusiastic about Stevens' succeeding picture, *The More the Merrier,* which he produced and directed for Columbia in 1943: "Columbia hit a gem of a notion when it got the bright idea of having George Stevens make a comedy based on wartime housing conditions in Washington"; the film was "warm and refreshing" and "brilliantly directed." Barnes of the *Herald Tribune* found that "a great director and knowing performers can work wonders with wisps of material on the screen. . . . Stevens has wisely supplemented bright chitchat with droll pantomime" unfolded "in a series of brilliant sequences." For his direction of *The More the Merrier* Stevens received a scroll of honor in the annual voting of the New York film critics.

It was in 1943 that Stevens entered the United States Army Signal Corps, with the rank of major, to head the Special Motion Picture Unit assigned to photograph the activities of the Sixth Army for the national archives. Recording six major campaigns (said *Variety*), Stevens and "his men were on the beaches D-Day, in Paris . . . Liberation Day, and across France and Germany to the link-up." A unit citation awarded by General Eisenhower for D-Day work read, in part: "Throughout this period members of this unit displayed unusual determination and zeal frequently in disregard of personal danger. As a result a distinct contribution has been made to archives of this major phase of war against Germany. This achievement is most praiseworthy." Besides serving in the European theater, where Stevens' unit filmed the liberation of Denmark and of the concentration camps at Dachau, and the capture of Berchtesgaden, it also saw duty

GEORGE STEVENS

in Africa and the Middle East. When discharged in 1945 he was a lieutenant colonel.

As his first film after the war, Stevens produced and directed the screen version of John van Druten's play, *I Remember Mama,* based on the novel by Kathryn Forbes. When the RKO picture was released early in 1948, Richard Watts, Jr., of the New York *Post* judged that "George Stevens, one of the most skillful of the Hollywood film makers, has provided an attractive and frequently touching motion picture." Bosley Crowther was struck by Stevens' "unfaltering control of the directoral reins. His soft scenes are never too sloppy. . . .And the humor is kept in an area of reasonable levity." The New York *World-Telegram*'s Alton Cook was particularly impressed by "ingenious camera work by director George Stevens and his crew. . . .Mr. Stevens has created illusion of movement where little exists either in action or plot." The same quality was admired by Howard Barnes: "What sets *I Remember Mama* apart as a film of distinction is Stevens' handling of his material. . . .There is no formalized directing. . . .The camera moves all over the place, but it achieves its purpose beautifully." Barnes also noted another characteristic of what he considered a "memorable motion picture," namely, that "since the producer-director is celebrating a saga of the San Francisco in which he grew up, he has filled the production with a realism which is too often lacking on the screen."

"I think it is the best thing I've ever done," was Stevens' own comment on his next motion picture, the adaptation of Theodore Dreiser's *An American Tragedy.* "We try to tell it easily and honestly, without dramatic contrivances." Released in 1951 under the title of *A Place in the Sun,* the picture starred Montgomery Clift, Elizabeth Taylor, and Shelley Winters. "As produced and directed by George

STEVENS, GEORGE—*Continued*

Stevens," wrote the *New 'Yorker*'s John Mc-Carten, "the movie is first-rate all along the line. . . .Among the worth-while things about *A Place in the Sun* are a laudable attention to detail—and photography with a clarity that is very easy on the eye." Bosley Crother drew attention to the director's use of the close-up to aid in the "sharp dissection of the pitiful working of the minds and the moods of three young people correlated by varieties of loneliness, ambition, and love." At the close of the year, *A Place in the Sun* was named the outstanding picture of 1951 by the National Board of Review of Motion Pictures. In early March 1952 Stevens was cited for an Achievement Award by *Look* magazine for his "brilliant direction of *A Place in the Sun*," for which he also was honored by the Screen Directors' Guild. In March 1952 his direction of that picture also won an award of the Academy of Motion Picture Arts and Sciences.

In 1951 Stevens was also responsible for the production and direction of *Something to Live For*, a study of reformed alcoholics with Ray Milland and Joan Fontaine in the lead roles. *Variety* found that "George Stevens' production and direction put the dramatic devices together with his usual meticulous touch, dealing as realistically as possible with what is, basically, a soap-opera formula along tear-jerker lines." Stevens' Western film, *Shane*, to be released in 1952, was filmed in Technicolor on a Wyoming range and stars Alan Ladd, Jean Arthur, and Van Heflin. Unlike the usual Hollywood Western, *Shane*, which is approached in terms of character study, is a realistic presentation of pioneer life in the 1880's, based in factual detail upon the director's extensive research. While completing the editing of *Shane* at the end of 1951, Stevens was also considering the possibility of filming several Ambrose Bierce stories. In 1951 Stevens announced he was severing his connections with Paramount.

Vogue, in analyzing the work of several outstanding men in Hollywood, attributed Stevens' achievement to the "triple strength of character, realism, and camera angles. . . .To his admirers, Stevens' greatest contribution is that he makes little beauties act." The director himself has said of his work: "I'm one of those who feels everything that goes into a picture affects the viewer, although the viewer doesn't realize the impact of tiny, minor things being worked up for him." Kate Cameron of the New York Sunday *News* wrote: "Stevens works on every section of a picture, sits in on story conferences and even after a film is completed, he passes exploitation ideas on to the advertising department."

In 1946 Stevens was president of the Screen Directors' Guild and in 1950 a member of the board. Hunting and fishing provide Stevens with recreation. He is also a "rabid baseball fan." The tall and broad-shouldered director has been described by *Time* as "unassuming, rugged . . . with a fine flow of good humor."

References

Time 39:84 F 16 '42
International Motion Picture Almanac, 1951-52

STONE, ABRAHAM Oct. 31, 1890- Physician; association official

Address: b. c/o Planned Parenthood Federation of America, Inc., 501 Madison Ave., New York 22; h. 40 Park Ave., New York 16

When the Government of India late in 1951 decided to introduce birth control in that country, it secured, through the World Health Organization, the advisory services of Dr. Abraham Stone, a pioneer in the American birth control cause. Through his work as medical director of the Margaret Sanger Research Bureau and as vice-president of the Planned Parenthood Federation of America, Dr. Stone has devoted more than forty years of study to that subject. With his late wife, Dr. Hannah M. Stone, he began a marriage counseling service which served as model for subsequent centers.

Abraham Stone was born October 31, 1890, to Miron and Amelia Stone in Russia, where his father was a merchant. At the age of twelve the boy was sent to live with an uncle in the United States. With the ambition, since early childhood, of becoming a doctor, Stone received his medical degree from New York University and Bellevue Medical College in 1912. After serving his internship at Knickerbocker and St. Mark's hospitals from 1912 to 1915, he obtained his Bachelor of Science de-degree in 1916 from New York University.

While he was an intern at Bellevue Hospital, Dr. Stone met Hannah Mayer, a bacteriologist and serologist on the hospital's staff, whom he married in 1917, just before he became a lieutenant in the United States Army Medical Corps. During his absence in World War I service, Mrs. Stone undertook the study of medicine, so that upon his return to civilian life they were able to set up practice together, a collaboration that lasted until Dr. Hannah Stone's death in July 1941. At the first International Birth Control Conference held in New York in 1921, the Stones came into contact with Mrs. Margaret Sanger, pioneer of the control movement, who four years later invited Dr. Hannah Stone to accept the medical directorship of the Margaret Sanger Research Bureau. After the death of his wife Dr. Abraham Stone succeeded her in this post, which he continues to hold. (Their daughter, Gloria, Mrs. Gerard Aitken, also studied medicine.)

A specialist in urology, Dr. Abraham Stone became instructor in 1923 in that field at the New York Post-Graduate Medical School and Hospital, where he remained for four years. Some time later, in 1933, he began to serve as chief in that specialty for the Union Health Center of New York; and in 1935, he was appointed associate in urology at New York's Sydenham Hospital, both of which posts he retains in 1952.

About 1929, the Stones were asked by Will Durant, then directing the educational services of the Labor Temple, to give lectures on marriage and family relations there. These talks were so heavily attended that Dr. John Haynes Holmes of the Community Church offered the use of his facilities to the Stones, who in 1931 set up the Marriage Consultation Center at the church. Subsequently the Stone center, providing services of a type available in Germany and Austria, but not previously in the United States, became a model for other such centers in the country. Similar work is also done by the Planned Parenthood Federation of America, established in 1939, and by its thirty-three affiliated State organizations. In addition, says the *Social Work Year Book* (1947), it makes "birth control information available under medical auspices to those who desire and need it," helps "childless couples obtain treatment for infertility," and promotes research "in the physiology of human fertility." Educational and clinical services are other divisions of the federation.

In January 1947 Dr. Stone and Dr. Alan F. Guttmacher were recipients of the Lasker Awards of the Planned Parenthood Federation of America, of which Dr. Stone is vice-president. Established by the Albert and Mary Lasker Foundation, the awards—a medallion and $500—were given to Stone and Guttmacher, reported Albert Deutsch in *PM*, because they had "through their writings, teachings, counseling and clinic services, led the way in making possible better health for mother and children, children for the childless, fewer mother and baby deaths, fewer juvenile delinquents, and fewer broken homes." A year previous to receiving the award, disturbed by the postwar increase in divorce and marital problems, Dr. Stone had inaugurated an experiment in marriage counseling at the Margaret Sanger Bureau, where groups of husbands would meet with one counselor, wives with another. "They gained insight rapidly through this mutual exchange," Dr. Stone told Deutsch. To another reporter, Mary Braggiotti of the New York *Post,* he later remarked, "Marriage and family life are essential to the life of the nation, and anything that will contribute to their maintenance should be encouraged and promoted."

At the request of the United States Department of State, Dr. Stone in July 1947 was named, by the National Research Council, a delegate to the first world conference on family and population, convened in Paris by the French Union of Family Association. From this meeting emerged the International Union of Family Organizations (with which the Planned Parenthood Federation of America is affiliated). Stone was elected vice-chairman of the union. Upon his return to the United States, he asked for aid in helping German doctors learn the latest advances in family planning, denied to them under the Nazi regime, while planned parenthood had advanced in the Scandinavian countries, Great Britain, and the United States. He also spoke of the existence of "a much more progressive and liberal attitude in Europe toward family planning than

ABRAHAM STONE

before the war." After attending the August 1951 congress of the International Union of Family Organizations in Brussels, Dr. Stone spoke before the annual conference of the National Council on Family Relations held in Wisconsin at the end of that month. His subject was the possibility of establishing family unions in the United States. Regarding that council, of which he is a board member, Dr. Stone has observed: "The National Council of Family Relations is merely interested in spreading family education. It is not like the French family unions which are lobbies like a labor lobby. American family organizations are for education and for furthering the stability of marriage and family life, rather than the purely social and economic values." Stone, who has declared himself against cash allotments to families similar to those given in France, Belgium, and Italy, believes that other forms of aid would encourage stable marriages and families—infant and maternity services, family clinics, and particularly revised rentals in relation to increases in the size of the family. (The latter method has been used successfully in Sweden.)

Upon the request of the World Health Organization, a United Nations affiliate, Dr. Stone in October 1951 visited India to formulate plans for implementing mass birth control education there. The previous July India's Prime Minister Nehru had suggested, in his five-year plan, the establishment of state birth control clinics and state-supervised sterilization facilities, in order to meet the problem of an annual 4,000,000 increase in India's population, a pressure that leads to famine when food supplies are inadequate. Dr. Stone, called by *Time* the man who "probably knows more about family planning than any other scientist," spent two months on a survey, conducted with the aid of India's woman Minister of Health, Rajkumari Amrit Kaur, and with that of Indian specialists

STONE, ABRAHAM—*Continued*

in the fields of hygiene and social work. As a start toward mass education, Dr. Stone aided in the establishment of five experimental centers.

Much of Dr. Stone's research and writing has been concerned with the problem of sterility and infertility in marriage: as medical director of the Margaret Sanger Research Bureau, he has extended its benefits to childless couples. A member of the American Society for the Study of Sterility, Dr. Stone has summarized a number of the most recent findings in that field for the September 1947 issue of the *American Journal of Nursing*. He is, as well, a member of the editorial boards of *Fertility and Sterility* and of *Marriage and Family Living*. Dr. Stone from 1935 to 1947 was editor of *The Journal of Human Fertility*, in which a number of his articles have appeared. He has also contributed to *Survey*, *Lancet*, and *Mental Hygiene*.

With Dr. Hannah Stone, Abraham Stone wrote *A Marriage Manual*, which, after its publication in 1935, went into more than twenty-three printings: a 1952 edition is planned, as the volume is frequently used as a college textbook. Upon its publication, the *Saturday Review of Literature* observed: "It is impossible to find the least fault with this book. It is, in the opinion of this reviewer, the most useful book of its kind that has thus far appeared." H. M. Parshley, reviewer for the New York *Herald Tribune*, thought that the "book is beyond criticism in style, ethical and aesthetic outlook, explictness and scientific authority." In collaboration with Dr. Norman Himes, Dr. Abraham Stone wrote *Practical Methods of Birth Control* (1938), of which the 1951 edition appeared under the title, *Planned Parenthood*.

Besides holding the vice-presidency of the Planned Parenthood Federation, Dr. Stone serves as a member of its board of directors and its executive committee. He is also a founder and president of the American Association of Marriage Counselors; director of studies in marriage and the family at the New School for Social Research in New York; and associate clinical professor of preventative medicine at New York University-Bellevue College of Medicine. The American Medical Association and the New York Academy of Medicine have elected him a fellow, and he is a member of the New York Academy of Science and of the American Association for the Advancement of Science. His fraternity is Alpha Omega Alpha.

The physician's week ends are spent at his farm in New Jersey, where he raises poultry and cows. Books, plays, and music help him to relax. His summer sport is canoeing, his winter sport is ice-skating. Dr. Stone has dark hair and brown eyes, and stands about five feet six inches tall.

References

N Y Post Mag p31 Mr 11 '47

American Association for the Advancement of Science Directory, 1940-48

STRACHAN, PAUL A(MBROSE) (strā' hān) Feb. 26, 1892- Organization official

Address: b. c/o American Federation of the Physically Handicapped, Inc., National Press Bldg., Washington 4, D.C.; h. 1341 E. Capitol St., Washington 4, D.C.

Paul A. Strachan is the national president of the American Federation of the Physically Handicapped, a nonprofit educational and beneficent organization, which he founded in 1940 to protect and advance the interests of the handicapped. Prior to that time he had been engaged in various entertainment enterprises, and had served as legislative and general representative for several labor organizations. He offered a resolution which Congress passed in 1945 to provide for the observance of an annual "National Employ the Physically Handicapped Week." A member of the President's committee on the annual event, Strachan also is a special consultant on the affairs of the handicapped to the United States Department of Labor.

Born in Perry, Michigan, on February 26, 1892, Paul Ambrose Strachan is the son of James Alexander and Lulu May (Calkins) Strachan. His father, a native of Scotland, was a watchmaker, printer, and writer, who in the United States took an active part in politics with William Jennings Bryan. As a "crusading country editor," he published newspapers in several Michigan towns and in Elkhart, Indiana. His wife, who was of Welsh-Scotch-Irish descent, was associate editor of several of the papers which he published. Young Paul grew up in Georgia, where the elder Strachan had been invited to establish a newspaper. The boy attended high school in Atlanta, but, in his own words, he found "the world was more attractive than study." At the age of twelve he got his first job, he says, as "demonstrator" of typewriters. In the years that followed, he traveled around the world while working as a stevedore, sailor, prospector for gold with two sourdoughs in Alaska, steamboat agent in the Orient, and at other jobs.

Returning to the United States, Strachan was for a time an assistant office manager for Griffing Brothers, nurserymen, in Port Arthur, Texas, and then an index expert for Walker, Evans & Cogswell, of Charleston, South Carolina. Between the years 1914 and 1916 and again from 1922 to 1931, he was associated with various theatrical enterprises as a producer, tour manager, press agent, and theater operator, as well as film salesman, regional manager, and correspondent for theatrical papers. According to Robert S. Allen (of the Washington *Post*), after Strachan was barred from military service in World War I because of physical disability, he assisted in setting up the Bureau of War Risk Insurance and was one of its first officials. Later, as a result of this work, he was active in organizing a union of Government employees. This in turn led to an interest in vocational training, and he reportedly helped draft and put through Congress the Federal Vocational Training Act of 1920. From 1917 to 1922, and after 1931 he served as a legislative and general representative for several labor and other groups, and he was an organizational promotion executive from 1919 to 1932.

An automobile accident severely disabled Strachan and sent him to Johns Hopkins Hospital, where in 1940 he decided to devote his efforts to furthering the cause of the handicapped. He has explained that "in view of the then impending war conditions and the need for all kinds of workers in the war production program there was clearly a great necessity for an intensive effort to develop and launch a program on behalf of all physically handicapped people." In the hospital he thought of the possibility of a week set aside as a period in which to enlist public interest in employment of the handicapped. "It was born of recollections of World War I," he has said, "when disabled veterans were pushed around and ignored as soon as the parades stopped . . . [of a memory] of thousands of other handicappeds I had seen who were the discards of society. It was born of personal experience, as one of the 85 per cent physically disabled, and who, because of that disability, was cast upon the human scrap pile, despite a fierce and intense desire to live, to work, and to achieve."

After being discharged from the hospital Strachan founded the American Federation of the Physically Handicapped (AFPH) on September 30, 1940. Two years later, on August 20, it was formally chartered in Washington, D.C., as a nonprofit, educational, and beneficent organization, "of, for, and by the physically handicapped," with Strachan as national president. The federation is dedicated to "justice, opportunity, equal rights," and "unity" for all the handicapped. Membership includes the blind, deaf, hard of hearing, victims of infantile paralysis, tuberculosis, arthritis, heart disease, amputations—all those disabled by a congenital physical defect, injury, or disease, as well as shut-ins. (Nonhandicapped may join as associate members.) The AFPH represents their joint interests before the Congress, State legislatures, county boards, and municipal governments, the branches of private industry, and the general public. It conducts a continuous campaign to make the public and industry conscious of the value of the handicapped, as workers, and also offers counsel and guidance to the handicapped themselves. By 1946 the AFPH had eighty-nine lodges throughout the country; it also has an extensive at-large membership.

On the legislative front Strachan "pounded the corridors and thumped the desks of Capitol Hill," wrote Sam Stavisky in the Washington (D.C.) *Post*, and "buttonholed legislators and bureaucrats, industrialists and labor leaders," who might be in line to further the cause of the disabled. In order to develop an over-all picture of the problem, it was first necessary to secure more facts on the conditions and needs of the handicapped; Strachan was responsible for the establishment in 1942 of the House Labor subcommittee to investigate aid to the physically handicapped. During the next three years, this subcommittee, in Strachan's opinion, "compiled more information on the handicapped than in all previous history." Meanwhile,

Strachan campaigned for Congressional enactment of legislation establishing "National Employ the Physically Handicapped Week." He himself drafted the resolution, which was first presented to the House in 1942. Three years later the measure finally passed both House and Senate by unanimous vote, and was signed by President Truman on August 11, 1945. The resolution set aside the first week in October each year for the observance, during which "appropriate ceremonies are to be held throughout the nation, the purpose of which will be to enlist public support for and interest in the employment of otherwise qualified but physically handicapped workers." At the time of the first "Week" (October 7-13, 1945) it was estimated that there were 25,000,000 persons in the United States who were physically handicapped to some degree by disease, accident, or war.

Strachan was named to serve on the Federal Inter-Agency Committee on Employment of the Physically Handicapped, which was set up in July 1946 by the head of the Department of Labor's Retraining and Re-employment Administration. Representatives of all agencies active in the field of counseling, restoration, training, education, and placement of the physically and mentally handicapped met in this committee to coordinate plans for a nationwide pooling of Federal, State, and community efforts to promote employment of the handicapped in peacetime jobs. In September 1947 Strachan helped organize the President's Committee on National Employ the Physically Handicapped Week—to operate a year-round program of public information and education on employment of the handicapped. This committee is composed of some 250 representatives of the nation's leading industrial and business, labor, veterans, women, farm, educational, religious, scientific, professional, civic, fraternal, welfare, and other organizations. Strachan was responsible for writing the committee's policy and administrative procedure. That same year the Department of Labor, for which Strachan serves as special consultant on the affairs of the handicapped, requested all State governors to appoint committees to aid in the nation-wide program. In July 1949 President Truman signed a bill authorizing $75,000 a year to finance the committee's activities.

The "Week" has reportedly made it possible for more than 500,000 handicapped men and women to obtain gainful work, and, according to Strachan, has accelerated the drive to make 2,255,000 placements of handicapped persons since 1940. In 1951 figures were presented to show that hirings of the handicapped during 1950 via placement through local Government placement offices totaled 277,000—a new record. This represented an increase of 100,000 over the previous year, a fact attributed by speakers to the growing awareness of industry that handicapped persons, when properly placed, are safe, reliable, and efficient workers. The annual campaign in 1951 was centered on the need for more workers to meet an expected labor shortage as defense production increases.

(Continued next page)

Harris & Ewing

PAUL A. STRACHAN

The AFPH president took part in the campaign culminating in the passage of the omnibus medical research bill, on August 15, 1950, providing for Federal grants for the study of a number of crippling diseases. He has also been engaged in promoting a full-fledged service program of rehabilitation, training, and aid for the physically handicapped of all kinds: this legislative program consists of twelve bills to establish a single Federal Agency for the Handicapped, and is reportedly the most comprehensive piece of legislation ever introduced in the handicapped field. As executive director of the affiliated AFPH Educational Fund, Strachan is further promoting the AFPH Institute for Human Engineering, which will be based in Florida. This project will provide for the first time an institute wherein handicapped may be medically treated; educated and trained; vocationally guided; and led to suitable employment, through selective placement, in occupations where their particular handicap is not a factor.

A contributor of articles on problems of the handicapped to various journals, Strachan is the author of *The Model Plan for Employment of Our Physically and Mentally Handicapped.* Organizations in which he holds memberships include the National Press Club, American Cancer Society, and several labor organizations. On January 4, 1919, he married Avery Pearl Beall, who was then a Government employee; they have four sons, William James, Robert Wallace, Frank LeRoy, and Bruce Carroll. The gray-haired, brown-eyed executive stands six feet two inches tall, weighs 220 pounds. His political party is the Democratic, his church the Methodist. For recreation he turns to baseball, fishing, and agricultural pursuits.

References

Newsweek 28:62-3 O 7 '46
Washington (D.C.) Post p2 O 4 '48;
   p11B Ag 13 '49 pors
Washington (D.C.) Times-Herald Ja 3
   '48
Who's Who in the East (1948)
Who's Who in the South and Southwest
   (1950)

STRAUS, JACK I(SIDOR) (strous) Jan. 13, 1900- Department store executive
Address: b. c/o R. H. Macy & Company, Inc., 151 W. 34th St., New York 1; h. 19 E. 72d St., New York 21; Jericho, New York

The chief executive of what has been described as the "world's largest store" is Jack I. Straus, the third in successive generations of the Straus family to head R. H. Macy & Company, Inc. Associated with the New York store since his graduation from college, Jack Straus became its president in 1940 after serving in administrative capacities in most of the departments and as vice-president from 1933 to 1939. For a year previous to assuming his present position he was acting president in charge of all operations of the institution. In the subsequent years, as department stores in other cities in the United States were acquired by Macy, Straus became director of these wholly owned subsidiaries and divisions. The business executive, known also for his service in civic affairs, has been since 1942 the director of the Greater New York Fund.

Jack Isidor Straus was born in New York City on January 13, 1900, one of three children of Jesse Isidor and Irma (Nathan) Straus. He is the grandson of Isidor Straus, who in 1854 came as a small boy to the United States from Rhenish Bavaria, worked as supply agent for the Confederate States in 1863, and in 1866 joined his father and his brothers, Nathan and Oscar Solomon Straus, in forming the firm of L. Straus and Sons, importers of pottery and glassware. In 1888, with his brother Nathan, he became one of the partners of the R. H. Macy & Company department store in New York City and later a member of the firm of Abraham & Straus of Brooklyn, New York. Jack I. Straus's father, Jesse Isidor Straus, was also an executive of Abraham & Straus and from 1919 to 1933 was president of R. H. Macy & Company. During the last few years of his life he was United States Ambassador to France. Other members of the Straus family have also been business executives, have held government positions, and have been directors of philanthropic societies. In this environment of business and philanthropy the member of the third generation of Straus executives spent his early years.

For his secondary education Jack Straus attended the Westminster Preparatory School, in Simsbury, Connecticut, graduating in 1917. He then entered Harvard College, of which his father was an alumnus, and chose English as his major study. At Harvard Straus was a member of the Hasty Pudding Club and the

Delta Kappa Epsilon fraternity. He also joined the Reserve Officers' Training Corp in 1918, receiving his commission as second lieutenant in the United States Army the next year and in 1923 becoming a member of the United States Army Reserve. In 1921, with his B.A. degree from Harvard, he entered the family business as a member of Macy's training squad. From this he passed through executive posts in the other departments of the firm. For a while he was assistant general sales manager, then a buyer, and then merchandise councilor. In 1926 he became executive vice-president in charge of the merchandise division and two years later a member of the board of directors. From 1929 to 1933 he also served as secretary of the board and at the end of that time was appointed vice-president. He held the latter title until 1939, when, as acting president, he was placed in charge of all operations of the 34th Street store. In 1940, when Percy Straus, a member of the second generation of the family and president for the previous seven years, became chairman of the board of directors, Jack I. Straus was elected president.

The company over which Straus presides was founded in 1858 by Rowland H. Macy, a whaler from Nantucket who in that year opened a retail store in New York City, innovating aggressive advertising and cash sales as the guiding principles for success. Some thirty years later, members of the Straus family became associated with the firm and since then have held the controlling interest in what is generally agreed to be one of the most important mercantile firms in the United States. The main store, occupying almost the entire area between Broadway and Seventh Avenue and 34th and 35th Streets in New York City, is physically the largest store in the world, with approximately 2,150,000 square feet, and containing departments which in themselves are larger than many individual stores specializing in these items. Reorganized in 1919 as R. H. Macy & Company, Inc., the firm has since 1923 gradually acquired ownership of large department stores in Toledo, Atlanta, Newark, San Francisco, and Kansas City, and has built branch stores in suburban areas of New York.

The Straus executives have closely adhered to the original Macy policies of wide-scale advertising and cash sales, with claimed savings to customers of 6 per cent for the cash purchase of all items not price-fixed by the manufacturer. An average of 250,000 customers are attracted to the Manhattan store in one day, and combined yearly sales in the stores amount to $300 millions. To facilitate cash sales, Macy's has its own bank, with Straus as a director and vice-president, into which customers may deposit money and from which they draw as they make their purchases. Approximately $9 millions are credited to these deposit accounts.

During his presidency Straus has held fast to the low-price policy. In May 1946 he urged retention of the Office of Price Administration and the next spring, at a press conference and in full-page advertisements in leading New York papers, he asked for a general reduction

Pach Bros.

JACK I. STRAUS

in the prices of consumer goods, warning of a business recession if manufacturers and distributors did not cooperate in such reductions. He suggested that the increase in industrial efficiency be translated "into lower prices rather than into additional profits," advised the public of the availability of most consumer items, and, according to a report of the conference in the New York *Herald Tribune*, concluded that "the only way we [Macy's] know to retain prosperity for the nation and business is to keep full production going by producing more units at lower prices." The next year at a conference of the Alumni Association of the Harvard Business School he again spoke for lowered prices: "We must fight for a lower level of prices on which depends the maintenance of a standard of living adequate to support a prosperous United States. . . .Price-fixing and price-maintenance are devices aimed at keeping prices up and, as such, are dangerous to the community and inimical to the interests of the consumer" (quoted in the New York *Times*, June 13, 1948). When, in the spring of 1951, the United States Supreme Court ruled that nonsigners of fair trade agreements were not bound by State fair-trade laws, Straus was able to put into practice his theories by announcing reductions in the prices of the "fairtrade" items. Other retailers joined in the price cutting and for some ten weeks a "price war" prevailed, in which many items were sold not only below the manufacturers' list price but below wholesale prices. A summary of the outlook for 1952, made by the New York *Herald Tribune*, carried remarks by Straus in which he continued his opposition to price-fixing, arguing that such methods denied consumers the privilege of buying at competitive retail prices and contributed to inflation.

Former director, beginning in 1941, of General Teleradio, Inc. (station WOR and WOR-

STRAUS, JACK I.—*Continued*

TV in New York City), Straus was elected
to the board of directors of Lee Enterprises in
January 1952, upon completion of the merger
of General Teleradio with the Yankee and Don
Lee networks. Other business affiliations of
the Macy executive are as director and member of the executive committee of Davison
Paxon Company, Atlanta (since 1941) ; director
of Bamberger & Company, Newark (since
1929), Lasalle & Koch Company, Toledo (since
1946)., Macy's store in San Francisco (since
1946), and Macy's store in Kansas City (since
1947). His associations in banking have been
with the Irving Trust Company (member of
the advisory board, 1926-32), International Acceptance Trust Company (director, 1928-29),
Bank of Manhattan Company (member of the
executive committee, 1930), and Greenwich
Savings Bank (member of the board of trustees since 1942).

Also active in civic affairs, Straus was a
member in 1937 of Mayor La Guardia's Traffic
Commission, from 1940 to 1947 a member of
the Mayor's Business Advisory Commission,
for a period during World War II a member
of the New York City Council of Defense,
and from 1935 to 1949 a member of the board
of trustees of the Jewish Board of Guardians.
Since 1939 he has belonged to the Council of
the Boy Scout foundation of Greater New
York and since 1942 director of the executive
committee of the Greater New York Fund.
For the four-year period beginning in 1950
Straus is a member of the board of overseers
of Harvard University; since 1938 has held
membership on the visiting committee of the
Graduate School of Business Administration
of Harvard; and in 1942-43 was on the visiting
committee of the university library. In other
public activities he has given his service on
the board of sponsors of American Baseball
Academy (since 1951), board of directors of
the Lenox Hill Neighborhood Association
(since 1951), and the board of trustees of
Roosevelt Hospital (since 1944).

The department store executive is six feet tall,
wears glasses, and has brown hair. He married,
on April 29, 1924, Margaret Hollister, and has
one son, Kenneth Hollister, and two daughters,
Patricia (Straus) Toohey and Pamela. In 1951
Belgium awarded him the Cross of Officer of
the Order of Leopold II and the same year
he was named Chevalier in the French Legion
of Honor. For his efforts to create more trade
between Italy and the United States Straus
was honored at a dinner given in November of
1951 by the Chamber of Commerce for Trade
with Italy. He belongs to the Harvard Club
of New York City as well as to the Faculty
Club of Harvard University; and to the Sands
Point Club of Port Washington, and the Nassau Country Club of Glen Cove, both in Long
Island. He names as his favorite recreations
golf, tennis, and piano playing.

References

> N Y Post p23 My 1 '40
> Who's Who in America, 1950-51
> Who's Who in Commerce and Industry
> (1951)
> Who's Who in New York, 1947

STRAUS, MICHAEL W(OLF) Mar. 20,
1897- United States Government official
Address: b. c/o Bureau of Reclamation, Department of the Interior, Washington 25, D.C.;
h. 2714 Quebec St., N.W., Washington, D.C.

Commissioner of the United States Bureau of
Reclamation since 1945, Michael W. Straus has
the administrative responsibility of supplying
9,000,000 people in seventeen Western States
with water and power by means of 96 dams,
16,000 miles of canals, and over 3,000 miles of
electric transmission lines. The bureau headed
by Straus also shares with the Army Corps
of Engineers responsibility for flood control
measures. Prior to his years in Government
service, Straus had been a reporter and editor
in Chicago and a national affairs correspondent
in Washington, D.C.

Michael Wolf Straus was born in Chicago,
Illinois, on March 20, 1897, the son of Michael
and Mary (Howe) Straus. His father, a
German-born emigrant, was grain exporter,
with a seat on the Chicago Board of Trade,
and a dealer in real estate; his maternal grandmother was Fanny Howe, whose progressive
social and economic theories are said to have
had a strong influence on her grandson.

Following his graduation from high school in
a Chicago suburb, Straus attended for three
years (1914-17) the University of Wisconsin,
where his special study was chemical engineering. In 1918 he enlisted in the Navy, serving
for a year as a deck officer. In 1920 he became a reporter on the Chicago *Evening Post*,
later advancing to the posts of city editor and
managing editor of that newspaper; he also
at various times wrote on music, sports,
and drama. Aside from newspaper work Straus
taught from 1922 to 1924 in the Northwestern
University School of Journalism. When the
Chicago *Evening Post* ceased publication in
1932, he went to Washington, D.C., as a writer
on national affairs for Hearst's Universal News
Service; he later wrote for the New York
Evening Post.

After covering the last period of Herbert
Hoover's Administration and the beginning of
Franklin Roosevelt's first term in office, Straus
was appointed in 1933 an assistant to Harold
Ickes, whom he had known in Chicago. Ickes,
at that time both the Secretary of the Interior
and the director of the Federal Public Works
Administration, appointed Straus the director
of information for PWA. The experience
Straus gained in that post from 1933 to 1938
was the basis of a book that he wrote in collaboration with Talbot Wegg (a Federal Housing architect) in 1939: *Housing Comes of Age*.
A survey of America's first slum clearance
and low-rent housing program, the book gave a
detailed account of how the opposition of local

interests was met by the Federal Housing Authority, how land was secured, and how care was taken that no graft or price-gouging be allowed to discredit the housing program. This "history of the PWA from the viewpoint of insiders," as the *New Republic* called it, was praised by the New York *Times* reviewer as "informative, unimpassioned" and by the *Saturday Review of Literature* as "simply, clearly, and succinctly" written.

From 1938 to 1941 Straus was information chief for the Department of the Interior, performing the same duties in regard to press relations and publicity that he had had in the PWA. Donald Nelson, then head of the War Production Board, "borrowed" Straus from the Interior Department, where during 1941-42 the latter set up between six and seven thousand "production drive" committees, later known as labor-management committees. Straus returned to the Interior Department on February 18, 1943, when President Roosevelt appointed him first Assistant Secretary of the Interior, a position which made him responsible for liaison with Congress and for supervision of personnel. Upon the retirement of Harry Bashore as Commissioner of Reclamation in 1945, Straus, applied for the post. "It was a step downward in the Department's hierarchy," explained Paul F. Healy in an article on Straus for the *Saturday Evening Post* (April 19, 1952), "but it would give him more executive authority, and, when Ickes retired, more security." He was named Commissioner of Reclamation (in 1952 a $14,800-a-year appointment) by President Truman on December 12, 1945.

Called by the New York *Times* "an indispensable part of Western life," the Bureau of Reclamation since its establishment in 1902 has had the function of planning and constructing irrigation projects for the reclamation of arid and semiarid lands of about seventeen Western States (including Texas since 1906). To the Bureau is also assigned the development of power resources, the marketing of power, and the maintenance of power systems. Other programs of the reclamation service are flood control, drainage, and the creation of wildlife refuges. Of the total investments by the Government in reclamation work, over 75 per cent is returned to the Treasury by water users and from the sales of electric power. Paul F. Healy estimated that Michael Straus administers "an annual budget ranging in recent years from around $250 millions to more than $300 millions. His bureau supplies 9 million people with water and power by means of 96 dams, 16,000 miles of canals and over 3,000 miles of electric transmission lines."

Notable among the achievements of the Bureau of Reclamation is the Columbia Basin project in southeastern Washington. This, "the largest single irrigation development ever undertaken," (in the words of Cabell Phillips of the New York *Times*) is designed to take water impounded in the Franklin D. Roosevelt Lake behind the Grand Coulee Dam and convey it through a hundred miles of tunnels and canals to irrigate about a million acres of new farm land in Oregon. Another undertaking nearly

Wide World Photos

MICHAEL W. STRAUS

as large is the Central Valley Project in California, which carries surplus waters from Sacramento River through canals into the San Joaquin River. The Colorado-Big Thompson project in eastern Colorado provides irrigation for some 615,000 acres of sugar beet and grazing lands in the Platte and Big Thompson river valleys. A feature of this development is the Grand Lake-Big Thompson tunnel, believed to be the longest irrigation tunnel in the world.

Straus, as head of the Bureau of Reclamation, became the center of a controversy in May 1948, when a rider was attached to the Interior Department Appropriation Act for 1949 stipulating that the Reclamation Commissioner and all regional directors must have at least five years' experience as engineers. In order to avoid having Straus and Richard L. Boke, regional director in California, removed from their posts after January 31, 1949, President Truman asked Congress to repeal the rider, stating, "The positions which they occupy are primarily administrative in character and do not necessarily require a professional engineering background." Secretary of the Interior J. A. Krug charged that the rider was due to "financial and political pressure" from opponents of the Department's policy of close adherence to a law which restricts reclamation benefits to family-size farms of 160 acres. While the matter was being debated in the Senate, Straus and Boke continued in their work without salary until, in October 1949, a new Congress reinstated them on the payroll.

In late 1950 Straus started a four months' tour abroad as a representative of the State Department, the Economic Cooperation Administration, and the Point IV Program. He traveled some 26,000 miles around the world, visiting several reclamation projects. The

STRAUS, MICHAEL W.—*Continued*

following year in October on a tour of South American countries, he delivered a series of 16 lectures in Santiago, Chile. (He is also the author of many publications issued by the Bureau.) Since the beginning of the Korean War, which increased the demands for electric power, Straus has emphasized the need for Congressional grants to extend reclamation activities. In the light of budget cuts, however, he has told the House Appropriations Committee that the Reclamation Bureau will be "essentially out of business" by 1956. The vital need for expanded flood protection measures both by the Reclamation Bureau and the Army Engineers was seen at the time of the floods of the Missouri and Mississippi rivers in the spring of 1952. The House of Representatives on May 20 approved and sent to the Senate an emergency appropriation of $55 millions to be used to repair flood control projects damaged in those floods.

At the dedication of the Hungry Horse Dam in Montana in 1949, Straus was made an honorary member of the Blackfoot Tribe with the title of "Little White Beaver, Engineer of the Wilderness." The Commissioner is six feet three inches tall, weighs 220 pounds, and has gray hair and dark-brown eyes. He married Nancy F. Porter on May 24, 1924; they have three children, Margaret, Michael, and James. (A fourth child, Lucy, is deceased.) He belongs to the Tavern Club in Chicago and the National Press Club in Washington, and names his church affiliation as Unitarian. His sports are sailing and tennis.

References

N Y Times p23 D 13 '45
Sat Eve Post 224:46+ Ap 19 '52 pors
Time 33:34 Ja 16 '39 por
Washington (D.C.) Post p2 Je 17 '48 por
American Men in Government (1949)
Who's Who in America, 1952-53
Who's Who in the Nation's Capital, 1938-39

STRAUS, ROGER W(ILLIAMS) Dec. 14, 1891- Industrialist
Address: b. c/o American Smelting and Refining Company, 120 Broadway, New York 5; h. 6 E. 93d St., New York 28

Roger W. Straus is chairman of the board of the American Smelting and Refining Company, which has been described by *Barron's* as "the largest smelter and refiner in the world," with affiliates in the United States, Mexico, Peru, Australia, and Canada. He joined the company in 1914 as an employee in the labor and welfare department, was named a director in 1916, became assistant to the president in 1920, and was elected president in 1941 and chairman of the board in April 1947. Long active in the movement to promote interfaith understanding, he helped found the National Conference of Christians and Jews and has been its Jewish cochairman since its establishment in 1928.

The birthplace of Roger Williams Straus, the son of Oscar Solomon and Sarah (Lavanburg) Straus, is New York City; his birth date is December 14, 1891. (Isidor and Nathan Straus, merchants and philanthropists, were his uncles.) His Bavarian-born father, who came to the United States as a young boy, after a successful career in law left that profession to become a merchant. Later, withdrawing from business activities, he entered Government service: he was twice appointed United States Minister to Turkey and once Ambassador; he was a member of the Permanent Court of Arbitration at The Hague, and Secretary of Commerce and Labor in Theodore Roosevelt's Cabinet from 1906 to 1909. Thus Roger Straus "grew up in the atmosphere of statecraft" (as Alden Hatch phrased it in *Harper's Magazine*) and inherited a family tradition of civic and philanthropic endeavor. He received his preparatory training at Collegiate School in New York City and the Lawrenceville (New Jersey) School, and graduated from Princeton with the degree of Litt.B. in 1913. Shortly afterward he joined the American Smelting and Refining Company as an employee in the labor and welfare department, and two years later, in November 1916, he was named a member of the company's board of directors.

In World War I as a lieutenant in the Army Signal Corps from June 1917 to August 1918, Straus was assigned to the Military Intelligence Division of the General Staff; and from August 1918 to February 1919 as assistant intelligence officer, with the rank of captain, he served on the commanding general's staff in Siberia. (From 1920 to 1934 he held the rank of major in the Officers Reserve Corps.) Upon his discharge from active service, he rejoined the American Smelting and Refining Company as a member of the executive committee of the board of directors, to which he was appointed on April 2, 1919. A year later, on April 7, he was made assistant to the president, a post which he held until 1941, becoming during that period also a member of the finance committee of the board of directors (January 19, 1923), vice-president (April 4, 1923), and vice-chairman (April 1940). Succeeding Simon Guggenheim, he was elected president of the company on November 27, 1941, at which time he was also named chairman of the board's executive committee. Since April 22, 1947, Straus, while remaining chairman of the executive committee, has been chairman of the board.

The American Smelting and Refining Company, which fifty years ago was for a time under control of the Guggenheim family, has expanded steadily, until today, according to *Barron's* (in 1950) "it owns 58 per cent of the lead smelters, approximately 15 per cent of zinc and 31 per cent of the copper smelting capacity in the United States and Mexico." Until a few years ago it concentrated on smelting and refining; it is now laying greater stress on its mining program, to the extent that about 60 per cent of its net income is derived from its own mines. Among other operations, it controls uranium-buying stations for the Atomic Energy Commission at Monticello and

Marysdale in Utah and at Shiprock in New Mexico.

Roger Straus is in contact with industrialists all over the globe. "In eighteen months, shortly after World War II," Hatch reported, "he traveled 60,000 miles, checking up on company properties and informing himself on political and economic conditions everywhere." At a stockholders' meeting in April 1952, he announced that the company was considering the development of properties in southern Peru at a cost of more than $75 millions. Straus is chairman of the executive committee and a director of the General Cable Corporation and of Revere Copper and Brass, Inc.; a director of Federal Mining and Smelting Company and the New York Life Insurance Company; and a former director of Pacific Tin Consolidated Corporation and Gallup American Coal Company. He is a member of the American Institute of Mining and Metallurgical Engineers.

The industrialist has long been prominent in furthering religious tolerance. When the National Council of Christians and Jews was established in 1928, Straus, one of the founders of the organization, became its Jewish national cochairman. (In this position he serves in 1952 with cochairman T. E. Braniff, the Catholic representative, and Benson Ford, the Protestant representative.) He was instrumental in 1947 in forming a new international organization to promote religious tolerance, World Brotherhood. In order to broaden the area in which the concept of mutual understanding was applied, he proposed that the National Conference of Christians and Jews work out a program of human relations for labor and management to help overcome prejudices and discrimination in industry. With Newton D. Baker and Carlton J. H. Hayes, Straus edited *The American Way* (1936); Straus is author of the pamphlet *Religious Liberty—Civilization's Barometer* (1935) and of *Religious Liberty and Democracy; Writings and Addresses* (1939).

In 1936 Straus was awarded *The American Hebrew* medal for his work in fostering better understanding between Christians and Jews. In applauding the award, *Commonweal* made this statement: "He has been an effective, interested, and most capable worker in a cause which must be considered as one of the major social missions of the time." In recognition of his contributions to Judaism, Straus in April 1952 was awarded the annual Man-of-the-Year citation of the Metropolitan Conference of the National Federation of Temple Brotherhoods, of which he was the first president and is now honorary president. He is a member of the executive board of the Union of American Hebrew Congregations and a trustee of the Emanu-El Congregation in New York City, member of the executive committee of the American Jewish Committee, member of the board of governors of the American Financial and Development Corporation for Israel, and from 1940 to 1951 was honorary vice-chairman of the United Jewish Appeal of Greater New York. Other welfare organizations have his interest. He is president of the Fred L. Lavanburg Foundation, whose object it is "to provide sanitary housing accommodations at

Harris & Ewing
ROGER W. STRAUS

low rentals for persons of small incomes, primarily those living in New York City and vicinity"; he is also a trustee of the John Simon Guggenheim Memorial Foundation, the Daniel and Florence Guggenheim Foundation, the Roosevelt Memorial Foundation, and of the National Foundation for Infantile Paralysis; and is member-at-large of the National Council of Boy Scouts of America.

Straus, a Republican, "has always been a generous G.O.P. contributor," according to *Time*. While an undergraduate at Princeton, he organized a Bull Moose club to support Theodore Roosevelt's Presidential candidacy in 1911-12. A close friend of Governor Thomas E. Dewey since 1935, he was Dewey's New York City manager in the 1938 gubernatorial campaign and was named vice-chairman of the Republican National Campaign Committee in 1944. In 1948 he was mentioned as a probable choice for a Cabinet post in the event that Dewey were elected; but Straus, who has never been a candidate for political office, stated that he did not desire any post.

Academic honors bestowed upon the industrialist are the Class Cup (Princeton 1913) in 1936, and honorary degrees from Bucknell University (L.H.D., 1936), Hebrew Union College (D.H.L., 1943), and Jewish Theological Seminary (LL.D., 1950). He is regent-at-large of the University of the State of New York. His clubs are the National Republican, Princeton, Bankers of America, Lotos (New York), and Cosmos (Washington, D.C.); he is a member also of the American Legion. Mrs. Straus is the former Gladys Guggenheim. Married on January 12, 1914, they have three children—Oscar S. 2d, Roger Williams, Jr., and Florence G. (Mrs. Max A. Hart). The industrialist is described in *Harper's* as "a

STRAUS, ROGER W.—*Continued*

handsome, gray-haired man . . . with a warm, friendly manner." Fishing is one of his recreations.

References

N Y Herald Tribune p7 F 11 '47
N Y Times p33 N 28 '41
N Y World Telegram p3 Ag 29 '44 por
Time 22:21-2 My 29 '44 por

Business Executives of America (1950)
Who's Who in America, 1952-53
Who's Who in American Jewry, 1938-39
Who's Who in New York, 1947

SULLIVAN, ED(WARD VINCENT)
Sept. 28, 1902- Newspaper columnist; television personality

Address: b. c/o New York Daily News, 220 E. 42d St., New York 17; c/o CBS Television Network, 485 Madison Ave., New York 22; h. Hotel Delmonico, 502 Park Ave., New York 22

Ed Sullivan, the former sportswriter who has conducted the *Little Old New York* column appearing in the New York *Daily News* and syndicated to newspapers throughout the country since 1932, was also a radio and vaudeville performer and the organizer and master of ceremonies of war- and peacetime benefit shows before he entered the television field in 1948. His Sunday night CBS-TV program, *Toast of the Town,* launched in June of that year, is currently rated among the best and most popular of TV variety entertainments.

Edward Vincent Sullivan was born in Manhattan on September 28, 1902, one of the seven children of Peter Arthur Sullivan, a customs house employee, and the former Elizabeth Smith. The greater part of his boyhood was passed in Port Chester, New York, to which the family moved after the death of his twin brother, Daniel, and a younger sister, Elizabeth. There he attended St. Mary's Parochial School before completing his formal education at Port Chester High School. At the latter he won twelve "letters" in athletics and captained the championship baseball team in the Westchester County Interscholastic League. "Ed was too interested in winning his letters in sports to make good high school grades," his wife stated in an article in *Collier's*, "but he was an omnivorous reader and because he has always been blessed with a photographic memory he remembered what he had read." Books aroused a desire to become a writer, an ambition encouraged by his mother and a sister; and while still in his middle teens he wrote high school sports news for the Port Chester *Daily Item.* On graduation he became a reporter on the *Item*'s staff and was assigned to cover police courts, weddings, deaths, and social, club, and athletic events until he left to join the Hartford (Connecticut) *Post* in 1919.

The Hartford *Post* went out of business only a few days after Sullivan arrived, with the consequence that he worked for a while as a wrapping clerk in a Hartford department store before beginning his metropolitan newspaper career on the now defunct New York *Evening Mail* in 1920. His big opportunity came when one night he was assigned to cover the Westminster Kennel Club Show at Madison Square Garden. Because of his novel treatment of this event, he was given a by-line, and in ensuing months at the *Mail* sports desk he continued to use unusual human-interest angles in his "stories." Subsequently, while covering a tennis tournament, he was the first to give the nickname "Little Poker Face" to Helen Wills, the Californian champion.

In 1924 the *Evening Mail* was absorbed by the *Sun.* The sportswriter's next position was on the *World,* which he left in 1925 for the *Morning Telegraph,* a daily chiefly devoted to sports and show business. (Sullivan's book, *Mister Lee,* is a biography of the producer and theater chain operator, Lee Shubert.) After about two years with the *Morning Telegraph* Sullivan was engaged in 1927 as sports editor of the New York *Evening Graphic,* the tabloid which had been established by Bernarr Macfadden in 1924 and on which Walter Winchell was building up a following with his *Broadway Hearsay* column. When Winchell moved to the *Daily Mirror* in 1929 the *Graphic* made Sullivan a Broadway columnist, an assignment he did not at first highly esteem. Thus, while Sullivan's "first column as a night-club reporter was a blast at gossip columnists" (the quoted words are Mrs. Sullivan's) he was seen challenging Winchell in their common domain, and a strong personal rivalry developed. The *Graphic* columnist, who had originated the paper's annual sports award dinners also became known for his charitable work in staging and introducing benefit variety shows to aid various causes: in April 1932 he was induced to appear at the Paramount Theatre in New York as master of ceremonies of a tabloid revue, *Gems of the Town.*

With the suspension of the *Graphic* in July 1932, Ed Sullivan joined the New York *Daily News,* in which his column has since appeared uninterruptedly under the heading *Little Old New York,* currently being syndicated to twenty-seven other newspapers. Also in 1932, he launched over Columbia Station WABC (now WCBS) his first radio show—he is credited with having introduced on the airwaves such showmen as Irving Berlin, Jack Benny, Jack Pearl, and the late George M. Cohan and Florenz Ziegfeld. In ensuing years he led from time to time his own vaudeville units, contributed sketches to Broadway musical shows, and tried writing and acting for the motion pictures. Sullivan was the author of the original story from which the light comedy film *There Goes My Heart* was developed in 1938, and of the screenplay *Big Town Czar* (1939), an underworld melodrama in which he played himself. Another example of his filmwriting was *Ma, He's Making Eyes at Me* (1940).

During the earlier period of American participation in World War II the *News* columnist staged two "monster" benefit shows at Madison Square Garden, the first of which raised $226,000 for Army Emergency Relief, while the second brought in $249,000 for the American Red Cross. (For these achievements he received a citation from the Catholic War Veterans.) Ed Sullivan was (stated a Columbia Broadcasting System release) "the first to organize and produce shows for wounded servicemen in New York," and for such activity there and elsewhere he has been cited four times by the United States Government. Another honor for war work was the commendation for distinguished service bestowed by the Halloran General Hospital on Staten Island. In addition to appearing at hospitals and camps, Sullivan's vaudeville units played Loew's State Theatre in New York City sixteen times and other houses in Manhattan and out of town before October 1942, when the columnist was re-signed by CBS to head the Monday evening radio program *Ed Sullivan Entertains*. His column in the *News* continued without interruption through the war period. For his emphasis on tolerance, Sullivan received the fourth annual journalism award of the Philadelphia B'nai B'rith Council in January 1951.

"Ed got into television by accident," Mrs. Sullivan has explained in her article in *Collier's*. "For a number of years he had been master of ceremonies of the gigantic dance competition, the Harvest Moon Ball, put on annually in the Garden by the *Daily News*. In 1947, although Ed did not know it at the time, CBS televised the Harvest Moon Ball." Worthington Miner, the Columbia manager of television program development, was so impressed by the columnist's showmanship at this and a subsequent Garden entertainment that Sullivan was engaged to head the hour-long televised variety show *Toast of the Town*, first projected on June 20, 1948. The master of ceremonies has been described by John Crosby in the New York *Herald Tribune* as "totally innocent of any of the tricks of stage presence." However, what Richard B. Gehman has characterized in a *Coronet* article as his "talent for spotting fresh personalities" was soon evident—"I believe in getting the best acts I can, introducing them quickly, and getting off," Sullivan told the *Coronet* writer. The celebrities whom he has introduced to television during the past four years have included Margaret Truman, Faye Emerson, Hedy Lamarr, Ethel Waters, Gloria Swanson, Sam Levenson, Victor Borge, and Bob Hope. In *Cue,* Philip Minoff pointed out that the Sullivan show has been "the first TV program to establish a permanent dancing line; first to use rear-screen projections; first to go on the road for occasional telecasts. . .and the first to introduce celebrities from the studio audience." In January 1951 Sullivan's contract with CBS was renewed for an additional five years, and in the same month he received the 1950 *Look* award as television's "best

Wide World Photos
ED SULLIVAN

master of ceremonies." In the 1951-52 season *Toast of the Town* made a feature of "television biographies" of famous show-world personages, among them Oscar Hammerstein 2d and Helen Hayes.

The columnist and television showman is a member of the Catholic Institute of the Press and of the Notre Dame, Westchester Country and Winged Foot Golf clubs in or near New York City. He has been married since April 28, 1930, to the former Sylvia Weinstein, whom he met at a Broadway night club to which she had been taken to celebrate her graduation from high school. Their daughter, Elizabeth, is now Mrs. Robert Henry Precht, Jr. For the past thirteen years the Sullivans have found it convenient to live in hotel suites. The columnist-TV showman, whom Gehman (in *Coronet*) has described, has a height of five feet ten inches and weighs 155 pounds; his eyes are blue and his wavy hair is dark brown. His solemn gaze has been the subject of comment. Golf, which he learned to play while caddying for Gene Sarazan on links near his boyhood home, remains Sullivan's favorite outdoor diversion, and he also likes horseracing and dogs. For reading he prefers biography.

References

Collier's 129 :47+ Je 21 '52 pors
Coronet 31 :53-8 Mr '52 por
Cue 21 :12-14+ Je 21 '52 pors
Look 21 :46+ Ap 11 '50 pors
N Y Times II p11 Mr 23 '52 por
Pathfinder 57 :54 Jl 1 '50 por
Time 57 :49 Je 25 '51 por; 59 :66 Ja 7 '52 por

International Motion Picture Almanac, 1950-51
World Biography (1948)

SUMMERFIELD, ARTHUR E(LLS-WORTH) Mar. 17, 1899- Postmaster General-designate; political party leader; automobile dealer

Address: b. c/o Republican National Committee, 923 15th St., N.W., Washington 5, D.C.; c/o Summerfield Chevrolet Company, 2712 N. Saginaw St., Flint 5, Mich.; h. 2952 Parkside Dr., Flint 3, Mich.

Arthur E. Summerfield of Flint, Michigan, was chosen chairman of the Republican National Committee (to succeed Guy Gabrielson) in July 1952, the day after the nomination of General Dwight D. Eisenhower as the party's

Wide World Photos
ARTHUR E. SUMMERFIELD

Presidential candidate. At the Chicago convention Summerfield gave the Eisenhower candidacy powerful aid when he brought most of the Michigan delegates to the support of the General. After the Republican victory in November, Eisenhower announced that in January he would appoint Summerfield Postmaster General. Summerfield, whose party organization work began in 1940 at the time of Wendell Willkie's campaign, has been chairman of the strategy committee of the national party organization and is known as a successful fund raiser. The new Republican leader is the president of one of the largest automobile agencies in the United States.

The son of William Henry and Cora Edith (Ellsworth) Summerfield, Arthur Ellsworth Summerfield was born March 17, 1899, in Pinconning, near Bay City on the lower peninsula of Michigan. At the age of thirteen, after completing grammar school (which he had attended in three Michigan towns), the youth worked on the production line of the nearby Weston-Mott Company. His next employment was at the Buick Motor Company. During World War I young Summerfield was the inspector of the ammunition department of the Chevrolet plant in Flint. By the age of twenty he was a married man and had entered the real estate business (in 1919).

In 1924 Arthur Summerfield became the Pure Oil Company distributor in Flint and, according to a 1952 release from the Republican headquarters, developed his business into one of the largest individual oil distributing companies in Michigan. In September 1929, just before the stock market crash started the depression years (in which Summerfield suffered heavy losses), he also went into the automobile field when he launched the Summerfield Chevrolet Company, which now has branches in Clio and Grand Rapids. The company's president since its establishment, he now owns one of the largest retail automobile agencies in America. In 1937 Summerfield gave up his Pure Oil business and the following year became president of the Bryant Properties Corporation—he is a director of the Genesee County (Michigan) Real Estate Association, as well as of the State and national automobile dealers associations. Two other business connections are in the insurance field: he is a member of the board of directors of the American Motorists Insurance Company and of the Lumbermen's Mutual Insurance Company.

His entrance into political organization work is said to have been the result of the failure of a Wendell Willkie rally during the 1940 Presidential campaign—attendance was small and the Republican candidate was given a mixed reception. Displeased at what he considered the ineptness of the local Republican organization, Summerfield organized a Genesee County campaign committee, which helped Willkie to carry the county and the State that November. Many of the problems facing Willkie campaign committees were similar to those Summerfield was later to encounter in managing the campaign of Dwight D. Eisenhower. Among them were the difficulty of coordinating the activities of the many different groups backing Willkie, and the resentment of regular Republican party workers at what they regarded as favored treatment for the "amateur" and volunteer workers and Democrats for Willkie.

Summerfield, who from 1942 to 1949 was Michigan director of the National Automobile Dealers Association (he has also been a regional vice-president), was appointed Michigan chairman of its automobile committee in charge of wartime recruitment for the Army Ordnance Department. The committee channeled more than five thousand mechanics into war production and recruited several hundred officers, an achievement for which the automobile dealer was cited by the Chief of Ordnance. Summerfield also served on the board of the Flint War Chest, was occupied with postwar planning as chairman of the National Automobile Dealers Association postwar planning committee in 1943-44, and in 1944 as a member of the similar committee of the Chamber of Commerce of the United States.

In the political arena Summerfield sought the Republican nomination for Michigan Secretary of State in 1942, but lost in the primaries to Herman Dignam. Appointed finance director of the Republican State Central Committee in 1943, Summerfield reorganized his party's fund-raising activities in Michigan. "Throwing out the old system under which a few men and the candidates paid most of the campaign costs," reported the New York *Herald Tribune,* "Mr. Summerfield divided the State into districts, asked each donor to make only one contribution and budgeted political expenses for the first time. His system proved so successful that leaders from other states visited Michigan to study 'the Summerfield plan.'" At the 1944 Republican National Convention, Arthur Summerfield was elected committeeman from Michigan over the opposition of Frank D. McKay of Grand Rapids, who had been a long-time strong leader of the party in Michigan. Two years later national committeeman Summerfield was also named regional vice-chairman of the party's national finance committee for the North Central Division, which comprises Michigan, Wisconsin, Illinois, Indiana, and Ohio. There, according to a *Herald Tribune* editorial, his "fame as a money raiser" approached the "legendary."

When Michigan Senator Arthur S. Vandenberg won re-election in 1946 by a 2-to-1 majority without campaigning, Summerfield began to work for the Senator's nomination for the Presidency. According to Arthur S. Vandenberg, Jr., in *The Private Papers of Senator Vandenberg,* Summerfield, who surveyed public opinion in the United States from 1946, found strong support for Vandenberg, some of it in the Democratic Southern States. While Vandenberg decided not to be a candidate, Summerfield organized the Michigan Republicans for Vandenberg with the thought of drafting him for the Presidential nomination. Summerfield had headed a committee which tried vainly to induce Vandenberg to seek the nomination, and although he received no encouragement from the Senator and much inducement to join the Dewey forces, he selected a "Draft-Vandenberg" delegation. Afterward Summerfield was discussed for the Republican national chairmanship to head the Dewey campaign, but declined, he has told, in favor of Representative Hugh D. Scott, Jr.

In July 1949, after Scott resigned under pressure from the chairmanship of the Republican strategy committee, Arthur Summerfield was appointed to the chairmanship. According to the New York *Herald Tribune,* he accepted the post "with some reluctance, after he had been urged to do so by other members of a group of party leaders designated to fill the job." The strategy committee described in the *Christian Science Monitor* as "not policy-forming," was to "set up a program of fundamentals for the 1950 campaign," these to be approved by Congressional leaders and presented to the National Committee by a specially appointed policy committee. Within a month after his appointment

Summerfield was involved in the factional dispute within the National Committee between "Old Guard," pro-Taft elements, who backed Guy Gabrielson for the national chairmanship, and pro-Dewey elements who voted for Axel E. Beck (Gabrielson won by a vote of 52 to 47). Summerfield's vote was cast for Beck. That December he called for a program "clearly and unmistakably in opposition to that now offered by our opponents" (the Democrats), and urged that his party "divest itself of 'me-tooism.'" In July 1950 Summerfield resigned from the strategy committee chairmanship, stating that although neither Scott nor Gabrielson had provided the committee with any funds, it had worked out "a very well conceived and constructive program" but that nevertheless Gabrielson was forcing it to "die on the vine" (New York *Times,* July 28, 1950).

Prior to the 1952 National Convention, Summerfield, as the leader of Michigan Republicans, maintained a position of neutrality between the Taft and Eisenhower proponents. He brought Senator Taft to Michigan to meet party leaders and visited General Eisenhower at SHAPE headquarters in Paris to arrange his coming to Michigan. Summerfield succeeded in keeping the delegation uncommitted. At the convention he joined Governor Fine of Pennsylvania, leader of another large uncommitted delegation, in an attempt to restore party harmony and to prevent a floor fight on contested delegations. Some bitterness was aroused, within the Michigan delegation and between Summerfield and reporters for Michigan newspapers, by the leader's refusal to allow his delegates to be polled as to their preferences for the nomination. At the last moment, while he was carrying an Eisenhower banner in the demonstration that followed the placing of the General's name before the Convention, Summerfield publicly announced his position. Thirty-five of his forty-six delegates also voted for Eisenhower on the first ballot. The Michigan leader was credited with having a major part in the maneuvers which brought Governor Fine and most of Pennsylvania's delegates behind the General.

Summerfield was one of the proponents of the "bonus rule," adopted at the 1952 Convention, which provided for an additional seat on the National Committee to States that succeeded in electing Republicans to major offices. At the first meeting of the enlarged committee, his was the only name proposed for the national chairmanship—according to custom, since he was the choice of the Presidential nominee. His election, on July 12, was unanimous. Summerfield was described by a New York *Times* correspondent then as "a comparative newcomer to big-league politics." Wrote another *Times* correspondent, "In some quarters it was muttered that this [change in committee personnel] was the passing out of the Old Guard. Closer inspection seemed to indicate, however, that the G.O.P.'s Old Guard was still largely on hand, but was all-out for General Eisenhower." The immediate problems facing the new national chairman were considered to be the healing of pro-Taft feelings embittered by

SUMMERFIELD, ARTHUR E.—*Cont.*

events at the convention, and the coordinating of the regular Republican organization work with the 2,500-club Citizens-for-Eisenhower movement and the "draft-Eisenhower" organization which had been built up by Senator Henry Cabot Lodge, Jr. Eisenhower appointed a personal campaign staff because, Russell Porter reported, "Arthur Summerfield. . .as chairman of the Republican National Committee, will be far too busy helping Congressional committees and State and local committees in their election campaign to do the coordinating job essential to avoid a Willkie debacle."

On November 25, 1952, President-elect Eisenhower announced that he had selected Summerfield to be Postmaster General. Before he takes his oath of office for this position (presumably in January 1953), Summerfield will resign as chairman of the Republican National Committee.

Summerfield and the former Miriam W. Graim, who were married July 22, 1918, have a daughter, Gertrude Miriam (Mrs. William C. Davison) and a son, Arthur E., Jr., who is in his father's business. The Republican is a Mason and an Elk and in Flint he belongs to the Kiwanis, the City Club (he is president of the latter), and the Golf Club; in Detroit he is a member of several clubs—the Economic, the Detroit, and the Detroit Athletic. Since 1946 he has been a trustee of Cleary College in Ypsilanti and since 1950 has served as Michigan director of the Boys' Clubs of America.

References

N Y Herald Tribune p7 Jl 13 '52; II pl
    Jl 20 '52 por
N Y Times p8 Jl 11 '52
Who's Who in America, 1952-53

TABER, GLADYS (LEONAE BAGG)
Apr. 12, 1899- Author
Address: b. c/o Ladies' Home Journal, 1270 6th Ave., New York 20; h. "Stillmeadow," Southbury, Conn.

Reprinted from the *Wilson Library Bulletin*, April 1952.

"We are always pursuing happiness and security. Now and then, rarely, we find them, if only briefly," writes Gladys Taber in one of the several books she has written about "Stillmeadow," the farm at Southbury, Connecticut, where she lives in a slightly remodeled house built in 1690, with her sister "Jill" (Mrs. Eleanor Mayer), a dozen or more cocker spaniels, Maeve (an Irish setter), and Esmé, the royal Siamese cat named for a character in Saki. "But for me," continues Mrs. Taber, "a small home in a green valley is security and the opportunity to make a happy life."

Though Mrs. Taber's novels have been written primarily for women, and her *Diary of Domesticity* department has been one of the most widely read features of the *Ladies' Home*

Journal since 1938, it is indisputable that many men have enjoyed her books about "Stillmeadow" and perhaps learned some home truths from *Especially Father* (1949), the best-selling biography of her impetuous parent ("Father went through life like a jet plane, and he expected everyone around him to do the same.")

Gladys Leonae Bagg—her middle name was derived from her uncle Leonidas, a Civil War officer—was born April 12, 1899, in Colorado Springs, Colorado, the second daughter of Rufus Mather Bagg, Jr., a descendant of Increase and Cotton Mather, the Massachusetts Puritan divines, and Grace Sibyl (Raybold) Bagg. "Father" was a man of tireless energy who whisked his family from one part of the country to the other. Gladys wrote an historical novel at nine, verse at ten. From Appleton High School, she was packed off by Father to Wellesley, taking her B.A. degree in 1920. Returning to Appleton, she taught English at Lawrence College, receiving her master's degree in 1921 in spite of a dearth of research material caused by Father's continuous warfare with the college librarian over a 75-cent fine—an incident which crops up in *A Star to Steer By* (1938). She married another teacher, Frank Albion Taber, Jr., in 1922. The Tabers have a daughter, Constance (the "Cecily" of the "Stillmeadow" books), now a teacher of linguistics at Columbia University.

Mrs. Taber published a book of poems, *Lyonesse*, in 1926, and her first novel, *Late Climbs the Sun*, in 1934, a story of feminine revolt praised by the New York *Times* for its competent style, humor, and "bright, convincing detail." By that time the Tabers, with Mrs. Mayer and her two children, were living at "Stillmeadow," with its forty acres, and finding that "a home in the country is no place for idlers. It takes you over." These first years were "years when Jill and I had no underwear" and one good dress apiece. But their days were crowded with activity, including the raising of pedigreed cocker spaniels and the care of a large garden. Garden produce goes into the deep freeze to take care of the many guests who are also fed from recipes collected in *Stillmeadow Kitchen* (1946, revised 1950), which Virginia Kirkus called "one of those cookbooks you start out to sample and soon find yourself reading just for the joy of it."

Harvest at Stillmeadow (1940), called by the New York *Herald Tribune Books* a "mellow, reassuring record," was a first collection of Mrs. Taber's informal essays on year-round living, working, and meditating there. *The Book of Stillmeadow* (1948) is "a book to recommend to people who need—for the space of a few hours—to find peace," according to Virginia Kirkus, who said of *Stillmeadow Seasons* (1950), "There is a serenity, sparked with humanity, that gives these books their unfailing charm." Some critics, however, have complained good-naturedly that Mrs. Taber's quick transitions from Shakespeare to casseroles are sometimes a bit confusing. *Especially Spaniels* (1945) is a practical book on the selecting and training of dogs, with photographs by "Jill," which the New York *Herald*

GLADYS TABER

Tribune Weekly Book Review described as extremely useful and a book which "can be happily read by the dogless." Similarly, the local flora served as inspiration for *Flower Arranging for the American Home* (1947), which Mrs. Taber wrote in collaboration with Ruth Kistner. This the *Weekly Book Review* called "a volume that is unique in charm, in stimulation, and in sincere down-to-earth advice."

Before and between these books came novels of romance and family life. *Tomorrow May Be Fair* (1935), *Evergreen Tree* (1937), *This Is for Always* (1938), *Nurse in Blue* (1944), *The Heart Has April Too* and *Give Us This Day* (1944), and *Give Me the Stars* (1945), called by Lisle Bell, "a solid and entertaining novel, nebulous only in title." An historical novel is now in progress. In addition Mrs. Taber has written two books for children: *The First Book of Dogs* (1949) and *The First Book of Cats* (1950). Her own reading tastes run to the soundly romantic—Keats, De la Mare, Yeats, and Millay in poetry—and *Wuthering Heights* in the novel.

A caller at "Stillmeadow" one afternoon last year found its chatelaine short, auburn-haired, blue-eyed, absorbed in a new litter of puppies, but ready to discuss a common enthusiasm, the novels of Joseph Shearing. "It gives me a good deal of pleasure to recognize many of my traits as pure, unadulterated Yankee," she once wrote, and it was evident that Mrs. Taber gave no more than a backward thought to New York, "which is a very special locale."

TALAL 1909- Former King of Jordan
Address: Amman, Jordan

The second ruler of the Hashemite Kingdom of Jordan, Talal, came to the throne in Sep-

tember 1951, a little less than two months after the assassination of his father, King Abdullah. In the period between Abdullah's death and his son's elevation there had been much discussion of whether Talal's health would debar him from succeeding to the kingship and speculation about his views on the political controversies disturbing the Middle East. In the summer of 1952, Talal, removed from the throne by Jordan's Parliament because of his mental illness, was succeeded by his son, Crown Prince Hussein.

The elder of Abdullah's two sons and his second child, Talal was born in Mecca in 1909. Talal's paternal grandfather, Hussein, ruled as hereditary sherif of Mecca and king of the Hejaz, heading the Hashemite family, direct descendants of the prophet Mohammed and claimants to the caliphate of Islam. During his childhood and youth, stated the London *Daily Telegraph* in a biographical sketch by R. J. C. Broadhurst (equerry to Abdullah from 1941 to 1948), the future Jordanian king was privately educated in Arabic literature, law, and philosophy under the supervision of King Hussein; and the boy participated as a spectator in state councils and on inspection trips through his grandfather's domain.

Soon after joining the Arab Legion as a lieutenant in 1927, Emil (Prince) Talal went to England to study at the Royal Military College at Sandhurst, from which he graduated in the rank of lieutenant in 1929. Back in the Middle East, he became an aide to King Hussein, who was at that time in Cyprus, having in 1924 been driven from Hejaz by Ibn Saud; and later he accompanied his grandfather to Amman, where Abdullah had established the capital of his country, then called Trans-Jordan. In the Arab Legion, Talal was advanced to a major in 1933, a major general in 1941, and to a full general in 1948. He also saw a token period of service in the Iraqi army. The crown prince did not participate in the Jordanian government and often found himself unoccupied, but while some thought that this was because Abdullah preferred his younger son, Emir Naif, Broadhurst stated that the King had simply followed the Oriental practice of letting his heir go without training in statecraft.

When Abdullah was assassinated in Jerusalem on July 20, 1951, there was much speculation about the effect of his death on Middle East and on world affairs. At a time when Arab leaders were turning against Great Britain, Abdullah remained that country's stanch ally. His Arab Legion, maintained by British subsidy, had been the only Arab force in the Middle East to take part in World War II. While he had joined the Arab countries' action against Israel in 1948, he later seemed disposed to effect a *modus vivendi* with the Jewish state. In his ambition to unite his country with Syria, Lebanon, and Iraq under Hashemite rule, Abdullah was in disagreement with Egypt and Saudi Arabia and in other policies showed a general tendency to diverge from the Arab League.

(Continued next page)

Wide World Photos

TALAL

Upon Abdullah's death it was much debated whether or not his successor was to be pro-British and to continue espousing a "Greater Syria." Since Talal was in Switzerland undergoing treatment for a nervous disorder at the time of his father's death, Emir Naif was named regent and was himself believed by some observers to be a candidate for the throne. Other sources suggested that the Hashemite family planned to make Feisal II, the young king of Iraq and Abdullah's nephew, joint ruler of the two countries, thus initiating the scheme of a "Greater Syria." In addition, certain Hashemite leaders from Iraq were mentioned as possibilities, as was Talal's eldest son, Hussein.

His claim to the throne (according to *Time*) backed by the British because of his known popularity in the Arab world, Talal returned to Amman, accompanied by Naif, on September 5, 1951, and the following day took the oath of office, having been proclaimed King of Jordan by the Council of Ministers. Later in the month he approved the formation of a new Cabinet headed by Premier Abdul Huda Pasha. At a pause in Athens on his trip back from Switzerland he had seemed to affirm his father's pro-British policy in assuring journalists that the "old friendly relations" with England would continue. A change in Jordanian policy toward the other Arab states was forecast when Talal returned in November to his native Arabia to visit his father's enemy Ibn Saud. An apparent improvement in relations with Syria was also thought proof that Talal had renounced ambitions respecting the "Greater Syria" plan associated with Abdullah. The new King, who reportedly disagreed with some of his father's ideas, is also said to be on good terms with the Grand Mufti of Jerusalem. After a reign of less than a year, Talal on August 11, 1952, was removed from the throne by the Parlia-

ment of Jordon on the grounds that he was mentally unfit to rule. His son, Crown Prince Hussein, was proclaimed his successor.

Talal and the Sherifa Zaïn, a Hashemite princess, daughter of Sherif Jamil, were married on November 27, 1934. They have three sons and a daughter. A writer who describes Talal as somewhat melancholy, points out that the former ruler has Abdullah's charm and considerateness. Talal speaks English fluently, is well read in Arabic literature, and enjoys gazelle hunting, collecting ancient manuscripts, and playing chess.

References

Daily Telegraph (London) p4 S 10 '51
N Y Times p6 Ag 31 '51 por; p16 S 6 '51
Newsweek 38:41 S 17 '51 por
Almanach de Gotha, 1937
International Who's Who, 1951

TASSIGNY, JEAN (JOSEPH MARIE GABRIEL) DE LATTRE DE *See* Lattre de Tassigny, J. J. M. G.

TAYLOR, ELIZABETH Feb. 27, 1932-
Motion picture actress

Address: b. c/o Metro-Goldwyn-Mayer Studios, Washington Blvd., Culver City, Calif.

At the age of twelve, in 1944, Elizabeth Taylor won approval for a leading role in the motion picture *National Velvet*. Then, after several years of relative obscurity, she emerged as an adult player in *The Conspirator* (1949), *Father of the Bride* (1950), and *A Place in the Sun* (1951). For her performance in the last-named film, a new version of Theodore Dreiser's *American Tragedy*, she received high praise from critics.

Elizabeth Rosemond Taylor was born February 27, 1932, in London, England, of American parentage. Francis Taylor, her father, had established himself abroad as a buyer for his uncle's art business. Her mother, known on the stage by her maiden name of Sara Sothern, had appeared in American and British productions. (The Taylors' elder child, born two years before Elizabeth, is a son, Howard.) While she was still a small child, the future actress began to study ballet under Vaccani, who for two generations was dancing teacher to the royal family. At the age of three she was one of the small dancers in a performance given before royalty at the Hippodrome. Shortly after, she began to receive her first instruction in horesback riding; in this she was encouraged by her godfather's gift of a horse. Her godfather, Colonel Victor Cazalet (who was killed in World War II), owned a place in Kent, where the Taylor family spent their summer vacations, occupying a fifteenth-century lodge. In the winter they lived in Hampstead, while Elizabeth attended school at Byron House.

Before the outbreak of World War II Francis Taylor sent his family to live with Mrs. Taylor's parents in Pasadena, California, where he subsequently joined them. Through their circle of acquaintances in Hollywood, the Taylors came to know J. Cheever Cowdin, who was instrumental in obtaining a one-year contract for eight-year-old Elizabeth with Universal, chiefly because of her fine singing voice. Taylor, who at first objected to his daughter's accepting the contract, later wrote in an article for *Parents' Magazine*, "We allowed the picture career because we believe that children should not be forced. They should be allowed and encouraged to develop on their natural lines." At Universal Elizabeth received training, particularly in singing, but made no pictures; at the end of the year she was released. Some time afterward her father was asked by Sam Marx of Metro-Goldwyn-Mayer whether his little girl was available for motion picture work—the studio was seeking a child with an English accent to appear with Roddy McDowall in *Lassie Come Home*. Upon the film's release in 1943, *Variety* observed: "Elizabeth Taylor, a pretty moppet, shows up to good advantage." She also appeared in a minor role in *White Cliffs of Dover*, which was followed by a "loan-out" to Twentieth Century-Fox for *Jane Eyre*. The young actress, who had been attending the Hawthorne School in Beverly Hills, subsequently became a student at the Metro-Goldwyn-Mayer School. She was graduated from the University High School in Hollywood in 1950.

For a number of years, MGM had owned the film rights to Enid Bagnold's *National Velvet*, which was withheld from production because of the company's inability to find a young girl suitable for the role of Velvet Brown. Anxious to secure the part (she related in "The Role I Liked Best"), she asked producer Pandro S. Berman for it, only to receive the reply that she was too small, although she was fitted for it by her speech and riding skill. To bring herself up to the required measurements, the child began eating steaks daily, said *Life*, developed her muscles by roller skating, and succeeded in four months in adding three inches to her height. During the same period, she practiced jumping horses on the polo field at the West Los Angeles Riviera Country Club. With this preparation, she made a test for *National Velvet* and was given the leading role. *Look* said that her performance placed her "among the screen's outstanding child actors." Alton Cook of the New York *World-Telegram* commented: "The performance of Elizabeth Taylor is a lovely conception . . . a burning eagerness tempered with sweet, fragile charm." To the New York *Post*'s motion picture reviewer, Archer Winsten, she seemed as "natural and excellent a little actress as you would ever hope to see." Bosley Crowther of the New York *Times* felt that Clarence Brown, the director, had drawn fine performances from the actors, "especially little Elizabeth Taylor. . . . Her face is alive with youthful spirit, and her voice has the softness of sweet song and her whole manner in this picture is one of refreshing grace." *National Velvet* was one of the first motion pictures selected in 1945 for the United States Library of Congress' newly instituted film archives. King Charles, the horse

ELIZABETH TAYLOR

ridden in *National Velvet* by Miss Taylor, was given to her by the studio as a birthday gift.

Miss Taylor's succeeding picture was *Courage of Lassie* (1946), in which the New York *Times* reviewer found her "refreshingly natural." The *World-Telegram*'s critic thought she did "a pleasant enough job, although her dialogue is limited to endless cries of 'Oh, Bill!'" After that she portrayed the title role of *Cynthia* (1947), in which Howard Barnes of the New York *Herald Tribune* considered her work "brilliant. . . . She plays an unwilling invalid with grave charm." "Miss Taylor breathes plenty of life into the title role," said *Variety*, "as a sheltered young girl who has never had a date or other fun generally accepted as matter-of-fact by teen-agers." In the same year (1947) Miss Taylor was in the cast of *Life With Father*, in which she was described as "very appealing" (New York *Times*) and "sweetly feminine" (*Variety*).

As a transition to more adult parts, Miss Taylor was in 1948 cast as "a spoiled beauty" in *A Date With Judy*. "The fact that she has always been a more than capable actress," wrote Archer Winsten, "assures us that we now witness the beginning of a new and brilliant career." The *World-Telegram*'s comment was: "It is pleasant to report that she handles the job with charm, character, and a new firmness in her style which suits her very well." This was followed by her role as the young wife in *The Conspirator*, filmed in England, where sixteen-year-old Miss Taylor, still subject to the educational laws of California, was accompanied by a teacher. Little warmth was shown by the critics for *The Conspirator* or its stars, *Time* remarking, "Elizabeth Taylor reveals several outstanding attributes of a beautiful woman but few of an actress."

A remake of *Little Women* in 1949 found Elizabeth Taylor in the part of Amy, in which, said Bosley Crowther, she was "appropriately

TAYLOR, ELIZABETH—*Continued*

full of artifice." To Howard Barnes she seemed "lovely and properly spoiled." She was next cast as costar with Van Johnson in *The Big Hangover*, an early 1950 production. "Miss Taylor is warm and appealing as the amateur psychiatrist," *Variety* judged, "in a role more mature and adult than usual for her." Her work, described as "competent" by the New York *Times*, was rated less high by the New York *Herald Tribune*'s Otis L. Guernsey, who said: "Elizabeth Taylor hovers on the edges of this comedy. . . .She has merely to appear interested or affectionate." Assigned next to play with Spencer Tracy and Joan Bennett in *Father of the Bride*, the young actress demonstrated, thought Alton Cook, "that she is still in the promising young actress stage of her career. For quite a time to come, she is likely to stir up more fuss off screen than on." Otis Guernsey found that "her good looks aid her in creating the illusion that in each successive scene the audience, like the father, is seeing her for the first time." *Father's Little Dividend* (1951), a sequel, contained the same cast, with Miss Taylor, according to Bosley Crowther, again mirroring "a real American type, slightly prettified and idealized, we'll grant you, but never sugared or overdone."

With the release of *A Place in the Sun* in mid-1951, Miss Taylor received almost unanimous praise from the critics: "Remarkably well cast" (the New York *Herald Tribune*); "an actress of emotional force" who gave a "wonderfully expressive performance" (New York *World-Telegram-Sun*). *Variety* attributed her good interpretation to the influence of director George Stevens: "The histrionics are of a quality far beyond anything she has done previously." The New York *Times* considered her portrayal of "the rich and beauteous Angela . . . the top effort of her career. It is a shaded, tender performance, and one in which her passionate and tender romance avoids the pathos common to young love as it sometimes comes to the screen." Two 1952 releases in which Miss Taylor appears are *Love is Better Than Ever* and *Ivanhoe*. At the time she signed a new, seven-year contract with MGM in mid-1952, she was to begin work on *The Girl Who Had Everything*.

Elizabeth Taylor was married on May 6, 1950, to Conrad Nicholas Hilton, Jr., son of C. N. Hilton, the hotel magnate. This marriage was terminated by divorce January 29, 1951. When the decree became final a year later, Miss Taylor was married again, in a February 21, 1952, ceremony in London to Michael Wilding, British film star. Five feet four and a half inches tall, the actress weighs 108 pounds. Frances Levison in *Life* has described her as a "violet-eyed beauty with magnificent deep coloring, a sharp delicate face framed in very dark hair, thick, honest brows, and curly double eyelashes." At the age of fourteen Miss Taylor wrote a story, *Nibbles and Me* (1946), illustrated by herself with pictures of her pet chipmunk. Subsequently, reported Dorothy Masters of the New York *Sunday News*, the young actress' pets have been rabbits, turtles, an owl, a horse, ducks, and several cats and

dogs. Painting and sculpturing are her hobbies. Aside from riding, which remains a favorite recreation of hers, she enjoys skeet shooting, badminton, and swimming.

References

Am Mag 146:42-3 Jl '48
Life 26:78-9 F 21 '49
Look 15:13 F 13 '51
N Y Herald Tribune IV p3 D 31 '44; V p1 F 27 '49
Parents Mag 24:36-7 O '49
Time 54:50+ Ag 22 '49

International Motion Picture Almanac, 1950-51

TAYLOR, ROBERT Aug. 5, 1911- Motion picture actor
Address: b. c/o Metro-Goldwyn-Mayer Studios, Culver City, Calif.

When Robert Taylor, who made his screen debut in 1934, became widely known several years later, he was greeted with an adulation remindful of the applause Valentino had won as a "matinee idol." In the course of the next few years Taylor played opposite Norma Shearer, Greta Garbo, and other famous stars. In the early 1950's, having arrived at "forceful maturity," he plays a variety of "types." Among his recent motion pictures are *Quo Vadis, Westward the Women*, and *Ivanhoe*.

Robert Taylor was born Spangler Arlington Brugh, the son of Spangler A. and Ruth Adelia (Stanhope) Brugh, in Filley, Nebraska; his birth date is August 5, 1911. The elder Brugh, a grain dealer, studied medicine in his later years in an attempt to cure Mrs. Brugh's heart condition, and Arlington was expected to take over eventually his father's practice in Beatrice, Nebraska. At grammar school the superintendent, who also led the school orchestra, persuaded him to give up the banjo and saxophone for the cello; later the youth earned money toward his college expenses by playing the cello in a trio which broadcast over Nebraska radio station KMNJ. As a high school student young Brugh was on the track team, and won the State oratorical championship. On vacations he shocked wheat and had other jobs.

During his freshman year at Doane College in Crete, Nebraska, he abandoned his plan to study medicine because he disliked science; as a sophomore he enrolled in economics courses, but discontinued that study too. When his music teacher, Herbert E. Gray, moved to Pomona College (in Claremont, California), young Brugh followed him. There he played in the college orchestra, continued his study of oratory, and took up dramatics, appearing in college productions of *M'lord the Duke, Camille*, and *The Importance of Being Earnest*. A talent scout from Metro-Goldwyn-Mayer saw him in the leading role of Captain Stanhope in *Journey's End* in February 1934—a part the student took under protest because it kept him from a public speaking contest in Oregon. Two days later the Pomona senior signed a seven-year MGM contract starting at thirty-five dollars a week.

Twice a week for three weeks Brugh drove to Culver City to study with MGM dramatic coach Oliver Hinsdell. Noticing that Hinsdell's interest waned, he postponed further training until his college graduation. After commencement the young Nebraskan moved to Hollywood and then inquired if MGM wanted him back. When the favorable reply arrived in October, he was called to Nebraska by the death of his father. He then took his mother and grandmother back to Hollywood with him.

Before he had his first part the young actor received encouragement from Louis B. Mayer, the studio head, who supplied him with a new wardrobe and changed his name to Robert Taylor. Seven days a week for six months Taylor worked with Hinsdell, learning not to overact or "mug." Loaned to Fox for Will Rogers' *Handy Andy*, Taylor was disappointed at being sent outside MGM for his debut, but soon found that being a guest gave him a higher status. Back at MGM, he was given the lead in *Buried Loot*, the first of the series of "Crime-Does-Not-Pay" shorts; an action picture, it allowed him to "mug a little" without damage. Also, in 1934 Taylor supported Frank Morgan and Binnie Barnes in *There's Always Tomorrow*, and Mady Christians and Jean Parker in *A Wicked Woman*. It was the second lead in *Society Doctor* that first brought him much fan mail.

In 1935 Taylor supported Wallace Beery, Robert Young, and Maureen O'Sullivan in *West Point of the Air*. This major feature was followed by two low-budget program pictures, *Times Square Lady* (starring Chester Morris and Virginia Bruce) and *Murder in the Fleet*, in which Taylor played opposite Jean Parker and received top billing. Then came the romantic lead opposite Eleanor Powell in the glittering musical *Broadway Melody of 1936*, which also starred Jack Benny. Taylor's biggest chance came when Universal borrowed him to play opposite Irene Dunne in *Magnificent Obsession* (1935). It was released on New Year's Eve, and Robert Taylor suddenly became a famous Hollywood star. With Jean Harlow he attended the President's birthday ball in Washington. In nearby Baltimore he was mobbed by fans, an experience that was to be commonplace in Taylor's life for the next few years, during which he was, in *Time*'s words, "the nation's most admired matinee idol since the late Rudolph Valentino."

During 1936 Taylor was cast opposite "top-flight" female stars: Janet Gaynor in *Small Town Girl*, Joan Crawford in *The Gorgeous Hussy*, Loretta Young in *Private Number*, Barbara Stanwyck in *His Brother's Wife*, Greta Garbo in *Camille*, Jean Harlow in *Personal Property*. One poll showed him the favorite male actor, with Clark Gable in second place. The exhibitors voted Taylor the fourth biggest box-office star of 1936, after Shirley Temple, Gable, and the Astaire-Rogers dance team. His weekly salary mounted to $3,500, his weekly mail to 7,000 items, and his Sundays reportedly were devoted to autographing the 3,000 pictures requested each week by his ad-

ROBERT TAYLOR

mirers. His courtship of Barbara Stanwyck, whom he married on May 14, 1939, was followed by the newspapers.

There was some decline in Taylor's box-office appeal during the years 1937-38. In England he made *A Yank at Oxford*, in which Vivien Leigh had a supporting role. *Three Comrades*, *The Crowd Roars*, and *Stand Up and Fight*, all in 1938, introduced a new, "tougher" Taylor; in two of the roles he was a mule driver and a prize fighter. In 1939 he was cast opposite two promising newcomers, Hedy Lamarr and Greer Garson, in *Lady of the Tropics* and *Remember?*, respectively; and in *Lucky Night*, with Myrna Loy.

Waterloo Bridge (1940), with Vivien Leigh, restored Taylor's popularity and started him on a series of successes: *Escape* (anti-Nazi melodrama with Norma Shearer), *Flight Command* (from which dates Taylor's interest in flying), *Billy the Kid*, and *When Ladies Meet* (a sparkling drawing-room comedy with Joan Crawford, Greer Garson, and Herbert Marshall). Taylor, who has named Billy the Kid as his favorite role, took special pains with the details. In *Johnny Eager*, also made in 1941, Taylor played a killer who died nobly for the love of Lana Turner. As before, opinions differed on the convincingness of Taylor's performance—one reviewer maintained, "Such a clean-cut young man is out of place amid the dark and forbidding characters who naturally inhabit gangster films."

Of *Her Cardboard Lover*, a 1942 "remake" with Norma Shearer, Bosley Crowther (New York *Times*) remarked, "Mr. Taylor, who had finally gotten somewhere as an actor, is back . . . compelled to make the most inane remarks." Taylor's performance in *Stand By for Action*, as a brash young executive officer of a warship, was well received. In the "grim . . . uncompromising . . . starkly tragic" war film

TAYLOR, ROBERT—*Continued*

Bataan, Taylor was "first rate" as a hard-bitten sergeant who died fighting at the edge of the grave he had dug for himself. The actor's last part before entering war service was in *Song of Russia*; he had been sworn in as a lieutenant (j.g.) in the Navy's aviation volunteer transport division in February 1943, but was deferred to complete the film. Reviews were generally favorable.

Although Taylor and his wife had legally assumed their professional names in 1942, it was as Lt. S. A. Brugh that he reported for duty, during which, he says, he was usually unrecognized. "Too old" for combat flying at thirty-two, he was slated for duty as a flight instructor, and in training for this was graduated in the top fifth of his class; he states that none of the cadets he trained were "washed out." Before Taylor's discharge from the Navy in November 1945, he also directed seventeen training films and spent four days speaking the narration for the battle film *The Fighting Lady* in what Alton Cook called "a stern, self-effacing voice with no trace of the movie star."

Taylor's return to the screen was in the "heavy" role of a jealous industrialist, opposite Katharine Hepburn in *Undercurrent*. Reviewers commented on his "new presence and dignity . . . handsome, forceful maturity . . . strong performance." After finishing *Undercurrent* in April 1946, Taylor refused many scripts. (Under his seventeen-year contract, his salary continued each week nevertheless.) In his one 1947 picture, *The High Wall*, he gave a "workman-like" performance as a sullen, secretive mental patient. During this period the actor's name was in headlines because of his testimony before a visiting subcommittee of the House Un-American Activities Committee inquiring into Communist activity in Hollywood. One of several film figures charging the presence of Communist influence in motion pictures, Taylor spoke specifically about *Song of Russia*, which he considered pro-Communist.

In *The Bribe*, released in early 1949, Taylor acted the part of a United States secret service man who falls in love with a "torch singer," played by Ava Gardner. For several years, beginning with 1949, he spent most of his time "on location" far from home. During his four months at Elstree, England, making *Conspirator*, he shared with rationed Londoners the steak and other scarce delicacies Barbara Stanwyck sent over to him. Reviewers said that Taylor, as a British Army major spying for Soviet Russia, and Elizabeth Taylor, as his American wife, were "working under a considerable handicap" because of the script. In Taylor's next two pictures he portrayed both sides of the classic Western movie story: in *Ambush* he was a brusque frontiersman guiding the cavalry against Apaches; in *Devil's Doorway* he was a noble Shoshone Indian and Congressional Medal of Honor winner leading his tribesmen in defense of their homes against encroaching white settlers. Both performances were said to be handled expertly and with restraint. Most of 1950 Taylor spent in Italy, playing the Roman centurion, Marcus Vini-

cius, to Deborah Kerr's Lygia in the six-million-dollar *Quo Vadis*, which was regarded by most reviewers as a money-making spectacle rather than a critical success. The year 1951 found him in the part of a bearded trail boss leading a wagon train of prospective brides across the desert in *Westward the Women*. After this, Taylor returned to England for three months' work in the twelfth century costumes of the title role of *Ivanhoe*, to Elizabeth Taylor's Rebecca and Joan Fontaine's Rowena.

There is a sprinkling of gray in Taylor's dark hair, and he now carries 175 pounds on his six-foot frame; he has blue eyes. His marriage to Barbara Stanwyck was terminated by a divorce decree which became final on February 25, 1952. Taylor is described by Sidney Skolsky as a conservative dresser and an excellent correspondent who always travels with a portable typewriter. The actor collects model racing cars as a hobby, enjoys skeet shooting, hunting and fishing trips, and flying his own six-passenger plane. With a business partner, Morgan Maree, he breeds prize-winning field dogs and horses.

References

Collier's 98:55 O 3 '36 por
Ladies' Home J 53:8-9+ S '36 pors
N Y Herald Tribune IV p1 N 15 '51
N Y Post pM5 D 16 '51 por
Photoplay 18:70 Mr '41 por
Time 29:25 Ja 18 '37 por
Who's Who in America, 1950-51
Who's Who in Los Angeles County (1950-51)
Who's Who in the West (1951)
World Biography (1948)

TAYLOR, MRS. WILLIAM BOLLING
See Young, M.

TEAGUE, OLIN E(ARL) (tēg) Apr. 6, 1910- United States Representative from Texas

Address: b. c/o House Office Bldg., Washington, D.C.; h. 4743 Bradley Blvd., Chevy Chase, Md.; College Station, Tex.

A many-times decorated veteran of World War II, Democrat Olin E. Teague, United States Representative from Texas since 1946, has been identified in Congress with veterans' affairs. In February 1952, as chairman of the special House committee investigating the GI educational program, Teague reported that, though the program on the whole had been beneficial, there had been instances of inefficiency and waste; and he asked for a new bill to provide education for veterans of the Korean war. Before the beginning of World War II Teague was an employee of a United States Post Office in Texas. In 1940 he began a six-year period in the United States Army as an officer. On his discharge, in Sept,mber 1946, he was chosen to fill a vacancy in the Seventy-ninth Congress caused by the resignation of the

Representative from the Sixth Congressional District of Texas. Teague was elected to the Eightieth Congress and in 1948, 1950, and 1952 was re-elected to subsequent Congresses.

Olin Earl Teague was born April 6, 1910, to James Martin Teague, a native Texan, and Ida (Sturgeon) Teague. Though Woodward, Oklahoma, is his birthplace, Teague has spent most of his life in the neighboring State. From 1928 to 1932 he was a student at the Texas Agricultural and Mechanical College, in College Station. After completing his studies he was employed in the United States Post Office there for eight years, from 1932 to 1940. When he resigned to volunteer for duty with the United States Army he had risen to the position of superintendent of the South Post Office Station in College Station.

Teague enlisted in the United States Army in October 1940 and was commissioned a first lieutenant. Previously he had served for three years as an enlisted man in the National Guard. In World War II the future Congressman saw action as commander of the 1st Battalion, 314th Infantry, of the 79th Division. In combat six months, he was wounded several times, in the attack on the Siegfried Line in Southern Germany suffering shrapnel wounds that necessitated removal of a portion of his left ankle. When he was discharged from the Walter Reed General Hospital in September 1946, he held the rank of colonel. For his services he was decorated eleven times, receiving among other honors the Silver Star with two Clusters, the Purple Heart with two Clusters, the Army Commendation Ribbon, and the Croix de Guerre with Palm.

Teague left the army hospital to fill the vacancy created by the resignation of Luther A. Johnson as United States Representative from Texas to the Seventy-ninth Congress. Soon after taking his seat, in the 1946 elections held to choose a Representative to the Eightieth Congress Teague was elected by the voters of the Sixth District. In 1948 and again in 1950 the Democrat was re-elected. The district which Teague represents comprises eight counties lying south of Dallas, with a population of 262,735 in 1940.

In 1947, as a member of the subcommittee of the House Foreign Affairs Committee, with other members of the group he toured the frontier regions of Greece. During the fighting between the Greek Army and guerrilla forces, he was cut off for several days from the Government-held region and was under fire.

Since taking his seat in the House of Representatives Teague has served as a member of the House Veterans Affairs Committee, as such offering legislation designed to benefit the ex-soldier. However, in the spring of 1949 he opposed the original veterans' pension bill, proposed by Representative Rankin. Teague suggested one which he believed to be more within the nation's capacity to pay. It was his motion which sent the first bill back for changes in committee. When the second bill was offered, reducing to $72 a month the pension to veterans of sixty-five years of age, he fought to

OLIN E. TEAGUE

have the payments limited to those in need and unemployable, to extend the benefits to veterans of World War II, and to provide $60 monthly pensions at the age of fifty-five to veterans with 60 per cent disability and at sixty years of age to those with 50 per cent disability. The bill's unemployability provision was defeated; however, the reduced payments and the need clause were incorporated in the bill, which was passed by the House in June of 1949. It limits pension benefits to those veterans who do not have an annual income of more than $1,200, if single, or $2,500, if married.

The next year Teague began his investigations of the education and training program for veterans. In May of 1950 he proposed a bill to prevent veterans from receiving tuition for attendance at trade schools that had been in existence for less than one year, and to ban such recreational and avocational courses as dancing, music, and photography. The bill was passed. In December of that year he was appointed chairman of a special House committee to investigate abuses in the veterans' training program. By January 1951 he had submitted his finding of alleged criminal practices in connection with the $11 billion-dollar legislation to the Justice Department for possible action. During 1951 his committee was continued, its scope enlarged to include investigations into the program of home loans to veterans. A year's study, said Teague, had revealed graft, waste, and inefficiency. Though the educational program on the whole had been beneficial, particularly at the college level, he criticized the smaller vocational schools and those veterans who had taken courses only in order to receive the subsistence payments.

As an alternative to the existing legislation, which the American Legion wishes to have extended to veterans of the Korean War, Teague has offered a bill that would require, he believes, greater self-help from the veteran-stu-

TEAGUE, OLIN E.—*Continued*

dent. Teague's bill would entitle veterans of the Korean War to one and one-half days of free schooling for each day of army service, with thirty-six months of education as the maximum. Monthly payments of $110 for a single person and $150 for men with dependents would be given directly to the veteran; out of this he would have to meet his tuition, as well as his living costs. Regulations of such provisions as changes in courses of study would be stricter.

On other legislation, the Texas Democrat has been in general agreement with his party's stand. In 1947, 88 per cent of his votes were with the party majority on partisan roll calls. Thus, he was against the Constitutional amendment limiting the Presidential tenure to two terms, voted to increase the school lunch appropriation; favored overriding the President's veto of labor-management bill; opposed statehood for Hawaii; was against legislation which would permit a voluntary 15 per cent rent increase; agreed to the Greek-Turkish aid bill. In 1948 the following significant legislation had his approval: the Selective Service Act (of June 1949), the repeal of the oleomargarine tax, the Mundt-Nixon anti-Communist bill, the income tax reduction, the draft bill, and ERP aid to Western Europe. He opposed the voluntary price-curb bill as well as the bill that would give Congress access to secret files of certain departments.

In 1949 the Texan voted in favor of the long-range housing bill (June) and the coalition (versus Administration) minimum wage bill (August). He also supported extending the coverage and benefits of the Social Security Act; he opposed lifting of the poll tax. On a foreign policy question he voted for the Mutual Defense Assistance Act of 1949, providing arms aid to Atlantic Pact nations. In the following year (1950) Teague gave his approval of the Foreign Economic Assistance Act, but rejected, along with the majority, the bill to aid Korea. He opposed the admittance of Alaska as a State. On issues of government expenditure he favored a $600 million cut in Federal spending and voted "nay" to a measure that would cancel the economy cut in postal service.

In the first session of the Eighty-second Congress (1951), the following "yeas" were recorded for Teague: The cut of $10 million for reclamation funds, reasonable profits under price ceilings, the tidelands oil bill, the $5.7 billions increase in taxes, the continuation of temporary rent control, the limiting of public housing in 1952 to 5,000 units. He cast his votes against decreasing the government's civil payrolls and the building of defense plants by the government. As to foreign aid, he approved the $7.5 billions for the foreign assistance bill. Teague won election to the Eighty-third Congress on November 4, 1952.

Olin Teague and Freddie Dunman (also of Texas) were married December 30, 1932, and became the parents of three children—James M., John O., and Jill Virginia. His church affiliation is Baptist. In College Station he is a member of the Lions Club and the Jefferson Club. In Washington he plays on the Congressional Democrats' baseball team.

References

Biographical Directory of the American Congress, 1774-1949 (1950)
Congressional Directory (1951)
Who's Who in America, 1950-51
Who's Who in United States Politics (1950)
World Biography (1948)

TEMPLER, SIR GERALD (WALTER ROBERT) Sept. 11, 1898- British High Commissioner for Malaya
Address: b. c/o Government House, Kuala Lumpur, Malaya

Appointed January 15, 1952, to the position of High Commissioner for Malaya, General Sir Gerald Templer has the authority to direct all military, police, and civil affairs in the British colony. His most important immediate task is to win for the British the now more than three-year war against the Communist guerrillas in the tin-and-rubber-rich peninsula, thus making possible political development among the Chinese, Malayan, and Indian populations. Templer, a veteran of both world wars, became vice-chief of the Imperial General Staff in 1948, after having filled postwar assignments as director of the British military government for West Germany and director of military intelligence in the War Office. For two years before his appointment to succeed Sir Henry Gurney in Malaya, Templer was General Office Commander in Chief of the British Eastern Command.

Gerald Walter Robert Templer was born September 11, 1898, in Colchester, England, the son of Lieutenant Colonel Walter Francis Templer. The Templers are "an Anglo-Irish military family." Gerald Templer, after receiving his early schooling at Wellington College, became a student at the Royal Military College at Sandhurst. In 1916 he joined the Royal Irish Fusiliers, in which he fought on the Western Front during World War I. When hostilities ended in Europe he was transferred to the Caucasus, the scene of action against Bolshevik guerrillas; for his later service (1919-21) in northwest Persia and Mesopotamia, he was awarded a medal and two bars.

In 1935, with the rank of brevet major, he was assigned to Palestine, where disorders between Arabs and Jews had broken out. His record there won for him the Distinguished Service Order in 1936, and in 1938 he was promoted to the rank of lieutenant colonel. At the outbreak of World War II, Templer, then a major, was assigned to Field Marshal Viscount Gort's headquarters as an intelligence officer and later served with "Mac Force," a special formation assembled to give protection to the right flank of the British Expeditionary Force. After the British evacuation from Dunkerque, Templer was put in command of an infantry brigade and an infantry division,

He was then given command of a corps and promoted to lieutenant general, at forty-four the youngest officer of that rank in the British Army.

In 1943 Templer voluntarily gave up his newly achieved rank, reverting to a major general in order to gain experience as a division commander. He was placed in command of the 56th London Division, operating in Italy, and, according to a report in the New York *Times*, converted what had been known as a "hard-luck" outfit into a creditable military force. While in command of the 6th British Armoured Division, he was seriously injured when a loaded army truck crashed into the jeep in which he was riding. As a result, incapacitated for combat duty, he was transferred as a staff officer to Field Marshal Montgomery's headquarters. At the end of the war in 1945 he became director of the Military Government of the 21st Army Group, in charge of both civil and military affairs in the area of northwest Germany occupied by the British. The Germans received "no soft treatment," reported the New York *Herald Tribune* (April 25, 1945), as on short notice he requisitioned houses, hospital facilities, and food for displaced persons. In 1946 he left Germany to assume direction of military intelligence for the War Office in London. After two years he became vice-chief of the Imperial General Staff and in 1950 was named commander of Britain's Eastern Command.

On January 15, 1952, General Sir Gerald Templer (he had received that military rank and a knighthood by that time) was appointed British High Commissioner in Malaya by Prime Minister Winston Churchill to succeed the late Sir Henry Gurney, who had been ambushed and killed by Malayan guerrillas in October of 1951. Less than a month later Templer arrived in Malaya and on February 7, 1952, was sworn in as High Commissioner of the Federation of Malaya and as Supreme Commander of all land, sea, and air forces in the area. With the advantage of possessing more power than any of his predecessors, Templer gave assurance of his desire to fulfill the British directive aimed at making Malaya a fully self-governing nation and a member of the British Commonwealth.

The 50,680-square-mile peninsula whose civil and military affairs Templer directs has been the scene for almost four years of an undeclared war between an estimated force of 4,000 Chinese Communist guerrillas and a British force of some 40,000 regulars and 140,000 native police and troops. Described by a New York *Times* correspondent as "one of the last strongholds of traditionalism in Southeast Asia," the Federation of Malaya, created in 1948 from the nine states of the Malay peninsula and two British settlements of Penang and Malacca, is Britain's richest colony and the world's largest producer of tin and rubber —consequently an important source of raw material needed for Western defense. It has a population of more than five million, with Malayans predominating; about two million Chinese control much of the colony's business activities but have no voice in political affairs.

Wide World Photos
GEN. SIR GERALD TEMPLER

Racial conflicts, outmoded forms of colonial administration, and economic competition between the Malayans and the Chinese have aided the efforts of the small group of guerrillas to prevent production of rubber, tin, and food. As the writer of the New York *Times Magazine* article on the conflict pointed out, the chief political problem is to gain the co-operation of the Chinese in combating the guerrillas without alienating the Malayans, who fear Chinese competition.

Templer's program has involved both a "tough" policy of dealing with the guerrillas and those who aid them with food and shelter, and a conciliatory policy of resettling Chinese in protected areas and working toward greater political equality. Soon after his arrival in Malaya, he announced, on March 3, 1952, that the War Council, previously set up to coordinate police and troop action against the Communist guerrillas, would be merged with the Civil Federal Executive Council to form a single policy-making body. Later in March Templer demonstrated the firmness of his administration by imposing severe punishment on the villagers of Tanjong Malim, where guerrillas had ambushed and killed two British officers and a number of police and Malay citizens. For thirteen days residents were restricted to their homes for twenty-two hours a day, with reduced rice rations, until they agreed to help ferret out townsmen suspected of aiding the guerrillas. Similar curfews have since been imposed in other areas where guerrillas are known to find assistance from residents. A plan to resettle Chinese in what Templer calls "new villages" has been inaugurated with a good measure of self-government in an attempt to organize a democratic system at the local level instead of establishing it from above. Templer has also been critical of the traditional attitude of the British resi-

TEMPLER, SIR GERALD—*Continued*

dents and has asked for their cooperation in a redress of Chinese grievances. A plan to include Chinese into home-guard units has also been mapped out by Templer.

Templer has received the honors of the Distinguished Service Order (1936), Officer of the Order of the British Empire (1940), Companion of the Bath (1944), Companion of St. Michael and St. George (1946), Knight Commander of the Order of the British Empire (1949), and Knight Commander of the Bath (1950). In 1946 he was also made Commander of the Legion of Merit (United States), Commander of the Order of the Crown with Palm and Croix de Guerre with Palm (Belgium) and Knight Grand Officer of the Order of Orange Nassau with Swords (Holland).

Templer belongs to the Army and Navy Club and the Marlborough-Windham. With Templer in Malaya are his wife, the former Ethel Margery Davie, whom he married in 1926, and a son and daughter. The general, who has been described as "swift and definite" in making decisions, has the reputation of being a "model of soldierly efficiency." He is six feet tall and is of slight build.

References

N Y Herald Tribune p10 Ja 16 '52
N Y Times p1 Ja 16 '52
N Y Times Mag p12+ My 4 '52
Newsweek 39:39 Ap 28 '52
Time 59:26 Ja 28 '52
U S News 32:65 Ja 25 '52
Washington (D.C.) Post p3B Mr 2 '52
Who's Who, 1951

TEWSON, SIR (HAROLD) VINCENT
Feb. 4, 1898- International labor leader
Address: b. Transport House, Smith Sq., London S.W. 1, England; h. 37 King's Rd., Barnet, Hertfordshire, England

Sir Vincent Tewson, general secretary of Britain's Trades Union Congress, was elected the second president of the International Confederation of Free Trade Unions in July 1951. One of the labor leaders who left the Communist-dominated World Federation of Trade Unions in 1948, he was secretary of the 1949 Geneva conference at which the I.C.F.T.U. was planned. Tewson, who has worked in the labor movement since the age of fourteen, in 1925 became secretary of the organization department of the T.U.C., in 1931 assistant general secretary, and in 1946 general secretary. The T.U.C. represented in 1951 nearly eight million British workers, while the I.C.F.T.U. represented fifty-five million workers in sixty-six countries.

Harold Vincent Tewson was born in Bradford, Yorkshire, England, on February 4, 1898, the son of Edward Tewson, a nursery gardener. At the age of fourteen he left Bradford's elementary school to work as an office boy in the headquarters of the Amalgamated Society of Dyers, the principal union in the wool textile industry. By the time he was eighteen, he had been promoted to organizing work in the union. After World War I broke out he volunteered as a private, gained a commission in the West Yorkshire Regiment. In 1918, as a second lieutenant he was awarded the Military Cross for personal gallantry, initiative, and leadership. The citation read: "When his men came under very severe machine-gun fire he dashed in front and so encouraged them by his fearless example that they drove the enemy back and captured the objective; when the fire became so heavy that a gap was caused on his flank, he ran along the front of the line, rallied his men and formed a defensive flank, thus saving a critical situation."

After the war Tewson returned to the Bradford union office to continue his organizing duties and to engage in piece-rate negotiations for the dyers. He devoted his free time to local civic affairs, with the result that he was elected the youngest member of the Bradford City Council in 1923. When Walter Citrine, assistant general secretary of the T.U.C., formed a new organization department in 1925, Tewson was selected from a long list of candidates to manage the office. In London, the Yorkshireman now had his office at Transport House as secretary of the organization department until 1931. He was then chosen (against "stiff opposition," said a report from the Economic Cooperation Administration) the assistant general secretary of the T.U.C. and as such served as deputy to General Secretary Sir Walter Citrine for the next fifteen years, with full responsibility for the office for those periods Sir Walter was abroad during World War II. Trade union duties sent Tewson twice to Greece in the spring of 1945 to help organize the Greek trade union elections. When the World Federation of Trade Unions was formed in 1946, Tewson visited France and Russia on missions connected with it and was appointed to its executive board as T.U.C. representative.

With the appointment of Lord Citrine to the Labor Government's Coal Board in July 1946, Tewson became acting general secretary of the T.U.C. His was the only name submitted for the position of general secretary by the affiliated unions at the T.U.C. conference in October 1946. Commenting on Tewson's unanimous election, *Newsweek* wrote that he was a man who viewed "one function of the union as consultant to the Government on technical as well as policy matters." According to the ECA release, Tewson welcomed the idea of the Marshall Plan in 1947 and took steps to give the European Recovery Program the full cooperation of free trade unions in the participating countries. Together with Arthur Deakin (general secretary of Britain's Transport and General Workers' Union and former president of the W.F.T.U.), Evert Kupers of the Dutch labor federation, and Paul Finet of Belgium, Tewson called a meeting in March 1948 of free labor leaders from Marshall Plan countries. It established the ERP Trade Union Advisory Committee for coordinating trade union cooperation in the economic rehabilitation of Europe. It also led to the break of trade

unions from the W.F.T.U. In the words of
the ECA release, Tewson was one of the first
to see that the W.F.T.U. was "becoming nothing more than another Moscow propaganda
tool." Soon after he and Deakin in 1948 announced the T.U.C.'s withdrawal from the
W.F.T.U., other trade unions withdrew from
the W.F.T.U. In June 1949 Tewson was secretary of the Geneva conference of free labor
leaders who made plans for a new world-wide
union of free labor organizations in opposition
to the W.F.T.U. Out of the Geneva conference thus came the International Confederation
of Free Trade Unions, which held its first congress in London in December 1949. At that
time Tewson was elected to the organization's
twenty-man executive board.

Sir Vincent (he was knighted in 1950) encountered Communist-led opposition within his own
T.U.C. at its eighty-second annual convention
in September 1950, when a small majority of
the 900 delegates passed a Communist-sponsored
resolution against the Labor Government's
wage-freeze policy. The Communists, who, according to *Newsweek*, command about 500,000
direct supporters in the union, also led a fight
to ban the atom bomb by introducing a proposal, which though voted down, received considerable support. However, a resolution moved
by Tewson for approval of the United Nations
Korean campaign was passed by a 12-to-1
majority, with delegates shouting approval of
Tewson's praise for the speedy action by American forces in Korea. At the September 1951
T.U.C. convention delegates supported the Labor Government of Britain in its rearmament
program, but passed a unanimous resolution
calling for the Government to break off diplomatic relations with Spain. It voted down resolutions calling for new negotiations with the
Soviet Union and a revival of trade with Russia and its satellites. It also voted down a motion calling for a reversal of the Government's
policy on Japanese and German rearmament.
In the heated debates on these issues, Tewson
and Deakin bore the brunt of defending the
Government policy.

The British labor leader was elected president of the I.C.F.T.U. for a two-year term at
its second conference, held in Milan, Italy, during July 4-12, 1951. Tewson, succeeding Paul
Finet, who resigned, received CIO support for
the presidency, but was opposed by the AFL
on the ground that the organization's head
should be neither British nor American. At
Milan he told representatives of some fifty-
five million trade unionists from sixty-six countries that he hoped the world would learn the
lesson of the Korean conflict—"a lesson spelt
out in human blood, not only that aggression
does not pay, but that aggression must not be
allowed to pay." He declared that the trade
unions desired peace, but peace with freedom,
and that they must never cease to expose the
"Communist-inspired 'peace' campaigns." The
I.C.F.T.U. has as one of its principal goals
the development of strong and democratic trade
unionism in backward regions of the world.
When a special fund of $700,000 was estab-

SIR VINCENT TEWSON

lished by the confederation to open training
centers in Asia, Africa, and the Middle East,
Tewson announced a T.U.C. contribution of
$168,000 and said: "The Confederation was not
called into existence merely to combat communism or to resist the dictation of international trade union policy by the Cominform.
More important work of a constructive character has to be done by the I.C.F.T.U. and its
affiliated national centers than just to counteract the dangerous subversive activities of the
W.F.T.U."

Since 1947 Tewson has been a member of
Britain's Economic Planning Board and since
June 1949 the labor representative on the Dollar Export Board established to promote British
sales to the United States and Canada. He is
a member of the Royal Institute of International Affairs and author of the foreword to a
British Institute of Management booklet published in 1950. The labor leader was made a
Commander of the Order of the British Empire in 1942 and on January 1, 1950, was named
a Knight Bachelor in recognition of his service
to the British nation and the trade union movement. In 1929 Tewson married Florence Elizabeth Moss, who had been his secretary at
Transport House. He served on the national
committee which looked after the Basque children evacuated to England during the Spanish
Civil War, at which time Mrs. Tewson organized a local committee in Barnet (where the
Tewsons have their home) to provide for some
of the children there. In the course of World
War II the Tewsons adopted two English
babies, Alan and Peter. Described in a British
press release as having the "genial equable
temperament and unhurried speech of the Yorkshireman," Sir Vincent is also known as a
"willing listener." *Newsweek* characterized him
as "well-dressed, well-informed, typical of the

TEWSON, SIR VINCENT—*Continued*

new generation of British union leaders." He finds recreation in gardening.

References

Newsweek 28:46 N 4 '46
International Who's Who, 1951
Kelly's Handbook to the Titled, Landed, and Official Classes, 1949
Who's Who, 1951

THEILER, MAX (tīl′ĕr) Jan. 30, 1899-
Physician; bacteriologist

Address: b. c/o Division of Medicine and Public Health, Rockefeller Foundation, York Ave. & 66th St., New York 21; h. Hastings-on-Hudson, N.Y.

For research which led to the development of two vaccines against yellow fever, Dr. Max Theiler was awarded the 1951 Nobel Prize in medicine and physiology on December 10, 1951. Theiler, a South African, has conducted his scientific work in the United States, first at Harvard Medical School and since 1930 in New York at the laboratories of what is now the Division of Medicine and Public Health of the Rockefeller Foundation.

One of the four children (two sons, two daughters) of Sir Arnold and Emma (Jegge) Theiler, Max Theiler was born in Pretoria, South Africa, on January 30, 1899. His father, of Swiss birth, was a well-known veterinary scientist, for whom a genus of protozoan parasites, the *Theileria*, has been named. After completing his preliminary medical training at Rhodes University College and the medical school of the University of Capetown (1916-

Wide World Photos
MAX THEILER

18), Max Theiler went to England to study at two branches of the University of London—St. Thomas' Hospital Medical School and the London School of Hygiene and Tropical Medicine—from which he received his medical degree in 1922. Theiler in the same year became a licentiate of the Royal College of Physicians of London and a member of the Royal College of Surgeons of England. (Later, in the United States, he became a member of the American Society for Experimental Pathology.)

In 1922 Theiler joined the Department of Tropical Medicine of Harvard Medical School as an assistant and advanced to an instructorship. His work there, reported in medical periodicals such as the *American Journal of Tropical Medicine* and the *Archives of Internal Medicine*, dealt largely with amoebic dysentery and with rat-bite fever. He investigated the controlled induction of that fever as a means of treating certain diseases. At Harvard he also worked with the yellow fever virus, in which he had become interested at the London School of Tropical Medicine, and is said to have contracted the fever in 1929.

The International Health Division of the Rockefeller Foundation offered Theiler in 1930 an assignment in its project of eliminating yellow fever from the regions where it was endemic, an undertaking in which the foundation had been engaged since 1915. At the beginning of the twentieth century Walter Reed and others had demonstrated that yellow fever could be controlled by mosquito destruction, and William C. Gorgas had shortly afterward succeeded in effecting mosquito control in Havana and Panama. When the Rockefeller Foundation began its project it was believed that the disease afflicted mankind exclusively and was spread only by the bite of the mosquito *Aedes aegypti*. Accordingly, the foundation took measures to destroy the insect and within about ten years seemed to have wiped out yellow fever. Then, however, the discovery was made that man was not the only species susceptible and that in certain mammals of Africa and South America there was a reservoir of infection capable of being transmitted to human beings by several varieties of mosquito. Since the knowledge of this so-called "jungle" yellow fever made insect control alone seem inadequate as a protective measure, the Rockefeller Foundation decided to concentrate upon identifying the causative agent and developing a vaccine. Theiler was one of those who devoted themselves to these two tasks.

Theiler and others had proved by 1927 that the organism responsible for yellow fever was not a bacterium, as Hidejo Noguchi had previously supposed, but a filterable virus. Study of the virus and its effects was hampered by the need to use a relatively expensive animal, the rhesus monkey, in the laboratories. When Theiler demonstrated shortly before coming to the Rockefeller Foundation that the disease could readily be transmitted to mice, the cost of research was much reduced. The susceptibility of mice led Theiler in 1931 to devise the "mouse-protection" test, in which an animal is inoculated in the brain with blood taken from a person suspected of harboring the yellow fever virus. Field surveys using this test were later able to map out the regions of the world where much of the population was infected, even though bodily resistance prevented the appearance of overt symptoms in many cases.

In working on a vaccine, Theiler experimented with two strains of the virus—the French, which thrives in the nervous system and hence is called neurotropic, and the Asibi, which is denoted viscerotropic because of its predilection for the viscera. Theiler demonstrated that after passage through the brain of many mice in succession the French strain usually would make a human being immune to yellow fever if injected under the skin. This, the first vaccine that he developed, was extensively used by France in its African territories, but being highly neurotropic it caused fatal encephalitis in some instances. In the hope that a safer preparation would be found, Theiler concentrated on the Asibi strain. Virus was grown in a variety of tissue cultures, of which part of the chicken embryo finally proved to be satisfactory for producing a standardized vaccine (17 D). One advantage of this vaccine is its suitability for mass production: it is estimated that since 1937 (reported the New York World-Telegram), the year Theiler announced his 17D vaccine, about 40,000,000 persons have been inoculated, including 8,000,000 American servicemen during World War II. Theiler has reported his work on yellow fever in papers written for the Annals of Tropical Medicine and in contributions to two books, Viral and Rickettsial Infections of Man (1948) and Yellow Fever (1951).

Public recognition of Theiler's contribution came on October 21, 1949, when he received one of the Lasker Awards of the American Public Health Association for research leading directly to production of the two vaccines. On October 18, 1951, the Swedish Royal Carolinian Medico-Surgical Institute of Stockholm announced that he had been awarded the 1951 Nobel Prize in medicine and physiology. It consists of a gold medal, a diploma, and a sum of money, which press reports stated would be $32,357.62. The presentation was made in Stockholm on December 10, 1951. In an interview for the New York Times (October 19, 1951), Theiler, when speaking about the development of the vaccine, said that credit should go to two of his associates, the late Dr. Wray Lloyd and Dr. Hugh H. Smith, an associate director of the foundation. Theiler himself is now the director of the laboratories of the Rockefeller Foundation's Division of Medicine and Public Health which was formed on May 1, 1951, by the merging of the Division of International Health and the Division of Medical Sciences. The laboratories are housed in, but are distinct from, the Rockefeller Institute for Medical Research.

Some of Theiler's other work for the Rockefeller Foundation has been concerned with the causes and immunology of certain disorders, including Weil's disease, which in common with yellow fever often affect the liver. These researches have been reported in papers written jointly with other scientists for the American Journal of Tropical Medicine and the American Journal of Tropical Diseases. He is also engaged in research on dengue fever and Japanese encephalitis. Another virus complaint, poliomyelitis (infantile paralysis), has much interested Theiler ever since he observed an apparently identical condition in laboratory mice. In order to distinguish the two diseases, he gave the mouse disorder the name encephalomyelitis (it is also called Theiler's disease). Applying his study of encephalomyelitis to human poliomyelitis, he speculated that the virus which causes the disease in mankind is widespread in the intestine, where it does no harm. Only in the rare instances when it enters the central nervous system are symptoms produced. His "Observations on Poliomyelitis" in Medicine summarizes his views.

Max Theiler and Lillian Graham of Massachusetts, who were married in 1928, have one daughter, Elizabeth. He maintains his South African citizenship. The scientist, who is of slight build, is described as a shy man. Among his free-time interests are books on philosophy and history and watching baseball games.

References

Life 38:61+ N 5 '51 por
N Y Herald Tribune p19 O 19 '51 por
N Y Times p1+ O 19 '51 por
N Y World Telegram p1+ O 18 '51 por
Newsweek 38:89 O 29 '51 por
Scholastic 59:8 N 7 '51 por

American Medical Directory, 1950

THOMAS, LOWELL (JACKSON) Apr. 6, 1892- News commentator; author; lecturer

Address: b. 50 Rockefeller Plaza, New York 20; h. Hammersley Hill, Pawling, N.Y.

NOTE: This biography supersedes the article which appeared in Current Biography in 1940.

In the front rank of American news commentators is Lowell Thomas, who made his radio debut in September 1930 and has been heard on the airwaves five evenings weekly for more than twenty-one years. Prior to his affiliation with broadcasting, he won fame as a world traveler and lecturer, particularly for his motion picture lectures on the World War I Palestine campaign of General Allenby and the career and exploits of Colonel T. E. Lawrence. He is the author and coauthor of more than forty books, ranging in character from topical biographies and recollections, such as With Lawrence in Arabia (1924) and Count Luckner, the Sea Devil (1927), through works of travel, to books for adventure-minded youth.

Lowell Jackson Thomas was born in Woodington, Ohio, on April 6, 1892, the only son of Harry George and Harriet (Wagner) Thomas. He is descended from Samuel Thomas, a Welshman who settled in Pennsylvania at the beginning of the eighteenth century. Both parents of Lowell Thomas had been teachers, but early in his career Harry Thomas turned to

CBS Photo.

LOWELL THOMAS

medicine, becoming a physician and surgeon, and later joining the United States Medical Corps in World War I. The first eight years of Lowell's life were passed at Woodington. In 1900 the family moved to Cripple Creek, Colorado, then a gold mining boom town. At the age of eleven the boy worked for a while in the gold mines and peddled newspapers. In his association with all kinds of adventurers his imagination was fired by stories they told of the far corners of the earth. The atmosphere of the Thomas home was one of culture: Dr. Thomas possessed what is said to have been, at this period, one of the finest private libraries west of the Mississippi. He also had a dislike for bad diction, and to his insistence on correct speech has been ascribed a good measure of his son's subsequent success on the lecture platform and in broadcasting.

When the future globe-trotter and newscaster reached college age he enrolled at the University of Northern Indiana, at Valparaiso, earning his expenses during and between school years as a cook, waiter, furnace tender, and cowpuncher, and completing a four-year course in two years. Receiving his B.S. degree in 1911, he returned to Cripple Creek, became a reporter on a local paper and soon thereafter city editor. In the autumn he proceeded to the University of Denver, where he took both the B.A. and M.A. degrees in 1912. The next stage in Thomas' educational progress was at the Kent College of Law in Chicago for two years (1912-14) of study, during which he was on the faculty as a teacher of oratory and as a reporter on the Chicago Journal. While at Princeton University, which he entered in 1914 for postgraduate work in constitutional law, his expenses were in part met through an instructorship in the English department. Thomas' M.A. degree from Princeton (1916) was the last of his regularly acquired degrees. Honorary degrees were later to be bestowed on him: Litt.D. by Grove City College (1933), St. Bonaventure University (1938), and Franklin and Marshall College (1942); the LL.D. by Albright College (1934), Lafayette College (1937), and Washington and Jefferson College (1942); the L.H.D. by Clark University (1941), Boston University (1943), and Union College (1944); and Doctor of Humanities by Temple University (1942). Thomas is also a Chevalier of the French Legion of Honor.

It was in 1915, between academic terms at Princeton, that Thomas made the first of his many expeditions to relatively little known parts of the globe. The place was Alaska, which he explored with notebook and camera, later arranging his material with the aid of Dale Carnegie in the form of an illustrated travelogue. The autumn he began on his first tour, appearing first before small groups, subsequently before such organizations as the Smithsonian Institution; and it so happened that one of his "shows" (Thomas has never liked the term "lecture") indirectly brought him to the attention of President Woodrow Wilson. The result was that Thomas was named head of a civilian mission assigned by President Wilson to prepare a history of World War I. With his staff Thomas was attached at various time to the Allied armies from the North Sea to the Persian Gulf, including the command of General Allenby in the Middle East. With Allenby at the capture of Jerusalem, he also met the fabulous Colonel T. E. Lawrence, the leader of the Arab revolt against the Turks. Toward the end of the war Thomas became one of the first persons to enter Germany, from which he brought back an eyewitness account of the revolution which overthrew Kaiser Wilhelm II; and at the Versailles Peace Conference he was called upon by President Wilson to make a special report to the delegates.

Returning to New York, Thomas engaged a theater there in the spring of 1919, which he "packed" nightly for three weeks with his motion pictures and talks entitled "With Allenby in Palestine" and "With Lawrence in Arabia." The presentations continued at Madison Square Garden, and in August they were repeated at the Royal Opera House, Covent Garden, London. A tour of the world followed, during part of which Thomas accompanied the Prince of Wales on his visit to India in 1922. The lecturer-showman's first and most famous book, With Lawrence in Arabia, was published in 1924; this "admirably well-poised history" (as Simeon Strunsky called it in the New York Times) went into thirty printings and sold a total of around 500,000 copies. It was followed in 1925 by Beyond Khyber Pass, about Afghanistan; and The First World Flight, a collection (edited by Thomas) of narratives by the participants in the encirclement of the globe in 1924 by United States Army airplanes. In 1927 appeared Thomas' The Boys' Life of Colonel Lawrence, a popular "juvenile" which was revised and republished in 1938 and again in 1950. Other early Thomas titles (he has in all more than forty books to his credit as author or coauthor) include *Count Luckner, the Sea Devil* (1927), *Raiders of the Deep* (1928), *The Hero of Vincennes* (1929), and *India: Land of the Black Pagoda* (1930). Thomas meanwhile continued to tour with his Lawrence-Allenby lecture, which is said to have been repeated more than 4,000 times.

The radio debut of Lowell Thomas on September 29, 1930, came about as the result of a sudden decision by the *Literary Digest* to replace the late Floyd Gibbons as broadcaster of the 6:45 P.M. (Eastern Standard Time) Monday-to-Friday news program the magazine sponsored on the Columbia Broadcasting System. President Paley of CBS asked Thomas on short notice to fill the gap. His virile-voiced, typically American, politically and otherwise carefully balanced commentaries, with their tag line "So long until tomorrow," quickly built up a following estimated at between 10,000,000 and 15,000,000 listeners. Friction with the *Digest* developed, however, and in 1932 Thomas transferred to the National Broadcasting Company and the sponsorship of the Sun Oil Company for what proved to be a fifteen-year association. In 1935 he became the "voice," too, of the 20th Century-Fox Movietone newsreel. Two years later (1937) Thomas covered the coronation of King George VI for NBC, and also reported from Paris and Rome on the mounting war threat in Europe; in 1939 he broadcast for NBC the first televised news program. His world peregrinations meanwhile took him into the bush country of Australia, among the pygmy tribes, to the Himalayan fastnesses of Upper Burma, and again into the Arctic regions; while to his literary record were added new titles. These include *Kabluk of the Eskimo* (1932), *Born to Raise Hell* (1936), *Adventures Among Immortals* (1937), a number of travel books such as *Seeing Japan With Lowell Thomas* (1937), and *How to Keep Mentally Fit* (1940).

In 1940 Thomas observed his tenth anniversary as a radio broadcaster. As a news commentator he is aided by Prosper Buranelli (former puzzle editor of the New York *World*) and Louis Sherwin (former dramatic critic of the *Globe*), who compile and write the newsscripts. Through the World War II period Thomas continued to be one of America's most widely heard newscasters; and in the latter stage of the conflict Thomas traveled around the world, broadcasting from London, Paris, Luxembourg, Rome, Cairo, New Delhi, the Philippines, Iwo Jima, Okinawa, and Chungking. His description of flaming Berlin as viewed from a P-51 Mustang plane was a factor in winning for him the A. I. du Pont radio award for the best news broadcasting of 1945. In 1947 Thomas left NBC to return to the Columbia Broadcasting System with a new sponsor (Procter and Gamble soap products), and in the same year was reported to have begun work on a 900,000-word history of the world (as conveyed by some 300 biographies of outstanding figures) to be entitled *Story of Mankind*. Otherwise his literary output in the 1940-50 decade was confined to some hundred articles; three small books of celebrity anecdotes and human interest stories (some with coauthors) taken from his news broadcasts, *Pageant of Adventure* (1940), *Pageant of Life* (1941), and *Pageant of Romance* (1943); an inspirational book for teen-agers, *Stand Fast for Freedom* (1940); and *These Men Shall Never Die* (1943), a collection of biographical sketches of war heroes.

In June 1949 Thomas received from the Dalai Lama an invitation to visit Tibet and its once forbidden capital of Lhasa. "It was for Thomas the realization of a lifelong ambition," stated a CBS release. "He had always wanted to go to the 'roof of the world,' but only about half a dozen westerners had ever been there and come out to tell about it." He made the expedition accompanied by his son, Lowell Thomas, Jr. (with whom he was to write in 1950 a six-installment article for *Collier's*, which was followed by his son's book, *Out of This World*, later that year). The return journey, however, almost cost the elder Thomas his life: he fell from his horse in the Karo Pass, broke his leg, and was saved from falling over a precipice only by the swift action of his son. Thomas celebrated the twentieth anniversary of his radio debut in September 1950. He made another lengthy trip to Europe and Latin America in the summer of 1951, resuming his New York broadcasts on August 27, on which occasion the trade weekly *Variety* noted that he "remains one of radio's standard personalities and one of its most enduring voices, despite a certain monotony of delivery." Actually, it should be noted, the newscasts are not made from CBS studios in New York City, but from Thomas' estate at Pawling, New York, which is fitted with complete broadcasting facilities. The scripts are compiled by Buranelli and a staff at CBS headquarters, and relayed to Pawling. The regular quarter hour 6.45 P.M. (EST) Monday to Friday broadcasts are repeated some hours later for Pacific Coast listeners.

Lowell Thomas and Frances Ryan of Colorado were married August 4, 1917; Lowell Thomas, Jr., is their only child. Thomas is president of the board of directors of the American School for Boys at Baghdad, a trustee of numerous educational institutions, and a member of Kappa Sigma, Tau Kappa Alpha, Phi Delta Phi, Sigma Delta Chi, and Alpha Epsilon fraternities. His clubs are the Explorers (of which he is a director), Princeton Players, Overseas Press (past president), and Advertising in New York City; while his physical recreations include handball, skiing, and riding. Five feet ten inches tall, he weighs 165 pounds; he has thick brown hair and blue eyes.

References

Coronet 26:167-72 Je '49 por
Lit Digest 121:24 Mr 21 '36 por
N Y World-Telegram p8 F 22 '40; p29 S 13 '40
Newsweek 30:54+ O 13 '47 por
PM p12 S 30 '40 por

(Continued next page)

THOMAS, LOWELL—*Continued*

Read Digest 28:61-3 Mr '36; 53:53-8
  D '48
Time 36:61-2 S 30 '40 por
Carnegie, D. Biographical Roundup
  (1945)
Himber, C. Famous in Their Twenties
  (1942)
Kunitz, S. J. and Haycraft, H. eds. Jun-
  ior Book of Authors (1934); Twen-
  tieth Century Authors (1942)
National Cyclopædia of American Biog-
  raphy Current vol E, 1937-38
Thomas, L. How to Keep Mentally Fit
  (1940); Pageant of Adventure (1940)
Variety Radio Directory, 1940-41
Who's Who, 1951
Who's Who in America, 1950-51
Who's Who in the East (1951)
World Biography (1948)

**THOMAS, SIR (WILLIAM) MILES
(WEBSTER)** Mar. 2, 1897- Airline executive

Address: c/o British Overseas Airways Cor-
poration, Airways House, Great West Road,
Brentford, Middlesex, England; h. Silver
Ridge, Wentworth, Virginia Water, Surrey,
England

The president of the International Air Transport Association for 1951, Sir Miles Thomas,
has been chairman of the British Overseas Airways Corporation since 1949 and chairman of
the Southern Rhodesian Development Co-Ordinating Commission since 1947. Considered one
of Britain's leading executives in the automobile industry, Sir Miles was associated for
twenty-three years with Morris Motors, Ltd.,
and its subsidiary companies, serving as vice-
chairman and managing director of the group
during 1940-47. Since he became chairman of
the government-owned B.O.A.C., the corporation realized a profit for the first time in its
history. At the 1951 meeting of I.A.T.A., he
predicted that commercial aviation would be
characterized in the immediate future by great
increases in speed and by lower tourist rates.

William Miles Webster Thomas was born in
Ruabon, Wales, on March 2, 1897, to William
Henry and Mary Elizabeth (Webster) Thomas.
After attending the Bromsgrove School in
Worcestershire from 1910 to 1914, he studied
engineering as a premium pupil with Bellis and
Morcom, Ltd., in Birmingham. During World
War I, following a brief period in 1915 in the
British Armored Car Squadron which fought
in the German East Africa campaign, he was
commissioned an officer in the Royal Flying
Corps and sent to Egypt. When he had fifty
hours in his log book he began doing stunt flying and was subsequently made an aerial fighting instructor at Heliopolis. His service in
Mesopotamia, Persia, and South Russia with
the RAF, won him a Distinguished Flying
Cross in 1918. After the war, he declined an
offer of a permanent commission to return to
civilian life. Combining a journalistic flair with
engineering knowledge, Thomas worked as a

reporter for *Motor* and later as editor of the
Light Car. He also concerned himself with the
development and use of multi-wheel vehicles
for cross-country and military purposes, publishing a pamphlet on the subject in 1924. Still
interested in flying, he participated in several
events in the early "barnstorming" days of civil
aviation.

Thomas' account of a press showing of automobiles produced by Morris Motors, Ltd., (one
of Britain's largest automobile manufacturers)
brought the young man an offer of a position as
editor of a magazine that Lord Nuffield (then
William R. Morris) was about to launch.
Thomas joined the Morris staff as adviser on
sales promotion in 1924 and founded the Mor-
ris-Oxford Press in 1926. During the twenty-
three years of his association with the Nuffield
organization, Thomas was named to a succession of positions: director and general sales
manager of Morris Motors, Ltd., in 1927;
director and general manager of Morris Commercial Cars, Ltd., in Birmingham in 1934, and
of Wolseley Motors, Ltd., in 1935; managing
director of Wolseley Motors, Ltd., in 1937.
From 1940 through 1947 Thomas was vice-
chairman and managing director of Morris Motors, Ltd., and its subsidiaries: Wolseley Motors, Ltd., Morris Commercial Cars, Ltd.,
M.G. Car Co., Ltd., Riley Motor Co., Ltd.,
Morris Industries (Exports), Ltd., S. V. Car-
buretor Co., Ltd., and Mechanizations and Aero,
Ltd. During World War II, when the group
was converted to munitions production, Thomas
administered a large aircraft repair organization which put 88,000 war planes back into the
fighting line. In 1941 he became chairman of
the cruiser tank production group and a member of the Government's advisory panel on tank
production, serving through 1945; he headed
the British Tank Engine Mission to the United
States in 1942-43.

After the war Sir Miles (who had been
knighted in 1943) urged tax adjustments to
spur the production of medium-sized cars for
home and foreign markets. By November 1946
he reported that Britain was nearer her prewar motor car output than the United States,
but that British cars had risen more in price.
Again, in January 1947, he advised a change in
the tax system to encourage manufacturers to
build bigger cars as the best means for Britain
to hold her "wonderful gains in export markets." The basis of Britain's automobile taxes
had been changed in 1944 from horsepower to
capacity of engines, but this change, according
to Sir Miles, had not proved sufficient to remove the obstacles to the manufacture of popu-
lar-priced large cars.

Thomas became chairman of the Southern
Rhodesian Development Co-Ordinating Commission in 1947 and in 1951 continues to hold
this office. Established to coordinate industrial
and commercial development, the commission
aims at effecting a compromise between free
enterprise and nationalization—or "rationaliza-
tion" as Sir Miles has termed it. Speaking before the Royal Empire Society on November
26, 1947, he said there was an opportunity for
the United Kingdom to build up dollar credit
in the United States by developing the mineral

resources of Africa for sale to American markets. From 1948 until early in 1951 he served as director of the Colonial Development Corporation, established in 1948 to promote economic growth in the Colonies with a view toward enlarging their productive capacity.

On April 1, 1948, Sir Miles joined the B.O.A.C. as deputy chairman; and in June 1949 he was appointed chairman. The corporation was formed in November 1939 to take over the facilities and operations of Imperial Airways and British Airways, whose undertakings during World War II were at the disposal of the Secretary of State for Air. In 1945 the functions of that Secretary regarding B.O.A.C. were transferred to the Minister of Civil Aviation, who has the duty of naming the members of the corporation. When civil aviation was nationalized in England in August 1946, B.O.A.C. was set up as one of three corporations to handle all British scheduled air services throughout the world. Responsible for all routes not within the sphere of the British European Airways and the British South American Airways, B.O.A.C. operates routes from the United Kingdom to the Commonwealth and Empire countries and North Atlantic and Far East areas. By June 1950 B.O.A.C. routes, thirty-two in number, with seventy weekly services in each direction, had reached a gross mileage of over 153,500 (*Whitaker's Almanac*). For the second quarter of 1951 the corporation showed the first quarterly profit in its history. "Our constant aim," Sir Miles has stated, "is to eliminate altogether the need for government grants" (*Christian Science Monitor* August 29, 1951).

Declaring faster and larger planes to be the key to the future success of British airways, Sir Miles announced in August 1951 that B.O.A.C. was planning a jet airliner service to be comprised of a fleet of fourteen four-jet, forty-eight-passenger De Havilland Comets capable of altitudes to 40,000 feet and speeds up to 500 miles per hour. According to British designers, the jet Comet is superior to anything the United States can develop in time to compete and will enable a traveler to circle the globe by air in three and a half days, compared to the eight days ordinarily required.

Elected president of the I.A.T.A. in October 1950, Thomas heads a nongovernmental organization of some seventy airline members, which was established in 1945 to provide machinery for cooperation among international airline carriers. In 1950 these lines operated a total of 2,500 planes and carried 30 million passengers—a 15 per cent increase over 1949. Sir Miles told the London meeting, over which he presided in September 1951, that the two main developments in commercial aviation in the immediate future would be increased speed and a larger number of passengers served through lower tourist rates. He said that Britain's two government-owned airlines (B.O.A.C. and British European Airways) were planning a drive to take air travel out of the luxury class by eliminating such "frills" as free meals and gifts, and by having more seats per plane.

British Inf. Services

SIR MILES THOMAS

In this way the airlines could compete with second-class rail and sea rates. The delegates to the I.A.T.A. meeting discussed plans for preparing the world's skyways for the use of jet airplanes in commercial aviation. It also sought to establish world-wide uniformity in immigration and landing procedures.

The British executive has given numerous radio talks. He is an honorary colonel of the 43rd Wessex Division, Royal Electrical and Mechanical Engineers; a member of the Institute of Mechanical Engineers and of the Society of Automotive Engineers (American). In 1947 he served on the Oxfordshire Council, Order of St. John. He was president of the Society of Motor Manufacturers and Trades during 1947-48 and is president of the British Advertising Association. He is a life-member of the court of governors of Birmingham University, chairman of the Royal Armored Corps Charities Trust, council member of the Society of Motor Manufacturers and Traders and of the English and Allied Employers National Federation, a member of the Management Committee of Horton General Hospital, and a fellow of the Institute of Motor Trade in Great Britain. His clubs are White's, Royal Automobile, Royal Motor Yacht, and Royal Air Force.

Miles Thomas and the former Hylda Nora Church, who were married on June 2, 1924, have a son, Michael, and a daughter, Sheila. According to the London *Sunday Times*, the airlines executive "seems to have a clear affinity with the internal combustion machine, and even to have borrowed its energy." A sense of humor, "insatiable" curiosity, and interest in people are outstanding characteristics of the tall, gray-haired official. He lists his recreations as motoring, golf, and shooting.

(Continued next page)

THOMAS, SIR MILES—*Continued*

References

Fortune 34:93 Jl '46 por
Sunday Times (London) F 11 '51 por
Burke's Peerage (1949)
International Who's Who, 1951
Who's Who, 1951
World Biography (1948)

THORNEYCROFT, (GEORGE ED-WARD) PETER July 26, 1909- British Cabinet member

Address: b. c/o Board of Trade, Horse Guards Ave., Whitehall, London, S.W.1, England; House of Commons, London, S.W.1, England; h. 68 Chester Sq., London, S.W.1, England

The Right Honorable Peter Thorneycroft a member of Parliament since 1938, was named to Winston Churchill's Cabinet as President of the Board of Trade when the Conservatives came to power in October 1951. A leader of the progressive group within the Conservative

British Inf. Services
PETER THORNEYCROFT

party, Thorneycroft has opposed Laborite attempts to nationalize industry, at the same time taking an active lead in postwar efforts to rebuild his country through increased production and exportation of merchandise.

George Edward Peter Thorneycroft was born in Dunston, England, on July 26, 1909, the son of Major George Edward Mervyn and Dorothy Hope (Franklyn) Thorneycroft. He has a twin sister, Elizabeth, who became a barrister. Thorneycroft was reared in Staffordshire and educated at Eton before entering the Royal Military Academy in Woolwich. In 1930 he was commissioned in the Royal Artillery but resigned his commission in 1933. With

the outbreak of World War II, he rejoined the Army, serving in the Royal Artillery and passing with distinction through the Staff College. As a member of the Joint Planning Staff, Captain Thorneycroft helped plan the North African landings.

Meanwhile, in 1935, he had been called to the bar at the Inner Temple and then for a time had practiced law in Birmingham on the Oxford Circuit. On June 10, 1938, he was elected as a Conservative member of Parliament in the Stafford by-election necessitated by the elevation of the former W. G. A. Ormsby-Gore to the peerage upon the death of his father, Lord Harlech. Thorneycroft's election was considered an important victory for the Chamberlain Government, seeming to indicate that Chamberlain's foreign policy had the general backing of the British public. Thorneycroft, who had taken the traditional three days off over Whitsun Holiday while his Laborite opponent, Frank G. Lloyd had continued campaigning, won the election in the face of vigorous opposition from Labor. A member of Parliament for Stafford for seven years, Thorneycroft was appointed Parliamentary Secretary to the Ministry of War Transport during the "Caretaker" Government of 1945, but lost his seat at Stafford in the general election of that year.

Returned to Parliament in October of 1945 by winning a by-election at Monmouth, Thorneycroft for a while continued his attempts "to stir up" the Conservative party, as the *Manchester Guardian* expressed it. (When he was chairman of the Tory Reform Group during the war he had begun this agitation, which earned him the coldness of more austere Tories.) His interests having soon found a new focus in trade and industry, he became known as a "constant and vehement critic" of the nationalization of the transport industry. On October 3, 1946, at the first postwar conference of the Conservative party Thorneycroft delivered a speech attacking both monopoly capitalism and socialism, while supporting Foreign Secretary Anthony Eden's proposal that a Conservative goal should be the "distribution of capital and ownership over a wide area." On November 21, 1946, in opposition to the Labor Government's legislation for the current Parliamentary session, he accused the Cabinet of spending all of its time nationalizing industries but failing to show how nationalization in itself would increase production.

When the Conservatives regained power in October 1951, Thorneycroft was named President of the Board of Trade and entered the Privy Council, at the age of forty-two becoming the youngest member of Winston Churchill's Cabinet. As head of the Board of Trade, he was immediately faced with the severe postwar problems of British commerce. Stating that in an attempt to solve these problems "the prime object is to make more capacity and materials available for export," Thorneycroft began supporting policies designed to increase Britain's export trade. In February 1952 he explained that it was the firm policy of the British Government to work for an increase of trade with Canada to "enable British capital and enterprise to participate as fully as financial and economic circumstances allow" in developing the rich resources of this Commonwealth country. The following month Great Britain was disturbed by South Africa's and Australia's curtailment of British imports, but Thorneycroft acknowledged that this move had been necessitated by the rapid rate with which these countries' sterling balances were falling.

With cotton mills closing down and unemployment increasing among textile workers, leaders of the Lancashire textile industry appealed for aid to the government in March 1952. In response to this appeal, members of Parliament from Lancashire called on Thorneycroft as President of the Board of Trade to submit a report on the English textile industry's widespread decline, which was, in its third month, beginning to take on the aspects of a serious depression. Thorneycroft pointed out that the causes for this slack included a "world-wide recession in the textile and clothing industries," competition from Japan, and the shortage of dollars restricting the amount of cotton Britain could buy from the United States. He went on to announce several meliorative measures, among them special discussions with the Cotton Board regarding competition from Japan, calling Australia's attention to instances where her plans to restrict imports would cause hardship to British textile companies, and canceling wherever possible orders made by the previous government for textiles abroad.

In April 1952 Thorneycroft sent a message to Lord Boyd-Orr (head of the self-appointed British delegation to the international trade conference in Moscow) to the effect that Great Britain would be willing to increase its trade with Russia and China by selling those nations consumer goods such as textiles but not restricted strategic materials like chemicals and metals. If the Russians and Chinese really wanted to do business, Thorneycroft charged, they need not have proposed it at an irregular conference but could have done it through ordinary official channels or by dealing directly with British manufacturers. (The New York *Herald Tribune*, April 10, 1952, reported that the British government and most British businessmen had refused to participate in the Moscow conference because they suspected it of being political in nature.)

The question of tariff regulations in trade relations between Britain and the United States has also been of concern to Thorneycroft. On July 22, 1952, he told the American Chamber of Commerce meeting in London that the British wait "in suspense" to learn whether or not American tariffs are to be raised, declaring that increased barriers against British goods "would strike a heavy blow against our solvency" (New York *Times*, July 23, 1952). A week later he made a statement to the House of Commons to the effect that during the Commonwealth Prime Ministers' economic conference scheduled for London in November, the General Agreement on Tariffs and Trade would be considered. Discussion of the agreement, frequently attacked in England because it re-

stricts preferential tariff rates within the British Empire, would reopen (according to Michael L. Hoffman, New York *Times*, August 2, 1952) "fundamental issues of world economic policy that were supposed to have been settled for this generation by British-United States agreements during the hectic days of 1944 and 1945."

Peter Thorneycroft married Sheila Wells Page in 1938 and by this marriage, which terminated in divorce in 1949, had one son, John Hamo. On April 2, 1949, he married Carla Malagola-Cappi, a former fashion editress; they have a daughter, Victoria Elizabeth Anne. Thorneycroft has written a number of articles on public affairs. His favorite recreations are painting and fishing, and he is a member of the Carlton Club and the Army and Navy Club. He belongs to the Anglican Church. He is six feet one inch tall and has brown hair and brown eyes.

References

Manchester Guardian O 31 '51
International Who's Who, 1952
Who's Who, 1952

TISHLER, MAX Oct. 30, 1907- Chemist
Address: b. c/o Merck & Company, Inc., Rahway, N.J.; h. 674 Shackamaxon Dr., Westfield, N.J.

Dr. Max Tishler, who is associate director of the research and development division of Merck & Company, manufacturing chemists, has been honored several times for his work in the synthetic development of cortisone. The Max Tishler Lectures at Harvard University and the Max Tishler Scholarship at Tufts College, both established in the fall of 1951, commemorate the first successful manufacture from easily obtainable substances of the steroid drug, which is used in the treatment of rheumatoid arthritis and several other chronic diseases. Tishler, who taught chemistry for nine years at Harvard before joining the Merck staff, has specialized in research leading to the isolation and synthesizing of such compounds of pharmacological use as vitamins, amino acids, alkaloids, steroids, and antibiotics.

Max Tishler was born in Boston, Massachusetts, on October 30, 1907, one of four children (three sons and one daughter) of Samuel Tishler, a cobbler of Roumanian birth, and Anna (Gray) Tishler, an Austrian. From the age of thirteen until the completion of his college education, Max Tishler worked after school hours in a pharmacy to contribute to the support of the family and to pay for his education. Upon graduation from the Boston English High School in 1924 he entered Tufts College at Medford, Massachusetts, where, under the influence of Professor C. F. H. Allen, he decided upon a career in chemistry.

In his first three years at Tufts College Tishler was aided by scholarships, and during his senior year, as a student-instructor, he taught elementary chemistry. He became a member of the Chemistry Club, the Economics Club, and the Pi Lambda Phi fraternity; and

Westfield Studios

MAX TISHLER

president of the German Verein, which he had organized. After receiving his Bachelor of Science degree *magna cum laude* in 1928, he spent the next nine years at Harvard University in teaching, research, and preparation for his graduate degrees. From 1929 to 1934, as Austin Teaching Fellow, he taught chemistry to undergraduate students, at the same time qualifying for his Master of Science degree in 1933 and for his Ph.D. degree the next year, with a thesis in organic chemistry, on the reactions of certain ketones. He was appointed a research associate in 1934 and in 1936-37, with the rank of instructor, taught advanced chemistry. Tishler has said that his work since leaving Harvard has been "profoundly inspired" by his association there with the late Dr. Elmer P. Kohler.

Tishler now entered the field of applied chemistry in 1937 as a research chemist at Merck & Company, in Rahway, New Jersey. Here he has held the successive titles of head of process development (1941), director of developmental research (1944), and associate director of research and development (1951). As the sole commercial producer of the drug cortisone, the Merck company was engaged in the search for a plentiful source of the steroid drug. First isolated in 1936, cortisone was synthesized by Dr. Lewis H. Sarett of Merck Research Laboratories in 1946, and was successfully manufactured from the desoxycholic acid from ox bile by Merck. The scarcity of its source, however (the bile from forty head of cattle is necessary to provide one day's dosage for one patient), provoked widespread attempts to discover cheap, plentiful sources that would make the drug better available for experimentation and application. When in 1949 cortisone, which had been used in the treatment of rheumatic fever, gout, certain eye diseases, and a number of other chronic illnesses, was

found efficacious in treating rheumatoid arthritis, these efforts were redoubled. Success of another investigation of a group of chemists directed by Tishler at the Merck laboratories was announced in May 1951 in the *Journal of the American Chemical Society.* Tishler and his colleagues, J. M. Chemerda, E. M. Chamberlain, and E. H. Wilson, produced a precursor of cortisone, starting with four easily obtainable materials: ergosterol, from yeast and other sources; stigmasterol, from soya beans; diosgenin, from the Mexican yam; cholesterol, from wool fat, egg yolk and other animal sources.

At an annual meeting of the American Association for the Advancement of Science in Cleveland, December 1950, Tishler reported that he and his assistants, N. L. Wendler, R. P. Graber, and R. E. Jones, had achieved the sythesis of a hormone of the adrenal gland, Compound F, a substance with the same antiarthritic activity as cortisone and ACTH. He also announced at this time that Merck could now start the synthesis of cortisone from cholic acid, a bile derivative more plentiful than desoxycholic acid. Simultaneously the *Journal of the American Chemical Society* reported that chemists at Harvard had reached the same preliminary goal, using as their basic source a coal tar derivative. On August 6 of that year both groups announced the culmination of their experiments, the manufacture of cortisone itself by their respective methods. It was emphasized at the same time that large-scale production of the drug would have to await further research and provision of manufacturing facilities.

In recognition of Tishler's achievement, the board of directors of Merck & Company voted him its Scientific Award, and in September 1951 the Max Tishler Lecture Series was set up at Harvard through a $15,000 grant made by Merck. By the terms of the award, scientists from the United States and abroad will lecture at Harvard on subjects related to organic and biological chemistry. A Max Tishler Scholarship was also established at Tufts College, Tishler's alma mater, to be awarded annually to outstanding students entering their senior year of chemical study. With James Bryant Conant, Tishler is the coauthor of the textbook *Chemistry of Organic Compounds* (1939); he also contributed to *Streptomycin* (1949), edited by Selman A. Waksman. He himself has written or collaborated on some seventy papers on chemical subjects in the *Journal of the American Chemical Society,* and is the holder or coholder of sixty-odd patents. His service during World War II was concerned with research on contracts from the Office of Scientific Research and Development. In 1952 he is a member of the national defense Research and Development Committee.

At Tufts College Tishler was elected to Phi Beta Kappa, scholastic honor society, and at Harvard to Sigma Xi, scientific honor society. He is a member of the American Chemical Society, the American Association for the Advancement of Science, the Swiss Chemical Society; is a fellow of the Chemical Society of

London and of the New York Academy of Science, and is a past president of the Association of Harvard Chemists. The scientist has brown hair and brown eyes, weighs 168 pounds, and stands five feet seven and a half inches in height. On June 17, 1934, he married Elizabeth Muriel Verveer, who had been a hospital psychologist. Their sons are Peter Verveer and Carl Lewis. Tishler calls himself an "independent" politically. He takes part in local United Campaigns Chest Fund drives and is a Cub Scout leader. His favorite sports are fishing and tennis, his hobbies stamp collecting and gardening.

References

American Men of Science (1949)
Chemical Who's Who, 1951
Who Knows—and What (1949)

OSCAR TORP

TORP, OSCAR (FREDRIK) June 8, 1893-
Prime Minister of Norway
Address: Oslo, Norway

Since the end of World War II Oscar Torp, who became Labor Prime Minister of Norway in succession to Einar Gerhardsen in November 1951, has been a leader in orienting his country into the Western trade, political, and defense orbit and is a strong supporter of the North Atlantic Treaty Organization. An active leader of the Norwegian Labor party since he was twenty-five years old, Torp held three different cabinet posts at Oslo prior to World War II, was prominent in his country's government-in-exile during the conflict, and for three years after the liberation made a notable record as Norway's Minister of Supply and Reconstruction. As Minister of Finance in the Nygaardsvold Labor Cabinet, he was credited with having saved Norway's gold reserve from Nazi confiscation on the day of the German invasion.

Oscar Fredrik Torp, the son of Anton Fredrik and Anne Bolette Andreassen (Gade) Torp, was born June 8, 1893, at Hafslund (Skjeberg) near Sarpsborg in Ostfold, the southeastern district or county of Norway. Almost all his life he has been associated with the labor movement: his father was a plant foreman, and he himself became a union official when only sixteen years old. While employed in his first trade as a woodworker, he trained as an electrician in a state evening technical school, and from apprentice electrician and mechanic rose steadily in responsibility at the Sarpsborg electrical works. In 1918 at the age of twenty-five, he became a member of the National Council of the Norwegian Labor party, which was then left-wing and Marxist and which joined the Communist Third International in the ensuing year. "In 1922," stated a short biography of the Norwegian Premier in the *Britannica Book of the Year* (1952), "Torp represented the Norwegian Labor party at the Comintern Congress in Moscow, but in 1923 the party withdrew from this organization." Oscar Torp became chairman of the National Council at that time, holding the post for the next seventeen years,

until the Nazi occupation of Norway early in World War II.

Having left Sarpsborg for Oslo on assuming the Labor Party National Council chairmanship, Torp became active in the municipal affairs of the Norwegian capital and in late 1934 was elected chairman of the Oslo Council. This post, equivalent to that of mayor, he held for only a few months, resigning in 1935 to become Deputy Minister of Defense and afterward Minister of Defense in the Government of Johan Nygaardsvold, Norway's first Labor Party Prime Minister. He moved to the Ministry of Social Affairs in 1936 and in the following year was elected for the first time to the Storting (Norwegian parliament) as a representative from Oslo.

After three years as Minister of Social Affairs, Oscar Torp again changed portfolios in the Nygaardsvold Cabinet, becoming Minister of Finance in July 1939. This was his position in the government when, early in the morning of April 9, 1940, a German invasion fleet steamed without warning into the Oslo fjord. The country's entire gold reserve—about $100 million in ingots—was then stored in vaults in the capital; but through Finance Minister Torp's swift decision, this reserve was secretly packed into 1,534 boxes. By the middle of the morning the gold was on its way to Lillehammer, ninety miles to the north, in twenty-seven trucks. Subsequently, under the guidance of Frederik Haslund, then parliamentary secretary of the Labor party, it was brought safely through German bomb and paratroop attack to the then unoccupied port of Andalsnes, and thence by fishing vessels and warships to England (as related by Webb Waldron in "The Wild Flight of Norway's Gold," *Liberty*, October 30, 1943). Once his country's gold assets were safe from the Nazis and the puppet government of Vidkun Quisling, Torp joined his colleagues of the Nygaardsvold Cabinet in

TORP, OSCAR—*Continued*

London, where he continued as Minister of Finance with the government-in-exile. (Torp, along with Prime Minister Nygaardsvold and Carl J. Hambro, former president of the Storting, was one of five prominent Norwegians whose citizenship was cancelled and whose property was confiscated by the Quisling regime in March 1942.) He became Minister of Defense again during 1942 and continued as such with the government-in-exile until the Germans withdrew from Norway early in 1945.

In June 1945 an interim coalition government headed by Einar Gerhardsen, successor to Nygaardsvold as leader of the Labor party, was set up at Oslo, with Torp as Minister of Defense. When, on October 8, the first postwar parliamentary election in Norway took place, the result was a majority for Labor over all other parties combined, and Prime Minister Gerhardsen accordingly formed an all-Labor Cabinet. Oscar Torp, who had been returned to the Storting by his Oslo constituency, took office as Minister of Supply and Reconstruction at the beginning of November, remaining as such for the next three years, during which time he did much to divert his country's economy away from dependence on trade relations with the Soviet Union and toward the Western bloc of Nations. Resigning from the Cabinet in 1948 to become Governor of the Vestfold district (to the southwest of Oslo), Torp nevertheless continued for a while as an Oslo member of the Storting, and during the same period assumed the leadership of the Labor bloc as chairman of the parliamentary group of the Labor party. The former Finance, Defense, and Supply Minister was returned to the Storting by the Vestfold district in the election of October 10, 1949, which resulted in another triumph for the Gerhardsen Government and the loss by the Communists of all eleven of their previously held seats. Increasingly influential in the formulation of foreign policy, Torp accompanied Foreign Minister Halvard Lange to Washington in 1949 for the discussions which led up to Norway's entrance into the North Atlantic Treaty Organization. (The descriptive paragraph on the Norwegian Labor party in the *Political Handbook of the World* classifies the party as "now basically reformist" with a program that "differs [little] from other Scandinavian Social Democratic parties" and stresses that it "strongly supports" rearmament, the Marshall Plan, and NATO.)

With the resignation of Einar Gerhardsen as Prime Minister on November 13, 1951, Oscar Torp was appointed by King Haakon to form a new government. Taking office six days later (November 19) the new Prime Minister made a statement to the Storting pledging continuation of "a policy of collaboration with the members of the North Atlantic Alliance" and promising that the country's defenses would be further strengthened as part of the common NATO effort. He emphasized that the pact was "purely defensive" and asserted that his government "would never take part in a policy of aggression." About two weeks later, in December, Prime Minister Torp attended a meeting in Stockholm, Sweden, of the executive council of the Nordic Interparliamentary Union, and (in the words of correspondent George Axelsson of the New York *Times*) "gave his blessing" to a "project to create a Nordic interparliamentary advisory council headed by premiers and foreign ministers of each country," one purpose of which would be to initiate and further "measures tending to co-ordinate and thereby simplify legislation and treaties in spheres of mutual interest." In September 1952 the Norwegian Prime Minister flew to the United States for what was described as an "unofficial" three weeks' visit. On arrival at Idlewild Airport in New York City he "vigorously denied recent reports that his country contemplated reduction" of its rearmament program (New York *Herald Tribune*). "There is nothing to indicate that Norway will curtail her military obligations to NATO that were assumed at the Lisbon conferences," he stated, although Norway was carrying "a very heavy economic load," and in this connection he expressed the hope that trade between the United States and Europe would be "stimulated by reduced tariffs." The Prime Minister's tour encompassed visits to Detroit, Duluth, Minneapolis, Chicago, Madison, Washington (where he conferred with President Truman and Secretary of State Dean Acheson), and New York City, where he unveiled in the Security Council chamber of the new United Nations building a large mural by the Norwegian artist, Per Krohg. The mural, he said, represented the gift of a small nation that looked to the United Nations as "the only torch in a dim world" (New York *Times*).

Mrs. Torp, who accompanied her husband on his American visit, is the former Kari Inga Hansen; the Torps were married in 1916. The Norwegian statesman is said to be companionable and unassuming. One of his recreations is watching soccer games.

References

N Y Herald Tribune II p1 S 28 '52 por
N Y Times p17 N 14 '51 por
Britannica Book of the Year (1952)
Hvem er Hvem? (1950)
International Who's Who, 1951
World Biography (1948)

TOWERS, GRAHAM F(ORD) Sept. 29, 1897- Canadian central bank governor

Address: b. c/o Bank of Canada, Ottawa, Canada; h. 260 Park Rd., Rockcliffe Park, Ottawa, Canada

Characterized as "one of the world's most successful central banks," the Bank of Canada, a public institution, has had since its creation in 1934 Graham Ford Towers as its governor. In that capacity Towers has also acted as chairman of Canada's Foreign Exchange Control Board (1939-51) and of the National War Finance Committee; and he is president of the Industrial Development Bank, and a director of the Central Mortgage and Housing Corporation, both Government agencies. In 1947 he was named executive director of the International Bank, and is alternate governor for Canada on the International Monetary Fund. Prior to his appointment to the Bank of Canada, Towers had been with the Royal Bank of Canada, a chartered bank, whose staff he joined as an economist in 1920.

Graham Ford Towers was born September 29, 1897, to William Crawford and Caroline (Auldjo) Towers in Montreal, Quebec, where his father was a wholesale dry goods merchant. The family is of United Empire Loyalist stock, their forebears, American colonists, having remained loyal to the mother country. Graham Towers, who received his early education in the city of his birth, attended Montreal High School from 1906 until 1911, when he was enrolled at St. Andrew's College, a boys' preparatory school at that time situated in Toronto, Ontario. Upon graduating from St. Andrew's in 1913, he returned to Montreal to enter McGill University.

Towers' university studies were interrupted by duty in the armed forces in World War I. He entered the Canadian Army Service Corps in 1915 as a lieutenant, having been in the McGill University officers' training corps. Sent to France as a railhead supply officer, he was attached to the British First Army Headquarters staff. In October 1918 he contracted influenza, and by Christmas of that year he was back in Canada as a convalescent. Upon his return he resumed his studies at McGill, and was granted the B.A. degree in 1919. He earned honors in political economics and won the Mackenzie Scholarship.

With the thought of making the law his career, the future banker entered the firm of Meredith, Holden & Company of Montreal. After a short time, however, hearing of a vacancy for an economist at the head office (in Montreal) of the Royal Bank of Canada, he applied for the position. He was accepted and was placed in the foreign trade department, where one of his duties was to make a survey of economic and banking conditions in the form of a monthly letter. In 1922, two years after he had joined the bank, Towers was sent, as accountant, to one of its biggest and most active branches, in Havana, Cuba. There he advanced to the position of assistant inspector of the Cuban branches in 1923. The following year he returned to head office as inspector of the Royal's foreign department, a position which entailed traveling to South America, the West Indies, and Europe, and which gave him opportunity to observe foreign banking. The position of chief inspector followed in 1929. In 1931 he was named assistant to the general manager, and in 1933, assistant general manager. The next year he resigned from the Royal Bank to accept the post of first governor of the newly established Bank of Canada (created by an Act of Parliament in 1934) offered him by Prime Minister R. B. Bennett.

Graham Towers was appointed governor for a term of seven years, and his term of office has been twice renewed. Before assuming his duties he spent some time in Europe studying various national and state banks. It was his task to organize a central banking institution "to regulate credit and currency in the best

Canada Nat. Film Bd.

GRAHAM F. TOWERS

interests of the economic life of the nation . . . to mitigate . . . fluctuations in the general level of production, trade, prices, and employment, so far as may be possible within the scope of monetary action" (preamble to the Bank of Canada Act). Canada's ten chartered banks (which have branches across the nation) are required by law to maintain, at the central bank, reserves of not less than 5 per cent of their deposit liabilities within the country; the central bank is not in competition with them in commercial banking fields, and cannot accept deposits from individuals.

The Federal Government's banker and adviser, the Bank of Canada issues its securities and performs other related tasks. (It may also act in a similar capacity to the Provincial Governments if requested.) Gradually the bank, which commenced operations March 11, 1935, has assumed control of bank note issue, exercising a complete and official monopoly in that field since January 1950, with the signatures of the governor and his deputy appearing on bills. Head office of the bank is in Ottawa, and it maintains agencies in each province. Sole shareholder in the bank, a public institution, is the Federal Government. The governor is its chief executive, and is aided by a deputy, assistant deputy, and a board of directors.

In 1938 the Bank of Canada assumed management of the national debt, until that time a responsibility of the Department of Finance. With the outbreak of World War II the bank gave advice on the setting up of the Foreign Exchange Control Board and contributed personnel to it; Towers acted as its chairman until it was dissolved in December 1951. Canada's war loans, issued every six months, were a concern of the central bank, and were handled by the National War Finance Committee, of which Towers was made general chairman in 1943. The central banker became a director

TOWERS, GRAHAM F.—*Continued*
of the Central Mortgage and Housing Corporation, a Government agency, in 1945.

In an article in *Saturday Night* (April 15, 1944) Carolyn Cox wrote: "Foreign exchange control and Government financing of the war have admittedly been done in this country with an imagination and forthrightness seldom equaled," and gave Towers the credit. Elsewhere in the same article the reporter said, "Today authorities best qualified to speak put it: 'Among central bankers Graham Towers is Number One.'" The Governor of the Bank of Canada is president of the Industrial Development Bank, a wholly owned subsidiary of the central bank with the function of lending to small industries of potential national value. In 1944 Towers received the order of the Companion of St. Michael and St. George for his services as governor of the bank and for that institution's contributions to the functioning of the war economy. The central banker was executive director of the International Bank for Reconstruction and Development during 1947-48. He is alternate governor for Canada on the International Monetary Fund. On the problem of checking inflation, Graham Towers in a press interview, February 13, 1951, gave it as his opinion that the application of direct controls should be a "last resort," pointing out the difficulty of imposing them on a peacetime economy. Maintenance of production, and taxation designed to prevent "competitive spending" he thought could be relied on to avert runaway inflation. He is author of the book *Financing Foreign Trade* (1921).

The Canadian banker is tall and of solid build, is clean-shaven, and wears rimless glasses. One observer has described him as "never untidy, never hurried, never enthusiastic," and as having a "clear and clipped" way of speaking. It is told that he has been known to speak of himself as "a product of the Victorian era." He is a member of the Rideau Club (Ottawa) and the Royal Ottawa Golf Club; his church is the Church of England. On February 1, 1924, Towers married Mary Scott Godfrey, of Montreal. Their recreations are golfing and skiing.

References

Maclean's Mag p12 O 15 '34
Montreal Gazette D 17 '49
Sat Night Ap 15 '44
Who's Who, 1951
Who's Who in America, 1950-51
Who's Who in Canada, 1949-50

TOY, HENRY, JR. Feb. 1, 1915- Organization executive

Address: b. c/o National Citizens Commission for the Public Schools, 2 W. 45th St., New York 19; h. 811 The Parkway, Mamaroneck, N.Y.

Henry Toy, Jr., is the executive director of the National Commission for the Public Schools, a nonprofit corporation which the New York *Times* has described as "the first independent national association of laymen dedicated to the improvement of the public schools in this century." A graduate of the Wharton School of the University of Pennsylvania, Toy served as manager of the priorities and surplus materials division of the purchasing department of E. I. du Pont de Nemours & Company from 1946 to 1949. He was the founder and first head (1946-49) of the Council for Delaware Education, which has been instrumental in achieving far-reaching school improvements in that State through community action. As a result of his work for the council Toy was appointed director of the National Citizens Commission in August 1949, about three months after that group had been organized.

Born in Easton, Pennsylvania, on February 1, 1915, Henry Toy, Jr., is one of the two children of Henry and Pauline (Pfenning) Toy. His father is a retired salesman. After attending public schools in Woodbury, New Jersey, young Toy began his career as an office boy with the Atlantic Refining Company in 1933, and held positions there, successively, for eight years as a file clerk, junior clerk, and accountant. In June 1939 he received a Certificate of Proficiency with honors from the Evening School of Accounts and Finance of the Wharton School of Finance and Commerce, at the University of Pennsylvania. He joined the staff of E. I. du Pont de Nemours & Company in February 1941 as a cost accountant, and the next month was promoted to procurement specialist. At the beginning of 1942 he was made supervisor of the priorities section of the explosives department at du Pont, a position he held for over three years. From August to December 1945 he was assistant manager of the priorities and surplus materials division of the purchasing department, and in January 1946 he advanced to manager of this division. Nine months later he was also given the post of assistant division purchasing agent.

Toy's interest in the public school dates from an evening in the fall of 1946, when his wife was competing in a bowling league contest, and he substituted for her at a Parent-Teacher Association meeting in Oak Grove, Delaware, the small Wilmington suburb where they lived and where their five-year-old son was starting in the first grade. He took part in the discussion and before it was over found himself appointed chairman of a local committee to study teachers' salaries. (Later he was elected president of the Oak Grove P.T.A.) His work on this committee soon led him to the realization that the parents could not accomplish major school reforms unless they obtained the support of most of the citizens of the State. Therefore, in November 1946 Toy and other parents, in cooperation with the Delaware Congress of Parents and Teachers, called a meeting to which were invited some 150 representatives of such organizations as the State Federation of Women's Clubs, American Legion, Veterans of Foreign Wars, Kiwanis, Rotary, Lions, church clubs, and P.T.A.'s from all parts of the State. This meeting marked the founding of the Council for Delaware Education, Inc., a group directed by an executive committee of ten parents with Toy as its president.

The Council for Delaware Education immediately launched an intensive campaign to improve the State's schools. To arouse public interest it summarized in layman's language the State's school laws, had them published in newspapers, and otherwise arranged for the dramatic presentation of all school issues in radio, press, and public meetings. Committees were sent out by the council to investigate conditions in every Delaware public school, and in 1948 a report on these conditions was written, published (with the cooperation of the American Association of University Women) and sent to educators, legislators, and civic groups in Delaware. According to *School Management*, the gubernatorial election in that fall was fought out largely on public school issues. As chairman of the legislative committee of the Delaware Congress of Parents and Teachers, Toy carried the fight for better schools to the legislature, before which council members appeared to argue for and against proposed bills during the 1949 session. After each bill was introduced, the committee issued a "Legislative Flash," showing how the bill would change existing conditions and the cost to the State.

As a result of this concerted action, the Delaware General Assembly passed more school legislation in 1949 than in any previous year, the legislation providing for prompt redistricting and closing of small schools, clarification of the school term, and more adequate and equitable allocation of State funds to school districts. A $19 millions school-building program, 60 per cent of which will be paid by the State, was adopted to meet the needs of the next several years and to provide proper facilities for Negro children. Legislation was also passed raising the average teacher's salary from $1,800 to $3,000 a year. The State now has a uniform salary schedule, and the pension laws for school personnel have been liberalized. But, in Toy's own words, "the major achievement of the council has been the reawakening of public interest in the schools . . . and the realization by the people of what the schools can do for them, and what they can do for the schools."

On August 9, 1949, it was announced that Toy had accepted the appointment as executive director of the National Citizens Commission for the Public Schools. At that time, Roy E. Larsen, president of Time, Inc., and chairman of the commission, stated that "as a businessman who realizes the vital importance of the public schools to each community," Toy would now be able to "give all his time and the full benefit of his experience to implementing" the commission's program. Discussing the origin of the commission in an article for *School Executive* (January 1952), Larsen explained that in the mid-1940's Dr. James Bryant Conant, president of Harvard, suggested to a small group of laymen, of which Larsen was one, the idea for such an organization. These educators "believed that our American system of education was in urgent need of reappraisal by citizens

HENRY TOY, JR.

at the local and national level." Over a period of two years this group of laymen met for frequent exploratory discussions, and it was finally decided that a national organization, patterned after Josiah Holbrook's American Lyceum in the nineteenth century, could make a real contribution toward the improvement of the public school system.

Accordingly, the National Citizens Commission for the Public Schools was launched on May 15, 1949, with the announcement, "The problems of public education concern all of us, and it is time for all of us to do something about them." Composed exclusively of laymen not professionally identified with education, religion, or politics, the commission had at its inception twenty-eight members (by 1952 thirty-three), many of them prominent in industry, labor, and business. The commission has set as its immediate goals: (1) "to help Americans realize how important our public schools are to our expanding democracy" and (2) "to arouse in each community the intelligence and will to improve our public schools." Convinced that the most successful efforts to improve the schools are conducted at the community level, the organization works to assist and encourage the formation of local nonpartisan citizens' committees to help solve their own school problems. The N.C.C.P.S. does not make any affiliations with these local groups, nor does it attempt to supervise or control them. Acting as a clearing house, it gathers and distributes information about what various community groups are doing to improve their schools. Among the most pressing problems in the estimation of the commission are: the shortage of trained teachers; the lack of clarity in educational goals; inadequate facilities, overcrowded classrooms, and outmoded buildings. The commission has received financial support from the Carnegie Corporation, the General

TOY, HENRY, JR.—*Continued*

Education Board, and the New York Community Trust.

Under Toy's direction, the N.C.C.P.S., in cooperation with the Advertising Council, Inc., the United States Office of Education, and the Citizens Federal Committee on Education, has been conducting a nation-wide "Better Schools" advertising campaign to arouse active public interest in the problem. Another effort to dramatize the urgency of the needs of the schools is represented by the film, *The Fight for Better Schools*, which the commission helped the March of Time to produce. The commission has also arranged a series of regional workshop conferences—for professional educators and laymen—to develop a process by which group experience and thinking can be turned to the improvement of schools. Committees of N.C.C.P.S. members have been formed to undertake special intensive studies: by 1951 there were committees on the American teacher, on community participation, on public education financing, and on boards of education. More recently, the commission has decided to embark on a series of objective reports on the "great issues" in public education, because available literature on educational problems is often highly technical or written from one point of view. In order to preserve the "grass-roots" character of the organization, the commission has set up six regional offices in the United States. By the beginning of 1952 it had received more than 42,500 inquiries, and the number of local, county, and State citizens' school-improvement committee with which it had established contact had grown from 150 (in 1949) to more than 1,500.

Henry Toy, Jr., was named "Young Man of the Year" in February 1949 by the Junior Chamber of Commerce in Delaware. The following June he won a membership competition of the National Association of Purchasing Agents. He has served as secretary of the Wilmington Purchasing Agents Association and on two committees of the Philadelphia Purchasing Agents Association. Greek letter societies in which he holds membership include Pi Rho Sigma and Sigma Kappa Phi. In Mamaroneck, New York, where he now resides, Toy is a member of the board of stewards, board of education, and official board of the Mamaroneck Methodist Church, and he recently became director of the 1952 local Community Chest campaign. His marriage, to Elizabeth Wray Voelker, took place on August 31, 1935. They have two sons: T. Jeffrey and C. Henry. According to the *Christian Science Monitor*, the commission director "combines the practical mind of an executive, the warmth of a family man, the enthusiasm of a grass-rooter, and the theory of an educator." Toy himself has commented: "My avocation is, temporarily at least, my vocation." For recreation he enjoys swimming and sailing and all kinds of spectator sports.

References

Am Mag 152:56 D '51 por
Christian Sci Mon II p9 S 1 '51 por

N Y Herald Tribune p7 Ag 10 '49 por
N Y Times p26 Ag 10 '49; p16 Je 12 '50
Sch Exec 71:41-3 Ja '52 por
Sch Manag 19:13 O '49
Time 52:58 D 6 '48

TRAUBEL, HELEN (trou'bĕl) June 16, 1903- Singer

Address: b. c/o Columbia Artists Management, 113 W. 57th St., New York 19; c/o Metropolitan Opera Association, 147 W. 39th St., New York 18

NOTE: This biography supersedes the article which appeared in *Current Biography* in 1940.

A notable indication of the increasing independence of the United States from Europe in the training of opera singers has been the career of Helen Traubel, the first American-born and entirely American-trained soprano to sing the parts of Isolde and the three Brünnhildes at the Metropolitan Opera. Since her performance for the Metropolitan in *Die Walküre* in 1939, Miss Traubel has become the leading interpreter of these and other roles in the German repertoire. She has also made extensive transcontinental concert tours, has appeared on radio and television programs, and has recorded for both Columbia and RCA-Victor.

Helen Traubel was born in St. Louis, Missouri, on June 16, 1903, the daughter of Otto and Clara (Stuhr) Traubel, both of German descent. Her maternal grandfather was the founder of the Apollo Theater in St. Louis, which presented the first serious German drama in the Middle West; and Clara Stuhr had won local fame as a concert and church singer before her marriage. With this background, and because her father, a druggist by trade, was a man of many interests, Miss Traubel and her brother, Walter, were present at almost every musical, theatrical, and sports event in St. Louis. In her sophomore year she left high school in order to devote all her time to vocal training, which she had begun at the age of thirteen, with Madame Vetta Karst as her teacher, her only teacher over a twenty-year period.

At the age of twelve Helen Traubel had substituted for her mother in a church choir. After her professional debut a few years later with the St. Louis Symphony Orchestra under the baton of Rudolph Ganz, she made several tours with the orchestra in the Middle Western States and as far south as New Orleans. In 1926, when Ganz was engaged as a guest conductor for the New York Philharmonic in a Lewisohn Stadium concert, he took Miss Traubel with him as soloist. Gatti-Casazza, then director of the Metropolitan Opera, summoned her to his office after the concert to discuss a contract. Feeling that she was not yet ready for opera, she decided not to accept the offer. She did return to the East a few months later for a series of concerts with the Philadelphia Orchestra and at the Worcester (Massachusetts) Festival, but went back to St. Louis before the tour was completed.

While continuing her studies in St. Louis, Miss Traubel earned her living as soloist in the choirs of the Pilgrim Congregational Church and the United Hebrew Temple. In 1935, when Walter Damrosch went to St. Louis to conduct the National Sängerfest, he heard her sing the "Liebestod." Asking her to appear in his new opera, *The Man Without a Country*, he added the soprano role of Mary Rutledge to the score for her. It was in this role that she made her operatic debut during the Metropolitan spring season of 1937, singing it in the five performances that year. "A woman of noble and gracious beauty," observed the New York *Herald Tribune*, "brings to the role of Mary Rutledge a voice of power and fine quality and [her] embodiment of the heroine was moving through its restraint and sincerity." After this debut Miss Traubel remained in New York about a year, appearing on sustaining radio programs over NBC. Then, still not satisfied with her voice, she took further training.

In the spring of 1939 the singer rejected an offer of a fifteen-week appearance at Radio City Music Hall at a salary of $1,000 a week. In the fall of that year, however, deciding that she was ready for the career toward which she had been working, she made her New York recital debut on October 8 in Town Hall. The success of the recital, in which, commented the music critic of the New York *Herald Tribune*, "Miss Traubel . . . displayed one of the finest voices to be heard anywhere today," brought other offers as well as critical acclaim. On the following Sunday she appeared on radio's *Ford Sunday Evening Hour*, and a week later she sang Brünnhilde's "Immolation" from *Die Götterdämmerung* on a broadcast with John Barbirolli and the New York Philharmonic. She also went to Chicago to make her first appearance in Wagnerian opera as Sieglinde in *Die Walküre* with Kirsten Flagstad as Brünnhilde and Lauritz Melchior as Siegmund. Shortly afterward, on December 28, 1939, she gave her first performance in a regular winter season of the Metropolitan Opera, again as Sieglinde. Olin Downes of the New York *Times* found her occasionally uneasy in the role during the first act, but of her performance in the second act, he wrote: "Miss Traubel gave one of the most moving and piteous portrayals of the distraught Sieglinde that we have seen in years." Later in the season she added the role of Elisabeth in *Tannhäuser* to her repertoire.

In her second New York recital, in October 1940, Miss Traubel offered a widely varied program: "Divinites du Styx" from *Alceste,* "Suicidio" from *La Gioconda,* a number of French, German, and English selections, and two Negro spirituals. In the 1940-41 season she made her first transcontinental concert tour, with Coenraad V. Bos as her accompanist. There was little opportunity to enlarge her operatic repertoire during her first two seasons with the Metropolitan Opera since Kirsten Flagstad had already established herself as the

HELEN TRAUBEL

company's greatest box office attraction in most of the Wagnerian operas. However, with the departure of Madame Flagstad for Europe in 1941, Miss Traubel succeeded the Norwegian soprano as the leading singer of German operas. She sang Elsa in *Lohengrin* and Brünnhilde in *Die Walküre* for the first time in December 1941. Of her interpretation as the *Götterdämmerung* Brünnhilde on February 13, 1942, Olin Downes remarked that it was "a distinguished portrayal, histrionically as well as vocally, surpassing any previously attempted by her." When *Tristan und Isolde* was returned to the stage of the Metropolitan in December 1942 after the absence of a year, Miss Traubel sang her first Isolde "very carefully, very intelligently, always with a lofty purpose and with a sincerity that was manifest in every measure" (New York *Times*).

With ten performances of the same role at the Teatro Colon in Buenos Aires, Miss Traubel made her first operatic appearances outside the United States in the summer of 1943. (She had earlier sung in recitals in Canada and in Cuba.) *Time* reported that the Argentine audiences, which had awaited the appearance of an American Isolde with considerable skepticism, were enthusiastic over her first performance. In 1945 she sang during the summer season of the Opera Nacional in Mexico City and in the fall of that year made her San Francisco Opera debut. At the Metropolitan Opera in March and April of 1950, she sang Kundry in two performances of *Parsifal,* her only appearances thus far in this role. When Kirsten Flagstad rejoined the Metropolitan Opera Association for the 1950-51 season, Miss Traubel and she were given equal status as the company's leading sopranos. During that season Miss Traubel sang for the first time the role of the Marschallin in Richard Strauss's *Der Rosenkavalier.* Some critics

TRAUBEL, HELEN—*Continued*

found her interpretation the finest since that of Lotte Lehmann and noted that she was almost completely successful in whittling her voice from Valkyrie dimensions to the warm lyricism of Strauss's princess. *Der Rosenkavalier* has been, so far, Miss Traubel's only departure from the Wagnerian music dramas since *The Man Without a Country*.

Helen Traubel's singing has been described by Howard Taubman of the New York *Times* as having "everything—vocal magnificence to match any demand made by the music, a grasp of the musical line, a capacity to shade and color the voice and the emotional penetration to bring out the essential humanity of [Wagner's] music." After hearing her sing at a Carnegie Hall concert in March 1949, a New York *Post* reviewer wrote: "When Miss Traubel is in the vein, there is probably no one in the Wagnerian domain who can match the power and splendor of her singing. Her upper notes flood the auditorium with vibrant tone. And Miss Traubel is a singer, not a screamer. The magnificent instrument can be diminished to a whispered pianissimo."

One of Miss Traubel's earliest recordings, for RCA-Victor, was the "Immolation," in which she was the first singer ever to record with Arturo Toscanini and the NBC Symphony Orchestra. Among her other recordings are three songs from Wagner's *Fünf Gedichte* song cycle, and Shubert's *Frauenliebe und Leben*, also for Victor; the "Wedding Night Scene" from *Lohengrin* with Torsten Ralf; excerpts from *Tristan und Isolde* including "Isolde's Narrative," the "Love Duet" from the second act with Ralf and Herta Glaz, and the "Liebestod"; the complete third act of *Die Walküre* with Herbert Janssen, Irene Jessner, and a Metropolitan opera ensemble; and a group of Italian operatic arias for Columbia.

From February 1949 to June of the following year Miss Traubel was the musical supervisor for Margaret Truman, the daughter of the President of the United States. Among the other musical activities of Miss Traubel are her performances as guest artist on radio and television programs, notably in 1951-52 her appearances on Jimmy Durante's NBC-TV show. Her interests outside the world of music having expanded in recent years, Miss Traubel in October 1950 became part owner of the St. Louis Browns, the baseball team she has applauded since her father first took her to games in her childhood.

At Christmas 1950 Miss Traubel presented her friends with copies of her first effort as an author, a privately printed short mystery entitled *The Ptomaine Canary*. This story, syndicated by the Associated Press, then appeared in newspapers in the United States, Europe, and Asia. Her first full-length mystery novel, *The Metropolitan Opera Murder*, in which a prompter is murdered by poison intended for a star, was published in October 1951. Critical appraisal of the book, a Mystery Guild selection, was somewhat mixed: James Sandoe of the New York *Herald Tribune* found "Miss Traubel's plot . . . conventionally

lively" but that she tended to use clichés in her prose; the reviewer for the San Francisco *Chronicle* commented that her "writing is admirably simple, and scenes backstage or those dealing with music are fine, but outsiders clutter up the plot."

The New York Tau Alpha chapter of Mu Phi Epsilon, an honorary music society, presented Miss Traubel with an award for the most outstanding performance of the year in 1939 and again in 1942. Other honors she has received include unanimous selection as "The Woman of the Year in Music" for two successive years by the Associated Press, the New York Newspapers' Headlines Award, Citation of Merit of the National Association for American Composers and Conductors, the King Christian X Medal of Liberation, and the New York Jewish Philanthropies Federation Division Award. The University of Southern California and the University of Missouri have presented her with honorary doctorates in music.

Helen Traubel has been married since October 1938 to William L. Bass, who is her business manager. She was previously married, at the age of nineteen, to Louis F. Carpenter, a St. Louis automobile salesman, from whom she was separated after a few months and later divorced. Said to be as heroic in appearance as the Valkyrie and the Irish princess she impersonates in opera, Helen Traubel stands five feet nine and a half inches tall, has large green eyes and a mass of red-blond hair. Charles O'Connell, former musical director of RCA-Victor, has described her as "beautiful in the best sense of the word." The singer has a home in South Laguna, California. Aside from attendance at baseball games, which is limited because her enthusiastic shouts make her hoarse, she finds diversion in walking, swimming, and shopping.

References

Collier's 109:19 Ja 31 '42 por
Mus Rec 11:7 S '41 por
Opera N 4:3 D 25 '39 por
Sat Eve Post 221:26 O 2 '48 pors
Ewen, D. ed. Living Musicians (1940); Men and Women Who Make Music (1949)
National Cyclopædia of American Biography Current vol G, 1943-46
O'Connell, C. The Other Side of the Record (1947)
Peltz, M. E. Spotlight on the Stars (1943)
Thompson, O. ed. International Cyclopedia of Music and Musicians (1949)
Who is Who in Music (1951)
Who's Who in the East (1951)
World Biography (1948)

ULBRICHT, WALTER (ŏŏl'brĭкt väl'tĕr) June 30, 1893- East German Communist leader

Address: b. Lothringerstrasse 1, Berlin, Germany; h. Viktoriastrasse 23, Berlin-Niederschönhausen, Germany

In his dual position as secretary-general of the Socialist Unity (SED) party's central committee and as Deputy Premier in the Otto Grotewohl Cabinet of the German Democratic Republic, Walter Ulbricht is considered one of the most influential Germans in the Soviet-controlled East German zone. A member of his country's Communist party since its founding in 1919, Ulbricht, whose Moscow training in Communist ideology began in the mid-1920's, is reportedly one of the few German leaders trusted by the Russians. Since his return to Germany in 1945 after some twelve years of exile in Moscow, his objectives have been the unification of Germany, nationalization of industry, economic and political cooperation with Eastern Europe and the Soviet Union, and prevention of West German remilitarization in alliance with the Western democracies.

Walter Ulbricht was born in Leipzig (Saxony), Germany, on June 30, 1893, the son of a tailor. With the completion of his elementary school education in his native city, he was apprenticed to a woodworker for training in carpentry and cabinetmaking. When he was fifteen years old, reported Ernest Leiser in an article for Collier's (May 27, 1950), he became a member of the Workers' Youth Organization of the Socialist party; by the age of seventeen, in 1910, he was a full trade unionist in the woodworkers' union and in 1912 joined the Socialist party. A member of the Lenin-inspired Spartacus Society and thus a follower of Karl Liebknecht and Rosa Luxemburg, who established the German Communist party in 1919, Ulbricht has been counted by some political observers as among the party's founders.

After working a few years as a Communist party organizer in Thuringia and Saxony, Ulbricht in the mid-1920's was called to Moscow for training in the cell system of party structure, which he was afterward to apply to the German Communist party organization. From 1928 until the rise of Hitler in 1933, he was Communist deputy in the Reichstag of the Weimar Republic and a leader of the politburo of his party. He spent the years of Nazi supremacy and World War II for a short time in Czechoslovakia and then in Russia, except for a period during the Spanish Civil War when he was assigned to set up a German section of the Communist police in Albacete, Spain. For part of these years he was also a member of the National Committee for Free Germany. An article written by Ulbricht in February 1940 for the Comintern magazine Die Welt put responsibility for the outbreak of the war on Great Britain and France and urged workers in Germany not to collaborate with these countries (Christian Science Monitor, October 16, 1950). Upon the defeat of Germany in 1945 he returned to his native land with Marshal Georgi K. Zhukov in the rank of colonel in the Russian Army. Shortly thereafter he joined Communist Wilhelm Pieck and Socialist Otto Grotewohl in effecting a merger of the strong Social Democratic party (SPD) and the Communist party (KPD) to form the Social Unity party (SED). The following year (1946) Ulbricht, who in May was elected to the central secretariat of the SED, made a number of speeches attacking Allied

policies in the Western zones of Germany on the ground that the occupying powers were "supporting all the old fascist forms of economic organization" (New York Times, March 4, 1946) and criticizing the "dilatory program on land reform" in the United States zone (New York Times, August 14, 1946).

In a speech before the Sachsen-Anhalt Diet, to which he had been elected in October 1946, Ulbricht in December 1946 opposed the economic merger of the British and American zones in West Germany and proposed a "national plebiscite for re-establishment of Germany's unity" (New York Herald Tribune, December 6, 1946). The formation of an all-German government became the chief objective of the National Front, a Communist-controlled bloc of East German political parties, which in 1949 Ulbricht, then the chairman of the Secretariat of the SED as well as the dominant member of the politburo, described as nonpartisan and open to former Nazis. While pressing for the abolition of the occupation statute for Western Germany, the Communist leader, who became president of the economic committee of the German People's Council in April 1948, was also occupied in drafting and executing a two-year economic plan to revive German industrial production and to communize industry. This plan, adopted in July 1948 and fulfilled in July 1950, was followed by a five-year plan, the outlines of which Ulbricht announced in the summer of 1950, stating at that time that Germany would seek admission to the Council for Mutual Economic Aid (the Russian counterpart of the Marshall Plan). Following a policy of closer integration of East Germany with the Soviet Union and Eastern Europe, in June 1950 Ulbricht headed the delegations which negotiated cultural and trade agreements with Poland (renouncing East German claims to territory east of the Oder-Neisse line), with Czechoslovakia (renouncing claims to the Sudetenland), and with Hungary; and in September 1950 with Rumania and Bulgaria. With raw materials supplied by Russia, Poland, and Czechoslovakia and exploitation of new iron mines in the Russian zone of Germany, East German production by 1955 was expected to double the area's 1936 figures. Ulbricht also made known at this time that by 1955 East Germany would build twenty-two ships for its new merchant fleet.

Meanwhile, in October 1949, Ulbricht had been appointed Deputy Premier of the German Democratic Republic in the Cabinet of Premier Grotewohl. "Despite his ostensibly secondary post as Deputy Premier," reported Kathleen McLaughlin in the New York Times, "Ulbricht actually wields greater influence with the Kremlin than either Herr Grotewohl or President Wilhelm Pieck." In evaluating Ulbricht's prestige with the Russians, political experts have noted that it is he who in December 1949 appeared on the podium in Moscow during celebrations of Joseph Stalin's birthday and who has been called to Russia several times a year to consult with Soviet leaders on German policy. To further strengthen his

Wide World Photos
WALTER ULBRICHT

power, the SED in July 1950 established a central committee of 151 members with Ulbricht as its secretary-general. The German Communist leader was thus given a position corresponding to Stalin's in the Soviet Union, since the political head in East Germany, in the view of Western observers, also controls the government. A few months after becoming secretary-general, Ulbricht announced an investigation into the activities of all Communist members in East Germany, this mass inquiry succeeding a general party purge which Ulbricht had begun in 1949 and which had resulted in the expulsion of thousands of officials of the SED and the dismissal of a number of Cabinet members. The *Christian Science Monitor* and other newspapers saw as one aim of the Deputy Premier the elimination from prominent positions of pre-1933 Communists, some of whom had become "Western-tainted" through their exile in the democratic countries during World War II.

Throughout 1951 the SED secretary-general reiterated in speeches and newspaper articles the goal of the party to secure German unity along Communist lines, warned that the militarization of Western Germany would precipitate a war, and pointed to the Soviet Union as the country to which Germany must look for guidance. At a Communist Youth World Festival in Berlin in August 1951 he called upon Communists in West Germany to resist cooperation between Germany and the Western powers through industrial sabotage and strikes, outlining a program of action he had advocated a year previously and was to enunciate

again in January 1952. Rejecting in December 1951 a proposal for a United Nations investigation (requested by West German Chancellor Konrad Adenauer) of conditions for free elections in Germany, Ulbricht headed an East German committee to draft a nation-wide law, based on the 1924 Weimar Republic election law, to guarantee a free election for an all-German assembly.

As the date drew near for conclusion of treaties to admit West Germany into the European defense program (which agreements were signed in Bonn on May 26 and 27, 1952, subject to ratification), Ulbricht issued a number of statements described by United States Secretary of State Dean Acheson as being of "a somewhat bellicose nature." The SED leader threatened that arming of West Germany constituted violation of agreements against rearmament and that reprisals would be felt immediately in West Berlin.

East Germany's Deputy Premier Ulbricht bears noticeable resemblance to Lenin, which, it is said, he has encouraged by cultivating a Lenin-like beard. He reportedly speaks Russian as fluently as German.

References

Christian Sci Mon p6 O 16 '50 por
Collier's 125:7 My 27 '50 por
N Y Herald Tribune p14 Jl 13 '50; p1 Jl 26 '50
Washington (D.C.) Post p2B Ag 27 '50 por
International Who's Who, 1951
Wer ist Wer? (1948)

VAN HEUVEN GOEDHART, G(ERRIT) J(AN) *See* Heuven Goedhart, G. J. van

VAN HOUTTE, JEAN See Houtte, J. van

VELASCO IBARRA, JOSÉ MARÍA (vä-läs′kō ē-bä′rä hō-sä′ mä-rē′ä) Mar. 19, 1893- President of Ecuador
Address: Presidential Palace, Quito, Ecuador

For the third time in seventeen years, José María Velasco Ibarra was inaugurated as President of Ecuador, on September 1, 1952, succeeding on that date Galo Plaza Lasso, who was the first constitutionally elected President of Ecuador since 1924 to serve the full four-year term. A scholar and professor of international law and political theory, Velasco Ibarra has written several books on governmental affairs and has held a number of important public offices. Before his first term as President in 1934-35, from which he was deposed, he was leader of the Chamber of Deputies. Returning to Quito after almost ten years in exile, he again became President of Ecuador and in 1947 he was again deposed. An independent candidate with the backing of the People's Force, Velasco Ibarra won the Presidency in June 1952 by the largest vote in Ecuador's history.

The son of wealthy parents, José María Velasco Ibarra was born in Quito, Ecuador, on March 19, 1893, to J. Alejandro Velasco and Delia Ibarra de Velasco. He attended the Colegio de San Gabriel and the University of Quito in his native city and later continued his studies at the University of Paris. The young lawyer first entered public service as secretary of the Public Welfare Society, from which he advanced successively to secretary of the Council of State, attorney general of Quito, and president of the Chamber of Deputies.

As leader of the Chamber of Deputies in 1933, Velasco Ibarra found himself in a position to speak out against Juan de Dio Martínez Mera, the Liberal president who had assumed office in December 1932. Opposition and repeated votes of lack of confidence in Congress against Mera were supported on the outside by rivalries among Liberal leaders, Communist agitators, and the Conservative party. When, following impeachment charges against him, Congress voted to remove Mera from office, Velasco Ibarra, backed by the Conservative party, became a candidate for the Presidency. In a two-day election, in mid-December 1933, Velasco Ibarra was victorious, defeating his Socialist opponent and succeeding acting President Abelardo Montelvo. For the first time since 1895, Conservative forces replaced the Liberal Radical party in power. Although his supporters were Conservatives, Velasco Ibarra stated that he would maintain the standards of the Liberal group, and on December 17, 1933, his election was confirmed. The new President-elect expressed himself as opposed to state monopolies and said his new government would plan to divide and develop the large landed estates. Before his inauguration, on a goodwill tour of Argentina, Chile, and Peru in July 1934, he asked for an early settlement with Peru of Ecuador's boundary dispute and for inter-American unity.

Upon being installed as President of Ecuador on September 1, 1934, Velasco Ibarra found Congress unsympathetic to his expressed desire to change the economic *status quo* of the people of his country. When Congress failed to pass legislation in support of his economic program, Velasco Ibarra turned in his resignation as President on October 3, 1934, but with the refusal of Congress to accept his resignation, he agreed to withdraw it. During the early days of his first term as President, on September 28, 1934, Ecuador joined the League of Nations.

Because of his failure to win the support of Congress for his policies, Velasco Ibarra is reported to have moved closer to the right and to dictatorial powers, seizing and imprisoning many leaders of the opposition, and subjecting the newspapers to police control. By November 1934 his position as President of Ecuador was insecure, but with his refusal to resign his administration was upheld by Congress. He also had the support of part of the army and the backing of the Accion Civica, described as a Fascist group. Further adding to his personal power, he closed Congress by a Presidential proclamation. When he seized Senator Carlos Arroyo del Rio, a leader of the opposition who

Wide World Photos

JOSÉ MARÍA VELASCO IBARRA

later became president, powerful army forces at Quito arrested him and forced his resignation, after calling him a dictator. He was later released to go into exile in Colombia, where he directed a boys' school.

In an unsuccessful attempt in 1938 to get back to Ecuador from exile, Velasco Ibarra was imprisoned for plotting a return to his country. In November of 1939, upon the death of President Mosquera of Ecuador, former Senator Carlos Arroyo del Rio, who had led an opposition party against Velasco Ibarra, was nominated for the Presidency by the Liberal-Radical party. Velasco Ibarra entered himself as a Presidential candidate, but the Conservative party, which had previously backed him, now refused its support. When, in January 1940, Carlos Arroyo del Rio won the election, Velasco Ibarra led his followers in a revolt which resulted in the arrest of Velasco Ibarra and his exile again to Colombia on January 15, 1940.

About two weeks later, on January 28, 1940, Velasco Ibarra asked permission to return to his native country and face charges of sedition. His petition having been refused, in September 1943 he applied to the Ecuadorian Embassy for a visa, stating that he was proposed as a candidate of the Conservative and Socialist parties for the June 1944 Presidential elections. President Carlos Arroyo del Rio refused this permit (*Time*, September 6, 1943). Acting upon the wide support he had among the lower classes and the students at the universities, Velasco Ibarra, as leader of the newly organized Alianza Democrática (Democratic Alliance), was able to carry on a furtive campaign for the Presidency from his position in exile in Pasto, Colombia. Four days before elections, the followers of Velasco Ibarra in Guayaquil, Ecuador, started a revolt in which they put the municipal authorities in jail. On May 29, 1944, this dem-

VELASCO IBARRA, JOSÉ MARÍA—
Continued

onstration was enforced in Quito by a call from workers and students for a general strike. On that day, unrest among the members of the National Committee of Ecuadorian Workers and among many private citizens having flared into further revolt, President Carlos Arroyo del Rio and his cabinet resigned under pressure.

Velasco Ibarra returned from exile to Quito on May 31, 1944, to seize control of the government. As reported by *Newsweek* (June 12, 1944), he promised that he would not be a dictator and that his government would co-operate with the United Nations. The various parties making up his victorious alliance, the Alianza Democrática, ranged from Catholic Conservatives to Communists, with Socialists between. Velasco Ibarra hoped to secure from the National Assembly, which had a leftist majority, the necessary legislation to break up the great landed estates in Ecuador. But when the leftist elements wished to go further and transform Ecuador virtually into a Socialist state, the Conservatives grew alarmed and the heads of the army and judiciary began attacking the National Assembly. Only by stepping out on the balcony of the presidential palace and persuading the mob to disperse could the President restore order. It was the kind of a demonstration that Velasco Ibarra, who referred to himself as "the President of a liberal country," had wished to avoid (*Time*, December 18, 1944).

In a February 1945 declaration Velasco Ibarra advocated nationalism in Ecuador: "Now is the time for invigoration of nationality to face the future" (*Christian Science Monitor*, February 14, 1945). He recognized the military regime in Argentina without consulting the neighboring countries and refused to recognize American "governments" established in exile. In need of money for public works (*Time*, July 23, 1945), he requested $6,500,000 from the Central Bank of Ecuador, which it was holding to back the country's currency. The bank's board of directors, who refused this request, were forced to resign. Velasco Ibarra took the money, unaware of the economic implications, and by July 15, 1946, Ecuador, as *Time* expressed it, was "broke." On August 10, 1946, a revolutionary *coup* made against the regime of Velasco Ibarra resulted in his resignation from the Presidency. The following day Ecuador elected a new Constituent Assembly (Conservative in composition since Liberals and Socialists refused to participate in the election), which renamed Velasco Ibarra constitutional President until September 1, 1948.

Basically liberal, in the opinion of some political observers, Velasco Ibarra turned to the old Conservative party in order to stay in power. As he began a virtual dictatorship in April 1946, which he stated was necessary to maintain order, the difficulties with his Liberal supporters increased, and one by one they deserted him (*Newsweek*, September 1, 1947). While economic hardships in the country turned public opinion against him, the university students and professors, who had been largely responsible for putting him in office two years

before, became his opponents. Newspaper editors and radio broadcasters were imprisoned and in February 1947 the electoral law was changed to allow the clergy, largely Conservative, to intervene in political affairs. Suggesting a sympathy for dictators, Velasco Ibarra defended the government in its refusal to intervene against Franco's regime in Spain. Early in 1947 Velasco Ibarra's Liberal Defense Minister, Colonel Carlos Mancheno, fearing the President would remove him from office and taking advantage of a rumor that Velasco Ibarra was about to resign in favor of Mariano Suárez Veintimilla, the Conservative Vice-President, went to the presidential palace with the army and police and demanded Velasco Ibarra's resignation.

With the resignation of Velasco Ibarra secure, Colonel Carlos Mancheno announced himself as the new President of Ecuador and forced his predecessor's departure into exile. Nine days after Colonel Carlos Mancheno took over the government of Ecuador, he was removed from office by an army revolt on September 2, 1947. To maintain continuity of government until Presidential elections in May of that year, former Vice-president Mariano Suárez Veintimilla led the country for three weeks. Then, by vote of a special Congress, Carlos Julio Arosemena, a banker and economist without party connections, was chosen to serve until the elections. The candidate of the Alianza Democrática, Galo Plaza Lasso, who was victor in the Presidential elections in Ecuador in 1948, gave the country a democratic rule for the next four years.

Upon the demand of his supporters, the People's Force, and the permission of President Galo Plaza Lasso (who wanted the 1952 elections to reflect the popular wishes), Velasco Ibarra returned to Ecuador from his five-year exile in Argentina in March 1952 to enter the Presidential campaign. He ran as an Independent Liberal and repudiated charges of Perónista tendencies, although the principal party supporting him, the People's Force, was said to be "Peronist-inclined" and another group backing him, Arne, was described as "Fascist in nature" (*New York Times*, June 4, 1952). On June 1, 1952, Velasco Ibarra won the Presidency by the biggest balloting in Ecuador's history, with 153,934 votes against 118,180 for his closest competitor Conservative Ruperto Alarcon Falconi. The following month, on July 18, Velasco Ibarra was formally proclaimed President-elect by the Supreme Electoral tribunal.

Immediately after his inauguration as President on September 1, 1952, Velasco Ibarra began "a big shake-up of Ecuadorean diplomats abroad" (*New York Times*, September 5, 1952). He accepted the resignations of Antonio Quevedo, Ambassador to the United Nations, of the Ambassadors to Chile, Argentina, Spain, Colombia, and France, and of Alfonso Moscoso, Ambassador to the Organization of American States. While United States newspapers reported that the newly elected president had inherited from his predecessor increased productivity and other improvements in Ecuador, Velasco Ibarra stated that he found the country "in very bad shape," and asked for special powers for his office to bring about a reform. He requested price controls, aid to agriculture, additional public works, and an overhaul of industry and trade.

Velasco Ibarra is the author of several books on statecraft and a contributor to several reviews and periodicals. Among his works are *Estudios Varios, Democracia y Constitucionalismo, Meditaciones y Luchas, Cuestionnes Americanas,* and *Conciencia o Barbarie.* He describes himself as "neo-liberal," with policies representing a "third position between capitalism and Communism" (*Time,* June 16, 1952). Velasco Ibarra is married and reportedly lives austerely, riding in outmoded automobiles and possessing little personal property. The tall, slender President is described by *Time* (June 16, 1952) as a man with a "spellbinding personal appeal."

References

N Y Herald Tribune II p3 Je 4 '44
N Y Times p1 Ag 25 '47; p11 Je 4 '52;
    IV p6 Je 8 '52
Newsweek 30:44 S 1 '47
PM p9 Ag 25 '47
Time 59:38 Je 16 '52; 60:44 S 15 '52
Washington (D.C.) Post p8 Je 9 '52
International Who's Who, 1952
Who's Who in Latin America pt 3
    (1951)

VON BRAUN, WERNHER (vŏn broun wĕrn'ĕr) Mar. 23, 1912- Engineer; rocket expert

Address: b. c/o Ordnance Guided Missile Center, Redstone Arsenal, Huntsville, Ala.; h. Route 4, Box 22-A, Huntsville, Ala.

One of the most important of the German weapons specialists during World War II, Wernher von Braun, is now technical director of the guided missile project of the United States Army Ordnance in Alabama. Von Braun, whose field is supersonic aerodynamics (rockets, guided missiles, jet propulsion), developed the V-2 flying bomb which the Nazis turned against England in 1944. Since his youth von Braun has been interested in interplanetary travel—he calls it his "scientific hobby."

Born March 23, 1912, in Wirsitz, Germany, Wernher von Braun comes from a landowning family in the former Prussian province of Silesia. His father, Baron Magnus von Braun, was an official of the pre-Hitler government and served for a time during the Weimar Republic in the Ministry of Food and Agriculture. The second of three children (all boys) born to him and Baroness Emmy (von Quistorp) von Braun, Wernher von Braun is seven years older than his brother Magnus, a chemist who works with him on the rocket project. The boys' childhood was spent in a number of German cities, wherever their father happened to be stationed.

Wernher von Braun studied engineering at the technological institutes of Berlin and of Zurich, Switzerland. In 1930 the eighteen-year-old youth's imagination was stirred by an

WERNHER VON BRAUN

article on travel to the moon. "It filled me with a romantic urge," he was to tell interviewer Daniel Lang of the *New Yorker* (April 21, 1951), "to soar through the heavens and actually explore the mysterious universe!" He chose rocketry as his lifework, von Braun said later, under the influence of the writings of Robert H. Goddard and Hermann Oberth on the potentialities of rocket propulsion for the exploration of outer space. By the summer of 1930 von Braun was assisting Professor Oberth in some of his early experiments with rockets using liquid fuel.

That fall the engineering student was one of the group of spaceship enthusiasts, the Verein für Raumschiffahrt, who established a rocket launching field in an abandoned proving ground at Ploetensee on the outskirts of Berlin, which the authorities allowed them to use for twenty-five cents a year. Unemployed mechanics traded their labor for living quarters in the warehouses and other buildings, and the needed material was usually "wangled" from diverse sources. As the rockets were improved, the society began to finance itself by charging small fees for admission to the launchings of its thirteen-pound-thrust rockets.

By the time von Braun received his B.S. degree in engineering in June 1932 he had made eighty-five tests, and his rockets had reached an altitude of a mile in free flight. That spring three visitors from the German army ordnance came to watch a launching. Everything went wrong—the rocket did not leave the ground. Nevertheless, the military men recognized the possibility of building the rocket into a weapon that was new and hence not restricted by the terms of the Versailles Treaty. "We didn't care much about that, one way or the other," von Braun is quoted by Lang as saying. "We were interested solely in exploring outer space . . . but we needed money." When the entire rocket program was transferred to the German

VON BRAUN, WERNHER—*Continued*

army ordnance in the fall of 1932, the twenty-year-old "boy wonder" was made chief of the experiment station at Kummersdorf. In 1933 (the year Hitler came to power) von Braun's organization produced a rocket stabilized by one large gyroscope in the nose, and the next year a rocket which had the gyroscope in the center made a 2,000-meter flight. In June 1934 the program chief was granted his Ph.D. degree in physics by the University of Berlin.

When Hitler became interested in rockets in 1936, twenty million marks and priorities on labor and materials were poured into construction of the vast rocket research center at Peenemünde on the Baltic Sea, where von Braun's men were expected to produce "a field weapon capable of carrying a large warhead over a range much beyond that of artillery." By 1938 von Braun had developed what may be regarded as the first successful model of the flying bomb which in six years became the V-2 (*Vergeltungswaffe Zwei* or "Revenge Weapon No. 2"). It was launched vertically, steered itself automatically by rudders or jet vanes in the gas stream, and had a range of about eleven miles.

In 1940 (the year von Braun joined the Nazi party) Hitler lost interest in guided missiles, with the result that Peenemünde priorities were lowered and von Braun lost technicians to the army. In the summer of 1942, related the *New Yorker*, he and his superior, General Dornberger, visited Hitler in East Prussia in a vain attempt to regain his support. A year later they were able to report such success that Hitler became enthusiastic again and began demanding mass production of the V-2, which was now twenty times the size of the 1938 model. In its five-minute flying time, this rocket carried nearly a ton of explosive a distance as far as 190 miles, could not be stopped or turned once it had been fired, and could be launched from any 25-foot square of hard level ground.

As a result of Hitler's personal interest in the rocket program, Gestapo chief Heinrich Himmler sought in February 1944 to take over the project himself. A few weeks after von Braun's refusal to join in this plan, he was suddenly arrested and imprisoned by the Gestapo at Stettin on charges that he planned to fly to England with secret documents. The expert's release was due to a direct order from Hitler, which General Dornberger had obtained. Another delay in production, caused by Allied bombing of Peenemünde and other installations, delayed the firing of the first V-2 against London by four months, von Braun estimates; but, he said in the *New Yorker* interview, when it was launched on September 7, 1944, "we felt a genuine regret that our missile, born of idealism . . . had joined in the business of killing. We had designed it to blaze the trail to other planets, not to destroy our own." Altogether (according to Stephen White in a New York *Herald Tribune* article, December 4, 1946), some $500,000,000 were spent in developing the V-2, and some 3600 were fired into English cities and Antwerp by batteries which

had been trained by the Peenemünde staff. Before the end of the war the Nazis were working on a weapon planned to carry some twenty tons of explosive more than 3,000 miles (to New York and other American targets).

When Russian forces came within 100 miles of Peenemünde in March 1945, Dornberger and von Braun, preferring to fall into American hands, moved to the Bavarian redoubt, where they and about 400 of their most skilled colleagues settled down in resort hotels to "hide out from the S.S." while awaiting capture. Before the end of hostilities, according to records of the United States 44th Division, von Braun sent his brother Magnus to arrange a surrender to the nearest American troops. According to the division's former public relations sergeant, Bill O'Hallaren, there was doubt that von Braun was really the inventor of the V-2— "he seemed too young, too fat, too jovial." Soon, however, he was at a special interrogation camp for German scientists at Garmisch-Partenkirchen, and in August was flown to London, where British rocket experts were eager to discuss technical problems.

A major find of the American search for former enemy technical experts (known as Operation Paperclip), von Braun signed a one-year contract (later renewed) with the United States Army, and in September 1945 was flown to America—"the next time, I wanted to be on the winning side," he has said. Von Braun's first assignment as technical director at Fort Bliss, Texas, was to help teach Army personnel to handle captured V-2s at the White Sands proving ground near El Paso. This required eight months, not only because "shooting a V-2 is a complicated and dangerous business," but also because the captured rockets were dried-out and rusty and the facilities were "disappointing." Von Braun's work in the United States, as it was in Germany, is highly secret. Since 1950 he has been stationed at Redstone Arsenal, Huntsville, Alabama, to which the Army Ordnance Guided Missile Center was moved in that year from Fort Bliss. Here as civilian director of rocket research-and-development projects, he is in charge of the work of a civilian staff, "the core of which," reported the *New Yorker*, "consists of a 117 German scientists, engineers, and technicians who worked under him in the old days."

In 1948, by crossing and recrossing the short bridge into Mexico, von Braun and other German scientists received visas and became eligible to apply for United States citizenship, as all of them did. In 1948, too, he began attending scientific conventions and preparing papers on interplanetary travel. A paper read for him at the Second International Congress of Astronautics in London in September 1951 presented a detailed description and timetable for an 869-day future expedition to Mars. A novel which he wrote about the Mars project is scheduled for publication as *Men Between the Planets*.

Permitted to return briefly to Bavaria in March 1947, von Braun there married Maria Louise von Quistorp, his eighteen-year-old second cousin; they have a daughter, Iris Careen, who was born in Texas. The scientist's par-rents, whose Silesian estate was confiscated by the Russian authorities, also live in Huntsville. Formerly a nominal Lutheran, von Braun told an interviewer, "I go to church regularly now. . . .As long as national sovereignty exists, our only hope is to raise everybody's standard of ethics." Honored by Hitler with the Knight's Cross and the title of Research Professor, von Braun was also made an honorary member of Gesellschaft für Weltraumforschung, Stuttgart, Germany, and of Norwestdeutsche Gesellschaft für Weltraumforschung, Friedrichstadt, Germany. The British Interplanetary Society made him an honorary member in August 1949; he holds memberships in the American Rocket Society and the Explorers Club, both of New York. The blond, blue-eyed scientist stands six feet one inch tall, weighs 186 pounds, and has been described as "startlingly handsome" and exuberant. In Alabama, as in Germany, his favorite hobbies are flying and sailing.

References

N Y Herald Tribune p14 D 4 '46
New Yorker 27:75 Ap 21 '51; 27:106 My 26 '51
Who Knows—And What (1949)

WADSWORTH, JAMES W(OLCOTT) Aug. 12, 1877—June 21, 1952 Former United States Congressman from New York; member of the New York State Assembly (1905-10); United States Senator from New York (1915-27); member of the House of Representatives (1933-50); opposed prohibition, woman's suffrage, and New Deal domestic legislation; advocate of military preparedness; engaged in live stock and farming business. See *Current Biography*, 1943.

Obituary

N Y Times p1+ Je 22 '52

WALD, JEROME IRVING *See* Wald, Jerry

WALD, JERRY Sept. 16, 1911- Motion picture producer

Address: b. c/o Columbia Pictures Corporation, 1438 N. Gower St., Hollywood 28, Calif.; h. 615 N. Beverly Dr., Beverly Hills, Calif.

Executive producer of Columbia Pictures and former executive producer of Wald-Krasna Productions, an independent unit at RKO-Radio Studios, Jerry Wald is ranked among the most prolific and successful makers of motion pictures in America. He began his career as a radio columnist, joined the writing staff at Warner Brothers in 1934, and during the next seven years collaborated on original stories or screen plays for thirty motion pictures. Promoted to an associate producer at Warners in 1941 and to a full producer the next year, he supervised the production of thirty-two films between 1942 and 1950, including such hits as *Destination Tokyo*, *Mildred Pierce*, *Johnny*

Belinda, The Inspector General, and *The Glass Menagerie*. In 1948 Wald received the Irving Thalberg Memorial Award, the film industry's highest honor, for distinguished achievement in motion picture production.

Born in Brooklyn, New York, on September 16, 1911, Jerome Irving Wald is the eldest son of Rudolph and Bella (Dungeo) Wald. One of his brothers, Malvin, is also a screen writer and producer. His father was a dry-goods salesman. Following his graduation from James Madison High School in Brooklyn, where he managed the soccer team and edited the school paper, young Wald entered New York University in September 1929 as a journalism major. A year later he persuaded Ted Von Ziekursch, then managing editor of the New York *Evening Graphic*, to give him a job as a radio columnist at a beginning salary of $12.50 a week. His column, first called *Not on the Air*, later was changed to *The Walds Have Ears*. After two years at New York University, Wald decided to abandon his studies, and he left the *Graphic* shortly before that tabloid was discontinued in 1932. Through his radio connections he then persuaded Warner Brothers to allow him to make *Rambling 'Round Radio Row*, a series of short subjects featuring radio stars.

During this period Wald also contributed articles to fan magazines and other periodicals. A "profile" he wrote on Russ Columbo was brought to the attention of Dick Powell, who thought this life story of the orchestra leader and singer would make a good screen musical. The idea was sold to Warner Brothers-First National, and in the fall of 1933 Wald and Paul Finder Moss went to Hollywood to assist in preparing the story as the basis for *Twenty Million Sweethearts* (1934), starring Powell, Ginger Rogers, and Pat O'Brien. To William Boehnel (New York *World-Telegram*), this satire on radio broadcasting seemed the best of the many musical films Warners had produced up to that time. Later Wald went to Universal to collaborate with Philip G. Epstein on the original story for *Gift of Gab* (1934), which also dealt with the broadcasting business.

Joining the writing staff at Warners in 1934, Wald collaborated on original stories or screen plays for thirty pictures during the next seven years. Among them were *Maybe It's Love*, *In Caliente*, and *Stars Over Broadway* (1935); *Sons o' Guns* (1936); *Ready, Willing and Able* (1937); *Gold Diggers in Paris* and *Brother Rat* (1938); *On Your Toes* and *The Roaring Twenties* (1939); *Flight Angels*, *Torrid Zone*, and *They Drive by Night* (1940); *Million Dollar Baby* and *Manpower* (1941). A number of Wald's early scripts were for musicals which one critic described as "fast and furious girlie shows with the creative element held to a minimum." According to Dwight Whitney (*Collier's*, August 27, 1949), it was not until the late 1930's and early 1940's, in pictures such as *The Roaring Twenties*, *Torrid Zone*, and *They Drive by Night*, that Wald's real talent began to assert itself. The late Mark Hellinger worked on these films as a

JERRY WALD

writer or producer, and reportedly taught Wald "the difference between being merely flashy and lending certain overtones of detachment and interpretation to his flash."

On Hellinger's recommendation, Wald was promoted to associate producer at Warners in 1941. Under Hal B. Wallis, Wald and Jack Saper worked as the associate producers on *Navy Blues* (1941), a musical which Wald also helped to write; *The Man Who Came to Dinner* (1941); *Larceny, Inc.* and *Juke Girl* (1942); then they were listed as the `coproducers of *Across the Pacific* (1942). That same year Wald was elevated to the rank of a full producer with the sole responsibility for the production of *George Washington Slept Here* and *The Hard Way*. For his accomplishment in his first years as a producer, Wald was named the "box-office" producer of the year by the *Motion Picture Herald*.

Wald's reputation as a "top" producer was established by a series of timely films depicting the activities of various branches of the armed service in World War II. Critics found these pictures notable for the blending of fiction and a factual, documentary treatment, the avoidance of "tried, true, and trite" formulas, and the absence of heroics. The first of the series, *Action in the North Atlantic* (1943), detailed life in a convoy. This was followed by *Destination Tokyo* (1943), the story of an American submarine that slipped into Tokyo harbor to get weather data. "For sheer intensity of melodrama it certainly must take its place with any film to come out of this war," was the verdict of *Variety*'s reviewer. *Objective, Burma!* (1945), which dealt with a group of American paratroopers, was found by Thomas Pryor (New York *Times*) to be "without question one of the best war films yet made in Hollywood." Next came *Pride of the Marines* (1945), which told of a blinded war hero.

Bosley Crowther (*Times*) felt the subject was treated "with uncommon compassion, understanding and dignity, as well as with absorbing human interest." The last of the group was *Task Force* (1949), a review of the development of United States naval aviation. (Although Wald did not produce *Air Force*, he conceived the idea for the 1943 film, which one critic ranked among "the greatest of all aviation epics.") In the opinion of Ezra Goodman (*Harper's,* May 1948), "Wald's films did more to celebrate the average man as the hero of World War II than those of any other single Hollywood producer."

While Wald likes to think of himself as a "front-page" producer of topical pictures, he is not averse to varying his schedule by making films based on novels and plays. He persuaded Joan Crawford to undertake her first matronly role as the heroine of James M. Cain's novel, *Mildred Pierce* (1945), in which her performance won the Academy Award. Later vehicles he produced for Miss Crawford were *Humoresque* in 1946, *Possessed* in 1947, *Flamingo Road* in 1949, and *The Damned Don't Cry* in 1950. Two other novels Wald successfully transferred to the screen were Dorothy Baker's *Young Man with a Horn* (1950); and *The Breaking Point* (1950), based on Ernest Hemingway's *To Have and Have Not*. Among the stage plays he has turned into motion pictures are Maxwell Anderson's *Key Largo* and a musical version of James Hagan's *One Sunday Afternoon* (1948); Norman Krasna's *John Loves Mary* and Gogol's *The Inspector General* (1949), starring Danny Kaye; and Tennessee Williams' *The Glass Menagerie* (1950), which marked the American screen debut of Gertrude Lawrence. Thanks to Wald's "earnest and painstaking production" and Jane Wyman's portrayal of the deaf-mute girl, *Johnny Belinda*, which had failed on the stage, was converted into "the freshest hit" of the 1948 season. It won for Miss Wyman the 1948 Academy of Motion Picture Arts and Sciences Award as the year's best actress; that same year Wald received the Irving Thalberg Memorial Award from the Academy "for the most consistent high quality of production achievement." Other pictures Wald produced at Warners were *Background to Danger* (1943); *In Our Time* and *The Very Thought of You* (1944); *The Unfaithful* and *Dark Passage* (1947); *To the Victor* and *Adventures of Don Juan* (1948); *Always Keep Them Laughing* (1949); *Perfect Strangers, Caged*, and *Storm Warning* (1950).

On June 19, 1950, it was announced that Howard Hughes, managing director of RKO-Radio Studios, had paid Warners $150,000 to release Wald from his contract. In the same month Wald joined with screen writer Norman Krasna to form an independent producing company, Wald-Krasna Productions, Inc. Following two months of negotiations with Hughes, the team reached an agreement which *Time* called "the juiciest independent producing deal in movie history." The terms provided that within the next five years the Wald-Krasna unit was to make $50 millions worth of pictures for RKO release at the rate of twelve a year, and would divide the profits from these films with RKO. Hughes retained the right to approve the basic stories and the stars to appear in them and to veto any budget in excess of $850,000; otherwise, Wald and Krasna were to have a free hand as autonomous executives at that studio. They immediately announced plans to employ stars, writers, and directors on a profit-participation basis; to set up a special staff of leading feature writers to research timely story material; and to complete a whole picture on paper before starting the camera. Wald and Krasna also committed themselves to a policy of "winning back glamour for Hollywood to recapture the 'lost' audience." As Wald commented, "We've got to return to the things that made this business great—imagination, showmanship, and excitement."

Because of various delays, the Wald-Krasna unit produced only two pictures by the end of its first year of operation: *Behave Yourself* and *The Blue Veil*. When these films were released in the fall of 1951, one comment, from Arthur Knight in the *Saturday Review* was that Wald and Krasna had followed "Hollywood's most conventional kind of film making." The production unit's contract with RKO was extended for one year on January 7, 1952. Under the terms of this continuance agreement, the team was to deliver eight pictures in 1952 (one of them was entitled *Clash by Night*). Wald took over complete production responsibility, while Krasna was designated as a writer-producer. "Norman and I didn't feel there was enough work for the two of us to be executive producers," Wald explained. On October 27, 1952, Wald who had earlier bought out Krasna's interest in Wald-Krasna Productions, disclosed that the contract between that company and RKO had been terminated. The following day it was announced that Wald had been appointed a vice-president of Columbia Pictures and the executive producer of Columbia Productions.

Many of the ideas for Wald's productions originate in his reading of newspapers and magazines, in a "tireless hunt for story material." The producer reportedly subscribes to some seventy periodicals and the leading newspapers published in this country and England; he reads perhaps a dozen selected books in a week, in addition to synopses of current novels and plays. All ideas derived from his reading are carefully indexed and filed. Once he gets enough "slants" on a subject, he writes a twenty or thirty page screen treatment. If this is approved, he works closely with the scenarist and director, "kicking things around until one day we all agree that we have a workable script." He does not, however, take writing credit on the pictures he originates. "I only block out the stories, the other fellow does the real work." Wald maintains that the writer is the most important contributor to the success or failure of a picture, and he "casts" writers as carefully as if they were actors. Second in order of importance, he says, are the performers; third, the director and, lastly, the producer, "who is the coach on the sidelines, cheering the team on and doing a general supervisory job." Actually, *Time* has said, this

"supervision" calls for a ten-hour day of "directing his writers, writing his directors, casting his actors, cutting and editing film, reviewing musical scores, sets, and costumes, compromising the clashes between the commercial mind and the artistic temperament."

Summing up Wald's accomplishment, Ezra Goodman stated: "As a middleman between business men and artists, Wald has largely managed to satisfy both factions and still keep his audiences with him. He has slightly extended the boundaries of a lethargic mass medium." Together with Richard Macauley, Wald edited *The Best Pictures of 1939-40* (1940). He is a member of the Academy of Motion Picture Arts and Sciences and has served as board chairman of the Actors Theater in La Jolla, California. His first marriage, to Eleanor Rudolph in 1935, was dissolved. On December 25, 1940, he married Constance Polan, a former model; they have two sons, Robert and Andrew. The producer stands six feet tall and weighs 205 pounds. He talks in a rapid and persuasive fashion (he is described as loquacious and good-natured), does not smoke or drink, and cares little for parties or other embellishments of Hollywood life. Although he occasionally plays tennis, he finds most of his recreation in his work. "If I were a wealthy man," he once remarked, "I would make this business my hobby."

References

Collier's 124:25+ Ag 27 '49 por
Harper 196:413-23 My '48
Life 31:115 D 10 '51
N Y Times II p5 Ja 19 '47 por
PM Mag p6 Je 22 '45 por
Time 54:72+ O 3 '49
International Motion Picture Almanac (1951-52)
Who's Who in America, 1952-53
World Biography (1948)

WALKER, PAUL A(TLEE) Jan. 11, 1881-
United States Government official
Address: b. c/o Federal Communications Commission, 12th St. & Pennsylvania Ave., N.W., Washington 25, D.C.

The appointment on February 28, 1952, of Paul A. Walker as chairman of the Federal Communications Commission brought him to the head of the Government agency with which he has served since its establishment in 1934. Before he joined the Commission, regulation of communications and utilities had been his field since 1915: he had been successively attorney, special counsel, member, and chairman of the State Corporation Commission of Oklahoma.

One of the eight children (four sons, four daughters) of Joseph Lewis and Hannah Jane (Pepper) Walker, Paul Atlee Walker was born January 11, 1881, in West Pike Run Township, Pennsylvania. At that time his family lived in a log house. On his father's side he is of Virginia Quaker stock and, more remotely, of Welsh. To prepare himself for teaching, the youth enrolled at Pennsylvania's Southwestern

Harris & Ewing

PAUL A. WALKER

State Normal School; on his graduation in 1899 he was class orator, speaking on the evils of monopoly.

Shortly after graduation from normal school Paul Walker entered the Chicago Institute, which, while he was a student, merged with the University of Chicago. With an interest in dramatic activities and speech, he was awarded a quarterly scholarship in debating and the Ferdinand Peck prize in declamation. He was also a charter member of the Illinois Theta Chapter of Sigma Alpha Epsilon. Walker, who for a time also attended John B. Stetson University in Florida, was to earn the Ph.B. degree at Chicago in 1909, about nine years after he first became a student there.

The first major interruption in his studies occurred in 1904, when he taught and was athletic coach in the high school at Charleston, Illinois. The following year he moved to Shawnee, Oklahoma—since then he has been a legal resident of that State—to become principal of its high school. During his tenure a system of student self-government was introduced.

In 1909, having left his high school position the year before, Walker entered the first class of the University of Oklahoma Law School; as the university debating coach he continued teaching during his law school days. Also the chairman of a students' committee, at one time he helped persuade the State legislature and Governor to approve an appropriation for the law school building, and at the dedication exercises—in 1914, two years after he was awarded the LL.B. degree—he spoke for the alumni. Extending his fraternal activities, Walker took part in organizing the university chapters of Delta Sigma Rho (debating and oratorical) and Phi Delta Phi (legal). After his graduation he was elected to Phi Beta Kappa.

A practicing attorney at Shawnee from 1912 to 1915, during that period Walker also held office as justice of the peace, and in 1914 was the unsuccessful Democratic candidate for judge of Pottawatomie County. In 1915 he began his long association with the State Corporation Commission of Oklahoma, which that year made him counsel, a position he held until 1919. In that post he stressed measures for conservation of oil and natural gas and helped draft legislation to further conservation. One of his duties in 1917-18 was to edit the laws governing the commission. In 1919 he was appointed referee by the Supreme Court of Oklahoma under the statute which provided an assistant to the court to enable it to dispose of cumulated undecided cases.

At the conclusion of his services with the court in 1921, he resumed his work for the State Corporation Commission, as special counsel. Among his duties was the conduct of litigation before the commission and the Interstate Commerce Commission. Walker directed the proceedings and litigation resulting in revised shipping rates applied to Oklahoma on livestock, grain, cotton, and petroleum. Later, as prosecutor of the Consolidated Southwestern cases, which were concluded before the Interstate Commerce Commission in 1927, he helped obtain other reductions in haulage charges.

A Democratic candidate for membership on the Corporation Commission of Oklahoma in 1930, Walker won the office by popular vote, and the year following was chosen chairman by the other commissioners. As chairman he conducted a general investigation into the rates charged for natural gas, electricity, telephone service, and cotton ginning in Oklahoma. During this period he participated as well in a rate investigation by the Interstate Commerce Commission, sitting as chairman of the legal committee which represented the Southwestern State Commission and Shippers' organization.

A major problem he encountered as State Commissioner was the regulation of local utility companies which were wholly owned by corporations organized in other States. The controlling corporation often refused to produce its books for inspection on the grounds that the commission's jurisdiction did not extend beyond Oklahoma. This situation convinced Walker that Federal measures were indispensable in utility regulation. As early as 1925 Walker, a member of the National Association of Railroad and Utilities Commissioners, had been chairman of its committee on cooperation with the Interstate Commerce Commission. (He remains a member of the association's committee on legislation.) Some of his experiences are reflected in his article "How Cooperation Works in Communications Regulation," which was published in *Public Utilities Fortnightly* for September 2, 1943. Walker resigned from the Oklahoma Corporation Commission and from the chairmanship within the National Association of Railroad and Utilities Commissioners in 1934, when he was called to Washington, D.C.

Before 1934, Federal regulation of interstate communications was in the hands of the

Interstate Commerce Commission and such bodies as the Federal Radio Commission. To provide a unified organization for handling the problems nation-wide in scope which arose in relation to radio, telegraph, and telephone operations, the Communications Act of 1934 was adopted; Walker was one of the witnesses who testified in its favor at the Congressional hearings. He was among the seven commissioners originally appointed to the newly formed Federal Communications Commission by President Roosevelt and was chosen chairman of the telephone division.

Early in 1935, with a special Congressional grant, Walker's division began an investigation of the American Telephone and Telegraph Company's structure and rate system. The subsequent FCC hearings on the company produced about 8,000 pages of testimony and over 2,000 exhibits. The final report, issued in 1939 and signed by Walker, recommended rate decreases in long distance telephone charges and reductions in most of the succeeding years until the end of World War II brought the basic cross-continental daylight rate down to $2.50. Among important effects of the investigation, Walker himself has listed the following: "Unity in accounting rules and requirements . . . and the basis laid for an actual, rather than a fictitious, valuation of telephone properties for rate-making and taxation purposes."

As FCC member, Walker also took part in investigations of radio, opposing contracts requiring local stations to take all their programs from one network. In 1943 the Supreme Court upheld the Commission's view that abrogation of such contracts was not deprivation of free speech. Walker several times urged that radio and television advances be made available to the people as a whole and not limited to commercial exploitation. He especially emphasized the opportunity presented by low-cost FM stations to broadcast programs of educational value or those dealing with local problems.

In April 1945 Walker was promoted to vice-chairman of the Federal Communications Commission, and at several later periods was the acting chairman. When he was elevated on February 28, 1952, to the chairmanship, he was the only one of the original seven members still in office. His new position will see him concerned to a great extent with the development of a nation-wide system of television, including the establishment of noncommercial educational stations and the advancement of color broadcasting. Walker had voted in 1950 with a majority of the commissioners in favor of the method of color telecasting sponsored by the Columbia Broadcasting System.

In Oklahoma Walker has given service in fields other than utility regulation. He was made a major in the State National Guard in 1918; with the rank of lieutenant colonel he was the organization's judge advocate general from 1919 to 1934 and edited the *Oklahoma Military Code* (1923). Maintaining his connection with the State university, in 1923 he successfully argued a case to safeguard university funds in the budget from the Governor's attempted veto. He has been president of the alumni association and of the university's alumni club in Washington. In 1937 he was its commencement speaker. Oklahoma gave Walker a place in the State Hall of Fame in 1945, and the following year he received the first plaque awarded by the Oklahoma Association for Education by Radio. For his assistance in the fifth Voice of Democracy competition, winning students gave him a plaque. Besides holding membership in scholastic fraternities, Walker belongs to a number of Masonic lodges.

Paul Walker and Myra Evelyn Williams were married in Oklahoma on June 2, 1914. Mrs. Walker is a former teacher. Their four children are Paul Atlee, Jr., Robert Williams, Myra Julia, and Virginia Jane. A Presbyterian, Walker has served the sessions of the First Presbyterian Church in Oklahoma City and of the National Presbyterian Church in Washington, D.C., and he has also taught Bible classes in these two churches. Aside from literature in his vocational field, his favorite reading is history. For his recreational interests he names horseback riding, travel, and watching football. The Oklahoman stands five feet ten inches tall, weighs 171 pounds, and has brown hair and brown eyes.

References

N Y Times p8 F 29 '52
U S News 29:34 O 27 '50
Emery, W. B., Paul A. Walker of the Federal Communications Commission (1945)
International Who's Who, 1951
Who's Who in America, 1950-51
Who's Who in Commerce and Industry (1951)
Who's Who in the South and Southwest (1950)
World Biography (1948)

WALLENSTEIN, ALFRED (FRANZ) (wäl'ĕn-stīn) Oct. 7, 1898- Orchestra conductor

Address: b. c/o Los Angeles Philharmonic Orchestra, 427 W. 5th St., Los Angeles, Calif.

NOTE: This biography supersedes the article which appeared in *Current Biography* in 1940.

As conductor and musical director of the Los Angeles Philharmonic Orchestra, Alfred Wallenstein, who assumed that post in 1943, is regarded as having restored that orchestra to the pre-eminence it formerly enjoyed. Besides extending the services of the orchestra to an ever-increasing number of adult listeners in Los Angeles and surrounding communities, the conductor has been instrumental in developing Symphonies for Youth, a project integrated into the Los Angeles public school system. At an early age "the finest of all United States cellists," according to *Time*, Wallenstein played first cello for a number of years with the Chicago Symphony Orchestra and with the New York Philharmonic Symphony. The musician was among the pioneers of classical mu-

ALFRED WALLENSTEIN

sic presentations on the radio as general music director of Station WOR of the Mutual Broadcasting System.

Born in Chicago, Illinois, on October 7, 1898, Alfred Franz Wallenstein is the son of Franz Albrecht and Anna (Klinger) von Wallenstein. On the paternal side, Wallenstein (who dropped the "von" designation of nobility to which his family is entitled) is a collateral descendant of Albrecht von Wallenstein, general in the Thirty Years' War ,who was chosen by Schiller as hero for a trilogy of plays. When his father's contractors supply house was destroyed by fire in 1905, young Wallenstein accompanied his parents to California, where he attended the public schools. Given his choice between a gift of a cello or a bicycle, at the age of eight Wallenstein chose the cello, with the result that he was sent to study music with Mme. Grofé, mother of the composer Ferde Grofé.

About a year later the boy was able to make his initial appearances in public as a cellist, reports *Who's Who in the West*, playing in his school orchestra and other local orchestral groups in Los Angeles, where the family was living, besides concertizing and performing in the orchestra at Grauman's Hollywood theater. In the course of 1913, the year after his "official" debut, Wallenstein was featured at a benefit concert sponsored by the Gamut Club of Los Angeles. Subsequently, the fifteen-year-old boy, billed as "The Wonder Boy Cellist," toured the Orpheum vaudeville circuit throughout the United States. After playing with the San Francisco Symphony Orchestra under Alfred Hertz for the winter season of 1916, Wallenstein was engaged by ballerina Anna Pavlova for a Central and South American tour which lasted for a year and a half.

Second cellist with the Los Angeles Philharmonic Orchestra for a while thereafter, Wallenstein returned briefly to the vaudeville circuit before acquiring enough money to continue his studies in Germany, under Julius Klengel. "It was in Leipzig that he became interested in surgery," wrote Stanley Walker in the *Woman's Home Companion*, "and actually studied it for a time." Upon his return to the United States in 1922, Wallenstein joined the Chicago Symphony Orchestra, directed by Frederick Stock, with which he remained until he was engaged by Arturo Toscanini in 1929 to fill the position of first cellist with the New York Philharmonic-Symphony Society. There, said *Time*, "he was made a member of the Philharmonic board of directors, received the highest salary in the orchestra." Until the year 1936, when Toscanini resigned, Wallenstein played at least one solo performance each season. During this period he also gave a "highly successful" recital in Carnegie Hall, appeared as soloist with Leopold Stokowski's Philadelphia Orchestra, and in 1932 made his first appearance as a symphony orchestra conductor at the Hollywood Bowl, conducting the concert without a score.

Wallenstein, who had given three recitals over Chicago's Station WGN in 1926, began more intensive radio work in 1931, when he was named to conduct a thirty-five-member orchestra to play the first all-classical program commercially sponsored. Four years later he took over the musical directorship of Station WOR of the Mutual Broadcasting System, which in 1933 had begun to present his *Sinfonietta*. It was in that program that he presented a Bach cantata series and Mozart's piano concertos, which met with strong public approval despite predictions that they would have no appeal to radio listeners. As the station's programs were developed by Wallenstein, the public heard rarely played concertos in the *Master Musicians* hour, compositions for the harpsichord, operettas on the *Impressions* hour, a cycle of Mozart operas, three hundred first performances of modern European and American music (including Honegger's *Harvest Suite*), and folk songs delivered by the Song Spinners, a group discovered by Wallenstein. Until he left Mutual in 1945, Wallenstein made a policy of encouraging young American musicians and composers, among the latter Morton Gould. "We have a large percentage of excellent raw talent here waiting to be utilized," he has said. "We have the orchestras, the audience, the technical equipment to ensure good performance, so my aim is to find a place for contemporary as well as classic music." Besides his radio work for Mutual, Wallenstein also conducted the *Voice of Firestone* program for the National Broadcasting Company network.

At a considerable financial loss to himself, said a publicity release, Wallenstein in 1943 accepted an offer from the Los Angeles Philharmonic Orchestra to become its conductor and musical director. When he signed the three-year contract, *Time* described his style as a conductor: "He has a passion for clarity and neatness." His association with the Los Angeles Philharmonic, said Kimmis Hendrick of the *Christian Science Monitor*, made him unique "because he was the first American-born, American-trained musician to become musical director of a major United States symphony orchestra." During his first six seasons with the Philharmonic, reports John Orlando Northcutt in a brief history of the Los Angeles Philharmonic Orchestra, Wallenstein "performed more works by Americans than had appeared on Philharmonic programs in the entire twenty-four years before his engagement," but at the same time he did not "neglect the classics which form the background of symphonic repertoire."

With the steady improvement of the orchestra under Wallenstein, it returned to the level of superiority it had previously had under such conductors as Walter Henry Rothwell, Artur Rodzinski, and Otto Klemperer, following its establishment in 1919 with funds given by copper millionaire William Andrews Clark, Jr. In 1950 Wallenstein received a new five-year contract from the Southern California Symphony Association. In one of the opening concerts of the 1950 season, his direction of Schubert's Symphony No. 4 in C Minor brought this comment from *Musical America*: "Wallenstein conducted the work with fine perception of its lyric content, and the playing, especially by the woodwinds, was notable for subtlety and finesse." At the end of that thirty-first season, C. Sharpless Hickman of the *Christian Science Monitor* said: "The season has found the orchestra technically the best it has ever been in Mr. Wallenstein's reign." Albert Goldberg of the Los Angeles *Times* found that in the playing of Mahler's Second Symphony on the last program, "the conductor demonstrated not only his mastery in controlling widespread forces but possession of the deep emotional power to plumb a huge work into meaningful form." Wallenstein's Beethoven-Wagner program which opened the thirty-second season in December 1950, said Hickman, was marked by "spirited precision"; and in the orchestral background to soloist Kirsten Flagstad, "Mr. Wallenstein showed acute understanding of the role of the orchestra in telling its own tale through the music's *leitmotivs*." Citing the "marked improvement in both playing and conducting" of subsequent programs, Hickman particularly made note of the third January 1951 concert devoted to Mozart and Strauss: "Mozart's early Quartette Concertante again underscored Mr. Wallenstein's skill in reading classical chamber orchestra works with unsentimentalized clarity." The performance in April 1952 of Beethoven's *Missa Solemnis* brought this praise from Raymond Kendall of the Los Angeles *Mirror*: "Alfred Wallenstein toiled, cajoled, demanded responsiveness from his soloists, chorus, and orchestra to produce the most exciting, full-of-contrasts reading of the Solemn Mass I can ever remember hearing."

One of Wallenstein's major achievements with the Los Angeles Philharmonic has been the development of what Kimmis Hendrick describes as "a school-integrated program said to be unique in the nation." In cooperation with William C. Hartshorn, head of the music department of the Los Angeles public school system, Wallenstein worked out the details for Symphonies for Youth, presented in the Philharmonic Auditorium to audiences of school children and also over a national radio hook-up of the Mutual Broadcasting System, as well as over stations in Hawaii and Canada. A *Collier's* article, "Symphonies for Small Fry," reported that Wallenstein's program choices concentrate "on precisely the same music offered to adult concertgoers," with each performance preceded by "an informal and lucid commentary" by the conductor. Sponsored jointly by the Southern California Symphony Association, the Los Angeles public school system and County Board of Supervisors, and the Los Angeles Junior Chamber of Commerce, Symphonies for Youth gives prizes for its intermission quiz on music which are supplied by the Junior Chamber of Commerce. Philharmonic clubs organized in the Los Angeles public schools are frequently addressed by Wallenstein, who has also initiated a special admission rate for college students to Philharmonic performances. "I like to think that the Symphonies for Youth represent an investment in the cultural future of our country," Wallenstein has said, "which will return dividends when the millions of children who listen to the concerts today become the concertgoers of tomorrow." Polls conducted by *Musical America* among seven hundred radio editors found Symphonies for Youth in second place in 1945 "for the best musical broadcasts of an educational nature," and in first place in 1946 and 1947. Similar praise has come from parent-teacher organizations in the United States.

As guest conductor, Wallenstein has appeared with the Chicago, Seattle, Cleveland, and NBC orchestras; and, for the first time as an opera director, he in 1951 conducted the orchestra of the San Francisco Opera Company in its Los Angeles appearances. As part of Utah's centennial celebration, Wallenstein in 1947 conducted the Los Angeles Philharmonic Orchestra in a series given at Brigham Young University. Besides winning the National Federation of Women's Clubs prize five times as well as the first honors award of the National Federation of Press Women, Wallenstein was third choice in the 1940 radio editors poll to determine those who had made "the most eventful musical contributions to radio," the others being Toscanini and John Barbirolli. The George Peabody Radio Award was given him in 1942 for "pioneering in a quiet way for good music and encouraging and originating various unique broadcasts." For his encouragement of American composers, Wallenstein in 1951 received the annual award of the National Music Council. From 1927 to 1929 the conductor was head of the cello department of the Chicago Musical College. He has honorary Doctor of Music degrees from the University of Wooster (1943) and from the University of Southern California (1951). His club is the Lotos in New York City.

(Continued next page)

WALLENSTEIN, ALFRED—*Continued*

At a forum held in 1950 at Columbia University, "The Composer's Place in industry and Society Today," Wallenstein suggested that, in order to augment orchestral earnings, American musicians make nonprofit records for lower fees to meet European competition, and, as compensation, receive a share of royalties on the records sold. This idea met with the opposition of the American Federation of Musicians.

Alfred Wallenstein has been described by Stanley Walker as "brown-haired, trimly built." Married on May 10, 1924, to Virginia Wilson, concert pianist, Wallenstein has been encouraged by his wife in his work to develop music appreciation among children. Photographs of their home on the West Coast in *House Beautiful* show the facilities for making and classifying music and the televison set on which the conductor can watch his favorite sport of prize fighting. For his outdoor sports Wallenstein enjoys tennis and deep-sea fishing; for indoor recreation he likes poker and billiards.

References

> Christian Sci Mon Mag p5 O 28 '50
> Time 42:40 Ag 23 '43
> Baker, T. ed. Biographical Dictionary of Music (1940)
> Ewen, D. Dictators of the Baton (1943)
> Thompson, O. International Cyclopedia of Music and Musicians (1946)
> Who's Who in America, 1950-51
> Who's Who in the West (1951)
> World Biography (1948)

WALTER, FRANCIS E(UGENE) May 26, 1894- United States Representative from Pennsylvania

Address: b. c/o House Office Bldg., Washington 25, D.C.; Drake Bldg., Easton, Pa.; h. 806 Hamilton St., Easton, Pa.

Representative Francis E. Walter of the Twentieth Pennsylvania District was elected to the Seventy-third United States Congress on March 4, 1933. As second-ranking Democrat on both the House Judiciary Committee and the House Un-American Activities Committee, Walter has given his attention to a wide range of public concerns, notable among them being the immigration of displaced persons left homeless by World War II and the presence of Communist party membership within the United States and its Territories.

Francis Eugene Walter was born in Easton, Pennsylvania, on May 26, 1894, the son of Robley D. and Susie E. Walter. His early years were spent in Easton, but in 1910 he entered the Princeton (New Jersey) Preparatory School, from which he was graduated in June of 1912. After two years of study at Lehigh University in Pennsylvania, he enrolled in George Washington University in Washington, D.C., from which he received his B.A. degree. He served for a time in the Naval Air Force during World War I. Returning to Washington for graduate study, he

attended Georgetown University and there took his LL.B. degree in 1919.

With his admission to the Pennsylvania bar in 1919, he opened his law office in Easton. In 1928 he was appointed a delegate to the Democratic National Convention held in Houston. In the same year he also became Solicitor of Northampton County, Pennsylvania, a position he held until his election to Congress five years later.

In 1933 Walter took his seat in the Seventy-third United States Congress as Representative of the Twentieth Pennsylvania District, composed of the counties of Carbon, Monroe, and Northampton. His early years in Congress were marked by an interest in the concerns of his home State. In the summer of 1935 a series of floods in eastern Pennsylvania, resulting in loss of life and property, led Walter to propose the construction of a three-million-dollar dam at Easton, the point of junction of the Lehigh and Delaware rivers. In March of the following year he introduced a bill proposing the fourfold development of the Delaware River Valley to provide for flood control, water conservation, hydroelectric power, and navigation; and on April 6, 1936, the House passed the Walter bill authorizing the Delaware River Joint Toll Bridge Commission of New Jersey and Pennsylvania to construct and operate a toll bridge across the Delaware River near Delaware Water Gap.

As a member of the House Judiciary Committee Walter became interested in the methods and procedures of courts and Government agencies in the late 1930's. This led to his co-authorship of the Logan-Walter bill providing for judicial review of regulations issued by New Deal agencies. The controversial bill, introduced into the Senate by the late Senator M. M. Logan and into the House by Representative Walter during the first session of the Seventy-sixth Congress (1939), was passed in 1940, vetoed by President Roosevelt, and passed over the veto in the House but not in the Senate. A measure with similar aims, however, was to become the Administrative Procedure Act of 1946.

With the threat of World War II involving the United States, in the course of the first session of the Seventy-seventh Congress (1941) Walter introduced into the House a measure aimed at curtailing strikes that threatened national defense. This he proposed done by conferring upon Federal courts jurisdiction over all threatened labor walkouts. The following year he was called to six months of active service in the United States Navy, but was back in Congress in July of 1942. Early in the Seventy-eighth Congress Walter supported the Hobbs antilabor racketeering bill adopted by the House on April 9, 1943. A few months later he introduced a bill (passed by the House in June of 1944) proposing that the regulation of insurance remain within the control of the several States and that the Federal antitrust laws not be applicable to that business. Another Walter bill, dealing with the settlement of claims arising from terminated war contracts, was approved on May 11, 1944, by the special House

Post-War Planning and Policy Committee, to which Walter had been appointed. As a member of this committee he also traveled to Europe in the spring of the following year to inspect war equipment and supplies.

In the Seventy-ninth Congress the Pennsylvania Democrat opposed a bill for a permanent Committee on Un-American Activities (January 1945) and supported extension of trade agreements (May 1945), appropriation of a second $1.35 billions for UNRRA (December 1945), $400 millions housing subsidies (May 1946), the President's strike control bill (May 1946), and the $3.75 billions British loan (July 1946). In the second session of the Seventy-ninth Congress in 1946 he coauthored the Mc-Carran-Walter Act requiring the publication in the Federal Register of all rules, regulations, delegations of authority, organization descriptions, and other such data. And in the summer of 1946 he began his support of the coal industry in its opposition to the use of oil pipelines for the transportation of natural gas to the East, a dispute which was carried over into the Eightieth Congress of 1947.

At the outset of the Eightieth Congress Walter was elected chairman of the newly formed group of War Veterans in Congress, which held its first organizational meeting on January 13, 1947. Later in the year he sailed for Europe as a member of the House Committee on Foreign Aid headed by Representative Christian A. Herter, a committee which recommended a $4.5 billions European Recovery Program early in 1948. Walter's area of investigation was confined to the British Isles, where he was favorably impressed by the reconstruction work Britain was doing under its Socialist Government. Towards the close of the Eightieth Congress he became interested in the revision of legislation for displaced persons. In July of 1948 he had first introduced into the House a bill doubling the number of DP's to be allowed entry into the United States in the ensuing four years. This bill was revised in December 1948 and reintroduced with variations in the Eighty-first Congress early in 1949. In the late summer of 1949 Walter made another European trip, this time as head of a delegation of the Committee on Immigration Affairs, to study problems of displaced persons. His voting record in the Eightieth Congress shows that he favored the Greek-Turkish aid bill (May 1947), the *Voice of America* bill (June 1947), the subversive activities control bill (May 1948); he voted against the extension of rent control (May 1947 and March 1948).

The year 1949 also saw the beginning of Walter's activities as second-ranking Democrat on the House Un-American Activities Committee, "a post he took reluctantly and only at the urging of other Administration Democrats" (New York *World-Telegram*). In March he introduced a bill to deprive Communist party members of United States citizenship irrespective of their place of birth. In June he was among the five out of nine members of the Un-American Activities Committee to oppose Chairman John S. Wood's action in calling for the examination of textbooks for traces of Communist teaching. During 1949 Walter also

Wide World Photos
FRANCIS E. WALTER

introduced a bill providing for a sixteen-month moratorium on antitrust actions. He voted "Yea" that year to rent control extension (March), Marshall Plan extension (April), and to the Administration's national housing bill (June); his "Nay" vote went to a proposed 50 per cent cut in European Arms aid (August).

With the opening of the second session of the Eighty-first Congress in January 1950, Walter resumed his activities as chairman of the House Judiciary subcommittee on immigration affairs by introducing a bill to amend the Nationality Act so as to enable several thousand Americans to regain the United States citizenship they had lost by voting in Italy's postwar election. This was soon followed by a bill substantially to increase the number of war refugees allowed admission to the United States. In March 1950 he introduced into the House a resolution urging President Truman to set up a new international organization to deal with the twelve million displaced persons of German ethnic origin. In August a Walter bill to remove the last racial barriers to naturalization was passed by the Senate and sent to the White House.

During 1950 Walter was also active in investigations of Communists, serving in April as chairman of the subcommittee of the House Un-American Activities Committee that held a series of hearings in Hawaii to determine the extent of the Communist problem in the islands. In August he coauthored a bill requiring the Communist party to register all of its members and report on their activities, on the premise that Communism is an international conspiracy to overthrow democracy. In December Walter presided at hearings investigating suspected Communist operations in an Ameri-

WALTER, FRANCIS E.—_Continued_

can Federation of Labor unit in the District of Columbia. On economy measures in 1950 he voted to cut Federal spending by $600 millions, but supported a bill to cancel a cut in postal services.

In the Eighty-second Congress the Pennsylvanian continued to take prominent part in probes into Communism as acting committee chairman at the extensive Hollywood hearings in the spring of 1951. His work on immigration problems was also continued, when in late November he served as a United States delegate to the twenty-six-nation conference in Brussels that designed an experimental program to resettle 115,000 people from overpopulated countries of Europe, forming itself into a group with the name Provisional Intergovernmental Committee for the Movement of Migrants from Europe. Another immigration issue with which Walter was concerned was the number of Mexicans illegally entering the United States, for the control of which an inquiry was planned to work out amendments to the immigration law that would make it a crime to harbor and employ such immigrants.

During the first session of the Eighty-second Congress Walter also took a leading part in planning an inquiry into the dealings between the Securities and Exchange Commission and the United Corporation. He introduced into the House a bill giving ownership of the oil-rich off-shore submerged lands to the coastal States up to three miles from their boundaries and to the Federal government the control of the lands from this three-mile limit out to the edge of the continental shelf. On measures of Government spending he cast a vote for a cut of $10 millions from Reclamation funds (May 1951) and against a cut of $350 millions from economic aid to Europe (August 1951).

In January of the following year Walter supported a contempt-of-Congress citation against Sidney Buchman, Hollywood writer and producer, and a Republican resolution to investigate Attorney General J. Howard McGrath. In March he sponsored a proposal to remove Newbold Morris, President Truman's special investigator into corruption in government, to put the inquiry into the hands of J. Edgar Hoover, Director of the Federal Bureau of Investigation. Walter's major action in the early days of 1952 was the introduction into the House, in January, of an extensive new immigration bill aimed at a thorough revision of American law governing admittance to the country and the granting of citizenship. The controversial bill, a companion to that introduced into the Senate by Senator Pat McCarran of Nevada, was passed by the House on April 25, 1952. In the November 1952 election Representative Walter was again returned to Congress by the voters of Pennsylvania.

Francis E. Walter has been married to May (Doyle) Walter since December 19, 1925, and is the father of two daughters, Barbara and Constance. He holds the rank of lieutenant commander in the Naval Reserve Corps. A trustee of the Easton Hospital since 1929, he also holds the positions of director of the Easton National Bank and vice-president of the Broad Street Trust Company in Philadelphia. Walter is a member of Phi Delta Theta, Phi Alpha Delta, the Elks, the Independent Order of Odd Fellows, the Junior Order of United American Mechanics, and the Eagles. His religious affiliation is Lutheran. A personal account in the _United States News_ (1947) has described him as "tall, gray, and relaxed, with an easy, slangy way of talking."

References

Biographical Directory of the American Congress, 1774-1949 (1950)
Congressional Directory (1951)
Who's Who in America, 1952-53

WALTON, ERNEST THOMAS SINTON
Oct. 6, 1903- Physicist; university professor

Address: b. c/o Trinity College, Dublin, Ireland; h. 26 St Kevin's Pk., Dartry Rd., Dublin, Ireland

"For their pioneer work on the transmutation of atomic nuclei by artificially accelerated atomic particles" in 1932, Sir John Cockcroft and Professor Ernest Thomas Sinton Walton were jointly awarded the 1951 Nobel Prize in physics some twenty years later. The importance of their 1932 experiments is threefold: they were the first to make nuclear changes by methods wholly under the control of man; they released enormous amounts of atomic energy per reaction; and they provided the first major proof that, as Einstein theorized, mass and energy are equivalent. Walton, a fellow of Trinity College, Dublin, since 1934, was in 1946 appointed Erasmus Smith's professor of natural and experimental philosophy at the Irish university.

Of Irish Protestant family, Ernest Thomas Sinton Walton was born in Dungarvan, County Waterford, on October 6, 1903. His father, the Reverend John Arthur Walton, reared in County Tipperary, was to be president of the Methodist Church in Ireland in the years 1934 and 1935. The clergyman's wife, Anna Elizabeth (Sinton) Walton, was from Ulster—her family had lived in the same house in County Armagh for at least two hundred years. With his sister and his stepbrother, Ernest Walton was reared in various places in Ireland, as their father occupied different pulpits.

For his secondary education young Walton was sent in 1915 to the Methodist College at Belfast, Northern Ireland, and after his graduation in 1922 he returned to what was then the new Irish Free State to enter Trinity College, Dublin (its full name is the College of the Holy and Undivided Trinity of Queen Elizabeth, University of Dublin). "Always interested" in physics and mathematics, Walton majored in those subjects and was an officer of the mathematical society and the experimental science association. His expenses were defrayed in large part by the college through a foundation scholarship, which included board, half the room rent, and most of the tuition fee, and which also entitled the holder, a fellow, to sit on the governing board of the institution. Among the prizes won by the science student were the Townsend, the Roberts, and the Mc-Cullagh. "For exercise," Walton says, "I did a little cross-country running and played a little tennis."

To quote the British scientific journal *Nature* (1946), Walton "made a good experimental record in classical physics at Trinity College." A FitzGerald Memorial Scholarship aided him in remaining, after he had received the B.A. degree in 1926, to earn his M.Sc. degree. The first scientific paper to bear his signature dealt with hydrodynamics: it was "Formation of Vortices Behind a Cylinder Moving Through a Liquid," which appeared in the January 1928 issue of the *Proceedings of the Royal Dublin Society*. Meanwhile, the author had gone to England, to the Cavendish Laboratory of Cambridge University, as a research student of the nuclear physics under Lord Rutherford, the 1908 Nobel Prize winner. Walton's work there was supported in 1927-30 by an 1851 Overseas Scholarship, in 1930-34 by the senior research award of the Department of Scientific and Industrial Research, and in 1932-34 also by a Clerk Maxwell scholarship. As one of Rutherford's assistants, he found himself on a team which the great scientist "drove, or rather led, to the point of exhaustion" (quoted from the *Dictionary of National Biography*).

The first task suggested to the new arrival by Rutherford was to investigate the possibility of accelerating electrons by spinning them in a circular electrical field surrounding a changing magnetic field. First Walton "investigated theoretically" the conditions necessary to keep the electrons spinning in stable orbits, and arrived at two equations which are now well known among physicists, one for flux conditions and one for radial field variation conditions. The apparatus he built was described in "Production of High Speed Electrons by Indirect Means" (*Cambridge Philosophical Society Proceedings*, October 1929), and used a heated tungsten filament in a glass vacuum tube as an electron source. The induction field was obtained by discharging a condenser into an induction coil wound around the tube. Although Walton's apparatus did not accelerate electrons enough to produce the X rays, which would have indicated success, his theory, according to *Nature*, "was a guide leading to the later success of Wideroe and Kerst" in developing the betatron. Working by himself, Walton also built an early model of the linear accelerator, later to become standard atom-smashing equipment.

Another of Rutherford's assistants, J. D. Cockcroft (later Sir John Cockcroft, head of the British Air Defense Research Establishment and Atomic Energy Establishment) was engaged in inventing an apparatus to accelerate positive ions—electrified atoms, which were far heavier "bullets" than electrons, to hurl at atomic nuclei. In response to Rutherford's call for "a million volts in a soapbox," Walton joined Cockcroft in this research, and the two worked together during the rest of the Irish physicist's stay at Cambridge. It had been

ERNEST THOMAS SINTON WALTON

thought that only particles of very high energies could be used to break up nuclei; but the new Gamow-Condon-Gurney quantum theory of radioactivity indicated that charged particles of relatively low energy could do so. Gamow, who was then (1929-30) at the Cavendish Laboratory on a Rockefeller fellowship, worked out what he called a "rather simple formula permitting [the physicists] to estimate the proportion of projectiles that would penetrate the nuclear interior, expressed in terms of the charge, mass, and energy of the projectiles used." On the basis of such calculations, Cockcroft and Walton believed that "moderate potentials, of the order of a few hundred kilovolts"—a few hundred thousand electron-volts—would suffice to disintegrate the lighter elements; and during the years 1929-32 the pair developed the voltage quadrupler steady potential generator for this use. The early model equipment with which they accelerated hydrogen ions (protons) to 280-kilovolt levels is described in their paper "Experiments With High Velocity Positive Ions," in the *Royal Society Proceedings* of November 3, 1930. Their bombardment of lithium with the 280-kilovolt protons was fruitless, however.

Continuing the experiment, the Cockcroft-Walton team redesigned their generator and proton acceleration tube, and were able to raise the particles to about 800,000 electron-volts. Before the publication of their paper describing this (June 1, 1932), the two research students had completed the work which was to win them the Nobel Prize twenty years later. On April 16, 1932, the two physicists wrote to *Nature* announcing that by using "voltages up to 400 kilovolts, with a proton current of a few microamperes" (a few millionths of an ampere), they had successfully disintegrated atoms of lithium, transmuting each lithium nucleus into two helium nuclei (alpha-particles). While each proton impact had re-

WALTON, ERNEST THOMAS SINTON
—Continued

leased about 60 per cent more atomic energy than it used up, for each such impact some ten million bombarding particles were wasted, so that there was a net loss of energy. The experiment was front-page news when Lord Rutherford announced at a Royal Society meeting that two of his laboratory workers "had successfully disintegrated the nuclei of lithium and other light elements by protons entirely artificially generated by high electric potentials" (quoted by *Manchester Guardian*, November 16, 1951). Its importance lay in the fact that for the first time matter had been transmuted by means entirely under the experimenter's control. As the Nobel laureate physicist Sir William Bragg said in 1938, "The experiments ... opened up a new line of work of outstanding interest and importance." And, as the Smyth report adds, "These experimental results prove that the equivalence of mass and energy was correctly stated by Einstein."

Further work by Cockcroft and Walton showed that, under the same conditions, about twenty-five times as many particles were obtained from boron as from lithium. Working with P. I. Dee, Walton confirmed the Oliphant-Kinsey-Rutherford theory of double-body disintegration (in "Transmutation of Lithium and Boron," published in *Royal Society Proceedings*, September 1, 1933). In "High Velocity Positive Ions, Part 3: Disintegration of Li, B, and C by Diplons" (same *Proceedings*, May 1, 1934), Cockcroft and Walton reported that the emission of a fast group of protons always appears to be connected with the change of one isotope of an element into the next heavier isotope. "Part 4: Production of Induced Radioactivity by Protons and Diplons" (*Proceedings*, January 1, 1935), by Cockcroft, C. W. Gilbert, and Walton, reported on bombardment of boron, carbon, and nitrogen targets by protons and the nuclei of the heavy hydrogen isotope, and included low-temperature experiments in the condensation of the radioactive gases formed.

In 1934 Dr. Walton returned to Dublin, where he has been a fellow of Trinity College ever since. When he was appointed Erasmus Smith's professor of natural and experimental philosophy in 1946, in succession to R. W. Ditchburn, *Nature* commented that the appointment would be "welcomed by all those who know Dr. Walton's work." In addition to his teaching duties, Professor Walton is a member of the Industrial Research Committee of Ireland's Institute for Industrial Research and Standards. The 1951 Nobel Prize award in physics, amounting to about $16,180 each for him and Cockcroft, came, Walton said, as "the greatest surprise" to him. "The atom bomb certainly could have been developed without the work we did," he commented, "but our experiments did open up a new field."

Dr. Walton has been described as "quiet, undemonstrative, little given to talk." Physically, he is a man of five feet eight inches, weighs 175 pounds, has graying brown hair, and blue eyes. In August 1934 he married Winifred Isabel Wilson, a kindergarten teach-er; their children (two sons and two daughters) are named Alan, Marian, Philip, and Jean. He is a Methodist, and has no political affiliation. Jointly with Cockcroft, Walton received the Hughes Medal of the Royal Society in November 1938. He holds membership in the Royal Irish Academy, the Royal Dublin Society, and serves on the board of governors of the Royal City of Dublin Hospital. He has, he says, little time for recreational interests.

References

Manchester Guardian p7 N 16 '51
N Y Times p20 N 16 '51
Nature 142:1045 D 10 '38; 158:476 O 5 '46
Who's Who, 1951

WAMPLER, (ELREY) CLOUD   June 7, 1895-   Business executive

Address: b. c/o Carrier Corporation, 300 S. Geddes St., Syracuse 1, N.Y.: h. 320 Sedgwick Dr., Syracuse 3, N.Y.

Cloud Wampler is president of the Carrier Corporation of Syracuse, New York, which in 1952 celebrated the fiftieth anniversary of the air conditioning industry started by its founder, Willis H. Carrier. Under Wampler's ten-year leadership Carrier Corporation, the largest industrial conditioner, "has about 15 per cent of the home market, has quadrupled its gross to $80 million, and tripled its net to $3.6 million" and expanded its operations in foreign countries (*Time* magazine). Wampler joined the company as a director in 1935, became chairman of the finance committee in 1938, was elected executive vice-president in 1941, and has been president since June 1942. Previously he had been associated with banking investment firms in Chicago.

One of the two sons of Thomas Calvin and Elizabeth (Cloud) Wampler, ElRey Cloud Wampler was born in Hallsville, Illinois, on June 7, 1895. His father, formerly superintendent of schools of Hallsville, later became a businessman. His brother, Charles E. Wampler, is now (1952) vice-president of American Telephone and Telegraph Company. Young Wampler attended public schools in central Illinois and was graduated from Clinton High School in 1912, four years later receiving his B.S. degree from Knox College in Galesburg, Illinois. He then entered the employ of the Harris Trust & Savings Bank, Chicago, where he specialized in investment banking until the outbreak of World War I in 1917. Joining the Army that year Wampler attended the first Officers Training Camp at Fort Sheridan, Illinois, where he was commissioned a first lieutenant of Infantry. The youngest general staff officer in the United States Army, he served as Assistant Chief of Staff in charge of Intelligence of the 86th and 41st Divisions, went overseas, and was honorably discharged in 1919 with the rank of captain.

On his return to civilian life, Wampler rejoined the Harris Trust & Savings Bank. Then after nine years in the private banking business in Chicago, which he entered in 1920, he became vice-president and a director of Lawrence Stern and Company, Inc., an investment house with wide real estate interests. It was in the early 1930's that Wampler first became interested in the Carrier Corporation, as Herbert Corey related in *Nation's Business:* "The Carrier Corporation had tenanted space in a Chicago building owned by Wampler's firm. In the early days of the depression the Corporation wanted to relinquish a part of this office. Times were hard and getting harder and a curtailment of expenses seemed desirable. 'Perhaps that isn't the answer,' said Wampler. 'Let's have a look.'" Wampler arranged and supervised a study of the company's finances and grew increasingly impressed with the possibilities of the air conditioning industry.

Invited to become a financial adviser to Carrier, he was soon afterward elected a director, in 1934, and shortly thereafter named a member of the executive committee. When Wampler became president in 1938 of Lawrence Stern, Inc., the company changed its name to Stern-Wampler & Company, Inc; that same year he also became chairman of Carrier's finance committee. Toward the end of 1941 he resigned from Stern-Wampler to work full-time at Carrier as executive vice-president at $25,000 a year; was chosen president ten months later in June 1942, upon the death of J. Irvine Lyle, who had been president since the Carrier Corporation was organized in 1930.

Willis Carrier had created and developed the first air conditioning system in 1902, when as an engineer employed by the Buffalo Forge Company, he designed an instrument to control humidity in the Sackett-Wilhelm lithographing plant in Brooklyn, New York. In 1915 Carrier and six of his close associates struck out on their own to form the Carrier Engineering Corporation, with an initial investment of $35,000. From 1915 to 1930, as Wampler stated in his Newcomen Address in April 1949, "the employees of Carrier Engineering Corporation increased from thirty-eight to many times that number, and its net worth from $35,000 to almost $4,000,000." The present company, Carrier Corporation, was formed in 1930 through the merger of Carrier Engineering Corporation with Brunswick-Kroeschell Company and York Heating and Ventilating Corporation.

"Under Mr. Wampler's guidance," a study of the company prepared by two investment houses stated, "there was inaugurated a long-range program calling for modern production facilities and stressing mass production, widened sales activities, better employer-employee relations and the elimination of unprofitable lines." During World War II Wampler obtained large defense contracts to air condition ships, defense plants, and government buildings, including the Pentagon, in which Carrier installed the largest air conditioning system in the world. "Once, on a hurry-up job for two synthetic rubber plants," *Time* reported, "Wampler yanked out the air conditioning system in Manhattan's swank Tiffany and Company jewelry store and shipped it to Oklahoma and Texas." In recognition of its wartime contributions Carrier received the Army-Navy "E" six times, an honor achieved

Fabian Bachrach

CLOUD WAMPLER

by only fourteen companies. At the end of the war Carrier management decided to forego immediate profits in order to implement a program of expansion, which included the purchase of a large plant from the War Assets Administration for $4 million and the enlargement of sales and distributing facilities. At the celebration of Carrier's fiftieth anniversary on February 26, 1952, Wampler announced that in 1951 consumer purchases for the first time had exceeded $1 billion. "And while it is impossible for any one to do any accurate forecasting for fifty years," he added, "I feel sure that before the next half century passes air conditioning will be a $5 billion business."

One of Wampler's most noted contributions to Carrier has been his emphasis on training not only employees for replacements of top personnel but all employees who wish to advance themselves. A major educational project is the Carrier Institute of Business, where employees are offered an intensive course in general economics, with lectures by leading educators and businessmen and discussion groups led by Carrier management personnel. During 1951 more than half of Carrier's regular employees participated in some phase of the training program. Carrier has never had a strike or work stoppage in its plants. "Management at the Syracuse plant," Corey reported in *Nation's Business,* "tries to keep on its toes and to make changes before employees ask for them. It does not always work out that way, but the average is pretty good, and Mr. Wampler himself sparks other executives into keen observance of things that are wrong and can be corrected." In 1945 Carrier adopted a policy of doing "everything possible to provide jobs for physically handicapped war veterans not formerly employed by the organization." When the company was cited in 1948 by the American Legion as the leading employer of

WAMPLER, CLOUD—*Continued*

handicapped veterans · in New York State, Wampler in accepting the citation said: "The company has adhered to the policy to the letter and the success which resulted has been gratifying in the extreme. . . . While the program has been highly successful in providing satisfactory employment for the physically handicapped, the Carrier Corporation has been the real beneficiary. These men and women make splendid employees, and our organization is better for having them a part of it." In August 1950 Wampler was one of fifteen persons named by Governor Thomas E. Dewey to the New York State Commission on the Employment of the Handicapped.

A frequent speaker before various bodies on government, industrial developments, and labor relations, Wampler addressed the Congress of American Industry in December 1948, pointing out that industrial peace and national unity require that labor and capital give each other a "square deal." In November 1949, at a meeting of the American Society of Chartered Life Underwriters in Chicago, he warned against expansion of the Federal Government and against excessive spending at home and abroad. Early in 1950 he described Carrier Corporation's good labor relations record to a group of Eastern bankers: "I believe this [record] is due chiefly to two things," he was quoted by Ralph Hendershot (New York *World-Telegram,* January 30, 1950) as stating. "First, utter frankness on the part of management. Second, a whole-hearted attempt on the part of management to educate employees, while at the same time giving employees, without limitation, opportunity to educate management." Wampler spoke in Chicago in February 1950 before the conference of the American Management Association, at which he voiced a plea "that American business establish more effective systems of two-way communication between management and employees for the sake of better intracompany relations and to combat a trend in government 'in the direction of collectivism'" (New York *Times,* February 16, 1950). On July 30, 1952, at the dedication of the world's largest private air conditioning system in the new Gateway Center in Pittsburgh's Golden Triangle business center, Wampler described air conditioning as "an economic necessity" for business and industry; while granting that prices of units are still high, he added that "the luxuries of yesterday have an uncanny ability to become the necessities of tomorrow."

Wampler has received honorary LL.D. degrees from Hobart College in 1946, from Knox College in 1946, and from Syracuse University in 1951. He has served as national vice-president and director of the National Association of Manufacturers, as president of the Manufacturers Association of Syracuse, and as governor of the Investment Bankers Association of America. He is a director of the Marine Midland Trust Company of New York, and the Syracuse Trust Company; he is also a director of Junior Achievement, Inc., a trustee of the Tax Foundation, Inc., a member of the founding group of the Citizens Foundation, and chairman of the Onondaga County Industrial Committee for United States Savings Bonds. His clubs are the Century Club and Onondaga Golf and Country Club of Syracuse, the Links Club and Cloud Club of New York City, the Chicago Club and the Attic of Chicago, and the Exmoor Country Club of Highland Park, Illinois. His fraternities are Phi Gamma Delta and Delta Sigma Rho. He is a Republican and a Presbyterian. Wampler married Eugenia Trask on June 29, 1918; they have two children, Elizabeth Jean (Mrs. William Macfarlane Jones) and Eleanor Rey. With a height of more than six feet, the executive weighs 200 pounds. Fishing and collecting etchings are his hobbies.

References

> Bsns W p 54 O 25 '47 por; p 26 Jl 23 '49 por
> Nation's Bsns 33:31 Mr '45 por
> N Y Times p 33 Je 26 '42
> Rotarian 62:33 My '43
> Time 66:80 Ag 11 '52 por
> Business Executives of America (1950)
> Who's Who in America, 1952-53
> Who's Who in Commerce and Industry (1951)
> Who's Who in New York, 1952
> Who's Who in the East (1951)
> World Biography (1948)

WARNE, WILLIAM E(LMO) (wôrn) Sept. 2, 1905- United States Government official

Address: b. c/o United States Technical Co-operation Mission, Tehran, Iran

In the post of the United States director of technical cooperation in Tehran, William E. Warne has since November 8, 1951, supervised the Point IV Program in Iran, which has as its objective the improvement of the living standards of the Iranian people. The economic specialist, who holds the personal rank of Minister, had by July 1952 set up some sixty-four projects to promote agricultural expansion, health standards, and rural education throughout the country. For sixteen years prior to his appointment as head of the $25 million aid program in Iran, Warne had been employed by the United States Department of the Interior, where as Assistant Secretary, beginning in July 1947, he was in charge of the Bureau of Reclamation, Fish and Wild Life Service, and the Alaskan division of the Office of Indian Affairs. Motivated by what he has called "a general interest in the development and prudent use of natural resources," Warne, a former newspaperman, joined the Interior Department's Bureau of Reclamation as an editorial assistant in 1935.

Descended from American pioneers who had farmed first on an early land grant in New Jersey, later in western Pennsylvania, and in Ohio, William Elmo Warne has received an extensive personal experience of many problems in the sphere of agriculture. He was born September 2, 1905, in Seafield, Indiana, one of five sons of William Rufus and Nettie Jane (Williams) Warne. In his early childhood the family moved to an irrigated farm in the Imperial Valley of California, where the five boys did their share of the farm chores during the years that they attended the local schools. In 1923 Warne graduated from the Holtville (California) Union High School and then entered the University of California in Berkeley, at which he majored in English. In extrascholastic campus activities he was a member of the Student Affairs Committee, associate editor of the *Daily Californian*, editor of the *Weekly Californian*, and assistant editor of *Blue and Gold*.

During his junior and senior years in college Warne worked as a reporter for the San Francisco *Bulletin* and the Oakland *Post-Enquirer*; on receiving his B.A. degree in 1927 he joined the staff of the Brawley (California) *News*. The next year he became editor and night manager for the Los Angeles Bureau of the Associated Press and continued in this position until 1931. Between 1931 and 1933 he was employed in San Diego as a reporter for the A.P., which in 1933 transferred him to Washington, D.C. Two years later he left the A.P. to join the United States Department of Interior as an editorial assistant in the Bureau of Reclamation, where he served from 1935 to 1942 as director of information.

The Bureau of Reclamation, established in 1902, is chiefly responsible for the construction and operation of irrigation projects in fifteen Western States and is also concerned with flood control, navigation, waterfowl and wildlife refuges, recreation, and fish propagation on each of its projects, as well as with the economic and social welfare of settlers on the irrigated lands. The year 1935, in which Warne was appointed Chief of Information, Congress authorized the Columbia Basin Reclamation Project, including the Grand Coulee Dam. While part of Warne's information activities was connected with the other dams and irrigation projects under the bureau's control, his major efforts were concentrated on planning and supervising the public relations programs for the Columbia Basin Project. The most important of these programs was the planning and publication of the reports of the Columbia Basin Joint Investigation Committee, which studied the agricultural, economic, and sociological problems arising from the development of this vast area.

Such questions as the amount of acreage necessary and desirable for each farm, the development of market facilities, the best cultivation methods and types of crops, the amount of financial assistance which should be extended settlers, the ownership of electric distribution systems were studied and the results were published by the Bureau's Information Division. Besides serving as codirector of the committee and as editor in chief of the reports, Warne acted as chief investigator of Problem No. 7, which concerned the question of the need for provisions on the area of special land units of small size for seasonal laborers and nonfarm workers desiring small plots for combined residence and subsistence farming. During this

WILLIAM E. WARNE

period he also was a member of the staff of the Third World Power Conference, an associate to the reviewing committee for the National Resources Commission on Drainage Basin Problems, and editor of the *Reclamation Era*, a monthly publication of the Department of Interior.

For a seven-month period beginning in March 1952 Warne acted as Assistant Chief of the War Production Drive Headquarters in charge of planning the promotion drives of the War Production Board. He then returned to the Department of Interior as Assistant to the Director of the Division of Power, with the responsibilities of executing plans for the utilization of the power resources of the United States and assisting in the formation of policies governing sale and utilization of power. From March 1943 to July 1943 he was Director of the Interior's Division of Information, where he co-ordinated publications, press releases, and other public relations activities of the department. As Assistant Commissioner of the Bureau of Reclamation, to which post he was appointed in July 1943, he had charge of co-ordinating the investigation programs of the Columbia Basin project as well as of the other projects. He also had supervision of the scheduling of construction projects, of the electric power development and marketing programs, and of the land classification and antispeculation programs. From 1944 to 1946 he was chairman of the President's Committee on the San Diego Water Supply.

Nominated by President Truman as Assistant Secretary of the Department of Interior, in July 1947 Warne was accepted by the Senate as the Interior official directly responsible for the Bureau of Reclamation. In this post he became a champion of the "Pick-Sloan Plan" for multiple-purpose co-ordinated development of the Missouri Basin, a plan sponsored jointly by the Bureau of Reclamation, the United States

WARNE, WILLIAM E.—*Continued*

Army Corp of Engineers, and the Soil Conservation Service and originally presented in 1944 when Warne was Assistant Commissioner of the Bureau of Reclamation. It was offered as an alternative to the much discussed plan for a Missouri Valley Authority, similar in purposes and organization to the Tennessee Valley Authority. In 1948 Warne was named chairman of the Federal Inter-Agency River Basin Committee and chairman of the Committee on Alaskan Development.

Among other concerns of the Assistant Secretary of the Interior was the welfare of the American Indian. In a session of the annual meeting of the Home Council of North America in January 1948 in Buck Hill Falls, Pennsylvania, Warne pointed out that discrimination against the Indian could be overcome "only through a reversal of public attitudes and by his gradual assimilation into the urban and industrial life of the country" (in the words of the New York *Times*, January 7, 1948). In September 1948 he spoke before the Seattle Chamber of Commerce on the subject of opportunities in Alaska for European displaced persons. In answer to questions relating to the Alaskan natives and Indians in other parts of the United States, Warne (chairman of the United States delegation) told the Second Inter-American Conference on Indian Life, held in Cuzo, Peru, in August 1949, that the way of life of these peoples must yield to the culture of the white man. Representing President Truman at the dedication of the Shasta Dam in California, the second largest in the world, in June 1950, Assistant Secretary Warne commemorated the authors of Federal reclamation laws and attacked the opponents of the dam as "selfish interests who sought to block the protection of the people against land monopoly" (New York *Herald Tribune*, June 18, 1950). He attended the Fourth World Power Conference in London, England, in 1950. In one of his last acts as an official of the Department of the Interior, Warne testified in September 1951 before the House Interior and Insular Affairs Committee in favor of a proposed $2,750,000 project, sponsored by the government, to turn wind into electricity.

Having resigned as Assistant Secretary of the Interior November 7, 1951, Warne the following day took the oath of office as director of technical cooperation for Iran, with the personal rank of Minister, to supervise the President's Point IV Program in that country. In its comment on the significance of the selection of Warne for this position, a Washington *Post* editorial (November 11, 1951) pointed out, "Warne is a public servant of great ability who has had unusual experience with water development and reclamation—the foremost needs of the Iranian economy." The aid program for Iran called for an expenditure in the first two years of some $25 million, of which $1,406,383 was allocated for 1950-51 and $23,-450,000 for 1951-52 (New York *World-Telegram and Sun*, February 16, 1952), in an effort to raise the living standards of the Iranian people and thus to stem the spread of Communism. On April 15, 1952, the United States Department of State announced that Warne and Iranian officials had signed agreements providing for three large development projects in agriculture, public health, and education. Under Warne's direction, by July 1952 some sixty-four projects, integrated by a system of regional offices, had been set up throughout the country.

In an effort to transform the Iranian farmer from a feudal tenant into an independent landholder, the United States technical aid mission in August 1952 joined in implementing a large-scale program of land reform whereby the Imperial estates would be distributed among the peasants who would pay for the land in twenty-four years at 20 per cent of its value. The Point IV Program agreed to contribute $500,000 to the bank set up by Shah Mohammed Riza Pahlevi to help the development of new rural villages; Warne said that he expected the Ford Foundation to allocate an additional $250,000 to the bank. As part of its contribution, the Point IV Program would train supervisors to aid the farmers in becoming self-sufficient landowners. Further encouragement was given to the objectives of the United States aid program when Premier Mohammed Mossadegh in mid-August announced a new tax bill affecting the wealthy landord class and the establishment of village councils which would allow the majority of the peasants to control the affairs of the community. The New York *Times* (August 17, 1952) reported that the officials of the technical aid program "were delighted." Warne, "referring only to the decree setting up the village councils and providing for cooperative village improvements, health facilities and the like from 10 per cent of the landlords' income and a 3 per cent village tax, said, 'Without this type of active participation by the Government of Iran, the Point IV Program could not have been successful.' "

While a newspaper reporter in California, Warne July 9, 1929, married Edith Margaret Peterson. Their three children are Jane Ingrid, William Robert, and Margaret Edith. The brown-haired, brown-eyed economic expert weighs 180 pounds and has a height of five feet ten and one half inches. Warne was president of the Group Health Association, Inc., from 1947 to 1952. He is a member of Sigma Delta Chi, Lambda Chi Alpha, and the National Press Club. His political party is the Democratic.

References

N Y Times p13 My 8 '47; p6 N 6 '51
American Men in Government (1949)
Who's Who in America, 1952-53
Who's Who in the South and Southwest (1952)
World Biography (1948)

WEAVER, WARREN July 17, 1894 Organization officer; mathematician

Address: b. c/o The Rockefeller Foundation, 49 W. 49th St., New York 20

Warren Weaver is the director of the division of natural sciences at the Rockefeller Foundation. A philanthropic organization, the foundation at present contributes some fifteen million dollars annually to universities, laboratories, and research institutes, and supports fellowships for postdoctoral study and research. Prior to his appointment to this post in 1932, Weaver served successively as assistant, associate, and full professor of mathematics at the University of Wisconsin for twelve years. During World War II he was chairman of the Fire Control Division (1940-42) and chief of the Applied Mathematics Panel (1943-46) of the National Defense Research Committee, the Office of Scientific Research and Development.

Born in Reedsburg, Wisconsin, on July 17, 1894, Warren Weaver is the son of Isaiah and Kittie Belle (Stupfell) Weaver. (He had an elder brother.) Isaiah Weaver was a druggist. In 1909 the family moved to Madison, where young Warren graduated from Central High School three years later. Entering the University of Wisconsin, he majored in mathematical physics, with a minor in physics. He has stated that the two chief influences on his choice of lifework were the late Dr. Charles Sumner Slichter, at that time professor of applied mathematics at Wisconsin, and Dr. Max Mason, professor of mathematical physics at the same university. Receiving his Bachelor of Science degree in 1916, Weaver was awarded a graduate scholarship and obtained his civil engineering degree at Wisconsin the following year.

Weaver began his career in the summer of 1915 as teacher in a civil engineering camp at Devils Lake, Wisconsin. He was appointed assistant professor of mathematics at Throop College, in Pasadena, California, in 1917, and remained there a year. During World War I he served as a second lieutenant in the United States Army Air Service from 1917 to 1919. Following his discharge he joined the faculty of the California Institute of Technology as an assistant professor of mathematics, and in 1920 returned to his alma mater in the same capacity. He was awarded a Ph.D. degree in mathematical physics by Wisconsin in 1921, writing his dissertation on electromagnetic theory. From associate professor in 1925, he was advanced to a full professor of mathematics and chairman of the department there three years later. His undergraduate teaching was in engineering mathematics, while his graduate teaching and research were concerned with electromagnetic theory, probability, and diffusion theory. In the summer of 1928 he lectured at the University of Chicago.

In 1932 Weaver succeeded Herman A. Spoehr as director for the natural sciences at the Rockefeller Foundation, a position he still holds. With funds provided by John D. Rockefeller, Sr., the foundation was incorporated in

Harold Haliday Costain

WARREN WEAVER

1913 "to promote the well-being of mankind throughout the world." The advance of knowledge—with research as the chief tool—and its effective application to human interests has been the definite objective and method of foundation action for several decades. The foundation selected public health and medicine as the field for its initial undertakings. Following the reorganization of 1929, the scope of its support was broadened to include public health, the medical sciences, the social sciences, the humanities, and the natural sciences. (This latter division took over that part of the program of the General Education Board, which was concerned with the promotion of scientific research in the United States, as well as the foreign program of the International Education Board.) Except for the field of public health, the foundation is for the most part a disbursing rather than an operating agency; the other four divisions conduct no researches of their own, confining their work to grants to other organizations—universities, laboratories, and research institutes—and to the support of a system of fellowships and grants in aid of special research projects. According to *Time*, the foundation had in 1952 the income from $131,480,000 to spend on its activities. During the same year that he joined the foundation's staff, Weaver also became director of the division of natural sciences of the General Education Board, which, though also founded by Rockefeller for the promotion of education in the United States, is an independent corporation, having no legal connection with the foundation. Weaver remained with the General Education Board until 1937.

During the last two decades, the Rockefeller Foundation's division of the natural sciences, under Weaver's direction, has given its major support to the different fields included in the broad area of experimental biology. Special

WEAVER, WARREN—*Continued*

emphasis has been placed on studies and investigations in endocrinology, nutrition, genetics, embryology, biology of sex and reproduction, psychobiology, general and cellular physiology, as well as on the application of the techniques of the physical and chemical sciences to the problems of living matter. As part of its interest in the relation of agricultural science to improved human nutrition, the division has, within the last decade, entered the field of agricultural research on an operating basis, assigning staff specialists to cooperate with the agricultural authorities of the Mexican Government in long-range experimental projects to improve the volume and quantity of that country's basic food crops and to develop additional trained Mexican personnel for careers in agriculture. A similar cooperative program in applied agriculture was begun in Colombia in 1950. In December 1951 the name of the division Weaver heads was changed to Natural Sciences and Agriculture, when it was decided substantially to expand the work in agriculture.

Among the many outstanding contributions of the Rockefeller Foundation in the field of the natural sciences have been funds to complete the erection of the 200-inch telescope on Mount Palomar in California; support of Sir Howard W. Florey's investigations that resulted in the development of penicillin; and aid to Niels Bohr and his associates at the Institute for Theoretical Physics at the University of Copenhagen for biological studies with radioactive atoms. Such prominent scientists as Enrico Fermi and Ernest O. Lawrence have benefited by the fellowship program, which in the field of the natural sciences, had by the end of 1951 included some 1,260 appointments. Since 1932 the foundation's appropriations for natural science projects have amounted to over $30 millions, ranging from $599,000 in 1943 to $3 millions in 1938. Funds appropriated for the natural sciences in 1951 totaled nearly $3 millions.

From 1940 to 1942 Weaver served as chairman of Section D-2 (Fire Control Division) of the National Defense Research Committee of the Office of Scientific Research and Development. This section had responsibility for developing new and improved high-speed and automatic mechanisms for aiming antiaircraft guns, as well as for developing improved computing sights for guns located in aircraft and for bombsights. He went to London during the blitz in 1941 to join an official scientific mission headed by Dr. James Bryant Conant, which was collecting information on new weapons then being developed by Britain. From 1943 to 1946 he was chief of the Applied Mathematics Panel of the National Defense Research Committee, and after the war in 1946-47 he was chairman of the Naval Research Advisory Committee and a member of the Research Advisory Panel of the War Department. When he received the Medal for Merit, the highest civilian award, in June 1948, he was described as having "revolutionized" antiaircraft fire control and having made bombers "more effective." That same

year the British Government awarded him the King's Medal for Service in the Cause of Freedom.

One of Weaver's special interests is the theory of probability, the subject of articles he has contributed to *Scientific Monthly, Scientific American,* and other periodicals. He is the coauthor of three books: *Elementary Mathematical Analysis* (1925; with Charles S. Slichter); *The Electromagnetic Field* (1929; with Max Mason); and *The Mathematical Theory of Communication* (1949; with Claude E. Shannon). As chairman of the advisory committee of the Intermission Science Series of the New York Philharmonic-Symphony Society broadcasts, he edited a volume of the Sunday afternoon talks, *The Scientists Speak* (1947), in which eighty-one American scientists presented various aspects of modern science to the layman. Reviewing this collection for the New York *Herald Tribune Weekly Book Review,* R. A. Millikan said: "It is a matter of extraordinary interest and importance to the people of the United States to have this series of broadcasts covering the whole range of sciences in printed and inexpensive form for the benefit of the whole population. In no other way can the public obtain such an extraordinarily authoritative and up-to-date picture of the present status of science in our country."

Organizations in which Weaver holds membership are the American Physical Society, American Mathematical Society, Mathematical Association of America, American Philosophy Society, American Society of Naturalists, and the American Society for Symbolic Logic. He is also a corresponding member of the Christian Michelsens Institut, in Bergen, Norway. A fellow of the American Association for the Advancement of Science since 1928, he became a member of its executive committee in 1950. That same year he was made a member of the visiting committee to the department of physics of Harvard University. From 1936 to 1939 and again from 1944 to 1947 a member of the National Research Council's Division of Physical Sciences, he was in 1951 appointed to the Council's committee on high-speed computing machines of its Division of Mathematics. In that year, too, he joined the board of scientific consultants of the Sloan-Kettering Institute for Cancer Research.

The Rockefeller Foundation officer was awarded an honorary LL. D. degree by the University of Wisconsin in 1948 and that of D.Sc. by the University of Sao Paulo, Brazil, in the following year. Along with several of his associates on the foundation's staff, he was made an officer of France's Legion of Honor in April 1951. His Greek-letter societies are Phi Kappa Sigma, Tau Beta Pi, and Sigma Xi. He belongs to the Candlewood Lake Club, in Brookfield, Connecticut; the Cosmos Club, in Washington, D.C.; the Century Club, in New York City; and the Town Club, in Scarsdale, New York, where he is active in community affairs, the topic of his speech at the New York *Herald Tribune* Forum in October 1951. On September 4, 1919, he married Mary Hemenway, who at that time was a teacher. They have two children, Warren, Jr., and Helen Hemenway. The scientist, who is five feet eight inches tall and weighs 153 pounds, has brown hair and brown eyes. He names his political party as the Republican, his church as the Congregational. Weaver's hobby is collecting the writings of Lewis Carroll, with special emphasis on the translations into foreign languages of *Alice in Wonderland*; his Carroll collection, comprising some 700 items, is presumably among the six or eight best in the world.

References

N Y Herald Tribune IX p62 O 28 '51
American Men of Science (1949)
International Who's Who (1951)
Who's Who in America, 1950-51
World Biography (1948)

WEBSTER, H(AROLD) T(UCKER) Sept. 21, 1885—Sept. 22, 1952 Cartoonist; noted for his delination of human nature; best known for his creation of Caspar Milquetoast, hero of *The Timid Soul*, and for his other daily cartoons, *The Thrill That Comes Once in a Lifetime* and *Life's Darkest Moment*; began career with Denver *Post* in 1902; first book of collected cartoons, *Our Boyhood Thrills and Other Cartoons*, published 1915; on New York *Herald Tribune* staff since 1931; in that year produced another book, *The Timid Soul*. See *Current Biography*, 1945.

Obituary

N Y Times p33 S 23 '52

WEIZMANN, CHAIM Nov. 27, 1874-Nov. 9, 1952 President of Israel; chemist; Zionist leader; left his native Russia for study in Germany (1894); lecturer in organic chemistry at University of Geneva (1901-06), then at the University of Manchester in England, where became leader of "Manchester Group" of Zionists; as head of British Admiralty Laboratories (1916-19), created synthetic acetone for British explosives; rewarded by Balfour Declaration, Britain's promise to help Jewish people establish a national home in Palestine; president of World Zionist Organization (1920-31 and 1935); headed delegation from Jewish Agency to United Nations Special Committee on Palestine (1947); first President of Israel beginning 1948. See *Current Biography*, 1948.

Obituary

N Y Times p1+ N 9 '52

WHEELWRIGHT, JERE (HUNGERFORD, JR.) (jĕr'ĕ) Sept. 8, 1905- Author

Address: b. c/o Charles Scribner's Sons, 597 5th Ave., New York 17; h. 14 Greenview Way, Upper Montclair, N.J.

Reprinted from the *Wilson Library Bulletin*, April 1952.

Readers who enjoy historical novels with authentic backgrounds and believable heroes find the books of Jere Wheelwright tailored to their tastes. Mr. Wheelwright says he tries never to put a twentieth century hero into a sixteenth century setting, nor to twist the facts into a crusade or a preachment. Although he has written his stories primarily for men, he has been gratified to find how many women enjoy them too.

Jere Hungerford Wheelwright, jr., was born September 8, 1905, in Lake, Maryland, now incorporated in the city of Baltimore. He was named for his father, an industrialist and coal operator. His mother, Eleanor Polk (Kalkman) Wheelwright, was a descendant of Von Kalkman, a Baltimore shipowner who in 1812 owned shares in Thomas Boyle's famous privateer, *Chasseur*. An ancestor on his father's side was John Wheelwright, celebrated New England pioneer minister. Both his grandfathers fought in the Confederate cavalry, and his childhood was enlivened by old soldiers' tales and refighting the battles of the Civil War. This may well have started young Jere on his lifelong interest in naval and military history.

While attending the Gilman Country School in Baltimore, he worked on the school magazine and paper, and was on the track team. Later, at Princeton, his extracurricular interests were dramatics and humorous writing. He received his B.A. degree in 1927 with honors in history.

After a year of graduate study at Harvard Law School, Wheelwright moved to New York to learn banking, starting with the Chatham-Phoenix National Bank and Trust Company, and eventually becoming assistant trust officer at the Manufacturers Trust Company. In 1934 he opened his own office as industrial consultant, where, he says, "I occupied my too-abundant leisure in writing a novel. While it was not accepted, to my surprise publishers were friendly." But as business picked up, writing was put aside for lack of time. In 1939 he married Beatrice Jacquelin Stout, and they have two children, Eleanor and Elizabeth.

Then came World War II, and he went into the Navy in 1942 as a lieutenant, serving in the Pacific until 1945. A service assignment may have influenced his future career. He prepared "Sense" pamphlets—"Dunking Sense", "Fuel Saving Sense," etc.—a series which gave technical information in a lighter vein.

Upon his discharge with the rank of lieutenant commander, he found impaired health made it impossible for him to go back into business life, so again he turned to writing. In this he was encouraged by such professionals as Robert Taylor, Hannibal Coons of *Collier's*, and the late Roark Bradford.

In 1945 Wheelwright's first book appeared—*The Strong Room*, a novel of Tudor England concerning a young aristocrat imprisoned by Henry VIII, pardoned by Queen Mary, but later condemned to death for taking part in a court intrigue. This novel was the Family Book Club selection for February 1948. Bonaventure Schwinn, in *Commonweal*, said of it: "Two features . . . rather unusual in contem-

Glidden

JERE WHEELWRIGHT

porary fiction, distinguish this novel. It has a good, although slightly melodramatic, plot cleverly woven into the historical events of the period. And it has . . . a hero with really admirable qualities, who wins the sympathy and holds the rapt interest of the reader." Virginia Kirkus gave a more qualified approval. Richard Match, in the New York *Times,* described it as "a 'swashbuckler' which just doesn't swashbuckle," but the San Francisco *Chronicle* pronounced it "exciting reading and a fairly palatable way of brushing up on one of the more confusing periods of English history."

A juvenile, *Gentlemen Hush!* was published in the fall of 1948, and was the October selection of the Junior Literary Guild. *Wolfshead* (1949) is a sequel to *The Strong Room.* It deals with the adventures of the hero, John Aumarle, as an outlaw in France and on the high seas during Mary Tudor's reign. The novel closes with the accession of Elizabeth bringing an end to Aumarle's piracy. E. B. Davis wrote in the New York *Herald Tribune Weekly Book Review,* "Wheelwright's virtue is that he can make material as casually real as the green of grass. . . . His scholarship is never pretentious nor presumptuous."

In his latest book, *Kentucky Stand* (1951), Wheelwright tells a story of the American frontier during the Revolution. "A readable, wholesome tale," Virginia Kirkus called it, and the *Library Journal* commented: "First-rate historical novel which should appeal to all teenage boys and girls." He is in 1952 busy on his fifth book, another historical novel.

Currently the author enjoys breeding horses, as he once rode a great deal; likes professional baseball; but has foresworn his love of cruising, saying he "swallowed the anchor" after the Pacific! Among authors, he favors Conan Doyle for his humor and cleanness and well-outlined characters.

Gray-eyed and brown-haired, he is five feet ten inches tall and weighs 220 pounds. He is a Republican and an Episcopalian, and belongs to the Maryland Club, in Baltimore; the Princeton Club, in New York; the Naval Historical Society; and the Authors' Guild.

WHERRY, KENNETH S(PICER) Feb. 28, 1892—Nov. 29, 1951 United States Senator from Nebraska, first elected on Republican ticket in November 1942; had previously been a lawyer, mortician, and businessman; in Congress served as minority whip (1944-46) and Republican floor leader (beginning 1949); with few exceptions, consistently opposed Democratic Administration policies in domestic and foreign affairs. See *Current Biography,* 1946.

Obituary

N Y Times p1+ N 30 '51

WHIPPLE, FRED LAWRENCE Nov. 5, 1906- Astronomer; college professor

Address: b. c/o Harvard College Observatory, 60 Garden St., Cambridge 38, Mass.; h. 12 Randolph Ave., Belmont, Mass.

The chairman of the Harvard University Department of Astronomy, Fred Lawrence Whipple, is a recognized leader in the field of meteor and comet research, an authority on meteor photography, and the independent discoverer of six comets. Advancing from his position in 1931 as staff member of Harvard College Observatory, Whipple became instructor in astronomy at Harvard University in the following year, lecturer in 1938, associate professor in 1945, and professor five years later. In World War II he was active in the Radio Research Laboratory of the Office of Scientific Research and Development and since 1946 has taken part in a project on upper-atmospheric research via meteor photography sponsored by the armed forces. He is the author of some ninety papers, published or in press, on astronomical subjects.

A native of Red Oak, Iowa, Fred Lawrence Whipple was born on November 5, 1906, to Harry Lawrence and Celestia (MacFarland) Whipple. He was reared and educated in Red Oak until 1922, when he entered the Long Beach (California) High School, from which he was graduated a year later. Following one year (1923-24) of study at Occidental College, Whipple enrolled at the University of California at Los Angeles to take his B.A. degree three years afterward, in 1927. While attending graduate school at the University of California at Berkeley from 1927 to 1931, Whipple was engaged as a teaching fellow at that institution from 1927 to 1929 and as a fellow at the Lick Observatory during the year 1930-31. In the summers of 1929 and 1931 he was, respectively, an instructor at Stanford University and at the University of California. Up to that time he had prepared a number of papers on comets in collaboration with L. Berman, E. C. Bower, and others. Among these publications were several on elements and ephemerides of a number of comets, and on observations of minor planets.

Upon receiving his Ph.D. degree from the University of California in 1931, the young astronomer became a member of the staff of the Harvard College Observatory. The next year he was promoted to a position which gave him charge of the Oak Ridge Station of Harvard College; this responsibility he discharged until 1937. Also in the year 1932 he was appointed instructor at Harvard University, afterward advancing to lecturer (1938-45), associate professor (1945-50), professor (since 1950), and chairman of the Department of Astronomy (since 1949). From 1947 to 1949 he was as well chairman of the committee on concentration in the physical sciences. Early in his career at Harvard, in 1936, Whipple succeeded in securing precise velocities and deceleration of meteors through his development of the double-station photography of meteor trails (*Nature*, November 19, 1949).

As research associate of the Radio Research Laboratory of the Office of Scientific Research and Development during World War II (1942-45), Whipple had charge of the development of confusion reflectors, or "windows," used extensively by the Air Force and Naval Air Force as a radar countermeasure. In this post he was sent on consulting missions twice to Great Britain and once to the Mediterranean theater of war. For his scientific work in the war he was awarded the Presidential Certificate of Merit. The Harvard astronomer was called upon after the war to fill a number of government positions that he still occupies in 1952: since 1946 he has been a member of the V-2 Rocket Scientific Panel and a member of the United States National Advisory Committee on Aeronautics; and since 1947 a member of the United States Research and Development Board Panel.

Simultaneously Whipple has taken part as an active leader in the project on upper-atmospheric research via meteor photography sponsored by the Bureau of Ordnance of the United States Navy from 1946 to 1951 and by the Air Research and Development Command of the Air Force and by the Office of Naval Research since 1951. In the summer of 1944, reported the New York *Herald Tribune*, Whipple and his associates at the Harvard Observatory conducted a line of research in which photographs of meteors were made simultaneously from a telescope camera at Cambridge and one at Oak Ridge Observatory, the distance of twenty-four miles between the two cameras being used as the base line to determine the heights of the meteors. In 1951, after the photographic meteor program directed by Whipple had been financed by the Navy for some years, Harvard Observatory acquired a new Super-Schmidt camera (installed near Las Cruces, New Mexico) capable of photographing forty times as many meteors as cameras previously used. Knowledge of the behavior of meteors and nature of the upper atmosphere is of interest to the armed rocket experiments, as press reports pointed out, because of the similarity in performance between meteors and military projectiles. In an

FRED LAWRENCE WHIPPLE

effort to determine the size of meteors, Whipple announced in November 1946, plans were made to project iron missiles from an Army V-2 rocket in a test conducted under the joint auspices of the Army Ordnance Department, Johns Hopkins University, California Institute of Technology, and Harvard. The flights of the missiles were to be photographed by Harvard's aerial cameras and calculations made from the photographic plates.

For his independent discovery of six new comets, Whipple was the recipient of Donohue Medals. The sixth of these comets, reported in December 1942, was described as being the brightest to appear in recent years and as having a tail 500,000 miles long. In recognition of his leadership in meteor research he was awarded the J. Lawrence Smith Medal of the National Academy of Sciences (1949). *Nature* (November 19, 1949) pointed out that Whipple was honored "especially for his derivation of the variations of air temperatures with altitude based on his studies of meteors and for his investigation of other phenomena of the upper atmosphere, the results of which correspond closely to the values obtained up to heights of 65 km. by V-2 rockets." Other achievements of Whipple mentioned by *Nature* were his research leading to the identification of the Taurid meteor stream with Encke's comet and the development of a comet model which showed the physical and genetic association of comets and meteor streams. At a meeting, in Zurich in August 1948, of the commission on meteors of the International Astronomical Union, Whipple, chairman of the commission, had stated that interpretation of meteors observed by radar was being handicapped by lack of simultaneous watching of the same meteor.

Among Whipple's published studies on meteors are "Photographic Meteor Studies II; Non-linear Trails' and "Photographic Meteor

WHIPPLE, FRED LAWRENCE—*Cont.*

Studies III; The Taurid Meteor Shower" for the *Proceedings of the American Philosophical Society* (1940), "Meteor Problems and Photographs of the Perseids" for *Sky and Telescope* (1947), "Meteors as Probes of the Upper Atmosphere" for *Compendium of Meteorology of the American Meteorological Society* (1951), and "Results of Rocket and Meteor Research" for *Bulletin of the American Meteorological Society* (in press, 1952). A member of the editorial board of *Astrophysical Journal* (1952) and author of *Earth, Moon and Planets* (1942), Whipple has also written papers on orbits of comets and asteroids; spectrophotography of apheid variable stars, novae and supernovae; colors of external galaxies, interstellar medium; planetary nebulae; earth's upper atmosphere and nature of meteors by two-camera photographic method; and stellar and solar-system evolution—which appeared in *Proceedings of the National Academy of Sciences, Harvard College Bulletin, Publications of the American Philosophical Society*, and *Bulletin of the American Meteorological Society*, among other journals. He is also the author of a number of popular articles on astronomical subjects such as "The Heavens Open" for *Collier's*, March 22, 1952.

Whipple, who was a delegate to the Inter-American Astrophysical Congress meeting in Mexico in 1942, has been since 1949 a member of the United States National Committee of the International Scientific Radio Union and is the voting representative of the United States in the International Astronomical Union in 1952. He became research associate of the Institute of Meteorites at the University of New Mexico in 1947 and in the same year was selected to deliver the Lowell lecture at Lowell Institute in Boston. Chairman of commission 22 (shooting stars) of the International Astronomical Union since 1946, Whipple is also a member of the union's commission 20 (positions and motions of asteroids) and commission 36 (spectrophotometry). Other organizations of which he is a member are the American Standards Association (committee on standardization in the field of photography), American Astronomical Society (vice-president, 1948-50), American Academy of Arts and Sciences, American Association for the Advancement of Science, American Geophysical Union, and the American Meteorological Society. At the first annual Symposium on Space Travel at the Hayden Planetarium in October 1951, Whipple advised future space travelers to equip their space ships with an outer, second "skin" to prevent meteors from damaging the ship's aluminium body.

Whipple is the recipient of an honorary M.A. degree from Harvard University, conferred in 1945. His societies are Pi Mu Epsilon, Phi Beta Kappa, and Sigma Xi. By his first marriage, to Dorothy Woods in 1928, he is the father of Earle Raymond; the marriage was terminated by divorce in 1935. In 1946 he married Babette F. Samelson, formerly a teacher at Wellesley College; their children are Dorothy Sandra and Laura. The astronomer turns to painting for recreation.

References

Nature 164:861-2 N 19 '49
American Men of Science (1949)
Who Knows—and What (1949)
Who's Who in America, 1950-51
Who's Who in the East (1951)
World Biography (1948)

WHITE, WALLACE H(UMPHREY), JR. Aug. 6, 1877—Mar. 31, 1952 Former United States Senator from Maine; lawyer; began career in 1899 as assistant clerk of the Senate Committee on Commerce; Republican member of the House of Representatives from Maine (1917-31); Senator from Maine (1931-49); majority floor leader in the Eightieth Congress; initiated legislation on shipping, merchant marine, and Federal Communications Commission. See *Current Biography*, 1948.

Obituary

N Y Times p29 Ap 1 '52

WHITMAN, WALTER G(ORDON) Nov. 30, 1895- United States Government official; chemical engineer; university professor

Address: b. c/o Research and Development Board, Department of Defense, The Pentagon, Washington 25, D.C.; c/o Massachusetts Institute of Technology, Cambridge, Mass.; h. Nashawtuc Rd., Concord, Mass.

Appointed chairman of the United States Defense Department's Research and Planning Board by President Truman on July 13, 1951, Professor Walter G. Whitman has taken a leave of absence from his position as head of the Department of Chemical Engineering at the Massachusetts Institute of Technology. In his new post he heads the government organization established to "create a complete and integrated program of research and development for military purposes" and to "advise the Joint Chiefs of Staff" on the interaction of this program and strategy. During World War II Professor Whitman was director of the Basic Chemicals Division of the War Production Board, and subsequently he headed the Atomic Energy Commission's Lexington Project for the investigation of nuclear power for aircraft.

The son of John Turner and Ida May (Alexander) Whitman, Walter Gordon Whitman was born November 30, 1895, in Winthrop, Massachusetts, and was brought up in that suburb of Boston. On graduation from the Winthrop High School in 1913 he entered the Massachusetts Institute of Technology in nearby Cambridge, majored in chemical engineering, and received his B.S. degree in 1917. Remaining to study for a master's degree, he was engaged as an assistant in chemical engineering and advanced to an instructorship in 1918. On taking his M.Sc. degree two years later he was promoted to assistant professor and placed in charge of the newly established station of

M.I.T.'s School of Chemical Engineering Practice at Bangor, Maine. In the following year he became the director of the Boston station, and in 1923 was appointed assistant director of M.I.T.'s Research Laboratory for Applied Chemistry. In that administrative post, either alone or in cooperation with his colleagues, he conducted research work in the fields of gas absorption, corrosion of iron and steel, flow of heat, hydration of lime and elimination of salt from salt water ice. Reports on these researches appeared in such publications as *Industrial and Engineering Chemistry*, *Journal of the American Chemical Society*, and the *American Journal of Science* at various intervals between 1923 and 1926.

Whitman left the Massachusetts Institute of Technology in 1926 to join the Standard Oil Company of Indiana as assistant director of research, and three years later was made associate director of research in charge of development work. In June 1934 Whitman added academic duties to his administrative functions when he was appointed head of the Department of Chemical Engineering at M.I.T. in succession to the late Professor William P. Ryan. In the course of the ensuing seven years he conducted courses and continued the study of petroleum and other fuels which had occupied him in Indiana. (He addressed the American Chemical Society on synthetic additions to petroleum products in December 1940, and in the following July published, in *Industrial and Engineering Chemistry*, a paper entitled "Synthetic Chemicals in Fuels and Lubricants.")

Obtaining leave of absence from M.I.T. for World War II service, he joined the War Production Board, first as assistant director and later as director, of its Basic Chemicals Division, and concurrently was chairman of the Subcommittee on Aircraft Fuels and Lubricants of the National Advisory Committee for Aeronautics. As early as November 1942 he opposed, in his official capacity, the granting to the liquor industry of a suggested "vacation" from wartime regulations banning the use of alcohol for distilling purposes; and again in May 1944 he was "understood" to be the "lone dissident among Federal officials to a plan suggested by the liquor industry as a means of replenishing stocks, whereby the Petroleum Administration . . . would allot 25,000,000 gallons of gasoline in exchange for Cuban industrial alcohol" (New York *Times*). Whitman told a special Senate committee investigating the industry that developments during the coming months might double the country's estimated requirements of industrial alcohol for military and lend-lease purposes, and added that "we are not going to be caught with 'too little, too late.'"

After the war Whitman returned to his teaching and administrative duties at the Massachusetts Institute of Technology, where in 1948 he was put in charge of the Atomic Energy Commission's Lexington Project for the investigation of nuclear power for aircraft. In September 1949 he became a member of the Research and Development Board's Committee on Fuels and Lubricants, and a further out-

WALTER G. WHITMAN

come of his work in this field was the publication, in the American Petroleum Institute's *Proceedings* for November 7-10 of that year, of the paper of which he is said to be especially proud—"Liquid Fuel Supply and National Resources." It estimated "the probable requirements for liquid fuels in another war" and "possible techniques" for supplying them; and already (according to an article in the *Chemical and Engineering News*) has proven in some respects prophetically accurate. On August 11, 1950, Whitman was appointed to the General Advisory Committee of the Atomic Energy Commission. At M.I.T. in the meantime he became the first chairman of the institute's committee on undergraduate policy, the mission of which he has defined as "to improve the scope and depth of general education for undergraduates."

The Research and Development Board of the Department of Defense, to the chairmanship of which the chemical engineer was named by President Truman on July 13, 1951, was created by the National Security Act of 1947 as a part of the National Military Establishment; it took over the personnel and records of the Joint Army and Navy Research and Development Board instituted in the previous year. The National Military Establishment became the Department of Defense on August 10, 1949, and the Board's functions are now defined (in part) by the *United States Government Organization Manual* as to "prepare a complete and integrated program of research and development for military purposes," to "recommend measures of coordination . . . among the military departments," to "consider the interaction of research and development and strategy, and to advise the Joint Chiefs of Staff in connection therewith." The Board is responsible to the Secretary of Defense, and consists of the chairman, two representatives each of the Army, Navy, and Air Force, an executive sec-

WHITMAN, WALTER G.—*Continued*

retary and his deputy, and the directors of the Board's planning and programs divisions. Whitman's appointment as chairman, which was confirmed by the Senate on July 27, followed the resignation of William Webster, vice-president of the New England Electrical System, whose tenure of the post dated from March 1950. (Earlier chairmen were Professors Vannevar Bush and Karl Compton.)

Commenting editorially on the appointment of the M.I.T. professor, the Washington *Post* pointed out that "RDB is potentially one of the most important agencies in the defense setup, albeit at the policy rather than the operating levels," but that recently it had "been next to impossible to get decisions" out of the Board, which had already lost the services of an able executive secretary, Dr. E. A. Walker, as the result of friction. "It is time this costly hiatus was ended," this editorial continued. "The new chairman . . . will have a big job in knitting the pieces back again—but it is a task which, in view of the enormous defense expenditures, is increasingly vital." Whitman was sworn in on August 1, 1951.

As chairman of the Research and Development Board, Whitman is *ex officio* a member of the National Advisory Committee for Aeronautics. Nongovernment organizations to which he belongs include the American Chemical Society (the industrial engineering division of which he is a past chairman), the American Academy of Arts and Sciences, and the American Institute of Chemical Engineers (council member). His fraternities are the Tau Beta Pi, Alpha Chi Sigma, and Sigma Xi; his clubs are the Chemists in New York and the Social Circle of Concord, Massachusetts, where the Whitmans live; his church is the Unitarian. Mrs. Whitman was Martha Thurmond Key; married in 1921, they have one daughter, Elizabeth Ann (Mrs. Sam Hosmer), and two sons, John Turner 2d and William Key. The scientist finds diversion in playing his guitar, and he names as his hobby the collecting of phonograph records of all kinds.

References

Chem & Eng N 29:3084 Jl 30 '51 por
American Men of Science (1949)
America's Young Men, 1936-37
Chemical Who's Who, 1951
International World Who's Who (1949)
Who Knows—and What (1949)
Who's Who in America, 1950-51
Who's Who in Engineering, 1948
Who's Who in New England (1949)
Who's Who in the East (1951)
World Biography (1948)

WILLIAMS, CAMILLA Singer

Address: b. c/o Columbia Concerts, Inc., 113 W. 57th St., New York 19; h. 4826 Aspen St., Philadelphia 39, Pa.

Acclaimed as one of the finest Cio-Cio-Sans in recent years, Camilla Williams created a sensation at her debut with the New York City Center Opera Company on May 15, 1946, as the first Negro soprano to sing with a major opera company in the United States. Besides the *Madama Butterfly* role, she has appeared in *La Boheme, I Pagliacci*, and *Aida*, and concert tours have taken her to cities in the United States and other countries of the Western Hemisphere.

Camilla Ella Williams was born about thirty years ago in Danvill, Virginia, the youngest of the four children of Cornelius Booker Williams, a chauffeur, and Fannie (Carey) Williams. Her grandfather, Alexander Carey, was a singer and a choir leader. She herself was singing in the Danville Calvary Baptist Church at the age of eight. "All my people sing," Miss Williams has said. "We were poor, but God blessed us with music." She also describes Danville as a "singing, musical town."

Upon her graduation in 1937 as class valedictorian from the John M. Langston High School in Danville, Miss Williams received an Alpha Kappa Alpha scholarship and went on to Virginia State College. There her major was public school music. She was named the outstanding graduate of her class when she received her bachelor of science degree in 1941. During the four years at Virginia State she served as president of the women's senate and as secretary, in her junior year, and president, in her senior year, of the college choir. She was a member of the Lindsay Treble Clef Club and Alpha Kappa Alpha Sorority. In 1942 she took a postgraduate course in Italian at the University of Pennsylvania.

Miss Williams, whose initial goal was teaching, was appointed a third-grade teacher and an instructor in music in the Danville elementary school system. In 1942, after her one year of teaching, the Virginia State College *a capella* choir invited her to be the guest soloist in a concert in Philadelphia. This was followed by an offer, from the Philadelphia Alumni Association of the college, of a scholarship if she chose to come to Philadelphia for voice training. Accepting the opportunity, the young soprano began her studies under Madame Marian Szekeley-Freschl in 1943. During 1945 and 1946 she took further training, in New York under Cesare Sodero; and she has continued to coach or study with Ralph Berkowitz of Philadelphia, Rose Dirman of New York City, and Borislava Bazala of East Orange, New Jersey.

While she was preparing herself for the concert stage Miss Williams supported herself by working in the evenings as an usherette in a Philadelphia theater. She also received assistance from Dr. W. R. Laird, a former employer of her mother, and from Virginia State College, which established the Camilla Williams Fund at the suggestion of Miss T. P. Whiting, the dean of women. In 1943, shortly after she began her studies, and again in 1944, Miss Williams won the Marian Anderson Award (of $750), given to outstanding young musicians. Also, in 1944, she signed a contract to record exclusively for RCA-Victor, and she made her radio debut in July of that year as a guest artist on Victor's *The Music*

America Loves Best. Emerging as winner from the Philadelphia Orchestra Youth Concert auditions, she was engaged as soloist for a concert with the Philadelphia Symphony Orchestra on November 14, 1944, in which she sang three arias, the "Alleluja" from the Mozart motet *Exultate, Jubilate,* "Dove Sono" from Mozart's *Marriage of Figaro,* and "Casta Diva" from Bellini's *Norma.*

After one of the young singer's early concert appearances in Stamford, Connecticut, on December 16, 1945, the former Metropolitan Opera soprano, Geraldine Farrar, wrote to Miss Williams' concert manager, Arthur Judson: "I was quite unprepared for this young woman's obvious high gifts. . . .I should like to voice my unsolicited appreciation, and the hope that under careful management and encouragement, the rich promise she shows will mature to even higher artistic endeavors." An audition in January 1946 with Laszlo Halasz, director of the City Center Opera Company, led to a contract with the company. Miss Williams learned the role of Cio-Cio-San in *Madama Butterfly* in two months and made her debut on May 15, the first Negro soprano to appear with an important opera company in the United States. (She was the second Negro singer, Todd Duncan having appeared at the City Center in *I Pagliacci* and *Carmen* the year before.) Miss Farrar, who had created the role of Cio-Cio-San on the Metropolitan Opera stage, was present at the debut, and, when asked by a *Newsweek* reporter about Miss Williams' talents, replied, "I would say that already she is one of the great Butterflys of our day." In the New York *Times* Noel Straus pronounced her "an instant . . . success in the title role," and found in her performance "a vividness and subtlety unmatched by any other artist who has essayed the part here in recent years." *PM's* critic, Robert A. Hague, called her voice one of "great natural beauty which she uses with considerable expressiveness and dramatic effect."

In the fall season of 1946 Miss Williams appeared in her second role, Nedda in *I Pagliacci,* of which the New York *Times* critic said that she "sang her new role with freshness of voice, charm, and personal sincerity." The New York critics, however, found her debut recital in Town Hall on January 12, 1947, less satisfactory than her operatic performances. Francis D. Perkins reported in the New York *Herald Tribune* that she "displayed a noteworthy voice, in volume and quality . . . but the recital as a whole did not repeat the impression made by her notable impersonation of Cio-Cio-San. . . .She was most persuasive in songs of a buoyant and outspoken character." Her program included the two Mozart arias she had sung with the Philadelphia Orchestra, songs by Schubert, Brahms, Strauss, Fauré, and Bizet, and a group of Negro spirituals.

With her first appearance as Mimi in *La Boheme* on October 26, 1947, the singer received her greatest critical acclaim since her debut. "Miss Williams was the heroine of the evening," said the New York *Times* critic. The critic of *PM* wrote, "Her Mimi is one of the most truly touching and believable embodi-

J. Abresch

CAMILLA WILLIAMS

ments of the role I've yet seen and heard. The lovely quality of her voice, the purity and radiance of her high notes, the sensitivity and deep emotional sincerity of her acting . . . all contribute to the fidelity and beauty of her portrayal." The following year, on October 28, 1948, a new production of *Aïda* at the City Center brought the young singer forward in another title role. The consensus of some of the New York critics was that Miss Williams' voice was too light in texture for the music; John Briggs reported in the New York *News* that she "brought down the house with a performance of 'O Patria Mia' that would have done credit to anyone now before the public," and Olin Downes found her "the most moving singer on the stage. . . .The voice is now somewhat small for the part . . . if [it grows] there will be a great *Aïda.* If not, Miss Williams has a high artistic accomplishment to her credit, and other roles for her greatest successes. Always she sang as a musician and an artist."

In 1950 Miss Williams went on a three-week concert tour of Panama, the Dominican Republic, and Venezuela, and the following year she traveled again to Venezuela for her first South American appearances in opera. In 1951, too, she appeared with the Little Orchestra Society on April 24 in Town Hall, singing the role of the Princess Ilia in a concert version of Mozart's seldom-heard opera *Idomeneo,* the first complete performance of the work in New York City. Olin Downes of the New York *Times* found her singing "of high excellence. Camilla Williams . . . has a lovely quality and *bel canto,* admirable taste, affecting sentiment."

The soprano's second Town Hall recital, on January 8, 1952, found critics still divided on her capabilities as a concert singer. Robert Bagar wrote in the New York *World-Telegram:* "After hearing her in opera and in re-

WILLIAMS, CAMILLA—*Continued*

cital I come to the conclusion that she is much better suited to the former." Irving Kolodin (of the *Saturday Review*) found in her singing "much musicality and obvious aptitude for this difficult genre of performance." The New York *Times* critic, Howard Taubman, felt that in striving for variety Miss Williams included in her program music not suited to her voice; her lieder singing, however, was "worthy to be compared with that of the most sensitive interpreters." She has also appeared in concert in Canada, Alaska, and the Dutch West Indies, in opera with the New York City Center Company in Chicago, Atlantic City, and Montreal, and has sung with the New York Philharmonic and the Chicago Symphony Orchestras.

For RCA-Victor Miss Williams has recorded the Negro spirituals "O What a Beautiful City" and "City Called Heaven," and she sings the role of Bess in the complete Columbia recording of Gershwin's folk-opera *Porgy and Bess*. Other recognition of Miss Williams' artistry has been the New York Newspaper Guild "Page One" Award as "First Lady of American Opera for 1946" and the 1950 Chicago Defenders' Trophy for contributions to music and opera. She is a member of the American Federation of Radio Artists, the American Guild of Musical Artists, Alpha Kappa Alpha Sorority, the National Association for the Advancement of Colored People, and the Virginia State College Alumni Association. She is a Baptist.

On August 28, 1950, Miss Williams was married to Charles Beavers, an attorney. The five-foot two-inch singer weighs 120 pounds. Her favorite hobby is collecting old folk songs, and she also finds enjoyment in reading, the theater, handicrafts, sports, and cookery.

References

> N Y Herald Tribune p19 My 15 '46 por
> N Y Post Mag p37 O 3 '46 por
> Opportunity 25:42 Ja '47 por
> Time 48:68 S 30 '46
>
> Who is Who in Music, 1951
> Who's Who in Colored America, 1950
> Who's Who in the East (1951)

WILLIAMS, EMLYN (ĕm'lĭn) Nov. 26, 1905- Actor; playwright; producer

Address: h. 15 Pelham Crescent, London, S.W. 7, England; Park End, North Moreton, Didcot, Berks, England

> NOTE: This biography supersedes the article which appeared in *Current Biography* in 1941.

For more than twenty years British and American theater and motion picture audiences have seen Emlyn Williams, the Welsh actor, who is also a playwright and a director. Beginning as an actor in a small part in a London stage production in 1927, Williams the next year had his first play produced, and five years later made his first screen appearance. By 1935 he was acting in and directing his own

plays and since then has often functioned simultaneously in these three capacities, both on the stage and on the screen. Of his twenty-odd plays, *Night Must Fall* and *The Corn is Green*, the latter an autobiographical account of the author's early years in a Welsh mining community, are the best known to American audiences. His performances in *Jamaica Inn*, *Major Barbara*, *Hatter's Castle*, and *Dolwyn*, particularly, have made him a familiar figure on the screen.

Born November 26, 1905, in Mostyn, a small mining village in Flintshire, North Wales, Emlyn Williams is the son of Richard and Mary (Williams) Williams. Like other boys of his village he spoke his native Welsh language, using no English until he was eight years old. His origin was a humble one: his father was successively a stoker, greengrocer, innkeeper, iron worker, and coal miner; thus the boy could anticipate a future similar to his father's life. In that time and in that part of Wales it was common for children to begin working in the mines when they were twelve. However, when Williams was ten years old he entered the local Holywell County School and here came under the influence of Miss S. G. Cook, a London social worker who in 1915 established the school for the miners and their children. Miss Cook recognized the talents of the Welsh boy, undertook to make him fluent in English, and for the next seven years guided him in his studies and stimulated his ambitions to be a schoolmaster. On a scholarship he studied at St. Julien's, in Switzerland, and in 1922 the seventeen-year-old youth won a scholarship (in French) to Christ Church College, Oxford. There he saw his first play, Somerset Maugham's *The Camel's Back*, and determined to make the stage his lifework. The choice was not surprising: Williams recalls that as a boy he would dramatize Bible stories and bits from *Pilgrim's Progress*. Further, he says, "I'm Welsh, and the theater is one of the fundamental instincts of my people."

While Williams was still an undergraduate, his first play, *Full Moon*, was produced by the Oxford University Dramatic Society (of which he was an active member) under the direction of J. B. Fagan. It was Fagan who in 1927, after Williams had received his M.A. degree, gave the young stage enthusiast his first chance to earn his living in the theater by assigning him a role in the London production of *And So to Bed*, which opened on April 4, 1927. Later that year he made his first trip to the United States to create the same role in the New York production. He returned to London, acted in the short-lived *The Pocket-Money Husband*, and in December 1928 appeared in a short run of his own play, *Glamour*. The next two years were difficult for Williams. He was working on his own dramatic creations and playing in a series of unsuccessful stage presentations, from 1929 to 1931 appearing in eleven productions. In 1929 *Full Moon* was produced in the commercial theater, where it was un-

successful, but in 1930 he had his first recognition as a playwright and director when
A Murder Has Been Arranged was presented at a special Sunday night showing.
It so impressed theater managers that he
received for it an advance of a thousand
pounds.

Williams' first success as an actor came
in August 1931 when he created the role of
Lord Lebanon in the Edgar Wallace mystery, *The Case of the Frightened Lady*. In
1932 the drama had a successful run in New
York, with Williams in the leading role; that
year he again created the part (his favorite,
according to *Who's Who in the Theatre*)
for the motion picture version. During this
period Williams also acted in the presentation of his fifth drama, *Port Said*. The London critic for the New York *Times* wrote
that in the play Williams showed himself to
be "among the most interesting and original
of our younger actors" and as a playwright,
"an imaginative writer." In May 1935, with
the warm reception given to his play *Night
Must Fall* and his performance in it, Williams' reputation as both actor and playwright was firmly established. The creation
of Danny, the psychopathic bellhop, had its
origin in a chance attendance by Williams at
the appeal trial of a murderer whose non-
chalance was notorious. The play ran for
a year in London and then went to New
York in September 1936, where, however,
it did not have a long run although critics
acclaimed the play and the actor. (Later a
screen version was made, with Robert Montgomery in the stellar role.)

On his return to England, Williams costarred
with John Gielgud in a brief production of his
He Was Born Gay, and then joined the Old
Vic Repertory Theatre, appearing in Shakespeare's *Richard III* and *Measure for Measure*
and in Ibsen's *Ghosts*. In September 1938 his
second notable play, *The Corn is Green*, opened
in London. Before producing this autobiographical drama, Williams submitted the manuscript
to Miss Cook for any deletions she might wish.
She found it a fine piece of work, but could
not see how anyone would be interested in the
life of a schoolteacher. The story of Morgan
Evans, the young Welshman rescued from the
mines and a life of ignorance by a crusading
woman who sought to bring education and en-
lightenment to a remote Welsh countryside, was
applauded by critics and public alike. It ran
for two years, closing only because of the 1940
London blitz of World War II. In this, as in
all his subsequent creations, Williams played
the principal part. The play moved to New
York in November 1940, where, although Williams was prevented by the circumstances of
World War II from appearing, it was acclaimed. Ethel Barrymore's creation of the
role of Miss Moffat, the schoolteacher, is considered her most successful. In New York the
production had 470 performances, on a subsequent road tour, 383. In 1943 it was revived
for seven weeks, with Miss Barrymore again
in the female lead; and in January 1950 Eva
LeGallienne played in a revival by the New

EMLYN WILLIAMS

York City Theatre. Brooks Atkinson, writing
in the New York *Times*, described the play
as a "stirring, high-minded drama that won the
hearts of the audience and illuminated something precious in the long story of man's 'blind
struggle in the network of the star.'" The play
won the New York Drama Critics' Circle
Award for the best foreign play for 1941.

With the reopening of the London theaters
in May 1940, Williams had two plays on the
stage—*The Corn is Green* and a new production, *The Light of Heart*, the story of a
"drunken, down-at-the-heels actor who gets his
last chance to stage a comeback in a mythical
production of *King Lear*." *Time* referred to
the author as the "reigning London playwright."
The next year he wrote, produced, and appeared in *The Morning Star*, a drama of wartime England. Two years later came *A Month
in the Country* and then *The Druid's Rest*, the
latter called by the *Theatre Arts* critic "a lively
dramatic idea, which perhaps could only be
worked out in a Celtic setting and realized by
a Welsh cast." The following year Williams
was again author, actor, and producer of *The
Wind of Heaven*, considered one of his best
productions by his English admirers. Philip
Hope-Wallace, in a detailed analysis of the
playwright in *Theatre Arts* (January 1948),
judged Williams' portrayal of "a vulgarian
who sees strange wonders in a Welsh village,"
his "best and most ambitious presentation of
a character." During these war years Williams
also went on extended tours to the posts of
the Allied Overseas Forces. In 1946 he made
one of his rare appearances in a play not his
own when he created the part of Sir Robert
Morton in Terence Rattigan's *The Winslow
Boy*. This was followed by a performance in
his own *Trespass*, a melodrama of "fright and
terror . . . edged with a laugh."

On October 31, 1949, Williams returned to
New York to take the leading part in Lillian

WILLIAMS, EMLYN—*Continued*

Hellman's *Montserrat*. Though the New York *Sun* critic found the drama lacking in "sustained impact," he felt that Williams' role was "fascinatingly played." The New York *Herald Tribune* reviewer wrote that Williams played "in a bravura style, keeping the action taut when it [threatened] to scatter all over the stage." Returning to London, Williams began to develop into a theatrical presentation an enthusiasm for the works of Charles Dickens which he had had since childhood. Stimulated by the warm reception his children gave to his nightly readings of Dickens' *Bleak House,* he mastered sections of that novel, borrowed Dickens' own desk from a museum, and at a benefit show in London gave a ten-minute performance of Dickens reading his own work. Then followed two years of preparation and testing, with a few performances before small groups, including dinner guests. By the end of 1951 Williams was ready for a public reading in London, which was so successful that he was called upon to give a hundred performances. On February 4, 1952, almost a century after Charles Dickens had given readings from his novels before American audiences, Williams began a six-week engagement in New York. In the guise of the nineteenth century author he read from *Our Mutual Friend, Dombey and Son, Pickwick Papers, A Tale of Two Cities,* and *Christmas Stories.*

Dressed in formal Victorian attire, wearing a beard cut in the Dickens' manner, and using a duplicate of the lectern designed by Dickens, Williams creates the illusion of the novelist reading to his audiences. Williams has summarized his own performance: "I am playing the people in the stories as I imagine Dickens would have played them—playing them through him." The reviewer for the *Christian Science Monitor* wrote: "The whole thing, including the subtly used lighting, is extraordinarily theatrical and effective. . . .Theatrical style and prose style are admirably matched." The *New Yorker* critic thought the production edifying and entertaining. In the New York *Times* Brooks Atkinson described the "magnificent" solo performance as "fluent and dramatic." Possibly the most enthusiastic report came from Walter F. Kerr of the New York *Herald Tribune*: "Williams is an actor of striking range and great virtuosity as well, and the result is a combination of personal charm and adroit theatrical minicry which rivets audience attention to him for two solid hours and which, miraculously, becomes increasingly compelling as it goes along."

In addition to his stage work, Williams has appeared in numerous cinema productions, beginning in 1932. Some of the more notable of these are *The Stars Look Down, This England, Major Barbara, You Will Remember, Hatter's Castle,* and in 1949, *Dolwyn,* which Williams wrote and directed. Reporting on the last-named, the New York *Times* critic found the story of a Welsh village "full of tenderness and charm." The New York *Post* thought that Williams' "choice of a real village, his feeling for gloomy landscape, the use of Welsh singers

and their songs, and the very effective employment of local people create an atmosphere of rare quality." In *Another Man's Poison* (with Bette Davis), Williams, said the reviewer for the New York *Times*, "effortlessly . . . adds a professionally polished characterization as the [inquisitive] veterinary."

Williams, who is a boyish-looking, not very tall man with gray hair, is described as "amiable, approachable, and persuasively articulate." Married in 1934 to Molly O'Shann, he has two sons. His club is the Garrick and his favorite recreations are reading and walking. In 1948 Williams was presented with an honorary LL.D. degree by the University of Wales.

References

Esquire 16:88+ N '41
N Y Times X p1 D 1 '40
Theatre Arts 20:824-5 O '36; 32:16-19 Ja '48
Theatre World 19:218 My '33 por; 24: 34-5 Jl '35 por; 24:125 S '35 por; 27: 34 Ja '37 por; 30:179 O '38 por
Time 28:52 O 12 '38 por; 35:71 My 6 '40
International Motion Picture Almanac, 1951-52
Who's Who, 1951
Who's Who in the Theatre (1947)
World Biography (1948)

WILLIAMS, JOHN J(AMES) May 17, 1904- United States Senator from Delaware

Address: b. Senate Office Bldg. Washington 25, D.C.; h. Millsboro, Del.

The senior United States Senator from Delaware, Republican John J. Williams, was elected to that office in 1946. In the Senate, Williams, who in 1951 was instrumental in exposing scandals involving tax collectors in the Bureau of Internal Revenue, is considered an uncompromising foe of what he regards as widespread waste and corruption in the Federal government. His stand on domestic and foreign issues is almost always in accord with the majority of his party. Before going to Washington, Williams was in the feed and grain business.

The ninth in a family of eleven children, John James Williams was born on a farm near Frankford, Delaware, on May 17, 1904, to Albert Frank and Anna (Hudson) Williams. He attended public schools at Frankford and is a graduate of the local high school. In 1922 he moved to nearby Millsboro to enter chicken farming and the feed and grain business. According to *Pathfinder,* he served for a time on the Millsboro town council.

"Fed up with what was going on in Washington" (quoted by *Pathfinder*), Williams decided to run for the Senate in 1946 against the incumbent James M. Tunnell, a New Deal Democrat. As a critic of the OPA, he campaigned on a platform for removing Federal controls over the nation's economy. Williams won the election by 62,603 votes to 50,910, and took his seat on January 3, 1947, in the Republican-controlled Eightieth Congress. He was appointed to the Public Works and Civil Service committees and to the Special Committee to Investigate the National Defense Program, which questioned airplane-builder Howard Hughes about his "flying boat." On the Public Works Committee, Williams helped frame the majority report recommending disapproval of Gordon R. Clapp to succeed David Lilienthal as chairman of the TVA. In his first two years in the Senate, Williams opposed wool price support, appointment of Lilienthal to head the Atomic Energy Commission, aid to Greece and Turkey, implementation of ERP (Marshall Plan), repeal of Federal taxes on oleomargarine, the Federal aid to education bill, a new TVA steam plant, and granting the President stand-by powers to continue rationing and to control prices and wages. During the same period he supported a proposal to limit the Presidential term to two years, the Taft-Hartley Act, a measure permitting a 15 per cent increase in controlled rents, the shelving of the St. Lawrence project, the peacetime military draft, and the admission of over 200,000 displaced persons to the United States. He voted for a cut in river-harbor and flood control funds and against a boost in the 1949 soil conservation funds.

In the predominantly Democratic Senate of the Eighty-first Congress, which assembled in January 1949, Williams was assigned to the Committee on the District of Columbia and the Finance Committee. In that Congress Williams voted against the ruling of Vice-President Barkley that cloture could be applied to debate on a procedural motion, against a measure forbidding segregation in public housing (1949), and against an extension of Federal rent control (1950). In favor of a cut in Federal spending of 5 to 10 per cent in 1949, he also voted for a cut in river-harbor appropriations (1949) and for a 10 per cent cut in nondefense spending (1950). On issues of defense and foreign affairs, while supporting the North Atlantic Security Pact bill in 1949, he voted against the foreign military aid bill and for a cut of 50 per cent in European arms aid. He also opposed, in 1950, a measure providing $45 millions for the Point Four Program and a $100 millions loan for Spain.

One of the matters which Williams discussed at length on the Senate floor in the Eighty-first Congress was the alleged inefficiency of the Commodity Credit Corporation, the government agency which has as major responsibilities purchasing agricultural surpluses and supplying cereals for ERP. He maintained on March 25, 1949, that the Corporation's books for 1943-45 were not balanced, and later he charged that food was purchased from farmers at exorbitant rates and often immediately resold at a fraction of the cost for animal feed. Another government agency whose operations he criticized was the Maritime Commission, charging, for example, that the subsidies which the Commission granted pursuant to statute for the construction of passenger ships were too large and that the Commission had sold surplus vessels after the war at an excessive loss to the government. Attacking the government's price-

support policies for leading to the high cost of food, Williams made a vain attempt in June 1949 and again in 1950 to have reduced to a lower level the guaranteed return to the farmer of 90 per cent of parity. The Senate in August 1950 adopted three amendments proposed by Williams to the defense production bill: to punish Federal employees, including members of Congress and the armed forces, who speculate on commodity exchange; "to discourage attempts to drive prices of poultry and poultry products at the producer level below government ceilings"; "to prevent establishment of ceilings allowing a greater margin of profit than was enjoyed during a representative period prior to June 25, 1950" (New York *Herald Tribune*, August 16, 1950).

With the convening in January 1951 of the Eighty-second Congress, Williams continued on the Finance Committee; leaving the Committee on District of Columbia, he went to the Committee on Interstate and Foreign Commerce. A member, with Harry F. Byrd and Clyde R. Hoey, of an investigating subcommittee of the Finance Committee, Williams was brought much into contact with matters affecting tax collections. In an interview for *United States News & World Report*, he has explained that in 1946, before he was a Senator, he began to suspect corruption within the Bureau of Internal Revenue: he learned that checks (including one of his own) which a Bureau employee in Delaware had used to cover a defalcation, were not properly credited to taxpayers' accounts even after the embezzlement became known to officials. Williams, whose method was described by Glenn D. Everett in the Washington *Post* as a "quiet, thorough investigating technique . . . [which] seems innocuous and unexciting," opened his campaign against suspected dishonesty in the Bureau early in February 1951. He produced data which he had been investigating since late 1949 and which he said showed that one district collector had taken bribes, and that the Treasury and Justice Departments had withheld information from a Federal grand jury which could have led to the indictment of another collector. Later he made additional accusations. It was said that largely because of Williams' charges and the investigations which followed them sixty-some collectors resigned or were suspended or indicted.

The Delaware Senator also presented evidence which, he maintained, showed response to political influence on the part of the Reconstruction Finance Corporation, a government agency which makes loans to industries. He charged several officials with exerting pressure on the agency to grant benefits to businesses in which they were interested.

Besides his determination to eliminate frauds in tax collection, Williams is also interested in measures for lightening the tax load and for equalizing burdens. He has favored proposed tax reductions and has generally opposed increases. In 1951 he insisted that the tax-free expense accounts of Presidents, Vice-Presidents, and members of Congress favored them

Wide World Photos

JOHN J. WILLIAMS

as against other persons. To remedy this, he introduced an amendment to the legislation which increased most taxes in November 1951 to give these officials a wholly taxable salary equal to their 1951 salary and expense account combined; as in the case of all other taxpayers, only actual business expenses might be deducted from this income. The amendment, which will go into effect in 1953, was incorporated in the new law. Throughout 1951 Williams voted consistently for reduction in Government spending, including cuts in some payrolls, a $10 millions decrease in reclamation funds, and a proposal to cut funds for the United States armed forces to $55 billions; he opposed the $5½ billions tax increase.

Williams and Elsie E. Steele were married on May 4, 1924; they have one daughter, Mrs. Blanche W. Baker. During the Eighty-second Congress Mrs. Williams became chairman of the special events committee of the Congressional Club. The Senator stands an even six feet tall, weighs 190 pounds, and has gray eyes and brown hair. He is a Methodist, and belongs to the Masons (Thirty-second Degree), the Shriners, Rotary, the Knights Templars, and the Junior Order United American Mechanics. "Gentle, retiring, slow-spoken" is a phrase applied to the Senator, who names hunting as a favorite sport.

References

Look 15:69 D 18 '51 por
N Y Herald Tribune II p2 Ag 26 '51
Pathfinder 58:43 O 17 '51 por
U S News 31:44 O 12 '51 por
Washington (D.C.) Post p3B S 30 '51 por

Biographical Directory of the American Congress, 1774-1949 (1950)
Congressional Directory (1951)
Who's Who in America, 1950-51
Who's Who in the East (1951)
Who's Who in United States Politics (1950)
World Biography (1948)

WILSON, DONALD R(ANDOLPH) May 17, 1917- Veterans organization official; lawyer
Address: b. c/o American Legion National Headquarters, 700 N. Pennsylvania St., Indianapolis, Ind.; c/o Steptoe & Johnson, Clarksburg, W.Va.

At its thirty-third annual convention, held in Miami, Florida, in October 1951, the American Legion chose Donald R. Wilson the national commander for 1951-52. Wilson, a West Virginia lawyer, joined the Legion a few weeks after his discharge from service in World War II, in which he had been Staff Judge Advocate, in charge of administrative details on a hospital ship. As a Legionnaire he advanced through posts on the county, State, and national levels, becoming conspicuous in formulating and presenting the Legion's stand on the foreign policy of the United States.

Donald Randolph Wilson, the only child of A. B. and Edna Lucille (Lehr) Wilson, was born May 17, 1917, in Detroit, Michigan. The Wilson forebears, who were Scotch-Irish, had settled in Virginia in colonial times; the Lehrs were of German descent. From the Michigan city the Wilsons moved to Clarksburg, West Virginia, when their son was three years old. An electrical engineer, the elder Wilson was employed there in the research division of the Weirton Steel Company. Donald Wilson, who attended the local schools, was graduated in 1935 from the Washington Irving High School, where he had taken the academic course. A member of several honor societies, he was president of the junior and senior classes, the editor of the school paper, and a leader in debating and dramatics groups.

Looking forward to a career in law, Wilson in 1935 enrolled at Princeton University for courses he considered the best background for that profession: he majored in politics and international affairs and again became active in debating events and in public affairs discussion groups. He was varsity debating manager during his last two years at Princeton, a member of the Clio (historical) society, and president of the Whigs during the latter part of his sophomore year and all of his junior year. In the junior year he won an oratorical contest on the subject of "The Case for Administrative Tribunals"; and he attained the highest average in the international affairs course. His athletic interests were fencing, boxing, and tennis. One summer he was news commentator on the Clarksburg radio station, another he worked at the Weirton company, and another he gave to research on a study of Anglo-American diplomacy during the years 1895-1902. As a senior he did some tutoring in politics and economics. He graduated with the B.A. degree and a Phi Beta Kappa key in 1939.

For his law studies Wilson attended the University of Virginia for three years. Extracurricular activities included an instructorship in public speaking, service on the honor committee (the university maintains the honor system), membership in the Raven Society (an honorary scholastic group) and in Sigma Nu Phi, and on the board of the *University of Virginia Law Review*. The LL.B. degree was conferred on him in 1942, and the next year he passed the Virginia State bar examination. (The war delayed his admittance to the West Virginia bar until 1946.)

Within a few weeks after leaving the university Wilson enlisted as a private in the Army and was assigned to the Medical Replacement Training Center at Camp Pickett, Virginia. Commissioned a second lieutenant in the Medical Administrative Corps at Carlisle Barracks, Pennsylvania, on February 27, 1943, he served for a time as platoon leader at Camp Pickett. This duty was followed by further training in hospital administration at Camp Campbell. Attached to the 216th Hospital Ship Complement early in 1944, in June he sailed for the Mediterranean as adjutant of the Medical Administrative Corps and Staff Judge Advocate of the *John J. Meany*. He was in charge of the administrative details of that hospital ship, which was constantly engaged in the evacuation of the wounded from the landing operations in Southern France and the battles in Northern Italy; and after V-E Day in shuttling back and forth between French ports and the United States, bringing home the wounded until September 1945. When separated from the service on October 24, Wilson had the rank of captain, and now holds a reserve commission as captain in the Judge Advocate General's Corps.

Wilson now became an associate in the Clarksburg law firm of Steptoe & Johnson (with twenty-two partners, it is the largest in West Virginia), by whom he had been employed as a law clerk during one of the summers he was a student at the University of Virginia. Wilson, who became a partner in the firm in 1949, is concerned chiefly with civil trial work, especially with cases of negligence.

As a seventh-grade pupil young Wilson had his first contact with the American Legion, when he was a Boy Scout in a group sponsored by the Legion. His hospital ship experience having convinced him of the importance of a rehabilitation program for the veteran, he decided the Legion was the organization most essential to the re-establishment of former servicemen in civilian life. In early 1946 he accordingly was present at a local meeting of the Legion, at which the sparse attendance evoked some sharp criticism from him. The result was his appointment as a delegate to the district (county) convention in June of that year. The same year saw his election as vice-commander of the Third West Virginia District and as commander of the local post, the Roy E. Parrish Post No. 13; 1947 his election to the commandership of the State's Third District; and 1948 (at thirty-one) as the

Noble Bretzman

DONALD R. WILSON

unanimous choice as the first World War II commander of the West Virginia Department (the State level). One of his first accomplishments was to guide successfully the American Legion's mandate for a veterans' bonus referendum in West Virginia.

A delegate to the Legion convention at Miami, Florida, in 1948, Wilson served as vice-chairman of the convention foreign relations commission, his first appointment on the national level. For the year 1948-49 he was named to the national membership and post activities committees; and for the year 1949-50 he was appointed vice-chairman of the national legislative commission. Invited to speak at the May 1949 banquet of past Legion commanders, Wilson chose as his topic the foreign policy of the United States, tracing its development, criticizing it, and demanding a "crystallized" policy. Impressing his hearers with his speaking, organizing, and administrative abilities, he was next asked to present the Legion's stand before the Senate Foreign Relations Committee in 1949, in support of the North Atlantic Treaty. Another national office came to him in 1950 when he received the top post in the American Legion's international policy-making division as 1950-51 chairman of the national foreign relations commission.

At the 1949 convention, in Philadelphia, Wilson's name came forward as a possible national commander candidate, but no serious effort was made by his admirers to win support. This happened again, in 1950. After that year, however, a campaign for his election was launched. In 1951, at the thirty-third annual convention, in Miami, Wilson was elected the 1951-52 national commander of the American Legion on October 18, succeeding Erle Cocke, Jr. There was no rival candidate for the office —his choice was by acclamation, without being put to a vote. In his speech of acceptance Wil-

WILSON, DONALD R.—*Continued*

son reiterated his belief in "aggressive Americanism, international realism, and no compromise with communism." Describing the State Department as "incompetent" in a December address before a group of businessmen, he called for steps necessary to end the Korean War successfully "with whatever means at our disposal."

Wilson, who takes part in civic affairs in Clarksburg, has been active in the Harrison County Red Cross and has been president of the Lions Club. In the Baptist Church he teaches a large Bible class. Mrs. Wilson, who was the former Mary Virginia Hornor, met her future husband when they were high school students; they were married March 1, 1943, and have two sons, Donald Randolph, Jr., and Thomas Hornor. The veterans leader is of medium height (about five feet ten inches) with an approximate weight of 170 pounds; he has light hair and blue eyes. Not a man of "flamboyant" tastes, said an associate, he preferred a quiet homecoming after his election as the Legion's national commander to a public Clarksburg welcome. His success as a speaker is attributed to the "meticulous care" with which he prepares his material and his "persuasiveness" in delivery. He is described as having a "level gaze." In golf, a sport he particularly enjoys, he rates himself "the world's worst player."

WILSON, I(RVING) W(HITE) Sept. 26, 1890- Business executive

Address: b. c/o Aluminum Company of America, Gulf Bldg., Pittsburgh, Pa.; h. 1201 Murrayhill Ave., Pittsburgh, Pa.

In April 1951 I. W. Wilson became president of the Aluminum Company of America, an organization with which he had been associated for forty years, having joined it immediately after his graduation from the Massachusetts Institute of Technology. During World War II, as head of Alcoa's defense efforts, he directed the company's $300 millions expansion program and the $450 millions plant construction project undertaken by Alcoa for the United States Government. He has also been prominent in Alcoa's defense against monopoly charges.

The son of J. J. S. and Lucy (White) Wilson, Irving White Wilson was born in Bloomington, Illinois, on September 26, 1890. He studied electrochemistry at the Massachusetts Institute of Technology, from which he received the B.S. degree in 1911. Later in that year Wilson started to work for the Aluminum Company of America at its plant in Niagara Falls, New York, at a time when Alcoa had just completed an expansion program. From his first job as research technician, the young electrochemist was in a short time advanced to assistant research director.

After his first four years with Alcoa, Wilson was named assistant superintendent of reduction at the Massena (New York) plant, where he remained until he joined the United

States Army in 1917. Placed in charge of detachments of the Chemical Warfare Service in Philadelphia, Pennsylvania, and Astoria, Long Island, Wilson rose to the rank of major. Following his demobilization in 1919, he was assigned again by Alcoa to the Niagara Falls plant. He spent 1920 at the main offices of Alcoa in Pittsburgh, Pennsylvania. The thirty-one-year-old executive was appointed general superintendent of all the company's reduction plants in 1921, vice-president in charge of operations in 1931, a director in 1939, and a senior vice-president in March 1949. On April 20, 1951, he was elected its president, to succeed Roy A. Hunt.

The Aluminum Company of America, which was founded as a Pennsylvania corporation under the name of the Pittsburg Reduction Company in 1888, now controls throughout the United States a large number of mining developments, hydroelectric installations, smelting and casting works, and research laboratories, along with thirty-four wholly owned subsidiaries. In the forty years of his association with Alcoa, recorded *Time*, Wilson has seen the growth of the company "from a $21,000,000-a-year business into an empire whose 1950 sales were $476,000,000."

As director of Alcoa's share in defense production during World War II, Wilson, a member of the aluminum subcommittee of the Aluminum and Magnesium Committee of the War Munitions Board, was in charge of the $300 millions expenditure made by the company for expansion. He was as well supervisor of the $450 millions project through which twenty-two plants were built and operated by Alcoa for the Government without profit to the company. For his contributions to the war effort, Wilson in 1949 received a Presidential Certificate of Merit. Mr. Wilson played a leading role in the fourteen-year-old antitrust litigation brought by the United States against Aluminum Company of America in 1937 and terminated in 1951. During the trial he was one of the key witnesses in the company's defense. In 1945 the United States Circuit Court of Appeals for the Second Circuit ruled that the company had monopolized the aluminum ingot market (but no others) prior to the war. The court directed that no relief should be granted to the government until it was first determined whether competitive conditions were restored by the sale of the aluminum plants built and operated by the company for the government during the war, but owned by the government and subject to sale at the war's end. Wilson had a prominent part in putting the government in a position to sell these plants advantageously. To that end, Aluminum Company of America made available to its competitors all of its competitively significant patents, some royalty free and others on a reasonable royalty basis.

With the outbreak of war in Korea in 1950, the United States Government began encouraging further expansion in the aluminum industry, which had already made two fourfold expansions: from 1917 to 1940 and from 1940 to 1943, the last-named year being that of all-time high production of 1,640,000,000 pounds. The Aluminum Company of America planned to add two new plants to its already existing six, with new power facilities supplied by natural gas rather than the hydroelectric power hitherto employed. Wilson is quoted by New York *Times* as stating: "We have high hopes that after the emergency a number of promising new markets for aluminum can be developed. It will require a period of time to develop some of these potential uses. We are, however, optimistic about being able to make use of the increased productive facilities which will be available and feel that aluminum markets should grow both in size and scope if costs, and thus prices, can be kept down." *Business Week*, in a study of Alcoa's expansion program published February 9, 1952, reports that 270,000,000 pounds of new aluminum output will be contributed by the company to a free market: 30 per cent of the entire industry's extra production. New uses for aluminum have been found in the engineering, refrigeration, air conditioning, automobile, building, and electrical industries, which will absorb the increased output. Danger of overproduction was slight, according to Wilson: "In fact, in a free market with a normally good world economy, we are more likely to need new capacity than we are to find ourselves with excess plant." By the spring of 1953, Wilson estimated, Alcoa would have spent $300 millions as its contribution to added plants in the industry, thus increasing its own capacity 55 per cent.

Addressing the New York Society of Security Analysts in May 1952, Wilson called for a liberalizing of the Government's Controlled Materials Plan, with early elimination of existing controls in order to help meet civilian as well as military needs for aluminum. In another speech shortly afterward, delivered to the National Association of Purchasing Agents, he said, "Sensible relaxation of controls may seem to be a good way to arrive at a free market, but relaxation certainly cannot be an acceptable or justifiable substitute for a free market." With other major American industrialists, Wilson has expressed an interest in advances in industrial hygiene. At the twelfth Annual Congress of Industrial Health in January 1952, he pointed out that "occupational disease is almost a thing of the past. Exacting requirements of modern industrial methods have reemphasized the need for employe health. . . .It is probable that more medical examinations are conducted by industry than by any other group."

Wilson is associated with a number of other business organizations. He is president and director of the American Magnesium Corporation as well as being the vice-president of the Aluminum Ore Company, second vice-president and director of the Alcoa Power Company, Ltd., vice-president and director of the Carolina Aluminum Company, and director of Aluminum Colors, Inc., the Aluminum-Seal Company, and the United States Aluminum Company. Utilities concerns with which Wilson is connected are the Cedar Rapids Transmission Company, Ltd., as first vice-president; the Knoxville Power Company, as vice-president and director; the St. Lawrence River Power Company, as vice-president and director;

I. W. WILSON

and the Massena Securities Corporation, as vice-president and director. Wilson holds directorates as well in the Republic Carbon Company, the Firth Sterling Steel Company, and in Kensington, Inc. *Modern Metals* magazine in 1950 named him the aluminum industry's "Man of the Year" for his contributions to the planning and execution of Alcoa's expanded production programs "to serve the nation's needs."

A resident of Pittsburgh, the industrialist belongs to three clubs in that city, the Duquesne, the Longue Vue, and the Fox Chapel. He married Katherine Whalen on June 27, 1917. Three daughters were born to them: Katherine (Mrs. Edward P. White), Anne, and Margaret Lucy. *Iron Age* remarked of Wilson that it is not strange he is "so easy to beat in golf or bridge. He's got too many other things on his mind."

References

    Bsns W p80 F 9 '52
    Iron Age 167:83 My 3 '51
    N Y Times p39 Ap 20 '51
    Time 57:102 Ap 30 '51
    Business Executives of America (1950)
    Who's Who in America, 1952-53
    Who's Who in Commerce and Industry (1951)
    World Biography (1948)

WILT, FRED(ERICK LOREN) December 14, 1920- Athlete; Government employee
Address: b. c/o New York Athletic Club, 7th Ave. & 59th St., New York 19; h. 1 Stuyvesant Oval, New York 3

Fred Wilt, a special agent for the Federal Bureau of Investigation, is by avocation a runner who has competed in a number of major postwar track meets. Although he has frequently and

WILT, FRED—*Continued*

successfully taken mile events, Wilt considers himself primarily a two-miler, and it is as such that he has established new United States and world records. In recognition of his record, Wilt has received several awards, including the James E. Sullivan Memorial Trophy.

Frederick Loren Wilt was born in Pendleton, Indiana, on December 14, 1920, one of four children (two boys and two girls) of Jesse and Inez C. (Franklin) Wilt. His paternal great-grandfather, a farmer by occupation, came to the United States from Germany. Interested in all forms of athletics from an early age, Wilt at Pendleton High School, as he later recalled for Margery Miller of the *Christian Science Monitor*, "went out for basketball, as well as baseball and track . . . was guard on the basketball team four years and a catcher in baseball four years." While in high school, from which he was graduated in 1938, he worked out his own training routine on the track, a practice he continued when he entered Indiana Central College. There, after Wilt had competed in a cross country meet, the athletic coach received a letter from E. C. Hayes of Indiana University, offering suggestions on the young runner's training. "After three semesters at Central, I switched to the university," Wilt continued in the *Monitor* interview. "Hayes ran the legs off me, but he made me a real runner. . . .Within two months of arriving at the university I ran a 9:22 two-mile and a 4:22 mile."

Competing as an Indiana sophomore in the National Collegiate Athletic Association meet in Palo Alto, California, Wilt took the two-mile championship, and in the N.C.A.A. cross-country meet at East Lansing, Michigan, the four-mile. At the university, where Wilt was a member of Delta Chi Fraternity and the Sphinx Club, he specialized in education, biology, and physical education and took his B.S. degree in 1943. Upon graduation he entered the United States Navy, from which he was honorably discharged in 1946. For a year (1946-47) he studied law at the University of Tennessee before accepting a position as a special agent for the Federal Bureau of Investigation. In the course of his assignments for the FBI, he found himself in Pullman, Washington, where the indoor field house of Washington State College caused him to resume track training. That was in 1948, an Olympic year, and Wilt prepared sufficiently to obtain a place on the 10,000-meter Olympic team. In the international contest in London he placed eleventh.

"When, later in 1948, the FBI transferred me to New York, I continued my work in track," Wilt has said. A relatively obscure racer at the beginning of 1949, he emerged early in the season as strong competition to European contestants in two-mile meets, clocking 8:55.7, a time theretofore made by only two other Americans, Greg Rice and Gil Dodds. His seven indoor track triumphs included a mile in 4:10.9. Entering two European competitions that year, Wilt took the mile victory from French contestant Marcel Hansenne in London at 4:09.7. In Dublin and Glasgow he defeated Irish John Joe Barry in the one-mile (4:10.4) and in the two-mile (9:05.2). On his second

trip to Europe in 1949 (after the United States National Athletic Association Union meets), Wilt took second place in the 5,000-meter event of the international meet with Scandinavian countries. In the meantime, at the N.A.A.U. competitions in Fresno, California, Wilt had secured the 5,000- and the 10,000-meter championships, reported Jesse Abramson of the New York *Herald Tribune*, "on the flat and the cross-country title. . . .Winning the five and ten was a remarkable double in itself. He set an American citizens' record of 31 minutes 5.7 seconds in the 10,000 meters . . . and the next afternoon took the 5,000 meters in the good time of 14:49.3."

Running under the emblem of the New York Athletic Club, Wilt commenced the 1950 season by winning the Philadelphia *Inquirer* Mile in 4:11.8, a record clocking for that event, eight yards ahead of nearest contender John Joe Barry. "In Boston the next night," reported *Time*, "he ran away with the Knights of Columbus two-mile for his fifth straight win." At the end of January Wilt competed in the Wanamaker Mile at New York's Madison Square Garden, an event of the Millrose Athletic Club games, in which he and Don Gehrmann reached the tape simultaneously. The disputed decision went originally to Gehrmann; was reversed by the registration committee of the Metropolitan Association A.A.U. in February; and again was awarded to Gehrmann by the national convention of the N.A.A.U. at the end of the year.

Defeated in a Boston two-mile meet by Curtis Stone early in February 1950, Wilt came through the following week ahead of the same runner in the Toussaint two-mile feature of the New York Athletic Club games in Madison Square Garden, with time of 8:59.3. He went down before Stone in the three-mile event of the annual N.A.A.U. indoor track and field championships shortly afterward. Late that month Wilt made his then fastest time for the two-mile, 8:55.2, in a special feature held at the Intercollegiate A.A.A.A. indoor track and field meet in the Garden. The beginning of March 1950 saw Wilt defeated by Barry in the two-mile intercollegiate Heptagonal championships in Boston, a defeat repeated two nights later in the Columbian Mile event of the annual New York Knights of Columbus games: Wilt came in fourth. On March 10 he made the relatively slow time of 4:25 to beat Barry in the mile run at the 369th Regiment Armory in New York, in competitions held for the third year by the Pioneer Club. His second defeat by Gehrmann came shortly after, in the Bankers Mile of the fourteenth annual Chicago *Daily News* Relays, which found Wilt, said Joseph M. Sheehan of the New York *Times*, "chained to the track." In May the FBI man was the victor in the Benjamin Franklin Mile of the Penn Relays (4:14.6) and in the Boardwalk Mile at Atlantic City, in which he set an American record of 4:05.5 for the outdoor mile. He followed this with an American record for the outdoor two-mile run at the Brown University interscholastic track and field meet, clocking 9:01.5 to break the fourteen-year-old record. At the annual spring games of the

New York Athletic Club held at Travers Island in June, Wilt was upset near the end of the fifth and last lap of the mile feature by Sweden's Alf Holmberg. In November Wilt successfully defended his senior Metropolitan Amateur Athletic Union cross-country championship by heading the six-mile event held in New York's Van Cortlandt Park by the "excellent" time of 30:43.5.

At the outset of the 1951 season, Wilt distinguished himself in both the mile and the three-mile features of the annual Metropolitan Amateur Athletic Union senior championship, registering the "sizzling" time of 4:12.2 in the first, and a satisfactory clocking of 14:34.9 in the second. Seven yards was the measure of his defeat by Don Gehrmann at the seventh annual Philadelphia *Inquirer* games later in January. "Wilt rated himself off the pace for a half, then took over and was not challenged" in the indoor mile run at the American Amateur Athletic Union indoor track and field championship in mid-February, with what Abramson called "a fine 4:09.4 performance." A split decision was awarded to both Wilt and Gehrmann for their dual finish in the Intercollegiate Four A special mile late that month— Wilt ultimately being named second. His victory over Gehrmann in the Columbian Mile of the thirty-second annual Knights of Columbus games in early March was clear cut: a six-yard margin and time of 4:08.4. (Wilt's margin was attributed to the impediment offered by his fellow N.Y.A.C. runner, Stewart Ray, to Gehrmann, which Ray denied in an interview with the *Times*'s Sheehan.) The following week, Wilt again beat Gehrmann in the mile event of the Milwaukee *Journal* indoor games, with time of 4:08.9; and the following month, he took the Glenn Cunningham Mile of the Kansas Relays from Gehrmann by 4:16.8. Both American racers fell to Roger Bannister of England in the late April Penn Relays, with Wilt coming in second. At the 1951 N.Y.A.C. annual games, Wilt, winning the James A. Norton Invitation Mile in 4:10.3, set a record for the Travers Island track. Toward the middle of June, he repeated his victory of the previous year in the Metropolitan Amateur Athletic Union three-mile competition, this time clocking 14:17.8. And in the Metropolitan A.A.U.'s cross-country meet that November, Wilt shared top honors with Horace Ashenfelter of the N.Y.A.C., to tie for time of 31:14.6.

For the fourth year in succession, Wilt took the Conklin Cup at the January 1952 two-mile event of the Columbus Council Knights of Columbus games in Brooklyn, New York, to set a record of 8:59.5, "an astonishing performance in flat shoes on a hardwood floor," said Abramson. Then, for the third successive year, he secured the Metropolitan A.A.U. senior championship mile event. At first far ahead in the Philadelphia *Inquirer* Mile in mid-January, Wilt was overtaken and beaten by Gehrmann, and at the early February Milwaukee *Journal* games, it was Gehrmann again "in the mile, skimming home in front of Fred Wilt by twelve yards in 4:08.4." One night later Gehrmann made "a ten-yard 4:08.9 victory over straining

FRED WILT

Fred Wilt in the Hunter Mile" at the sixty-third annual Boston Athletic Association games. Wilt reversed the process the following week at the New York Athletic Club games; the two runners, who seemed to break the tape at the same time in the Baxter Mile, had to await a decision by the Bulova Photo-Timer, which gave the verdict to Wilt. Returning to the event which he prefers, Wilt in late February covered the two-mile track at the Intercollegiate A.A.A.A. track and field championships for a world record of 8:50.7, breaking the 1943 record established by Greg Rice. In the early March 1952 Columbian Mile of the thirty-third annual Knights of Columbus games in New York Wilt, "with three laps to go, bolted to the front and immediately it was no contest at all": he won in 4:11.4. The withdrawal of Gehrmann from the Cleveland Knights of Columbus indoor track meet in mid-March left a clear field for Wilt, who came up at the end to clock 4:10.8 for the mile. His ensuing victory, in the Regimental Mile of the National Amateur Athletic Union meet in Buffalo, was made in time of 4:10.1. Wilt "withered a lap and a half from the finish" of the mile feature of the late March Olympic Carnival in New York, to come in second to Warren O. Dreutzler. On a rain-soaked outdoor track two months later, Wilt made the comparatively good clocking of 4:14.4 to win the Reading (Pennsylvania) Gerry Karver Mile for the third time (he had lost it in 1951). In June Wilt ran in the N.Y.A.C. annual two-mile at Travers Island and in the Metropolitan A.A.U. championships before going to Helsinki to compete in the 10,000-

WILT, FRED—*Continued*

meter event of the 1952 Olympics. He came in twenty-first.

A resident of New York City, F.B.I. man Wilt trains by running a mile in the morning before work and a mile and a half in the evening after work. Because he would like to devote more time to his wife, the former Eleanor Christensen, to whom he was married December 23, 1950, and to his small daughter, Barbara, Wilt intends to cease running in indoor competitions after the Olympics. He has received a number of awards for his sportsmanship: the Mayor William O'Dwyer Trophy (1950); the James E. Sullivan Award, given each year to the outstanding amateur athlete of the United States by the Amateur Athletic Union (1950); the N.Y.A.C. Veterans Association Progress Award (1950); and the Impellitteri Trophy of the Bronx County Democratic Committee for his performance in the Metropolitan A.A.U. championships (1951). He belongs to the New York Athletic Club. The blue-eyed athlete is "blond and wiry," stands five feet eight inches tall, and weighs 145 pounds. His religion is Protestant. Music, reading, dancing, and keeping up with current events are listed as his recreations.

Reference

Christian Sci Mon p17 Mr 12 '52

WINTERS, SHELLEY Aug. 18, 1923-
Actress

Address: b. c/o Universal-International Studios, Universal City, Calif.

Shelley Winters has been one of the best-known Hollywood actresses from the time of her success in *A Double Life* in 1948. Since then she has played a series of "unladylike" roles. Somewhat different was her portrayal of the drab, rejected factory girl in *A Place in the Sun* (1951), for which she received critical acclaim.

One of two daughters of men's clothing designer Johan Schrift, Shelley Winters was born Shirley Schrift in East St. Louis, Illinois, on August 18, 1923. Her mother, Rose Winter, sang with the St. Louis Municipal Opera. According to the biography supplied by her studio, at the age of three the future actress managed to get on the stage at an amateur talent contest for teenagers. "The more they tried to get me off, the louder I sang," she recalls. "Finally, in desperation the master of ceremonies gave me a size-fourteen knitted sweater that hung down to my feet." When Shirley was eleven, the family moved to Brooklyn, New York, where their daughter attended Thomas Jefferson High School. There she became editor of the school paper and took part in dramatics (she sang Katisha in *The Mikado*). Then, to pay for lessons in acting the schoolgirl worked in a five-and-ten-cent store. In 1939, six months before graduation, she left school to go to work as a dress model in the garment district. Recalling her early

awkwardness, she says that the first time she paraded before customers she stumbled and fell.

During the evenings, the young girl studied acting at the New Theater School, where she decided upon Shelley Winter as a stage name, which later (in 1947) became Winters. She worked in the chorus at La Conga night club, played in summer stock for ten dollars a week, and spent most of a year applying at the offices of theatrical managers, who came to know her as "that aggressive blonde without talent." When their offices were closed to her, she rode up and down the elevators of their office buildings for hours, hoping to gain the attention of a producer.

Eventually the aspirant's persistence was rewarded by a small singing-acting part in *Conquest in April*. Next came other small stage roles in *Meet the People, Night Before Christmas, Of V We Sing*, and in 1942 she had a supporting role with Dorothy Sarnoff in *Rosalinda*. The operetta part brought her a $150-a-week contract with Columbia Pictures, which put her into bit parts in *What a Woman, The Racket Man, Two-Man Submarine*, and *Stepping Out*. Eventually the name Shelley Winter received fifth billing in *Knickerbocker Holiday* (Nelson Eddy was the star) and fourth billing in a "B" picture, *Sailor's Holiday*, then dropped to lower billings in *She's A Soldier, Too, Tonight and Every Night* (starring Rita Hayworth), and *A Thousand and One Nights* (starring Cornel Wilde, Evelyn Keyes). All of these were released in 1944 and 1945. Miss Winters has said that during the year and a half of her Columbia contract, she "constantly bemoaned" her own deficiencies. Columbia tried to remake her in patterns which had been efficacious with others, but was unsuccessful; the contract came to an end in 1944.

Applying herself then to the task of self-improvement, the actress wore corrective braces on her teeth, took dancing lessons to learn grace, studied acting and speech in classes conducted by Charles Laughton. During this period she appeared in the stage productions *The Taming of the Shrew, Of Mice and Men*, and *The Merry Widow*; had unsuccessful screen tests at Metro-Goldwyn-Mayer, Twentieth Century-Fox, and Warner Brothers; and played a small part in a minor picture, *The Gangster* (1947).

In the early part of 1945 the actress asked Garson Kanin if she might understudy Judy Holliday in his new comedy, *Born Yesterday*. Kanin suggested that she apply for the somewhat similar role in *A Double Life*, which his brother Michael was casting in Hollywood. A test was arranged, but proved so disappointing that Miss Winters went instead to New York, where she was to take over Celeste Holm's former singing comedy role of Ado Annie in *Oklahoma!* for the summer. Deciding to make her return to the stage permanent, she resumed the search for Broadway parts. At this time director George Cukor sent for her for more tests for the *Double Life* part. The result was that she was given the role.

To prepare herself for the small but effective part of the waitress whom Ronald Colman murders, she took a job as a waitress for a week. She was so much in awe of Colman that their scenes together had to be retaken many times until he put her at her ease with stories of his own early nervousness. *A Double Life*, released in February 1948, brought Shelley Winters a nomination by the Academy of Motion Picture Arts and Sciences as the best supporting actress and such critcal comments as "the new girl, Shelley Winters, leaves a vivid impression in her brief appearance. . . . [The interpretation] is toughly sympathetic . . . intriguing."

This was followed by another role for Universal-International, that of the "gun moll" Tory in the medium-budget melodrama *Larceny*. According to *Time*, the young director let Miss Winters play the part her own way— "she gave it a strong blend of sex, humor, loneliness, and desperation." Reviewer Alton Cook wrote of her, "She emerges as one of the definitely important actresses of the year . . . a dramatically vigorous ingenue." Other critics were less enthusiastic, but her "solid hit" brought contract offers from MGM (which wanted her to remake the old Jean Harlow pictures) and three other studios. She accepted the Universal offer, and for it she gave a "vivid supporting characterization" in *Cry of the City*, in which she sheltered a fugitive gangster.

In Paramount's *The Great Gatsby* (1949), starring Alan Ladd and Betty Field, Shelley Winters' role of Myrtle Wilson was a small one. In *Take One False Step*, with William Powell, she played the part of a girl who "went a little crazy." Reviewers' comments varied: "There is slight indication that she has arrived as a knowing actress, but she is well worth watching"; "A little more of Miss Winters . . . might have rendered a rather drab picture more decorative"; "She offers tantalizing promise of the sweep with which she would play an important [role]." A similar role was hers in *Johnny Stool Pigeon*, in which she was billed after Howard Duff, the lead; one reviewer praised her for "a credible performance."

In her first starring role, in *South Sea Sinner*, Miss Winters sang a song called "One-Man Woman." In the last months of 1949 she worked on Paramount's *A Place in the Sun*, which was not released until two years later. Determined to play the lonely, graceless, factory girl, Alice Tripp, in the film version of Dreiser's *An American Tragedy*, she read everything she could find about the book and the author and talked to people who had known Dreiser—novelist Norman Mailer was one of them. When she persuaded director George Stevens to test her for the role, he specified that she dye her hair dark brown, use no makeup, and refrain from curling her eyelashes. Miss Winters also visited nearby factories to study the girl workers before taking the test.

The three 1950 pictures in which Shelley Winters appeared included two Westerns— *Winchester '73*, opposite James Stewart, in which *Variety* called her "just sufficiently hard-boiled and cynical," and *Frenchie*, which had been Marlene Dietrich's comeback role eleven years earlier. In *Frenchie*, opposite Joel Mc-

SHELLEY WINTERS

Crea, Miss Winters played a gambling-house proprietor. During the summer of 1950 she played Billie Dawn in *Born Yesterday*, "expertly to packed houses in six [Eastern summer] theaters at $1,500 a week." In January 1951 she settled in New York and began studying acting, singing, and dancing at the Actors Studio, under Elia Kazan and Michael Chekhov. There she remained until that May, when Universal suspended her salary until her return to work.

Described by one reviewer as Miss Winters' "first full-length part that makes adult sense" was the role of Peg Dobbs in *He Ran All the Way*. As the boy-shy girl who unwittingly brings a murderer (John Garfield) into the household, she was described as "a lonely, appealing waif, full of horror . . . and frightened." When *A Place in the Sun* was released in September 1951, Shelley Winters, Montgomery Clift, and Elizabeth Taylor were all praised for excellent performances, with Miss Winters' portrayal of the drab, tragic figure as "particularly moving." That December, Shelley Winters lost out to Vivien Leigh on the fifth ballot for the New York Film Critics award; she was also nominated for a 1952 Academy Award on the strength of that performance; and she received the *Holiday* award as "the woman in the motion picture industry who has done most in the past year to improve standards and to honestly present American life to the rest of the world."

When Miss Winters went to Europe in September 1951 four pictures which she had made in the preceding six months were awaiting release. These were *Behave Yourself*, with Farley Granger, in which she had her first real comedy role as a scatterbrained wife; *Meet Danny Wilson*, with Frank Sinatra; *Phone Call from a Stranger*, in which she was billed over Bette Davis; and *The Raging Tide*.

(Continued next page)

WINTERS, SHELLEY—*Continued*

The blonde, blue-eyed actress is five feet four inches tall and weighs 120 pounds. For exercise she swims, dances, and plays tennis. She likes to wear slacks and cotton shirts, uses no make-up, and is known for her "jet-propelled energy and four-alarm personality." Interviewers remark on her outspokenness and humor. She enjoys lectures, concerts, and the theater, and is an avid reader. Married in 1942 to textile salesman Mack Mayer, Miss Winters was divorced in 1948. On April 28, 1952, she was married to the Italian actor Vittorio Gassman.

References

Collier's 124 46 Jl 30 '49
Motion Pict & Television Mag 82:42 D '51
N Y Herald Tribune p21 Je 20 '50
N Y Journal American Pictorial p1 Mr 27 '49
N Y Post p5 Mag O 14 '51
N Y World-Telegram p26 F 2 '52
Photoplay 40:52 D '51
Silver Screen 22:22 D '51

WIRTH, CONRAD L. (wûrth) Dec. 1, 1899- United States Government official; landscape architect

Address: b. c/o National Park Service, Department of the Interior, Washington 25, D.C.; h. 10 E. Leland St., Chevy Chase 15, Md.

In December 1951, after a twenty-year association with the National Park Service of the Department of the Interior, Conrad L. Wirth was named director of the Service, which is responsible for the administration of national parks, monuments, historic sites, and other reservations. Wirth's earlier positions with the National Park Service were as associate di-

CONRAD L. WIRTH

rector for an eight-month period in 1951 and as assistant director in charge of planning from 1931 to 1951. A landscape architect by training, Wirth began his career in California and later followed that profession in Louisiana. Before joining the Federal office he was employed from 1928 to 1931 as a landscape architect for the National Capital Park and Planning Commission.

Conrad L. Wirth was born December 1, 1899, in Hartford, Connecticut, the son of Theodore Wirth, who is of Swiss origin, and Leonie Augusta (Mense) Wirth. Until 1906 the future park official lived in his native city, where his father was the superintendent of parks. In that year Theodore Wirth was appointed superintendent of parks for the city of Minneapolis, a position he held until 1937, and here the young Conrad spent his boyhood. On completion of his elementary education, Wirth became a student at St. Johns Military Academy in Delafield, Wisconsin. Here he was director of one of the school's clubs and was active on the football, track, and crew teams. He graduated from the secondary schol in 1919, and, stimulated by his father's career, entered Massachusetts University at Amherst to begin the study of landscape architecture under the direction of Professor Frank A. Waugh. Wirth's extracurricular activities were football and track, membership in Kappa Sigma, and a position as class officer. In 1923, after he had received his B.S. degree, he moved to San Francisco, where he took his first position as a landscape architect with a firm.

Wirth remained in California until 1925. In that year he moved to New Orleans, where with a partner he formed the firm of Neale and Wirth, engaged in landscaping and town planning. Three years later Wirth accepted his first government appointment when he became a landscape architect for the National Capital Park and Planning Commission. This Federal agency has the responsibility of planning and acquiring an adequate system of parks, parkways, and playgrounds for the national capital and its environs, as well as the task of preserving the forest and natural scenery around the city, and preparing a coordinated city and regional plan for the District of Columbia. The landscape architect stayed with the commission until 1931, when he received the appointment of assistant director of the National Park Service. For the next twenty years Wirth served in this capacity, with most of his work centering around the planning aspects of the service.

In April 1951 he was named associate director, and in December of 1951, on the retirement of Arthur E. Demaray, who had served in the chief executive position for a few months, Wirth was appointed director by the Secretary of the Interior, Oscar L. Chapman. At the time that Wirth moved from his post as an assistant director to that of associate director, the Washington *Post* carried an editorial on the subject of this and other changes in top-level positions and on Chapman's views on the function of the National Park Services. Wirth, who, according to the Washington *Post*, is "sympathetic to Secretary Chapman as well as competent," presumably will endeavor to prevent any encroachment on the parks that would injure their original purposes and will attempt to gain administration by his agency of recreational areas developed in connection with dam and river projects.

The agency which Wirth directs was created by Act of Congress in 1916 in order, according to the wording of the Act, "to conserve the scenery and the natural and historic objects and the wildlife therein" of areas set aside for their unusual scenic qualities and historic significance, and "to provide for the enjoyment of the same in such manner and by such measures as will leave them unimpaired for the enjoyment of future generations" (quoted from the *United States Government Organization Manual*). In order to carry out this objective, the National Park Service has jurisdiction over more than 171 areas comprising 28 national parks, located throughout the United States as well as in Hawaii and Alaska; the five national historical parks; the eleven national military parks; six national battlefield sites; the two national battlefield parks; the more than 80 national monuments, including the 1,860,138 acres in Death Valley and the 85,304 acres of the Petrified Forest of Arizona; the three national parkways, the 750 units of the National Capital Parks in the District of Columbia and vicinity; and other miscellaneous areas preserved for their historic, scenic, recreational, or memorial attributes. In addition to protecting these areas from fire, stream pollution, and other injuries to the unique features of the public grounds, and from commercialization of their resources, the National Park Service provides for the needs of the public which uses the parks. Thus, the agency builds roads, trails, campgrounds, and other recreational facilities for the enjoyment of the areas. Concessionaires, operating under contract with the National Park Service, offer accommodations to visitors. An information program, composed of field studies of flora and fauna, research reports on historic sites, pamphlets for the use of visitors, and guided tours, is also conducted by the agency. In addition, the National Park Service is responsible for the maintenance of the White House and its grounds.

Aside from his work with the National Park Service, Wirth from 1933 to 1942 represented the Department of the Interior as an advisory board member on the Civilian Conservation Corp and in 1945 was policy adviser to the United States Allied Council in Austria. He was the recipient in 1947 of the Pingsley Gold Medal presented by the American Scenic and Historic Preservation Society and in 1949 was granted by Congress the Selective Service Medal. He is a director of the National Conference on State Parks as well as of the American Shore and Beach Preservation Association. He is a fellow of the American Society of Landscape Architects; an active leader in the Federal Inter-Agency Committee on Recreation; and a member of the American Planning and Civic Association, the Cosmos Club of Washington, D.C., and the Kappa Sigma fraternity.

The park executive has hazel eyes and brown hair, is five feet ten and one-half inches in height, and weighs 195 pounds. His faith is the Catholic. On June 30, 1926, he married Helen Augusta Olson, a student at the time. Their two sons are named Theodore Julian and Peter Conrad. Gardening is a diversion of the government official.

References

Recreation p194 Jl '47
Who's Who in Government, 1932-33

WOODWARD, R(OBERT) B(URNS)

Apr. 10, 1917- University professor; chemist
Address: b. c/o Department of Chemistry, Harvard University, Cambridge 38, Mass.; h. 24 Kenmore Rd., Belmont 78, Mass.

Three of the major chemical achievements of the twentieth century have come from the Harvard laboratory of R. B. Woodward, who found the first total synthesis of quinine (1944), the first complete polymerization of "protein analogues" (1947), and the first total synthesis of a steroid (1951). On Woodward's discoveries may be predicated a number of hitherto impossible advances in medicine, pharmacology, antibiotic research, and plastics development. Devoted to the study of organic chemistry from his early youth, Woodward at twenty received his doctorate from the Massachusetts Institute of Technology. By the age of thirty-four, he was a full professor on the Harvard University faculty.

The son of Arthur Chester and Margaret (Burns) Woodward, Robert Burns Woodward was born in Boston, Massachusetts, on April 10, 1917. Through the gift of a chemistry set, the child's interest in chemistry was aroused early, and his parents—who were not scientifically inclined, but sympathetic to his interest—allowed him to set up a laboratory in the basement of their home. By the time Woodward graduated from the Quincy (Massachusetts) High School in 1933, he was reported to have had a greater knowledge of chemistry than most science majors in college. At the Massachusetts Institute of Technology the young student of organic chemistry "flunked out" in his sophomore year.

Recognizing in Woodward a student of unusual capabilities, the faculty allowed him to formulate his own curriculum, with the requirement that he take the examinations. Further help was given him through a thousand-dollar fellowship, to eliminate the necessity of his working at part-time jobs to earn his expenses, and the allocation of a laboratory for his exclusive use in research in hormones. His third year in college found Woodward taking fifteen courses. James Flack Norris of the M.I.T. faculty remarked, "We did for Woodward what we have done for no other student in our department. We think he will make a name for himself in the scientific world." At the age of nineteen young Woodward received his Bachelor of Science degree, and at the age of twenty, in 1937, his doctorate. After instructing for the summer at

R. B. WOODWARD

the University of Illinois, Woodward joined the faculty at Harvard as postdoctoral assistant to E. P. Kohler, chairman of the organic chemistry department.

Appointed a junior fellow of the Society of Fellows at Harvard in September 1938, Woodward was a member of that body until 1940, when he was named instructor in chemistry. His promotion to assistant professor came in 1944, to associate professor in 1946, and to full professor in 1951. *American Men of Science* recorded that his early research concerned oestrogenic hormones, santonin, dimerization, absorption spectra, diene addition reaction, cantharidien, triisobutylene, and the resolution of camphor.

Woodward had been engaged in June 1942 as a consultant by the Polaroid Corporation, manufacturers of optical materials. Because of wartime quinine shortages, Polaroid had found it necessary to assign its chemists to seek a substitute for quinine crystals (needed for lenses), a problem quickly solved in its laboratories. Woodward, however, suggested further research on the total synthesis of quinine. Under a financial agreement with Polaroid, he and Dr. William E. Doering (later of Columbia University) began work February 1, 1943, in Harvard's Converse Memorial Laboratory. Fourteen months later, on April 11, 1944, they were able to send a communication to the May issue of the *Journal of the American Chemical Society*: "We wish to announce the first total synthesis of quinine." Woodward, as quoted by *Newsweek*, stated: "It was a problem of molecular architecture . . .We started with a coal tar derivative known as benzaldehyde, a cheap, common bulk material containing the essential ingredients." Basing their work on research done by German chemists Rabe and Koenigs in 1908 and using no extraordinary materials or equipment, Woodward and Doering converted the benzaldehyde

into a substance named 7-hydroxy-isoquinoline. Then, explained William L. Laurence of the New York *Times*, through sixteen further conversions "finally they obtained a product with a skeletal molecular structure resembling quinine," from which ultimately the total synthesis was derived by rearrangements of its atomic architecture. The New York *Herald Tribune* quoted a Polaroid release as saying: "Their new synthetic material is a precise duplicate of natural quinine: it cannot be distinguished from natural quinine." The total yield from five pounds of chemicals, reported *Business Week*, was small, less than 1 per cent, composed of a half gram of quinine, a little more of quinidine. Cinchonidine and cinchonine were also found. Polaroid, patent-owner, planned to lease manufacturing rights to other firms and employ the profits for future scientific research, in the event that means of commercial production could be worked out.

In his next discovery, stated the *New Republic*, Woodward came "closer to duplicating nature's process of growth than anyone else who ever lived." With C. H. Schramm of Harvard, he announced the synthesis of "protein analogues"—materials resembling the natural proteins found in animal and plant life—in the June 1947 issue of the *Journal of the American Chemical Society*. *Science News Letter* summarized this report: Schramm grew "simple amino acid anhydrides into complex polymers" [giant molecules] with benzene as chemical solvent and water as the start of reaction. Using only two amino acids of the thirty or so possible, the collaborators in this polymerization process succeeded, by throwing off carbon-dioxide between the molecules, in forming chains of 10,000 units of the acids. (The longest previous chain, achieved by German chemist Emil Fischer, had been only eighteen units.) Besides the importance of the improved polymerization process to the chemical industry, the "protein analogues" would also be of use, said the *New Republic* and *Science News Letter*, in plastics manufacture (synthetic materials indistinguishable from natural silk, wool, or fur); in antibiotic research (artificially made antibiotics similar to gramacidin, tyrocidin, etc., used in treating virus infections); and in medical research (clarification of the processes used by the body in absorbing protein). Complete commercial possibilities of the finding had not been determined in 1947, but both Stephen White of the New York *Herald Tribune* and Waldemar Kaempffert of the New York *Times* suggested that the plastic film derived from Woodward's solution would bring about a number of new products in the industry.

At the April 1951 meeting of the Chemical Society in London, Professor Woodward announced that he and six associates at Harvard had, after sixteeen months of experimentation, achieved "the first total synthesis of a steroid" —that group of chemicals which number, among others, cortisone, digitalis, vitamin D, and the sex hormones. With financial help from the Research Corporation of New York and the Merck Company, and with materials from Monsanto Chemical Company, the Harvard group had evolved a synthetic steroid nucleus from orthotoluidine, a coal-tar derivative. The twenty steps involved in the process yielded one twenty-eighth of an ounce of a genuine steroid from 22 pounds of raw material. "The possibility of converting this steroid into one of the natural steroids," said a Harvard release, "lies in effecting relatively simple further changes in the atoms attached to the steroid nucleus." Woodward emphasized that cortisone had not yet been made. Since orthotoluidine is much less expensive than the animal bile acids ordinarily employed in cortisone production, it was thought that the possible total synthesis of an artificial cortisone steroid based on Woodward's compound would profoundly affect medicine by making available the rare drugs needed in the treatment of arthritis, heart disease, and certain types of cancer. The National Academy of Science at its 1951 spring meeting welcomed his discovery "as one of the greatest in the history of chemistry." In a communication in the *Journal of the American Chemical Society* of August 1951, Woodward, F. Sondheimer, and D. Taub recorded "the completion of the final links in the total synthesis of cortisone."

In order to release Woodward from his teaching duties, Harvard named him Dupont Research Professor for 1949-50. For three months in 1951 he toured Scotland and Ireland, lecturing on his subject, and at the invitation of the Chemical Society he gave its Centenary Lecture that year. Besides being a member of the Chemical Society, Woodward belongs to the American Association for the Advancement of Science, the American Academy of Arts and Sciences, and the New York Academy of Science. During World War II he was consultant to the committee on medical research of the Office of Scientific Research and Development, and to the War Production Board. He has been recipient of an honorary doctorate in science from Wesleyan University (1945) and of the John Scott medal of the Franklin Institute (1946). Woodward has contributed articles to *Science* and (in collaboration with Gurbakhsh Singh) to *Nature*. He has prepared more than fifty papers in the general field of organic chemistry.

Woodward, who has been married twice (in 1938 and in 1946), is the father of three daughters, Sirii, Jean, and Crystal. His wife, Eudoxia, has also been a consultant to the Polaroid Corporation. The Harvard chemist is five feet eleven and a half inches tall and has blond hair and blue eyes. He prefers to wear gray flannels and "quiet" ties. While at work he sustains himself with many cigarettes and thermoses of coffee. For relaxation he may play softball or touch-football.

References

Chem and Eng N 25:2137 Jl 28 '47
N Y Times p1 Ap 26 '51
Newsweek 29:57 Je 23 '47; 37:93-5 My 7 '51

American Association for the Advancement of Science Directory (1940-48)
American Men of Science (1949)

WOUK, HERMAN (wōk)   May 27, 1915-
Author
Address: b. c/o Harold Matson, Rockefeller Plaza, New York 20

Reprinted from the *Wilson Library Bulletin*, March 1952.

"Setting aside the years at war, I have had no other aim or occupation than that of writing; and it is the ambition I had when I was a boy. It is hard work; and in the good hours when words are flowing well it seems there is

HERMAN WOUK

hardly a pleasanter way to spend one's time on earth. Never mind the bad hours. There is no life without them." Thus Herman Wouk, author of the best-selling novel, *The Caine Mutiny* (1951), sums up a literary career which, though brief in years, has been crowded with activity. The count (as of early 1952) of only the major work includes three novels, two motion pictures, and a Broadway play.

Herman Wouk is the son of Russian-Jewish immigrant parents, Abraham Isaac and Esther (Levine) Wouk. His father began work in this country as a laundry laborer at $3 a week and eventually became a well-known industrialist in the power laundry field. Herman was born in New York City, May 27, 1915, and spent his early years in the Bronx—"that romantic (and much over-ridiculed) borough," he loyally calls it. After graduation from Townsend Harris Hall High School, he entered Columbia University, majoring in comparative literature and philosophy.

By 1934 Wouk had managed to acquire not only the conventional B.A. degree but the invaluable experience of editing the college humor magazine and writing two of the famous varsity shows (following in the hallowed tradition of Rodgers, Hart, and Hammerstein). This extracurricular activity led to his being

WOUK, HERMAN—*Continued*

hired after graduation to work as a "gagman" grinding out material for radio comedians. Wouk recalls: "My first literary task was copying old jokes out of tattered comic magazines on to file cards." From there he advanced rapidly to script-writing, working happily for five years with Fred Allen—one of the rare figures in radio, Wouk says.

With the outbreak of World War II in Europe, Wouk went to work for the United States Treasury, writing and producing radio shows to promote the sale of bonds. Soon after Pearl Harbor he enlisted in the Navy, serving as an officer. In 1943 on the *Zane* in the Pacific, Wouk tried to enliven the tedium of sea duty by writing a novel, *Aurora Dawn.* He sent the early chapters to Irwin Edman, under whom he had studied at Columbia, and Edman was sufficiently impressed to forward them to a publisher. With a publishing contract to inspire him, Wouk worked on the book during off-hours, completing it in 1946.

Readers familiar with Wouk's three novels will be quick to recognize the extraordinarily close parallel between them and his life. *City Boy,* which appeared in 1948, describes in exact, sometimes pathetically realistic detail, the coming-of-age of a fat, eleven-year-old Bronx schoolboy, tracing his adventures in school, camp, home, and—most delightful—in his lively imagination. A modern Tom Sawyer (as J. H. Jackson described him in the San Francisco *Chronicle*), Wouk's young hero, Herbie Bookbinder, is characterized by humor but also by warmth and understanding. *City Boy* was a Family Book Club choice and was filmed by Columbia Pictures. (In 1948 Wouk wrote another film, *Slattery's Hurricane,* a story of Navy weather fliers.)

Similarly, in *Aurora Dawn* Wouk draws upon his experience by setting his novel in the frenetic, ulcer-ridden atmosphere of radio advertising. The protagonist may well be Aurora Dawn itself—no hero or heroine, but a soap for which a fantastic but not untypical sales campaign is launched by the merely mortal characters in the book. It was a Book-of-the-Month Club selection.

With *The Caine Mutiny* Wouk turned to the more serious scene of World War II to produce a novel which rings true not only as a war story but also as the account of the maturing of a sheltered young Princetonian. While the book benefits immeasurably from Wouk's Navy service, it is not autobiographical. Hailed by reviewers as one of the best novels of the war, it was chosen by the Literary Guild and sold a quarter of a million copies besides. It is also being made into a motion picture. Authentic, it impressed readers most perhaps with its freshness after the sordid world-weary, monosyllabic war novels which had appeared since 1945.

The success of *The Caine Mutiny* tends to overshadow Wouk's career as a playwright. In 1949 his melodrama *The Traitor* was produced on Broadway with Lee Tracy and Walter Hampden. The play deals with the tragic decision of an idealistic and brilliant scientist to give atom bomb secrets to his country's enemies. Unwittingly, Wouk points out, he had anticipated the Klaus Fuchs case.

In 1952 Wouk is busy on another play, *Modern Primitive,* and an untitled novel, a love story set in Manhattan. He lives in New York with his wife, a former Californian, Betty Sarah Brown, whom he married in 1945, and their son Nathaniel. Reading is his favorite recreation, with *Don Quixote* heading the list. Wouk admits to a special fondness for Anthony Trollope, from whose autobiography he learned valuable lessons in literary craftsmanship, especially rigorous self-discipline. He is also interested in Hebrew studies and is a member of the board of directors of the Orthodox Jewish Council of Congregations.

WRIGHT, ANNA (MARIA LOUISA PERROTT) ROSE Oct. 13, 1890- Author

Address: b. c/o Houghton Mifflin Company, 2 Park St., Boston, Mass.; h. 113 Bellevue Ave., Upper Montclair, N.J.

Reprinted from the *Wilson Library Bulletin,* March 1952.

Swimming, sailing, collecting box turtles, and reading are secondary interests of Anna Rose Wright. Of greatest importance has been the taking into her home of children faced with real handicaps or problems, and helping them to reach good, wholesome, happy adjustments.

Anna Maria Louisa Perrott Rose was born in New York City, October 13, 1890, the daughter of Charles Frederick Rose and Kate Ashley (Loomis) Rose. Her father, born in Stratford upon Avon, studied architecture in England, Paris, and Rome, and was established in business in New York City. When his people had settled in Virginia, Mrs. Wright's paternal grandfather became a tobacco planter. It was about one of those farms (which she inherited) that she wrote in *Summer at Buckhorn,* a book for children. Some of Mrs. Wright's happiest childhood days were spent on this Virginia farm. Her mother's people, also of English descent, were teachers, professors, and writers. Mrs. Wright's maternal grandfather, Dr. Mahlon Loomis, sent the first wireless message in America, experimenting in the Blue Ridge Mountains of Virginia.

Two brothers and two sisters completed the Rose family. They all grew up in Upper Montclair, New Jersey, where the children attended public schools, "as did my husband and our children."

In 1914 Vassar College conferred the B.A. degree upon Mrs. Wright. She had majored in English and once received a prize for a story in the college magazine. Mrs. Wright yielded this information recently with characteristic embellishment: "But this did not indicate any great achievement." Two years in a creative writing course at Columbia University finished off general schooling. For several years she worked in publishing houses and print-shops, and taught typography at Columbia. Stenography, typing, teaching, and tutoring also played a part in a kaleidoscopic career, but "Juvenile writing is my favorite work."

On August 21, 1920, Anna Rose married Arthur Wright, chemical engineer. Their three children, Ann, Tom, and Ellen, gradually were supplemented by Carolyn, Jack, Harry, Paul, and Albert, who were taken into the Wright home partly in order to achieve "a nicely balanced family," but mostly because each of these additional youngsters was badly in need of a home. Mrs. Wright has stated four specific problems which face foster parents who take a disturbed or destitute child into their homes. "Each child as he comes does the selfsame thing. He lies frantically; he brags unbearably; he screams every night in wild nightmares; and he wets the bed. Confronted by these things, some foster parents give up in despair. Those who hold on find that these troubles begin to fade out after the first six months, but it takes at least a year before a child really settles down."

The story of the "nicely balanced family" appeared in *Room for One More,* the best-seller published in 1950 and made into a motion picture in 1952. The part about Jimmy John had appeared in the *Ladies' Home Journal* and evoked one of the largest reader responses in the *Journal's* history.

Because they practiced their faith that laughter and fun are as important to childhood as food, the Wrights' pattern for rearing an augmented family has gained wide attention as a successful experiment in living. "You often read horrors about 'black-market baby farms,'" wrote Mrs. Wright, "but you seldom hear of the good work of that vast army of American foster mothers which, in cooperation with legitimate agencies and for very low board, is quietly doing constructive work with children." So unique and unpredictable have been experiences related in books, magazine, and newspaper articles, that time and again Mrs. Wright has been called upon by doubting editors to substantiate to their satisfaction the anecdotes she has reported. (She has satisfied the editors.)

Mrs. Wright first published at the age of twelve when she sent an article to *Harper's Bazaar* on "The Best Thing Our Club Has Ever Done." It won a five-dollar prize. *Reader's Digest, Parents, Child Life,* and other magazines have since published her articles. Her books include *Life of Hugo the Horse* (1935), *Children of the Nineties* (with Richard Jones, 1936), *Barefoot Days* (1937), *Summer at Buckhorn* (1943), and *Hungry Hollow.* *Barefoot Days* and *Summer at Buckhorn* were both Junior Literary Guild selections. *Room for One More* was a Family Book Club choice.

Summer at Buckhorn is the story of the five lively Rose children spending the summer in Virginia while their mother was ill. *Whirligig House* (1951) again is a family story of five children without their mother. Left in the care of Andy, cook and general factotum of their home, the children form their own private army, "The YEBO." They deal out their own punishments and make their own rules, chief of which is to obey ("YEBO" spelled backwards). Drawings in the book are by the author's own children.

Room for One More begins: "We tried an experiment in our family and when we began people said 'You're crazy!' 'You can't afford it!' 'You're making a big mistake!' We went ahead anyway, and everything turned out all right. This is a true record of the way it worked." The book was written in answer to those who said they longed to take a child but couldn't find a suitable one. Mrs. Wright's belief was that children are not very "suitable" anyhow; one had better take unsuitable ones and go on from there. Edward Barry in the Chicago *Sunday Tribune* observed that she ". . . does not pretend that raising children (one's own or somebody's else) is all sweetness and light and gaiety and joy. She duly stresses the exasperation, the physical and mental ordeals, and the need for unlimited endurance." To this the *Christian Science Monitor* added that the book "teaches, by example, practically the whole art of parenthood." Ernestine Evans, in the New York *Herald Tribune,* commented that the author ". . . understands social work and organizations, and the details of legal responsibility."

Mrs. Wright has served as board member on child welfare organizations and has written publicity for them. She is an Episcopalian, and has taught Sunday school for twenty-five years, "which sounds tamer than it was." In politics she considers herself a mugwump; when it comes to clubs and organizations, she is no joiner. She strongly dislikes publicity. Her eyes are blue, her brown hair is beginning to turn gray, she is five feet five inches tall. "I weigh 195 pounds and can't sink, hence my confidence in the water—preferably salt water."

WRIGHT, FRANK LLOYD   June 8, 1869-
Architect

Address: "Taliesin," Spring Green, Wis.; "Taliesin West," Paradise Valley, Phoenix, Ariz.

NOTE: This biography supersedes the article which appeared in *Current Biography* in 1941.

One of the founders of modern architecture, Frank Lloyd Wright is regarded by many as the greatest architect of the 20th century. He was trained as an engineer, worked for nearly six years under Louis Sullivan, and established himself in Chicago as an independent architect in 1893. Since that time his innovations in the field of domestic architecture and his engineering feats in such structures as the Larkin Building, the Imperial Hotel in Tokyo, and the Johnson Wax Company buildings have won him world-wide fame and influence. By 1952 he had designed over 600 executed buildings of all types. He remains in the vanguard of contemporary architectural development.

Frank Lloyd Wright was born on June 8, 1869, in Richland Center, Wisconsin, one of the three children of William Russell Cary and Anna Lloyd (Jones) Wright. His father was a musician and preacher from New Eng-

FRANK LLOYD WRIGHT

land; his mother, the daughter of a Welsh Unitarian who had settled in the Wisconsin River Valley, was a school teacher. When Frank was three years old, his father was called to a pastorate in Weymouth, Massachusetts. Around 1880 the family returned to Wisconsin and the boy then divided his time between working on his uncle's farm and attending secondary school in Madison, where his father had opened a music conservatory. From the very beginning Anna Wright wanted her son to become an architect. Since the University of Wisconsin offered no courses in architecture, he enrolled as a prospective civil engineer in 1884. As an undergraduate, he gained some practical experience by working part-time in the private office of Allen D. Conover, the dean of the engineering school, who was at that time supervising the construction of several of the university's buildings.

In the spring of 1887 Wright left the university without graduating and went to Chicago, where he obtained a job as a draftsman at $8 a week in the office of J. L. Silsbee. While employed there, he designed his earliest executed work—the house for his aunts at Spring Green, Wisconsin (1888). That same year he entered the offices of Dankmar Adler and Louis Sullivan, the most progressive architectural firm in the country, and immediately achieved a position of importance as a designer. He was subsequently given a five-year contract which made it possible for him in 1889 to start building his own home in suburban Oak Park and to marry Catherine Lee Clark Tobin the following year. They had six children: Lloyd, John (both of whom became architects), Catherine, David, Frances, and Llewelyn. Inasmuch as Sullivan (the only

architect to whom Wright has ever acknowledged a debt) was interested mainly in commercial buildings, it fell to Wright to design all the domestic work which came to the firm. To help provide for his growing family, he also did outside designing on his own. This led to a break with Sullivan, and in 1893 Wright began the independent practice of architecture in Chicago. Important landmarks in his progress towards an individual style during this period are the Charnley (1891) and Harlan (1892) houses in Chicago; the Winslow House at River Forest (1893)—Wright's first commission after leaving Sullivan; the wooden windmill and watertower at Spring Green (1896); and the River Forest Golf Club (1898).

In 1900 Wright designed the first of his celebrated "Prairie houses," for which "no precedent existed anywhere." According to H. R. Hitchcock (*Modern Architects*), in these houses Wright accomplished "something of as much consequence in the history of the dwelling as the architects of the 15th century who turned the defensive castle into the residential mansion." Hitchcock has thus summed up their characteristic features: "Room flowed into room, in the plan, and the supports were increasingly isolated as the windows ceased to be mere holes in the wall and were grouped together in long rows. The strong horizontals of the projecting eaves and the second floor window sill were emphasized, but through the weft of lines parallel to the earth, verticals indicated the main lines of support. Interior and exterior flowed into one another to create an abstract design in space relationships. The integrity with which various materials were used and the functional plasticity of the parts provided the chief decoration." Among the outstanding examples of the Prairie-type house Wright built in and around Chicago during this decade are the Heurtley and Willitts houses (1902), the Isabel Roberts House (1908), and the Gale and Baker houses (1909). In the opinion of Sigfried Giedion, the Robie House in Chicago (1909) has had "perhaps the most far-reaching influence" of all Wright's works. The large Coonley House in Riverside (1908) is regarded by many critics as the culmination of this period, and Wright himself calls it "the most successful of my houses from my standpoint."

During these years Wright also designed two of his most famous nondomestic works: the Larkin Company's Administration Building in Buffalo (1904) and Unity Temple Church in Oak Park (1905-06). The former was the first office building in the United States to use metal-bound, plate-glass doors and windows; all-metal furniture; and air conditioning. Enclosed within a massive shell of severe brick walls, the interior of this structure was a large space five stories high surrounded by galleries, forming a great nave open to the skylight. In the latter building, Wright employed poured concrete for the first time in a monumental public edifice.

The year 1910 initiates a new phase in Wright's artistic development. It was then that a large portfolio of his work, *Ausgeführte Bauten und Entwürfe,* was published in Berlin; this monograph was the principal vehicle of his important influence on the younger generation of modern architects in Europe. Wright visited Europe for the first time in the spring of that year. On his return in 1911, he built a new house for himself, near Spring Green, which he called Taliesin ("shining brow" in Welsh). Built around a hilltop and constructed of native materials, Taliesin was designed to serve not only as a private residence, but also as a studio, a farm, and eventually as a school. The house was burned in 1914 and had to be rebuilt. In the meantime, Wright completed Midway Gardens (1913-14), a richly ornamented, open-air casino in Chicago, where he incorporated abstract sculptural and painted decorations as an integral part of the design. His most notable undertaking of this period, however, was for the Imperial Hotel in Tokyo (1915-22). This commission presented a difficult engineering problem, for the vast structure had to be made to withstand earthquakes. He solved the problem through a unique use of concrete supports cantilevered floors, and a foundation floating on a cushion of soft mud, and the hotel survived the disastrous earthquake of 1923 without damage. Between his trips to Japan, Wright worked on the Barnsdall House in Hollywood (1917-21), a poured-concrete house of almost monumental dimensions and character.

Early in the 1920's Wright developed a new method of construction, using precast concrete blocks threaded through with metal reinforcement. This system was employed in a series of houses he built in Southern California, of which the first and most representative was the Millard House in Pasadena (1923). During the latter half of the decade, Wright's fame was in eclipse and his personal fortunes at their lowest ebb. He received few commissions; the depression prevented the execution of several important projects; and some critics regarded his work as concluded. When Taliesin was again destroyed by fire in 1925, Wright exhausted his resources to rebuild it. The house fell into the hands of creditors, and he got it back only after a group of old clients and friends came to his assistance in 1929. Meanwhile, his first wife having granted him a divorce, in 1922 he married Miriam Noel, a sculptress. The marriage was dissolved in 1927. Wright devoted much of his time in the early 1930's to writing and lecturing. From this period dates his polemics against the so-called "International Style" of the European modernists, which was then being introduced into the United States, and he has continued to oppose his own "Organic Architecture" to what he considers the mechanistic and antidemocratic "negativities" of this European influence. In 1932 Wright organized the Taliesin Fellowship as a studio-workshop for apprentices (some 60 were participating in 1952), who pay to work with him and assist him with his commissions. At that time he also presented his answer to the evils of urbanization in the project for Broadacre City, a decentralized, self-contained community in which the distinction between town and country is obliterated.

With the revival of building activity in the mid-thirties, Wright designed two much publicized buildings that helped to re-establish his reputation in the United States and led to many subsequent commissions. One was the Kaufmann House, cantilevered over a waterfall at Bear Run, Pennsylvania (1936); many critics rank this as the most beautiful of all his houses. The other was the Administration Building for the S. C. Johnson and Son Company in Racine, Wisconsin (1936-39), with its streamlined exterior of brick walls broken only by horizontal bands of glass-tubing and its interior with the famous mushroom-shaped columns. In 1937 Wright built the first of his many recent "Usonian" homes—the Herbert Jacobs House, near Madison. "Usonia" is Wright's name for an ideal, democratic America, and these houses are the result of his researches into the problem of how to construct medium-sized homes at a moderate cost with the least expenditure of material and labor, and at the same time to retain the artistic excellence of his more expensive residences. The Taliesin Fellowship in 1938 began construction on Wright's winter headquarters, Taliesin West, near Phoenix, Arizona. This desert camp consists of a system of stone walls surmounted by exposed redwood trusses and canvas ceilings.

Since 1940 Wright's production has been more extensive and varied than at any time in his career. His largest recent commission is for the $10 million campus of Florida Southern College in Lakewood. The general plan dates from 1936; eight units had been constructed by 1952; and the whole group of sixteen buildings is scheduled for completion by 1960. Other notable works include the unconventional V. C. Morris gift shop in San Francisco (1949), with its bare brick front; the crescent-shaped Herbert Jacobs House II, near Madison (1942); and the circular Friedman House (1949-51), near Pleasantville, New York, in a cooperative community development known as Usonia Homes, for which Wright made the site plan. In 1950 the fifteen-story Research and Development Laboratory Wright designed for the Johnson Wax Company was completed. The floors of this round-cornered tower are cantilevered from a central core anchored to a concrete foundation that penetrates over fifty feet into the ground. Plans were filed with the city authorities in 1952 for Wright's first building in New York—the Solomon R. Guggenheim Memorial Museum on Fifth Avenue. This unprecedented concrete structure has the form of a spiral ramp to afford continuous gallery space.

"Of all present-day architects whose span of work reaches back into the 19th century," observed Sigfried Giedion (*Space, Time, and Architecture*), "Wright is without doubt the most farsighted, a genius of inexplicably rich and continuing vitality." According to Bruno Zevi (*Towards an Organic Architecture*), the principal elements in modern architecture for which Wright is responsible are "the space within as a reality"; the free plan; the organic

WRIGHT, FRANK LLOYD—*Continued*

growth of the house from interior to exterior; the blending of the house with its natural surroundings; the use of various building materials with respect for their inherent characteristics; and the problem of the house "as shelter." More important, he believes that Wright's historic contribution lies in the fact that "after the industrial revolution and the progress of engineering had driven architecture to take refuge in applied decoration," Wright "effected a completed artistic synthesis."

The architect has written a number of books, including *The Japanese Print* (1912); *Experimenting with Human Lives* (1923); *Modern Architecture* and *Two Lectures on Architecture* (1931); *An Autobiography* and *The Disappearing City* (1932); *Architecture and Modern Life* (1937, with Baker Brownell); *An Organic Architecture* (1939); *Selected Writings on Architecture* (1941, edited by Frederick Gutheim); *When Democracy Builds* (1945); and *Genius and Mobocracy* (1949). Awarded the Royal Gold Medal for Architecture by King George VI of England in 1941, he has also received the Gold Medal of the American Institute of Architects (1949), the Italian Star of Solidarity (1951), and the Gold Medal of the City of Florence (1951). Honorary degrees have been bestowed upon him by Wesleyan, Princeton, Florida Southern, and the University of Venice. Organizations in which he holds honorary membership include the Académie Royale des Beaux Arts of Antwerp; Akademie der Kunst in Berlin; Royal Institute of British Architects; and National Academies and architectural societies in Mexico, Portugal, Uruguay, Cuba, Brazil, and Finland. He is a member of the American Academy of Arts and Letters, National Academy of Design, American Institute of Decorators, and Phi Delta Theta. On August 25, 1928, Wright married his third and present wife, Olga Lazovich, of Montenegro, and they have one daughter, Iovanna. The architect stands five feet eight inches tall and has white hair and light gray eyes. A complete individualist by temperament, he has been variously described as a poet, a romantic philosopher, and a social reformer. He collects Oriental art, enjoys music, and plays the piano. "Give me the luxuries of life and I will willingly do without the necessities," has always been one of his favorite sayings.

References

Arch Forum 68:sup 1-102 Ja '38; 88: 65-155 Ja '48; 94:7-108 Ja '51
L'Architecture Francaise no 123-24 '52
Life 21:85-8 Ag 12 '46 pors
Time 31:29-32 Ja 17 '38 pors
Gutheim, F. ed. Frank Lloyd Wright on Architecture (1941)
Hitchcock, H. R. In the Nature of Materials (1942)
Hitchcock, H. R., & Johnson, P. Modern Architects (1932)
International Who's Who, 1952
Kaufmann, Edgar, Jr. Taliesin Drawings (1952)
National Cyclopædia of American Biography, Current vol D (1934)
Who's Who, 1952
Who's Who in America, 1952-53
Who's Who in Commerce and Industry (1951)
Who's Who in the Midwest (1952)
Wijdeveld, H. T. Life-Work of the American Architect Frank Lloyd Wright (1925)
Wright, F. L. An Autobiography (1943)
Wright, J. L. My Father Who Is On Earth (1946)
World Biography (1948)
Zevi, B. Frank Lloyd Wright (1947); Towards an Organic Architecture (1950)

WRISTON, HENRY M(ERRITT) July 4, 1889- University president

Address: b. c/o Brown University, Providence 12, R.I.; h. 55 Power St., Providence 6, R.I.

Henry M. Wriston became the eleventh president of Brown University in 1937, after twelve years as president of Lawrence College and, earlier, eleven years as instructor and professor at Wesleyan University. Among other positions of academic distinction held by Wriston were the Albert Shaw lectureship at Johns Hopkins University; the chief secretaryship of the Round Tables of the Institute of Politics, Williamstown, Massachusetts, and the presidency of the American Association of Universities.

Born on July 4, 1889, in Laramie, Wyoming, Henry Merritt Wriston, is one of two sons of Henry Lincoln Wriston, a Methodist minister from West Virginia who was a member of the first graduating class of the University of Denver. Jennie Amelia (Atcheson) Wriston, the daughter of a New York ship carpenter, as a child crossed the prairies in a covered wagon; before her marriage to the minister she had taught school. The boy was reared in New England, where the elder Wriston had assumed the pastorate of Asbury Methodist Church in Springfield, Massachusetts. After graduating in the class of 1907 from Central High School, Henry Wriston entered Wesleyan University in Connecticut. For four years a William Rice scholar, he majored in English literature, was editor of the *Wesleyan Argus*, and won the Briggs prize for debating. From Wesleyan he received his B.A. and M.A. degrees in 1911 and 1912, respectively.

At the end of three years' study at Harvard University, as a university scholar (1911-12) and later as an Austin teaching fellow (1912-14), Wriston joined the faculty of Wesleyan. He was advanced from instructor in history to associate professor in 1917 and to professor in 1919. Meanwhile, in 1918 he served as executive secretary of the $3 millions Wesleyan University Endowment Fund and in the same year as assistant manager of the Connecticut State Council of Defense, in which office he wrote the council's report. Taking a leave of absence from his duties at Wesleyan, Wriston engaged in research at Harvard and in the archives of the Department of State in Washington in the year 1920-21 to qualify for his Ph.D. degree in history at Harvard in 1922. During the following year (1923-24) he delivered the Albert Shaw Lectures on diplomatic history at Johns Hopkins University. These were later expanded and published in book form under the title of *Executive Agents in American Foreign Relations* (1929). From 1922 to 1926 he was chief secretary of the Round Tables conducted by the Institute of Politics, Williamstown, Massachusetts.

Dr. Wriston became the youngest college president in the United States when in 1925 he was installed as president of Lawrence College in Appleton, Wisconsin. In line with his policy of meeting the depression "in a head-on manner," Wriston raised Lawrence's standards for admission and increased the tuition on the strength of better facilities available. Among the first to present free educational opportunities to a qualified group of unemployed, Lawrence shared in a grant from the Federal Emergency Relief Administration. In an effort to bring industry closer to the educational scene, Wriston was instrumental in organizing, in 1929, the Institute of Paper Chemistry, financed by the paper industry through grants for education and research. From its founding until 1937 Wriston filled the office of director of the institute.

When Henry Wriston, a Methodist layman, succeeded the late Clarence Augustus Barbour in February 1937, he was the first non-Baptist to become president of Brown University and the third non-alumnus to fill this position. Brown University, the third oldest college in New England, is privately controlled. It was established by Baptists in 1764 as the Rhode Island College, located in Warren; in 1770 it was moved to Providence and its name was later changed to Brown University. The university now consists of three major subdivisions: the college (for undergraduate men), Pembroke (for undergraduate women, founded in 1891 as Women's College in Brown), and the graduate school (a coeducational division established in 1887). In the year 1949-50 the enrollment was 3,021 undergraduate men, 883 undergraduate women, and 525 students in the graduate school. During the years of Wriston's administration the university's endowment has been substantially increased and its facilities expanded. The Metcalf Research Laboratory has been completed; a new infirmary for men and a health center for women have been established; library resources have been enlarged; five dormitories, a new faculty club, faculty house, education buildings, and other property have been acquired; and a gift of $480,000 for the restoration of University Hall, the original college edifice, has been received. In 1946 a $10 millions housing and development project was started to enable Brown to offer its liberal arts facilities to a greater number of students. At the close of 1950 ten buildings were under construction in the contemplated expansion program which will double the value of Brown's physical plant.

Fabian Bachrach

HENRY M. WRISTON

Described as forthright in his views and dynamic as a speaker, Wriston has been quoted widely by the press in statements on educational and national affairs. As spokesman for Brown, Wriston joined other university presidents in 1945 in an effort to avoid overemphasis in intercollegiate football. Earlier, while president of Lawrence, he had made public statements against subsidies to football. In 1948 he recommended to the White House that no educational deferments be granted to potential draftees, but rather that the armed services assign servicemen to educational training; he also opposed in April 1951 a plan whereby students would be deferred from the draft on grounds of scholarship as setting up a wrong basis for determining who should go to college. Expressing his objection to the idea of Federal money for the country's colleges, Wriston maintained in 1948 that Government grants would destroy incentive; and the following year he stated that the demand of the House of Representatives for a list of textbooks used by institutions of higher learning imperiled the integrity of the democratic idea of higher education. Another example of Wriston's interest in public affairs is his membership in a group of scholars, business, and professional men who are studying "a new approach to the problem of restating of America's basic ideals in terms more understandable at home and abroad." On April 14, 1952, he served as moderator of the discussions on the moral and religious bases. (Several individuals, the Advertising Council of America, and the Ford Foundation are financing the project.)

A member of the editorial advisory board of *Foreign Affairs*, Wriston is also a frequent contributor to periodicals devoted to current events and education. Among his articles are "Academic Tenure," *American Association of University Professors Bulletin*, June 1941;

WRISTON, HENRY M.—*Continued*

"Why Not Try Freedom," *Harper's Magazine*, August 1943; "What Good Is a College Degree?" *American Magazine*, vacation number, 1947; "Brown University Curriculum," *Journal of Higher Education*, March 1948; "Outlook for the Independent College," *Association of American Colleges Bulletin*, May 1951. Two recent speeches delivered by Brown's President, "Education for Democracy" and "What Is It All About?" appear in *Vital Speeches* for July 15, 1950, and October 15, 1951, respectively. Wriston is also author of *War Chest Practice* (1918), *Nature of a Liberal College* (1937), *Prepare for Peace* (1941), *Challenge to Freedom* (1943), and *Strategy of Peace* (1944). In his review of *Challenge to Freedom* John Chamberlain of the New York *Times* observed, "Believing in an orbit of freedom within a framework of law, Dr. Wriston naturally attacks those who set 'security' or 'full employment' as overmastering goals. Dr. Wriston wants both security and full employment, but not at the expense of democracy or liberty."

During World War II Wriston served as chairman of the Citizens Emergency Committee on Nondefense Expenditure, president of the Rhode Island United Campaign of Community Chests, and vice-president of the National War Fund. He is a trustee of the World Peace Foundation and of the Carnegie Endowment for International Peace, and has been chairman of the educators committee of the United China Relief. Since 1933 he has been a trustee and member of the executive committee of the Carnegie Foundation for the Advancement of Teaching and completed a term on the executive committee of the American Council on Education. His election in November 1948 as president of the American Association of Universities made him the first individual to hold that office (from which he retired at the end of 1950), the presidency having previously been filled by institutions. Active in a number of other educational organizations, Wriston has also been president of the North Central Association of Colleges and Secondary Schools (1933-34) and of the Association of American Colleges (1935-36), vice-president of the American Association for Adult Education, chairman of the committee on the status of the liberal arts and sciences for the National Phi Beta Kappa Society, and a trustee of the Educational Records Bureau since 1939.

Wriston, who was a delegate in 1939 to the International Studies Conference in Bergen, Norway, has been associated with several organizations concerned with international relations: Fletcher School of Law and Diplomacy (member of the board of counselors, 1939-40), Council on Foreign Relations (president since October 1951), Diplomatic Affairs Foundation (member), American Society of International Law (member), Providence Committee on Foreign Relations (member), and World Affairs Council of Rhode Island (member of advisory committee). He has been a trustee of the American Federation of Arts, a fellow of the American Academy of Arts and Sciences; member of the College of Electors of the Hall of Fame, of the American Historical Association, the American Political Science Association, the Century Association, Rhode Island Historical Society, board of directors of Rhode Island Public Expenditure Council, and the Providence Art Club. In another field he is trustee of the Northwestern Mutual Life Insurance Company, a public governor of the New York State Exchange, and a member of the Corporation of the Providence Institution of Savings. Wriston has been a trustee of the Teachers Insurance and Annuity Association Stock since 1943 and was an incorporator of the recently established College Retirement Equities Fund. His Greek-letter societies are Phi Beta Kappa, Delta Sigma Rho, and Delta Tau Delta.

Honorary degrees that Wriston has received are: the LL.D. from Ripon College (1926), Wesleyan (1931), Tufts (1938), Rutgers (1940), Rhode Island State (1942), Lawrence (1944), Princeton (1946), Harvard (1949), New York (1950), Colgate (1950), Middlebury (1950), Providence (1950); the Litt.D. from Columbia (1937); and the L.H.D. degree from Wesleyan (1943) and Western Reserve (1950). In 1947 he was made honorary commander of the Order of the British Empire.

The blue-eyed, gray-haired educator is six feet tall and weighs 195 pounds. On June 6, 1914, Wriston married Ruth Colton Bigelow (now deceased), who became the mother of his two children, Barbara and Walter Bigelow. In June 1947 he married Marguerite Woodworth, dean of women at Oberlin College and previously dean of women at Lawrence College. In political alignment Wriston is a Republican—in April 1952 he announced his support of General Eisenhower as Presidential nominee. He names his recreations as swimming and photography; people who know him say that he is a competent critic of art and music.

References

St. Louis (Mo.) Post Dispatch p1+ S 13 '42
Time 28:54+ O 19 '36
Author's and Writer's Who's Who (1948-49)
Directory of American Scholars (1951)
Director of the American Political Science Association, 1948
Leaders in Education (1948)
Providence (R.I.) Journal & Bulletin Wriston of Brown (1951)
National Cyclopædia of American Biography Current vol F, 1939-42
Who's Who in America, 1950-51
Who's Who in New England (1949)
World Biography (1948)

YAMUT, NURI 1891- (yä-mōōt' nōō'rē) Turkish military leader

Address: b. c/o Office of the Chief of Staff, Ministry of Defense, Ankara, Republic of Turkey

As Chief of Staff in the Republic of Turkey, General Nuri Yamut commands armed forces which form a bastion of the North Atlantic Treaty Organization's defenses in the Near East. The veteran of a number of Turkish military campaigns, he was appointed to this post June 6, 1950, when he was promoted from his position as commander of the country's land forces. Emphasizing the need for modernization of equipment and tactics, Yamut has built an army, a navy, and an air force which have been ranked by some observers as equal to the best in Europe. Meetings in 1952 with General Dwight D. Eisenhower have enabled the Turkish Chief of Staff to coordinate the fighting plans of his 400,000-man military force with the comprehensive strategy of the Western powers.

Born in 1891 in Salonika, then held by Turkey, Nuri Yamut is the son of a grain merchant, Mahmut, and his wife Emire. He has a sister. At the Military College in Istanbul, which he attended after graduation from the Military High School in the same city, he became particularly interested in geography, geology, and archeology. His postgraduate study was undertaken at the Military Academy in Istanbul. At the time that Yamut was a student, the close ties betwen Germany and Turkey resulted in the influence of Prussian methods on the training of the Turkish Army. Enver Pasha, the Turkish commander in chief in 1914, had been schooled in Germany and had been deeply influenced by German ideas. Turkey entered World War I on the side of the Central Powers.

In that conflict Yamut saw service in various military theaters, including the Balkans, Dardanelles, Caucasus, Iraq, and Syria. The first major Turkish campaign in World War I was in the Caucasus, following Russia's declaration of war against Turkey on October 30, 1914. An invasion of Persia by Turkey was repulsed on January 30, 1915, and further Russian victories prevented the Sultan's forces from obtaining control of the Caspian oil fields. However, the Turkish Army, under the command of the German General von Sanders, inflicted severe losses upon the British and French at the Dardanelles, driving the invaders off the peninsula in December 1916, after more than a year of campaigning. Arabia, then a Turkish province, was also the scene of action: a British army under Townsend was forced to surrender on April 29, 1916, but a second English expedition pushed up the Tigris River, capturing Bagdad on March 11, 1917. The loss of Syria and Palestine began with the fall of Gaza, after which the British gained victories at Jaffa and Jerusalem.

Yamut, who had risen in rank to the post of commander of the army, was chosen on June 6, 1950, to replace Colonel General Abdur Rahman Nafiz Gurman as Chief of Staff. General Yamut's advancement occurred shortly after the candidate of the Democratic party, Celâl Bayar, was elected on May 22, 1950, to the presidency of the republic, defeating the former president, Ismet Inönü, who represented the Republican People's party. The latter organization had been the party of Kemal Atatürk, former dictator, modernizer, and national

GEN. NURI YAMUT

hero of Turkey. In the words of *Time* (February 16, 1951) General Yamut "was upped from command of the Turkish land forces when a bevy of high-ranking generals was retired for being overage, overweight, or overzealous in their support of Republican Inönü."

As Chief of the General Staff, Yamut is a member of the Supreme Council of National Defence. This body was created by the Grand National Assembly of Turkey in June 1949, when the armed forces were reorganized. The other members of this council are the heads of the economic ministries, the Minister of National Defense, and the Prime Minister, who acts as chairman. The purpose of the council is to mobilize the country's resources in the event of hostilities. Yamut heads land, air, and naval forces which are available for training an average of 175,000 men every year. Youths are called up for two years at the age of twenty, and for three years under extraordinary circumstances. One of the aims of the new Chief of Staff is to eliminate the German methods of training soldiers which had become traditional in the Turkish military forces.

In 1951 the United States, France, Great Britain, and Turkey established a four-power Middle East defense command, with Turkey as the keystone. The vital strategic significance of Turkey was pointed out by Karl Marx one hundred years ago: "Let Russia get possession of Turkey and her strength is increased nearly half and she becomes superior to all the rest of Europe put together. Such an event would be an unspeakable calamity to the Western cause." Western observers still regard this opinion valid. Turkey has fought the Russians thirteen times in the past four hundred years; and since November 7, 1945, when Russia ended a treaty of neutrality, nonaggression and international cooperation between the two countries, no new agreement has been worked out.

(Continued next page)

YAMUT, NURI—*Continued*

The United States has allocated large funds to the building up of Turkey's armed forces, funds which in the opinion of former Defense Secretary Marshall, "brought larger returns than received from any similar venture." When Yamut's country became a full member in the North Atlantic Treaty Organization in 1951, she had received more than $350 millions in military aid. Since Turkey prefers regular NATO membership to being part of a separate Balkan command, Yamut strongly approved the action of Greece and Turkey in entering the treaty organization.

The General, as quoted by the New York *World-Telegram*, envisages the Soviet strategy in the event of war as follows: "First would be an attack toward Europe, on the west. Second would be a move to invade the Middle Eastern area between the Black and Caspian Seas." To meet a future crisis the Chief of Staff of the Republic of Turkey commands forces with all modern equipment, including motorized infantry, tanks, tank destroyers, antiaircraft batteries, and heavy artillery. According to the *Statesman's Year Book* (1951) Turkey's army has twenty-two infantry units, as well as six armoured and three cavalry units. The air force has about 750 planes, World War II models which are being converted into jets, and the navy comprises two cruisers, eight destroyers, eleven submarines, twenty-four minesweepers, along with other auxiliaries. Yamut has about 400,000 men under his command, of which approximately 360,000 are in the army, with 20,000 each in the naval and air forces. Another 600,000 men who have ended military service within the last six years are also available. Visiting American press correspondents stated in the fall of 1951 that Turkish forces appeared in a "most favorable light," creating a "much better impression" than either the French or Italian troops.

General Yamut has said that the Russians will run into "supermen" if they invade his country. The United States assists Turkey by maintaining near Ankara the Joint American Military Mission for Aid to Turkey, with a staff of 1,250 personnel headed by Major General William H. Arnold. General Yamut participated in conferences with General Eisenhower on March 3, 1952, in Ankara and on April 4, 1952, in Paris on problems relating to Turkey's role in the event of an invasion.

In 1951 Yamut was awarded the United States Legion of Merit (degree of Commander) for "outstanding service in contributing to the successful mission of the United Nations in the struggle for freedom." Presented at ceremonies in Ankara by Major General Arnold, the medal was accompanied by a citation by President Truman, which stressed General Yamut's "wholehearted cooperation, professional ability, and devotion to the cause of freedom."

Nuri Yamut, a Moslem, married Cavidan Yamut in 1924. They have one daughter, Güsfent Sahingiray, who is married. Military clubs comprise his club memberships. His favorite sports are football, wrestling, and horseback riding. He has blue eyes and light hair, and, of stocky build, has a height of five feet eight inches and a weight of 162 pounds.

YOUNG, MARIAN Nov. 21, 1909- Radio commentator

Address: b. c/o Martha Deane, WOR Radio Station, Mutual Broadcasting System, Inc., 1440 Broadway, New York 18

Marian Young has been broadcasting since 1941 as radio's Martha Deane on New York's Station WOR of the Mutual Broadcasting System. Drawing on her background as a former women's editor and foreign correspondent, she presents a daily-except-Sunday morning comment and interview program heard in nine States, which has three times brought her the Ohio State University Education by Radio Institute award as "the best woman commentator" on the air. Of some 850 women radio commentators Miss Young has been described as representing "the ultimate to those in her profession" (*Newsweek*) by reason of her high income and her large listener response. In private life she is Mrs. William Bolling Taylor.

One of the two daughters of Edwin Young and the late Mary Elizabeth (Zuber) Young, Marian Young was born November 21, 1909, in Star Lake, New York, about thirty miles from the Canadian border, where her father was a silver fox rancher. (Both girls were to become radio personalities: Marian Young's sister, Dorothy Parr, is the Harriette of *Harriette Meets the Ladies* on station WWNY in Watertown, New York.) Marian attended high school in the larger community of Gouverneur, New York, where she played basketball. After being graduated in 1925 she attended St. Lawrence University in Canton, New York, for two years, majoring in English. To earn money for an attempt at a journalistic career she returned to her home town to teach in a one-room country school for a year (1928-29) and "loved it." Her twenty-six pupils were distributed among eight grades and an algebra class.

Going to New York in 1930, she took a job as a switchboard operator with the Newspaper Enterprise Association (NEA), the Scripps-Howard feature syndicate. She resigned after six months, three months later returned to the NEA as assistant to the women's editor, and in 1934 became women's editor. For four of the eleven years she was to remain with NEA she served as foreign correspondent. Her first assignment abroad was to Nazi Germany in 1935, for an account of the youth program and of women under the Hitler regime. To obtain material for part of that article she spent a month living in a German women's farm labor camp; she was also the only reporter ever given an interview by Magda Goebbels (the wife of Joseph Goebbels), and the only woman present in the Reichstag the morning in March 1937 on which Hitler announced that his troops had invaded the Rhineland.

While women's editor of NEA she won the 1937 New York Newspaper Women's Award

for the consistently best column in a specialized
women's field—a beauty column she wrote under the name Alicia Hart. Not a home economist ("although I don't underrate domestic
science—it's just not my field"), as editor Miss
Young sought the "good story," giving space
to food or fashion items on the basis of news
interest; her test was whether the story would
interest a man as well as a woman. Magazine
articles she wrote in this period appeared
largely in *Everyweek*, a Scripps-Howard Sunday newspaper supplement. She also taught
evening courses in journalism from 1935 to 1937
at Centenary Junior College in Hackettstown,
New Jersey, and from 1939 to 1941 was employed as merchandising consultant for Krene,
at that time a plastic material manufactured by
the National Carbon Company.

When Miss Young in 1941 returned to New
York from a trip to Nassau, where on a routine NEA assignment she had interviewed the
Duke and Duchess of Windsor, she was asked
by radio station WOR whether she would like
to make an audition record for its program
known as *Martha Deane*. She was on the air
a week later; and for twelve weeks held two
positions simultaneously, training a new wom-
en's editor for NEA most of the day and at
night preparing the *Martha Deane* afternoon
broadcast. Her two predecessors had been
Mary Margaret McBride, the first Martha
Deane, and Bessie Beatty, who moved to a
morning broadcast under her own name. Four
years later, when Miss Beatty died, the program was moved from its afternoon spot to
what had been Miss Beatty's morning time,
10:15 to 11 o'clock daily, except Sunday. At
the time of the change, for three weeks Miss
Young broadcast mornings and afternoons, interviewing two guests each day.

From the beginning Miss Young conceived
of her program as built around news, dealing
with topics broadly political or social in nature
as well as the so-called "women's interests."
"There's hardly a 'controversial' issue that
Marian Young . . . is afraid to tackle and in
vigorously liberal fashion, too," a *PM* writer
noted in May 1945. About 40 per cent of the
program is devoted to Miss Young's comments
and her commercial announcements for twelve
sponsors; the rest is given over to the interview. Guests have been authors, educators,
scientists, statesmen, admirals, generals, and
ambassadors, as well as personalities in the
field of entertainment and specialists in food
and fashion. Herbert Lehman, John Foster
Dulles, and Harold Stassen have appeared, as
have Margaret Mead, James Stewart, and
Christian Dior. A 1951 series of interviews,
"Why We Behave As We Do," with social
scientists, psychiatrists, and philosophers brought
the largest mail response. Another 1951 series
was "What is Woman's Place?" Miss Young
believes her listeners are interested most in
human relations—"how to get along with one
another." As for the "woman's angle," Miss
Young maintains that it does not exist: "A
story is either good or it isn't—there's no sex
in brains, intelligence, perception."

MARIAN YOUNG

Martha Deane received the Ohio State University Education by Radio Institute award
for the first time in 1944, for "stimulating
presentation of ideas and information" and
again in 1948 and 1949. The 1949 citation commended her "interesting and mature presentation
which astutely blends educational and entertainment values." Earlier, in 1942, radio editors of the United States and Canada, polled
by *Motion Picture Daily*, named the program
"the best in the women's field." Her radio
pleas for CARE brought that organization
$32,000 for packages for European orphanages,
the most successful CARE collection on record
at that time. Further evidence of the success
of her program came from WOR, which in
1950 announced that in nine years she had
brought the station $3,000,000 in gross business.
At that time Martha Dean, who reserves the
right to refuse to advertise products about
which she feels she cannot talk with honest
enthusiasm, had twelve sponsors, who were paying "the highest rate in the field," *Newsweek*
noted.

To prepare for her program Miss Young
reads six newspapers a day, about six books
a week, and many magazines, and sees important plays and motion pictures. She pays
the salaries of the six people on her staff; she
does not employ a manager or a press agent.
Occasionally she calls on a "Listeners' Panel,"
which is composed of members of local women's
clubs and civic organizations, for round-table
discussion programs. Guided by notes rather
than by a regular script, her own comment is
largely extemporaneous in style. She has said
that she refuses to live "hectically," but depends on her capacity to work anywhere (buses
and airplanes she finds conducive to concentration), to "catnap" any time, to put off for tomorrow what cannot be readily done today.
When her children were born, WOR allowed

YOUNG, MARIAN—*Continued*

her to record for broadcast by transcription her Friday and Saturday shows. Miss Young has pointed out that she is "her own boss," has never had difficulties with either the station management or her sponsors.

The radio commentor calls hers the "ideal job for a woman," since it permits her to work at home much of the time. She was married on March 6, 1937, to William Bolling Taylor, who in 1951 resigned from his position as executive with William Esty advertising company to raise beef cattle in Florida. Their twins, William Bolling, Jr., and Marian Nicole, were born on New Year's Eve of 1943. When the birth was announced on her program, listeners sent many gifts, including 248 pairs of bootees. The family lives in Florida four months a year, Miss Young often commuting from New York for weekends, and in Shelter Island, New York, the other eight months. Her church is the Presbyterian.

Miss Young, who stands five feet six and one half inches tall and weighs 130 pounds, has red-brown hair and brown eyes. Her voice has been called "calm, yet extremely alive." She dislikes "personal appearances" and does not think of herself as a celebrity—"I'd say I was a reporter with a good radio job."

References

N Y Times p9-11 Ag 26 '51
Newsweek 35:44 Je 26 '50 por
Who's Who in America, 1952-53
Who's Who in the East (1951)

YOUNG, NANCY WILSON ROSS *See* Ross, N. W.

ZALDÍVAR, FULGENCIO BATISTA Y
See Batista y Zaldívar, F

ZECKENDORF, WILLIAM June 30, 1905
Business executive

Address: b. c/o Webb & Knapp, Inc., 383 Madison Ave., New York 17; h. 30 E. 72d St., New York 21

Webb & Knapp, Inc., New York real estate firm which handles property all over the United States as well as in Canada, Mexico, and England, is headed by William Zeckendorf. The highly diversified holdings of his company and its extension of its practice into allied fields are the results of policies launched by Zeckendorf. His most widely known negotiation is perhaps the New York area sold to John D. Rockefeller, Jr., who presented it to the United Nations. Zeckendorf's name has also been associated with plans for urban development—such as rooftop airports, garages, and apartment buildings constructed on new principles—and with plans for a revision of real estate financing practice.

William Zeckendorf was born June 30, 1905, to Arthur William and Byrd (Rosenfield) Zeckendorf in Paris, Illinois, where his father

was then operating a general store. His paternal grandfather, with four merchant brothers, had come to the United States from Germany at the time of the 1848 revolution. When William was three years old the family moved to Long Island, New York, where Arthur Zeckendorf went into the shoe business. After the family settled in Manhattan about ten years later, the youth attended De Witt Clinton High School. From 1922 to 1925 he was a student at New York University, where he joined the varsity football team, playing the position of guard during his sophomore and junior years. "Having found the academic life unappealing," wrote E. J. Kahn, Jr., in the *New Yorker*, Zeckendorf left at the end of the third year.

The young man now obtained a position with an uncle, Samuel Bochard, a real estate agent, who placed Zeckendorf in his firm as assistant purchasing agent and as manager of an office building on lower Broadway. Within a year Zeckendorf had succeeded in renting all except two of the offices of the many that were available when he took over the management. Zeckendorf then suggested to Leonard S. Gans, a general real estate broker, that he establish a management department in his concern, which Zeckendorf headed from October to December 1926; he next persuaded Gans to allow him to act as a broker. It was nearly a year later that he completed his first sale, an East Side hotel. At the age of twenty-five, in 1930 Zeckendorf handled the three-million-dollar sale of a West Side property which resulted in the building of a large, fashionable apartment house, netting him a $21,000 commission. That year Gans took him into partnership, an association which lasted nearly nine years.

As a broker, Zeckendorf in 1937 had taken part in the sale of a New York office building for the firm of Webb & Knapp, a real estate concern founded in 1922 and housed in its own building at 383 Madison Avenue. At the time that Zeckendorf was invited to join the company in 1938, Webb & Knapp controlled, owned, or managed about fifty million dollars' worth of property, in New York and elsewhere. A relatively conservative firm, it began to expand considerably when Zeckendorf brought the influence of his ideas to bear. In May 1947 Zeckendorf became its president, while partner John H. P. Gould became chairman of its board. Two years later, Zeckendorf found himself in a position (partly "by extensive borrowing," wrote E. J. Kahn, Jr.) to buy out his partners for six million dollars in cash and collateral and thus become sole stockholder. Under his initiative, Webb & Knapp's holdings had increased to a reported hundred million dollars—including office buildings, stores, an Idaho jail, a New Jersey railroad, hotels, warehouses, nightclubs, factories, oilwells, airports, supermarkets, and undeveloped tracts—acquired through deals in thirty-five States, in Canada, Mexico, and England. Each permanent project handled by Webb & Knapp, *Time* reported, is separately financed, since Zeckendorf does not believe in financial pyramids. Robert Sellmer, of *Life*, said in 1946 that Webb & Knapp has come to function "not only as broker, but consultant, manager, designer, builder, agent, and principal."

Zeckendorf, who had previously retained Wallace Harrison, Le Corbusier, and William Lescaze as architectural consultants, in 1949 engaged I. M. Pei, assistant professor of architecture at Harvard, to head Webb & Knapp's heretofore small architectural department. Among other innovations he introduced were the installation of a public relations office and the production of a Kodachrome film about Webb & Knapp operations for distribution to civic and other groups. Clients for whom Zeckendorf has handled negotiations have included Allied Stores, Gimbel's, Macy's, Montgomery Ward, Time, Inc., Walgreen's, Woolworth's, the Guaranty Trust Company, the Israeli Government, the Rockefeller family, and the New York Philharmonic-Symphony Society. "What I like to do," Zeckendorf told writer Kahn, "is to recognize a great piece of land and conceive a suitable edifice for it. . . . I usually estimate the value of properties by checking factors like the ratio between the real estate taxes on them and their gross rent potentials." A commentary on this came from Charles F. Noyes, another realtor: "Zeckendorf has no equal in the perception of potential values in property."

In 1942 Zeckendorf was suggested to Vincent Astor as capable of handling the $50,000,000 portfolio of the Astor Estate while Astor was in the Navy. Through 150 separate negotiations made between then and early 1946, Zeckendorf sold a number of parcels of real estate traditionally held—at a loss—by the Astors in the New York area and began the nation-wide expansion of Astor holdings. By eliminating the profitless items, Zeckendorf succeeded in adding $5,000,000 of assets to Astor's estate. In the first year alone of handling this account, Zeckendorf received $400,000 in commissions for it.

During much of this same period, 1941-46, Zeckendorf was engaged in assembling a number of real estate parcels in the downtown area of Flushing, Long Island, on which he hoped to see erected a shopping center, hospital, underground walks, and a hotel. Although the Metropolitan Life Insurance Company had invested an initial $2,000,000 in this project, Zeckendorf was unable to obtain condemnation and acquisition of a key small area, so that the final project was limited to an $8,000,000 shopping district (yet to be constructed). Toward the end of 1946, in September, Webb & Knapp bought a large section of the Hoboken (New Jersey) waterfront for $8,000,000, thus acquiring warehouses, piers, buildings, and a railway. Part of these were sold shortly afterward for the same price as the whole original had cost, while Webb & Knapp retained the railroad and warehouses.

Zeckendorf's eye for the potentialities of property led him, early in 1946, to buy a large piece of land in midtown New York on the East River, then occupied by slaughterhouses and old tenements. Paying about seventeen dollars a square foot, or a total of slightly more than $6,000,000 for the eight acres, he obtained

Fabian Bachrach

WILLIAM ZECKENDORF

title to an area on which he proposed to construct a $150,000,000 "X City" (described in *Life,* October 28, 1946), consisting of an office building, opera house, convention hall, hotel, concert hall, and yacht and helicopter landings. Shortly afterward, upon hearing that Mayor O'Dwyer of New York was eager to bring the United Nations headquarters to that city, Zeckendorf offered the use of his site, "at any price the U.N. was willing to pay," said the New York *Herald Tribune.* Wallace K. Harrison, U.N. architect, signed the option for the land, and it was bought by John D. Rockefeller as a gift to the U.N. Rockefeller's purchase price of $8,500,000 allowed Zeckendorf and Webb & Knapp to realize approximately $2,000,000 on the transaction. At the time he purchased the area, Zeckendorf had also begun to acquire surrounding land at prices between five and nine dollars a square foot, part of which he offered to the city for use as an approach to the United Nations site. The necessity for condemning this six-block area, however, was not approved by the city.

In 1947 Zeckendorf expended $3,000,000 for a twelve-thousand-acre tract just within the city limits of Los Angeles, California, on which he hopes eventually to see constructed a large residential development. For a midtown Los Angeles parcel he owns, Zeckendorf projects the building of a sixty-eight-acre shopping center "in the tradition of both the Greek agora and the Chinese market place," designed by Pei. Another of Zeckendorf's California holdings is the summit of San Francisco's Nob Hill, where someday will be built the spiral apartment house evolved in 1949 on Pei's drawing board, the "Helix," in which what *Newsweek* has called "pie-shaped" apartments spread outward to the periphery of the building from a central utilities core.

(Continued next page)

ZECKENDORF, WILLIAM—*Continued*

Possibilities of unused New York property have been recognized by Zeckendorf in several other instances, among them an old riding academy and a boxing arena which were subsequently sold for television studios; and potentialities of Long Island's old Roosevelt Air Field as an "industrial estate"—similar to those in England—which Zeckendorf bought in 1950, because of its proximity to the large residential area of Levittown. The following year he announced plans for the extension of the campus of Long Island University (he is president of the board of trustees), in accordance with a plan developed by Webb & Knapp.

Zeckendorf, who believes "that cities will eventually strangle themselves through unregulated growth," has frequently suggested revolutionary ideas to forestall such conditions. One idea is a rooftop airport project to be built on a fifty-block stretch along the Hudson River; another is a plan for an automatic garage. His concern for New York has been voiced in a 1946 speech to the New York Chapter of the American Institute of Real Estate Appraisers, in interviews with the New York *Star* (August 29, 1948) and the New York *Post* (December 5, 1946), and in two talks delivered at the Harvard School of Design in 1951. Recorded on tape and expanded for publication in the *Atlantic Monthly*, "New Cities for Old" and "Baked Buildings" contain Zeckendorf's pleas for a new approach to city planning and for liberalization of investment capital to permit these new building and planning ideas to be put into effect.

In another move to integrate all phases of his firm's operations, Zeckendorf announced on February 23, 1952, the establishment of the Webb & Knapp Construction Corporation, a wholly owned subsidiary, for the purpose of acting as general contractors on its own developments and in some instances on the projects of others. Zeckendorf is chairman of the board of the new unit. In another business affiliation he is president of the Hoboken Railroad Warehouse and Steamship Connecting Company. He holds memberships in the Real Estate Committee of New York City and the Real Estate Board of New York; and directorates in the First Avenue Association, the Thirty-Fourth Street Midtown Association, the Manhattan Hospital, and the American Broadcasting Company. He is also a member of the Mayor's Business Men's Advisory Committee and of the War Memorial Association. In 1951 he was named an Honorary Deputy Commissioner of Commerce by New York's Mayor Impellitteri. Early in 1952 he served as chairman of the New York Heart Association's fund-raising campaign. His fraternity is Phi Lambda Phi. When questioned about his political affiliation, Zeckendorf replied, "I vote both ways." In religious faith he is Jewish.

By his marriage, on September 20, 1928, to Irma Levy, William Zeckendorf is the father of two children, William 3d and Susan. This marriage was terminated by divorce in 1934. Zeckendorf was married a second time, on December 10, 1941, to Marion Griffin, who,

reported *Life*, "assists at the birth of nearly all his projects." They live in a penthouse, where Zeckendorf is able to garden on the terrace. Four or five times a year the Zeckendorfs go abroad—he takes pleasure in air travel. He also enjoys "superlative" cooking. About six feet tall, he has a weight of 250 pounds. *Life* has said that "banks and insurance companies consider Zeckendorf's word as good as a signed contract."

References

Bsns W p28+ Ag 16 '47
Fortune 33:218 Ap '46
Life 21:67-70+ O 28 '46
N Y Post Mag p57 D 5 '46
New Yorker 27:46+ D 8 '51; 41+ D 15 '51
Newsweek 32:61 S 6 '48
Who's Who in America, 1950-51

ZUCKERT, EUGENE M. Nov. 9, 1911-

United States Government official; lawyer

Address: b. c/o United States Atomic Energy Commission, 19th St. & Constitution Ave., N.W., Washington 25, D.C.; h. 141 Hesketh St., Chevy Chase, Md.; 1499 Hope St., Stamford, Conn.

Eugene M. Zuckert was appointed to the Atomic Energy Commission by President Harry S. Truman on January 21, 1952, to fill the unexpired term of Sumner T. Pike. Zuckert had been Assistant Secretary of the United States Air Force since that branch of the armed forces became coequal with the Army and Navy in 1947. After three years (1937-40) in his first Federal position, as an attorney for the Securities and Exchange Commission, the Yale Law School graduate became teacher and administrator at Harvard University, where during part of World War II he also served as consultant to the Army Air Force and an instructor of an Air Force school conducted at the university.

Born in New York City on November 9, 1911, Eugene M. Zuckert is the son of Harry M. Zuckert, who maintains a law practice there, and of Eugenie Adrienne (Pincoffs) Zuckert. He attended grammar and high school in New York suburbs and the Salisbury (Connecticut) preparatory school, where his roommate was Mennen Williams, now Governor of Michigan. For undergraduate study he enrolled at Yale University, where he edited the sports section of the *Yale Daily News*. Upon receiving the B.A. degree in 1933 he enrolled at the Yale Law School for an experimental course sponsored by William O. Douglas, now a member of the United States Supreme Court, which was designed to give the law student a better knowledge of the business problems of his future clients. The course consisted of one year of study at the Yale Law School, one year at the Harvard Graduate School of Business Administration, and the final two years at Yale with several courses taught by the Harvard Business School faculty. Zuckert was assistant director and then director of the Yale Moot Court during his last two years of study. In 1937 he received his LL.B. degree and a certificate of completion of the combined law-business course.

A member of the bar of New York and of Connecticut, Zuckert has practiced law in both States when he has not been occupied by public duties. His first Government appointment, in 1937, was as attorney for the United States Securities and Exchange Commission, which had been established three years earlier to "protect the interests of the public and investors against malpractices in the securities and financial markets." The young lawyer served the agency in New York and Washington, D.C., for three years. Joining the faculty of the Harvard Graduate School of Business Administration in 1940 as an instructor in the relations of government and business, he advanced during a four-year association with the school to assistant professor and later to assistant dean. A newly instituted advanced management course, administered by Zuckert, was the subject of an article in *Fortune* (December 1943), which stressed the value of the training given in this class to industry whose administrative ranks were depleted by the war and whose production was complicated by government contracts and wartime exigencies. During the same years (1940-44) Zuckert, as a special statistical consultant to the commanding general of the United States Army Air Force, was assigned to various Air Force bases in the United States. He also taught in the Army Air Force statistical control school, conducted at Harvard, in which over 3,000 Air Force officers were trained in business practices and administration.

In 1944 Zuckert went to the Office of the Chief of Naval Operations in Washington, where for a year he worked on the Navy's inventory control plan with the rating of lieutenant (junior grade) in the United States Naval Reserve. After being relieved of this duty, in September 1945, he took the post of executive assistant to W. Stuart Symington, head of the Surplus Property Administration. When Symington became Assistant Secretary of War for Air in February 1946, he named Zuckert as his special assistant.

Following the passage of the National Security Act, which in September 1947 established the Air Force as an independent unit of the armed forces, Symington was named first Secretary of the Air Force and Zuckert and Cornelius Vanderbilt Whitney were appointed Assistant Secretaries. In his assignment to the management aspects of the new force, Zuckert was called upon to supervise the military and civilian personnel policies, the long-range plan for the reserve forces, the financial management program, and the contract financing program, and worked on the development of the organizational policies of the Air Force. It was also his responsibility to develop the comptroller system in the Air Force, which was the first of the three services to have a comptroller. This innovation in a military organization was later enacted into law for all three services as a result of the Hoover Commission amendments to the National Security Act. His con-

Air Force Photo.

EUGENE M. ZUCKERT

tribution to the development of the performance-type budget, he has said, was "to steer it over some of the hurdles prior to its being accepted." His own evaluation of his position in the Air Force has been quoted as "a combination of part coach and part blocking back."

Zuckert's period of service in the Air Force has been in what he himself has described as "tumultuous" years, "with changes up and down, cut-backs, and expansions of program." "We are faced with the problem of building a large-scale, atomic-age war machine," Zuckert said in 1951, "while, at the same time, maintaining a strong civilian economy, and the tax revenues it produces to pay the tremendous military bills." Speaking in the House of Representatives on March 12, 1951, Congressman Leo E. Allen of Illinois said, "There are few men in Government who—because of their innate ability, character, and integrity—merit the confidence of this Congress more than does Eugene Zuckert, Assistant Secretary of Air." During his term of office, Zuckert served as the Air Force representative on the management committee, the munitions board, and the personnel policy board of the Department of Defense. In 1948 he was a member of the Commission for Unified Court-Martial Procedure established by James V. Forrestal, then Secretary of Defense.

Simultaneous with an announcement of an expansion of atomic energy facilities was President Truman's nomination of Zuckert to the Atomic Energy Commission on January 21, 1952. As provided for in the Atomic Energy Act of 1946, this five-man board, appointed by the President with the advice and consent of the Senate, has five major responsibilities: a program of "assisting and fostering" private research in the atomic field; a program for control of scientific and technical information; a program of federally conducted research and

ZUCKERT, EUGENE M.—*Continued*

development; a program for "government control of the production, ownership, and use of fissionable material"; and a program of administration (*United States Government Organization Manual*). Operations supervised by the Commission are conducted partly by industrial concerns and private and public institutions under contract, partly at the facilities owned by the Commission. Primarily production is carried on at the Commission's facilities at Oak Ridge, Tennessee, at Hanford, Washington, at Paducah, Kentucky, and at Aiken, South Carolina. Major research and development facilities are at Oak Ridge, Los Alamos, the Argonne National Laboratory at Chicago, the Brookhaven National Laboratory at Upton, Long Island, and the Knolls Atomic Power Laboratory at Schenectady, New York. The proposed expanded program of the Commission calls for a total expenditure for the fiscal year ending June 30, 1952, of $1.725 billions.

Zuckert was sworn into office on February 25, 1952, after his nomination to the Commission had been approved by the Senate earlier in the month. His term, which he fills in place of Sumner T. Pike, who resigned from the Commission, will run until June 30, 1954. The Washington *Post* commented editorially: "A great deal of logic supports President Truman's choice of Eugene M. Zuckert . . . as a member of the Atomic Energy Commission,"

and George Zielke, Washington correspondent of the Toledo *Blade,* called it one of "a series of appointments far removed from what is commonly called the realm of practical politics."

While teaching at Harvard University Zuckert was the author of publications on the subjects of venture capital and indemnification of corporate directors. He retains his connection with the Harvard Graduate School of Business Administration as a member of its executive council. He belongs to the Beta Theta Pi law fraternity. On June 24, 1938, he married Kathleen Barnes, who died in January 1945; they had two children, Kathleen and Robert Barnes. Married a second time, on May 5, 1945, to Barbara E. Jackman, he has another daughter, Gene Prentiss. The Commissioner has been described as a "friendly but quiet and self-effacing man" who "dresses and looks the part of a young banker." He is five feet, seven and a half inches tall, "balding, graying." Among his recreations is golf. He is a Democrat and names his church affiliation as Episcopal. His slogan, and avowed goal as a public administrator, is, "Be objective."

References

Chem & Eng N 30:3276 Ag 11 '52 por
N Y Times p26 Ja 22 '52
Toledo (Ohio) Blade Ja 26 '52
American Men in Government (1949)
Who's Who in America, 1950-51
World Biography (1948)

CORRECTION: page 209. The statement was made in error that Don Gehrmann competed in the 1952 Olympics in Helsinki. The section of the Yearbook containing this page was already on the press when information was received that the only Olympic game in which Gehrmann has competed thus far was the one held in London in 1948.

BIOGRAPHICAL REFERENCES CONSULTED

The publication dates listed are those of volumes in CURRENT BIOGRAPHY's reference collection.

American Catholic Who's Who, 1952-53
American Medical Directory, 1950
American Men in Government (1949)
American Men of Science (1949)
American Women, 1939-40
America's Young Men, 1938-39
ASCAP Biographical Dictionary of Composers, Authors, and Publishers (1952)
Author's and Writer's Who's Who (1948-49)

Baker, T. ed. Biographical Dictionary of Musicians (1940)
Baseball Register (1952)
Biographical Directory of the American Congress, 1774-1949 (1950)
Blue Book of American Aviation (1942)
British Film Annual, 1949
Burke's Peerage (1949)
Business Executives of America (1950)

Canadian Who's Who, 1949-51
Catholic Who's Who, 1952
Chemical Who's Who, 1951
Chi è? (1948)
Congressional Directory (1951)

Dictionnaire Biographique des Artistes Contemporains, 1910-30
Dictionnaire Biographique Français Contemporain (1950)
Dictionnaire de Biographie Française (1933-)
Dictionnaire National des Contemporains (1936)
Directory of American Scholars (1951)
Directory of Medical Specialists (1949)
Directory of Medical Women, 1949
Directory of the American Political Science Association, 1948

Ewen, D. ed. Composers of Today (1936); Living Musicians (1940); Men and Women Who Make Music (1949)

Grove, G. Dictionary of Music and Musicians (1927-28); Suppl vol (1940)

Hoehn, M. ed. Catholic Authors (1947)
Hvem er Hvem? (1950)

Indian and Pakistan Year Book and Who's Who, 1948
International Motion Picture Almanac, 1952-53
International Press Who's Who: New Zealand, 1938
International Who's Who, 1952
International Who's Who in World Medicine, 1947
International World Who's Who (1949)
Italian-American Who's Who (1946)

Japan Who's Who, 1950

Kelly's Handbook to the Titled, Landed, and Official Classes, 1951
Kraks Blaa Bog (1949)
Kunitz, S. J., and Haycraft, H. eds. Junior Book of Authors (1951); Twentieth Century Authors (1942)

Leaders in Education (1948)

Musicians' International Directory and Biographical Record (1949-50)

Nalanda Yearbook and Who's Who in India and Pakistan, 1950-51
National Cyclopædia of American Biography Current Volumes A-G (1926-46)
Near and Middle East Who's Who, 1945-46
Nobel Prize Winners (1938)

Prominent Personalities in American Methodism (1945)

Quem é Alguém (1947)

Religious Leaders of America, 1941-42

Salter, J. T. ed. Public Men in and Out of Office (1946)
Slavonic Encyclopaedia (1949)
South African Who's Who, 1949

Thompson, O. ed. International Cyclopedia of Music and Musicians (1949)

Universal Jewish Encyclopedia (1948)

Variety Radio Directory, 1940-41
Vem är Det, 1949
Vem och Vad, 1948

Webster's Biographical Dictionary (1951)
Wer ist Wer? (1948)
Wer ist's? (1935)
Who's Who, 1952
Who Knows—and What (1949)
Who's Important in Medicine, 1945
Who's Who, 1952
Who's Who in Alaska, 1947
Who's Who in America, 1952-53
Who's Who in American Art, 1940-47
Who's Who in American Education, 1947-48
Who's Who in American Jewry, 1938-39
Who's Who in Australia, 1950
Who's Who in Aviation, 1942-43
Who's Who In Canada, 1949-50
Who's Who in Central and East-Europe, 1935-36
Who's Who in Chicago and Illinois (1950)
Who's Who in Colored America, 1950
Who's Who in Commerce and Industry (1951)
Who's Who in Egypt and the Middle East, 1949
Who's Who in Engineering, 1948
Who's Who in Government, 1932-33
Who's Who in India, 1946-47
Who's Who in Japan, 1940-41
Who's Who in Labor (1946)
Who's Who in Latin America Pts 1-7 (1946-51)
Who's Who in Law, 1937
Who's Who in Library Service (1943)
Who's Who in New England (1949)
Who's Who in New York, 1952
Who's Who in New Zealand (1951)
Who's Who in Railroading, 1946
Who's Who in Switzerland, 1950-51
Who's Who in the Clergy, 1941-42

Who's Who in the East (1951)

Who's Who in the Major Leagues (1947)

Who's Who in the Midwest (1949)

Who's Who in the Nation's Capital, 1938-39

Who's Who in the South and Southwest (1950)

Who's Who in the State of Israel, 1949

Who's Who in the Theatre (1952)

Who's Who in the United Nations (1951)

Who's Who in the West (1951)

Who's Who in Transportation and Communication, 1942-43

Who's Who in United States Politics (1950)

Who's Who of the Allied Governments, 1943

Wie is Dat? 1948

Wier, A. E. ed. Macmillan Encyclopedia of Music and Musicians (1938)

Winchester's Screen Encyclopedia (1948)

Women of Achievement (1940)

World Biography (1948)

World Diplomatic Directory (1951)

Yearbook of the United Nations, 1950

Yost, E. American Women of Science (1943)

PERIODICALS AND NEWSPAPERS CONSULTED

A. L. A. Bul—American Library Association Bulletin $1.50; free to members. American Library Assn, 50 E Huron St, Chicago 11

Adult Ed J—Adult Education Journal $2. American Association for Adult Education, 167 Public Square, Cleveland 14
Formerly Journal of Adult Education

Adv Age—Advertising Age $2. Advertising Publications, Inc, 100 E Ohio St, Chicago 11

Adv & Sell—Advertising and Selling $4. Moore-Robbins Pub Co, Inc, 9 E 38th St, New York 16

Am Artist—American Artist $4. Watson-Guptill Publications, Inc, 345 Hudson St, New York 14
Formerly Art Instruction

Am Assn Univ Women J—Journal of the American Association of University Women $1. American Assn of University Women, 1634 I St, N W, Washington 6, D.C.

Am Collector—American Collector $4. Collectors Pub Co, Inc, 19 W 44th St, New York 18

Am Federationist—American Federationist $2. American Federation of Labor, 901 Massachusetts Ave, Washington 1, D.C.

Am Hist R—American Historical Review $5; free to members of the American Historical Assn. Macmillan Co, 60 Fifth Ave, New York 11

Am Home—American Home $2.50. American Home Magazine Corp, Forest Hills, New York

Am Mag—American Magazine $3. Crowell-Collier Pub Co, Springfield, Ohio

Am Mercury—American Mercury $3. American Mercury, Inc, 251 W 42d St, New York 18

Am Phot—American Photography $2.50. American Photographic Pub Co, 421 Fifth Ave S, Minneapolis 15, Minn.

Am Pol Sci R—American Political Science Review $6.60; free to members of the American Political Science Assn, University Hall, Ohio State University, Columbus, Ohio

Am Scand R—American Scandinavian Review $3; free to members. American Scandinavian Foundation, 116 E 64th St, New York 21

Am Scholar—American Scholar $3. United Chapter of Phi Beta Kappa, 415 First Ave, New York 10

Am Sociol R—American Sociological Review $5. American Sociological Society, 427 W 117 St, New York 27

America—America $6. America Press, 70 E 45th St, New York 17

Américas—Américas $3. Pan American Union, 17th St and Constitution Ave, NW, Washington 6, D.C.

Ann Am Acad—Annals of the American Academy of Political and Social Science $5; free to members. 3817 Spruce St, Philadelphia 4

Apollo—Apollo, the Magazine of the Arts for Connoisseurs and Collectors 42s. 10 Vigo St, Regent St, London, W 1. ($6. 18 E 48th St, New York 17)

Arch Forum—Architectural Forum $12; $5.50 to firms and governments. Time, Inc, 540 N Michigan Ave, Chicago 11

Arch Rec—Architectural Record $4.50. F. W. Dodge Corp, 119 W 40th St, New York 18

Art Bul—Art Bulletin $10. College Art Assn, Inc, 625 Madison Ave, New York 22

Art Digest—Art Digest $4. Art Digest, Inc, 116 E 59th St, New York 22

Art N—Art News $9. Art Foundation, Inc, 136 E 57th St, New York 22

Arts & Arch—Arts and Architecture $5. John D. Entenza, 3305 Wilshire Blvd, Los Angeles 5

Arts & Dec—Arts and Decoration (discontinued)

Asia—Asia and the Americas.
Merged with United Nations World, February 1947

Asiatic R—Asiatic Review £1. East and West, Ltd. 3 Victoria St, London, SW 1

Atlan—Atlantic Monthly $6. Atlantic Monthly Co, 8 Arlington St, Boston 16

Automotive Ind—Automotive Industries $2. Chilton Co, 56th & Chestnut Sts, Philadelphia 39
Formerly Automotive and Aviation Industries

Aviation W—Aviation Week $6. McGraw-Hill Pub, Co, Inc, 330 W 42d St, New York 18

Banking—Banking $4. American Bankers Assn, 12 E 36th St, New York 16

Bet Hom & Gard—Better Homes & Gardens $2.50. Meredith Pub Co, 1714 Locust St, Des Moines 3, Iowa

Book-of-the-Month Club N—Book-of-the-Month Club News Free to members. Book-of-the-Month Club, Inc, 385 Madison Ave, New York 17

Books Abroad—Books Abroad $3. University of Oklahoma Press, Norman, Okla.

Bronx Home News. See N Y Post

Bsns W—Business Week $6. McGraw-Hill Pub Co, Inc, 330 W 42d St, New York 18

Bul Bibliog—Bulletin of Bibliography and Dramatic Index $3. F. W. Faxon Co, 83 Francis St, Boston 15

Bul Museum Modern Art. See New York City. Museum of Modern Art Bul

Bul Pan Am Union. See Américas

Calif Arts & Arch—California Arts & Architecture. See Arts and Architecture

Canad Forum—Canadian Forum $2. Canadian Forum, Ltd, 16 Huntley St, Toronto 5

Canad Hist R—Canadian Historical Review $3. University of Toronto Press, Toronto 5

Cath Lib World—Catholic Library World $5; free to members. Catholic Library Assn, P.O. Box 25, New York

Cath N—Catholic News $3. C. H. Ridder, 22 N William St, New York 7

Cath School J—Catholic School Journal $3. Bruce Pub Co, 400 N Broadway, Milwaukee 1, Wis.

Cath World—Catholic World $4. Paulist Press, 401 W 59th St, New York 19

Chem & Eng N—Chemical and Engineering News $6. American Chemical Society, 1155 16th St, N W, Washington 6, D.C.

Christian Cent—Christian Century $6. Christian Century Press, 407 S Dearborn St, Chicago 5

Christian Sci Mon—Christian Science Monitor (Atlantic edition) $14, including the Magazine. Christian Science Pub Soc, 1 Norway St, Boston 15

Christian Sci Mon Mag—Christian Science Monitor Weekly Magazine Section. Christian Science Pub Soc, 1 Norway St, Boston 15

Civil Eng—Civil Engineering $5. American Society of Civil Engineers, 33 W 39th St, New York 18

Col Engl—College English $4. University of Chicago Press, 5750 Ellis Ave, Chicago 37

Collier's—Collier's $5. Crowell-Collier Pub Co, Springfield, Ohio

Commonweal—Commonweal $7. Commonweal Pub Co, Inc, 386 Fourth Ave, New York 16

Cong Digest—Congressional Digest $6. Congressional Digest Corp, 1631 K St, N W, Washington 6, D.C.

Connoisseur—Connoisseur 43s. Connoisseur, Ltd, 28 & 30 Grosvenor Gardens, London, SW 1 ($7.50. Connoisseur and International Studio, 572 Madison Ave. New York 22)

Contemp—Contemporary Review $9.50. British Periodicals Ltd, 46-47 Chancery Lane, London, WC 2

Coronet—Coronet $3. Esquire, Inc, 65 E South Water St, Chicago 1

Cosmopolitan—Cosmopolitan $3.50. Hearst Magazines, Inc, 57th St & Eighth Ave, New York 19

Cue—Cue (Manhattan edition) $4.50. Cue Publishing Co, Inc, 6 E 39th St, New York 16

Cur Hist ns—Current History $4. Events Pub Co, Inc, 108-10 Walnut St, Philadelphia 6

Cur Opinion—Current Opinion (discontinued)

Dance—Dance Magazine $3.75. Rudor Pub Co. 503 W 33d St, New York 1

Design—Design $4. Design Pub Co, 337 S High St, Columbus 15, Ohio

Dublin R—Dublin Review 15s. Burns Oates & Washbourne, Ltd. 28 Ashley Pl, London, SW 1 ($4 International News Co, 131 Varick St, New York 13)

Ed & Pub—Editor and Publisher $5. Charles T. Stuart, 1475 Broadway, New York 18

Educ—Education $4. Palmer Co, 370 Atlantic Ave, Boston 10

El Engl—Elementry English $3.50. National Council of Teachers of English, 211 W 68th St, Chicago 21
Formerly Elementary English Review

Engl J—English Journal $4. University of Chicago Press, 5750 Ellis Ave, Chicago 37

Esquire—Esquire $6. Esquire, Inc, 65 E South Water St, Chicago 1

Etude—Etude $3. Theodore Presser Co, Bryn Mawr, Pa.

Facts on File—Facts on File $45. Person's Index, Facts on File, Inc, 516 Fifth Ave, New York 9

Far Eastern S—Far Eastern Survey $6. 1 E 54th St, New York 22

Finance—Finance $5. Finance Pub Corp, 20 N Wacker Dr, Chicago 6

Flying—Flying $3. Ziff-Davis Pub Co, 185 N Wabash Ave, Chicago 1

For Affairs—Foreign Affairs $6. Council on Foreign Relations, Inc, 58 E 68th St, New York 21

For Policy Rep—Foreign Policy Reports $5. (to libraries subscription includes Foreign Policy Bulletins and 6 headline books); $4. to F. P. A. members. Foreign Policy Assn, Inc, 22 E 38th St, New York 16

Forbes—Forbes $4. B. C. Forbes & Sons Pub Co, Inc, 120 Fifth Ave, New York 11

Fortnightly—Fortnightly $6.50. Fortnightly Review, 4, 5, & 6 Soho Sq, London, W 1

Fortune—Fortune $12.50. Time, Inc, 540 N Michigan Ave, Chicago 11

Forum—Forum $4. Events Pub Co, Inc, 108-10 Walnut St, Philadelphia 6
Forum combined with Current History from May 30, 1940, to August 31, 1945; resumed publication as an independent magazine in September of 1945.

Free World—Free World.
Merged with United Nations World.

Good H—Good Housekeeping $3.50. Hearst Magazines, Inc, 57th St & Eighth Ave, New York 19

Harper—Harper's Magazine $5. Harper & Bros, 49 E 33d St, New York 15

Harper's Bazaar—Harper's Bazaar $5. Hearst Magazines, Inc. 572 Madison Ave, New York 22

Holiday—Holiday $5. Curtis Pub Co, Independence Square, Philadelphia 5

Home & F See House B

Horn Bk—Horn Book $3. Horn Book, Inc, 248 Boylston St, Boston 16

House & Gard—House and Garden $5. Condé Nast Publications, Inc, Boston Post Road, Greenwich, Conn.

House B—House Beautiful $5. Hearst Magazines, Inc, 572 Madison Ave, New York 22

Illus Lond N—Illustrated London News £5 1s. 1 New Oxford St, London, WC 1 (American edition $16. British edition $18. International News Co, 131 Varick St, New York 13)

Ind Woman—Independent Woman $1.50. National Federation of Business and Professional Women's Clubs, Inc, 1819 Broadway, New York 23

Inland Ptr—Inland Printer $4. The Inland Printer, 309 W Jackson Blvd, Chicago 6

Inter-American—Inter-American.
Merged with United Nations World, February 1947.

J Am Med Assn—Journal of the American Medical Association $8. Am Med Assn, 535 N Dearborn St, Chicago 10

J Home Econ—Journal of Home Economics $5. American Home Economics Assn, Victor Bldg, Washington 1, D.C.

J Negro Hist—Journal of Negro History $4. Association for the Study of Negro Life and History, 1538 Ninth St, N W, Washington 1, D.C.

Knickerbocker—The Knickerbocker $3. The Netherlands Pub Co, 50 Rockefeller Plaza, New York 20

Ladies' Home J—Ladies' Home Journal $3. Curtis Pub Co, Independence Sq, Philadelphia 5

Liberty—Liberty $2.25. Liberty Magazine, Inc. 37 W 57th St, New York 19

Library J—Library Journal $6. R. R. Bowker Co, 62 W 45th St, New York 19

Life—Life $6. Time, Inc, 540 N Michigan Ave, Chicago 11

Life & Letters To-day—Life and Letters Today 20s. 430 Strand, London WC 2 ($5. International News Co, 131 Varick St, New York 13)

Lit Digest—Literary Digest (discontinued)

Lon Studio. See Studio

Look—Look $3.50. Cowles Magazines, Inc, 511 Fifth Ave, New York 17

Mademoiselle—Mademoiselle $3.50. Street & Smith Publications, Inc, 122 E 42d St, New York 17

Mag Art—Magazine of Art $6; free to members. American Federation of Arts, 1262 N Hampshire Ave, N W, Washington 6, D.C.

Mag of Wall Street—Magazine of Wall Street $12.50. Ticker Pub Co, 90 Broad St, New York 4

Mo Labor R—Monthly Labor Review $4.50. Supt. of Documents, Washington 25, D.C.

Motion Pict—Motion Picture $1.20. Fawcett Publications, Inc, 67 W 44th St, New York 18

Mus Am—Musical America $4. Musical America Corp. 113 W 57th St, New York 19

Mus Courier—Musical Courier $3. Music Periodicals Corp, 119 W 57th St, New York 19

Mus Q—Musical Quarterly $4. G. Schirmer, Inc, 3 E 43d St, New York 17

Musician—Musician $3. Fellowship Concerts Service, Inc, 545 5th Ave, New York 17

N Y Herald Tribune—New York Herald Tribune $22, including Sunday edition. New York Tribune, Inc, 230 W 41st St, New York 18

N Y Post—New York Post $16.50, including Sunday edition. New York Post, Inc, 75 West St, New York 6
Bronx Home News consolidated with N Y Post February 16, 1948

N Y Star—New York Star (discontinued January 28, 1949)

N Y State Ed—New York State Education $2. New York State Teachers Assn, 152 Washington Ave, Albany 6

N Y Sun. See N Y World-Telegram

N Y Times—New York Times $19.50, including Sunday edition. New York Times Co, 229 W 43d St, New York 18

N Y Times Book R—New York Times Book Review $3. New York Times Co, 229 W 43d St, New York 18

N Y Times Index—New York Times Index $35. New York Times Co, 229 W 43d St, New York 18

N Y Times Mag—New York Times Magazine $7.50. (Complete Sunday edition; not sold separately) New York Times Co, 229 W 43d St, New York 18

N Y World-Telegram—New York World-Telegram and Sun $15. N Y World-Telegram Corp, 125 Barclay St, New York 15
  N Y Sun consolidated with N Y World-Telegram January 5. 1950

Nat Ed Assn J—Journal of the National Education Association $5. free to members. National Education Assn, 1201 16th St, N W, Washington 6, D.C.

Nat Geog Mag—National Geographic Magazine $5. National Geographic Soc, 1146 16th St, N W, Washington 6, D.C.

Nat R—National Review 36s. Rolls House, 2 Bream's Bldgs, Chancery Lane, London. EC 4 ($8.50 International News Co, 131 Varick St, New York 13)

Nation—The Nation $7. The Nation Associates, Inc, 20 Vesey St, New York 7

Nation's Bsns—Nation's Business $15 (3 years). Chamber of Commerce of the United States, 1615 H St, N W, Washington 6, D.C.

Natur Hist—Natural History $5. American Museum of Natural History, 79th St and Central Park West, New York 24

Nature—Nature £4 10s; single numbers 1s 6d. Macmillan & Co, Ltd, St Martin's St, London, WC 2 ($22.50; single numbers 50c. Macmillan Co, 60 Fifth Ave, New York 11)

Nature Mag—Nature Magazine $4. American Nature Assn, 1214 16th St, N W, Washington 6, D.C.

New Eng Q—New England Quarterly $4. New England Quarterly, Hubbard Hall, Bowdoin College, Brunswick, Me.

New Repub—New Republic $6.30. Editorial Publications, Inc, 1416 F St, NW, Washington, D.C.

New Statesm & Nation—New Statesman and Nation—Week-end Review 32s 6d. 10 Great Turnstile, London, WC 1 ($7 International News Co, 131 Varick St, New York 13)

New York City. Museum of Modern Art Bul—Bulletin of the Museum of Modern Art 15c to 25c a copy; free to members. Museum of Modern Art, 11 W 53d St, New York 19

New Yorker—New Yorker $7. F-R. Pub Corp. 25 W 43d St, New York 18

Newsweek—Newsweek $6.50. Weekly Publications, Inc, Newsweek Bldg, 152 W 42d St, New York 18

19th Cent—Nineteenth Century and After $8.75. Constable & Co, Ltd, 10 Orange St, London, WC 2

Opera N—Opera News $4; free to members. Metropolitan Opera Guild, Inc, 654 Madison Ave, New York 21

Outlook—Outlook (discontinued)

Parents Mag—Parents' Magazine $3. Parents' Institute, Inc, 52 Vanderbilt Ave, New York 17

Parnassus—Parnassus (discontinued)

Pathfinder—Pathfinder $2. Farm Journal, Inc, Washington Square, Philadelphia 5

Photoplay—Photoplay $3.60 (two years) Macfadden Publications, Inc, 205 E 42d St, New York 17
  Combined with Movie Mirror

PM—PM (changed to N Y Star, June 23, 1948)

Poetry—Poetry $5. 232 E Erie St, Chicago 11

Pol Sci Q—Political Science Quarterly $6; free to members. Academy of Political Science, Columbia University, New York 27

Pop Mech—Popular Mechanics Magazine $3.50. Popular Mechanics Co, 200 E Ontario St, Chicago 11

Pop Sci—Popular Science Monthly $3. Popular Science Pub Co, Inc, 353 Fourth Ave, New York 10

Progres Educ—Progressive Education $4.25. American Education Fellowship, 34 E Main St, Champaign, Ill.

Pub W—Publishers' Weekly $6. R. R. Bowker Co, 62 W 45th St, New York 10

Q R—Quarterly Review 31s 4d. J. Murray, 50 Albemarle St, London, W 1. ($6.50 International News Co, 131 Varick St, New York 13)

Queen's Q—Queen's Quarterly $3. Queen's University, Kingston, Canada

R of Rs—Review of Reviews (discontinued)

Read Digest—Reader's Digest $3. Reader's Digest Assn, Inc, Pleasantville, N.Y.

Reader's Scope—Reader's Scope $3. L. S. Gleason, Pub, 114 E 32d St, New York 16

Ref Shelf—Reference Shelf $7 per volume of six bound numbers, published irregularly. H. W. Wilson Co, 950-972 University Ave, New York 52

Rotarian—Rotarian $2. Rotary International, 35 E Wacker Dr, Chicago 1

Roy Inst Brit Arch J—Journal of the Royal Institute of British Architects £2 postpaid. The Institute, 66 Portland Pl, London, W 1

Sales Management—Sales Management $6. Sales Management, Inc, 386 Fourth Ave, New York 16

Sat Eve Post—Saturday Evening Post $6. Curtis Pub Co, Independence Sq, Philadelphia 5

Sat Night—Saturday Night $4 (in Canada) $6 (in United States). Consolidated Press, Ltd, Birks Bldg, Montreal, Canada

Sat R—Saturday Review $6. Saturday Review Associates, Inc, 25 W 45th St, New York 19

Sch & Soc—School and Society $7; free to members of the Society for the Advancement of Education, Inc, 15 Amsterdam Ave, New York 23

Sch R—School Review $4.50. University of Chicago Press, 5750 Ellis Ave, Chicago 37

Scholastic—Senior Scholastic (High School Teacher edition) $2 (teacher ed. only); school group rate (two or more subscriptions to one address) $1.20 for special eds. $1.50 for combined ed. Scholastic Corp, 7 E 12th St, New York 3

Sci Am—Scientific American $5. Scientific American, Inc, 24 W 40th St, New York 18

Sci Mo—Scientific Monthly $7.50. American Assn for the Advancement of Science, 1515 Massachusetts Ave, N W, Washington 5, D.C.

Sci N L—Science News Letter $5.50. Science Service, Inc, 1719 N St, N W, Washington 6, D.C.

Science ns—Science (news series) $7.50. American Assn for the Advancement of Science, 1515 Massachusetts Ave, NW, Washington 5, D.C.

Scrib Mag—Scribner's Magazine (discontinued)

Sign—The Sign $3. Passionist Missions, Inc, Union City, N.J.

So Atlan Q—South Atlantic Quarterly $3. Duke University Press, Durham, N.C.

Spec—Spectator 30s. 99 Gower St, London, WC 1 ($7 International News Co, 131 Varick St, New York 13)

Sport—Sport $3. Macfadden Publications, Inc, 205 E 42nd St, New York 17

Sporting N—Sporting News $8. Sporting News Pub Co, 2012-18 Washington Ave, St. Louis, Mo.

Stage—Stage (discontinued)

Stage Pict—Stage Pictorial (discontinued)

Studio—Studio $6. Studio Publication, Inc, 381 Fourth Ave, New York 16 (30s; The Studio, Ltd, 66 Chandos Pl, London, WC 2)
Sunset Mag—Sunset Magazine $2. Lane Pub Co, 576 Sacramento St, San Francisco 11
Survey—Survey $5. Survey Associates, Inc, 112 E 19th St, New York 3
Survey Graphic. See Survey
Survey Midmonthly. See Survey

Theatre Arts—Theatre Arts $5. Theatre Arts, Inc, 130 W 56th St, New York 19
This Week—This Week Magazine. Distributed each Sunday with different newspapers. United Newspapers Magazine Corp, 420 Lexington Ave, New York 17. In New York included in Sunday edition of New York Herald Tribune.
Time—Time $6. Time, Inc, 540 N Michigan Ave, Chicago 11
Town and Country—Town and Country $7.50. Hearst Magazines, Inc, 572 Madison Ave, New York 22
Travel—Travel $4.50. Travel Mag, Inc, 115 W 45th St, New York 19

U N Bul—United Nations Bulletin $4.50. International Documents Service, Columbia University Press, 2960 Broadway, New York 27
U N World—United Nations World $4. U N World, Inc, 319 E 44th St, New York 17
U S Bur Labor. See Mo Labor R
U S Bur Labor Bul—United States Bureau of Labor Statistics. Bulletins. Free to libraries. Bureau of Labor Statistics, Washington, D.C. Purchase orders, Supt. of Documents. Washington 25, D.C.

U S News—United States News & World Report $5. United States News Pub Corp, 24th & N Sts, NW, Washington 7, D.C.
U S Office Educ Bul—United States Office of Education. Bulletins. Free to libraries. Office of Education, Washington, D.C. Purchase orders, Supt. of Documents, Washington 25, D.C.

Va Q R—Virginia Quarterly Review $3. University of Virginia, 1 West Range, Charlottesville, Va.
Variety—Variety $10. Variety, Inc, 154 W 46th St, New York 19
Vital Speeches—Vital Speeches of the Day $5. City News Pub Co, 33 W 42d St, New York 18
Vogue—Vogue (Incorporating Vanity Fair) $7.50. Condé Nast Publications, Inc, Greenwich, Conn.

Washington (D.C.) Post—Washington Post $10.80. P. L. Graham, Pub, 1337 E St, N W, Washington 4, D.C.
Wilson Lib Bul—Wilson Library Bulletin $2. H. W. Wilson Co, 950-972 University Ave, New York 52
Woman's Home C—Woman's Home Companion $2.50. Crowell-Collier Pub Co, Springfield, Ohio
World Rep—World Report. See U S News
World's Work—World's Work (discontinued)
Writer—The Writer $3. The Writer, Inc, 8 Arlington St, Boston 16

Yale R—Yale Review $3.50. 143 Elm St, New Haven 7, Conn.

NECROLOGY—1952

This is a list of biographees' obituaries for the year. Deaths which occurred in late 1952 are recorded in the January and February 1953 issues of CURRENT BIOGRAPHY; references to those obituaries are included in this list.

Avenol, Joseph (Louis Anne) (biog 1940)

Björnsson, Sveinn (biog 1944)
Blake, Francis G(ilman) (biog 1943)
Borgese, G(iuseppe) A(ntonio) (biog 1947)
Brickell, (Henry) Herschel (biog 1945)
Chubb, L(ewis) Warrington (biog 1947)
Cox, E(dward) Eugene (biog 1943)
Cripps, Sir (Richard) Stafford (biog 1948)
Croce, Benedetto (biog 1944)

Davidson, Jo (biog 1945)
Davis, Harvey N(athaniel) (biog 1947)
Dewey, John (biog 1944)
Duncan, Sir Andrew Rae (biog 1941)

Feller, Abraham H(oward) (biog 1946)

Garfield, John (biog 1948)
George VI, King of Great Britain (biog 1942)
Giannini, L(awrence) M(ario) (biog 1950)
Gow, James (Ellis) (biog 1944)
Green, William (biog 1942)

Haskell, William N(afew) (biog 1947)
Hedin, Sven Anders (biog 1940)
Higgins, Andrew J(ackson) (biog 1943)

Horney, Karen (biog 1941)
Hume, Edgar Erskine (biog 1944)

Ickes, Harold L(e Claire) (biog 1941)
Ingram, Jonas H(oward) (biog 1947)

Karfiol, Bernard (biog 1947)
Kenny, Elizabeth (biog 1942)
Kirby, Rollin (biog 1944)
Kollontay, Alexandra (Mikhailovna) (biog 1943)

La Cava, Gregory (biog 1941)
Lattre de Tassigny, Jean (Joseph Marie Gabriel) de (biog 1945)
Lawrence, Gertrude (biog 1952)
Lee, Canada (biog 1944)
Linlithgow, Victor Alexander John Hope, 2d Marquess of (biog 1942)

McCarthy, Leighton (Goldie) (biog 1942)
McDaniel, Hattie (biog 1940)
McMahon, (James O')Brien (biog 1945)
Matthews, Francis P(atrick) (biog 1949)
Minor, Robert (biog 1941)
Montessori, Maria (biog 1940)
Montgomery, James Shera, Rev. (biog 1948)
Morgan, Anne (Tracy) (biog 1946)
Moulton, F(orest) R(ay) (biog 1946)

Murray, Philip (biog 1949)

Orlando, Vittorio Emanuele (biog 1944)
Oursler, Fulton (biog 1942)

Patterson, Robert P(orter) (biog 1941)
Perón, (Maria) Eva (Druate) de (biog 1949)
Piñero, Jesús T(oribio) (biog 1946)
Poole, DeWitt C(linton) (biog 1950)

Quo Tai-chi (biog 1946)

Robinson, Boardman (biog 1941)
Rosenbach, A(braham) S(imon) W(olf) (biog 1946)

Sabath, Adolph J(oachim) (biog 1946)
Santayana, George (biog 1944)
Schumacher, Kurt (biog 1948)
Senanayake, Don Stephen (biog 1950)
Sforza, Carlo, Count (biog 1942)
Short, Joseph (Hudson, Jr.) (biog 1951)
Smith, Ida B. Wise (biog 1943)

Wadsworth, James W(olcott) (biog 1943)
Webster, H(arold) T(ucker) (biog 1945)
Weizmann, Chaim (biog 1948)
White, Wallace H(umphrey), Jr. (biog 1948)

CLASSIFICATION BY PROFESSION—1952

Agriculture

Andrews, Stanley
Bennett, Henry G(arland) obit
Capper, Arthur obit
Cowden, Howard A(ustin)
Duggar, Benjamin Minge
Hannah, John A(lfred)
Lysenko, T(rofim) D(enisovich)
O'Neill, J(ohn) E(dward)
Senanayake, Don Stephen obit
Senanayake, Dudley (Shelton)
Warne, William E(lmo)

Architecture

Gropius, Walter (Adolf)
Wright, Frank Lloyd

Art

Davidson, Jo obit
D'Harnoncourt, René
Disney, Walt
Enters, Angna
Gropius, Walter (Adolf)
Karfiol, Bernard obit
Karsh, Yousuf
Kirby, Rollin obit
Kirstein, Lincoln (Edward)
LeBrun, (Fede)rico
Levi, Carlo
Milles, Carl (Wilhelm Emil)
Packer, Fred L(ittle)
Robinson, Boardman obit
Webster, H(arold) T(ucker) obit

Aviation

Braniff, T(homas) E(lmer)
Nuckols, William P(reston)
Nyrop, Donald W(illiam)
Rickenbacker, Edward Vernon
Thomas, Sir (William) Miles (Webster)
Yamut, Nuri

Business

Ball, Stuart S(coble)
Bender, George H(arrison)
Braniff, T(homas) E(lmer)
Brophy, Thomas D'Arcy
Capper, Arthur obit
Chapman, Albert K(inkade)
Charles-Roux, François (-Jules)
Christenberry, Robert K(eaton)
Cocke, C(harles) Francis
Coppers, George H(enry)
Cowden, Howard A(ustin)
Doan, Leland I(ra)

Dowling, Robert W(hittle)
Duffy, Bernard C(ornelius)
Eccles, David (McAdam)
Fellows, Harold E(verett)
Field, Marshall, 3d
Gallup, George (Horace)
Grede, William J(ohn)
Hilton, Frank C.
Irwin, Helen G.
Johnson, Joseph T(ravis)
Killion, George (Leonard)
King, Cecil R(hodes)
Lee, Laurence F(rederick)
Loynd, Harry J.
McConnell, F(owler) B(eery)
McKinney, Frank E(dward)
Matthews, Francis P(atrick) obit
Mehta, G(aganvihari) L(al-lubhai)
O'Neill, J(ohn) E(dward)
Payne, Frederick G.
Pinay, Antoine
Rackmil, Milton R.
Rosenbach, A(braham) S(imon) W(olf) obit
Seixas, E(lias) Victor, Jr.
Shelly, Warner S(woyer)
Sloan, George A(rthur)
Smith, John L.
Strachan, Paul A(mbrose)
Straus, Jack I(sidor)
Summerfield, Arthur E(llsworth)
Toy, Henry, Jr.
Wampler, (ElRey) Cloud
Wherry, Kenneth S(picer) obit
Williams, John J(ames)
Zeckendorf, William
Zuckert, Eugene M.

Dance

Enters, Angna
Greco, José
Jeanmaire, Renée
Kirstein, Lincoln (Edward)
Petit, Roland

Diplomacy

Ali, Mohammed
Araki, Eikichi
Avenol, Joseph (Louise Anne) obit
Björnsson, Sveinn obit
Borberg, William
Charles-Roux, François (-Jules)
Donnelly, Walter J(oseph)
Erkin, Feridun C(emal)
Hawkins, Harry C(alvin)
Kollantay, Alexandra (Mikhailovna) obit

Litvinov, Maxim (Maximovitch) obit
McCarthy, Leighton (Goldie) obit
MacVeagh, Lincoln
Matthews, Francis P(atrick) obit
Matthews, W(ilmot) Donald
Mehta, G(aganvihari) L(al-lubhai)
Muniz, Joao Carlos
Paz, Hipólito Jesús
Poole, DeWitt C(linton) obit
Popovic, Vladimir
Quo Tai-Chi obit
Radhakrishnan, Sir Sarvepalli
Sen, B(inay) R(anjan)

Education

Adler, Mortimer
Allen, Raymond B(ernard)
Anderson, Leroy
Aydelotte, Frank
Backman, Jules
Bacon, Selden D(askam)
Belkin, Samuel
Bennett, Henry G(arland) obit
Blake, Francis G(ilman) obit
Brophy, Thomas D'Arcy
Burdell, Edwin S(harp)
Calkins, Robert D(e Blois)
Carlson, William S(amuel)
Carr, William G(eorge)
Cherwell, Frederick Alexander Lindemann, 1st Baron
Clift, David H(orace)
Compton, Wilson (Martindale)
Daniel, Robert Prentiss
Dewey, John obit
Downs, Robert B(ingham)
Duggar, Benjamin Minge
Faust, Clarence H(enry)
Feinsinger, Nathan P(aul)
Figueroa, Ana
Finkelstein, Louis, Rabbi
Gallup, George (Horace)
Goldstine, Herman H(eine)
Gore, Albert (Arnold)
Gould, Ronald
Gropius, Walter (Adolf)
Handlin, Oscar
Hannah, John A(lfred)
Hawkins, Harry C(alvin)
Heald, Henry Townley
Holland, (George) Kenneth
Hook, Sidney
Horne, John E(lmer)
Horsbrugh, Florence
Irwin, Robert B(enjamin) obit
Kimble, George H(erbert) T(inley)

Kotschnig, Walter M(aria)
Lawrence, Ernest O(rlando)
Layton, Mrs. Roy F(rancis)
Lloyd, Wesley P(arkinson)
Mackay, John A(lexander)
McMillan, Edwin M(attison)
Mansfield, Michael J(oseph)
Meyer, K(arl) F(riedrich)
Milles, Carl (Wilhelm Emil)
Millikan, Robert A(ndrews)
Montessori, Maria obit
Padover, Saul K(ussiel)
Paton, Alan
Poole, DeWitt C(linton) obit
Radhakrishnan, Sir Sarvepalli
Rosenfield, Harry N(athan)
Salazar, António de Oliveira
Santayana, George obit
Scoggin, Margaret C(lara)
Sears, Robert R(ichardson)
Sforza, Carlo, Count obit
Shapiro, Harry L(ionel)
Shapley, Harlow
Shulman, Harry
Sperry, Willard L(earoyd)
Toy, Henry, Jr.
Walton, Ernest Thomas Sinton
Weizmann, Chaim obit
Whipple, Fred Lawrence
Whitman, Walter G(ordon)
Woodward, R(obert) B(urns)
Wriston, Henry M(erritt)

Engineering

Boyer, Harold Raymond
Byroade, Henry A(lfred)
Chubb, L(ewis) Warrington
obit
Heald, Henry Townley
Mackenzie, C(halmers) J(ack)
Thomas, Sir (William) Miles
(Webster)
Von Braun, Wernher
Weaver, Warren

Finance

Araki, Eikichi
Cashman, Robert
Cocke, C(harles) Francis
Cook, Donald C(larence)
Dawson, John A(lbert)
Draper, William H(enry), Jr.
Field, Marshall, 3d
Giannini, L(awrence) M(ario)
obit
Johnson, Joseph T(ravis)
Locke, Edwin A(llen), Jr.
McKinney, Frank E(dward)
Matthews, W(ilmot) Donald
Rooth, Ivar
Sloan, George A(rthur)
Towers, Graham F(ord)

Government—
Foreign

Abdullah, Mohammad
Ali, Mohammed

Araki, Eikichi
Asgeirsson, Asgeir
Batista (y Zaldívar), Fulgencio
Björnsson, Sveinn obit
Blank, Theodor
Cherwell, Frederick Alexander
Lindemann, 1st Baron
Chevrier, Lionel
Cripps, Sir (Richard) Stafford
obit
Duncan, Sir Andrew Rae obit
Eccles, David (McAdam)
Erkin, Feridun C(emal)
Faure, Edgar
Figueroa, Ana
Forsyth, W(illiam) D(ouglass)
George VI, King of Great
Britain obit
Guillaume, Augustin (Léon)
Heuven Goedhart, G(errit)
J(an) van
Hilaly, Ahmed Naguib
Horsbrugh, Florence
Houtte, Jean van
Ibáñez (del Campo), Carlos
Johnson, David M(offat)
Kollantay, Alexandra (Mikhail-
ovna) obit
Letourneau, Jean
Linlithgow, Victor Alexander
John Hope, 2d Marquess of
obit
Litvinov, Maxim (Maximovitch)
obit
Lloyd, (John) Selwyn (Brooke)
Lloyd-George, Gwilym
Lysenko, T(rofim) D(enisovich)
McCarthy, Leighton (Goldie)
obit
Mackenzie, C(halmers) J(ack)
Magloire, Paul E(ugène)
Magsaysay, Ramón
Maher, Aly
Malenkov, Georgi M(aximilian-
ovich)
Matthews, W(ilmot) Donald
Mehta, G(aganvihari) L(al-
lubhai)
Morrison, William Shepherd
Muniz, Joao Carlos
Naguib, Mohammed
Paton, Alan
Perón, (Maria) Eva (Duarte)
de obit
Pinay, Antoine
Popovic, Vladimir
Quo Tai-Chi obit
Radhakrishnan, Sir Sarvepalli
Ruiz Cortines, Adolfo
Salazar, António de Oliveira
Sandys, (Edwin) Duncan
Schumacher, Kurt obit
Sen, B(inay) R(anjan)
Senanayake, Don Stephen obit
Senanayake, Dudley (Shelton)
Sforza, Carlo, Count obit
Talal, Former King of Jordan
Templer, Sir Gerald (Walter
Robert)
Thorneycroft, (George Edward)
Peter

Torp, Oscar (Fredrik)
Towers, Graham F(ord)
Ulbricht, Walter
Velasco Ibarra, José María
Weizmann, Chaim obit

Government—
United States

Adams, Sherman
Allen, Raymond B(ernard)
Andrews, Stanley
Bender, George H(arrison)
Bendetsen, Karl R(obin)
Bennett, Henry G(arland) obit
Boyer, Harold Raymond
Brickell, (Henry) Herschel obit
Burdick, Usher (Lloyd)
Byroade, Henry A(lfred)
Capper, Arthur obit
Chelf, Frank L(eslie)
Christenberry, Robert K(eaton)
Clark, Joseph S(ill), Jr.
Clark, Robert L(incoln)
Compton, Wilson (Martindale)
Cook, Donald C(larence)
Cooper, Joseph D(avid)
Cordon, Guy
Davidson, William L(ee)
Donnelly, Walter J(oseph)
Draper, William H(enry), Jr.
Feinsinger, Nathan P(aul)
Forbes, John J. (V.)
Fowler, Henry H(amill)
Gore, Albert (Arnold)
Gorrie, Jack (Osborne)
Graves, Alvin C(ushman)
Hawkins, Harry C(alvin)
Hendrickson, Robert C.
Hoopes, Darlington
Horne, John E(lmer)
Humphrey, Helen F.
Ickes, Harold L(e Claire) obit
Kersten, Charles J.
King, Cecil R(hodes)
Kotschnig, Walter M(aria)
Langer, William
Locke, Edwin A(llen), Jr.
McGranery, James P(atrick)
McKeldin, Theodore R(oose-
velt)
McMahon, (James O')Brien
obit
MacVeagh, Lincoln
Maggiolo, Walter A(ndrew)
Mansfield, Michael J(oseph)
Matthews, Francis P(atrick) obit
Mays, Ewing W(oodrow)
Mitchell, Stephen A(rnold)
Montgomery, James Shera, Rev.
obit
Morano, Albert Paul
Morris, Newbold
Nyrop, Donald W(illiam)
Padover, Saul K(ussiel)
Patterson, Robert P(orter) obit
Payne, Frederick G.
Perlman, Philip B(enjamin)
Pine, David A(ndrew)
Poindexter, Joseph B(oyd) obit

Putnam, Roger L(owell)
Rabaut, Louis Charles
Rosenfield, Harry N(athan)
Sabath, Adolph J(oachim) obit
Sargeant, Howland H(ill)
Schoeppel, Andrew F.
Shafer, Paul W(erntz)
Short, Joseph (Hudson, Jr.) obit
Spence, Brent
Steelman, John R(oy)
Straus, Michael W(olf)
Teague, Olin E(arl)
Wadsworth, James W(olcott) obit
Walker, Paul A(tlee)
Walter, Francis E(ugene)
Warne, William E(lmo)
Wherry, Kenneth S(picer) obit
White, Wallace H(umphrey), Jr. obit
Whitman, Walter G(ordon)
Williams, John J(ames)
Wilt, Fred(erick Loren)
Wirth, Conrad L.
Zuckert, Eugene M.

Industry

Boyer, Harold Raymond
Bransome, Edwin D(agobert)
Britton, Edgar C(lay)
Chubb, L(ewis) Warrington obit
Compton, Wilson (Martindale)
Coppers, George H(enry)
Doan, Leland I(ra)
Duncan, Sir Andrew Rae obit
Ford, Benson
Grede, William J(ohn)
Higgins, Andrew J(ackson) obit
Homer, Arthur B(artlett)
Loynd, Harry J.
McCarthy, Leighton (Goldie) obit
Maloney, Walter E(dward)
Manning, Harry
Putnam, Roger L(owell)
Randall, Clarence B(elden)
Rickenbacker, Edward Vernon
Sloan, George A(rthur)
Straus, Roger W(illiams)
Thomas, Sir (William) Miles (Webster)
Wampler, (ElRey) Cloud
Wilson, I(rving) W(hite)
Zeckendorf, William

International Relations

Ali, Mohammed
Andrews, Stanley
Araki, Eikichi
Asgeirsson, Asgeir
Avenol, Joseph (Louise Anne) obit
Aydelotte, Frank
Bennett, Henry G(arland) obit
Blank, Theodor

Borberg, William
Byroade, Henry A(lfred)
Calderone, Frank A(nthony)
Carr, William G(eorge)
Charles-Roux, François (-Jules)
Cowden, Howard A(ustin)
Cripps, Sir (Richard) Stafford obit
Donnelly, Walter J(oseph)
Draper, William H(enry), Jr.
Erkin, Feridun C(emal)
Figueroa, Ana
Forsyth, W(illiam) D(ouglass)
Gould, Ronald
Guillaume, Augustin (Léon)
Hawkins, Harry C(alvin)
Heuven Goedhart, G(errit) J(an) van
Hilaly, Ahmed Naguib
Holland, (George) Kenneth
Johnson, David M(offat)
Kollantay, Alexandra (Mikhail-ovna) obit
Kotschnig, Walter M(aria)
Letourneau, Jean
Litvinov, Maxim (Maximovitch) obit
Lloyd, (John) Selwyn (Brooke)
Lloyd, Wesley P(arkinson)
Locke, Edwin A(llen), Jr.
MacVeagh, Lincoln
Maher, Aly
Mehta, G(aganvihari) L(allu-bhai)
Muniz, Joao Carlos
Paz, Hipólito Jesús
Poole, DeWitt C(linton) obit
Popovic, Vladimir
Quo Tai-Chi obit
Rooth, Ivar
Sandys, (Edwin) Duncan
Sargeant, Howland H(ill)
Schwebel, Stephen M(yron)
Sen, B(inay) R(anjan)
Sforza, Carlo, Count obit
Templer, Sir Gerald (Walter Robert)
Tewson, Sir (Harold) Vincent
Warne, William E(lmo)

Journalism

Ahlgren, Mrs. Oscar A(lexander)
Alsop, Joseph W(right), Jr.
Alsop, Stewart (Johonnot Oliver)
Andrews, Stanley
Birnie, William A(lfred) H(art)
Brickell, (Henry) Herschel obit
Cooke, (Alfred) Alistair
Cowles, Fleur (Fenton)
Dix, Dorothy obit
Field, Marshall, 3d
Gallup, George (Horace)
Gorrie, Jack (Osborne)
Heuven Goedhart, G(errit) J(an) van
Hightower, John M(armann)
Kilgallen, Dorothy

Killion, George (Leonard)
Leviero, Anthony H(arry)
Markel, Lester
Nuckols, William P(reston)
Oursler, Fulton obit
Packer, Fred L(ittle)
Patterson, Robert P(orter) obit
Pusey, Merlo J(ohn)
Reid, Helen Rogers
Ross, Harold W(allace) obit
Shafer, Paul W(erntz)
Short, Joseph (Hudson, Jr.)
Sullivan, Ed(ward Vincent)
Thomas, Lowell (Jackson)
Warne, William E(lmo)
Webster, H(arold) T(ucker) obit
Young, Marian

Labor

Blank, Theodor
Clark, John
Croft, Arthur C(larence)
Feinsinger, Nathan P(aul)
Haywood, Allan S(haw)
Humphrey, Helen F.
Knight, O(rie) A(lbert)
Lundeberg, Harry
Maggiolo, Walter A(ndrew)
Murray, Philip obit
Shulman, Harry
Steelman, John R(oy)
Tewson, Sir (Harold) Vincent

Law

Ball, Stuart S(coble)
Bendetsen, Karl R(obin)
Burdick, Usher (Lloyd)
Charles-Roux, François (-Jules)
Chelf, Frank L(eslie)
Chevrier, Lionel
Clark, Joseph S(ill), Jr.
Cocke, C(harles) Francis
Cook, Donald C(larence)
Coppers, George H(enry)
Cordon, Guy
Cripps, Sir (Richard) Stafford obit
Erkin, Feridun C(emal)
Faure, Edgar
Feinsinger, Nathan P(aul)
Fowler, Henry H(amill)
Gore, Albert (Arnold)
Granik, (S.) Theodore
Hallinan, Vincent (W.)
Hendrickson, Robert C.
Hilaly, Ahmed Naguib
Hoopes, Darlington
Houtte, Jean van
Humphrey, Helen F.
Johnson, David M(offat)
Kersten, Charles J.
Langer, William
Lee, Laurence F(rederick)
Lloyd, (John) Selwyn (Brooke)
McCarthy, Leighton (Goldie) obit
McDaniel, Glen

McGranery, James P(atrick)
McKeldin, Theodore R(oosevelt)
Maggiolo, Walter A(ndrew)
Maher, Aly
Maloney, Walter E(dward)
Matthews, Francis P(atrick) obit
Mitchell, Stephen A(rnold)
Morris, Newbold
Morrison, William Shepherd
Muniz, Joao Carlos
Nyrop, Donald W(illiam)
Paz, Hipólito Jesús
Perlman, Philip B(enjamin)
Pine, David A(ndrew)
Poindexter, Joseph B(oyd) obit
Rabaut, Louis Charles
Randall, Clarence B(elden)
Root, Oren
Rosenfield, Harry N(athan)
Salazar, António de Oliveira
Schoeppel, Andrew F.
Shafer, Paul W(erntz)
Shulman, Harry
Spence, Brent
Walker, Paul A(tlee)
Walter, Francis E(ugene)
Wherry, Kenneth S(picer) obit
White, Wallace H(umphrey), Jr. obit
Wilson, Donald R(andolph)
Zuckert, Eugene M.

Literature

Adler, Mortimer
Babson, Naomi Lane (WLB)
Bell, Margaret Elizabeth (WLB)
Brickell, (Henry) Herschel obit
Bro, Margueritte Harmon (WLB)
Dejong, Meindert (WLB)
Dewey, John obit
Dickson, Marguerite (Stockman) (WLB)
Emery, Anne (Eleanor McGuigan) (WLB)
Enters, Angna
Finkelstein, Louis, Rabbi
Graham, Elinor (Mish) (WLB)
Havill, Edward (WLB)
Jagendorf, Moritz (Adolf) (WLB)
Kahmann, (Mable) Chesley (WLB)
Kanin, Garson
Lagerkvist, Pär (Fabian)
Lauritzen, Jonreed (WLB)
Leighton, Margaret (Carver) (WLB)
Levi, Carlo
Montgomery, Elizabeth Rider (WLB)
Moore, Marianne (Craig)
Oursler, Fulton obit
Paton, Alan
Rosenbach, A(braham) S(imon) W(olf) obit
Ross, Nancy Wilson (WLB)
Runbeck, Margaret Lee (WLB)

Santayana, George obit
Saunders, Hilary A(idan) St. George obit
Shay, Edith (WLB)
Shay, Frank (WLB)
Taber, Gladys (Leonae Bagg) (WLB)
Thomas, Lowell (Jackson)
Wheelwright, Jere (Hungerford, Jr.) (WLB)
Wouk, Herman (WLB)
Wright, Anna (Maria Louisa Perrott) Rose (WLB)

Medicine

Allen, Raymond B(ernard)
Armstrong, George E(llis)
Blake, Francis G(ilman) obit
Calderone, Frank A(nthony)
Graham, Evarts A(mbrose)
Haber, Heinz
Hume, Edgar Erskine obit
Lawrence, Ernest O(rlando)
Meyer, K(arl) F(riedrich)
Montessori, Maria obit
Porter, Mrs. Elizabeth K(err)
Sleeper, Ruth
Stone, Abraham
Theiler, Max

Military

Armstrong, George E(llis)
Batista (y Zaldívar), Fulgencio
Bendetsen, Karl R(obin)
Bennett, Ivan L(overidge)
Boatner, Haydon L(emaire)
Byroade, Henry A(lfred)
Chase, William C(urtis)
Erskine, Sir George (Watkin Eben James)
Guillaume, Augustin (Léon)
Harding, Sir John
Harrison, William K(elly), Jr.
Haskell, William N(afew) obit
Hilton, Frank C.
Hume, Edgar Erskine obit
Ibáñez (del Campo), Carlos
Lattre de Tassigny, Jean (Joseph Marie Gabriel) de obit
Magloire, Paul E(ugène)
Magsaysay, Ramón
Mathewson, Lemuel
Mays, Ewing W(oodrow)
Naguib, Mohammed
Nuckols, William P(reston)
Patterson, Robert P(orter) obit
Shepherd, Lemuel C(ornick), Jr.
Smith, John L.
Speidel, Hans
Templer, Sir Gerald (Walter Robert)
Von Braun, Wernher
Wilson, Donald R(andolph)
Yamut, Nuri

Motion Pictures

Allyson, June
Arnaz, Desi

Ball, Lucille
Brando, Marlon
De Sica, Vittorio
Disney, Walt
Douglas, Kirk
Garfield, John obit
Garland, Judy
Gow, James (Ellis) obit
Henie, Sonja
Hunter, Kim
Jeanmaire, Renée
Kanin, Garson
Kaye, Danny
Krasna, Norman
La Cava, Gregory obit
Lahr, Bert
Lawrence, Gertrude
Lee, Canada obit
Levant, Oscar
McDaniel, Hattie obit
Merrill, Robert
Moorehead, Agnes
Rackmil, Milton R.
Simmons, Jean
Stevens, George (Cooper)
Taylor, Elizabeth
Taylor, Robert
Wald, Jerry
Williams, Emlyn
Winters, Shelley

Music

Anderson, Leroy
Arnaz, Desi
Eckstine, Billy
Garland, Judy
Levant, Oscar
Merrill, Robert
Mitchell, Howard (Bundy)
Mitropoulos, Dimitri
Rackmil, Milton R.
Sloan, George A(rthur)
Traubel, Helen
Wallenstein, Alfred (Franz)
Williams, Camilla

Naval

Andrewes, Sir William (Gerard)
Brind, Sir (Eric James) Patrick
Cassady, John H(oward)
DeLany, Walter S(tanley)
Gardner, Matthias B(ennett)
Ingram, Jonas H(oward) obit
Lemmonier, André (Georges)
McCormick, Lynde Dupuy
Matthews, Francis P(atrick) obit
Shepherd, Lemuel C(ornick), Jr.
Yamut, Nuri

Politics

Abdullah, Mohammad
Adams, Sherman
Asgeirsson, Asgeir
Batista (y Zaldívar), Fulgencio

Bender, George H(arrison)
Björnsson, Sveinn obit
Blank, Theodor
Burdick, Usher (Lloyd)
Capper, Arthur obit
Chelf, Frank L(eslie)
Cherwell, Frederick Alexander
  Lindemann, 1st Baron
Chevrier, Lionel
Clark, Joseph S(ill), Jr.
Cordon, Guy
Cripps, Sir (Richard) Stafford
  obit
Davidson, Jo obit
Eccles, David (McAdam)
Faure, Edgar
Gore, Albert (Arnold)
Hallinan, Vincent (W.)
Hendrickson, Robert C.
Hilaly, Ahmed Naguib
Hoopes, Darlington
Horsbrugh, Florence
Houtte, Jean van
Ibáñez (del Campo), Carlos
Ickes, Harold L(e Claire) obit
Kersten, Charles J.
Killion, George (Leonard)
King, Cecil R(hodes)
Kollantay, Alexandra (Mikhail-
  ovna) obit
Langer, William
Litvinov, Maxim (Maximovitch)
  obit
Lloyd, (John) Selwyn (Brooke)
Lloyd-George, Gwilym
Lord, Mrs. Oswald B(ates)
McGranery, James P(atrick)
McKeldin, Theodore R(oose-
  velt)
McKinney, Frank E(dward)
McMahon, (James O')Brien
  obit
Magloire, Paul E(ugène)
Magsaysay, Ramón
Maher, Aly
Malenkov, Georgi M(aximilian-
  ovich)
Mansfield, Michael J(oseph)
Matthews, Francis P(atrick) obit
Mitchell, Stephen A(rnold)
Morano, Albert Paul
Morris, Newbold
Morrison, William Shepherd
Payne, Frederick G.
Perón, (Maria) Eva (Duarte) de
  obit
Pinay, Antoine
Priest, Ivy (Maud) Baker
Rabaut, Louis Charles
Radhakrishnan, Sir Sarvepalli
Root, Oren
Ruiz Cortines, Adolfo
Sabath, Adolph J(oachim) obit
Salazar, António de Oliveira
Sandys, (Edwin) Duncan
Schoeppel, Andrew F.
Schumacher, Kurt obit
Senanayake, Don Stephen obit
Senanayake, Dudley (Shelton)
Shafer, Paul W(erntz)
Spence, Brent

Steelman, John R(oy)
Summerfield, Arthur E(llsworth)
Ulbricht, Walter
Velasco Ibarra, José María
Walker, Paul A(tlee)
Walter, Francis E(ugene)
Weizmann, Chaim obit
Wherry, Kenneth S(picer) obit
White, Wallace H(umphrey),
  Jr. obit
Williams, John J(ames)
Teague, Olin E(arl)
Thorneycroft, (George Edward)
  Peter
Torp, Oscar (Fredrik)

Publishing

Birnie, William A(lfred) H(art)
Capper, Arthur obit
Cowles, Fleur (Fenton)
Croft, Arthur C(larence)
Field, Marshall, 3d
Horne, John E(lmer)
MacVeagh, Lincoln
Reid, Helen Rogers
Ross, Harold W(allace) obit

Radio

Arnaz, Desi
Ball, Lucille
Cooke, (Alfred) Alistair
Fellows, Harold E(verett)
Field, Marshall, 3d
Garland, Judy
Garroway, Dave
Lee, Canada obit
Kaye, Danny
Kilgallen, Dorothy
Kollmar, Dick
Levant, Oscar
McDaniel, Glen
Merrill, Robert
Moorehead, Agnes
Perón, (Maria) Eva (Duarte) de
  obit
Scoggin, Margaret C(lara)
Thomas, Lowell (Jackson)
Traubel, Helen
Young, Marian

Religion

Belkin, Samuel
Bennett, Ivan L(overidge)
Cashman, Robert
Cushing, Richard J(ames),
  Archbishop
Daniel, Robert Prentiss
Dawson, John A(lbert)
Faust, Clarence H(enry)
Finkelstein, Louis, Rabbi
Ford, Benson
Grey, J(ames) D(avid)
Mackay, John A(lexander)
Macy, Mrs. Edward W(arren)
Miller, Irving

Montgomery, James Shera, Rev.
  obit
Sperry, Willard L(earoyd)

Science

Blodgett, Katharine Burr
Britton, Edgar C(lay)
Cherwell, Frederick Alexander
  Lindemann, 1st Baron
Chubb, L(ewis) Warrington obit
Davidson, William L(ee)
Dubos, René J(ules)
Duggar, Benjamin Minge
Goldstine, Herman H(eine)
Graves, Alvin C(ushman)
Haber, Heinz
Harvey, E(dmund) Newton
Kimble, George H(erbert)
  T(inley)
Lawrence, Ernest O(rlando)
Loynd, Harry J.
Lysenko, T(rofim) D(enisovich)
McMillan, Edwin M(attison)
Meyer, K(arl) F(riedrich)
Middlecoff, (Emmett) Cary
Millikan, Robert A(ndrews)
Sears, Robert R(ichardson)
Shapley, Harlow
Theiler, Max
Tishler, Max
Walton, Ernest Thomas Sinton
Weaver, Warren
Weizmann, Chaim obit
Whipple, Fred Lawrence
Whitman, Walter G(ordon)
Woodward, R(obert) B(urns)

Social Science

Ahlgren, Mrs. Oscar A(lexand-
  der)
Backman, Jules
Bacon, Selden D(askam)
Burdell, Edwin S(harp)
Calkins, Robert D(e Blois)
Charles-Roux, François (-Jules)
Compton, Wilson (Martindale)
Cooper, Joseph D(avid)
Croft, Arthur C(larence)
Dewey, John obit
Eccles, David (McAdam)
Feinsinger, Nathan P(aul)
Finkelstein, Louis, Rabbi
Forsyth, W(illiam) D(ouglass).
Handlin, Oscar
Heuven Goedhart, G(errit)
  J(an) van
Hook, Sidney
Houtte, Jean van
Irwin, Helen G.
Kimble, George H(erbert)
  T(inley)
Kotschnig, Walter M(aria)
Layton, Mrs. Roy F(rancis)
Lloyd, Wesley P(arkinson)
Mansfield, Michael J(oseph)
Muniz, Joao Carlos
Padover, Saul K(ussiel)
Paton, Alan

Porter, Mrs. Elizabeth K(err)
Pusey, Merlo J(ohn)
Putnam, Roger L(owell)
Radhakrishnan, Sir Sarvepalli
Rosenfield, Harry N(athan)
Salazar, António de Oliveira
Saunders, Hilary A(idan) St.
  George obit
Schwebel, Stephen M(yron)
Shapiro, Harry L(ionel)
Sleeper, Ruth
Speidel, Hans
Stone, Abraham
Wriston, Henry M(erritt)

Social Service

Braniff, T(homas) E(lmer)
Burdell, Edwin S(harp)
Dowling, Robert W(hittle)
Faust, Clarence H(enry)
Field, Marshall, 3d
Haskell, William N(afew) obit
Heuven Goedhart, G(errit)
  J(an) van
Irwin, Robert B(enjamin) obit
Layton, Mrs. Roy F(rancis)
Lord, Mrs. Oswald B(ates)
Macy, Mrs. Edward W(arren)
Mays, Ewing W(oodrow)
Morgan, Anne (Tracy) obit
Paton, Alan
Perón, (Maria) Eva (Duarte)
  de obit
Root, Oren
Rosenfield, Harry N(athan)
Sloan, George A(rthur)
Smith, Ida B. Wise obit
Stone, Abraham

Strachan, Paul A(mbrose)
Straus, Roger W(illiams)
Weaver, Warren

Sports

Berra, Lawrence (Peter)
Bushnell, Asa S(mith)
Christenberry, Robert K(eaton)
Gehrmann, Don(ald Arthur)
Henie, Sonja
Hornsby, Rogers
Ingram, Jonas H(oward) obit
Marciano, Rocky
Mathias, Robert Bruce
Middlecoff, (Emmett) Cary
Paige, Leroy (Robert)
Reynolds, Allie
Savitt, Richard
Seixas, E(lias) Victor, Jr.
Wilt, Fred(erick Loren)

Technology

Andrews, Stanley
Bennett, Henry G(arland) obit
Chapman, Albert K(inkade)
Heald, Henry Townley
Mackenzie, C(halmers) J(ack)
Von Braun, Wernher
Whitman, Walter G(ordon)
Wilson, I(rving) W(hite)

Television

Arnaz, Desi
Ball, Lucille
Cooke, (Alfred) Alistair
Fellows, Harold E(verett)

Garroway, Dave
Granik, (S.) Theodore
Kilgallen, Dorothy
Kollmar, Dick
Lahr, Bert
Levant, Oscar
McDaniel, Glen
McDaniel, Hattie obit
Merrill, Robert
Rackmil, Milton R.
Sullivan, Ed(ward Vincent)
Traubel, Helen

Theater

Allyson, June
Brando, Marlon
Cornell, Katharine
Douglas, Kirk
Dowling, Robert W(hittle)
Garfield, John obit
Gow, James (Ellis) obit
Henie, Sonja
Hunter, Kim
Kanin, Garson
Kaye, Danny
Kirstein, Lincoln (Edward)
Kollmar, Dick
Kramm, Joseph
Krasna, Norman
Lagerkvist, Pär (Fabian)
Lahr, Bert
Lawrence, Gertrude
Lee, Canada obit
Mack, Nila
Moorehead, Agnes
Oursler, Fulton obit
Strachan, Paul A(mbrose)
Williams, Emlyn
Winters, Shelley

CUMULATED INDEX—1951-1952

This is a two-year cumulation of all names which have appeared in CURRENT BIOGRAPHY from 1951 through 1952. The dates after names indicate monthly issues and/or Yearbooks in which biographies and obituaries are contained.

For the index to 1940-1950 biographies, see CURRENT BIOGRAPHY 1950 Yearbook; that eleven-year cumulated index is also available separately at fifty cents a copy.

Fuller, Charles E(dward), Rev. Dec 51
Funston, G(eorge) Keith Jul 51
Furman, N(athaniel) Howell Dec 51
Fyan, Loleta D(awson) Dec 51
Fyfe, Sir David (Patrick) Maxwell Dec 51
Fyfe, H(enry) Hamilton obit Jul 51

Gaer, Joseph (WLB) Yrbk 51
Gainza Paz, Alberto Apr 51
Gallup, George (Horace) Dec 52
Gamow, George Oct 51
Garbett, Cyril Forster, Archbishop of York Feb 51
Gardner, Matthias B(ennett) Jun 52
Garfield, John obit Jul 52
Garland, Judy Dec 52
Garroway, Dave May 52
Garroway, David Cunningham See Garroway, Dave May 52
Gasparotti, Mrs. John J. See Seifert, E. (WLB) Yrbk 51
Gauss, Christian obit Dec 51
Gehrmann, Don(ald Arthur) Oct 52 See correction page 664 Yrbk 52
George VI, King of Great Britain obit Mar 52
Giannini, L(awrence) M(ario) obit Oct 52
Gilbreth, Mrs. Frank Bunker See Gilbreth, L. E. M. Sep 51
Gilbreth, Lillian (Evelyn) M(oller) Sep 51
Gilmer, Elizabeth Meriwether See Dix, D. obit Feb 52
Glubb, John Bagot Sep 51
Goedhart, G(errit) J(an) van Heuven See Heuven Goedhart, G. J. van Oct 52
Goldsborough, T(homas) Alan obit Jul 51
Goldstine, Herman H(eine) Nov 52
Golschmann, Vladimir Apr 51
Goodwin, Robert C(lifford) May 51
Gore, Albert (Arnold) Jan 52
Gorrie, Jack (Osborne) Mar 52
Goshorn, Clarence B(aker) obit Jan 51
Gould, Ronald Nov 52
Gow, James (Ellis) obit Mar 52
Graham, Billy, Rev. See Graham, W. F., Rev.
Graham, Elinor (Mish) (WLB) Yrbk 52
Graham, Evarts A(mbrose) Feb 52
Graham, Frank P(orter) Jul 51
Graham, William Franklin, Rev. Apr 51
Granik, (S.) Theodore Dec 52
Graves, Alvin C(ushman) Dec 52
Greco, José Mar 52

Grede, William J. Feb 52
Grey, J(ames) D(avid) Sep 52
Grieder, Naomi Lane Babson See Babson, N. L. (WLB) Yrbk 52
Griffin, R(obert) Allen Feb 51
Grogan, John Joseph Dec 51
Gropius, Walter (Adolf) Mar 52
Gross, Ernest A(rnold) Feb 51
Guillaume, Augustin (Léon) Jan 52
Gumpert, Martin Dec 51

Haber, Heinz Dec 52
Hahn, Otto Mar 51
Hallinan, Vincent (W.) Oct 52
Handlin, Oscar Jul 52
Handy, Thomas T(roy) Sep 51
Hannah, John A(lfred) Oct 52
Harber, W. Elmer Mar 51
Hardie, S(teven) J(ames) L(indsay) Jul 51
Harding, Allan Francis See Harding, Sir J. Oct 52
Harding, Sir John Oct 52
Harnoncourt, René d' See D'Harnoncourt, R. Sep 52
Harriman, E(dward) Roland (Noel) Mar 51
Harrison, William K(elly), Jr. Jul 52
Harvey, E(dmund) Newton May 52
Haskell, William N(afew) obit Sep 52
Havill, Edward (WLB) Yrbk 52
Hawkins, Harry C(alvin) Apr 52
Hayden, Carl T(rumbull) Jul 51
Haywood, Allan S(haw) May 52
Heald, Henry Townley Feb 52
Hébert, F(elix) Edward Nov 51
Heidenstam, Rolf (Magnus) von Oct 51
Hektoen, Ludvig obit Sep 51
Hendrickson, Robert C. Nov 52
Henie, Sonja Jan 52
Herod, William Rogers Mar 51
Hershey, Lewis B(laine) Jun 51
Heuven Goedhart, G(errit) J(an) van Oct 52
Hickman, Herman (Michael, Jr.) Nov 51
Higgins, Andrew J(ackson) obit Sep 52
Higgins, Marguerite Jun 51
Hightower, John M(armann) Nov 52
Hilaly, Ahmed Naguib Jul 52
Hilton, Frank C. Jul 52
Hinshaw, (John) Carl (Williams) Jul 51
Holland, (George) Kenneth Mar 52
Hollenbeck, Don Feb 51
Holliday, Judy Apr 51
Holt, Hamilton obit May 51
Homer, Arthur B(artlett) Jul 52
Hook, Sidney Oct 52
Hoopes, Darlington Sep 52
Horne, John E(lmer) Dec 52
Hornsby, Rogers Sep 52

Horsbrugh, Florence Feb 52
Houtte, Jean van Mar 52
Howard, Elizabeth (WLB) Yrbk 51
Howorth, Mrs. Joseph Marion See Howorth, L. S. Oct 51
Howorth, Lucy Somerville Oct 51
Hudleston, Edmund C(uthbert) May 51
Hulcy, Dechard A(nderson) Sep 51
Hume, Edgar Erskine obit Mar 52
Humphrey, Helen F. Nov 52
Hunt, Lester C(allaway) Mar 51
Hunt, Mabel Leigh (WLB) Yrbk 51
Hunter, Croil Jul 51
Hunter, Kim May 52

Ibáñez (del Campo), Carlos Dec 52
Ibarra, José María Velasco See Velasco Ibarra, J. M. Nov 52
Ickes, Harold L(e Claire) obit Mar 52
Impellitteri, Vincent R(ichard) Feb 51
Ingram, Jonas H(oward) obit Oct 52
Inverchapel of Loch Eck, Archibald John Kerr Clark Kerr, 1st Baron obit Sep 51
Ironside, Henry Allan obit Feb 51
Irving, Frederick A(ugustus) Mar 51
Irwin, Helen G. Oct 52
Irwin, Robert B(enjamin) obit Jan 52
Iverson, Kenneth R(oss) Apr 51

Jackson, C(harles) D(ouglas) Oct 51
Jackson, William H(arding) Mar 51
Jagendorf, Moritz (Adolf) (WLB) Yrbk 52
Jansen, William Oct 51
Jeanmaire, Renée Nov 52
Jenner, William E(zra) Jun 51
Jennings, B(enjamin) Brewster May 51
Jensen, Mrs. Oliver See Stafford, J. (WLB) Yrbk 51
Johnson, David M(offat) Jul 52
Johnson, Joseph T(ravis) Feb 52
Johnson, Lyndon B(aines) Jan 51
Johnston, Alvanley obit Nov 51
Johnston, Olin D(eWitt) Nov 51
Johnston, Wayne A(ndrew) May 51
Jooste, G(erhardus) P(etrus) Apr 51
Jordan, Mildred (WLB) Yrbk 51
Jouvet, Louis obit Oct 51
Joy, C(harles) Turner Jun 51
Juan Carlos, Count of Barcelona Oct 51

Matthews, Francis P(atrick) obit Dec 52
Matthews, W(ilmot) Donald Sep 52
Mature, Victor Dec 51
Maynor, Dorothy Dec 51
Mays, Ewing W(oodrow) Jan 52
Mead, Margaret May 51
Mehta, G(aganvihari) L(allubhai) Nov 52
Merrill, Robert Mai 52
Meyer, K(arl) F(riedrich) Mar 52
Middlecoff, (Emmett) Cary Jul 52
Mies van der Rohe, Ludwig Oct 51
Miller, Edward G(odfrey), Jr. Jun 51
Miller, Irving Nov 52
Miller, J. Cloyd Dec 51
Milles, Carl (Wilhelm Emil) Dec 52
Millikan, Robert A(ndrews) Jun 52
Mitchell, Howard (Bundy) May 52
Mitchell, Stephen A(rnold) Oct 52
Mitropoulos, Dimitri Mar 52
Mizner, Elizabeth Howard See Howard, E. (WLB) Yrbk 51
Monckton, Sir Walter (Turner) Dec 51
Monroney, A(lmer) S(tillwell) Mike Nov 51
Montessori, Maria obit Jun 52
Montgomery, Elizabeth Rider (WLB) Yrbk 52
Montgomery, James Shera, Rev. obit Sep 52
Moody, (Arthur Edson) Blair Sep 51
Moore, Bryant E(dward) obit Mar 51
Moore, Marianne (Craig) Dec 52
Moorehead, Agnes Jun 52
Morano, Albert Paul Mar 52
Morgan, Anne (Tracy) obit Mar 52
Morgan, Edward P. May 51
Morison, Samuel Eliot Oct 51
Morrill, J(ames) L(ewis) Feb 51
Morris, Newbold Mar 52
Morrison, Herbert (Stanley) Feb 51
Morrison, William Shepherd Jan 52
Mossadegh, Mohammed May 51
Muccio, John J(oseph) Jan 51
Mulai Mohammed, Sultan of Morocco See Sidi Mohammed Oct 51
Muniz, Joao Carlos Sep 52
Murphy, Thomas F(rancis) Mar 51
Murray, Philip obit Dec 52
Murrell, Ethel Ernest Oct 51
Murrell, Mrs. John Moore See Murrell, E. E. Oct 51

Naguib, Mohammed Oct 52
Nahas, Mustafa Jul 51
Nam Il Sep 51
Newsom, Herschel D(avis) Apr 51
Ngawang Lobsang Yishey Tenzing Gyatso See Dalai Lama Jul 51
Niebuhr, Reinhold, Rev. Nov 51
Nielsen, A(rthur) C(harles) Dec 51
North, John Ringling Jun 51
Nu, Thakin Dec 51
Nu, U See Nu, T. Dec 51
Nuckols, William P(reston) May 52
Nyrop, Donald W(illiam) Jun 52
Nystrom, Paul H(enry) Mar 51

Ogilvie, Elisabeth (May) (WLB) Yrbk 51
Oliphant, Marcus L(aurence Elwin) Dec 51
O'Neill, J(ohn) E(dward) Jun 52
Oursler, Fulton obit Jul 52

Packer, Fred L(ittle) Jul 52
Padover, Saul K(ussiel) Oct 52
Paige, Leroy (Robert) Sep 52
Paige, Satchel See Paige, L. R. Sep 52
Paley, William S(amuel) Dec 51
Palmer, Lilli May 51
Papagos, Alexander Nov 51
Parker, Roy H(artford) Oct 51
Pate, Maurice Jun 51
Patel, Vallabhbhai (Jhaverbhai) obit Jan 51
Paton, Alan Jun 52
Patterson, Robert P(orter) obit Mar 52
Payne, Frederick G. Dec 52
Paz, Alberto Gainza See Gainza Paz, A.
Paz, Hipólito Jesús Jan 52
Peng Teh-huai Dec 51
Perkins, R(ichard) Marlin Oct 51
Perlman, Philip B(enjamin) Jul 52
Perón, (Maria) Eva (Duarte) de obit Sep 52
Perrin, Francis (Henri) Jul 51
Pétain, Henri Philippe obit Sep 51
Petit, Roland Apr 52
Petsche, Maurice obit Nov 51
Pholien, Joseph Feb 51
Pibul Songgram, Luang Sep 51
Picon, Molly Jun 51
Pinay, Antoine Apr 52
Pine, David A(ndrew) Jun 52
Plaza (Lasso), Galo Oct 51
Poindexter, Joseph B(oyd) obit Jan 52
Poole, DeWitt C(linton) obit Oct 52
Popkin, Zelda (WLB) Yrbk 51
Popovic, Vladimir Feb 52
Porter, Mrs. Elizabeth K(err) Oct 52
Porter, Mrs. Eugene Vandergrift See Porter, Mrs. E. K. Oct 52

Powers, Marie Jan 51
Priest, Ivy (Maude) Baker Nov 52
Priest, Mrs. Roy F(letcher) See Priest, I. M. B. Nov 52
Pugh, (Herbert) Lamont Mar 51
Pusey, Merlo J(ohn) Jul 52
Putnam, Roger L(owell) Jan 52

Quo Tai-chi obit Apr 52

Rabaut, Louis Charles Jan 52
Rackmil, Milton R. Nov 52
Raddall, Thomas (Head) (WLB) Yrbk 51
Radhakrishnan, Sir Sarvepalli Jun 52
Ralls, Charles C. Jan 51
Ramspeck, Robert (C. Word) Jun 51
Randall, Clarence B(elden) Jun 52
Randolph, A(sa) Philip Oct 51
Rappard, William E(mmanuel) Oct 51
Rathbone, Basil Mar 51
Rau, Sir Benegal Narsing Dec 51
Razmara, Ali obit Mar 51
Reed, Ralph T(homas) Apr 51
Reichstein, Tadeus Feb 51
Reid, Helen Rogers May 52
Reid, Mrs. Ogden Mills See Reid, H. R. May 52
Remorino, Jerónimo Sep 51
Renner, Karl obit Jan 51
Reynolds, Albert Pierce See Reynolds, Allie Jun 52
Reynolds, Allie Jun 52
Richards, James P(rioleau) Sep 51
Richter, Conrad (Michael) Jun 51
Rickenbacker, Eddie See Rickenbacker, E. V. Feb 52
Rickenbacker, Edward Vernon Feb 52
Riddell, R(obert) Gerald obit Apr 51
Ridenour, Nina Apr 51
Riiser-Larsen, Hjalmar Nov 51
Riley, William E(dward) Nov 51
Robinson, Boardman obit Oct 52
Robinson, Ray Mar 51
Robinson, Sugar Ray See Robinson, R. Mar 51
Robson, Flora Jan 51
Rockefeller, Nelson A(ldrich) Mar 51
Rodgers, Richard Apr 51
Romberg, Sigmund obit Dec 51
Root, Oren Jul 52
Rootes, Sir William (Edward) Nov 51
Rooth, Ivar Dec 52
Rosenbach, A(braham) S(imon) W(olf) obit Sep 52
Rosenberg, Mrs. Anna M(arie) Jan 51
Rosenfield, Harry N(athan) Apr 52